THE LIFE OF MARK TWAIN
THE FINAL YEARS

The Life of

MARK TWAIN

THE FINAL YEARS

1891–1910

Gary Scharnhorst

UNIVERSITY OF MISSOURI PRESS
Columbia

University of Missouri Press, Columbia, Missouri 65211
Printed and bound in the United States of America

Library of Congress Cataloging-in-Publication Data

Names: Scharnhorst, Gary, author.
Title: The life of Mark Twain : the final years, 1891-1910 / by Gary Scharnhorst.
Description: Columbia : University of Missouri Press, [2022] | Series: Mark Twain and his circle | Includes bibliographical references and index.
Identifiers: LCCN 2021026148 (print) | LCCN 2021026149 (ebook) | ISBN 9780826222411 (hardcover) | ISBN 9780826274687 (ebook)
Subjects: LCSH: Twain, Mark, 1835-1910. | Twain, Mark, 1835-1910--Homes and haunts. | Authors, American--19th century--Biography. | Humorists, American--19th century--Biography.
Classification: LCC PS1331 .S24 2022 (print) | LCC PS1331 (ebook) | DDC 818/.409 [B]--dc23
LC record available at https://lccn.loc.gov/2021026148
LC ebook record available at https://lccn.loc.gov/2021026149

∞™ This paper meets the requirements of the American National Standard for Permanence of Paper for Printed Library Materials, Z39.48, 1984.

Typefaces: Clarendon and Jenson

This book was published with the generous support of

The Mark Twain Foundation

The Missouri Humanities Council

The State Historical Society of Missouri

Mark Twain and His Circle
Tom Quirk and John Bird, Series Editors

Contents

Illustrations

THE LIFE OF MARK TWAIN
THE FINAL YEARS

CHAPTER 1

Exits and Expatriates

I have been an author for 20 years & an ass for 55.

—*Mark Twain's Notebook*

NOT EVEN SAMUEL Clemens knew how deeply he was in debt, though he had staunched the gush of red ink from the publishing company he owned. When he sailed with his family to Europe in June 1891, he believed that Charles L. Webster and Company, his publishing house, owed its creditors about $80,000, not including over $70,000 his wife Olivia had advanced the firm. He later learned that the figure, including Livy's loan, was closer to $200,000, nearly $6 million in today's money. He spent most of the next decade escaping from this "bondage of debt."[1]

He was rumored to be as wealthy as Croesus, or as Huck Finn once said, "as Creosote"—so filthy rich that, if the quality of his writing had declined, "it is because," noted the *Chicago Inter Ocean*, "he has deteriorated into a millionaire." In an effort to hide the truth, Sam claimed that he and Livy had decided to educate their three daughters in Europe, "especially in German, French, and Italian literatures and languages." However, Susy, their nineteen-year-old daughter, was largely unschooled while abroad and Jean—the youngest, at ten—would be homeschooled. Only Clara, the middle daughter, was placed in private schools during their European residence, and then only intermittently, to study music. Sam added that he was taking Livy to a warmer climate for her heart, as well as seeking treatment for rheumatism in his writing hand—claims with a modicum of truth. "His hand has given out from overwork in signing checks and making deposit accounts," according to one news report. (Privately Sam conceded that "every pen-stroke gives me the lock-jaw.")[2] More adept at self-promotion than book promotion, his reputation as a shrewd businessman was largely his own creation. Few people knew the real reason for the Clemens family's departure: to reduce housekeeping costs for a few years. To be sure, the family continued to spend lavishly, albeit less extravagantly, while abroad. At least they were no longer required to stable horses or employ a retinue of servants to run the house in Hartford, Connecticut. Eventually they rented out the mansion to pay some of their expenses, including the caretaking of the grounds.

So at the age of fifty-five Sam began, like the patriarch Ishmael, to roam the earth. On June 14, 1891, after an eight-day voyage, the first of his fourteen transatlantic crossings over the next four years, Sam; Livy; daughters Susy, Clara, and Jean; Livy's sister Susan Crane; and maid Katy Leary, along with twenty-five steamer trunks, landed at Le Havre, France, and registered at the beachfront Hotel Frascati. On June 18 the family railed to Paris and registered at the Grand Hotel Terminus near the opera house. Sam's fortunes did not change with the scenery, however. He crossed paths with the artist W. H. McEntee, who expressed "the hope that he was enjoying" the City of Lights. Sam replied that he was "not over here enjoying myself; I'm over here heaping maledictions upon the rheumatism, which has got hold of my right arm." Later, as McEntee "was strolling through the Salon in the Champ de Mars," he "observed Mark standing in more or less rapt contemplation before one of the pictures. Art had evidently made him lose sight of his rheumatism." Sam was notified by cablegram soon after his arrival, moreover, that the proposed sale of his interest in the trouble-plagued Paige typesetter to brothers George and Marshall Mallory of New York had fallen through, so he advised Fred Hall, president of Webster and Company, "to modify your instalment system" of sales "to meet the emergency of a constipated purse; for if you should need to borrow any more money I would not know how or where to raise it."[3] The company foundered under the weight of producing the multivolume *Library of American Literature*, for which subscribers paid only on delivery.

After excursions to Saint-Cloud and Versailles, the family left Paris on June 26 for Geneva. There the older girls were installed in a private home where they might polish their conversational French. The next day Sam and the rest of the clan railed to the health resort of Aix-les-Bains, the so-called paradise of rheumatics in eastern France, to take the waters for a month at the Pavillon des Bains. "Mr. Clemens was having kind of paralysis in his arm then," Katy recalled, "and thought some baths would be a good thing and Mrs. Clemens wanted to take the baths too." Sam "was suffering a great deal of pain and he liked those big men that used to rub him." Two half-naked men escorted him "into a stone-floored basin about fourteen feet square, which had enough strange-looking pipes and things in it to make it look like a torture chamber," Sam recalled. They "seated me on a pine stool and kept a couple of warm-water jets as thick as one's wrist playing upon me while they kneaded me, stroked me, twisted me, and applied all the other details of the scientific massage to me for seven or eight minutes." During his first course of baths he "developed plenty of pain, but the subsequent ones removed almost all of it." He recovered the use of his right arm and, comparing his convalescence to the washing of ore in the Nevada mines, bragged that the baths "sluiced out of me every important ailment known to medical science." While in Aix-les-Bains he also resurrected his Thomas Jefferson Snodgrass pseudonym after thirty-five years to satirize publicly a philistine who wrote dramatic criticism for the London *Speaker*. Between hydrotherapy treatments he and Livy loitered in the casino, the "gambling hell" that, Sam thought, ranked "next to Monte Carlo for high play and plenty of it." They also cruised around Lake Bourget and railed to the medieval villages of Annecy and Talloires "through a garden land that has not had its equal for beauty perhaps since Eden." On these side trips they "stepped from the sparkling water and the rush and boom and fret and fever of the nineteenth century into the solemnity and the silence and the soft gloom and the brooding mystery of a remote antiquity."[4]

Sam reminisced about this trip to Aix-les-Bains in the first of six travel letters from Europe he submitted under contract to the McClure newspaper syndicate. He was paid $1,000, or about $300 per thousand words, for each of these articles, "perhaps the highest rate ever paid for newspaper correspondence," according to the *Portland Oregonian*, and they were widely distributed, appearing in the United States in the New York *Sun*, *Boston Globe*, *Chicago Tribune*, *San Francisco Examiner*, *San Francisco Call*, *Kansas City Times*, *Philadelphia Inquirer*, *Galveston Daily News*, *Dallas Morning News*, *Omaha Bee*, *St. Louis Post-Dispatch*, *Pittsburgh Dispatch*, *Louisville Courier-Journal*, *Atlanta Constitution*, *Detroit Free Press*, *Montgomery Advertiser*, *Minneapolis Star Tribune*, *Indianapolis News*, and *Buffalo Courier*. They likewise appeared abroad in the *Illustrated London News*; *New Zealand Times*; Otago *Evening Star* (New Zealand); *Auckland Star*; *Adelaide South Australian Register*; *Melbourne Age*; *Sydney Echo*; Orange *Leader* (New South Wales, Australia); and Rockhampton *Bulletin* (Queensland, Australia). Despite their popularity, Edward Bok, editor of the *Ladies' Home Journal*, sniffed in his syndicated column that Sam was in the twilight of his career. Bok pronounced his first travel letter from Europe "a disappointment. . . . The simple fact is that Mark Twain has no longer that control of his pen and wit which he once had, and these letters, I think, will demonstrate the fact."[5]

Sam, Livy, Jean, Susan Crane, and Katy Leary left Aix-les-Bains on July 28 for Geneva, where they were joined by Susy and Clara. The tribe of seven then traveled the next three days via Lausanne, Zurich, Stuttgart, and Nuremberg to the Wagner festival at Bayreuth. Sam joked about the trip in another syndicated letter he entitled "Playing Courier." As he told the story, despite his best efforts to guide the group their journey became a perfect storm of misadventures: he neglected to reserve hotel rooms; lost his letter of credit, a valise, and fourteen of their trunks; bought discounted (fake) rail tickets at a cigar shop rather than the train depot; habitually arrived late at the station after misreading the schedules; was briefly detained by the police; and generally offended all of his fellow travelers through his ineptitude.[6]

Nothing Sam described in this comedy of errors can be trusted, of course. The Clemenses had in fact cabled for rooms and ordered tickets for seats in the Festspielhaus in Bayreuth months in advance. To be sure, they found the restaurants there overrun by "music-mad strangers" and other Wagner devotees. "Why, you couldn't hardly get anything to eat," Katy Leary remembered. The family routinely dined on bratwursts—Leary called them "hot dogs"—purchased from the ubiquitous street vendors. In yet another syndicated letter, Sam urged prospective pilgrims to the festival in future to "bring your dinner-pail with you. If you do, you will never cease to be thankful. If you do not, you will find it a hard fight to save yourself from famishing." His family had tried to dine in "all kinds of places—some outside of the town, a mile or two—and have captured only nibblings and odds and ends, never in any instance a complete and satisfying meal." Jean complained in her diary that the food in Bayreuth was "awful."[7]

The Bayreuth Festival, held at least every other year since 1876 in an amphitheater designed by Wagner and seating over sixteen hundred, attracted music devotees who traveled "from the very ends of the earth to worship their prophet in his own Kaaba," as Sam put it. He did not pretend to be among the enthusiasts, though he certainly had long been familiar with Wagner's *Lohengrin, Tannhäuser,* and *Das Rheingold.* "I am not a musical critic and did not come here to write essays about the operas and deliver judgment upon their merits," he explained in another of his syndicated travel letters. He merely accompanied "four or five pilgrims" to the festival. To judge from his travel letter, "At the Shrine of St. Wagner," he heard only two operas in their entirety and part of another during the eleven days he was in attendance, the first of the two being *Parsifal* on August 2. Richard Wagner's widow Cosima, director of the festival, permitted *Parsifal* to be staged only in Bayreuth, where its three acts and two intermissions required seven hours. Katy Leary recalled that the Clemens women "liked Parsifal" but she didn't think Sam "really liked it very much," though he insisted he enjoyed it "in spite of the singing." He was unable, he said, "to detect in the vocal parts of 'Parsifal' anything that might with confidence be called rhythm or tune or melody," and he lamented in particular the role of "a hermit named Gurnemanz who stands on the stage in one spot and practices by the hour, while first one and then another character of the cast endures what he can of it and then retires to die." On August 3 he watched the last act of *Tannhäuser*, "the only operatic favorite I have ever had—an opera which has always driven me mad with ignorant delight whenever I have heard it." On Wednesday, August 5, he saw *Tristan and Isolde* and was struck by the solemnity of the performance. Whereas at the Metropolitan Opera House in New York the audience "sit in a glare and wear their showiest harness; they hum airs, they squeak fans, they titter, and they gabble all the time," in Bayreuth the listeners "sit in the dark and worship in silence." A tragedy of doomed love, the opera "broke the hearts of all witnesses who were of the faith." Sam conceded he was "strongly out of place" in "the Wagner temple." Sometimes he felt "like the sane person in a community of the mad" or "the one groping savage in the college of the learned and always, during service, I feel like a heretic in heaven." But he likewise refused to "overlook or minify the fact that this is one of the most extraordinary experiences of my life."[8]

The family left Bayreuth on August 11 and railed some sixty miles east to Marienbad, in Bohemia, where they spent the remainder of the month. Sam was enchanted by the landscape along the route; he had "never made so picturesque a journey before," he reported, "and there cannot be another trip of like length in the world that can furnish so much variety and of so charming and interesting a sort." But he did not make the trip to enjoy the scenery. His rheumatic right arm was sore again and he sought treatment by taking the baths there. (Katy Leary reminisced that "we went to take some of them mud baths, as they called them," and "regular mud, it was.") As he wrote Clarence Buel of the *Century* shortly after his arrival, "I soaked my rheumatic arm 5 weeks at Aix-les-Bains, but never could use a pen at all until the fifth week, & then only an hour or so at a time. The pain all left me; but after a fortnight it returned & I am trying these baths, & getting small relief from them." From Sam's perspective, part of the problem with "Mary's bath," which was affiliated with a convent, was its emphasis on asceticism. The rules allowed the patient to satisfy his hunger "so long as he is careful and eats only such things as he doesn't want," to "drink one glass of any kind of liquor that he has a prejudice against," and to "smoke one pipe if he isn't used to it." Two weeks into the regimen, which included soaking in a tub "with two kinds of pine juice in it," the aching had not abated. "What I have been through in these two weeks," he declared in his syndicated letter from Marienbad, "would free a person of pretty much everything in him that wasn't nailed there—any loose thing, any unattached fragment of bone, or meat or morals, or disease or propensities or accomplishments, or what not." Yet his arm was still crippled, and "I do considerable cussing over it." He had "to save all my muscle for my literary drudges." He was so determined to finish his essays for the McClure syndicate that he began to write them with his left hand. While in Bohemia he also befriended a pair of prominent British Liberal Party politicians: Henry Campbell-Bannerman, "a great and brave statesman and a charming man," and the controversial Henry Labouchère. Sam occasionally "helped that picturesque personality [Labouchère] walk off his mineral water up and down the promenade."[9]

Late in August, Livy, in company with Susan Crane and Susy Clemens, traveled to Berlin to scout for a winter residence for the family. She rented a five-room apartment on the second floor of a house in the western part of the city near the Tiergarten. Sam, who remained at the resort with their two younger daughters, befriended Charles Waldstein, an eminent Anglo-American archeologist and director of the American School of Classical Studies in Athens. He was often visited by Frank Mason, the U.S. consul general in Frankfurt, whom he had known in 1878. During her mother's absence, seventeen-year-old Clara, who later reminisced that like the rest of the clan she had fallen "in love with Marienbad, which, as a watering-place, can hardly be surpassed," attended a military ball one evening in a frock that was "so slightly *décolleté* that I blushed with shame"—because it was cut *too low* or *not low enough?*—and she attracted the earnest attentions of a young German officer. As a result, Sam locked her in her room until Livy came back from Berlin or, as Clara later put it in a miracle of understatement, her father expressed an "ingrained objection to foreign suitors." She thought at first that her punishment was "some kind of joke. Surely I could not be incarcerated like a damsel of the Middle Ages. Yet that was just what happened." It would not be the last time Clara rebelled against the moral strictures of her father, who subscribed to conventional ideologies of gender and adhered to a strict code of mid-Victorian propriety, including the cult of true womanhood. These views were implicit in his essay "In Defense of Harriet Shelley," a "brilliant article," according to the *San Francisco Call*, published in the *North American Review* for July 1894.[10] In this review of Edward Dowden's biography of Percy Bysshe Shelley, in which Sam condemned sexual license and male predatory behavior, he betrayed both his prudishness and his progressivism.

The family left Marienbad soon after Livy, her daughter Susy, and her sister Susan returned from Berlin. They scurried west, first to Nuremburg, then Heidelberg, where they spent two days in the same rooms at the Schloss-Hotel they had occupied in 1878. Sam reveled in the opportunity to show Katy Leary the nighttime view of the gaslit city from the bluff overlooking the Neckar River—"the most beautiful string of diamonds in the whole world"—but he was disappointed to discover that in the intervening fourteen years he had been forgotten by the young daughters of the family who lived in the Molkenkur, an inn atop the Königstuhl. He pardoned them on the grounds that he had been "a skittish young thing of 42 in those days." He also found the time to drive over the Philosophenweg, the trail on the Heiligenberg, a wooded hill across the Neckar from the castle. From the university town they railed south to Switzerland, first to Lucerne, where they paused for four days, then continued by carriage from Alpnach through Brienz and over the Brünig Pass to Grindelwald, Lauterbrunnen, and the Victoria Hotel at Interlaken. Sam chronicled this leg of the trip in his next syndicated letter, which included a salute to the beauty of the Jungfrau, "the most engaging, and beguiling, and fascinating spectacle that exists on the earth." On September 14 they left for Berne and Geneva, arriving at the Hôtel Beau-Rivage in Lausanne-Ouchy on the north shore of Lake Geneva three days later. In "The Cradle of Liberty," his syndicated letter to the New York *Sun* about his foray through Switzerland, Sam mused on his experience: "After trying the political atmosphere of the neighboring monarchies, it is healing and refreshment to breathe an air that has known no taint of slavery for 600 years and to come among a people whose political history is great and fine, superlatively great and fine, and worthy to be taught in all schools and studied by all races and peoples."[11]

Sam left the others there to take a ten-day, two-hundred-mile voyage down the Rhône River, a jaunt he planned to chronicle in a book tentatively titled "The Innocents Adrift." The purpose of the excursion, he explained, was "not to see sights, but to rest up from sight-seeing." He hired Joseph Verey, the courier who had guided the family on its grand European tour in 1879, to accompany him. Verey bought a flat-bottomed skiff some fifteen or twenty feet long in Bourget, France, for the equivalent of five dollars, engaged a boatman to escort them, and rendezvoused with Sam at the Castle of Chatillon on Lake Bourget. Eleven years later, Verey recalled that Sam "was in search of absolute quietude, in order to get on with his book. . . . Throughout that long river trip Mr. Clemens sat in the stern of the boat writing from morning to night, and smoking his favorite 'Durham' tobacco." Whereas he had been a "perfect" courier in 1879, however, Verey proved to be woefully imperfect in 1891. He had "picked up all the bad qualities acquirable on Earth and imported others from Hell," and particularly boozing, according to Sam, who suspected Verey of swindling him and the boatman. Before the Rhône trip ended, Sam "was ready to offer him to Satan as a gift." After Sam fired the courier—the first time—on the weekend of September 25, Verey found his way to Ouchy where, according to Livy, he was "in a constant state of inebriation and . . . the center of all eyes in the dining room" of the Hôtel Beau-Rivage.[12]

Still, Verey hardly figures in Sam's humorous account of the trip, which features an imaginary cast of fellow travelers named the Admiral (the boatman), Fargo, Harris, Stavely, Uncle Abner, and an unnamed courier in a decidedly minor role. In this version of events, Sam drifts with the current past such bucolic and "slumberous" villages as Chanaz and Massignieu de Rives and the cities of Lyon and Valence; breakfasts in the open air; happily dines "on the choicest chickens, vegetables, fruit, butter, and bread, prepared in French perfection and served upon the whitest linen"; sleeps at inns with such inviting names as the Hôtel des Voyageurs and Hôtel du Rhône Moine. He visits the Grotte de la Balme, the "worn and vast and idiotic ruins of a castle" at Bourg-Saint-Andéol "built by two crusaders 650 years ago"; the papal palace of Avignon; the Bridge of the Holy Spirit in the village of Pont-Saint-Esprit; and various châteaus along the way. The journey ends on September 29 at Aries, where Sam gave away the boat, then traveled to Nîmes to explore the Roman ruins before catching a train back to Ouchy on October 4. In a letter from Nîmes to his friend Joseph Twichell he compared his voyage in 1891 to his walking tour with the minister in 1878:

> I have been ten days floating down the Rhone on a raft, from Lake Bourget, & a most curious & darling kind of a trip it has been. You ought to have been along—I could have made room for you easily—& you would have found that a pedestrian tour in Europe doesn't begin with a raft-voyage for hilarity, & mild adventure, & intimate contact with the unvisited native of the back settlements, & extinction from the world & newspapers, & a conscience in a state of coma, & lazy comfort, & solid happiness. In fact there's nothing that's so lovely.

Unfortunately, the manuscript of "The Innocents Adrift"—written despite the discomfort in his right arm and offered in July 1893 to John Brisben Walker, owner-editor of *Cosmopolitan*, for serial publication—has never been printed in its entirety. Albert Bigelow Paine, Sam's literary executor, edited only about half of the 174 pages for publication in 1923 under the title "Down the Rhône."[13]

Two days after Sam rejoined the family in Ouchy, they decamped for Berlin via Basel, Strasbourg, and Frankfurt. Katy Leary had been summoned back to the United States to care for her ailing mother—"the first time I ever left them," she said—so Sam rehired Verey in her stead. The Clemenses moved into their second-floor rooms in a tenement on Körnerstrasse in

Berlin around October 10. Though Livy had sought accommodations "in einer möglichst ruhigen Strasse" (in the quietest street possible), according to a reporter for the Berlin *National-Zeitung,* she had unwittingly rented "a cheap apartment in a disagreeable quarter of the city," as Clara recalled. She remembered "noisy children who played in the muddy streets" and the "unkempt, half-clad women"—apparently prostitutes—who "were continually leaning out the windows opposite us, their elbows propped on comfortable cushions." With a warehouse across the street and a lumberyard three doors away, the rooms were "not merely noisy in a general citified way," Sam complained. "The night was made up of deep stretches of silence broken to smash at irregular intervals by the thundering rush of heavy wagons that made the house quake and brought us broad awake and quivering. . . . Yes it was a noisy street—unquestionably the noisiest one in the whole earth." In his notebook, Sam described the neighborhood scornfully as a "Rag-picker's Paradise" and a "slum-land." In the end, however, the greatest problem with the apartment was neither noise nor crime. Asked by the *National-Zeitung* how long he would remain in Berlin, Sam replied, "until your taxes drive me away." Germany had recently adopted a tax law that soaked resident foreigners at the rate of 5 percent of their income, and Sam was widely thought to be a millionaire. The German press reported that he earned, with reprint fees, about $100,000 for twenty syndicated travel letters.[14] A few hours after Sam filed "the customary declaration as to my income" as part of his application for an *Aufenthaltserlaubnis,* or residency permit, he was "visited by a brass-buttoned gentleman, who declared that I was woefully wrong in my calculations. He produced a newspaper clipping saying I received in the neighborhood of a thousand marks every time I wrote a line, and that my regular income from my books was about as large as the revenues of the Kaiser himself." When Sam protested, the tax official "proved conclusively to me that I was a liar." There was "no use denying the facts."[15]

Predictably, while they lived in such shabby quarters, the Clemenses rarely entertained at home. Perhaps the only exception was a luncheon they hosted on November 21 for Almira Russell Hancock, the widow of General Winfield Scott Hancock; William Walter Phelps, the U.S. ambassador; and other prominent Americans resident in Berlin. Clara was enrolled in the exclusive American School for Young Girls founded by Mary Bannister Willard in Schöneberg; studied music with Moritz Moszkowski, a well-known pianist and composer; and bragged in her memoirs about attending "one or two parties at the American Embassy." As an A-list celebrity, moreover, Sam was a welcome guest, an ornament at any social gathering, especially at diplomatic events. He renewed his acquaintance with Henry

Labouchère and met such journalists as Heinrich Opper von Blowitz of the London *Times*, the Civil War hero Wager Swayne, and other "authors, ambassadors, and scientists of rank." He attended the seventieth birthday celebration for Rudolf Virchow, director of the Institut für Pathologie in Berlin, and Hermann von Helmholtz, professor of physics at Humboldt University, at the Kaiserhof Hotel on October 13, only a few days after settling in the city, and a grand official dinner at the U.S. embassy hosted by Phelps on October 31. Among the other guests were the American journalist Poultney Bigelow; Sir Edward Malet, the British ambassador to Germany; the German foreign secretary Baron Adolf von Marschall; and the imperial ministers of finance and commerce. Sam often traveled in the same circles as Henry W. Fisher, a fellow Connecticut journalist, who accompanied him to the Salamonski Circus and the Berlin Royal Library, where they examined "a volume of grossly indecent verses by Voltaire addressed to Frederick the Great"; and together they met Ward Hill Lamon, Abraham Lincoln's friend and biographer.[16]

Despite his professed distaste for opera, Sam whetted his appetite while in Berlin by attending performances of Wolfgang Amadeus Mozart's *Don Giovanni* and Wagner's *Tannhäuser* and *Lohengrin*. Ever the avid theatergoer, he also saw Johann Wolfgang von Goethe's *Götz von Berlichingen*, to which he had alluded in *A Tramp Abroad* (1880), and was introduced to the actress Anna Haverland at the home of the journalist and industrialist Henry Villard. He heard Haverland recite the poetry of Heinrich Heine in German and, she quipped, he "was good enough to say that he almost liked German—when I spoke it." Sam delivered a humorous address before an audience of over two hundred at a conference of the local American Physicians Association at the English Haus on Thanksgiving; he joked to Hall that his arm was "so much better that I was able to make a speech last night to 250 Americans." Accompanied by Phelps, he read some of his sketches before the English and American Club at the Gewerbehaus in Dresden on December 18. He closed by reciting "The Awful German Language" from *A Tramp Abroad*, which was received "with roars of real American laughter," the *New York Tribune* reported. But "the German officers present took offence and a score of them left the room in high dudgeon." At the reception afterward, Sam learned he had unwittingly precipitated the walkout. "Well," he drawled, "I never could see anything funny in that speech myself.'" In early January 1892 he and Murat Halstead were the guests of honor at a dinner hosted by the secretary of the U.S. embassy and Sam lectured on behalf of the Berlin YMCA. On January 13, the day after he and Livy returned from a brief visit to Ilsenburg, Germany, in the Hartz

Mountains, he also spoke on behalf of the Berlin American Church—Livy had been active in its Ladies' Union—and his talk raised 1,257 German marks, the equivalent of several thousand dollars, for the church building fund. But he caught the flu and spent the next month in bed. Livy was abruptly transformed from patient to nurse. As she wrote Alice Day, "I was really frightened," noting that his condition was "so unnatural that it was frightful." Sam reflected later that "on a very cold winter's night I lectured for the benefit of an English or American church-charity in a hall that was as hot as the Hereafter. On my way home, I froze. I spent thirty-four days in bed, with congestion of the wind'ard lung. That was the beginning. That lung has remained in a damaged condition ever since." While he recuperated, he followed the news about the legislative debates—in German—in the Reichstag and savored "a booming time all to myself."[17]

By late 1891, after living for almost three months in a seedy neighborhood, Sam could no longer tolerate the crime, noise, and taxes. As he jotted in his notebook for December 12, "It's all up with Kornerstrasse, too much police." The police and the tax commissioners "drove me out of house and home," he told a reporter for the New York *Press*, so the Clemenses leased an eight-room suite in the upmarket Hotel Royal on Unter den Linden a few hundred yards east of the Brandenburg Gate, where they paid a higher rent but "where they can tax me only in accordance with the income I actually spend for rooms and board and incidentals." Clara remembered that on the last day of the year "we moved with gay hearts to a comfortable, if simple, hotel." The next day, as if to signal their overnight rise in status, they were dinner guests of J. B. Jackson, the second secretary of the U.S. legation.[18]

The relocation signaled a corresponding bump in Sam's social status. Through the agency of Poultney Bigelow, Phelps, and Sam's distant cousin Mollie Clemens von Versen, who was married to General Maximilian von Versen, commander of the Third Prussian Army Corps, Sam was invited to dine with Kaiser Wilhelm II at the home of the Versens at 36 Mauerstrasse near the Hotel Royal the evening of February 20, 1892. "Greatly pleased that his Majesty was familiar with my books," Sam sat at the right hand of the emperor. Among the others at the table were Wilhelm's brother, Prince Henry of Prussia; the imperial chamberlain Prince Radolin; and Rudolf Lindau and Friedrich Rottenburg of the German foreign ministry. After dinner the men chain-smoked until midnight, as Sam recalled, "when the Emperor shook hands and left." Poultney Bigelow, who was not present, later claimed that "both enjoyed the meeting," though the truth belies the assertion. Sam admitted to Albert Bigelow Paine many years later that he "committed an indiscretion" during the conversation by disagreeing with Wilhelm about the "generous soldier pensions" granted Civil War veterans; Sam considered them bribes for votes, whereupon the table fell silent. "The Emperor refrained from addressing any remarks to me afterward," he recalled, "and not merely during the brief remainder of the dinner, but afterward in the kneip-room, where beer and cigars and hilarious anecdoting prevailed until about midnight. I am sure that the Emperor's good night was the only thing he said to me in all that time." Sam thought he had been unfairly rebuked and wrote W. D. Howells in a pique of lese majesty that he considered the kaiser "a cockahoop sovereign." Fifteen years later he learned that Wilhelm was still puzzled that Sam had failed to converse over dinner and cigars.[19]

In fact, Sam was still recovering from his bout with influenza when he met the kaiser. A week later, on the recommendation of his physician, Sam and Livy left their daughters in the care of Susan Crane and, in company with Joseph Verey, railed to Menton on the French Rivera. They stayed at the Hotel des Anglais for over three weeks, until March 25, when they left for Italy, first to Pisa, while Verey returned to Berlin to "fetch the tribe"—all but Clara, who remained in residence at the Willard School. Sam assured Susy, with a hint of past disapproval, that the courier "has never uttered a scolding word to anybody, this time, but has made himself pleasant & welcome with all servants." Meanwhile, Sam visited the obligatory Pisan sights in the Square of Miracles—the Leaning Tower; the cathedral displaying the lamp of Galileo; and the Camposanto Monumentale, featuring Buonamico Buffalmacco's "hideous" fourteenth-century frescoes, including one depicting the crucified "Christ emerging from a bath-tub coffin." Sam and Livy reunited with the rest of the family at the Hotel Molaro in Rome, where they stayed "a charming five weeks," and he attended another Mozart opera, *The Marriage of Figaro,* dined with the sculptor Horatio Greenough, renewed his friendship with the painter Elihu Vedder, visited the studio of the sculptor Harriet Hosmer, and went sightseeing with Clara and Jean to the dome of St. Peter's Basilica. Jean recalled that "the view was very fine indeed, from there we could see entire Rome, the Mediterranean Sea, and the Claudius Aqueduct." Sam met Anthony Trollope's younger brother Tom, who allowed that he had "been laughing with you for years." In all, as Susy wrote her Bryn Mawr College friend Louise Brownell, she had "never seen a place so busy as Rome." She also betrayed a brand of ethnocentrism and snobbery: "The ancient parts of the city are just as tremendous as I had imagined them but the modern city is disappointing." Moreover, "the Italians are not *one bit* as I expected. There is no brilliancy and intellectual vivacity in their faces, but only beastliness and dirt." She added, "I don't see how Italy can ever have any very great charm while the people are what they are. I keep contrasting them with the Germans, the *clean*, honest, kindly, dignified, self respecting Germans."[20]

In early May the family migrated north to Florence, where they stayed at the Hotel Grande Bretagne, which, despite the luxury room rates, was little more than "a vast confusion of halls and sleeping-holes, a huge congeries of rats' nests, furnished with rubbish, probably bought at pauper-auctions," Sam griped. "Everything on the cheapest & shabbiest scale, except the bills," and "Everywhere the dirt of antiquity, everywhere gigantic fleas that threaten your life." His complaints were compounded by Joseph Verey's shirking of his duties; as Sam noted in his notebook, "These days Joseph has been about as idle & hard to find as ever." Still, Sam and Livy were so beguiled by Florence that they decided to winter there, partly because, as their daughter Clara put it later, "it was possible to live like princes on limited means." They also had a group of friends in residence there. On May 5 they traveled to Fiesole with professor Willard Fiske of Cornell University. Later in the week they lunched with Sir George Bowen, Lady Edward FitzMaurice, the young Lord Granville Leveson-Gower, and Marchesa Spinola. Before they left Florence, with the help of Fiske and the English expatriates Henry and Janet Ross, Sam and Livy agreed to rent the furnished Villa Viviani near Settignano, three miles from the city, beginning in September for 250 francs a month. Later in May they tarried in Venice for ten days, registering at the swank Hotel Danieli. "We had a most perfect trip from Florence," Susy reported to Brownell on May 29. "We got into Venice by moonlight between eleven and twelve at night. Last night we were all up late on the grand canal hearing the serenades."[21]

While in the city, Sam by chance encountered Annie Fields, Sarah Orne Jewett, and Robert Underwood Johnson, the associate editor of *Century*, "in front of one of the restaurants in the Piazza of his patron saint," St. Mark's. "The great humorist did most of the talking," Johnson recalled in his autobiography, with "the others only putting in a few words now and then by way of keeping him going." On his part, Sam noted that they "drank red cherry syrup & water in big glasses & told dreams & ghost stories till midnight." During this recess from travel Sam "gave an evening of readings from Browning for a few friends at Danieli's hotel" and Johnson commended in particular his "sympathetic interpretation" of "Andrea del Sarto." From the City of Bridges the Clemenses returned to Germany "by a tangled route" with "superb scenery" via Florence; Milan; Cadenabbia, on Lake Como; Lugano;

Lucerne; Basel; and Frankfurt. On June 6 they arrived at the Hotel Bellevue in the resort town of Bad Nauheim—which Sam promptly dubbed "Bath No-harm"—near Frankfurt. "These sprudel baths are just darlings," he tittered to Phelps. "I am taking them, not for physical deterioration but for moral decay. They take right hold. Ordinarily a single course removes the enamel from the conscience, but it has been thought best for me to double up." Sam wrote Clara that "two doctors have pronounced Mamma's case curable & *easily* curable. They say these baths will do it, & that these are the only baths in the world that can." Livy hoped to benefit from the regimen, too. "I am here taking the 'cure' trying to make myself a very strong woman for next Winter," she wrote a friend.[22]

Sam sent Verey packing about this time. A decade later, Sam's secretary Isabel Lyon remarked in her diary that "S. L. C. had to discharge him 3 times before he could get rid of him." Verey would resurface in New York in November 1895 with plans to marry a rich Cincinnati widow, or so he claimed. Verey had crossed the Atlantic in steerage, though he protested to a Gotham reporter that he had booked cheap passage "because I felt it was more in keeping with my humble mode of life and have been so comfortable that I am glad now I did not come first-class." By all appearances a vulgar fortune hunter, he bragged that his "courier days are over." He had met the widow while guiding her party on a tour of the Continent and "before her steamer put off" to return to the United States "we were betrothed." The two of them were "so 'simpatica,'" he insisted, "that life with us will be one golden dream." In the interview Verey expressed pity for "poor Twain," whose own fortunes had suffered. "He was better at writing than sightseeing, and no matter what he saw or did not see, I never knew what he would write about it." Verey's "golden dream" soon turned to ashes, however. By September 1902 he had returned to London where, according to the *Daily Mail*, he "had been resident . . . for some time." He had "fallen on evil days," though he averred he was "not so desperate as to demand public charity." Still, the British travel writer Robert Allbut solicited money for Verey and appealed to Sam to donate. "We hear a good deal about Verey these latter months from London," Sam observed. "He has descended to the grade of hog (he hadn't far to go) and is dying like one."[23]

In March 1892 Webster and Company issued a collection of seven of Sam's short writings entitled *Merry Tales* in its Fiction, Fact, and Fancy series. Peter Messent has observed that the book "has more signs of being hastily put together and carelessly planned than any other" of Sam's books. Sam did not christen the volume; five years later he urged the Harpers to "squelch that title & call the mess by some other name—almost *any* other name." The potboiler was designed for no other purpose than to improve the company's cash flow in a vain attempt to stave off bankruptcy. Incredibly, there was no comparable British edition. Unfortunately, it attracted lackluster sales and mostly mediocre reviews in, for example, Boston's *Mahogany Tree,* which claimed that the author had allowed "his natural wit to degenerate into the veriest buffoonery and horse-play"; the *San Francisco Chronicle,* noting that Sam "should exercise better judgment in making his selections for republication"; the *Overland Monthly,* which called it "amusing without being laughable"; the *Hartford Times,* which mentioned "some funny" sketches but "one or two not so droll"; and the *Boston Post,* which asserted that "none of the pieces are up to the author's best." The *Cultivator & Country Gentleman,* while conceding that "in excellence they vary," singled out the "ridiculous but unsavory" tale "The Invalid's Story" for special condemnation. Whereas the *Boston Transcript* declared there was "nothing in the language funnier," the *Atlantic Monthly* indicated that "the fun is at times stupendous," the *Kansas City Times* pronounced "all of them good," and its rival the *Kansas City Star* declared that "some of these stories are merely tiresome, others are depressing, not one is good cause for merriment." The Boston *Literary World* complained that "if one likes this sort of humor, this is just the sort he will like" and revived an old charge: that "Mr. Clemens is nothing if not irreverent of the most sacred things in human life."[24]

Meanwhile, the McClure syndicate had serialized *The American Claimant* between January 3 and March 30, 1892, in dozens of American papers, including the New York *Sun, Chicago Inter Ocean, Charleston News, Kansas City Times, Omaha World-Herald, Milwaukee Sentinel, Pittsburgh Dispatch, Indianapolis News, Philadelphia Inquirer, St. Louis Republic, San Francisco Examiner, Helena Independent-Record, Buffalo Courier, Boston Globe,* New Orleans *Times-Democrat, Cincinnati Commercial Gazette,* and *Detroit Journal.* It also ran in Australia in the *Melbourne Age, Adelaide Observer, Sydney Evening News,* in New Zealand in the *Auckland Star,* and in the United Kingdom in *Idler* between February 1892 and June 1893. Ironically, though perhaps the poorest of Sam's novels, *The American Claimant* in syndication enjoyed the widest circulation of any of them. Webster and Company issued it in hardcover with illustrations in mid-August 1892, though as in the case of *Merry Tales,* sales were disappointing and reviews mixed. In fact, virtually no reviews of the novel appeared in the American press because Hall apparently mismanaged the release and mailed out no review copies. The only known notice was printed in the *San Francisco Chronicle* and it was hostile, deeming that the author's name was "more likely to attract attention" than "the intrinsic merit of the book."[25]

The British edition of *The American Claimant*, issued by Chatto & Windus in mid-September 1892, months before the completion of its serialization in *Idler*, fared better—but not by much. At least it was not ignored by the critics, though most of them panned it. Whereas the London *Review of Reviews* asserted that "Mr. Clemens' hand has not lost its cunning," for example, the *London Morning Leader* dissented: "Mr. Clemens' hand has lost its cunning." The *Scotsman* ("full of fresh fun") and the London *Literary World* ("some excellent good fooling") detected some glimmers of light, but they were among the exceptions. The *Manchester Guardian* ("we have seen no book of his before which had so small an allowance of [drollery] to so large an allowance of aimless narrative"), London *Bookman* ("wearisome and fatuous, occasionally something worse"), *Glasgow Herald* ("slightly tedious"), *Athenaeum* ("only rather amusing"), *Leeds Mercury* ("little in the book that is in any sense remarkable"), London *Morning Post* ("not one of Mark Twain's best works"), and London *World* (the author "was not particularly amusing even when he was new") were no less equivocal. Edward Bok pronounced the death sentence of the novel in his syndicated column: *The American Claimant* "was a dire failure," though Sam sold serial rights to the story for $12,000. But the papers that printed it "were not so fortunate." Bok attributed the failure of the novel to Sam's "unwise revival of the character of Mulberry Sellers." The crackpot investor in *The Gilded Age* (1873) became a crackpot inventor in *The American Claimant*. "When the impractical and flighty Colonel first stepped out of the pages of 'The Gilded Age' he was a fresh character and at once took hold of the reading public. . . . But there he should have been allowed to remain, for his creator to rehabilitate him in a new story was a grievous mistake," Bok noted.[26]

Bret Harte alluded to the sales failure of these potboilers in his story "An Ingénue of the Sierras" (1893) in a way so coded that perhaps almost no one except Sam would have recognized the slur. Harte's tale features a notorious road agent who poses as a bill collector named Charley Byng, mirroring the alias (Carl Byng) under which Sam had allegedly masqueraded in writing the poem "Three Aces" (1870). Even the mustachioed villain's real name, Martinez, suggests Mark Twain—the sobriquets share six letters in sequence. The Martinez gang is "about played out," not "from want of a job now and then but from the difficulty of disposing of the results of their work."[27] In the shorthand of the story, that is, Martinez—like Sam—could no longer fence his swag.

Soon after the Clemens clan settled in Bad Nauheim, a pair of "bath physicians" determined that Livy had "no heart disease, but has only weakness of the heart-muscles & will soon be sound & well again. That was worth going to Europe to find out," Sam notified his brother Orion. The doctors prescribed the continued use of laudanum and analgesics, and although Livy was also diagnosed with erysipelas, a skin infection, Sam was optimistic about her eventual recovery—so optimistic that he chose to leave Livy and Jean at the spa, Clara back at Miss Willard's School in Berlin, and Susy and Susan Crane "prowling around Switzerland" while he returned to the United States on business. As Livy wrote Grace King, "Our affairs over there are in such a very unfortunate position, that he is obliged to go back and try to get things in a better condition." The Paige typesetter remained an albatross around Sam's neck, though Livy assured King that "Mr Clemens has great faith in the machine and believes in time it will take us out of our difficulties."[28]

On June 14, 1892, Sam sailed from Bremen on the North German Lloyd steamship *Havel*—"the delightfulest ship I was ever in"—and upon arriving in New York on June 22 he registered at the Union League Club. He spent June 24–25 in Hartford on business; the next two days in Elmira, New York, visiting friends; and the two days after that in Chicago, where he registered at the Metropole Hotel under a pseudonym. James Paige had moved his operation, including the only working prototype of the typesetter, from Hartford to the Windy City the previous March at the urging of a group of investors incorporated as the Connecticut Company. Paige professed to have received orders for four thousand machines priced at $20,000 apiece and announced that he would transfer to Chicago the skilled employees who worked on the project in Hartford. No collaborating evidence exists for either claim. Still, the venture capitalists hoped to showcase the machine at the Chicago World's Fair, or World's Columbian Exposition, the next year and were attempting to build a factory in which to manufacture it. While Sam no longer subsidized its development, he was still entitled to royalties on future sales of the machine. While in the city, he snubbed the inventor, whom he suspected was conning the investors. As Sam confided to his notebook, "Nothing *but* a Co[mpany] can manufacture & P[aige] is determined there never shall be one, except on his own terms—& they will never be granted." But his concerns were calmed by his investigation, and on July 1 he returned to New York, where he dined with the once and future president Grover Cleveland, the editorial cartoonist Thomas Nast, General William Tecumseh Sherman, and the journalist John Russell Young.[29]

On July 5 Sam embarked from New York aboard the *Lahn* to return to Bremen. Among his fellow passengers were fifteen Yale University students, including Howell Cheney, scion of a wealthy Hartford family; Pierre Jay, who would become the first chairman of the Federal Reserve Bank of New

York in 1913; Lee McClung, a future treasurer of the United States who captained the undefeated Yale football team in 1891 and who was later inducted into the College Football Hall of Fame; and Charles B. Sears, a future New York Supreme Court justice who would preside at one of the Nuremburg war crimes trials in 1947. At sea Sam "made merry" in the entertainments and "told some of his most extraordinary stories," which resulted in his mock arrest and trial before a jury of Yalies on a charge of "inordinate and unscientific lying" on July 14. Sam mounted an insanity defense, claiming he "had no recollection of ever having written anything about a lineup frog," and the ship physicians testified "that in all their experience they had never met a man who talked so irrationally as Mark Twain did." Nevertheless, Sam was found guilty and sentenced to read aloud from his own works in the ship's saloon every evening for the duration of the voyage. According to a fellow passenger, he threw himself upon the mercy of the court and begged: "Anything but that! Hang me if you will, but do not compel me to read my own works. That is a slow and horrible death!" Like a good sport, he "served his sentence faithfully" for three hours every night, and the entertainment raised about $600 for the Seaman's Fund. Still, as he wrote from Bad Nauheim on July 18, he "came away thoroughly disgusted" with the fruitlessness of his "flying visit."[30]

Apart from the six travel letters he promised to the McClure syndicate, Sam undertook no new writing projects during the first months of his European exile. "I do not expect to be able to write any literature this year," he notified his partner Fred Hall. "The moment I take up a pen my rheumatism returns." In August 1891 he had proposed that Hall reprint the McClure letters in a cheap pamphlet of thirty-five or forty thousand words under the title "Recent European Glimpses," but even this plan fell through. Despite their attempts to "scrimp & economise," Sam still needed to earn about $20,000 (about $580,000 in modern dollars) a year to support his family in the style to which they had become accustomed. Within a month of his return to Bad Nauheim, no longer tortured by the rheumatism in his right arm, he finally returned to work. In fact, during the summer of 1892, as Tom Quirk observes, Sam composed nine essays and five sketches and began two novels. Among the stories was "The £1,000,000 Bank Note," a parable about the liquidity crisis and the risk of fiat currency or greenbacks unsecured by specie. He likewise puttered on a "howling farce" about a pair of conjoined or "conglomerate" twins similar to his early sketch "Personal Habits of the Siamese Twins" (1869), inspired in this case not by Chang and Eng Bunker but by Giovanni and Giacomo Tocci, whose picture he had seen in a recent issue of *Scientific American.*

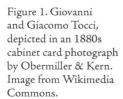

Figure 1. Giovanni and Giacomo Tocci, depicted in an 1880s cabinet card photograph by Obermiller & Kern. Image from Wikimedia Commons.

Unlike the Bunkers, who were joined at the abdomen and each of whom had four limbs, the Toccis were joined at the waist and together had four arms and two legs. As Sam originally conceived the tale, the Capello twins exhibit diametrically opposite traits: the fair Angelo (angel) is a teetotaler, sings tenor, and is a Methodist in religion and a Whig in politics; the brunette Luigi (Lucifer) is a habitual drunk, sings bass, and is a Free-Thinker and a Democrat. In his rough notes for the story, they also play four-handed piano, "sing duets & do Romeo & Juliet—balcony scene—one lays head on other's shoulder & they do a languishing waltz—sailor's hornpipe, both pulling on imaginary ropes." Sam laid this story aside in early August, however, after Mary Mapes Dodge, editor of the children's magazine *St. Nicholas* and author of *Hans Brinker; or, The Silver Skates* (1865), offered him $5,000 for serial rights to a fifty-thousand-word juvenile tale. In a note to Hall on August 10, Sam explained that he had "dropped" the earlier project,

> because I saw a more effective way of using the main episode—to wit: by telling it through the lips of Huck Finn. So I have started Huck Finn and Tom Sawyer (still 15 years old) and their friend the freed slave Jim around the world in a stray *balloon* . . . and somewhere after the end of that great voyage he will work in the said episode and then nobody will suspect that a whole book has been written and the globe circumnavigated merely to get that episode in an effective (and at the same time apparently *unintentional*) way. I have written 12,000 words of this narrative, and find that the humor flows as easily as the adventures and surprises—so I shall go along and make a book of from 50,000 to 100,000 words. It is a story for boys, of course, & I think will interest any boy between 8 years and 80.

Initially given the working title "Huck Finn in Africa," and soon retitled "New Adventures of Huckleberry Finn" and then "Huckleberry Finn & Tom Sawyer Abroad," and finally published as *Tom Sawyer Abroad* (1894), the sequel is set again in a fantasy world where fishhooks and marbles are coin of the realm. It begins with the return of Huck, Tom, and Jim to St. Petersburg at the end of *Huckleberry Finn*. In lieu of a raft drifting "free and easy" down the Mississippi River to Arkansas, however, they embark on a "breezy and pleasant" balloon trip from St. Louis across the Atlantic to desert Africa—a narrative arc reminiscent of Jules Verne's *Five Weeks in a Balloon* (1863).[31]

More to the point, Sam took the opportunity in the novella to satirize imperialism, colonialism, and protective tariffs. Tom yearns to launch a "crusade" to recapture the Holy Land from the paynim, or Arabs. "Our folks, our Jews and Christians, . . . made it holy, and so they haven't any business to be there defiling it. . . . We ought to march against them and take it away from them." He approves the seizure of western land formalized by the Treaty of Guadalupe Hidalgo ("we've took California away from the Mexicans"). Similarly, Tom is miffed that foreigners fail to apologize "for insulting the [American] flag." Huck asks "if countries always apologized when they had done wrong," and Tom answers, "Yes; the little ones does." Louis J. Budd suggests that this episode alludes to a squabble in 1891 between Chile and the United States "over the mobbing of some American sailors." After Tom and Huck decide to haul back some Sahara sand to sell on the souvenir market because "they can't raise Sahara sand in America," Tom has second thoughts and declares they needed to abandon the plan "on account of the [import] duties." According to Budd, this mockery of "protection" was the comment the whole book had been rewritten to include in an "effective (and at the same time apparently unintentional) way." Certainly Sam was always a fierce opponent of tariffs; as he wrote in his notebook in 1895, "The man that invented protection belongs in hell."[32]

He completed forty thousand words on the story in a month before ending it abruptly, but he insisted to Hall that the manuscript be offered to Dodge anyway. *Caveat emptor.* "If Mrs. Dodge wants it," Sam noted, "let her have it. It falls nearly 10,000 words short of what she wanted for $5,000; but if she isn't willing to pay $5,000, let her pay $4,000. It is finished, and doesn't need another finish. . . . I tried to leave the improprieties all out; if I didn't, Mrs. Dodge can scissor them out." At the time he considered *Tom Sawyer Abroad* potentially the first in a line of pulp juvenile novels akin to the Frank Merriwell or Bobbsey Twins tales. He simply needed to add "'Africa,' 'England,' 'Germany,' etc., to the title pages of each successive volume in the series. It is easy work, & I enjoy it."[33]

Unfortunately, Dodge and her minions used pruning shears rather than sewing scissors on the story prior to serializing it. They "modified or completely omitted" references "to death, perspiration, profanity, and religion" and attempted "to improve my spelling and punctuation," Sam complained. Nor did the bowdlerization end there. Dan Beard, whose illustrations for the serial Sam considered "mighty good," reported that the *St. Nicholas* editor thought "it was excessively coarse and vulgar to depict" the characters "with *bare feet*" and so Beard was "asked to cover their nakedness with shoes." In the end, Dodge's Huck is a much more bourgeois figure than Sam's Huck, and Jim is transformed by blue pencil into a minstrel show stereotype, according to Guy Cardwell. Sam, of course, was dismayed by the liberties taken with his text and drew the line at tampering with it. "When Mark read the proof," Beard remembered, "he was exceedingly wroth and, entering the sanctum sanctorum, the holy of holies, or the editorial department of *St. Nicholas,* he shocked the gentle creatures and terrified the associate editors by exclaiming, 'Any editor to whom I submit my manuscripts has an undisputed right to delete anything to which he objects but'—and his brows knit as he cried—'God Almighty Himself has no right to put words in my mouth that I never used!'" Or as Sam told the journalist Frank Marshall White, he would rather editors "put street sweepings" in his manuscripts—this when horse-drawn vehicles were the standard mode of urban transportation—than "put words into my mouth." Sam's stenographer, Mary Louise Howden, confessed years later that she "was never allowed to add so much as a comma" to his dictation.[34]

Sam's interlude in Germany during these weeks was noteworthy, too, for the celebrities he met. He crossed paths with Oscar Wilde, resplendent in "a suit of soft-brown with a pale pink flowered vest, a blue necktie and some strange picturesque white flower in his button hole" in Bad Nauheim, and on a day-trip to Homburg he and Susy dined in a small group with the popular novelist Marie Corelli, though the encounter was unpleasant. As Sam recalled years later, he "took a dislike to her at once, a dislike which expanded and hardened with each successive dinner course until when we parted at last, the original mere dislike had grown into a very strong aversion." In late August, while Joe and Harmony Twichell were visiting the Clemens clan, Sam and Joe railed to Homburg, some twenty miles from Bad Nauheim, where by chance Sam renewed his acquaintance with Sir Edward Malet, the British ambassador to Germany, who in turn introduced him to the Prince of Wales, later King Edward VII. The prince was "one of the heartiest & pleasantest Englishman I have ever seen, absolutely un-English in his quickness in detecting carefully concealed humor," Sam jotted in his notebook, "& he was a wholly unembarrassing man & swept away stiffness & restraint with admirable art." On his part, Twichell concurred: "The meeting was a most cordial one on both sides, and presently the Prince took Mark Twain's arm and the two marched up and down, talking earnestly together, the Prince, solid, erect, and soldier-like, Clemens weaving along in his curious, swinging gait in a full tide of talk, and brandishing a sun-umbrella of the most scandalous description." Four days later Sam dined at the Kursaal with the prince and five other men, including Chauncey Depew and the British comic actor J. L. Toole. For two hours they enjoyed "much talk, many yarns, everything sociable, pleasant, no formality."[35]

On September 10 the family finally left for Italy, though they dallied en route so that Livy could rest—with layovers in Frankfurt, Basel, Lucerne, Milan, and Bologna before arriving in Florence on the September 24. As Sam kidded Susan Crane, who had returned to the United States the month before, "Next year we will walk." Before they moved into the Villa Viviani, Janet Ross, the daughter of Sir Alexander Duff-Gordon and Lady Duff-Gordon, hired servants and, as Sam reported, "had the house scoured from cellar to roof, the curtains washed & put up, all beds pulled to pieces, beaten, washed & put together again, & beguiled the Marchese into putting a big porcelain stove in the vast central hall." On her part, Ross recalled in her autobiography that "the Clemens family were very pleasant neighbours. He used to drop in at all hours" and frequented the salon at her home, the Villa di Poggio Gherardo, where according to local legend Giovanni Boccaccio composed the *Decameron*. Ross recalled that on at least one occasion Sam sat at her piano and sang black spirituals: "Without much voice and with little or no knowledge of music (he played the bass notes with one finger) he moved us all in a wonderful way." Lina Duff-Gordon, Ross's eighteen-year-old niece, likewise reported that Sam visited "at all hours of the day, generally entirely ignorant of what he has come to ask until he pulls out a large notebook."[36]

Sam reveled in his temporary home in the hills above the city. It was "a plain, square building, like a box," two stories tall and surrounded by vineyards and olive orchards, pine and fig trees. A veritable fortress, and centuries old, its main walls were "about 3 feet thick. I have several times tried to count the rooms of the house, but the irregularities baffle me. There seem to be 28. There are plenty of windows & worlds of sunlight." The salon at the center of the house was "a spacious & lofty vacuum" that extended "through both stories & its roof." From the garden Sam could view a panorama of the city, "pink & gray & brown, with the ruddy, huge dome of the cathedral dominating its center like a captive balloon, & flanked on the right by the small bulb of the Medici chapel & on the left by the airy tower of the Palazzo Vecchio; all around the horizon is a billowy rim of lofty blue hills, snowed white with innumerable villas." The "most conspicuous towers & domes down in the city," he wrote Susan Crane, "look today just as they looked when Boccaccio & Dante used to contemplate them from this hillock five & six hundred years ago." He thought it

> the fairest picture on our planet, the most enchanting to look upon, the most satisfying to the eye & the spirit. To see the sun sink down, drowned in his pink & purple & golden floods, & overwhelm Florence with tides of color that make all the sharp lines dim & faint & turn the solid city into a city of dreams is a sight to stir the coldest nature & make a sympathetic one drunk with ecstasy.

"They are the most superlatively magnificent sunsets ever dreamed of," he added in his diary. "I don't believe they have finer ones in hell." As he wrote Susan Crane a month after their arrival, "No view that I am acquainted with in the world is at all comparable to this for delicacy, charm, exquisiteness, dainty coloring, & bewildering rapidity of change. It keeps a person drunk with pleasure all the time. Sometimes Florence ceases to be substantial, & becomes just a faint soft dream, with domes & towers of air." More to the point, he rejoiced that Livy was "progressing admirably" in the temperate climate, noting, "This is just the place for her." In all, as Susy wrote at the time, "Father is very happy here. He is devoted to the villa and the quiet and his writing. All things considered the villa seems the best living arrangement we have found since leaving our beloved home in America."[37]

Though Sam vowed after they were settled in the villa that he planned to live in "absolute seclusion here—a hermit life," the Clemenses were soon as socially active as ever. Jean averred that some or all of the family "once a day and sometimes twice" rode into Florence on one of the horsecars that left the nearby village of Ponte a Mensola every half hour. Sam toured the Pitti Palace at least once and, much as he had reviled Leonardo da Vinci's *The Last Supper* and other paintings of the Old Masters in *The Innocents Abroad* (1869), he disputed the genius of Raphael's *Madonna della seggiola* in his notebook: "Madonna, child & child St. John. *Three* children, for the Madonna is a physically developed woman 9 years old. St John is wretchedly drawn. The whole picture is poor. With Raphael's name removed it would be dear at $1.50." Among their foreign guests were Grace King and her sister Nan, who visited for several weeks that fall. King remembered that "the morning excursions into Florence became a rule" and that, in particular, "Mrs. Browning's house and her tomb in the Protestant cemetery awakened in us the usual sentimental outbursts of feeling." In late October, Sam noted that "late in the afternoons friends come out from the city & drink tea in the open air & tell what is happening in the world." He and his oldest daughter received so many invitations from others "that for Susy's sake" and despite "doctor's orders," Livy opened the Villa Viviani to receive people on Wednesday afternoons. Among the other Americans in Florence who dined with Sam that winter were the financier Robert Fulton Cutting, Laurence Hutton, and William James, a philosopher and the brother of novelist Henry James. In a note to his Harvard University colleague Josiah Royce on December 18, James remarked, "Mark Twain is here for the winter in a villa outside the town, hard at work writing something or other. I have seen him a couple of times—a fine, soft-fibred little fellow with the perversest twang and drawl, but very human and good. I should think that one might grow very fond of him and wish he'd come and live in Cambridge."[38]

To be sure, the family's life was not all sweetness and light during this period. Jean began to exhibit the erratic behavior symptomatic of the epilepsy she would suffer as an adult. In January 1893 wild child Clara was reproached by her father for "an offence against propriety" by mingling with forty German officers without other women present at a dinner hosted by the Versens in Berlin. He reprimanded her for failing to "leave the room the moment you found yourself the only representative of your sex in it." Their relations were so strained that Mary Willard, the founder of Clara's private school, hastened to assure Sam that his daughter "never goes out unattended, to any place of amusement, or on any trivial errand." But, as if in retaliation for his scolding, Clara later made it a point to announce publicly that her father's books bored her: "I haven't read half he's written . . . and what I have read didn't interest me in the least." While living in Florence, moreover, Clara once attracted the attention of young men at a restaurant and Sam afterward pruned the plastic fruit from her hat—a figurative act of neutering—because he believed it too alluring.[39]

The greatest drawback by far to the Clemenses' otherwise idyllic life in the hills above Florence was totally unexpected: Susy hated living there. Sam and Livy's oldest daughter, idolized by her parents and idealized in the lore about the family, was in fact a spoiled snob. In Berlin she had attended a "court ball, a most brilliant function," in a silk dress sewn for her "by a great modiste," but she had not enjoyed the function. It had bored her, in fact. She "loathed the memory of it," according to Grace King, and Livy allowed that Susy thought Berlin "too gray." Her manner at the Villa Viviani was no less bratty. She condescended to the domestic staff of five ("the unselfishness of good servants is so wonderful, so beautiful, so pitiful, somehow") and remained aloof from the rest of the family and their guests. As King remembered, Susy "dwelt apart from us and joined us for the drive into Florence but seldom." Susy chafed under the strain of "the family discipline," she admitted to Clara. "I have been to the usual number of teas this week," she once whined, "and as usual was almost always the only young person present. Florence society consists of old people's teas. It's too funny! No dances, no lunches, no dinners—just teas!" Her gripe ironically echoes the lament of Henry James's overindulged ingenue Daisy Miller ("The only thing I don't like . . . is the society. There isn't any society; or, if there is, I don't know where it keeps itself. Do you? I suppose there is some society somewhere, but I haven't seen anything of it"). Though Susy's father was invited to dinners, "I am almost never included." Certainly she missed her friends in the United States, especially Louise Brownell. But she exaggerated her grievances against the birthplace of the Renaissance, as when she wrote Clara in April 1893 that she had "decided that Florence is the most uninteresting tiresome city on the face of the earth!" Her boredom—she once referred to "that faithful friend of mine, the ennui"—was little more than adolescent affectation. In fact, she studied French with an Italian tutor and took singing lessons in the city, though she denigrated her own talent. She also frequented "the theatre & the opera," as her father remarked to Mary Mason Fairbanks, including a performance of Pietro Mascagni's *Cavalleria rusticana,* which helped "to ease the dulness of eternal study." She befriended Lina Duff-Gordon and, like her father, frequented the Ross home, where she was introduced to the British writer Vernon Lee (aka Violet Paget) in early November 1892. As in Berlin, Susy attended "the social event of the season—the ball of the Princess Corsini" at the Palazzo Corsini. "The dressing was most beautiful and the old palace magnificent" and she exhibited a "deep obeisance to the princess." In February 1893, "out at dinner" with "Lina and papa," she met the famous actor Tommaso Salvini, who was "so courtly so gentle so almost caressing in his manner and at the same time so large and dignified and powerful" that she felt she was "sitting near someone very *great*"—and she was not referring to her father. She relished the visit of Grace King, "whose breadth and enthusiasm and high ideals for life & art are such an inspiration," she wrote Brownell. "Exquisitely pretty," according to King, Susy was also smitten with the married Count de Calry, with whom she often flirted at gatherings in Florence (though she never mentioned him in any of her letters to Brownell). Much as Daisy Miller regards the fortune-hunting *cavaliere* Giovanelli in superlatives ("he's the handsomest man in the world" and "she thinks him the finest gentleman in the world"), Susy insisted the count was "altogether the most fascinating person I have met in Europe." From Berlin, Clara commiserated with her sister: "You poor thing: It must be hard! It's funny I can't remember even what it feels like to be gone on a man, & I hope I never shall be again."[40] Nothing came of Susy's crush.

If the Paige typesetter was an albatross, Webster and Company was a millstone around Sam's neck. In 1891 he plowed all the profit from his own books back into the business to help it remain afloat, even though by early 1893 the subscribers to the *Library of American Literature* still owed the firm some $62,000 in uncollected payments. The *Library* was less a cash cow than a cash-eating cow and, worse yet, the editor E. C. Stedman had requested an increase in his royalties. "By your magnificent management & by my sacrifices of money together with grinding & painful economies on the part of my family," Sam advised Hall, Stedman's *Library* "has been saved." But, he whined, had Stedman "ever come forward & said, 'You are in deep waters—let me help what I can—stop my royalties & take them as a loan for a while'"? On the contrary, "he has contributed nothing but criticism & dissatisfaction. . . . The man has no bowels," the ostensible seat of sympathy, and "his inside is upholstered with gas pipe." If their agents could sell a thousand sets per month, Sam allowed, the company cash flow would improve and, continuing the scatological metaphor, "our financial bowels would soon begin to move." But such a prospect was unlikely, so Sam struck on an alternative: to entice Andrew Carnegie, the second-richest man in America, his friend and a fellow member of the Lotos and Authors' Clubs, to invest in the company or at least to subsidize production of the *Library* until it could turn a profit. "I think that the association with us of someone of great name and with capital would give our business a prodigious impetus," he explained, and he sent Hall a letter of introduction to present to Carnegie.

After they became acquainted Hall could ask the industrialist "to lend us money enough at 6 or 8 per cent to run the *L. A. L.* up to 1000 sets per month—not a heavy sum, but only enough per month to cover the necessities of the month. Show him that the possibilities are 2,500 sets a month, & that the history of the book shows that the collections are as sure as they are slow, & not attended by loss." Like the best laid plans of mice and men, the scheme fell through. Just as he had refused to invest in the typesetter, Carnegie declined to gamble on the publishing company. Instead he offered Sam this financial advice: "Put all your eggs in one basket and then watch that basket"—a maxim Sam quoted without attribution in his next novel, *The Tragedy of Pudd'nhead Wilson* (1893).[41]

CHAPTER 2

Identifying Mark

The symbol of the race ought to be a human being carrying an ax, for every human being has one concealed about him somewhere, and is always seeking the opportunity to grind it.

—Mark Twain, quoted in Albert Bigelow Paine, *Mark Twain: A Biography*

UNDER SERENE CIRCUMSTANCES, Samuel Clemens resumed work in the fall of 1892 on "Those Extraordinary Twins," the "extravagantly fantastic little story with this freak of nature for hero—or heroes" he had begun over the summer in Bad Nauheim, Germany. He had "laid it aside to ferment while I wrote 'Tom Sawyer Abroad,' but I took it up again on a little different plan lately, and it is swimming along satisfactorily now," he wrote Fred Hall in early September 1892. From all indications, including Sam's own testimony, however, he had a "hard time with that tale, because it changed itself from a farce to a tragedy while I was going along with it,—a most embarrassing circumstance." He was victimized by the improvisational method of composition that had served him so well in the past. He eventually realized that the manuscript contained "not one story but two stories tangled together"—one about the Italian twins and the other a domestic romance featuring a fair-haired wastrel named Tom Driscoll and the silly "light-weight heroine" Rowena Cooper—that "obstructed and interrupted each other at every turn and created no end of confusion and annoyance. I could not offer the book for publication, for I was afraid it would unseat the reader's reason." He finished a sixty-thousand-word draft of this monstrosity at the Villa Viviani on December 10 and reported to Fred Hall two days later that the "last third of it suits me to a dot. I begin, today, to entirely re-cast & re-write the first two-thirds—new plan, with two minor characters made very prominent, one major character cropped out, & the Twins subordinated to a minor but not insignificant place. *The* minor character will now become the chiefest" and "I will name the story after him." Or as he later explained, "I pulled one of the stories out by the roots, and left the other one—a kind of literary Cæsarean operation." But he was "a butcher rather than a surgeon in performing" this operation, according to Robert A. Wiggins. The domestic romance had morphed into a hybrid, a race novel complicated by a murder mystery starring the detective Pudd'nhead Wilson. On February 3, 1893 Sam alerted Hall that his 82,500-word narrative was "type-written and ready for print" but he was "in a quandary. Give me a lift out of it. I will mail the book to you and get you to examine it and see if it is good or if it is bad."[1]

Even Hall, though not a professional editor, concluded the manuscript was not ready for prime time. It contained too many characters, too many subplots, and incongruities aplenty. For one thing, as Hershel Parker notes, "the surviving vestiges" of the role of conjoined twins was "a distracting embarrassment." After all, how could twins who share both a common heredity and a common environment (so long as they are bound together by a ligature of flesh) exhibit such diverse traits? The farcical elements of the convoluted plot warred with the race narrative of the changelings, Tom Driscoll and Valet de Chambre (named for a personal servant). Though they are born of different parents and one is a white aristocrat and the other a slave "by a fiction of law and custom," they are another set of twins in all but name, so identical in physical appearance they are swapped in their cradles. Over the next six months Sam "tooth-combed" the manuscript again. As he wrote Hall on July 30, he "pulled the twins apart and made two individuals of them." The Capellos were "mere flitting shadows now." The farce had been elided and "the whole story" now "centered on the murder and the trial" featuring three major characters: detective Pudd'nhead, murderer and masked slave Tom Driscoll, and his mother Roxy, the most eroticized woman character in Sam's oeuvre. The length had been cut from about eighty-one thousand words to fifty-eight thousand by deleting "everything that delayed the march of the story—even the description of a Mississippi steamboat." This revision was "a success! Even Mrs. Clemens, the most difficult of critics, confesses it, & without reserves or qualifications," Sam crowed to Hall. Years later he told a gaggle of reporters, "I rewrote one of my books three times and each time it was a different book. I had filled in and filled in until the original book wasn't there. It had evaporated through the blanks, and I had an entirely new book."[2]

But there are still anomalies in the text, as Philip Cohen, Parker, and others have shown. For one, Pudd'nhead Wilson solves the murder mystery, which is set in small-town antebellum Missouri, by identifying the killer by his fingerprints. But Francis Galton published his book proposing that such "natal autographs" offered "a means of differentiating a man from his fellows" in 1892, after Sam began to write the novel and long after the novel is set temporally. Galton's argument "changed the whole plot & plan of my book," Sam later admitted. Despite the incongruity—like introducing a prop telephone into a William Shakespeare tragedy—the gimmick solution to the mystery was "virgin ground" for his readers: "absolutely *fresh*, and mighty curious & interesting to everybody."[3]

In the course of converting the farce into the murder mystery fingering Tom, Sam introduced another, even more serious, complication that has puzzled generations of readers. He seemed to offer a racist explanation for Tom's refusal to fight a duel with Luigi Capello. Raised in a privileged, old Virginian family, Tom ought to have welcomed the opportunity to defend his honor. Instead, he behaves like a downtrodden inferior; for example, "The 'nigger' in him went shrinking and skulking here and there and yonder." In a controversial passage Sam deleted in revision this explanation seems still more explicit: "Why was he a coward? It was the 'nigger' in him. The nigger *blood?* Yes, the nigger blood degraded from original courage to cowardice by decades and generations of insult and outrage inflicted in circumstances which forbade reprisals, and made mute and meek endurance the only refuge and defence." Critics have tried to argue away the apparent bigotry of such statements in a variety of ways: that they should be read ironically, like the racist rant of Pap Finn about the "mulatter" college professor in *Huck Finn;* or that they are Tom's masochistic thoughts just after he has learned Roxy is his mother and thus are triggered by his new race consciousness; or that Sam was simply confused and contradicted his long-held belief that "training is everything." As Robert Moss puts it, "Far from clearing up the question of heredity versus environment, these passages serve only to muddy the waters." Or as Barry Wood suggests, perhaps Sam deliberately obfuscated: "Any definitive explanation for [Tom's] moral corruption is out of reach" and "Twain appears to have intended that it remain so."[4]

From Sam's Lamarckian perspective, however, heredity versus environment was a false binary. In his view, heredity or race *was* the product of training or environmentally acquired traits transmitted over many generations. The concept of race was thus inseparable from training or, as Anne Wigger notes, the inherent cruelty of race-slavery "acting on generations of slaves and slaveowners is the corrupting force in Tom's nature." The Old Man in Sam's so-called bible, *What Is Man?* (1906), defines *instinct* as "inherited habit," a notion akin to racial or genetic memory. For example, according to Jean Baptiste de Lamarck, a woman who learns to play the piano prior to pregnancy is more likely to bear a child who is musically gifted than is a mother without musical training. "If you were buying babies, investing in young human stock as you would in colts or calves, for the value of the beast, a sturdy English baby would be worth more than an equally vigorous young Fuegian," Charlotte Perkins Gilman once asserted. "With the same training and care, you could develop higher faculties in the English specimen than in the Fuegian specimen because it was better bred." Sam's belief in the transmission of acquired characteristics permitted him to subscribe to a theory of racial degradation that was, at bottom, racially biased. Native Americans and African Americans had suffered so many "decades and generations of insult and outrage" that they had become debased stock. Blood always tells, especially if it contains a drop of black, as in the case of the usurper Tom Driscoll. Roxy's explanation for her son's cowardice and criminality—"It'd de nigger in you"—is usually regarded as another instance of Sam's irony, but the comment should not be read at all ironically. Indeed, Roxy may be said to speak for the author. Black people *were* inferior, he thought, based on his Lamarckian perspective, because they had been brutalized over the centuries by slavery and other forms of oppression until, like the offspring of feral animals, they were born wild. "The negroes at present are merely freed slaves, and you can't get rid of the effects of slavery in one or even two generations," he rationalized. Despite his undoubted nineteenth-century racial progressivism, Samuel Clemens believed in racial hierarchies, though he did not affirm the native or innate inferiority of any people because their degraded condition could be ameliorated. His opinions rationalized and justified racial uplift, not discrimination. "We have given the negro the vote," he told an interviewer, "and he must keep it."[5]

A jumble of competing narratives, each with its own purpose, *Pudd'nhead Wilson* (1894) fairly qualifies as a *mélange des genres*. It is a murder mystery, with Wilson in the role of detective, though Sam admitted to his wife Olivia that he had "never thought of Pudd'nhead as a *character*, but only as a piece of machinery," not even a deus ex machina but simply a *machina* in a formula fiction—"a button or a crank or a lever, with a useful function to perform in a machine, but with no dignity above that."[6]

It is also a passing novel, set entirely in slave territory before the Civil War. Sometime in the late 1880s, probably after writing *Huck Finn*, Sam outlined a novel, never completed, with the working title "Man with Negro Blood." The protagonist, a young man who by ancestry is one-sixteenth black, resolves to pass as white after realizing that "even the best educated negro is at a disadvantage, besides being always insulted." The plot obviously anticipated the welter of fin de siècle passing novels published at the nadir of race relations in the United States that includes W. D. Howells's *An Imperative Duty* (1891) and Frances E. W. Harper's *Iola Leroy* (1892). *Pudd'nhead Wilson* is set in the village of Dawson's Landing which, like St. Petersburg and Bricksville in *Tom Sawyer* and *Huck Finn* and even Camelot in *A Connecticut Yankee*, is modeled on Sam's actual hometown, though located "half a day's journey below St. Louis," a full day's journey downriver from the actual Hannibal. As a result, Leslie Fiedler contends, Dawson's Landing seems like "a *Southern* town." The story is comparable in many respects to the antislavery novel *Uncle Tom's Cabin*, the best-selling American novel of the nineteenth century by Sam's former Hartford neighbor Harriet Beecher Stowe. Leland Krauth observes that the popularity of *Uncle Tom's Cabin* "became a benchmark for [Sam's] own books." As early as December 1869 he had compared the sales of *The Innocents Abroad* (1869) and *Uncle Tom's Cabin* in a letter to Livy. In February 1874 he again compared the sales of *The Gilded Age* (1873) to those of Stowe's novel in a note to Dr. John Brown. In August 1880 he was reportedly collaborating with Stowe in a new dramatization of *Uncle Tom's Cabin* scheduled for production in New York the next month, though the play never appeared. Though Fiedler once speculated that it was "improbable" that Sam "ever read *Uncle Tom's Cabin*," in May 1891, seventeen months before beginning to convert his farce about the conjoined twins into a narrative about race, Sam twice mentioned the novel in his notebook.[7]

Moreover, he borrowed racial tropes and plot incidents for *Pudd'nhead Wilson* from the earlier novel, in particular modeling the character of Roxy upon Stowe's "tragic mullata" Cassy. As Kenneth S. Lynn has argued, Roxy's "personality comes too close to that of Cassy in *Uncle Tom's Cabin* to be mere coincidence." A slave mother in chapter 12 of Stowe's tract drowns her child and takes her own life rather than allow him to be sold down the river, a passage to the Deep South tantamount to a death sentence, and Cassy similarly smothers her son to save him from a life of bondage. Roxy's fear that her son may suffer the same fate becomes the engine of Sam's narrative. In chapter 3 she considers killing Valet de Chambre ("yo' po' mammy's got to kill you to save you, honey") much as Cassy committed infanticide. Instead she switches him with Tom Driscoll in their cribs to save him—a subversive act that, as Michael Kiskis observes, "is ultimately the most dangerous threat imaginable to white power and authority." Sam learned from Stowe how vulnerable the slave mother was to threat, coercion, and extortion and, like Cassy, Roxy must forfeit her maternal role to protect her son. Sam might even have discovered the device of contrasting twin boys in Stowe's novel. Like Thomas à Beckett Driscoll and Valet de Chambre, Stowe's St. Clair twins, Augustine and Alfred, "were in all points a contrast." One "had black, fiery eyes, coal-black hair, a strong, fine Roman profile, and a rich brown complexion" and was "active and observing." The other "had blue eyes, golden hair, a Greek outline, and fair complexion" and was "dreamy and inactive."[8] In short, Stowe's *Uncle Tom's Cabin* everywhere looms in the background of Sam's novel.

Pudd'nhead Wilson is also a prototypical Western, as outlandish as this claim may seem. For purposes of the race theme, Dawson's Landing may be a southern town, but it is also a western town, located on the Missouri side of the Mississippi River, the cusp or frontier between eastern civilization and what Ralph Waldo Emerson called "unhandselled savage nature" in the West. The geography of the setting is critical: upon his arrival Wilson settles "in a small house on the extreme western verge of the town"; that is, not only is he a detective-hero, he is a type of Western hero who straddles the East and the West, mediating between order and chaos. Roxy and Tom meet repeatedly and clandestinely in a haunted house that stands three hundred yards farther west of Wilson's abode. There, in a liminal territory ungoverned by civil law, Roxy confesses to her son the primal crime that first upset the social order, swapping him with the legitimate Driscoll heir; Tom pays her every month the extortion money she demands to keep his secrets; and the two conspire to break other laws, including Tom's theft while in disguise—all threats to the stability Wilson restores in the trial that concludes the novel. Sam had lived in California and Nevada for over five years in the 1860s, of course, before writing the western travelogue *Roughing It* (1872), so he was familiar with such tropes in Western writing as the gunfight. In the space beyond Wilson's house, Luigi and Judge Driscoll fight the proxy duel that triggers an inexorable chain of events: the humiliation of Tom, the murder of the Judge, the trial and exoneration of Luigi, and the restoration of order in Dawson's Landing with the mayoral election of Wilson. It remained for Owen Wister, who first read *Roughing It* as a student at St. Paul's, a preparatory school in New Hampshire, to formalize the gunfight as a standard element of the formula Western.[9] The climactic chapter of his novel *The Virginian* (1902) features a shootout between hero and villain on the main street of Medicine Bow, Wyoming—a plot device that may be traced from Wister back to Sam Clemens.

Immediately after completing a draft of *Pudd'nhead Wilson* in mid-December 1892, Sam turned to a project he had long contemplated: a historical romance titled *Personal Recollections of Joan of Arc*. The impetus to undertake this project has long been a puzzle to Twain scholars. As Susan K. Harris frames the paradox, Sam was a religious skeptic and he generally despised the French, "so he writes a book about a French-catholic-martyr? Ostensibly, it doesn't make a lot of sense." Nor did he plan the book to make money, however desperately he needed it. As he explained to his friend Mary

Mason ("Mother") Fairbanks, *Joan of Arc* was undertaken "not for print" or "for lucre" but "for love" and "to entertain the family with, around the lamp by the fire." Even after he decided to publish the fictionalized biography he insisted that it appear initially without his name so that readers inured to the "Mark Twain brand" would not be misled by its serious subject and tone. "The name Mark Twain was the trouble," he admitted, because readers "were certain to see nothing but humor in the story if it came out with that fateful name tagged to it." As a result, as Jason Horn aptly puts it, the "anonymous author" (Sam) "cites a fictional translator" (Jean François Alden) of a pretend manuscript in the National Archives of France by "an imaginary narrator" (Sieur Louis de Conte) "who shares the initials of the anonymous author." Nor was his decision to pen the book an impulsive one. Certainly Sam was planning it no later than September 1891 while he floated down the Rhône River. During the voyage he read Marius Sepet's *Jeanne d'Arc* (1894) and jotted a note in his diary to ask Chatto & Windus to send him more "Joan of Arc books." In the end he listed a total of eleven French and English sources for his story, among them J. E. J. Quicherat's *Procès de condamnation et de réhabilitation de Jeanne d'Arc* (5 volumes, 1841–49), Jules Michelet's *Jeanne d'Arc* (1853), La Comtesse Clémentine de Chabannes's *La Vierge Lorraine* (1874), Janet Tuckey's *Joan of Arc the Maid* (1880), and Ronald Gower's *Joan of Arc* (1893).[10] Though he invented some characters, Sam generally hewed to verifiable fact in recounting Joan's experience. "I never attributed an act to the Maid herself that was not strictly historical," he insisted in his autobiography, "and I never put a sentence in her mouth which she had not uttered."[11]

So why did Sam choose to devote months if not years to working such an uncharacteristic and potentially unrewarding vein? The easiest answer is that he considered *Joan of Arc* a companion piece to *The Prince and the Pauper* (1881) and *A Connecticut Yankee in King Arthur's Court* (1889)—another historical novel set in medieval Europe. Put another way, the former novel was a metabiography much as the latter novels were metahistories of the period. The topic also resonated with Sam because, as Susan Gillman explains, as "a tribute to a 'stainlessly pure child'" it presupposed "an utterly conventional attitude toward female purity." That is, like "In Defense of Harriet Shelley" (1894), *Joan of Arc* illustrated a mid-Victorian sexual ideology Sam practiced in his parenting. Joan was the most desexed of all his heroines not only because she dressed in male attire but, as Sam was at pains to assure his readers, she physically remained a child and never menstruated. The novel was the only book he ever dedicated to his wife Livy and, more to the point, he later insisted that he had modeled the eponymous heroine on his idealized oldest daughter: "Susy at 17—Joan of Arc at 17. Secretly I drew Joan's physical portrait from Susy at that age, when I came to write that book." *Joan of Arc* was the last of Sam's books that Susy heard her father read to the family, and she had been moved by it. Sam sometimes wept as he recited from his manuscript, and Susy admitted that she once "held up the reading so she could go fetch a handkerchief." Listening to her father declaim from his manuscript, she wrote Clara, "is an uplifting and revealing hour to us all."[12]

But, even more, Sam genuinely admired Joan. Unlike the usurper Tom Driscoll, the debased heir of centuries of brutality, Joan was the beneficiary of generations of exalted ancestry; as he insisted, "It took six thousand years to produce her." In 1907 Sam told Elizabeth Wallace, a dean at the University of Chicago, that "for years he had been impressed by the spirit of the French heroine, and year by year, for twelve years, he had laid by in his memory, and in his notes, every impression he could get of her. The most thrilling historical document he had ever read, he said, was the official account of her trial." From Sam's point of view, Joan was a type of divinity, the locus of a "secular Mariolatry," according to Carl Van Doren. She was the only person who "has lived in this world whose merits are beyond the reach of overpraise," Sam noted, and,

> When we praise other heroes, there are limits beyond which we cannot go & not strain the truth, but with her it is not so. She was finer than any words can convey; she was nobler than the noblest words can set forth; she was greater than any standard of greatness that can be framed in speech. The grace, & beauty, & sweetness & modesty & purity & steadfastness of her nature, the sublimity of her spirit, the loftiness of her purposes & inspirations, the absence of all pettiness, malice, envy, of all trace of ignoble ambition, of all suggestion of self-seeking in her words & deeds—these together form a complete & rounded & majestic character that has not its peer in human history.

Quoting Sam, his secretary Isabel Lyon observed in her stenographic notebook in January 1906 that the "sacrifice of Jesus Christ was trifling compared with that of Joan of Arc. God knew what he was going to do" when he was crucified, unlike Joan in her martyrdom. That is, she was arguably holier than Jesus. Though convicted on a trumped-up charge of heresy and burned at the stake, Joan was gradually rehabilitated in the Catholic Church after Quicherat published the unabridged transcript of her 1430–31 trials translated from Latin. She was venerated in 1904, beatified in 1909, and ultimately canonized in 1920. In any case, by writing a hagiography of Joan of Arc, Sam marched in lockstep with an Anglo-American literary culture that, for whatever reason, fostered a spate of Jesus and Joan books at the end of the century, including Archibald McCowan's *Christ, the Socialist* (1894), William T. Stead's *If Christ Came to Chicago* (1894), Elizabeth Stuart Phelps Ward's *A Singular Life* (1894), Andrew Lang's *A Monk of Fife: A Romance of the Days of Jeanne d'Arc* (1895), Francis C. Lowell's *Joan of Arc* (1896), Margaret Oliphant's *Jeanne d'Arc: Her Life and Death* (1896), and Charles M. Sheldon's *In His Steps* (1896). Incredible as it may seem, according to Booker T. Washington, at one time Sam apparently planned "to write a life of Christ," too, but his friends persuaded him "not to do it for fear that such a life might prove a failure or would be misunderstood."[13]

In addition, *Personal Recollections of Joan of Arc* may fairly be considered an experiment in point of view. Much as Huck Finn tells his story in the first person, Joan's life is ostensibly chronicled sixty years after her death in the voice of an eighty-two-year-old friend who had known her in childhood. Sam readily allowed in his autobiography that he struggled to find the best narrative strategy:

> In the story of "Joan of Arc" I made six wrong starts, and each time that I offered the result to Mrs. Clemens she responded with the same deadly criticism—silence. She didn't say a word, but her silence spoke with the voice of thunder. When at last I found the right form I recognized it at once that it was the right one, and I knew what she would say. She said it, without doubt or hesitation.

By mid-January 1893 Sam had completed about a hundred thousand words of the novel, through the lifting of the Siege of Orléans, when he laid the manuscript aside. "I have ground out mighty stacks of manuscript in these 3½ months, & someday I mean to publish some of it," he wrote Mother Fairbanks. Similarly, he notified Fred Hall on January 28 that he had "written 1800 MS pages since the 5th of last August, & 1500 of them are still in my possession (one completed book & one half-completed make 1350 of the 1500)"—that is, the completed *Pudd'nhead Wilson,* the half-completed *Joan of Arc,* and two or three minor sketches for good measure. These months at the Villa Viviani were among the most productive of his career. As he crowed to Laurence Hutton on February 5, "I've never enjoyed being alive more than I enjoy it now."[14]

Early in January 1893 Charles L. Webster and Company, and then in the spring Chatto & Windus in England, released a mishmash of nine pieces titled *The £1,000,000 Bank-Note and Other New Stories* apparently designed for no better purpose than to improve Sam's cash flow. In the title story, Sam recounts how a mendicant lives for an entire year upon the goodwill and confidence inspired by his possession of a borrowed and unbreakable million-pound banknote. The second piece, "Mental Telegraphy," originally written in 1878 and rejected by the *North American Review* because it documented mere "coincidences" than instances of genuine clairvoyance, was finally published in *Harper's Monthly* in December 1891. "Some people do not believe in mental telegraphy, but I have had twenty-one years of experience of it," Sam wrote later, "and I know considerable about it." A devout believer in the paranormal, Sam even predicted that "someday people *will* be able to call each other up from any part of the world & talk by mental telegraph—& not merely by impression, the impressions will be articulated into *words*." In "Mental Telegraphy" he called for the invention of the "phrenophone," a device to read minds—not that he had any idea how prospective inventors might research and develop such an instrument. The volume was padded with two of the six travel essays Sam had written for the McClure syndicate in 1891.[15]

Reviews of the volume were predictably mixed. The American critics were generally favorable—for example, the theatrical manager Lynden Behymer in the *Los Angeles Herald* ("very entertaining and written in Mark Twain's well known humorous style"), the *American Monthly Review of Reviews* ("rises . . . to his wonted pitch of audacity and humor"), the *Hartford Courant* ("an amusing extravaganza in the writer's most genial manner"), the *Fort Worth Gazette* ("happily commingles pathos and pleasantry"), and the New Orleans *Times-Democrat* ("original and cleverly carried out in that extravagant spirit of humor peculiar to the author"). The *Chicago Tribune*, however, voiced a dissenting opinion: "Mark Twain's literary style never had any staying power" and this volume was "dull and dreary." The notices in the United Kingdom trended mostly from tepid to cool. The London *Telegraph* ("his rich vein of humour is by no means exhausted"), *Woman* ("delightful"), *Manchester Guardian* ("recalls the best old vein of *The Tramp Abroad*"), *London Post* ("abundant variety"), and Glasgow *North British Mail* ("sure of a hearty welcome") were upbeat. On the other hand, George Saintsbury averred in *Academy* that he missed the "fun in this volume," if it contained any. Similarly unflattering reviews appeared in the *Westminster Gazette* ("more than usually slight"), London *Times* ("unworthy of a laughing philosopher"), *Saturday Review* ("will not prove to be a joyous book"), *Athenaeum* (this brand of humor "has lost its freshness"), London *Bookman* ("passable" but overall "disappointing"), London *Graphic* ("trifling"), London *Literary World* ("a poor book" that the author's "friends will be glad to forget" as "quickly and as effectually as possible"), and the *Scotsman* ("hardly up to the author's usual level" and "somewhat disappointing"). The *New Zealand Mail* likewise considered the book "a disappointment."[16]

One of Sam's occasional short pieces dating from this period belongs to a cluster of biblical satires often designated "the Genesis stories." He had puttered on "Methuselah's Diary," the initial chapter in this series, in 1873. He wrote the next installment, "Extracts from Adam's Diary," in early 1893 at the Villa Viviani. He thought the story was "a gem, if I do say it myself." Excerpts from this first of four iterations of the diary appeared in syndication on April 30 prior to its publication in the souvenir *Niagara Book* on June 3, after which this version disappeared on account of poor sales. Sam received only half of the thousand dollars he was promised by the publisher, who lost money on the book. In one of the few notices of the sketch in the United States, the *Catholic World* warned that "his jokes have an ancient-fish-like smell," prompting the rumor that Sam at the age of nearly sixty had exhausted his vein of humor:

> So Mark, just heed my verse and turn,
> Its moral please remember;
> And don't ring in the jokes of June
> While living in December.

"Extracts from Adam's Diary" is perhaps most noteworthy for its irreverence and satire of biblical text. Edward Bok, who claimed to have read the essay in manuscript, scorned it in his syndicated column on April 29, noting that "it may prove, should the screed receive publication, that Mark Twain has overstepped himself in his latest attempt to be funny" and "it will require an editor of more than average bravery to publish" the item. Sam was predictably graveled by Bok's mot. Livy had read "Adam's Diary" and approved it, he wrote Mother Fairbanks: "Bok has not read a line of it, & *dis*approves it, I suppose. Never mind about Bok: even assassins must live." Bok "has overreached himself this time," he added in a note to Hall, and he briefly considered filing suit for libel. "I shall tackle Adam once more," he asserted, "& do him in a kind of a friendly and respectful way that will commend him to the Sunday schools."[17]

Upon its publication in England, "Adam's Diary" was met with almost unanimous scorn by reviewers. The *Manchester Guardian* ("blasphemous" and "scurrilous vulgarity") and *St. James's Gazette* ("profane" and "lumbering provincial priggishness") considered it sacrilegious. The London *Bookman* (the author "at his feeblest and vulgarest") and *Spectator* ("too far-fetched, grotesque in fact") were scarcely more complimentary. The notice in the *Thanet Advertiser* was a rare exception: "We do not regard it as sacrilegious, though we think it vastly amusing."[18]

Came the wobble, then the crash. On February 20, 1893, the Philadelphia and Reading Railroad, one of the largest corporations in the world, declared bankruptcy, prompting nationwide bank runs and closures and a credit squeeze. It was the first domino in what became a cascade of collapses. The looming financial crisis threatened the stability of businesses around the world, including the Paige Compositor Company. When Webster and Company again began to hemorrhage red ink, Sam hurried to the United States to inspect the damage in person. He jotted in his notebook, "March 19, '92, you owed [the] Barrow [family] $15,000 & the M[ount] Morris [bank] $16,000. That was the whole debt except ours, which was about $40,000. One year later, it is $200,000," including about $140,000 owed the Clemenses. Sam's alarm was palpable. All his progress in repaying old debts and avoiding new ones had vanished in the volatile markets. Hall warned Sam that the Panic of 1893 had so diminished the value of the company that he could not "sell your interest for anything like the amount of money you have invested in it nor could you find a purchaser at that price or any other price just at present." In January, moreover, Hall had taken out a second $15,000 loan from the Mount Morris Bank and sent the papers to Italy for Sam to sign. Thinking he was simply renewing the initial loan, Sam "endorsed them without examining them and sent them back." Only later did he discover "that additions had been made to the borrowings, without my knowledge or consent."[19] Livy urged Sam to sell the Hartford house, assign his copyrights to his creditors for whatever they would bring, and "reduce the indebtedness in every way you can think of—then get to work and earn the rest of the indebtedness, if your life is spared. And don't be afraid. We shall pay a hundred cents on the dollar yet." The empty mansion had become a money pit, costing nearly $3,000 a year to maintain, and Sam implored Franklin G. Whitmore to "rent, or sell, or burn" it.[20]

Accompanied by William Walter Phelps, the former U.S. ambassador to Germany, Sam railed to Genoa and embarked on the *Kaiser Wilhelm II* for New York via Liverpool on March 22.[21] As usual, he told stories in the salon in the evening and attended a "nice hall on deck with colored electric lights" one night when he "waltzed with [an] overcoat" and "danced a Virginia reel." His fellow passenger Countess Di Brazza, the former Cora Slocum of New Orleans and wife of the president of the Italian delegation to the Chicago World's Fair, told reporters upon arrival on April 3 that Sam was "too lovely for anything." With only a small hand satchel, he registered at the Glenham Hotel on Fifth Avenue as "George Jones, Gibraltar." His cover was blown, however, when he sent a telegram to Livy notifying her that he had arrived safely, and his presence in the city was soon announced in the local press.[22]

Over the next few days Sam dined with Andrew Carnegie, Hall, Howells, Charley Stoddard, and John Brisbane Walker. Mary Mapes Dodge hosted a dinner party for Sam, Howells, and Rudyard Kipling, the *Hartford Courant* reported, and "for over an hour the three literary lions were closeted together in the most spirited literary discussion and conversation." Sam chatted privately about his Joan of Arc project with Howells, who solicited the manuscript for anonymous publication in *Harper's Monthly*. "Let it make its big *Ben Hur* reputation before revealing the authorship," Howells argued, and "I agreed. He says it ought to repeat *Ben Hur*'s popularity." With his fellow future anti-imperialist Carnegie, Sam discussed the case "for absorbing Canada into our union." The steel tycoon even expressed the bizarre wish "to add Great Britain and Ireland."[23]

On Monday afternoon, April 10, Sam visited the offices of the Connecticut Company at Eighteenth Street and Broadway. He learned that fifty of the Paige typesetters were under construction, with the first one scheduled for completion on July 1. The company had received a written offer from a concern near Chicago of acreage, two million dollars in bonds, and five million dollars in working capital "if they will build a factory on their land." Sam was assured that his royalty on sales "will be collectible on all fifty machines" and that "by the end of this year the company will be making one machine a day, next year two—the year after, five." Every one of these statements was a gross exaggeration. The company had in fact secured castings to build fifty machines, but in the end it only completed one.[24]

Sam left for Chicago accompanied by Hall on April 12 to inspect the machine plant, but he came down with the grippe while en route. He had also hoped to visit the World's Fair at Jackson Park but "saw not a vestige" of it. Rather than spend only two days in the city as planned, he was confined to his room in the Great Northern Hotel for eleven days, which "crippled all the rest of my business & made my visit to America almost useless," he admitted to his sister Pamela. On his part, Hall was left with "but a faint remembrance" of the typesetter. "As a matter of fact," he claimed, "I knew very little about it." Despite doctor's orders to curtail his smoking, Sam puffed cigars in bed and spun yarns with friends, including the poet Eugene Field. Sam's brother Orion also traveled from Keokuk, Iowa, to see him, and it would be the last time the brothers would meet. James Paige called twice, on April 20 and 23, and Sam's notes of their conversations reveal his gullibility, his almost undeniable eagerness to be "sold." Sam asked Paige "if his conscience troubled him any about the way he had treated me." Paige replied that "he could almost forgive me for that word. He said it broke his heart when I left him and the machine to fight along the best way they could, etc. etc." Paige promised that, whatever he received from the company that contracted to build the machine,

> he will take in cash and send me one-half. When his European patent affairs are settled, he is going to put me in for a handsome royalty on every European machine. . . . He is a very extraordinary man—the smoothest talker I ever saw. I tried to impress upon him that I would compromise and square matters for two or three hundred additional royalties on the machine—and for less than that indeed . . . but then I wanted some trifling evidence . . . that I had not been dealt with in an absolutely shameless conscienceless way. In reply I got an abundance of gilt-edge promises but nothing more. . . . Paige shed even more tears than usual. What a talker he is. He could persuade a fish to come out and take a walk with him. When he is present I always believe him—I cannot help it. When he is gone away all the belief evaporates. He is a most daring and majestic liar.

Yet the very next day, before boarding an eastbound train, Sam admonished Orion and Mollie in Keokuk in effect to save their Confederate money: "Don't lose or sell that $1 royalty" he had given them on sales of the typesetter. "From all I can see, it ought to begin to pay more than $50 a month after this time next year." Sam's letters from Chicago with news of the machine likewise excited Livy, who replied, "It does not seem credible that we are really again to have money to spend." Not until 1909, a few months before his death, did Sam finally acknowledge that "all through my life I have been the easy prey of the cheap adventurer." Bernard DeVoto was even more blunt: he was "a predestinate sucker for all salesmen of gold bricks."[25]

Back in New York, Sam registered at the Murray Hill Hotel, though Sam's physician friend Clarence C. Rice convinced him to continue his recuperation at his own home on East Nineteenth Street at Irving Place. While in the city Sam sold about $14,000 of stock to leave with Hall as an emergency account, though Hall immediately paid the money to subscription agents selling the *Library of American Literature*. A week later, on May 2, Sam beat a hasty retreat to Elmira, New York, and the Langdon family home, Quarry Farm, to rest "until I am sound & hearty again." He canceled his plans to spend a couple of days in Hartford, as he wrote his niece Ida Langdon, because "I was there last year, but I wouldn't have missed my visit to Elmira for anything. It was an ideal visit. I learned to know every one of you better; I got closer to you all." He returned to New York on May 11 and sailed on the *Kaiser Wilhelm II* the morning of May 13. The best part of the seven-week trip was the journey home. He bought a couple of books, Howells and Hall presented him with two more, and his friend William M. Laffan, publisher of the New York *Sun*, "gave me two bottles of whisky and a box of cigars—I go to sea nobly equipped." His only reservation: the bill of fare. "If this ship pays *anything at all* for its potatoes, oranges, grapes, apples, & pears, it gets cheated," he claimed. "Positively they are not worth picking up in the gutter. The bananas were good—they gave out yesterday." The evening prior to arrival, Sam entertained the passengers at the customary concert with "a long meter anecdote with a snapper at the end." The steamer docked in Genoa on May 25 and Sam arrived back at the Villa Viviani two days later. Ironically, he arrived home "in tolerable condition—nothing left but weakness, cough all gone," not that his recovery compensated for all his trouble in America. A few days later he griped to Joseph Twichell that he had "accomplished nothing that I went home to do." To add insult to inanity, during Sam's illness-plagued business trip he was the target of character attacks in the press. In an editorial widely reprinted in religious papers, he was accused of debauching "the youth of his country" with his fiction. Such stories as *Tom Sawyer* "illustrate the author's view that to escape being 'a Sunday-school milk sop' a boy must be a fit candidate for the workhouse." Other reports circulated that he was "a bitter, jealous man" and that his "parsimony" was "growing more pronounced." To counter the bad press, Livy advised Sam to "be generous . . . even if we are as poor as church mice."[26]

Then they became even poorer than church mice. The Panic of 1893 precipitated the longest and most severe economic depression in American history excepting only the Great Depression of the 1930s. Some sixteen thousand businesses, including 119 railroad companies and six hundred banks, failed before the end of 1893 as a consequence of the stringency. Webster and Company was hardly immune from the virus. "When the panic of 1893 arrived, followed by severe business depression," Hall remembered, "our failure became inevitable unless we secured funds to pay our obligations and carry on the business. General conditions made it impossible to borrow enough money on our notes to meet our needs." Hall wrote Sam on May 19 that "the condition of the money market . . . is something beyond description. You cannot get money even on government bonds." But Sam had been aboard the *Kaiser Wilhelm* in the mid-Atlantic and was unaware of the severity of the crisis, and upon his return he helped the family pack to leave for Germany. Instead of asking Hall if he needed any help to balance the company books, Sam wrote him a note that focused on his own problems: "We are skimming along like paupers & a day can embarrass us. I am terribly tired of business. I am by nature and disposition unfitted for it & I want to get out of it." He faced repayment of $8,000 in notes in September "with help from the machine a long ways off." He urged Hall to contact "Harper, or Appleton, or Putnam" and offer any or all of them his "two-thirds interest in the firm" for $200,000. "I don't want much money," he protested. "I only want first class notes—$200,000 worth of them at 6 per cent, payable monthly;—yearly notes, renewable annually for 3 years, with $5,000 of the principal payable at the beginning and middle of each year. After that, the notes renewable annually and (perhaps) a larger part of the principal payable semi-annually." He might as well have tried to sell the Brooklyn Bridge. With upwards of $200,000 in liabilities and $50,000 in assets, as Fred Kaplan notes, Sam's share of the company "had not the slightest hope of a buyer." Nevertheless, he plaintively begged Hall, "Get me out of business! And I will be yours forever gratefully." That is, Sam notified Hall in no uncertain terms that he was liable to lose his financial "angel."[27]

The same day, several time zones to the west, Hall penned a similarly frantic note to Sam. "You can scarcely conceive of the condition of business generally," he wailed from New York. There had been "a constant succession of crashes since you left" and "failure after failure." Webster and Company's cash-flow problems were serious enough before the Panic, but since then "we cannot collect money from our very best customers. It is like pulling teeth to get any money at all." A week later Hall was even more agitated. "I am worried half to death," he whined. Since Sam sailed in late May, "the whole bottom seems to have dropped out of everything." Livy—significantly, not Sam—replied to Hall's alarm. "Mr Clemens did not realize what trouble you would be in when his letter should reach you or he would not have sent it just then," she explained, adding,

> I hope you will not worry any more than you can help. Do not let our interests weigh on you too heavily. We both know that you will, as you always have, look in every way to the best interests of all. I think Mr Clemens is right in feeling that he should get out of business, that he is not fitted for it; it worries him too much. But he need be in no haste about it and, of course, it would be the very furthest from his desire to imperil, in the slightest degree, your interests in order to save his own.

Livy assured Hall that she and Sam could draw on her brother Charley Langdon and her own interest in J. Langdon and Company "for money for a few weeks until things are a little easier with you." Sam had no idea what Livy wrote to Hall, nor did Livy know what Sam wrote him soon thereafter: "I have never felt so desperate in my life—and good reason, for I haven't got a penny to my name, and Mrs. Clemens hasn't enough laid up with Langdon to keep us two months." In truth, Livy's profit from her inheritance amounted to about $6,000 a year—several times what the average American household earned in 1893 but only a small fraction of the Clemens family income at their height of their affluence. But "with what you can comfortably earn in addition without taxing yourself," she assured her husband, "we can live perfectly well for our requirements."[28] Nevertheless, Hall knew better than to beseech Sam and Livy to bail out the company.

He struck on another alternative: the sale of the *Library of American Literature,* the multivolume boondoggle that was devouring the equity of the firm. "The one great mistake we have made and the mistake that has caused us all so much uneasiness," Hall admitted to Sam in mid-June, was "in trying to swing a book like the 'Library of American Literature.' Before we touched it we should have been in a position to lay aside at least two hundred thousand dollars" to pay sales commissions and production costs. "Although our installment business gave every promise of good returns, we could not carry it on without capital, so we decided to sell it," Hall recalled. Sam preferred the sale of the *Library* to "the other scheme," selling the entire business for interest-bearing bonds. Unlike Webster and Company as a whole, the *Library* was unencumbered by debt and had "large money owing to it. A proposition to sell that by itself to a big house could be made without embarrassment. We merely confess that we cannot spare capital from the rest of the business to run it on the huge scale necessary to make it an opulent success," Sam wrote Hall. With the *Library* "out of the way & the firm out of debt we could drive the trade business & make it profitable." Sam had ambitious plans, never realized, to "start a magazine—*inexpensive* & of an entirely unique sort," to be edited by his nephew Sam Moffett and called *The Back Number.* It would contain "nothing but ancient news" and "narratives culled from mouldy old newspapers and mouldy old books," such as excerpts from Samuel Pepys's diary and Jean-Jacques Rousseau's *Confessions,* unprotected by copyright and thus free for the taking. Sam urged Hall to sell the book series "in the fall, as soon as business freshens up and times are easier and less scary." The economic depression lingered well into the late 1890s, however. Hall proposed six weeks later reviving the dormant *Library* as a prelude "to disposing of it," but Sam vetoed the idea. "We are not in shape to venture that," he feared. "It would require more borrowing and we must not do that."[29] Neither of them ever ventured to name a price the *Library* was worth, moreover. Eventually, the idea was pushed to a back-burner.

Though the Clemenses hosted a farewell reception for their friends and neighbors on June 3, their departure from the Villa Viviani was delayed until June 15 when Livy fell ill. After brief stopovers in Bologna, Verona, Trento, and Innsbruck, they arrived at the Rheinischer Hof, "a fine & expensive hotel," in Munich on June 24. There Livy consulted a heart specialist, who concluded that she suffered from no systemic disease "that cannot be cured," Sam reported. "This is a relief, after two years of the other opinion. The uplift is not to be described. Mrs. C. is now making good & steady progress. . . . Two American & three European doctors [told her that] she had incurable heart disease." On June 28 Sam railed to Berlin, where he retrieved his daughter Clara and was the guest of J. B. Jackson for four days before returning with Clara to Munich. On July 12, on the recommendation of the heart specialist, they headed to the health resort of Krankenheil-bei-Tölz in the Bavarian Alps, where they remained five weeks. In mid-July Sam returned to Berlin to lecture, and on the leg of his trip from Leipzig to the city he was seated by chance next to the astronomer Professor E. E. Barnard of the Lick Observatory. "I found myself alone in a car with a man whose picture it struck me I had seen somewhere," as Barnard recounted after his return to the United States. "It chanced that it was Mark Twain and we sat and talked for three hours together."[30]

The family had originally planned to tarry in Krankenheil until the end of September and then settle in Paris for the winter, but Livy's doctors and Susy's voice coach "changed our plans" by directing them to spend several weeks in another spa town, Franzensbad, in Bohemia. In mid-August, even before the move there, however, Sam decided he needed to return to the United States on business. All the while, Sam was suffering from a slow crescendo of anxiety. He admitted to Hall from Munich that he felt "panicky." In mid-July, after returning from Berlin to Krankenheil, he outlined to Hall a "scheme to protect the family against the almshouse for one more year." Three weeks later he implored Hall to "do your best for me, for I do not sleep, these nights, for visions of the poorhouse." Once his side job, writing had again become his only source of income. But his worries—what Huck Finn would call the "jimjams"—affected his writing, as Livy was quick to note. "I have never seen him when he worked with so much difficulty," she reported. "He often comes down at night with his head so sore and tired that he cannot bear to have the simplest questions asked him, or be compelled to talk at all." With loan payments to the Mount Morris Bank falling due in mid-September, Sam's presence was imperative should he be needed to keep the wolf at bay. "I am very glad indeed if you & Mr. Langdon are able to see any daylight ahead," he grumbled to Hall from Krankenheil on August 14. "To me none is visible. I strongly advise that every penny that comes in shall be applied to paying off debts. I may be in error about this, but it seems to me that we have no other course open." He was distressed by the possibility that he would be forced to relinquish his copyrights in bankruptcy court. His books still sold about twenty thousand copies annually in the United States and about twelve thousand per year in England. If he lost the income on these, he fretted, "I am a beggar. I would sail today if I had anybody to take charge of my family and help them through the difficult journeys commanded by the doctors. I may be able to sail ten days hence; I hope so, and expect so."[31]

Sam still harbored evergreen hopes for the Paige typesetter. Since visiting Chicago in April he had expected a cable almost daily notifying him that the machine was finished and ready for mass production. By late July he was plagued by a recurrence of his old doubts: "I wonder what they call 'finished.'" After Paige pronounced it "perfect," it would still need to be tested for at least a month in a printshop to prove its mettle. By early August he conceded to Hall that it was "unquestionably the boss machine of this world, but it is the touchiest one on prophets [*sic*] . . . that has ever seen the light."[32] He was obliged, he thought, to be on the scene in the United States not only to protect his not-so-silent partnership in Webster and Company but to safeguard his remaining interest in the compositor.

He accompanied Livy and their daughters via Munich to Franzensbad, leaving on August 20 and arriving three days later. Sam and Clara, who was suffering from a persistent cough her parents thought would be remedied by an ocean trip, left for Leipzig on August 26; they embarked on the North German Lloyd steamer *Spree* from Bremen for New York three days later. Despite the dire circumstances of his return, Sam was feted like a VIP on holiday during the voyage. After landing on September 7, Clara headed to Elmira and Sam lodged with the Rices. He resisted all entreaties to speak with reporters. "You can't interview me," he told one of them. "I lost my voice while abroad." He had caught Clara's cough and spoke "with difficulty."[33] But the worst was yet to come.

CHAPTER 3

Courting Bankruptcy

I wasn't worth a cent two years ago and now I owe two millions of dollars.

—*The Gilded Age*

"I DON'T WANT [*PUDD'NHEAD Wilson*] to go into a magazine," Samuel Clemens had cautioned Fred Hall in February 1893, before the Panic. As late as July 30 of that year he counseled Hall, "I don't want any more syndicating—nothing short of $20,000, anyway, and that I can't get." The same day Sam arrived in New York aboard the *Spree*, he sold serial rights to *Pudd'nhead Wilson* to the *Century* for $6,500. "It'll furnish me hash for a while I reckon," he mused. "I am almost sorry it is finished; it was good entertainment to work at it & kept my mind away from things." The *Century* editors, Richard Watson Gilder and Robert Underwood Johnson, were "vastly pleased with the story & they say Roxy is a great & dramatic & well-drawn character," Sam bragged to his wife Olivia. The installments appeared in the magazine between December 1893 and June 1894—simultaneously, as it happened, with the serialization of *Tom Sawyer Abroad* in *St. Nicholas* between November 1893 and April 1894. The day of Sam's arrival he also sold his story "The Esquimau Maiden's Romance" to the upstart *Cosmopolitan* for $800. But he devoted most of this "pen-money" toward family living expenses—his own and Clara's in the United States and that of Livy and their two daughters in Europe, mostly in Paris. He was still short $8,000 of the $10,000 in loan payments that would fall due on September 18. He raced to Hartford to touch Charley Langdon and Susan Crane for a loan, but to no avail: they had no ready cash. They offered to cosign a note but, as Sam explained to Livy, "money cannot be had, at any rate of interest whatever, or upon any sort of security, or by *anybody*." Others he approached in Hartford "were not moved, not strongly interested, & I was ashamed that I went." On September 14, back in New York, he "raced around Wall street" to assail bankers and brokers but "couldn't get anything." "Bless your life they're *bitter* hard times!" he moaned to Livy. "You have never seen anything to remotely compare with them." He had "never lived any such days" in his life as September 11–15. Still, he was determined to weather the financial storm. "I shall stay right here until this business cyclone abates," he added. "I experience great satisfaction in being on the spot in these troublous times."[1]

Then Sam caught a series of lucky breaks. The same evening he sold *Pudd'nhead Wilson* to the *Century*, he had dined with its editor Johnson and Clarence C. Rice at the Players Club. Rice then treated him for the sore throat he had contracted on the *Spree*—perhaps the most fortuitous throat infection in history—and learned about his financial plight. Sometime over the next few days Sam saw Henry H. Rogers, vice president and chief operations officer of Standard Oil (or "Slandered Oil," as Sam once called it), a centimillionaire and another of Rice's patients. Rogers admired *Roughing It* (1872), had once heard Sam speak, and may have met Sam a year or two earlier. In any case, Rice convinced Rogers to intercede on Sam's behalf. As legend has it, on Friday, September 15, Sam and Rice encountered Rogers by chance. Despite evidence that Rice engineered the meeting, Sam believed it was entirely unplanned. "I stumbled accidentally upon H. H. Rogers one evening in the lobby of the Murray Hill Hotel," he remembered, "whither Dr. Clarence C. Rice and I had gone." Rogers "interested himself in my troubles at once, and set himself the task of piloting me out of them." On his part, Rogers recalled that he "was standing in the lobby of the old Murray Hill Hotel in New York. Up came Dr. Clarence Rice, the famous throat specialist with Mark Twain in tow. Rice said: 'I have just told Clemens that if any man can pull him out of the hole it is yourself.'" Rogers invited Sam to meet him in his office at the Standard Oil building on Broadway to discuss the situation. "We were strangers when we met," Sam remembered, "and friends when we parted half an hour afterward." Sam and Fred Hall left Rogers's office the next afternoon with a check and an agreement in principle to sell the *Library of American Literature* to Rogers's wealthy son-in-law William Evarts Benjamin, a part-time publisher, for $50,000. "The amount received was far less than the business was worth under normal conditions," Hall allowed, "and only a fraction of what had been expended in developing it, so we were still left staggering under a burden of debt." But in the short term, with this last-minute reprieve, "our worries were over," Sam assured Livy, at least until the next loan payment fell due. Rogers was "the best new acquaintance I've ever seen," he chortled. "We skinned through" after making the deal. "We've got another reef to cross 5 days hence"—he invoked a steamboating metaphor—"& another one 4 days after that," but "I think we'll get over—& without the help of any old friend or relative."[2]

Rogers asked Sam to let him handle all of his affairs, and he served as his financial guru for the remainder of his life. Rogers "took hold with avidity and said it was no burden to work for his friends, but a pleasure," Sam concluded. "Obstructions and perplexities which would have driven me mad were simplicities to his master mind and furnished him no difficulties," Rogers was a "singularly clear-headed man," as was apparent at their "every meeting. And no grass grows under his feet. He takes his steps swiftly, yet no step is bungled or has to be taken over again." "He's a pirate," Sam conceded, but the jolly Rogers "owns up to it and enjoys being a pirate. That's the reason I like him." Meanwhile, Sam began to live even more economically if no less comfortably. In late September, when Rice left town, he moved to a "deliciously quiet" room "with an open fireplace, two mirrors, six electric lights, seven gas burners" that cost only $1.50 per day on the top floor of the Players Club. He kept bachelor's hall in the comfortable house in Gramercy Park and "relished its friendly informality," according to Brander Matthews.[3]

Much as Sam protested changes to the manuscript of *Tom Sawyer Abroad* prior to its publication in *St. Nicholas,* he objected to the editorial alternations he discovered in *Pudd'nhead Wilson* before its serialization in *Century.* The proof "was fairly small-poxed with corrections of my punctuation—my punctuation, which I had deeply thought out & laboriously perfected!" he complained, whereupon "my volcano turned itself loose, & the exhibition was not suited to any Sunday school." Robert Underwood Johnson blamed the "peerless imported proof-reader" who had been imported from Oxford University and in consequence "whatever he did was sacred" in the eyes of the publisher. Sam replied that he "didn't care if he was an Archangel imported from Heaven, he couldn't puke his ignorant impudence over *my* punctuation, I wouldn't allow it for a moment." An agnostic about commas, Sam was nothing if not protective of his prose. Likewise his colloquial dialogue. "Look here! *Now* they've gone to mending my dialect for me—I can't *stand* it." he carped to an editor. "Won't you tell them to follow copy *absolutely,* in *every detail,* even if it goes to hell?"[4]

Despite its haphazard production, the serialization was generally welcomed by reviewers. The New Orleans *Times-Democrat* ("many sparkles of the author's old-time fun") and the *Nation* ("vigorously sketched tale") were unequivocal in their praise. The *Windsor Review* ("the usual amount of blood-and-thunder"), London *Middlesex Courier* ("we should prefer his work if he would only treat the English language with greater clemency"), and *Leeds Mercury* (the plot device of heirs switched in the cradle was "somewhat hackneyed") were more ambivalent. William Livingstone Alden observed in *Idler* that the novel faithfully depicted antebellum life in the South, though the twins were "as little like Italians as they are like Apaches." Martha McCulloch Williams in *Southern Magazine* ("tremendously stupid and malicious and misleading") was one of the few critics who carped. The *New York Times* played the last card of the desperate reviewer by hailing not the content but the production values of the final installment, praising its "faultless typography and unsurpassed engravings."[5]

Even before the serial had run its course, Frank Mayo, Sam's old actor friend from his days in Virginia City, Nevada, and San Francisco, proposed adapting *Pudd'nhead Wilson* to the stage and producing and starring in the play. "On a cold drizzly day in February 1894," Mayo remembered later, he crossed paths with Sam while walking to the Players Club, and Sam agreed to sell Mayo dramatic rights to his newest novel and to send him the advance sheets. Sam and Mayo chatted again in his room at the Players Club after midnight on February 7 and signed a contract granting Mayo first rights to dramatize the novel in early March. The actor began to script it in mid-June 1894, as soon as the final installment appeared in the *Century*, and he finalized a contract with Sam on September 29 that assigned the novelist 20 percent of the net profits of the production. Mayo tweaked the plot slightly, adding a love story featuring (secretly free white) Valet de Chambre and Rowena, thus eliding the interracial romance between (secretly slave-born) Tom and Rowena. The play was first produced on April 8, 1895, at Proctor's Theater in Hartford and soon became a fixture on the fin de siècle American stage.[6]

After settling into his room at the Players Club, Sam's dance card filled quickly. He rarely spent an evening alone. He was entertained at dinner by some fifty members of the Oxford Club of Brooklyn, including William Cullen Bryant, Murat Halstead, and John Brisben Walker, on the night of October 17. On his part, Sam was "exceedingly fastidious. He told good stories and laughed at other people's stories immensely." After spending October 25–30 at the home of Charles Dudley Warner in Hartford, where Sam also visited his daughter Clara, he returned to a blizzard of dinner invitations in New York—with the Uncut Leaves Society on November 4, William Laffan and his wife Georgiana the next night, Laurence and Eleanor Hutton two nights after that, and the Rices on November 8.[7]

He was the guest of honor at a Lotos Club banquet at its new home on Fifth Avenue the evening of November 11; it was attended by about two hundred members, including such old guard as Andrew Carnegie, Edward Eggleston, Richard Watson Gilder, John Hay, W. D. Howells, Seth Low, St. Clair McKelway, Rice, Rogers, E. C. Stedman, Bram Stoker, Walker, and Warner. Sam was in top form in replying to the after-dinner toasts. He was "glad to see a club in these palatial quarters," he quipped. "I knew it twenty years ago when it was in a stable." The dinner was so successful that within a week the club received some thirty applications for new memberships. Edward Bok, however, took this opportunity to publicize in his weekly column the buzz in the air in late 1893 that Sam had been financially embarrassed in the backwash from the Panic. According to Bok, the banquet had been arranged by friends who were "sorry for Mark in his recent losses" and it "confirms the rumors which have been rife in New York for some weeks past" that he was flirting with bankruptcy. Some journalists still doubted the gossip. "The rumor that Mark Twain is financially embarrassed is funnier than most of Mark Twain's recent jokes," the *Boston Globe* opined. "The story must have been started by somebody who struck Mr. Clemens for a loan." Others rallied to his defense, like the *St. Louis Republic,* which claimed that Sam had "always been deemed rich, and correctly so, and if he has suffered losses he is in no immediate danger of becoming a pauper."[8]

Two days later Sam attended the memorial services for the actor Edwin Booth at the Madison Square Concert Hall. Many of the usual suspects joined him in the boxes: Thomas Bailey Aldrich, Mary Mapes Dodge, Daniel Frohman, Gilder, Nat Goodwin, Laurence Hutton, Henry Irving, Low, Matthews, Sol Smith Russell, Stedman, Ellen Terry, and Warner. That evening he dined with the Huttons and Irving, who gave him a free lifetime pass to his theaters. Sam and Howells then attended Abbey's Theater to watch Irving in the title role of Alfred, Lord Tennyson's *Becket* on the evening of November 16.[9]

Over the next two weeks Sam viewed a fencing demonstration; was entertained by Charles Dana, the editor and part owner of the New York *Sun,* and his wife Eunice, and by the Manhattan Club; played billiards with Laffan at the Racquet Club; and attended a dinner in honor of the aging bonanza king John Mackay at the Players Club. After taking a cab to the home of H. C. Bunner, the editor of the humor magazine *Puck,* in Nutley, New Jersey, on December 10, however, Sam fell ill with a severe cold (again). In consequence, he was confined on Rice's orders to his room and forced to cancel talks before the St. George's Church Men's Club on December 14 and the New York State Society of the Sons of the American Revolution at Delmonico's on December 16. The New York *Sun* carried an item on December 15 about his "hacking cough," which was "almost convulsive" and caused him to bend "almost double under [its] violence." Sam was worried that Livy would learn he was "laid up again," so he preemptively lied to her. "Dear heart," he wrote her the same day the *Sun* story appeared, "they say there is another newspaper report that I am sick. It is a lie. Pay no attention to such things. They aggravate me beyond expression." He freely admitted the deceit to a Hartford friend on December 17: "I have been cabling Mrs. Clemens that I am in perfect health—it being my duty to do that, to prepare her to disbelieve the newspaper reports—but I was out of doors today for the first time since last Thursday."[10] His rationale anticipates his defense of white lies in his sketch "Was It Heaven? or Hell?" a decade later.

Sam had recovered sufficiently by December 19 that he lunched with Rogers and fifty others at the Standard Oil building. Among them was the flamboyant journalist Richard Harding Davis whom, Sam wrote Livy, "I have come to like very much." The next evening he responded to the toast "Our Host" at a dinner at Sherry's restaurant honoring Brander Matthews, professor of literature at Columbia University. Among the forty other guests were Aldrich, Hjalmar Hjorth Boyesen, Columbia president Nicholas Murray Butler, Daniel Frohman, Gilder, Henry Harper, Howells, Hutton, Irving, Johnson, Low, Charles Scribner, Stedman, Stoker, Warner, and the architect Stanford White. "I was so prejudiced against speaking that I came near not going," Sam admitted to Susy, and in his toast he merely ridiculed at length the sound of Matthews's "somber and awful . . . lurid and desolating name." Yet his performance was the hit of the evening. Matthews gushed to him a few days later that "New York is simply *resounding* with your speech. I hear of it from morning till night. But *those* people can't rise to the size of it. They only know the *words*—unsurpassable words, that's true, but the *delivery*!—oh, it was just masterly!"[11]

The Panic of 1893 and the ensuing economic depression also represented a setback for the manufacture of the Paige typesetter. Sam wrote Livy the day of his arrival in New York City that "the whole United States stopped work two or three weeks ago, the machine along with the rest," adding in the same tone of naïveté that always marked his magnificent obsession with the machine: "It still lacked 3 *weeks* of being done." Before the end of the month he reiterated the point: "The type-setter is standing dead still. Neither here nor in Chicago can they raise any money to finish the machine" and the investors were "feeling dismal & disheartened." Within a week after they met in the lobby of the Murray Hill Hotel, Sam had enlisted Rogers's help with this project, too. As he reported to Livy,

> I have got the best & wisest man in the whole Standard Oil group of multi-millionaires a good deal interested in looking into the type-setter. . . . He has been searching into that thing for three weeks, & yesterday he said to me, "I find the machine to be all you represented it—I have here exhaustive reports from my own experts, & I know every detail of its capacity, its immense value,

> its construction, cost, history, & all about its inventor's character. I know that the New York Co & the Chicago Co are *both* stupid & that they are unbusinesslike people, destitute of money and in a hopeless boggle.

Sam provided Rogers with a letter of introduction to Towner K. Webster, one of the leaders of the investment group, so that he might conduct his own firsthand inspection of the compositor and the facilities to manufacture it. "I want Mr. Rogers to know all about the machine," he advised Webster. "I do not need to explain to you who Mr. Rogers is, since whoever knows the Standard Oil knows *him*." A week later, with Rogers intervening on his behalf, Sam was bursting with optimism. "We are millionaires if we hold the royalties 12 months," he crowed to his daughter Susy. "And we shall hold them if I stand by until they are safe from getting into trouble through Webster & Co's debts." Under the worst-case scenario he would scrape together "twelve or fifteen thousand dollars to live on for the next ten or twelve months; & if more should be necessary I will turn out & earn it."[12]

By early December 1893 Rogers had tied off the loose threads that had dangled from the typesetter for years. He agreed to represent the common interests of the investors in all negotiations. To see Rogers "apply his probe & his bung-starter & remorselessly let the wind & the water" out of the investors' inflated assumptions was, Sam wrote Livy, more entertaining "than a circus." Rogers "sweetly and courteously . . . stripped away all the rubbish" of their illusions of quick profit and "offered to buy the other shares at 20 cents on the dollar," in the end investing $78,000 of his own money in the company. He also bargained directly with Paige. Rather than a series of patchwork agreements signed over a period of years, the oil magnate proposed an arrangement whereby Sam had the right "to demand & receive any time during 3 years $240,000 cash or $500,000 stock" in the Paige Compositor Company or retain his royalty option. He and Sam would share equally in the profits. In a show of good faith, Rogers and Sam left New York for Chicago the afternoon of December 21 to discuss the settlement in person with the inventor. They traveled in a "mighty nice and comfortable" private rail car belonging to the vice president of the Pennsylvania Railroad. "In its parlor it had two sofas, which could become beds at night," a personal cook and waiter, as well as

> a very nice bedroom with a wide bed in it; which I said I would take because I believed I was a little wider than Mr. Rogers—which turned out to be true; so I took it. It had a darling back-porch—railed, roofed and roomy; and there we sat, most of the time, and viewed the scenery and talked, for the weather was May weather, and the soft dream-pictures of hill and river and mountain and

> sky were clear and away beyond anything I have ever seen for exquisiteness and daintiness.

During the twenty-five hours they were traveling to the Windy City, Rogers planned their Paige campaign while Sam "walked the floor and smoked and assented." They remained in the city only twenty-four hours. While Sam toured the World's Fair, Rogers made "promising progress" with Paige. "I am full of pity & compassion for [Paige] & it is sincere," Sam wrote Livy. "If he were drowning I would throw him an anvil." Leaving Chicago the evening of December 23, Rogers and Sam "were 30 hours returning [to New York]. Brisk work, but all of it enjoyable." Despite Sam's attempt to pay his share of the travel expenses, he "was not allowed." Rogers continued to dicker with Paige and his attorneys "by means of tedious long telegrams & by long talks over the long-distance telephone." On the contract they were hammering out depended "our very bread & meat," Sam cautioned Livy. "If it fails we are ruined," or "badly crippled, at least. If it is signed, it means the banishment of the wolf from the door permanently."[13]

Sam lingered in New York for the next several weeks with quick trips to Elmira, Hartford, and Boston while Paige dithered. His Christmas dinner at the Laffan home was unpleasant because "just at the last moment, when dinner-time was 15 or 20 minutes over past, & I was perfectly happy & joyous & tongue-free & hungry, the bell rang & in came the one woman in this world whose every single detail, from her trivial head to her invisible heels, is hateful to me & maddening"—Lilian Aldrich. "Lord, I loathe that woman so!" he confessed to Susy. "She is an idiot—an absolute idiot—& does not know it. She is sham, sham, sham—not a genuine fibre in her anywhere—a manifest & transparent humbug—& her husband, the sincerest man that walks, doesn't seem aware of it. It is a most extraordinary combination; he fine in heart, fine in mind, fine in every conceivable way, sincere, genuine, & lovable beyond all men." Two nights later, at dinner with the Huttons, Eleanor Hutton likewise allowed that Lilian Aldrich was "my pet detestation, too.'"[14]

On the night of December 30, Sam, Rice, Rogers, and John Archbold, another director of the Standard Oil Company, attended a boxing card at the gymnasium of the New York Athletic Club on upper Sixth Avenue. The main event featured Frank Craig, a black middleweight nicknamed the Harlem Coffee Cooler, who defeated a white sluggard by a knockout in the seventh round. After a weekend in Elmira, where he saw a play written and produced at Unity Hall by some of the young women of the Saturday

Morning Club, he dined with the painter Edwin Austin Abbey, the architect Stanford White, and other artists at White's apartment in the Tower of Madison Square Garden and attended a lecture on anatomy by the German bodybuilder Eugen Sandow. Sandow explained to the audience that the ordinary man "can expand his chest two inches," though he bragged he could expand his fourteen inches, "and then he did it," exclaimed Sam; he then mocked his own lack of physical prowess to a reporter for the New York *Sun*: "I guess I'll go out and expand my chest the usual two inches."[15]

He traveled to Boston the afternoon of January 25 for an authors' reading at the Hollis Street Theater sponsored by the New England Women's Press Association to benefit the poor and unemployed. Among the other participants were Robert Grant, Edward Everett Hale, Thomas Wentworth Higginson, Julia Ward Howe, and Louise Chandler Moulton, and the event raised about $1,000. As usual, Sam asked to speak third because "after that, the people begin to die." With fellow guest Oliver Wendell Holmes he dined that evening at the home of Annie Fields and Sarah Orne Jewett on Charles Street. Holmes was "in splendid form," his conversation "brilliant & beautiful," Sam thought. He soon proposed to Chauncey Depew a plan "to raise $50,000 cash for the unemployed poor of New York," in part by auctioning stage boxes at local theaters, though nothing came of the idea. He watched "Gentleman Jim" Corbett spar for three rounds at Madison Square Garden the evening of January 27 and, afterward, with Stanford White, he visited the world heavyweight champion in his dressing room. "Corbett has a fine face & is modest and diffident," he wrote Livy, "besides being the most perfectly & beautifully constructed human animal in the world." In early February he dined with the painter Frank Millet and his wife Elizabeth and the opera star Madame Lillian Nordica; and on the evening of February 6 he partied at the studio of impressionist painter Robert Reid with an eclectic all-male group, including the actors Benoît-Constant Coquelin and John Drew, the writer Richard Harding Davis, the inventor and electrical engineer Nikola Tesla, and the Swedish painter Anders Zorn. But such amusements failed to offset the "5 months of daily & nightly fussing with business" he endured during this period, Sam moaned. "I shall not feel any interest in literature or anything else until I have had a half-year of rest & idleness."[16]

Meanwhile, Sam nurtured his bond with Rogers. "He is not common clay, but fine—fine & delicate—& that sort do not call out the coarsenesses that are in my sort," he assured Livy from afar. "You perceive that he is a pleasant text for me. It is easy to write about him. When I arrived in September, lord how black the prospect was—how desperate, how incurably desperate! . . . It was from Mr. Rogers, a stranger, that I got the money & was by it saved. And then—while still a stranger—he set himself the task of saving my financial life." In February, George Warner tried to interest him in "a book that will go like wildfire" should it be issued by Charles L. Webster and Company—"a book that arraigns the Standard Oil fiends & gives them unmitigated hell, individual by individual." The book was almost certainly Henry Demarest Lloyd's *Wealth against Commonwealth*, a classic muckraking exposé. "There is a fortune in it," Warner promised Sam, "& I can put you in communication with the author." The sales success of such a book would have set Webster and Company on a firmer financial footing, but in the end Sam refused to pursue the opportunity in deference to Rogers. He declared that "the only man I care for in the world, the only man I would give a damn for, the only man who is lavishing his sweat & blood to save me & mine from starvation is a Standard Oil magnate." As Matthew Seybold remarks, "What Lloyd did not and could not know was that he had unwittingly brought the first genuine expose of Standard Oil" to Rogers's newest best friend.[17] Lloyd's book was subsequently issued by Harper & Brothers in October 1894 and has never lapsed from print.

Sam's fealty to his new best friend was also evident in his willingness to appear at the dedication of the town hall in Fairhaven, Massachusetts, Rogers's birthplace, on February 22. Rogers had donated a half million dollars to construct the French Gothic building and invited him to speak at the ceremony. "He was as shy & diffident" about requesting the favor "as if he were asking me to commit suicide," Sam joked to Livy, but if Rogers "should ask me to swim the Atlantic I would at least try." Speaking last to a capacity audience in an eight-hundred-seat hall, he wrapped his chestnut "stolen watermelon" story around a tribute to the father of our country on George Washington's birthday and "convulsed the audience." In the months and years to come, Sam repeatedly testified to his affection and admiration for Rogers. "You have been to me the best friend that ever a man had," he wrote Rogers two weeks after his trip to Fairhaven. "I never had a friend before who put out a hand and tried to pull me ashore when he found me in deep waters," he reiterated ten months later. Rogers was "not only the best friend I have ever had" but "the best man I have known." "Jesus! but I had a narrow escape," he wrote Rogers as late as 1905. "Suppose you had gone into humor instead of oil—where would I be?"[18]

During his many-months-long business trip to the United States in early 1894 Sam was obliged to raise some money both to cover his own expenses and support his family at the Hotel Brighton in Paris, "one of those arcaded little hotels in the rue de Rivoli," as Howells described it. On February 8 Sam drafted his essay "How to Tell a Story," an attempt to theorize his brand of humor, in his room at the Players Club. He finished the piece a month later and sold it for $500 to *Youth's Companion,* where it was printed in October 1895. He considered submitting the long-pigeonholed manuscript of "Captain Stormfield's Visit to Heaven" for publication—"it is a raging pity that that book has never been printed," he wrote Livy, "and yet if it were printed it would spoil it as a dinner-table yarn." Fred Hall priced Sam's writings at $150 per thousand words and John Brisben Walker of *Cosmopolitan* offered Sam $140 per printed page to publish excerpts from his letters to Livy, though he wisely resisted the invasion of their privacy.[19]

Instead, almost as unwisely, he contracted to perform on stage at the Madison Square Garden Concert Hall on February 26–27 with the Hoosier poet James Whitcomb Riley for $250 per night on the "condition that Riley leave all of the humorous parts to me & restrict himself to the serious." By Sam's own admission he was out of practice and, worse yet, the audience the first evening was trifling due to a snowstorm. Though the *New York Times* was unflattering ("Mark Twain loitered through several of his back numbers"), the *New York Herald* reported he was "drier and funnier than ever" in his delivery of the jumping frog sketch and received several encores. The next evening the odd couple entertained a "large audience" and "met a ready response." Sam later joked that the phrase "large audience" almost universally meant the house was two-thirds full. To compensate for the poor box office receipts on the first night, Sam and Riley appeared together a third time on Saturday, March 3, in a packed Chickering Hall, when Sam recited "My First Duel" and "The Golden Arm." His performance was uninspired, if only because he had been busy over the previous two days with a gathering of the Kinsmen Club with Henry Irving and Bram Stoker that lasted until 4:00 a.m. and "the annual round-up of the Aldine Club." The readings replenished Sam's pocketbook, but on the whole he was dissatisfied with them. He derided "those botches at Madison Square Garden with Riley" in a letter to Rogers and admitted he had been "a fool to go on the platform—but I had to have money." Nevertheless, he and Riley appeared pro bono on "story night" the next evening at the Aldine Club on Lafayette Place.[20]

Paige finally agreed in principle on January 15, 1894, to the settlement Rogers had negotiated with the other shareholders in the typesetter company the month before. Sam wrote Livy upon returning to his room at the Players Club that evening, "the realization burst upon me and overwhelmed me: I and mine, who were paupers an hour ago, are rich now and our troubles are over! I walked the floor for half an hour in a storm of excitement. Once or twice I wanted to sit down and cry." That night he jotted in his notebook,

"This is a great date in my history. Yesterday we were paupers, with but 3 months' rations of cash left and $160,000 in debt, my wife and I, but [Paige's] telegram makes us wealthy." As usual, he read his financial ledger through rose-colored glasses. By the end of the month he was nearly despondent again. "Sometimes when I reflect that our great scheme may still at any moment go to ruin before our eyes & consign me & mine to irretrievable poverty & want, my three months' work are but acts of a tragedy," he confided to Livy, "but all the rest of the time it is a comedy—& certainly the killingest one, the darlingest one & the most fascinating one that ever was." William Hamersley, his former friend in Hartford who had originally introduced him to Paige and enticed him to invest in his machine in 1886, tried to renew his rights in the typesetter and Sam was not amused by the inopportune claims of "that inveterate blatherskite," that "fat fraud, that crater cask of slumbering steaming rancid guts." Like a prisoner feeding birds through the bars of his cell, Sam nursed a futile hope that the Paige compositor would make him a millionaire. "By the power & pluck and genius of a better man than I am or than any other man than I am acquainted with, the typesetter *is* on its feet, and permanently," he chortled in late February. "It cost us 3 or 4 months of difficult labor, but the reward will arrive before many months." Put another way, as in Nevada in 1862 when he owned a paper fortune in mining stock he could not sell for money enough to buy groceries, he and Livy were "rich people who haven't any ready cash." All he wanted, he insisted, was the means to "be comfortable for another six months; then the new machine will be out & will make things easy for us."[21]

On January 31, 1894, Sam cabled a coded message from Rogers's office on Broadway to Livy in Paris that he had nearly reached a deal with Paige: "A ship visible on the horizon coming down under a cloud of canvas." The next day the inventor formally signed a contract and Sam sent his wife the welcome news on their twenty-fourth wedding anniversary: "Our ship is safe in port." He acknowledged to Rogers that he was "glad Paige has signed. I wish it was his death warrant." Rogers founded the compositor company that superseded all previous holding companies, its fifty thousand shares, each theoretically worth $10,000, divided among the investors. Paige owned ten thousand shares, Rogers seven thousand, and Sam twenty-five hundred. "It is the strongest company that—well, there couldn't be a stronger company," Sam wrote Bram Stoker, whose investment in the firm he was soliciting. "It has the best business man among the millionaires of America at its back, & he has chosen its President, its board of directors, its executive committee & the Chief Engineer of the factory himself. Work was resumed on the machines last Monday, & ten of them will be pushed to completion with all dispatch, without wasting energy on the other forty unfinished ones." Of course, all of the company stock was merely a paper asset, but Sam was genuinely appreciative. "You have saved me & my family from ruin & humiliation," he wrote Rogers on March 4. Two days later Sam signed a power of attorney authorizing Rogers to handle all his business affairs, and the next day he sailed on the *New York* for France to rejoin Livy after a separation of seven months, the longest of their marriage. "I wanted to see for myself just how she was," he explained, "and that's the reason I went." Two days after Sam left, Rogers assigned all of Sam's worldly goods, including his copyrights, to Livy as one of the preferred Webster and Company creditors, insulating them from the other claimants to his assets. "I owe more to Henry Rogers than to any other man whom I have known," he acknowledged eight years later. "He released me from my entanglements with the scoundrel Paige and stopped that expensive outgo; when Charles L. Webster & Co. failed he saved my copyrights for Mrs. Clemens when she would have sacrificed them to the creditors."[22]

During the voyage Sam befriended his fellow passengers Charles Francis Adams Jr., the great-grandson and grandson of two U.S. presidents and the brother of Henry Adams, and William T. Stead, editor of the London *Review of Reviews*. "We had a capital passage," Stead remembered, and he enjoyed "long and pleasant conversations every day on deck" with Sam, who spent his mornings writing in his cabin. Sam paused in England long enough to tell reporters that "the only proper way for an American to go to France in comfort was via Southampton, which enabled him to speak and be spoken to in his own language for a part of the journey." He also announced that he had three unnamed books "almost ready for publication" (*Tom Sawyer Abroad*, *Pudd'nhead Wilson*, and *Joan of Arc*), though a columnist for the *San Francisco Call* upon hearing the news declared that the American public "would gladly see him protect his own name by consigning these unfinished works to the flames." On March 15 Adams traveled across the English Channel to Paris with Sam, who found Livy "very much improved."[23]

For the next three weeks he enjoyed a temporary respite from the business crisis in the United States. According to the *Brooklyn Eagle*, he was seen daily walking along the Champs-Élysées. He met Poultney Bigelow for lunch at the restaurant Rue Royale, where he dined on Japanese eggs and beer and praised George Kennan's book *Siberia and the Exile System* (1891). It was, he insisted, "the most remarkable book and in all respects the book of our time best worth reading." On April 5, at the invitation of Lord Dufferin, the British ambassador to France, Sam read selections from his works for two hours in the British embassy ballroom for the benefit of "a school for destitute English and American children." The charity priced the tickets at an exorbitant four dollars each, which "frightened me," he confessed to his brother Orion. "But it turned out all right—had a full house," including Lord Terence and Lady Hermione Blackwood, Lord and Lady Dufferin, the journalist Theodor Herzl (the father of modern Zionism), and Countess Hoyos.[24]

Two days later, alerted to the imminent foreclosure of the Mount Morris Bank loans to Webster and Company, Sam embarked on the *New York* for Gotham. Despite the trials awaiting him upon his arrival, Sam enjoyed the "delightful" voyage. The weather was so pleasant that the passengers "were on deck most of the most," and among them was Max Judd, a chess champion and American diplomat. The ship crossed from Southampton in a record six days and twenty-two hours, and the evening before its arrival on April 14 Sam delivered a speech at the customary concert. After the ship docked, Sam "found my old room" at the Players Club "swept & garnished & ready for me."[25]

Webster and Company had long been teetering on its last legs. In February, Rogers had suggested that Sam "assume the debts & close up the concern & turn over my books to the Century Company on the best terms I can get," prompting him to complain to his sister Pamela that the firm had been "insanely managed from the day it got the Grant book till now." As usual, he blamed Charley Webster for the predicament but, he added, "the blatherskite is dead, let him rot in peace." On April 16 the Mount Morris Bank served notice that notes for $10,000 of the $30,000 owed by Webster and Company would fall due two days later, a predictable move given the continuing financial misery in the country. The demise of the company was no less predictable. The voluntary assignment of Webster and Company on April 18, 1894, was as inevitable as the creation of the Paige companies had been. Its liabilities were estimated at between $70,000 and $250,000, most of it good money thrown after bad. Its assets were valued at between $25,000 and $200,000, a difference of some $45,000 or $50,000 excluding Livy's claims. (How could one appraise the value of unsold books in a warehouse?) Among its approximately one hundred creditors were the Mount Morris Bank ($29,500), the family of the New York politician George Barrow ($15,420), the printing firm of Thomas Russell & Son ($4,623), and the estate of Ulysses S. Grant ($2,943). Fred Hall nearly wept when the bankruptcy papers were signed. "I half thought he would go off & drown himself," Sam scoffed. "In all my days I have never seen so dull a fool." News of the assignment made a splash in the papers, of course. It "was very sudden and unexpected," Hall admitted to the press. "We had expected to get money from certain sources which we had counted upon to meet certain maturing obligations, but we were very much disappointed in not obtaining this money and consequently could not meet the obligations referred to, and we thought the best course for all concerned was to make an assignment." Bainbridge Colby, the assignee, attributed the failure to "the depression in business. The firm, under existing circumstances, could not raise money to meet some obligations which were due. The course pursued has been fair and honorable and all of the creditors will be treated alike."[26]

In the end, however, all of the company's creditors were not treated alike; some were more equal than others. Rogers had arranged for Livy to be declared a preferred creditor and for her to be assigned all thirty-six of Sam's copyrights and his stock in the Paige Compositor Company, potentially worth several hundred thousand dollars, to protect them from attachment by other creditors. The Mount Morris Bank was designated merely a secured creditor. "Nobody finds the slightest fault with my paying you with all my property," Sam assured Livy. "There is nothing shady or improper about it. We make no concealment of it." To be sure, in negotiations with the bank, "It was confoundedly difficult at first for me to be always saying 'Mrs. Clemens's book,' 'Mrs. Clemens's copyrights,' 'Mrs. Clemens's typesetter books,' & so on but it was necessary to do this, & I got the hang of it presently. I was even able to say with gravity, 'My wife has two unfinished books, but I am not able to say when they will be completed or where she will elect to publish them when they are done.'" Elsewhere Sam laconically allowed that he had never been a real publisher. "I simply gave those fellows some of my money to play with—and they did."[27]

The myth persists in Twain studies that the bankruptcy of Webster and Company was the result of Sam's overzealous investments in the Paige compositor. Arthur G. Pettit, for example, asserts that the publishing firm was starved to death because "its capital [was] too quickly siphoned off to feed the Paige typesetting machine," and Alan Pell Crawford echoes the point: "Funds from the publishing company's earnings had been used to keep the compositor company operating." Neither statement is accurate. Sam was no longer subsidizing the development of the machine when the company hit the skids. The truth is that Webster and Company collapsed under its own weight as a result of a fatally flawed business model and the credit crunch that followed the Panic of 1893. The *Library of American Literature* depleted its cash reserves; and its backlist, with such titles as *Reminiscences of Winfield Scott Hancock* (1887), a minor Civil War general and defeated Democratic nominee for president in 1880, and *The Life and Letters of Roscoe Conkling* (1889), a powerful former U.S. senator from New York, simply failed to sell.

As Sam's lawyer Charles Rushmore reported soon after its closure, "the firm was loaded down with a lot of riff-raff, biographies, and memoirs of people in whom the public had absolutely no interest."[28]

Issued in hardcover by Webster and Company on April 18, 1894, *Tom Sawyer Abroad* had been at least partly reset from the original manuscript rather than from the heavily redacted version published in *St. Nicholas*. Webster and Company had declared bankruptcy the same day. As a result, virtually no notices of the American edition appeared, the book was not promoted in the United States, and sales were negligible. A little taffy appearing several months after its release in the *Los Angeles Herald* ("the interest never lags and the humor is delightfully spontaneous") and by novelist-playwright (and Sam's friend) Israel Zangwill in *Critic* ("as much set upon scarifying the superstitions of his day as Rabelais") were rare exceptions. Zangwill even defended the contrived conclusion of the novella as a "flash of [Sam's] old genius."[29]

Unlike the American edition, the British version published by Chatto & Windus was widely reviewed—sometimes warmly—in such venues as the *London Chronicle* ("thirty or forty pages abounding in the best kind of work which Mark Twain has given us"), London *Daily News* ("with its Jules-Verne-like invention and quaint oddity of thought and expression" it "ought to be an especial delight to boy-readers"), *Glasgow Herald* ("stronger and better in every way than" the original *Tom Sawyer*), London *Telegraph* ("an entertaining sequel" and a "sedulously funny book"), Glasgow *North British Mail* ("thoroughly Twainian"), *Hearth and Home* ("one of the most amusing of Mark Twain's many laughable books"), *Black and White* ("delightfully inconsequent, erratic and funny"), and *Dundee Advertiser* (written in the "author's usual quizzical and light-hearted style"). The review in the *Scotsman* ("no end of fun in the book") was safely noncommittal. Other notices were lukewarm to chilly—for example, the *Pall Mall Gazette* ("a nonsense story"), *St. James's Gazette* ("worthy neither of its author nor its hero"), *Athenaeum* ("a dull book" and "not an adventure worth remembering"), London *Bookman* ("desperate exhaustion of his author's invention"), *Spectator* ("amusing, but not, in our judgment, so amusing, by a long way, as Tom Sawyer's adventures on the Mississippi"), *Academy* ("not . . . particularly funny"), London *Morning Post* ("a disappointing production"), London *Sketch* ("a more unequal work never came from the pen of Mark Twain"), *Manchester Guardian* ("slang and slipshod spelling will serve in the place of humour"), and London *Sketch* (Tom Sawyer "was once a bright, winning, and promising boy" but "too much attention has turned his head and spoilt him"). Both the London

Literary World (it had "a lame and impotent conclusion") and *Saturday Review* ("anything more flat and unprofitable or more shabby to the reader was never devised") were particularly critical of the abrupt close of the novella. Even so, in 1946 Bernard DeVoto ranked *Tom Sawyer Abroad* "among the very best" of Sam's writings.[30]

Sam initially expected the creditors to allow Webster and Company to continue to operate in the short term. Two days before the assignment he wrote Livy that Rogers was "so much encouraged about Websterco's probable ability to pull through alive" that he advised that "we hold on & try to work out paying a hundred cents on the dollar" and close the company "without any stain upon its name." The timing of the assignment Sam thought propitious. "Earlier we should have made a poor showing; but now we shall make a good one" by settling the debts, he wrote Livy. "I meet flocks of people, and they all shake me cordially by the hand and say, 'I was so sorry to hear of the assignment, but so glad you did it.'" Poultney Bigelow sent him a check for $1,000 out of the blue, after which Sam wrote, "I had been meeting him every day at the Club and liking him better and better all the time. I couldn't take his money, of course, but I thanked him cordially for his good will." The bonanza king John Mackay called at the Players Club to assure Sam that "it's nothing to be ashamed of." At least he was free "of Mr. Hall's stupid & extravagant mismanagement" and he was "no longer harassed for money to pour down that hole." He likewise apprised Mary Mason Fairbanks that he was "not losing any sleep" over the assignment because "I think the creditors will let us resume business; in which case they will get their money. The strongest & wisest friends in the world are at my back, & I make no move until they have decided what it shall be."[31]

In the aftermath of Webster and Company's voluntary bankruptcy, however, the Mount Morris Bank effectively closed it. The firm might have paid its debts "if allowed to go on," and "all the creditors but the bank are quite willing to take that chance," Sam thought. But the bank balked at any settlement that renewed the loans. As a result, each of the nearly one hundred creditors was entitled to a percentage of the company assets, which eventually paid 27.7 percent of a declared debt of $79,000, not including the money owed Sam and Livy. "In time you & I can pay" the balances due, "*excluding* the bank," Sam insisted to her. "I shall be a very old person before I pay the bank any more than half of their claim unless it can be clearly shown that I *owe* more." Sam fumed to Hall, "I was not consulted beforehand when the $30,000 (the cause of our ruin) was borrowed" from the Mount Morris Bank. "The bank should have asked you if you knew me to be willing—& it should have declined the loan until you found out." After meeting with the bank officers on May 3, Sam reiterated to Livy his "strong suspicion that a good half" of the $30,000 the company owed the bank "is bogus paper & that we don't really owe it more than $15,000." On his part, Hall vociferously denied any duplicity. All notes were endorsed by Sam and regular statements were sent to him; that is, as he wrote Albert Bigelow Paine in 1909, the confusion and Sam's conflation of the Mount Morris loans "can only be explained by [his] ignorance of commercial matters and extreme impatience [with] business details."[32]

At a court-mandated meeting in New York on June 4 most of the creditors were, Rogers remembered, "willing to agree to any equitable arrangement" but a few were hell-bent "on devouring every pound of flesh in sight," including Sam's copyrights and the Hartford house, "and picking the bones afterward." Exasperated, Rogers finally addressed them: "Gentlemen, you are not going to have this thing all your way. I have something to say about Mr. Clemens's affairs. Mrs. Clemens is the chief creditor of this firm. Out of her own personal fortune she has lent it more than sixty thousand dollars. She will be a preferred creditor, and those copyrights will be assigned to her until her claim is paid in full. As for the home in Hartford, it is hers already." Sam offered to "pay fifty cents on the dollar" when the company was finally liquidated—and more, later, if possible. Nevertheless, he was ordered by the court to discharge his debts immediately to the bank, the Barrows, and Thomas Russell & Sons. That is, as Richard Zacks notes, the court "in one swoop" required him to pay $31,986. Most of his creditors, Sam assured Livy, were "acting handsomely. . . . Mind you, dearheart, nobody can charge me with dishonorable conduct; I have not been guilty of any; I shall *not* be guilty of any until I desert my family to take care of those others." In her reply, Livy endorsed his behavior: "Now is the time for you to add to or mar the good name that you have made. Do not for one moment let your sense of our need of money get advantage of your sense of justice & generosity."[33]

In truth, Sam was more relieved than embarrassed by the bankruptcy. No one, he admitted, knew "what a burden has been lifted from me & how blithe I am inside." On April 20 he wrote Livy that he had "read everything the newspapers had to say about it" and "discovered not one unkind or unpleasant or fault-finding remark. As I hadn't done anything to be ashamed of, I wasn't ashamed." On the other hand, Livy was mortified. "I have a perfect horror and heart-sickness over it. I cannot get away from the feeling that business failure means disgrace," she wrote her sister. "Sue, if you were to see me, you would see that I have grown old very fast during this last year. I have wrinkled. Most of the time I want to lie down and cry. Everything seems to me so impossible. . . . I feel that my life is an absolute and irretrievable failure. Perhaps I am thankless, but I so often feel that I should like to give it up and die." She would be mollified only by the full restitution of the creditors—dollar for dollar. "What we want," she told Sam, is that they

> get all their money out of Webster and Co. and surely we want to aid them all that is possible. Oh my darling, we want those debts paid and we want to treat them all not only honestly but we want to help them in every possible way. It is money honestly owed and I cannot quite understand the tone which both you & Mr Rogers seem to take—in fact I cannot understand it at all. You say Mr Rogers has said some caustic and telling things to the creditors. . . . I should think it was the creditors' place to say caustic things to us.

To his credit, Sam tried to comfort her: "You only seem to see rout, retreat, & dishonored colors dragging in the dirt—whereas none of these things exist." To his credit, he would eventually agree that his good name and reputation required him to discharge his debts honorably. He still hoped to recoup his fortune with earnings from the typesetter. As he informed his sister Pamela, "The new machine will be finished in June. We already know it will work like an angel. Mr. Rogers's doubts are all gone—he believes the machine's great future is secure."[34]

After closing Webster and Company, but before returning to France, Sam bid au revoir to a few friends. He had no idea, after all, when he would next return to the United States. He traveled to Massachusetts with Rogers for the annual meeting of the Fairhaven Improvement Association on April 19 and spoke briefly. Before they parted, Rogers urged Sam to draw on him should he need money. A week later Sam dined with the Rices. After a quick trip to Elmira in early May to visit Susan Crane and others, he embarked on May 9 on the *New York* in company with his old friend William Winter, the drama critic for the *New York Tribune*. During the voyage he wrote a first draft of his iconoclastic tour de force "Fenimore Cooper's Literary Offenses," mostly devoted to *The Deerslayer* (1841), "the most idiotic book I ever saw." Sam planned it as the first in a series of essays in which he would "review (& blackguard) all the novelists the last two generations of Englishmen & Americans admired" from the perspective of a "Professor of Belles Lettres in the Veterinary College of Arizona." He thought such a collection "ought to make a vicious & entertaining book," but he "had to *make*" the editors of the *North American Review* "take it at the revolver's muzzle. They said the subject was so *old*; & that nobody cared to read about Cooper in our day or have his dry bones dug up & inspected."[35]

The initial response to this satirical classic was not what might have been expected. Critical opinion of it was sharply divided. It was hailed in the *Kansas City Gazette* ("the best thing he has written for years"), *Buffalo Express* ("the best thing in the July magazines"), *Wilkes-Barre Record* (one of "the best things that the humorist has ever written"), *Chicago Chronicle* ("proves . . . Cooper was destitute of all artistic literary ability"), and *San Francisco Examiner* ("a very funny article"), and the *New York Tribune* offered tepid approval ("some of Mark Twain's criticisms . . . are not unjust"). On the other hand, the essay was reviled in the *Chicago Tribune* (Twain "wouldn't know a literary man if he should see one"), *Elmira Star-Gazette* ("it is idol Twain and not idol Cooper that is smashed by this article"), *Rochester Post-Express* (Cooper's novels "will be read long years after the writings of Mark Twain are forgotten"), *Chicago Record* (Cooper's "artistic blemishes flavor his excellencies; he is to be taken without minute inspection"), Austin *American-Statesman* (Cooper's novels are "too sacred for the carping criticism of modern flatboat men of Mr. Mark Twain's stamp"), *Brooklyn Life* (written "in a most unamiable spirit"), and Philadelphia *Public Ledger* (the "bitter iconoclast" has "struck a false note" and "should never have published" the essay). The New Orleans *Times-Picayune* scored with an obvious comeback: while Sam may have demonstrated that Cooper lacked "artistic literary ability," the author of the Leatherstocking Tales nevertheless "made lots of money. There is certainly something about his work which the ambitious (for cash) author may well imitate."[36]

After landing at Southampton on May 16, Sam hurried to London where, that night, he was the guest of honor at a dinner hosted by U.S. Consul General Patrick Collins at the Albemarle Hotel and, the next night, a guest at a dinner aboard the cruiser USS *Chicago*, commanded by Captain Alfred Thayer Mahan, where he "made the speech of the evening." During the two days Sam lingered in the city James B. Pond offered him £2,000 (or $10,000—i.e., $1,000 per appearance) to lecture ten nights, though he refused "because the London season would be over in 3 weeks, therefore there was not sufficient time to advertise." Bram Stoker, for one, advised him to decline, though Sam agreed to reconsider Pond's offer in the fall.[37] He finally shuttled across the channel and rejoined his family in Paris on May 19.

CHAPTER 4

Rent in Twain

A literary man's reputation is his life; he can afford to be money poor, but he cannot afford to be character poor.

—*Autobiography of Mark Twain*

THE CLEMENSES HAD originally planned to decamp for Aix-les-Bains when Sam returned to Europe so that his wife Olivia could take the baths for gout. Instead he delayed their departure to spend a week with W. D. Howells in Paris and then, on orders of his daughter Susy's doctors, on June 23, 1894, the family headed to La Bourboule, a spa town in central France, where they registered at the Grand Hôtel des Iles Britanniques. They had no sooner settled into their rooms than they learned that Marie François Sadi Carnot, the president of the republic, had been murdered in Lyon by an Italian anarchist. "We live in strange times," Sam lamented to Henry H. Rogers. "While the French and the Italians were celebrating the anniversary of [the battle victory at] Solferino [that ended the Second Italian War of Independence in 1859] and weeping on each others' necks by telegraph, the bottom Italian of the period stabs the top Frenchman of the period to death." The assassination sparked anti-Italian rioting throughout the country. The night of June 29, as the family was preparing to retire, Sam heard "shoutings of a great crowd" about a hundred yards from the hotel. As he recounted in his essay "A Scrap of Curious History," the mob sang the "Marsellaise," threw rocks at hotel windows, and demanded the landlord surrender the Italian servants to be beaten or lynched. When the landlord refused, Sam feared that the hotel would be firebombed. Susy was too ill to travel, so the clan was forced to remain in Bourboule.[1] The turmoil subsided after Carnot's funeral on July 1.

Buoyed by Rogers's news that all was well at the the Paige Compositor Company and by his promise that the "perfected" compositor was scheduled for a trial run in the print shop of the *Chicago Herald*, Sam decided to return to the United States as soon as he could travel safely. He left the family in Bourboule—they would retreat a couple of weeks later to the Chalet des Abris in the resort town of Étretat on the Normandy coast for the summer—for Paris on July 5 and crossed the English Channel to London.

There he was awarded an honorary membership in the Foreign Press Association of the city and, on July 7, he embarked for New York on the steamer *Paris* from Southampton. He was more optimistic about the typesetter's prospects than he had been in years, albeit for no good reason. In early June he had given his brother Orion five (of his twenty-five hundred) shares in the Paige Compositor Company together with an admonition: "This is the best stock in the United States & should not be lightly fooled away." Rogers's executive assistant Katharine Harrison, one of the highest salaried women in the nation, admitted to Sam on June 1 that a foreman in the *New York Herald* print shop whom Sam had authorized to sell the stock to his fellow pressmen was "finding it pretty hard work" because "the majority of those printers are such poor fellows. . . . As yet, they have reported no sales." But Sam garbled the essence of Harrison's message when he tried to summarize it in a letter to Orion three weeks later: "The compositors in New York offices are buying this stock; they borrow money to buy it with; they devote to it their hoardings in the savings banks. But they have never bought a share in any other composing machine. They know what they are about."[2]

The voyage to New York aboard the *Paris* was even more pleasant than usual. "We have 200 first cabin passengers," Sam reported to Livy, and they were by and large "considerably above the quality of folk who travel by the German ships." Among them were Nancy Barnum, the widow of P. T. Barnum, and Natalie Hammond, wife of John Hays Hammond, the American manager of Cecil Rhodes's mining operations in South Africa. While en route, Sam tinkered with the manuscript of *Personal Recollections of Joan of Arc*, which he had not touched in nearly two years. He had originally ended the tale triumphantly with the lifting of the Siege of Orléans and the surrender of the British—at which point, like Ulysses S. Grant at Appomattox, Jean allows the defeated soldiers to keep their horses if they depart in peace. But Henry Mills Alden, the editor of *Harper's Monthly*, persuaded Sam that he needed to extend the narrative. "You have told the story of a success and have abandoned it at the culminate point of triumph," Alden explained. "It is as if the story of the Saviour stopped with his entry into Jerusalem amid the hosannas of the children." Sam agreed, and decided to continue the story to its tragic conclusion with the trials and martyrdom of Joan at Rouen. He had written the first two-thirds of the novel as a "labor of love" to be read only to the family. In the throes of a personal financial crisis, however, he revised the manuscript for publication because he was even more desperate for money to pay his bills than he had been in early 1893. Soon after docking early in the morning of July 14, Sam submitted the partial manuscript of *Joan of Arc* to the editors at Harper & Brothers. Within two weeks he received a "pretty nearly satisfactory" offer of $5,000 to serialize the first part of the story without signature in *Harper's Monthly*, though he chose to wait before accepting the offer because "the Century would give more, I think." Before the end of the month Sam decided to decline the offer, though he was persuaded to discuss the matter with J. Henry Harper, the head of the firm. When he returned to the Harper offices on August 3 "to take [the manuscript of] Joan away, he and Harry Harper—"a very lovely man"—reached "an understanding in five minutes." Harper sweetened the deal, eventually paying over $9,000, or about seventy-five dollars per printed page, for rights to the story. Sam imposed only one condition on the agreement: that the production people, long the bane of his existence, refrain from "improving" or tampering with his prose. He asked Harper to

> make an order in writing & attach it to my MS., & sign it & back it with your whole authority, requiring the *compositor & proof-reader* to follow my copy EXACTLY, in every minute detail of *punctuation, grammar, construction* and (in the case of proper names) spelling. . . . I am thus urgent because I know that the Century proof-reader is insane on the subject of his duties & it makes me afraid of all the guild. That man changed every punctuation point in the Introduction to *Pudd'nhead Wilson—did it in the MS* before it went to the printer & it came mighty near being set up so. Do you know what that bat was trying to do? He was trying to make *sense* of a lot of stuff which I had taken enormous pains to deprive of all semblance of sense.

Throughout the negotiation Sam held also held firm to Livy's principle that the creditors would "lose no penny" by the assignment but would be paid "100 cents on the dollar," with the caveat that he would need to "adopt the wisest & best way to accomplish this."[3]

His living arrangements in the United States were lush compared to the cramped quarters the family had occupied in Bourboule. While he took a room at the Players Club, he only stayed there during the days he was in the city on business. He spent his nights as Rogers's guest at the Oriental Hotel on Manhattan Beach at the southern tip of Brooklyn. As a courtesy to the other patrons of the hotel, including Eugene Mitkiewicz, a colorful figure who purported to be a Polish count, Sam read from his works a couple of times, including "Reverend Samuel Jones' Reception in Heaven" on July 23 and "Playing Courier" three nights later. He crammed excursions to Fairhaven. Massachusetts, with Rogers and to Hartford into his schedule the next week. He took the second of these trips to discuss with Frank Bliss the issue and subscription sale of *Pudd'nhead Wilson* by the American Publishing Company. He also toyed with trying to "sell a big block of stock" in the Paige

Compositor Company to whomever was in the market to buy, but Rogers discouraged him from such a desperate move "till the machine is at work in the *Chicago Herald* office a month hence" and the value of the stock increased. In any case, Sam swore to Livy in late July that he felt "the strain letting up—letting up a great deal, in fact. I begin to feel pretty confident that the Webster creditors are safe in our hands & will not lose a penny." He assured her they would "come out [of the bankruptcy] without a smirch, don't you doubt it for a moment." He was even amenable to paying the entire Mount Morris Bank claim "to please you," though he soon changed his mind on this point. "I've *got* to stay here a while longer," he notified her a week later. Bainbridge Colby, he explained, "thinks he is getting the Webster affairs into promising shape & getting the creditors into a gentler frame of mind than ever." Soon there was even better news: over a year after last touching the manuscript of *Pudd'nhead Wilson*, and long after its serialization in *Century* was complete, Sam sold the "refuse matter" he had deleted from the novel—the afterbirth from the Caesarian operation titled "Those Extraordinary Twins"—to the American Publishing Company for $1,500, roughly equivalent to the Clemenses' living expenses for a month. The deal was comparable to the sale of sweepings from a barber shop floor to a wig maker. In any event, on August 24—after Sam sailed for France—Colby finalized a contract with Bliss to issue the two works in a single volume sold by subscription.[4]

Sam embarked on the *Paris* on August 15 in company with the painters Henry Abbey and Frank Millet; Thomas Gilroy, the mayor of New York City; and the theatrical producer Bolossy Kiralfy. Interviewed by a scrum of reporters before boarding, Sam explained that he was headed to Étretat, where Livy was "supporting a couple of doctors." He added, "Over there when a doctor gets hold of a good patient he keeps him," so "I don't dare to have even a headache after I land on the other side." This voyage was Sam's eleventh transatlantic crossing since June 1891 and he was "getting real fond of sailing now. After the first five or six days I rather enjoy the trip." The evening before the ship docked in Southampton, Sam read a pair of his sketches at the customary concert, which raised about $150 for the Seaman's Orphanage and the Blue Anchor Society on Staten Island.[5]

He reached Étretat on August 23 and found Livy "in great spirits" and "ever so much better in health and strength" than when he left. The rented cottage was "remote from noise and people and just the place to write in," he reve(a)led to Rogers August 25. He resumed work on *Joan of Arc* that afternoon. For the next month he mercilessly "drove the quill," as he put it. Within a week he had added over ten thousand words to the manuscript.

The story "tells itself; I merely have to hold the pen," he crowed. He even anointed an illustrator for the book: Frank Vincent Du Mond, an American artist living in France whose "views and sympathies are right." By September 24, a month after he returned from the United States, he had completed thirty-five thousand words, of which "only 300 have been condemned by Mrs. Clemens and short of 3,000 destroyed by myself." Livy then packed their trunks to winter in Paris, much to Sam's regret: "This place is a kind of paradise; it is beautiful, and still, and infinitely restful."[6]

The Clemenses left Étretat on October 1 but had traveled only four hours, as far as Rouen, before Susy fell ill with fever and the family registered at the Hôtel d'Angleterre. This pause in their plans might have been opportune for purposes of Sam's research into Joan's life had the city where she was burned at the stake not been scrubbed of all references to her over the centuries. The site of her execution was not even clearly marked. Or as Sam wrote Rogers on October 5, "There is no scrap or stone in Rouen that she ever saw. Even the spot where she was burned is not as definitely located as one would expect it to be." After eighteen days the family finally reached Paris and took their former rooms in the Hotel Brighton for two weeks before Sam sublet for $250 a month a "lovely house in the Latin Quarter" (as Clara put it) belonging to the British sculptor Frederick Pomeroy. "Large, rambling, quaint, charmingly furnished and decorated, built upon no particular plan, delightfully uncertain and full of surprises," Sam once described it in print. Privately, he was not so admiring. The "little" house had "two stories, eight staircases, no end of cells and passages, and little or no room. It was built by an idiot, I think." A dozen years later he complained to an interviewer that it "was one of the most curious [houses] that I ever have seen in my life. I was always afraid to take a walk in it after my meals for fear I should get lost. There were corridors and corridors leading to everywhere and nowhere."[7] At least it was conveniently located on the Left Bank on the rue de l'Université in the seventh arrondissement near the Hôtel des Invalides.

Pudd'nhead Wilson was finally issued as a book by Chatto & Windus in England and, accompanied by *Those Extraordinary Twins*, by the American Publishing Company in the United States in late November 1894 to mixed reviews. (The first British edition of *Those Extraordinary Twins* would not appear until 1899.) In general the English critics overlooked its formal flaws and praised its satirical force, particularly its commentary on character and race—for example, the *London Morning Post* ("remarkable . . . in the presentation of two characters [Roxy and the milksop Tom Driscoll] and their relations with one another"); London *Graphic* ("the full life and force of the story is the portrait of 'Roxy,' the white slave-woman"); *Saturday Review* ("the sketch of Roxy, the negress, is by far the finest thing in the book"); *Elgin Courant and Morayshire Advertiser* ("the most complete study of character which the author has ever attempted"); *Spectator* ("a somewhat gloomy but powerful tale of the slavery times"); and *Westminster Budget* (a "remarkable 'study in color' "). The *Athenaeum* similarly critiqued the social construction of race ("the best thing . . . is the picture of the negro slave Roxana") while acknowledging that the Italian twins "seem to have very little *raison d'être* in the book" and "the story at times rambles on in an almost incomprehensible way." In contrast, while William Livingston Alden agreed in *Idler* that "the introduction of the two alleged Italian noblemen" struck a false note, he argued that "in point of construction" *Pudd'nhead Wilson* was "much the best story" Sam had written. On the other hand, the *London Chronicle* ("an array of wood figures and utterly absurd people") and *Liverpool Post* ("impossible characters" and "equally impossible plot") were outspoken in their scorn.[8]

Perhaps because *Pudd'nhead Wilson* was published in the United States between the same covers as *Those Extraordinary Twins*, it was apt to be read not as a social satire but as a more generic human comedy. That is, the American notices rarely commented on Sam's treatment of race or his portrayal of Roxy specifically. To be sure, the *Springfield Republican* commended his "vivid picture of the South of slavery," adding that "the extraordinary Italian twins" seemed "absurdly out of place" in that world. But most of the American notices of the novel focused almost exclusively on its aesthetic qualities. The *Critic* applauded its "local color and dialect," the sine qua non of a work of Southwestern humor, then betrayed a bias against humor writing by asserting "it cannot be called in any sense *literature*." The *Book Buyer* ("full of the wildest fun") and the *Boston Globe* (it exhibited "fully the author's power in quality and influence of humor") highlighted its comic merits. Several reviewers described the story with superlatives—for example, the *Cincinnati Commercial Gazette* (Wilson "is one of the wittiest and most original characters Twain has produced" and the novel was "as full of the characteristic humor of Twain as is the best of his work"); *Public Opinion* ("much the best piece of work he has produced"), *Hartford Times* ("one of the queerest" of his stories), *New York Times* ("two of Mark Twain's most interesting stories"), and Hjalmar Hjorth Boyesen in *Cosmopolitan* (Sam had "published no book comparable in interest" since *Tom Sawyer*). At least two notices explicitly contrasted the two tales: *American Hebrew* (whereas *Pudd'nhead Wilson* was "the most coherent story that has issued from [Sam's] pen for many years," *Those Extraordinary Twins* was "as quaint, whimsical and preposterous as anything the author has ever written"); and the *Washington Star* (the tragedy of *Pudd'nhead* was "all right" but the comedy of the *Twins* was "probably less satisfactory than anything else Mark Twain ever wrote"). Then there were the equivocal notices, such as in the *Congregationalist* ("The author was not at his best when he wrote these stories") and the *Chicago Inter Ocean* ("Twain has done better literary work"), and the outright disdainful review in the New York *Outlook* ("excessively melodramatic," "confused," and "not always probable").[9]

Rather than fiddle in Rouen, where Joan burned, Sam spent his time there on an unrelated project: a full frontal assault on the xenophobia of the French writer Paul Bourget in his recent travelogue *Outre-Mer: Impressions of America*. Bourget ridiculed American customs in a style comparable to Sam's satire in *The Innocents Abroad*—not that this similarity mattered. As Tom Quirk remarks, Sam's "What Paul Bourget Thinks of Us," first printed in the *North American Review* for January 1895, was "an indignant and largely patriotic response" to the Frenchman. Bourget opined that "the poetry of a past is wanting" in the United States; that American culture to the extent it existed at all was distilled from European (i.e., French) culture; and, in a particularly odious aside, that bored or un(der)employed Americans could always devote a few years to discovering "who their grandfathers were." A long-standing and unapologetic Francophobe, Sam was insulted by the imputation and by some readers' willingness to tolerate such "weighty and well timed" observations and attacked both the author and the "oracular owls" who thought Bourget's slurs "'important.' What the hell makes them important, I should like to know!" Sam raged. American civilization a mere derivation of French civilization? His retort: "I like that! France hasn't any to speak of, except what she got at second-hand. American might profitably research "who their grandfathers were"? Sam called tit and raised a tat: "I reckon a Frenchman's got his little stand-by for a dull time, too; because when all other interests fail he can turn in and see if he can't find out who his father was!" Privately, too, he disparaged *Outre-Mer*: it was "wretchedly small game, & not much short of idiotic; but I kind of love small game," though he protested for months afterward that he would not engage in a "row with a shabby Frenchman."[10]

Predictably, critical opinion of Sam's rejoinder was split. Julian Hawthorne thought that it "amuse[d] past mirth" and the *Hartford Courant* hailed it as "a wholesome word" about the "offensive" tendency of foreign tourists to generalize about their experiences in the United States. The *St. James Gazette* diffidently excused Sam's "humorous attack" on Bourget, while the *Saturday Review* sniffed that it was "diverting though somewhat overdrawn" and the *New York Times* dismissed its "somewhat shallow as well as savage" humor. The London *Sporting Times* averred that it was "a bit unkind of Mark" and the *London Globe* dismissed the "very odd and not particularly amusing article" as "a lot of incoherent nonsense in his worst 'Tramp Abroad' style." The distinguished French physician Frédéric Labadie-Lagrave was less forgiving in *Le Figaro*: "Among the literary men of the United States it would be difficult to meet one who by his cast of mind is less fitted than Mr. Mark Twain to pass judgment impartially on Paul Bourget's work."[11]

The most celebrated riposte to Sam's review, penned by Max O'Rell, the pseudonym of the French journalist Léon Paul Blouët, appeared in the *North American Review* for March 1895. The retort was reasoned, if not always fair. As "a humorist" and "a genial, good-humored writer," O'Rell declared, Sam should not have concocted the "unkind, unfair, bitter, nasty" piece. "In this case," he opined, Bourget "is the humorist and Mark Twain the dull man." Nor should Sam have hurled "a gratuitous charge of immorality" at Frenchwomen, because the remark was both "unworthy of a man who has the ear of the public" and "a gross insult to a nation friendly to America." But O'Rell then indulged in some sour grapes of his own. He attempted to prove statistically that there was "more low, repulsive, unheard-of vice in a square block of Chicago and San Francisco than in a square mile of Paris," as if urban crime statistics were the best metric of national morality. Whereas, according to O'Rell, only 9 percent of births in Paris were illegitimate, that figure reached 12 percent in New York and 15 percent in Chicago, and the rate was even higher in San Francisco. O'Rell followed the jab with a cheap shot at Sam's personal finances: "In France . . . a man who had settled his fortune on his wife to avoid meeting his creditors would be refused admission into any decent society. Many a Frenchman has blown his brains out rather than declare himself a bankrupt." And he ended with a haymaker, to the effect that Bourget was "a great man of letters" and "a gentleman" whose book "ought to have achieved at least one object—Mark Twain might certainly have derived from its perusal a lesson in politeness and good manners."[12]

There is little wonder that the rumor circulated that Sam and O'Rell hated "each other like poison." Sam even suspected that O'Rell and Bourget were the same person. In a response apparently declined by the *North American* that remained unpublished until April 1897, he accused Bourget of trying to conceal his identity. On the whole, the critics were underwhelmed by this little contretemps. The *Chicago Tribune* considered Sam's initial rejoinder "personal, dead-in-earnest, ill-natured, undignified" and regretted that the second had "seen print at all." The *New York*

Times concluded that the tempest in a teapot did "not reflect much credit on Mr. Clemens." The normally anti-American *Saturday Review,* however, opted on this occasion to be even more Francophobic, deeming Sam's articles on Bourget "the smartest, the wittiest and keenest piece of literary fencing we have met for a considerable time."[13]

In early March, O'Rell doubled down by publicly challenging Sam to a duel. In Chicago, a safe distance from his erstwhile adversary, O'Rell announced that Sam "could have satisfaction of any kind he desired." The dispute was front-page news across the country. Though the ruckus might have escalated into a something approaching Sam's farcical feud with James Laird in Virginia City, Nevada, in 1864, Sam mocked the kerfuffle from the first as nothing more than a publicity stunt ("O'Rell wanted an advertisement") and the press covered it with all the gravity it deserved. A number of editors suggested that, if the two humorists chose to fight, they should fling jokebooks at each other. After all, as the challenged party, Sam was entitled to select the weapons. The *Chicago Herald* proposed that they should "discharge original witticisms at each other. If the seconds are kept well out of earshot, no innocent person would suffer." Then a would-be bard as talented as Bloodgood Cutter loosed the doggerel of war in an anonymous ditty memorializing the putative clash:

> I dreamed the other night and thought
> I heard M. Blouet shoot a shot
> From out a cannon, smoking hot,
>   At my old friend Mark Twain;
> The gun, it seemed was but a shell,
> The powder blew it all to—pieces,
> And Mark escaped, but Max O'Rell—
>   That is Blouet, was slain.

Flouting the better part of valor, O'Rell repeated his challenge to Sam in an interview on March 13, and Sam's response was volcanic:

> I wouldn't fight a duel with a thing like that. . . . Even now while I am talking of him my mouth has a bad taste. He wants me to reply to him so that he may be advertised. O'Rell is a nobody in France. He came over here to get some of our American dollars by lecturing. He says all Americans care for is to grab the dollar, and yet he does the very same thing he condemns. Why does he do it? Because he can't get a dollar in his own country.

Sam asked James Pond, O'Rell's lecture manager, why he permitted "that jackass of yours to bray so much." Pond laughed and replied that O'Rell's actions "helped to advertise the lectures." Sam was not mollified. On the contrary, he publicly accused O'Rell of plagiarism: "If he ever did find a good thing he spoiled it when he attempted to palm it off as his own after having stolen it and changed it around so that the original author couldn't swear that the article was stolen bodily." O'Rell's prose was so purple that Sam was surprised that the editors of the *North American Review* "should have allowed [him] to deface its pages." He concluded, "I cannot say anything more about O'Rell. The discussion of him acts like an emetic to me."[14]

This controversy continued to simmer for months, to judge from questions interviewers lobbed at Sam as late as September 1895. Had he met Bourget in Paris? "I did not," he replied. "He was there, I believe, but we did not meet. We had nothing to say to each other." What about the duel with O'Rell? "I daresay you have heard of our little breeze. But it was he who did all the talking; after I had answered him in his own fashion I let him alone." After all, "I'm far too old a soldier for that sort of thing."[15]

Fortunately, this episode in Sam's life has a happy ending. Over four years later, on June 16, 1899, he and O'Rell crossed paths at a Whitefriars Club dinner at the Hotel Cecil in London. Though they apparently had no interchange, Sam received a rousing welcome from the audience of two hundred when he rose to speak. Coincidentally, they met again a week later at the new Grand Hotel at Broadstairs on the Kent coast in southeastern England, where, with a little prompting from the artist, actor, and playwright Weedon Grossmith, they agreed to bury the hatchet. As Grossmith remembered the encounter, "they looked at each other for a few moments without speaking or moving" when "simultaneously they extended their hands" and shook "most heartily." They "seemed delighted to put an end to their grievances" and spent the next hour or two "engrossed in each other's conversation: they were evidently making up for many years of silence and were thoroughly happy." Back in London on June 28, O'Rell was present when Sam spoke at St. Paul's School and two days later, with Henry and Dorothy Stanley, Sam had tea at O'Rell's home.[16] For one of the few times in his life, he was reconciled with someone whom he once considered an enemy.

As early as April 1893, during one of his intermittent trips to the United States and when he was more dependent than ever on the income from his pen for a livelihood, Sam began yet another Huck Finn–Tom Sawyer sequel. "I have been out all day mapping out an adventurous summer for Huck and Tom and Jim," Sam reported to Livy on April 7. "As a result I have two closely written pages of notes, enough for the whole book. There will be two mysterious murders in the first chapter. The book will be devoted to finding out who committed them." From all indications, however, it was a false start. He seems to have laid his notes aside until the following November, when he wrote his brother Orion from the Players Club in New York that he had "mapped out a long novel" and "will bury myself in it tomorrow & be heard of no more & answer no letters till the back of it is broken, some weeks hence." A week later he identified the working title of the story, eventually dubbed *Tom Sawyer, Detective* (1896), in a letter to Livy: "I am making good progress with 'Tom's Sawyer's Mystery,' for I have written 10,000 words. . . . It is delightful work & a delightful subject. The story tells itself." The same day, November 10, he notified Mary Mason Fairbanks that he could not "put my book down at this stage lest I lose the thread of the story & get side-tracked."[17]

During late June and July 1893, in the interim between drafting notes for the narrative in April and beginning it in earnest in November, Sam had twice been a guest of the U.S. legation in Berlin, where he apparently discussed the story line with Lillie Greenough de Hegermann-Lindencrone, the American-born wife of the former Danish minister to the United States. While the evidence is entirely circumstantial, it suggests that Lady Lillie synopsized for him Steen Steensen Blicher's *The Rector of Veilby* (1829), based on an actual 1626 crime in the village of Vejlby, Denmark. In a footnote on the first page of *Tom Sawyer, Detective* (1896) Sam explained, "Strange as the incidents of this story are, they are not inventions, but facts—even to the public confession of the accused. I take them from an old-time Swedish criminal trial, change the actors, and transfer the scenes to America. I have added some details, but only a couple of them are important ones." Or as he noted when he pitched the story (to no avail) to the Bacheller & Johnson Newspaper Syndicate, the tale "transfers to Arkansas the incidents of a strange murder committed in Sweden in old times." Never mind that Sam confused a Danish murder with a Swedish murder; the plot complications are similar. That is, much as Francis Galton's *Finger Prints* (1892) inspired Sam with the plot twist necessary to resolve the murder mystery in *Pudd'nhead Wilson,* Lady Lillie's summary of Blicher's story apparently supplied the *donnée*—a snarl of mistaken identities more suited to a screwball comedy than a detective story—that Sam needed to develop a murder mystery. In both tales an innocent man is framed for murder; in Sam's novel it is Tom's Uncle Silas. When presented with overwhelming eyewitness evidence of his guilt, however, the alleged killer confesses, though eventually the truth is revealed. The alleged victim had in fact engineered the hoax to exact revenge on the accused. Ironically, the only novel for which Sam prepared a detailed outline in advance—he was keen on exploiting the genre formula popularized by

Arthur Conan Doyle and Edgar Allan Poe—is also "painfully plot-ridden," as Everett Emerson remarks. He completed the twenty-four-thousand-word manuscript in Paris in January 1895 and sold it for $2,600 to Henry Mills Alden of *Harper's Monthly,* where it was serialized with illustrations by A. B. Frost in the August and September 1896 numbers. The Wellington *Evening Post* in New Zealand thought it "all too short," and the New Orleans *Times-Democrat* pronounced the concluding episode "quite amazing," though not necessarily in a good way—rather like a dime-novel parody.[18]

The saga of the Paige typesetter ended not with a clang but a whimper. In late September 1894 a prototype of the machine—the only one manufactured by the Paige Compositor Company—was installed in the press shop of the *Chicago Herald* for a sixty-day field test. The initial results were promising. "I haven't ever seen such nice work as the Compositor does," Sam wrote Rogers two weeks into the trial. Even if the *Herald* chose not to adopt the typesetter in its shop, the Paige company could leverage a deal with the Mergenthaler Linotype Company if the trial went well. "Someday the Mergenthaler people will come and want to hitch teams with us," Sam predicted. "And we'll do it if they've got a long-life patent left then." He was more convinced than ever that the Paige was vastly superior to its competition. "When a bastard cripple like the Mergenthaler can fight its way up through ridicule & hostility during seven years to prosperity & a goodly share of respect," he announced to Rogers, "there's no occasion for the Paige Compositor to have any doubts about the future." Before the end of October he exulted that "things couldn't well be going better at Chicago than they are. There's no other machine that can set type 8 hours with only 17 minutes' stoppage." In November, Rogers traveled to Chicago to inspect the machine and immediately intimated to Sam that all was not well. The problem was not simply that the typesetter was failing the field test. On the contrary, as the mechanical engineer Charles E. Davis later insisted, "the Paige compositor, with all delays counted against it, delivered more corrected live matter to the imposing stone, ready for the forms, per operation employed, than any one of the thirty-two Linotype machines which were in operation in the same composing department. . . . This record may fairly claim never to have been equaled by any composing machine on its maiden trial." The problem was that the proprietors of the *Chicago Herald* simply chose not to exercise their option to buy Paige machines for the pressroom. As Joseph Csicsila observes, "the Paige did not impress the *Chicago Herald* enough for the newspaper to take a chance with it."[19] With line justification and an automatic type sorter, the typesetter was a technological wonder, an invention ahead of its time, like the jetpack or the electric car, though in truth its time never arrived. It was not a failure so much as it was impractical compared to the cheaper and more reliable Mergenthaler Linotype.

Rogers understood the problem after observing the machine break type in Chicago. He was dubious whether it would ever be commercially viable and decided to suspend further investments in it. The Paige "was a marvelous invention," he conceded, and it

> was the nearest approach to a human being in the wonderful things it could do of any machine I have ever known. But that was just the trouble; it was too much of a human being and not enough of a machine. It had all the complications of the human mechanism, all the liability of getting out of repair, and it could not be replaced with the ease and immediateness of the human being. It was too costly; too difficult of construction; too hard to set up. I took out my watch and timed its work and counted its mistakes. We watched it a long time, for it was most interesting, most fascinating, but it was not practical—that to me was clear.

Sam's first response to this warning was to propose some fraudulent insider trading: before publicly abandoning the Paige, he wanted to divert as much money as possible "into Mergenthaler stock at as low a figure as possible." Then "Paige will be crowded for bread and will be obliged to sell his patents to the Merg[enthaler] for a song. . . . That will boom the Merg. stock, for their machine will then be cock of the walk and *permanently,* without possibility of rivalry. I might be of use in privately purchasing that stock (through Dean Sage as go-between)." A week later he added another stroke to the scheme, writing to Rogers, "I wish Paige and the rest would give you full control of the patents, so that they could be traded to the Mergenthaler Co for stock" on "easy terms." The Mergenthaler stock would prove to be "an absolutely sure investment with the Paige patents suppressed." He admitted in hindsight that were he "back at the starting-place" he wouldn't "wouldn't spend any money on a machine." But then, as reluctant as ever to surrender his dream of wealth, he had a bright idea: "Has the notion of putting the *old* machine in the *Herald* in place of the new one [been considered]?"[20]

Rogers was more clearheaded, and before the end of the year he shuttered the Paige Compositor Company. He notified Sam, as well as the other stockholders, of the closure; the news "hit me like a thunderclap," Sam allowed. "It knocked every rag of sense out of my head" for several days, though he conceded there did not "seem to be any other wise course." Oddly, the evening after he received the bad news he attended "a masked ball blacked up as Uncle Remus" and "had a good time," the only time he is known to have worn minstrel blackface. At Livy's insistence he reimbursed his friends John Brusnaham (the foreman of the print shop of the *New York Herald*), Henry Irving, and Bram Stoker a total of about $1,500 from his own pocket because he had persuaded them to invest in the machine. But pipe dreams die hard. Sam promptly urged Rogers to "make a new deal with Paige and continue the Co. 6 or 12 months with Paige and Davis under reduced wages, and no others. That would trouble the Mergs, who are expecting our immediate dissolution of course." Rogers might then negotiate at least the sale of Paige's patents, perhaps even a sale of the company. Or perhaps attempt a radical redesign of the machine—by making brass rather than lead type to prevent breakage, or even by reducing the number of characters on the keyboard from 108 to fifty-nine to reduce its weight and complexity.[21]

Rogers complied with none of these suggestions, prompting Sam on January 2, 1895, to confess that his "ten-year dream is actually dissolved." Not only should he "have knocked C. L. Webster & Co. in the head 3 years ago," but that moment "would have been a good time to shove the machine out of my dreams, too." Not exactly. An obscure entity, the Regius Manufacturing Company, emerged from the ashes by exchanging one of its shares for ten shares of the Paige Compositor Company. The new company was capitalized at $200,000 and ostensibly had a contract to manufacture twenty thousand typesetters. "Please hang on tight to every share of Mrs. Clemens's Paige stock," Sam implored Rogers in May 1895, and "let's lay for that new Co[mpany]." The Regius paid at least one dividend before it, too, collapsed two or three years later. The Mergenthaler Company eventually bought Paige's patents for $20,000 to preempt any potential litigation by James W. Paige or his agents. In his autobiography Sam claimed he had "been robbed of a hundred and seventy thousand dollars" through "the ignorance and maladministration of Charles L. Webster" and the bankruptcy of Paige. Albert Bigelow Paine calculated that Sam's loss on the project amounted to about $190,000. Ron Powers estimates his total loss at "between $170,000 and $300,000 in late-19th century dollars," or between $5 million and $9 million in modern money. But as he had long wished, Sam at least was out of business. He was left counting his dollars, if not his pennies. Livy's share of the profit from her late father's coal and timber company amounted to about "$3,000 a year for herself and $1,000 for the children." Sam's royalties from the American Publishing Company and Chatto & Windus totaled about $3,500 a year. If he could earn $5,000 a year with new work, the combined incomes would "keep the tribe alive."[22]

The myth persists in Twain studies that the Paige compositor was an abject failure. Even Sam fed this myth when, in 1904, he declared that when "the machine failed to stand the test" his "fortune went up in air." But the Paige company failed, not the typesetter. "Marvelously ingenious and perfect, from a mechanical standpoint; worthless commercially," it was "the costliest machine ever built," the *St. Louis Republic* reported in retrospect in 1898. The compositor tested at the *Chicago Herald* "easily set up type at the rate of 8,500 ems an hour," eight times the production of most skilled manual typesetters. Of the two prototypes, the second became the property of the Mergenthaler Linotype Company in 1898 when it purchased Paige's patents. It was donated to the Sibley College of Engineering at Cornell University and, after disassembly, its scrap parts were apparently melted down during a World War II metal drive.[23] The original machine is on display in the basement of the Mark Twain House in Hartford. Paige died in a poorhouse near Chicago in 1917 and his body is interred in an unmarked grave.

As the Paige Company spiraled into insolvency, Sam rushed to complete *Joan of Arc*. "At 6 minutes past 7, yesterday evening, Joan of Arc was burned at the stake," he announced to Rogers on January 29, 1895. "With the long strain gone, I am in a sort of physical collapse today, but it will be gone tomorrow." He had

> never done any work before that cost so much thinking & weighing & measuring & planning & cramming or so much cautious & painstaking execution. For I wanted the whole Rouen trial in, if it could be got in in such a way that the reader's interest would not flag—in fact I wanted the reader's interest to increase; & so I stuck to it. . . . The first two-thirds of the book were easy; for I only needed to keep my historical road straight; there I used for reference only one French history & one English one—& shoveled in as much fancy-work & invention on both sides of the historical road as I pleased. But on this last third I have constantly used five French sources & five English ones, & I think no telling historical nugget in any of them has escaped me.

Ten days later he finished polishing the manuscript. "I have been at it off & on for more than two years," he noted to Mother Fairbanks, "& have written two other books [*Pudd'nhead Wilson* and *Tom Sawyer, Detective*] in the meantime." Or as the narrator the Sieur Louis de Conte declares on the final page, "I have finished my story of Joan of Arc, that wonderful child, that sublime personality, that spirit which in one regard has no peer and will have none—this: its purity from all alloy of self-seeking, self-interest, personal ambition. In it no trace of these motives can be found, search as you may, and this cannot be said of any other person whose name appears in profane history." Sam might have been speaking in his own voice. Within a day or two he composed a short piece celebrating his completion of the novel. "All the litter and confusion are gone. The piles of dusty reference books are gone from the chairs, the maps from the floor; the chaos of letters, manuscripts, notebooks, paper knives, pipes, matches, photographs, tobacco jars, and cigar boxes is gone from the writing table."[24] At about 170,000 words, *Joan of Arc* was by far the longest of his novels.

It was also an anomaly in his oeuvre, the least characteristic of his books, fundamentally at odds with his long-held belief, derived from William E. H. Lecky, that self-interest or selfishness is at root the motive for all human behavior. Who save a knave would believe that the same author wrote *Adventures of Huckleberry Finn*, the story of an untouchable in antebellum Missouri, the Mysterious Stranger, the story of a satanic visitor to earth, as well as *Personal Recollections of Joan of Arc*, the story of a martyred medieval Catholic saint who leads the French Army to victory at Orléans? Little wonder that Sam insisted that *Harper's Monthly* publish it without his signature or the imprimatur of the Mark Twain brand. He and his editors agreed that "if at any time" during its serial publication his pseudonym "should be appended to it as author" he was to receive an increment in his payment for it. "When I sold to the Harpers the serial rights," he reflected in his autobiography, "I did not want the authorship to be known because I did not wish to swindle the public. At that time, my *nom de guerre* placed upon a book meant to everybody that the book was of a humorous nature; to put it upon a serious book, like the *Joan*, would beguile many persons into buying it who would not have been willing to spend their money upon serious books from my pen." Its anonymous publication was also a clever marketing ploy, sparking a guessing game like the unsigned releases of Henry Adams's *Democracy* (1880) and John Hay's *The Bread-Winners* (1883). The editors at Harper & Brothers promoted the gossip, hinting only that the author was "the most popular of living American magazine writers." Among the suspected authors were Marion Crawford, Doyle, Hay, Howells, Thomas A. Janvier, Rudyard Kipling, Howard Pyle, Julian Ralph, Frank Stockton, and Charles Dudley Warner.[25]

In the end, however, not many readers were fooled. Arthur Stedman, for example, publicly speculated that Sam was the author of *Joan of Arc* in mid-February 1895, even before the first of thirteen installments hit the newsstands. In April the *New York Tribune* "outed" Sam ("if the style is to be considered, only one man, Mark Twain, could have written it"), then insisted his authorship was an open secret. Similarly, the New York correspondent of the Boston *Literary World* contended in April that, to judge from its "earmarks," Sam was the writer, an item soon reprinted in the London

Anglo-American Times. (The New York *World* quibbled with the argument, opining that *Joan of Arc* was "a better piece of work than Mr. Clemens has ever before been credited with.") In early May, three weeks after the appearance of the second installment, Edward Bok announced in his syndicated newspaper column that "the consensus of literary opinion in New York" held that Sam was the writer. Not all readers, especially some Catholics, were pleased. Sam was "unfit" to chronicle the life of the beloved Joan, according to the Boston *Sacred Heart Review* in October. The editor who commissioned the serial had committed "the most glaring literary mistake of modern times," analogous to assigning "a variety show reporter to 'do' the Passion Play at Ober-Ammergau," Germany. When asked by interviewers during these months whether he had written *Joan of Arc*, Sam was always evasive, though he never explicitly denied that he had written it. As he told one reporter, "I always make it a point to claim everything that is without an owner, whether it is tangible property or the more subtle product of the mind, but I can't answer that. It wouldn't be fair." Or in response to the same question from another reporter two months later: "I have always said that I considered it wise to leave an unclaimed piece of literary property alone until time has shown that nobody is going to claim it. Then it's safe to acknowledge that you wrote that thing whether you did nor not." Or as he said on still another occasion, "I am always willing to adopt any literary orphan that is knocking about looking for a father, but I want to wait until I'm sure that nobody else is going to claim it." Finally, in January 1896, ten weeks before the serial concluded in *Harper's Monthly*, Sam's authorship was formally acknowledged when the sketch of his life in the *National Cyclopedia of American Biography* listed *Joan of Arc* among his publications. The *Boston Globe* thought the admission unnecessary, nor did critical opinion of the novel shift appreciably after he revealed his authorship.[26]

Sam embarked on February 23, 1895, from Le Havre aboard the *New York* to consult with Pond and Rogers about his personal finances and to deliver personally the manuscript of *Joan of Arc* to Frank Bliss. Among his fellow passengers was Howard Gould, the son of railroad magnate Jay Gould. The steamer landed in New York on March 2, and Sam lingered most of the next two weeks at Rogers's mansion on Fifty-Seventh Street. Lloyd Bryce, the editor of the *North American Review*, asked Sam to submit an article for the next issue within ten days, a condition he rejected out of hand despite his financial hardship. "I *couldn't* undertake [to write] an article at ten days' limit. That's for O'Rell's kind—the kind that *puke* an article & think it's *literature*." Instead he solicited advice from both Pond and Rogers about an audacious project he was contemplating: to "hire myself out to Mrs. Clemens as a platform-reader" and "go around the world on a lecture trip . . . not for money, but to get Mrs. Clemens & myself away from the phantoms & out of the heavy nervous strain for a few months" and "thus escape trouble from my creditors." Such a staying action would limit their household expenses while his copyrights earned money and news of the trip whetted the public appetite for the travel book he would write. Though he could not repay all his debts from the proceeds of the journey, he was persuaded that he had "to mount the platform next fall or starve." Such a speaking tour, moreover, was "our last chance to go around the world. If we don't do it now we never shall." The American Publishing Company was interested in issuing the travelogue, moreover, and offered Sam half the profits above the cost of manufacture and a cash advance of $10,000 for the book.[27]

He had first considered circumnavigating the globe in the fall of 1893, when he was living alone in the Players Club in New York and desperately trying to borrow money to pay the notes owed the Mount Morris Bank. "When the worst comes to the worst I can go to India & Australia & lecture," he had assured Livy. "If I have to go, I would rather begin with India & Australia, & not reach the American platform till times are better." Two weeks later, he again mentioned the possibility and plaintively asked her, "Do you think you could go with me? I do hope it will not have to be, but often it seems to me that there is going to be no other way out." Clara recalled her father saying to her mother around this time, "Do you remember . . . the hellish struggle it was to settle on making that lecture trip around the world? How we fought the idea, the horrible idea, the heart-torturing idea?" A year later, on the eve of the trial run of the Paige typesetter in the printshop of the *Chicago Herald*, he contacted Pond about the prospect of an Australian lecture tour. Pond in turn queried Robert Sparrow Smythe, who had managed Henry Stanley's Australian engagements in 1891–92 and who promptly announced to the world that Sam was "likely to visit these colonies soon." Sam's audacious initial plan, as he shared it with Rogers in February 1895, was to

> start west in September, read twice in Kansas City, four times in Chicago, four times in San Francisco, two or three times around about there, & sail for Australia about Oct. 1. Read 60 times in Australia, New Zealand and Tasmania; once in Colombo, Ceylon; 4 times in Bombay; maybe read also in Calcutta or around there somewhere; then go on to the gold & diamond mines of South Africa & put in 20 or 25 readings there; then to Great Britain & read in London, Dublin, Edinburgh, & so on. 20 or 30 times; then home & read a few times in Boston, New York, Philadelphia, Baltimore, Washington

> and Richmond. . . . If I go on that trip I may possibly get a book of travel out of it; & books of travel are good sellers in the subscription trade.

"If we go," he added, he and Livy expected Jean and Susy to remain with Livy's family in Elmira, New York, and with Joseph Twichell's and Charles Dudley Warner's families in Hartford. The Clemenses would return to the United States in May 1895, "spend June, July and August" at Quarry Farm, where Sam would "prepare my lectures; then lecture in San Francisco and thereabouts during September and sail for Australia before the middle of October and open the show there about the middle of November."[28]

On March 18 Sam railed to Hartford with the manuscript of *Joan of Arc* in hand. He bunked at the home of the Twichells, and Joe noted in his journal that "he seemed tired and downhearted by reason of recent pecuniary losses, yet we enjoyed seeing him, and especially because he was under a cloud were glad he came." He also inspected the Farmington Avenue mansion and, as he admitted to Livy, "as soon as I entered this front door I was seized with a furious desire to have us all in this house again & right away, & never go outside the grounds any more forever—certainly never again to Europe." Sam felt "as if I had burst awake out of a hellish dream, & had never been away, & that you would come drifting down out of those dainty upper regions with the little children tagging after you."[29]

Back in New York on March 24, Sam was introduced to the fourteen-year-old Helen Keller at Laurence and Eleanor Hutton's apartment. Deaf and blind since the age of nineteen months, Keller had been taught to communicate by both spoken word and sign language, to read braille, and to "hear" speech with her fingers by her teacher Anne Sullivan. Sam christened Sullivan "the miracle worker," a nickname that would stay with her for the rest of her life. At their first meeting, in the presence of Howells, Rogers, and the poet Margaret Sangster, Sam "made me laugh . . . till I cried," Keller remembered. Howells told her a story with "her fingers against his lips" and "you could see each detail of it pass into her mind and strike fire there and throw the flash of it into her face." She read from Sam's lips "one or two of his good stories. He has his own way of thinking, saying and doing everything. I feel the twinkle of his eye in his handshake." He asked her permission "to swear, taking away her fingers [from his lips] when he did so." She told him "that *Life on the Mississippi* was my favorite story of adventure" and he replied, "That amazes me. It wouldn't have occurred to me that a woman would find such rough reading interesting. But I don't know much about women. It would be impossible for a person to know less about women than I do." Sangster later recalled that Sam "impetuously dash[ed] the tears from his eyes as he looked into her sweet face." Keller kissed Sam goodbye when he left and wrote her mother that he "knew with sure intuition many things about me; how it felt to be blind and not be able to keep up with the swift ones. . . . He never embarrassed me by saying how terrible it is not to see, or how dull life must be, lived always in the dark." She later wrote that Sam "was interested in everything about me—my friends and little adventures and what I was writing. I loved him for his beautiful appreciation of my teacher's work. Of all the people who have written about me, he is almost the only one" who understood Anne Sullivan's importance in her life.[30]

A few months later, at the behest of Eleanor Hutton, Sam helped raise a $50,000 endowment for Keller and Sullivan. He contacted the Rogerses to seek a subscription to the fund. "It won't do for America to allow this marvelous child to retire from her studies because of poverty," he insisted. "If she can go on with them she will make a fame that will endure in history for centuries. Along her special lines she is the most extraordinary product of all the ages." Within a month the "business shark" and his wife contributed "far and away" more than "the sum I expected"—enough to pay Keller's college expenses and to leave her an annuity. Sam promised to keep the news of their contribution private so that they would not "be flooded with begging letters," the bane of philanthropists. He was relieved "everything has come out so well for Helen Keller. If she doesn't go into the publishing business she'll be all right, now." In an aside in *Following the Equator* (1897), Sam hailed Keller's achievements: "She doesn't know merely things, she is splendidly familiar with the meanings of them. When she writes an essay on a Shakespearean character, her English is fine and strong, her grasp of the subject is the grasp of one who knows, and her page is electric with light."[31]

The day after his first meeting with Keller, Sam traveled to Philadelphia to speak at a luncheon following the launch of the seven-thousand-ton steamer *St. Paul* at the shipyards of William Cramp and Sons. According to the New York *Sun*, Sam was almost giddy at the event. "He actually laughed at several jokes of others, smiled suspiciously at one or two of his own, and in his enthusiasm" he asked the *Sun* reporter, "have you stood directly in front of the bow of that boat? I have, and I tell you that that bow is a beauty, and so sharp that you have to actually shut one eye to see it." Trouble is, instead of gliding into the Delaware River, the *St. Paul* failed to slip its moorings despite the efforts of Cramp's engineers to release it over a period of hours. Sam handed a copy of his speech to a journalist and left while the representatives of the afternoon Philadelphia papers "scrambled over each other in their haste to copy it and send it to their offices."[32]

Figure 2. Helen Keller, Anne Sullivan, Samuel Clemens, and Laurence Hutton (left to right), 1902. From Laurence Hutton, *Talks in a Library with Laurence Hutton* (New York: G. P. Putnam's Sons, 1905).

Sam embarked on the *Paris* from New York to return to Europe two days later. He sailed with Andrew Carnegie, the bonanza king John Mackay, congressman and future New York mayor George B. McClellan Jr., and Clarence C. Rice's artist wife Jeanne Durant-Rice and her three children. On the evening of April 2, the night before landing in Southampton, Sam again recounted his "dream about my trip to heaven & hell with Rev. Sam Jones & the Archbishop of Canterbury" during the customary concert, Carnegie in the chair. "It was good fun," he insisted, "but just scandalous. When Mrs. Clemens finds it out there will be a scalp lacking in the Clemens family." The night after landing, Sam attended a dinner in his honor at Henry Stanley's home in London, "a grand mansion in the midst of the official world right off Downing street & Whitehall." Stanley "had an extraordinary assemblage of brains & fame there to meet me—thirty or forty (both sexes) at dinner, & more than a hundred came in after dinner. Kept it up till after midnight. There were cabinet ministers, ambassadors, admirals, generals, canons, Oxford professors, novelists, playwrights, poets, & a number of people equipped with rank *and* brains. I told some yarns & made some speeches." Sam's reception convinced him that, when he returned from Australia, he ought to "lecture there a month or two." Among the "many delightful ladies" who greeted him was Lady Bridge, wife of Rear Admiral Cyprian A. G. Bridge of the Royal Navy and commander in chief of the Australian Station, who told him that "her husband was able to throw wide all doors to me in that part of the world" and that "she would write him we were coming."[33] The next day, Sam rejoined his family in Paris to pack for their return to the United States after an absence of almost four years.

Sam's speaking tour of the Antipodes during September and October 1895, the spring season "down under," had been all but scheduled by the time he arrived at their house on the rue de l'Université. He wrote Rogers in mid-April, scarcely ten days after his return, that he was "tired to death all the time, and my head is tired and clogged, too, and the mill refuses to go. It comes of depression of spirits, I think, caused by the impending horror of the platform." Before the Clemenses moved to the Hotel Brighton at the end of April upon the expiration of the lease on the house, but only after consulting with Henry Stanley, Sam signed a contract with Smythe "for a six to nine months' reading tour," departing from the West Coast of the United States in mid-August, tracking through "the Sandwich Islands, New Zealand, Australia, Ceylon, Madras, Calcutta, Bombay & other Indian cities, then South Africa & the Mauritius." After a few months in England, where he planned to write most of the travelogue based on the trip around the world, he expected to "read in England a spell," then "gabble" across America to the Pacific coast "& then back again through the Southern States. And then die, I reckon." He wailed to his friend Poultney Bigelow the same day he cabled his agreement to the terms of the contract that he was obliged "to turn out in my lazy old age and go on the platform again." Livy and Clara had agreed to accompany him around the world, but Susy refused "because she hates the sea" and Jean declined "because she can't spare the time from school." Clara thought they simply "preferred the comforts of home to uncertain joys in India or Africa." In any event, the sisters remained in Elmira with friends and family, Susan Crane and Katy Leary among them. If all went according to plan, he informed Bigelow, he would complete the barnstorm "by next March & reach London early in April."[34]

Then he revived his old hope of once more performing in San Francisco. "I've a notion to read a few times in America before I sail for Australia," Sam advised his former manager Pond, who promptly notified authorities in both Salt Lake City and San Francisco to expect him to speak in their cities during the summer. For years Pond had been hounding Sam, who "has more calls to lecture than any other American," to tour the United

States again and had tendered him a standing offer of $300 a night.[35] Sam had worried, however, that his creditors would attempt to seize the box office receipts at any venue in the States where he appeared.

During his last days in Paris, Sam proofread some of the pages of *Joan of Arc* in advance of their publication in *Harper's* and discovered "a couple of tip-top platform readings" he might declaim on his tour if his authorship were known. "The fact is," he decided, "there is more good platform-stuff in *Joan* than in any previous book of mine, by a long sight." The evening of May 2, Sam, Livy, and two of their daughters attended a performance of *La Comtesse de Lisne* by Victor Mapes, the Paris correspondent of the New York *Sun*, at the Theatre Mondain. Among the others in the audience were the American actress Georgia Cayvan and the U.S. ambassador to France, James Biddle Eustice.[36] On May 10 the clan crossed the Channel to Southampton and the following day they embarked on the *New York* for New York City. It was Sam's fifteenth transatlantic crossing since June 1891 and would be his last for more than five years.

"It wasn't much of a trip," Sam remembered later. He did no work during the voyage. "I simply went over because my family wanted to come home" and he "brought 'em." The crossing was so uneventful, he joked later, that he had "placed a lemon in the center of the table in my stateroom on Saturday evening and it didn't roll off until the following Wednesday afternoon." He spent part of his time conversing with fellow passenger James J. Hill, president of the Great Northern Railway, which ran from St. Paul to Seattle. Sam and Hill, who like Jay Gould and Henry Rogers was considered one of the "robber barons" of the period, had been distantly acquainted thirty-five years earlier when Sam was piloting on the lower Mississippi and Hill worked as a bookkeeper for a steamboat company on the upper Mississippi. They mostly discussed, Sam said, "the pilots of the Mississippi. Most of them have gone to —— and a few to heaven, but only a few of us are left." At the customary concert to benefit the American Seaman's Friend Society the evening before the ship arrived in New York, Sam read two of his works. The ship docked the morning of May 18 and Sam was met at the pier by Howells and a troupe of Hartford friends.[37]

Though he was expected to "remain in New York only twenty-four hours," the report was wrong. In fact, the Clemenses registered at the Everett House on Union Square. Charley Langdon had invited them to be his guests at the Waldorf-Astoria but Livy was sensitive to the impression such luxury would leave if they accepted: "People would think that we were splurging there on our own footing and it wouldn't look modest for bankrupts." They dallied in the city for four days so that Sam could attend two of the final performances of *Pudd'nhead Wilson* starring Frank Mayo at the Herald Square Theater before it went on the road. Mayo played the title role with a Mark Twain–type drawl, and the production featured Frank Campeau—who would later star on Broadway in the role of Trampas in Owen Wister's *The Virginian*—as Tom Driscoll. Sam had telegraphed Mayo from Paris on April 15 to "cable me the jury's verdict"; the audience at the New York premiere, no doubt with some prompting, had shouted that it was "a success!" He soon wrote James Pond that Mayo "has done a great thing for both of us; for he has proved himself a gifted dramatist as well as a gifted orator, and has enabled me to add another new character to American drama. I hope he will have grand success." Sam again telegraphed Mayo from Southampton on May 11, the day he embarked on the *New York*, that he would arrive in time to see the play before it closed on Broadway.[38]

In fact, he occupied a box at the Herald Square Theater the very evening of his arrival on May 18 and was called by the audience to deliver an impromptu speech at the end of the third act. "Never in my life have I been able to make a speech without preparation," he began, "and I assure you that this position in which I find myself is one totally unexpected. I have been hemmed in all today by W. D. Howells and other frivolous persons. . . . I will only say that I congratulate Mr. Mayo. He has certainly made a beautiful play out of my rubbish." The evening of May 22, Sam again occupied a box at the Herald Square Theater with Livy and over a dozen of their friends, including Richard Watson Gilder, Murat Halstead, Howells, St. Clair McKelway, Pond, Rogers, and E. C. Stedman. An "uncommonly large audience," among them Robert Ingersoll, was attracted to the theater that night by the announcement that Sam "would be present and would probably make a speech." He again obliged at the end of the third act, this time delivering a prepared ten-minute address before the curtain, the gist of which was simple enough: "Mr. Mayo has been able to manage those difficult twins. I tried" but "failed," as if the subplot about the Italian twins was the focus of the play.[39]

Frank Mayo staged the play over 360 times during the next year and met "with great success," as he bragged in an interview with the *San Francisco Call* in April 1896. Sam (or more correctly Livy, as the holder of dramatic rights to the novel after the bankruptcy of Charles L. Webster and Company) received generous royalty checks from Mayo as long as it was acted—$1,457 in April 1896, the month it was produced in San Francisco, for example. Unfortunately, Mayo died two months later at the close of the theatrical season.

The next year, Edwin Mayo tried to replace his father in the title role, albeit with little success. As Sam lamented in March 1897, "Why didn't the useless *son* die, instead of the useful father?"[40]

Sam and the clan retreated to Elmira and Quarry Farm by the end of the same week *Pudd'nhead Wilson* closed on Broadway. Pond soon joined them there to finalize the itinerary of the speaking tour. "I have very little time in which to select and prepare my readings," Sam wrote Orion from the Langdon mansion on Main Street, "but I will make up by working double tides till I start west." Pond was still toying with the itinerary for the North American leg of Sam's tour and negotiating over locales where he would perform. Pond initially proposed four appearances in San Francisco—a city "of half a million people," Sam noted. "I filled 3 great houses there 27 years ago when the population was 100,000," and Tom Maguire, whose Academy of Music he rented in 1866, "lost his temper & called me a fool because I didn't talk ten nights." Sam insisted on nine appearances, including matinees, during a week in San Francisco, with Pond receiving only 20 percent of the profits there versus 25 percent elsewhere. Pond initially accepted the terms, then reneged. The city would be deserted in the August heat, he maintained (the coldest winter Sam ever spent was a summer in San Francisco?) so he scheduled no dates there at all. Sam was "thoroughly disappointed," he admitted to his nephew Sam Moffett. "I wanted to talk half a dozen times in San Francisco, & I expected to have a good time & stay ten days & see everybody I ever knew; but Pond says the town empties itself before the first week of August, & I must not go there earlier than October." In the end, Pond arranged for Sam to speak in one- and two-night stands in twenty-one North American towns and cities between mid-July and mid-August while en route to the West Coast. This itinerary included neither San Francisco nor Salt Lake City—cities where he obviously preferred Sam to appear during the traditional late fall and winter lecture season rather than in midsummer. In mid-June 1895 Pond "postponed" most appearances by Sam in western venues below the 49th parallel "until the season of 1896–97, when he will make a general tour" throughout the United States. The plan was to "lecture all over America, north & south," Sam notified Rogers, but he was reluctant to trust Pond to manage such an assault on the lyceums. Despite his reputation, the bureau manager was "an idiot," "an incompetent," and "a business-coward" with "no idea of proportions." He scheduled Sam to lecture "twice in the little town of Winnipeg" yet had postponed his appearances in New York and Chicago. Still, Sam eventually acceded to Pond's plans. After all, he needed to cover expenses on the transcontinental trip, even if some of the engagements in the mining towns of the upper-tier states were not very remunerative. "We cross the continent in July by one of the northern routes," he explained to Moffett, "in the hope that the higher north the road is, the cooler the weather will be & the wholesomer for your aunt Livy, whose health fails under heat." In fact, the entire tour was scheduled to avoid the worst of the warmth in India during the summer there. Better to endure "midsummer heat in Cleveland," he decided, "than tropical temperatures" in Delhi later.[41] Pond and his wife Martha would accompany them to the West Coast in order to manage publicity, travel, interviews, bookings, and the box office.

As soon as Sam's world tour was announced, *Cosmopolitan*, *Century*, and Frank Bliss of the American Publishing Company each offered him an exclusive contract to detail the trip in its pages. *Cosmopolitan* tendered $10,000 for a dozen articles about Australia, the *Century* $12,000 for twelve humorous essays, and Bliss a $10,000 advance for a travel book. "The *Century* people actually proposed that I *sign a contract to be funny* in those 12 articles," Sam marveled to Rogers. "That was pure insanity. Why, it makes me shudder every time I think of those articles. I don't think I could ever write one of them without being under the solemnizing blight of that disgusting recollection." He fully expected to "write a subscription book of travels without any effort" in a year, "but to write travels for serial publication is hideous hard work. I am not committed to any magazine yet—and I believe it will be wisest to remain unfettered." He could always "sell some of [the travelogue] to a magazine," but he was "not going to make any previous contract with any magazine." In the wake of the bankruptcy of Webster and Company and the failure of the Paige Compositor Company, Sam was also gun-shy about all legal agreements. "I've signed a lot of contracts in my time," he admitted to Rogers, "and at signing-time I probably knew what the contracts meant—but 6 months later everything had grown dim and I could be *certain* of only two things, to-wit: 1. I didn't *sign* any contract; 2. The contract means the opposite of what it *says*."[42]

In the end, Sam accepted Bliss's tender, however reluctantly. He preferred that his final travelogue be sold by subscription rather than by Harper & Brothers through the trade, and as little as Sam trusted Bliss he believed the American Publishing Company to be the right distribution channel. "I think that my reason for wanting my travel-book in Bliss's hands is sound," he assured Rogers, adding,

> Harper publishes very high-class books & they go to people who are accustomed to read. That class are surfeited with travel-books. But there is a vast class that isn't—the factory hands & the farmers. *They* never go to a bookstore; they have to be hunted down by the canvasser. When a subscription book of

> mine sells 60,000, I always think I know whither 50,000 of them went. They went to people who don't visit bookstores. I planned this book, from the beginning, for the *subscription* market. I am writing it according to that plan. If it doesn't pay me $30,000 in the first six months, it will be because the new Blisses lack their own father's push and efficiency.

Lest Rogers "think me foolish about the subscription business," Sam reiterated that he had "tried it & I have tried the trade, too—& really there is no comparison between them. The sub[scription] plan can outsell the 'trade' five to one with any book of mine whose subject is *foreign travel*."[43]

While residing at Quarry Farm during the spring of 1895, Sam hoped to develop three distinct programs for his talking tour so that he might attract some admirers as many as three times in any city he visited. But he was soon afflicted with a strange illness—"I am in bed, & must stay there two or three weeks yet—gout in my starboard an[k]le, a boil as big as a turkey's egg on my port thigh," he complained—that significantly slowed his preparation. By early June the "boil" was diagnosed as a carbuncle. "I could have done without it, for I do not care for jewelry." ("Carbuncle" may also refer to a red gem, usually a garnet.) "I have discouraged and squelched three others in their infancy and am discouraging still another," Sam griped to Rogers on June 4. "I've got one on the back of my right hand which has crippled it for a week." He spent the entire month of June incapacitated, and as a result "lost all interest in life and work and lecturing and everything else." During the month the carbuncle finally burst and "sloughed out a big hunk of decayed protoplasm like a Baltimore oyster . . . & left a corresponding raw cavity in my leg."[44]

Worse yet, in late June he was presented with a subpoena to testify under oath on July 5 in New York. The firm of Thomas Russell & Son had filed suit against him to recover over five thousand dollars in printing, binding costs, and interest charged to Webster and Company and awarded by the court the year before. Rogers suggested that he ignore the subpoena, though Sam understood better than Rogers the public relations disaster it would entail. "It would [be] a bad advertisement for my lecture-trip to have all the papers here and in Australia saying I have dodged the courts and fled the country," he replied. "I mustn't do it." Instead he asked for a postponement of the court date to July 11 for reasons of health. In the interim he tried but failed to negotiate a settlement with Russell because Livy was "dead set against having me keel-hauled and fire-assayed in that court for the benefit of the newspapers." Instead, a reluctant witness, he railed to New York on July 10 accompanied by a nurse, hauling along his personal financial records, including the paperwork executed in the transfer of his copyrights to Livy, and over the next two days he was questioned in the Wall Street office of his attorneys. As he was grilled, according to the *New York Herald*, he was "suffering physical pain" from his recent ailments yet "bore the ordeal resignedly." Russell's lawyers asked specifically for the reasons Sam's copyrights had been transferred to Livy, how much they were worth, and whether the transfer was liable to be revoked. These "supplementary proceedings" publicized for the first time the fact that Sam was "virtually penniless" even though he had "requested that the matter of the examination be not used by the press." No stranger to bad publicity, Rogers tried to comfort Sam: "Your examination is like one of New York's nine days' wonders and will be forgotten within the prescribed time." But Sam was embittered by the entire affair. Russell "had made a neat little fortune out of Webster & Co., but that didn't signify: he wanted his money; he could not wait on my slow earnings, so he persecuted me with the law." And in Elmira, Livy was disconsolate that Sam's name and news of their financial embarrassment "had gotten into the papers." The response of the Concord, Massachusetts, *Enterprise*, which blamed Sam's problems on greed, proved her fears well-founded. Had he been satisfied with the "pretty pile of money" he made on Grant's memoirs, Sam would not have gotten into financial trouble. Then again, Sam blamed his woes, his "shame," and "the humiliations of these days" on Charley Webster, his favorite scapegoat.[45]

To add insult to injury, the attorneys Bainbridge Colby and Charles E. Rushmore (after whom Mount Rushmore in South Dakota is named)—or "this idiot and his associate-idiot," as Sam called them—charged $700 to represent him. "What cheap, cheap material one can make a New York lawyer of," he grumbled. Colby was "a mere nine-days' miscarriage, just a pulpy foetus. I reckon he wants that $700 to buy a sugar-teat with." Sam blamed them for mishandling the case from the beginning. The "jackasses allowed me to come to New York" for questioning, though the court "had no more authority over me than the Mikado of Japan," a maneuver by the plaintiff that "made a compromise at less than par wholly unnecessary." Yet while crossing the United States on his speaking tour Sam's baggage or the gate receipts from his public appearances were still liable to be attached for debt, so the day after the proceedings ended, without waiting for the assignee to arbitrate a settlement with his creditors, Sam instructed his attorneys to pay Russell and all legal fees in full and draw on Charley Langdon (that is, on Livy's account with J. Langdon and Company) for the money. Only then was Sam satisfied that the Russell lawsuit had been "silenced."[46]

On July 12, the same evening the "supplementary proceedings" ended, Sam rehearsed one of his talks at the House of Refuge on Randall's Island in New York City before a captive crowd of about seven hundred juvenile delinquents. The venue was not his first choice. He had hoped to try out his readings before live audiences at Cornell University in Ithaca, only thirty miles north of Quarry Farm, and/or the new Town Hall in Fairhaven, Massachusetts, but his ill health had precluded those appearances. Instead, as a told a reporter for the New York *Sun*, "I'm going to try my new lecture" on the inmates of the reform school "and by the way it takes here I will be able to tell how it will take on the other side of the world." He was escorted by his Elmira nurse and Katherine Harrison, Rogers's assistant, and suffered a monumentally "comical defeat" by "delivering a grown folks' lecture to a sucking-bottle nursery! No, only *trying*—I didn't do it—& couldn't. No man could have done it." The boys had paid little attention. Rogers once again tried to comfort him. "It was not a comical defeat at Randall's Island," he countered. "It may have been a mistake to go up there to talk to a lot of hoodlums, nine-tenths of whom perhaps have never seen the inside of a book, but Miss Harrison says anybody of sense would have appreciated and enjoyed it." To be sure, the *Sun* reporter praised his performance—"the boys were in a roar of laughter from the time they found out that it wasn't against the rules"—while conceding that "some of the jokes they could hardly understand," as when Sam "referred to a potato bug as a mollusk."[47]

Before leaving New York, Sam was the guest of honor at a luncheon of the Lantern Club, "a little Bohemian club" of New York journalists, including Irving Bacheller, Stephen Crane, Richard Watson Gilder, and Edward Marshall. This luncheon, at their clubhouse near Park Row likely in the afternoon of July 13, may have been the only time that Sam and Crane ever met in person.[48]

Not easily discouraged by his flop at the House of Refuge, Sam returned to Elmira and achieved "a roaring success" with a different program on July 14 before another captive audience of seven hundred convicts at the prison there. He rehearsed for the first time the lineup of stories he would relate at one-night stands for the next several weeks: first the jumping frog sketch; then a passage from *Roughing It* (1872), either the anecdote about Sam's discovery of the dead man in his father's office or "Jim Blaine and His Grandfather's Old Ram"; then something about Huck and Tom, either their rescue of Jim from the ash hopper from *Adventures of Huckleberry Finn* (1885) or Tom's argument to liberate the Holy Land in a crusade from *Tom Sawyer Abroad* (1894); and ending with the tale of Sam's theft of an unripe watermelon or, alternatively, the tale of the clergyman who christens a child and/or "The Golden Arm." If summoned for an encore, Sam declaimed "The Whistling Story." In its next issue, the prison newspaper noted that during Sam's performance many of the men were "on the verge of apoplexy," presumably from laughter. Little wonder that in later years Sam joked that his favorite audiences were "college men and convicts."[49]

Accompanied by Pond and his wife, the three Clemenses—Sam, Livy, and Clara—headed west for Cleveland the evening of July 14 on the first leg of the yearlong trip that would take them around the world. As the train departed the Elmira station, Sam looked back and saw Susy on the platform "brimming with life & the joy of it" in "the blaze of the electric light" while "waving her good-byes to us as the train glided away, her mother throwing back kisses and watching her through her tears."[50] It was the last time they saw her alive.

They arrived in Cleveland in the cool of the morning on July 15 and registered at the Stillman Hotel. That evening, "with the mercury trying to crawl out of the top of the thermometer" at ninety-plus degrees, Sam performed before a capacity audience of 4,200 "sweltering people" at the Music Hall for the benefit of the local Newsboys Home. He was "badly fatigued, . . . nervous and weak," according to Pond. Nor had he been advised in advance that his reading was to be preceded by a concert of amateur violin and flute soloists whose families "kept encoring them," so he did not appear until 9:40 p.m.—and then with five hundred newsies seated behind him "on a lofty tier of benches which made them the most conspicuous objects in the house" with "nobody to watch them or keep their quiet." It was a recipe for disaster. "With their scufflings and horse-play and noise," the gamins and ragamuffins in the bleachers behind him were "a menagerie," he reported to Rogers the next day. "They flowed past my back in clattering shoals, some leaving the house, others returning for more skylarking." At one point, moreover, Sam was interrupted by a barking terrier.[51]

To be sure, as Sam "hobbled upon the stage," Pond remembered, "there was a grand ovation of cheers and applause, which continued for some time. Then he began to speak and before he could finish a sentence the applause broke out again." In his talk, Sam proposed a novel method to achieve moral perfection: to commit all 462 possible sins: "When you have committed your 462 you are released of every other possibility and have ascended the staircase of faultless creation." He illustrated the ameliorating influence of theft with his stock watermelon anecdote. "I got *started* magnificently, but inside of half an hour the scuffling boys had the audience's maddened attention and I saw it was a gone case; so I skipped a third of my program and quit" after an hour. Sam considered it "another Randall's Island defeat." The next day the *Cleveland Leader* ("rich entertainment") and *Plain Dealer* ("humor is just as vigorous and his style as entertaining as ever") were "kind," Sam thought, though another Cleveland reviewer considered the reading an "oddly constructed affair" and the *Buffalo Enquirer* a week later dismissed it as "one of the queerest jumbles that ever passed for a lecture." Ever the impresario, Pond insisted that the size of the crowd and the favorable notices proved that Sam "still has a strong hold on the people and that they like him on the platform as well as in books." After Sam left town, however, a columnist for the *Plain Dealer* flayed his performance. While he had been greeted by a "tumult of applause," Sam had obviously been distracted by the newsboys on the stage and "literally skimmed over his subjects. . . . Toward the latter part of the lecture he seemed to lose all his physical strength." Fortunately, Pond had already collected the $300 speaking fee in advance.[52]

They lingered in Cleveland a second day so that the Clemenses could dine with Timothy and Eliza Crocker and Solon and Emily Severance, Sam's fellow passengers on the *Quaker City* cruise in 1867. Sadly, the Fairbankses were not present; they had lost their fortune and closed the *Cleveland Herald* in 1880. Abel had since died, and Mary had moved to Newton, Massachusetts, to live with her daughter.[53]

Early in the morning of July 17, the Clemens party embarked on the Great Lakes steamer *Northland*. Sam was delighted by the accommodations, so luxurious that it was equipped to produce several tons of ice per day. "I have seen no boat in Europe that wasn't a garbage scow by comparison," he marveled. Interviewed in Detroit during a stop, Sam announced that he hoped "to start and complete a book" during his world tour, though he allowed he was "not under contract to furnish anybody with anything, and am thus free to write or loaf as I please." Sam spoke in Sault Ste. Marie, Michigan, on the St. Marys River between Lakes Huron and Superior, on the evening of July 18. One yahoo in the audience reportedly laughed so loudly she had to be carried from the Grand Opera House. The five travelers backtracked to Mackinac Island, where Sam spoke the next evening to an audience of four hundred who paid a dollar apiece as admission. ("Mark was simply immense," according to Pond.) The women remained at the swank Grand Hotel on the island while Sam, his manager in tow, ventured to Petoskey the next day, where the opera house was crammed like an overstuffed sofa with an audience of over 750 despite a seating capacity of only five hundred; among them were Sam's old acquaintances Hjalmar Hjorth Boyesen and George Kennan. Sam "had a satisfactory time." The local paper reported the next day that he "kept the vast audience in a constant ripple of laughter from first to last" despite the lingering pain in his legs. The box office receipts totaled $548, over twice the previous record for the house. Sam and Pond spent the night at a cottage on Harbor Point, Michigan, on Little Traverse Bay.[54]

They rejoined the women on Mackinac Island the next day and in the morning of July 21 sailed on the steamer *Northwest* for Duluth, 430 nautical miles distant. Not surprisingly, the ship arrived at 9:00 p.m., an hour after the scheduled start of Sam's performance. He was the first passenger to disembark and, driven hastily to the First Methodist Church, where 1,250 people were waiting for him in the hundred-degree heat, he began his lecture by diffidently declaring that "it looked for a time as if I would be a few minutes late." The *Duluth Evening Herald* remarked the next day that the audience as a whole was subdued given the late hour.[55]

At midnight the party left by train for Minneapolis and a sleep day at the West Hotel before Sam's appearance at the Metropolitan Opera House the next evening—the same hotel where Sam and George Washington Cable had lodged and the same theater where they performed while on tour a decade earlier. According to Pond, the arena was "filled to the top gallery with a big crowd of well-dressed, intelligent people" and the box office receipts totaled about $450. The *Minneapolis Journal* reported that Sam's selections were "permeated by a quiet humor that made them entertaining" and "an underlying vein of philosophy pointing to some moral," in all "a judicious blending of the pathetic and homely with those occasional scintillations of wit that flashed like dew drops in the morning sun." Sam was honored after the reading with a public reception jointly hosted by the Commercial Club and the Press Club, though with a twist. The plan was to provide the guests with "punch and light sandwiches" and Sam with an opportunity "to express himself in any way that he sees fit." That is, he was expected to sing for his sandwich. Before a "large and select audience" at the People's Congregational Church in St. Paul the next evening, the *St. Paul Globe* reported, he "read some of his best stories and did it in such an inimitable way that people laughed till their sides ached." Obviously, "he has not lost a particle of the popular hold which he has upon the reading public." The St. Paul *Pioneer Press* largely concurred, concluding that while "his delivery is not so animated as it used to be" it "lacks none of the former charm on that account."[56]

After a swing through the "splendid country" of eastern Dakota the next day, crossing the Canadian border at Gretna, Manitoba, Sam spoke to large audiences at Selkirk Hall in Winnipeg on the evenings of July 26 and 27. The audience the first night was "splendid," according to Pond. Sam's "pungent and witty remarks were thoroughly appreciated," the *Winnipeg Tribune* reported, and his reading contained "anecdotes enough to give his audience a lasting and pleasing recollection of a well spent evening," declared the *Winnipeg Free Press*. The second night Sam tested a new program with mixed results because, as he discovered, it was "35 minutes too long." On both evenings Sam and Pond were entertained after the lecture at the Manitoba Club, consisting of the leading men in the city, including Isaac Campbell, the Winnipeg solicitor, queen's counsel, and president of the Law Society of Manitoba. Sam was impressed by "Mud City," as Winnipeg was nicknamed: "I have never seen real mud since I left Missouri until today," he told an interviewer. "Here I am at home again."[57]

Sam and his entourage left Winnipeg on July 28 and during a brief stop he was hurriedly interviewed by the Grand Forks, North Dakota, *Herald*. While expressing his regret that he had no speaking date in Grand Forks, he voiced his awe for the oceans of grain in the region. "This country of yours out here . . . astonished me beyond all imagination," he stated. "Never in my life have I seen such fields of grain extending in all directions to the horizon. This country appears to me to be as it were a mighty ocean." He jotted the same sentiment in his notebook: "that wonderful wheat ocean—by gracious it is bewitching; there is the peace of the ocean about it, & a deep contentment, a heaven-wide sense of ampleness, spaciousness, where pettiness & all small thoughts & tempers must be out of place, not suited to it, & so not intruding. The scattering far-off homesteads, with trees about them were so homelike & remote from the warring world, so reposeful & enticing." The Clemenses and Ponds arrived in Crookston, Minnesota, after sundown and were the first people ever to register at the new Hotel Crookston, the first lodge in town with hot and cold running water, which would not officially open for another three days. As a result, they remained in the dark—"as dark as the inside of a cow," in a phrase he had coined in *Roughing It*—"until the electrician could get the incandescent lights adjusted" in their rooms. The next day, Pond noted, people from the surrounding countryside "filled up the town from all directions to see and hear 'Mark'" at the Grand Opera House that evening. As usual, the theater was "filled to capacity" and Sam "kept the audience in a constant uproar." He introduced a new reading from "Adam's Diary," much to the approval of the *Polk County Journal*, which pronounced it "the drollest of all his writings," and the *Crookston Times*, which opined that it exhibited "more originality than any of the other selections," though the watermelon story "was probably the most humorous." The reviews in the *Warren Sheaf* ("rich and varied stories of wit and humor"), *Fosston Thirteen Towns* ("droll" and "inimitable"), and *Crookston Tribune* ("selections were all taken from his books and while humorous each contained some deep thoughts") were no less complimentary.[58]

They were scheduled to leave Crookston early in the morning of July 30 for the eight-hundred-mile journey to Great Falls, Montana, but the train was late. As usual, Sam was impatient with the disruptions in their schedule.

Pond remembered that he grumbled, "I'm tired of this business. Pond contracted with me to travel, and here I am waiting for late trains that never arrive. . . . I contracted to travel and I insist upon his keeping the contract." So Pond pushed Sam around the platform in a wheelbarrow, and Clara took a snapshot of their antics with Pond's Kodak camera.

Despite the delay, they arrived the next morning and registered at the Park Hotel a full twelve hours before Sam's reading that evening at the Great Falls Opera House. In consequence, they were cursed with a tour of the region led by Paris Gibson, the founder of the town, with visits to the Giant Springs, the smelter at Black Eagle, and Rainbow Falls, a fifty-foot cascade on the Missouri River that in June 1805 Meriwether Lewis had pronounced "one of the most beautiful objects in nature." Of course, Sam diplomatically decreed Great Falls "one of the prettiest towns in the West" after the circuit of the sights.[59]

But that evening he exhibited his travel fatigue. Though the "best audience that ever attended a performance" in Great Falls "thoroughly enjoyed" his lecture, he was "in poor voice." To make matters worse, the box office receipts totaled only about $220. Sam and Pond were guests of honor at the Electric Club after the reading, and the Clemenses and Ponds left the next morning for Butte, where he "entertained a large and fashionable audience" for ninety minutes with his "quaint humor and native wit" at Maguire's Opera House that evening. The Butte correspondents for the *Helena Independent-Record* ("a great success") and *Anaconda Standard* ("the people laughed until laughing became painful") both commended the reading, and the *Butte Post* added that it was "always worth a dollar to see a great national character." Pond averred that Sam "more than made up for last night's disappointment. He was at his best." On his part, Sam was pleased by the "*beautiful* audience. Compact, intellectual & dressed in perfect taste." Expecting a crowd of rustic bumpkins in a rural backwater, he was surprised "to find this London–Parisian–New York audience out in the mines."[60] At Livy's suggestion he had interjected more serious material into his program to alter its rhythm, and the experiment succeeded. As usual, Sam and Pond were hosted after the reading by the local Silver Bow Club.

The next afternoon Sam and Pond railed to Anaconda, only twenty-five miles distant, for Sam's date that evening at Evans' Opera House. Their late arrival was fortuitous because a welcoming party expected them in the morning and had planned an elaborate lunch followed by another "lively day" of sightseeing. Instead, as Pond noted, Sam missed this demonstration and was in "good condition for the evening." As the *Anaconda Standard* reported, his reading "was as original in style as are the writings of the man."

Unfortunately, it did not draw a crowd in a town with a population of only about six thousand. "There were not enough people interested in high-class entertainments to make up a paying audience," and the local promoter "was short about sixty dollars" of his expenses, including Sam's speaking fee, so Pond "took what he had, and all he had." When Sam learned about his loss a few days later, he insisted that Pond refund a hundred dollars to cover the deficit: "I'm not going around robbing poor men who are disappointed in their calculations as to my commercial value," he told Pond. "I'm poor, and working to pay debts that I never contracted; but I don't want to get money in that way." When the promoter expressed his thanks for the godsend, according to Pond, Sam was delighted and wished that "every hundred dollars I ever invested had produced the same amount of happiness!"[61]

After they reunited in Butte the next day, the Clemenses and Ponds traveled seventy miles north to Helena, where Sam appeared that night at Ming's Opera House. After the obligatory tour to the local mineral springs, he was again greeted by a meager audience—the Helenians "did not care for lectures," as Pond put it—though among those present was Senator Wilbur Sanders. Sam's performance again was lackluster, to judge from the bland notice in the local paper: for two hours "the humorist" offered "his best efforts to entertain." During the customary reception at the Montana Club after the reading, moreover, Sam was confronted by an old nemesis from Nevada who, according to Pond, had traveled to Helena "to settle an old score" and accused Sam of playing "a d——d dirty trick" on him thirty years earlier. After a moment of "deathly silence," Sam disarmed his adversary in this battle of wits by drawling out: "Let's see. That—was—before—I—reformed, wasn't—it?"[62]

The next morning, Sam, Livy, Clara, the Ponds, and Senator Sanders caught a train for the five-hour, 115-mile trip to Missoula. By chance, at the depot they crossed paths with Eunice Beecher, Henry Ward Beecher's widow, en route to the West Coast to visit her son. That evening, according to the *Missoula Missoulian* and the *Missoula Republican*, Sam entertained a "select and fashionable" audience at the Bennett Opera House "with his droll manner and ever ready wit. No more enjoyable occasion could be imagined than an evening with Mark Twain and it is needless to say that none went away disappointed." After the reading, many of the attendees, officers at Fort Missoula and their families, lingered in the hall until midnight. Sam and his party were invited to the fort, four miles from the city, for lunch and to review the troops of the Twenty-Fifth U.S. Colored Regiment the next day by Colonel Andrew Burt, the commandant. Sam in particular was impressed by the military drills there. While most of the officers of black regiments at the time were white, the Twenty-Fifth had a black chaplain, as Sam noted, who was "saluted, like other officers." He was convinced that "the negro has found his vocation at last." The "splendid buffalo soldiers" were "obedient, don't desert, don't get drunk," were "proud of their vocation," and were reportedly "great in battle." On his part, Pond was more overtly racist in framing the point: "the colored soldiers were more subordinate and submissive to rigid drill and discipline than white men" and "there were very few desertions from among them." The Clemenses and Ponds left that afternoon, rode the rails overnight, and arrived in Spokane, two hundred miles west, shortly before noon on August 7. Sam was slowly recuperating from his long illness and "enjoying everything," Pond observed, so the local reporters from the *Chronicle* and *Spokesman-Review* who awaited him at their hotel, the Spokane House, "had a good time" interviewing him. Unfortunately, the publicity did not translate into popularity at the new Spokane Opera House that evening. The box office receipts at the two-thousand-seat theater totaled only $262. "The manager was greatly disappointed," according to Pond, because "he had counted on a full house. Where he expected the people to come from I don't know." Sam was no less dismayed "and manifested no delicacy in so expressing himself." Even the *Spokesman-Review* noted the next day that the audience "was not so large as it should have been," though Sam's "quaint and original humor delighted" the people in attendance. To all appearances a boomtown, with "asphalt streets, electric lights, nine-story telegraph poles, and commercial blocks that would do credit to any Eastern city," Spokane was in truth suffering from an economic depression. While walking around the town, Sam and Pond discovered "buildings ten stories high with the nine top stories empty" and "many fine stores" with "to rent" signs hanging in their plate-glass windows.[63]

After only twelve hours in Spokane, the five travelers boarded the Great Northern for the overnight trip to Seattle, followed by a Puget Sound ferry to Tacoma, "another overgrown metropolis," as Pond moaned. They took an apartment at the Hotel Tacoma late on August 8 and the following morning Sam was interviewed by his nephew Sam Moffett of the *San Francisco Examiner*. Sam "blaspheme[d] for a few minutes," according to Pond, and "cursed the journey, the fatigues and annoyances" and insisted that he "was not travelling for pleasure."[64]

In midafternoon Sam and Pond left the women in Tacoma and railed to Portland for his speaking date at the Marquam Grand Opera House downtown that evening. They arrived to a standing-room-only theater—"splendid house, full to the roof," Sam noted—twenty minutes after the lecture was scheduled to start. It was a "great compliment to have a lofty gallery packed with people" and the "floor & dress circle full too, many standing." The receipts totaled over $800, the largest box office of Sam's North American tour. Pond thought "his entertainment had reached perfection," that Sam's performance this night "surpassed all" and was "a grand success." The notice of his performance in the *Portland Oregonian,* filed by Lute Pease, later a Pulitzer Prize recipient, was also sterling, commending Sam's "droll, quiet manner, his peculiar pronunciation, his inimitable drawl" and asserted that the audience was convulsed with "one ripple of laughter from the beginning to the end" and recalled him for an encore. Pond considered the review "one of the best notices" Sam received during the trip. The *Portland Telegram* was less enthusiastic, dismissing the reading as "somewhat tiresome and vapid."[65]

After the lecture Sam was the guest of honor at a supper at the Arlington Club hosted by his old friend Charles Erskine Scott Wood, the former adjutant to the superintendent of the U.S. Military Academy at West Point, the original publisher of the ribald tale *1601* in 1882, and now a high-dollar railroad lawyer. According to the *Oregonian,* Sam regaled about two dozen prominent men in the community with yarns; Pond added that "they will remember that evening as long as they live." The next morning, as he was boarding a train for Olympia, Sam briefly chatted with Pease; the young journalist transcribed their talk in a two-column interview Sam declared "the most accurate and the best that had ever been reported of him." In the course of their conversation, Sam allowed that "through the diabolical machination of Major Pond" he was compelled to leave the Rose City "after but a glimpse. I may never see Portland again, but I liked that glimpse."[66]

His experience in Olympia was a letdown by comparison. He and Pond were met at Tumwater by a delegation of Olympians led by John Miller Murphy, the editor of the *Washington Standard,* and escorted to the "very pleasant" Olympia Hotel in an open trolley car. His audience that evening was a disappointment, however, and "by no means commensurate with the reputation of the man," according to Murphy's notice in his paper. Though the *Olympian* averred that Sam's "recitations and stories were greatly enjoyed and applauded," ticket sales barely covered the expense of transportation and lodging. Though Sam jotted in his notebook that the "nice little theatre" was "half full of the right kind of people," he cleared only fifty-two dollars, the smallest payday of his entire trip. Nor had the organizers arranged a reception for him after the lecture. The forests of the Northwest were ablaze in wildfires, moreover, filling the sky with wood smoke and limiting visibility. He was unable to spy either Mount Hood from Portland nor Mount Rainier from Puget Sound through the haze.[67]

Figure 3. Lute Pease (left) and Samuel Clemens (right), Portland, Oregon, August 10, 1895. Photograph by James B. Pond, *Pacific Monthly* 24, August 1910.

Sam and Pond left the next morning by train to rejoin the women. In the afternoon of August 12, the Clemenses and Ponds were invited to a tea at the Hotel Tacoma hosted by Sarah Turner and Nellie Allyn—the widow and daughter, respectively, of George Turner, Sam's old friend in Virginia City and the late chief justice of the Nevada Territory Supreme Court. Clara entertained at the piano, and Sam crossed paths with Lieutenant Commander (later Rear Admiral) Albion V. Wadhams of the USS *Mohican*, whom he had met in Washington, D.C., in February 1885. The *Mohican* was anchored in the Seattle harbor, and Wadhams invited the Clemenses and Ponds to dine aboard the warship the next afternoon. That evening Sam lectured before a "large and enthusiastic audience" at the Tacoma Theater, where he enjoyed a "great time" though the Tacoma *Ledger* was slightly ambivalent in its review: his performance was "not exactly a lecture nor yet readings from his works"; nevertheless, the throng of listeners "spent a most delightful evening." Afterward, the Tacoma Press Club hosted a banquet for him in its rooms, "which proved to be a very bright affair," according to Pond. Sam delivered a brief postprandial address in which he complimented the chair of the event for calling upon him to speak after all the "irresponsibles." Among the other guests were Wadhams and the artists Candace Wheeler and her daughter Dora Wheeler Keith, friends from the Onteora colony in the Catskills.[68]

The next evening Sam again triumphed before a standing-room-only crowd of over twelve hundred at the Seattle Theater. He was hoarse—the forest smoke had begun to affect him—but Pond thought the throatiness of his voice augmented its volume. Wheeler attended with her daughter and recalled that his performance "was not exactly a reading, but a repetition from some of his own books, interpolated constantly with personal thought or story as he proceeded" and "delighted his audience." Sam jotted in his notebook that he had treated a "splendid house" to a "most splendid time" and the *Post-Intelligencer* remarked that the audience "heard him for an hour and a half with unwearying enjoyment." The Seattle *Times* was not so sanguine, however. "If Mark Twain is the representative American humorist," it carped, "American humor is rather a sorry product. That he is funny no one can deny; that his exaggerations are grotesque is also true; but that his wit is brilliant or his humor suggestive cannot be truly claimed." In any case, after the lecture the Rainier Club hosted a reception for Sam that lasted until the wee hours of the morning. Pond noted that Sam again "met many of his friends and admirers," among them Wadhams, and that he was discovering from such soirées "that his misfortunes are his blessings." Or as Sam conceded in a message the next day to Sam Moffett, "my eyes have been opened by this lecture trip across the continent. I find I have twenty-five friends in America where I thought I had only one."[69]

Sam and Pond left the women and Sam Moffett at the Rainier Hotel in Seattle the next morning for a speaking date that evening in New Whatcom, Washington, the twin city of Fairhaven, two towns that in 1903 would merge with two others to form Bellingham. Sam spoke to a full house of six hundred in the Lighthouse Theater, located on the fourth floor of a building without fire escapes. He was so raspy, however, that "he got through the lecture," according to Pond, "with great difficulty," or as Sam wrote Rogers, "I had very great difficulty in pumping out any voice *at all*." "I could scarcely talk," he jotted in his notebook, and he even left the stage for an impromptu intermission in the middle of his performance, though in the end he "captured the crowd," was recalled for an encore, and was entertained afterward with a reception at the Commercial Club in Fairhaven—or rather, as Pond put it, "he delightfully entertained the club for an hour or more."[70]

They left the next afternoon for Vancouver, British Columbia, where they rendezvoused with the women, who had been escorted there by Sam Moffett. Sam spoke that evening before a crowded Vancouver Opera House, though he was off his game. His throat was "in very bad condition," according to Pond, and "it was a great effort to make himself heard." But "he is a thoroughbred. A great man,—with wonderful will power, or he would have succumbed." Sam kept a stiff upper lip despite his "Pullman carbuncles," as he began to call them, and his bronchitis. "I knew the Vancouver audience would be English, and therefore no trouble to talk to," he wrote Rogers; "otherwise it would have been insane for me to try to succeed with such a dilapidated voice. I went through all right—by whispering mainly." Sam apologized from the stage for his croakiness, which the *Vancouver News-Advertiser* allowed "may have detracted from the perfect effectiveness" of his delivery, though the *Vancouver World* ("90 minutes of almost uninterrupted laughter") did not discern any problem with the lecture.[71]

Sam, Livy, and Clara had originally been booked to sail for Sydney on August 16 from Vancouver aboard the SS *Warrimoo* of the Canadian Pacific line, but in the haze from the fires the steamer had run aground on an uncharted reef in the narrow Juan de Fuca Straits a week earlier. Sam explained to Rogers that "she was not greatly damaged," but "she had to be docked and repaired." Nor did he blame the captain for the accident: "The smoke is so dense all over this upper coast that you can't see a cathedral at 800 yards." Pond likewise groused about the weather. "There is a rumor afloat that the country about us is beautiful, but we can't see it," he allowed, "for there is smoke, smoke everywhere, and no relief. My eyes are sore from it." While the ship was in drydock in Victoria, British Columbia, Pond quickly arranged for Sam to read in the city on August 17, a speaking date not on the original itinerary. On the advice of a doctor, who "said it would be very perilous for Mr. Clemens to read that night" because "he was in a condition that could easily develop pneumonia or lung fever," Livy persuaded him to postpone his appearance until August 20. Sam spent most of his unexpected free time lying in bed at the Hotel Vancouver, though he granted interviews while he was there, authorizing Pond in his role as publicist to schedule them by appointment. "A quartet of bright young English journalists came" to his room at Pond's invitation. "They all had a good time, and made much of the last interview with 'Mark Twain' in America" before he left for a year.[72]

Finally, Sam and the others boarded the *Charmer* the morning of August 20 for the six-hour, 115-mile voyage to Victoria for his reading that evening, only to learn from the captain that "he had 180 tons of freight to discharge" and that the ship would not depart until midafternoon. Pond was forced to telegraph and postpone Sam's appearance until the following night. Sam was livid or, as Pond put it, he was "not in condition to relish this news" and "took occasion to tell the Captain" in "unpious language his opinion of a passenger carrying company that for a few dollars extra would violate their contract and obligations to the public. They were a lot of —— somethings and deserved the penitentiary." As usual, he soon apologized to the officer for his outburst and they "became quite friends." They arrived in Victoria after midnight on August 21, registered at the Hotel Driard, and the next night Sam attracted "a splendid crowd" to the lecture at the Victoria Theatre. Every seat on the main floor was taken and the gallery well filled. The *Victoria Times* commended Sam's "highly interesting" performance the next day and added that while some in the audience were disappointed, "most people were charmed." The *Victoria Colonist* pronounced it "a decided success." Only the *Victoria Province* sounded a discordant note, suggesting that Sam was "a first-rate reader but only a second-rate speaker." Pond conceded that Sam's voice "showed fatigue toward the last" but the "audience, which was one of the most appreciative he ever had, was in great sympathy with him as they realized the effort he was obliged to make, owing to his hoarseness." From his perspective, Sam thought the evening had been "in every way pleasant." Among the "elite of Victoria" who attended were the governor-general and his wife, the Lord and Lady Aberdeen, who entered the theater to "God Save the Queen," congratulated Sam backstage after the reading, and "offered to write to friends in Australia about it." Lady Aberdeen confided in her diary rather archly, however, that she was "not v[ery] sure if I liked him." His "best bit" was Huck's rumination on helping Jim escape "& the final victory of his better instincts," but "he ended with an essentially stupid ghost-story. We saw him for a few minutes afterwards. He has the strangest slopingish sort of head at the back with long hair about his neck."[73]

Thus ended, Sam later wrote, "a snail-paced march across the continent, which had lasted forty days." Counting the tryouts on Randall's Island and in Elmira, he had appeared twenty-two times over five and a half weeks. Despite the tumultuous start in Cleveland, he had earned some $5,300 toward expenses and the liquidation of his debts, an average of over $200 per speaking date. On the eve of his departure for Australia, he released a press statement through his nephew Moffett in which he discussed the bankruptcy of Webster and Company and publicly announced for the first time his resolve to pay its creditors dollar for dollar. The news was splashed from coast to coast the next day in such major metropolitan papers as the *Buffalo Courier, Washington Times, New York Tribune, New York Times,* New York *Sun, Brooklyn Eagle, Hartford Courant,* New Haven *Journal and Courier, San*

Francisco Call, Boston Advertiser, Boston Journal, Chicago Inter Ocean, and *Oakland Tribune.* "It has been reported that I sacrificed, for the benefit of the creditors, the property of the publishing firm whose financial backer I was, and that I am now lecturing for my own benefit. This is an error," Sam explained. "I intend the lectures, as well as the property, for the creditors." Honor "cannot compromise for less than a hundred cents on the dollar, and its debts never outlaw." He was "confident that if I live I can pay off the last debt within four years"—that is, after two lecture seasons in the United States, one in England, and one around the world. Then

> at the age of sixty-four, I can make a fresh and unencumbered start in life. I do not enjoy the hard travel and broken rest inseparable from lecturing, and if it had not been for the imperious moral necessity of paying these debts, . . . I should never have taken to the road at my time of life. I could have supported myself comfortably by writing, but writing is too slow for the demands that I have to meet; therefore I have begun to lecture my way around the world. . . . In my preliminary run through the smaller cities on the northern route, I have found a reception the cordiality of which has touched my heart and made me feel how small a thing money is in comparison with friendship.

Privately, Sam was not so confident. Livy admitted to her sister Sue that "underneath he has a steady, unceasing feeling that he is never going to be able to pay his debts. I do not feel so—I am sure if his life and health are spared to him that it will not be long until he is out of debt." But the press release he issued through his nephew was arguably the most important public statement of his entire life. The *Boston Journal,* for example, applauded his "courageous resolve." To be sure, not all the editorials were flattering. "Because Mark Twain announces his intention to pay his debts, a lot of newspapers are slobbering all over him, just as if it were anything extraordinary," the *Bakersfield Californian* sniffed. In England, the *Saturday Review* likewise claimed that Sam hath protested

> too much. It is a matter of simple honesty to pay one's debts in full, and the obligations of honor run further than Mr. Samuel L. Clemens seems to imagine. Curiously enough the first and only time we met Mr. Samuel L. Clemens he dwelt at length upon the dishonesty of a contemporary writer, a compatriot of his [no doubt Bret Harte], to whom all English readers owe many delightful hours, in such a way that we confess to but scant sympathy with him in his monetary troubles. . . . There is too much self-pity here and too

> much self-applause. Mr. Mark Twain would have us believe that to be honest deserves a martyr's crown.

Nevertheless, Sam's sister Pamela wrote her son that she was "prouder of your Uncle Sam's determination to pay off all the debts of the firm a hundred cents on the dollar than of his fame as a writer." A week later, Moffett published what seems to be Sam's addendum to his announcement, concluding, "Lecturing is gymnastics, chest-expander, medicine, mind-healer, blues-destroyer, all in one. I am twice as well as I was when I started out. I have gained nine pounds in twenty-eight days, and expect to weigh 600 before January. . . . My wife and daughter are accumulating health and strength and flesh nearly as fast as I am. When we reach home a year hence I think we can exhibit as freaks."[74]

All that remained was to prepare for the voyage across the Pacific—the longest cruise of his career, some nine thousand nautical miles over twenty-four days, from Vancouver to Honolulu to Fiji to Sydney—and to bid the Ponds farewell. Sam shopped for the trip the morning of August 23 and stockpiled the necessities: books, cigars, and pipe tobacco. "He bought 3,000 manila cheroots" (ten months' supply) and "four pounds of Durham smoking tobacco," according to Pond. "If perpetual smoking ever kills a man, I don't see how 'Mark Twain' can expect to escape."[75]

The *Warrimoo* left drydock on August 22 and anchored in Victoria the following afternoon, when the Clemenses boarded. Livy and Clara were underwhelmed. The 3,300-ton steamship "looked dingy, smelled oily & musty and I think Mrs. Clemens was very homesick & almost heartbroken" by the prospect of sailing on it for the next several weeks, according to Pond. Livy's worst fears were realized, moreover: she later acknowledged that their "food and beds" were "poor." Clara also "indignantly inquired if that was the great line of steamers that run to Australia," particularly since one-way fares for the three Clemenses from Victoria to London, England, cost $1,800 (over $50,000 in modern dollars). But Livy was resolute: "She tells me she is going to brave it through for she must do it" for her children. On the other hand, at least to all appearances, Sam was reconciled to the voyage. As he reported in the first chapter of the travelogue he began to write a year later, the *Warrimoo* was "a reasonably comfortable ship, with the customary sea-going fare—plenty of good food furnished by the Deity and cooked by the devil. . . . The ship was not very well arranged for tropical service; but that is nothing, for this is the rule for ships which ply in the tropics. She had an over-supply of cock-roaches, but this is also the rule with ships doing business in the summer seas."[76]

The leave-taking was poignant, especially on Pond's part. The trip across the continent had been, in his opinion, "the most delightful tour I have ever made with any party and I wish to record it as one of the most enjoyable of all my managerial experiences. I hardly ever expect another." He admired Livy, "the great magnet" who had held the group together. "What a noble woman she is!" he exclaimed. The Ponds lunched with the Clemenses aboard the *Warrimoo* before its departure and they posed for pictures.

Figure 4. The Clemenses and the Ponds (left to right: James B. Pond, Olivia Clemens, Samuel Clemens, Clara Clemens, Martha Pond) prior to their departure aboard the *Warrimoo*, August 23, 1895. Photograph from J. B. Pond, *Eccentricities of Genius: Memories of Famous Men and Women of the Platform and Stage* (New York: G. W. Dillingham, 1900).

Sam inscribed a copy of *Roughing It* to the Ponds: "Here ends one of the smoothest and pleasantest trips across the continent that any group of five has ever made." James and Martha Pond then "went ashore and the old ship started across the Pacific Ocean with three of our most beloved friends on board. We waved to one another as long as they kept in sight." Sam recalled that "after the distressful dustings and smokings and swelterings of the past weeks" he expected the voyage to "furnish a three-weeks holiday. . . .

We had the whole Pacific Ocean in front of us, with nothing to do but do nothing and be comfortable." A month later, however, Sam slammed Pond, describing him to Rogers as "superannuated" and lacking "any sand or any intelligence or judgment." He was determined not to contract "with him to perform me through America next year if I can do better."[77]

In the absence of an underwater cable connecting the mainland and Hawaii, the delays in the sailing of the *Warrimoo* went unreported on the islands. (Ironically, Sam's managers in Australia learned of the holdups by cablegrams forwarded through Europe and Asia on August 26.) Sam's reading at Independence Park, the largest hall in Honolulu, had been slated for August 24, literally the day after the ship sailed from Puget Sound. His lecture was advertised as late as the day it was originally scheduled and some 250 tickets had been sold. On August 29 the local Honolulu press announced that the *Warrimoo* "will arrive in a few days—there seems to be some uncertainty in regard to the date." The next day the *Honolulu Advertiser* reported that the ship "was to leave Victoria on the 22d, and if she left on that date, should be along sometime today." The island promoters held out hope as late as August 30 that Sam would arrive in time to lecture the next night. In fact, the *Warrimoo* anchored in Pearl Harbor a mile from the docks at around 10:00 p.m. the evening of August 30, but no through-passengers were allowed to land because of a cholera scare, with five deaths on the islands reported that day and another five the next.[78]

As a result, Sam's appearance was canceled and over $1,600 in advance ticket sales refunded. The passengers who wished to debark were permitted to leave; but no new cargo or passengers were allowed aboard; and the cargo shipped to Hawaii was unloaded onto smaller craft—in particular, the *Waialeale*. Sam helped secure the bowline from the *Waialeale* when some of the *Warrimoo* crew refused to touch it lest it carry infection, and he even shook hands with the captain of the other ship. Otherwise, there was little or no contact between ship and shore despite the siren call of paradise. Sam contemplated Oahu from a distance and reminisced about his once-upon-a-time joie de vivre. "If I might I would go ashore and never leave," he wrote in his notebook. "The mountains right and left clothed in rich splendors of melting color, fused together. Some of the near cliffs veiled in slanting mists—beautiful luminous blue water; inshore brilliant green water." He admitted later to his old friend Henry Whitney that he "was perishing to get ashore at Honolulu, and talk to you all, and see your enchanted land again, and be welcomed and stirred up. But it was not to be, and I shall regret it a thousand years; for of course I shan't get another chance to see the islands again." Instead, the *Warrimoo* hauled anchor on Sunday morning, September 1, and sailed for Fiji.[79]

Ten days later, after Sam and Clara had played innumerable games of hearts and "horse-billiards" (as he called shuffleboard) for recreation, the *Warrimoo* wended its way into the harbor at Suva, the capital of the British island colony. As soon as he escaped from the clouds of smoke that blanketed the Northwest, Sam recovered from his bronchitis. "Mr. Clemens seems entirely well again," Livy wrote her sister Sue. "I do trust that he is not going to be subject to those colds." He reveled in the half day he spent on the "lovely island" amid its "splendid stalwart natives," not only the seminude young Polynesian girls, "blithe and content, easy and graceful," who were "a pleasure to look at" but the "wrinkled old women, with their flat mammals flung over their shoulders, or hanging down in front like the cold-weather drip from the molasses faucet."[80]

Early in the morning of September 17, after nearly a month at sea, the *Warrimoo* docked at Circular Quay, Sydney Harbor. The ship had encountered "no rough weather, no rain, a rich abundance of sunshine and moonlight" on its voyage a third of the way around the world. Fortunately so. Unknown to them at the time, as Clara noted years later, "the steamer even after repairs was not seaworthy" and might have capsized in a storm. A few dozen steel plates on the hull, damaged on the rocks near Vancouver in early August, had not been replaced in drydock and water had seeped into one of the compartments belowdecks. According to Robert Cooper, "the money spent to repair the vessel was almost one-third as much as the initial cost of building it."[81] Sam had not been in such danger of drowning since his boyhood in Hannibal.

CHAPTER 5

Girdling the Earth

> I have filled the post—with some credit, I trust—of self-appointed Ambassador at Large of the U.S. of America—without salary.
>
> —*Mark Twain's Notebook*

"Life started with a vengeance" as soon as the *Warrimoo* docked and Samuel Clemens and his family registered at the Australia Hotel on Castlereagh Street, his daughter Clara remembered. They were corralled by "newspaper reporters, photographers, callers from all circles; and beggars of every description, slovenly and distinguished." Unfortunately, Sam stumbled out of the blocks by committing a pair of tactical mistakes his first day in Australia. During an interview with the Sydney *Daily Telegraph* on September 16, 1895, he hewed to the free trade line. "I don't profess to be learned in matters of this kind," he said, "but my instinct teaches me that protection is wrong." A few minutes later, shown a portrait of Sir Henry Parkes, the revered former premier of New South Wales and a champion of the protective tariff, Sam remarked that Parkes had "a truly splendid head" and that "it was hard to believe . . . he could make the bitter speeches . . . attributed to him." As innocuous as these statements may seem, Sam was immediately accused of interfering in Australian politics. The *Australian Star* in Sydney damned Sam in its next issue for his "slanderous matter concerning Sir Henry Parkes." He "came to Australia to lecture," not to "discuss party politics, and if he had a tithe of the common sense he is credited with possessing he would have decided to leave the subject of party politics severely alone. Nor would he have been guilty of the meanness of making disparaging remarks, on hearsay, concerning Sir Henry Parkes, who is not nearly so black as he has been painted by Mark Twain." The paper warned that Sam's comments might cause hundreds of people "to keep away from the entertainments." Luckily, Sam's faux pas was easily corrected with Parkes's help. The two men met two nights later at a dinner in Sam's honor at the Athenaeum Club. Before a hundred members and guests, Edmund Barton, who would later become the first prime minister of a federated Australia, proposed a toast to "Our Guest" which Parkes answered with "a magnificent reception." A couple of days later, Sam jovially told the *Sydney Times* that "your Sir Henry—he has the pull on me. I reverence that man's hair." He not only admired "the honey locks of the veteran" but "Sir Henry's oratory." Parkes also hosted a luncheon for the Clemenses during their stay in Sydney.[1]

Sam committed another gaffe his first day in Australia that was almost as perilous as defending free trade when he maligned Bret Harte in the press. He told Herbert Low of the *Sydney Herald* that he considered Harte "sham and shoddy" because "he has no pathos of the real, true kind." He had written "nothing that is genuine," though Sam allowed that his opinion was slanted because "I do not care for the man." His "venomous attack," as the *Melbourne Advocate* called it, provoked a backlash across Australia, where Harte remained popular. It was considered "bad form" at the least to "slang-wang a rival funny man" and Sam retracted his remarks on the grounds they were not intended for publication. His comments were "stupid," he admitted, and he had "no right to state those opinions publicly in unparliamentary language," though he added that his aversion to Harte "would always make it difficult for me to say rational things about him." He promised in the future to "modify my language" if "not my opinions." He reiterated that his criticism of Harte "could have no value as it would be tainted with prejudice." Sam did, however, apologize to the "unoffending public" for his "spiteful utterances" and expressed the hope that he would "never do anything to lose their good will." Livy even interrupted his interview with the *Sydney Times* to tell her husband, "I think it would be better if your wife saw your interviews in print before they were published." The brouhaha subsided after this interview, though on September 28 the *Freeman's Journal*, a Catholic magazine, opined that Sam was "a quite uninteresting and almost insufferable old man—a tedious knifegrinder with no story to tell," and the *Sydney Bulletin* claimed he "could make a considerable sum by giving private back views of himself in his shower-bath at a guinea a head." As late as mid-October, Sam told an Adelaide reporter that his disparagement of Harte had been "one of those hasty things I had no business to have said and it should never have appeared" in print. Harte heard about the ruckus and, on his part, told an interviewer that Sam had "attacked me in a most savage and unprovoked manner—denounced me as a feeble sentimentalist, and altogether gave it to be understood that Art and I were strangers." Sam's jibe had been "foolish" because "I have a great many friends in Australia and it was inevitable that all this should come to my ears." Thirteen years later, Herbert Low remembered that the "one tinge of bitterness" in Sam's visit to Australia had been "his dislike of Bret Harte, to whose genius he could not be brought to grant praise of any sort."[2]

Sam concluded to be more discreet in his public utterances. When asked for his impressions about Australia by an interviewer for the *Ballarat Star* in mid-October, he declared that he had "an almost insatiable craving to remain and feast his eyes upon its picturesque spots, which abound in every colony and to associate with men and women who love their country and can stand by a stranger." Two months later, safely aboard a steamer in the Indian Ocean, he vented his true opinion in his notebook: "One must say it very softly, but the truth is that the native Australian is as vain of his unpretty country as if it were the final masterpiece of God." He "is as sensitive about her as men are of sacred things" and "can't bear to have critical things said about her."[3]

Despite the controversies, Sam's four appearances between September 19 and 24 at Protestant Hall in Sydney, with a seating capacity of over two thousand, were wildly successful. Under the management of Robert Sparrow Smythe, all four were sellouts, "packed to suffocation," with estimated ticket sales of over £300, or $1,500 per night. At his first appearance on the stage, the audience welcomed him with a "burst of applause" and "an outburst of uncontrollable enthusiasm as but rarely comes within the experience of the average man." The Sydney *Daily Telegraph* (a "string of inimitably funny stories"), *Sydney Herald* ("passages of real eloquence, albeit simple and natural"), and *Melbourne Argus* (a "medley of anecdotes and personal experiences to which were appended some moral put in the quaintest way") hailed his performances. The *Sydney Bulletin* asserted that Sam repeatedly paused during his readings to hear "Smythe in the back-room counting the proceeds." Certainly he was convinced that, if his readings continued to prosper and his next travelogue sold well, he would liquidate his debts a year earlier than he had predicted only a month before.[4]

During his third performance before the Sydneysiders, Sam introduced the so-called Australian Poem he featured in readings over the next couple of months and recited in public as late as February 1898. Though he claimed he wrote the poem "in haste while traveling in Australia as I knew the poetlaureateship was vacant," he in fact composed a first draft while en route across the Pacific aboard the *Warrimoo*:

> Come forth from thy oozy couch,
>   O Ornithorynchus dear
> And greet with a cordial claw
>   The stranger that longs to hear
> From thy own lips the tale
>   Of thy origin all unknown:

Thy misplaced bone where flesh should be
And flesh where should be bone,
And fishy fin where should be paw,
And beaver-trowel tail,
And snout of beast equip'd with teeth
Where gills ought to prevail;
Come, Kangaroo, the good & true,
Foreshortened as to legs,
And body tapered like a churn,
And sack marsupial fegs
And tell us why you linger here,
Thou relic of a vanished time,
When all your friends as fossils sleep
Immortalized in lime.
Hail! & peace be unto you!

Adding lines to the poem later, Sam complained that "nothing would really rhyme with ornithorhynchus," though much as Emily Dickinson once slant-rhymed "Syria" and "too near," Sam rhymed "ornithorhynchus" and "link us." Similarly, he protested that it was "kind of hard to make anything rhyme with long three syllable words." He "could get nothing to rhyme with kangaroo, except kangaroo," though he joked later that Bret Harte had suggested "cockatoo." The *Adelaide Herald* eventually published a poem of twenty-six lines, every one of which rhymed with "kangaroo" (e.g., "hullabaloo," "mountain dew," "fang or two," and "Warrimoo"). The Melbourne *Australasian* printed a lyric in Sam's honor that rhymed "dingo" and "lingo," "emu" and "adieu," and "boomerang" and "whizzed and sang." Not to be outdone, the *New Zealand Mail* challenged Sam to invent a rhyme for the Maori word *paikakariki*.[5]

Meanwhile, he happily discharged his social duties as a guest in the city, first at a tea on September 18 aboard the British warship *Orlando* hosted by Admiral Cyprian Bridge (whose wife Sam had met in London the previous April), where Sam befriended Louis Becke, the author of *By Reef and Palm*; he toured a sheep slaughterhouse and refrigerating plant at the New South Wales Fresh Food and Ice Company the afternoon of September 20 and attended a ball that evening at the invitation of Lieutenant Governor Frederick and Lady Darley at Government House, adjacent to the botanical gardens. "We have had a darling time here for a week—and really I am almost in love with the platform again," Sam crowed to Henry H. Rogers on September 25. Escorted by Smythe, the Clemenses left that afternoon on the overnight express train to Melbourne and, inexplicably, the London *Era* reported that he left "the impression that his talent as a writer far exceeds his lecturing powers." Later the *Sydney Herald* recalled that Sam had seemed like "an old man fallen on evil times" during his engagement—an allegation that would dog his steps throughout the remainder of his tour. Still, he found time to take a fishing trip while in the city.[6]

Sam spoke five times in Melbourne over the next six days. He was welcomed "enthusiastically" by a crowd of two hundred the next morning at the Spencer Street Station, including U.S. Consul General Daniel Maratta, and he drew audiences "like a mustard plaster" to the Bijou Theater. He was introduced the afternoon of his arrival to the teenage British-Russian pianist Mark Hambourg, whose recital at the town hall he attended that evening. Sam delivered his first "At Home" the next night before an audience that included a pair of former premiers of Victoria, Sir James Patterson and James Service. The reviews were unanimously laudatory in the *Melbourne Argus* ("all his odd, quaint turns were presented in his proper setting"), *Melbourne Leader* ("pithy sentences and sparks of humor"), *Melbourne Age* (his performance was replete with "originality," "freshness," and "abundant humor"), *Melbourne Herald* ("some of his funniest, though some of his oldest, stories"), and *Australasian* ("shrewd and quaint and homely"). After his reading Sam was feted by the Yorick Club at the Cathedral Hotel. The next evening he again received a "very cordial reception" from a capacity crowd and was again entertained with a supper by about eighty-five members and guests of the Yorick Club. On Monday evening, September 30, the "gigantic crowd" at the Bijou "packed like sandwiches into the boxes" for Sam's third reading and heard him perform "in wonderful style" and "fine wit." Sam closed the engagement on the evening of October 2 with a performance the *Melbourne Age* commended for its "measured tones, brimful of quiet humor." His share of the box office receipts for his nine appearances in Sydney and Melbourne averaged about $230 per night. At a farewell dinner at the Yorick Club the evening before leaving Melbourne, Sam addressed the simmering border dispute between British Guiana and Venezuela that threatened to escalate into war between the Great Britain and the United States. "The Americans and the English and their great outflow in Canada and Australia are all one," he declared in an appeal for Anglo-Saxon unity. "Blood is thicker than water, and we are all related. If we do jaw and bawl at each other now and again, that is no matter at all. We do belong together, and we are parts of a great whole."[7]

Then Sam fell ill with another "damned carbuncle" that required him to postpone his appearances in Horsham, Bendigo, and Geelong and cancel his dates in Brisbane and the rest of Queensland. In his room at the Menzies Hotel on Latrobe Street he was treated by "one of the very best surgeons in the world" who "made brisk work" of the infection by freezing and lancing it and then injecting it with opium. As he later wrote Rogers, "I was laid up a week in Melbourne with a new carbuncle & this damaged my Australian campaign a good deal, & also shortened it." Sam joked at the Yorick Club that he was "entertaining a carbuncle unawares. I have got it on my port hind leg, and it reminds me of its company occasionally. I have a greater respect for it than for any other possession I have in the world. I take more care of it than I do of my family." While still bedridden, he sent Rogers £437, or almost $2,200 (about $64,000 in modern dollars), toward the liquidation of his debts, and he took notes on such subjects as the Sunday blue laws and the Melbourne Cup horse race that he later worked into his travelogue.[8]

After a farewell luncheon at Government House on October 11, Sam, Livy, Clara, and Smythe boarded an overnight express to Adelaide, the capital of South Australia, where he was welcomed the next day by the U.S. consular agent, Charles A. Murphy; a delegation of reporters at the South Australian Club Hotel; and a limerick in the *Adelaide Advertiser*:

> There's a veteran writer, Mark Twain;
> His admirers observe it with pain
>   Though the art can he teach
>   Of post-prandial speech,
> He can't write a "Tom Sawyer" again.

During his five days in the city, October 12–16, Sam delivered four "At Home" talks that were "received with much laughter and applause" by the audiences at the Theatre Royal or, as the Adelaide correspondent of the *Newcastle Herald* put it, he "illuminated the Theatre Royal as a passing meteor." On opening night, the lieutenant governor of the state was present and an overflow of some forty people was seated on the stage. As in Sydney and Melbourne, Sam was welcomed with a thundering ovation when he stepped onto the stage and was extolled the next day by the critics—for example, the *Adelaide Advertiser* ("pathos and humor were charmingly blended"), the *South Australian Register* ("unique in person and performance"), and the *Quiz and Lantern* ("more 'goody-goodies' "). He was entertained after his appearance by a group of "lively friends" until after midnight. On October 14 he was toasted before his performance in the Mayor's Parlor by twenty men, including Murphy, Smythe, the mayor, and Premier Charles C. Kingston. The next night he dined at the local government offices before his reading and was entertained by the Adelaide Club after it. Horace George Stirling, a columnist for the *Adelaide Journal* who wrote under the pen name Hugh Kalytus, spent "a considerable deal" of time with him in the city and reported that Sam

> will drink with you, smoke with you, yarn with you, and talk about anything from carbuncles to Christianity, from literature to liquor, or any mortal thing, with an air of good camaraderie quite taking; but you must not make the mistake of taking him for a "new chum"—he has your measure. Take him as man to man, and leave his books out of the conversation, and you will enjoy him; but refer to his lectures or his books and he loses interest in the subject.

While in the city Sam toured the zoological gardens, where he "saw the only laughing jackass that ever showed any disposition to be courteous to me" and, accompanied by Murphy and Smythe, Sam observed Parliament in session for a half hour on October 15 from the Speaker's Gallery. He also tolerated unseasonably hot and humid weather while in the city. "I guess we are so near our destination," he told a reporter, "that it heats through the partition." Still, as the Melbourne *Table Talk* remarked, Sam "scored a greater success in Adelaide than in either Sydney or Melbourne" despite the heat and the "real and obvious pain" he suffered from carbuncles.[9]

After leaving Adelaide the afternoon of October 16, the Clemenses' long march through Australia continued to five provincial towns—the first Horsham, with a population of about three thousand—where they arrived early the next morning and registered at the White Hart Hotel. That evening Sam spoke to a "delightful audience" at the Mechanics' Institute, as he observed in his notebook, with a buoyant review the next day in the *Horsham Times*: "the lecture, or address, or friendly chat, or whatever it was, was simply unreportable." For almost two hours Sam "held the undivided and expectant attention" of the crowd. Livy reported to Susy that "Papa never talked to a more enthusiastic audience. . . . They were entirely uproarious, taking a point almost before he reached it." The next evening in Stawell, in gold mining country some forty miles distant, a large number of the town's fifty-three hundred citizens attended Sam's "At Home" at the town hall, and the *Stawell Times* reported the reading was "as caviar to a few." The next stop was Ballarat, about four hours by train from Stawell, where the Clemenses were joined by Carlyle Smythe, Robert's son, who ushered the family for the duration of the tour. Sam, suffering from yet another carbuncle, was interviewed while "stretched at full length on a comfortable couch" at Craig's Hotel by the *Ballarat Courier* on October 20. A few in the audience who left the Mechanics' Institute after his "At Home" the next evening, according to the *Ballarat Echo*, declared that Sam was not "worth listening to," though most testified they had not "laughed so much for a long time." The *Ballarat Star* was more generous, asserting that "none who went last night would say they did not get full value for their money." In company with the Australian minister of mines, on October 21 the Clemenses toured Hans W. H. Irvine's Great Western Vineyard and wine vaults.[10]

The next day they traveled another nine hours to Bendigo, where Sam performed twice at the Royal Princess Theater. The *Bendigo Advertiser* pronounced his readings "a feast of intellectual fun," and the family went sightseeing with the local newspaper publisher. The family traveled from Bendigo to Maryborough, a town of about fifty-two hundred, on October 25 for Sam's "At Home," then returned the next day to Melbourne for a matinee performance at Athenaeum Hall that the *Melbourne News* pronounced "an undoubted success in every particular." That evening he again heard the piano prodigy Mark Hambourg perform in concert, and he attended a smoker hosted by the Australian Institute of Journalists at the Cathedral Hotel. On October 28 Sam railed fifty miles to Geelong with the younger Smythe to read in the Exhibition Theatre, where he offended some folks of German heritage by ridiculing the "terrors of the German language," though the *Geelong Advertiser* granted that his reading was also "full of dry humor" and "put the audience in a laughable mood." The next day he performed before a full house in the one-thousand-seat town hall in Prahran, a suburb of Melbourne, and in its review the *Prahran Telegraph* commended his "inimitable drollery" that kept "the vast audience in a constant simmer of merriment."[11]

The Clemenses and Carlyle Smythe sailed from Melbourne early in the afternoon of October 31 for New Zealand via Hobart, Tasmania, formerly "a convict-dump," aboard the *Mararoa*, a 2,600-ton tramp steamer. Among his fellow passengers was the Irish nationalist politician Michael Davitt. Sam and Davitt had crossed paths at the Athenaeum Club in Sydney in mid-September when Davitt "had the pleasure" of "listening to one of the wittiest and best all-round after-dinner speeches which ever mitigated the dyspeptic penalty of a public banquet," and during the five-day voyage they forged a friendship. Sam had been reading Marcus Clarke's convict colony novel *For the Term of His Natural Life* (1872), later describing it in his journal as "the book that stands at the head of Australian literature. . . . It reads like a dream of hell." In company with Davitt and Henry Dobson, a former premier of Tasmania, during the brief stop in Hobart he visited the Refuge for the Indigent, the "spacious and comfortable home" of 223 ex-convicts, a crowd "of the oldest people" Sam had purportedly ever seen. It was "one of the most interesting but saddening experiences" of his life. During the voyage he became "a favourite of everybody on board" and "entertained us in the smoke-room of the *Mararoa* with some capital anecdotes"—this despite the carbuncles that continued to afflict him. "The only good times I have had—times, that is to say, when I have been entirely free from pain," he told a journalist in Hobart, "have been on the platform, talking to my audiences." Ironically, his scheduled "At Home" talks in Hobart and Launceston were canceled on account of his late arrival and poor health.[12]

The ship docked at the southern port of Bluff, New Zealand, on November 5 and the Clemens party railed north twenty miles to Invercargill. There Sam spoke, according to the *Otago Witness*, before "one of the largest audiences that ever paid for admission to any entertainment" in that city. His visit, the *Southland Times* added the next day, "will live long in the recollection of the town and his lecture will be among our most pleasant and treasured memories." On November 6 they traveled 140 miles northeast to Dunedin—a town, he wrote later, that "justifies Michael Davitt's praises." The forty miles between Lawrence and Dunedin on South Island reminded Davitt of the landscape of southeast Scotland and the city "suggests Edinburgh." Ironically, Davitt cited Sam's opinion of Dunedin in his own travelogue of the region: "a place which was visited by some people from Scotland who were on their way to Heaven, and who, believing they had reached their destination, remained." Sam spoke at the city hall in Dunedin the evenings of November 6–8 to mostly glowing notices—for example, in the *Dunedin Star* ("this merciless exposer of humbug, this bright and wholesome humorist" with "wit of the inimitable and perennial joke"), *Otago Times* (Sam "told his stories in a matter-of-fact way as if utterly unconscious of their drollery"), and *Tuapeka Times* ("full of quaint witticisms and side-splitting absurdities of manner and speech and incident"). The Dunedin correspondent of the *Grey River Argus* commended in particular Sam's deadpan delivery, noting that he was "never guilty of a ghost of a smile—he is as solemn as a wart on an undertaker's nose." Only the *Dunedin Triad* struck a sour note, claiming that "nine out of every ten who heard Mark Twain were hugely disappointed with him."[13]

While in the city Sam also examined a collection of Maori art and artifacts—his first exposure to indigenous culture during a visit to the South Sea Islands. Museums became virtually his only contact zone with aboriginal peoples in Australia and New Zealand. He viewed the artifacts with an "imperial gaze," however. Only a week earlier he had expressed relief in his notebook that "all these native races are dead and gone, or nearly so. The work was mercifully swift & horrible in portions of Australia." Extermination or deracination or decimation "seemed to be the proper medicine for such creatures," he elsewhere observed. The whites "did not kill all the blacks, but they promptly killed enough of them to make their own persons safe. From the dawn of civilization down to this day the white man has always used that very precaution." The native Tasmanians should have been permitted to intermarry with whites, he mused. "It would have improved the whites and done the Natives no harm."[14] So much for Sam's reputation as a modern racial progressive. His comments are reminiscent of his remarks in *Roughing It* (1872) about "Cooper Indians" and the desirable "extermination" of Native Americans. During his tour of the southern hemisphere, as he was exposed firsthand to the historic consequences of colonialism, however, he gradually abandoned some of his more draconian opinions.

On November 9 the Clemenses and Smythe headed to Timaru, where Sam spoke at the Theatre Royal that evening, while Livy and Clara continued on the train another 150 miles to Christchurch. Although some people left in the midst of his "At Home," the *Timaru Herald* saluted Sam's performance the next day ("his humour is but the foam floating upon a deep stream of serious thought and of liquid wisdom"). After resting his infected leg on the Sabbath, on November 11 Sam retreated fifty miles to "browse at random among the pastures of his published work" before a sparse crowd at the Theatre Royal in Oamaru. The next day Sam and Smythe joined Livy and Clara in Christchurch. They were welcomed by members of the Savage Club and stayed at Coker's Hotel four days. Sam appeared three times before houses crowded cheek by jowl at the thousand-plus seat Theatre Royal to fulsome reviews, as in the *Christchurch Star* ("a rare treat"), *Christchurch Press* (a "perfect simmer of laughter"), and *Lyttelton Times* ("some splendid specimens of his peculiar style of humour"). The day of his third "At Home," Sam was entertained at lunch by the Canterbury Club, and an unsung poet celebrated Sam's visit to the city in a local paper:

> Hail, King of Smiles. Your health we quaff,
> The last, the best of merry-men;
> Yours 'tis to rouse the hearty laugh,
> That brings life's golden prime again. . . .
> With you we've laughed this many a year,
> We've met your jokes in black and white,
> We knew you not, we held you dear,
> We're pleased that you're 'At Home' tonight.

After Sam's reading that evening, some fifty members and guests of the local Savage Club hosted a supper for the Clemenses in the Canterbury

Provincial Council chamber. "We have had a good time these last few days," Sam declared in his after-dinner speech, "and I have felt what a good time Christchurch must have been having, too." During this visit he toured the Canterbury Museum, where he saw an exhibition of "lovingly carved" Maori totem poles. He had enjoyed an exceptionally hospitable welcome to the city; he had won, according to the *Auckland Star*, "an unprecedented social success in the fullest sense of the word"; and he carried away a raft of gifts, including many Maori artifacts, mementos of his family's visit to South Island. After supper on the evening of November 16, Sam, Livy, Clara, and Smythe traveled to the nearby port town of Lyttelton to catch the 1,273-ton British steamship *Flora* at midnight for Auckland, the largest city in New Zealand.[15]

Lamentably, it was not the good ship *Flora*. Sam later called it, in a passage deleted from the British edition of his travelogue lest it invite a slander suit, "the foulest I was ever in," "dangerously overpacked," and "the equivalent of a cattle-scow." He did not sleep a wink all night. Licensed to carry 125 passengers, Sam alleged, the "floating pig-sty" may have "had all of 200 on board" the night they sailed. As he complained,

> All the cabins were full, all the cattle-stalls in the main stable were full, the spaces at the heads of companionways were full, every inch of floor and table in the swill-room was packed with sleeping men and remained so until the place was required for breakfast, all the chairs and benches on the hurricane deck were occupied, and still there were people who had to walk about all night! I had a cattle-stall in the main stable.

No food or drink was available in the saloon, Clara remembered, "because the tables and floor had to be used for beds." The corpulent passengers "were selected to sleep on the tables in the belief that they would be less likely to roll off. Curtains were strung from wall to wall, separating the men and women, who had mattresses on the floor." At the first opportunity, at Wellington at around 5:00 a.m. the next morning, the Clemenses abandoned ship—Sam "praying with all my heart that she would sink at the dock"—and they booked "good rooms in the *Mahinapua*, a wee little bridal-parlor of a boat . . . clean and comfortable; good service; good beds; good table, and no crowding." After stops on November 18 in Nelson and the next day in New Plymouth, the party arrived in Auckland on the afternoon of November 20 and registered at the upscale Star Hotel. Back in Nelson, a city neglected, a reporter sniffed that it "must be rather pathetic than otherwise to hear Mark Twain" as he "wanders about the world . . . delivering lectures made up out of scraps of his own books."[16]

Over the next two days Sam twice spoke to "thronged houses" of over a thousand Aucklanders at the city hall. The *Auckland Star* reported that New Zealanders were not only unaccustomed to his "style of humorous delivery" but that "one must see the man and hear him to enjoy him to the full. . . . Nothing short of some ingenious combination of photography and the phonograph . . . could furnish even a faint representation of his appearance." The *New Zealand Herald* declared that as a raconteur he was "more delightful . . . than as a writer," though on the other hand the *New Zealand Observer* complained that he "was scarcely more entertaining than a speaker at an average Sunday school bun scuffle." While in the city he was an avid sightseer or, as he wrote later, he enjoyed the "charming drives all about," from the "grassy crater-summit of Mount Eden" to a Kauri gum processing plant, despite the onset of yet another carbuncle under his arm. A friend who accompanied the Clemenses, however, remembered that Sam sat "buried in gloom" and no doubt in pain during these excursions. Auckland "preferred him on rather than off the stage." As Livy wrote her sister Susan on November 24, Sam "does not seem to have as much strength as I could wish to see him have." If only Australia and New Zealand "had as many big cities as America has he could make his fortune," she observed, "but the trouble is that there are so few cities, just a *very few* along the coast. I think there are only seven or eight in New Zealand large enough for it to make it worth his while to lecture in them." Given his travel fatigue and his popularity in Auckland, Sam canceled a scheduled one-night stand 150 miles away in Rotorua, the center of the so-called thermal district, to deliver a third "At Home" at the Auckland Opera House at "popular [i.e., cheaper] prices" on November 25.[17]

The next day the Clemenses and Smythe sailed for their next stop, Gisborne, on the east coast of North Island, aboard the *Rotomahana,* "a nice ship, roomy, comfortable, well ordered, and satisfactory." After a voyage of twenty-three hours, Sam's "At Home" there was canceled because high seas prevented the ship from docking and Sam from disembarking. The next day they arrived at the port town of Napier, where Sam was scheduled to speak at the Theatre Royal on the evenings of November 28 and 29. Though he was discouraged by doctors from appearing on stage, Sam's first "At Home" went well. He bragged in his notebook about his "lovely time with the audience," and the *Hawke's Bay Herald* admired "the facility with which a heaven-born genius . . . could so twist words and contort phrases as to keep an audience in an agony of amusement." He then canceled his second performance on account of his health. As he wrote Joseph Twichell from his bed at Frank Moeller's Masonic Hotel overlooking the bay,

> I lectured last night without great inconvenience, but the doctors thought best to forbid tonight's lecture. . . . Livy is become a first-rate surgeon, now; she has been dressing carbuncles once & twice a day almost without a holiday ever since the 25th of last May. . . . I think it was a good stroke of luck that knocked me on my back here at Napier, instead of in some hotel in the centre of a noisy city. Here we have the smooth & placidly-complaining sea at our door.

Sam spent November 30, his sixtieth birthday, resting comfortably in his room. He wrote James Pond that Livy and Clara "have had a very pleasant time of it" since embarking from Victoria and "*I've* had an exceedingly good time, barring the carbuncles. One couldn't have more delightful audiences; & the journeys, both water & land, have been full of interest." While in Napier he visited a barber who subsequently sold locks of his hair.[18]

The party of four left two days later for Palmerston North on an express train, the Ballarat Fly, that averaged about thirteen miles an hour. On December 2 Sam saw Manawatu Gorge and read that evening in the city, then traveled forty-five miles the next day to Wanganui, a town of about three thousand, where he performed before a capacity crowd at Oddfellows Hall that included "many comely girls" in "cool and pretty" summer dresses and a delegation of "very polite" Maori. On December 4 the Clemenses toured a Maori village—more evidence of Sam's increasing sensitivity to cultural differences—and he delivered a second "At Home" in Wanganui. The local press reported that he received a "hearty welcome" from "a large and appreciative audience" that was "convulsed . . . with laughter for nearly two hours" by "a magnificent entertainment—intellectual and humorous."[19]

Sam and Smythe left Livy and Clara in Wanganui on December 5 for an engagement at Drill Hall in Hawera that evening (according to the *Hawera Star*, Sam was "a nonentity" who "pleased about 10 percent of those who heard him"). His "At Home" in New Plymouth the next night (the *Taranaki Herald* noted that Sam's "droll witticisms kept the audience in a perpetual state of half-subdued laughter, disturbed now and then by a spontaneous and uncontrollable outburst") was followed by a reception at the all-male Taranaki Club. They rejoined Livy and Clara in Wanganui on December 7, when Sam jotted in his notebook one of the few criticisms he expressed of New Zealanders; he derided "the most comical monument in the whole earth" that honored white militants "who fell in defense of law and order against fanaticism and barbarism" by prosecuting a genocidal war against the Maori and an adjacent monument to those natives who died "fighting with the whites and against their own people." This comedy of terrors, he asserted, "cannot be rectified. Except with dynamite."[20]

The party of four departed via express train for Wellington the morning of December 9, though the 120-mile trek took over nine hours and they arrived late in the city, forcing the postponement of the first of Sam's two "At Home" talks at the opera house until the next evening. They arrived in time to attend a dance party at Government House for the officers of HMS *Goldfinch*, however. On December 10 Sam visited Lord David Glasgow, the governor-general of New Zealand, who with the Countess of Glasgow attended his reading that night. As usual, he performed before bumper crowds and to radiant reviews. The Wellington *Evening Post* praised his "quiet power of description," and the *New Zealand Times* his "stories of a riotously humorous character" and "the liveliest lecture (so called) one could ever wish to hear." After his first appearance he was hosted by the Wellington Club; after his second he was honored with a dinner at the Club Hotel hosted by a small party of eminent Maori; and on December 12 the Clemenses and Smythe toured the "magnificent" botanical gardens in the suburb of Lower Hutt. Sam wrote Henry Rogers that evening the he, Livy, and Clara had enjoyed "a most delightful 6-week lecture campaign in New Zealand."[21]

On December 13 they embarked aboard the *Mararoa* on a return voyage to Sydney, and while they basked for three days in "summer seas and a good ship," as Sam boasted publicly, he grumbled in his notebook that they traveled with the "damnest menagerie of mannerless children I have ever gone to sea with" and prayed privately for "a storm and a heavy one" to confine them to their rooms. They docked the morning of December 17 and within a day or two attended a dramatic adaptation of Clarke's *For the Term of His Natural Life* at Her Majesty's Theatre. Clara thought the play "gruesome," though "we did not . . . regret" seeing it. Sam considered the chain gang scenes "a most pathetic sight. . . . That old convict life . . . [was] invented in hell and carried out by Christian devils." On December 19 Sam and Smythe left Livy and Clara at the Australia Hotel and railed 180 miles to Scone for an "At Home" ("a delightful treat," according to the *Maitland Mercury*), returning to Sydney the next day for the first of two performances at the School of Arts. He arrived late and blamed the weather. "I have been travelling in a railway carriage," he explained from the stage, "and the heat—whew! It was sweltering." Over the previous two days, moreover, President Grover Cleveland had threatened war with England over the border dispute in South America. The crisis was eventually settled by arbitration, but for several days Sam worried about the talk of war, another indication of his increasing reservations about European colonialism. He ended his first reading in Sydney on the night of December 20 with the hope that "we shall soon cease to be annoyed by all this unpleasant, unprofitable, and unbrotherly war talk," and he exited the stage the second night to prolonged cheers after wishing "that these two mighty nations will continue to march shoulder to shoulder in the van of peace and civilisation." Despite the talk of war, Sam's listeners throughout the talking tour

> were as friendly and as hospitable to me as if there were not a suggestion of gunpowder in the air. Neither in social gatherings nor in the lecture hall did anyone say anything which could remind me that friction existed between England and America. The newspapers never spoke of this episode with anything like bitterness but were always moderate in tone, rational, kindly. . . . When Mr. Cleveland's sizzling message came I thought that the people of the British colonies would feel a little chilly toward me. But I was mistaken. They didn't let it interfere with our relations, and laughed at my jokes just as much as ever. I even think they strained a point to laugh, or they laughed sometimes where I didn't intend that they should. I found that they had learned to like me a little through reading my books, and that friendship was warm enough to carry me smilingly through the crisis.

Certainly Sam thought that Cleveland had overreacted to what seemed to him "such slight, such inadequate grounds." The president, he thought, had taken "a strained view of the Monroe doctrine."[22]

On December 23 the Clemenses and Smythe sailed from Sydney aboard the 6,610-ton Peninsular and Oriental steamer *Oceana*—"a stately big ship, luxuriously appointed," Sam noted, "much the cleanest ship I ever saw" with "spacious promenade decks" and "large rooms." They arrived back in Melbourne on Christmas morning for a three-day layover. They dined on Christmas night at Highgate-on-the-Hill with the Smythe family and stayed at Stonington Mansion in Malvern, the ranch home of John Wagner, a partner in the Cobb & Company coach service, founded by American expatriates, that according to Clara "lacked no comforts or luxuries." In an interview with the *Melbourne Herald* at the ranch, Sam reiterated his belief that President Cleveland would never "degrade his high office" by threatening war with England for domestic political purpose. "Whether he be mistaken or not, I am sure he believes that he is doing what is right for the honour of the nation." On December 26—Boxing Day in Britain and its territories—Sam read at Athenaeum Hall to benefit the widow of Marcus Clarke, and he performed there again the next night before large crowds and to a favorable notice in the *Melbourne Age* ("concluded amidst loud applause"). He closed his engagement by again affirming the destiny of Anglo-Saxons around the globe: "Let us chaff and jaw and criticize one another as we please, when all is said and done, the Americans and the English, and their great outflow in Canada and Australia, are all one. . . . The English is the greatest race that ever was, and will prove itself so before it gets done—and I would like to be there to see it." Sam's nearly fifty appearances during his fifteen weeks in Australia and New Zealand were the most profitable of his entire world tour.[23]

The Clemens party sailed on Proclamation Day, December 28, for Adelaide aboard the *Oceana*, which anchored in Largs Bay two days later for a two-day visit. Accompanied by the consular agent, Murphy, Sam attended a luncheon in suburban Glenelg on December 30 and was greeted with applause and a toast from the two hundred guests, including Premier Kingston and Sir Thomas Fowell Buxton, the governor of South Australia. In a brief speech he again decried the war scare.[24]

The Clemens party sailed at noon on January 1, 1896, on a two-week voyage to Ceylon (today Sri Lanka) aboard the *Oceana*. Their itinerary had originally called for them to leave for India from Sydney on December 23 via the northern Queensland mail route and the Torres Straits and for Sam to open his tour of the subcontinent in Rangoon and Calcutta. Instead they detoured through Melbourne, Adelaide, and Albany to bid friends au revoir and to shield Sam's carbuncles from the scorching heat; they thus took a roundabout passage to India, voyaging twenty-five hundred miles south around the continent and then northwest a week behind schedule. "I have been persecuted with carbuncles and colds," Sam wrote Rogers while at sea, "until I am tired and disgusted and angry." All the while, Sam wondered whether Britain and the United States were at war over Venezuela, though, he added, "a ship is a world of its own—one does not trouble himself about other worlds & their affairs." He was ashore in Colombo, Ceylon, for only a few hours on January 13, time enough to visit the market and seaside esplanade, and he later told an interviewer it was "the most enchanting day I ever spent in my life. Everything was absolutely new—all that beautiful nakedness and colour." He confided to his journal, however, that the city was "unspeakably hot." Clara remembered that the family "only stayed long enough in Ceylon to see some of the tropical gardens and sandy roads by the sea." Sam postponed his speaking date in Colombo in order to catch the steamer *Rosetta* for Bombay (or Mumbai) to make up for lost time. The rusty tub—"this is a poor old ship," Sam remarked, "and ought to be insured and sunk"—completed the thousand-nautical-mile voyage along the west coast of India in five days. He spent three of them in his berth with a cold.[25]

The *Rosetta* arrived in Bombay on January 18, and Sam was greeted at the dock by Samuel Comfort, one of Rogers's Standard Oil lieutenants. The itinerant lecturer was bewitched by the city, he later reported in his travelogue; it was "the Arabian Nights come again." Rather than meeting with a round of welcomes, however, he was promptly confined to his room at Watson's Hotel with bronchitis and a fever for the next six days. In interviews on January 22 with the Bombay *Gazette* and the *Times of India*, he expressed his eagerness to see the fascinations of the city and spoke again of the distant drumbeat of war, the festering border crisis in South America. "I think it would be criminal now to interrupt the old friendly relations" between the mother country and the United States, Sam insisted. He could not "conceive of any greater disaster to the world than a war between these two great countries. There can never be a sufficient excuse for so great a crime; neither the Monroe Doctrine or anything else." He had sufficiently recovered from his fever on January 24 and delivered his first of three "At Home" talks to a full house of fourteen hundred at the Novelty Theatre. The *Advocate of India* noted that the audience consisted chiefly of "all the Americans in Bombay," "all the English who had been able to get places," and a "fair sprinkling of Hindoos and Parsees." The *Times of India* reported that Sam "gazed on a house the like of which has perhaps never been seen in any of our local theatres" and spoke in a "manner, voice, gesture, and the indescribable something which, in manifold ways, is always characteristic of genius." The *Bombay Gazette* reported that he was "unquestionably a great humorist," had "the power of moving people to tears as well as to laughter," and had been welcomed "not as a stranger in a strange land but as an old friend to well nigh everyone in the audience—a friend who has accompanied them in many a journey and been with them in many hours of joy and suffering, brightness and despair, health and sickness." His Bombay audience was mostly European but included a smattering of Hindus, Muslims, and Parsis, though his appearances in India were generally ignored by the leading native-language newspapers.[26]

Over the next few days Sam finally was able to see some of the sights, including the Jain temple on Malabar Hill, escorted by Virchand Raghavji Gandhi, who had been a delegate to the Congress of Religions at the Columbian Exhibition in Chicago in 1893.[27] He also enjoyed "an hour in the mansion of a native prince," Kumar Shri Samatsinhji Bahadur; and lunch at Government House on Malabar Hill with the governor and his wife, Lord and Lady Sandhurst. Late in the afternoon of January 26, escorted by Sir Jivanji Jamshedji Modi, a Parsi scholar, the Clemenses toured the Towers of Silence and witnessed a Parsi (or Zoroastrian) ritual exposure of the dead, which Sam equated with the Western practice of cremation. When a corpse was carried into one of the towers, a flock of vultures descended upon it and devoured the carrion—an antiseptic method of disposing of bodies that neither risked contamination of groundwater nor wasted arable land. He considered it an effective system "for the protection of the living from the contagion derivable from the dead—I mean one marvels to see this proof that modern science is behind the ancients in this so important matter." The next day Sam and Clara visited the collections of the local natural history society and attended a ball at the Royal Bombay Yacht Club. During this week, too, Sam was introduced to the eighteen-year-old Aga Khan III, imam of the Shia Ismai Muslims. "I spent a whole afternoon in his company and finished by having dinner with him at Watson's Hotel," the imam recalled in his autobiography. It was "a memorable experience of my later boyhood."[28]

On the evenings of January 27–28 Sam also delivered "At Home" talks before full houses at the Novelty Theatre. The next day Sam and Carlyle Smythe hurried to Poona for a performance at Gymkhana Hall, returning to Bombay the next day. One of the attendees remembered seventy years later that Sam's audience was "predominantly European," mostly Englishmen in suits or military uniforms, and that their laughter was so riotous Sam repeatedly quieted them "so that he could go on with the talk." Still, the bishop of Bombay walked out of the lecture, apparently offended by Sam's irreverence.[29]

Then Sam accepted an invitation to deliver something like a command performance that became a near disaster. The Gaekwad of Baroda asked him to speak, and although he would cancel appearances at Ferozepur, Peshawar, Amritsar, Ambala, Delhi, and Meerut over the next few weeks, Sam shoehorned this extra payday into his schedule. Sam, Livy, Clara, and Smythe railed overnight about 260 miles north to Baroda (today Vadodara), arriving the morning of January 31 for his reading that afternoon at the Makarpura Palace. The trouble was that while the Gaekwar was fluent in English and "a fine and cultivated gentleman," almost none of his two hundred guests (mostly native women) responded to Sam's stories. As Clara remembered, some of them "understood English very well, but laughed so little that our impression was that their sense of humor was certainly not of the American variety, if they possessed any at all." It was "a deadly affair for the poor humorist." Befitting his flop, Sam "slept all the way back to Bombay" that night on the train.[30]

They arrived at 7:00 a.m. on February 1 and departed fifteen hours later for Allahabad (or "Godville," as Sam called it), 860 miles and more than two days distant by train. As the saying went, the sun never set on the British Empire. Sam insisted to a Calcutta reporter a week later that he had "nothing to complain about in the journey," evidence of his charm offensive with the press while on tour. The Clemens party arrived on the morning of February 3 and Sam spoke that evening before a packed house at the Railway Club Theatre. As the *Lucknow Pioneer* described his style of humor, "in a casual, incidental way he introduces a circumstance that puts quite a new color on a detailed story, and as he tells it—as if the thought had just occurred to him—it is wonderfully telling in its unexpectedness." During the Clemenses' brief visit they witnessed thousands of Hindu pilgrims bathing in the confluence of the Ganges and Yamuna Rivers. They also saw the Pillars of Ashoka and explored Allahabad Fort, built by the Mughal emperor Akbar in the sixteenth century and occupied by troops of the British East India Company, a proxy for the British government, during the Indian Mutiny, or Sepoy Mutiny, of 1857.[31]

On the afternoon of January 4 they railed some ninety miles to Benares (today Varanasi), a Hindu holy city on the Ganges. Sam, Livy, and Clara spent the entire next day reconnoitering, mostly following tips in Arthur Parker's *Guide to Benares* (1895)—a trip on the river, where they gazed upon a funeral pyre onshore and "comely young maidens waist deep in the water"; tours of Moslem mosques and Hindu temples, including the Mosque of Aurangzeb and "the temple of the Thug goddess Bhowanee, or Kali, or Durga"; and a visit to the hovel of a reclusive local god, Sri Swami Bhaskarananda Saraswati, "a man who is worshipped for his holiness from one end of India to the other." Sam "had never realised till then what it was to stand in the presence of a divinity," he admitted to an interviewer, and "he is a divinity. Not even an angel. At the age of seventeen, I am told, he renounced his family ties, and embraced the asceticism in which he has lived these forty years and over. . . . He is minus the trappings of civilisation. He hasn't a rag on his back. But he has perfect manners, a ready wit, and a turn for conversation." Sam added that "I had heard of him and he said he had heard of me. Gods lie sometimes, I expect." They traded copies of their books—the holy man gave Sam a copy of his *Upanishad Prasada, i.e., An Easy Translation of 10 Upanishads* (1894), a meditation on Vedic verse, and Sam gave him a copy of *Adventures of Huckleberry Finn* (1885). "I knew that if it didn't do him any good it wouldn't do him any harm," he explained. "I thought it might rest him up a little to mix it in along with his meditations of Brahma, for he looked tired." In all Sam's travels, "I have never seen anything so remarkable as Benares or anybody so wonderful as that recluse," he conceded. "It has struck me that a Westerner feels in Benares very much as an Oriental must feel when he is planted down in the middle of London. Everything is so strange, so utterly unlike the whole of one's previous experience." He later echoed the observation in his travelogue: "Benares was not a disappointment. It justified its reputation as a curiosity."[32]

It could have been a watershed moment. He had begun to question the beneficence of imperialism in general. The time was ripe for his doubts, given the Japanese invasion of Manchuria in 1894 during the first Sino-Japanese

War; the British Guiana–Venezuela border dispute, the result of a violation of the Monroe doctrine, according to Grover Cleveland; the Hottentot Uprising in German South West Africa; and the unending clashes between Native Americans and the U.S. Army. As Sam told an interviewer in early February 1896, "In the United States there are continual rows with the Government, which invariably end in the red man being shot down," a transparent allusion to the massacre of Lakota Indians at Wounded Knee in December 1890. Added to these events was a festering crisis in South Africa. He had first heard about the Jameson Raid in Albany, his last port of call in Australia, from telegrams reporting that Leander Jameson, a colonial British functionary, and six hundred mercenaries under his command "were crossing the Border [from the Bechuanaland Protectorate, today Botswana] and were making for Johannesburg. Nobody could tell where this 'Border' was, or how long Jameson would take to cross it. We had a long interval to wait for the second chapter—until we reached Ceylon. Then we got the announcement that Jameson had fought his way so far, and had surrendered, and he and his men been taken prisoners." Sponsored by the British arch-colonialist Cecil Rhodes, prime minister of the Cape Colony, the raid was a spectacularly pathetic attempt to spark a revolution by the Uitlanders or "outsiders" in the Transvaal and overthrow the government of President Paul Krüger, ironically a product of Afrikaner or Dutch colonial practices. In this proxy war between the Boer overlords and the colonial British, about a quarter of Jameson's recruits were killed or wounded and the others jailed in Pretoria; and sixty-four henchmen in Johannesburg were arrested, tried, and sentenced to death. In a passage deleted from his travelogue, Sam described the raid as an "immortal farce," though in context it seems a dress rehearsal for the Boer War three years later.[33]

Under the circumstances, Sam might have experienced an epiphany. Instead, trapped in an intellectual blind spot, he continued to commend the civilizing influence of British colonialism. No one, he insisted in February 1896, "can deny the obvious advantages which the British have conferred on India. When one looks at the industrial and educational activity which has been set in motion all over the country, and when one considers its security and prosperity one cannot help coming to the conclusion that the British Government is the best for India, whether the Hindus or Mohammedans like it or not." The British race had not only migrated to all corners of the world but was "vigorous, prolific, and enterprising. Above all it is composed of merciful people—the best kind of people for colonising the globe." He extended the argument to the beneficent treatment by Brits of American Indians north of the border. "Look at the difference between the position of the Canadian

Indians and the Indians with whom the United States Government has to deal," he pleaded. "In Canada the Indians are peaceful and contented enough" because they had been treated honorably by the Canadian government.[34]

Even in his travelogue Sam held fast to this opinion, which was t(a)inted by his Lamarckianism and expressed in terms indistinguishable from the rhetoric of capture and conquest often deployed by his sometime bête noire Theodore Roosevelt. Viewing the world through a social Darwinist lens, the imperialist par excellence Roosevelt declared that "at the present time peoples of European blood hold dominion over all America and Australia and the islands of the sea, over most of Africa, and the major half of Asia." Indeed, over the previous millennium, "substantially all of the world achievements worth remembering are to be credited to the people of European descent." On his part, an ardent believer in Anglo-Saxon superiority and of a natural world red in tooth and claw, Sam continued to defend the system of British domination. He told an interviewer for the English-language Madras *Standard* while he was in country that subcontinent Indians "as a nation" lacked "inventive genius in the various practical arts." In his travelogue, he echoed the same theme: "When one considers what India was under her Hindoo and Mohammedan rulers, and what she is now; when he remembers the miseries of her millions then and the protections and humanities which they enjoy now, he must concede that the most fortunate thing that has ever befallen that empire was the establishment of British supremacy there." Sam predicted with xenophobic conviction that "all the savage lands in the world are going to be brought under subjection to the Christian governments of Europe" and "the sooner the seizure is consummated, the better for the savages." This derisive term for native or aboriginal or indigenous peoples was, unfortunately, neither accidental nor casual but recurrent and deliberate. "The great bulk of the savages must go," he declared in his travel book. "The white man wants their lands, and all must go excepting such percentage of them as he will need to do his work for him upon terms to be determined by himself." Such comments cannot be repaired. His support for British colonial government in India extended to British colonial ambitions in South Africa, where "from Cape Town to Kimberley and from Kimberley to Port Elizabeth and East London, the towns were well populated" with "tamed and Christianized" blacks. Of all the colonial powers, he believed, England—not Belgium, France, Germany, Japan, Russia, or the United States—was the most benevolent.[35]

On February 6 the Clemenses and Smythe railed to Calcutta—the capital of Bengal and, boasting a population of about a million, the largest city in

India. As usual, Sam was ill when he arrived and remained in his room at the Hotel Continental most of the next two days, meeting with a trio of reporters for the local English-language newspapers the next afternoon. "I am shut up," he wrote Susy in Hartford, "so instead of river parties & dinners & things, all three of us must decline & stay at home." He emerged from his confinement in time to dine at the eighteenth-century mansion, Belvedere House, on the evening of February 8 with the lieutenant governor, Sir Alexander MacKenzie. The environs around Calcutta were "rich in British achievement," as Sam put it, and he was eager to tour the sites associated with "that brace of mighty magicians" Robert Clive and Warren Hastings, who had been instrumental in establishing British colonial authority in India. Over the next few days Sam visited the ruins of Fort William and the site of the infamous Black Hole of Calcutta, where over a hundred English prisoners of war died under torturous conditions in June 1756; toured the "great botanical gardens," the Calcutta garrison, and Indian Museum; took a pleasure cruise on the Hooghly River; called on Sir William Elles, commander in chief of the Bengal Army; and attended a meeting of the Imperial Legislative Council chaired by Lord Elgin. On the evenings of February 10, 12, and 13 he delivered talks before packed houses at the Theatre Royal to favorable notices in the *Englishman* ("irresistible" and "inimitable") and *Indian News* ("humor is of that quiet, sly kind"). Only the Calcutta correspondent of the *Madras Mail* struck a discordant note: "Mark Twain as a lecturer is rather disappointing. He has a sing song methodical kind of delivery that becomes monotonous as he proceeds." Still, "he is a very funny man and most interesting. He has a refined intellectual face beaming with kindness and good nature, though sometimes wearing an expression of sadness and weariness that was touching."[36]

Sam and the others departed for a stop added late to their itinerary—Darjeeling, a resort town of the British Raj in the foothills of the Himalayas—on January 14. They ferried across the Ganges River at Siliguri and traveled to Kurseong, where Sam delivered an "At Home" and the family spent the night. They covered the remaining miles on the narrow-gauge miniature Darjeeling Himalayan Railway—Sam considered it "the most remarkable forty miles of railroad in the world"—and arrived in time for him to speak before a full house that evening. They lingered in the region the next day to admire the view. While Livy and Clara traveled to a lookout point outside the town, Sam absorbed the vista of Mount Kanchenjunga, the third highest mountain in the world, and other peaks from his room at the hotel and at the Planters' Club, where he also played billiards. They returned to Calcutta on January 17 by descending part of the way in a small handcar. "We came down the mountain at a dizzy toboggan gait on a six-seated handcar & never enjoyed ourselves so much in all our lives," Sam reported to Rogers. "We started in rugs & furs & stripped as we came down, as the weather gradually changed from eternal snow to perpetual hellfire." He echoed the point in his published travelogue: "For rousing, tingling, rapturous pleasure there is no holiday-trip that approaches the bird-flight down the Himalayas in a hand-car. It has no fault, no blemish, no lack, except that there are only thirty-five miles of it instead of five hundred."[37]

Sam and Smythe left later that day for Muzaffarpur, about 350 miles northwest of Calcutta, where Sam read the evening of January 19 to a full and "enthusiastic" audience. He dined afterward at the local British club, as was his wont. He explained, "In every town and city in India the gentlemen of the British civil and military service have a club; sometimes it is a palatial one, always it is pleasant and homelike." It was always exclusive, too: "a central symbol of imperial rule" because, with rare exceptions, Robert Cooper explains, "only white men belonged to it." Sam and his manager rendezvoused with Livy and Clara the next day on the train to Benares, where Sam spoke that evening. The next week was chockablock with events: a reading before a full house at the Mahomed Bagh Club in Lucknow, where he was "received with hearty applause from start to finish"; a "most enthusiastic banquet" in his honor at Chattar Manzil, or the Umbrella Palace, that "did not break up until a very late hour"; and a second reading in Lucknow. Meanwhile, as he traveled through the state of Uttar Pradesh where the Indian Mutiny of 1857 had been centered, especially while he was in Lucknow, Cawnpore, and Agra, he was determined to tour the (to the British) "sacred" sites. After passing through Jaunpur City en route to Lucknow on February 21, he jotted a note that "no doubt all those native grayheads remember the Mutiny." Apart from his readings in Lucknow, according to Coleman Parsons, "what drew him most" there was the sixty-acre site of the Residency, the command post of the East India Company and one of the major targets of the rebellion. Many of the buildings are still standing, albeit in ruins, though in February 1896, when Sam saw them, they were "draped with flowering vines" and "impressive and beautiful. They and the grounds are sacred now and will suffer no neglect nor be profaned by any sordid or commercial use while the British remain masters of India. Within the grounds are buried the dead who gave up their lives in the long siege." On January 23, during an interlude between his readings, and the same day that he was banqueted at Chattar Manzil, he retraced the route the forces of Colin Campbell, commander in chief of the British military during the mutiny, had taken in December 1857 to recapture Lucknow. While he was in the neighborhood, Sam also visited the Bara Imambara, one of the architectural wonders of the region.[38]

On January 25 the three Clemenses and Smythe railed forty miles to Cawnpore (now Kanpur), where Sam again spoke that evening. But he spent most of two days paying homage to the British victims of the mutiny at sites around the city, including Sati Chaura Ghat on the shore of the Ganges, site of the massacre of the betrayed garrison of British soldiers who had been promised safe passage from the city; the Koyleshwar Shiva temple, where the signal to ambush was allegedly blown on a bugle; and the Bibighar Well, into which the bodies of about two hundred British women and children, most of them relatives of the troops, were cast after they were executed by the sepoy rebels. Sam eventually became an outspoken opponent of imperialism, declaring in October 1900, for example, that "We have no more business in China than in any other country that is not ours."[39] Yet he apparently remained blind to the parallels between the mutiny against British colonialism in India in 1857–58 and the Boxer Rebellion against Western influence in China because he admired British discipline and efficiency.

On January 27 the Clemens party traveled 140 miles to Agra, where they stayed at Government House, the residence of the local British administrator. Livy was delighted by the "most beautiful and delightful" accommodations—"good food, nice, interesting, homelike people, great comfort, & great independence." While in the city Sam delivered an "At Home" before a packed Metcalfe Hall, and he visited the Taj Mahal, "the most celebrated construction in the earth," by day and moonlight and even during a lunar eclipse. He admitted, however, that the Taj he saw and touched was a disappointment compared to the Taj he had imagined, "built of tinted mists upon jeweled arches of rainbows supported by colonnades of moonlight," but he also conceded that the bejeweled mausoleum "is man's ice storm," a line reminiscent of Goethe's definition of architecture as "frozen music." They traveled another 140 miles on February 29 to Jeypore (Jaipur), where Sam promptly fell ill again. His physicians initially feared he had contracted smallpox. He was quarantined in his room in the Kaiser-i-Hind Hotel for most of the next two weeks lest he spread the contagion and was ordered to cancel all speaking dates for the foreseeable future. As a result, his appearances in Umballa, Meerut, and Delhi were scratched from his schedule. Livy later calculated that the "ten days of rest cost him nearly \$2000" in speaking fees. She predicted that "we shall not make very much out of India, perhaps a thousand dollars besides our expenses," but "we have enjoyed every minute" of this leg of the trip. Similarly, Sam wrote Rogers that "we have had a good time in India—we couldn't ask a better. They are lovely people there, both in the civil & the military service, & they made us feel at home." Ironically, in England and the United States, Sam was widely reported to be "dangerously" sick, perhaps even dying. In truth, he wrote Rogers, he suffered from severe diarrhea. His English physician urged him "to fly for Calcutta" with his family and leave India "immediately because the warm weather could come at any time now and it would be perilous for us."[40]

They left Jeypore on March 15 for Delhi, where they lingered only about twenty-four hours. "We saw almost nothing of that very interesting city," Livy wrote her sister Susan, both because "we expected to return there" and "there was so much smallpox that it was deemed better not to go about among the natives." As a precaution against the disease, both Livy and Clara were vaccinated. The family then headed to Lahore in the present-day Pakistani province of Punjab, where Sam spoke at the Railway Club Theatre on March 18–19, and to Rawalpindi, where he lectured on March 20. They then began to retrace their steps, first almost fifteen hundred miles to Calcutta, where they arrived on March 24—and where some two hundred people were dying from cholera every day. They embarked for Ceylon aboard the *Wardha* two days later. During more than two months in India, Sam delivered only eighteen readings—partly because there was a paucity of appropriate venues, but mostly because of his repeated illnesses. During Sam's stop in Madras late in March, he appeared to a local reporter to be pale, tired, and old. As Livy wrote Jean, had her father "been well he would have delivered 30 lectures or more in India." As pleasant as the abbreviated tour had been, they were ready to leave. Clara declared that "we had about enough of hot dusty traveling," and Livy wrote that "India was getting too hot for us to stay." Sam complained, too, that "it was always summer in India; at least we found it so—particularly in the winter." (The hottest summer he ever spent was a winter in India?) Still, he recalled years later that India was "the only foreign land I ever daydream about or deeply long to see again." The heat had exacerbated his aches and pains and he was troubled by his uncertain progress toward paying his debts. As Livy wrote Susan Crane, Sam had

> not as much courage as I wish he had; but, poor old darling, he has been pursued by colds and inabilities of various sorts. Then he is so impressed with the fact that he is *sixty* years old. Naturally I combat that idea all I can, trying to make him rejoice that he is not *seventy*. He does not believe that any good thing will come, but that we must all our lives live in poverty. He says he never wants to go back to America. I cannot think that things are as black as he paints them.

On April 3 they arrived back in Colombo, Ceylon, where he spoke in the half-empty public hall the evening of Good Friday and again the next afternoon. The *Ceylon Observer* rather equivocally observed that "his stories are so good that they will, in our opinion, bear neither extempore amplification nor much repetition."[41]

They departed the next evening on the *Wardha* for Mauritius. Clara and Livy slept on deck "on account of the heat & cockroaches in the cabins. The cockroaches are as large as mice & more familiar." Sam, on the other hand, said the ship "just suits my mood at present. I am in no hurry to get along. The more salt air I breathe the better I feel." Like Huck on the raft, at sea he experienced "no weariness, no fatigue, no worry, no responsibility, no work, no depression of spirits. There is nothing like this serenity, this comfort, this peace, this deep contentment, to be found anywhere on land. If I had my way I would sail on forever and never go to live on the solid ground again." The Clemenses "had a perfectly delightful voyage . . . from Calcutta by Madras & Ceylon to Mauritius," Sam wrote Rogers. "That was a holiday, but not enough of it."[42]

Early in the morning of April 15 they landed in Port Louis, where the daytime temperatures hovered above 120 degrees. They fled the village that afternoon for two weeks at the mountain resort of Curepipe—"it is on high ground, is cool, & rains all the time, & is very damp & pleasant"—where Sam recovered from his latest bronchial infection. Though he belittled the island for producing nothing more than "sugar, molasses, & mongrels," and though he was disgusted by the "ugliness & savage discomfort" of the hotel, he was at least blissfully free from carbuncles, his old bugaboo. He was also favorably impressed by the variety of "nationalities and complexions" he encountered there: "ebony, old mahogany, horse chestnut, sorrel, molasses-candy, clouded amber, clear amber, old-ivory white, new-ivory white, fish-belly white—this latter the leprous complexion frequent with the Anglo-Saxon" and, ironically, the same phrase Huck uses to describe Pap's skin tone.[43] In Mauritius, unlike India, moreover, Sam was "never pestered by a beggar." They returned to Port Louis on April 28 and embarked for South Africa aboard the *Arundel Castle*, "the finest boat I have seen in these seas" and "a perfect passenger boat. Everything that one could hope for; and the table is most excellent." The ship moored in Delagoa Bay, Mozambique, a Portuguese colony, the afternoon of May 4, and during shore leave—the first time he had set foot on the continent of Africa since the *Quaker City* cruise—Sam was reminded (just as unfavorably) of his stop in the Portuguese Azores in 1867. He told a South African reporter, "Portugal doesn't seem to be able to take care of herself in a very effective way, let alone manage a Colony."[44] Unlike, say, England.

The ship docked in Durban, South Africa, two days later, and the Clemens party registered at the historic Royal Hotel, which met with Sam's unqualified approval. As he noted, it was "comfortable" and offered a "good table, good service of natives and Madrasis" (an ethnic slur for South Indians). He particularly luxuriated in the moderate climate in the province of Natal; as he wrote Rogers, "here in Durban it is cool. . . . The days are warm, but not too warm; coolness begins with sunset; an hour later you must put on an overcoat; and your bed must have several blankets on it." They were entertained over the next several days by members of the Durban Savage Club, who hosted Sam at dinner on May 8 and escorted them to the Mariannhill Trappist monastery near Pinetown three days later. Predictably, Sam scorned the asceticism of the monks; he considered their rustic raiment, vows of silence and celibacy, and vegetarian diet "a sweeping suppression of human instincts." After nearly a week of leisure time, Sam read before full crowds at the Theatre Royal, which seated about a thousand, on the evenings of May 12 and 13 and he was afterward hosted at suppers both nights by the Savage Club. The Durban *Natal Mercury* commented that the second "At Home" in particular was "in every way thoroughly enjoyed."[45]

Sam and Smythe departed on May 14 for a five-week whistle-stop tour through South Africa, leaving Livy and Clara in Durban. Their first stop was Pietermaritzburg, the capital of Natal, where Sir Walter Hely-Hutchinson, the governor-general, and his wife Lady Hely-Hutchinson attended the first of Sam's two "At Home" talks the next evening. The Theatre Royal was packed both nights with, among others, as Sam noted, a "wonderful lot of pretty girls & young misses." He also garnered glowing notices, though one critic observed, in an allusion to *Macbeth*, that Sam was "falling into the sere and yellow leaf"—that is, getting old. The same note would be struck increasingly in the reviews of his performances over the next several weeks. After his first appearance in Pietermaritzburg, however, he was entertained at a joint meeting of the Victoria and Savage Clubs, and he assured Livy that he was "satisfied with myself & with the noise that was made" after dinner. While in Pietermaritzburg, Sam also lunched at Government House with the governor-general and toured Maritzburg College, a boys' school, whose headmaster reported that in his experience "some men are not so good as their books while others are better." Max O'Rell, who had recently toured South Africa, fell into the former category, and Sam, "the most genial-hearted man I ever met," into the latter.[46]

Sam's next stop was Johannesburg, the largest city in the country, with a population of over a hundred thousand. He delivered four talks between May 18 and 21 there at the cozy Standard Theatre, with a seating capacity of only about six hundred. He was greeted on opening night "with a perfect furor of applause" by "one of the most crowded houses" the theater had ever seen. The next day Sam gleefully announced to Livy that he had "had a grand time." He reported to Livy after his third performance that his lecture "came out just as handsomely as the others." The Johannesburg correspondent of the *Bloemfontein Friend* concluded that "the mighty master of wit" had "done more for the salvation of the human family than ten score of priests." On the other hand, the Johannesburg *Star* observed that some in the audience "confessed that they felt disappointed with the lectures," and the Johannesburg *Standard* opined that "in the art of saying nothing in an hour he easily surpasses the most accomplished of our parliamentary speakers."[47]

Sam's visit to South Africa coincided, as he put it, with a brisk "boil" in the "political pot." He wished he might "bum around these interesting countries another year & talk." He told reporters he "could not have come to South Africa at a better time, excepting that I should like to have arrived earlier, and been 'on the spot' throughout the whole crisis." The South African people "have had a fearful time here lately—what with wars, revolutions, rinderpest, locusts, drought—and me. I guess you can go no further with plagues. Now that I've come, you must make a change for the better." In any event, "I take a great interest in the political situation, but at the same time I consider politics here an inextricable tangle." The so-called Reformers, the sixty-four conspirators, including several Americans, convicted of treason for complicity in the Jameson Raid, had been imprisoned in Pretoria, the capital of the Transvaal. One of them committed suicide while Sam was appearing in Johannesburg, an event that stirred "tremendous excitement" in the press. During his week there he reconnected with Natalie Hammond, his fellow Missourian and shipmate aboard the *Paris* in July 1894 and the wife of the mining engineer John Hays Hammond, one of the jailed Reformers. Coincidentally, Sam had also known him years earlier. When he was a student at Yale University, Hammond noted in his autobiography, they had met "a number of times at Hartford, Connecticut, where I often went to spend weekends" with William B. Franklin. Mrs. Hammond introduced him to U.S. consular agent Robert Chapin and his wife Adèle Chapin, and these friends persuaded him to intervene on behalf of the jailed Americans. "My sympathies were soon with the Reformers," Sam explained in his travelogue, "with their friends, and with their cause" because as Uitlanders, or outsiders. they paid huge taxes "yet got little or nothing for it"—not even the vote. He compared the Jameson Raid to the Battles of Lexington and Concord, fought to guarantee the British colonists' rights. Rather than revolution, the Uitlanders wanted "reform—under the existing government," and Sam predicted they would eventually win the day without armed conflict. But he also conceded that "the cause of political reform" had "been retarded a decade by the Jameson fiasco."[48]

On May 23, Sam, Mrs. Hammond, and Carlyle Smythe traveled forty miles to Pretoria. That afternoon, accompanied by the Chapins, Mrs. Hammond, and Smythe, Sam visited about fifty of the prisoners in the Pretoria Gaol. Natalie Hammond and Carlyle Smythe described the facility in starkly different terms. Mrs. Hammond remembered that the cell where the four leaders, including her husband, were confined was only eleven feet square, windowless, with an earthen floor "and overrun by vermin." The prisoners were racially segregated. To Smythe, however, it seemed like a proverbial country club jail. "When we entered the prison quadrangle," he recalled, "it seemed from the laughter and bright clothing that we were attending some tennis [match]." The prisoners' larder was "stocked with such unusual prison delicacies—unusual, as far as my experiences goes—as Yorkshire hams, Scandinavian sardines in piles, Bologna sausage, pate-de-foie gras, and French olives." John Hays Hammond, who was by some accounts the chief architect of the raid and who "talked Rhodes into backing it," introduced Sam to the other Reformers, albeit at a distance. Sam explained that a Boer guard "barred the way . . . and wouldn't let me cross a white mark," or "deathline," on the ground. He was "allowed to see some of the cells and examine their food, beds, etc.," and he was told "Hammond's salary of $150,000 a year" had been continued by Rhodes. None of the prisoners appeared to be undernourished or to have been abused, they looked "healthy & well-kept," they had "a lot of books to read," and "they play games and smoke."[49]

Still, they all faced long prison terms and suffered "times of deadly brooding and depression." Sam was asked by Natalie Hammond to bolster their morale with a speech, and he proceeded to offend at least some of them by suggesting they savor their situation. That is, he seemed to share Smythe's view of their privileged circumstances: "I told them that they didn't seem to appreciate the privilege of being confined in a jail." After a few months, he assured them, "they would prefer the jail and its luxurious indolence to the sordid struggle for bread outside." John Bunyan, for example, "would not have written the *Pilgrim's Progress* if someone had not shut him up in a cell" and "we should not have had the pleasure of reading *Don Quixote* if Cervantes had not spent several years in prison." So "you see being in jail is not so bad after all." Sam declared that he "would willingly change places with any one" of them and even promised to ask Krüger "to double their jail terms" when he met the president. "I have seen the prisoners and made them a nonsensical speech," he wrote Rogers. Sam profoundly misjudged his audience, of course. "Some of the fellows smiled sadly," he admitted. "Some of them laughed, and they all appeared good natured, notwithstanding the fact that some others did not even smile at my joke on them."[50]

It was, in fact, an old gag. In a letter to Mary Mason Fairbanks twenty years earlier, Sam had claimed that he envied Bunyan because "solitary imprisonment" was "the one perfect condition" for writing. But many of the Reformers were not amused. The distinguished South African physician Alfred Hillier, one of the inmates, merely noted that "some of us failed to look at it in this philosophic light." Percy FitzPatrick, secretary of the Reform Committee, considered Sam a has-been, a "poor old chap" who was "now ruined and broken in health!" John Hays Hammond resented Sam's condescending comments for the rest of his life. "I am not one of Mark Twain's admirers," he told the author William Dana Orcutt years later. During Sam's South African lecture tour, "Mark Twain reported that he was amazed to find conditions as they were" in the jail where Hammond was confined and "that the food and accommodations were fully equal to the Waldorf-Astoria in New York" so that he thought the prisoners should request life sentences. Not that Sam was deterred. He told reporters that, compared with the conditions in the Nevada mining camps thirty years earlier, Hammond was "now living in luxury." He believed the prisoners' confinement "an ideal rest cure" for "tired businessmen." The next day the Boer papers hostile to Krüger sharply criticized the lax conditions in the jail and, as Hammond recalled, "the prison authorities responded by diminishing our rations, which had been none too liberal before." One of Cecil Rhodes's sisters later told Smythe that "the prisoners were furious" because Sam "praised their lodging comforts," which prompted a crackdown. To be sure, Sam had meant "to be humorous, but a wave of indignation swept over South Africa" and, Hammond told Orcutt, "since then I have failed to see anything 'funny' in anything Mark Twain says or does."[51]

Sam insisted, however, that he sympathized "with the Reformers in the Pretoria jail, with their friends, and with their cause." Accompanied by Consul Chapin, he met Krüger in his office on May 26 and insisted that his comments at the prison had been made in jest. "I had heard so much about [Krüger] everywhere, read so much about him," and "had painted his picture in my brain so often," Sam recalled, "that I knew him before I saw him. He did not astonish me. He was exactly as I had fancied him." Attired "in ordinary everyday clothes," the president stated that he was "disposed to be lenient" with the imprisoned Americans, whereupon "the severity of the discipline was once more relaxed." Yet as late as mid-June, when asked by an interviewer whether he had heard "any complaints from the prisoners as to their treatment" when he visited them, Sam replied, "Oh, no; I have been in many worse jails in America." Nevertheless, a few days after Sam's meeting with Krüger, all of the Reformers were released upon payment of an indemnity, £2,000 each for most of them, and £25,000 each for the four leaders—fines officially paid by the British government but likely funded by the warmonger Rhodes. The reputed transaction confirmed for Sam what he had long suspected: "that Brer Rhodes meant to overturn the government; it also looks suspiciously like the leading Reformers were accessories." On his part, Krüger was so impressed by Sam's appeal on behalf of the Reformers that he acquired a complete edition of his works.[52]

Sam read at Caledonian Hall in Pretoria the nights of May 23, 25, and 26. After the first "At Home," the Pretoria *Transvaal Advertiser* mused that he was "a first-class raconteur, and possesses in full the ability to say the drollest and most mirth-provoking things without appearing to be in the slightest degree aware that that he has said anything but the most ordinary thing in the most ordinary manner." On his part, Sam wrote Livy that his audience had been "composed chiefly of Africanders & direct descendants of the old Boers, hard to start but promptly & abundantly responsive after I once broke through their ice." In contrast to his Indian auditors, Sam's South African listeners were overwhelmingly white. Meanwhile, he yearned to finish his tour and, as he wrote Twichell, "sail for England; and then we will hunt up a quiet village and I will write and Livy edit, for a few months, while Clara and Susy and Jean study music and things in London." He had been planning his final travelogue since landing in Sydney and he was amenable to reverting to the journalistic practices he had once observed as the city editor of the Virginia City *Territorial Enterprise*: "I'm writing a book and I want information. I don't care if it's true or not." After all, "one does not get his mind strengthened by hard facts."[53]

But first came a series of platform performances in rapid-fire succession. After his second appearance in the capital he was hosted at a supper by the Pretoria Club. Sam and Smythe left Pretoria the morning of May 27 for Krugersdorp, where Sam spoke that night at Freemasons' Hall, though the *Krugersdorp Times* was underwhelmed: his yarns were deemed "too lengthy and too prosily told."[54]

Sam returned to Johannesburg the next day for his fifth appearance there—and his ninth performance within a forty-mile radius in ten days. Carlyle Smythe informed the local press that "Mark Twain would rather

. . . deliver a serious lecture than a humorous one. The only poets he ever reads are Browning and Shakespeare, and there is not much frivolity about Browning." Sam appeared there before a "packed audience of fashionables," including the consul of the United States at the Masonic Hall there. According to the *Johannesburg Times*, the "large and thoroughly appreciative assemblage followed his lecture with rapt attention." The Johannesburg *Standard & Diggers' News* considered his reading "the best wine of his marvelous cellar," in apparent contrast to the first four, perhaps because he opined on his parley with the Reformers:

> He had been to Pretoria, and saw the Reformers gathered there in the charge of the Government, and it seemed to him such a pity to see all that energy and talent and nerve-power and will-power and all those multitudinous capacities—(immense applause)—locked up even for a trifling time—(renewed applause)—lost to this wonderful country with its great mines, the richest in all the world. To carry on the work without them was something like running the cyanide process without the cyanide. (Hear, hear, and applause.)

Sam's friend Poultney Bigelow remembered that the audience "crowded every square inch" of Freemasons' Hall and that, though he "was a sick man," Sam "made his audiences roar with laughter. He was good at a laugh himself, when in his normal health, but never laughed at his own stories. Indeed, his very sepulchral solemnity when perpetrating a violently comical tale was not the least part in its ultimate success." After the lecture, Sam dined with Bigelow; Bigelow's friend Adolf Goetz, a mining engineer; and Goerz's "winsome Viennese *bonne à tout faire*," followed by "the real day of joy for [Sam]—an easy chair and outstretched legs, pockets full of cigars," and "a long tumbler of steaming toddy."[55]

The next evening, Sam and Smythe left for a weekend in Bloemfontein, capital of the Orange Free State. They arrived midafternoon on May 30 and, after registering at the Free State Hotel, Sam read that evening to an overflow audience at the town hall. Before departing on June 3, Sam read a second time and, armed with a letter of introduction from Bigelow, called on the president of the province, Martinus Theunis Steyn. The British settler Dora Ortlepp Poultney remembered in her autobiography that Sam warned the South African presidents that they should "give Cecil Rhodes plenty of rope to hang himself or he will swallow up your Republics." After his next appearance "before the best-paying house ever" in Queenstown the evening of June 5, the Queenstown *Representative* declared that Sam "can be as funny on the platform as on paper." Yet the next day, in a spasm of despair, fearing that the book-form publication of *Joan of Arc* had been delayed or canceled,

Sam confessed to Rogers that he did not "think it is of any use for me to struggle against my ill luck any longer. . . . If I had the family in a comfortable poor-house I would kill myself." On June 7 Sam and Smythe railed to King William's Town, where Sam spoke the two following nights before "enthusiastic" audiences at the town hall. His humor was, according to the King William's Town *Cape Mercury*, "more droll than intensely funny." The *Kaffrarian Watchman* similarly noted that "the gifted Yankee" left his "large and appreciative audiences" regretting "that the 'At Homes' were not longer."[56]

Before he left town Sam also floated a trial balloon for Livy to consider: "How would you like me to be U.S. Consul at Johannesburg for a year? Mr. Chapin wants to quit, & I suppose I could have the place for the asking. I might make a fortune, I might not. But a Consul there must have mighty good chances. I've not said anything to Chapin, but I would like you to telegraph me yes or no." Livy immediately deflated the idea. On June 10 Sam and Smythe traveled fifty miles to East London, where Sam spoke at Mutual Hall each of the next three evenings, though the first of his performances was "meagerly attended" on account of weather. On June 16 they sailed aboard the *Norham Castle*, "a large and very fine ship," south to Port Elizabeth, where the next day they finally reunited with Livy and Clara at the Grand Hotel and Sam spoke to crowded audiences the evenings of June 22–24. On the first of these dates, Smythe later reported, a woman "began to laugh and continued to laugh so loud and so often that she grew a nuisance and became finally so intolerable that she had to be taken out."[57]

Sam's fatigue from his weeks on the stump began to become apparent, and the reviews of his performances were generally hostile—for example, the Port Elizabeth *Leader* deemed his talk "generally disappointing," and the Port Elizabeth *Looker-On* "decidedly disappointing," "strained," and "extremely insipid." Coleman Parsons concludes that "the words 'disappointing' and 'disappointed' appeared increasingly in news reports" of Sam's readings in South Africa as he "grew weary," and Sam conceded to Rogers that he "got horribly tired of the platform toward the last" of his tour—"tired of the slavery of it; tired of having to rest up for it, diet myself for it, take everlasting care of my body & my mind for it, deny myself in a thousand ways in its interest. . . . I hope I have trodden it for the last time; that bread-and-butter stress will never crowd me onto it again." It was a familiar refrain. Sam had complained to Livy as early as June 10 that lecturing was "tiresome" and "hateful." Carlyle Smythe conceded that "everything makes him tired, even sleeping." On June 25 the Clemenses and Smythe traveled to Grahamstown, where Sam spoke at the Albany Drill Hall the evenings of June 26 and 27 to a "grand success," according to *Grocot's Penny Mail*.[58]

Then followed a long haul to the South African diamond fields, four hundred miles away. They departed on June 28, paused two nights at the Victoria Hotel in Cradock, and arrived in Kimberley two days later. Sam spoke that evening and again two nights later at Kimberley Town Hall. While in the region he toured the local diamond mines—including the infamous "Big Hole," which he thought "roomy enough" to admit the Roman Colosseum—owned by Rhodes's De Beers Company, and from which an average of $50,000 in diamonds per day, or $400,000 a week, were excavated by black laborers. Sam was told by a mine manager, "We don't own our black slaves, but that is what they are and that is what we mean they shall remain." Sam would later claim that during his tour he found "a diamond about as big as the end of my finger, but there were so many people watching me that I didn't bring it away."

Then followed another slog of six hundred miles over two days to the legislative capital, Cape Town, on the west coast, arriving the morning of July 5. Over the next seven days Sam dined at the Castle of Good Hope with William Howley Goodenough, commanding general of British forces in Cape Colony; toured Table Rock, Table Bay, and St. Simon's Bay; and thrice delivered talks at the opera house to upbeat notices, though one critic thought he resembled a "good grizzled old worker . . . as if he had been at it a thousand years." The *South African Telegraph* of Cape Town cooed that his lectures were "like his books, full of geniality and quaintness" and he was "by far the most successful [humorous lecturer] who ever visited South Africa." Edward Vincent of Cape Town's *Cape Argus* observed that his "method of approaching his audience is unstudied to a degree. It suggests the idea of a retiring man taking a quiet stroll and . . . finding himself suddenly confronted by an animated crowd anxious to pay him homage."[59] On July 13, almost exactly a year to the day after he opened his world tour at the House of Refuge on Randall's Island in New York City, and after over 130 appearances on four continents, Sam performed for the final time at the town hall in Claremont, a suburb of Cape Town, and was hosted afterward at a reception by the Owl Club there.

Though Sam had originally planned to begin his book about the world tour in South Africa, he decided instead in light of "the disturbed state" of the country "and the possibility of war" there to leave for England immediately. On July 15, Sam, Livy, Clara, and Smythe boarded the *Norman*, "a beautiful ship, perfectly appointed," for Southampton, England, where the Clemenses had departed on their trip around the world the year before. Among the other four hundred passengers were Barney Barnato, Cecil Rhodes's chief rival in the mining fields of South Africa; and three of the

Reformers recently released from jail in Pretoria. "I seemed to have been lecturing a thousand years, though it was only a twelvemonth," Sam reflected during the voyage. Lamentably, the tour had not been as financially remunerative as he had hoped. He collected only about $20,000 over expenses,[60] roughly the same sum he had received during his "raid on the lyceums" with George Washington Cable in 1884–85. But he had profited enough to liquidate about 30 percent of his debt, with prospects for more lectures around Great Britain over the summer and in the United States the following fall. And best of all, Sam, Livy, and Clara anticipated a reunion with Susy and Jean within days of their arrival in England.

CHAPTER 6

Falling to Earth

The secret source of Humor itself is not joy but sorrow. There is no humor in heaven.

—Mark Twain, *Following the Equator*

AFTER SIXTEEN DAYS of sailing from Cape Town and a brief stop in Madeira, the *Norman* docked in Southampton on July 31. Interviewed upon his arrival, Sam pronounced "the Transvaal the country of the future" and praised the U.S. consular officials he had met in Australasia and South Africa. Privately, he wrote James Pond that, while "I managed to pull through that long lecture campaign," he was "never very well from the first night in Cleveland to the last one in Cape Town, and I found it pretty hard work on that account. I did a good deal of talking when I ought to have been in bed." The Clemenses rented Highfield House on Portsmouth Road in Guildford, some twenty-five miles southwest of London in the Surrey Hills, for five weeks. Livy began to scour the countryside for a place, as Sam wrote W. D. Howells on August 5, "in some quiet English village away from the world & society, where I can sit down for six months or so & give myself up to the luxury & rest of writing a book or two after this long fatigue & turmoil of platform-work & gadding about by sea & land." He then added, "Susie & Jean sail from New York today, & a week hence we shall all be together again."[1]

Critical opinion about *Personal Recollections of Joan of Arc* upon its publication in May 1896 was sharply divided by nationality. Relatively few notices were equivocal. On the one hand, the Chatto & Windus edition was well received in England, not surprisingly given its implicit censure of French aristocracy, but no doubt in part because "Mark Twain" was listed on the title page only as the editor. As a result, many British reviewers were flummoxed, reading the narrative as a faithful transcript or translation from medieval French of a genuine memoir by Sieur Louis de Conte about a French martyr rather than as a work of fiction. Or as Sam explained, "I find that people are misled by the words '*Edited* by.' They seem to take it entirely for granted that Joan is not my book & that I am simply lending my name to somebody else's book for such commercial value as it may possess." The *Scotsman*, for example, asserted that "Sieur de Conte's original work" has been "translated by Jean François Alden, whose work has been edited by Mark Twain." The London *Morning Post* opined, moreover, that "readers of this moderately interesting telling of the famous story will be rather puzzled to know what part Mark Twain had had in its preparation, seeing that he contributes nothing in the way of preface, introduction, or annotation." This reviewer raised the possibility that Sam was in fact "Louis de Conte and Jean François Alden rolled into one" but cautioned that such a conclusion "would be premature."[2]

In any event, British critics routinely praised, if sometimes faintly, the book for its portrayal of a nascent French Catholic saint. Walter Besant in the *Queen* ("a most amazing book" and "a most moving portraiture"), Andrew Lang in the *St. James's Gazette* ("honest, spirited, and stirring"), and Richard Le Gallienne in the *Idler* ("a great imagination" and "a great heart") were all approving. Many other unsigned reviews were similarly complimentary, as in the London *Speaker* ("the best book he has ever written" and "one of the best things done by anybody in fiction for a long time past"), *London Chronicle* ("never did Mark Twain display his artistic sense to better end"), London *Daily News* ("abounds in wisdom, insight, and reverence" and "Clemens vindicates himself as an artist"), London *Times* (an "honest fervor of admiration . . . fires Mark Twain's narrative"), London *Sketch* ("very readable"), London *Bookman* ("very fresh, and much finer in texture than, we confess, we had expected from its writer"), London *Morning Post* ("considerable success"), *London Leader* ("a dignified, ennobled, hero-worshipping Mark Twain" whose "language has undergone a startling change"), *Glasgow Herald* (an "enthusiastic" panegyric "chivalrous in tone"), and *Dublin Herald* ("a close and loving study of Joan's character and of the age in which she lived").[3]

Joan of Arc was also received with predictable approbation by the religious press in both England and the United States. The *American Hebrew* ("has proved by this book that he is a great writer"), *Northern Christian Advocate* ("one of the best of recent books"), New York *Evangelist* ("charming" and "a revelation"), and *Christian Work* ("a new and fascinating chapter of French history") were no less admiring. The Reverend George H. Hepworth suggested in the *New York Herald* that Sam had completed a "difficult" task "astonishingly well." Despite some misgivings about Sam's humor in a devotional tract, the Boston *Congregationalist* similarly concluded that he "has given us a most satisfying book and one that must live as literature."[4]

To be sure, some British reviewers expressed more serious reservations. The London *Standard* argued that the novel betrayed a distressing lack of "historical reading and knowledge." The *Manchester Guardian* damned the book with faint praise—it had "a good many second-rate qualities and, at the worst, is readable, but it seems rather too much like a magnified obituary notice"—and groused that "the style that amuses us in *Huckleberry Finn* jars upon us" here. The *Pall Mall Gazette* launched a fusillade of charges—that the novel was "abnormally dull," "ill-composed," and "a failure." The *Athenaeum* opined that "the verisimilitude of the narrative is rather spoilt by the Americanisms which intrude too frequently in the book" and that it was "rather long-winded and didactic in tone," and the *Sydney Herald* speculated that "the majority of his readers would prefer Mark Twain to have chosen another subject." Later Frank Harris complained that *Joan of Arc* was "a dreadful book" because Sam "makes a Puritan maiden of the great Frenchwoman" and George Bernard Shaw declared Sam's Joan "an unimpeachable American schoolteacher in armor" and, in an epitomic ambiguity, "a credible human goodygoody."[5]

The American edition of *Personal Recollections of Joan of Arc* issued by Harper & Brothers, which included the author's name embossed on the cover and spine but not printed on the title page, attracted plenty of defenders in its own right—a surprising number, given its mediocre modern reputation. The publisher J. Henry Harper argued that "the trial scene, where Joan stands up alone, fighting for her existence and confuting the best legal talent of the day, is a superb picture, and it is all based upon the facts gleaned in his painstaking research." Many of the reviewers in the United States similarly emphasized the thoroughness of Sam's research, among them the *Boston Beacon* ("rests upon a foundation of historical learning that is absolutely marvelous for its range and profundity") and New York *Outlook* ("fidelity to the original documents and records"). Others, such as the *Independent* ("a great historical picture"), *Chicago Tribune* ("among the best examples of English historical romance"), *Brooklyn Times* ("an excellent and thoroughly exhaustive biography"), *Cleveland Plain Dealer* ("a wonderful story about the most wonderful woman in history"), *Hartford Times* ("one of the great stories of the world" told "in such a fashion that it makes a congruous whole and seems real to the reader"), New York *Critic* ("a good, straightforward, hearty story of a great and noble life"), New York *Evening Post* ("a romantic character sketch"), and George Hamlin Fitch in the *San Francisco Chronicle* ("no one, old or young, can read it without getting spiritual benefit from this fine study of one of the greatest characters of all history"), stressed its power as a work of history or biography. Still others, incredibly enough, highlighted its humor; these included the *Chicago Inter Ocean* ("characterized by the simplicity and quaint humor which have given the author his pre-eminent distinction"), Chicago *Advance* ("vivid, abounding with life and color, with pathos, with humor"), New York *Sun* ("the occasional passages of characteristic humor will prove to be more popular than the serious parts"), and Colorado Springs *Gazette* ("humor . . . abounds throughout the book").[6]

Some critics tried to situate the novel in the context of Sam's career. The notice in the *Emporia Gazette*, probably penned by its owner-editor and Sam's friend William Allen White, suggested not only that *Joan* was "one of the great books of the year" but that it qualified its author no longer to be considered merely the great American jokesmith but the great American novelist. The *Brooklyn Eagle* ("certainly a striking proof of his versatility and may turn out to be the book upon which his title to fame will rest"), *Boston Transcript* ("a wonderful testimony to the versatility and vitality of his industry and his talents"), *Boston Journal* ("certainly Mr. Clemens greatest work"), and *Philadelphia Times* ("the most earnest and serious if not the most important thing that Mr. Clemens has ever done") followed suit. There were brief announcements, as quotable as cover blurbs, in such papers as the *Boston Post* ("one of the notable books of the year"), *Boston Advertiser* ("the volume is one of rare interest"), *Indianapolis Journal* ("a very ingenious and interesting work"), *Salt Lake Tribune* (a "luminous and most agreeable" work that "cannot fail to please the public"), *Book Buyer* ("pathetic power of the narrative is great"), *New York Mail and Express* ("one of the most delightful books of the time"), *Saturday Evening Gazette* ("style is quaint and exquisitely adapted to the story"), *Philadelphia Inquirer* (likely to become "one of the most popular of books among young readers"), *Charleston News* ("much pleasure"), and *Baltimore Sun* ("remarkable scenic painting"). The poet Vachel Lindsay conferred a certain cachet on Sam's novel years later, too, with a brief ditty entitled "Mark Twain and Joan of Arc":

> Mark Twain, our Chief, with neither smile nor jest,
> Leading to war our youngest and our best.
> The Yankee to King Arthur's court returns.
> The sacred flag of Joan above him burns.
> For she has called his soul from out the tomb.
> And where she stands, there he will stand till doom.

On his part, Sam famously repeatedly claimed that he liked "*Joan of Arc* best of all my books; and it is the best; I know it perfectly well. And besides, it furnished me seven times the pleasure afforded me by any of the others: 12

years of preparation & 2 years of writing. The others needed no preparation, & got none."[7]

This verdict, however, was not unanimous. Many American reviewers tempered their opinions or simply offered hollow praise or nondescript notices of *Joan of Arc*, Sam's friends Howells, Laurence Hutton, and Brander Matthews foremost among them. All three of them commended the book the best they could, though none of them extolled it. Howells declared it was "a vast frolic, in certain aspects," but conceded that he would have preferred that Sam "had frankly refused to attempt it at all. I wish his personal recollections of Joan could have been written by some Southwestern American, translated to Domremy by some such mighty magic of imagination as launched the Connecticut Yankee into the streets of many-towered Camelot." He was particularly troubled by "the outbursts of the nineteenth-century American in the armor of the fifteenth-century Frenchman." Hutton mustered a few banalities, such as "Never since the days of Hollynshed has the maiden seemed so earthly as Mr. Mark Twain has made her." Matthews blamed the blemishes in the novel not on Sam's personal shortcomings but on the shift in literary fashion: "Mark Twain as a historical novelist is not at his best; and the reason for this is, I think, that in this last decade of the nineteenth century the historical novel is an outworn anachronism." (In fact, the period occasioned a renaissance in the genre with the publication of such works as George du Maurier's *Trilby* [1895], Henryk Sienkiewicz's *Quo Vadis* [1896], Charles Major's *When Knighthood Was in Flower* [1898], Mary Johnston's *To Have and to Hold* [1899], and Maurice Thompson's *Alice of Old Vincennes* [1900].) A glut of other critics hedged their views about the novel; for example, in the *New York Tribune* ("had Mark Twain possessed a streak of poetic genius his 'Personal Recollections' of the Maid would have been a masterpiece"), *New York Times* ("a bold effort to reimpose delusions upon us and the joke may lie in seeing how far it will succeed"), *Portland Oregonian* ("more of an effort than an accomplishment"), Boston *Literary World* ("apart from its tediousness the book is well worth reading"), *Hartford Courant* ("a remarkable work such as only a man of genius could have written" despite "certain faults of construction"), *St. Paul Globe* ("may not be a great work of art but . . . a great work of affection"), and *Minneapolis Star Tribune* ("not artistic but who cares?").[8]

In the end, it is fair to say, American readers were more overtly hostile to the novel than their British counterparts. The gist of the objections, ironically, was that the story was insufficiently faithful to the historical circumstances of its setting. Ironically, Raymond Roth in the San Francisco *Wave* asserted that Sam's decision to eschew "the heroic medieval style of address" was one of the primary virtues of the book, but most critics disagreed. As Howells complained, de Conte too often is made to speak (even if ostensibly translated from medieval French) in colloquial American, as when he declares that "there was one English gun that was getting our position down fine" or "the court had a fashion of coming back to a subject every little while and spooking around it" or when he describes Joan's father as an "old land-crab." Or as the *Buffalo Courier* ("one breathes the atmosphere of two distinct and irreconcilable ages"), *Providence Journal* ("the everpresent atmosphere of Connecticut humor spoils the effect"), and the *Dial* ("labored spontaneity" and "artificial style") argue, the diction of the novel is marred by historical anomalies. The Milwaukee *Weekly Wisconsin* similarly complained that the defects in wording "remind us that Mr. Clemens is not primarily a man of letters"—a line cribbed from W. P. Trent's review in the New York *Bookman* ("the chief defects" of *Joan of Arc* lie "in the fact that he is not primarily a man of letters"). In any case, the critics for many periodicals concluded that the novel was claptrap and drew their long knives, as in the *San Francisco Call* (Sam "must have been hard up for material"), *Bachelor of Arts* ("does not add much to history or to literature or to Mark Twain's reputation"), and *Nation* ("we hope that if he makes another excursion into this field of historical idealism he will keep incident and panegyric within artistic bounds"). Julian Hawthorne, who had long championed Sam's genius, "began to search for the joke" in the book "as soon as we learned that it was [written by] Mark Twain" and was "almost offended when none appeared." Sales of the book were disappointing and, in the end, it was deemed a financial failure. Still, Basil Wilberforce, the canon of Westminster Abbey, wrote Sam that he believed "nothing can approach your book" about Joan "for power vividness and appreciation of her character," and the actress Sarah Bernhardt considered it "an admirable work, sincere, full of life."[9]

On August 10, when Susy and Jean, escorted by Katy Leary, should have been aboard ship in the mid-Atlantic, two or three days from arriving in England, Sam wrote James Pond that his daughters were "not on their way hither" and "we do not yet know why." Pond had seen Susy at the mansion on Farmington Avenue a month earlier, when he attended the funeral of Harriet Beecher Stowe in Hartford and thought she seemed "quite happy where she is. She says it seems very much like home to her." Charley Langdon had notified Sam and Livy in early August that Susy was "slightly ill—nothing of consequence." They cabled for an update on her condition on the fourteenth, only to receive a reply hours later: "Wait for cablegram in the morning." Early the next day they railed to Southampton, ready to sail for the

United States should they receive alarming news, where they received word that Susy's "recovery would be long but certain. This was a great relief to me," Sam remembered, "but not to my wife. She was frightened." So Livy and Clara boarded the *Paris* for New York should they be needed in the United States to nurse Susy. Sam remained behind "to search for another and larger house" for the family to occupy when they all returned. He planned to follow soon if "if the cablegrams do not improve meantime." The next day he addressed an oddly prescient note to Livy, which she would receive after her arrival in the United States.

> You & Clara are making the only sad voyage of all the round-the-world trip. I am not demonstrative; I am always hiding my feelings; but my heart was wrung yesterday. I could not tell you how deeply I loved you nor how grieved I was for you, nor how I pitied you in this awful trouble that my mistakes have brought upon you. You forgive me, I know, but I shall never forgive myself while the life is in me. If you find our poor little Susy in the state I seem to foresee, your dear head will be grayer when I see it next.

He alternately blamed himself and Charley Webster for Susy's trouble. Had he not lost his fortune, or had Webster not cost him his fortune, he would not have been forced by financial exigency to lecture around the world to pay his debts and the family would have remained together in Hartford. His "crimes made [Susy] a pauper & an exile." Awash in self-reproach and alone in London, he was humbled as Livy hurried to their daughter's bedside: "Livy darling, you are so good & dear & steadfast & fine—the highest & finest & loveliest character I have ever known," he wrote; "& I was never worthy of you. You should have been the prize of a better man—a man up nearer to your own level. But I love you with all my heart, from my proper place at your feet." On August 18, the day after posting this letter, he received encouraging news to the effect that Susy's "illness has moderated." He decided "not go to America next week, as I was expecting to do, but will wait a little in the hope that a cablegram will soon tell me that the family are on their way to England."[10]

No one—not her parents, Katy Leary, Charley Langdon, Susan Crane, or even her doctors—yet realized that Susy was fatally ill. She had contracted spinal meningitis, a malady that was almost always fatal before the advent of antibiotics, and her illness was not diagnosed until August 15. She wandered through the rooms of the Hartford house, as Livy later reported to Grace King, "with her tortured mind in delirium and pain." She lost her sight the next day and, touching "a dress of her mother's hanging in a closet," she asked for Livy, "broke down and cried." On August 16, she slipped into a coma and did not move again. She died on Tuesday, August 18, three days before Livy and Clara landed in New York after a year-long separation. At her bedside were Katy Leary, her uncle Charley Langdon, and her aunt Susan Crane.[11]

Langdon immediately cabled Sam in England with words that cut "like a sword: 'Susy could not stand brain congestion and meningitis and was peacefully released today.'" He was "not expecting that awful news—there had been no preparation for it whatever," he confessed to his brother Orion, "& when the cablegram announcing it was put in my hands I supposed it was going to be something pleasant." "It is one of the mysteries of our nature that a man, all unprepared, can receive a thunderstroke like that and live," he reminisced over a decade later in his autobiographical dictation. "I was not dreaming of it," he wrote Livy the day after he received the cable. "It seemed to make me reel. I loved Susy, loved her dearly; but I did not know how deeply, before. But—while the tears gushed I was still able to say 'My grief is for the mother—for myself I am thankful; my selfish love aside, I would not have it otherwise.'" If only "three little days could have been spared them," Sam bitterly reflected a month later, "poor Susy would have died in her mother's arms." Yet he took some consolation that she had "died in our own house, not in another's, died where every little thing was familiar & beloved" in the city "where she had spent all her life," that "her dying eyes rested upon nothing that was strange to them, but only upon things which they had known and loved always and which had made her young years glad," and that she had not lingered, that "the beautiful fabric of her mind did not crumble to slow ruin, its light was not smothered in slow darkness, but passed swiftly out in a disordered splendor. These are mercies. They will help us to bear what has befallen." He begged Joseph Twichell to comfort him. "The others break my heart," he explained, "but you will not. You have a something divine in you that is not in other men. You have the touch that heals, not lacerates. And you know the secret places of our hearts."[12]

Over the next several days Sam compulsively ranted in grief-stricken letters addressed mostly to Livy, incommunicado in the mid-Atlantic en route to New York. "Oh, my heart-broken darling," he raged the day he received the news of Susy's death—"no, not heart-broken yet, for you still do not know—but what tidings are in store for you!" Then later: "You will see her. Oh, I wish I could see her & caress the unconscious face & kiss the unresponding lips—but I would not bring her back—no, not for the riches of a thousand worlds. She has found the richest gift that this world can offer; I would not rob her of it. . . . How lovely is death; & how niggardly it is doled out." (Five years later, in his brief allegory "The Five Boons of Life" [1902],

Sam also decreed Death the greatest blessing, ranking it above Fame, Love, Riches, and Pleasure.) "Oh, poor Livy darling," he raved on August 21, "at 8 tomorrow morning your heart will break, the Lord God knows I am pitying you. . . . Hour by hour my sense of the calamity that has overtaken us closes down heavier & heavier upon me. . . . I eat—because you wish it; I go on living—because you wish it." He soon wrote her again: "I know what misery is at last, my darling. I know what I shall suffer when you die. I see, now, that I have never known sorrow before, but only some poor modification of it." His self-reproach slowly shaded into survivor guilt, much as he had blamed himself for the deaths of his brother Henry in 1858 and his son Langdon in 1872. He longed to receive any kind of message Susy may have left him before she became delusional but conceded he did not deserve it. "My remorse does not deceive me," he wrote Livy while she was still in mid-ocean. "I know that if she were back I should soon be as neglectful of her as I was before—it is our way. . . . My selfishness & indolence would resume their power & I should be no better father to her, no more obliging friend and encourager & helper than I was before." He decided that under the circumstances "there is but one thing to do—hide in an English village away from the sight of the human face" and mourn.[13]

Livy and Clara learned of Susy's death when they arrived at quarantine in New York harbor the morning of August 22. That is, Sam knew his daughter had died almost 3,400 miles away three days before her mother and sister were told the news when their ship docked, only a hundred and twenty miles from Hartford. He began to play "billiards, and billiards, & billiards" around the clock "to keep from going mad with grief." He cabled Rogers in New York to arrange for the physician Clarence C. Rice, their mutual friend, to meet the ship and break the sad news. Rogers in turn ordered the Standard Oil tugboat *Astral* to convey Rice, Joe Twichell, and Livy's brother Charley Langdon to the *Paris* at quarantine on August 22. Even before the trio reached the ship, however, the captain of the *Paris* showed Clara a copy of Susy's obituary in a New York paper. "The world stood still," Clara recalled. "All sounds, all movements ceased. Susy was dead. How could I tell Mother? I went to her stateroom. Nothing was said. A deadly pallor spread over her face and then came a bursting cry, 'I don't believe it!' "[14]

After the ship docked, Livy retreated to the Waldorf-Astoria to rest a few hours. There Katy Leary described Susy's last hours to her mother. "I told her how that last night I was lifting Susy in her bed, how she put her arms around my neck and rubbed down my face with her two little hot hands, and she laid her cheek against mine and said, 'Mamma, mamma, mamma!' She thought I was her mother then. When I told this, Mrs. Clemens was sitting in a big chair" and "she just stretched out her two hands and held mine hard." Sam was comforted that, "in that forlorn hour of wreck and ruin, with the night of death closing around her," Susy "should have been granted that beautiful illusion—that the latest vision which rested upon the clouded mirror of her mind should have been the vision of her mother, and the latest emotion she should know in life the joy and peace of that dear imagined presence."[15]

Livy and the others caught a train later that afternoon for Elmira, where Susy's body had already been taken. The next day, in the parlor of the Langdon mansion on Main Street, Thomas K. Beecher and Annis Eastman, co-minister of the Park Church, conducted Susy's funeral, followed by her burial in the family plot in Woodlawn Cemetery. Grace King claimed that Livy, "always a frail woman, never recovered from the shock" of Susy's death. As bitter as her death was for Sam, even he wondered "what must it be to my wife." Certainly Livy protested that, while other families had lost children, they had had never "lost a Susy Clemens." "We are a broken-hearted family," she wrote Mary Mason Fairbanks, "yet such we are and such I think we must always remain. This is of course the first terrible staggering blow that we have had and I realize that for me there can be but one worse."[16]

Similarly, Susy's death was arguably the most traumatic event in Sam's life—more devastating than the deaths of his father in 1847, of his brother Henry or his son Langdon, of his mother in 1890, or even of Livy a few years later. His son, mother, and wife had long been ill and their deaths were not unexpected. Susy's death was sudden and unforeseen. Moreover, she was the chosen and cherished child, the most gifted of his daughters, a bookworm and by right of primogeniture his literary heir. She was "a rare creature," as he wrote Twichell in late September, "the rarest that has been reared in Hartford in this generation. I merely knew that she was my superior in fineness of mind, in the delicacy and subtlety of her intellect, but to fully measure her I was not competent." She was "a poet—a poet whose song died unsung" and Sam mourned "the books that Susy would have written and that I shall never read now. This family has lost its prodigy. Others think they know what we have lost" but "only we of the family know the full value of that unminted gold; for only we have seen the flash and play of that imperial intellect at its best." "To *us* she was a prodigy," he averred. "We of the family believed, & still believe, that she had no equal among girls of her own age in this regard. Even the friends thought highly of her gift." Soon enough, Sam blamed a host of those others for Susy's death. As early as December 1896 he alleged that if she "had had only *one* wise and courageous friend among the crowd of friends in Hartford, we should not have lost her." A month later he again scapegoated Charley Webster for bankrupting him, prompting him to lecture around the world and separating Susy from her mother. As he wrote his sister Pamela, Webster was "the primal cause of Susy's death & my ruin. I am not able to think of him without cursing him. . . . The thought of that treacherous cur can wake me out of my sleep." Webster "was all dog. And he put me where I am, & Susy where she is."[17] If only he had, like Pamela, opposed Webster's marriage to Annie Moffett in 1875, he would never have gone bankrupt and been forced to travel around the world with her mother and sister, leaving Susy to die in Hartford.

Livy, Clara, Jean, and Katy Leary embarked on the *St. Louis* for Southampton on September 2. Rogers booked them into an "airy and spacious and homelike" suite of cabins that spared Livy the "necessity of going outside her door the whole voyage to encounter the eyes of either the curious or the compassionate." They arrived in Guildford a week later, just in time to help Sam locate a house for $1,350 a year on Tedworth Square in the upscale neighborhood of Chelsea in London in London, where they might "shut ourselves up" and "bar the doors and pull down the blinds and take up the burden of life again." Sam canceled his plans to lecture around England that fall and around the United States that winter because, as he wrote Orion, "the unspeakable bereavement which had befallen me in Susy's death has necessarily quenched all desire to continue on the platform." The *Paris Messenger*, among other papers, reported that "the death of his bright young daughter in America" had prompted Sam to withdraw from public view. He explained to his second cousin James Ross Clemens, a surgical intern at St. Thomas' Hospital in London, that in their "deep bereavement" for Susy "we are hermits and keep our address secret." A publicity hound under normal circumstances, he readily sat for reporters' questions when free advertising was to his advantage, as when he was on tour. But while in mourning he sought seclusion. He was "inundated with would-be interviewers" but refused them all "very firmly, though politely." The London correspondent of the *Sheffield and Rotherham Independent* found him "hard at work on his new book" but Sam declined to be quoted for the record and the reporter conceded that "the good people of Guildford appear to see very little of him" and "some of them are totally unaware of his existence" in their town. Without remarking on the reason he was reclusive, the London *Fun* joked about his eagerness to remain out of sight:

> The petty humorist, we know, would fain
> Be interviewed twelve times, and yet again,
> Until quite turned was his little brain!

> But the Great Humorist bids men refrain
> From writing him up in their well-known strain—
> Just *Mark* the difference betwixt the *Twain*!

In early October the Clemenses moved to Chelsea, two blocks from the house on Tite Street where Oscar Wilde had lived until his arrest in April 1895. Katy Leary remembered that the house had "big rooms and a lovely porch and a fine billiard room." No one save Sam's closest friends knew their location; otherwise, he could be reached through Chatto & Windus, his British publishers. "We keep in hiding because we are four broken hearts," he explained to Poultney Bigelow, "and I do not go out and my wife and daughters never see anybody—they cannot bear it yet." He admitted to his sister Pamela after the move that "neither Livy nor I pretend to be happy or ever expects to be again." Clara recalled that "it was a long time before anyone laughed in our household after the shock of Susy's death" and "we did not celebrate Thanksgiving day or Christmas" that year. Indeed, "it was a long time before anyone laughed in our household." Sam remembered that it was a desultory period, the first since his marriage that holidays "came and went without mention. No presents were exchanged and we studiously pretended to be unaware of the day."[18]

During this period of mourning, apparently in hopes of reuniting with Susy, Sam nourished a belief in the hereafter. A year before, he had facetiously ridiculed immortality in a poem he addressed to Julia Beecher, Thomas K. Beecher's wife:

> If you prove right and I prove wrong,
> A million years from now,
> In language plain and frank and strong
> My error I'll avow
> (To your dear mocking face).
> If I prove right, by God His grace,
> Full sorry I shall be;
> For in that solitude no trace
> There'll be of you and me
> (Nor of our vanished race).
> A million years, O patient stone!
> You've waited for this message.
> Deliver it a million years—
> Survivor pays expressage.

However, he wrote Howells in September 1896, a month after his daughter's death, that he "without *shadow* of doubt" would "see Susy" again, and soon after the holiday season of 1896 the grieving family failed to celebrate he discussed in his notebook the notion of "a spiritualized self" or "dream body" that could "*detach itself* and go wandering off upon affairs of its own." His "other self, my dream self, is merely my ordinary body and mind freed from clogging flesh and become a spiritualized body and mind," and he predicted that "when my physical body dies my dream body will doubtless continue its excursion and activities without change, forever." He soon abandoned his lukewarm faith in an immortal soul—"the Bible of Nature tells us no word about any future life, but only about this present one," he jotted in his notebook on May 27, 1898—but he acquiesced to Livy's occasional attempts to contact Susy beyond the pale. "I have never had an experience which moved me to believe the living can communicate with the dead," he admitted in March 1901, "but my wife and I have experimented in the matter when opportunity offered and shall continue to do so." Near the end of his life he told his biographer Albert Bigelow Paine that he was "wholly indifferent" to the question of an afterlife. "If I am appointed to live again," he explained, "I feel sure it will be for some more sane and useful purpose than to flounder about for ages in a lake of fire and brimstone for having violated a confusion of ill-defined and contradictory rules said (but not evidenced) to be of divine institution. If annihilation is to follow death I shall not be aware of the annihilation, and therefore shall not care a straw about it."[19]

Sam was not entirely inaccessible after the family moved to Tedworth Square. Coincidentally, Poultney Bigelow lived nearby, and they sometimes met "of a sunny morning for a smoke and chat—sometimes for a stroll on the Embankment." Bigelow also took Sam along on a visit to Mary Collier, Lady Mary Monkswell, who was "mightily pleased to see him." In mid-December, Sam by chance again crossed paths with his friend Michael Davitt. Over the months he and Henry Stanley visited Parliament together a few times, including one day in March 1897 when they heard, according to Harold Frederic, the novelist and London correspondent of the *New York Times*, "a debate on the recent disbanding of a Scotch volunteer regiment, which was certainly funnier than anything they ever did in Missouri during the war." To judge "by the sunny twinkle" in Sam's eye he considered it "a congenial subject." He called on his old friend John Hay, now the U.S. ambassador to England, at the U.S. embassy on June 23 "and spent a couple of hours in reminiscent chat." Among the other people with whom he socialized were Bram Stoker; publisher Andrew Chatto; Andrew Lang; the novelist and playwright Anthony Hope; C. F. Moberly Bell, editor of the *Times* of London; Rudyard Kipling; John Y. W. MacAlister; the journalist Julian Ralph; Lord Lorne, the former governor-general of Canada, whom Sam met in

1883 when he was in Ottawa to secure Commonwealth copyright on *Life on the Mississippi*; and his friend Adèle Chapin, the wife of the former U.S. consul in Johannesburg.[20]

All the while he took solace in his work. "I shall write the book of the voyage—I shall bury myself in it," he declared to Rogers. "But if I only had time and money and no bread-and-butter pressure upon me I would write a certain other book"—a tribute to Susy—"and make this one wait." He began to organize his notes on October 4, soon after the family moved to Chelsea, and completed the first chapter of the travelogue, tentatively titled "Around the World," "Another Innocent Abroad," "The Surviving Innocent Abroad," "The Last Innocent Abroad," "The Latest Innocent Abroad," or "Imitating the Equator," on October 24. "I work seven days in every week," writing on average about eighteen hundred words a day, "and seldom go out of the house," he reported to Rogers. "I don't rush, and I don't get tired, but I work every day and sleep well every night." Since Susy's death he had focused upon his books.

> They will be the only support of my family in case of my death; yes, & their only support while I remain alive, for I am done with the platform. For a year or more, at any rate. I wish to make the list of books as large as I can. And so, after I finish the present subscription book, I shall go straight on & clear out my skull. There are several books in there & I mean to dig them out, one after the other without stopping. . . . Since I am cut off from the platform I am thinking much more about creating an income for my family than I am about paying creditors.

He was not miserable, he advised Howells, but "worse than that, indifferent. Indifferent to nearly everything but work. I like that; I enjoy it, & stick to it. I do it without purpose & without ambition; merely for the love of it." He originally planned to end the travelogue with his departure from India, preferring to discuss his tour of South Africa in a separate volume "if there is material enough in that rather uninteresting country to make the job worthwhile." Sam privately predicted that in half a century "the Rand mines will have become exhausted," Johannesburg will be "a deserted wilderness," nobody but the Boers will care to inhabit the Transvaal and the Orange districts," and the Cape and Natal "will be prosperous British communities." He completed a rough draft of the travelogue on March 1 and spent a week gutting a third of the manuscript before beginning "a careful revising & editing of the remaining two-thirds." He crowed on March 25 that he was "more than satisfied" with the work and "wouldn't trade it for any book I have ever written" and the next day that "if it isn't a rattling good book *I* don't know one when I see it." He notified Orion around this time that four-fifths of the manuscript was complete "& is now undergoing Livy's second revision & my third."[21]

Trouble is, the Blisses wanted to issue a single volume that chronicled the entire trip, including its final leg. They feared that Sam was withholding "the best stuff to sell to another publisher" and they were scared they had wasted their $10,000 advance. Ironically, both Livy and Rogers sided with the Blisses, to Sam's dismay. To extend the narrative "to take in South Africa—a big addition to the job, I can tell you, after I supposed I was done"—would require him "to dig 300 pages of MS out of the present book to make room" and "it is not any easier to take a complete book apart than it is to take an Indian rug apart." Nevertheless, he resumed work in late April on a manuscript he had considered finished. He reported to Rogers on April 28 that he had written seven thousand words over two days and expected to have the project completed "once more in two or three weeks." After adding a total of about thirty thousand words to the text, he finished another draft of the book on May 18. To shorten the British edition, however, as late as July 1 he and Andrew Chatto "ripped out a raft" of material from the narrative. He had padded it with citations to some fifty published sources, not all of them necessary in Chatto's view.[22]

He completed the 190,000-word manuscript in less than eight months and, at least to its American publisher and a few others, professed to be satisfied. Bliss traveled to England in early July to pay Sam the promised advance and to collect the first part of the typewritten manuscript. In an interview, Bliss reported that Sam was "working hard" and "will take a rest when he gets the book off his hands." Privately, however, Sam was circumspect. "I should have never written the Equator book if I could have gotten out of it," he told Rogers. "I would rather be hanged, drawn and quartered than write it again. . . . All the heart I had was in Susy's grave and the Webster debts. And so, behold a miracle!—a book which does not give its writer away." He was even more candid with Howells: "I wrote my last travel-book in hell; but I let on, the best I could, that it was an excursion through heaven. Someday I will read it, & if its lying cheerfulness fools me, then I shall believe it fooled the reader. How I did loathe that journey around the world!—except the sea-part & India." But he had little choice: he "owed a fortune" and wrote it not for pleasure but "purposely to get money wherewith to reduce that burden." To be sure, he enjoyed writing parts of it, such as "chaffing [Cecil] Rhodes and making fun of his Jameson Raid." He purported to admire the mining magnate and notorious imperialist Rhodes and declared tongue-in-cheek that "when his time comes I shall buy a piece of the rope for a keepsake"—an apparent allusion to the sale of inch-long specimens of the rope used to lynch the slave Glascock's Ben near Hannibal, Missouri, in 1849.[23]

However, he was not yet a wholehearted critic of imperialism and colonialism in the travelogue, published in the United States under the title *Following the Equator* and in a slightly longer version in the UK as *More Tramps Abroad*. Such criticism may be cherry-picked from the book, such as this passage:

> All the territorial possessions of all the political establishments in the earth—including America, of course—consist of pilferings from other people's wash. No tribe, howsoever insignificant, and no nation, howsoever mighty, occupies a foot of land that was not stolen. When the English, the French, and the Spaniards reached America, the Indian tribes had been raiding each other's territorial clothes-lines for ages, and every acre of ground in the continent had been stolen and re-stolen 500 times. The English, the French, and the Spaniards went to work and stole it all over again; and when that was satisfactorily accomplished they went diligently to work and stole it from each other.

While such paragraphs seem remarkably modern, as Peter Messent argues, they nevertheless presume "that western culture is the central source of meaning, worth, and authenticity against which foreign difference must be measured." Put another way, Sam's comments on colonialism are undergirded by racist notions of European cultural superiority. A believer in a global Manifest Destiny, he shouldered his share of the white man's burden with his friend Kipling. Whereas on the one hand Sam asserted that "the world was made for man—the white man," he only twenty-five pages later described as "humorous" the "white man's notion that he is less savage than the other savages."[24] That is, both imperialists and anti-imperialists might selectively cite *Following the Equator*—a hybrid text comprised variously of anecdote, folklore, memoir, travelogue, world history, fish story, ethnography, political commentary, and social satire—to support their ideas.

Critical opinion about *Tom Sawyer, Detective*, despite its long gestation, was sharply divided. The novel was considered by many British critics little more than a slapdash potboiler upon its publication in the United States by Harper & Brothers and in Great Britain by Chatto & Windus in December 1896. It was scorned, for example, by the *Manchester Guardian* ("poorly conceived and badly put together"), *St. James's Gazette* ("a vastly unpleasing tale—extravagant, incredible, not at all amusing"), London *Bookman* ("we have liked Tom Sawyer and Huckleberry Finn better in other circumstances"), Athenaeum ("a tendency to dullness"), and London *Standard* ("Mark Twain should give us the adventures of new boys"). On the other hand, a few reviewers were charitable, such as the critics for the *Boston Transcript* ("an exciting narrative of adventures"), *Chicago Inter Ocean* ("another of the author's imperishable creations"), *Charleston News and Courier* ("his satire is as keen as it is bitter"), London *Telegraph* ("leaves little to be desired"), London *Academy* ("humour is as fresh and entertaining as ever"), London *Speaker* ("very amusing and interesting"), London *Times* ("a capital story full of fun"), *London Chronicle* ("will serve to send the judicious into the sort of laughter that, as the French say, makes a pint of good blood"), *Spectator* ("inimitable"), and Sydney *Daily Telegraph* ("dashing and dramatic"). The British edition of *Tom Sawyer, Detective and Other Tales* also included the first publication of "A Little Note to M. Paul Bourget," Sam's second rejoinder to the French travel writer. The essay was hailed and assailed Down Under by the *Daily Telegraph* ("a satire in Mark Twain's best style"), *Sydney Herald* ("tone is provincial and bitter"), and *Australian Town and Country Journal* (the humorist "meant to be very funny and very sarcastic but did not exactly succeed in being either").[25]

Over a decade later, Sam's reputation was tainted by the accusation that he had plagiarized the plot of *Tom Sawyer, Detective* from Steen Blicher's "The Vicar of Weilby"—a case of the potboiler calling the kettle black. Never mind that Sam had always acknowledged in a footnote that he had borrowed some plot incidents. The Danish schoolteacher Valdemar Thoresen asserted in the *Maaneds-Magasinet* that Sam stole the germ of his novel, even though Blicher's story had not yet been translated into English. Through his secretary Isabel Lyon, Sam denied in December 1908 that he was a deliberate plagiarist or that "this or any other matter that has appeared under Mr. Clemens's name is based upon the work of any other." Thorensen was astonished by this response but accepted it.[26]

Unfortunately, the seclusion upon which Sam insisted after Susy's death sparked a rumor in spring 1897 that his world tour had been a financial failure and he was dying in "a dingy London lodging-house" in squalor somewhere on Grub Street. The item was printed in the London *Evening Globe* on March 2 and widely copied across the United States. His cousin James Ross Clemens sent him a copy of the original article in the *Globe* and Sam quickly tried to squelch the rumor. He replied that "part of what it says is true"—the part that reported he was "hard at work on a book" to pay debts "contracted for me by others. But the rest is an error. My wife has a modest (but sufficient) income from property inherited from her father, & so we do not have to live in a lodging house." Joe Twichell sent Sam a clipping from a U.S. paper that indicated he was "living in penury in London and that *my family has forsaken me.* This would enrage and disgust me if it came from a dog or a cow or an elephant or any of the higher animals, but it comes from a man and much allowance must be made for man." Frank Marshall White, European correspondent of the *New York Journal,* tracked down Sam on June 2 to verify the story only to discover that

> he was living with Mrs. Clemens and their two daughters in a comfortable home in Chelsea, was in good health, and working ten or twelve hours per day. It was a house of mourning, however, for only a few months before death had removed the oldest daughter from the family of five . . . and the visitor felt a prevailing sadness in the atmosphere, in the subdued voices of the servants, in the silence of the darkened rooms. Mrs. Clemens had not left her own apartment for many days, and her daughters were constant in their attendance upon her.

Sam told White "he did not know whether to be more amused or annoyed" by the rumor, which soon mushroomed into a minor scandal, and he famously explained how he suspected it originated: "James Ross Clemens of St. Louis, a cousin of mine, was seriously ill two or three weeks ago in London but is well now. The report of my illness grew out of his illness." Sam later joked that White's New York editor had cabled him: "If Mark Twain is dying in poverty send five hundred words. If he has died in poverty send one thousand words." In any case, White sent a dispatch about Sam's situation to his paper

> that night, in which I embodied in his own words what he had written about his cousin in the morning. The operator who cabled it left out all punctuation marks, as is usual unless they are specifically marked for transmission. The copyeditor in New York, preparing the dispatch for the printer, began a paragraph with the last clause of the second and last paragraph of the note he had written in bed "The report of my death is an exaggeration," and this by process of repetition became "The reports of my death are grossly exaggerated."

After picking up the story but without first seeking Sam's approval, the *New York Herald* established a fund on his behalf, contributing $1,000 before passing the hat. Andrew Carnegie donated another $1,000 on the condition that none of his money would be diverted to Sam's creditors. Less than a week later, the *Herald* explained that subscribers were underwriting his living expenses, not his debt relief. When White informed him of the campaign, Sam "was taken entirely by surprise" but he was "very much pleased."

He thought "a sufficient fund could be raised to lighten my debt very greatly, possibly even discharge it."[27]

But he failed to anticipate the public backlash. As soon as the charity was established the London *Sun* expressed regret that Sam had been "reduced to such a position as the *Herald* fund indicates." The *Hartford Times* averred that some of Sam's "most intimate friends" in his former hometown were "greatly puzzled by the continued talk about his poverty." Not only was he traveling in Europe with his family accompanied by "two or three servants," it was inconceivable "that he proposes to accept a dollar of gift money from anybody." That is, the paper implied, the *New York Herald* had established a late-nineteenth century equivalent of a fraudulent Go Fund Me page. The New York *Town Topics* editorialized that "neither the *World* nor the *Journal* in the moments of deepest and most desperate degradation have been guilty of anything half so vile and vicious as the *Herald*'s abominable assault on the dignity and proud name of 'Mark Twain.'" The "impudent attempt" by James Gordon Bennett, the founder, owner, and editor of the *Herald*, "to represent one of the foremost of American authors as a pauper in need of a charity fund to keep him from the poorhouse is a condemnable outrage.... Bennett's methods of relieving his alleged distress will do no more than to arouse widespread disgust and regret that one of the most brilliant lights in American letters has been made the victim either of rank ignorance or contemptible revenge." Sam was even the target of a mocking ditty in *Town Topics*:

> But just remember Mark is tired
>   And wants to take a rest,
> And hence has haply been inspired
>   To make this little jest.
> So though you may not see the point,
>   Just laugh away a lot
> Laugh till your bones are out of joint
>   Then send him all you've got.

According to *Life*, the *Herald* had insulted Sam, who should rebuke Bennett for his "impudent proposition." The newspaper had "no more right to declare him a pauper than to punish him as a thief."[28]

Sam was oblivious to the insult but when Livy learned of the charitable fund she was mortified that her husband had become an object of pity and demanded that Sam shut down the fundraising. If they ever needed money he could return to the lecture circuit "in the old way and at the ordinary prices." He admitted to Rogers that he had concealed the scheme from her because she "would have forbidden me" to accept charity and on the June 19 he explained to Bennett that after "three days of strenuous effort . . . the family" (i.e., Livy) had "convinced me that I have no right to take your money & other men's to smooth my road." The family had implored him "to write & ask you to close the subscription list & return the money to the contributors, with their thanks & mine for the kindness which they had tried to do me." Henry Rogers also advised Sam by cable to "withdraw graciously" from the fund because "All friends think Herald movement [a] mistake." Sam drafted a contrite letter to Bennett for publication in the *Herald* so "that I may once more stand well with the household." The letter ran in the newspaper under the headline "Mark Twain Declines Help" on June 27:

> I made no revelation to my family of your generous undertaking in my behalf and for my relief from debt, and in that I was wrong. Now that they know all about the matter they contend that I have no right to allow my friends to help while my health is good and my ability to work remains; that it is not fair to the friends and not justifiable; that it will be time enough to accept help when it shall be proven that I am no longer able to work. I am persuaded that they are right. While they are grateful for what you have done and for the kindly instinct which prompted you, they are urgent that the contributions be returned to the givers, with their thanks and mine. I yield to their desire and forward their request and my endorsement of it to you. I was glad when you initiated that movement, for I was tired of the fret and worry of debt, but I recognize that it is not permissible for a man whose case is not hopeless to shift his burdens to other men's shoulders.

Far from quieting the controversy, this letter stirred the pot. Though the *Brooklyn Eagle* suggested that it required some moxie on his part "to refuse . . . the money that has been raised for him," the *Indianapolis News* pronounced it "pitiable. It indicates that he was willing to accept this method of escape from the financial difficulties that beset him, but that his desires have been overridden by his family." He should have long since recognized the "obvious fact" stated in his last sentence. Whereas the *Chap-Book* had initially considered the fund a "blundering indignity" inflicted on Sam, the magazine concluded after the appearance of this letter that a "pathetically flaccid and groveling figure" betrayed "his own lack of scruples" by begging for alms.[29]

Ironically, the "Herald business," as Sam later called it, was both an embarrassment and an unmitigated disaster, apparently because the public distrusted the fund manager. When the drive was suspended after four weeks, contributions totaled only $2,938—the $2,000 subscribed by the *Herald* and Carnegie, $650 from five major contributors, and $288 from all other donors, including children who gave as little as ten cents. To mask the paltry sum raised, Sam proposed a stunt to Rogers: to "collect $40,000 privately for me" and report it to the press, knowing all the while it would be returned. The ruse would "give me a handsome boom," "nobody will ever be the wiser,"[30] and he saw no harm in the ploy, though nothing came of it.

A postscript: James Ross Clemens had also read in the London *Evening Globe* in March that Sam "was residing in London in straitened circumstances" and, not realizing he had been confused with his famous cousin, wrote him a letter, care of Chatto & Windus,

> in which I introduced myself as another of the Clemens tribe and asked for the honor and privilege of being allowed to aid him in his distress. Several days passed and then one evening there came a knock at my street door and in walked Clemens himself. Fortunately the report of his bankruptcy proved false but he seemed altogether at a loss how to express adequately his appreciation of my letter and was visibly touched. From that time on to the day of his death I was always his "Dr. Jim." I was often invited to his home . . . and met at his table all of England's literary lions.

In early June, as the Clemenses' stay in London was drawing to a close, Sam's friend William Gillette invited him to a performance of his play *Secret Service* at the Adelphi Theatre on the Strand. Sam was joined by his cousin "Dr. Jim" and, as he later told the story, in the second act a black cat walked across the stage whereupon Sam predicted that "poor Gillette is in for some misfortune or other this evening." When they went backstage at the end of the act "we found Gillette binding up a forefinger which he had cut about to the bone." A month later, Gillette hosted a supper in Sam's honor at the Savoy Hotel after another performance of the play attended by Henry Irving, Chauncey Depew, Beerbohm Tree, Charles Frohman, and Richard Harding Davis.[31]

How to Tell a Story and Other Essays, Sam's latest book, appeared from the press of Harper & Brothers in March 1897. Apparently assembled by the publisher without the help or advice of the author, it was not issued in a British edition. Fortunately, it reprinted none of Sam's "old time stuff," all of which Sam believed "should be allowed to remain dead." The volume contained eight essays, all previously published, including the title piece, "Fenimore Cooper's Literary Offenses," "The Private History of the 'Jumping Frog' Story," and the two rejoinders to Paul Bourget. The earliest notices of the collection were uniformly favorable; an "admirable edition" (New York *World*), "a very acceptable edition" (*Hartford Courant*), "needles of Mark Twain's satire are sharp and incisive" (*Washington Times*), "clever" (*San Francisco Call*), "we are so certain of his abundant humor that we never open his pages without having a laugh ready" (*Brooklyn Eagle*), "distinctly humorous" and "very pleasant reading" (*Chicago Inter Ocean*), "presents ideas which are well worth listening to and heeding" (Laurence Hutton in *Harper's Monthly*), "inimitable" (*Northern Christian Advocate*), and "enlivened with the humor and the whimsies which the world expects to find in everything Mark Twain writes" (*Buffalo Express*). Only after the book had been in print for several months did some reviewers find fault with it; the West Chester, Pennsylvania, *Citizen* called it "depressing," the *New York Tribune* "dull," and the *Dial* "a miscellany of uneven quality."[32]

After interviewing Sam during the *Herald* fund debacle, Frank Marshall White had a bright idea: to hire Sam to cover Queen Victoria's Diamond Jubilee in London on June 22–23, 1897, the celebration of her sixtieth anniversary on the throne, for the Hearst syndicate. By his own admission, White "might not have ventured to make the proposition to one whom many regarded as America's first man of letters had I not believed that money would be an object to him." White assured him that "anything he might write" for his paper would appear "word for word as he wrote it" and that he would view the Jubilee procession from a grandstand at the Hotel Cecil overlooking the parade route on the Strand. They also negotiated Sam's fee: £400 or $2,000, about $48,000 today, for two articles. White remembered that their bargain "was not secured on either side by so much as the scratch of a pen," though in the end Sam delivered more copy than required. On June 23, he was escorted by a member of White's staff "from Chelsea by the underground road and through the Embankment Gardens into the rear entrance of the Hotel Cecil" and to "the front corner seat facing the head of the line of march" on the viewing stand. There "he sat with a large pad on his knee and made many notes." After the spectacle had passed, he remarked that he had not expected "so stunning a show. All the nations seemed to be represented. It was a sort of an allegorical representation of the Last Day, and some of us who live to see that day will probably recall this one—if we are not too much disturbed in mind at the time." He then retired "to a friend's chambers in Henrietta Street, Covent Garden," where according to White "he deftly turned out his copy, which reached the cable office and eventually the newspaper in ample time."[33]

Unfortunately, neither of the pieces Sam submitted for syndicate publication transcended the banal. The first was little more than a history lesson and the second was a superficial account of the parade, which he slighted as "a spectacle for the kodak, not the pen." He offered a formulaic tribute to Victoria (she "has seen more things invented than any other monarch that ever lived . . . and more than Methuselah himself") that he had first invoked in a speech aboard the *Quaker City* in 1867 and later recycled in his homage to Walt Whitman upon the poet's seventieth birthday in 1889. He endorsed in passing the adoption of the eight-hour workday, one of the triumphs of the age. And he joked about the number of soldiers who paraded about the London stage on any given night. Trouble is, as an Englishman on the staff of the *San Francisco Examiner* complained, Sam failed to understand that "the soldiers in the theater are the same old soldiers marching around and around" and "there aren't more than a hundred soldiers in the biggest army ever put on the stage." Still, Sam's articles were widely syndicated across the United States in the *New York Journal, Cincinnati Enquirer, Buffalo News, Pittsburgh Post, Chicago Tribune, St. Louis Post-Dispatch, St. Louis Republic, Boston Globe, San Francisco Examiner,* Philadelphia *Press, Denver Post,* and *Indianapolis News*. But the American playwright, actor, and theatrical manager Howard Paul, for one, regarded Sam's reports of the Jubilee the "weakest" of all the dispatches from London that appeared in the New York press to mark the occasion.[34]

In early July 1897, upon the expiration of the lease on the Chelsea house, the Clemenses moved for a few days to the new Hans Crescent Hotel in the Knightsbridge neighborhood of West End London. Sam was interviewed there by Hamlin Garland, who had "never met him, although I knew a great deal of him through his friends and had heard him speak several times." Garland was "shocked by the changes which had come to him. His shaggy hair was white and a stoop had come into his shoulders. It appeared that in growing old he had diminished. He appeared smaller than I had remembered him on the platform, but his fine head and rough-hewn features were more impressive than ever before." As Sam talked, according to Garland, "he appeared to forget me. He looked over my head at some far-off landscape. His eyes, hidden by his bushy eyebrows, were half closed and I saw them only occasionally. I was surprised to find them blue and keen." He insisted he was "going home" to Hartford "as soon as I have made a little more money. I am nearly clear of those obligations I assumed as a partner in Webster & Co." At length he reminisced about his bankruptcy and cursed the memory of Charley Webster "with heart-felt fervor and Oriental magnificence." Webster, he claimed, "chouselled me out of fifty thousand dollars, thus bringing about the ruin of my publishing house." He spoke "with such deadly hatred in face and voice," Garland recalled, "that I was able to share in some degree the disgrace he had been called upon to bear and the burden he had voluntarily assumed."

On a happier note, he and his family planned to spend the remainder of the summer in a Swiss village and move in the fall to Vienna where, he hoped, Clara would study music with Theodor Leschetizky, whom Sam considered "the greatest pianist in the world."[35]

The family was joined in London the first week of July by Susan Crane, Julie Langdon Loomis, and Susan's "butler" (as Sam called him) Ernst Köppe. On July 12 the seven of them plus Katy Leary left London for Switzerland, overnighting at the Grand Hotel des Bains in Flushing (Vlissingen), Belgium, and the Victoria Hotel in Cologne, Germany, near the train station and the cathedral, arriving at the Hotel Union in Lucerne on July 15. Three days later they settled in the Villa Bühlegg in the village of Weggis, population fourteen hundred, six miles east of the city by ferry on Lake Lucerne and about a hundred feet above the lake surface. The terms were modest, as Sam noted: "6 francs a day per person, rent & food included, also candles & 2 lamps; & 14 fr[ancs] extra per week to have the meals brought up & served in the house," the equivalent of about $70 a week, for "feeding, liquoring, lighting, and housing of 7 persons." Their expenses increased when they rented a rowboat, a piano for Clara, and a writing studio for Sam in the nearby Villa Tannen; bought bicycles; and added a daily tea service, but he saved money on cigars: he bought them for $5 a thousand, or half a cent apiece, whereas they cost $4 a hundred or four cents apiece in London. "Through these profitable economies I could get rich if we could stay long enough," he joked.[36]

Best of all, they relished the bucolic surroundings, a frequent refrain in their comments about the ten weeks they resided in Weggis. As Susan Crane wrote Sam Moffett four days after they arrived, they were "delightfully situated in a small cottage near Lake Lucerne, where we command a wonderful view of lake & mountains particularly Mt. Pilatus, while the Rigi rises up behind us. It's a soothing & most restful place." Katy Leary remembered that they lived in "a cottage near the hotel down by the water." Sam "was very happy there" and "we had a suite generally, bedroom, sitting-room, and dining-room. Always just like Royalty." On his part, Sam informed his friend Wayne MacVeagh, former attorney general of the United States and former U.S. ambassador to Italy, that he resided with his family in "a snug & comfortable little villa, submerged in a sea of green woods on a slope of the Rigi overlooking the lake & the passing boats & widely frontiered by mountain crags & domes & steeped in eternal stillness and repose." More importantly, "we are gathering cheerfulness and healing of the spirit, & that is the best profit of all. Susy would have loved this place." He was even more graphic in his notebook entries, as on the day of their arrival: Pilatus was "a sublime mystery which is full charged with beautiful secrets which only a lifetime of daily observation" might reveal.

> Every slight change of the ceaselessly changing atmosphere washes the mountain with new distributions of light & shade, new dreams of enchanting color. On a bright day all the great mass is a glory of all shades of green, & hazy blacks & blues, with vagrant films of white clouds creeping about it & mottling it with their shadows; & as evening approaches it is drowned in soft & rich & luminous mists, blue & purple & golden—& presently the sun is gone & the mountain's vast silhouette, looms stupendous in the sky, its base fused with the night, its jagged summit backed strong & black against a sunset explosion of rich dyes, a conflagration of flaming splendors.

Clara, Jean, and Julia Langdon biked "20 & 30 miles a day" and rowed "us old people about the lake in the evenings." One day Clara, Jean, and Köppe climbed Rigi Kulm and returned with "plenty of skinned feet & blisters," inspiring Sam "to go up the Rigi myself someday." For the first time since Susy's death, he professed to be "a cheerful man" and before he left the village at the end of the summer he swore to Rogers that he "would as soon spend my life in Weggis as anywhere" in the world and to Twichell that "we shall always come here for the summers if we can."[37]

Coincidentally, the Clemenses crossed paths with other friends while in Switzerland. George Williamson Smith, the president of Trinity College, met Livy by chance on the Lucerne ferry on July 30 and lunched with them the next afternoon. Their three hours together were "more refreshing & uplifting & enjoyable than any sixty hours we have known for months," Sam gloated to Twichell. But the highlight of their summer in Weggis no doubt was the visit of the Fisk Jubilee sextet the weekend of August 12–13, when the singers performed publicly at the Hotel Löwen and privately for the Clemenses. Not only was their music "diviner, even, than in their early days" when Sam first heard them, they "are as fine people as I am acquainted with in any country." He remembered seeing one of them in the Hanover Square Rooms in London in 1873.

> Three of the 6 were born in slavery, the others were children of slaves. How charming they were—in spirit, manner, language, pronunciation, enunciation, grammar, phrasing, matter, carriage, clothes—in every detail that goes to make the real lady and gentleman, and welcome guest. . . . The Singers got up and stood—the talking and glass jingling went on. Then rose and swelled out above those common earthly sounds one of those rich chords the secret of whose make only the Jubilees possess, and a spell fell upon that house. It was fine to see the faces light up with the pleased wonder and surprise of it.

> No one was indifferent anymore; and when the singers finished, the camp was theirs. It was a triumph.

The next day, the singers came to the Clemenses' cottage "and we had a pleasant time."[38]

Less than a week later, on August 18, the family marked the first anniversary of Susy's death. Livy and Sam spent the sad day alone and apart, Livy at an inn somewhere on the shore of the lake where she read Susy's letters, Sam "under the trees on the mountain side" in Weggis, where he wrote a sentimental elegy, sixty-eight lines of vers libre, including this stanza:

> And then when they
> Were nothing fearing, and God's peace was in the air,
> And none was prophesying harm—
> The vast disaster fell:
> Where stood the temple when the sun went down,
> Was vacant desert when it rose again!

"This lament was written to beguile me through the heavy hours of the first anniversary of our Dark Day & not for print," Sam wrote Henry Mills Alden when he submitted the poem to *Harper's Monthly*, "but I have always meant to say some day a modest public word in memory of our lost Susy." It appeared in the November 1897 number of the magazine and upon its publication Twichell for one tried to console Sam, commending "its unspeakable heart-breaking sadness; its aching, choking pathos. It sets all chords of memory and of love atremble. It renews the pain of the sense of Life's inscrutable mystery, and of the mystery of human experience." Always the muscular Christian, though he sometimes veiled his orthodoxy behind cigar smoke and brandy snifters, Twichell had "long known that it was in you to chant the music of the hidden soul conversing with the Fathomless Elements, and as I followed your yearning throbbing song of Grief and inextinguishable Regret, my inward comment was 'It is he: none other than my Mark Twain.'"[39]

Meanwhile, Sam read the proof of *More Tramps Abroad*, the British title of his travelogue, as it arrived from the presses of Chatto & Windus. Though Chatto omitted some long excerpts from secondary sources and some potentially libelous material about the filthy South Pacific steamships, the English edition also retained more of Sam's original manuscript and thus was longer by several chapters than the U.S. edition issued by Bliss.[40] As usual, however, Sam fulminated at the alterations to his prose. As early as July 22 he refused to read any more proof, which was "perfectly lousy with errors and foolishnesses which are not in Bliss's copy," until his original punctuation (or lack thereof) had been restored. The printers had failed to pay "strict enough attention" to his manuscript. "Their commas are too handy; I hate commas." In fact, as a former printer he had learned "more about punctuation in two minutes that any damned bastard of a proof-reader can learn in two centuries," whereas Chatto's printer was a "damned half-developed foetus!" Most of "the labor & vexation put upon me" by the printers "consists of annihilating their ignorant & purposeless punctuation & *restoring* my own." Nor would he "permit 'an' hospital," he advised Chatto on July 24. "Unless that *n* is removed, you must allow me to append a disclaimer in the form of a footnote. Please see that it is removed. One might as well say an horse or an whore." He fussed over Chatto's proof for another month before he finally declared "that slavery is over."[41]

"When I left America I thought $40,000 would set me clear of debt," Sam wrote Rogers soon after arriving in England at the close of his world speaking tour. However, an audit of his accounts revealed that his debt "was nearer $70,000 than $40,000." The profit from his tour had reduced his liabilities by only perhaps a fourth. He harbored a vain hope that William Jennings Bryan would be elected president and a majority of Democrats elected to Congress in November 1896 on a platform of free silver so that he might pay his remaining debts with "soft" or inflated money. He was content that the Mount Morris Bank and the Barrow family "still stand out against the 50 per cent" settlement reached with the other creditors and, as he wrote Rogers in September 1896, "I shall be glad if they never consent. It was the Bank's criminal stupidity that caused my destruction & I never greatly liked Barrow. I don't want to pay those two anything until all the others have been paid in full—if that day ever comes." He was still combative a month later. "If ever I get the others paid I will then tackle the Barrows debt, and pay that if I can. But I expect to be dead before I get a chance to begin on the Bank; and First-Assistant Archangel before I begin on the Grants." He reserved a special animus for the Grant sons. He planned to "pay Fred Grant off full in my Autobiography" with a blast at his character. "I saved that family considerably over $200,000, and in return Fred Grant robbed the firm of many thousands by going back on an oral agreement." They were "a poor lot, those Grants." By November 1897, months after completing the travelogue, Sam directed Rogers to begin paying off the debts owed the small creditors.

> I cannot bear the weight any longer. It totally unfits me for work. I have lost three entire months, now. In that time I have begun twenty magazine articles & books—& flung every one of them aside in turn. The debts interfered every time & took the spirit out of the work. . . . A man can't possibly write the kind

> of stuff that is required of me unless he have an unharassed mind. My stuff is worth more in the market today than it ever was before—& yet in 3 months I have not succeeded in turning out fifty acceptable pages.

These stillborn projects included "Hellfire Hotchkiss" or "Sugar-Rag Hotchkiss," set in a fictionalized Hannibal and featuring a fictionalized Orion Clemens and Lillie Hitchcock, his tomboy friend from San Francisco thirty years earlier, in the title role; "Tom Sawyer's Conspiracy," a tiresome reprise of the "evasion" chapters that conclude *Adventures of Huckleberry Finn*; and "Which Was the Dream?," originally outlined in Paris in 1894.[42] All of these works died aborning.

Nevertheless, he wrote a total of 28,000 words of "Tom Sawyer's Conspiracy" before tossing it aside. The story originated in a note Sam jotted down while in South Africa in the spring of 1896: "Have Huck tell how one white brother shaved his head, put on a wool wig & was blackened & sold as a negro. Escaped that night, washed himself, & helped hunt *for himself*." A year later, he refined this *donnée*: "Tom is disguised as a negro and sold in Ark[ansas] for $10, then he & Huck help hunt for him after the disguise is removed." Whereas in *Huck Finn* Tom and Huck schemed to free a slave who was already free, here they scheme to free a slave who does not exist. Sam redeployed many of the plot elements in the earlier Tom and Huck books; Huck narrates their adventures, the boys retreat to Jackson's Island, Tom testifies at a trial, the Duke and King reappear, etc. Sam incorporated a few other details from his adolescence in Hannibal to the narrative—for example, Tom learns to set type—and one bizarre memory from his adulthood: the local detective announces that a killer in the town "was a gigantic intelleck" and "prob'ly the worst man alive." The allusion is not to Arthur Conan Doyle's villain Moriarty but to the moral monster Edward H. Rulloff, the gifted philologist convicted of murder in New York in 1870. Sam had facetiously proposed that the sentimentalists opposed to Rulloff's execution on grounds that he was a genius should recruit a substitute to take his place on the gallows. After Rulloff was executed, his oversized brain, one of the largest on record, was donated to the "brain collection" of the psychology department at Cornell University. Not so coincidentally, in the spirit of his thirty-year-old joke Sam reportedly agreed in 1903 to donate his skull to Cornell after his death. "I am getting pretty old," he was quoted as saying "and shall probably not need the skull after next Christmas, I dunno. But if I should, I will pay rent." The gift, one wag quipped, the first time that anyone had gotten a head of Mark Twain.[43]

Despite his lack of finished writing that summer, Sam declined a generous proposal to lecture that fall and winter. Pond had offered him £10,000 or $50,000 for 125 appearances across the United States—Sam to speak and Clara to play the piano—and he had been sorely tempted. "I was strongly minded to write Pond & agree to do 20 or 30 nights," he admitted, but he realized that "honest people do not go robbing the public on the platform except when they are in debt." Livy vetoed the idea, moreover, for not only health reasons but also financial ones: like Sam, she distrusted Pond's business sense, and with a variety of income streams—profits from the world tour, royalties on his old books, Bliss's payment of the promised advance on *Following the Equator,* and dividends on Rogers's investments and Livy's inheritance—they were nearly solvent again. "Your splendid news that the Bliss money & what is in your hands foots up to $27,000 & that you are doing a little gambling [stock investing] for Mrs. Clemens has set us both up in spirits & we are feeling pretty fine," Sam chortled to Rogers. As soon as possible he wanted to pay all his creditors except the Mount Morris bank, which he still believed was trying to steal from him $9,000 that Webster and Company had never borrowed. Perhaps "a year from now" he would prepare "a farewell shout" from the platform "& then retire" and "stop worrying." He no longer needed to dance to the tune of the organ-grinder. In mid-September, as he was preparing to leave Weggis, he reiterated to Rogers that he never expected "to go on the platform" again if he could settle his debts without lecturing and to Pond his determination never again to perform for pay: "I feel quite sure that in Cape Town, 13 months ago, I stood on a platform for the last time. Nothing but the Webster debts could persuade me to lecture again, & I have ceased to worry about those." Pond again offered Sam $1,000 a night for ten lecture dates in 1899, though Sam again declined because "I do not like the platform & will not lecture so long as I can earn a living in honest ways."[44]

Pond found another way to capitalize on his business relationship with Sam. He sold an unsigned essay to Edward Bok for publication in *Ladies' Home Journal* entitled "The Anecdotal Side of Mark Twain" that included Pond's reminiscences of the North American leg of Sam's lecture tour, personal photographs, and paraphrased interviews. Sam was unexpectedly drawn into fighting a rearguard action against Pond for violating his privacy. "I haven't a doubt that it was Pond who emptied that sewage down the back of the Chambermaid's House Journal," Sam observed to Rogers. "It's in his taste." He was appalled by the very tenor of Bok's magazine: "Why, bless my soul, it is a merely literary night-cart. I would rather steal nickels for a living than earn it writing for such a rag as that. It is full of Wanamaker [the Philadelphia department store mogul] and his Sunday schools and other hypocrisies. It ought to be medicated, and restricted [to] the Bleeding Piles Hospital." Two years later, Pond notified Sam that he planned to devote a chapter to him in his book *Eccentricities of Genius* but would refrain from printing any of his letters "in full." Sam ordered Pond in response not to "print a single paragraph from any private or business letter of mine without my personal consent;—& that is not at all likely to be given. I do not allow the public to read my private letters over any man's shoulder. Pond, I cannot understand how you are made that you should want to do such insane things."[45] The rebuke seemed to have worked. The chapter contained brief excerpts from several of Sam's letters but mostly consisted of copious passages from Pond's diary.

On September 19 Sam, Livy, Clara, Jean, and Katy Leary left Weggis for Vienna with intermediate stops in Lucerne, Zurich, Innsbruck, and Salzburg. In the latter city, Sam was dismayed by the extravagance of the church compared to the poverty of the people. As he jotted in his notebook, "Money represents labor, sweat, weariness. And that is what these useless churches have cost these people & are still costing them to support the useless priests & monks."[46] The family arrived in the capital of the Austro-Hungarian Empire eight days later, as Clara remembered, "on a cold, rainy evening" without reservations and asked for rooms at seven hotels before they found a suitable overnight vacancy in "a dreadful little hotel called the Hotel Müller" at the end of the Graben. The next morning Sam visited eight hotels before he found a suite of "cheerful rooms" on the third floor of the Hotel Metropole on Morzinplatz adjacent to the Danube Canal. For 2,200 francs or about $450 a month they rented a parlor, a study, a music room for Clara, and four bedrooms, plus a balcony, service, heat, and meals. With the imminent publication of the travelogue and Rogers's wise management of their assets (that is, his insider trading) they were affluent again and abandoned all pretense of austerity. "We like this hotel so much & are so roomily & comfortably situated in it that we expect to remain in it until next June & not keep house at all," Sam wrote James Ross Clemens back in London. Ironically, when they moved a year later to an even more luxurious Viennese hotel, Sam disparaged the "rusty and rather shabby Metropole."[47] After the Anschluss in 1938, the Metropole became the headquarters of the Nazi Geheime Staatspolizei, the largest Gestapo post outside Berlin. The hotel was leveled by Allied bombing during World War II.

CHAPTER 7

Vienna Sausage

When in doubt tell the truth. It will confound your enemies and astound your friends.

—Mark Twain, *Following the Equator*

WITH A POPULATION of about 1.7 million, Vienna in 1897 was the fourth largest metropolis in Europe after London, Paris, and Berlin and the second-largest German-speaking city in the world. It was a musical and theatrical center, a cosmopolitan hub and, truth be told, a welter of anti-Semitism.

Sam and his family soon settled into a routine. Though he was confined to their rooms at the Metropole for most of their first ten days in the city with gout or what he called "toothache of the toe," he was enthusiastically welcomed in the local press. Within two days of the announcement of his arrival, he was interviewed by the journalist Sigmund Schlesinger for the *Illustriertes Wiener Extrablatt* and the humorist Eduard Pötzl for the *Neues Wiener Tagblatt* and over the next two weeks he was interviewed by Ferdinand Gross of the Concordia Press Club for the *Fremden-Blatt* and Vincenz Chiavacci for the *Wiener Bilder*. As Albert Bigelow Paine translated his remarks, Pötzl declared that seldom has "a foreign author" found "such a hearty reception in Vienna as that accorded to Mark Twain, who not only has the reputation of being the foremost humorist in the whole civilized world, but one whose personality arouses everywhere a peculiar interest on account of the genuine American character which sways it." Gross's interview in the *Fremden-Blatt* was, according to Carl Dolmetsch, "the most significant, certainly most penetrating, of the myriad of interviews and articles appearing about Mark Twain in Viennese newspapers during the early days of his stay" and Sam commended Gross for his comments: "What you have written . . . has gratified me more than I can say, because of the friendly & hospitable feeling which pervades it." But Sam also joked with Henry Harper that "some of these newspaper interviews," while in English, "make me talk German" in print—"which I won't do. My German is bad, but not *that* bad."[1]

That all four of his initial interviews in Vienna were conducted by Jewish journalists reinforced the popular impression that Sam was also Jewish. He was caricatured in the anti-Semitic humor magazine *Kikeriki* for October 10 surrounded by Jewish stereotypes named "S. Cohn" and "P. Lowenstein" peddling bolts of cloth and a caption that reads in English, "He must be careful that he doesn't receive shoddy wares." As early as December 1896, nine months before he landed in Vienna, the *Chicago Tribune* had in fact asserted that with his aquiline nose "his face is Jewish" and, as Dolmetsch explains, "Austrian Catholics never use Old Testament names" and "thus Samuel is an impossible name for an Austrian gentile." Soon the *Reichpost* "and other newspapers with an overtly racist bias were routinely referring" to Sam as "der Jude Mark Twain" or "der jüdische amerikanische Humorist." His friend Theodor Herzl of the *Neue Freie Presse* sarcastically remarked that Sam sported "a thick mustache hanging under a hooked nose."[2]

Sam had professed an admiration for Jewry throughout his life even though, as he wrote in "Journey to an Asterisk," an unpublished fragment omitted from "Captain Stormfield's Visit to Heaven," "Christians always are . . . trained to a prejudice against Jews." During his boyhood a Jewish family named Levin owned a haberdashery in Hannibal. "To my fancy they were clothed invisibly in the damp and cobwebby mould of antiquity," he reminisced in his autobiography. "They carried me back to Egypt, and in imagination I moved among the Pharaohs and all the shadowy celebrities of that remote age." While on the *Quaker City* cruise in 1867 he discovered that in some of the European cities he visited Jews were "treated just like human beings instead of dogs. They can work at any business they please; they can sell brand new goods if they want to; they can keep drug-stores; they can practice medicine among Christians; they can even shake hands with Christians if they choose; they can associate with them, just the same as one human being does with another human being." In early 1879 he noted in his diary that Jews "have the best average brain of any people in the world. The Jews are the only race in the world who work wholly with their brains, and never with their hands. There are no Jew beggars, no Jew tramps, no Jew ditchers, hod-carriers, day-laborers, or followers of toilsome mechanical trade. They are peculiarly and conspicuously the world's intellectual aristocracy." One of the little-noticed heroes in *Adventures of Huckleberry Finn* is the Jewish lawyer Levi Bell, who unmasks the fraudulent Duke and King and saves the Wilkes daughters from penury. "I have never felt a disposition to satirize the Jews," he wrote his longtime friend Charles E. S. Wood a few months later. "I have never seen a Jew begging his bread; and have never seen one procuring it by manual labor. The one fact must mean that the Jews take care of their unfortunates with a fidelity known to no other race; and the other fact must mean that the Jews are the only race with whom brains are a *universal* heritage (by contrast consider the Irish race)." Had only he resisted the temptation to slander the Irish! Sam likewise admired the writings of Israel Zangwill, whose novel *The Master* (1895) he read soon after its publication. He heard Zangwill's "very fine & bright" lecture "on the Jewish Ghetto" at the Hampstead Conservatoire in London the evening of November 11, 1896, and congratulated him afterward. During the winter of 1896–97 Sam composed a short tale, "Newhouse's Jew Story," for inclusion in *Following the Equator,* though he subsequently chose to omit it. He recounted in it the action of a courageous Jewish passenger aboard a steamboat who prevents an unscrupulous gambler from winning a slave girl in a poker game. But during the twenty months Sam resided in Austria in 1897–99, anti-Semitism "ceased to be an academic question" for him. It became personal. He was persuaded by his daily contact with Jews in Vienna that the descendants of Jacob were a racially superior type—another twist in his Lamarckian ideas. As he claimed to Twichell a month after settling in Austria, "The difference between the brain of the average Christian and that of the average Jew—certainly in Europe [thus excepting the Middle Eastern Jews he had met in 1867]—is about the difference between a tadpole's and an Archbishop's. It's a marvelous race—by long odds the most marvelous that the world has produced, I suppose." And, as Sam later added, "It will not be well to let that race find out its strength. If the horses knew theirs, we should not ride anymore."[3]

Unsurprisingly, ethnic tensions between Jews and gentiles spilled over into governing the country. Sam attended a session of the city council on October 15 at which the anti-Semitic mayor Karl Lueger presided. In *Mein Kampf,* Adolf Hitler described Lueger, the head of the Christian Socialists, as "the last great German to be born in the ranks of the people," "a statesman greater than all the so-called diplomats of the time," and "the greatest German mayor of all times." As Dolmetsch observes, scuffles broke out "in the gallery as the meeting concluded. . . . It was an unusually raucous meeting even for this notoriously fractious, unwieldy body of 138 members." A week later, Sam wrote Twichell that local politics were strained by conflicts between Christian and Jew, "the advantage with the superior man, as usual—the superior man being the Jew every time & in all countries."[4]

Sam soon drifted into the orbit of the Jewish intelligentsia in the Kaiserstadt. By invitation he was the guest of honor at a *Festkneipe* hosted by the actors, musicians, publishers, and writers in the Wiener Journalisten und Schriftsteller-Verein the evening of October 31 in the *Festhall* of the Kaufmännische Verein (merchants' association). The Concordia boasted 348 members in 1897, as Dolmetsch reports, of whom "at least 150 were identifiably Jewish," including such prominent figures as Herzl; Pötzl; the composer and conductor Gustav Mahler; authors Felix Salten, Peter Altenberg, and Richard Beer-Hofmann; music critic Eduard Hanslick; and journalists Sigmund Schlesinger, Theodor Hertzka, and Moritz Szeps. Both Charlemagne Tower, U.S. ambassador to Austro-Hungary, and U.S. consul general Carlton Hurst were present at the meeting of the club. Livy and Clara sat in the gallery, reserved for the female guests of the all-male group, along with the British journalist and art historian Amelia Levetus and Bettina Wirth, Vienna correspondent of the London *Daily News*. After the dinner Sam delivered a funny speech "in a mixture of German, French, and English" entitled "Die Schrecken der Deutschen Sprache" (The horrors of the German language), a sort of companion piece to "The Awful German Language" in *A Tramp Abroad*. The local reviewers in the *Neues Wiener Tagblatt* and the *Illustrierte Zeitung* concluded, according to Edgar Hemminghaus, that Sam "had acquired a very satisfactory grasp of idiomatic but not scholarly German" and his address was soon translated into English for publication in the United States.[5]

During his residence in Vienna, Sam moved in the upper circles of Austrian society, perhaps surprisingly. After railing against elitist privilege most of his life, Sam had glossed in a book in 1894, "I am an aristocrat (in the aristocracy of mind, of achievement), and from my Viscountship look reverently up at all earls, marquises, and dukes above me, and superciliously down upon the barons, baronets, and knights below me." He confided to his notebook shortly after settling in Vienna that some of his new friends there "make me regret—again—that I am not a prince myself. It is not a new regret but a very old one. I have never been properly and humbly satisfied with my condition. I am a democrat only on principle, not by instinct—nobody is *that*." Among the nobility with whom he mixed was a fellow guest at the Metropole, Princess Pauline von Metternich, granddaughter of Queen Victoria, who told Sam that his books had "given me great enjoyment." Through her agency Sam met several peers of the realm, including Countess Misa Wydenbruck-Esterházy; the pacifist leader Baroness Bertha von Suttner, recipient of the Nobel Peace Prize in 1905; Archduchess Maria Theresa, the stepmother of Archduke Franz Ferdinand; the "charming and lovable German princess and poet" Pauline Elisabeth Ottilie Luise of Wied, aka Carmen Sylva, queen of Romania; Princess Charlotte of Prussia, the younger sister of Wilhelm II and another granddaughter of Queen Victoria; Princess Feodora of Saxe-Meiningen, daughter of Princess Charlotte, and her fiancé the German prince Heinrich XXX Reuss of Köstritz; Count Erich Kielmansegg, the governor of Lower Austria; Karl Max, Prince Lichnowsky, first secretary of the German embassy and future German ambassador to the UK; the Duke of Frias, one of the secretaries of the Spanish Legation; and Baron Gustav von Springer.[6]

Sam was invited to dine in late November with twenty other guests at the home of the railroad executive Vincenz Anton Josef Ritter von Dutschka and his "large and stately and beautiful" wife. He thought it "a remarkable gathering—no commonplace people present, no leatherheads. Princes & other titled people there, but not *because* of their titles, but for their distinction in achievement. It was like a salon of old-time Paris." In addition, Sam was introduced during his months in Vienna to Baroness Langenau, British widow of the Austrian ambassador to Russia and "a person I have strong fondness for, for we violently disagree on some subjects & as violently agree upon others"; Albert, the eighth Prince of Thurn and Taxis, who "speaks English nearly perfectly and is a fine man, worthy representative of that ancient house"; Countess Ilka Pálmay, a singer and actor in light opera, of whom "there could have been few more charming or sweeter women"; Count Philipp Friedrich Alexander von Eulenburg, the German ambassador to Austro-Hungary; and Count Bernhard von Bülow, state secretary for foreign affairs and later chancellor of the German Empire.[7]

On his part, Sam greeted visitors to his home as warmly as he was welcomed in society. "It came to be a daily habit in the family," Clara recalled, to host callers in their hotel suite "from five o'clock on, and our list of acquaintances augmented so rapidly . . . that our drawing-room was often called the second U.S. Embassy." Much as they had formally received visitors every Wednesday while in Florence, they hosted "tea parties every single Sunday night" while in Vienna. Among their guests during these months were Clara's piano teacher Theodor Leschetizky; the Russian pianist Ossip Gabrilowitsch, Clara's fellow student and her eventual husband; Henry Campbell-Bannerman, Sam's friend from Marienbad and the future prime minister of England; the Swedish playwright August Strindberg; Czech composer Antonín Dvořák; German painter Franz Ritter von Lenbach; Hungarian artist Maurus Jókai; Norwegian explorer Fridtjof Nansen, a future Nobel Peace Prize laureate; and Count Claës Lewenhaupt, Hjalmar Hjorth Boyesen's friend, who had dined with them in Hartford in October 1886. Ignace Jan Paderewski, a celebrated Polish pianist and composer who had been Leschetizky's student, remembered that "the beautiful impression [Clemens] made upon me abides with me still. He was a purely American product, someone that only America could have produced, in the quality of his mind, his humor and character. I think he remains an undimmed figure in your history. The years will not diminish his towering qualities and virtues." Mark Hambourg, the musical prodigy whom Sam had befriended in

Melbourne two years before, reminisced that the Clemenses "would provide hearty meals for us artists" but Sam "would take nothing but a glass of claret. He would then walk around the table while we ate, telling stories in his slow drawl. One day, when I came to call unexpectedly I heard an extraordinary noise overhead. Something like a dog howling, which turned out to be Mark Twain singing and strumming queer old river songs of the Mississippi on the piano" he had rented for Clara. Not many people ever heard Sam sing, Hambourg joked, "and it certainly was a unique performance." Sam supplied Hambourg, prior to his departure for a concert tour in the United States, with a letter of introduction that noted he "plays the piano better than any of the Clemens family but his complexion is not as good as mine.[8]

At the age of twenty-three, Clara was one of the most eligible belles in the city and, as Gabrilowitsch remembered, "enjoyed great popularity in musical and social circles." By his own admission he "was by no means the only young man in Vienna whose head was turned and whose heart sorely needed mending." Katy Leary, too, recalled that "Miss Clara had lots of officers for beaux" when they lived in Austria. Clara testified years later that "I did not allow my work to interfere with Viennese pleasures, which included dancing into the break of dawn," and that she and Jean "had gay companions among the titled layer of society." She was rumored at one point to be engaged to a poor fortune-hunting Austrian count until he learned that Sam was deep in debt. The American journalist Josiah Flynt was similarly said to be smitten with her. Clara was the topic of so much gossip that eventually Leschetizky joked with a group of his male students that he thought they were "all suffering from the same trouble—'Delirium Clemens.'"[9]

In the midst of a busy social season in Vienna, Sam received some sad news. His brother Orion died in Keokuk on December 11, 1897, at the age of seventy-two. "He had gone down to the kitchen in the early hours" and "built the fire," Sam learned, and "then sat down at a table to write something, and there he died, with the pencil in his hand and resting against the paper in the middle of an unfinished word—an indication that his release from the captivity of a long and troubled and pathetic and unprofitable life was mercifully swift and painless." Later that day, Sam sent condolences to Orion's widow Mollie:

> We all grieve for you; our sympathy goes out to you from the experienced hearts; & with it our love; & with Orion, & for Orion, I rejoice. He was good—all good, and sound; there was nothing bad in him, nothing base, nor any unkindness. It was unjust that such a man, against whom no offence could

> be charged, should have been sentenced to live 72 years. He has received life's best gift. It was beautiful, the patience with which he bore it. The bitterness of death—that is for the survivors; & bitter beyond all words.

Like Susy, Orion was "at peace, & no loyal friend should wish to disturb them in their high fortune." Sam and Livy continued to support Mollie financially with a $50 monthly stipend for the remainder of her life.[10]

Sam had the great (mis)fortune of arriving in Vienna just as the long-simmering Dreyfus affair was reaching a boil. A case study in anti-Semitism, this episode in French history has epitomized the rampant hatred of Jews that ravaged the continent. In December 1894 Alfred Dreyfus, a Jewish captain from Alsace-Lorraine in the French army, was convicted on trumped-up charges of spying for Germany and imprisoned on Devil's Island in French Guiana. The actual culprit was tried but acquitted by a military tribunal two years later amid the strong odor of whitewash and the scandal grew into a cause célèbre. As Sam asserted with his tongue firmly in cheek, "By the decision of the French courts in the Dreyfus matter, it is established beyond cavil or question that the decisions of courts are permanent and cannot be revised." The French nation had saved "its honor by condemning an innocent man to multiform death and hugging and whitewashing the guilty one." He lived in Paris when Dreyfus was originally convicted and, as Clara recalled, he "was among the first few who were incensed" by the "unfair trial." In mid-November 1897, soon after settling in Vienna, he started a book about the Dreyfus affair—"the finest real-life romance," he thought, since an Australian butcher masqueraded as the Tichborne Claimant. He was excited by the project because, as he wrote Rogers, "Of all the work which I have begun since last August I have finished *not one single thing*."[11]

He then reimagined the project: a compilation of editorials in French newspapers about *l'affaire Dreyfus* translated into English with an introduction he would write. He initially pitched the idea to his British publisher Andrew Chatto:

> My idea is this: that you send to Paris & gather up and translate the insanest of the newspaper articles which appeared there between the first announcement of the Dreyfus business & his arrival in his Pacific island captivity. To these should be added some of the insanest of these *recent* articles protesting against the re-opening of the case. . . . A book of those windy French editorials ought to be luxurious reading-matter now & be a selling book. Is this your opinion too? . . . I shall want rough galley-proofs as fast as the book goes into type from which to build my introduction.

Then Sam "went to work; & just as I was finishing the first chapter" Chatto replied, "discouraging the idea & saying there was but a mild interest in the Dreyfus matter in England." Sam was disappointed because "the like of that opportunity couldn't come again in five centuries." After Zola on January 13, 1898, published "J'accuse," his open letter to the president of the French Republic in which he defended Dreyfus, accused the government of obstructing justice, and protested anti-Semitism in France, the novelist was arrested and convicted of criminal libel. Though Sam had sometimes criticized Zola for wallowing in the sewer in his fiction, he now paid homage to him for heroism. Within a week he sent a letter to the *New York Herald*, subsequently widely reprinted, saluting Zola for "standing there all alone fighting his splendid fight to save the remains of the honor of France. I feel for him the profoundest reverence, and an admiration which has no bounds." Sam credited Zola, "the manliest man in France," with Dreyfus's eventual exoneration from all accusations and his restoration to the French army at his former rank. But he was not pleased that his own defense of Dreyfus had been declined. "The book would be in print, now, & on the market, if I had stuck to my project," he wrote Chatto on February 8, three weeks after the publication of Zola's open letter, the same day Zola's trial began "before that court of chicken-livered French monkeys."

> I laid my MS away unfinished & dropped the matter out of my mind. Sho! it would have been a most killingly readable book. The first chapter—the only one finished—fits into today's news as snugly as if it had been written since breakfast this morning. I'm trying hard not to cry over the spilt milk, but I *am* crying over it just the same; for I knew, at the time, that we were wasting the opportunity of the century, & of course I know it all the better, now.

Almost three years later, Sam conceded that, had his proposed work appeared, it might have sparked a backlash. "Jews did wisely in keeping quiet during the Dreyfus agitation," he wrote the Jewish activist Simon Wolf, because "the other course would have hurt Dreyfus's cause, and I see now that *nothing* could have helped it." But he never qualified his conviction that Dreyfus, like Joan of Arc, was a victim of a gross miscarriage of justice. "From the beginning of the Dreyfus case to the end of it," he asserted, "all France, except a couple of dozen moral paladins, lay under the smother of the silent assertion-lie that no wrong was being done to a persecuted and unoffending man."[12]

After the sinking of the *Maine* in Havana Harbor—ostensibly by a Spanish mine—and the loss of 261 American lives the night of February 15, 1898, and subsequent U.S. declaration of war with Spain on April 25, Sam championed military action to liberate the island from colonial occupation. Though he attended rallies of the Österreichische Gesellschaft der Friedensfreunde (Austrian Society of Friends of Peace) in Vienna in 1898, he had become an anti-imperialist but not a pacifist. His appearances were motivated more by friendship with its leader, Bertha von Suttner, than by shared conviction. He believed the Japanese retaliation to Russian aggression in the Far East had been justified, for example, and that the mere threat of war sometimes served a salutary purpose, such as by reminding "the two English-speaking families that they are kin" during the Venezuelan border dispute. He scoffed at the notion that war with Spain would raise the price of his cigars and he doubted the worth of the international peace movement. "I am indeed in *sympathy* with the movement," he wrote von Suttner,

> but my head is not with my heart in the matter. I cannot see how the movement can strongly appeal to the selfishness of governments. It can appeal to the selfishness of nations, possibly, but nations have no command over their governments, & in fact no influence over them, except of a fleeting & rather ineffectual sort. If you could persuade the Powers to agree to settle their disputes by arbitration you would uncover their nakedness. You would never persuade them to reduce their vast armaments; & so even the ignorant & the simple would then discover that the armaments were not created chiefly for the protection of the nations but for their enslavement.

In mid-May, Sam wrote former U.S. senator Cornelius Cole of California, whose son George, a medical student in Vienna, was courting Clara, that in his opinion "we ought to have taken hold of the Cuban matter & driven Spain out fifty years ago." When he was invited by the journalist Theodore Stanton, son of the suffragist Elizabeth Cady Stanton, to a Decoration Day banquet in Paris in late May, he replied that, while he was unable to accept, he valued the opportunity to honor the Civil War veterans and to pay "homage to our soldiers and sailors of today who are enlisted for another most righteous war, and utter the hope that they may make short and decisive work of it and leave Cuba free and fed when they face for home again." This letter to Stanton was widely copied in the press.[13]

In mid-May, Sam began to beat the drums of war. "From the beginning the family have been rabid opponents of this war & I've been just the other way," he wrote Andrew Chatto. "I have never enjoyed a war—even in written history—as I am enjoying this one," he exclaimed to Twichell a month later. "For this is the worthiest one that was ever fought, so far as my knowledge goes. It is a worthy thing to fight for one's own freedom; it is another sight finer to fight for another man's. And I think this is the first time it has been done." The same day, he echoed the sentiment in a note to Pond: "This is a good war with a dignified cause to fight for. A thing not to be said of the average war." He anticipated by a month John Hay's praise for the "splendid little war begun with the highest motives." Likewise, when the war with Spain spread to the Philippines, he acquiesced to the stated goal of the U.S. government to spread democracy through the region: "I said to myself, Here are a people who have suffered for three centuries. We can make them as free as ourselves, give them a government and country of their own, put a miniature of the American Constitution afloat in the Pacific, start a brand-new republic to takes its place among the free nations of the world. It seemed a great task to which we addressed ourselves." He accused the Spanish authorities of war crimes in Cuba for permitting the bodies of American casualties to be maimed. As he wrote Bettina Wirth of the London *Daily News* on June 19, "the mutilation of our soldiers killed on picket is denied in Madrid. I wish the denial might be true, but as an American Admiral made the charge that ends the matter. The mutilations were probably done by guerrillas. It's part of their trade, but as Spain recognizes the guerillas their acts are Spanish acts and official." Sam's remarks again were widely circulated in the press. "When the United States sent word to Spain that the Cuban atrocities must end," he insisted years later, "she occupied the highest moral position ever taken by a nation since the Almighty made the Earth." He celebrated American victories in the naval battles of Manila Bay on May 1 and Santiago de Cuba on July 3 and the defeat of the Spanish army of occupation by American soldiers and Filipino regulars led by Emilio Aguinaldo. He attributed the U.S. military successes to the fighting spirit of Anglo-Saxons, a belief rooted in his Lamarckian view of national character. "The Austrians used to tell me the Spaniards would whip us a few times at the start, because we were ignorant of war," he wrote, but, he replied, "We are merely Britishers under another name, and, ignorant or not, you will see the blood show up." Sam tentatively planned "to put Huck & Tom into the Spanish war, but I was so slow about it" that the five-month war was over "before I got them in."[14]

As the intensity of the war waned, Sam responded to a call by Czar Nicholas II for an international disarmament conference at the Hague. "The Czar is ready to disarm: I am ready to disarm," he joked in a letter to his friend William T. Stead. "Collect the others, it should not be much of a task now." On a more serious note, Sam wondered, in a piece Stead printed in the second issue of his magazine *War against War,* whether the great military powers of the world might "reduce the armaments little by little—on a prorate basis," say by "ten percent a year"? Universal peace might be a pipe dream, only to be realized when humans were extinct, he conceded, "but I hope we can gradually reduce the war strength of Europe till we get it down to what it ought to be—20,000 men, properly armed. Then we can have all the Peace that is worthwhile, and when we want a war anybody can afford it."[15] While he was sympathetic to the goals of their movement, he considered the pacifists impractical idealists.

Around this time Sam facetiously proposed a plan to Secretary of State Hay to force the world to disarm by threatening to "kill the massed armies of the world & every living thing" or "to exterminate the human race" with a doomsday weapon; for instance, by withdrawing all oxygen from the atmosphere. He figured either of his friends Jan Szczepanik or Nikola Tesla could devise the necessary technology and he even offered to hawk the weapon. "Have you Austrian & English patents on that destructive terror which you have been inventing?" he asked Tesla.

> If so, won't you set a price upon them & commission me to sell them? I know cabinet ministers of both countries—& of Germany, too; likewise William II. Here in the hotel the other night when some interested men were discussing means to persuade the nations to join with the Czar & disarm, I advised them to seek something more sure than disarmament by perishable paper-contract—invite the great inventors to contrive something against which fleets & armies would be helpless & thus make war thenceforth impossible. I did not suspect that you were already attending to that & getting ready to introduce into the earth permanent peace & disarmament in a practical & mandatory way.

On a more serious note, unlike some modern military strategists, Sam repudiated the deterrent effect of "mutually-assured destruction." As he explained to his daughter Jean, he doubted "that these formidable new war-inventions will make war impossible by and by" because the human animal "will always thirst for blood and will manage to have it. I think he is far and away the worst animal that exists; and the only untamable one." On October 19, he declared at a meeting of the Austrian Society of Friends of Peace that he doubted "whether the world would ever be able to put a stop to war," a sneer at the czar, and in consequence his speech was not translated from English. He was a victim of censorship, as Bettina Wirth reported, allegedly "because the Government representative had not been informed" of his remarks in advance. The following spring, Sam admitted to Twichell that he "*used* to attend the Society's meetings here, although I was not interested," and "it is no place *at all* for me now."[16]

The Treaty of Paris that the United States and Spain signed to end the war on December 10, 1898, however, convinced Sam that the administration of President William McKinley had played a game of bait and switch. What was billed as a war of liberation in Cuba had become a war of conquest in the Philippines, "a land-stealing & liberty-crucifying crusade." While freeing Cuba, the treaty sold the Philippines—"islands it no longer possessed"—for $20 million and surrendered Puerto Rico and Guam to the United States. The treaty also stipulated that the surrender of the Spanish overlords did not affect "the peaceful possession of property" by "ecclesiastical or civic bodies or any other associations"; that is, it did nothing to limit the authority or landowning of the hundreds of Catholic friars, all of them European, most of them Spanish, who effectively governed the Philippines at the time through a kind of clerical colonialism. In "A Word of Encouragement for Our Blushing Exiles" (1898)—which remained unpublished until 1923, apparently because Sam was loath to criticize American foreign policy while he lingered on foreign soil—he explicitly charged that emancipating Cuba had been "a sham humanitarian pretext" for war with Spain. Or as he wrote Twichell privately, "Apparently we are not proposing to set the Filipinos free and give their islands to them; and apparently we are not proposing to hang the priests and confiscate their property." "I have read carefully the treaty of Paris," he told an interviewer after his return to the United States, "and I have seen that we do not intend to free but to subjugate the people of the Philippines." Rather than liberate the Filipinos, "we conceived the divinely humorous idea of *buying* [the islands] from Spain! It is quite safe to confess this" since no "sane person will believe it." He later referred to the $20 million purchase price as America's "entrance fee into society—the Society of Sceptred Thieves." For the record, almost a third of the members of the U.S. Senate voted against ratification of the treaty and as late as December 1900 Sam proposed testing its "constitutionality & legality" before the Supreme Court.[17]

Worse yet, McKinley assumed the Filipinos were incapable of self-government and issued a Benevolent Assimilation Proclamation on December 21 that sanctioned U.S. occupation of the Philippines and authorized the War Department to maintain "the strong arm of authority to repress disturbance and to overcome all obstacles to the bestowal of the blessings of good and stable government upon the people of the Philippine Islands under the free flag of the United States." On his part, Sam disputed the claim that the Filipinos were incapable of self-government. After the American fleet under the command of Admiral George Dewey defeated the Spanish navy at Manila Bay, he argued, Dewey should simply have sailed away. He "should have gone about his affairs elsewhere, and left the competent Filipino army to starve out the little Spanish garrison and send it home, and the Filipino citizens to set up the form of government they might prefer, and deal with the friars according to Filipino ideas of fairness and justice." Those ideas were "of as high an order as any that prevail in Europe or America." That is, given the civic corruption in New York and the "church-going negro burners" across the country—religious hypocrites on a grand scale—he argued that Filipinos could govern themselves at least as well as Americans. Moreover, he thought that the atrocities the United States performed during the war proved that the Filipinos were more civilized that the Americans. He condemned the water torture of Filipino insurgents—forcing water down their throats—by U.S. soldiers. Those who did it were, he said, "Christian butchers."[18]

In January 1899, in response to the Treaty of Paris and the Benevolent Assimilation Proclamation, the Filipinos adopted a constitution, declared the First Philippine Republic, and elected Aguinaldo as their first president. At the battle of Manila on February 4, hostilities erupted between the republic and the United States. With peace ostensibly "established in all parts of the archipelago except in the country inhabited by the Moro tribes," Theodore Roosevelt formally declared the insurgency formally defeated on July 4, 1902, by presidential proclamation—he might have declared "Mission Accomplished"—though sporadic fighting continued until 1913. Even during the official forty-one-month war, however, American casualties amounted to over 4,200 dead and 2,800 wounded, and about 20,000 Philippine guerillas and 200,000 civilians were killed in the fighting or by famine and disease. As Stephen Kinzer concludes, "Far more Filipinos were killed or died as a result of mistreatment than in three and a half centuries of Spanish rule."[19]

In April 1899, with the Dreyfus affair boiling and at virtually the same moment the United States declared war on Spain after the sinking of the *Maine*, Sam began to compose the personal "gospel" in which he elaborated many of the ideas first advanced in "What Is Happiness?" (1883), a talk delivered before the Monday Evening Club of Hartford. Tentatively entitled "Selfishness" or "What Is the Real Character of Conscience?" and now better known as the "Vienna typescript," this first draft comprises almost half the essay eventually published in a limited edition under the title *What Is Man?* In the most simple sense, Sam argued in the essay that the human mind was "merely a machine & not even in the slightest degree under the control of its owner or subject to his influence." "A piece of automatic mechanism" like a clock, the mind "can no more dictate or influence" behavior "than can a watch." As he recalled in his autobiographical dictation, "I wrote out and completed one chapter, using the dialogue form in place of the essay form. I read it to Frank N. Doubleday, who was passing through Vienna and he wanted to take it and publish it, but I was not minded to submit it to print and criticism."[20] According to Alexander E. Jones, the chapter "still exists among the Mark Twain Papers. Unlike the rest of *What Is Man?* it is characterized by a mood of pessimism that sometimes approaches misanthropy." In truth, Livy was appalled by the treatise and forbade its publication. "I've often tried to read it to Livy," Sam admitted to Twichell, "but she won't have it; it drives her mad & makes her melancholy." He similarly conceded to Howells that "Mrs. Clemens loathes, & shudders over, & will not listen to the last half nor allow me to print any part of it." She was wary that its sacrilege would harm his reputation and/or "have a harmful influence on many people." She even questioned his mental health around this time: "Where is the mind that wrote the Prince & P[auper], Jeanne d'Arc, The Yankee, &c &c. &c. Bring it back! You can if you will—if you wish to. Think of the side I know; the sweet, dear, tender side—that I love so. Why not show this more to the world?" After completing several thousand words of his "bible," Sam laid the manuscript aside in July because, as he wrote Howells, "I don't wish to be scalped any more than another."[21]

Like Jonathan Edwards's *Freedom of the Will,* Sam's treatise argues that the human animal is a creature of fate, incapable of independent action. In effect, Sam espoused a type of a vestigial Calvinism or a secularized doctrine of original sin, with evil engrained in human nature and the human race inevitably damned. In a Socratic dialogue between an Old Man and a Young Man, he embraced a type of mechanistic determinism that equated people with machines; in a word, that "whatsoever a man is, is due to his make, and to the influences brought to bear upon it by his heredities, his habitat, his associations. His is moved, directed, *commanded,* by exterior influences solely. He originates nothing, not even a thought." Privately, Sam was even more candid: "The human being is a stupidly-constructed machine. He may have been a sufficiently creditable invention in the early & ignorant times, but today there is not a country in Christendom that would grant a patent on him." Sam occasionally added a paragraph or two to the manuscript or returned to it for his own edification. "Whenever I wish to account for any new outbreak of hypocrisy, stupidity or crime on the part of the race," he confessed, "I get out that manuscript and read it and am consoled." In any case, Livy loathed the essay because she understood it perfectly well. The mechanistic determinism Sam promulgates, as Hamlin Hill concludes, "is a desolating doctrine; it is not inspiring, enthusing, uplifting. It takes the glory out of man, it takes the pride out of him, it takes the heroism out of him, it denies him all personal credit, all applause; it not only degrades him to a machine, but allows him no control over the machine."[22]

Robert Ingersoll's influence on Sam is evident even in this précis of the treatise. As John Bird has argued, *What Is Man?* echoes Ingersoll's claim in "The Gods" (1872) that "Man has no ideas, and can have none except those suggested by our surroundings." Sam and Ingersoll undoubtedly admired each other after their first meeting in 1879. When the *New York Herald* launched its aborted fundraiser on Sam's behalf in 1897, the Great Agnostic endorsed the effort: "Mark Twain has a warm place in every American heart," he averred. "He is not only the greatest of living humorists, but he is a philosopher. In all he writes—back of the laugh, behind the joke—you will find the keenest logic, the best of sense." On his part, when he learned of the death of "the great agnostic" in November 1899, Sam wrote Ingersoll's niece with his condolences: "Except my daughter's, I have not grieved for any death as I have grieved for his. His was a great and beautiful spirit, he was a man—all man from his crown to his foot soles. My reverence for him was deep and genuine; I prized his affection for me and returned it with usury. . . . I knew him twenty years and was fond of him, and held [him] in as high honor as I have held any man living or dead." In his memoir *My Mark Twain*, Howells recalled that his friend "greatly admired Robert Ingersoll, whom he called an angelic orator and regarded as an evangel of a new gospel—the gospel of free thought."[23]

While Sam never compiled his proposed Dreyfus book, the affair became a subtext in his best-known short story, "The Man That Corrupted Hadleyburg," which he began to write soon after he laid aside the manuscript of *What Is Man?* In the most superficial sense, as he told Isabel Lyon, the tale argues against sheltering "the young from temptation; let them be tempted, & let them fall early, that they may know by experience what things are to be avoided." But at a more subtle level, Hadleyburg represents a microcosmic Hapsburg Empire, its nineteen leading citizens or Nineteeners corresponding to the nineteen states represented in the Reichsrath. As Cynthia Ozick observes, "we can recognize in Hadleyburg," corrupted by a satanic stranger's scheme to expose the avarice and provincialism of the townspeople, "the dissolving Austria-Hungary of the 1890s" riven by ethnic hatreds. The uproar in the town meeting likewise suggests the pandemonium of Reichsrath sessions in the winter of 1897–98.[24] While Sam was writing the story, moreover, the *Chicago Tribune* reported that it was "said to be partly political in character. The scene is laid in Austria and parliamentary struggles appear in it." Peter Messent also notes that, in collecting the fable in *The Man That Corrupted Hadleyburg and Other Stories and Essays* (1900), Sam followed it with four pieces that refer directly to the Dreyfus scandal a total of six times.[25] He jumped at an offer from Harper's to pay $2,000 for the story in December 1898 and it was printed in the *Monthly* a year later.[26]

"The Man That Corrupted Hadleyburg" was almost unanimously applauded upon publication in periodicals on both sides of the Atlantic. A partial list: "a fair example of the humorist at his best" (London *Literary World*), "a fine piece of humour" (*Manchester Guardian*), "one of the most original stories Mr. Clemens has ever written" (*Public Opinion*), "a most curious and ingenious conception" (*American Monthly Review of Reviews*), "admirably constructed" (*New York Times Saturday Review of Books*), "one of the best stories Mr. Clemens ever wrote" (*New Orleans Picayune*), "among the cleverest of its writer's many clever studies in human character" (*London Post*), "a fable designed to drive home an ethical lesson" (*London Leader*), "a moral apologue of great value and most admirably written" (London *Speaker*), "conceived in his best vein of elaborate satire" (*Liverpool Post*), "a masterpiece" (*Baltimore Sun*), and "one of Mr. Clemens' profoundest studies of human nature" (*Zion's Herald*). Only a few notices were equivocal—the humor "seems rather forced," though the tale "is very clever, striking, and entertaining" (*Salisbury and Winchester Journal*)—or adverse: "too long" (*Athenaeum*), "thin and weak but may be read while waiting for breakfast" (*Saturday Review*), and "does him little credit" (St. Louis *Christian Evangelist*).[27]

In November 1897, as the Dreyfus affair was blazing across Europe, anti-Semitic firestorms were erupting in the Austrian Reichsrath in Vienna. At issue was a proposal by Kasimir Felix Badeni, prime minister of the Austrian part of the empire, to recognize Czech, the native idiom of Jews in Bohemia and Moravia, as a lingua franca in those states, a move the anti-Semites regarded as tantamount to granting the "Auslander-Juden" a special privilege. According to Dolmetsch, Badeni's proposal would have required "all German-speaking judges, lawyers, and bureaucrats" in these two of the nineteen states in the empire to become bilingual by 1901 or lose their jobs. The ethnic Germans in Austria were also outraged by the proposal, fearing "the *Czechisierung* or Czechifying of Vienna and of the *Verjudung des Richerstandes* (Jewifying of judgeships)" and the attraction of more Jewish immigrants to the region. The ethnic Germans comprised "but a fourth part of the empire's population," Sam reported, "but they urge that the country's public business should be conducted" exclusively in German.[28]

Badeni's task of reforming the language ordinance was complicated by the looming expiration of the Ausgleich (Compromise), the 1867 treaty that unified the empire but required ratification every decade, with the most recent renewal due before the last day of calendar year 1897. "Otherwise," as Sam observed, "the two countries [Austria and Hungary] would become separate entities" and "both countries would be weakened" and "suffer damage"—a sort of late nineteenth-century equivalent of Brexit. Badeni's proposed compromise on the language issue was designed to secure the support of the Bohemian and Moravian representatives to reratify the Ausgleich—in effect, to condition the ratification of the treaty on the approval of the language measure. Ironically, as Dolmetsch observes, Sam's speech before the Concordia about "the horrors of the German language" could not have been delivered at a worse moment.[29]

Sam chronicled the events that transpired in the Reichsrath during late October and November in his essay "Stirring Times in Austria," a classic piece of political reportage published the following March in *Harper's Monthly*. Howells thought the essay made "the whole thing delightfully intelligible"; one reviewer called it "one of the best magazine articles of the month"; another with remarkable insight observed that it recorded scenes that would shame "a French court of justice"; and on the basis of the piece, the *Springfield Republican* pronounced Sam "perhaps the best reporter alive." In it he outlined the dynamics of the problem, specifically the many parties represented in the parliament. Moreover, as he explained, "the deputies come from all the walks of life and from all the grades of society. There are princes, counts, barons, priests, peasants, mechanics, laborers, lawyers, judges, physicians, professors, merchants, bankers, shopkeepers. They are religious men, they are earnest, sincere, devoted." Though riven by such diversity, they share one common trait: "they hate the Jews."[30]

The government, in particular the parliamentary leader of the pan-German Nationals, Georg Ritter von Schönerer, another of Hitler's idols, schemed to circumvent a vote on Badeni's compromise by parliamentary maneuvers, to approve the Ausgleich immediately, then to defeat the compromise. To frustrate this strategy, Otto Lecher, a delegate from Moravia and president of the Brünn (aka Brno) Board of Trade, delivered a twelve-hour filibuster on the floor of the Reichsrath from the evening of October 28 until the next morning, "the longest flow of unbroken talk that ever came out of one mouth since the world began." As a result of Lecher's speech, the opposition minority prevented the government from forcing a vote on the Ausgleich as planned. Still, the all-night session accomplished nothing and, in the view of the Vienna correspondent of the London *Times*, "was the most disorderly ever witnessed in any parliament. Some of the anti-Semite expressions were of such an improper character as to defy reproduction."

Seated in the visitors' gallery next to the Russian painter Vasily Vereshchagin, Sam said it reminded him of "an American lynching meeting to punish a horse thief." He sympathized with the minority delegates, of course, especially after meeting Lecher by chance in the Reichsrath restaurant on November 3. He asked Lecher "to give him notice of his next 12 hour speech and said he would be there and sit it out. Herr Lecher took the observation seriously and replied that he hoped next week to repeat the performance and perhaps to improve upon it." The *Boston Journal* editorialized that Sam probably "never spent a pleasanter hour than when watching the German and Czech Deputies in the Austrian Reichsrath the other evening shaking their fists at each other and exchanging indescribable epithets." Certainly he followed the "customary pandemonium" closely in the press, if not in person from the gallery of the Reichsrath, over the next few weeks. He frequented "a certain large café on the Ringstrasse" near the Parliament Building and cited the texts of some of the parliamentary debates that appeared in the *Arbeiter-Zeitung* and *Neue Freie Presse* in "Stirring Times in Austria." "During the whole of November things went from bad to worse," Sam reported. "The all-important Ausgleich remained hard aground, and could not be sparred off"—the metaphor here from Sam's steamboating days—and "Badeni's government could not withdraw the Language Ordinance and keep its majority and the Opposition could not be placated on easier terms."[31]

The crisis finally came to a head in late November with Sam in the galleries, where "I lost none of the show." As he told a reporter later, "I think I had most fun in Vienna with the poor old Reichsrath. . . . It was one of the biggest jokes I have ever seen, and I enjoyed it immensely." On November 24 several fights broke out in the chamber, as he noted in his journal, including "hammerings with fists, choking, threatenings with chairs, a wound made with a penknife." The next day—Thanksgiving Day in the United States—"the harried, bedeviled, and despairing government went insane," as Sam put it. "In order to free itself from the thraldom of the Opposition it committed this curiously juvenile crime: it moved an important change of the Rules of the House," specifically to abolish roll-call votes, "forbade debate upon the motion, put it to a stand-up vote instead of ayes and noes, and then gravely claimed that it had been adopted; whereas, to even the dullest witness—if I without immodesty may pretend to that place—it was plain that nothing legitimately to be called a vote had been taken at all." In the bedlam of the Reichsrath, Sam explained, many of the members stood much of the time "to have a better chance to exchange epithets and make other noises." Then by voice vote the government passed a motion permitting "the use of force to maintain order."[32]

The stage was set for a confrontation. The next day, November 26, with Sam present again and "no vacant seats in the galleries," "everyone felt that *something* was going to happen." Early in the afternoon, a group of ten Social Democratic delegates stood "against the ministerial desks, in the shadow of the Presidential tribune," when without warning a battalion of sixty uniformed and spike-helmeted police burst into the chamber—"the most thrilling theatrical surprise I ever saw." These former soldiers marched "in double file down the floor of the House—a free parliament profaned by an invasion of brute force. It was an odious spectacle—odious and awful." They "went at their work with the cold unsentimentality of their trade. They ascended the steps of the tribune, laid their hands upon the inviolable persons of the representatives of a nation, and dragged and tugged and hauled them down the steps and out at the door; then ranged themselves in stately military array in front of the ministerial estrade, and so stood. It was a tremendous episode. The memory of it will outlast all the thrones that exist today."

Four of the Socialist delegates were arrested and "imprisoned on the premises." After an hour the violence of the moment seemed to have passed, so Sam returned to his hotel and sent a dispatch about the melee to the New York *World* that was widely reprinted across the United States. Somehow the story got around that Sam had shouted "Hoch die Deutschen!" when the police invaded the Reichsrath and been clubbed by a Czech delegate and evicted. "The next time he wants to give vent to his feelings in that chamber he will probably use English, which seems to be the only tongue not represented in the Reichsrath," the *St. Louis Republic* opined. But, as Sam lamented to Twichell, "what a pity it is that one's adventures never happen!" He wrote Rogers three weeks later that, while the papers had reported that "a Czech hit me over the head in the Reichsrath," they had "suppressed what I did to the Czech. There are orphans in that family now." The contretemps reverberated across the country for weeks. It precipitated (as Sam reported) "a popular outbreak or two in Vienna; there were three or four days of furious rioting in Prague, followed by the establishing there of martial law; the Jews and Germans were harried and plundered, and their houses destroyed; in other Bohemian towns there was rioting—in some cases the Germans being the rioters, in others the Czechs—and in all cases the Jew had to roast, no matter which side he was on." Sam half expected a revolution in the country when the Reichsrath reopened and joked with Rogers that if one should erupt, "we shall pull out & go to Cuba" or "to Spain or some other health-resort."[33] Instead, the Badeni government resigned and as a result Austro-Hungary was governed mostly by executive fiat for the next several years.

Early in the new year 1899, Sam published a sequel to "Stirring Times in Austria" entitled "The 'Austrian Parliamentary System'? Government by Article 14" in *Lords and Commons,* an ephemeral London weekly that promised him £100 for two thousand words, double the rate of *Century* and more than double the rate of *Harper's.* He focused on a clause in the Austrian constitution—written in German—that "provides for the creation of urgent new laws by the executive between Sessions and the Legislature and for the continuance of the usual functions and industries of the Government—and thus the Executive itself becomes a Legislature." The genius of article 14, according to Sam, is that "it means anything you please; but it does not mean the same thing to any two people." He also noted that barely a sixth of the members of the Reichsrath were elected by over four million Hungarian and other voters; that is, that suffrage in the empire was "a gilded and handsome phantom."[34]

In the midst of these other rows, Sam was obliged to squelch reports that he had satisfied the claims of all his creditors. This "free of debt" rumor was the opposite of the "dying in poverty" rumor that had circulated in the spring and it was just as untrue. The assertion seems to have originated in New England, when on October 23 the *Boston Journal,* New Haven *Journal and Courier, Hartford Courant,* and *Hartford Times* announced that Sam had "paid all his debts by money he has earned the last two years." His income during his period ostensibly amounted to $82,000, most of it earned by his writings. On November 4, literally the same day he witnessed the dustup in the Reichsrath, Sam cabled Bliss that the report was a "lie" and he was "still deeply in debt," though he explained to Bliss in a letter written the same day that he expected to "be out of debt within the next twelvemonth" if his travelogue sold well. As his liabilities diminished, he crowed to Rogers that "for the first time in my life I am getting more pleasure out of paying money out than pulling it in. When I get everybody paid but the Bank & the Grants I shall be as full of spirit as a distillery." A month later, he again wrote Rogers that "since we began to pay off the debts I have abundant peace of mind again—no sense of burden. Work is become a pleasure again—it is not labor any longer." Rogers also rallied around this flag. Sam had "paid nearly 75 percent of the indebtedness incurred" when Webster and Company failed, he told the *New York Tribune.* "He has, considering that he is sixty-four years old, done something that I consider remarkable, and I am confident that he will in the end keep his promise and settle, dollar for dollar, every claim against the old firm."[35]

In early May 1898, as he was liquidating the last of the "legitimate" debts owed by the defunct Webster and Company, Sam was suddenly sent an eight-year-old invoice from Pratt & Whitney in Hartford on the Paige account for

$1,744. "I always paid the P. & W. bills when I received them, difficult as it was sometimes to accomplish it," he ranted to his business manager Franklin Whitmore. Sam never learned what the bill was for, whether for rental space in the Pratt & Whitney factory or for special tools Paige had ordered. The company continued to strike for payment until at least May 1901, though Sam resolved "never [to] pay that bill till I'm forced" and he apparently never did, much as he never fully liquidated the claims of the Grant family and the Mount Morris Bank.[36]

Bliss in fact orchestrated a slow rollout of *Following the Equator* in the United States. He had hired Dan Beard to be its principal illustrator months before, and he began to recruit subscription agents to sell the book door-to-door in mid-September 1897. The first prepublication notice of it appeared in the *Hartford Courant* on October 4. The *Atlanta Constitution, Boston Globe, Boston Journal, Buffalo News, Chicago Tribune, Cincinnati Commercial Tribune, Detroit Free Press, Louisville Courier-Journal, New York Herald,* New York *World, Philadelphia Inquirer, Portland Oregonian, Springfield Republican, St. Louis Post-Dispatch,* and *St. Louis Republic* all excerpted several hundred words from the advance sheets, which duplicated the canvassing copy, on October 10; the *Hartford Courant, Elmira Star-Gazette, San Francisco Examiner,* San Francisco *Argonaut,* New Orleans *Times-Democrat, Omaha Bee, Los Angeles Times, El Paso Herald, Butte Post,* and *Seattle Post-Intelligencer* all printed excerpts before the end of the month; and without Sam's knowledge Bliss sold three chapters for $1,000 to *McClure's,* which carried them under the title "From India to South Africa" in its November 1897 number. Even these previews of the book were received with some vacillation, however. The *New York Tribune* was underwhelmed, for example, declaring that the excerpts consisted of "more description than fun" and "the general effect is not so lively as was expected." Horatio Alger, author of books for juveniles, lamented privately that the excerpts were "not up to his Innocents Abroad." On the other hand, the *San Francisco Call* predicted that the book "will be as great a success . . . as anything he has written"; the *Idaho Statesman* forecast that it "will be worth its cost many times over, but if it were trash the public should buy it and place the old favorite on his feet"; and the Dalles (Ore.) *Chronicle* concluded that the passages proved "his pen has not lost its trickery or his mind its store of plausible fiction." The *New York Herald* remarked in its reprinting of the advance sheets that Sam was an "observer first and humorist afterward," though when he got wind of the printing of these excerpts Sam groused to Bliss that apparently "the *Herald* has stolen your whole canvassing book—a harm ten thousand times more damaging than if you had allowed me to publish the same chapters in the *Century*."[37] Sam was so troubled by Bliss's duplicity in selling chapters to *McClure's* that he apologized to Richard Watson Gilder, editor of the *Century*. His contract with the American Publishing Compa-nystrictly forbade *me* to print any word of the book or the *subject* in a periodical, but it put no restraint upon Bliss—a detail which I didn't notice. But he knew perfectly well that by the unwritten laws of honor you were entitled to a say in the matter of advance-selections before anybody else in the world. I am sorry about this thing, and ashamed of it. Bliss has acted within his rights, but it is shabby, just the same." Worse yet, Bliss delayed for months forwarding $1,000 *McClure's* had paid for the excerpts even though, as Sam protested, the advance publication of the three chapters "cost you & me ten times" that amount in book sales.[38]

Still, the travelogue in its various incarnations became the most eagerly anticipated and widely reviewed book Sam ever wrote upon its publication by the American Publishing Company in Hartford on November 13 and Chatto & Windus in London on November 26, 1897. Many of the initial notices in the United States commended the work without flattering it. The *Boston Herald* epitomized this brand of equivocal appraisal: *Following the Equator* was "as funny as ever" but lacked "a certain unnamable tone" and consequently "will never become a classic." Among the papers that followed suit: the *New York Tribune* ("may not quite have the aplomb of his earlier and more famous productions" but "is characteristic of his fun and is likely to live as long as anything he has written"), the *Hartford Times* (contains "a great deal of information" but "is not dull"), the *Chicago Inter Ocean* ("the reader will . . . find much that is valuable"), the *Literary Digest* ("philosophic and bravely irreverent"), the *Springfield Republican* ("does not rank with the author's best work like *Huckleberry Finn*" but "is lively and entertaining"), *Critic* ("the diary of a skilled observer and writer, with originality and humor, but with too much of the reformer to find the world anything but a tragedy to those who think"), *Overland Monthly* ("a traveler's miscellany—a globetrotter's hotchpotch"), *Buffalo News* ("it is "Mark Twain from cover to cover and perhaps that is enough to say of it"), *Nebraska State Journal* ("a good deal of inadvertent amusement"), *Dallas Morning News* ("not his best book" but "an authentic description of the lands through which he has just traveled"), and Topeka *American Bimetallist* ("a good book for dyspeptics"). No less innocuous was Robert Bridges in *Life* ("anyone who has acquired the art of judicious skipping can get a great deal of fun out of the book"). Laurence Hutton was especially gracious in *Harper's Monthly* ("much to interest, amuse, and instruct the reader here"), concluding that if the book "is more grave and subdued than *The Innocents Abroad* or *A Tramp Abroad*, the cause is easily found in the loss of Susan Clemens just as the world tour came to an end." Sam wrote to thank Hutton for his "good notice," relieved to read such pleasantries "about a book which was written in blood & tears under the shadow of our irremediable disaster—a book whose outside aspect had to be cheerful, but whose secret substance was made all of bitterness & rebellion."[39]

Given its middling modern reputation,[40] *Following the Equator* was hailed with superlatives by a surprising number of critics. The New York *Sun* pronounced it not only "one of the freshest, most vigorous, and altogether delightful series of notes of travel and personal impression of our time" but Sam's best book. Sam wrote Rogers that this notice in the *Sun* "delighted me all over." Similarly unqualified in their acclaim were Hiram M. Stanley in the *Dial* ("a first-rate specimen of the eminently sagacious mixture of sense and nonsense which is so characteristic" of the author), the *New Haven Register* ("the best of Mark Twain"), *Louisville Courier-Journal* (his "greatest" book in "size and scope"), *Catholic World* ("one of the best of his books"), *Minneapolis Star Tribune* ("the most serious work of travel the author has ever attempted"), *Los Angeles Herald* ("full of the very keenest observations"), and Rockford, Illinois, *Star* ("his masterpiece, the crowning effort of his life"). Several readers ranked it above *The Innocents Abroad* among Sam's travel books, including the reviewers for the *Omaha Bee* ("a book of far greater value"), Cottonwood Falls (Kans.) *News-Courant* ("a new and more enjoyable feast"), *San Francisco Call* (humor "even keener" than his early books), and *Boston Globe* ("One is often amazed at the worldwide truth he condenses in a sentence"), Charles de Kay in the *New York Times Book Review* ("shows a great advance . . . in taste and in the wisdom of the jester"), and Sam's old friend George Hamlin Fitch in the *San Francisco Chronicle* ("as interesting" as *The Innocents Abroad* and "better written").[41]

Others judged the book in scarcely less complimentary terms, such as the New York *Commercial Advertiser* ("abounds in picturesque and often rather striking description"), *American Monthly Review of Reviews* (humor "permeates his latest volume as it did his first"), *New Orleans Picayune* ("more laughs to the square inch . . . than in any other book of its size"), *Munsey's* ("a delightful book of travels"), *Independent* ("Mark Twain has never done any better work"), *Chicago Tribune* ("almost if not entirely as good as anything this prince of humorists has ever written"), *Hartford Courant* ("delightfully fresh, piquant, and vivid"), Washington *National Tribune* ("will be hailed with delight by thousands"), Burlington *Free Press* ("very readable"), *Salt Lake Tribune* ("a thousand of Mark's drolleries"), Little Rock *Arkansas Gazette* ("full of quaint descriptions"), *Augusta Chronicle* ("thoroughly interesting"), *Lexington Herald* ("unusually interesting, amusing" and "instructive"),

Vancouver *Province* ("bristles with the humour which has made Clemens famous"), and *Christian Observer* ("information and amusement in the same breath"). The U.S. edition of *Following the Equator* was sold by subscription in Brazil and favorably noticed in the *Rio News*: "His hand has lost nothing of its cunning, nor of its versatility." Henry Rogers assured Sam that he enjoyed the book and James Whitcomb Riley wrote him that "if you've ever done anything better, stronger, or of more wholesome uplift I can't recall it." Howells lauded the travelogue both privately and publicly. He told Sam that it was "enormously good. . . . At the right times there is a noble seriousness; and at all times, justice and mercy. There isn't a mean thought, a shabby lie, a cowardly bravado in the whole book." In 1901, in a survey of Sam's entire career, Howells declared that Sam's analysis of the factionalism in South Africa in 1896 that led to the Boer War was "prophetic," and as late as August 1906 he pronounced the travelogue a "wonderbook" and "a delight truly unspeakable." In brief, only a few American reviewers panned *Following the Equator*. The *Providence Journal* thought it "repellant rather than attractive" and the *Chap-Book* reviled it: "Viewed as a work of art, this volume is monstrous and as a book of travel it is impossible. The only way to view it is as a bundle of haphazard thoughts" interlarded with long passages of "hackwork and cyclopedic padding."[42]

The reception of *More Tramps Abroad* in the British Commonwealth was more nuanced, especially on the topic of colonialism. Sam was repeatedly commended, as the *Pall Mall Gazette* put it, for the "generous tribute he pays to England and Englishmen, to the wisdom of our rule no less than to our splendid supremacy," for conceding "that the most fortunate thing that has ever befallen that Empire was the establishment of British supremacy there." The *Gazette* concluded that the travelogue "will be held in popular esteem with the best books of its author." Several prominent publications echoed the point: the *St. James's Gazette* pronounced it "the most brilliant notebook of the kind that has ever been written" and praised in particular Sam's "just and generous . . . appreciation of British rule in India and of the events of the Mutiny." *Literature* noted that while "the book is greatly inferior to *Tom Sawyer* and *Huckleberry Finn*," its author "has nothing but admiration for the equity and tact of British rule in India." The London *Morning Post* was "convinced" by Sam's "judgment on our rule in India" that it was "the most fortunate thing that has ever befallen" the subcontinent. The London *Review of Reviews* added that "he is sure that the American colonies would never have revolted last century if they had been treated as the Australians are today" and expressed an appreciation in his "first-class book of travel" for "the order and just government that has been established" in India. The *Scotsman* went so far as to declare Sam's travels apparently "made him a thorough Imperialist and convinced him of the beneficent effects of British rule."[43]

To be sure, a couple of British critics took exception to Sam's criticism of the Jameson raid in South Africa. Those chapters were "the least satisfactory" part of the book, according to the London *Globe*, and his comments upon the raid were "in every sense impertinent." The *Saturday Review* was even more terse: Sam's remarks "on the South African business" exemplified "insolently irresponsible journalism." Many of the reviews in Australia and New Zealand were likewise tepid, as witness the Sydney *Daily Telegraph*, Melbourne *Age*, and *Wagga Wagga Express* ("absolutely commonplace and [to Australians] uninteresting"), *Coolgardie Miner* ("unmitigated bosh"), *Wellington Mail* ("dismisses the Empire City in about half a dozen lines"), *Wellington Evening Post* ("travel-impressions of an exaggerative humorist turned philosopher"), *Clare's Weekly* ("more of pathos than fun"), and Adelaide *Weekly Herald* ("the book is feeble, the matter jumbled together, and the effect disappointing").[44] Even some modestly favorable notices in British magazines and newspapers agreed that *More Tramps Abroad* paled in comparison to Sam's earlier and livelier travel books, among them the *Academy* ("the proportion of fun to hard sense and hard facts is smaller than usual and the quality less high"); London *Morning Post* ("far below the work that suggested its name"); *London Mail* ("a certain falling off of late"); London *Speaker* ("we confess to have been slightly bored with much of this latter-day elaborate fooling"); London *Bookman* ("the new series will never reach the popularity of the old"); *Glasgow Herald* ("though the stream runs perhaps less clearly than of yore, it is still far from having come to the muddy bottom"); and *Auckland Star* (Mark Twain has become "more the philosopher" than "exuberant humorist"). Other Commonwealth papers were not so restrained in their criticism, for example the *Liverpool Post* ("there is a pathos in the thought of a man in the autumn of life courageously responding to the spur of necessity and settling to work to repeat if possible the triumphs of his vigorous youth"); *Sydney Herald* ("something pathetic in this attempt" of this "old man fallen on evil times" to "draw water from the ancient springs that once welled forth so spontaneously"); *Australian Star* of Sydney ("Mark Twain furbishing up old jokes to pay his debts while his erstwhile wit is upon its deathbed"); *Westminster Budget* ("the unflagging good spirits which carried us along in old days are unhappily not at the author's disposal"); *Westminster Gazette* ("a desultory book"); London *Globe* ("tracts of dullness which only the most determined spirits will have the courage to cross"); Otago, New Zealand, *Witness* ("he has not observed the proper proportions of a book of humor, which should consist of a minimum of padding with a maximum of humor"); and A. G. Stephens in the *Sydney Bulletin* ("Mark Twain *was* Mark Twain: now he is M. T. And old, sick, tired, he still plods round the weary literary whim-path—has to, it seems; for a creditor's lash drives him. . . . The volcano was in its day a good volcano . . . [but] there now remain only ashes"). In the same vein, a few notices simply noted a blunt truth: the book was sometimes boring. The London *Literary World* complained that "the reader who is looking for passages to arouse his laughter will have to plod through much sand before he comes across an oasis"; the *Athenaeum* called the book "too long" and "too diffuse"; and the *Spectator* found it "often as tiresome to read as it must have been to write." The London correspondent of the Sydney *Daily Telegraph* allowed that "whether I am stupid or Mark Twain is dull I shouldn't like to be certain. I can only say the book, at a casual glance, seems to me absolutely commonplace."[45] This notice was widely reprinted in newspapers in Perth, Adelaide, Melbourne, Geraldton, Riverine, Bendigo, Wagga Wagga, Brisbane, and Tasmania.

The favorable reviews of *More Tramps Abroad* in the Commonwealth were predominately shallow and ornamented with a few vapid adjectives. The London *Daily News*, for example, extolled "the observant, humourous, witty, and wise record of a lecturing tramp around the world," the London *Telegraph* the "pleasant work of travel," the *Manchester Guardian* the "really admirable piece of craftsmanship" and its "several delightful stories," *Colonies and India* the "interesting and instructive narrative," and the *Birmingham Post* its "fine, sunny, delightful" tone. The *London Chronicle* ("free from the cant of secondhand criticism"), *London Leader* ("full of good stories and high spirits"), London *Clarion* ("many good things"), *Melbourne Argus* and Perth *Daily News* ("a great deal" that is "amusing and much that is serious and instructive"), *Pall Mall Gazette* ("the work of a shrewd and impartial observer, a man of keen common sense, of the most brilliant wit, and of genial and extravagant humor"), London *Graphic* ("eloquent in its own whimsical way"), Adelaide *Critic* (an "inimitable" storyteller), Melbourne *Australasian* ("as imperturbable and audacious a raconteur as ever"), and Chiltern *Leader* ("fully sustains the character of the author" as "a man of exceptionally keen and accurate observation") were no more specific or concrete in their praise or approval. The London *Times* paid it a dubious compliment ("quite up to the mark of" *A Tramp Abroad*); *Publishers' Circular* considered it therapeutic ("a more effective remedy for the blues has not been offered in England for many a day"); and both the *Manchester Guardian* and *Booksellers' Review* urged readers to "make haste" to buy it to help Sam pay his debts. Sam was unconcerned, writing Rogers that the London and Vienna papers like the book "and so do my personal friends in England."[46]

Despite its wavering critical reception, the travelogue was a best seller, in part as the result of an organized campaign by women's clubs across the United States to promote its sale. Their members were encouraged to buy the book to help lift the author out of debt. During its first six weeks in print during the holiday season, it sold over twenty thousand copies in the United States, on which Sam received a 12.5 percent royalty. The American Publishing Company paid him about $11,400 in 1897, mostly on sales of the travel book. Another ten thousand copies were sold in the United States during the first month of 1898, and the publisher issued a second edition in early February and at the end of the year paid Sam an additional $10,000. *More Tramps Abroad* reportedly sold over seven thousand copies in its first four days in press, ten thousand copies across the Commonwealth during its first month, and was issued in a fourth edition by spring. The combined royalties ostensibly enabled Sam to liquidate most of his remaining liabilities from the Webster bankruptcy early in the new year 1898. In his autobiographical dictation, he recalled that "at the end of '98 or the beginning of '99" Rogers cabled him that his creditors had "all been paid a hundred cents on the dollar" with "eighteen thousand five hundred dollars left" in his account.[47]

But Sam either misremembered or deliberately misrepresented events. Rogers actually wrote Sam on January 6, 1898, that he was holding a cash balance of $29,982, and after paying a final $6,648 to all the creditors except the Barrow family, the Grant family, and the Mount Morris Bank, "we will have remaining $23,334.62." The balance still owed the Barrows ($11,147), the bank ($21,244), and the Grants ($1,471) totaled $33,862. In reply, Sam instructed Rogers to repay the Barrows' principal. "Barrow is an ass & disgruntled," he thought, "but I don't care for that. I am responsible for the money" Hall had borrowed from the family "& must do the best I can to pay it." But he refused to grant George Barrow the accrued 6 percent interest he demanded. "So far as I know [Barrow] is the only similarly-situated creditor in all history since Shylock's time who has demanded blood in addition to flesh," Sam complained. In the end, Barrow forgave the interest. Sam also directed Rogers to pay all the other creditors except Grant and the bank—he had no intention to pay their full claims—and "we shall still have about $12,000 left in cash. This is exceedingly bully; the best music we have heard lately." Before the end of January, the financially strapped Mount Morris Bank agreed to settle its demands for $6,612. Sam was elated, of course, and he pledged to Rogers that he would pay the bank "a small sum yearly—$1,000 or $2,000—until I have paid $10,000, then quit." A month later, he had revised the amount downward. He planned to pay the bank "about $6,000 more . . . a little at a time, at my leisure. When they prove to me that they never collected the $9,000 false notes, I will pay that, too. But the burden of proof is upon them—they must do the proving, themselves. And I don't quite know how they will do it."[48] Nothing came of these hasty promises.

Sometime over the next few weeks, moreover, the Grants apparently forgave Sam's debt to them—at least no record of any future invoice by them or payment to them survives. Sam was determined never "to pay them a cent *anyhow*." He had been generous to the family over the years, lending Jesse Grant $500 in 1885 "when the family were still poor" and neither the principal "nor any interest has ever been paid." But the "puny little weasily, good-for-nothing" Fred Grant had brought suit against Colby as assignee for royalties on unbound copies of the memoirs sold during the liquidation of Webster and Company's assets. Rogers and his assistant Katherine Harrison mailed the last of the checks to creditors in late February 1898, and Sam finally emerged from bankruptcy—but not because he had paid all his creditors in full.[49]

Punning on Henry Rogers's first name, Sam repeatedly commended his financial angel for setting a "fertile old hen" on the nest to hatch out "those big broods" of profits and dividends even months before he repaid his creditors. "Dear me, our wealth piles up faster under your handling of it than it did under my labors on the platform," he wrote Rogers in September 1897. "Mrs. Clemens asks me to say to you that she is 'perfectly delighted & very grateful.' So am I." His windfalls amounted to as much as $10,000 within a two-week period or $17,000 in a month. In early 1899 Livy calculated that she and Sam had liquid assets of about $107,000 in addition to the equity in the Hartford house, enough that they could again afford to live in the United States. "I have been out and bought a box of 6 cent cigars; I was smoking 4½ before," he advised Howells. (The joke soon went around that his favorite book was his bank book.) In August 1899, Sam thanked Rogers for managing his financial affairs—"By George they were ill enough when you took hold of them"—by astute insider trading in such companies as Brooklyn Union Gas, Federal Steel, and the Anaconda Copper Mining Company. Asked by a reporter in March 1898 how it felt to be out of debt, Sam was quick to reply, "I'm glad it's over; what a worry it has been." At long last he was "able to look forward to the day when I can return home and live in the house which I and my family so dearly love." Katy Leary remembered that "he was so happy when all them debts was paid that he said he felt just like a boy again—free and out of school." In the course of the fiscal year, Sam adjured Rogers not to exclude him from investment opportunities: "I want to be in, with the other capitalists."[50]

As legend has it, Sam behaved in the throes of bankruptcy with the same brand of moral courage as his bête noire Walter Scott, who, after the failure of his publisher in 1826, painstakingly repaid the firm's indebtedness of £130,000. *Publishers' Weekly* broke the news in its issue for February 19, 1898, with the publication of a letter from Katherine Harrison under the title "Mark Twain Pays in Full." Sam's friend John Y. W. MacAlister spread the news in a piece that appeared in the London *Times* and was widely copied around the world. Sam had

> discharged the load of debt which the unfortunate collapse of the firm of Messrs. Charles L. Webster and Co. placed upon his shoulders, or rather I should say which he took upon his shoulders . . . with the exception of the historical case of Sir Walter Scott, he does not think there is to be found in the records of literature anything quite equal to Twain's conduct in insisting upon taking on himself the debts of the company when he might under limited liability provisions have left the creditors to satisfy themselves with a mere dividend.

Sam quickly expressed his appreciation to MacAlister for the favorable publicity: "I see that you took the trouble to bring to notice the fact that I have worked myself out of debt. You could not have done me a greater favor than that, & I sincerely thank you for it." The London *Daily News* reported at virtually the same moment that Sam's liquidation of his debts was "a fine example of the very chivalry of probity . . . rank[ing] with the historic case of Walter Scott." Andrew Carnegie likewise extolled Sam's conduct by insisting (incorrectly) that, like Scott, he had "triumphed, paying every creditor . . . every cent of his debt. There comes to men in life critical moments which test whether they be of clay or the pure gold. Mark Twain proved himself the latter." In his autobiography, Carnegie embellished the simile, comparing Sam to the biblical Shadrach, Meshach, and Abednego: "Our friend entered the fiery furnace a man and emerged as a hero." Howells echoed the encomium. "Clemens's behavior in this matter redounded to his glory among the nations of the whole earth," he declared, "and especially in this nation, so wrapped in commerce and so little used to honor among its many thieves. He had behaved like Walter Scott, as millions rejoiced to know. . . . No doubt it will be put to his credit in the books of the Recording Angel." Even on the fringe of Sam's circle of friends, Owen Wister applauded his achievement: "His gallant lecture journey round the world was over, his heavy load of debt paid off by the sole exertion of his genius." His heroism was acclaimed in verse and song by poets such as Horace MacGrath:

> Mark Twain, a name known near and far,
> At Sunday school, at hotel bar,
> On mountain peaks, in valleys deep—
> Mark Twain, whose books made Darwin sleep!
> They've fed him oft in London town,
> This humorist of great renown;

They wined him in the gay Paree
Where Mark first learned to say his 'Oui.'
They've beered him well in old Berlin,
The Kaiser kindly took him in,
And Mark he told him how he thought
The German language should be taught.
Vienna, too, has fed him some
He struck the Reichsrath stark and dumb
When he got up and told them how
They ought to run a friendly row.
He took Australia in Transvaal,
Meandered round the Chinese wall,
Waltzed grandly through the Hindo land
And shook the Rajahs by the hand.
He paid his debts (we wish we could!)
And now he says he will be good
And quit the platform once for all,
And give some other men the call.
And now he's home again once more,
Again upon the mother shore;
His friends do nothing else but treat,
While Mark's done nought but eat and eat.
Oh, may the day be far from here
When Mark shall take his final bier,
And he himself be but a name
Emblazoned in the Hall of Fame.

Sam promoted the legend of his own financial valor, too, in interviews ("I was able to pay off every cent") and speeches. Thirty years later Hamlin Garland remembered Sam's welcome-home dinner at the Lotos Club when "he feelingly announced to us that he had paid off the debt with which for so long a time he had been burdened. It was humorous, of course, but it was more than that; it was a brave and manly and exultant speech." As late as July 1907, at a banquet in his honor in Liverpool, he wept as he recalled that "it was my wife who insisted upon my going into the world again to earn 100 percent for every dollar I owed."[51] The implication that he had done so was also almost faithful to the facts.

Sam played the part of the literary lion throughout the twenty months he resided in Vienna. He sat for two busts during his stay, both begun late in

1897, one executed by Ernst Hegenbarth in his studio in the Prater, the other by Teresa Feodorowna Ries, "a quaint & naïve & interesting" Russian sculptor" whose work was later displayed at the 1900 Paris Exhibition.

Figure 5. Samuel Clemens posing for Teresa Feodorowna Ries in Vienna. Illustration from *McClure's*, May 1898.

He became a regular theatergoer and his movements were routinely reported in the local press. On October 19, soon after settling in the city, he toured the new Burgtheater and "expressed himself with great enthusiasm about the gorgeous playhouse." He returned later to the theater—"that wonder of the world for grace and beauty and richness and splendor and costliness," as he called it—for performances of Arthur Schnitzler's *Liebelei* (Love games), Alfred von Berger's *Habsburg*, Adolf von Wilbrandt's morality play *Der Meister von Palmyra*, and Gerhart Hauptmann's *Die versunkene Glocke* (The sunken bell). On Thanksgiving—the same day the Austrian government "went insane" in the Reichsrath, coincidentally—the Clemenses were among the two hundred Americans who attended the holiday reception at the Palais Springer, Ambassador Tower's residence, where they heard a recital by the concert pianist Mary Elizabeth Hallock of Philadelphia, another of Leschetizky's students. As Sam reported to a Viennese newspaper, the reception revealed that twice as many Americans lived in the city as had been supposed, the men all medical students, the women all students of the maestro. Katy Leary went even further, reminiscing that the piano master "made wives of most of his students." Because Leschetizky routinely invited the Clemens family to join him in his box at the Hofopera, Sam frequented the Viennese opera, attending productions of Richard Wagner's *Die Walküre*, Pietro Mascagni's *Cavalleria rusticana*, Georges Bizet's *Carmen*, Wolfgang Amadeus Mozart's *Die Zauberflöte* (*The Magic Flute*), Giuseppe Verdi's *La Traviata*, Ludwig von Beethoven's *Fidelio*, Bedřich Smetana's *Dalibor*, and Lorenzo Perosi's oratoria *La risuzzezione di Cristo*. In early December 1897, Sam witnessed the premiere of Charles Weinberger's operetta *Blumen Mary* (*Mary's Flower Shop*), with book and lyrics by Alexander Landesburg and Leo Stein, Gertrude Stein's older brother, at the Theater an der Wien. Archduke Franz Ferdinand, whose assassination at Sarajevo in 1914 triggered World War I, was seated in an adjacent box. Before the end of the year, Sam, Clara, and Jean attended a performance of Johann Strauss's newest waltz "An der Elbe" conducted by the seventy-two-year-old Waltz King at the Große Musikvereinssaale and were introduced to the composer. On January 5, 1898, Sam saw the premiere of Herzl's Jewish-problem play *Das neue Ghetto* at the Carltheater—both he and Sigmund Freud received complimentary tickets, though there is no evidence the two men actually met. Sam decided soon afterward to translate the play into English, though after a false start or two he dropped the idea.[52]

Nevertheless, his decision to adapt Herzl's drama reflected his broader desire to develop several plays during his stay in Vienna. As he wrote Howells, "I don't know that I can write a play that will play; but no matter, I'll write half a dozen that won't." According to Frank Marshall White, Sam had started to write a stage comedy before he left London the previous July. If so, it was either a script entirely lost to scholarship or, more likely, an early theatrical adaptation of his short story "Is He Living or Is He Dead?" White suggested that it "might be suitable for publication" in a literary supplement to a newspaper, though Sam resisted the idea:

> It wouldn't do to print the Comedy because it would destroy the stage-rights in England & could damage it in America. That would be rather sorrowful, after all the work I have put on it. I don't mean that I have done such a power of work in writing the Comedy, but in trying to cut it down so that it will play

> inside of a week. I am still at that—chopping off at one end & adding on at the other. I have got it now where one end is short enough, but I am in more trouble than ever about the other. There seems to be something wrong about my method.

In mid-January 1898, he returned to the three-act comedy now simply titled *Is He Dead?* Both story and play are premised on the idea that, whatever their merit or lack thereof, objets d'art increase in value after the death of the artist. Sam illustrated the idea by burlesquing the career of the French painter Jean-François Millet, a founder of the Barbizon school, most of whose canvases became pricey collectors' items only after his passing. In the play, Millet both dashes off dozens of paintings and fakes his death to boost their sale price. Sam even slipped into the script an allusion to the Dreyfus affair, with Millet declaring at one point, "When France has committed herself to the expression of a belief, she will die a hundred thousand deaths rather than confess she has been in the wrong." Sam finished the play in late January and bragged to Rogers that Livy "thinks it is very bully. I think myself that for an ignorant first attempt it lacks a good deal of being bad." He sent the manuscript to his Bram Stoker and on February 3 several papers in the United States announced it would be "simultaneously produced in London and New York." But then Stoker delivered his verdict. "On a first reading" he did not "much believe in my play," but he promised "to examine it more closely." A week later, Stoker reported that while the play might succeed in America, it was unsuited to the English stage, in his opinion, whereupon Sam asked Rogers to be his theatrical agent because Stoker was "too slow and uncertain and unsatisfactory." Some New York producers eventually reported that, were the script doctored "by some clever and practical dramatist, particularly in the last act," it might be performed satisfactorily. The premise was "certainly unique and the treatment of some of the scenes very humorous." Rather than toy with the project any longer, however, Sam instructed Rogers to put the script "*in the fire*. God will bless you. I too. I started in to convince myself that I could write a play or couldn't. I'm convinced. Nothing can disturb that conviction."[53]

But in the interim Sam squandered weeks of work on other plays. He turned first to Philipp Langmann's *Bartel Turaser*, a three-act proletarian drama that had created a stir in Vienna. He mailed his completed translation to Rogers on March 22 and it was advertised in early May for production in London and New York during the fall season, but it was never staged. After attending a performance of Oscar Blumenthal and Gustav Kadelburg's *Hans Huckebein* in March, he considered adapting it for the American stage but F. C. Burnand had already secured English translation rights to it. Meanwhile, Sam translated under contract a farce by Ernst Gettke and Alexander Engel entitled *Im Gegenfeuer* (In purgatory), finishing it in late July. Charles Frohman rejected the script on the grounds it was "all jabber and no play." In early June Sam reportedly planned to translate Blumenthal and Kadelburg's *Im Weissen Rössl* (The White Horse Inn), but no reference to this project again appears in the record. Little wonder Sam wrote Rogers around this time that he had wearied of translating "dull & stupid work & I'll do no more of it." Over the months Sam also collaborated with Sigmund Schlesinger on a pair of plays set in America to be staged at the Burgtheater: *Der Gegenkandidat, oder die Frauen Politiker* (The opposing candidate, or women politicians) and *Die Goldgräberin* (The woman gold miner), the former apparently in English and completed, the latter in German and never completed. According to Edgar H. Hemminghaus, neither Schlesinger nor Sam was sufficiently fluent in the other's language to facilitate their work together so they agreed to delay further collaboration "until they understood each other's tongue 'more perfectly.'"[54] In any case, both scripts have been lost.

During the summer of 1898, Sam and the American playwright Sydney Rosenfeld, on holiday in Vienna, agreed to collaborate on a comedy. This play may have been "Shackleford's Ghost," an undated fragment of which survives in the Mark Twain Papers, about an entrepreneur who develops a potion that makes people invisible. According to news reports at the time, Sam "evolved the scheme of it," gave Rosenfeld a "rough draft of the play as it has emerged from his foundry," and Daniel Frohman expressed interest in it, though in the end they postponed the partnership until Sam returned to the United States. They met on October 24, 1900, reportedly "went through several manuscripts" by Sam, conceived a play "in embryo," and as late as December 1903 Rosenfeld told an interviewer that he thought he and Sam could "cook up a few jokes between us."[55] But in truth they never resumed the collaboration. Perhaps they simply lost interest, but the pages of "Shackleford's Ghost" that are extant hint at the formidable obstacles that would have hampered the production: the dearth of action on an often empty stage occupied only by invisible actors and the need to develop a daunting array of special effects, such as the sudden appearance of footprints on the set.

Sam's repeated playwriting failures did not prevent him from expressing an opinion about Wilbrandt's masterpiece or about the state of the stage in America. In "About Play-Acting," published in the *Forum* for October 1898, he mused that *Der Meister von Palmyra* was "a great and metaphysical poem, and deeply fascinating," a play in which the heroine appears in a different form in each act, each of the five acts "contains an independent tragedy of its own," and Death in person stalks the stage. (After seeing the production a second time, Sam wrote Howells that "Death, with his gentleness and majesty, made the human grand-folk around him seem little & trivial & silly!") He lamented the frivolity of American theater, with its buffoonery and circus. "It seems to me," he argued, "that New York ought to have one theatre devoted to tragedy. With her three millions of population, and seventy outside millions to draw upon, she can afford it, she can support it." Instead, "you find her neglecting what is possibly the most effective of all the breeders and nurses and disseminators of high literary taste and lofty emotion—the tragic stage."[56]

"I have always felt friendly toward Satan," Sam announced in a fragment of autobiography written in Vienna during the winter of 1897–98. Inspired by *The Master of Palmyra*, he decided to undertake the "rehabilitation" of Satan's reputation. In fall 1897 he began to draft the first "mysterious stranger" manuscript, sometimes called the "pre-Eseldorf" version or "St. Petersburg fragment," about a satanic type who visits the fictionalized Hannibal of Sam's boyhood. After writing a few thousand words, he incorporated some of the elements in this draft into a second version begun in November and titled by editor William M. Gibson "The Chronicle of Young Satan," set in "Eseldorf" or "Asstown," a medieval village in Austria, visited by a young Satan named Philip Traum (or "dream" or perhaps better yet "trauma"). Sam's description of Eseldorf, with its "tranquil river" beyond which loomed "a tumbled expanse of forest-clothed hills cloven by winding gorges where the sun never penetrated" and "a precipice [that] overlooked the river," may owe as much to his adventures in Weggis, Heidelberg, and Vienna as to his memories of Hannibal. This version reincarnates the Manichean "two Providences" of the Widow Douglas and Miss Watson in *Adventures of Huckleberry Finn* (or the Deism of Thomas Paine and the Calvinism of his Presbyterian upbringing) in the characters of pious priest Father Peter and evil priest named Father Lueger after the anti-Semitic mayor of Vienna, later renamed Father Adolf; features an honest Jewish moneylender, rather than a stereotyped Shylock, named Solomon Isaacs; and is narrated by Theodore Fischer, leader of the village gang of boys, whom Sam associated with Huck Finn in his working notes (Fischer = Finn). Little Satan declares on good authority that "Man is made of dirt—I saw him made" and, moreover, "is a museum of disgusting diseases, a home of impurities; he comes today and is gone tomorrow, he begins as dirt and departs as a stench; I am of the aristocracy of the Imperishables. And man has the *Moral Sense*." Sam explained the meaning of the last phrase in a letter to the editor of the *Wiener Bilder* published on October 17, 1897: "There is a Moral Sense and there is an Immoral Sense. The Moral Sense teaches us what morality is and how to avoid it; the Immoral Sense teaches us what immorality is and how to enjoy it."[57] He worked on "The Chronicle of Young Satan" intermittently through the end of 1897 before laying the manuscript aside.

The evening of February 1, 1898, at the request of Countess Wydenbruck-Esterházy and Princess von Metternich, Sam performed before a packed house with "lots of standees" at five dollars per head in the Bösendorfer Saal to benefit the Alland Charity Hospital for Consumptives. A musical performance, including a piano recital by the fifteen-year-old prodigy Artur Schnabel, another of Leschetizky's students, preceded his lecture and, to Sam's consternation, doubled the length of the program he headlined. He finally opened his forty-five-minute reading with a few comments in his broken or "kitchen German," then recited his anecdote about the first watermelon he ever stole, "Jim Blaine and His Grandfather's Old Ram," "The Golden Arm," a short essay Paine later titled "Beauties of the German Language" (to avoid alienating the German speakers present with a repeat of "the horrors of the German language"), and closed with his comic ballad about the ornithorhyncus. The crowded audience included Countess and Princess Metternich, Prince and Princess Alois Liechtenstein, two other members of the imperial family "and four princes of lesser degree," "almost the whole of the English and American colonies" in Vienna, and three other patrons of the hospital: U.S. ambassador Charlemagne Tower, his wife Helen Tower, and Sigmund Freud. "I taught the whole of them how to steal watermelons," Sam bragged. Freud reported afterward that he had "treated myself to listening to our old friend Mark Twain in person, which was a sheer delight." However, as a British critic remarked, "only the English and Americans enjoyed him to the full. The others had to be satisfied with the varying expression and the eloquent mimicry of the great humorist. Many carried bitter disappointment home with them." After his reading, Sam was introduced to Countess Bardi, a princess of the Portuguese royal house by marriage and sister to the Austrian archduchess Maria Theresa. The countess was "a beautiful lady, with a beautiful spirit," Sam reported to Twichell, "& very cordial in her praises of my books & thanks to me for writing them; & glad to meet me face to face & shake me by the hand—just the kind of princess that adorns a fairy tale & makes it the prettiest tale there is."[58]

Even as he emerged from bankruptcy, Sam fairly itched to invest in other harebrained get-rich-quick schemes rooted in new but unproven technologies. "I was born with a speculative instinct," he allowed in his notebook, and he never repressed it. "Why didn't Laffan tell me about that Monotype Machine!"

he complained to Rogers. "I could have helped to get up that Company in London." He was briefly obsessed with the profit potential of a machine that converted peat moss mixed with cotton or wool into cheap fabric. It produced low-grade "stuff enough" to make "a suit of clothes for 36 cents" or cloth for "a cent or two a yard." In mid-March 1898 he learned that the American patents on Jan Szczepanik's Raster, a device for electronically copying images onto cloth and carpeting, "were not yet sold" and he began negotiations with the twenty-five-year-old former Austrian schoolteacher. One of Szczepanik's assistants remembered the morning in March 1898 when Sam "made the first of his many visits to the laboratory. Szczepanik showed him our several inventions, both finished and in preparation," including the "telectroscope" or "Fernseher," a forerunner of television. "The writer's grasp of the mechanical difficulties was amazingly accurate. He was deeply absorbed in the demonstrations." Sam was impressed by Szczepanik, who was "well born, educated, dresses nicely," and was "not a Paige, but a gentleman." Szczepanik sometimes visited Sam at the Metropole to drink beer and talk "till midnight." Sam was no less impressed by Szczepanik's laboratory, which occupied multiple floors of a commercial building in midtown Vienna, and the "Austrian Edison" had "inventions enough in his head to fill it to the roof." On March 18 they "entered into an agreement," as Sam jotted in his notebook—an option on the Raster "for 2 months at $1,500,000" payable in installments, with "the term of the Option to be extended if I should need it & ask for it." The machine "automatically punches the holes in the jacquard cards, and does it with mathematical accuracy. It will do for $1 what now costs $3" and "saves $9 out of $10 and the jacquard looms *must* have it." As Paine observes, "Again the air was full of gold—even the typesetter had never held out such prospects as this. The whole industry of carpet-making was to be revolutionized. When he had his option property signed, sealed, and delivered, he accounted himself a billionaire."[59] But Sam's enthusiastic calculations were based on outdated statistics—and that was only a small part of the problem.

From his perspective, he simply needed to raise investment capital to underwrite the development and sale of the designing machine. He turned first, of course, to his friend Rogers, who was unimpressed. The machine was only really profitable in factories that employed the Jacquard method of producing textiles with patterns, so its long-term profitability depended upon the spread of the method in the industry, a risky proposition. In fact, Rogers sent Sam a report in early April that "the number of Jacquard looms in use in America" was so limited that there was no reason "to develop the invention here." Rogers not only declined to invest money in the patent rights, he discouraged Sam from investing as well. Nor was Charley Langdon tempted to join when he and his son Jervis visited the Clemenses in Vienna for nine days in April. Two Gobelins or tapestries woven by Szczepanik's new loom, one of them with Sam's portrait, were exhibited at the Vienna Jubilee Exhibition that summer but attracted scant attention.[60]

During his months in Vienna, Sam was introduced to yet another product he thought would make his next fortune: "Vienna albumen" or plasmon, a powdered, high-protein concentrate derived from skim milk. He claimed that a single teaspoonful of plasmon, a purported miracle food, contained nutriment "equivalent to an ordinary beefsteak" and a pound of it the equivalent of sixteen pounds of beef. The only "needful thing is to get the Plasmon into the stomach—dissolved or in clods or petrified or any way, so it gets there. The stomach will praise God and do the rest." It cured the dyspepsia from which he suffered for years, he claimed, and for a man of little faith he vouchsafed extraordinary confidence in its healing properties. An ingredient even today in some prepared European foods, including biscuits, oats, and chocolate, plasmon never produced the medicinal wonders Sam claimed for it. Nevertheless, he promoted its benefits as unwaveringly as a peddler of patent medicines or a snake oil salesman. Howells "was not surprised to learn" from Sam in 1900

> that "the damned human race" was to be saved by plasmon, if anything, and that my first duty was to visit the plasmon agency with him, and procure enough plasmon to secure my family against the ills it was heir to for evermore. I did not immediately understand that plasmon was one of the investments which he had made from "the substance of things hoped for," and in the destiny of a disastrous disappointment. But after paying off the creditors of his late publishing firm, he had to do something with his money, and it was not his fault if he did not make a fortune out of plasmon.

Like the dehydrated foods storehoused by survivalists a century later, plasmon sold well, especially in "belly-plagued England." While in Vienna he was unable to invest in the product but he kept track of it and in April 1900 he bought £5,000 worth of stock in the Plasmon Company of London and was appointed to a seat on its board of directors. He asked Rogers to send him half the money he required without revealing the nature of his purchase or the total amount he had spent. "Pretty soon I will tell you what it is I have bought," he assured his financial adviser, and "then you will see that I am thoughtful and wise."[61]

The Clemenses summered in 1898 in Kaltenleutgeben, a town famous for its baths located in the Vienna Woods a dozen miles from the center of the city. Sam had begun half facetiously to advocate for an eclectic approach to medical treatment: "A flight to Marienbad to get rid of fat; a flight to Carlsbad to get rid of rheumatism; a flight to Kalteneutgeben to take the water cure and get rid of the rest of the diseases." The latter resort was so close "you can stand in Vienna and toss a biscuit" there "with a twelve-inch gun," he joked. "You can run out thither at any time of the day; you go by phenomenally slow trains, and yet inside of an hour you have exchanged the glare and swelter of the city for wooded hills, and shady forest paths, and soft cool airs, and the music of birds, and repose and the peace of paradise." Their reasons for the retreat were as therapeutic as they were recreational. Not only was Livy in frail health—she had rarely socialized outside the Metropole in the eight months since their arrival in the city—but Jean's condition was increasingly worrisome. For years she had experienced "blackouts" or fainting spells, later diagnosed as petit mal seizures, but in February 1896, while her parents were traveling in India, she suffered her first grand mal seizure and a second "quite near the first." She was sedated daily with toxic bromides which seemed to alleviate the epilepsy until the spring of 1897, when they began to recur, with two in the summer, one in late September 1897 soon after the Clemenses' arrival in Vienna, and another on January 2, 1898. Sam sought the advice of Heinrich Obersteiner, a prominent Viennese neurologist, and the physician Wilhelm Winternitz, the "father of Austrian hydrotherapy" who owned the *Wasserheilanstalt* in Kaltenleutgeben. Winternitz even made a house call to the Metropole on March 28 to ask whether the medicinal waters would "suit the complexion of [the Clemenses'] ailments." Sam notified Rogers a month later that the family had rented at "economical cost" a "pleasantly situated" house with a garden, "satisfactorily furnished, at a little health-resort an hour from Vienna—beautiful woods all about," where "Mrs. Clemens & Jean will take the baths."[62]

They moved to the Villa Paulhof on May 20, immediately hired four servants, including a cook, and remained there almost without interruption for the next six months. Though a few of their Viennese friends also summered in the village, including Countess Wydenbruck-Esterházy, Carmen Sylva, Mme von Dutschka, and Countess Bardi, they were relatively isolated and alone most of the time. Their Hartford friends the Reverend Edwin P. Parker and A. C. Dunham, president of the Hartford Electric Light Company, visited for two days in the first week in July. Otherwise, Sam exploited the seclusion to write, much as he had spent his summers at Quarry Farm. Livy reported that she had "not known Mr. Clemens for years to write with so much pleasure and energy as he has done during this past summer." One of the first pieces he composed was a humorous sketch about the resort, "At the Appetite Cure," finished on May 30 and published in the August 1898 number of *Cosmopolitan*. The humor of the piece is implicit in the title: if appetite is a disease, the "appetite cure" is starvation. The bill of fare at the resort was "packed with dishes calculated to gag a cannibal," he joked, and "the idea of coaxing a sick man's appetite back with this buzzard-fare is clear insanity."[63]

During this period Sam also tinkered with his "gospel" *What Is Man?*, drafted several chapters of his autobiography, and sent a public letter declining an invitation to attend the Fourth of July banquet for American dignitaries in Leipzig. "It costs me a pang to lose this Fourth in solitude when the fortunate may get on their feet and shout," he admitted to the U.S. consul there, but he was tied to his desk. "Ordinarily I should not care, but I care this time, for this is not an ordinary Fourth. On the contrary, it is a memorable one—the most memorable which the flag has known" since the end of the Civil War. "This one marks the burial of the estrangement which has existed so long and so perniciously between England and America, a welcome condition of things, which, if wisely nursed and made permanent, can be of inestimable value to both nations and incidentally to the world."[64]

Sam devoted much of July 1898 to writing "Concerning the Jews," his analysis of anti-Semitism in Austro-Hungary. On the surface, he professed a brand of philo-Semitism. As Clara insisted, her father "always grew eloquent in defense of Christ's race" and, as if to prove it, Sam noted in his journal tongue-in-cheek that "I hold in just as much reverence that little Jew baby that was born in Bethlehem nineteen centuries ago as if it had been a Christian baby." More recently, Dan Vogel has asserted that "there was no anti-Jewish prejudice in Mark Twain." In the first part of the seven-thousand-word essay Sam indeed affirmed that "the Jew is not a disturber of the peace of any country. Even his enemies will concede that." Dreyfus, "the most famously misused Jew of modern times," was a perfect example. "He is not a loafer, he is not a sot, he is not noisy, he is not a brawler nor a rioter, he is not quarrelsome. . . . That the Jewish home is a home in the truest sense is a fact which no one will dispute. . . . The Jew is not a burden on the charities of the state nor of the city." But, Sam suggested, "the Jew has his other side." Though "a frequent and faithful and capable" civil servant, he exhibits "an unpatriotic disinclination to stand by the flag as a soldier." Sam attributed Jewish persecution not to religious prejudice but to their superior business acumen, a common and historic anti-Semitic trope. A natural-born capitalist, according to Sam, "the Jew is a money-getter and in getting his money he is a very serious obstruction to less capable neighbors who are on the same quest." He asserted "that in Russia, Austria, and Germany"—he pointedly omitted the United States—"nine-tenths of the hostility to the Jew comes from the average Christian's inability to compete successfully with the average Jew in business—in either straight business or the questionable sort." Anti-Semitism was "a trade union boycott in disguise"—the resistance of workers to their Jewish employers. Only in Scotland were Jews equaled in avarice by Christians, according to Sam, who thus libeled two ethnic stereotypes with one stone. Nor do Jews assimilate, according to Sam: "A Jew will never be a citizen; he will simply live in the cities of others," he thought. "By his make and ways he is substantially a foreigner wherever he may be, and even the angels dislike a foreigner." Yet he also opposed Theodor Herzl's Zionism, the movement to repatriate Palestine and establish a Jewish state. "Were the Jews to segregate themselves in the way suggested," Sam feared, "they would afford an easy means to their own extermination." He was delighted with the essay when he completed it. "The Jew article in my gem of the ocean," he wrote Rogers.

> I have taken a world of pleasure in writing it and doctoring it and polishing it and fussing at it. Neither Jew *nor* Christian will approve of it, but people who are neither Jews nor Christians will, for they are in a condition to know truth when they see it. I really believe that I am the only one in the world who is equipped to write upon the subject without prejudice. For I am without prejudice. It is my hope that both the Christians and the Jews will be damned.

Henry Mills Alden pronounced the article "timely" when he accepted it, but he might as well have damned it as too topical. He paid Sam a mere $500 for the manuscript and held it for a year before publishing it in the September 1899 number of *Harper's Monthly*.[65]

Despite his profession of philo-Semitism, and however well-intentioned it may have been, Sam reinforced and perpetuated a number of stereotypes in the essay. Though he claimed he was "quite sure that (bar one) [the French] I have no race prejudices," according to Jordan Lesslie "very strong proof can be adduced . . . that he is very much beset by race prejudice." Rabbi Mayer S. Levy of San Francisco sharply rebuked Sam for disseminating information "not only tinged with malice and prejudice" but "incorrect and false." Both Levy and Simon Wolf challenged the claim that Jews were disinclined to serve in the military, Levy citing Jewish heroes who served in the American War of Independence and the Civil War, Wolf referring Sam to his book *The American Jew as Patriot, Soldier, and Citizen* (1895). As a result, Sam retracted the charge, confessed his ignorance of the truth, and issued an apology in a "Postscript—The Jew as a Soldier" (1904) usually reprinted as an appendix to his original essay. Rabbi E. N. Calisch of Richmond corrected Sam's mistaken notion that most anti-Semitism was caused by business rivalry; rather, "it is the identification of the Jewish people" as "Christ-killers," a point reiterated by Cyrus L. Sulzberger, the great-grandfather of *New York Times* publisher Arthur Ochs Sulzberger Jr., in *American Hebrew*. *Die Welt*, the Zionist weekly in Vienna founded and edited by Sam's friend Herzl, regretted that even "this freest mind of a free country is tainted with several prejudices" and that Sam "repeated in his essay more than one false and long since disproven assertion." His comments about the "rapacity of the Jews" and their "unpatriotic dislike against bearing arms . . . could have been written just as well by some European anti-Semites." The *Jewish Chronicle* ("Of all such advocates, we can but say 'Heaven save us from our friends'") and *Jewish World* ("a well-intentioned article weakened by sundry jokes by no means aimed against Jews but which prevent many people taking the author seriously") in London, as well as the *Indianapolis Journal* ("However clearly he may see some things, he fails to see others in the right light"), in effect threw up their hands. Surprisingly, Sam's essay favorably impressed Freud, who published a precis of it in "A Comment on Anti-Semitism" in the Parisian immigrant paper *Die Zukunft* in November 1938. But only gentiles praised the essay without qualification. Frank Bliss called it "a bang-up thing . . . one of the best serious articles you have ever done." The Congregationalist paper the Chicago *Advance* averred that it "contains much humor, much right feeling toward the Jews, and much shrewd sense." The London correspondent of the *Jewish Herald* of Victoria (written "with impartiality, scrupulous fairness, and insight") and the *Southern Cross* of Adelaide (exhibits "with true courage and humanity") echoed the approval. But no amount of praise can obscure the fact that American Nazis and others cited the essay in anti-Semitic propaganda during the 1930s.[66]

After completing "Concerning the Jews" and while still in Kaltenleutgeben, Sam hit upon a new way to write the narrative eventually entitled "Which Was the Dream?" His original plan "was a totally impossible one—for *me*; but a new plan suggested itself & straight way the tale began to slide from the pen with ease & confidence," as he wrote Howells. The first section of about twelve thousand words—which was all he completed—"will be comedy" but a "tragedy-trap" for the unsuspecting reader. Sam allegorized his bankruptcy and blackguarded Webster, here renamed Sedgewick, whom the narrator "trusted . . . as no human being ought to be trusted" and who "destroyed me." When he learns that he is penniless, he protests that "I shall try my best while I live to do that and clear away the debts put upon me by a trusted subordinate; but I am *not* a dishonest man, whatever you may think." In the wake of his financial ruin, he declares—as Sam might have said—"Almost every paper in the land used me generously. There was but one man

[Thomas Russell] who was bitter against me; even the injured bankers made no trouble, and ceased from saying harsh things about me."[67]

In his journal for August 10, 1898, moreover, Sam recounted a dream he had the night before about "a whaling cruise in a drop of water. Not by microscope, but *actually*. This would mean a reduction of the participants to a minuteness which would make them nearly invisible to God, and He wouldn't be interested in them any longer." He soon began a horror story, never completed, which Bernard DeVoto entitled "The Great Dark." The narrator peers through a microscope at a drop of "stale water from a puddle in the carriage-house" and spies monstrous protozoa. Translated to microscopic size in a dream—or is it a dream?—he voyages for years in darkness with his family aboard a ship in the drop of water, on seas "unknown, uncharted, unexplored" and filled with monsters. He is shadowed by "the Superintendent of Dreams" who, as DeVoto observed, resembles the Deity in *What Is Man?*[68] The ocean in a drop of water evaporates under the Great White Glare, the light from the reflector on the microscope, whereupon the fragment abruptly breaks off.

The same day Sam wrote Howells about his new dream narrative, he left with his family on a vacation from their vacation, a ten-day excursion to the Salzkammergut. He had been disappointed with the water-cure in Kaltenleutgeben. "I expected it to do great things for Mrs. Clemens," he wrote Rogers, "but I think she is not as strong as she was when she began." After a long and uncomfortable train trip, they landed in the Hotel Post in Bad Ischl and spent a week gadding about "among the lakes and mountains to rest-up Mrs. Clemens." On August 22 Leschetitzky shepherded them to Hallstatt, where the musician had a summer house near the Hallstätter See, a "beautiful lake in a cup of precipices" and a "surface littered with refuse & sewer-contributions." Traveling back to Kaltenleutgeben on August 27, Sam paused in Vienna to finalize an agreement with Josef Krantz for winter quarters in the new Hotel Krantz, "a kind of Splendid Waldorf" overlooking the Neuer Markt in the center of the city. "I used to be a little ashamed when Ambassadors & dukes & such called on us in that rusty & rather shabby Metropole," he admitted to Rogers, "but they'll mistake us for millionaires next fall & will probably lend us money." He had negotiated for a suite on the fourth floor—"a dining room, a parlor, a music-parlor, a study, and 4 bedrooms" with "bathrooms attached to 3 of the bedrooms"—plus meals for five for a rent of 2,800 francs or $560 a month, only about $60 a month more than the Metropole had charged for fewer rooms and amenities but over $16,000 per month today. As extravagant as this arrangement may seem, Sam insisted that "we couldn't get the half of it in New York for the same money." Josef Krantz knocked down the price because, as he told Sam, his residence in the hotel "would be the best advertisement they could have." As good as his word, Krantz advertised Sam's presence in his house over four thousand miles away in the *New York Tribune*.[69]

Figure 6. Advertisement for the Hotel Krantz in Vienna, *New York Tribune*, April 19, 1899.

On September 10, 1898, the sixty-year-old Empress Elisabeth of Austria was assassinated at the Hôtel Beau-Rivage in Geneva by an Italian anarchist. Sam learned the news that evening from Countess Wydenbruck-Esterházy, his Kaltenleutgeben neighbor and a personal friend of the empress, who "burst in at the gate in the deep dusk of the evening" and announced "in a voice broken with tears, 'My God the Empress is murdered.'" Livy reported that the countess "looked so white & was so breathless that I thought she would faint. I gave her some brandy to steady her a little." Sam was unnerved by the calamity, informing Twichell that the "good & unoffending lady" had been "killed by a mad-man & I am living in the midst of world-history again. The Queen's jubilee last year, the invasion of the Reichsrath by the police, & now this murder, which will still be talked of & described & painted a thousand years from now." The buildings in Vienna were soon draped in black and, as Sam wrote Rogers, "the lamentings (particularly in Hungary) are deep & universal. I have not seen anything like it since General Grant died." On September 17 Sam observed from the windows of the Hotel Krantz the empress's funeral at the old Capuchin Church across the Neuer Markt. Sam described the events of the day in his bitter essay "The

Memorable Assassination," in which he raged at the killer: "without gifts, without talents, without education, without morals, without character, without any born charm or any acquired one, without a single grace of mind or heart or hand," this "mangy, offensive, empty, unwashed, vulgar, gross, mephitic, timid, sneaking human polecat," this "sarcasm upon the human race," knifed and killed a lady who was "a grace to the human race and almost a justification of its creation." A month later, the Clemenses moved from the Metropole to their new quarters at the Krantz. But, more to the point, in his growing despair Sam increasingly misjudged the mainstream magazine market. "The Memorable Assassination" was declined by *Ladies' Home Journal*, *Harper's Monthly*, and *Century* and was not published until a generation later in *What Is Man? and Other Essays* (1917).[70]

Sam attempted at this moment to publish a bawdy parody of Edward FitzGerald's translation of *The Rubáiyát of Omar Khayyam* (1859) under the title "Omar's Old Age." He submitted a sample of sixteen quatrains marked "Confidential" to Andrew Chatto and proposed publishing a total of fifty quatrains in a small edition for collectors. "Read them, then *burn* them at once," he cautioned Chatto, and "don't let any see them or hear about them." In one of the quatrains, "A Weaver's Beam," the aging "Omar" laments his impotence:

> Ah, now in Age a feeble stream we Piss,
> And maunder feebly over That & This,
> Thinking we Think—alas, we do but Dream—
> And wonder why our Moonings go amiss.
> Our sphincters growing lax in their dear Art,
> Their Grip relinquishing, in Whole or Part,
> We fall a Prey to confidence misplaced,
> And fart in places where we should not fart.
> A Weaver's beam—Handle of a Hoe—
> Or Bowsprit, then—now Thing of Dough:
> A story Change, lamented oft with Tears
> At Midnight by the Master of the Show.
> Behold—the Penis mightier than the Sword,
> That leapt from Sheath at any heating Word
> So long ago—now peaceful lies, and calm,
> And dream unmoved of ancient Conquests scored.

Chatto was impressed—he preserved the manuscript rather than destroy it as Sam had requested—but he also threw cold water on the project. "As a scathing satire on the crazy literary taste of today" he considered the sample of quatrains

> a work of great genius—But in all my experience I have never known a case in which the writer of works of like inspiration did not at some time in after life regret the printing of them. It would be an easy matter of course for us at a moderate expense to have such a *brochure* set up in *Edition de Luxe* for private circulation amongst a select few limited to say 30 copies which number I think could be distributed amongst collectors at perhaps £10 to £20 each.

But such an edition would hardly be worth the trouble and expense and, worse yet, Chatto concluded, "all the press men would expect free copies!"[71]

In early November 1898 Sam began a third version of "The Mysterious Stranger" set back in St. Petersburg and featuring Huck and Tom. He outlined the plot of this "Schoolhouse Hill" or "Hannibal" draft in his notebook:

> Story of little Satan Jr. who came to Hannibal, went to school, was popular and greatly liked by those who knew his secret. The others were jealous and the girls didn't like him because he smelled of brimstone. He was always doing miracles—his pals knew they were miracles, the others thought they were mysteries. . . . In the early days he takes Tom & Huck down to stay over Sunday in hell—gatekeeper doesn't recognize him in disguise & asks for tickets—then is going to turn them out (it is raining) when L[ittle] S[atan] privately tells him who he is & is obsequiously received.

Much as young Satan brags that Lucifer was his uncle, Sam joked a few weeks later that he too was Satan's nephew, as if he identified with the amoral trickster figure. He worked on this draft only for a few weeks before laying it aside. But months later he reiterated to Howells his intent to "tell what I think of man, & how he is constructed, & what a shabby poor ridiculous thing he is" in some version of the narrative.[72]

Sam never again lectured for money after his 1895–96 world tour but he never abandoned the "gratis" platform. "I don't like lecturing," he bluntly informed James Pond from Vienna in the spring of 1899. "I like to talk for nothing about twice a year; but talking for money is *work*, and that takes the pleasure out of it. I do not believe you could offer me terms that would dissolve my prejudices against the platform. I do not expect to see a platform again until the wolf commands." On March 8, 1899, at the request of Countess Wydenbruck-Esterházy, Sam again read at a benefit for the Alland Charity Hospital for Consumptives on the same program as the

Viennese actress Auguste von Wilbrandt-Baudius, wife of the playwright Adolf von Wilbrandt, in the crowded festival hall of the Kaufmännische Verein. Though a practiced performer, and though she opened the program, Frau von Wilbrandt failed to time her presentation, much to Sam's disgust. She "was wholly ignorant of the length of her pieces. I told her she must restrict herself to 30 minutes, so that I could have 40," and "she came loaded with an hour's ammunition & confessed that she was only guessing at its bulk. She occupied the stage just an hour, & then I came before a perishing audience that had the death-rattle in its throat." He spoke German "with his native nasal accent" for five minutes before shifting to English. He saved the day only by omitting "The Genuine Mexican Plug" from his planned readings. According to press accounts, the audience, including Charlemagne and Helen Tower, was "kept laughing throughout the whole reading" and Sam was presented with "a superb laurel wreath" at the close. But Bettina Wirth of the London *Daily News* filed a dissenting report: "I am afraid the princesses, countesses, and baronesses, though they did honor to their English governesses, did not quite understand what it was all about."[73]

Two weeks later, on March 23, the Clemens clan railed to Budapest, where he was booked "for a lecture & a dinner-speech & some private parties & things." He admitted to Laurence Hutton that he had repeatedly "sworn off from the platform" but "already I have fell again. Nothing has saved me from being a harlot but my sex." Aboard the train he was interviewed in German by a reporter for the *Pesti Napló* and during the week he was in the city he was treated as a celebrity, with a luncheon at the Journalists Club; another lunch with Ferenc Kossuth, son of Louis Kossuth, leader of the Hungarian Revolution of 1848; and an afternoon tea party he attended with Clara and Jean. As Anna Katona notes, "There was music, the girls learned Hungarian dances, and above all, there was lively conversation, at least part of it in English." Sam "must have enjoyed the party; he stayed from quarter past three to eight in the evening," and he hastened to assure Howells that "those Hungarians are lovely people." The evening of March 25 he lectured for expenses only in the great hall of the Lipótvárosi Kaszinó before the Hungarian Journalists' Association at a banquet marking the fifty-first anniversary of freedom of the press in Hungary. Before many members of the Hungarian government he had planned to joke about the Ausgleich and propose from the podium that they negotiate and ratify its terms then and there: "If you will act for Hungary I shall be quite willing to act for Austria." Sam was "willing to make any concession you want, just so we get it settled. . . . In return for these concessions I am willing to take anything in reason, and I think we may consider the business settled and the

Ausgleich ausgegloschen at least for ten solid years, and we will sign the papers in blank and do it here and now." But when he rose to speak, as he admitted to Twichell, "I got to talking with interest on a text dropped by the introducer, & I had a very good time; but when I got down to my 'set' speech it had wholly disappeared out of my memory," which "is old and rickety and cannot stand the strain." Nevertheless, according to the press reports, "his humorous sallies were keenly appreciated." Unfortunately, Livy was ill on the trip so the farewell banquet in Sam's honor on March 29 was canceled and the family returned to Vienna the next day in a special Pullman car provided by the Hungarian railroad.[74]

Sam was not only an unofficial U.S. envoy in Austria during his residence there, he was a fixture at the official U.S. embassy and a favored guest of Ambassador Charlemagne Tower at diplomatic functions. Though his secretary Isabel Lyon purported a decade later that "the King," as she called Sam, was snubbed socially by Tower during his tenure in Vienna, that the ambassador "never treated the Clemenses very well," all contemporary evidence belies the claim. Sam attended an embassy dinner on February 10, 1898, where he met the German, Italian, Portuguese, Swedish, and Romanian ambassadors, and he was obliged "to shake hands incessantly" at the annual Thanksgiving celebration for Americans in late November that year. As if he were an actual U.S. diplomat, Sam became an A-list guest in Austrian ambassadorial circles; for example, he was invited by Agenor Maria Gołuchowski, the Austrian minister of foreign affairs, to attend his annual dinner for envoys in the spring of 1899, the first time "a civilian, without official rank or title, was ever invited to so exclusive an affair." When Tower was reassigned to St. Petersburg as the ambassador to Russia, moreover, Sam was sincerely sorry he was leaving. At the farewell banquet in Tower's honor at the Hotel Bristol on February 28, 1899, Sam proposed the toast of the evening, declaring that Tower was "the best ambassador the American nation has ever sent forth." A multilingual and well-traveled sophisticate, Tower had been "the right man in the right place" when he headed the U.S. embassy in Vienna.[75]

Not so his successor Addison Harris, a Republican apparatchik from Indiana appointed chief of the U.S. mission in Vienna by William McKinley. Harris was too poor or miserly to rent the palatial house where Tower had lived, instead resuming "the shabby American tradition" among its diplomats, as Sam put it, by residing in a single apartment at the Krantz. He spoke no German and bemoaned his ignorance of European history. Sam was unimpressed and, in what Dolmetsch declares "probably the most scathing, vitriolic essay of his career," the still-unpublished "American Representation in Vienna," he denounced Harris for his lack of qualifications, concluding dismissively: "I wonder where our Government fishes for its average foreign-service officials."[76]

Harris's arrival on the scene may have been a factor in Sam's decision to leave Vienna. He admitted to a reporter for the New York *World* in March 1898 that he yearned to return to the United States. He was resolute that his family would never again live in the house in Hartford haunted by memories of Susy, but he thought they might afford to live in Princeton or Richmond or Washington or even New York. Sam wrote Twichell early in May that "business calls me to London indefinitely" and "the family have decided to go along." Clara had abandoned her piano studies in late 1898, soon after the Clemenses moved to the Krantz—after years of lessons she had decided "her hands were so small she didn't have any stretch—couldn't reach an octave," and so she could never become a great concert pianist—and was instead training for a singing career under the tutelage of the operatic contralto Marianne Brandt in Vienna.[77]

On May 21, on the eve of the Clemenses' scheduled departure from the city, Sam was invited to meet Emperor Franz Josef the afternoon of May 25. The overture came out of the blue, perhaps managed from behind the scenes by the Towers or a minor royal Sam had befriended over the months or, less likely, Addison Harris. Sam had never sought such an audience—it "had never occurred to him" to ask for one—but he happily lingered in the city an extra few days to honor the invitation. Arrayed in "swallow-tail coat, pin-striped trousers, silk hat, white gloves," Sam arrived at the Hofburg Palace at 1:00 p.m. in a carriage loaned to him by Harris and was immediately ushered by palace officials into the emperor's private study. Franz Josef welcomed him in English and "at once started talking quite freely," Sam told the Viennese press afterward, "and I wholly forgot, at first," that he had prepared an eighteen-word speech in German. Instead, "we were absorbed in a friendly conversation, which was quite informal." "Old Mutton Chops," as the emperor was nicknamed, complimented Sam on his literary successes and

> after a while in the course of our talk I remembered and told the Emperor I had prepared and memorized a very good speech but had forgotten it. He was very agreeable about it. He said a speech wasn't necessary. He seemed to be a most kind-hearted emperor, with a great deal of plain, good, attractive human nature about him. . . . I was greatly impressed by him, and I liked him exceedingly. His face is always the face of a pleasant man and he has a fine sense of humor. . . . He is a man as well as an emperor.

After listening to Sam utter "some strange and wonderful" sentences in German, the emperor complimented him on his mastery of the language.

They exchanged pleasantries for twenty minutes before "his Majesty bade Mr. Clemens farewell in a most kindly manner." Sam told the reporters back at the Hotel Krantz that "it was merely a pleasant and unembarrassed private conversation upon subjects not connected with the world's politics" and that the audience "will be numbered among my finest memories," a fitting coda to one of the most productive and rewarding periods of his life. During his final hours in the city, Sam told reporters, "I can truthfully say that in all my travels I have never felt so well as in this wonderful *gemütlichen* Vienna, a city from whose splendid yet graceful proportions I have derived so much inspiration." No one can live long there "without being caught completely by the spell of this city and her people. One gets settled in Vienna very soon, is happy there, and would never like to leave it."[78]

The Clemenses reluctantly left the next day for England. "The station seemed full of our beloved friends," Clara remembered, "and among them most distinguished men and women," including Leschetizky and Adolf von Wilbrandt. "My sister and I did not hide our feelings, but wept frankly with all the tragedy and youthful suffering in our hearts. While the inexorable revolution of the wheels started our journey we knew we were gazing on those dear faces for the last time."[79]

CHAPTER 8

London Fog

> **We live in a strange and unaccountable world; our birth is a mystery, our little life is a mystery and a trouble, we pass and are seen no more; all is mystery, mystery, mystery; we know not whence we came, nor why.**
>
> —Mark Twain, "Which Was the Dream?"

THEY RAILED FIRST to Prague, where they spent two days at the Chateau Lautschen at the invitation of the nobleman Prince Albert I of Thurn and Taxis. After stops in Nuremburg, Cologne, Brussels, Calais, and Dover, they arrived in London the evening of May 31 and registered at the Prince of Wales Hotel in De Vere Gardens, Kensington. As Katharine Clemens, James Ross Clemens's wife, remembered, they "had a charming big drawing room, very English in style with a large, round table in the center, consoles on the side, big English chairs and an open fireplace." On his part, Sam reported to Rogers that there was no convenience "known to civilization which it doesn't lack; there isn't a detail pertaining to its business which it isn't ignorant of." But after only two days, Clara was ordered by her doctor to the seashore for a week and the family decamped for Broadstairs, where, as Sam quipped, "it costs a shilling to look at a cup of coffee & two to drink it."[1]

Upon his return to London on June 9, Sam began to be wined and dined almost every day. At the Savage Club the evening of his arrival, he was awarded an honorary lifetime membership—one of only four the club had conferred in its history—and, in his toast, teased that he was "sorry to hear my name mentioned as one of the great authors, because they have a sad habit of dying off. Chaucer is dead. Spenser is dead, so is Milton, so is Shakespeare, and I am not feeling very well myself." The next day, along with the Prince of Wales, the Duke and Duchess of York, Ambassador Joseph Choate, Lord Herbert Kitchener of Khartoum, and Poultney Bigelow, he and Livy were guests at a garden party hosted by the Marquess of Salisbury at Hatfield House. He and Sir Spencer Walpole were banqueted by the Authors Club the evening of June 12 and in his post-prandial remarks Sam expressed relief that the South American border dispute between British Guiana and Venezuela had not erupted into a war between England and the U.S. The bond between the

English-speaking nations had been strengthened, he declared, by an "outburst of sympathy" across boundaries when Rudyard Kipling fell ill while in New York the previous February, and Sam concluded his remarks with a pun he claimed was eight days in the making: "Since England and America have been joined together in Kipling, may they not be severed in Twain." Over the next few days he supped with James Ross Clemens and Katharine Clemens in the dining room of the Queen's Gate Hotel in South Kensington; attended another dinner hosted by the National Club; and consulted with his London publishers Chatto and Windus about the forthcoming deluxe edition of his works. But he repeatedly declined the overtures of a reporter for the *London Leader* who pestered him for an interview. "You shall talk of authors, Austrians, Arkansaw, anything in the wide world & we will taboo Mark Twain," she sought to assure him. "Isn't that sweetly generous, and I won't ask the size of your socks or how many times a day you don't brush your hair." Sam was put off by her feigned familiarity and jotted on the envelope "Preserve this bitch's letter." He also cautioned his friend Howells, whom James Pond had offered to sponsor on a lecture tour, to beware of the manager's promises. In fact, Howells had already agreed to the deal so that he might take a break from the demands of writing but he soon regretted his decision. The following October, Sam consoled Howells, who was in the midst of a series of wearisome one-night stands across the midwest: "*I* know how you feel! I've been in hell myself. . . . Nothing is so lonesome as gadding around platforming."[2]

On June 15, Sam, Livy, Clara, and Jean dined at Bram Stoker's along with Henry Irving, Ellen Terry, Sarah Bernhardt, and Finley Peter Dunne before attending Gilbert and Sullivan's *H.M.S. Pinafore* at the Savoy with William Gillette.[3] The next day, Sam lunched with Choate and was dined by the Whitefriars at the Hotel Cecil in the evening. Attended by U.S. senator Chauncey Depew; Rear Admiral Sir Edward Chichester, the English naval commander at Manila; Winston Churchill, a hero of the Boer War and a rising Tory politician; M.P., journalist, and Irish nationalist T. P. O'Connor; novelists Beatrice Harridan and G. A. Henty; and about two hundred others, the formalities were chaired by Bigelow. "Received on rising with prolonged cheers" after the dinner, Sam spoke "in his happiest vein, causing much laughter and applause." After the dinner, Churchill sought out Sam and "inveigled him" into a separate room, where they chatted for several minutes. As they parted, Sam reportedly shook Churchill's hand and declared, "Well, I'm very glad to have met you, and am very interested in all you have said. I should like to meet you in a few years time—when you are a little younger."[4]

In the evening of June 19 Sam and Livy attended a performance of Victorien Sardou's *Robespierre* starring Irving and Ellen Terry at the Lyceum Theatre with complimentary tickets sent them by Bram Stoker. The next day he lunched with James Bryce, an influential member of parliament, and on June 21 he not only received an honorary membership in the Sesame Club and privileges at its clubhouse in Piccadilly but was invited by Irving to a midnight supper at the Beefsteak Room of the Lyceum, where he "told a series of stories with inimitable humor." The next day Sam and Livy were guests of the Archbishop of Canterbury for tea at Lambeth Palace in company with Walter Besant, Arthur Conan Doyle, and Henry Lucy. He attended meetings of the Savage Club and Kinsmen the next two evenings; a dinner at the U.S. embassy on June 28 with senators Mark Hanna and Henry Cabot Lodge and British politicians Joseph Chamberlain, George Wyndham, and Lord Charles Beresford; and a gathering of the New Vagabonds on "Ladies' Night" at the Holborn Restaurant on June 29 at which he spoke at length. He crossed paths again with Hanna during a visit to Windsor on July 1 and again with Hanna and Lodge at the embassy on the Fourth of July. That evening, Sam made the closing speech around midnight at the Hotel Cecil for the American Society before an audience of about four hundred, among them Booker T. Washington. He lamented the "business aspect" of the holiday for causing "loss of life, the crippling of thousands with its fireworks, and the burning down of property," and treaded lightly on the topic of the war in the Philippines.[5]

Sam and Livy originally intended to remain in London until the end of July and unwind over the summer either in the Scottish Highlands or on one of the Channel Islands before returning to the United States in the fall. But Jean's seizures had increased in frequency, often occurring twice a day, so the family changed their plans in order to seek treatment for her. Sam had experienced a bout of dysentery and, at the suggestion of Poultney Bigelow, who had recovered from a severe case of the ailment after treatment at the Swedish Institution in Eaton Square in London, he consulted Jonas Henrik Kellgren, its director. Sam was initially skeptical because Kellgren's so-called gymnastics or movement therapy proscribed all medicines, drugs, lotions, ointments and blisters, plasters, antiseptics, anesthetics, and even special diets—"no anything but the manipulations & exercises" of tissue and bones by the practitioner. Initially, this prohibition "prejudiced me against the system," he admitted, "for it smacked of Christian Science pretentiousness," but, always an advocate of alternative medicines, he "tried the treatment" and "saw that it would prop a person up physically, whether it could cure disease or not." After repeatedly visiting his sanitarium, Sam concluded that Kellgren and his assistants worked miracles: "These people cure a deadly *acute* malady with splendid swiftness & certainty—scarlet fever, diphtheria, lung-fever, bronchitis, peritonitis, broken bones, bad wounds, shoulders out of joint, &c." Better yet, Kellgren claimed he could cure nonhereditary epilepsy. In fact, he "was the first man who said he could cure her. He said it without hesitation." The treatment "might take a longer time then our patience could stand—a year, two years, three years—he could make no guess—but he could certainly cure her," because "he has cured cases like hers." Yet the only published study of the results of his treatment of grand mal seizures indicates he cured a total of only four patients. Jean's health had deteriorated over the previous three years, Sam complained to Rogers, although they "had tried the baths, and the doctors and everything—all no good." Plainly, no conventional doctor "will ever do her any good" given that "the best in the world have had charge of her for 3 years and haven't made an inch of progress toward a cure." So "what should we do? For one, I was willing to try anything that might turn the tide—except Christian Science." He described the therapy, which consisted mostly of physical massage similar to osteopathy, as a form of "vigorous exercise, *and other people do it for you*." Upon Kellgren's recommendation, they booked passage to his sanitarium in Sanna, Sweden.[6]

Sam, Livy, and Jean embarked on July 7 for Göteborg or "Godalmightyville (if that is the correct translation)," as he wrote the novelist Edmund Gosse. Clara continued her voice training in London until the end of the month. The next day they railed about four hours to Jönköping on the shores of Lake Vättern and rode by carriage three miles to Sanna, a health resort owned by Kellgren much as Kaltenleutgeben, the village where they had summered in 1898, had been managed by Winternitz. "I always felt so fresh & fine & young there that I grew insanely fond of the place," Sam remembered. Upon their arrival Kellgren stipulated that he would not treat Jean "if she took another dose of medicine of any kind"—this after she "had taken 2 doses of bromide every day for the previous 18 months,—frequently 3, less frequently 4, on two occasions 5, & on three occasions 6,—a grand total of 1300 doses of poison. The doctors didn't allow her to venture a day without the protection of 2 doses." They were "gradually destroying her" but "the great European & American specialists know no other way to modify the disease." Sam and Livy were alarmed by Kellgren's ban because "we did not know what might happen. Livy smuggled two doses to Jean on the 11th, the day before she was to begin; then we held our breath & stood from under." After only a week, as he confided to his notebook, the improvement in her condition was "so astonishing that we hardly venture to talk together about it lest it presently turn out to be only a transient flurry with nothing substantial about it." She had suffered no grand mal seizures and been "absent-minded only twice, instead of 15 or 20 times, as formerly. Kellgren says bad attacks are in store, but that she must weather them without resorting to drugs." Unfortunately, on July 20 she "fell in a spasm striking her head on the slop jar. A bad convulsion; she lay as if dead—face purple & no light in the eyes" and five days later she "had a convulsion in bed at noon—fortunately the Director [Kellgren] had just entered the room. It was tolerably severe. He relieved her. At 5 she had another while sitting on the porch, Livy & I present." Kellgren was unalarmed by the apparent setback and advised Sam and Livy in late August to "keep your grip." Jean was "full of life & go & energy & activity" and experienced no grand mal seizures for the next several weeks. Her "health booms along here in the most surprising & gratifying way," Sam reported to Rogers on August 22. "For the first time in 3 years we go to bed untroubled, & get up the same. We can pretend that trouble must come, & several times before her cure is perfect, but we do not bother about that—she is on the safe road." In mid-September, Sam gleefully reported to Sam Moffett that Jean had not "tasted medicine of any kind" in sixty-six days.[7]

The Clemenses also struggled with—and, truth be told, shared—the widespread prejudice that was associated with epilepsy. At the time the disease was considered a form of mental illness or even insanity, and epileptics were often ostracized not unlike lepers. As a result, Jean's diagnosis was a closely guarded secret. Sam never mentioned her malady in print or public interview, though this common prejudice may explain why Isabel Lyon later told Connecticut neighbors that Jean was "crazy." Sam revealed the nature of her affliction to his sister Pamela, nephew Samuel Moffett, Susan Crane, and Henry Rogers only in the strictest confidence. He never understood that epilepsy was a neurological disorder rather than some sort of brain fever or infection. As he wrote his nephew from Sanna, Jean was obliged to continue "the gymnastic treatment till the disease is eradicated." Over time, in the way Sam and others discussed Jean's malady it seemed to assume a life of its own. One of her physicians said she "had long been possessed by this hideous disease" as if the disease were a demon. After one of her convulsions, Sam wrote Rogers that he had seen "it" and that he had "seen it only three times before," as if it were a demonic presence. On at least one occasion he wrote "leprosy" when he meant "epilepsy" before striking it out. Another time he rejoiced that "the corner is turned, the back of the thing is broken." Even Jean in her diary remarked that "slight things" like "pleasure, distresses, annoyances and excitements" tended to "feed the disease and keep it in a thriving condition," as if it were a beast of prey.[8]

While residing in Sanna, despite insisting "there's nothing the matter with me," Sam took the movement cure simply "for the mental & physical refreshment it furnishes" and because it "makes me feel fine & gay all day. I have never taken any exercise, & I never shall; but I find that exercise *is* good, provided someone else takes it for me." Or as he wrote Richard Watson Gilder, "it takes all the old age out of you & sends you feeling like a bottle of champagne that's just been uncorked." Coincidentally, one of the assistants in Sanna who cared for Sam was Count Claës Lewenhaupt, who also served as their host and escort during their stay. Lewenhaupt or one of his coworkers remembered that Sam was "in excellent humor all summer. It was a real pleasure taking care of him. Three of us were in attendance. We took his pulse every morning" and then for about twenty minutes "we would give him a leg-roll, in which you hold the leg at the knee and at the foot and swing it around rapidly. The exercise always delighted him." During an excursion on Lake Vättern aboard the steamer *Per Brahe* on August 1, the sixty-three-year-old Clemens danced a sailor's jig "alone and with youthful vigor to the music of a concertina."[9]

Sam became a true believer in the therapy while living in Sanna. "This establishment here does not pretend to cure cancer & the other incurable diseases," he allowed in late July, but it undertakes to cure any curable disease, no matter what its nature is. By conversation with old patients I am becoming convinced that the claim is well based. Here they take a man who has been tied up in knots for years, & who can't sit & can't stand, & they work the knots out of him & make him walk. Sometimes it takes years, but in one case it has taken only two weeks; I am a witness to it." One formerly crippled man had "not been on his feet for 6 years, but he hobbles around on them now without a cane & has been doing it a week." Sam was not only convinced that Kellgren could "cure any disease that any physician can cure" but that "in many desperate cases he can restore health where no physicians can do it & where no physician will claim to be able to do it. . . . He does not make extravagant promises, but he *makes* promises, & if the patient" remains for the entire regimen of treatment "he makes the promise good." Sam spent half an hour daily in Kellgren's hospital "every day for 2 months" and "watched the miracles & seen them done." Kellgren "will take a chance at any ailment known to man"—Sam specifically mentioned typhoid, diphtheria, plague, cholera, scarlet fever, influenza, chronic bronchitis, lumbago, gastralgia complicated with jaundice, hemorrhoids, fractured bones, heart disease, and of course epilepsy—and "cure any that is curable."[10] Kellgren added to the list: pneumonia, migraines, peritonitis, sciatica, and tonsillitis. The only exceptions were "surgical cases where the knife must be used & dentistry." Sam even concluded that Susy had died of "assassination through ignorance. Kellgren would have cured her" of spinal meningitis "without any difficulty." In January 1900, he compiled "a list of 52 human ailments—common ones—and in this list I count 19 which the physician's art cannot cure. But there isn't one which Osteopathy or Kellgren cannot cure, if the patient comes early." After "watching the Kellgren business" for six months, Sam lost his respect "for the physician's trade," "convinced that of all quackeries, the physician's is the grotesquest and the silliest. And they know they are shams and humbugs." He recommended Kellgren to Twichell, Henry Stanley, and William James, among others, and predicted that ten years hence "no sane man will call a doctor except when the knife must be used—& such cases will be rare. The educated physician will himself be an osteopath."[11]

Livy was less enthusiastic about movement therapy than her husband. Though she acknowledged that "Jean's general health is much improved" under Kellgren's care, she feared "the treatment has done nothing" to address the underlying disease. Nor could they learn from Kellgren or his assistants, as Sam conceded, "when Jean's cure is to begin, nor how many months or years it will take, for these idiots keep no record of their cases, & don't know any more about the phases & stages & other vital details of them than a cow might. I believe it is the most stupidly administered institution that exists in the earth." When Livy caught a cold in late December 1899 and was confined to bed, she asked Sam to summon a doctor, "the last man in the world I should want around at such a time," he admitted to Twichell. He told her that "we knew no good doctor and it could not be good policy to choose at hazard; so she allowed me to send for Kellgren." Her treatment at his hands was "nearly unendurable for violence" and "made her sore & lame & filled her mind with black thoughts & antagonisms toward the system." She protested that her two-week recovery was no faster than it would have been "in Vienna under the doctors" and called off the gymnastics, according to Sam to save expense, more likely to save pain and suffering. Still, Sam was convinced that, had he called a doctor, "she would have been promptly killed or permanently broken down in health & strength" and had she continued the Swedish treatment "she would be in excellent condition."[12] Both propositions were idle speculation.

"It was pretty dull for the madam at Sanna, but not for me: I was at work. It was a nice quiet place for scribbling," Sam wrote Rogers. He was "leading a hermit life & working like a pile-driver." Not surprisingly, given his enthusiasm for Kellgren and the Swedish Movement Cure, he had begun a series of essays in Vienna poking "remorseless fun" at the "pudd'nheaded little Godddlemighty" of the Christian Scientists, "Mrs. Eddy, & her jackass 'Key' to the Scriptures." In Sanna he was keen, if not to contrast the two leaders and their therapeutic methods, at least to denigrate Eddy and her brand of mind-cure. "Damn all the other cures," he wrote Gilder two weeks after arriving in Sweden, "including the baths & Christian Science & the doctors of the several schools—*this* is the satisfactory one!" Kellgren was "no ignorant Christian Science village schoolmarm out of a job, but a man whose countenance & ways compel respect at once; a man who knows the human machinery as minutely as does any anatomist that lives, & knows its *real* functions *better* than any anatomist or doctor that lives." To be sure, Kellgren's cure shared a trait in common with Eddy's: it prescribed no medicines. But Kellgren's system was so superior that his patients testified to "such wonderful things that you half believe you have wandered into an asylum of Christian Science idiots." The practitioners in Sanna "actually *do* several of the great things the Christian Scientist pretends to do." In a cynical moment, Sam even equated traditional Western medicine with Christian Science "when it is a question of ignorance & quackery."[13]

Sam sent the first of his articles ridiculing Eddy and her "fraud" in late July to John Brisben Walker of *Cosmopolitan*, where it appeared in the October number under the title "Christian Science and the Book of Mrs. Eddy." The comic essay challenges the core belief of the Scientists that "nothing exists but mind" and therefore physical pain is unreal. The narrator pays the practitioner who fails to help him with "an imaginary check and she is suing me for substantial dollars. It looks inconsistent." Sam marshaled internal evidence that Eddy did not write *Science and Health*, the textbook of the cult, and accused her of rivaling the prolixity of Jim Blaine in telling the story of his grandfather's old ram ("the effect which Christian Science has upon the verbal bowels . . . makes one think of a dictionary with the cholera"). He likewise alleged that the "Eddy Trust," like the papacy, operated like a business. His friend Edward Everett Hale commended Sam upon its publication: "You have tackled a problem which all the rest of us have shirked." The *Omaha Bee* pronounced it "the most remarkable magazine article of the month, if not of the year," and the *Hampshire Advertiser* thought it "very humorously written." In England, T. P. O'Connor thought Sam treated "the practices of the Christian Scientists" with "satirical respect." The essay proved so popular that Walker paid Sam $1,000 for it rather than the promised $800. But the former rabbi Max Wertheimer of Dayton, Ohio, a convert to Christian Science, charged Sam with misrepresenting "Mrs. Eddy's wonderful mental revelation." Then again, Wertheimer later denounced the Church of Christ Science, too.[14]

Sam's strongest objection to Christian Science by far was its secular machinery, its commercialization and nascent capacity to wield political power like Roman Catholicism. "The thing is on a cash-&-piety basis," Sam replied to Hale, "its powers & authorities are centralized in a close (& irresponsible) corporation, & it is as well organized a Trust as the Papacy itself. It will give hordes of people of both sexes an easy chance to make money, without having to waste a week on education or apprenticeship." He predicted that, after Eddy's death, her "relics are going to cure a hundred cripples to Lourdes's one. And take the business. I believe I would be willing to live until 1910, just to see the C. S. begin to run legislatures & make laws for the doctors to obey & swear about. A century from now I wouldn't trade C. S. Trust Stock for Papal stock, dollar for dollar. The human race was born crazy." He riffed on this final point in a note to Twichell. "The human race is made up almost exclusively of people wholly destitute of anything really resembling a thinking-equipment, & that of the scattering few who have it hardly two in a million ever use it," he wrote with predictable hyperbole. Christian Science

> has pirated the one feature which has kept Romanism alive & strong all the centuries—the money-lust & money-grubbing—& has added some taking things that will make for perpetuity. Among them a fresh new god to worship. That seems to me to be a mighty good asset, & that it will be a still better one when that old cow dies & her bones begin to work miracles in presence of trains of pilgrims. I would rather own her burial lot than the bank of England. Lourdes isn't going to stand any chance against her. I am selling my Lourdes stock already & buying Christian Science Trust. I regard it as the Standard Oil of the future.

Or as he conceded to Frederick W. Peabody, a Boston lawyer and author of *Complete Exposure of Eddyism or Christian Science* (1898), "The absurdity the human race can't swallow hasn't been invented yet, and the more silly it is the more certain are they that it came from the Most High," though he found a "private delight" in watching people make fools of themselves.[15]

While in Sanna during the summer of 1899, as he wrote Howells, he "put the pot-boiler pen away." For years he had wanted "to write a book without reserves—a book which should take account of no one's feelings, and no one's prejudices, opinions, beliefs, hopes, illusions, delusions. . . . I judged that that would be an unimaginable luxury, heaven on earth. It is under way, now, and it *is* a luxury! an intellectual drunk." Sam added several thousand words to his old "Chronicle of Young Satan" manuscript, including a passage satirizing Christian Science in which an elderly woman is burned at the stake because "she had cured bad headaches by kneading the person's head and neck with her fingers." About the same time, in a letter to Gilder, he pronounced Kellgren "a genius; in the Middle Ages they would have burnt him." He also began the longest of the dream-narratives, never completed, entitled *Which Was It?* Set in another manifestation of Hannibal called Indiantown, the fragment fictionalizes the themes of Sam's "bible" *What Is Man?* by illustrating how so-called human nature, especially incarnated in the characters of the mulatto Jasper and his master Harrison, is the product of heredity and circumstance, all human behavior is invariably selfish, and the human animal is uniquely afflicted with the "Moral Sense." The utterly forgettable potpourri of plots, including a parodic detective story, exposes a series of swindles: a Ponzi scheme, fake charities, slave-master role reversals, mistaken identities, and a séance at which the spiritualists hold hands under the table and communicate in the language of the deaf, a plot twist no doubt inspired by Sam's friendship with Helen Keller. As usual, he lobbed a brick in the direction of Christian missions, which were always profitable "regardless of the condition of the financial weather." One steadfast believer working "in the interest of Turkey" over thirteen years "had saved one Turk and part of another."[16]

On September 27, as the weather turned cool, the Clemenses quit Sanna and followed Kellgren to England. "Since we came here early in July to get Jean doctored up we have found out that she will have to continue the treatment in London," Sam notified Hutton, "& possibly keep it up all winter before her cure is perfect. She has made astonishing progress in these 2½ months." He likened their departure to "leaving heaven. I've never spent such a delicious summer." This paradise was not cheap, however. Kellgren charged Sam £300 or the equivalent of over $40,000 in modern dollars for their treatments, rent, and meals during their three months in residence. The family sailed south to Germany, paused in Berlin for a day or two, and by September 30 were back in London, where they registered at the Queen Anne Residential Mansions while "hunting for comfortable quarters which shall not overstrain the purse: & they are not easy to find, for we need to be near Kellgren's place & that is in a high-priced region." Two weeks later, after signing a seven-month lease and paying half the rent, Sam and the rest of the clan moved to a furnished flat in Wellington Court in Knightsbridge near Hyde Park, less than a mile from Kellgren's Swedish Institution on Eaton Square, where Jean continued her therapy. Pond soon dangled another of his occasional offers to manage Sam on a U.S. lecture tour—$10,000 for ten nights—but Sam declined on the grounds that "we must remain in London & continue Jean's cure till it is perfected, if it takes a year—& the chances are that it *will* take the best part of it. She will come out all right, by & by, & then we shall go home & *stay* there." He was convinced Jean was steadily improving under Kellgren's care. "Her natural disposition," which she had lost to her disease, he reported to Rogers, "has returned. Her physical condition is good," he exulted. "Her mind is sound and capable."[17]

Less than six weeks after settling in London, Sam learned from his sister Pamela that a close cousin of Kellgren's movement cure was practiced "all over America" under "the new name of 'Osteopathy.'" Had he only known the therapy was available in New York, he complained in early November, "we should all have been located in New York the 1st of October" rather than lease an apartment in London. After all, they were in England "*only* to have the Kellgren treatment for Jean," yet she could have received similar treatment in the United States. Andrew Taylor Still, a rural Kansas physician, began to develop his system "in 1874, only five years after Kellgren began the same work," a coincidence Sam characteristically attributed to mental telepathy between the two men. During the previous three years, he discovered, osteopathy had been "legalized in 14 States in spite of the opposition of the physicians" and the "medical gymnasts" had founded "20 Osteopathic schools and colleges," including institutes in Boston and Philadelphia, with some "75 allopathic physicians" enrolled, another "100 students in the parent college (Dr. Still's at Kirksville, Missouri)," and "about 2,000 graduates practicing in America. Dear me, there are not 30 in Europe." After their long exile from the United States, even Livy was willing to grasp at this straw. She wanted to know what success the osteopaths had enjoyed with treating epilepsy and which of Still's graduates "on the Atlantic seaboard he would recommend." For whatever reason—Sam claimed they were "damned fools incredibly indifferent & incompetent"—none of the people he contacted in the United States could answer these questions. "Thus far we get no information of a clear and definite sort concerning the osteopaths," he complained to Rogers in mid-April 1900, "and we cannot venture to take Jean away from Kellgren until we can transfer her to reasonably competent hands." He reiterated the problem to his sister about the same time: "We have moved heaven & hell & the earth, trying to find out something *definite* about Osteopathy—something to justify us in venturing to cross the ocean with the prospect of finding it as good as Kellgren's method." Sam was convinced there was little difference "between Kellgren's science and osteopathy; but I am sending to America to find out. I want osteopathy to prosper; it is common sense & scientific, & cures a wider range of ailments than the doctor's methods can reach."[18]

Finally, early in the new year 1900 he asked Sam Moffett to investigate. "What we need is *all* the information we can get," he admonished his nephew. "I have worn my soul out trying to get hold of *some*body who had sense enough to ask straight questions & send me *informing* answers, but I have struck nothing but fools & incapables. Now don't *you* fail me!" Moffett replied with information and an enclosure from George J. Helmer, D.O., an 1896 graduate of Still's American School of Osteopathy in Kirksville, whose offices were located on Madison Avenue in New York. Helmer furnished "some definite particulars at last—all he had in stock, no doubt," but they were sufficient to satisfy Sam and Livy. "When we elect to go home, now, we can go with confidence. In Dr. Helmer Jean would have competent help, I believe." Meanwhile, in early May, even as Moffett was examining the credentials of American osteopaths, Kellgren suddenly announced Jean had "turned the corner—an event" her parents "had been anxiously" awaiting "for 6 or 7 months." The change in her behavior was "very marked. Tomorrow it will be 4 weeks since she had a convulsion," Sam wrote on May 17. The family delayed their return to the United States not only because Jean was "in fine condition & we are well content," but because Helmer planned to visit London in August, when he would "diagnose Jean's case & deliver an opinion. If he has doubts, we shall stay here until Kellgren cures her."[19]

But make no mistake: Sam and Livy were anxious to return to the United States so long as they could maintain a comfortable living standard. As early as January 1895 Livy calculated that "without horses and coachman" they could live in Hartford for about the same amount as in Paris—$1,000 a month. Sam wrote Poultney Bigelow in December 1897 that they hoped to "go home to America at the end of the summer and see if we can *afford to live there*." He admitted to Rogers in January 1900 that he was "tired to death of this everlasting exile." Around the same time Livy allowed to Grace King that they needed either to sell the Hartford house "or go back & live in it. We cannot afford to keep it and not live in it. . . . Of course we could not live in our old expensive way but I think with care & if we kept no horses that we could live there with our present income."[20]

At virtually the same moment, S. S. McClure tendered Sam an inviting proposition: the editorship of a monthly magazine he planned to launch in the fall at a salary of $5,000 a year for five years, plus $150 per thousand words of anything he wrote for its pages, plus 10 percent of its ownership when he signed the contract and 5 percent more of its stock at the beginning of each of its second and third years. The magazine, to be titled the *Universal*, would be mostly run "by a staff of sub-editors," with Sam merely approving the contents of each number, which would only "occupy me one or two days per month." He would be "free & independent in my movements," moreover, "live where I please, & go & come as I choose, arranging the duration of my absences to suit myself." As he wrote Rogers, "I am very much in love with the idea." But he also stipulated some conditions in his response to McClure, above all that it was *"not to be a comic magazine"* like *Puck* or *Judge* but "simply a good, clean, wholesome collection of well-written & enticing literary products" like the *Atlantic* or *Century*. He agreed to contribute to

> this magazine every time the spirit moves me; but I look for my largest entertainment in editing it. I have been edited by all kinds of people for more than thirty-eight years; there has always been somebody in authority over my manuscript & privileged to improve it; this has fatigued me a good deal, & I have often longed to move up from the dock to the bench & rest myself and fatigue others. My opportunity is come, but I hope I shall not abuse it overmuch. I mean to do my best to make a good magazine; I mean to do my whole duty & not shirk any part of it.

His enthusiasm soon began to wane, however, because, as he wrote Rogers "I do not like slavery & work," but he was prepared to "remain in this editorship" for a year. He had "stuff lately written & laid away for use in that magazine in case the cat jumps that way." Undeterred by such caution flags, McClure continued to entertain grandiose plans for the prospective editor as soon as he committed to the project. On March 30 he proposed to Sam to "have a special train . . . take you over the American continent under the most luxurious conditions and have you write a series of articles reporting the United States. . . . You could be the guest of the principal railroads and we could have the whole country placed under our eyes." But at the age of sixty-four Sam preferred not to work that hard. The plans for the magazine were eventually scuttled when McClure not only insisted that it appeal specifically to the humor market but increased the amount of time he expected Sam to devote to it—that is, the amount of material he expected the editor to contribute. McClure "mapped out an excursion for me" that "won't take place" because "it is too circusy for my tastes." "I can conceive of many wild and extravagant things when my imagination is in good repair," Sam later confessed, "but I can conceive of nothing quite so wild and extravagant as the idea of my accepting the editorship of a humorous periodical. I should regard that as the saddest (for me) of all occupations." He subsequently declined an offer of $10,000 a year to devote an hour per week to editing the American humor magazine *Puck*.[21]

When the lease on the apartment in Wellington Court expired in June 1900, the Clemenses moved for the summer to a house on Dollis Hill, only three hundred yards northwest of the London city limits. With "6 acres of hay and sheep," a "spacious" lawn that stretched toward Hampstead to the east and Harrow to the west and "plenty of old forest trees for shade," it had once been the home of Lord Aberdeen and the frequent retreat of William Ewart Gladstone. In a familiar refrain, Sam averred that "Dollis Hill House comes nearer to being a paradise than any other home I have ever occupied," though it had "no telephone," which "sometimes made life in it a biting aggravation." While roomy, the house was also "wretchedly furnished" and "certainly the dirtiest dwelling-house in Europe—perhaps in the universe" when they rented it, but it was conveniently located for commuting to the city. Thrice a week Jean and her maid traveled forty-five minutes each way to Kellgren's institute and the Clemenses were often visited by friends, including Dean and Sarah Sage, Willard Fiske, Brander Matthews, George Standring, James Ross Clemens, and Robert Jones Burdette. Sam was also once interviewed at Dollis Hill by the journalist W. H. Helm, with whom he shared "his absolute conviction that man was so bound by inherited ideas and early environment that he had scarcely a particle of control over his destiny."[22]

Meanwhile, Sam kept up appearances. As clubbable as ever, he was active in the Whitefriars, the Blackfriars, the Kinsmen, and the Liberal, Savile, Savage, Beefsteak, and Lotos both for the bonhomie and the cachet. He occasionally visited the House of Commons and attended a meeting of the Boz Club at the Athenaeum in Pall Mall, where he met Charles Dickens's son Henry. He dined with one of his favorite historians, William E. H. Lecky, and Basil Wilberforce, the canon of Westminster Abbey; and in company with Anthony Hope, Israel Zangwill, and other literati he spoke at the opening of Poultney Bigelow's new house in the Elm Park suburb of London. He testified before the copyright committee of the House of Lords in defense of the idea of intellectual property and in favor of an act that would have granted perpetual copyright to authors, though the gag went around that Sam was "unlikely to live that long." He not only disputed the equation of copyright with protective tariffs, he insisted that "the value of real estate was as much dependent on an idea as any book was" (though he also joked that his brain had once been assessed for tax purposes at the same rate as "gas works"). At various social events around the city he was introduced to Oscar II, the king of Sweden and Norway, and the Duke of York, the future King George V. He attended at least two dinners at the home of the painter Edwin Austin Abbey on Tite Street, where he again met Robert and Adèle Chapin, Richard Watson and Helena de Kay Gilder, the artists James McNeill Whistler and John Singer Sargent, Henry Lucy, and Lord and Lady Alma-Tadema.[23]

The evening of May 2, at the annual dinner of the Royal Literary Fund at the Hotel Cecil, Sam announced his mock candidacy for president of the United States. (In truth, he never stood for election to any public office.) Before an audience of about a hundred and twenty, including the Lord Chief Justice, he joked in the toast to literature that he would return "to my own country to run for the presidency because there are not yet enough candidates in the field." He laid out a broad platform: "I am in favor of anything and everything—of temperance and intemperance, morality and qualified immorality, gold standard and free silver." His declaration attracted the attention of newspapers across the United States. The *Los Angeles Herald* noted that he had worked his way up from "editor, publisher, author, lawyer, and burglar"; the *Sioux City Tribune* opined, "he will have to be more original before he can wrest the honors from some of the shining lights already in the field"; the *Minneapolis Times* called "Mark Twain's candidacy . . . not much more of a joke that some others that have been sprung this season"; and the *New York Press* claimed that "the difference between Mark Twain and Dewey is that Mark was only joking." Among his suggested vice presidential running mates were the heavyweight boxer "Gentleman Jim" Corbett; the humorist Finley Peter Dunne, aka "Mr. Dooley"; and E. W. Howe, author of *The Story of a Country Town*.[24]

The evening of June 9, Sam attended a banquet at the Savoy Hotel, hosted by Richard D'Oyly Carte, welcoming Sir Henry Irving back to England. Some two hundred men attended, including Edwin Austin Abbey, Lawrence Alma-Tadema, Joseph Choate, Charles Frohman, George Grossmith, Bret Harte, Anthony Hope, Arthur Wing Pinero, and Bram Stoker. In his toast to "the Drama," Sam joked that he had sent playscripts to Irving and added, "with a merry twinkle in his eyes, 'look where he is now.'" Nor had Pinero had "written as many plays as I have . . . but he has that God-given talent, which I lack, of working them off on managers." His remarks were "received with continuous laughter" and Pinero remembered that he met Sam only this one time when "I had the misfortune to be put up to respond to a speech of his." Sam and Harte were together in the same room for the first time since 1877, moreover, though there is no evidence they interacted. A week later, Sam was present at the premiere of William Gorman Wills's play *Olivia* starring Irving and Ellen Terry at the Lyceum Theatre. Before the end of the month, Sam also participated in the ceremonial opening of a new West End line of the London Underground. In a midnight address before the American Society on July 4 at the Hotel Cecil, he both paid tribute to London bobbies and subtly protested the influence of business culture in the conduct of the war in South Africa. "I want to stand in the middle of the street," he announced, and "know that no cabman or truck driver dares to run me down. I want to stand out there and hold up my right hand and feel that I am paralyzing the commerce of the globe for five minutes."[25]

Several months before the appearance of "The Man That Corrupted Hadleyburg" in *Harper's Monthly* in December 1899, Sam began to discuss with Frank Bliss the contents of his next collection of stories and essays. He calculated in February 1899 that he had banked some hundred thousand words of copy—"half as much more as *Huck Finn* or *Tom Sawyer* contains. Half of it has not yet been in print, & half of *that* half is especially good & *ought* to be put into a magazine"—but he did not "much care, one way or the other." As it happened, neither did he much care whether Bliss issued the book or not. *The Man That Corrupted Hadleyburg and Other Stories and Essays* appeared from the presses of Harper & Brothers in the United States in mid-June, and *The Man That Corrupted Hadleyburg and Other Stories and Sketches* from Chatto & Windus in the United Kingdom in mid-September 1900. Only eight items were common to both editions, however, among them the title story, "About Play-Acting," and "Is He Living or Is He Dead?" The fourteen pieces in the U.S. edition also included "Adam's Diary" and the twenty in the UK volume reprinted "Christian Science and the Book of Mrs. Eddy," "Concerning the Jews," and "Stirring Times in Austria." Nevertheless, the critical responses to the two books were remarkably similar, a point illustrated by comparable reviews of them by William Archer in both the *London Leader* and the New York *Critic*. Sam's recent writings "are full of ethical suggestion," Archer wrote in the former venue; many of his new stories and sketches are "designed to drive home an ethical lesson," he noted in the latter.[26]

In fact, the stark distinction between the two groups of critics regarding the merits of the editions pivots not on their various contents or cultural differences but on the incongruities between humorous or "old" and serious or "new" material. On the one hand, many of the notices acknowledged their heterogeneity without registering a complaint, among them the *Pall Mall Gazette* ("a book more varied in range than any Mark Twain has published"), the *American Monthly Review of Reviews* ("there is nothing common to all" of the selections "except the distinctive genius" of the author); *Brooklyn Eagle* ("all are worth re-reading") and *New York Observer* ("worth reading more than once"); *Boston Post* ("he is more than a humorist nowadays; he is a satirist, a philosopher"); *San Francisco Chronicle* ("the freshness and variety of the stories in this book will excite surprise"); *New York Tribune* ("Mark

Twain's new book might fairly be regarded as a summary of his life's philosophy"); Chicago *Standard* ("a smattering of everything representing the varied genius" of the writer); *Book Buyer* ("Mark Twain's humor has grown more quiet with the passing of the years but more subtle as well"); *Cleveland Plain Dealer* ("a medley of wit, wisdom, and 'Twaineries' "); *Littell's Living Age* (the author "has for some time been suspected of serious moral purposes and his latest volume confirms the suspicion"); *Hartford Courant* ("plenty of good ore on the lower levels yet—nor has the percentage of gold diminished"); *Public Opinion* ("affords a peculiar combination of amusement and food for thought"); *Washington Times* (a "miscellaneous collection of shrewd satires, keen comment and analysis, and clever character sketches"); *Christian Advocate* (a "solid and well-filled," "widely varied" collection); *Minneapolis Star Tribune* ("a collection of stories written with Mark Twain's characteristic humor but with an undercurrent of philosophy and seriousness"); *Detroit Free Press* ("abound in the author's characteristic vein of humor and original plot-making"); and *Buffalo Express* (readers "often overlook how large a portion of what he says is nothing but hard sense"). These opinions were echoed in the United Kingdom by the London *Review of Reviews* ("a tribute to Mr. Clemens' many-sidedness and versatility"), London *Morning Post* ("may be very miscellaneous" but "abounds in good sense and happy touches"), *Scotsman* ("the whole collection makes first-class reading"); *London Chronicle* ("as rich and various and diverting as ever"), *Spectator* ("Mark Twain at sixty-five is just the same fearless, alert, and whimsical philosopher that he was when he made his 'debut as a literary person' some thirty-four years ago"), London *Daily News* ("most of the stories . . . are in the old playfully humorous and quaintly paradoxical manner of the author"), *Academy* ("the new Mark Twain . . . is not a whit less readable than the old and he is more provocative of thought"), London *Globe* ("the writer's personality shines through everywhere"); London *Evening News* ("the author has lost none of that quiet, sedate humor"), and *Belfast News-Letter* ("entirely worthy of his well-deserved fame and literary reputation").[27]

On the other hand, some critics disparaged the cacophony and dissonance, among them the *New York Times Saturday Review of Books* ("the book's contents are so various in character that a coherent comment on them is extremely difficult"); New York *Sun* ("a pity that Mr. Clemens should have taken to using over again old material"); *Brooklyn Life* ("the Austrian sketches in particular are remarkable for a quality not characteristic of the author—dullness"); New York *Outlook* (contains "many things" that "ought to perish"); London *Outlook* ("most of this volume reads like a third-rate imitation of the Mark Twain whom we knew and loved of old"); *Athenaeum* ("diffuseness, indeed, spoils most of the matter in this book"); *Saturday Review* (even readers "whose distorted sense of humour is tickled by his bald exaggerations and rough slang will be disappointed by this miscellany of reporter's scrap-book and ponderous preaching"); *Illustrated London News* ("our general impression is one of dissatisfaction with this motley assemblage of sketches, stories, satires, and recollections"); *Manchester Guardian* ("Mark Twain is at his worst . . . when he is serious"); *Literature* (the author "has of late years allowed the tendency to what Americans call 'preachments' to have its way, sometimes at the expense of both his humour and his readers"); *Blackwood's* (the "new" Mark Twain "is too fond of being didactic, of pointing morals, or drawing lessons"); Melbourne *Arena* ("a very disappointing book"); *Hampshire Telegraph and Naval Chronicle* (the reader lays the book down "with the feeling that, perhaps, it is too much to expect of any author to look for the best from him always"); and *Sydney Herald* (the humor "has become mordant, unkind, cynical in places"). Whereas Howells and most modern critics hail Sam for his departure from the genteel tradition in American letters, for writing the way ordinary people speak, the *Independent* plowed a unique claim in its review, accusing him of "slipshod workmanship," of punctuating his writing with "split infinitives, slang, loose English and an obvious straining after humorous effects." The *Literary Digest* similarly complained that Sam had "blotched and smeared with modern slang and vulgarisms" the "heroic and stupendous tragedy" of Joan of Arc. These indictments of Sam's style were a common refrain throughout the final stage of his career. William Norman Guthrie, professor of literature at the University of the South, allowed that while Mark Twain was "unquestionably . . . a genius and has written some things that makes one laugh," nevertheless "a lot of his stuff is rot." Guthrie preferred authors "who will retain the natural refinement of our language."[28]

The betrayal of the Filipinos kindled a major shift in Sam's views of colonialism and wars of conquest. He was equally critical of imperialism across the board—whether of the United States in the Philippines, Germany in China, Russia in Manchuria and Japan, Japan in Manchuria, China in Korea, or Belgium in the Congo. He sympathized with the opponents to Western cultural imperialism, especially to the influence of Christian missionaries by the Boxers in China during the Boxer Rebellion of 1899–1901. While in South Africa in June 1896, Sam had praised the efforts of the Salvation Army. "They are the missionaries for me," he observed, because "they feed the poor, they employ the idle & the ex-prisoner, they reform the drunkard & the wanton." But four years later, in an unsent letter addressed to the editor of the London *Times*, C. F. Moberly Bell, and entitled "The Missionary in World-Politics," he revised his views to indict the zealots and proselytizers.

> I do not know why we respect missionaries. Perhaps it is because they have not intruded here from Turkey or China or Polynesia to break our hearts by sapping away our children's faith & winning them to the worship of alien gods. . . . Wherever the missionary goes he not only proclaims that his religion is the best, but that it is a true one while his hearer's religion is a false one; that the pagan's gods are inventions of his imagination. . . . The missionary has no wish to be an insulter, but how is he to help it? All his propositions are insults, word them as he may.

The Boxer Rebellion reached a crescendo in in mid-June to mid-August 1900, when the Legation Quarter in Beijing was surrounded by the Boxers and the Imperial Army, trapping nearly a thousand westerners and some three thousand Chinese Christians. Sam followed the "ghastly news" closely, predicting in mid-July that the European powers would eventually "sup in hell, there in China, I think—& will richly deserve it. I believe Europe will get by the ear, there; I hardly think she can escape it—unless she withdraws & leaves her booty behind her. It's a robber-gang which will be loath to do that. I believe the human race is filthier today than it ever was before; & that is saying much." Even when the siege was finally lifted by an eight-nation military invasion, Sam defended the Chinese, who had "been villainously dealt with by the sceptered thieves of Europe, & I hope they will drive all the foreigners out & keep them out for good. I only wish it; of course I don't really expect it." Yet there was a nativist t(a)int to his defense of the Boxers. "Foreigners are the cause of all the trouble" in China, he insisted, because "the Chinese don't want them any more than we want the Chinese. They have as much right as a nation to exclude foreigners as we have to exclude them." Were the foreigners expelled, "the trouble would be all over. Now my sympathies are with the Boxers. The Boxers are the only patriots China has got. The newspapers call them hard names, but all they are after is to get the foreigners out of their country and I hope they may have all success in doing so. If I am opposed to the Chinaman being here then I am a Boxer." Much as he believed Dewey should have simply sailed away from Manila Bay after defeating the Spanish fleet, he thought "all the foreign powers" should depart China "and leave her free to attend to her own business." He certainly approved the withdrawal of the United States because "we have no more business in China than in any other country."[29]

He was more ambivalent about the prosecution of the Boer War, fought by Afrikaners or the descendants of the original Dutch colonists in the

Orange Free State and the Transvaal against the British over the mineral deposits in South Africa. In mid-September 1899, a month before the outbreak of hostilities, Sam insisted that "England is more in the wrong than is the Transvaal." (He once joked that Jesus had mentioned the British people in the Beatitudes: "Blessed are the meek.") He blamed the civic "murder" of South Africans on Joseph Chamberlain, the colonial secretary of Great Britain, and "the lackeys of Cecil Rhodes & his Forty Thieves, the South Africa Company." By mid-January 1899, as their defeats mounted and enthusiasm for the war waned among the Brits, Sam told Howells that "every day I write (in my head) bitter magazine articles" about the "sordid & criminal" conflict. Yet he never put pen to paper in opposition to the war, "for England must not fall." Defeat "would mean an inundation of Russian & German political degradations which would envelop the globe & steep it in a sort of Middle-Age night & slavery which would last till Christ comes again—which I hope he will not do; he made trouble enough before. Even wrong—& she is wrong—England must be upheld. He is an enemy of the human race who shall speak against her now." His "heart & such rags of morals as I have are with the Boer," he said, but "my head is with the Briton." And so, as he explained to Twichell, "I am for England; but she is profoundly in the wrong" and "no (instructed) Englishman doubts it." Public opinion in London was riven by controversy over the conduct of the conflict, and "Boer sympathisers—respectable men, taxpayers, good citizens, and as much entitled to their opinions as were any other citizens—were mobbed at their meetings, and their speakers maltreated and driven from the platform by other citizens who differed from them." During the first months of the war, Clara remembered, her father "found it best to accept no more [personal] invitations" except to "the houses of those with whom he was on intimate terms." Or as he acknowledged, "the private dinner parties (we go to no public ones) have been Lodges of Sorrow, & just a little depressing sometimes."[30]

Only after British victories in the battles of Magersfontein, Paardeberg, and Tugela Heights did the public mood shift. "London is happy-hearted at last," he noted in early March 1900. The military triumphs "swept the clouds away & there are now no uncheerful faces." He marked the relief of Mafeking in mid-May ("All London was in the streets, gone mad with joy"), though he continued to regard the prosecution of the fighting as a "black blot upon England." But the Mother Country was "the best friend we have got in Europe and we are the only friend she's got on earth," he explained to an interviewer. Under any circumstances it was "best for England, best for America and best for the world that the Union Jack and the Stars and Stripes should wave together." In an act of charity—or self-advertising—the Plasmon Company of London, a month after Sam became a director in April 1900, donated two tons of the powdered milk albumen to the War Department of the British government for distribution among the military hospitals in South African because, as he claimed to Rogers, "the sick soldiers prefer it to the other food."[31] The war finally ended with British annexation of the two South African republics in May 1902.

During these months, with wars of conquest erupting around the globe, Sam began to vent in private more and more about the "bastard human race." Whereas Emerson insisted that "man is a god in ruins," with emphasis on the divine, Sam Clemens opined that each individual is "a nest of disgusting & unnecessary diseases, a tub of rotten offal." "I believe it was about the year 1900," Howells later remembered, "that his sense of our perdition became insupportable and broke out in a mixed abhorrence and amusement which spared no occasion." Sam derided to Howells "the nasty, stinking little human race" as "a poor joke—the poorest that was ever contrived—an April-fool joke, played by a malicious Creator with nothing better to waste his time upon." The largest class of people, some "9 in 10," Sam ranted to Twichell, consisted of "the fools, the idiots, the puddnheads." So-called civilization was "a shabby poor thing and full of cruelties, vanities, arrogancies, meannesses, and hypocrisies." Twichell in response teased the agnostic who had become "quite orthodox on the Doctrine of Total Human Depravity." "The way you throw your rotten eggs at the human race doth greatly arride me," he jibed. "We preachers are extensively accused of vilifying human nature, as you are aware; but I must own that for enthusiasm of misanthropy you beat us out of sight."[32]

Sam took a holiday from writing for publication while living at Dollis Hill during the summer of 1900. More to the point, he basked "in writing two books simply for the private pleasure of writing." One was his autobiography, addressed to "the remote posterity of a hundred years hence." The other, "The Chronicle of Young Satan," he did not expect to "be published at all." Or as he wrote Gilder on July 31, "I am 25,000 words deep in a story which I began a good while ago (in Vienna, I think) & I mean to finish it now." Not only did he take a page from his "gospel" in describing every person as "a suffering-machine and a happiness-machine combined," he peppered this third mass of manuscript with a number of topical allusions, particularly to imperialism, before abandoning it in September. In oblique reference to the Boxer Rebellion, for example, young Satan suggests that "the Christian missionary will exasperate the Chinese; they will kill him in a riot. They will have to pay for him, in territory, cash, and churches, sixty-two million times his value. This will exasperate the Chinese still more, and they will injudiciously rise in revolt against the insults and oppressions of the intruder. This will be Europe's chance to interfere and swallow China." He predicted that fin de siècle England would wage a shameful war at the behest of colonialists and that "two or three centuries from now it will be recognized that all the competent killers are Christians." The 55,000-word manuscript ends abruptly after young Satan carries Theodor Fischer to nineteenth-century India, where he requires a "foreigner" in white linen and a pith helmet to water the roots of a fruit tree on his property every hour for the rest of his life lest it and he die—a cautionary tale about the obligation of British colonists to preserve the indigenous (agri)culture.[33]

Whether or not Jean had turned the corner in her recovery from epilepsy, Sam was determined by mid-1900 to return with his family to the United States. He was persuaded that the differences between osteopathy and Kellgren's movement therapy were "not serious." In the only known letter Sam wrote to A. T. Still, he acknowledged the "differences in the application" of the method, but insisted "the principles underlying your system & Kellgren's are the same." In August he notified Twichell that the family would "sail for home sometime in October, but shall winter in New York where we can have an osteopath of good repute to continue" Jean's treatment—"any osteopath, good or bad." But one of the differences between Kellgren and osteopathy may have been in the treatment of epilepsy. Kellgren never publicly described a procedure for ameliorating the disease, whereas Still explicitly instructed osteopaths to treat seizure victims, whom he gendered as female, with physical violence: "Proceed to punish her with a wet towel, well twisted and administered freely, . . . and spank her very much. The American School of Osteopathy . . . has issued orders to 'wallop,' and 'wallop' very freely." After all, in Still's opinion, "the cause of her disease is a failure of the passing of the blood, chyle, and other substances to and from the abdomen to nourish and renovate the abdominal viscera, that are diseased owing to a lapsed diaphragm, which would cause resistance to the blood-flow in the aorta, through which passes the arterial blood, and the vena cava, through which the venous blood returns." That is, Still considered epilepsy a disease caused by restricted blood flow to and from the abdomen.[34]

Sam attributed Jean's seizures not to a fever she had suffered as a toddler but to a "bad knock" to her head in a fall "when she [was] 8 or 9." But what if Helmer and the other osteopaths who treated Jean for the rest of her life believed her epilepsy was the result of a fall that damaged the uterus? The etiology of epilepsy, according to Still and other osteopaths, located the origins of the disease not in the brain but in the pelvis. Women who suffered seizures and other "female troubles" not inherited from their mothers were usually victims of injury "to the womb . . . hurt in a fall." In order to diagnose and address the condition, an osteopath needed to know the "frequency, regularity, amount, duration, and attendant pain of menstruation," and Jean routinely tracked her cycle in her diary, repeatedly noting the day "grandmother arrived." More to the point, Marion Edward Clark, an instructor at Still's osteopathic school in Kirksville, identified a disease she termed "hystero-epilepsy," a type of epilepsy "due to disease of the generative organs," in her textbook *Diseases of Women: A Manual of Gynecology Designed for the Use of Osteopathic Students and Practitioners*. Blackouts or petit mal seizures in hystero-epileptics were caused by "a knot or constriction starting from the ovary and traveling upward" to the throat, producing "the spasm or unconscious spell." Grand mal seizures occurred most frequently "near the menstrual period and especially just following the cessation of the menstrual flow." The standard treatment of "female convulsionaries" who suffered from "hysteria" or "womb disease"? Intravaginal massage or "manual massage of the vulva" or adjustment of the displaced or "retroverted" uterus and/or ovaries. That is, Jean's treatment for epilepsy at the hands of osteopaths during the final decade of her life may well have included what would today be considered physical and sexual abuse. After the age of twenty she may well have been routinely molested in the name of medical science. Her frequent outbursts of anger during her adult years, amounting sometimes to acts of physical violence, may well have been the result of the torment to which she was routinely forced to submit. Paradoxically, however, she was also warned by an osteopath not to ride a bicycle lest the activity trigger her seizures. She was also cautioned by George Helmer to stop masturbating. On November 16, 1900, a year after she became his patient, Helmer "gave me pretty violent treatment alone," and "as mamma was in another room" and "there was no maid about" he "took the opportunity" to ask her "about that old habit of mine. It has been so entirely out of my thoughts for so long that I really didn't know what he meant for a second or so when it flashed across me. He said there were still the symptoms of that old difficulty in my back, and when I asked him if that could be still effecting [sic] my memory, he said that it most decidedly could and doubtlessly was."[35]

On September 27, Sam delivered a type of valedictory public speech at the opening of a reading room in Kensal Rise. Before a large audience, he told a story about a young girl who wrote that she liked the name "Mark" because "Mark Anthony" was a character in the Bible. Sam replied that as "Mark

Anthony had got into the Bible, I am not without hopes myself." Three days later, with the expiration of the summer lease on the house on Dollis Hill, the Clemenses moved to Brown's Hotel in Mayfair near Piccadilly. "Brown's is as interesting as the Tower of London & older I think," Sam joked with his friend John Y. W. MacAlister. "The bedrooms are hospitals for incurable furniture" and "the lift was a gift of William the Conqueror." Ten days later Sam attended a Whitefriars Club dinner in honor of Winston Churchill at Anderton's Hotel on Fleet street. Churchill delivered an entertaining speech, "a happy blend of American truth and British exaggeration," according to Sam, who promptly upstaged the headliner with "perhaps the most brilliant and delicious speech which has ever fallen from him," as the *Westminster Gazette* reported. "Mr. Clemens, who declared that his two years' stay in England had been a period of 'exceeding felicity,' was in delightful form."[36]

Their exile at an end, the next day the Clemenses embarked from Tilbury aboard the new steamship *S.S. Minnehaha,* with first-class cabins on the promenade deck, for the nine-day cruise to New York. On the eve of their departure, Sam kidded a reporter that his family had "been away from America so long I'm afraid they may have forgotten the language." It had been "nine years since they left . . . and though I have been back several times, this is their first return trip." Sam believed Livy's "health and strength were in better condition than they had ever been before since she was sixteen years old." They planned to remain in New York for the winter and return to Hartford in the spring, but they would soon discover again that even the best-laid plans often go awry.[37]

Sam entrusted Rogers with solving a series of difficult and potentially prickly problems: negotiating contracts that would allow Harper & Brothers to market a complete and uniform edition of his works while recognizing the residual rights of the American Publishing Company to the eight books it had issued and the rights of Charles Dudley Warner, his collaborator on *The Gilded Age*. His long-term financial health depended on negotiating deals satisfactory to all parties. In late May 1895, even before leaving on his world speaking tour, he transferred the rights to his books published by Webster and Company to Harper & Brothers, who had agreed to issue a uniform edition. But Frank Bliss balked at the plan. He asserted that the American Publishing Company was entitled to renew copyrights on the Mark Twain books on its list and refused to allow the Harpers to include them in its edition. In late 1896, as Sam struggled to pay his debts, Rogers arranged a settlement between the Clemenses and Blisses that allowed for the continued sale of the subscription books as well as the forthcoming *Following the*

Equator and that acknowledged Warner's coauthorship of *The Gilded Age*. He also clarified in a separate contract the respective rights of Livy, Sam's preferred creditor, and Harper & Brothers, the trade publisher. "I am very glad indeed that the contract is accomplished at last, both for your patient indomitable sake & for my sake—I can work the better now," Sam wrote Rogers. "And I am glad of what you say of Harry Harper. He always seemed to me to be a frank and straightforward man & a man of a good heart & an obliging disposition." Sam continued to write books, of course, and the respective rights to them continued to be a point of contention among the parties. Ideally, he wanted the claims of the two presses to his intellectual property to be sharply distinguished: "If you *can* only 'make an arrangement with the Harpers to publish the whole of my books for the trade & with Bliss to publish them by subscription' that will be very jolly," he adjured Rogers in August 1898. But Bliss was adamant, insisting that "he ought to have 18 months [to market] his uniform edition" before surrendering his rights. "I was hoping for that new arrangement whereby you would handle all my books in the trade & Bliss the uniform sets—& it didn't materialize," Sam conceded to Henry Harper.[38]

He readily approved a Chatto & Windus proposal to issue six hundred sets of a twenty-two volume deluxe edition of his works, printed on special paper manufactured from pure cotton rag and bound in linen covers for sale in the United Kingdom. To his credit, Rogers was able to negotiate a temporary truce between the dueling American publishers that granted Bliss the option of issuing a limited "Popular Edition of the Works of Mark Twain." "I hope Bliss is in earnest, and I am persuaded that he *is*," he advised Rogers. "He gets nothing out of the old books; so I think he believes he can mend his fortunes with the Uniform." At least Sam was no longer "sweating any more over the Bliss-Harper deadlock." He asked Rogers to "look at the stock-report & see what the latest rates are for a Tinker's Damn." Bliss was unable to marshal the resources required to execute such an ambitious project, however, and subcontracted with the R. G. Newbegin Co. of New York to publish and market a uniform edition. Sam was untroubled; he was contractually guaranteed "$16,000 a year for 4 years on the 'Popular Edition' of my books" no matter the publisher and, in fact, during the two years (1901–3) "the Newbegin scheme was able to keep its head above water, it paid me $44,000." To enhance its sale, Sam contributed a humorous preface to the edition in which he struggled to explain his reasons for writing such a preface:

> Aside from the ordinary commercial reasons, I find none that I can offer with dignity. I cannot say without immodesty that the books have merit; I cannot

> say without immodesty that the public wants a Uniform Edition; I cannot say without immodesty that a Uniform Edition will turn the nation toward higher ideals and elevated thought; I cannot say without immodesty that a Uniform Edition will eradicate crime, though I think it will. I find no reason which I can offer without immodesty except the rather poor one that I should like to see a Uniform Edition myself.

A columnist for the *Brooklyn Eagle* was unamused by the much-heralded publication of the works attired in "fine linen" and grumbled that "the chance . . . Mark Twain will be a name to conjure with a hundred years hence is slight." Meanwhile, Harper & Brothers issued a total of four new books by Sam for the trade market between 1898 and 1902, including *The Man That Corrupted Hadleyburg and Other Stories and Essays* and *How to Tell a Story and Other Essays*. Sam's income from both publishers in 1902 was about $60,000 and from all sources over $100,000.[39]

But this arrangement was at best only a short-term solution. Sam lost confidence in the Newbegin Co. in September 1901 when it began to advertise its "Popular Edition" of his works fraudulently. Rogers sent him a copy of a newspaper advertisement the company was running in the New York *Sun* and elsewhere that Sam considered "a mighty cold-blooded piece of rascality." It reproduced a purported personal testimonial in Sam's handwriting for the Newbegin edition that the author had never seen, much less written: "This is the authorized Uniform Edition of all my books. Mark Twain." Such a statement obviously compromised the marketing of Sam's new releases by Harper's.

> The Newbegin Co wanted me to give them something just about like this. (They applied first through Bliss & he brought me the draft of it) but of course I didn't consent. But I sent them something through you (which you approved) & never got even a thank-you. I didn't suit, I guess. So now they resort to plain forgery. They forge my signature, & then they put into my mouth a shameless personal letter no word of which ever had its source in either my mouth or my head, & then they add sacrilege to impudence & counterfeit my *style*! Now then, am I not right? *Sue these rascals at once.*

As it stood, Bliss in cahoots with Newbegin had a monopoly on the sale of Sam's earliest books and might "charge for them any price he might choose," while Harper was the exclusive publisher of all his new articles and books.[40] This cockeyed bargain was simply unsustainable over time, but a long-term resolution to the problem would not be negotiated for many months to come.

CHAPTER 9

Crossing Guard

The political and commercial morals of the United States are not merely food for laughter, they are an entire banquet.

—*Autobiography of Mark Twain*

SAM WAS MET at the gangplank by a gaggle of reporters when the *Minnehaha* docked at the West Houston Street pier the evening of October 15, three weeks before the presidential election of 1900. It was the most intensely covered press event of his career and one of the most newsworthy. He announced to the gathering his conversion to anti-imperialism during his years abroad. The *New York Herald* even entitled its report of the press conference "Mark Twain Home, an Anti-Imperialist." He was asked what he meant by imperialism. "I am at the disadvantage of not knowing whether the American people are for or against spreading themselves over the face of the globe," he responded. "I should be sorry if they are, for I don't think that it is wise or a necessary development." Twain applied the lessons of the border dispute in South America and his understanding of the Monroe doctrine to the eastern hemisphere. When he left on his round-the-world lecture tour in 1895, he told them, he had been a "red hot imperialist" who "wanted the American eagle to go screaming into the Pacific. It seemed tiresome and tame for it to content itself with the Rockies." Upon his return, he protested, the United States had pledged "to maintain and protect the abominable system established in the Philippines by the Friars. It should, it seems to me, be our pleasure and duty to let them deal with their own domestic questions in their own way. And so I am an anti-imperialist. I am opposed to having the eagle put its talons on any other land." Then, in the most explicit condemnation of jingoism he ever voiced, printed the next day in dozens of newspapers around the country, he said:

> I have tried hard, and yet I cannot for the life of me comprehend how we got into that mess. Perhaps we could not have avoided it—perhaps it was inevitable that we should come to be fighting the natives—but I cannot understand it, and have never been able to get at the bottom of the origin of our antagonism to the natives. I thought we should act as their protector—not try to get

> them under our heel. We were to relieve them from tyranny to enable them to set up a government of their own, and we were to stand by and see that it got a fair trial. It was not to be a government according to our ideas, but a government that represented the feeling of the majority of the Filipinos, a government according to Filipino ideas. That would have been a worthy mission for the United States. But now—why, we have got into a mess, a quagmire from which each fresh step renders the difficulty of extrication immensely greater. I'm sure I wish I could see what we were getting out of it, and all it means to us as a nation.

Sam made it clear that his political opinions in this case were shaped by the situation in South Africa he had observed at first hand. "If we desire to become members of the international family," he told the reporters, "let us enter it respectably and not on the basis at present proposed in Manila. We find a whole heap of fault with the war in South Africa, and feel moved to hysterics for the sufferings of the Boers, yet we don't seem to feel so very sorry for the natives in the Philippines." He also joked about running for political office. He was not sure if he was eligible to vote, though he had been paying property taxes in Hartford. As he remarked, "If I find that I cannot vote, I shall run for President. A patriotic American must do something around election time, and that's about the only thing political that is left for me."[1]

In short, he returned to a hero's welcome, greeted by the editors of dozens of newspapers across the country the next day. George Harvey, the new president of Harper & Brothers, contracted to buy anything he wrote "of whatever character" over the next year for ten cents a word, soon doubled to twenty. On Long Island, "poet lariat" Bloodgood Cutter hailed Sam's return to the American strand with a hackneyed rhyme:

> I will you now congratulate
> On your present prosperous state,
> And on your safe arrival here,
> To meet your friends, who you do cheer.
> The daily papers do us tell
> How you are looking very well,
> And when they do you interview,
> They say you are so cheerful, too.

The popular Chicago newspaper poet S. E. Kiser published a ballad more creditable to the occasion:

> What if the skies be dull and gray?
> He's home again at last.

And though he stoops somewhat today.
    And though his noon is past,
Beneath the frosted mane there lies
The same old twinkle in the eyes—
Come, for a space have done with sighs—
    Let's toot a merry blast!
Once more the grand old man of mirth
    Stands on his native shore.
From straying far upon the earth
    Where fun was not before!
The sun is slipping down the west—
Come, Mark, till sunset be the guest
Of those who like your lore and jest—
And let us laugh some more!

The family settled into an apartment in the Hotel Earlington on Twenty-Seventh Street near Madison Square Park and immediately began to hunt for a "furnished house that will not bankrupt us" to lease for the winter. Sam expected to "spend the time very quietly," devoting his time "to reading, smoking" and working as little as possible.[2]

As it happened, his life back in the United States was anything but quiet. "I could fill a book with just the doings that winter," Katy Leary remembered. "It was like a fairy story, and it was just as exciting to me to hear about them things as it was to the rest of the family. . . . Everybody was so glad to have Mark Twain back again they was just chasin' him everywhere. He was flooded with invitations from the highest and grandest in the town." The evening of October 17, only two days after his arrival, Sam spoke at the close of a three-day bazaar at the Waldorf-Astoria that raised over $25,000 for the victims of the hurricane that had struck Galveston Island the month before, specifically for the children orphaned by the storm.[3]

His former neighbor and collaborator Charles Dudley Warner died on October 20, and Sam hurried to Hartford three days later for the funeral and to serve as an honorary pallbearer. "Mr. Warner was one of my oldest, one of my dearest friends," he told an interviewer the day after Warner's passing. "I am unable to talk about his death or discuss our pleasant labor together. The suddenness of his death was such a shock to me that it would be impossible to go over the past in which he figured." Sam and Clara railed to Hartford on the day of the obsequies and remained only a few hours for what became a type of melancholy reunion of his circle of old friends, at least of the ones who survived. He visited George Warner, Charles's brother, and Charley Clark, Charles Warner's fellow editor at the *Courant*. Joseph Twichell and Edwin P. Parker conducted the funeral at the Asylum Hill Church, and William Hamersley, General Joseph R. Hawley, Laurence Hutton, Sarah Orne Jewett, and Franklin Whitmore attended. Another upshot of the sentimental journey: it convinced Sam he could never live in the mansion on Farmington Avenue again. "There was a pathetic pleasure in seeing Hartford and the house again," he conceded, "but I realize that if we ever enter the house again to live, our hearts will break. I am not sure that we shall ever be strong enough to endure that strain." He echoed the point on the final pages of his autobiography, dictated over nine years later: "Susy died in the house we built in Hartford. Mrs. Clemens would never enter it again. But it made the house dearer to me. I have entered it once since, when it was tenantless and silent and forlorn, but to me it was a holy place and beautiful."[4]

Back in New York, Sam and Livy rented a furnished house at 14 West Tenth Street, near Washington Square Park, for $2,500 a year. "We were very lucky to get this big house," Sam allowed. "There was not another one in the town—procurable—that would answer us. But this one is all right—space enough in it for several families, & the rooms all of old-fashioned great size." The evening of October 27, four days before moving from the hotel to their new home, Sam saluted Helen Keller, "that marvel of marvels of which there has been no precedent in human history," in a talk before the Women's Press Club at Carnegie Hall. Two weeks later, he was honored with a banquet at the Lotos Club attended by such Republican luminaries as Senator Chauncey Depew of New York; Benjamin B. Odell Jr., governor-elect of New York; and Thomas B. Reed, former Speaker of the U.S. House of Representatives. Also present were such cognoscenti as Thomas Bailey Aldrich, Moncure Conway, W. D. Howells, St. Clair McKelway, Sam Moffett, Clarence C. Rice, Booker T. Washington, and Sam's friends Henry Rogers and George Harvey. In the course of his remarks, Sam hinted at his disdain for Theodore Roosevelt, the newly elected Republican vice president ("If we could only give him some—some more—rope—") and ironically claimed to favor free silver, anathema to the "sound money" Republicans in the audience ("We have watched by its cradle, we have done our best to raise that child; but every time it seemed to be getting along nicely along came some pestiferous Republican and gave it the measles or something"). But his sober critique of conflict in the Philippines was apparently misunderstood for sarcasm. "By the grace of God . . . we have set Cuba free," he declared, and "we started out to set the Filipinos free" but "why our righteous purpose appears to have miscarried, I suppose I will never know. (Laughter.)" Howells remarked to Aldrich after the dinner that Sam appeared "younger and jollier than I've seen him for ten years. He says it is all Plasmon, a new German food-drug he's been taking, but I think it's partly prosperity."[5]

The evening of November 12, Sam was entertained by the New York Press Club at the Morton Building on Nassau Street, and three evenings later by the Society of American Authors at Delmonico's. The next day he railed to Princeton, where he spent the weekend with Laurence Hutton. With a coterie of Princeton professors including Hutton he attended the Princeton-Yale football game, won by a Yale team captained by F. Gordon Brown, who was inducted a half century later into the College Football Hall of Fame. "This beats croquet," Sam said, adding that he thought the country "safe when its young men show such pluck and determination as are here in evidence." On November 20, the day after returning from New Jersey, Sam dined with the Nineteenth Century Club at Sherry's Restaurant on West Thirty-Seventh Street, where he spoke on "The Disappearance of Literature."[6]

The same day Sam appeared before the Nineteenth Century Club, Katy Leary returned from Hartford, where she had been "to get some things." At Grand Central Station she hired a cab to carry her to the Clemens home on West Tenth, a distance of thirty-two blocks or less than two miles. By city ordinance the fare should have been between seventy-five cents and a dollar. "Well," Leary recalled, the hackman

> just took me all over New York instead! I didn't know the city very well then, but I did know that I shouldn't be ridin' all through Central Park! Up and down he took me, all over Central Park! Finally, after I hollered to him, he took me down to Tenth Street. I was pretty mad, but I only said, "How much is it?" Then he said, very sharp, "Seven dollars!" Well, I nearly fainted! I didn't have only two dollars in my purse, so I says: "Just you wait a minute. I'll go and get the money for you." I rang and the butler let me in, but Mr. Clemens, it happened, was standin' right there in the hall when I opened the door, so I just burst out and says: "Oh, Mr. Clemens! That cabman outside wants to charge seven dollars for bringing me down here."
>
> "What?" said Mr. Clemens. "Bring him right inside, Katy." Then he put his head out the front door and shouted to the man, "Bring in your tariff!"
>
> Well, the cabman brought it in and Mr. Clemens looked at it and says, "Young man, you're entitled to exactly seventy-five cents—for bringing this woman down here—just seventy-five cents," he says.
>
> "Yes," I said, "and you told me it would be *seven dollars!*"
>
> The cabman was pretty scared by that time, for he said: "Oh, you didn't understand me! I only said *five* dollars."

"Well," says Mr. Clemens, "we can't hear no more about it," he says. "You can just take this dollar and be off! But," he says, "I think I'd better know who you work for." The cabman was mad, but he told him, of course. Then Mr. Clemens says, "Is this your own cab?"

"No," says the man, "I'm working for my boss."

"Well," says Mr. Clemens, "you take this dollar and if your boss ain't satisfied with that, report to me in the morning." And then Mr. Clemens added, "If you don't report to me, I'll report *you*, for the way you've acted."

The man started to go and he kind of muttered to himself, "The old damned fool!"

Oh! Then Mr. Clemens said, "I heard you, I heard you, and you'll hear in the morning from me!"

The next day, Sam filed a complaint at City Hall with the Bureau of Licenses, which scheduled a public hearing for November 22.[7]

Some background: As early as April 1893, on his trip to Chicago to inspect the facilities to manufacture the Paige machine, Sam met an army major who contended that "every citizen of the republic ought to consider himself an unofficial policeman and keep unsalaried watch and ward over the laws and their execution. He thought that the only effective way of preserving and protecting public rights was for each citizen to do his share in preventing or punishing such infringements of them as came under his personal notice." In May 1895, Sam argued that the most effective means of contesting poor customer service was to "kick" the authorities. "If we want courteous treatment we have got to see to it that complaints of abusive treatment are made to the proper people," as he insisted to an interviewer. "Let each man kick his neighbor and receive a kick in return, until we have peace with courteousness." A year later he observed that "in London if you carry" a spat with a hack driver "into court the man that is entitled to win it will win it. In New York—but no one carries a cab case into court there. It is my impression that it is now more than thirty years since any one has carried a cab case into court there." In October 1897, soon after settling in Vienna, Sam was overcharged by a cabman. With assistance from staff at the American consulate, he filed a grievance with the police and, according to a news report, "gave assurance that the driver would be arrested the following day." Sam "went home happy in the thought that he would have an opportunity for seeing justice dealt out in an Austrian police court. But the trial never came off."[8]

So when Katy Leary was overcharged by New York cabman William Beck in November 1900, hardly a month after the Clemenses returned to the

United States, Sam was loaded for bear. His outrage did not erupt in a vacuum. Leary remembered that Beck initially demanded $7, or the equivalent in modern currency of about $200, for the short ride, which he soon reduced to "only" $5, or about $150 today. Sam jotted in his notebook the day of the incident that the cabbie wanted "$1.50 to bring maid from G[ran]d Central to 14 W. 10. His real fare was probably 75 c[ents]." Beck offered to compromise for $1.25, and Sam gave him a dollar. At the City Hall hearing on November 22, Sam sought to recover the amount of the overcharge and/or persuade the hearing officer to cancel Beck's license. As a result of the publicity given the case, Leary recalled, "the room was just crowded. Lots and lots of reporters. They was even settin' up on the windows and on everything." Beck readily confessed his guilt in the matter, though he explained that competition among the cabbies was so stiff that they had "to get square somehow. . . . We have to get all we can out of our fares." Beck later conceded—an explanation transcribed in dialect to emphasize his working-class status—that he

> was in the wrong and did charge [Clemens] too much. But he certainly was very crabbed the night I took his "gal" home. When I see him coming out to pay me with his fine white hair all over his head I says to myself, "Here's a nice soft old guy'll stand an extra half." And when he began to make a holler I thought he was jist one of those old cranks with lots of dough that's always tryin' to pinch out an extra cent because he doesn't need it. I don't blame him for kicking, but as a rule a 'cabbie' thinks a man that can afford to ride in a cab is able to stand a rise now and then. It was my idea if he could afford to have his hired gal riding around he wouldn't be looking twice at a half dollar before giving it up.

In the end, the hearing officer commended Sam for performing his civic duty, adding that "if there were more citizens like Mr. Clemens there would not be so much overcharging," and he suspended Beck's license. Afterward, Sam told a representative of the cabdrivers' union that his grievance had not been a matter of personal rancor but one of "practical business. You cannot imagine that I am making money wasting an hour or two of my time prosecuting a case in which I can have no personal interest whatever. I am doing this just as any citizen should do" in his role of "a non-classified policeman." Beck was "not the criminal here at all. The criminal is the citizen of New York and the absence of patriotism." Editorialists around the country praised Sam for his "courage in standing up for the rights of the citizen against extortion," for "acting on resolute lines," and "placing the obligations of the citizen above the amiabilities of the man of letters."[9]

This story of the cabman's loss of his license has a coda if not a sequel. Within a week after the hearing, Sam learned that Beck was supporting both his immediate family and a widowed mother. He summoned the driver to the house on Tenth Street, played billiards with him, gave him a $10 bill, and withdrew his complaint with the city so that his hack license was restored. Sam "gave him good advice and talked to him for about an hour," according to Katy Leary, "and I guess he made a real good man" of him. Beck wrote a letter of apology and in response Sam allowed that he had "gained my point and that is entirely satisfactory to me. I was not fighting the cab drivers but the system of charging extortionate fares." The cabbies' union was not so forgiving, however. Months later its president declared that, so far as its membership was concerned, "He's a dead one. He's in the Potter's Field. I don't think much of a cheap man who will try to have an honest cabman's license revoked, all on account of a quarter. Mark Twain ain't got nothin' to do with us." Still, the episode ended happily. As one wit waxed poetically,

> Where'er Mark Twain doth ride abroad
> The cabmen look askance;
> They show that they are overawed
> In every frightened glance.
> And when they've done the rattling tour
> And trembling name the fare
> They feel their pockets to make sure
> Their license still is there!

Sam's fame might wane "in another century," the *Boston Advertiser* editorialized, "but he will go down to countless ages as the one man who made a New York hackman apologize."[10]

During the final decade of his life, after his return to the United States, Sam Clemens was more than a social satirist and man of letters. He became a cultural critic, public intellectual, and political sage. In other words, he found a new polemical voice. In late November he addressed the Public Education Association at the Berkeley Lyceum, though by his own testimony he was neither a product of nor an authority on public schools. In early December he was the guest of honor at an Aldine Club dinner at its headquarters in the Constable Building on lower Fifth Avenue before an audience that included Winston Churchill, Frank Doubleday, Richard Watson Gilder, George Harvey, Howells, Laurence Hutton, Joe Jefferson, Brander Matthews, Silas Weir Mitchell, James Pond, Rice, Isidor Straus, and Owen Wister. When he accepted the invitation to the banquet, Sam stipulated that journalists be excluded from the gathering, much to the consternation of the press. The *Boston Globe,* for example, decried Sam's effrontery "in refusing to allow his speeches to be reported. If it were not for the newspapers comparatively few people would ever have heard of him."[11]

The protest seems to have struck a nerve. Two nights later, when Sam responded to the toast to "Our City" before an audience of five hundred at the St. Nicholas Society annual dinner at Delmonico's, his speech was fully reported. For several minutes, he mused aloud about the "great improvement in the city of New York" during the nine years he had lived abroad. But toward the close he became "more and more solemn until his voice fairly trembled in its earnestness." Or as the *New York Tribune* averred, he entertained the company before concluding with "a few neat uppercuts of satire and sat down before his hearers had time to recover their breath." His peroration dripped with sarcasm: "Gentlemen, you have the best municipal government in the world and the purest and most fragrant. The very angels envy you and wish they could establish a government like it in heaven. You got it by a noble fidelity to civic duty." The banqueters laughed, misunderstanding the term *fragrant* (that is, fetid). Then the final coup de grâce: "The angels of heaven, when you approach the final resting place, will gather at the gates and cry out: 'Here they come. Show them to the archangels' box and turn the limelight on them.'" The word "sarcasm" was whispered "in various quarters" of the room at this point, and "on reading the thing over next morning," some society members wondered "what he meant by making such a speech on an occasion designed strictly for the joy of self-laudation."[12]

A week later, in one of his finest hours, Sam introduced Winston Churchill, who was inaugurating a U.S. speaking tour under Pond's management, before an audience of twelve hundred in the grand ballroom of the Waldorf-Astoria. At Pond's invitation, Sam agreed to preside because, as he said, "I like that young man very much." The youngest member of the British Parliament at age twenty-six, Churchill later remembered the occasion. "My opening lecture in New York was under the auspices of no less a personage than 'Mark Twain,'" whom he had met at least twice before in England. The two men shared a birthday, albeit thirty-nine years apart, but not a point of view anent the Boer War. "Of course we argued about the war," Churchill recalled. "After some interchanges I found myself beaten back to the citadel. 'My country right or wrong.' 'Ah,' said the old gentleman, 'when the poor country is fighting for its life, I agree. But this was not your case.'" In presenting his "honored friend" Churchill to the assembly, Sam again upstaged one of the great orators of the twentieth century. As he "walked to the front of the platform," according to the New York *Sun*, "he got the reception of the star of the evening, the applause being long and hearty." "Mr. Churchill and I do not agree on the righteousness of the South African war, but that is of no consequence," he began. He preferred to emphasize the common cause of England and the United States.

> For years I have been a self-appointed missionary to bring about the union of America and the mother land. This union of friendship and esteem and fellowship, an alliance of the heart, should permanently and beneficently cement the two peoples together. I've warmed this mission of mine up with compliments to both peoples wherever I've been. They ought to be united. . . . I think that England sinned in getting into a war in South Africa which she could have avoided without loss of credit or dignity—just as I think we have sinned in crowding ourselves into a war in the Philippines on the same terms. . . . We have always been kin: kin in blood, kin in religion, kin in representative government, kin in ideals, kin in just and lofty purposes; and now we are kin in sin.

Sam "was cheered as much when he sat down" after this remarkable introduction "as when he arose," according to the *Sun*, "although there were evidences of mystified celebration in some quarters of the room." On his part, "Churchill seemed ill at ease" when Sam "turned him over to his audience and traces of his nervousness remained throughout the evening." At the end of the talk, Sam thanked Churchill for extolling both British and Boer valor, and Churchill in reply thanked Sam "for coming here to give to my lecture an importance and a dignity which it could not otherwise have obtained." Afterward, Churchill put the best face possible on these events. Sam was not displeased by his lecture, he thought, because "he was good enough at my request to sign every one of the thirty volumes of his works for my benefit; and in the first volume he inscribed the following maxim intended, I daresay, to convey a gentle admonition: 'To do good is noble; to teach others to do good is nobler, and no trouble.'" The press response to Sam's role that night was decidedly mixed, however. On the one hand, the New York *Evening Post* thought "he drew the razor of his satire across several of the most flaunting and destructive humbugs of the age," while on the other, the *Detroit Free Press* suggested that "Churchill might better have gone without being introduced than to have had Mark Twain do it in that fashion."[13]

Clara Clemens debuted as a professional concert singer at the Columbia Theater in Washington, D.C., the evening of January 22, 1901, and at Chickering Hall in Boston on February 16. Sam was present at the first of these appearances, though neither performance was particularly successful. The reviewers for the *Washington Star* and *Chicago Tribune* noted that she suffered from "evident nervousness" and "stage fright" and "partial paralysis of the vocal cords." Within a week of her Boston performance she decided to cancel the balance of her winter concerts. Livy admitted to Grace King that she and Sam were relieved: "We do not oppose her, for of course that is not best, but we are very sorry indeed that she wants this public life."[14]

The fin de siècle Samuel Clemens was no less an American iconoclast than an American icon. On December 30, 1900, two days before the start of the new epoch, he published a satirical "Salutation Speech from the Nineteenth Century to the Twentieth" in the *New York Herald*: "I bring you the stately matron named Christendom, returning bedraggled, besmirched, and dishonored from pirate-raids in Kiao-Chou, Manchuria, South Africa, & the Philippines, with her soul full of meanness, her pocket full of boodle, and her mouth full of pious hypocrisies. Give her soap and a towel, but hide the looking-glass." William M. Gibson has called it "perhaps [his] most perfect single piece of persuasive writing." He was much less diplomatic in a pair of private letters he wrote the last day of the year. To Abner Goodell: "I find but few men who disapprove of our theft of the Philippines & of our assassination of the liberties of the people of the Archipelago." And to John Y. W. MacAlister: "Oh, the Philippine mess! I wish I had been here two months before the Presidential election. I would have gone on the stump against *both* candidates, b'gosh! McKinley's war [in the Philippines] is as discreditable as [Joseph] Chamberlain's [in South Africa]. I wish to God the public would lynch both of those frauds."[15]

Sam courted more controversy and risked dissipating the goodwill he had accumulated over years a week later when he addressed almost two hundred members of the City Club of New York, a pro-civic-reform, "goo-goo" (good government), anti–Tammany Hall organization. He was expected to criticize local political corruption but he delivered more than advertised. In an impromptu aside he excoriated American foreign policy in the Philippines. Toward the close of his speech Twain discussed the recent presidential campaign and allowed that he had voted for neither candidate. He joked that "if we'd had an 'Anti-Doughnut Party'"—meaning a mugwump third party "of sixty thousand or eighty thousand voters in New York"—neither William Jennings Bryan nor William McKinley "would have been nominated" because the mugwumps would have forced the other parties to choose their best men. He had abstained from voting because he supported neither Bryan's "wildcat financial theories" nor McKinley, the man who sent "our bright boys as volunteers out to the Philippines to fight with a disgraced musket under a polluted flag." Most of the New York papers quoted these fighting words in their columns the next day, but only the prowar New York *Sun* included context in an obvious attempt to embarrass Sam. According to the *Sun*, "The statement about the President, his Philippines policy, and the polluted flag was not received with enthusiasm," and the applause when Sam sat down, "in marked contrast to that which he received when he got up," was "less than at any other time" during his speech. If, as the saying goes, sunshine patriots wrapped themselves in the flag, Sam unwrapped himself from the flag during his City Club speech. The next speaker, St. Clair McKelway, editor of the *Brooklyn Eagle* and a McKinley Republican, chided Sam for his remarks: "Candidly and absolutely I protest against his estimate of the able and dignified soldier and statesman who is the President of these United States and I believe that our gallant Army is fighting behind no dishonored muskets and under no polluted but under a glorious flag." The response to McKelvey's comment "was very pronounced. The audience rose and cheered, and cheered again and again, and not until some time had passed could the speaker proceed" while on the dais, in full view of the hostile crowd, Sam "simply puffed away at a stub of his cigar." In the audience, the physician Frank Van Fleet recalled that "we did not take him seriously. If we had, some of us might have mobbed him, and rightly, too."[16]

Sam's City Club address sparked a backlash across the country rivaling the controversy over his Whittier birthday speech in 1877. His first impulse was to walk back his comments, though not to retract them. As he told a reporter the next day, "I said a thing last night in a speech that I didn't mean to say. It just slipped out because I had been writing an article on the subject. I didn't intend to say it there." He was so outspoken that he offended even his mugwump friends, and he could not put the gin back in the bottle. The *New York Times* warned that Sam risked serious consequences to his popularity and reputation by such improper remarks; the *Boston Herald* noted that McKelvey's rebuke "was the one incident of the evening which came dangerously near to being an unpleasantness"; and the *Washington Times* admitted that Sam's talk "left his hearers with mingled feelings." Nevertheless, Sam considered "the round of cursing I have got from one end of the country to the other on that speech's account as a valuable compliment to me," and Conway hailed his "utterance as a *sursum corda* to the intellectual leaders and public teachers of America. The summons is needed" to rally "an uprising of intellectual forces in America." Horace White, the anti-imperialist editor of the New York *Evening Post*, noted that "some men profess to be indignant at Mark Twain for declaring that our flag in the Philippines is 'polluted'!

If Spain's flag was polluted, ours is, for we are doing the same things Spain did." Jervis Langdon, Sam's nephew, recalled that his uncle raged about the start of the war in Asia: when the United States "snatched the Philippines and butchered the boats of a poverty-struck, priest-ridden nation of children, she stained the flag. That's what we have today—a stained flag." Later in 1901 he expressed a different view, albeit reluctantly and privately. "In order not to seem eccentric I have swung around now and joined the nation in the conviction that nothing can sully a flag," as he wrote in an unpublished piece. He had suffered under the "illusion that a flag was a thing which must be sacredly guarded against shameful uses and unclean contacts lest it suffer pollution," and so when the Stars and Stripes "was sent out to the Philippines to float over a wanton war and a robbing expedition I supposed it was polluted, and in an ignorant moment I said so. But I stand corrected. I concede and acknowledge that it was only the government that sent it on such an errand that was polluted."[17]

In the wake of the controversy over Sam's City Club speech, Edward W. Ordway, secretary of the Anti-Imperialist League of New York, invited him to become an honorary officer in his organization. Sam readily accepted so long as he was not required to stuff envelopes. He was "glad to be a Vice President of the League" if the position was "a non-laboring one" because he was "prodigally endowed with sympathy with the cause." Over the next couple of years he signed a statement addressed to the American people circulated by the league protesting the prosecution of the war as well as a "Petition from Sundry Citizens of the United States Favoring the Suspension of Hostilities in the Philippine Islands and a Discussion of the Situation between the Government and the Filipino Leaders." Signed by dozens of prominent Americans, including Charles Francis Adams, John Burroughs, John Dewey, Edward Everett Hale, Howells, William James, Carl Schurz, and William Graham Sumner, the petition condemned U.S. atrocities in the islands, including the use of the "water cure," a form of torture a later generation of Americans would call "waterboarding," in particular the torture of a Filipino priest who had been killed by the "cure." On November 13, 1901, he also attended a meeting of the officers of the New York branch of the Anti-Imperialist League, at which he seconded a motion by Schurz that the organization "should for the time being confine itself to disseminating knowledge and sound opinion on the subject of the Philippines, keeping itself in the background as much as possible."[18]

At the time Sam addressed the City Club, he was writing "To the Person Sitting in Darkness," a bitterly ironic denunciation of Christian missionary efforts in China, prosecution of the Boer War by the British, the Russian invasion of Manchuria, and American policy in the Philippines. His title glossed on a verse in the Gospel according to Matthew ("The people which sat in darkness saw a great light") and alluded, in fact, to Americans, not benighted foreigners. The fundamental questions he posed in this essay were "Shall we go on conferring our Civilization upon the peoples that sit in darkness, or shall we give those poor things a rest? Shall we bang right ahead in our old-time, loud, pious way, or shall we sober up and sit down and think it over first?" He contrasted the *claims* of civilized nations with their *acts* in colonized countries. The phrase *cultural imperialism* had not yet been coined, so in the essay Sam invented his own terms to describe the phenomenon. He explained how "the Blessings-of-Civilization trust," as he called it, had packaged "civilization" for consumption abroad. "In the right kind of a light, and at a proper distance, with the goods a little out of focus," "the Blessings-of-Civilization trust" "furnishes this desirable exhibit to the Gentlemen who Sit in Darkness: love, justice, gentleness, Christianity, protection to the weak, temperance, law and order, liberty, equality, mercy, education, and so on." But in truth those goods are "merely an outside cover, gay and pretty and attractive, displaying the special patterns of our Civilization which we reserve for Home Consumption, while *inside* is the Actual Thing that the Customer Sitting in Darkness buys with his blood and tears and land and liberty." The Actual Thing, with the cover left off, included confiscation of property, extortion, "Glass Beads and Theology, guns, hymn books, and gin." The American president, the British colonial secretary, the kaiser, and the czar had been "exporting the Actual Thing *with the outside cover left off*." This was bad for business. "Is it possible," Sam wondered, "that there are two kinds of Civilization—one for home consumption and one for the heathen market?" That is, he implied that Christian missions in other nations simply established a beachhead for armed intervention. Nowhere was his iconoclasm more apparent than in his indictment of religious hypocrisy and his condemnation of military and cultural imperialism. The "Philippine temptation" had been "too strong" for the "Master of the Game" (McKinley) to resist. The entire essay, in fact, reeked of "playful & good-natured contempt for the lousy McKinley." The United States had returned Emilio Aguinaldo, "their leader, their hero, their hope, their Washington" from exile and exploited the Filipinos in various ways "until we needed them no longer; then derided the sucked orange and threw it away. . . . With our Treaty ratified, Manila subdued, and our Ghosts secured, we had no further use for Aguinaldo and the owners of the Archipelago. We forced a war, and we have been hunting America's guest and ally through the woods and swamps ever since." Sam proposed a special flag for "the Philippine Province," as he called it: "We can have just our usual flag, with the white stripes painted black and the stars replaced by the skull and cross-bones."[19]

Never one to suffer fools gladly, Sam was particularly incensed by the misconduct of Western missionaries in northern China during and after the Boxer Rebellion, "the indignant uprising of China's traduced patriots." He had long been critical of every stripe of proselytizing. "The symbol of the missionary (of *any* religion)," he confided to his notebook, "should be the polecat—an animal which does you no bodily harm but whose presence is unendurable. A missionary's presence on missionary ground is an insult—an insult as infamous as the invitation of a Catholic pulpit by a Protestant preacher & a proper matter for sharp punishment." The missionary practiced "a most strange vocation," one that resembles no other "unless party politics may be called reputable. In all lands the religious deserter ranks with the military deserter: it is considered that he has done a base thing & shameful. It is the mish's trade to make religious deserters." William Scott Ament, longtime missionary in China, had collected compensation—or, perhaps better stated, extorted tribute or war reparations or blood money—from Chinese for the deaths of Christians and the property damaged or appropriated during the rebellion. Ament's actions were reported on the front page of the New York *Sun* on December 24, 1900, and a month later the *New York Times* editorialized that the Christian missionaries in China were "the most implacable demanders of Chinese blood" and "as active in the looting of Chinese property" as "in instigating the promiscuous taking of Chinese lives." The column caused no demonstrable stir. In "To the Person Sitting in Darkness," however, Sam cited the *Sun* dispatch to the effect that Ament had "compelled the Chinese to pay" 300 taels, or about $200 in gold, "for each of these murders" committed by the Boxers, "compelled full payment for all the property belonging to Christians that was destroyed," and "assessed fines amounting to thirteen times the amount of the indemnity." Ament had denied that the missionaries were vindictive—an "impassioned assurance" Sam greeted with undisguised sarcasm: "Let us hope and pray that they will never become so," given that the "thirteen-fold indemnity" extorted from "the pauper peasants to square other people's offenses" condemned "them and their women and innocent little children to inevitable starvation and lingering death." Sam "never wrote anything more scorching, more penetrating in its sarcasm, more fearful in its revelation of injustice and hypocrisy" than this essay, according to Paine.[20]

Sam well understood the risk to his reputation and income. In early January, three weeks before the article appeared, he agreed to chair the ceremonies on Lincoln Day at Carnegie Hall. His friend and distant cousin Henry

Watterson, editor of the *Louisville Courier-Journal* and a former Confederate soldier, had also been invited to speak. "Think of it," Sam wrote Twichell—"two old rebels functioning there. . . . Things have changed somewhat in these 40 years, thank God." But he lodged one reservation with General Oliver O. Howard, who was organizing the event: "I'm venturing to accept on condition that you will be frank and disinvite me if you find you don't want a person of my stripe after you read my article in next *North American Review.*" (To his credit, Howard assured Sam after the article was printed that it was not "an obstacle. I have been as catholic as possible in inviting Bishops of different grades & divisions of the church to meet you, officers of the Army & Navy, & also Henry Watterson & many men of all parties & stripes among our citizens.") Similarly, Sam acknowledged to Twichell on the eve of the essay's appearance that he was "not expecting anything but kicks for scoffing at McKinley, that conscienceless thief & traitor, & *am* expecting a diminution of my bread and butter by it," but "if Livy will let me I will have my say. This nation is like all the others that have been spewed upon the earth—ready to shout for any cause that will tickle its vanity or fill its pockets. What a hell of a heaven it will be, when they get all these sons of bitches assembled there!"[21]

Twichell, who had risked his own career in 1884 by publicly opposing the Republican candidate for president, to Sam's dismay tried to dissuade him from publishing the article. Sam replied:

> *I* can't understand it! You are a public guide & teacher, Joe, & are under a heavy responsibility to men, young & old; if you teach your people—as you teach me—to hide their opinions when they believe their flag is being abused & dishonored, lest the utterance do them & a publisher a damage, how do you answer for it to your conscience? You are sorry for me; in the fair way of give & take, I am willing to be a little sorry for you. . . . You are supposing that I am supposing I am moved by a Large Patriotism, & that I am distressed because our idiot President has blundered in up to his neck in this Philippine privy; & that I am grieved because this great big ignorant nation, which doesn't know even the A B C facts of the Philippine is in disgrace before the sarcastic world—drop that idea! I care nothing for the rest—I am only distressed & troubled because *I* am befouled by these things.

Fortunately, both Livy and Howells, his fellow vice president of the Anti-Imperialist League, approved Sam's decision to publish the piece. Clara Clemens remembered that their opinions "enabled him to stand like the Statue of Liberty, unweakened by the waters of condemnation that washed up to his feet," though Howells facetiously suggested that Sam hang himself prior to its appearance to "save the public the trouble."[22]

In short, Sam fully expected the firestorm of vituperation that ensued. Coincidental with its publication in the *North American Review* for February 15, 1901, which hit the newsstands on January 31, the essay was widely excerpted, as in the *New York Tribune* (in a column ironically entitled "A Humorist's View"), the *St. Louis Republic*, and *San Francisco Call*. Livy wrote Grace King that "many of our friends do not approve" of the essay while "on the other hand very many do. He receives more letters of approval than of disapproval—in fact ten to one I should think." By midmonth the battle lines had been drawn, led by an attack in the *New York Times* on February 7 ("a grotesque picture of the Philippine transaction, true at no point and faithful in no detail") and a parry in the *Washington Post* three days later ("Mark Twain's credit with the American people is quite as good as that of the *New York Times*—even with the comparatively small number of persons who have ever heard of the latter").[23]

As Howells predicted, most editorialists were drawn to Sam's article like sharks to chum; the *Minneapolis Journal* called it "a very excellent specimen of flippancy" with an "utter disregard for truth and fact"; the *Boston Journal* opined that it "manifests both a mental and moral obliquity which astonishes and pains his New England neighbors and admirers"; the *Duluth News Tribune*, that "most people laugh at his Philippine tirade as a joke"; the *Nebraska State Journal*, that "there has been a screw loose in his head from the beginning and he has always been on the wrong side of National questions"; and the *St. Paul Pioneer Press*, that "a man who sees nothing but a hypocritical game of grab in our endeavors to carry the blessings of freedom and civilization to the Filipinos is lacking in moral sense." Dismissing the essay out of hand were the New York *Sun* ("he is in a state of mortifying intoxication from an overdraught of seriousness"), *Hartford Courant* ("the most meandering and wildest sort of history"), *Des Moines News* (Ament was "grossly misrepresented"), *Independent* ("hasty and blundering"), New York *Journal of Commerce* ("hasty" and "ill-informed"), *Brooklyn Eagle* ("unpatriotic"), *St. James's Gazette* ("a rather rabid and violent attack on Imperialism"), *Aberdeen Press and Journal* ("groundless slanders"), London *Sketch* ("hardly generous to a country which has treated him with great generosity"), and Chicago *Advance* ("as a humorist Mark Twain is a success; as a moralist he is clearly a failure"). The *Yorkshire Post and Leeds Intelligencer* hurled some of the harshest charges: Sam had published "a savagely ironical slander upon the Governments, and through them upon the peoples, of the United States and Great Britain." He misrepresented facts and "insinuates what is not true." No less than three Commonwealth papers described Sam's essay with the diminutive adjective "quaint": the *Westminster Budget*, the Wellington *Evening Post,* and the *Norwich Mercury* ("a scathing, albeit quaint, review of current wars and of the effects of the policy of expansion"). The leading religious magazines predictably reprimanded him for leaping to a conclusion, among them the New York *Outlook* ("condemns Dr. Ament without giving him a hearing or inquiring as to the facts"), the *Congregationalist* ("a snap judgment" based on "imperfect knowledge"), and *Zion's Herald* ("a Pecksniffian *poseur*").[24]

In an early application of the "equal time" principle of political debate, George Harvey of Harper & Brothers reprinted the substance of Sam's essay followed by a rejoinder by the satirist John Kendrick Bangs on facing pages of the February 9 issue of *Harper's Weekly* under the joint title "Is the Philippine Policy of the Administration Just?" Bangs, of course, argued in the affirmative. "For the first time in my life, or his," Bangs opined, "I seemed to find the great American somewhat astray in his Americanism; the great satirist wielding the bludgeon instead of the rapier; the great purveyor of sunshine to his fellow-men joining the ranks of the prophets of evil, spreading the gospel of discontent, and being governed by his disgusts rather than by his admirations." When Sam attacked "the President of the United States," Bangs was "inclined to find the most fault with him, because, in my judgment, his arrows are tainted with the poison of injustice." To the allegation the United States was meddling in the internal affairs of the Philippines, Bangs replied that "our authority" in the nation "is so clearly defined and our title to it so absolutely indisputable that the veriest child should be able to grasp the fact." How honorable was Aguinaldo, "the great leader of this rebellion"? He "sold himself to the enemy, deserted his people, robbed his fellow-conspirators, and did not even keep faith with those who bought him. . . . Publicly to endorse the act of a scheming adventurer in armed rebellion against the forces of the United States in other days would have been called treason." In an effort to extenuate Sam's alleged gaffe, Bangs blamed his "prolonged absence from his native land, during which time he may reasonably have been expected to get out of touch with things American." Bangs was disheartened "to find one from whom we have a right to expect so much" joining "the ranks of the merely captious—for Mr. Clemens indulges not at all in argument. A Philippine Philippic I should rather call this latest screed of his." Poultney Bigelow reacted to Bangs's rebuttal in a note to Sam: "It was something to see Bangs make an ass of himself while trying to teach you how to think—a l'Americaine! I didn't think Bangs could be such a provincial scribbler!"[25]

To be sure, others rallied to Sam's side, as in the *Baltimore Sun* ("little food for laughter but a great deal for serious reflection" and "Many people who are wearied of cant and humbug will welcome his blows"), Syracuse *Post-Standard* ("The strongest voice that has been heard in the anti-imperialist cause"), *Buffalo Courier* ("trenchantly impeaches the civilized nations for their treatment of 'heathen' peoples"), *Boston Herald* ("a savagely ironical review of the present policy"), Boston *Literary World* ("keen mingling of sarcasm, sense, and sentiment"), *Boston Post* ("combines wit, humor, argument and a variety of qualities which no other writer could put into one article"), *Boston Globe* ("undeniably strong"), and the *Hartford Times* (carries "the sad and shocking facts of the crime against the Filipinos home to hundreds of thousands of American from whom they have been hitherto hidden"). The *Springfield Republican* pronounced Sam "the most influential anti-imperialist and the most dreaded critic of the sacrosanct person in the White House that the country contains." According to the New Orleans *Times-Democrat*, he exposed the "true motives" of "rapacious nations" and "scourges their hypocrisy, their rapacity, their avarice, and their cruelty." William T. Stead declared in the London *Review of Reviews* that Sam had "never combined in a single article so much mordant humor and such merciless truth as are to be found in the inimitable essay"; Herbert Welsh, the editor of *City and State*, saluted the "burning and cutting satire . . . applied by the hand of a genius"; and Edwin Buritt Smith, chair of the executive committee of the American Anti-Imperialist League, thought it "the strongest indictment of imperialism with all its cant and humbug that has yet appeared." Horace White commended Sam's courage without stint in the *Evening Post*: "Mark Twain comes home to tell our flaunting Imperialists that he sees through their hypocrisies." Sam's cousin-by-marriage Henry Watterson echoed the paean of praise in the *Louisville Courier-Journal*: "A remarkable transformation, or rather a development, has taken place in Mark Twain. The genial humorist of the earlier day is now a reformer of the vigorous kind, a sort of knight errant who does not hesitate to break a lance with either church or State if he thinks them interposing on that broad highway over which he believes not a part but the whole of mankind has the privilege of passing." Daniel DeLeon, editor of the New York *Daily People*, the organ of the Socialist Labor Party, observed that Sam "mercilessly exposed the vandalism of the missionaries in China when he showed that they had looted the palaces and despoiled the temples and then sold their booty." John Ames Mitchell, editor and publisher of *Life*, cackled that Sam "had hung up the hide of the Reverend Ament" and dared the American Board to sue Sam "for defamation of Dr. Ament's character" because, while he "is not as rich as he ought to be, he is better able to pay for damage done to missionaries than the Chinese villagers are." Howells, who routinely paid court to Sam at his home on Tenth Street, wrote his sister Aurelia that "we agree perfectly about the Boer War and the Filipino war and war generally. Then, we are old fellows, and it is pleasant to find the world so much worse than it was when we were young. Clemens is, as I have always known him, a most right-minded man, and of course he has an intellect that I enjoy. He is getting some hard knocks from the blackguards and hypocrites for his righteous fun with McKinley's attempts to colonize the Philippines, but he is making hosts of friends, too." E. L. Godkin and Andrew Carnegie, two other vice presidents of the Anti-Imperialist League, congratulated Sam upon publication of the piece. Godkin commended it in the *Nation* ("His satirical weapons were never keener, or played about the heads of Imperialists with a more merciless swish"). Carnegie wrote Sam that he liked the "new Gospel of Saint Mark in the *North American* . . . better than anything I've read for many a day. I am willing to borrow a thousand dollars to distribute that sacred message in proper form, & if the author don't object may I send that sum, when I can raise it, to the Anti-Imperialist League, . . . the only missionary work I am responsible for. Just tell me you are willing & many thousands of the holy little missals will go forth. This inimitable satire is to become a classic. I count among my privileges in life that I know you." While Sam never reprinted the essay in any collection of his work during his life, the Anti-Imperialist League of New York, with his permission, distributed 124,000 copies of it in pamphlet format.[26]

Privately, Godkin advised Sam not to "retract or explain or do anything but to rub it in harder. To say a single word in explanation or apology would be treason to every good cause for which men have ever fought or fallen." Whether by accident or design, Sam poured salt in the wounds of the Christian lobby a few weeks later when he dusted off and revised "Extracts from Adam's Diary," a parody of the Higher Criticism of Ernest Renan and Adolf von Harnack, for publication in *Harper's Monthly*. The dour Henry Adams thought the fractured fairy tale contained "one or two good jokes," though he admitted he was "not an expert judge" of humor. The *Sheffield Telegraph* considered it in Sam's "very best vein," and the London *Review of Reviews* deemed it "good-hearted irreverence." The *Paisley & Renfrewshire Gazette* thought it therapeutic ("the best antidote to a heavy dinner among all the bright things in this month's magazines") and "vastly more human" and "considerably more entertaining" than the book of Genesis. However, the London *Daily News* scorned it ("very poor stuff and totally unworthy of the greatest living humourist"), and the Reverend M. S. Waters of the Evangelical Lutheran Church in Newark regarded Sam's burlesque of Holy Writ "flippant, cheap, coarse, and shameful."[27]

The missionary and religious enthusiasts in general were predictably incensed by Sam's lapses from orthodoxy. Erving Winslow, secretary of the New England Anti-Imperialist League, conceded that "the only unfortunate thing" about "To the Person Sitting in Darkness" was the "allusion to the missionaries which will prejudice a good many people against his arguments and was not really necessary and perhaps mistaken." The pamphlet circulated by the league omitted the sections on Ament's misconduct and on political corruption in New York. The Reverend Paul C. Curnick declared at a missionary conference in Detroit that Sam's "false attack" upon Ament was "the most unjust, unfair, and outrageous attack that has ever been made upon missionary work." The president of the Foreign Christian Missionary Society at its annual convention blamed Sam for a decline in donations. The Reverend Judson Smith, secretary of the American Board of Commissioners for Foreign Missions of the Congregationalist Church, in an open letter printed in several papers backed Ament and demanded that Sam recant his allegations. "You base all you have to say of him on a single press dispatch" in the *Sun*, Smith began, and "you assume the accuracy of this dispatch as though it were Dr. Ament's frank and full confession of deeds and motives," but "you are too experienced an author to rest so terrible an accusation . . . upon a single newspaper dispatch." In response, Sam noted that the *Sun* dispatch had been in print for over a month without a public denial of its accuracy—that is, "the American Board conceded the validity of the dispatch by silence"—but he pledged to investigate and publish his findings "at some length in the *North American Review*." Privately, he belittled "idiot Christian pirates like Ament & professional hypocrites & liars like Rev. Judson Smith." But as good as his word, he contacted Henry Chamberlain, the *Sun* reporter who had written the original article, for verification of his reporting. Smith "thinks I have committed an enormity in condemning a man upon a single newspaper dispatch," he explained. But he had "waited 39 days for the Board to produce from Mr. Ament a repudiation of the facts of the dispatch before I said anything." Sam was willing to drop the matter entirely "if I am left unmolested. But if molested I should like to be in shape to say with positiveness one thing or the other—that Ament did and said those things or didn't. If he shall prove innocent I wish to frankly say so; and if guilty as frankly say that."[28]

The same day that Sam sent this inquiry, the controversy over his essay became more contentious. Ament cabled that all reports about his collection of indemnities had omitted a decimal point: "Collected one-third, for church purposes, additional actual damages, now supporting widows and orphans. Publication thirteen times blunder cable. All collection received approval

Chinese officials." The American Board of Foreign Missions claimed vindication because the *Sun* and in turn Sam had "grossly exaggerated" the amount of money Ament levied on the Chinese. The board and others alleged that Sam had slandered the missionary, however inadvertently, and insisted he apologize or that Ament sue him for libel. The department store baron John Wanamaker of Philadelphia even offered to pay the legal costs of such a suit. Ament eventually replied to Sam at length, not in a religious periodical or other denominational venue, however, but in Orison Swett Marden's New Thought magazine *Success*. "It is a well-known fact that Chinese officials are corrupt. If they had collected the indemnity, from ten to fifteen percent of it would have remained in their hands and never would have reached the suffering people." Ament likewise argued that "The stories of the evil deeds of the troops have been grossly exaggerated. To be sure, there was much bad conduct—you cannot get forty thousand troops together without it." Smith urged Sam to "withdraw the criticisms that were founded on 'a cable blunder,'" and the Peking Missionary Association petitioned him to retract his statements "concerning monies [Ament] collected from rural Chinese in payment for properties destroyed and people killed during the Boxer rebellion" in a cable to the *North American Review*: "Peking Missionary Association demands public retraction. Mark Twain's gross libel against Ament utterly false." The *Boston Globe* and the *Hartford Post* adjured him to "make for the amen corner" and "offer a contrite apology" to Ament "for his scathing attack." The *Boston Journal* added that "it is not Dr. Ament, but Mark Twain whose reputation needs rehabilitating." Sam replied that his error in "one unimportant detail" had occurred in quoting the amount of indemnities Ament had demanded. The other facts remained unchanged: "Ament has twice confessed that he took money from A to pay B's debts," a method of extortion "despoiling the innocent to square the damages created by the guilty—& why? Because it is in accordance with *Chinese* law & custom! It seems incredible. For broad humor, the situation puts opera bouffe to shame." The principle at stake was the same. To his credit, Sam was hardly chastened by the downpour of vilification. Though he bubbled in "hot water with the clergy and other goody-goody people," he wrote, "I am enjoying it more than I have ever enjoyed hot water before." In a speech to the Lotos Club in New York on March 23, with Vice President Roosevelt in the audience, he even joked that he had been called a traitor because he "didn't go to fight in the Philippines" and so perhaps he should be "dangling from a lamp-post somewhere." A year after the piece appeared, Sam acknowledged that he had paid a price "in public approval (& consequently in money)" in publishing "a Satanic magazine article which got the missionaries in my hair—also some politicians—Yes, sir, I contributed that article, knowing quite well what I was going to catch." Even eight years later, he defended his decision to air his criticisms of the missionary trade to Twichell: "the horrors of the Boxer revolt in China were making Christendom gasp & shudder—a revolt largely—mainly?—caused by the Chinaman's quite justifiable hatred of the foreign missionary," and he had vented his opinion in the *North American Review*. The missionary "looters have never yet been whitewashed clean," he insisted, "& they never will be. Every attempt at it has failed; although the American Board did its best."[29]

Henry Rogers eventually requested a favor in kind from Sam for the financial advice that rescued him from bankruptcy. He learned in late December 1901 that Ida Tarbell, one of the original muckrakers, was preparing a history/exposé of the Standard Oil Company for publication in *McClure's*, and he asked Sam to intervene. "It would naturally be supposed that any person desiring to write a veritable history would seek for information as near original sources as possible," as he informed Sam.

> Miss Tarbell has not applied to the Standard Oil Company, nor to anyone connected with it, for information on any subject. On the contrary, I have reason to believe she is seeking all her information from those not disinterested enemies of the 'Standard' who have for years invented and published falsehoods concerning it. . . . I do not know whether you can be of any service in the matter, but it would be a kindness to Mr. McClure as well as myself if you could suggest to him that some care should be taken to verify statements which may be made through his magazine.

Sam contacted S. S. McClure on Rogers's behalf, and as Tarbell later recalled, McClure in turn "dashed into the office one day to tell me he had just been talking with Mark Twain," who had asked "what kind of history of the concern *McClure's* proposed to publish." Sam helped arrange for Tarbell to interview Rogers, and the two of them seem to have gotten along famously. In her history of Standard Oil, Tarbell described Rogers as "one of the ablest and frankest" executives of the company, who had testified before the Industrial Commission in 1899 "with delightful candour." She also reported that "Rogers is accused daily in Montana of having burned a refinery in Buffalo. As a matter of fact, no refinery was burned in Buffalo." When the book appeared, Sam chortled to Rogers that Tarbell "always gives you a good character, as a man, & this time she does it again, but she gives you no rank as a conspirator—does not even let you say any dark things; does not even let you sit mute & awful in a Buffalo Court like John D. [Rockefeller] & lower the temperature of justice. Henry H., the woman has been *bought*!" In her 1939 autobiography, Tarbell admitted to "heartily liking" the robber baron, "one of the great figures in the development of oil" and "as fine a pirate as ever flew his flag in Wall Street."[30]

With his daughter Jean in the care of George J. Helmer, the president of the New York State Society of Osteopaths, Sam became a public advocate for this brand of therapeutic practice. In his view, the liberty to select a regimen of treatment, like freedom of speech or religion, was a civil right. The government should not fetter the freedom of the individual to choose among types of medicine. "My body is my own," he insisted, or "at least I have always so regarded it. If I do it harm through my experimenting it is I who suffer, not the state." Every citizen had a "fair & legitimate right to do with his body as he does with his soul: choose healer & creed to suit himself." He publicly observed that the so-called anti–Christian Science bill before the New York State legislature carved out an exception permitting family members to treat illness. Grandmothers might "continue to dose the babe," and Sam asked the lawmakers to allow osteopaths "the same liberty" they gave grandmothers. On February 27, he testified for nearly an hour before the New York State Assembly committee on public health about a bill to license osteopaths and earned the enmity of his old foe, the *New York Times*. The next day the *Times* pronounced him "a defender of quacks" and declared that, "however unintentionally," he was "assuming the role of a public enemy." Sam was unfazed, of course, by the opposition of the medical establishment. "To ask a doctor's opinion of osteopathy," he noted in his journal, "is equivalent to going to Satan for information about Christianity."[31] The proposed legislation died in committee.

In "To My Missionary Critics," his promised reply in the April 1901 issue of the *North American Review*, Sam doubled down on his original flaying of Ament. He "did not want to write" the article, he professed, but "it was forced from him by the statements of missionaries." He hoped "they will like it," but he had doubts, and well he should have. In his response, Sam ridiculed Arent's alibi that he had only levied an indemnity of 1.3 rather than 13 times the damages, and the willingness of his defenders to accept that rationale as a form of self-defense. As he argued, "The girl who was rebuked for having borne an illegitimate baby excused herself by saying, 'But it is such a *little* one.' When the 'thirteen-times-extra' was alleged, it stood for theft and extortion, in Dr. Smith's eyes, and he was shocked. But when Dr. Ament showed that he had taken only a *third* extra, instead of thirteenfold,

Dr. Smith was relieved, content, happy, I declare I cannot imagine why." Put another way, "If a pauper owes me a dollar and I catch him unprotected and make him pay me fourteen dollars thirteen of it is 'theft and extortion.' If I make him pay only one dollar thirty-three and a third cents the thirty-three and a third cents are 'theft and extortion' just the same." Or still another: "There is no moral difference between a big filch and a little filch. . . . Morally there are no degrees in stealing." Ament's "curious" dispatch to the board had been nothing if not self-incriminating. He had confessed to extorting money from the Chinese not for the "propagation of the gospel" but for "church expenses." The board ought to have suppressed that revelation rather than allow it "to get into print." As the *New York Tribune* noted, someone might call "To My Missionary Critics" an apology only "if he be careless about the actual meaning of words." The *Sheffield Telegraph* pronounced it "a terrible exposure of a certain lop-sided view of moral questions which seems to have become dominant in missionary circles."[32]

Then another unexpected turn of the screw. In a series of interviews Ament granted in April and May, he tumbled from the moral high ground. The more he talked, the more he admitted to unrighteous retaliation. While in Japan en route to the United States to defend his reputation on a national fundraising tour, he allowed to the *Kobe Herald* that the Committee of Confiscated Goods, the so-called Loot Committee, pillaged stores "of people who had sought refuge in the legation during the siege" of Beijing and that his mission had received $75 from the sale of the goods. As he elaborated while in San Francisco three weeks later, Ament had confiscated and ransacked the abandoned home of a "broken down Mongol" prince, a Boxer ally, before it "would have been destroyed by the Russians," and sold the plunder, including furs and sables, over a two-week period "for about one-half or two-thirds of the value that they would have brought in ordinary times," a total of about $4,000 in gold. Ament did not fundamentally refute the charges leveled by Sam; he merely insisted upon extenuating circumstances that justified his actions. "We entered the residences of the Chinese who had fled from the city, and a great deal of valuable property was secured," he admitted. "On the Prince's grounds was found a large stable of mules and horses. There was very little feed for these animals, and something had to be done with them or they would starve to death." In the heat of the debate, what some called "looting," others called the "spoils of war," and still others "justifiable confiscation." Ament added, while in Chicago at the end of the month, that "the stories of barbarous practices by the allied troops" had been "greatly exaggerated," though he admitted that he approved the torching of a hut occupied by "one of the worst characters" in the region—obviously a

Boxer sympathizer—a terrorist act by U.S. Marines that "had a beneficial" effect on the other villagers. Ament never filed a libel suit against Sam lest he expose his own legal liability and submit to cross-examination on the witness stand. "I am enjoying Ament," Sam admitted to Twichell in June. "He is doing my work for me—damaging his nefarious cause. If ever he shows signs of quieting down I will stir him up again. He is doing good & must be kept at it. I believe China can be saved yet from Christianity of the American Board breed & I think that that old mud-turtle, Smith, & the talky Ament will accomplish it if some traitor doesn't gag them."[33]

The fallout among the clergy from Sam's uncustomary effrontery lasted for months. The Reverend Washington Gladden of the Congregationalist Church in Dayton, the leading American proponent of the Social Gospel, admonished Sam that "what Mr. Ament was doing not only 'follows Chinese custom' but *is* 'warranted' by every 'code of civilization' with which I am familiar." The Reverend Dr. David J. Burrell, a prominent Presbyterian minister, professed at Marble Collegiate Church his belief that Sam had "injured every missionary in China and in the world, and yet he has not had the grace to apologize." The Reverend Dr. Cortland Myers complained from the pulpit of the Baptist Temple in Brooklyn that Sam had "become a little Pharisaical" and "never was there more shallow and unjust criticism uttered" than "To the Person Sitting in Darkness." The Reverend E. P. Johnson of Albany at a regular session of the synod of the Reformed Church in America compared Sam to Satan "and gave all the honors to the Devil." The Reverend Dr. A. C. Bunn, rector of the Church Charity Foundation on Long Island, alleged that Sam "had maligned the missionaries through a misunderstanding." The Reverend Charles M. Sheldon, author of the best-selling novel *In His Steps* (1897) and a Congregationalist minister in Topeka, Kansas, complained that Sam's writings were often "marred by a coarseness of thought" and might "be funny" but were "not real entertainment." John J. Fullam of St. Mary's Catholic Church in St. Louis assailed Sam as a "scurrilous buffoon." The Reverend Dr. Wayland Spaulding, president of the Congregational Clerical Union, headquartered in New York, leveled perhaps the most disgraceful insult, an ad hominem attack on Sam's character. "All that can be said of Mr. Clemens," Spaulding said, "is that he is a man of low birth and poor breeding. He has not had the decency, now that there is shown to be no authority for the statement he made, to come out and retract." Sam waited less than a week to reply to Spaulding at a meeting of the Brooklyn Clerical Union. A minister he declined to name "has just called me low born and ill bred. I don't mind that so much. Shakespeare was low born, too; and there was Adam—I believe he was born out in the woods. But I'm glad the doctor didn't say it about Adam. When such a thing is said about the head of the family it hurts. Anyhow, I think I would prefer to be low born—in a republic—like the rest." Even his mild public riposte, however, prompted a rebuke by the editors of *Christian Work*: "We have an idea that the ministers of the country have had enough of Mark Twain."[34]

Fortunately, not all of them. William Jewett Tucker, president of Dartmouth College and an ordained Congregationalist minister, agreed that the cause of Christ had "been set back, nobody knows how far, by the behavior of the missionaries in China." The Reverend Franklin M. Chapin, a former associate of Ament in the Chinese mission, confessed "with great reluctance" in a letter to the *New York Tribune* that Sam was "in the right." And Henry Codman Potter, Episcopal bishop of the diocese of New York, implicitly defended Sam in an address at the University of Rochester, observing that he was "at a loss to account for the disregard of customs of these foreign countries by our missionaries."[35]

On June 21 Sam, Livy, Clara, Jean, and Katy Leary moved for the summer to a cabin, rented for $150 a month and soon nicknamed "the Lair," on the southern shore of Lake Colby two and a half miles from Ampersand, New York, near Lake Saranac. "It is as reposeful as the cemetery," Sam announced. He told an interviewer, with a backward glance at his summer in Weggis, that they enjoyed a "paradise" in the Adirondacks all summer: "One doesn't need to go to the Swiss Lakes to find that condition." He said to another interviewer, "In all my travels and sojourns among the Swiss lakes and mountains I have never come upon anything so perfectly delightful, so restful, so conducive to the forgetfulness of all thought of care, so free as this place. I am more than charmed with it, as is also Mrs. Clemens, and, indeed, I may say the entire family." In his autobiography, Sam recalled that the "repose and seclusion in the Adirondacks" during the summer "did [Livy] manifest good." One local resident, however, thought Livy enjoyed her invalidism and the attention it attracted.[36]

As usual, Sam took a vacation from his vacation the first two weeks in August. At Henry Rogers's invitation he spoke at the dedication of the new Unitarian Church in Fairhaven, Massachusetts, on August 5, and in company with Rice, former Speaker of the House Thomas Reed, the Reverends Robert Collyer and Minot Savage, and several others, he sailed along the coast of Maine, New Brunswick, and Nova Scotia on Rogers's 225-foot, 322-ton luxury yacht *Kanawha*. "Beautifully furnished," as Sam wrote Livy, and the fastest private steamer in the world with a top speed of over twenty-two knots, it carried a crew of forty. Interviewed near Bar Harbor, Maine,

Sam joked that the men on the floating poker game lived "by borrowing from one another, the amount of the loan being restricted by the denomination of the cards." He claimed two years later that he had been "robbed of large sums of money by Standard Oil millionaires," though former justice of the New York State Supreme Court William N. Cohen remembered that the card games had a ten-cent limit. As a gag, some of the other passengers threw Sam's cheap umbrella overboard, and Sam, playing along, spent the rest of the "stag party" searching the ship for it. But not all was fun and games aboard the craft. Rice remembered that Reed "undertook to belittle Mr. Clemens' opinion on some political happening in Washington," no doubt the controversy over the war in the Philippines. "The debate became very spirited, and Mr. Clemens easily came out ahead. After this we noticed that Mr. Reed was extremely careful in engaging Mr. Clemens in verbal controversy." Nevertheless, after the cruise, Sam wrote Rogers it had been "the most contenting & comfortable & satisfactory pleasure-excursion I have ever made." "We had a noble good time," he reiterated to Twichell, "& caught a China missionary & drowned him." A few days later, Sam watched the third and final America's Cup race off Sandy Hook in New York Harbor, won by the yacht *Columbia* against Sir Thomas Lipton's *Shamrock II*, from the deck of the *Kanawha*.[37]

Back at the Lair, for the remainder of the summer he wrote on average four hours and some eighteen hundred words with gusts up to four thousand words per day, including a parody of Arthur Conan Doyle's Sherlock Holmes fiction entitled "A Double-Barrelled Detective Story." The "seed" of the story had been planted "many years ago" when Twichell lent him a copy of *A Study in Scarlet* (1887) by "a new author, not heard of by me until then." Sam had "planned to make fun of that pompous sentimental 'extraordinary man' [Holmes] with his cheap & ineffectual ingenuities"[38] but "the plan wouldn't sprout; I have planned again, several times in past years, but each time the sprout withered on my hands." He attended a performance of William Gillette's play *Sherlock Holmes* at the Harlem Opera House on November 10, 1900, which no doubt roused his imagination. But by riffing on the opening installment of *The Hound of the Baskervilles* in the August 1901 issue of *Strand*, as he bragged to Twichell, "this time I've pulled it off," specifically by inventing a rival detective to Holmes born with the olfactory scent of a bloodhound. He completed the twenty-five-thousand-word burlesque "magazinable at 20 cents a word" in only a week—between August 29 and September 6. Its sale for $4,400 to *Harper's Monthly*, where it appeared in the January and February 1902 issues, "pays a third of our year's expenses & a little over," including the "tiresome" cost of maintaining their Hartford mansion.[39] A *tour de farce* of absurd situations, contrived clues, mock melodrama, and mistaken identities, the tale contains a cluster of characters, one named Ham Sandwich, hung on a plot as thin as a slice of prosciutto and irrelevant subplots that feature an inept Holmes, a forerunner of Peter Sellers's Pink Panther.

However slight and frivolous, the flapdoodle was welcomed by critics upon its serialization in *Harper's Monthly*. Reviewers for such papers as the New York *Evening Post* ("an intentional burlesque on the overwrought detective tale"), New Orleans *Times-Democrat* ("rich in startling incidents"), *Minneapolis Star Tribune* ("full of mystery"), and *Richmond Times* ("full of . . . satirical humor") lauded it judiciously.[40]

But the tenor of notices rose a key when the story was repackaged by Harper & Brothers in the United States and Chatto & Windus in the United Kingdom for sale as a single volume printed in large font with wide margins and seven full-page illustrations. The parody spread over about twenty-three double-columned pages in two issues of *Harper's Monthly* was transformed into a book of 179 rubricated pages. A few venues commended the story in this new format, including the New York *Sun* ("undeniably amusing"), *Cleveland Plain Dealer* ("admirable fooling"), *Book News* ("wonderfully diverting and highly amusing"), *London Chronicle* ("genial piece of fooling"), *New Zealand Mail* ("as a piece of satire . . . it is a pronounced success"), *Lyttelton Times* ("an elaborate and clever skit"), and Sydney *World's News* ("delightfully entertaining" and "ingeniously told."[41]

But most critics were hostile. The *Brooklyn Eagle*, which had asserted that the "weird," "unusual and uncanny" serial was "told with the greatest force," thought the story less than four months later "positively amateurish" with its descent into farce. Whereas the *Hartford Courant* claimed in January that the serial combined "a stroke of the imagination" with "convincing verisimilitude," the same paper called the tale "sad stuff" in May. Other notices of the book were equally scornful, considering it balderdash and (to echo Pap Finn) little more than "hifalut'n foolishness," among them the *Baltimore Sun* (a "perplexing . . . mixture of cleverness and inanity"), *Brooklyn Life* ("unworthy of the author"), *Public Opinion* ("too tame to be a burlesque and too far-fetched to be humorous"), *Providence Journal* (a "farrago of nonsense"), *Boston Transcript* ("a farrago of sensationalism, burlesque, sentimentality, farce and supposititious humor"), *Times Literary Supplement* ("not a real story"), *Manchester Guardian* ("a dull burlesque"), *Saturday Review* ("a feeble burlesque"), New York *Outlook* (a "revolting" burlesque), London *Daily News* (a "grim and uncanny story"), London *Standard* ("only worth publishing in a magazine"), *Truth* (an "incongruous blending of the methods of tragedy and comedy"), *St. James's Gazette* ("Whether these two barrels are meant for jest or earnest is not so evident as the unfortunate fact that neither of the Twain is up to the Mark"), *Yorkshire Post and Leeds Intelligencer* ("The successful humorist is not necessarily a good parodist"), *Chicago Tribune* (a story "distinctly not worth telling"), *Buffalo Commercial* ("the weakest book on the Harpers' list this year"), *Ithaca Journal* (a "jumble of grotesque nonsense"), *Dayton News* ("little in the book to recommend it"), *New York Tribune* ("nothing more than an ingenious piece of fooling"), *San Francisco Chronicle* ("very dismal reading"), *Brooklyn Standard Union* ("the average reader will be greatly disappointed"), Chicago *Dial* ("leaves the reader disappointed"), *Springfield Republican* ("a brilliant possibility spoiled by a caprice"), *New Orleans Picayune* ("savors somewhat of the gruesome"), *Grand Rapids Press* ("will add nothing to the fame of the author"), *Philadelphia Times* ("a bizarre mixture of blood-and-thunder and downright burlesque"), *Boston Advertiser* ("inferior to the author's previous work"), and Sydney *Daily Telegraph* ("a railway romance" that "will not bear looking into closely"). The reputation of the story was so low that in 1907 it was declared "literary junk" and expelled from the shelves of the Detroit Public Library, though it was returned to the shelves the next month by the librarian, who, bowing to public pressure, admitted "he had not read the book" before he removed it.[42]

At virtually the same moment Sam finished "A Double-Barrelled Detective Story" at his cabin in the Adirondacks, he heard a rumor that William McKinley had been shot in Buffalo. "But there are no newspapers," he complained to Henry Rogers, "& no one knows whether it is true or not. It may be only talk." The next day, a New York City paper "wandered into the camp" and confirmed the news, though Sam doubted if McKinley's injury was serious because he had been moved after surgery to a private home. After all, he added, "doctors (& politicians) always get all the advertising they can out of a case," though "if [McKinley] dies, I wish to withdraw these remarks." The president had in fact been gut-shot while touring the Pan-American Exposition in Buffalo by a twenty-eight-year-old unemployed anarchist, Leon Czolgosz—or, as Sam called him, "this ass with the unpronounceable name."[43] On September 10, four days after the assault, McKinley was reportedly on the mend.

Though he had long disparaged the temporary-insanity defense in criminal trials, Sam in a long disquisition to Twichell pondered the ripple effects of Czolgosz's act. He must have "been entertaining fiery and reason-debauching maggots in his head for weeks and months" and "was probably more insane than usual this week or two back." He might "get back upon his bearings by and by, but he was over the sanity-border when he shot the President." Sam feared the assassination attempt, like lynchings in the South, would breed copycat crimes just as every lynching "unsettles the brains of another set of excitable white men and lights another pyre." Even laws that would "punish with death attempts upon a President's life" would not deter the lunatic whose "mind-space is all occupied" but whose subsequent notoriety would disturb "the rickety minds of men who envy the criminal." The only way to "check the lynchings and ruler-murder" was "absolute silence" about the crimes that inspired them; that is, by "gagging every witness and jamming him into a dungeon for life; by abolishing all newspapers; by exterminating all newspaper men; and by extinguishing God's most elegant invention, the Human Race."[44]

McKinley lingered a week before dying of an abdominal infection the morning of September 14. Long opposed to the president's brand of imperialism, especially in the Philippines, Sam imagined in blank verse what ran through McKinley's mind on his deathbed.

> I erred through weakness, not intent. For I
> Was overborne by sordid counsels,
> Base ambitions, & from my head I took
> The precious laurel I had earned, & in its place
> I set this poor tin glory, now my wear,
> Of World-Power, Conqueror of helpless tribes,
> Extinguisher of struggling liberties! . . .
> O, not as it was in its great old days!
> The Stars are gone, a Skull & Bones
> Are in their place; the Red Bars are there,
> But soaked with guiltless blood;
> The White Bars are Black—
> Hide it from my sight!

Sam also joined in the public mourning and expressed sincere sorrow. McKinley "was the Head of the Nation, he fell in its service, the base hand that took his life struck dead the hostility in every feeling heart that harbored it, and he passes to the peace of the grave mourned not by such as were his friends, only, but by all who bear the American name." Four years later, in a letter to Twichell, Sam ranted that "even the jelly McKinley was a man" compared with his successor Theodore Roosevelt, a "kitten that masquerades in a lion's skin."[45]

Despite the controversy that swirled around "To the Person Sitting in Darkness" and "To My Missionary Critics" and his growing reputation as a reprobate, Sam was contacted in October 1901 by Mother Mary Alphonsa, aka Rose Hawthorne Lathrop, Nathaniel Hawthorne's daughter and Julian Hawthorne's sister. The year before, as a lay sister after the death of her husband George Parsons Lathrop, she had founded the Servants of Relief for Incurable Cancer, later the Dominican Sisters of Hawthorne, and she invited Sam to contribute to the magazine of the order. In his reply, Sam pledged to raise money on behalf of the charity:

> I wish I were not so hard-driven; then nothing could give me more contentment than to try to write something worth printing in your periodical *Christ's Poor*; indeed you pay me a compliment which I highly value when you invite me to do it, as holding me not unworthy to appear in its pages. But if I cannot write I can at least try to help in other ways, & I shall do that, for among the needs of your noble charity is money, & I know some people who have it & who have not been reluctant to spend it in good causes. And certainly if there is an unassailably good cause in the world it is this one undertaken by the Dominican Sisters of housing, nourishing & nursing the most pathetically unfortunate of all the afflicted among us—men & women sentenced to a painful & lingering death by incurable disease.

The same week, Sam received an honorary doctor of letters degree from Yale University. Joe Twichell, a longtime member of the Yale Corporation, the governing body of the university, was no doubt instrumental in his receipt of this accolade. Twichell wrote Sam on October 15, a week before the festivities, to warn him both that he would be offered the "*literary* decoration" and that "it will be tendered you by a Corporation of gentlemen the majority of whom do not at all agree with the views on important questions which you have lately promulgated in speech and in writing. . . . They grant, of course, your right to hold and to express those views, though, for themselves, they don't like 'em." Sam would be asked to speak while in New Haven and he ought not overplay his hand. Twichell was writing before Yale formally contacted him "to give you time—if you require it—to get ready the remarks with which I *suppose* you will be called on" to deliver.[46]

Sam heeded the caution. Rather than stay in the home of a Yale official, he avoided such a potentially ticklish situation by renting a house in New Haven for three days. On October 22, the day of his arrival, he skipped some of the pomp to tour the campus and when "a great crowd of students thundered the Yale cry, closing with "M-a-r-k T-w-a-i-n—Mark *Twain*!" he removed his hat and bowed, as he wrote Livy. Later that afternoon, he attended a performance of the oratorio *Hora Novissima* at the Hyperion Theater, where he was greeted by spontaneous applause. The next day, Sam was among a procession of sixty men who received honorary degrees, all of them "gowned and hooded for baptism," as he put it later, eight of them recipients of the D.Litt.: he and Aldrich, George Washington Cable, Gilder, Howells, Matthews, Thomas Nelson Page, and Woodrow Wilson. "We were four couples, but to the crowds that lined the streets seven of us vanished and became invisible as soon as the spectators caught sight of Mark," Matthews remembered. "They applauded, they laughed, they shouted his name, they cheered; and Mark took it all to himself, very much as if he were a king entering his capital for the first time." Receiving honorary degrees of LL.D. at the same commencement were his friends Joseph Choate, U.S. ambassador to the Court of St. James; John Hay, the U.S. secretary of state; and President Theodore Roosevelt, who upon recognizing Sam reportedly remarked sotto voce, "When I hear what Mark Twain and others have said in criticism of the missionaries, I feel like skinning them alive." During the ceremony Sam also crossed paths again with Booker T. Washington, a guest of Yale professor John Christopher Schwab.[47]

Nearly seven years later, Sam recounted in his autobiographical dictation an anecdote about Roosevelt and Washington that may be apocryphal. First, some background: the president of the United States and the principal of the Tuskegee Institute had dined in the White House on October 16, 1901, a week before the Yale ceremonies, at Roosevelt's invitation. As Sam remembered the controversy that ensued, Washington was "a man worth a hundred Roosevelts, a man whose shoe-latchets Mr. Roosevelt is not worthy to untie." But "a negro feeding at the White House table" provoked a storm "from one end of the country to the other" that "must have enthused the circus soul of the little imitation cowboy to the utmost limit for a few hours" until he discovered "that it wasn't all praise" and "that the Southern half of it was furious censure." The afternoon of the Yale graduation Roosevelt ostensibly asked Sam if he had been right to invite Washington to lunch. Sam "judged by his tone that he was worried and troubled and sorry about that showy adventure, and wanted a little word of comfort and approval." Sam's response, or at least the one he claimed to have made, was equivocal: "I said it was a private citizen's privilege to invite whom he pleased to his table, but that perhaps a president's liberties were more limited; that if a president's duty required him, there was no alternative, but that in a case where it was not required by duty, it might be best to let it alone since the act would give offense to so many people when no profit to the country was to be gained by offending them.""

On October 24, Sam lunched with Arthur Twining Hadley, the university president, and his wife Helen; his friends Robert Chapin, the former U.S. consul in Johannesburg and a Yale Law School graduate, and his wife, Adèle

Chapin; and Choate. After Sam returned to New York, Howells wrote "Dr. Clemens" from his home a few blocks away: "I have long been an admirer of your complete works, several of which I have read, and I am with you shoulder to shoulder in the cause of foreign missions. I would respectfully request a personal interview, and if you will appoint some day and hour most inconvenient [sic] to you I will call at your baronial hall." Howells was confident "our meeting will be mutually agreeable" on the basis of "the account of your courtesy given me by the Twelve Apostles, who once visited you in your Hartford home and were mistaken for a syndicate of lightning-rod men."[48]

Sam hewed the anti-imperialist party line for the next couple of years, though not all of his comments on the topic reached print during his life and as a result they cannot always be precisely dated. He parodied Julia Ward Howe's most famous ballad, for example, in "The Battle Hymn of the Republic (Brought Down to Date)," probably composed in 1901 but unpublished until 1958:

> Mine eyes have seen the orgy of the launching of the Sword;
> He is searching out the hoardings where the stranger's wealth is stored;
> He has loosed his fateful lightnings, & with woe & death has scored;
> His lust is marching on.
> I have seen him in the watch-fires of a hundred circling camps;
> They have builded him an altar in the Eastern dews and damps;
> I have read his doomful mission by the dim and flaring lamps—
> His night is marching on.
> I have read his bandit gospel writ in burnished rows of steel:
> "As ye deal with my pretensions, so with you my wrath shall deal;
> Let the faithless son of Freedom crush the patriot with his heel;
> Lo, Greed is marching on!"
> We have legalized the strumpet and are guarding her retreat;[49]
> Greed is seeking out commercial souls before his judgement seat;
> O, be swift, ye clods, to answer him! be jubilant my feet!
> Our god is marching on!
> In a sordid slime harmonious Greed was born in yonder ditch,
> With a longing in his bosom—and for others' goods an itch.
> As Christ died to make men holy, let men die to make us rich—
> Our god is marching on.

Similarly, in "The Stupendous Procession," unpublished in its entirety until 1972, Sam described an allegorical parade of floats representing the horrors of the world. The spectacle is led by "Monarchs, Presidents, Tammany

Bosses, Burglars, Land Thieves, Convicts, etc. appropriately clothed and bearing the symbols of their several trades," including Cecil Rhodes and Joseph Chamberlain, followed by "Christendom," a "majestic matron in flowing robes drenched with blood" wearing "a golden crown of thorns, impaled on its spine the bleeding heads of patriots who died for their country—Boers, Boxers, Filipinos," followed in turn by mutilated figures in chains labeled "Transvaal Republic," "Orange Free State," "Dreyfus," "Madagascar," and "Filipino Independence" and a "*Fat Spanish Friar* wrapped in the Treaty of Paris." The tail of the parade featured "a float displaying a polluted American flag draped with crepe," while the ghost of Abraham Lincoln, "towering vast and dim" in the sky, broods "with pained and indignant aspect." John S. Tuckey, the editor of the first complete printing of the allegory, speculated that Sam wrote it early in 1901, taking as a model the funeral parade for Queen Victoria in February that year. The hovering shade of Lincoln suggests a date of composition after the Lincoln Day celebration around the same time. But Sam might just as readily have found inspiration for the essay while at Yale on October 22 in an allegory "symbolic of successive events in the history" of the university performed by an acting troupe, or the pageantry of the graduation procession the next day, led by a color guard followed by Roosevelt, by the governor of Connecticut, and officers of the university.[50]

Sam well understood that racism lay at the root of both domestic terrorism and imperialism. His daughter Clara remembered that her father adamantly denounced lynching, even proposing that "the Government should borrow or steal enough money to police the South so thoroughly that wherever a negro steps he bumps into an officer of the peace, and these same officers must control the lynchers in their criminal defiance of the law." After the public lynchings of three black men in Pierce City, Missouri, on August 20, 1901, and reading an editorial reprinted from the *Chicago Tribune* that cited statistics to prove lynchings across the South had increased over the past two years, Sam resolved to assemble a reference book for subscription sale entitled *History of Lynchings in America* or *Rise & Progress of Lynching* in hopes of stopping "this epidemic of bloody insanities." According to the *Tribune* editorial, "the year is little more than half gone and yet there are eighty-eight cases, as compared to 115 for all of last year. The four Southern States, Alabama, Georgia, Louisiana, and Mississippi, are the worst offenders. Last year there were eight cases in Alabama, sixteen in Georgia, twenty in Louisiana, and twenty in Mississippi, over one-half the total. This year to date there have been nine in Alabama, twelve in Georgia, eleven in Louisiana, and thirteen in Mississippi, again more than one-half the total number in the whole

United States." On August 26 Sam asked Frank Bliss to hire a researcher to compile as much information as possible about all lynchings "from the earliest days down to the present. There may be 3,000 of them. . . . Nothing but such a book" as he planned "can rouse-up the sheriffs to put down the mobs & end the lynchings," which totaled 115 the previous year, with "half of the harvest" in "Alabama, Mississippi, Louisiana & Georgia"—the same figure and the same four states mentioned in the *Tribune* editorial. "The book ought to make a sensation—from here to Siberia," he added. "I shall write it in the way calculated to be most effective, whether it require one volume or six. . . . No book is so marketable as this one—the field is fresh, untrod[d]en, & of the strongest interest." He had already drafted an essay on the topic for publication in the *North American Review* entitled "The United States of Lyncherdom," in which he excoriated the mass of Americans for their "moral cowardice," "the commanding feature of the make-up of 9,999 men in the 10,000." He worried he might "live to see a negro burned in Union Square, New York, with fifty thousand people present, and not a sheriff visible, not a governor, not a constable, not a colonel, not a clergyman, not a law-and-order representative of any sort." He recommended that missionaries return from China and teach "their own Christian countrymen" to love thy neighbor, and at the same time urged Joe Twichell to stop raising money for missionaries in China because "their presence there is forbidden by the Bible" and "they have done vast mischief there. I would bar no other country, I believe, but they have no business in China. Besides, there is plenty for them to do at home."[51]

Within three days, "upon reflection," ironically, he changed his mind about the whole project. He decided not "to write that book" because after its publication "I shouldn't have even a half a friend left" in the South. "I shan't destroy the article I have written, but I see it won't do to print it. I shall keep it & wait," he notified Bliss, though he privately admitted a week later that "the lynching-book still haunts me." Sam compromised his principles and suppressed "The United States of Lyncherdom" at a moment when he was already under fire from critics of his anti-imperialism. The essay remained unpublished until 1923, when Paine printed a corrupt version of it.[52]

Soon after abandoning his history of lynching in the United States, Sam began a review, unpublished in its entirety until 1992, of Edwin Wildman's biography of Aguinaldo. Jim Zwick has called it his "most explicitly anti-racist essay" about the Philippine-American War. Whereas Aguinaldo was as downtrodden as a "despised young negro of Alabama," Sam also compared him to George Washington, Joan of Arc, "or any of that great breed" in his patriotism and capacity to lead and inspire his followers. He disparaged the tactics of Frederick Funston, his American captor, who hoodwinked

Aguinaldo into allowing him entry to his hideout by pleading starvation and begging the revolutionary leader for food relief, capturing him "by methods which would disgrace the lowest blatherskite that is doing time in any penitentiary." Put another way, "It was left to a Brigadier General of Volunteers in the American army to put shame upon a custom which even the degraded friars had respected."[53] Funston received the Congressional Medal of Honor in February 1900 for his military achievements in the Philippines.

CHAPTER 10

Lost and Found

When an election goes with us, we see & feel how intelligent this great nation is; when it goes against us we see & feel how hard it is to make this great nation understand the issues.

—*Mark Twain's Notebook*

THE CLEMENSES LEFT the Adirondacks on September 19, 1901, spent a week in Elmira with Susan Crane and the Langdons, and settled into their new home on Wave Hill in Riverdale-on-the-Hudson in the upper Bronx on October 2. They needed to live near New York so that Jean could continue her osteopathy treatments in the city, but Sam also wanted, partly for Livy's health, "the advantage of space and spreading lawn and trees, large rooms, and light" such as they had enjoyed at Dollis Hill in 1900. "We drifted from room to room on our tour of inspection, always with a growing doubt as to whether we wanted that house or not," Sam remembered, "but at last, when we arrived in a dining-room that was 60 feet long, 30 feet wide, and had two great fireplaces in it, that settled it." With "14 bedrooms (5 each on two floors, 4 on the third)" on eighteen acres "with the imposing Hudson sweeping by & the stately Palisades lifting their frosty precipices beyond," the estate was nevertheless only twenty-five minutes by rail from Grand Central Depot. "Sam "could see the steamboats on the Hudson" from the crest of the hill, yet the house was readily accessible. During one autumn week in 1901, the Clemenses hosted guests at seventeen of twenty-one meals. The humorist George Ade remembered a visit with Sam in 1902 in company with Clarence C. Rice. "Dr. Rice and I journeyed up the Hudson by rail" to the Riverdale station and traveled by carriage "to a delightful, rambling, homey-looking old house on a hillside, surrounded by huge, wide-branching trees" where they "spent a couple of hours" with Sam "on the front porch, rocking and smoking." Howells recalled that "I began to see [the family] again on something like the sweet old terms" when they lived in Riverdale. The house also boasted a storied history: as an adolescent Theodore Roosevelt had summered there with his family, and its visitors had included Charles Darwin and Thomas Henry Huxley.

Sam rented the furnished mansion and grounds from William Worthen Appleton, eldest son of the publisher William Henry Appleton, for $3,000 a year with an option to rent it a second year at the same price. The only problem: though an upscale suburb, Riverdale was suffering a crime wave. Appleton had moved from the mansion after it was burglarized. As a result, Sam bought "a highly polished revolver" as a precaution. Still, he thought it was "the pleasantest home" in "the pleasantest neighborhood in the Republic."[1]

Early in the new century, Sam became a prominent political actor, an ardent supporter of women's suffrage and a fierce opponent of Tammany Hall. In January 1901, three months after his return to the United States, he spoke "at great inconvenience and expense of precious time" at Temple Emanuel in New York on behalf of the Hebrew Technical School for Girls, where, he declared, if women could vote they would "elect a Mayor who would sweep corruption away." He was astonished, moreover, by the quality of the vocational training the students received at the "wonderful school." He authorized the production of his play *The Little Lady and the Lord General*, adapted from his story "The Death Disk," about an execution lottery, by the Children's Theatre in Carnegie Lyceum to benefit the school. In May he addressed the associate alumnae of the Normal College in Manhattan, where he admired a "bevy of beauty" and read from one of his books. That fall he joined a civic group called the Order of Acorns—they hoped to grow into a mighty oak—which endorsed Seth Low, the president of Columbia University, a former mayor of Brooklyn, and the Fusion candidate for mayor of the consolidated city of New York, supported by both the Citizens Union and Republicans, against the Tammany nominee Edward Shepard. He told the New York *Evening Post* on October 8, less than a week after settling in Riverdale, that he would "vote the Low ticket. I am only interested in voting this ticket, whatever it may be. I'll vote for anything that opposes Tammany Hall. I'd rather have Mr. Low than Satan on the ticket, but I'd vote for Satan himself if he were on the Low ticket." He vowed the next day to "do all in my power for the success of the ticket." In his first campaign speech, before an audience of three hundred at the Waldorf-Astoria on October 17, Sam eloquently impeached Tammany boss Richard Croker, who had ridiculed the Order of Acorns as "the Popcorns," for "high crimes and misdemeanors. I impeach him in the name of the people, whose trust he has betrayed. I impeach him in the name of all the people of America, whose national character he has dishonored. I impeach him in the name and by virtue of those eternal laws of justice which he has violated. I impeach him in the name of human nature itself, which he has cruelly outraged, injured, and oppressed, in both sexes, in every age, rank, situation, and condition of life."

Sam began to detect links between civic corruption and neocolonialism, between Tammany Hall and the East India Company. Both were political machines designed to exploit the people for profit—"to lie, forge, betray, steal, swindle, cheat, rob." The speech was soon printed in *Harper's Weekly* and distributed as a pamphlet. At an outdoor Low rally in lower Manhattan on October 29, eight days before the municipal election, Sam presented Low to the crowd by comparing Tammany Hall to a decaying banana: while one spot, Shepard, may appear "sound and wholesome," the "other nine-tenths is rotten. Shepard believes he can purify the whole banana; but he can't. If we want decent government; here we must get rid of the whole banana. . . . The only way to cure this city of its grievous ills is to have a good doctor and I've got him right here and will now introduce him to you—Dr. Seth Low." The same day, Sam volunteered to paste campaign posters for Low along the commuter train routes.[2]

On November 5, Low was elected mayor with over 50 percent of the vote in a five-person race, over five points more than Shepard. Sam was awarded the honorary degree of H.G.T. (Hale Grown Tree) by the Acorns, and he was sometimes credited with tipping the scale in Low's favor. He noted in his journal that he rejoiced in the victory and asked rhetorically, "Who won it? Modesty almost forbids." Yet he also moaned that while "the entire press, the entire pulpit, the women's organizations—every single moral influence existent in this vast city and in the nation, was arrayed against this criminal and infamous government in the fight," Low had "won by a margin so small that it may rightly be called contemptible." Still, at a celebration on Times Square and a parade through lower Manhattan sponsored by the Acorns the day after the election, Sam exulted that, just as he had predicted the deaths of the national Democratic Party in 1876 and the national Republican Party in 1884, "Tammany is dead and there is wailing in the land."[3] Unfortunately, to coin a cliché, his report of Tammany's death was greatly exaggerated.

Over the next few months Sam held serve in his back-and-forth with the politicos. Eleven days after the municipal election, at a Lotos Club dinner for the U.S. diplomat Joseph Choate, he spoke before an audience of nearly three hundred that included Chauncey Depew and Tom Reed about the need for talented foreign service officers. A week later, he spoke off the cuff at a meeting of the New York Teachers' Association. Before the end of the month, at Andrew Carnegie's invitation, Sam addressed the annual banquet at Delmonico's of the Sons of Scotland, aka the St. Andrew's Society, on the topic "Scotch Humor," with Carl Schurz and Seth Low among the five hundred men present. Howells lamented around this time that he hated to have his friend "eating so many dinners and writing so few books." In another of Sam's works with an interrogatory title (in company with *What Is Man?*, "Is He Living or Is He Dead?," and "What is the Real Character of Conscience?"), Sam answered the question "Does the Race of Man Love a Lord?" in the affirmative in the April 1902 issue of the *North American Review*. More to the point, he argued that people are innately predisposed to pander to their superiors in social rank, such as political bosses. Or as he put it, "As a race, we do certainly love a lord—let him be Croker, or a duke," or whomever. Americans worshipped titles—a case in point, the marriages of rich young American heiresses to impecunious European counts."[4]

Despite his own inclination to love a lord, Sam entertained a profound ambivalence for Carnegie, whom he once described as "the Jesus Christ of riches" and "the evangelist of the Omnipotent Dollar." Sometimes he thought the steel baron "amusing" and at other times "tiresome." A ruthless industrialist who hired private-security goons to break the strike at the Homestead steel factory near Pittsburgh in 1892, Carnegie was "always a subject of intense interest" for Sam. "I like him; I am ashamed of him; and it is a delight to me to be where he is if he has new material on which to work his vanities where they will show him off as with a limelight," as he reminisced in his autobiography. Carnegie's philanthropies, especially his funding of libraries that bore his name, were according to Sam merely an expression of his narcissism: "He has bought fame and paid cash for it; he has deliberately projected and planned out this fame for himself; he has arranged that his name shall be famous in the mouths of men for centuries to come." As a joke, Sam once begged Carnegie to loan him cash to buy a hymnal. "God will bless you," he assured the billionaire. In a postscript, he added, "Don't send the hymn-book, send the money." Long remembered in the annals of New York was a dinner Carnegie hosted in honor of Sir Sidney Lee on March 28, 1903, to which a couple of dozen of men of letters were invited, including John Burroughs, Hamlin Garland, Richard Watson Gilder, Howells, Brander Matthews, and Sam. In his after-dinner speech, Matthews recalled, Sam "soared aloft in whimsical exaggeration, casually dropping a reference to the time when he had lent Carnegie a million dollars. Our smiling host promptly interjected: 'That had slipt my memory!'" Sam "looked down on him solemnly" and ad-libbed a *jeu d'esprit*: "Then, the next time, I'll take a receipt."[5]

Since his return to the United States in 1900 at the age of sixty-five, Sam had begun to dial back his public appearances and the frequency of his speeches. He wrote Thomas Bailey Aldrich, for example, that he had pledged "to take no engagement outside the city & not more than 2 per month *in* it. They can't improve on this happiness in heaven." Invited to return to Yale, he replied that he was determined "not to speak anywhere outside New York City except at funerals." He was determined never "to stand on a platform again until the sheriff requires it." Urged by William Winter to read for charity in Yonkers, he again resisted: his "frontier" was the city limits. He sometimes read "for good causes *in* the City, but only in private houses, not in halls," and on the condition the money raised was "gathered by private ticket-sales & no advertising done." He had "read in a private house last year; the tickets were $5, the sale 300; & as there were no expenses for lecturer or advertising, it was all clear profit to the cause." Contacted by Pond with a lucrative offer for another lecture tour, Sam was unequivocal in refusing: "I wouldn't go on a platform & bring down another avalanche of invitations for the best $50,000 in America."[6]

Nevertheless, Sam succumbed to temptation on occasion. Upon the establishment in 1901 of the Rockefeller Institute for Medical Research, Sam befriended John D. Rockefeller Jr., heir apparent to the family fortune. The disease that had killed Sam's daughter Susy, cerebrospinal meningitis, was a particular focus of the research program of the institute. At the younger Rockefeller's invitation Sam twice addressed his Bible class at the Fifth Avenue Baptist Church in New York and was elected an honorary member of the class. In 1907 Simon Flexner, the first director of the Rockefeller Institute, developed a serum treatment for meningitis and, as Sam remarked in his autobiography, "at a single stroke earned its costly endowment ten times over."[7]

On March 13, 1902, Sam left Riverdale for the New Jersey docks, where he boarded the *Kanawha* for a month-long cruise through the West Indies. The seven passengers included many of the usual suspects and a few others: "Unreformed Congressman" Wallace Foote of New York, "Professor" Laurence Hutton, financier and "Reformed Pirate" Augustus G. Paine, "Czar" Tom Reed, "Surgeon to the Expedition" Clarence Rice, "Chaplain" Sam Clemens, and of course "Commodore" Henry Rogers. They sailed to Charleston, South Carolina, where the men boarded the Florida Special train in Sam's first foray through the Deep South—"a dreary & unpeopled & poverty-stricken piece of the earth," as he reported to Livy—and arrived in Palm Beach on the March 15. They registered at the Royal Poinciana Hotel, the largest wooden building in the world and one of the largest hotels, with room for two thousand guests, owned by Rogers's fellow Standard Oil tycoon Henry Flagler. The ocean "here is perfectly beautiful—divine in delicate colors of blue & green, snowed over with white-caps like snowflakes," Sam wrote Livy, though he admitted it "will be an immense relief" to return to the ship in south Florida and escape the "sweltering weather." On March 17 they railed to Miami, rendezvoused with the *Kanawha*, and headed out to sea, first to Key West and then Nassau, where they enjoyed "a fruit debauch" on Hog (aka Paradise) Island. "Our half dozen men must have eaten several barrels of fruit," Sam wrote Livy, before they went sea-bathing and called on the governor, Sir Gilbert Carter, at Government House. En route to Cuba, the shipboard entertainment consisted mostly of worshipping at the "poker chapel," though to lighten the mood Sam had also composed some bawdy verses entitled "The Mammoth Cod" that began:

> Of beasts, man is the only one
> Created by God,
> Who purposely, and for mere fun,
> Plays with his mammoth cod.

On March 23 the yacht anchored in Havana Harbor, where, Sam reported, the wreck of the *Maine* loomed above the water, a "wrenched & tangled battered bunch of rusty iron" resembling "a brobdignagian tarantula in his death-squirm." The floating feast arrived on Good Friday at Kingston, Jamaica, a city Sam found "rather uninteresting," though he ascended to the nearby summit of Blue Mountain Peak and marveled at the view. As a later story went, "he sat down on a moss-covered rock under a shady bamboo, filled his pipe and gazed at the landscape for the best part of an hour without talking. His Jamaican hosts asked him to come and have lunch, but he waved them aside impatiently. At last, when the mules were brought up for the return journey down the mountain, he arose to his feet, sighed deeply and said: 'I'd like to come here when I die, instead of going to heaven.' "

On the return voyage, the *Kanawha* touched at Santiago, Cuba, and Rum Cay, Bahamas, "a lonesome little out-of-the-way island" that Sam compared to heaven "in one respect—they neither marry there nor are given in marriage." On April 5 the *Kanawha* anchored in Charleston, where for six hours the ship recoaled and the troupe toured the South Carolina Inter-State and West Indian Exposition, a type of world's fair. According to the *Charleston*

News and Courier, Sam and his friends were "attired in blue yachting suits and white caps and white shoes" and were wheeled through the principal buildings, including the Cotton Palace and the South Carolina Building, in roller chairs. "I am very much pleased with it as far as we've seen," he told local reporters. His only regret, he added, that "he did not have time to visit the Woman's Building." Privately, however, Sam grumbled that the fair "resembled a funeral; nobody there; it is a dead failure."

On April 7 the ship moored in Old Point, Virginia, just south of Chesapeake Bay (pronounced Cheapskate, as Huck might say), where the men were guests of General Alexander McDowell McCook. The next morning they docked in Hampton Roads, where Sam and his friends visited Fort Monroe and lunched at the Chamberlain Hotel. They arrived back in New York the evening of April 9. Sam thanked Rogers in his next note for hosting "the grand trip in the yacht—it couldn't be improved on."[8] Except for his private letters to Livy, however, he never mentioned the trip in any of his writings, though it had offered plenty of grist for the mill.

Sam had other birds to roast, specifically Brigadier General Frederick Funston. In a speech to the Lotos Club on March 8 that Sam mercifully missed, Funston had alleged that American antiwar activists were encouraging Filipino resistance and prolonging the war. He also issued ex cathedra not a veiled threat but an explicit one: "I would rather see any one of these men hanged, hanged for treason, hanged for giving aid and comfort to the enemy, than see the humblest soldier in the United States army lying dead on the field of battle."[9] He mocked to "roars of laughter" the charge that he had captured Emilio Aguinaldo by "a dirty Irish trick." At the end he received a standing ovation and the blessing of George H. Daniels, a Civil War veteran and an executive of the New York Central railroad: "Funston has told us more truths and showed more common sense . . . in his simple speech than all the anti-imperialists ever said in their lives."[10]

While Funston did not mention Sam by name, he no doubt meant his reprimand to include Sam, who regarded the rebuke as a personal insult. To his credit, rather than remain silent and protect his reputation, Sam landed squarely on the right side of history. He discussed the speech with the men aboard the *Kanawha* during their voyage through the West Indies, and he notified Rogers five days after his return that he had written the last part of "the Funston article yesterday" for the May number of the *North American Review.* Much as Funston sarcastically dismissed the charge that he had committed a war crime, the very title of Sam's five-thousand-word essay—"A Defence of General Funston"—oozes irony, unlike the title of his earlier essay "In Defense of Harriet Shelley." A "master of mordant satire," as the London *Morning Post* called him, he replied expressly to "Funston's Lotos Club confession" of his cruelties, which, as Sam noted, "needs editing." He exposed Funston's vain lies about his battlefield exploits, cataloguing some of the most recent brutalities committed by Funston and his soldiers in the Philippines. These included the capture of Aguinaldo by treachery, the wholesale slaughter of civilians, and the torture and execution of Filipino prisoners. Among the "many ghastly" innovations in military strategy inspired by Funston's example was "the awful 'water-cure'" to make Filipinos "confess—what? Truth? Or lies? How can one know which it is they are telling? For under unendurable pain a man confesses anything that is required of him, true or false, and his evidence is worthless." Sam insisted that American soldiers who waterboarded were barbarians and added, "I think I may speak for the other Traitors, for I am sure they feel as I do about it." Citing his source for the term, he explained that "we get our title from the Funstonian Patriots." But make no mistake: "Funston is not to blame for his fearful deed" because "he did not make his own disposition. It was born with him." As Sam wrote, ostensibly in Funston's "defense," the general's disposition "took as naturally to moral slag as Washington's took to moral gold."[11]

The ruckus that ensued in the press mostly erupted among Funston apologists in Kansas, the general's home state. The *Emporia Republican* set the tone in early May: Sam's attack on Funston was "as groundless . . . as the one he made on the missionaries in China." The *Leavenworth Times* declared that "Mark Twain has made a fool of himself" and the *Chanute Sun* reprinted a comment from the *St. Louis Globe-Democrat*: "Twain is a clown grown tiresome and repulsive." The reviewer for the *Wichita Eagle*, who denounced Sam's "sinistruous and exceptious attack," apparently had to consult a thesaurus to find adjectives commensurate with his fury. The *Topeka Capital* was particularly incensed, printing no less than five hostile notices of the essay, on May 16 ("the anti-imperialists show the effects of the silly season"), May 21 ("the spectacle of Mark Twain wringing his hands like a hysterical girl and shouting out lamentations against General Funston is simply ludicrous"), May 25 (Twain "has developed into one of the most contemptible" slanderers), May 28 (Twain was "an ass" for his criticism of Funston), and May 30 (no longer "a joke," he was "now in the nuisance class"). The *Nebraska State Journal* ("a labored attack"), *Rochester Democrat and Chronicle* ("sourly sarcastic tone"), *Chicago Tribune* ("a doleful article"), and *Army and Navy Journal* ("contemptuous and malignant") were similarly disparaging. The *Duluth News-Tribune* compared the essay to "the prattle of childhood or the gibberings of dementia." Among the few newspapers that commended the piece were the *Buffalo Courier* ("a scathing, excoriating criticism of Funston"), *Kansas City Gazette* ("scathing and inexorable criticism" of Funston), St. Joseph (Mo.) *News-Press* ("the most withering condemnation of an army officer ever written"), Columbia (S.C.) *Sunday State* ("puts the rascally little Kansan just where he belongs"), *Charlotte Observer* ("an exquisite piece of irony"), and *Houston Post* ("admirably done").[12] In any case, neither Sam nor his literary executor and biographer Albert Bigelow Paine ever included "A Defence of General Funston" in any edition of Mark Twain's writings published in the United States. The controversial essay was not reprinted in the United States until 1962.

At Hutton's invitation, Sam railed to Princeton on April 19, only five days after completing "A Defence of General Funston," to spend the weekend at Laurence Hutton's home on Mercer Heights and, at Hutton's invitation, to address the Cliosophic Literary Society (aka the Monday Night Literary Club). He was still exercised by the Philippine question and read his Funston essay to an "overflowing" audience at Alexander Hall that included his friends Helen Keller and Woodrow Wilson. Keller remembered that the audience "listened breathlessly" as Sam "poured out a volcano of invective and ridicule. Only those who heard him can know his deep fervor and the potency of his flaming words." He then delivered a short coda, unpublished until 1992, which Jim Zwick has entitled "Notes on Patriotism." "If I were in the Philippines," Sam observed, under the terms of the treason act "I could be imprisoned for a year for publicly expressing the opinion that we ought to withdraw and give those people their independence—an opinion which I desire to express now." He "would hire a hall" to violate the law. In the course of his remarks Sam also turned on its head Funston's accusation that anti-imperialists were turncoats. "I am quite willing to be called a traitor—quite willing to wear that honorable badge," but he was "not willing to be affronted with the title of Patriot and classed with the Funstons when so help me God I have not done anything to deserve it." *Tu quoque*. A rough translation: You're another. After the reading, Sam was inducted into the society. Unrepentant to the end, he soon referred to "that military louse" Funston in a private note to Twichell and classified him with McKinley and Jay Gould among the "Holy Trinity," the "begetters of present American political, commercial & military morals. There's one good thing: we've struck bottom, & can't sink any lower."[13]

The morning after his address in Princeton, Sam chatted with Helen Keller, who "with a glow of joy" pressed her fingers to his lips to "listen" and with "every word he said imagined his great, loveable personality and brilliant thought." At the age of sixteen, Sam marveled, "this miraculous creature, this wonder of all the ages," "this marvelous child" had passed the Radcliffe College entrance examinations "in Latin, German, French history, belles lettres" without conditions, scoring an average of 90 compared to an average of 78 by the other applicants. A year before Keller graduated with honors from Radcliffe in 1904 at the age of twenty-three, she published an autobiography titled *The Story of My Life* and sent an inscribed copy to Sam. He was "charmed" with the book, he wrote in reply. "You are a wonderful creature, the most wonderful in the world." Sam boasted in his autobiographical dictation years later that Keller was "one of the best educated women in the world," "a competent scholar in Greek, Latin, German, French, and mathematics." One of the most distinguished Americans of her generation, Keller was acquainted with every U.S. president from Grover Cleveland to Lyndon Johnson, received the Presidential Medal of Freedom in 1964, and remained politically active until her death at age eighty-seven in 1968. She also credited Sam with helping to inspire her. "More than anyone else I have ever known except Dr. Alexander Graham Bell and my teacher," she once wrote, Samuel Clemens "aroused in me the feeling of mingled tenderness and awe."[14]

Early in the new century Sam organized a small group of schoolgirl and young women pen pals from around the world, a short-lived successor to the Saturday Morning Club in Hartford that he christened the Juggernaut Club. "I have a Club, a private Club, which is all my own," he explained to one of them.

> I appoint the Members myself, & they can't help themselves, because I don't allow them to vote on their own appointment & I don't allow them to resign! They are all friends whom I have never seen (save one), but who have written friendly letters to me. By the laws of my Club there can be only one Member in each country & there can be no male Member but myself. Someday I may admit males, but I don't know—they are capricious & inharmonious, & their ways provoke me a good deal.

The only qualification to join, he added, was "intellect and the spirit of good will." The members eventually included Hélène Picard from France, Muriel Pears from Scotland, and Elizabeth Wallace, dean of women and professor of French literature at the University of Chicago, whom Sam befriended in Bermuda, from the United States.[15]

His lifelong infatuation with schoolgirls also prompted him at the age of sixty-two to propose the revocation of laws governing the age of consent. In "Why Not Abolish It?" (1903), yet another one of his interrogatory-titled essays, he argued that such laws shift "the burden of guilt from the males (who seduce) to the females (who are seduced)."[16] His idiosyncratic argument was premised by a trio of dubious assumptions: that the reputation of a family is a form of property whose value might be reduced by scandal, that "there is no age at which consent shall in the least degree modify the seducer's crime or mitigate its punishment," and that even adult women cannot be trusted to govern their sexuality. It also missed a larger point: that age of consent laws entitle the state to prosecute the crime of underage sexual assault, and thus the abolition of such laws would in effect license child sexual abuse. Like "A Defence of General Funston," the essay was not collected in any edition of Sam's writing during his life.

Sam rarely returned to Missouri after he reached middle age. He had passed through Hannibal in 1882 while traveling the river before writing *Life on the Mississippi*. He performed there while on speaking tour with George Washington Cable in 1885. And he was present part of a day for his mother's burial there in 1890. The reasons he returned so rarely over the final thirty years of his life are simple enough: none of his family still lived in Missouri, and more to the point, he hated long-distance train travel. But during his cruise in the West Indies aboard the *Kanawha* he received an invitation from Richard Jesse, president of the University of Missouri, to receive an honorary doctor of laws degree at graduation ceremonies on June 4 in Columbia, and accepted with alacrity. "The distinguished honor offered me by the University of Missouri touches me deeply," he replied, "& is peculiarly gratifying, coming as it does from my native State." He was so honored that, as he put it, he was willing "to travel more than 1000 miles each way in my old age" to receive the degree. Or as he elsewhere explained, "I am glad of the invitation to come and get an honorary degree which I have not earned." He hoped to doctor as many laws as possible in future.[17]

He left Grand Central Station in New York the evening of May 27 on a New York Central express train for the thirty-hour trip to St. Louis. At the age of sixty-six, he journeyed alone. He arrived the morning of May 29 and, as he wrote Olivia, "I slept pretty well the second night on the train, & was up at 6 in the morning well rested; shaved & put on a white shirt; breakfasted in my room & was at the same time interviewed by a St. Louis reporter who had mounted the train after midnight" somewhere in Illinois. This enterprising reporter was Robertus Love of the *Post-Dispatch*, who shadowed him for the next eleven days. Love followed him so doggedly that Clemens began to introduce him to audiences as his son. He was met at Union Station by his cousin James Ross Clemens, who escorted him to the Planters'

House, where there was not "a ghost of a show for me to go to a room even if I should get one, so I'll stay up and save expenses." He lingered in the lobby from eight until noon talking with reporters and then retired to the rooms of the Pilots' Society, where he chatted "for half an hour with the old stagers—several of whom I knew 45 years ago." Among them: Beck Jolly, Dan Able, John Henton Carter, and his old master Horace Bixby. He was then accompanied to the Merchants' Exchange by its president "& made a 5-minute speech" to an assembly of businessmen. During the afternoon he also visited the editorial offices of the *Post-Dispatch*, where Love photographed him, before catching a train for Hannibal. On the train he encountered, quite by chance, a childhood friend: the former Mary Moss, daughter of Russell Moss, co-owner of Samuel & Moss, the largest packing house in Hannibal in the 1850s. The two old classmates "talked 3 hours" all the way to Hannibal. Sam arrived in town late that afternoon without fanfare, registered at the Windsor Hotel on Main Street near the station, dined alone, and was in his room when the first welcoming delegation called. He had not been expected in Hannibal—which had grown sixfold in population since he left in 1853, from about two thousand to twelve thousand—until the following week, after graduation ceremonies at the university, but the news of his arrival spread rapidly. The next morning he began a hectic round of activities lasting four days.[18]

First he visited his boyhood home on Hill Street, a public appearance that attracted a throng of spectators. "I went & stood in the door of the old house I lived in when I whitewashed the fence 53 years ago;—was photographed, with a crowd looking on," he recalled.

Built by his father in 1843, when Sam was only seven, the building seemed "small to me," he remarked in 1902. "A boy's home is a big place to him. I suppose if I should come back again ten years from now it would be the size of a bird-house." Next, apropos of Decoration Day, he was driven by his childhood friend and classmate Helen Kercheval Garth to Mount Olivet Cemetery, to the graves of his parents, his brothers Henry and Orion, and to the grave of Helen's late husband John, another of his childhood friends. "It is very beautifully situated, that cemetery," he told Love. "If I had the time I should look for the boys out there. That is where they are. I came here to see the people. I have met a good many more than I expected to meet. I find about 20 surviving, and am moved with gratification and gratitude for that. But most of them are out there in that cemetery."[19]

Sam spent the holiday afternoon listening to speeches at the Presbyterian Church, where he was also asked to address the thousand people in the audience. "When I stepped forward," he wrote Olivia, "the entire house rose; &

Figure 7. Samuel Clemens in front of his boyhood home in Hannibal, Missouri, May 30, 1902. Courtesy of the Library of Congress.

they applauded so heartily & kept it up so long, that when they finished I had to stand silent a long minute till I could speak without my voice breaking." "I am profoundly touched by my reception here," he declared. "I have not only been moved, moved a number of times, by the cordiality of my reception by the old, old men and women who knew me here when I was a boy." He spoke briefly about patriotism, a topic appropriate to Decoration Day and his own candid, recent criticism of Funston. "The patriot is the conscience-instructed man," he declared, or "the man who is true to his convictions." At the close of the formalities, he "shook hands with everybody." He dined that evening at Helen Garth's town house on South Fifth Street. He was joined there by Laura Hawkins Frazer, his schoolmate, his first sweetheart, and the model for the character of Becky Thatcher in *Tom Sawyer.* After the death of her husband, Frazer had returned to Hannibal and now managed an orphanage, the Home for the Friendless.[20]

After dinner, in company with Frazer and Garth, Sam attended the Hannibal High School graduation ceremonies at the Park Theater. At the invitation of Billy Nash, president of the school board and another of his boyhood chums, he had agreed to speak and to hand out diplomas to the sixteen graduates, thirteen of them young women. Seated onstage, he remembered that the curtain opened "upon a packed house, & there was great enthusiasm." He listened tolerantly for three hours of declamations in no way comparable to the torturous exercises he had described in *Tom Sawyer*. "These young ladies tonight had delivery, graceful and expressive, and they had written their own ideas." He closed the ceremonies by speaking for fifteen minutes, relating "some things [about] the young people of that earlier time that brought their laughter and their tears." At the conclusion of his remarks he was given an armful of diplomas to award the graduates, but they were in no particular order, so he distributed them in what was for him a predictable way—at random. He told the students, "Take one. Pick out a good one. Don't take two, but be sure you get a good one." None of them "received his or her own diploma." They sorted out the mess later. Finally, he "shook hands" for an hour before returning to his hotel. "Even when a boy . . . he was manly and good. He was kind-hearted and true to his friends," Laura Frazer told Robertus Love. "There is no wonder . . . that all of us love him."[21]

His dance card was not so full the next day. He visited Frazer at the Home for the Friendless and spent most of the afternoon with his sister-in-law Mollie, Orion's widow, who had traveled from Keokuk to see him. As it happened, they never met again. She died eighteen months later. He also met with the previous year's high school graduating class at the Windsor Hotel. That night he attended a reception on his behalf hosted by the Labinnah (Hannibal spelled backward) Club, where he reminisced about his boyhood before an audience of five hundred people and paid tribute to his mother. He praised the lovely young women of the town, whom he described "as his sweethearts of the third generation." As Love noted, "Mark Twain likes pretty girls almost as well as cigars." According to Paine, he spoke "in a very humorous and touchingly pathetic way, breaking down in tears at the conclusion." "As this is probably my last visit to you, my old, old friends, and you my new friends, and to Hannibal," he said, "I want to express my sincerest affection for you all and this town where I spent my boyhood."[22]

Sunday, June 1, was more eventful. Sam crossed paths with John RoBards, his childhood classmate and his fellow volunteer in the Marion Rangers in 1861. RoBards "was old then—though not quite so old as I—and the burden of life was upon him," he reminisced four years later. RoBards escorted him to various churches and Sunday schools around the town, where he waxed nostalgic. Sam had never entered any of them, but he pretended otherwise. "In each one he was asked to speak a few words, and he began by saying how good it was to be back in the old home Sunday-school again," which as a boy he had loved, and he would even point to his old seat. In particular, Everett Gill, the minister of the Fifth Avenue Baptist Church, had invited him to speak to his congregation. "I thought Mr. Clemens was only a humorist," Gill said, "but I have found that he is a philosopher and a man of the tenderest emotions." Sam agreed to address the group but not from the podium. As he replied to Gill, "I find it too formidable. I should not be able to sit in the pulpit on Sunday & feel that I was doing a right & decorous thing; I should be under my own censure all the time. Therefore I shall sit where any sinner may sit without offence, & where all sinners are welcome. I shall be comfortable there, & free of self-reproaches." True to his word, on Sunday morning he delivered a lay sermon to a thousand congregants from the floor of the church. "I thank the Reverend Dr. Gill for the privilege which he has offered by permitting me to say a few words," Sam began. "I will not take the pulpit, for I should be embarrassed with unsanctified tongue if I did. It might be well for me to stand there on a weekday, but on Sunday I think the place for layman is in the pew, so with your permission I shall remain here at my seat and tell you what I have to say." All of us preach all the time, Sam said, "even if we do not know it," if not by word then by deed and example "We forget that we carry influence. We ought to remember it, however, and make it a constant reminder. We had better see that our conduct is of a favorable nature." The journalist Joseph Fort Newton, who was present that day, recalled that "in a little speech at the end" of the meeting Sam

> took for his text a story of St. Francis, how he asked one of the Brothers to go with him into the village to preach. Arm in arm they walked down the hill, rejoicing in the soft spring sunlight, talking of the love of God, happy in their fellowship. On through the village they went, up the hill on the other side, then back again to the monastery gate, without stopping. "But are we not going to preach today?" asked the Brother. "We have preached," said Francis. "We have been happy in the love of God and the glory of His sunlight—that is our sermon for the day." It was plain that Mark Twain was thinking of what kind of a sermon he had preached as he had walked down the years.

He again paid tribute to his dead mother, who, he said, "lies buried out in the beautiful city of the dead on the hill south of the city. . . . Her preaching did not perish when she passed away, but goes on and on with me." Love reported with pardonable understatement that "Mark Twain's sermon at the Baptist Church . . . was a little different from what the people had expected." But Sam afterward told an interviewer that he spoke "in church on Sunday morning to my own satisfaction at least."[23]

After his church tour, Clemens performed an act of kindness that attracted no attention at the time, and that none of his biographers has ever mentioned. RoBards disclosed that his twelve-year-old granddaughter Sara "had read [Sam's] books and would like to see" him, and Sam granted her request. "It was a pathetic time," he remembered in his autobiography, "for she was a prisoner in her room and marked for death. And John knew that she was passing swiftly away. . . . In her I seemed to see that boy again. It was as if he had come back out of that remote past and was present before me in his golden youth. Her malady was heart disease." She died two days later, even before Sam left Hannibal. He expressed his condolences to the grieving grandfather: "The tidings you send me are inexpressibly distressing, & my heart goes out to you in your sorrow."[24]

After visiting RoBards's granddaughter, Sam reunited with still another childhood friend, John Briggs, the model for the character of Ben Rogers, Tom Sawyer's best friend. Briggs came to Hannibal from his home in New London, Missouri, just to see Sam. The two sexagenarians toured the town from Holliday's Hill in the north to Lover's Leap in the south. "They drove by the place where the haunted house [featured in both *Tom Sawyer* and *Pudd'nhead Wilson*] had stood. They drank from a well they had always known." They drove past Soap Hollow, where the tons of offal from the slaughterhouses once drained into Bear Creek before emptying into the Mississippi, and past Rockcliffe Mansion on West Bird Street. At the end of the afternoon, according to Paine, Clemens said to Briggs, "This day has been worth thousands of dollars to me. We were like brothers once, and I feel that we are the same now." Six months later, in a speech after a dinner at the Metropolitan Club in New York to celebrate his sixty-seventh birthday, Sam remembered the moment:

> I met in . . . Hannibal a schoolmate of mine . . . whom I had not seen for more than fifty years. . . . We spent a whole afternoon going about here and there and yonder, and hunting up the scenes and talking of the crimes which we had committed so long ago. It was a heartbreaking delight, full of pathos, laughter, and tears, all mixed together; and we called the roll of the boys and girls [we had known] so many years ago, and there were hardly half a dozen of them left; the rest were in their graves; and we went up there on the summit of that hill, a treasured place in my memory, the summit of Holliday's Hill, and looked out again over that magnificent panorama of the Mississippi River, sweeping along league after league, a level green paradise on one side and retreating capes and promontories as far as you could see on the other, fading

> away in the soft, rich lights of the remote distance. I recognized then that I was seeing now the most enchanting river view the planet could furnish. I never knew it when I was a boy; it took an educated eye that had travelled over the globe to know and appreciate it.

On Monday, his last full day in Hannibal, Sam met Joe Douglass, according to local legend the model for the character of Injun Joe in *Tom Sawyer*. Douglass walked a mile to the Windsor Hotel to present a bouquet of flowers to Sam, who received it with "honest thanks." Asked if Douglass was in fact the prototype for the villain in the novel, Sam replied "that he may as well have the honor as anybody else," a characteristic nondenial denial. On his part, Douglas always disavowed any resemblance on the grounds that, unlike the fictional scoundrel, "he had always lived an honorable life."[25]

That evening Sam was the guest of honor at a reception attended by some three hundred people at the Rockcliffe Mansion. It was, according to the *St. Louis Republic*, the "social function of the season. . . . For more than an hour" he "entertained the guests" with stories about his boyhood. The next morning, June 3, he met with the students at St. Joseph's Academy, a Catholic girls' high school, his final formal appearance in the city. Later that morning Clemens was escorted to the rail depot by Aaron Levering, the founder of Levering Hospital, John Garth's successor as president of the Farmers & Merchants Bank, and yet another of Sam's boyhood friends, to catch a train for Columbia.[26] A large crowd had gathered to bid him farewell, including the last of the boyhood friends he encountered on the trip. As a teenager Tom Nash had nearly drowned one winter when he broke through the ice while skating on the river. He contracted scarlet fever, lost his hearing, and in consequence "could not modulate his voice. . . . When he supposed he was talking low and confidentially, you could hear him in Illinois," as Sam put it. "When I was at the railway station ready to leave Hannibal," Sam recalled in his autobiography, through the crowd of people "I saw Tom Nash approaching . . . and I walked toward him, for I recognized him at once. He was old and white-headed, but the boy of fifteen was still visible in him. He came up to me, made a trumpet of his hands at my ear, nodded his head toward the citizens and said confidentially—in a yell like a fog-horn—"SAME DAMNED FOOLS, SAM!"[27]

Before boarding the train, Sam made a brief parting speech. "This visit . . . has been one of the happy events of my life," he stated. It "has been a most enjoyable one, and I do not recall a single instance when I ever had a better time. . . . I have met many of my boyhood friends and enjoyed pleasant chats with them."

Figure 8. Samuel Clemens at the Hannibal, Missouri, train station, June 3, 1902. Courtesy of the Mark Twain Papers and Project, Bancroft Library, University of California–Berkeley, PH00297.

As the train departed, he stood on the back platform and waved goodbye to the cheering crowd "as long as the train was in sight." He later told a reporter that "never had anything . . . hurt him more than his farewell to Hannibal." The *Hannibal Journal* editorialized that there was "not a man or woman in Hannibal who saw him while here but that feels better" that he came. Two weeks later, he declared that he "renewed my youth in Hannibal—all but the hair—& I would not trade those days for any others I have seen in a quarter of a century."[28]

His trip from Hannibal to Columbia aboard a Missouri, Kansas & Texas local was punctuated over the next few hours by ovations along the route. At every station—Rensselaer, Monroe City, Clapper, Stoutsville, Paris, Madison, and Moberly—the favorite son of Missouri was greeted by multitudes of well-wishers. As Paine reports, "At each place crowds were gathered when the train pulled in, to cheer and wave and to present him with flowers. Sometimes he spoke a few words," but more often he choked up and could not speak. At Stoutsville, eight miles from his birthplace in Florida, "quite a number of people appeared at the depot and cheered him." At Paris, upward of two thousand people "were on hand. Arrangements had been made to hold the train about ten minutes, so that Mark Twain might make a little speech. He had hardly begun when a little girl stepped up to the car and handed him" a bouquet of roses. "He broke down completely and was unable to continue." A year later, he joked that in every town along this route through the American heartland he was introduced to a "nice old lad[y]" who purported to be the original Becky Thatcher.[29]

He was in Columbia for less than two days. The evening of June 3, upon his arrival, he was the guest at two banquets honoring the recipients of honorary degrees from the university. The first was hosted by President Jesse, the second by the local chapter of Phi Beta Kappa, and both were attended, in addition to Sam, by Ethan Allen Hitchcock, the secretary of the interior; James Wilson, the secretary of agriculture; prominent Kansas City lawyer Gardiner Lathrop; and E. W. Stephens, a distinguished local newspaper publisher instrumental in the establishment of the University of Missouri School of Journalism and son of the namesake of Stephens College. At the second banquet, Sam spoke briefly and pledged to donate to the Missouri Historical Society a set of the complete twenty-two-volume Newbegin uniform edition of his books, which, he said, "he was certain contained everything that was not in any other books."[30]

The next day, at commencement ceremonies in the university auditorium, he received his honorary doctoral degree. Paine writes of the ritual: "Mark Twain was naturally the chief attraction." Attired in his Yale academic regalia, "he led the procession of graduating students and, as in Hannibal, handed them their diplomas," albeit this time in the appropriate order. When it came time to confer the honorary degrees, Gardiner Lathrop, son of the first president of the University of Missouri, introduced him to the several thousand people in the audience as

> a typical Missouri boy, a printer's apprentice, the Mark Twain of the Mississippi River, and later the Mark Twain of the civilized world, a journalist of note, successful in literature and the leading humorist in the annals of American literature and distinguished as a writer; a poet whose verses have been all too few, a ripe Shakespearean scholar, a philosophical man of generous heart and kindly character; an exceedingly courteous and a Christian gentleman. . . . The university honors itself by conferring upon him the highest degree in its gift. I will not refer to his humorous writings, for they are familiar to young and old, but he is equally a master of pathos. What more beautiful than his letter of advice to a young girl just budding into womanhood?

That is, Lathrop introduced Sam not as the cream of the jesters but in far more respectable terms: as a "master of pathos," a poet and scholar, a "Christian gentleman." He was the author not of that vulgar novel *Adventures of Huckleberry Finn* or the controversial "To the Person Sitting in Darkness," but of a "letter of advice to a young girl just budding into womanhood." That is, Lathrop depicted him in the mold of a refined, urbane man of letters, the proper sort of fellow who might be the guest of honor at a polite dinner party. After he was introduced, according to the *New York Times*, Sam stood, stepped to the center of the stage, "and paused. . . . Suddenly, and without a signal, the great audience rose as one man and stood in silence at his feet. He bowed, but he could not speak. . . . He said he didn't know whether he was expected to make a speech or not. They did not leave him in doubt. They cheered and demanded a speech," whereupon he delivered an extemporaneous twenty-minute address "full of quaint phrasing" and "happy humor." He said, in part, that soon after he received a degree of doctor of literature at Yale eight months before, "an envious man wrote to me asking what did I know about doctors and literature anyhow, and I replied that I knew enough to doctor my own literature at any rate. You can't give me too many honors. I deserve them all and am willing to accept anything in that line that you have to offer." Then he pivoted to the welcome he had received in his home state. In Hannibal, he said, "I looked in the faces of women"—he might have named Mary Moss, Helen Garth, and Laura Frazer—who "when I last saw them were beautiful with the peach bloom of early youth—now on the heads the frosts of age, and in their faces wrinkles and the weatherbeaten look"—but still beautiful. In Hannibal, "I experienced emotions that I had never expected, and did not know were in me. I was profoundly moved and saddened to think that this was the last time, perhaps, that I would ever behold those kind old faces and dear old scenes of childhood." His auditors "laughed and laughed again, but some of them cried" when he "said in tones that shook with suppressed emotion that he was bidding Missouri and old friends farewell forever." That evening, he was the guest of honor at a dinner party at the home of E. W. Stephens, his host while he was in Columbia, and a guest at a dinner for Secretary Wilson at the home of Henry Jackson Waters, the dean of the College of Agriculture. Asked by a reporter for the Philadelphia *North American* how it felt "to be an LL.D?" he answered that "it feels like official emancipation from ignorance and vice."[31]

The next day Sam returned to St. Louis. Again he was again greeted by well-wishers along the route. That evening he was the guest of honor at a smoker attended by about fifty men, "all the local notabilities," hosted by his cousin James Ross Clemens at his home on Washington Avenue, where

Sam bragged about his penchant for cheap stogies. He smoked "two grades of cigars," he said, "three-centers and seven-centers. He preferred the three-centers because they are 'just as good' and cost less.'" Over the years he had been given a few expensive cigars, "and I am keeping them in the hope that I can sell them to somebody." Later that night, at the invitation of David Francis, a former governor of Missouri and the president of the 1904 World's Fair committee, he attended a reception at the St. Louis Country Club for the visiting leaders of the French delegation to the upcoming fair, Count and Countess de Rochambeau.[32]

Before leaving Columbia, Sam had received a telegram from the mayor of St. Louis, Rolla Wells, to the effect that "there was a boat here without a name" and promising that if Sam would "make a trip on it with the other foreigners," the mayor "would name it after me." The day after his return, June 6, Sam rendezvoused at the pier with Wells, Governor Francis, and the count and countess for a spin on the river. The ancient tug had in truth been built and christened the *St. Louis* thirty years before. That is, Wells lured Sam to the river with a promise to rename the sidewheeler the *Mark Twain*. It was repainted for the occasion and Sam took part, knowingly or not, in a publicity stunt staged by the mayor—not that he cared. Before the boat was (re)launched, Mayor Wells supervised a brief (re)christening: he welcomed the "illustrious visitors from France," the countess smashed a bottle of champagne across the bow, and then in a short speech Sam praised the pioneering French explorers like Jolliet, Marquette, and LaSalle who had opened the river to commerce in the late seventeenth century.[33]

After the dignitaries boarded and embarked on the good boat *Mark Twain*, Sam took the helm and steered it around the harbor for half an hour. "This is the last time I will ever play pilot," he told his passengers. "Good enough water for anyone; you couldn't improve it without a little whisky." A would-be poet soon commemorated the event with a buttery rhyme in the *Chicago Tribune*:

There was cryin' and cursin', but Mark yelled out,
  Over all the infernal roar:
"I'll hold her nozzle agin the bank
  Till the last galoot's ashore!"
Through the thick, black smoke of the harbor boat
  Mark Twain's loud drawl was heard,
And they all had trust in his cussedness
  And knowed he would keep his word.
But soon as they run the gangplank out

They hurried to git ashore,
Fur they knowed Ole Mark hadn't steered a boat
For forty years or more.

There is, of course, no evidence that any of the passengers felt endangered. The count, in fact, declared that he would never forget his "meeting with Mark Twain" and that he had "invited him to visit us if he should ever come to France."[34]

Ironically, Mayor Wells was so eager to share the stage with Sam and bask in his reflection that he ran afoul of the city bureaucracy. He had no authority to rename the harbor boat. It was officially rechristened the *Mark Twain* by vote of the aldermen two months after Sam visited the city. The name change, as journalists around the country joked, invited such headlines as "Mark Twain in Need of Repairs," "Mark Twain's Boilers Explode," or "Mark Twain Scrapes Bottom on Sandbar." Nor does the story end there. Five years later, after it was decommissioned and its engine removed, the old boat was converted into a garbage scow. At almost the same moment, Rolla Wells, the incumbent St. Louis mayor, again invited Sam to speak in the city at the dedication of a Civil War monument erected by the Daughters of the Confederacy. Sam had the good sense to decline.[35]

Late that afternoon, many of the same dignitaries gathered in front of a building on South Broadway for yet another formal ceremony. Sam had been invited to unveil a bronze plaque inscribed "Here was born Eugene Field, the Poet" and mounted on the wall of a house located in the decaying tenement district of Walsh's Row near the river. Governor Francis, who apparently orchestrated these formalities, delivered a brief address to the effect that they had assembled to unveil a tablet to a beloved American poet, a son of Missouri, and that it was meet for Mark Twain to perform the honors. The men removed their hats, and Sam spoke: "My friends: we are here with reverence and respect to commemorate and enshrine in memory the house where was born a man who, by his life, made bright the lives of all who knew him, and by his literary efforts cheered the thoughts of thousands who never knew him. I take pleasure in unveiling the tablet of Eugene Field." He then pulled a rope to unveil the plaque. As he was leaving, Sam said to a reporter that he was pleased to participate "in this act of homage to the memory of Eugene Field. 'He was a lovable fellow. In his death I felt a personal loss.'" There was only one problem: the plaque had been bolted to the wrong house. According to Field's brother Roswell, they had hallowed not the house where Eugene was born but one where he lived later. He had been born in a house on Collins Street, since demolished, not the one on South Broadway.[36] That is, Sam unwittingly took part a second time this day in a publicity stunt engineered by a local politician eager to have his picture taken standing next to the most famous man in America.

He was initially disgusted by the news of the mistake. On June 12, by then back in New York, Sam wrote Field's son that "the tablet should be moved to the right house if the right house is still standing," but if it had been razed "I hope you will adopt the present house as the birthplace; for the sentiment is the main thing, after all, & it is better that a rose grow in an alien garden than that it grow not at all—as any will say who loved Eugene Field." On further reflection, however, Sam was undaunted. He didn't really care where the plaque was placed. After all, he never let the facts interfere with a good story. He eventually wrote Roswell Field, "Officially and for the purposes of the future, your brother was born" on South Broadway. For the record, the original plaque has never been removed or replaced or corrected. It remains on the building on South Broadway.[37]

The same day of the dedication of the wrong Eugene Field house, a Friday, Sam enjoyed a *meal maigre* at the St. Louis Club, the guest of Theophile Papin, a St. Louis socialite and descendant of the founder of St. Louis. Countess de Rochambeau was seated next to him. Afterward he was honored with a reception at the University Club hosted by Philip Scanlan, the St. Louis parks commissioner. In his speech he waxed philosophical, especially in an observation that anticipated Forrest Gump's tagline: "Life is just a sandwich of pleasures and heartaches. . . . You have to have the pains to appreciate the pleasures." He added that he would not have missed "that last week and my visit to Hannibal for anything." The next day, he was feted at lunch by the Noonday Club, and in the afternoon by a group of artists and art students at the Museum of Fine Arts, who conferred upon him the honorary degree of "Master Doctor of Arts"; he then dined (again) at the St. Louis Club. Afterward he returned to the home of his cousin James Ross Clemens for the night. The next day, Robertus Love celebrated his triumphant homecoming in rhyming tercets in the pages of the *St. Louis Post-Dispatch*:

Thou first Missourian, free-and-easy Mark
Back from thy half a century's lingering lark
We hail thee home—our loud hosannas hark!
To native haunts we bid thee welcome back,
New laughs to generate, new jokes to crack,
And tread again the Mississippi's track.
Though long a Yankee of Connecticut
We find that from thy heart thou hast not shut

Missouri, of thy genial jibes the butt.
Whilst thou with kings and queens hast joked and jawed
We know that Time's relentless tooth hath gnawed
Thy youth away, O Innocent Abroad!
But still to us who hold thee as our own
Thou art the selfsame Samuel we have known
These sixty years thy jovial eyes have shown.
And still we love thee for that thou hast told
That 'mid the dross of life there still is gold,
And, whilst we gather it, we grow not old.
For with Tom Sawyer, still we all are boys,
High jinks contriving, adolescent joys
Inventing, filling earth and sky with noise.
And still some of us have the hapless luck
Old clothes to wear and borrow bed and chuck
Like that immortal waif, the care-free Huck!
Though some mayhap have made a lucky hit
And high in commerce or in council sit,
The crowd, with thee, is mainly Roughing It.
With Prince and Pauper thou hast wept and laughed,
Beer of Bohemia, wine of luxury quaffed—
Prince of good fellows, king of writing craft!
So here's to thee, old printer, pilot, wit
And may thy days be long, thy nights be lit
With mirth, till thou among the immortals sit!
Age cannot wither thee, nor custom stale
The freshness of thy merry quip and tale;
Wherefore, old boy, immortal infant, hail!

Sam left for the East at noon that day aboard the Big Four Knickerbocker Express and arrived back at Riverdale the next evening.[38]

In one respect only might Sam's valedictory visit to Missouri be considered a disappointment: he wrote nothing for publication about the trip. According to his correspondence and an entry in his notebook in the summer of 1902, he began another Huck Finn/Tom Sawyer sequel. Set again in the fictionalized Hannibal he christened St. Petersburg, the first part chronicled events before the Civil War when the boys were still young. The second part would portray them as old men who return to the village a half century later. He summarized his plans in a letter to Howells, who replied that "what I shall enjoy most will be the return of the old fellows to the scene and their tall lying. There is a matchless chance there." As Howells remembered, that summer Sam read aloud from the manuscript of "an admirable story" featuring "characters such as he had known in boyhood" in Hannibal. But Sam never completed the tale. In fact, he destroyed the thirty-eight-thousand-word fragment lest "I might someday finish it"—a rare act in his career, given the abundant documents and manuscripts he preserved. But in this case he concluded that Huck, Tom, and Jim "had done work enough in this world and were entitled to a permanent rest." So he performed a kind of literary euthanasia and, for better or worse, consigned the fragment, tentatively titled "50 Years Later," to the flames.[39]

While Sam had little to show for his final homecoming to Missouri in a literary sense, from his personal perspective the sentimental journey was one of the highlights of his life. The honors "which came to me at Hannibal, Columbia, St. Louis, and at the village stations all down the line, are beyond all price and are a treasure for life," he remembered. On June 12, two days after his return to Riverdale, he wrote Laura Stephens, his hostess in Columbia, that "those eleven days in Missouri" were "a memorable time for me, a dream come true, after 50 years. Billions of boys have dreamed it—all boys of all times and climes and nationalities have dreamed it, but not two dozen have seen it come to pass, perfect, and unmarred by any alloy of reproach or remorse or bitterness."[40]

While renting the Appleton mansion in Riverdale, Sam and Livy shopped for a house to buy along the Hudson. As soon as they purchased one, Sam advised Franklin Whitmore in early March 1902, "you can advertise the Hartford house for sale." He spent one entire day the next week inspecting "12 country seats from garret to cellar," which "ended my usefulness and my strength." Livy continued to house-hunt while Sam cruised the West Indies on the *Kanawha*, and during his absence she purchased an estate named Hillcrest in Tarrytown, some fifteen miles north of Riverdale, for $45,000, the same amount the previous owners had paid for the land alone. It included a thirteen-room mansion and stables on about eighteen acres of land. Livy bought it "largely for Jean's benefit," with plans to make it her home for the rest of her life. Sam described the place as a farm where Jean might raise animals. He assured Rogers that "we are very well satisfied," though Livy "secretly reproaches herself for buying the new house before selling the old one."[41]

Of course, Livy had long resisted the sale of the Hartford mansion. Including upkeep and taxes, the house cost about $1,600 a year to maintain—"a burden which we've got to go on carrying yet awhile," Sam admitted in late 1901, because "the madam won't allow the house to be advertised for sale. That settles it! She would feel homeless if she sold that house before she *knew* there was some other place that she preferred to live." Privately, Sam counseled Whitmore to let him know "whenever you have an offer for the house." He doubted "if Mrs. Clemens can ever bring herself to sell, but it might happen—one never knows. I wish we had sold it ten years ago for what it would fetch, little or big. . . . Just on account of the taxes there has never been a time when I wouldn't have sold the house for anything it would fetch if the family [that is, Livy] had been willing."[42]

In April 1902, after buying the Tarrytown estate, they finally listed the Hartford mansion for sale for "$75,000—bottom price $60,000," and "Mrs. Clemens puts her foot down there." Sam advised Whitmore that the house, stable, and land "cost $110,000 cash," and the land alone was worth $31,000. "Do you think you could see the whole $111,000 worth for $60,000?" Livy hired John Howells, the architect son of W. D. and Elinor Howells, to design an addition to the Tarrytown house. "We are very anxious to get to building" because "we are too old to keep waiting to settle down," she explained to Whitmore, and "we feel that we better wait not until the Hartford house is sold." She urged Whitmore to sell the mansion on Farmington Avenue "as quickly as you can, but don't sacrifice too much. Of course you will not get your price $75,000, but I had hoped you might get $60,000.[43]

On his part, uncharacteristically, Sam was more cautious about family finances. "For a while I felt that we must sell the house even at a sacrifice, because we were planning to build an expensive addition" in Tarrytown, he wrote Whitmore in June, but "we have stopped the architect & shall do no building for some time yet." Instead, they would squeeze "into the little Tarrytown house next October. . . . And we mean to *stay* squeezed till the Hartford house is sold, whether the squeezing is comfortable or not." Unfortunately, when Whitmore finally listed the Farmington Avenue mansion for sale, even placing an ad for it in the *New York Tribune*, it attracted little interest among buyers.

Before the end of May, Sam dropped the price on the mansion to $40,000. State senator Henry Roberts offered $35,000 for the house, but Whitmore held out for a higher bid. Worse yet, the authorities in Tarrytown appraised the taxable value of Hillcrest at $70,000 after Sam bought the property, and Sam briefly considered offering to sell the property to the town at that price. The assessment was subsequently reduced to $50,000 after he challenged the figure. The next year, the property was taxed at a value of $80,000, again reduced to $50,000 after Sam's lawyers appealed.[44]

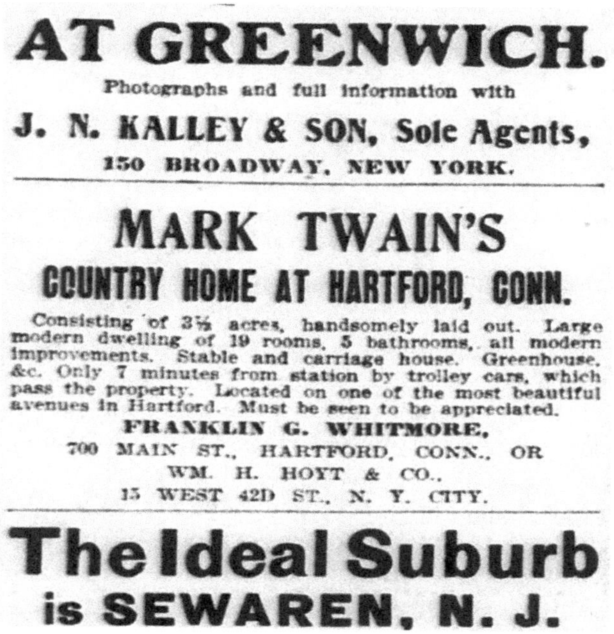
AT GREENWICH.
Photographs and full information with
J. N. KALLEY & SON, Sole Agents,
150 BROADWAY, NEW YORK.
MARK TWAIN'S
COUNTRY HOME AT HARTFORD, CONN.
Consisting of 3½ acres, handsomely laid out. Large modern dwelling of 19 rooms, 5 bathrooms, all modern improvements. Stable and carriage house. Greenhouse, &c. Only 7 minutes from station by trolley cars, which pass the property. Located on one of the most beautiful avenues in Hartford. Must be seen to be appreciated.
FRANKLIN G. WHITMORE,
700 MAIN ST., HARTFORD, CONN., OR
WM. H. HOYT & CO.,
15 WEST 42D ST., N. Y. CITY.
The Ideal Suburb
is SEWAREN, N. J.

Figure 9. Advertisement for the sale of the Clemenses' Hartford house, *New York Tribune*, April 27, 1902.

Meanwhile, Sam, Livy, and Jean planned to spend the summer of 1902 in a rented cottage located in a pine grove above the York River near Sewall's Bridge in York Harbor, Maine, a forty-minute trolley trip from Howells's vacation home at Kittery Point. Katy Leary recalled that they thought the sea air "would be cool and bracing for Mrs. Clemens." Livy had been suffering some heart palpitations and "for a while could only breath when sitting up." To minimize the stress of the trip on her, the family sailed aboard the *Kanawha* on June 27 to the Hotel Champernowne in Kittery. Jean suffered convulsions on the yacht—"if we had been in a train," Sam alerted Rogers, "it would have been equivalent to being in hell"—and again ten days later, which upset Livy's health more than the cruise. Each of her daughter's seizures "comes near to killing Mrs. Clemens," Sam wrote Rogers, "and there is not much left of her for a day or two afterward." Nevertheless, according to Leary, "Mrs Clemens felt a little better at first." Howells remembered that he and Sam "used to sit at a corner of the veranda farthest away from Mrs. Clemens's window, where we could read our manuscripts to each other, and tell our stories, and laugh our hearts out without disturbing her. At first she had been about the house" and "one gentle afternoon . . . she made tea for us in the parlor." Howells was more circumspect in a note to Charles Eliot

Norton: "How sad old men are!" He and Sam "meet, and strike fire and flicker up, and I come away a heap of cold ashes."[45]

In late July, Sam was presented with an attractive business proposal by the theatrical producers Marc Klaw and A. L. Erlanger. They had commissioned Lee Arthur to script adaptations of both *Tom Sawyer* and *Huck Finn* to be directed by Charles Dillingham and to star Arthur Dunn. They were ready to invest $60,000 in a production to be staged exclusively in the provinces. If Sam read and approved the script, perhaps even offered a suggestion or two, Klaw and Erlanger promised to credit him as its coauthor in their advertising. On July 27, Sam thanked the producers for pitching the idea, which pleased him "completely," and granted them permission to "announce the play as Mark Twain's 'Huckleberry Finn adapted for the stage by Mark Twain & Lee Arthur.'" The next day Dillingham and Lee Arthur arrived in York Harbor with a copy of the manuscript, which Sam judged "a pretty good play." He reported to the producers that it "did greatly please me," though he recommended a change or two. On August 7, newspapers across the country, including theatrical sheets in New York, broke the news that Sam and Arthur were collaborating on the project, though there is no extant correspondence between them. The *St. Louis Republic* added, however, that "it was not known until within the past two weeks that Mr. Twain had taken any active part in the writing of the play"—this for a very good reason. Klaw and Erlanger continued to plant stories in the press through the summer, as in the *New York Clipper* theatrical paper, that Arthur "has been hard at work with Mr. Clemens" on a dramatization "soon to be produced with Arthur Dunn in the title role." The three-act comedy, which boasted a company of eighty, went into rehearsal in the fall at the Knickerbocker Theater in New York. As the ostensible joint dramatist Sam was present at the final rehearsal on November 8 and declared he was "highly pleased" with it, though he dodged the premiere of the play in Hartford on November 11. Not until the end of the month, with the company on the road, did the truth leak out in a stage whisper: the play contained nothing written by Sam not in the novels; that is, he had sold his name for publicity purposes. Lee Arthur admitted that the only line in the script that appeared in the original novel had been omitted "to make room for another song and dance," and Sam privately groused afterward that the adaptation of the novel into a musical comedy disgusted him.[46]

Sam made but one public appearance during the entire summer in York Harbor: a brief speech at the local public library in early August to mark the two hundred and fiftieth anniversary of the founding of the town. With Howells, Sarah Orne Jewett, Thomas Nelson Page, Thomas B. Reed, and Dartmouth president William Jewett Tucker in the audience, he praised the climate in the region because he had been able to "work 34 days out of the 37" he had lived there. Then on August 9 the journalist Brand Whitlock "drank tea and smoked a cigar" with Sam "on the veranda of his summer home . . . while he convulsed us with story after story."[47]

The family holiday had already begun to sour in the summer heat. "In order to be able to breathe," Livy "had to sit upright in bed" all night. "In the daytime she feels fairly well," he wrote Rogers on August 7, but she "has to be watched all the time to keep her from making exertions herself which others could make for her." Early in the morning of August 12, she suffered an apparent heart attack. Her breathing became labored, and she told Sam she "was dying & I was not able to doubt it." He summoned a New York doctor summering in York Harbor who concluded that "nothing but absolute rest, seclusion, and careful nursing could help her." Immediately Sam wrote Susan Crane that Livy was "low-spirited & wants you. . . . She wants you & she is right. We mean well, but we make a poor job of it." Katy Leary remembered that Crane "come up from Elmira because Mrs. Clemens was really very sick and couldn't see anybody or hear the slightest noise" and on doctor's orders "hardly could see Mr. Clemens except a few minutes at a time." On August 21 Sam informed Whitmore that Livy was "still feeble & languid" and Rogers that she "feels doubtful all the time" about her recovery. "She was never like this before in her life." On September 6 he reported to John Y. W. MacAlister that Livy was "slowly recovering from an alarming illness . . . which continued to be alarming, by fits & starts, until 3 or 4 days ago." He notified Charley Langdon on September 11 that his sister was "very weak, but she improves a little per day." Meantime, Clara assumed control of the housekeeping, "seeing that everything was going to destruction for want of a centralized power & authority," and household conditions improved. She "seems to be as good a general as her mother," Sam wrote Twichell. Two days later Livy "lay & meditated long upon the situation—two or three hours" and then resolved "*to get well* & dismissed the subject." On September 20 George J. Helmer was summoned by telegraph from New York, and the next day the osteopath administered "a severe treatment" to Livy that left her "sore and lame." Livy's allopath in turn urged Helmer to stay away "for a few days" to allow Livy to "gather strength" before he treated her again, whereupon Sam protested that Helmer's massage had "*enabled her to take food.*" In any case, Livy's condition remained precarious for the rest of her life. As the result of her progressive heart disease, "the specialists cannot tell us whether the period of her tarrying with us is to be long or short. They only know that the situation is grave & will remain so." For better or worse, Livy was nourished with plasmon, though she detested it, and Sam wished he could transport "old Kellgren here from Sweden" because, he believed, "with his two hands he is worth fifty osteopaths and fifty million doctors. He would have had the madam on her feet & as sound as a nut in three days."[48]

One of the sources of Livy's heart trouble, as Sam allowed, was her stress and anxiety over the purchase of the Tarrytown house, though Sam assured her it would "hold its value" even if "the Hartford one doesn't seem to have any hold." Under the circumstances, it became even more imperative to dump the Hartford house. "I strongly want Whitmore to get rid of the house—sell it for a song," he wrote Rogers in late August, "so that I can tell Mrs. Clemens that that burden upon her spirits is gone." With "four doctors & two trained nurses all summer, with a war-price specialist from Boston now & then," he whined, the family expenses were "$10,000 a year heavier than they were a year ago." Sam was so unhappy with the inflated charges of one of the York Harbor physicians—$3 per visit "for the summer visitor" rather than the customary $1 "for the old resident"—that he threatened suit. Despite her heart attack, moreover, Livy was still "*determined* to build an addition at Tarrytown," but the construction would "not cost less than $30,000," and Sam would not "consent to put a dollar there that the Hartford house doesn't furnish. She'll have to take $30,000 for that house if she can't do any better." By early October, Sam asked Whitmore whether Roberts would pay "what the *land* cost ($32,000)," in which case "I should be quite willing to let him have the house, stable & greenhouse for nothing." In mid-January 1903 Sam dropped the price to $30,000, and in early March he proposed to tear the house down to reduce his taxes and maintenance costs on the property. A month later, in early April 1903, he wrote in exasperation that his monthly expenses, including Livy's round-the-clock nursing, amounted to $4,000. "For the Lord Jesus H. Christ's sake *sell* or rent *that God damned house*," he ordered Whitmore. "I would rather go to hell than own it 50 days longer." Their annual expenses were $8,000 or $9,000 more "than we can afford." He repeated the order another month later: "Rid me of the Hartford house. If any man wants to pay $25,000 cash for it, let him have it." Whitmore finally sold the house in early May to a vice president of the Hartford Fire Insurance Company for $28,800, about a fourth of its original construction cost and about a third of its initial listing price.[49]

Coincidentally, the same day that Livy suffered a severe heart attack in August 1902, Sam learned that the Denver Public Library had reignited the controversy over *Adventures of Huckleberry Finn* by purging the novel from its shelves on the grounds that it was "immoral and profane." Denver librarians were widely quoted in the press defending their decision to ban the novel because Huck "denounces the Sunday-school," "indulges in profanity," and "tells things more serious than fibs in order to wiggle expeditiously and safely out of embarrassing situations." Even before Sam commented on the ban, the *Portland* (Ore.) *Journal* protested that there was "surely something the matter with the microbes that serve" the Denver librarians and members of the Denver library board "for brains." The *Washington Times* similarly branded the exclusion of the novel "an offense against our national common sense." Sam suspected that Frederick Funston, by then the military commander of the Department of the Colorado, had engineered its suppression in retaliation for Sam's attack on his character in the *North American Review*. In the light of the circumstantial evidence and the absence of a denial, the allegation seems plausible. As Sam soon wrote the *Denver Post*, "a few months ago I published an article which threw mud at that pinchbeck hero, Funston, and his extraordinary morals." Whereas "Huck's morals have stood the strain in Denver and in every English, German and French speaking community in the world" for seventeen years, suddenly Denver, where "Funston commands," had expelled the novel from its library. "If Satan's morals and Funston's are preferable to Huck's," he concluded, "let Huck's take a back seat; they can stand any ordinary competition, but not a combination like that." Sam's defense of his novels was echoed in a tongue-in-cheek opinion piece in *Collier's Weekly* almost certainly written by his nephew and namesake Sam Moffett, who had recently joined the staff of the magazine. "In our own variegated youth," this editorialist declared, "a clerical uncle took us out of the house behind some bushes and cautioned us against the insidious effects of reading Mark Twain; but the warning fell on barren soil. We wished to be good, but not at the price of losing Tom and Huck."[50]

The proscription of *Huck Finn* in Denver triggered a cascade of new banishments of the novel and other books by Sam over the next few months from public libraries in Brooklyn; Council Bluffs, Nebraska; and Des Moines, Manchester, and Sioux City, Iowa. On the whole, Sam was unperturbed. "I wrote Tom Sawyer and Huckleberry Finn for adults exclusively," he insisted in a private letter to a Brooklyn librarian,

> and it always distresses me when I find that boys and girls have been allowed access to them. The mind that becomes soiled in youth can never again be washed clean; I know this by my own experience, and to this day I cherish an unappeasable bitterness against the unfaithful guardians of my young life, who not only permitted but compelled me to read an unexpurgated Bible

> through before I was 15 years old. None can do that and ever draw a clean sweet breath again this side of the grave. . . . If there is an unexpurgated Bible in the Children's Department, won't you please help . . . remove Huck and Tom from that questionable companionship?

Or as he reflected later, "When a Library expels a book of mine and leaves an unexpurgated Bible lying profusely around where people can get hold of it, the unconscious irony delights me."[51]

Funston never replied publicly to Sam's charge of censorship, though of course Funston's apologists responded forthwith, mostly from a safe distance in Kansas. The *Leavenworth Times* not only declared that his letter to the *Post* was "another foolish blunder" but that he "seems to have reached his dotage." The *Fort Scott Monitor* lamented his "malignant abuse" of Funston. But once again the *Topeka Capital* led the charge with a succession of rants: Sam's accusations were "laughed at" (August 20), he was "getting to be a good deal of a joke" (August 21), and his "silly" and cranky letter" was the "crazy outbreak of a humorist in his dotages" and made him "the laughing stock of the country" (August 22). The *Rochester Democrat and Chronicle* called for Sam to refrain from "further public exhibition of progressive asininity." The controversy over the censoring of *Huck Finn* in Denver prompted a reporter for the *Omaha World-Herald* to inquire into the status of the novel in the local library, only to discover it had been banned there several years earlier. He then telegraphed Sam, who replied by mail, as he said, to save time. "I am tearfully afraid this noise is doing much harm," he admitted. "It has started a number of hitherto spotless people to reading *Huck Finn*, out of a natural curiosity to learn what this is all about—people who had not heard of him before; people whose morals will go to wreck and ruin now." Ironically, a month later both *Tom Sawyer* and *Huck Finn* were removed from the shelves of the Alton, Illinois, public library.[52] During the same period when he was awarded honorary degrees from Yale and the University of Missouri, the so-called library authorities were blacklisting his books, forbidding children under fifteen from reading them without parental permission.

Despite the distractions, Sam wrote a fair amount during this period, mostly on two topics: the Philippine war and Christian Science. In such unfinished manuscripts as "Glances at History (Suppressed)," "Outlines of History (Suppressed)," and "History 1,000 Years from Now," imaginary histories of the decline and fall of the Great Republic from the perspective of a distant future, he railed about the fin de siècle events that had transformed the United States from democracy to dictatorship. A historian putatively observes in A.D. 2901 that "it is now a thousand years since the happy accident—or series of accidents" that "rescued our nation from democracy and gave it the blessed refuge and shelter of a crown." The "first of these incidents was the seizure of the group of islands now called the Vashington Archipelago," formerly the Philippines, and the prosecution of "an unjust and trivial war." In the longest of these fragments, "The Secret History of Eddypus," composed between spring 1901 and spring 1902, Sam again envisioned the new dark age a millennium hence, the dystopian "intellectual Night" or repressive theocracy that descends upon "all the globe" after the merger of Christian Science headquartered at Boston (now Eddyflats) and the Church of Rome (now Eddyburg) except (ironically) China, "the only country where an enlightened civilization now exists" because it had never succumbed to the pernicious influence of missionaries. The most reliable chronicle of ancient events to survive massive past book burning is a manuscript entitled "Old Comrades" by "the revered and scholarly Mark Twain, Bishop of New Jersey," aka "the Father of History," who was lynched in 1912. In consequence, "The Secret History of Eddypus" is a hilarious compendium of misinformation and fractured history ("Yellow journalism was invented by Ralph Waldo Emerson"). It is also a companion of sorts to *A Connecticut Yankee in King Arthur's Court.* Whereas the Yankee battles ignorance and superstition in Camelot thirteen centuries in the past, the narrator of "Eddypus" describes a world a millennium in the future governed by the same ignorance and superstition because "the damned human race" does not change. Ironically, much as the manuscript by "Mark Twain" was ostensibly discovered centuries after it was written, Sam's actual manuscript remained unpublished until 1972, over seventy years after it was written. In a similar essay entitled "The Philippine Incident," unpublished during his life, Sam was even more candid:

> We have bought some islands from a party who did not own them; with real smartness and a good counterfeit of disinterested friendliness we coaxed a confiding weak nation into a trap and closed it upon them; we went back on an honored guest of the Stars and Stripes when we had no further use for him and chased him to the mountains; we are as indisputably in possession of a wide-spreading archipelago as if it were our property; we have pacified some thousands of the islanders and buried them; destroyed their fields; burned their villages, and turned their widows and orphans out-of-doors; furnished heartbreak by exile to some dozens of disagreeable patriots; subjugated the remaining ten millions by Benevolent Assimilation, which is the pious new name of the musket; we have acquired property in the three hundred

> concubines and other slaves of our business partner, the Sultan of Sulu, and hoisted our protecting flag over that swag.[53]

For obvious reasons, Sam abhorred Theodore Roosevelt's "Big Stick" foreign policy.

Livy "will get well—they all say it. If we only *could* get home to Riverdale!" Sam yelped on October 13. "That would be the right medicine" for her. But the logistics of their return from York Harbor to Wave Hill at the end of the summer—Sam had renewed the lease on the house for another year—posed a problem. He initially thought they might sail on the *Kanawha* from Portsmouth to Boston, then rail in a private car to Elmira for a few weeks before landing back in Riverdale. But in mid-September Livy's doctors nixed "the idea of going by sea" and Sam scrapped the notion of a stay at Quarry Farm. Instead, he chartered a private rail car that was "hauled over various lines" around Boston to Grand Central Station in New York, where "a locomotive stood ready and waiting" to deliver them to Riverdale on October 16 "in fifteen minutes," reducing the length of the trip from thirteen to nine hours at a cost of $340, or nearly $10,000 in modern dollars.[54]

Sam was not allowed to see the bedridden Livy for the next several months lest the excitement of his visit provoke a relapse. She was "condemned to solitude" and received no visitors except the doctors, the nurses, and Clara. Every night during her convalescence Sam "slipped a letter under the bathroom door that opened near her bed—a letter which contained no information about current events and could do no harm. She responded, with pencil, once or twice a day—at first at some length, but as the months dragged along and her strength grew feebler, she put her daily message of love in trembling characters upon little scraps of paper." One of the few compensations in the "ghastly life that we are leading," Sam wrote Aldrich, is "that we do not despair" and "neither does she." Another was that, as Livy said, she was no longer a captive listener to his incessant rants about the "damned human race."[55]

CHAPTER 11

Vanity Fare

Twentieth Century Civilization—when we consider the innocent pride which we take in it—is surely the most sarcastic sarcasm which our race has put on the market for many centuries—perhaps a million.

—Samuel Clemens to Edward Everett Hale, 28 March 1905

One of Sam's last orders of business before leaving York Harbor was to hire a personal assistant for Livy. She could no longer manage the housekeeping staff or maintain her correspondence from bed, where she would be confined for months. Clara traveled for weeks at a time in pursuit of her musical career, and Jean was in fragile health. Harriet Whitmore, the wife of Sam's financial agent Franklin Whitmore, highly recommended Isabel Van Kleek Lyon, the Whitmore's former nanny, whom the Clemenses had known slightly years before in Hartford. Raised in Tarrytown, the daughter of a Columbia University classics professor, the eldest of three children, Lyon had long been employed as a governess for affluent families and most recently had worked for the Hartford Woman's Exchange. "I am going to want just such a person in the Autumn," Livy confirmed to Mrs. Whitmore in late June, even before her heart attack in York Harbor, and "I should probably want her to begin her work about the 1st of Oct[ober]." Apparently on the strength of Whitmore's recommendation, Sam hired Lyon, as the *Hartford Courant* reported on September 26, to "begin her duties on October 1" by preparing the house in Riverdale for their return. Sam was pleased with the Clemenses' newest employee, whom he described as "slender, petite, comely, 38 years old by the almanac, & 17 in ways & carriage & dress." Clara was likewise delighted, at least initially, and expressed her gratitude to Whitmore: "How thankful we are that you told us about Miss Lyon for she is really a treasure and enormous comfort. She not only is sweet and attractive entirely lacking any disagreeable qualities but she has a cheerful manner and way which are welcome in a house at times of illness & consequent depression. I am so glad we have her & I know my Mother will be when she knows her." In addition, Lyon worked for a modest salary, only $50 a month plus room, board, and clothing, and liked her employer and his daughters.

As she wrote Whitmore three weeks after the Clemenses returned from Maine, "I find him most lovely and possessed of great depth of soul, showing itself in small things," and "I find the girls charming, erratic, irresponsible, but possessed of much character." Lyon repeatedly thanked Whitmore for giving her "all this joy" and making her "the wealthiest woman ever." Lyon rarely saw Livy in person—not at all the last months of 1902, and only twice during the first half of 1903—but she soon became an indispensable part of the family. Sam began to dictate letters to her in early November 1902, and though she did not know shorthand, his drawl enabled her to transcribe his words in longhand. Over the years she assumed many roles in the Clemens house: majordomo, gatekeeper, interior designer, social secretary, hostess, amanuensis, companion, adviser, and nurse. Sam famously defended Lyon for years whenever one of his daughters insinuated that she had overstepped her place, as in this note to Jean: "I have to have somebody in whom I have confidence to attend to every detail of my daily affairs for me except my literary work. I attend to not one of them myself; I give the instructions and see that they are obeyed. I give Miss Lyon instructions—she does nothing of her own initiative. . . . She does all my matters well, and although they are often delicate and difficult she makes no enemies, either for herself or me."[1] The poet Witter Bynner, a member of the *McClure's* staff, christened her "the Lyon of St. Mark."

Sam's first order of business after settling back in the Riverdale house was to order fuel for the approaching winter. The anthracite coal miners in eastern Pennsylvania had been on strike all summer for an eight-hour day, a dollar per week increase in wages, and recognition of their union. On October 20, Sam gave a push to all sides in the dispute by ridiculing their collective failure to reach an agreement. He sent a letter, soon released to the press, to the secretary of the treasury, a sound-money Republican, complaining that the prices for wood and coal had "reached an altitude which puts them out of the reach of literary persons in straitened circumstances." He placed an order with the U.S. Treasury Department for "45 tons best old dry Government bonds, suitable for furnace, gold 7 percent 1864 preferred; 12 tons early greenbacks, range side, suitable for cooking"; and "8 barrels seasoned 25 & 50-cent postal currency, vintage of 1866, eligible for kindlings." He asked that his order be delivered "with all convenient dispatch at my house in Riverdale at lowest rates for spot cash." He promised to "be very grateful" and to "vote right" at the next election. This letter was telegraphed across the country by the Associated Press and received hostile reviews in Kansas; the *Lawrence Journal* called it "something pathetic," and the *Wellington Journal* "veriest rot" from an "old fraud." Interviewed by the New York *Evening World* the next day, Sam insisted he had not been joking, that he had "never made a more serious and urgent request in all my life." The family cook had informed him "there wasn't a lump of coal in the house" and he might have "underestimated the amount of fuel I will need this winter," though "I shall be grateful if I can even get this modest order filled." He could "cut down the trees about the place, except that I fear I should miss them next summer," or "gather together old leaves and dried grass" to burn, "or else chop up the furniture to obtain fuel. There is only one coal dealer here and I can't pay his prices."[2] Whether or not Sam's letter to the treasury secretary had any effect, the strike was finally settled by arbitration on October 23.

Three days later, Sam attended the inauguration of Woodrow Wilson as the thirteenth president of Princeton University. He and Robert Todd Lincoln, W. D. Howells, J. P. Morgan, and Thomas B. Reed were guests of former President Cleveland over the weekend, and he attended the Columbia-Princeton football game with Reed and ten thousand other sports fans.[3]

Before Sam left England in October 1900, he invented a scheme to exploit the vanity of public figures who, he thought, would pay to approve their own obituaries. He proposed a new type of magazine, to be called *The Obituary,* that would prepare the necrologies of prominent people before their deaths, subject to their endorsement, for prices ranging from £100 to £500, depending on the size "of the purse of the subject." The memoirs "were to be very thorough," he explained, "covering every spot in a man's life. Every man has some shady spots, you know." The idea "was to write the most scandalous things about a man while he was alive," and unless he paid cash on the barrelhead either to suppress or revise it, "the article would appear in *The Obituary* contemporaneously with the announcement of his death." He "could cut the proof, add to it, or polish it as much as he wished, but he had to pay." In other words, Sam conceived of a sophisticated form of extortion. He pitched the idea over after-dinner cigars at Edwin Austin Abbey's home one evening to the British humorist and political journalist Henry Lucy, who teased that the "division of profits were simplified" because "there were to be only two proprietors" and they "were to equally share the revenues." Of course, no copy of the magazine was ever published, Sam claimed, because every issue was "suppressed in advance," though when Lucy requested his share of the booty, Sam protested that "there's not profit enough for two, only just enough for Twain."[4]

He publicized a variation on the scheme in *Harper's Weekly* two years later. In "Amended Obituaries," he solicited copies of his *own* death notices from "such journals and periodicals as have obituaries of me lying in their pigeon-holes" to send them to his attention so that he could edit "not the Facts, but the Verdicts—striking out such clauses as could have a deleterious influence on the Other Side and replacing them with clauses of a more judicious character. I should, of course, expect to pay double rates for both the omissions and the substitutions; and I should also expect to pay quadruple rates for all obituaries which proved to be rightly and wisely worded in the originals, thus requiring no amendations at all." He "was much taken" with the idea, Paine recalled, and "naturally he got a shower of responses—serious, playful, burlesque."[5]

The evening of November 28, Sam was the guest of honor at a celebration of his sixty-seventh birthday at the Metropolitan Club hosted by George Harvey. "It was very grand & flatters one, & finely successful," he reported to Livy. Owen Wister wrote Sam to congratulate him on the occasion: there was "no living American of which I'm quite so proud as I am of you." On the other hand, the *Elmira Star-Gazette* admonished him not to "presume upon this liberality, not on his life," merely because "during the festivities" his "recent treason is temporarily forgotten." Among those men present at the banquet were George Washington Cable, Charles Frohman, Garland, Richard Watson Gilder, Henry Harper, John Hay, Howells, Brander Matthews, Tom Reed, Clarence C. Rice, Henry Rogers, Booth Tarkington, and Twichell. Eight of them toasted Sam that evening, including Howells, who declaimed "A Double-Barrelled Sonnet to Mark Twain," including these lines:

> The missionary may not love him quite,
> The imperialist may not think him wholly right,
> The predatory cabman free from blame,
> The moralist consider it the same
> To teach by joke as with a text in sight.

Sam did not rise to respond to their tributes until well after midnight. The *Brooklyn Eagle* remarked that "he was never brighter, he was never more sardonic, he was never sweeter, he never more successfully brought humor and pathos into close or finer relationship in all his life. He simply reveled in reminiscence, characterization and gratitude." Garland too thought "he made all other speakers seem tame." Howells, who had heard him speak dozens of times over the years, told him afterward that it was "the best speech you've ever made." "There are fifty-four men here," Sam began. "Of them thirty-nine are my dear personal friends. They know me and I know them. Of the remaining fifteen I am confident that I can borrow money." Sam ended his speech with a homage to Livy: "She has been the best friend I have ever had, and that is saying a good deal; she has reared me—she and Twichell together—and what I am I owe to them." His comments prompted a "*mighty* burst" of applause, and Howells told him later that "it was splendid to close, like that, with Mrs. Clemens."[6]

The day after his birthday celebration, Sam railed with Jean to Elmira to attend the wedding of Julia Langdon, the daughter of Charles Langdon, and Edward Loomis, the first vice president of the Delaware, Lackawanna and Western Railroad, in the parlor of the mansion on Main Street.[7]

A week later, early in the morning of December 7, Sam's friend Tom Reed, former Speaker of the House of Representatives, died unexpectedly. His passing represented "an incalculable loss to the nation," Sam told reporters. He wrote Reed's widow that everyone who knew him "is stricken with you & mourns with you. He could have achieved the age of the patriarchs if his friends could have been privileged to spare from their lives to lengthen his." Sam eulogized Reed in *Harper's Weekly* in similar fashion two weeks later. "He was transparently honest and honorable," he wrote, "and whoever came to know him trusted him and was not disappointed. He was wise, he was shrewd and alert," and "his life and character" were "fine and beautiful." Reed had delivered his final speech "at my birthday dinner at the end of November," and Sam had sent "my last word to him" in a letter the next day.[8]

When Sam finally returned to his writing desk in Riverdale, he began yet another draft of the Mysterious Stranger narrative he had thrice abandoned. He composed the first seven chapters of the "Print Shop" version he entitled "No. 44, the Mysterious Stranger" and resumed the harangue against Christian Science he had begun in 1899—no "Secret History of Eddypus" this time but a detailed nonfiction exposé of the motives of the founder of the sect. If he had deified Joan of Arc, he demonized Mary Baker Eddy. At least initially he reworked for publication a couple of Christian Science articles that he had prepared in Vienna in 1899 but that Livy had demanded he suppress because "I was trying to prove that all men are born crazy," thus accounting for the new religious fad. At the time "Christian Science was so new to me that I had not studied it at all, & was only interested to play around in the shallows with it & get a moment's fun out of it." He "actually studied the history of Christian Science, its claims & pretensions, & its bible" in 1902, "with the result that if I had had any hostility toward Christian Science itself previously, I lost that & in its place conceived a vast admiration for & detestation of Mrs. Eddy." By mid-September he had finished articles totaling between eighteen and twenty thousand words on the topic and offered them to Frederick Duneka, the general manager at Harper & Brothers, which printed them not in *Harper's Weekly* as Sam expected—a devout Catholic, Duneka was squeamish about anything that smacked of religious controversy—but in the December 1902 through February 1903 issues of the *North American Review*, more directly under the editorial control of company president George Harvey. The firm was, after all, contractually obliged to publish whatever its star contributor submitted.[9]

The essays were hailed by a few critics, as in the *London Leader* ("Mark Twain is not crusading against Christian Science by halves") and Toronto *Saturday Night* ("Mark has a keen scent for money-changers in the temple"). But in general the series was panned in the press; the *Pittsburgh Post* complained, "his wealth of wit is squandered recklessly"; the *Denver Republican*, that "Mark Twain the humorist long ago gave way to Mark Twain the critic and sometimes Mark Twain the scold"; the *Philadelphia Medical Journal*, that "of all the blatherskite he has ever written his latest is . . . the most senile"; and *American Medicine*, that "sane logic gives way to senile fantasy." William D. McCrackan, a journalist and Christian Science convert, assailed Sam in the March number of the *North American Review*, contending that Mrs. Eddy had developed her theology "by logical steps consistent with clear reasoning" and it was "therefore strictly scientific in the proper sense of the word." The only complaints about the alleged materialism of the church, he added, were leveled by persons who did not buy her books. Sam replied in the next issue of the *Review*, concluding that if McCrackan "will make an excursion through my book when it comes out, and will dispassionately examine her testimonies as there accumulated, I think he will in candor concede that she is by a large percentage the most erratic and contradictory and untrustworthy witness that has occupied the stand since the days of the lamented Ananias."[10] The exchange did not quell the controversy.

Sam always insisted that he was not opposed to Eddy's brand of "mental science" but to her profit- and racketeering. In fact, he wholeheartedly approved of Susy's conversion to the "rational & noble philosophy" of mind-cure, which he considered a form of hypnosis, and Livy similarly was "very glad indeed that Susy has taken up Mental Science." In poor health, he wrote his daughter while in India in February 1896 that he was "perfectly certain" his "exasperating colds & the carbuncles come from a diseased mind, & that your mental science could drive them away." He once attributed Ulysses S. Grant's cancer not to his tobacco habit but to his "mental miseries." He claimed in an interview in March 1901 that he had "tried" many types of medical treatment over the years, including "allopathy, homœopathy, hydrotherapy, osteopathy, and many other a pathy besides; and I've tried Christian Science, too. But I haven't much use for it."[11] In a more charitable moment, he pondered a distribution of illnesses by discipline: "surgery cases to the surgeons; lupus to the actinic-ray specialist; nervous prostration to the Christian Scientist; most ills to the allopath and the homeopath; (in my own particular case) rheumatism, gout and bronchial attacks to the osteopathist." He elsewhere conceded that Christian Science, stripped of its institutional and religious trappings, might "reduce the world's disease and pain about four-fifths." Put another way, "my irreverence and disrespect are pretty exclusively" for Mary Baker Eddy, "not for her flock. I believe the flock to be honest and sincere and that she is neither." "*I* am not combating Xn Science," he reiterated to the anti-Eddyite Frederick W. Peabody. "I haven't a thing in the world against it. Making fun of that shameless old swindler, Mother Eddy, is the only thing about it I take any interest in," though "at bottom I suppose I take a private delight in seeing the human race making an ass of itself again—which it has always done whenever it had a chance." Or again: Eddy, "the queen of frauds & hypocrites," has "a powerful interest for me, because I think that in one way or two ways she is the most extraordinary woman whom Accident & Circumstance have thus far vomited into the world. She is the monumental Sarcasm of the Ages; & it seems to me that when we contemplate her & what she has achieved, it is blasphemy to longer deny to the Supreme Being the possession of the sense of humor."[12]

He repeated the charge he had first leveled in 1899 that Eddy's original sin was plagiarism. He contended she had stolen the central ideas in *Science and Health* from the mid-nineteenth-century faith healer Phineas Parkhurst Quimby, whose patient she had been, and then hired ghostwriters and editors to polish her own awkward and stilted prose. To be sure, his evidence was circumstantial, based primarily on his argument that she exhibited little sense of style in her other works, particularly her *Miscellaneous Writings, 1883–1896* (1896). After reading "acres of what purported to be Mrs. Eddy's writings in the past two months," Sam concludes, "it is not believable that the hand that wrote [the] clumsy and affected sentences [of the *Miscellaneous Writings*] wrote the smooth English of *Science and Health*." Eddy's unedited works were studded with grammatical mistakes such as noun-verb disagreements, tense shifts, and dangling participles. For example, Eddy stated, "Many pale cripples went into the Church leaning on crutches who came out carrying them on their shoulders," as if the crutches were "carrying the cripples on their shoulders." As Sam added, "I think her proof-reader should have been shot." Eddy "has never been able to write anything above third-rate English," "is weak in the matter of grammar," and "has but a rude and dull sense of the values of words." Her "known and undisputed writings" exhibit "no depth, no analytical quality, no thought above school composition size, and but juvenile ability in handling thoughts." In short, Sam did "not believe that she ever wrote any part" of *Science and Health,* and the only reason Quimby had not protested was because she had "not exposed" his work "to print until after he was safely dead." In mid-April 1903, after his Christian Science articles had all appeared in the *North American Review,* Sam read the manuscript of Livingston Wright's pamphlet *How Reverend Wiggin Rewrote Mrs. Eddy's Book,* which he believed proved that the Unitarian minister J. Henry Wiggin authored the standard textbook of Christian Science. In any case, in May 1903 he asserted that Eddy "never wrote a line of *Science and Health*" and "therefore I have no respect for her; her claim is a falsehood and she is a criminal." Howells too recalled Sam's "disgust for the illiterate twaddle" and the "vacuous vulgarity" of Eddy's writings.[13]

Sam was also peeved that Eddy had seemingly acquiesced to her followers' identification of her as "a Redeemer, a Christ, and Christ's equal," a second Mother Mary, a fourth deity in the Godhead. Of all the allegations Sam leveled in his series of essays in the *North American Review,* Eddy replied only to this point in an Associated Press release on January 17, 1903. From her retirement in New Hampshire, she protested that "I begged the students who first gave me the endearing appellative 'mother' not to name me thus. But without my consent that word spread like wildfire." She asserted that she believed "in one Christ, teach one Christ, and know of but one Christ." Still, as late as April 1906, Sam restated that Eddy "stole 'Science & Health.' She is an ignorant twaddler. She can't write English; she can't write anything above nursery grade, she hasn't a vestige of reasoning power." Much as Sam alleged in *Roughing It* that Joseph Smith "smouched" the Mormon Bible from the Old and New Testaments and later expressed doubt that the plays attributed to Shakespeare were in truth written by him, Sam was a undeviating skeptic that Eddy authored *Science and Health.*[14]

His reservations about Christian Science were rooted in part in his conviction that it was a money machine or business venture masquerading as a church. As he put it, she inherited "a sawdust mine" and transformed it "into a Klondike." *Science and Health* had been published "in hundreds of editions" and sold "at a clear profit per volume, above cost, of 700 per cent—a profit which distinctly belongs to the angel of the Apocalypse." And not just the one text: "Many, many precious Christian-Science things" were available for sale—cash only, better cash in advance: "Bible Lessons; Church Manual; C[hristian] S[cience] Hymnal; History of the building of the Mother-Church; lots of Sermons," etc. The "Christian-Science Trust gives nothing away; everything it has is for sale," so much so that "its god is Mrs. Eddy first, then the Dollar. Not a spiritual Dollar, but a real one. From end to end of the Christian Science literature not a single (material) thing in the world is conceded to be real, except the Dollar. But all through and through its advertisements that reality is eagerly and persistently recognized." A putative religion, moreover, Christian Science paid no taxes and, he asserted, supported no charities, though Sam was sometimes challenged on this point. In a stunning hypocrisy, at least from his point of view, Eddy's Metaphysical College denied admission to anyone who was ill. Hamlin Garland, who dined with him in Riverdale in February 1903, heard his "scathing" rant about the "closed corporation" or "monopoly" Eddy had formed to sell religious indulgences. When Garland mentioned Sam's tirade to Howells the next day, "he agreed that Clemens, like many another humorist, was essentially sad. 'He realizes that his wife is hopelessly ill, and Jean is a constant care. He would like to believe in mental healing and is rather prejudiced in its favor, but is infuriated with the money-making side of the organization.'"[15]

But mostly Sam reviled Christian Science for the demagogy he worried it would wield in the not-too-distant future, though he fuzzed the dates. "Nothing can stay the Xn Science epidemic," he predicted in December 1902. "In a hundred [years] it will supplant all the other religions & boss all the governments." Two months later, he prophesied that "in America in 1910 the Christian Scientists will be a political force, in 1920 politically formidable, and in 1930 the governing power in the Republic—to remain that, permanently." But by the time this passage was reprinted in 1907, Sam postponed these benchmarks by a decade. In any case, Sam imagined an authoritarian future in the United States, if not the whole world, dominated by Christian Scientists. After all, Eddy was already "the only absolute sovereign in all Christendom." As Howells averred, "He believed that as a religious machine the Christian Science Church was as perfect as the Roman Church and destined to be more formidable in its control of the minds of men." By 1906 Sam was despondent on the subject: Eddy had founded "a religion which may last 3000 years & probably will. She has accomplished more in 30 years than any other fraud achieved in a century." He feared that, like a greedy Tom Sawyer, she had "a hunger for power and glory; and that while her hunger for money still remains, she wants it now for the expansion and extension it can furnish to that power and glory." Thousands of Americans "fully believe" the revelations in *Science and Health*, "although they can't understand a line of it," and "worship the sordid and ignorant old purloiner" Eddy, whom they "believe to be a member, by adoption, of the Holy Family."[16]

Sam initially anticipated that *Christian Science*, the last long work he completed, would be issued by Harper & Brothers in spring 1903, but he was mistaken. Duneka had the serialized chapters typeset and sent to Sam in the form of galley proofs, and urged him on January 28, 1903, to forward the balance of the manuscript as soon as possible so that the firm could send it to the compositors. Harper & Brothers even advertised it for sale. But when Sam carried the manuscript to Duneka, as he recalled years later, the editor

> did not break out into any enthusiasms about it, in fact he looked embarrassed. I inquired as to what might be the matter, and he developed the fact that he was afraid of the Christian Scientists. He said they were growing very strong, and would it be to my interest to publish such a book and antagonize this growing power? also, would it be to the interest of Harper and Brothers to antagonize that power? I said that if he was afraid, I didn't wish to push a dangerous book upon him, and I would publish it elsewhere; but he said "No; by no means no, if the book must be published, we wish to publish it ourselves."

Put another way, "they asked me not to insist upon its publication, they being afraid it could hurt their house by antagonizing the Scientists. I did not insist, but left them to choose their own time—which they did." But Sam's "back was hardly turned" before the company, on April 6, announced in *Publishers' Weekly* that it would not "publish in book form Mark Twain's papers on Christian Science. All orders for the book now on file will be cancelled." Duneka "is slippery beyond imagination!" Sam grumbled to Rogers. "I had been doing my very best to show in print that the Xn-Scientist cult was become a power in the land" and "here was *proof*: it had scared the biggest publisher in the Union!" He hoped at first the release had merely been postponed until the autumn, but as he soon realized, the book had been effectively suppressed. "My publishers have always been doubtful about the judacity of publishing the book," he admitted, and they "may take their time." He insisted that he was unconcerned. "Whenever I have finished a book the question of whether it should ever be pub[lished] or not is a matter of indifference to me," he claimed in February 1906. *Christian Science* "has been ready for publication some 3 or 4 y[ea]rs. If at any time the Harpers should conclude to issue it, there will be no occasion to consult me about it."[17]

Early in the new year he signed a petition with Gilder, Howells, and dozens of others demanding that the Congressional Committee on Philippine Affairs investigate conditions in the islands. But he declined to contribute or to raise money during an Anti-Imperialist League fund drive. "Must I pass that hat *besides?* Must I do *two* shares of the work, while some others do nothing?" he asked. "I hope to be deported to John Bunyan's heaven if I do." He remained fervent in his views, but with the formal end of the war in the Philippines in July 1902 the *raison d'état* of the league—and so donations to the cause it represented—began to evaporate despite the "excellent materials for a moral campaign":

> We have the grotesque Cuban swindle & the broken promise—the promise which was so full of noble and hallowed gush; we have the comical Philippine stupidity, where we crept slyly in, disguised as friends, hoping to rob the hen roost before our game was found out—& found ourselves in a hornet's nest, to our pathetic & childlike surprise; we have our Funston & our opportunity to train up young American lads on the new American idea of "heroism." . . . Why, we can get ourselves called Traitors by those wise & saintly self-appointed Official Inspectors & Judges of Patriotism who know a Traitor the minute they see him.

If self-anointed "Patriots" can publicly identify "Traitors," Sam concluded, they might as well "dictate to us how we shall vote, too."[18]

Between late August and mid-September, as the Clemenses' summer in York Harbor was drawing to a close, Sam "scribbled" a 7,500-word tale entitled "Was It Heaven?—or Hell?" for the December issue of *Harper's Monthly* for which he was paid $1,500. In the story, based on an anecdote Howells had told him in York Harbor, a pair of aged aunts lie to their ailing niece to shield her from the fact that her daughter is dying of typhoid; that is, Sam distinguished "between a lie that helps and a lie that hurts." The *Baltimore Sun* commended it as "full of pathos and of unorthodox philosophy." Sam anticipated by decades the "situational ethics" or moral pragmatism or anti-absolutism of such philosophers as Jean-Paul Sartre and Paul Tillich. "Little did he dream," Clara remembered, however, "that a similar drama would take place" in Riverdale shortly after the story was published. On December 22, Jean fell ill, and she was soon diagnosed with double pneumonia. Her "flaming fever" spiked to over 104 degrees, her holiday in Elmira was canceled, and all the time the truth was concealed from Livy, who "never suspected that anything was wrong." Sam "had a glimpse of" Jean a day or two after Christmas, and thought she resembled "a survivor of a forest fire." Every day Clara, the only member of the family permitted to visit her mother, had to improvise "the particulars of Jean's day: how many hours she was outdoors," what she wore, "how she was enjoying herself," and Jean abed "all the time, with a splotched face & fevered eyes, & all of us terrified—her mother the only placid & contented soul in the house. And reverently thankful, without a doubt!" Or as he reported to Twichell, "What a week! So full of comedy and pathos and tragedy!" Livy "would not live an hour if Clara lost her self-possession & let her secret be suspected," he feared. Sam was allowed to visit Livy "for the first time in 3½ months," since the family returned to Riverdale from York Harbor, for almost four minutes on December 30, and, as he wrote Howells, he was scheduled to see her again for 3½ minutes on New Year's Day. "She was in great spirits—like 25 years ago," he crowed, and he planned to lie to her should she ask whose voice she had heard in the house. He could not disclose to Livy that she had heard the doctor treating Jean for pneumonia. Twichell approved of Sam's "narratives of Holy Lying" and "of Clara's heroic untruth. 'Twas surely a brilliant performance." Fortunately, Jean fully recovered after a few weeks, and Livy never knew how close she had come to dying. But Sam quipped as late as April that "a fact would give her a relapse."[19]

Nor was Sam entirely callous when Bret Harte died in England in May 1902. To be sure, he never forgave Harte's dissipation and dishonesty. Garland recalled that, after dining in Riverdale in February 1903, Sam cursed the "whelp," "blackguard," and "blanketyblank two-faced hound." His "fury of invective was almost comical." But when Howells lauded Harte posthumously in *Harper's Monthly* ("he was a poet of a fine and fresh touch"), Sam was forbearing. "You have written of Harte most felicitously—most generously, too, & yet at the same time truly," he conceded, "for he was all you have said, & although he was more & worse, there is no occasion to remember it & I am often ashamed of myself for doing it." Howells was relieved that he had not offended Sam with his tribute. "It was sweet of you to write me those words," he replied, "and I am glad that the half-truth . . . didn't quite seem to you a half-lie." He conceded that he might have written "things that would have left blisters on [Harte's] fame."[20]

The first weeks of 1903 were fallow ones for the Clemens family. Jean and Livy both kept to their rooms. Sam canceled all engagements to remain in Riverdale, where he was allowed to visit Livy for fifteen minutes twice a day. "We are prisoners in this beautiful jail," he reported to Laurence Hutton in mid-March. Clara practiced the piano and "stands the afternoon watch with her mother," though she also contracted measles in the spring. Nor did they receive many visitors, though Ossip Gabrilowitsch paid a visit to the Clemens home before Clara got sick. Sam saw Howells occasionally and "the Rogerses every week or two," he noted, "but I hardly ever have a sight of other friends." Sam seldom left the house, and when he did, "I go to private things only & decline all public ones, of whatever kind." He was present the evening of March 26, however, at Miller Hutchison's laboratory on West Thirty-Second Street for a demonstration of the "acousticon," a portable, battery-powered hearing-aid. Unfortunately, when he returned to Riverdale he "caught a heavy cold which went to my bronchial tubes" and was confined to his bed for most of April and part of May. Not even the osteopath George J. Helmer could relieve the symptoms. "None of the family is robustly well," he acknowledged to William Winter, though by mid-spring he had begun to joke about his illness: "Why, that was a pleasant adventure, a sort of vacation, that gave me a legitimate excuse for spending five weeks in bed."[21]

While Sam was still on the mend, Livy's medical team "met in conspiracy" and recommended that she spend the next winter in a mild or "humaner" climate. She had been "a helpless victim of nervous prostration for fourteen months," Sam explained to Henry Lucy, "and we hope a year in Italy will put her on her feet. The doctors believe it." The family planned to travel, preferably to the neighborhood of Florence, in October if Livy was strong enough, as he notified Poultney Bigelow in April, and "if she isn't, we remain in this house." The advice "to clear for Italy in October" brightened Livy's spirits, and she began to plan their exodus "with lively interest & cheerfulness." Sam asked rhetorically, "Why *did* we ever return to America—it is a life & a climate that is not endurable by anybody but horses." By early May, Livy "of her own accord" suggested to Sam that he "spend a night at Fairhaven" the next time Rogers sailed there on the *Kanawha*. "*That* shows she is getting healthy," he bragged. In fact, Sam spent several days at Rogers's mansion in Fairhaven two weeks later, and afterward he thanked his friend for "the air, the billiards, the driving, the yacht trip, the social cussing & discussing, & the spiritual healing conferred by immersion in that simple Christian tank." He returned to Fairhaven to speak during Old Home Week in late June. "I had a perfectly gaudy time in Fairhaven," he allowed to Rogers on June 25, the day he returned by rail to New York, and "I wouldn't have missed that orgy for anything."[22]

Two weeks later, Sam, Livy, Livy's nurse Margaret Sherry, and Katy Leary left Riverdale for Elmira. They sailed down the Hudson aboard the *Kanawha* with the Rogerses for three-quarters of an hour to the Lackawanna Railroad dock at Hoboken, transferred to a special car Sam had hired, and arrived about eight hours later at Quarry Farm, where, as Sam wrote the Huttons, "all is repose & immense comfort." While the cruise down the river had been "refreshing," the rail trip "was unmitigated hell," "suffocating and awful," though Livy tolerated "it well for a person who has been bedridden nearly 11 months." Nevertheless, she arrived at the farm exhausted by the journey. She spent many of her waking hours over the next three months in a chair on the front porch "reading or enjoying the wide view of valley & town & the receding panorama of Pennsylvanian hills," and Leary thought that over the weeks "Mrs. Clemens seemed to get a little better." But she was also melancholy some of the time. "Everything here is so full of the past—the cherry tree, the air, the odors, the sound of summer everything is so suggestive of a time long ago, that one feels overwhelmed with a cloud of sorrows," she wrote Clara soon after she arrived. "At night it seems almost unendurable." Sam remained upbeat, at least in his correspondence with friends. "Livy is coming along," he notified Twichell on July 21. She "eats well, sleeps some, is mostly very gay, not very often depressed; spends all day on the porch, sleeps there a part of the night, makes excursions in carriage and in wheel-chair."[23] Clara and Jean joined their parents in early August.

Sam's last summer at Quarry Farm was largely uneventful. He returned to his octagonal study on the bluff a hundred yards from the house, where at Jean's urging he wrote a story entitled "A Dog's Tale" in defense of animal rights.

He had been elected an honorary member of the London Anti-Vivisectionist Society prior to his departure from England in 1900 and had rallied to the cause of abolishing this brand of torture. In a letter to the secretary of the group he detailed his opposition to it: "The pains which it inflicts upon unconsenting animals is the basis of my enmity toward it, and it is to me sufficient justification of the enmity without looking further. . . . I could not even see a vivisector vivisected with anything more than a sort of qualified satisfaction." Narrated by a collie, "A Dog's Tale" begins as a parody of the nature-fakir chronicles or animal fables popularized by Ernest Thompson-Seton and William J. Long but gradually morphs into a protest against animal abuse when the collie's pup is killed by her owner to prove a scientific theory.[24]

Originally published in the December 1903 issue of *Harper's Monthly*, the story was reprinted in pamphlet form by the National Anti-Vivisection Society in England and by Harper & Brothers in the United States. Howells thought it "most affecting and lovely," but in general critical opinion of it was almost evenly divided between pro- and anti-vivisectionists. On the one hand, the *San Francisco Chronicle* asserted that "when one recalls the human lives saved by the sacrifice of some animals" Sam's "sentimental argument falls to the ground," and Elia Peattie in the *Chicago Tribune* dismissed its "tenderness" as "sporadic" and "sensational." In Great Britain, where vivisection was a hot-button issue, the London *Standard* regarded the "trifle"

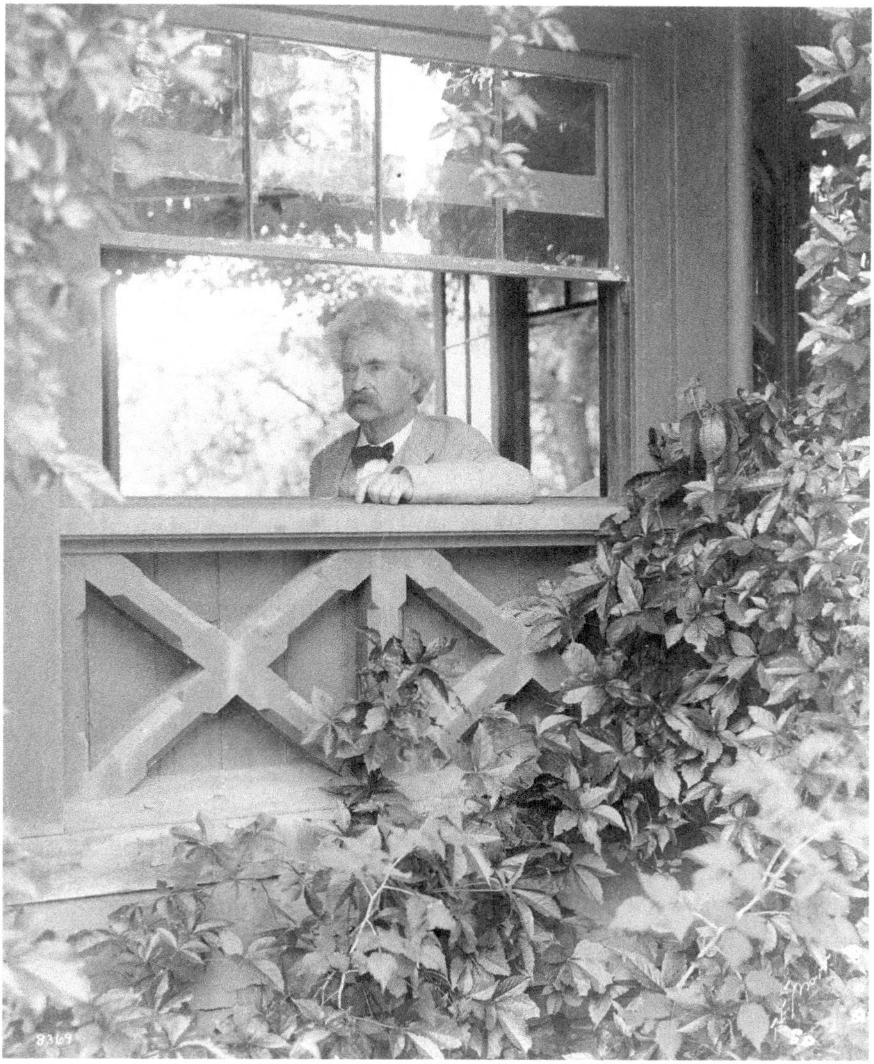

Figure 10. Samuel Clemens in his octagonal study at Quarry Farm, summer 1903. Courtesy of the Library of Congress.

unconvincing "as an anti-vivisectionist tract"; the *Saturday Review* mused that the "illustrations show more understanding of dogs than is to be found in the text, which will appeal only to confirmed sentimentalists"; the *Northern Chronicle and General Advertiser for the North of Scotland* opined that Sam "makes a mistake in meddling with a scientific subject." The *Sydney*

Herald similarly declared that the tale consisted of little more than "three decrepit jokes" and pathos.[25]

On the other hand, numerous newspapers sided with Sam, among them the *New York Tribune* (a "pathetic and altogether convincing satire on the vivisectionists"), *Charleston News and Courier* (a "terrible indictment of the vivisectionists"), Brooklyn *Standard Union* ("a passionate sermon against vivisection"), *Philadelphia Inquirer* (a "strong argument against vivisection"), *Congregationalist and Christian World* ("a most effective plea against the excesses of vivisection"), *Buffalo Express* ("a protest that cannot fail to appeal to children"), *Hartford Courant* (a "cruel satire on vivisection"), New York *Evening Post* ("a first-class anti-vivisection document"), *Pittsburgh Press* ("a powerful piece of fiction, which will make the same widespread appeal to lovers of dogs as did the book *Black Beauty* to lovers of horses"), New Orleans *Times-Picayune* ("exquisitely pathetic"), and *Salt Lake Tribune* ("a master story"). In England, the *Bath Chronicle and Weekly Gazette* called it "a very pathetic story" that "appeals with wonderful canine eloquence against vivisection," the *Newcastle Chronicle* opined that "the Anti-Vivisectionist Society should scatter it far and wide," and the *Yorkshire Post and Leeds Intelligencer* described it as "a very simple story, but the lover of animals will appreciate Mark Twain's perfect artistry when he reads it."[26]

The only noteworthy interruption in Sam's routine during the summer of 1903 occurred in late August, when he observed the America's Cup races in New York Harbor with Rogers from the deck of the *Kanawha*. The city was so hot and noisy at the time that he even slept aboard the yacht rather than in a hotel. The defeat of the *Shamrock III*, again captained by Sir Thomas Lipton, prompted Sam to pen a comic self-interview for the *New York Herald* under the title "Mark Twain, Able Yachtsman, on Why Lipton Failed to Lift the Cup." At the end of the third and final heat on August 25, the *Kanawha* outran the steam yacht *Hauoli*, owned by F. M. Smith, a fellow member with Rogers of the New York Yacht Club, in a race back to port. Sam was, according to the New York *Sun*, "one of the most earnest rooters."[27]

On October 5, the Clemens clan pulled up stakes in Elmira and returned to New York, registering at the exclusive Grosvenor Hotel at the corner of Fifth Avenue and Tenth Street, to pack boxes and finalize plans for their trip to Italy later in the month. Livy had so far recovered her strength that she was able to "walk several steps—about 6—without assistance." The mayoral campaign was in full swing, and though Sam had little time to politick, he addressed a letter in midmonth to the Women's Municipal League, soon printed in the *New York Tribune*, *Times*, and *Sun* and widely copied across the country, that laid out the case for reelecting Seth Low: "I should think that any humane and honest person would rather be convicted of one robbery and one murder than become a cold and deliberate confederate in wholesale robbery and wholesale murder by voting a Tammany ticket. Certainly, if anything is proven up to the hilt, Tammany's financial history and health statistics of 1901 prove that Tammany's especial and remorseless trade is wholesale pillage and wholesale destruction of health and life." Invited by the Acorns to take an active part in the canvass, he was forced to decline. He was "so overwhelmed with labor and errands that I could not find time to answer letters. Tomorrow I must work twenty-five hours, next day twenty-seven," but he knew "the cause is just as good as it was before" and wished he could have greeted the call to arms "with a word and a shout for the clean ticket of the Acorn platform." Just before boarding the ship that carried him to Italy, he repeated his hope "that Fusion will win this fall. I trust that every self-respecting citizen will vote to retain Mayor Low in office and keep the tiger from running wild again."[28] Instead, George B. McClellan Jr., son of the Civil War general fired by Abraham Lincoln, was elected with Tammany backing on November 3 while Sam was in mid-ocean. The Tammany tiger had been terrified but not tamed.

On the eve of his departure from the United States Sam was also eager to resolve the warring interests of his dueling presses by purchasing the rights to his six early books plus *Pudd'nhead Wilson* and *Following the Equator* from the American Publishing Company. Early in 1903, Robert Collier of *Collier's Weekly* and P. F. Collier & Son offered him a minimum of $10,000 per year at the rate of thirty cents a word for exclusive rights to publish his magazine material. In the end, however, Sam negotiated a more lucrative if more complicated deal with Bliss and Harper. He railed to Hartford in early June 1903, lunched at the Hartford Club with friends on June 4, spent a night at Whitmore's home, and met with Bliss. Three weeks later, Bliss traveled to Riverdale to continue their talks, leading to Sam's offer of $50,000 cash—half to be paid by him and the other half by Harper & Brothers—for rights to all eight of his copyrighted volumes. As Hill explains, "This proposal was in effect an 'offer' for the American Publishing Company to go out of business," and it was accepted. While the details remained to be spelled out—Bliss, Duneka, and Rogers did not sign the final contract until October 23—the agreement enabled Harper & Brothers to become Sam's exclusive publisher. For the first time in his career all of his books in print were listed in the sales catalogue of a single press. Though the press falsely reported that Sam had been promised an "annuity for life," his five-year deal with Harpers paid him a royalty of 20 percent on sales of individual titles,

17 percent on sales of uniform editions, and thirty cents per word on new magazine articles, and guaranteed him an income of $25,000 a year, equivalent to an annual income of about $725,000 in modern dollars. When Sam returned from his trip around the world in October 1900, George Harvey remembered, he "could barely earn $6,000 a year." By late 1903 he was paid "30 cents a word for everything he wrote, whether it was printed or thrown away," prompting a wag to compose a whimsical quatrain:

I sometimes write
Jokes without sense—
But every word
Brings 30 cents.

Under the terms of the new contract he was required to contribute only three new articles a year, two for summer issues and one for the Christmas number of *Harper's Weekly* or *Harper's Monthly*. Under these terms, his books were worth "a fortune." They "will yield twice as much" as the contract guaranteed "for many a year, if intelligently handled. Four months ago I could not have believed that I could ever get rid of my 30-years' slavery to the pauper American Publishing Co—a worthless concern which always kept a blight upon the books." In fact, the royalties Sam received from the Harpers during the first four years of the five-year deal totaled over $140,000.[29]

The night after reaching an oral agreement with Bliss and before departing for Italy, Sam was the guest of honor at a farewell dinner at the Metropolitan Club sponsored by J. Pierpont Morgan. As usual, only men were present, among them Hamlin Garland, Howells, Rogers, Bram Stoker, and a coterie of Harpers people, including the host George Harvey, Henry Mills Alden, Duneka, and J. Henry Harper. Alden later recorded all that is known of Sam's remarks at the private dinner, which was closed to the press. After recounting

> in his most humorous vein many vivid and laughter-provoking early experiences of his early life in the West, he spoke of his approaching departure to Italy with his wife in terms that clearly indicated his apprehension as to her health, and his hopes of its restoration through the change of scene and climate. . . . I thought then of this homely side of the man's nature, of which the world at large knew scarcely anything; I thought of what he had suffered, in reverses of fortune, in private griefs and solicitudes, and how these sorrows had developed those sweeter traits of the man's personality which bind all men more closely to him, and which should yield new graces and values to his imaginative work.

Howells believed Sam's parting was a permanent one. "Clemens, I suppose, will always live at Florence, hereafter," he wrote. "He goes first for his wife's health, and then because he can't stand the nervous storm and stress here. He takes things intensely hard, and America is too much for him. I envy his going to Italy to live."[30]

The next morning, October 24, the Clemens party of seven, including Katy Leary, and eighteen trunks left the Hotel Grosvenor and ferried across the Hudson River to Hoboken, where they boarded the 13,000-ton *Prinzess Irene* of the North German Lloyd Steamship Company for Genoa. (Isabel Lyon and her mother were to follow a week later.) Sam had booked rooms on the promenade deck, including Cabin Deluxe Number 1 for Livy—"new rooms up in the sky, open to sun and air"—for a total fare of $1,100. Coincidentally, the steamer carried 1,420 steerage passengers, the largest number who had ever embarked from New York on a single vessel to that date. After the ship sailed, a jingle maker commemorated the occasion:

> Mark Twain has gone, this very week,
> In Italy to live or die.
> 'Twas natural that he should seek
> A home beneath a smiling sky.

Three days into the voyage, Sam noted in his journal that Livy was enduring it "marvelously well." But the *Prinzess Irene* soon began to resemble a ship of fools. Sam complained the next day about a fellow passenger "talking nursery German" in a loud voice, and the following day about two men—"a giraffe" and "a Shetland pony"—who "tramped the deck after midnight talking loudly." By the time the family landed in Genoa on November 6, he had decided never to "take a promenade-deck room again, at any price: a madhouse is preferable," and never again to "travel in an emigrant ship." "The first-cabin savages" kept Livy awake "night & day. We shall travel in a *real* cattle-boat next time," he wrote woefully to Rogers. The voyage "was very hard upon her," and Sam hoped "to meet some of [the passengers] in hell yet." A Genoa newspaper reported, upon the family's arrival, that Clara and Jean were "lively girls with the real American freedom of manner," but Livy seemed wizened with a "dry and severe face" and "large spectacles bestride her thin nose."[31]

Sam had negotiated over seven months by mail and cable for "the kind of house we want" near Florence, but even a week before their departure he admitted he did not know if the Villa di Quarto in the hills three miles north of the city "is big enough, nor anything about it." Built by one of the Medici and occupied over the decades by the Grand Duchess Maria of Russia and a king of Württemberg, the fifteenth-century palace was owned by the diplomat Count Annibale Raybaudi-Massiglia, Italian minister to Siam, former consul at Philadelphia, and husband of the American divorcée Frances Paxton, aka Countess Massiglia. With stables, a surrounding twenty-five-acre park, and a magnificent view overlooking Florence and the Chianti hills, the property came highly recommended by Sam's friend George Gregory Smith, a Scottish literary critic, who brokered Sam's rental of it for $2,000 or 10,000 lire a year—the price "made Livy swear," he admitted. The 200-by-60-foot villa was cavernous, with over sixty rooms on three upper floors and a disarray of hallways, cells, and corridors in the basement.

Figure 11. The Villa di Quarto. Photograph from *Critic*, June 1904.

It was "a monster accumulation of bricks," Sam wrote to Howells, that "must have been built for fuss & show & irruptions of fashion, not for a home." After they were settled, Jean bought a horse and rode the villa grounds, and Clara began to perform in concert with the local Philharmonic Society and at the Teatro Alfieri. After one of her recitals, according to Yale professor William Lyon Phelps, who was passing through Florence, Sam "was forced to hold an informal reception before the Italians and foreigners in the room would let him depart to his villa on the hill."[32]

On his part, Sam was sufficiently satisfied, at least at first, upon occupying the villa in early November, by its "secluded & silent solitude, this clean, soft air & this enchanting view of Florence, the great valley & the snow-mountains that frame it." During his first week "in the deep and dreamy stillness of this woodsy and flowery place I was without news of the outside world, and was well content without it. It had been four weeks since I had seen a newspaper, and this lack seemed to give life a new charm and grace, and to saturate it with a feeling verging upon actual delight." He told an interviewer in April 1904 that Italy was "the best country in the world to live in" and he fully expected "the sunny kiss of the Florentine hills" to "revive the delicate health of my wife." He was also welcomed by the British and American colonists in Florence—among them George Gregory Smith, the retired Cornell librarian Willard Fiske, U.S. consul general Francis B. Keene, Admiral John C. Watson, and Janet Ross. Among Smith's guests at Thanksgiving, for example, were Jean and Sam, who "kept his end of the table in a roar." Sam was feted by the Ponte Vecchio Club, a group of American and English artists, and delivered a "witty and brilliant reply" to a toast in his honor that included the "Wapping Alice" story. He attended a tea party at the Palazzo Serristori hosted by Countess Serristori, and he sat for a portrait by Edoardo Gelli, professor at the Royal Academy of Fine Arts in Florence. It was exhibited at the 1904 St. Louis World's Fair, aka the Louisiana Purchase Exposition, and reproduced on a full page of *Harper's Weekly*. "You will find it excellent," Sam notified his friend David Francis, the former governor of Missouri and president of the fair. "Good judges here say it is better than the original. They say it has all the merits of the original and keeps still besides."[33]

In return for the hospitality they received, Sam, Clara, Jean, and occasionally Livy held a regular weekly reception day at the villa that became a crossroads for Americans visiting Italy. Over the weeks they welcomed the playwright and theatrical producer Kirke La Shelle; Andrew Dickson White, former U.S. ambassador to Germany and cofounder and ex-president

Figure 12. Portrait of Samuel Clemens by Edoardo Gelli, *Harper's Weekly*, September 3, 1904.

of Cornell University; art historian Bernard Berenson; businessman John D. Crimmins; book designer and author William Dana Orcutt; and philosopher William James, who informed his Harvard colleague Josiah Royce that Sam was "here for the winter in a villa outside the town, hard at work writing something or other. I have seen him a couple of times—a fine, soft-fibred little fellow with the perversest twang and drawl, but very human and good. I should think that one might grow very fond of him and wish he'd come and live in Cambridge." Sam also delivered a lecture on Italian grammar at the famous Teatro Rinuccini for the benefit of the postwar British Relief Fund.[34]

In late November Sam also announced his now quadrennial mock candidacy for president in an interview with the New York *World*. "The principal reason I came to Italy," he claimed, "is that next year I intend to be a candidate for election as President of the United States" and he wanted to be able to address Italian-American voters "in their melodious language." It was a gag, of course. He was not even sure if he was eligible to vote or, if so, where he might cast his ballot. Either joining in the joke or missing it entirely, however, *Collier's Weekly* expected "the party leaders on both sides to consider Mr. Clemens seriously." At its annual moot convention in New York, the suffragist Lillie Devereux Blake of the Past Parliament Club placed Sam's name in nomination to run for president on the same ticket as Carrie Nation. Even a year later, the Biloxi, Mississippi, *Herald* endorsed his candidacy. If he "will give us some sort of a guarantee that he is not joking . . . we will place at The Herald's masthead: 'For President—Samuel Clemens alias Mark Twain.'"[35]

Despite the distractions, Sam was productive for most of the months he lived at the Villa di Quarto. According to George Gregory Smith, during "the first six weeks he was there he wrote 39,000 words" and thereafter "he averaged about 1500 words a day." He wrote a pair of satirical pieces about Italian idiom reminiscent of "The Awful German Language" for *Harper's*. In one, he resolves to learn how to conjugate the verb *amare*, "to love." "I inquired into the character and possibilities of the verb, and was much disturbed to find that it was over my size, it being chambered for fifty-seven rounds—fifty-seven ways of saying *I love* without reloading; and yet none of them likely to convince a girl that was laying for a title." As he explained in the other piece, each morning he would learn a new word from the local newspaper:

> I have to use it while it is fresh, for I find that Italian words do not keep in this climate. They fade toward night, and next morning they are gone. But it is no matter; I get a new one out of the paper before breakfast, and thrill the domestics with it while it lasts. . . . Yesterday's word was *avanti*. It sounds Shakespearian, and probably means Avaunt and quit my sight. Today I have a whole phrase *sono dispiacentissimo*. I do not know what it means, but it seems to fit in everywhere and give satisfaction.

He resumed work on "No. 44, the Mysterious Stranger," the final "Print-Shop" version of the novel, writing some sixteen chapters between January and June. In this part of the narrative, Sam was implicitly critical of the striking typesetters in Eseldorf, much as he had reproached the striking Pennsylvania coal miners in 1902.[36]

Perhaps no other writing of the period silhouettes his state of mind so well as his sketch "Sold to Satan." It originated in a dream Sam had while in South Africa in spring 1896: "Tried to sell my soul to Satan. His polite objections & evasions. Certain lines of goods he was overstocked with. Never *had* paid the prices attributed to him by lying priests. (Lit his pipe with the end of his tail—make me shrink)." He returned to this germ of a story about a Faustian bargain in early January 1904, when he wrote it out and sent it to Duneka, who apparently objected to it on religious grounds and shelved it. The piece remained unpublished until 1923. In this iteration of the story of Mephistopheles, the narrator initially negotiates to sell his soul to Satan for money to invest in the stock market. He learns, however, that the Archfiend is made of radium worth billions in energy costs rather than mere fire and brimstone and is capable of destroying the earth "in a flash of flame and a puff of smoke," leaving a "snow-shower of gray ashes"—a vision of the end of the world even more terrible than the Battle of the Sand Belt at the end of *A Connecticut Yankee*. The narrator senses a lucrative business opportunity. He is tempted to kidnap the Prince of Darkness "and stock him, and incorporate him, and water the stock up to ten billions—just three times its actual value—and blanket the world with it." He resolves instead to invite the fallen archangel into partnership: "Quick—my soul is yours, dear Ancestor; take it—we'll start a company." Ironically, the Tempter is tempted and congratulates the narrator on his business acumen: "All through the Middle Ages I used to buy Christian souls at fancy rates, building bridges and cathedrals in a single night in return, and getting swindled out of my Christian nearly every time that I dealt with a priest . . . but none of those people ever guessed where the real big money lay." According to Stanley Brodwin, the burlesque is "a satire and exposure of Twain's own character" in the wake of his history of financial misdealings.[37]

In mid-January 1904 Sam also began to compose his autobiography in earnest. Isabel Lyon was "an inspiration," he crowed, "because she takes so much interest in it." He dictated about fifteen hundred words per day to her, and "if I live two years this Autobiography will cover many volumes." He originally planned to publish the memoir as notes to his earlier books in order to add twenty-eight years to his copyrights, though this legal strategy was hardly failsafe. After many false starts dating back to 1870, Sam believed he had finally "hit upon the right way to do an Autobiography," as he said: "Start it at no particular time of your life; wander at your free will all over your life; talk only about the thing which interests you for the moment;

drop it the moment its interest threatens to pale, and turn your talk upon the new and more interesting thing that has intruded itself into your mind meantime." That is, shun strict chronology in lieu of a scattershot method of free association akin to Freud's talking cure. "About January 14," Lyon noted in her diary, "Mr. Clemens began to dictate to me. His idea of writing an autobiography had never proved successful, for to his mind autobiography is like narrative and should be spoken. At Mrs. Clemens' suggestion we tried and Mr. Clemens found that he could do it to a charm." On January 16, Sam exulted to Howells that "you will never know how much enjoyment you have lost until you get to dictating your autobiography; then you will realize, with a pang, that you might have been doing it all your life if you had only had the luck to think of it." He was so convinced he had struck on a revolutionary method of life-storytelling that he announced in his dictation, with no little hubris, that he intended his autobiography to "become a model for all future autobiographies when it is published" and "that it shall be read and admired a good many centuries because of its form and method." Above all, it was "a portrait gallery of contemporaries with whom he [had] come into personal contact," the ultimate effort to protect his public image, settle a few scores, and guarantee he would get the last word after his death whatever his enemies might say about him.[38]

In early April, Harper & Brothers issued an 89-page version of *Extracts from Adam's Diary* with forty-five crude full-page illustrations by Frederick Strothmann. "I have deciphered some more of Adam's hieroglyphics," as Sam bragged in his introduction. The book received mostly plaudits, at least in North America. The *Boston Transcript*, for example, considered it "continuously and genuinely funny," the *Detroit Free Press* "light exercise for his pen," the *New York Times* "a revised and improved version of one of his earlier flights of humorous fancy," the *Louisville Courier-Journal* "a fresh laugh for all who choose to read," the *Montreal Gazette* "laughable from first to last," the *Brooklyn Standard Union* "one of the most laughable of all his books," the *Philadelphia Record* an "undoubted masterpiece," the *Philadelphia Inquirer* "rich" and "good," the *Des Moines Register* "most amusing," the *Pittsburgh Press* "brilliant," *Public Opinion* "peculiarly illuminating and humanizing," the *Hartford Courant* "delightfully characteristic," the *Manchester Guardian* "good fun," and the New York *Outlook* "a fantastical bit of topsy-turvydom." The *Independent* opined that while Sam "used to write very large books, now he writes very small ones, but they are just as funny," and the *Boston Journal* similarly noted that "the jokes are as good as any to be found in the author's earlier books." Even one prominent religious periodical, the *Congregationalist and Christian World*, thought it "good fooling." Both the *Syracuse*

Post-Standard ("The woman suffragist cannot fail to notice that . . . Eve was by far the more important half of that partnership in the Garden") and the *Brooklyn Eagle* ("nothing more nor less than a satire on women") put political spin on their comments, albeit in opposite directions. A few critics qualified their praise, such as the *San Francisco Chronicle* ("strains humor a little"), *Chicago Inter Ocean* ("grotesque humor"), *Washington Post* (pleasure "is denied the reader"), *Boston Advertiser* ("We are disappointed"), and New York *Sun* (What would "the man who wept at Adam's Tomb . . . do over these 'Extracts'?"). A few critics leveled harsher charges, such as the *Washington Times* ("picturesque but not in the least Biblical"). Columbia classics professor Harry Thurston Peck sniffed in the New York *Bookman* that the short book proved "just how far a man who was once a great humorist can fall. We thought when we read *A Double-Barrelled Detective Story* that Mark Twain could do no worse. But we were wrong. The other book may have been more ridiculous; but this one is more pitiable." Peck predicted with wild inaccuracy that "a hundred years from now it is very likely that 'The Jumping Frog' alone will be remembered" of all Sam's writings.[39]

Many Commonwealth reviewers were similarly dubious about the merit of the book, among them the *Manchester Guardian* ("irreverent"), London *Telegraph* ("represents the *ne plus ultra* of tastelessness"), *Spectator* ("the most irresponsible product of his pen"), London *Globe* ("only fitfully amusing and not very spontaneous with his fun even then"), *Yorkshire Post* ("will not for a moment bear comparison with Mark Twain's best-known work"), London *Daily News* ("not one of Mark Twain's happiest efforts"), and *Sydney Herald* ("a lamentable instance of a man insisting upon being funny when all the fun has gone out"). Both the *Westminster Gazette* ("happily it has the merit of brevity") and the London *Morning Post* ("the author was well advised to make the book as short as it is") commended it for its length. To be sure, the *St. James's Gazette* ("he has handled without transgression a subject in which the margin for error is very small indeed") and Sydney *World's News* ("some pages of the diary are as good as anything the American humorist has ever written") praised the book, and over the years Sam began a number of companion pieces to *Adam's Diary*, most of them fragments left unpublished at his death, such as "Eve's Diary," "Noah's Ark," "Satan's Diary," "Papers of the Adams Family," "That Day in Eden," "Eve Speaks," and "Shem's Diary."[40]

For a variety of reasons, the Clemenses' residence at the Villa di Quarto was hardly as bucolic as their abode at the Villa Viviani had been eleven years earlier. The weather was not as pleasant as Sam remembered it. "Florentine sunshine?" he complained in one letter. "Bless you, there isn't any.

We have heavy fogs every morning & rain all day." Nor were the sunsets what he recalled: "Late in the afternoon the sun sets down behind those mountains somewhere, at no particular time & at no particular place, so far as I can see." As he recounted in his autobiography, "The year spent in the Villa Viviani was something of a contrast" to the months lived in the "ducal barrack."[41]

To complicate matters, their landlady was a constant nuisance, repeatedly interfering in the family's daily routine. Countess Massiglia had pledged to depart for Paris when the Clemenses arrived and "her expensive house was off her hands," according to Sam, but if so she lied. "She could not endure life without the daily and hourly society of her handsome chief manservant and she was not rich enough to take him along," so she moved with him into an apartment over the stable some fifty yards from the villa. She also tried to persuade Sam to employ her "fattore" or (as Sam called him) her "paramour" or "temporary husband" to manage the estate and "throw pecuniary advantages" in his way. "She had expected that we would buy all supplies through him and thus extend to him the same opportunities to rob us which he was enjoying in robbing her." After Sam refused to hire her gigolo, George Gregory Smith recalled, the countess "did everything she could to inconvenience him. She declared she would drive him out." Or as Katy Leary remembered, "This American Countess was very disagreeable, and made everything awful hard for [the Clemenses]. She was mad at having to rent her villa, 'cause she had to live in the stable herself; so she done everything she could to make it uncomfortable for us." Isabel Lyon had known the countess in Philadelphia fifteen years earlier when she was married to her first husband and believed the count had left the villa in the hands of this "coarse" woman with "painted hair," "slitlike vicious eyes," "dirty clothes," and "terrible manners" for "the sake of [his] peace or freedom."[42]

"The American bitch who owns this Villa," Sam wrote Rogers, "found that she could afflict me with all sorts of trivial & exasperating annoyances because I couldn't raise a row lest it get to Mrs. Clemens & give her a fatal backset." Put another way, the countess played a number of sinister pranks on Sam and his daughters. As Smith reported, "She put stones and rocks in the roadways of the park so his daughters could not ride or drive as they liked. She cut off the water supply" to the villa and forced Sam to obtain drinking water from her "Roman steward." The toilets were inoperable, however, and the stench was so pervasive "the windows had to be kept open." She then attempted "to have the villa declared in an unsanitary condition by the authorities." The countess "even tried to arrange things so bells would ring near the house as often as possible while Mrs. Clemens was seriously ill." On another occasion, according to Leary, "she did an awful mean thing" to the girls.

> They was having a tea party out on the lawn one day and the Countess' big dog came over. He was very fond of Miss Clara and Miss Jean. He was playin' with them in the garden, snapping round with them, and when the Countess seen him, she called him into the house and put some grease all over his body and his head and his nose, and then she let him out again! Of course he ran right back to the girls and he began playing and rubbing up against them and rubbed all the grease right off onto their nice dresses!

When Sam attempted to install a telephone in the palace so that he could summon doctors from the city should Livy suffer a medical crisis, "the Countess ordered the telephone company to remove" it because he had not received her permission in advance. "It was one feather more than I could stand," as he wrote Rogers, so in retaliation "I got the weightiest lawyer in Italy & game was called." He bankrolled "some peasant-suits" against her for unlawful evictions from her property "& when those are through I have some more up my sleeve." In the spring of 1904 he filed suit against her for failing to maintain the property, which he had nicknamed "Calamity House," because the sewage from the villa went "directly into the cesspools under the house—almost under Mrs. C[lemens]'s room!" "I was losing my belief in hell until I got acquainted with the Countess Massiglia," he declared in his autobiographical dictation. She was "easily the most fiendish character I have ever encountered in any walk of life," which was saying a great deal. "I really never expected to wish to meet anybody in h—l," Smith remembered that he remarked, "but I'd like to meet that countess there, no matter at what personal inconvenience." Sam prosecuted the suits for a couple of years, inflicting as much pain on the countess as possible in legal costs before he dropped the cases. On her part, "the fragrant countess from the divorce-courts of Philadelphia," as he called her, spread rumors designed to destroy his character, though Sam was not bothered by the scheme because "the character that she could destroy is not worth saving." In early February 1904 he began to search for another house. "I climbed around, over and prowled through an average of six large villas a week but found none that would answer," he reflected. By the end of the month he "found the right one I think" and resolved to move as soon as Mrs. Clemens was ambulant. The "reptile with the filthy soul," he predicted, would "have a difficult time trying to rent" the villa after he left because "she knows I will prove to any applicant that he will be an ass to take it on any terms." In any case, he concluded in May, "We *can't* stay in the neighborhood of this fiendish Countess

Massiglia—an American adventuress & born skunk." He soon enshrined her in the pantheon of his other unforgiven and unforgiveable enemies like Charles Henry Webb, Bret Harte, Ned House, John T. Raymond, Elisha Bliss, Dan Slote, Charley Webster, and James Paige. He wished the countess would "move out of Italy; out of Europe; out of the planet. I should want her bonded to retire to her place in the next world and inform me which of the two it was, so that I could arrange for my own hereafter." As was his custom when he pilloried an enemy, he piled on the derogatory adjectives: "She is excitable, malicious, malignant, vengeful, unforgiving, selfish, stingy, avaricious, coarse, vulgar, profane, obscene, a furious blusterer on the outside and at heart a coward. Her lips are as familiar with lies, deceptions, swindles and treacheries as are her nostrils with breath. She has not a single friend in Florence, she is not received in any house. I think she is the best hated person I have ever known, and the most liberally despised." Her "soiled name, her execrable nature, and her residence in a stable with her manservant and the other cattle all count against her."[43]

Despite the hope that the Italian climate would have a salutary effect on Livy, her health began to fail almost as soon as they were settled. He complained to Duneka that "when we first arrived here she was twenty times better than she is now," and he admitted to Thomas Bailey Aldrich that "we were sent to Italy for Mrs. Clemens's sake, but she has never been as well here as she was when she left home." By mid-December she had relapsed to "where she was 8 or 9 months ago, & is discouraged, & depressed," he admitted to Mary Mapes Dodge. "I wish we had never come." Their living expenses during the first five weeks at the villa amounted to $2,100, not including "gas, fuel for the winter, nor doctor-bills." Worse yet, Livy was "hit with a week of tonsillitis" in December that "took away what was left of her strength & she cannot seem to get it back. For a year & a half, life for this family has been merely a bad dream." In early February, twenty-nine-year-old Clara inexplicably threw a tantrum that distressed her mother. By Clara's own account she was suddenly

> seized by something & began to scream & curse & knocked down the furniture etc. etc. 'till everyone of course came running & in my father's presence I said I hated him hated my mother hoped they would all die & if they didn't succeed soon I would kill them well on and on for more than an hour, I don't know all I said but mother hearing the noise & being told that I was overwrought got a heart attack and as you can imagine today I can hardly meet anyone's eyes.

In mid-February Sam reported to Susan Crane that Livy was "very very far from being as well as she was when she left America. It has been 9 or 10 weeks since she could leave her bed. She can't eat; the food will not digest. She is pale, she is a shadow, she is very weak. *I* don't know how she lives." One night in late February her pulse raced up to 192, and "nothing but a subcutaneous injection of brandy brought her back to life." "We have had a bad 3 months," he reported to John Y. W. MacAlister in March. Not only had he suffered his annual bout of bronchitis but during that time "Mrs. Clemens has not left her bed, and we have had more than one serious scare on her account." On April 8 Livy suffered another crisis, either a heart or serious asthma attack, from which she never recovered. Not only was Sam unable to call a doctor by telephone because "the wires had been cut," but the doctor when summoned by courier was unable to enter the grounds of the villa because the gates were locked on orders of the countess. Sam called on a lawyer and obtained what was in effect a restraining order to remove her "from our vicinity." Livy had another "awful night" on April 20, and Sam admitted two weeks later that he feared she would "never again be strong enough to travel." He visited her for two minutes one day in mid-May and saw her "blue lips, the pallor of the dead, and that pathetic something in the eye which betrays the secret of a waning hope." George Gregory Smith wrote his mother in late May that Livy was "no better nor do I believe she ever will be, poor woman." She was bedfast "& only sees her husband twice a day for 5 minutes at a time—Clara once a day, & Jean not at all. She is entirely on a milk diet and the end cannot be far off."[44]

About 7:30 p.m. the evening of June 5, Sam entered Livy's room for one of his rationed daily visits. He lingered for half an hour rather than the usual ten minutes "because she was so animated & was feeling so well." For the past five months he had been searching for "another and satisfactory villa, in the belief that if we could get Mrs. Clemens away from the Villa di Quarto and its fiendish associations, the happier conditions would improve both the health of her spirit and that of her body." Before departing this night, he told her that he had finally "found the villa that will content you: tomorrow you will examine the plans and give it your consent and I will buy it. Her eyes danced with pleasure." When Sam left, "she threw a kiss to me" and asked him to "come back again" to tell her good night. He

> was so hopeful & happy that it amounted to an exaltation. And so I was moved to do a thing which I have seldom done since Susy died: I went upstairs to the piano & broke out into the old Jubilee songs that Susy liked to hear me sing. Jean came straightway & listened—she never did it before. I sang "Swing

> Low, Sweet Chariot" & the others. And Livy, so far away, heard me & said to the nurse, "He is singing a good-night carol for me."

She had concealed from him the distress she had suffered that day. She told Katy Leary that she had "been awful sick all the afternoon." Katy replied, "You'll be all right now." She held Livy in her arms and "was fanning her and then—then she fell right over on my shoulder. She died right then in my arms. She drew a little short breath, you know, just once, and was gone!"[45]

CHAPTER 12

Slough of Despond

The coat-of-arms of the human race ought to consist of a man with an axe on his shoulder proceeding toward a grindstone.

—*Autobiography of Mark Twain*

"I WENT DOWN TO say good-night & entered the room suspecting nothing," Sam wrote Susan Crane. "Livy was sitting up in bed—as always—& Katy was supporting her on one side & the nurse on the other, the children standing at the foot, looking dazed." Katy and the nurse "were holding the oxygen pipe to her mouth," thinking she had fainted, "expecting to revive her." "I went & bent over & looked in her face, & was surprised that she did not greet me. I did not know she was dead. I did not suspect it until Clara said, 'Katy is it true? Katy, is it true?' Then Katy burst out in sobbings, & I knew!" Sam took Livy in his arms and held her "for the longest time, and then he laid her back and he said 'How beautiful she is—how young and sweet—and look, she's smiling!' " As Katy recalled, "He cried all that time, and Clara and Jean, they put their arms around their father's neck and they cried, the three of them, as though their hearts would break." At 9:15 Livy had been "bright & happy," Sam remembered, "and a single minute later she passed from life. All in an instant. Without a struggle, without a catch of the breath—peacefully, unconsciously, just as a tired child falls asleep. It was heart-failure. How grateful I am that she was mercifully spared the awful fate she has been dreading—death by strangulation." Years later, he reflected that "if I had been there a minute earlier, it is possible—it is possible that she might have died in my arms. Sometimes I think that perhaps there was an instant—a single instant—when she realized that she was dying and that I was not there." The night Livy died, Sam recorded in his notebook: "At a quarter past 9 this evening she that was the life of my life passed to the relief & the peace of death after months of unjust & unearned suffering." Then the first expression of the survivor guilt that would plague him for the rest of his life: "I was full of remorse for things done & said in these 34 years of married life that hurt Livy's heart." Much as he had blamed himself for the deaths of his brother Henry and son Langdon and daughter Susy, he blamed himself for Livy's death. He was as guilt- as grief-stricken.[1]

After the body was embalmed by Livy's physician, G. W. Kirch, Katy "put on her the dress she wanted, the beautiful lavender silk dress and the stockings and the little slippers that matched." Clara spent at least a part of the night lying under Livy's coffin, and Jean was unable to sleep at all, precipitating her first grand mal seizure in thirteen months. Early the next morning Sam crept downstairs "to worship that dear face, & for the first time in all these long years it gave no heed. How beautiful it was; & young, & smooth, & rounded, & how sweetly reposeful! I can carry that picture clear & fadeless in my heart until my own happy time shall come." Livy's death was "a thunder-stroke," he wrote Rogers—the exact word he used to describe Susy's death in his autobiographical dictation two years later. "Her miseries had lasted 22 months," he lamented to Thomas Bailey Aldrich, but "I am so grateful that her sweet spirit is at rest." Her manner of death had been "merciful," and he was grateful "it came without warning & was preceded by no fear" because she dreaded dying by strangulation. "Five times" during her last four months "she went through that choking horror for an hour & more & came out of it white, haggard, exhausted, & quivering with fright."[2]

As soon as the news reached the United States, he received a flood of condolence notes. "Letters have come to me from shop-girl, postman, & all ranks in life, down to the humblest," he noted. Twichell wrote him that "there is nothing that we can say. What is there to say? But here we are—with you all every hour and every minute—filled with unutterable thoughts; unutterable affection; affection for the dead and for the living." The Clemenses' former coachman Patrick McAleer "sent five dollars from his small savings to buy white roses for her coffin." Though she had never met Livy, Helen Keller urged Sam to "try to reach through grief and feel the pressure of her hand, as I reach through darkness, and feel the smile on my friends' lips and the light in their eyes." Sam replied that for nearly two years "my trembling family of four groped our way down the Valley of the Shadow of Death, at times heartened & made hopeful by fleeting rays of promise which were but lies & beguilements—& then the end came, in an instant & unexpected."[3]

Livy's death, unfortunately, required Sam to joust with the Italian bureaucracy. Even before he and his daughters could hold a simple funeral at the villa, sanitary officers insisted on compliance with a number of regulations. The embalmed body was placed in an oak casket and the U.S. vice-consul fixed the necessary seals upon it before it was put in a lead vault and sent to Genoa to be loaded on the steamer that returned the Clemens party to New York. "We shall carry her home & bury her with her dead at Elmira," Sam wrote Rogers. "Beyond that, we have no plans. The children must decide. I have no head, I am stunned; I was not expecting this. In these last days I was beginning to hope, & half-believe, she would get well." On June 8, Clara's thirtieth birthday, she remained in her bed "motionless & wordless—& has so lain ever since Sunday night brought our irremediable disaster." Sam saw Clara twice a day, Katy Leary stood watch at her bedside during the day, and Isabel Lyon slept in the room with her. A week after her mother's death, Clara "had not cried yet," Sam wrote W. D. Howells. "I wish she could cry." On June 17, Gregory Smith visited the family and reported that Clara "keeps her bed quite prostrated," though Sam had "in a measure recovered from the shock." Five days later the horses Livy had bought for her daughters were shipped to the States, and on June 24, after packing their trunks to sail for home, the family traveled to Rome, where Sam confronted Kirch for overcharging for Livy's medical care—$900, or over $26,000 modern dollars. "Kirch is a mere robber, & I told him so, & invited him to sue for his lacking 2200 francs." They then railed to Naples, "taking it by easy stages on account of Clara," who was "perilously near" a nervous breakdown. Sam had booked five staterooms on the SS *Prinz Oskar* of the Hamburg America Line rather than the larger and faster *Prinzess Irene* because they had had such a miserable outbound voyage on it eight months earlier.[4]

They were scheduled to embark the afternoon of June 28, but that morning Sam learned that the requisite certificates no longer accompanied the casket, and that if he could not produce them, it would be put ashore because it would not be allowed to land in America. Fortunately, the captain of the ship "was touched by my humiliating situation & he ventured a large & grave risk in my behalf. He accepted a written declaration from me in place of the certificates." Homer M. Byington, the American vice-consul in Naples, likewise "took a risk for me" by allowing the casket to remain after Sam "furnished him [with] a sworn statement" that all necessary health precautions had been taken. But Sam was convinced Kirch had deliberately "withheld & suppressed" the documents in an attempt to sabotage their repatriation. He was to have sent them "with the casket; but I had afterward repudiated his bill in the bank, and possibly this had moved him to avenge himself upon the living by putting a dishonor upon the dead." Kirch subsequently sued Sam for $400 to settle his bill, though the suit eventually died of disinterest. In any case, Isabel Lyon logged the only extant record of the voyage. As she wrote on July 5, "We have been 7 days at sea, skirting Sardinia, passing Gibraltar at night, and all today we have been coasting by & between the Azores." Clara "keeps to her room all the time and is driven frantic by the cockroaches. There are about 35 passengers."[5]

The family landed in New York on July 12 and were met at the dock by Livy's brother Charley, his son Jervis, daughter Julie Langdon Loomis, and her new husband Edward Loomis. Theodore Roosevelt and Leslie Shaw, the secretary of the treasury, had directed the customs office to permit the family to reenter the country without inspection, a courtesy Sam never forgot. Long a critic of the president, Sam refrained from public comment about him. "Roosevelt closed my mouth years ago with a deeply valued, gratefully received, unasked favor," he acknowledged to Clara, "& with all my bitter detestation of him I have never been able to say a venomous thing about him in print since—that benignant deed always steps in the way & lays its consecrated hand upon my lips." The family overnighted at the new uptown Wolcott Hotel—"a house with no associations," as Sam noted—while Isabel Lyon, her mother, and Teresa Cherubini, the maid, stayed at the St. Denis. The group traveled to Elmira the next day with Livy's body on Loomis's private rail car. Sam was grateful for the gesture. "I do not know how to thank you enough for the peace & comfort & the inestimable privacy of that car," he wrote Loomis later. It was "a benefaction beyond price to us in these days when exposure to the curious & the stranger in the nakedness of our sorrow is so hard to bear." Sam hoped to persuade Clara not to attend the obsequies in Elmira, though if she chose to be present "we shall make the strain upon her as brief as possible." On July 14 Livy's funeral was held in the parlor of the Langdon mansion on Main Street, where she had "stood as a happy young bride" thirty-four years earlier. Much as Twichell had blessed her marriage then, he "spread his hands in benediction & farewell & in a breaking voice commended her spirit to the peace of God." Afterward her body was interred in the family plot in Woodlawn Cemetery. As the coffin was lowered into the ground, Clara, in a paroxysm of grief like Laertes at Ophelia's burial, "gave a great cry" that "stabbed everyone's heart" and tried to leap into the grave. Katy Leary remembered that Sam caught her in his arms.[6]

While still in Florence, he had rented Glencoat, a summer house at Four Brooks Farm in the Berkshires near Lee, Massachusetts, owned by Richard Watson Gilder. Clara and Jean were "anxious to go there, as the Gilders are specially intimate friends of theirs," as he told Rogers. He had shipped their sixteen trunks, totaling well over twenty-five hundred pounds, from the New York Customs House directly to Lee. He stationed his daughters and Lyon in the cottage while he lived much of the time at the Grosvenor Hotel near Washington Square and searched for a house to lease in the city. Lyon arrived at Glencoat on July 15, the day after Livy's funeral, and Clara appeared there the next day, though she was so "pale, weak, exhausted" that Rodman Gilder, Richard's son, carried her into the house. Sam and Jean soon joined them. Clara's emotional health was so fragile, however, that in late July she was admitted to Angenette Parry's private sanitarium on Sixty-Ninth Street in New York. She notified her father that she was "comfortable" and "happily situated," and Sam in turn urged her to "stay as long as you wish; stay as long as the dear Dr. Parry will let you; & keep Katy with you; you cannot have a wiser nor gentler nor faithfuller sentinel to stand guard over you." Back at Glencoat on August 3, however, Clara became "hysterical," according to Lyon, "& alarmed me much." Clara and Katy returned to Parry's institute on August 6, and on September 8 she began a rest cure in Norfolk, Connecticut, where she was to be confined "4 or 5 weeks, in bed, without books, without companionship, writing no letters, reading no letters, seeing no one but physician & nurse—a horrid solitude, with grief and memory for company." Lyon noted in her journal that "the strain of living here has been too great. She cannot stand the sounds in the tiny house." Leary remembered that the summer after Livy's death the entire family were "pretty sad. . . . We could never get even a little bit used to the idea that she was gone. It left a great hole in all our lives." But Clara's Connecticut regimen was hardly as rigorous as the rest cure prescribed by the Philadelphia nerve specialist S. Weir Mitchell and depicted by Charlotte Perkins Gilman in her story "The Yellow Wallpaper" (1892). Clara apparently did not rest enough, so on October 23 she returned to Parry's sanitarium, where she was subjected to more stringent discipline. She was allowed "no company but a cat & a trained nurse & no visitor but the specialist," Sam reported. "This must continue until May. The shock of her mother's death was crushing." She was largely out of touch with her family for the next half year. Sam was not "allowed to have any communication with her," even by telephone." Twichell for one was distressed "to think of poor Clara's long, long imprisonment, however advisable and necessary it is. 'Twill be dismal and forlorn as an Arctic night."[7]

On his part, Sam preferred to grieve for Livy alone. "With Mrs. Clemens gone my life has lost color & zest," he conceded, but he did not spiral into deep despair. Richard Watson Gilder, who saw Sam routinely during this period, agreed that he was "most grim and unhappy, but full of life and abounding in scorn of a mismanaged universe." Soon after Livy's death,

Sam acknowledged to Twichell that he sometimes retreated into a nihilism that held

> that there is no God & no universe; that there is only empty space, & in it a lost & homeless & wandering & companionless & indestructible thought. And that I am that thought. And God, & the Universe, & Time, & Life, & Death, & Joy & Sorrow & Pain only a grotesque & brutal dream, evolved from the frantic imagination of that insane thought. By this light, the absurdities that govern life & the universe lose their absurdity & become natural, & a thing to be expected. It reconciles everything, makes everything lucid & understandable. . . . Taken as unrealities; taken as the drunken dream of an idiot Thought, drifting solitary & forlorn through the horizonless eternities of empty Space, these monstrous sillinesses become proper & acceptable, & lose their offensiveness. I suppose this idea has become a part of me because I have been living in it so long—7 years—& in that time have written so long a story embodying it & developing it; a book which is not finished & is not intended for print.

He expressed many of these same ideas in virtually the same words in the final chapter of "No. 44, the Mysterious Stranger," begun about this time, in which the Stranger descends into a type of solipsism. Twichell replied sympathetically: "I can't wonder—and I don't—that with the light of your life gone out you sit dazed in the dark seeing no meaning or reason in anything, the Universe appearing to you only a confusion of unintelligible phantasmagoria. . . . I am not ignorant of the thoughts you are thinking."[8]

Livy's sister became his closest confidant in bereavement. On July 25, only eleven days after Livy's funeral, still in the throes of survivor guilt, he wrote Susan Crane:

> Yes, she did love me; & nothing that I did, no hurt that I inflicted upon her, no tears that I caused those dear eyes to shed, could break it down, or even chill it. It always rose again, it always burned again, as warm & bright as ever. Nothing could wreck it, nothing could extinguish it. Never a day passed that she did not say, with emphasis & enthusiasm, "I love you so. I just worship you." They were always undeserved, they were always a rebuke, but she stopped my mouth whenever I said it, though she knew I said it honestly. I know one thing, & get some poor small comfort out of it: that what little good was in me I gave to her to the utmost—full measure, the last grain & the last ounce—& poor as it was, it was my very best & far beyond anything I could have give to any other person that ever lived. It was poverty, but it was all I

> had; & so it stood for wealth & she so accounted it. I try not to think of the hurts I gave her, but oh, there are so many, so many!

He was uncertain whether the family should have returned to the United States in 1900, though Livy seemed to be recovering her health at the time. Sam was convinced in August, at least briefly, that had they remained in Europe "she would have lived 15 years longer." Two months later, he decided the family should never have left the United States for Italy in 1903 on "a journey invented by insanity! And it is piteous to remember how eager she was to go, poor child. She so longed for health; it was returning to her by leaps & bounds." But her fate was sealed, "her date was set, & she would have perished on the 5th of June, let her be where she might." Still later, in another spasm of self-recrimination, he lamented "that I allowed the physicians to send Mrs. Clemens on a horrible ten-day sea journey to Italy when Bermuda was right here at hand and worth a hundred Italies for her needs." Rather than the "warm and soft and gentle climate" he expected, they suffered through "eight months of uncomfortable weather" in Florence "with much chilliness, two months of rain, and very infrequent splashes of sunshine. She was not able to outlive these disasters." He admitted to Helen Keller that he was "very lonely, sometimes, when I sit by the fire after my guests have departed. . . . My thoughts trail away into the past. I think of Livy and Susy and I seem to be fumbling in the dark folds of confused dreams. I come upon memories of little happenings of long ago that drop like stars into the silence. One day everything breaks and crumbles. It did the day Livy died." Gradually, however, he resurrected his old idea that death was one of the "boons" of life. As he affirmed to Susan Crane in May 1905, "there has not been a single week of the past 48 which has not brought me reason to say 'how grateful I am that Livy is out of it!' How did she ever live in this execrable world? & why did she love it & wish to stay in it?" Or as he wrote Rogers's daughter Mai Coe years later under similar circumstances, "My grief for the loss of a friend is soon replaced by gratitude that that friend is released from the ungentle captivity of this life."[9]

Jean was injured on July 31 while on a moonlight horse ride with Rodman Gilder along the highway in South Lee. A trolley car struck Jean astride her horse Rhea, throwing her some fifty feet, knocking her unconscious, and mortally wounding the animal. Gilder raced her to a doctor, who treated her for a torn tendon in her ankle and multiple contusions and released her around midnight. Sam slept through the commotion, though the next day he told Lyon "the whole affair was simply another stroke of a relentless God." Inexplicably, moreover, the young couple gave fictitious names to reporters: they claimed to be "Miss Julia Langdon" and "Joseph Drake" of New York. When the truth leaked out a day or two later, their defenders explained that they had simply tried to prevent Clara "and other relatives from being unduly alarmed." But this excuse fails on two counts: Why did Jean give the name of a cousin to the papers, and why did Gilder invent a name? Still, the episode inspired one of Sam's apothegms: "It is easier for a needle to go through a camel's eye than for a rich woman to sprain her ancle [sic] & keep it out of the papers." In any case, Jean's injuries were not serious. She was "full of bangs & bruises, both fore & aft, & has a leg in plaster of paris & will keep her bed for a fortnight, but she reads & writes & plays games & is having a pleasant time," Sam noted, and she was confined to the cottage for only three weeks.[10]

On August 17, Sam signed a three-year lease on a town house at 21 Fifth Avenue, a block from the Grosvenor Hotel and three blocks north of Washington Square, for $3,500 a year, though it required three months of renovations and repairs before it was habitable. "That will answer quite well," he thought, "for we are under no pressure of hurry. Jean, with the servants, is in the country home in the Berkshire hills," he was "in a very comfortable little hotel close to No. 21," and Clara was confined to rest cure hospitals. The house on Fifth Avenue was "the quietest place I could find, and Clara is going to need the quietest kind of quiet for many months to come, I think. She is no perceptibly better or stronger than she was when we arrived at this side. Katy says she is thinner than her mother was."[11]

Though he lived alone in the city most of the time, he did not live in seclusion. He spent several days in late August at George Harvey's country house Jorjalma on Deal Beach on the Jersey shore. He crossed paths there with Henry James, on his final visit to the United States, who wrote brother William that "delicious poor dear old M. T. . . . beguiles the sessions on the deep piazza" of a local hotel. In mid-September he welcomed Rogers back from Europe and two weeks later left with him aboard the *Kanawha* for Fairhaven, where, along with the Unitarian ministers Minot Savage and Robert Collyer, he attended the dedication of the Rogers Memorial Church, built in honor of the oil magnate's mother.[12]

"If I were to start over again I would be a Reformer. I certainly would," Sam admitted a month before his death. He certainly was catholic in the causes he supported. On October 17, 1904, he dined with E. D. Morel, founder of the Congo Reform Association in England, and afterward the two men talked for several hours in Sam's hotel room. "I can see him now," Morel remembered three years later, as Sam paced "up and down his bedroom in uncontrollable indignation, breaking out ever and again" in angry exclamations. The upshot was that Sam "promised he would do something to help to arouse the American public" on the subject. Morel not only recruited him "to use his pen for the cause" but supplied him with information on the topic, including his own book *King Leopold's Rule in Africa*. At the Berlin Conference of 1884–85 hosted by German Chancellor Otto von Bismarck, King Leopold II of Belgium had beguiled the other participants to grant him a fiefdom in central Africa ironically called the Congo Free State with a population of some twenty million, and he exploited both the land and his de facto slaves and serfs for personal profit. As Hunt Hawkins explains, in 1892 Leopold "instituted a brutal system of forced labor to collect ivory and wild rubber." During his sovereign regime, in a portent of the Holocaust, an estimated five to eight million people were murdered or starved to death and many others maimed in retaliation for their failure to meet production quotas. "I am whetting up for King Leopold of Belgium," Sam wrote Twichell eleven days after his initial conversation with Morel. "By January I shall have all the material (& venom) I want." In his annual Thanksgiving sentiment for 1904, Sam hailed "our free Republic," the "official godfather of the Congo Graveyard, first of the Powers to recognize its pirate flag & become responsible through silence for the prodigious depredation & multitudinous murders committed under it upon the helpless natives by King Leopold of Belgium in the past twenty years." In interviews, Sam compared Leopold to a vampire who "sits at home and drinks blood" and to such mass killers as Nero, Caligula, Attilo, Torquemada, and Genghis Khan. In his autobiographical dictation, Sam indicted the barbarous behavior of Leopold, a "bloody monster whose mate is not findable in human history anywhere," "probably the most intensely Christian monarch, except Alexander VI, that has escaped hell thus far." By "murder, mutilation, overwork, robbery, rapine," Leopold had exploited "the helpless native's very labor" and gave him "nothing in return but salvation and a home in heaven, furnished at the last moment by the Christian priest."[13]

But "the most effective and widely circulated piece of American propaganda in the cause of Congo reform," as Justin Kaplan describes it, was *King Leopold's Soliloquy*. Sam wrote the essay, the longest of his anti-imperialist writings, during the winter of 1904–5, though as early as December 1904 the lickspittle San Francisco lawyer Henry Kowalsky, an American lobbyist for the Belgian government, warned Leopold that Sam "must certainly" have been hired on a retainer by the British government given that the U.S.

campaign against atrocities in the Congo was "organized as it has never been before." In the soliloquy, a Browningesque dramatic monologue with stage directions, the king offers a pathetic defense of his barbaric behavior, all the while confessing his crimes. He earns "millions of guineas a year" from his Congo enterprises and, he admits, "every shilling I get costs a rape, a mutilation, or a life." While his apologists denied the claims that natives were brutalized under his rule, Leopold admits that "the incorruptible kodak" by documenting physical mutilations has become "a sore calamity to us" and "the most powerful enemy that has confronted us." Predictably, the published editions of the soliloquy featured photographs of amputees. Leopold similarly concedes in the soliloquy attributed to him by Sam that his minions had been "wrong to crucify" Congolese women, "clearly wrong, manifestly wrong, I can see it now, myself, and am sorry it happened, sincerely sorry. I believe it would have answered just as well to skin them. . . . But none of us thought of that; one cannot think of everything; and after all it is but human to err."[14]

Sam completed *King Leopold's Soliloquy* in late February 1905 and read it to Susan Crane and Isabel Lyon before mailing the manuscript to Harper & Brothers. Lyon noted in her diary that they sat "breathless" and "weak with emotion when he finished" reciting "the bald truthful statements that rolled from Leopold's vicious lips. Horribly—too horribly picturesque it is, & Mr. Clemens will cut out some of it—It's a pity too—but I suppose it would be too strong a diet for people & governments." Sam offered the "unfriendly article about the Butcher" of Belgium to Duneka, who accepted it as contractually required "and thought he ought to publish it as soon as possible" given its timeliness, but true to form he then sat on the piece, much as he had shelved *Christian Science*. Sam was not surprised, blaming the delay in its appearance on Duneka's Roman Catholicism, a religion he shared with Leopold. He had warned Morel that "the corporation" (Harper & Brothers) would "probably be doubtful about the commercial wisdom of dipping into Leopold's stinkpot, for they had been doubtful about dipping into Mrs. Eddy's." By early April 1905 Sam had received Duneka's permission to withdraw the essay and arrange for its publication in pamphlet form by the American Congo Reform Association "as a gratis contribution to the cause," and he thanked Duneka for agreeing to the compromise: "I shall feel sweeter inside after I have spewed out my opinion of Leopold."[15]

The American Congo Reform Association finally released the pamphlet on September 28 to uniformly favorable notices. Literally every reviewer who noticed the essay praised it, and it helped to rehabilitate Sam's reputation even among religious critics as a satirist on the right side of history if not the angels. "The great humorist never wielded his pen more pointedly in behalf of honesty and humanity," the *American Journal of Theology* averred; and Sam proved that Leopold "is the worst criminal of the centuries," according to the *Congregationalist and Christian World*. The *Baltimore American* ("a terrible arraignment of King Leopold"), *Washington Times* (a "forceful indictment"), *Chicago Inter Ocean* ("the most violent attack upon the Belgian monarch that has yet appeared"), *Montgomery Times* ("the most scathing arraignment of the century"), and *Sioux City Journal* ("one of the most terrible arraignments ever put into English") each made much the same point. The *Buffalo Commercial* ("blighting"), Chicago *Advance* ("a very fine and a most mirth-provoking bit of sarcasm"), New Haven *Journal and Courier* (horrors "vividly depicted" with "a caustic pen"), *Nashville Tennessean* ("a powerful voice" added "to the clamor for retribution"), and *New York Observer* (a "most effective" and "biting satire") were equally complimentary, and Tom Aldrich wrote Sam privately to commend his "noble piece of work!"[16]

Sam remained active in the American Congo Reform Association for several months after the publication of the pamphlet. He was appointed a vice president and permitted his name to appear on its stationery "so that he could be connected" with it and "could be of service" to it "without doing any work." Between late November 1905 and late January 1906, in fact, he traveled three times to Washington, D.C., to consult with President Roosevelt, Secretary of State Elihu Root, Assistant Secretary Robert Bacon, and other government officials about the crisis in the Congo. After discussing the issue with Roosevelt over lunch on November 27, Sam was convinced that if the president received "quietly trustworthy assurance" that the British would act, then the United States would follow suit. Sam soon became a diplomatic back channel between the State Department and the association. Bacon contacted him on December 4 to solicit information about the posture of the British in the Congo, and Sam replied that he would "take measures at once to get that information. It is my impression that England asked our Government some time ago to join her in a move, but I will inquire & find out what this impression is based upon." He spoke at a meeting of the association on December 21 and assured Aldrich that "it will be difficult to unseat Leopold, but it is worth trying and we shall go on trying." He never wavered in his conviction that Leopold was a mass murderer. Such charges "are proven to the hilt by unimpeachable testimony," he wrote. "There is not whitewash enough on the planet to modify Leopold's complexion." Booker T. Washington never knew Sam "to be so stirred up on any one question as he was on that of the cruel treatment of the natives in the Congo Free State."[17]

But by the end of the year Sam was exasperated by the ineffectiveness of the Congo Reform Association. Lyon noted in her diary that "the slowness of the Congo movement is troubling Mr. Clemens very much. There is no leadership to it & he can do no more than he has done." He withdrew from the organization in January 1906 when he discovered that the United States had never ratified the treaty with thirteen other nations, negotiated in Berlin in 1885, to supervise Leopold's administration of Congolese affairs. He had declared to an interviewer in December 1905 that "like every other citizen of the United States" he was obliged to protest the king's conduct, but he resigned from the association when he realized that he had argued from a false premise, and worse yet, that the reformers had lied to him:

> I began to suspect that the Congo Reform Association's conviction that our Government's pledged honor was at stake in the Congo matter was an exaggeration; that the Association was attaching meanings to certain public documents connected with the Congo which the strict sense of the documents did not confirm. A final visit to the State Department settled the matter. The Department had kept its promise, previously made to the President and to me, that it would examine into the matter exhaustively and see how our Government stood. It was found that of the fourteen Christian Governments pledged to watch over Leopold and keep him within treaty limits, our Government was not one. Our Government was only sentimentally concerned, not officially, not practically, not by any form of pledge or promise. Our Government could interfere in the form of prayer or protest, but so could a Sunday-school. I knew that the Administration was going to be properly and diplomatically polite, and keep out of the muddle; therefore I privately withdrew from the business of agitating the Congo matter in the United States.

He believed, moreover, "that the American branch of the Congo Reform Association ought to go out of business, for the reason that the agitation of the butcheries can only wring people's hearts unavailingly—unavailingly, because the American people unbacked by the American government cannot achieve reform in the Congo." In other words, in the absence of a treaty with Belgium and forty years before the notion that crimes against humanity justified the prosecution of war criminals in Nuremberg, the United States had no right to intervene in the domestic affairs of other nations: "Our Government is so entirely outside of the Congo matter that it could by no means initiate a move in it, nor even second a move made by one or all of the other Governments concerned, without laying itself open to the danger of undiplomatic intrusion. The strength of the Reform movement in America lay in the apparent fact that our Government was one of the responsible parties and therefore could be persuaded to come forward and do it duty." In reply to Sam's resignation from the Congo Reform Association, Thomas Barbour implored Sam to remain active in the group. "I do not think you can leave the Congo until you take the people with you," he pleaded. "That hour has seemed to me not far away. It has seemed near because you are there." But Barbour's appeal failed. The conclusion of the State Department that the United States had no formal responsibility to end the genocide in the Congo "relieves it and sets it free," Sam explained. Meanwhile, what should happen to the pamphlet Sam had written? "It still has value,—as an exposure of the butcher Leopold—but the rest of it is now not only valueless but pernicious, since it in effect charges our government with unfaithfulness to a duty" that had never existed.[18]

Unfortunately, much to Sam's consternation, the British Congo Reform Association dithered while Léopoldville (today Kinshasa) burned. It failed to issue an edition of *King Leopold's Soliloquy* in the Commonwealth until May 1907, even though it enjoyed the same right to publish it as the American Congo Reform Association, and it paid Sam nothing from the proceeds of its sale. In his introduction to the British edition, Morel thanked Sam "most deeply for having written it and for placing it so generously at the disposal" of the group. He added that "The cult of kid gloves and rose water is not the cult of Mark Twain." Reviewers of this edition were almost as enthusiastic as those in the United States: the *Athenaeum* called it "a trenchant satire," *T. P.'s Weekly* "a book of white-hot irony," and the *Pall Mall Gazette* "a valuable and trenchant contribution to the cause"; the London *Bookman* opined that there "has not in our time been a fiercer satire"; *Punch,* that it was "glad to see Mark Twain taking part in a campaign against the owner of the Congo Free State"; the *Bristol Western Daily Press,* that "nothing quite so searchingly severe has been published in this country for a very long time"; the *Newcastle Chronicle,* that it was "one of the most effective appeals that we have read" on behalf of the victims of "unspeakable atrocities" and "a most effective piece of propaganda"; *Truth,* that it was "a passionate plea for justice for the oppressed natives"; the London *Clarion,* that it "shows that [Sam] is in deadly earnest"; the *Sheffield Telegraph* and *Belfast News-Letter* both called it "a terrible indictment"; and the *Perthshire Advertiser* lauded its "stories of atrocities which are too well authenticated to admit of doubt." The term most often invoked by critics to describe the *Soliloquy* was "grim," as in the *Stroud News and Gloucestershire Advertiser* ("grim humour punctuating with terrible incisiveness the facts of the most terrible tragedy and crime"), Sydney *World's News* ("grim in the extreme—but necessary"), *London Reader* ("Mark Twain never jested in grimmer earnest"), *Manitoba Free Press* ("the grimmest kind of a monologue"), and *Aberdeen Press and Journal* (every page contains humor "of the grimmest sort"). Perhaps as the result of the recent colonial past in Australia, Sam's essay resonated with some editorialists Down Under, such as in the *Perth Western Mail* ("as merciless a piece of satire as any that has appeared of recent years"), *Adelaide Advertiser* ("as a satirist of political abuses Mark Twain was never perhaps more effective"), *Australian Christian Commonwealth* ("never has Mr. Clemens put his powers of sarcastic humor to better service"), *Melbourne Leader* ("drives home responsibility with relentless force" and "puts in bold relief the moral responsibility of America"), *Lithgow Mercury* ("stinging satire"), and Sydney *Daily Telegraph* ("scathing comments that lose nothing from the mordant humor in which they are clothed." Only a few Commonwealth papers struck a slightly sour note, such as the *Spectator* ("while we are wholly in sympathy with Mark Twain's purpose, we cannot approve of his method"), the London *Graphic* (an "intemperate" denunciation), London *Justice* ("the soliloquy is a failure" but "as an indictment of Leopold's rule on the Congo it is very telling"), and *Sydney Stock and Station Journal* ("an awful book"). The official Belgian government reply to Sam's attack was as temperate as a rabid dog. *An Answer to Mark Twain* pictures Sam and Morel on the cover as human-headed vipers; decries his "infamous libel against the Congo State" as an "ugly piece of work" that "met with no success in America"; and asserts that the accompanying photographs of amputees and other victims were faked or, in modern parlance, photoshopped. "No Belgian would take the trouble of discussing such filthy work," it concludes. On the contrary, the Congo, a country once "steeped in the most abject barbarity . . .today is born to civilization and progress."[19]

The genocide finally ended in 1908 with the annexation of the Congo Free State and the removal of Leopold as its sovereign leader by act of the Belgian parliament, though the renamed Belgian Congo remained a colony governed under a colonial charter until 1960. In the lingering controversy over Leopold's atrocities, moreover, Sam played a trump card. He proposed a fitting epitaph shortly before the monarch's death in December 1909: "Here under this gilded tomb lies rotting the body of one the smell of whose name will still offend the nostrils of men ages upon ages after all the Caesars and Washingtons & Napoleons shall have ceased to be praised or blamed & been forgotten."[20]

Two months before Leopold's death, Arthur Conan Doyle, at the behest of the officers of the Congo Reform Association, tried to recruit Sam to reenlist in the cause, albeit to no avail. Albert Bigelow Paine replied that his boss could not help because "any intimate consideration" of the Congo "excites and distresses him to a degree which we think dangerous." The officers reiterated their overture, eliciting Sam's final comment on the subject: "I would be glad if I were able to take an active part in your crusade but I am obliged to refrain. The condition of my health has made it necessary for my physician to advise me not to take any part in any public movement, particularly one like that affecting the Congo, the effect of which could not be otherwise than disturbing to my general mental and physical condition."[21]

The remodeling of the town house at 21 Fifth Avenue was sufficiently advanced by the second week of November that Katy Leary, promoted from maid to housekeeper after twenty-four years in the Clemenses' service, was able to move there and supervise the interior decorating. The furniture from the Hartford mansion was installed about the time she arrived. The family had "not seen it for 13 years," and Leary cried when it was carried into the house. She told Sam, "I had forgotten it was so beautiful, & it brought Mrs. Clemens right back to me—in that old time when she was so young & lovely." Lyon, Jean, and the other servants arrived from the Berkshires on November 29, though Sam remained at the Grosvenor, for his rooms in the town house were not quite ready. "The house is nicely oldish," Lyon noted, "with Gothic adornments over the doorways & windows on the main floor."[22]

To fill the house with song, Sam purchased an Aeolian orchestrelle, an eight-foot-tall player organ, and sixty-two paper rolls of music. A successor to the music box bought in Geneva in 1878 for the Hartford house, the orchestelle played mostly classical pieces, including some compositions by Johann Sebastian Bach, Edvard Grieg, and Felix Mendelssohn; Richard Wagner's "Wedding March" from *Lohengrin* and overture from *Tannhäuser*; the famous funeral march from Frédéric Chopin's Sonata no. 2 in B-flat Minor and his Nocturne in G Major, op. 37, no. 2; the Andante from Beethoven's Fifth Symphony and the Adagio cantabile from his *Sonata Pathétique*; the final Adagio lamentoso from Pyotr Ilyich Tchaikovsky's Symphony no. 6 in B Minor, op. 74; the aria "Largo" from George Frideric Handel's opera *Xerxes*; the intermezzo from Pietro Mascagni's *Cavaleria Rusticana*; the Pizzicato from Léo Delibes's *Sylvia*; Joachim Raff's "Cavatina for Violin and Piano"; Robert Schumann's "Träumerei"; the "Flower Song" from Charles Gounod's opera *Faust*; and Franz Schubert's "Impromptus," "Unfinished Symphony," and "Der Erlkönig" (or, as Sam called it, "Königstuhl," after the mountain overlooking Heidelberg), adapted from a ballad by Johann Wolfgang von Goethe about the death of a child. In addition, the instrument played some popular tunes, including waltzes; a medley of Scottish and Irish airs such as "Ye Banks and Braes O'Bonnie Doon," "Robin Adair," "Bonnie Sweet Bessie," and "The Campbells are Coming"; the German folk song "Die Lorelei," based on a poem by Heinrich Heine and composed by Friedrich Silcher; the melancholy "The Last Rose of Summer"; some "bugle call & war songs"; the "Chorus of Angels," probably the popular hymn "Angels We Have Heard on High";

and compositions by the Polish American prodigy Josef Hofmann. "My musical taste is vulgar & untrained, & is about up to the level of machine-music & ballads & Jubilee hymns," he conceded to Clara at her rest cure, "& to confess the truth I always had a passion for the common street-hurdygurdy. Without a doubt this machine has raised my level a little." In any case, "I am satisfied that the machine" and the "music which we bought with it are worth the twenty-six hundred dollars they cost." Though equipped with a keyboard, the orchestrelle was most often operated by a foot pump. Dorothy Quick, one of his "angelfish," remembered that Sam "was never happier than when he was listening to the orchestrelle, and he would sometimes have it played for him for several hours at a time—no mean task, as the foot pedals had to be pumped continuously." Lyon, his preferred victim, recalled that he often did not "hear the music, he couldn't for his wonderful brain is singing melodies all its own with the music that the aeolian is making for accompaniment. He has said that often it will start a train of thought that will rise and fall and go on and on with the strains of the music, but he doesn't know that I am there, it is just disembodied sound, and that's what I like best." Sam associated particular songs with his dead daughter and wife. The evening of March 2, 1906, Lyon recalled, she "took up the 'Largo' while Sam "sat in the green tufted chair quite near me, with his back toward me, and when I had finished it he said: 'If you're not tired, play the Susy one.' ('The Intermezzo' from 'Cavaleria Rusticana') When I had played it, he said: 'I can fit the words to both those pieces. As the coffins of Susy & her mother are borne through the living room, & the hall & the drawing room of the Hartford house, Susy calls to me in the Intermezzo, & her mother in the Largo.' " Much "as a masseur refreshes the body," according to Lyon, "so the Aeolion is his spiritual massage—it soothes and rests him." After his death, his daughter Clara donated the instrument to the Mark Twain Museum in Hannibal.[23]

"A child of the pavement," as he was called by James Dickie, the minister of the American Church in Berlin, Sam often took a morning stroll along Fifth Avenue. He frequented a few beaneries and greasy-spoon cafés around lower Manhattan, including Pat Dolan's dive on Park Row across from City Hall, a "little saloon on Fourteenth Street" where he once took his old Nevada friend Samuel Post Davis, and "a little, quiet place" Joe Goodman discovered on Seventh Avenue that "sold splendid beer at 5 cents per big schooner and gave you all the headcheese, corned-beef or bologna sandwiches you wanted."[24]

To lighten the burden he felt after Livy's death, Sam began to shed some ballast. She had borne the "privations of our poverty for years & never uttered a murmur nor allowed me to curse myself for causing it," he admitted to her brother Charley Langdon, "& just as the relief came she was stricken down & cruelly robbed of her reward." After her will was probated and he inherited her estate, estimated at about $35,000, he sold the Tarrytown property for $55,000, about $7,000 more than he had paid for it.[25] Like Saladin Foster, the protagonist in his story "The $30,000 Bequest," he was chastened by his dream of "vast wealth, acquired by sudden and unwholesome means." His unruly ambition to acquire fortune "did us no good, transient were its feverish pleasures; yet for its sake we threw away our sweet and simple and happy life." The *San Francisco Call* thought it "written in the vein of his old-time humor."[26]

During these same months, however, Sam refused to dump his investments in plasmon, a failure to divest that threatened to sink his financial ship. His initial returns were sufficiently lucrative to allow it to remain afloat. In March 1900, as a member of the board of directors of the British Plasmon Company he even proposed a publicity stunt: to sell two and a half million pounds of product to India for only £50,000 monthly. The plasmon would furnish everyone stricken by the famine there "the equivalent of ½ pound of best beefsteak per day" for the cost of only "one shilling per month." Not only would such a deal end the famine, the business would "clear £20,000 a month." Publicize "the fact, make a boom, & float the company." In April 1900 he urged Rogers and Standard Oil "to keep an eye" on Henry A. Butters, a California railroad and mining entrepreneur, who along with John Hays Hammond had founded Plasmon USA, and "buy control of the company" if "he makes a success of it." By April 1901, moreover, British Plasmon was selling upward of eight tons a month of powdered milk albumen, and Sam was receiving about £350, or $1,750, in quarterly dividends. If he still lived in England, he announced, "I would double my investment in plasmon, I have such a confidence in it." "My faith in Plasmon has remained strong all the time," he wrote five months later. "If I could afford to live out of the income for a while I shouldn't want anything better than another whack at it. As a speculation. Our income is exactly competent now, at last; so we don't really speculate anymore." Nevertheless, the temptation was too great, and by March 1902 he owned about four hundred shares, or about five percent, of the stock in the Plasmon Company of America, worth about $40,000.[27]

A year later, however, Sam had lost confidence in the management of the company, especially in Butters, who Sam believed had defrauded him. He suspected that in one transaction, rather than selling him $25,000 worth of stock, Butters had transferred $25,000 worth of his own assets to Sam and pocketed the money. A year later, "the thief Butters" tried to unload another "350 American Plasmon shares" on Sam "for $3,400—and I declined. I consider that the money I paid in there last year ($32,500) is totally lost." Butters "set his traps and played a 'confidence game' upon me," Sam reminisced in 1908. "To what end? Merely to swindle me out of an infinitely trivial sum of money." He considered Butters "easily the meanest white man, and the most degraded in spirit and contemptible in character I have ever known." He admitted to Rogers that had he refrained from investing in "American Plasmon I would now be a good businessman; but as it is, I am only half a good businessman." It had been "one of those investments of mine that I am ashamed of and would like to forget. Damn!" He likewise was "perfectly convinced that the chiefs" of the British branch "intend to rob me," he insisted. "They exhibit all the ways of thieves and none of the ways of honest men." Acting on a tip from Ralph Ashcroft, the "truthful, honorable, careful" (according to Sam) treasurer of British Plasmon, "a bright & good business man & very efficient manager," he confronted one of its officers: "I am warned from sources which I respect that the Company is crooked, and has private schemes which will not bear the light. The Company's deliberately dishonest course toward me for two years is good circumstantial evidence that the warning was well founded." He claimed to have received no annual reports or other documents routinely distributed to stockholders.[28]

By late 1904, Plasmon USA was foundering, gouged "out of its cash capital," as Sam later put it, by Butters and his (mis)management team. The company was riven by rival investment groups, one led by Hammond and Butters, the other by Sam and his man Friday Ashcroft. At a stockholders' meeting on September 1, a new board of directors was elected that hired Ashcroft to be the new general manager. Hammond soon notified Sam by telegram that he would "strongly oppose" Ashcroft because he was "incompetent or worse," and Sam shared the telegram with Ashcroft, who promptly filed suit against Hammond for $25,000, later raised to $100,000, in libel damages. The litigation, with Sam as a witness, lasted for over five years. Asked how he was acquainted with Hammond, Sam testified in his deposition—omitting that they had first crossed paths in Hartford when Hammond was a student at Yale—that he had "a delicacy about saying" because "I met him in jail" in Pretoria. He added, however, that he knew "nothing about the case." Meanwhile, Ashcroft "rained filth & fury and unimaginable silliness" upon Hammond; American Plasmon went bankrupt, wiping out Sam's entire investment; and Sam and his business manager quarreled acrimoniously. In January 1906, Sam resisted an invitation to help recapitalize the company. "I'll have no money in any new Plasmon Co—not on your life!" he insisted. "Not if there's a Hammond or a Butters" involved.

Hammond might be "square," but he was Butters's unwitting tool. Still, Sam put up $2,500, apparently in the vain hope that a revived company might eventually repay part of his losses. The legal wrangling finally ended in February 1910 with the dismissal of Ashcroft's case by the New York Court of Appeals on the grounds that it was based on a private or privileged communication "from one stockholder to another." Sam sneered that Ashcroft's suit "never cost him anything" because "he stole the money [to file it] from me." He wrote Hammond that he was "glad" Ashcroft had lost "that ridiculous suit" because his former business manager "couldn't be libeled, there being no possible combination of English words that could achieve that miracle." Sam had "never doubted" Hammond's honesty and "have long believed a day would come when you and I would meet—and then all misunderstandings would vanish."[29]

Despite passage of the Chace Act, or International Copyright Act, of 1891, the legislative battle for equitable copyright or the defense of his personal intellectual property was, from Sam's point of view, not yet won. In March 1901 he sued Butler Brothers, a Chicago publisher, in federal court for infringing on the copyright of *Mark Twain's Library of Humor* by advertising a volume entitled *Library of Wit and Humor by Mark Twain*, which he considered "the most impudent swindle I have ever seen." The parties settled out of court for damages, and the publisher agreed to melt the plates. Sam also appeared as an expert witness in a similar suit brought in federal court in New York by Rudyard Kipling against both R. F. Fenno and Company and G. P. Putnam's Sons for using Kipling's "trademark of authorship"—that is, his name—"without his authority." Sam reiterated on the stand his familiar claims that "there had been a considerable increase in the property of an author in trademarks" and there was "no difference between counterfeiting a label on a book, a box of blacking, or a bottle of whisky."[30] Kipling won the case.

Sam also argued in favor of extending copyright protections not only for the lives of authors but for a period of fifty years after their deaths to cover the lives of their children. He told a journalist who interviewed him for the London *Sketch* in March 1904 that he never expected the members of Parliament or Congress "to settle satisfactorily the intricate question of copyright" because the vast majority of them did not understand the issues at stake. In the absence of such protections, the law turned the doctrine of "survival of the fittest" on its head: the "fittest" books would not survive except in cheap or corrupt editions. In "Concerning Copyright," the lead essay in the *North American Review* for January 1905, he noted that the copyrights on Harriet Beecher Stowe's book had expired years before she did and, as a result, while "the profits on *Uncle Tom's Cabin* continue today, nobody but the publishers" collect them, while Stowe's "daughters receive nothing." They were "no longer able to live in their modest home" in Hartford "and had to move out and find humbler quarters." Put another way, under the current law "the author's copyright expires just in time to permit his children to starve." Sam proposed an alternative: perpetual copyright so long as a book remained profitable, royalties to be paid to an author's heirs. If such a law had existed "in the forty-second year of *Uncle Tom* there would have been one cheap edition instead of twenty, and it would have preserved the book, not paralyzed it; and the income from *Uncle Tom*, to both publishers and heirs, would have remained steady and ample to this day." Sam was soon elected to the executive council of a revitalized American Copyright League, joining George Washington Cable, Richard Watson Gilder, Howells, Brander Matthews, and twenty others. He endorsed a plan to test the possibilities in court of common-law judicial protections of authors' rights. He hoped "we can land a success," he wrote Edward Everett Hale, whose copyright on *The Man Without a Country* (1863) was about to lapse, "and empty all the puerile & mephitic copyright-laws down Congress's throat or some other sewer."[31]

Nor had Sam finished tilting at windmills. On Bloody Sunday, January 22, 1905, thousands of striking Russian workers marched to the Winter Palace in St. Petersburg to present a petition to Czar Nicholas II for higher wages, a reduced work week, and an armistice in the Russo-Japanese War. Never mind that the czar had fled the palace the day before. During the day an estimated thousand men, women, and children were massacred by the Imperial Guard, a killing spree that inspired Sam to write "The Czar's Soliloquy" along the same lines as *King Leopold's Soliloquy*. In this imaginary disquisition, delivered while standing naked before a mirror, Czar Nicholas II acknowledges that "there is no power without clothes." Without clothes he would be "as destitute of authority as any other naked person. Nobody could tell me from a parson, a barber, a dude. Then who is the real Emperor of Russia? My clothes." In modern parlance, he was nothing more than an empty suit. Like a decadent King Arthur, Czar Nicholas invokes a Lamarckian rationale for his tyrannical rule; in effect, he was to the manner born: "the blood that flows in my veins" was "blood informed, trained, educated by its grim heredities, blood alert by its traditions, blood which has been to school four hundred years in the veins of professional assassins, my predecessors." On January 30, only a week after Bloody Sunday, Sam had finished a draft of "The Czar's Soliloquy" and declaimed it to his family. Isabel Lyon noted that "he was wonderful" and "his voice shook with emotion." This version of the sketch included an admonition to Russian mothers to teach their children that as adults they should "knife a Romanoff wherever you find him, loyalty to these cobras is treason to the nation; be a patriot, not a prig—set the people free." Four days later he read a revision to them that omitted this line. Still, according to Lyon, George Harvey "said it was the strongest thing he had ever written."[32]

The essay was rushed into print in the March 1905 issue of the *North American Review,* though it was not as well regarded by critics as *King Leopold's Soliloquy*. On the one hand, the piece was praised by the *Minneapolis Journal* ("a hit at the worshippers of royalty"), Decatur *Herald* ("a lesson in the democracy and equality of mankind"), *Salt Lake Tribune* ("a scalding philippic"), *Oakland Tribune* ("more than enough to insure the genial author's immurement in the Siberian mines"), *Sydney News* ("a remarkable article . . .written after the manner of Carlyle"), and London *Standard* ("Mark Twain plays Teufelsdröckh to the Czar"). On the other hand, the article was received with much less fanfare by the New York *Evening Post* ("a dismal bit of humor"), *Buffalo News* ("a failure"), *Washington Post* ("frank expression in grimly saturnine fashion"), *Spectator* ("partisan oratory" and "personal invective"), *Australian Christian Commonwealth* ("a mordant article"), and London *Review of Reviews* (the author "does not appear at his best").[33]

As it happened, Sam composed his lemon-bitter "The War Prayer" not against the backdrop of U.S. jingoism during the Spanish-American War, which at first glance makes sense, but in the context of the Battle of Mukden, fought in Manchuria by Russian and Japanese armies between late February and early March 1905. Sam equated three recent wars of imperialism, in fact. "Did England rise against the infamy of the Boer war?" he asked Twichell rhetorically. "No—rose in favor of it. Did America rise against the infamy of the Philippine war? No—rose in favor of it. Did Russia rise against the infamy of the present war? No—sat still & said nothing. Has the Kingdom of God advanced in Russia since the beginning of time?" Over dinner on March 11, as Lyon noted in her diary, the family discussed "the great Russian-Japanese War, for at this time the Russians are suffering tremendous losses and the Japanese are lashing them with victory upon victory. They are capturing Mukden." He had read a finished draft of "The War Prayer" to his family only the day before. Lyon noted that it was "wonderful and strong, finishing with his eternal slap at the human race." In the piece, Sam satirized the hypocrisy of Christians who implore God to protect their loved ones in battle, failing to recognize that by their supplications they also express the wish that others' sons, husbands, and brothers will die. Those who beseech the Almighty to "watch over our noble young soldiers and aid, comfort, and encourage them in their patriotic work" silently pray at the same time to blight the lives of the enemy, "protract their bitter pilgrimage, make heavy their steps, water their way with their tears, stain the white snow with the blood of their wounded feet!" In his own voice, Sam savaged the notion that "the Almighty has been personally conducting this Russian campaign against the Japanese" and the claim of the Russian Orthodox Church that the war "is ordained of God." Sam mailed the manuscript on March 21 to Elizabeth Jordan, the editor of *Harper's Bazar,* who replied the next day that she thought it "not quite suited to a woman's magazine." Sam pigeonholed the article and wrote Dan Beard that he did not "think the prayer will be published in my time. None but the dead are permitted to tell the truth." It was not published in its entirety until 1923, though it was excerpted in the *Boston American* in early September 1914, scarcely a month after the start of the Great War in Europe.[34]

The popular unrest in Russia after Bloody Sunday and the defeat of Russian forces at the Battle of Tsushima by the Japanese fleet in late May led to a ceasefire in the Russo-Japanese War. Sam celebrated the Japanese victories and privately wished that "somebody would assassinate the Russian Family. So does every sane person in the world—but who has the grit to say so? Nobody." The approval of the Treaty of Portsmouth in August 1905 formally ended the conflict, and for his part in sponsoring the negotiations, Theodore Roosevelt received the Nobel Peace Prize the next year. From Sam's perspective, however, the armistice was premature, a "foolish brief truce," a setback to the causes of Russian freedom and reform. The war was halted one battle too soon. As he wrote the *Boston Globe,* in a statement distributed nationwide by the Associated Press,

> Russia was on the high road to emancipation from an insane and intolerable slavery. I was hoping there would be no peace until Russian liberty was safe. I think that this was a holy war in the best and noblest sense of that abused term and that no war was ever charged with a higher mission. I think there can be no doubt that that mission is now defeated and Russia's chains re-riveted—this time to stay. I think the Czar will now withdraw the small humanities that have been forced from him and resume his medieval barbarisms with a relieved spirit and an immeasurable joy. I think Russian liberty has had its last chance and has lost it. I think nothing has been gained by the peace that is remotely comparable to what has been sacrificed by it. One more battle would have abolished the waiting chains of billions upon billions of unborn

> Russians and I wish it could have been fought. I hope I am mistaken, yet in all sincerity I believe that this peace is entitled to rank as the most conspicuous disaster in political history.

The *Globe* editorialized the next day that Sam "seems to have thought beyond everybody else on the question what the effects of the peace just secured are going to be." Charles Francis Adams allowed that Sam's column "attracted my attention because it so exactly expresses the views I have myself all along entertained." Invited by George Harvey to a dinner party for the Russian diplomats who had reached the settlement, Sam demurred. He was crippled with gout, he politely protested, though in an unsent note he furiously objected to meeting "the illustrious magicians who with the pen have annulled, obliterated, and abolished every high achievement of the Japanese sword and turned the tragedy of a tremendous war into a gay and blithesome comedy."[35]

By 1905 or so, moreover, Sam had taken a decisive turn in his critique of modern Western civilization. Whether or not he was a believer in the inevitability of Progress in 1889 when he published *A Connecticut Yankee*, a topic of debate among modern scholars, he certainly was a nonprogressive thinker fifteen years later. More to the point, by 1905 he condemned the rapacity and materialism of twentieth-century America, which he blamed on such post–Civil War fat cats as John D. Rockefeller, Andrew Carnegie, and Jay Gould for fostering by setting new standards of avarice, greed, and conduct. Gould "was the mightiest disaster which has ever befallen this country," Sam asserted. "The people had desired money before his day, but he taught them to fall down and worship it." In a querulous letter to Twichell, Sam admitted that

> the 19th century made progress—the first progress after "ages & ages"—colossal progress. In what? Materialities. Prodigious acquisitions were made in things which add to the comfort of many & make life harder for as many more. But the addition to righteousness? Is that discoverable? I think not. The materialities were not invented in the interest of righteousness; that there is more righteousness in the world because of them than there was before is hardly demonstrable, I think. . . . All Europe & all America are feverishly scrambling for money. Money is the supreme ideal. . . . Money-lust has always existed, but not in the history of the world was it ever a craze, a madness, until your time & mine. This lust has rotted these nations; it has made them hard, sordid, ungentle, dishonest, oppressive.

Not surprisingly, under the circumstances Sam sometimes surrendered to a type of social Darwinist cynicism that was part of the Zeitgeist and tempered his anti-imperialism: "There is no such thing as morality; it is not immoral for the tiger to eat the wolf, or the wolf the cat, or the cat the bird, and so on down. . . . It is not immoral for one nation to seize another nation by force of arms, or for one man to seize another man's property or life if he is strong enough and wants to take it."[36]

In mid-March 1905, at virtually the same moment he condemned the materialism of an amoral age in his letter to Twichell, Sam began to write a story unpublished until 1972 originally titled "The House of Tragedies," later changed to "Refuge of the Derelicts." In this pastiche of autobiographical allusions, a hodgepodge of shards shored against the ruins of memory about people in his life, Sam took an occasional swipe at Christian Science and other targets of his (sat)ire. Most of these people were "shipwrecks," "old and battered and broken, that wander the ocean of life lonely and forlorn." Sam pitied them and "sometimes my feelings are so hot that I have to take the pen & pour them out on paper to keep them from setting me afire inside." To be sure, "all that ink & labor are wasted, because I can't print the result," as he wrote a few weeks later in "The Privilege of the Grave," ironically an essay that would not be published in its entirety until 2008. In his autobiographical dictation for August 30, 1906, Sam remarked that "Refuge of the Derelicts" was "half finished and will remain so."[37]

For only $200 a month, Sam rented Lone Tree Hill, Henry Copley Greene's house in remote Dublin, New Hampshire, an artists' colony on the slope of Mount Monadnock, for the summer of 1905. Jean, Katy Leary, and Isabel Lyon arrived in early May, and Sam joined them on May 18. Despite its bulk, Leary recalled, Sam shipped the orchestrelle there at "a lot of trouble and expense" because "it was a real comfort to Mr. Clemens." He cherished the "woodsy solitude" on the mountain and "the pleasantest summer home we have ever had on either side of the ocean." They were situated in "the best atmosphere outside of Fairhaven. Physically regarded, I mean. The moral atmosphere wasn't much to speak of before I came," he joked with Aldrich. Jean seemed to thrive in the mountain air, moreover. "She drives herself to death with a continuous carnival of riding, driving, walking, climbing, romping—I don't know how she has survived it," Sam wrote. She began to plan the next steps in her treatment for epilepsy—a brain X-ray and perhaps a surgical operation.[38]

Among his neighbors on the mountain, whose houses Sam could see "scattered in the forest distances," were the artist Joseph Lindon Smith;

Professor William Graham Sumner of Yale; Ethan Allen Hitchcock, the U.S. secretary of the interior; the geologist and explorer Raphael Pumpelly; Sumner B. Pearmain, a Boston stockbroker, and his wife Alice; Sam's friends Franklin MacVeagh and Thomas Wentworth Higginson; and the painters George de Forest Brush and Abbott Thayer. "I am astonished to find that I have known 8 of these 14 neighbors a long time," he marveled to Twichell; "10 years is the shortest; then seven beginning with 25 years & running up to 37 years' friendship. It is the most remarkable thing I ever heard of." He was invited to dinner "very often," and "once I came near going to church," he teased Helena Gilder. "I think it was in May, but it might have been June. They took up a collection." The actress Ethel Barrymore, who was playing in summer stock in Cornish, New Hampshire, sixty-five miles away, remembered first meeting Sam at the home of the Smiths. "They were having some kind of garden fete and I was to be a sprite coming up from a fountain" in a skit entitled "Jack Frost Comes in Midsummer," she recounted in her memoirs. "Mark Twain was one of the guests that night. He was always very nice to me. It was the first time I had seen him in white evening clothes." According to Corinna Lindon Smith, Sam jokingly told Barrymore that "the audience thought you were wonderful in it, because you are Ethel Barrymore, but frankly you tried too hard to be spontaneous."[39]

Sam began his last attempt at a novel two days after he arrived in Dublin. He had long been intrigued by microscopic life. As far back as 1895, while in Sydney, Australia, he had described the phantasmagoria in one of his dreams: "The visible universe is the physical person of God, "the vast worlds that we see twinkling millions of miles apart in the fields of space are the blood corpuscles in His veins," and "we and the other creatures are the microbes that charge with multitudinous life the corpuscle." While in Kaltenleutgeben, Austria, during the summer of 1898, he had composed the fragment "The Great Dark," about a whaling cruise in a drop of water. He once expressed the same idea to Paine, who quoted him to this effect: "The suns & planets that form the constellations of a billion billion solar systems & go pouring, a tossing flood of shining globes, through the viewless arteries of space are the blood-corpuscles in the veins of God; & the nations are the microbes that swarm and wiggle." He returned to the premise in his new manuscript, a variation on Swift's tale of Gulliver in Lilliput, with the working title "The Adventures of a Microbe," later changed to "3,000 Years Among the Microbes," the autobiography of a bacteriologist transformed by a botched scientific experiment into a cholera germ. The narrator Huck [short for Huxley] Bkshp [Blankenship], who declares man "a microbe and his globe a blood-corpuscle drifting with its shining brethren of the Milky Way down a vein of the Master and Maker of all things," inhabits the "unspeakably profane" body of an ethnically stereotyped Hungarian tramp named Blitzowski, who "never shaves, never washes, never combs his tangled fringe of hair; he is wonderfully ragged, incredibly dirty; he is malicious, malignant, vengeful, treacherous, he was born a thief, and will die one." He is host to over thirty thousand "swarming nations" of vermin, including "the mighty Republic of Getrichquick" or GRQ, a country analogous to the United States that had recently adopted a policy of "benevolent assimilation" toward a "collection of mud islets inhabited by those harmless bacilli which are the food of the fierce hispaniola sataniensis."[40]

Among the other targets of Sam's broad-brush satire in the manuscript are the usual suspects: Christian Science and Christian missions. A potential convert to the "Giddyites" (= Eddyites) reads the sect's gospel, a book entitled "Science and Wealth, with Key to the Fixtures," until "she was all spirit" and "the last vestige of flesh was gone." Elsewhere a clergyman argues that the gospel must be "carried to all the World and preached to every creature," including dumb animals. Despite his assertions to the contrary, Sam wrote the story largely for his own amusement. It is filled with private or inside jokes, such as a passing reference to a "bucket-shop dysentery-germ" named Butters. On May 22, he began to read a chapter of the "imaginative scientific little story" aloud to his family every night after dinner "like Paris in Joan-of-Arc days." Lyon asked him "how long he'd been turning those marvelous imaginings over in his mind, & he said that the idea had been there for many years—he tried to work it up from a drop of water & a scientist with a powerful microscope; but it wasn't right. He had to become the microbe & see & think & act & appreciate as a microbe." He admitted it was not "a story for babes," but "it will delight physicians & bacteriologists." Two evenings later she gushed that the "microbe story grows and grows in depth and wonder. It has grown into the thought that perhaps we too are microbes chasing around in a globule that is only a molecule of the universe." Sam bragged a week later that he had "written a third of a book here in 10 or 12 days," and after another week that he not only had completed thirty thousand words but expected the book to exhibit such scientific learning that it would "compel the gratitude of common schools & the public." The "atmosphere of the New Hampshire highlands is exceptionally bracing and stimulating and a fine aid to hard and continuous work," he wrote Duneka. "I came in May and wrought 35 successive days without a break." He wrote virtually every day in June, except June 5, the first anniversary of Livy's death. "I am deep in a new book which I enjoy more than I have enjoyed any other for twenty years," he announced on June 16, "and I hope it will take me the entire summer to write it; in which case it will be a giant for size judging by the stack of manuscript I have ground out on it since I arrived here." The evening of June 21, Sam read the latest installment of "the microbe satire" to the family, and Lyon pronounced it "strong, fearfully strong, touching on all the great events of the day and telling the truth about them too. It is so clever—and so scathing." But then Sam apparently lost interest in it. After writing a total of forty-six thousand words, he abandoned it two days later. A year later he admitted that, like "The Refuge of the Derelicts," the manuscript was "half finished and will remain so."[41]

He suffered not from a poverty of invention but a superabundance of it. After laying aside the microbe narrative, he again took up the manuscript of "No. 44, the Mysterious Stranger." On June 29 he mentioned to Clara that he had "spent the day reading the book I wrote in Florence. I destroyed 125 pages of it" because it was "too diffusive" and "expect to go over it again tomorrow and destroy 25 more." Better than his word, the next day he "burned 30,000 words & am now taking a fresh start" on it. The same day, Lyon gushed in her journal, "Oh, I have been steeped and steeped and steeped with joy over a manuscript that Mr. Clemens brought down stairs for me to read 'when I had leisure.'" He wrote chapters 26 through 32 of the extant manuscript over the next two weeks. "Mr. Clemens is going on with 'The Mysterious Stranger' and it is magic," Lyon wrote. "When Jean asked him how he could drop one story and work on another, he said it had always been his habit to write that way. While he was working on one story the 'tank is filling up for the one just stopped.'" On July 3, she noted that Sam "came down at 3:00 o'clock today with the day's work finished. In 3 days he has done the work of 5 days—and it is so delicious." By July 9 Sam's productivity had declined to eight pages a day, from thirty-two manuscript pages a day "a fortnight ago." Three days later he was visited by the devout Duneka, who (as Lyon put it) "shrivelled up over the first part of Forty Four" because it featured an evil priest. He wanted the character reformed or omitted.[42] Sam was apparently so discouraged by Duneka's hostility to the story that he again laid the manuscript aside.

But during the two weeks he worked on the manuscript, he skewered the doctrine of papal infallibility and "Kitchen Science" or "Christian Silence," specifically the "uninterpretable irrelevancies" in the "incomprehensible" teachings "of a complacent, commonplace, illiterate New England woman." But the primary target of his satire in these chapters are the striking printers who are replaced at the case by dehumanized "Duplicates" created by the printer's devil No. 44. The "Duplicates," who do "not need to eat or drink or sleep" and receive "no pay for their work," are not strike-breaking scabs so much as automatons who represent alienated workers or, at another remove, the mechanization of the Paige typesetter.[43]

Even after abandoning "3,000 Years Among the Microbes" and laying aside "No. 44," the two months between May 20 and mid-July 1905 were among the most prolific periods in Sam's career. He wrote "considerably more than 100,000 words." On July 28, he bragged that he had been in Dublin "59 days & can show 70 full days' work for it." Thomas Wentworth Higginson called on Sam one day and "found him in bed where he prefers to write, a strange picturesque object, in night clothes, with curly white hair standing up over his head. The bed was covered with written sheets" that Jean retrieved "at intervals, to be copied by her on typewriter." Higginson attested to his method of working on multiple projects at the same time: "He often leaves off anything in the middle and begins on something else and goes back to it. He has always worked in this way and likes it." A would-be poet also celebrated Sam's habit of writing in sleepwear:

> Mark Twain to us has often said
> He writes his best while propped in bed;
> And pictures of him we have seen,
> In bed, snow white, and nightie, clean;
> At work between the sheets at ease,
> His writing desk upon his knees;
> It seemed a most delightful way
> Of getting what is known as pay.

In late July he began "Eve's Diary," a seven-thousand-word companion or sequel to *Adam's Diary* that he completed in only five days. He concluded "Eve's love-story" with Adam's declaration at her grave, "Wheresoever she was, there was Eden"—a distinct echo of Sam's statement to Charley Langdon after Livy's death, "Wherever Livy was, that was my country." Duneka had effectively commissioned the piece for *Harper's Monthly*, and he was delighted with the result, even though Eve is a harebrained type, a precursor of the dingbat played by Gracie Allen a generation or two later. Duneka considered the sketch "fresh as the dawn, a very sweet and beautiful idyl." Upon its appearance in the December issue of *Harper's*, the *Scranton Republican* proclaimed "Eve's Diary" a "quaintly curious bit of foolery."[44]

Six months later Harper & Brothers released *Eve's Diary* as a 109-page booklet with fifty-three illustrations by Lester Ralph. Sam was delighted by the drawings. They were, he thought, "full of grace, charm, variety of invention, humor, pathos, poetry—they are prodigal in merits. It's a bonny Eve, a sweet & innocent & winning little lassie, & she is as natural & at home in the tale as if she had just climbed out of it. Now do you think draperies are indispensable to picture women? Isn't she cunning where she has been chasing Adam, & is looking after him in his flight? Do you note how dear & sweet & clean minded she is, & how charged with childlike wonder and interest? Clothes would vulgarize her."

Figure 13. Lester Ralph illustration for *Eve's Diary* (New York: Harper & Brothers, 1906).

Upon its publication, Sam sent a copy of the booklet to his friend Charlotte Teller Johnson, an editor at *Everybody's,* fiction writer, and aspiring playwright, with a note to the effect that she was "not obliged to read it, but you are obliged to admire the pictures, for they are just as sweet & cunning as they can be." Of course, he was equally capable of sarcasm on the topic of the illustrations. "I am sending you a small book," he wrote the artist Martha S. Bensley. "But I do not wish you to think I approve of the pictures, for I do not. I think they are scandalous. I tried hard to get the artist to put clothes on those people, but he would not do it at any price that I could afford. Please tear the pictures out, then you need not be afraid to leave the book lying around."[45]

With rare exceptions, reviewers welcomed the illustrated format. It was greeted in the United Kingdom by the *Glasgow Herald* ("blend of humor and tender sentiment"), *Birmingham Post* ("among the best things Mark Twain has done for a long time"), London *Outlook* ("might be called some harsh names by different kinds of mental invalids but nobody who used words correctly could call it frivolous"), and Belfast *Northern Whig* ("a deliberate, amusing absurdity"). The *Spectator* even extrapolated a sort of biblical moral from the story consistent with Sam's newfound disdain for materialism: "The love of money lies at the root of both [Adam's and Eve's] characters." Their "love of beauty is half of it love of possession," as when Eve wishes to adorn her body with stars or sets a forest on fire to admire the blaze. Put another way, original sin consists of what Whitman called "the mania of owning things." Across the United States, critics echoed the approbation; the *Brooklyn Eagle* called the book "a delightfully whimsical satire," the *Houston Post* "one of the cleverest and most amusing of Mark Twain's many absurdities," the *Fort Worth Telegram* "one of the best and therefore most amusing of the many absurdities . . .from the pen of Mark Twain"), the *New York Observer and Chronicle* "one of the most amusing of Mark Twain's many absurdities"; the *Cincinnati Enquirer* praised its "many humorous experiments"; the *Hartford Courant* opined that "seldom has the veteran written anything more delicately humorous," the *Philadelphia Inquirer* that it was "a work of genius"; the *Critic* found "no little ingenuity in the development of Eve's character"; the *New York Times Saturday Review of Books* found it "new and unique"; according to the *Independent,* "the only fault to find" is "that there is so little" of it; the New York *Outlook* described it as "full of interest," the *Springfield Republican* as "highly entertaining," and the *Boston Journal* as "full of amicable fun." The *Woman's Standard,* a suffragist paper ("absurd and amusing"), and the *Congregationalist and Christian World,* a denominational magazine ("if the fun is not quite so spontaneous and sympathetic as in [Adam's Diary], it is nevertheless what no other living humorist could have given us"), were no less complimentary. Down Under, the Sydney *Daily Telegraph* ("the writer's mind can still scintillate now and then with all the old fire"), Sydney *World's News* ("not so sparkling as" Adam's Diary "but it has all the elements in it for holding the attention of the reader"), *New Zealand Herald* ("a deliberate, amusing absurdity"), *New Zealand Mail* ("sure of a tremendous circulation"), *Perth Daily News* ("full of quaint, quiet humor"), and *Otago Witness* ("scorching" and "biting irony") joined the chorus. The New York *Sun* singled out for particular praise Lester Ralph's "very good" pictures. Only a few venues were lukewarm or cool, such as the *Athenaeum* ("the book is hardly to us a favourable specimen of the author's humour"), London *Telegraph* ("a naïve little book, odd and harmless"), *Zion's Herald* ("pictures are decidedly interesting but the wit is very forced and feeble"), and *Providence Journal* ("a silly piece of business," "simply dull and rather coarse"). The *Manchester Guardian* allowed that the book was "certainly peculiar," and the *Westminster Gazette* in London exhumed the old accusation that Sam was "somewhat irreverent," a charge to which he responded in his autobiographical dictation: "As to my irreverence, I am sure I was never irreverent in my life; I am also sure that no irreverent person has ever existed in the earth."[46]

Even as Duneka declined to publish "King Leopold" and shrank from "No. 44," he published a thin volume containing six of Sam's humorous pieces dating back to 1864 without his help or cooperation and with only the implied consent of their contract. Duneka titled the compilation *Editorial Wild Oats* without even consulting the author. When Sam saw a prepublication announcement of it in mid-September, he queried Duneka: "What's the new book? I hope it isn't old sketches that I've tried to keep out of print, for they could damage me." The editor replied that it was "made up of extracts from your various works relating to newspaper experiences" and were "in your best little vein"—that is, not polemical pieces—"and form a permanent contribution to American literature." In other words, Duneka was trying to resurrect Mark Twain the early literary comedian. For better or worse, the collection was so negligible that it raised hardly a ripple. The vast majority of the notices were brief but favorable: the *Brooklyn Eagle* ("the old irrepressible exuberance which makes you split your sides"), *Louisville Courier-Journal* ("whimsical"), *New Orleans Times-Picayune* ("whimsicality and adventure"), *Santa Cruz Sentinel* ("certainly funny"), *Boston Advertiser* ("such nonsense contributes to the gayety of existence"), *Elmira Star-Gazette* ("the first distinctively humorous volume" from the author in years), *Portland Oregonian* ("the humor is laid on thick"), *Brooklyn Standard Union* ("sure of a warm welcome"), *Chicago Tribune* ("something to add to the gayety of nations"), *Pittsburgh Press* ("several of

Mark Twain's funniest sketches"), *San Francisco Chronicle* ("some of the funniest stories that he has ever printed"), *Hartford Times* ("a collection . . . well worth bringing together"), *Public Opinion* ("full of enough laughs"), *Book News* ("sweetness and nourishment"), New York *Outlook* ("extravagant tales of newspaper life"), *Spectator* ("some amusing papers of the farcical kind"), and *Critic* ("humor seems inexhaustible"). However, the praise from the *Richmond Times-Dispatch* ("these papers, while humorous beyond question, are readily resistible") and the New York *Sun* ("they are funny, but some have been funny for nearly thirty years") came with caveats. A couple of notices in the Commonwealth were even overtly hostile, such as the *Adelaide Observer* ("a good deal of chaff" amid the oats) and *Queen* ("the laboured" humor "will not enhance the reputation of the writer").[47]

In the summer of 1905, Rogers quietly arranged to cancel Twichell's personal indebtedness, much as he had extended educational assistance to Helen Keller that was never disclosed. He laundered $1,500 through Sam, who forwarded the money to Twichell masked as a Wall Street windfall. "I want you to accept this $1500 conscience-money if you will," he wrote Twichell on July 13, "as it marks the turning of a reform-corner for me: I've been into Wall street again in a small way & am out again with a profit of $4,700 & am not going in any more. This profit is tainted money; & lies heavy on my conscience." Twichell replied with alacrity: "You have paid every earthly cent we owe, leaving us with a handsome, big balance on which to begin a new celestial life."[48] Sam had agreed to the ruse on the condition that Twichell as well as his daughters would eventually learn that their benefactor was Rogers.

After receiving an appeal in mid-September 1905 from the actress Minnie Maddern Fiske, an ardent animal rights activist, to write an anti-bullfighting tale, Sam drafted "A Horse's Tale" as the summer in Dublin wound to a close. "I shall certainly write the story," he assured Fiske, but "I may not get it to suit me, in which case it will go in the fire. Later I will try it again—& yet again—& again" until he got it right. On September 26 he read "70 pages of the new story" aloud after dinner to the family, and he finished an eighteen-thousand-word draft four days later. Fortunately, he was "satisfied with it, though it was not manufactured calmly but with an eight-day drive & rush—a dangerous process." He mailed a revision of the manuscript to Duneka on October 9 for publication in *Harper's Monthly*. "Although it doesn't preach," he insisted in his cover letter, "there's a sermon concealed in it." But his purpose in writing it had not been entirely didactic. "For an 8-day job it isn't a bad tale. Profitable, too—an average of $700 a day," as he wrote Clara. He had hoped "to crowd it into the Jan & Feb numbers" of the magazine "& that is what I have been rushing to accomplish." Instead, Duneka postponed its appearance until the August and September 1906 issues. A narratological experiment, the story is told from multiple points of view, among others by a young girl named Cathy, based on his daughters Susy and Jean, and Buffalo Bill's horse Soldier Boy, in a nod to Anna Sewell's *Black Beauty* (1877). In an aside, one of the characters slurs a "trap-robber, horse-thief, squaw-man, renegado" named Hank Butters. But more to the point, Soldier Boy laments the number of times he has been sold, each time "down a step lower, and each time I got a harder master. They have been cruel, every one; they have worked me night and day in degraded employments, and beaten me; they have fed me ill, and some days not at all." Once he "was the pride of the mountains and the Great Plains" but "now I am a scarecrow and despised. These piteous wrecks that are my comrades here say we have reached the bottom of the scale, the final humiliation; they say that when a horse is no longer worth the weeds and discarded rubbish they feed to him, they sell him to the bull-ring for a glass of brandy, to make sport for the people and perish for their pleasure." Sam needed to depict a bullfight in the final chapters, though he had never seen one, so he literally and liberally "smouched" the description of one from John Hay's *Castilian Days* (1871). Mary Boewe traces many of these borrowings or (to be more precise) plagiarisms to their source. Hay writes, for example, that "the great gate is thrown open, and the procession of the toreros enters. . . . First the marshals of the day, then the picadors on horseback, then the matadors on foot, surrounded each by his quadrille of chulos." Sam mimics the passage: "The great gate is flung open, and the procession marches in, . . . the marshals of the day, then the picadores on horseback, then the matadores on foot, each surrounded by his quadrille of chulos." "A Horse's Tale" ends after Cathy and Soldier Boy are killed by a charging bull in front of thousands of spectators. It had "a righteous purpose," Sam maintained in his autobiography. He had written it by request to convince the children of Spain "to renounce and forsake the cruel bull-fight."[49]

Like *King Leopold's Soliloquy* and "Eve's Diary," "A Horse's Tale" was almost universally well received by reviewers. Ironically, few of the critics explicitly noted its advocacy of animal rights, though one of the exceptions was the *New York Times Saturday Review of Books*: it combined "some of the best flavor of Mark Twain's peculiar humor with sentiment borrowed partly from standard nursery literature and partly from the tracts" of the SPCA. Many of the other notices paid lip service to his compassion, among them the *Birmingham Post* (the author "has lost nothing of his fine humanity, his gift of vivid description, his mastery of quaint American dialogue"), London *Bookman* ("not a book of humor but it is a book written by a humorist who knows the natures of children and horses"), *Independent* ("we feel the throb of the kindest heart in the world beating for the helpless, whether brute or human"), and New York *Sun* ("acceptable to sentimental lovers of animals"). Still others used eerily similar wording: "combined his most delicate veins of humor and pathos" (*Louisville Courier-Journal*), "in his best vein of humor and pathos" in the *Brooklyn Citizen*), "mingling of humor and pathos" *Nashville Tennessean*), "mingled humor and pathos" (*Northern Christian Advocate*), "blend of humor, pathos, and kindly love of humanity" (*Trenton Times*), and "tenderness and swift, unexpected pathos" (*New York Times*). Then there were the more or less generic accolades: *Book News Monthly* called it "one of the most important [books] published this fall in fiction," the *Pittsburgh Press* "one of the best things Mr. Clemens has done," the *San Francisco Examiner* "one of the most striking pieces of fiction the great humorist has done in years," *Life* a "bubbling and innocent story," the *Butte Miner* a "wonderful exposition of the workings of the mind of a child," the *Buffalo Express* "captivating"; the *Hartford Courant* declared that there was "no story fuller of sympathetic and pathetic humor," the *Chicago Inter Ocean* that it was an "interesting little story"; the *Brooklyn Eagle* praised its "quaint humor and clever fancy," and the Launceston *Telegraph* wrote that it had "humor in abundance, but . . . also a much deeper significance." Only a handful of reviewers read the tale against the grain, among them the Chicago *Advance* ("not nearly as clever as some of this author's other work"), *New Orleans Picayune* ("The story is patchy and the threads of probability that hold the patches together are not strong"), and especially the *Spectator* ("It is difficult to forgive the author for the final catastrophe" that concludes "what is otherwise a pretty and amusing little sketch on a note of horrible tragedy"). The notices of the story in the *Scotsman*, whose writer was unsure whether Sam was "emulating the writers . . . who compose weepy stories about heroic children" or "making fun of them," and *Field* ("a pretty little story with a sad ending") were more ambivalent.[50]

On his part, Butters was unamused by the reference to him in the tale and sued Sam for libel in the amount of $50,000 in the spring of 1908. Sam initially expressed regret at having "allowed myself, in a moment of passion, to carry my quarrel with Mr. Butters into the newspapers & call him a swindler," but true to character he later voiced defiance. Butters's reputation "couldn't be damaged by any process known to science," he insisted, because "there wasn't a place on it the size of a hydrogen molecule that wasn't already rotten." The suit was dropped a few months later when Butters died.[51]

"For seven years I have suppressed a book which my conscience tells me I ought to publish," Sam wrote of his so-called "bible" or "gospel" entitled *What Is Man?* "I hold it a duty to publish it," he admitted to Twichell. "There are other difficult duties which I am equal to, but I am not equal to that one." Nevertheless, he returned to the manuscript during his final weeks in Dublin during the summer of 1905. On August 31 he read part of "his unpublishable Gospel" aloud to Isabel Lyon, who was favorably impressed. She had "been afraid of it, but that was because my only knowledge of it was through Jean who hates it, and if you hate a thing you can't see any of its good. This is full of wonderful thoughts—beautiful thoughts, terrible truths, oh such a summing up of human motives and if it belittles—does it belittle?—every human effort, it also has the power to lift you above that effort, and make you fierce in your wish to better your own conduct." She eventually qualified her approval of the project; the following February, Sam read the latest installment to her, and she was struck by "how strong a fatalist he is," especially his Lamarckian belief that "we're nothing but a ragbag of disappeared ancestors" and his notion that "every deed is leading right on toward the next." He would elaborate this premise in "The Turning Point of My Life" (1910), the last essay he ever published, in which he argued in effect that he became a professional writer because he contracted measles as a child. But in truth he repudiated the notion of a "turning point" or watershed moment, given his belief that every act is a link in an inexorable and unbroken chain of events. Such nonteleological convictions were not new to him. "Life is only one long Accident, nothing more," he mused in 1902. "It begins with the Accidents of birth—place, sex, social degree & the formidable & much-determining Accident of Environment—& these helplessly breed the rest of the Accidents."[52]

Sam put the final touches on *What Is Man?* in June 1906. In a prefatory note he drafted at the time, he remarked that the initial "studies for these papers were begun twenty-five or twenty-seven years ago" and the initial version was "written seven years ago. I have examined them once or twice per year since and found them satisfactory. I have just examined them again, and am still satisfied that they speak the truth. Every thought in them has been thought (and accepted as unassailable truth) by millions upon millions of men—and concealed, kept private. Why did they not speak out? Because they dreaded (and could not bear) the disapproval of the people around them. Why have I not published? The same reason has restrained me, I think." Or, as Sam observed in his autobiography, "By anticipation I couldn't bear the reproaches which would assail me from a public which had been trained from the cradle along opposite lines of thought." "Of the three persons who have seen the manuscript," he joked, "only one understood it and all three condemned it." Frank Doubleday, who first read a draft of *What Is Man?* in Vienna, eventually persuaded Sam to allow 250 copies of his "pet book" to be printed privately, without signature, and not to be sold. George Harvey granted an exception to his exclusive contract with Sam on these conditions. "The Gospel is going to be a fine book. Keep the 250 copies safe & secure," Sam admonished Doubleday.[53]

Predictably, when the book was finally published in August 1906, it hardly caused a ripple. Doubleday sent a copy to Carnegie, who thought it "will startle the ordinary man, but I don't see that it goes much deeper than we were before." Elia W. Peattie referred to it in passing in the *Chicago Tribune* as "that extremely clever anonymous book, 'What Is Man?'" Over the months Sam sent copies of the book "to a couple of dozen prudent friends. Three or four of them understood it & believed in it, the others did not understand it, & couldn't be made to understand it; still, they had opinions about it just the same & the opinions were not complimentary to me." Such dissenting views hardly disturbed Sam; after all, as he declared soon after its publication, "I have talked my gospel rather freely in conversation for twenty-five or thirty years and have never much minded whether my listeners liked it or not." In a sort of footnote to *What Is Man?* Sam predicted in his autobiography that the United States was likely "to drift into monarchy by and by. It is a saddening thought, but we cannot change our nature: we are all alike, we human beings; and in our blood and bone, and ineradicable, we carry the seeds out of which monarchies and aristocracies are grown: worship of gauds, titles, distinctions, power."[54]

The critical reputation of the "gospel" has not fared well over the years, at least in the opinion of literary scholars and historians. Waldo Frank dismissed it, after Paine edited it for republication in 1917, as "the confession of [the author's] despondency." On his part, H. L. Mencken scorned it for its tremulous release: "Imagine a man writing so honest and excellent a book, imagine him examining it and re-examining it and always finding it good—and yet holding off the printing of it for twenty-five years, and then issuing it timorously and behind the door, in an edition of 250 copies, none of them for sale!" Justin Kaplan scorned its "shrill, philosophically shallow nihilism."[55]

Clara left the care of Angenette Parry in New York in early June 1905 to return to the rest-cure facility in Norfolk, Connecticut. Sam had not seen her since the previous October and would not see her again until August, though he received occasional updates about her health. She was "comf[ortable] &

satisfied," he assured a friend. "Her natural sleep is restored to her after being absent & mislaid for more than a year. She drives about with the horse she got from Italy. She has her piano & is allowed to work a little." She also joined the local Episcopal Church of the Transfiguration, to Sam's surprise, though he professed to be pleased by her piety. "Dear heart, I am gladder of the spiritual peace which has come to you than I can ever tell you. I was a criminal towards your mother in that matter & can never forgive myself, but for her sake—& yours & mine—I shall try to do my very best never to treat you so." Lyon noted in her diary that "A great faith has come to Santissima ["most sainted," Lyon's nickname for Clara at the time]. She had to reach out to something in her grief. . . . The woman who hasn't that human protector has got to turn to the spiritual one, and Santissima turned. She has such a pure beautiful flame burning out of her soul, & so much soul & intellect—I am allowed now to write to her."[56]

In early July, Jean and Teresa Cherubini visited Clara at her cottage Edgewood. They had "delightful times," Sam reported to Rogers, so he advised Jean "to take her time and not hurry" back to Dublin. Sam was not cleared by Clara's doctor Edward Quintard to see her until early August. He left Dublin on August 9, planning to remain "a week or ten days," but he was stranded in Norfolk by an attack of gout until the twenty-eighth. He issued a statement to the press making light of his ailment: "This gout is of no consequence. I have had it for forty years and am outgrowing it." The joke went around that Christian Scientists regarded his attacks of gout a form of revenge for his apostasy. While abed in Norfolk, Sam bitterly complained, not for the first time, about the human condition in his notebook: "We lice die & are dust our king-lice the same; & we put up statues so that we may not forget how they looked when they were living lice; & we honor them reverently as becomes the louse kind." As he recuperated, he was visited by his eighty-three-year-old former Hartford neighbor Isabella Beecher Hooker, a summer resident of Norfolk. She "sat by my bed an hour, & talked with all her old brightness, & deep earnestness, & passion," Sam wrote Twichell.

> Her mission was to put me in the way of learning what spiritualism really is, in the hope that I might come to believe in it & then use my reputation in its service. Joe, (this is the privacy) she has for 15 years had spiritual communication with a miscarriage in heaven! (I have never come nearer to smiling in my life & escaped.) This miscarriage has a name—the name its parents had intended to call it by if it had not miscarried. In heaven it has borne that name for 30 years. It knows English & talks it fluently & takes as much interest in Nook Farm affairs as any miscarriage that ever lived. I wish I could see it with its halo on.

When Beecher got wind of Sam's mockery a week later, she disinvited him to return her call. "My thought was that being a psychic yourself," Hooker wrote him on August 25, "& understanding in part the laws of spirit intercourse you were ready to enter the whole realm under the guidance of competent teachers such as Mr. Hooker & myself. . . . But I see you are not ready for such humble entrance." As if in compensation for the snub, Sam was hosted at lunch by the Serbian-born Columbia University professor of physics Mihajlo Idvorski Pupin before his return to Dublin. There he again took to his bed for a three-week self-prescribed rest cure. The journey had been "murderous," he explained to Rogers. "I expected it to knock me out, & it did."[57]

Sam was again active in the fall 1905 municipal campaign in New York, albeit from a distance. Weeks before the canvass, he endorsed the Republican candidate William M. Ivins for mayor and the independent incumbent William Travers Jerome, who had first been elected to the office on the Fusion ticket led by Seth Low in 1901, for district attorney. In an essay for *Collier's Weekly*—which he did not sign lest he violate his contract with Harper—he expounded on the choice New Yorkers would make at the next balloting: they "will presently have an opportunity to elect or defeat some straight, clean, honest men, of the sterling Jerome stamp, and some of the Tammany kind." On November 3, Sam sent a dispatch to be read to the crowd at an Ivins rally in Cooper Union: "I believe in Ivins and Jerome and hope to be allowed to vote my whole strength for them." The following Tuesday, however, Ivins finished third in the mayoral race, behind the incumbent George B. McClellan and the upstart William Randolph Hearst, with only about twenty percent of the vote. Jerome was reelected with the support of both Democrats and mugwumps.[58]

Sam failed to appear in person at the Cooper Union rally because, for the first time since Livy's death, he was in Boston to "talk several times to invited gangs" or, as he put it to Rogers, "to fill various social engagements (with my jaw)" between October 21 and November 5—"no gate-money permitted & no newspaper-mention." He stayed most of the time with his friends the Pearmains at their home on Beacon Street. His first evening in the city he attended a concert of the Boston Symphony Orchestra featuring the Russian pianist Waldemar Lütschg performing Franz Liszt. On October 24 he spoke before an audience of women at the College Club in Back Bay, and the next afternoon he was accompanied by Alice Pearmain to a meeting of the Boston Authors' Club at the Cambridge home of Harvard classics professor J. H. Wright. Among the two hundred attendees were Richard Henry Dana,

Edward Everett Hale, Thomas Wentworth Higginson, William James, John T. Trowbridge, and Julia Ward Howe, who regaled the crowd with "a scrap of rhyme" in welcome of the guest of honor:

> Mark the gracious, welcome guest,
> Master of heroic jest;
> He who cheers man's dull abodes
> With the laughter of the gods;
> To the joyless ones of earth
> Sounds the reveille of mirth.
> Well we meet, to part with pain,
> But ne'er shall he and we be Twain.

Afterward, Howe recalled, "M. T. jumped upon a chair and made fun, some good, some middling, for some three quarters of an hour." The next evening he was the guest of honor at a meeting of the Round Table Club at the Beacon Street home of the surgeon John Bapst Blake, where he crossed paths with Higginson, Aldrich, and the old Concord transcendentalist Frank Sanborn, friend of Ralph Waldo Emerson, Henry David Thoreau, the Alcotts, and the abolitionist John Brown. The next several days he relaxed with the Aldriches at their Massachusetts farmhouse. His two-week respite in the Bay State was climaxed by a speech at the Twentieth Century Club the afternoon of November 4. Accompanied by Sumner Pearmain, one of its founders, Sam waxed eloquent on the dubious prospects for universal peace (it would occur only when "a real genius" invented a method of sucking "all the oxygen out of the atmosphere for eight minutes" and then "it will be permanent") and evangelizing the Chinese (there "were 82,000 pagans born every day in China" and the Christian missionaries there "were converting them at the rate of 2½ a day" so it will "take quite a while"). Sam wrote his daughters from Boston that he had been entertained by "many hosts in my time, but the Pearmains are the only perfect hosts I have known." He "could not have felt more entirely at home if I had been under my own roof." On his part, Sumner Pearmain told reporters afterward that entertaining Sam over the past two weeks had been "the most enjoyable" experience "of his life and "a continuous feast of intellectual delight."[59]

Around this time Sam also wrote a pair of anti-imperialist fables, one of them published posthumously, the other never published at all. In "The Fable of the Yellow Terror," a takeoff on Bernard Mandeville's *The Fable of the Bees* (1714), a race of aggressive butterflies conquers a race of stigmatized "yellow" or Asian bees. The imperial(ist) butterflies "sent missionaries to all the pagan insects to teach them how to be tranquil and unafraid on a deathbed, and then sent trader-bugs to make them long for the deathbed, and then followed up the trader-bugs with diplomat-bugs and undertaker-bugs to perfect the blessings of the conferred civilization and furnish the deathbed and charge for the funeral." They also export honey to the bees. Eventually, however, the bees revolt and retaliate for their subjugation. The fable ends when a "prominent butterfly" observes, "Maybe you ought to have let the Yellow Peril alone, as long as there wasn't any." Similarly, in "Journey to an Asterisk," an unpublished fragment omitted from "Captain Stormfield's Visit to Heaven," the narrator sails to a miniature world on an asteroid or asterisk where "little animals were having wars all the time and raising armies and building navies." One of these militaristic species invaded any "savage country that needed civilizing" and "divided it up among the several enlightened monarchs" who introduced "Bibles and bullets and taxes. And the way they did whoop-up Morals, and Patriotism, and Religion, and the Brotherhood of Man was noble to see."[60]

These anticolonial parables may serve as backdrop to Sam's "A Humane Word from Satan," a letter ostensibly written by the Archfiend and published in *Harper's Weekly* in April 1905. John D. Rockefeller had recently contributed $100,000 to the American Board of Commissioners for Foreign Missions, and a debate was raging over the morality of accepting such "tainted" funds. The Reverend Washington Gladden argued that because Rockefeller had obtained the money in "flagitious" ways, it should be refused, though Henry H. Rogers defended Rockefeller. In Sam's essay, Satan notes that "the American Board accepts contributions from me every year" and then asks rhetorically, "Why shouldn't it [welcome donations] from Mr. Rockefeller? In all the ages three-fourths of the support of the great charities has been conscience money," no less tainted in its own way. Less than a month later, Sam in his own voice offered the same rationale for accepting the donation: "I don't know how I would vote on the Rockefeller donation as a congregational minister," he wrote Twichell, "but speaking for my own unsanctified self I would say like this, if it is tainted money take it, by all means and ship it to China—no other kind can legitimately be used in the missionary business there, when the Aments are sent to dance to the Golden Rule and bully better men into adopting a civilization which is inferior to our own."[61]

Sam remained unrepentant, with Christian missionaries a target of his wrath, to the end of his life. The proselytizer's prey were foreign children. He beguiles them "to forsake their parents' religion & break their hearts," he chided Twichell.

> Would you be willing to have a Mohammedan missionary do that with your children or grandchildren? Would you be able to keep your temper if your

> own government forced you to let that Mohammedan work his will with those little chaps? You can't answer anything but No to those questions. Very well, it closes your mouth. You haven't a shadow of right to uphold & bid Godspeed to the Christian missionary who intrudes his depraved trade upon foreign peoples who do not want him. "Do unto others, etc." is a Christian sarcasm, as long as Christian missionaries exist. . . . To my mind the Christian missionary is easily the most criminal criminal that exists on the planet, & the lowest down in the scale of malefactors.

He urged Twichell to "repent, reform," and recall to the United States his "dear & sweet" daughter Harmony, a professional nurse who had volunteered for a medical mission to Turkey.[62]

Meanwhile, Sam effectively left Isabel Lyon in charge of supervising the household move from Dublin back to New York at the close of the summer in 1905. In fact, Lyon during the months after Livy's death and during Clara's year-long absence had become well-nigh indispensable to the Clemens clan. "I think a very great deal of Miss Lyon," Sam stressed to Clara soon after she arrived in Norfolk in June, and while he soon appointed his daughters "to arrange & publish my 'Letters' someday" because "I don't want it done by any outsider," he added that "Miss Lyon can do the work & do it well," and "take a tenth of the royalty." Lyon was given access to his papers and authorized to manage the family accounts. By the end of the summer, she had become a surrogate sister/daughter/spouse and gatekeeper to the throne. She "lived with us & was necessarily pervasive," Sam allowed, "for she was to all intents & purposes a member of the family. She sat at table & in the drawing-room when there was company & when there wasn't; our intimates became her intimates; they visited her & she visited them; of her own motion & by her own desire she became housekeeper." She joined Sam and Jean and most of the other locals at the social event of the summer on September 2: the wedding of Higginson's daughter Margaret, a recent graduate of Radcliffe, to James Dellinger Barney, a former football star at Harvard and recent graduate of the Harvard Medical School, at the local Unitarian Church. A hundred and forty miles away, Clara feared her role had been usurped by Lyon and advised her father from Norfolk that upon her return to the family she expected to be placed in charge of the house at 21 Fifth Avenue. "You're merely owner," she once told him, invoking the customary chain of command aboard a steamboat. "I'm the captain—the commander-in-chief." Sam replied on October 18 that he was pleased she would "run the ranch" and acceded to her request to "assume full and sole authority in the house. Require that all complains be brought to you, none to anyone else. Allow no one but yourself to scold or correct a servant. All this for Jean's sake and to keep her out of trouble" with the servants. Lyon, Jean, Katy Leary, and the rest of the staff left Dublin for New York on November 1, and as "we drove up to the house," Lyon wrote, "the light in Santa C[lara]'s room went down. In a minute her sweet black figure appeared in the doorway. I had not seen her for more than a year." Clara soon delivered an ultimatum: Unlike Katy Leary, Lyon could no longer reside in the same house as the family. Sam rescinded the order when he arrived five days later. In the interim, Leary counseled Lyon to watch her back because Clara "hates you and don't you forget it." In a show of confidence in his secretary, Sam took Lyon to the Produce Exchange Safety Vaults and made her his "deputy" on December 8.[63] The domestic disputes that scarred Sam's final years had only begun to fester.

CHAPTER 13

Pier 70

Before 70 we are merely respected at best and we have to behave ourselves all the time or we lose that asset. But after 70 we are respected, esteemed, admired, and revered and don't have to behave unless we want to.

—Samuel Clemens to Sir Henry Campbell-Bannerman, 6 September 1906

SAM WAS NEVER more in demand as a public speaker, bon vivant, and advocate for liberal causes than over the next several months. Or as the *New York Herald* remarked in the spring of 1906, "He was the most popular man in New York all winter." Upon his return to the United States in October 1900, in addition to announcing that he was an anti-imperialist, Sam had declared he was a dyed-in-the-wool mugwump: "I am a mugwump now. I shall be a mugwump until I die—and afterward. It is the only entirely respectable party that ever existed." Later asked to define a mugwump, he said, "He is a Republican who usually votes the Democratic ticket." And what about a Democrat who votes Republican? "He is an ordinary fool." By November 1905 Sam had begun to agitate for a permanent third party:

> It must be composed of men who are willing to give up all affiliations with either of the great parties. No man in it can have any political aspirations. He must not have any friends whom he wishes to push forward for political preferment. The sole reason for the existence of this new third party must be to elect the candidates of either the democratic or the republican party who are believed to be the best fitted for the office for which they are nominated.

Accompanied by George Harvey of Harper & Brothers ("because he always pays all the bills"), Sam railed to Washington on November 24 to lobby members of Congress for reformed copyright legislation and to discuss the carnage in the Congo, and while in the city he toured the Library of Congress, guided by the retired librarian Ainsworth Spofford; was honored with a dinner at the Willard Hotel marking his seventieth birthday, hosted by Harvey and attended by Secretary of State Elihu Root and Secretary of War William Howard Taft; and lunched at the White House on November 27 with President Roosevelt, First Lady Edith Roosevelt, Secretary of the Navy Charles Bonaparte, Attorney General William Henry Moody, and the newspaper editor John Temple Graves. According to Lyon, he thought the First Lady "charming—simple & without any shred of self-consciousness—a lovely woman" and he "liked the President" in a personal setting "as much as he always does. 'You can't help liking him for he is a magnetic creature, and he shows his teeth in his forceful smile, just as much as ever.'" In the afternoon he had "a private word with [the President] on a public matter," probably the genocide in the Congo. The same day, Sam issued his annual Thanksgiving mock proclamation:

> The servants of the [Russian] government in patriotic obedience to its commands have lately killed and wounded 50,000 Jews by unusual and unpleasant methods, butchering men and women with knife and bayonet; flinging them out of windows; saturating them with kerosene and setting fire to them; shutting them up in cellars and smothering them with smoke; drenching the children with boiling water; tearing other children asunder by methods of the Middle Ages. Doubtless, the most that He can be thankful for is that the carnage and suffering are not as bad as they might have been. . . . He has noticed that the political smell ascending from New York, Philadelphia, and sixty or seventy other municipalities has been modified a little—temporarily—and is doubtless thankful for that reprieve. He has observed that King Leopold's destruction of innocent life in the Congo is not as great this year as it was last, by as much as 100,000 victims, because of diminishing material.

Sam's sarcasm did not fall on deaf ears, but it provoked petulant replies. "It is apparent that old age has overtaken Mark Twain," the *Portland Oregonian* responded, for example. "His recent attempts to be funny have been pathetic enough, but his sacrilegious remarks anent Thanksgiving are positively pitiful. He will be 70 in a few days, but nowadays a man is hardly old at 70. Something is the matter with Clemens."[1]

Sam's seventieth birthday was formally celebrated on December 5, 1905, five days after the fact, at a dinner hosted by Harvey in the Red Room at Delmonico's. In truth, Sam had invited Harvey to plan the event two months earlier: "Old man, art meditating a feed Nov. 30? If you aren't, then get to work & meditate beer & sandwiches & good friends & a good time in a snug place & late hours there too." Rather than a modest feast of beer and sandwiches, however, Harvey sponsored a lavish "sky-scraping banquet" for 172 "immortals," as W. D. Howells called them, nearly half of them women, mostly writers of fiction, including George Ade, Henry Mills Alden, Irving Bacheller, John Burroughs, George Washington Cable, Dorothy Canfield,

Bliss Carmen, Andrew Carnegie, Willa Cather, Charles W. Chesnutt, Samuel Post Davis, Frederick Duneka, Finley Peter Dunne, Mary E. Wilkins Freeman, Richard Watson Gilder, Henry Harper, Julian Hawthorne, Howells, Brander Matthews, Frank Millet, Agnes Repplier, Kate Douglas Riggs, Henry H. Rogers, Ruth McEnery Stuart, Joseph Twichell, Carolyn Wells, and Owen Wister. Also present was Albert Bigelow Paine, Sam's future official biographer and literary executor, though he and Sam this night had time for only "a brief exchange of words." Harvey also invited members of Sam's family and Isabel Lyon, who bought a dress for the occasion with $50 Sam had given her. She seems to have misunderstood his motives, however. As Sam wrote Carnegie, Lyon "was there, by kindness of the Colonel, to watch over my daughter [Clara], who is not very well."[2]

Figure 14. Samuel Clemens's seventieth birthday dinner at Delmonico's, December 5, 1905. Left to right: Kate Douglas Riggs, Samuel Clemens, Joseph Twichell, Bliss Carmen, Ruth McEnery Stuart, Mary E. Wilkins Freeman, Henry Mills Alden, and Henry H. Rogers. Photograph by Joseph Byron, *Harper's Weekly*, December 23, 1905.

There have been few more distinguished gatherings of writers in the history of American letters than the assembly at Delmonico's that evening. Not only was it the apotheosis of Sam's career, it marked a passing of the baton from the postwar generation of Clemens and Howells to the early modernists represented by Cather and Chesnutt. Each attendee was presented with a half-life-sized bust of Sam—Carnegie enshrined his on a mantel in his house—and the dinner was preceded by music performed by a forty-piece orchestra from the Metropolitan Opera House. After a two-hour dinner, the postprandial speeches began about 10:00 p.m. amid the "glutting and guzzling." President Roosevelt had sent a congratulatory letter, concluding with the wish that Sam might "live long and year by year . . . add to the sum of admirable work that he has done". Among the speakers who followed were Bacheller, Cable, Carnegie, Gilder, Howells, Matthews, and Riggs. Burroughs, a nature writer and conservationist, groused later that "I did not care for" Cable or Carnegie and "Bacheller was a bore." He wondered how Sam could "accept favors" from Rogers, the oil baron. Even the "small plaster cast" of the honoree presented to all the guests was "not very good." Similarly, Samuel Post Davis, the owner and editor of the *Carson Appeal*, recalled that too many of the speakers "attempted to be funny because they thought the occasion required it. . . . It is sufficiently sad even to think of them."[3]

When Sam finally rose to the podium at about 2:00 a.m. to respond to the toasts and well wishes, he was greeted for several minutes with cheers. By all accounts, he then delivered an hour-long tour de force about how to survive to old age. "When I think of my first birthday and compare it with this celebration,—just a bare room; no one present but my mother and one other woman; no flowers, no wine, no cigars, no enthusiasm,—I am filled with indignation," he began. He joked about his tobacco habit: he had resolved "never to smoke more than one cigar at a time" and "never to smoke when asleep and never to refrain when awake." Matthews remarked that "nothing could have been better—that is to say, more characteristic—in its matter or in its method than what he said." The speech featured

> his customary exaggeration, of course, and not a little of his humorous distortion of fact. It was all about himself, which was entirely satisfactory to us, for he could not but be the topic of every speech. It was genial and friendly; and at the end it attained a graceful dignity which sat well upon him as he stood there facing us, with his "good gray head that all men knew." He closed by telling us there was one satisfaction in attaining the scriptural limit of years;—there is no longer any necessity for pleading a previous engagement when we prefer to stay at home. We need only reply, "Your invitation honors me and pleases me because you still keep me in your remembrance, but I am seventy, seventy, and would nestle in the chimney corner, and smoke my pipe, and read my book, and take my rest, wishing you well in all affection, and that

> when you in your turn shall arrive at pier No. 70, you may step aboard your waiting ship with a reconciled spirit, and lay your course toward the setting sun with a contented heart."

When he at last "ceased erupting, the enraptured company dispersed to the cloakroom and departed, full of good fare and good cheer" at almost three in the morning. Though Sam had the speech recorded on wax cylinders, they later melted in the heat where they were stored. Still, a text of the entire proceedings was published as a supplement to *Harper's Weekly* for December 23. Harvey was criticized for hosting "the kind of dinner that he did for Mr. Clemens" and exploiting the event to advertise the magazines he published, but Sam did not seem to mind. After all, he had suggested the revelry in the first place, and he wrote afterward to express his gratitude to his publisher: "O Harvey the Magnificent! little by little I am recovering from its emotions & its splendors—the most satisfying & spirit-exalting honor ever done me in all my 70 years, oh by 70 times 70! By George, nobody but you could have imagined & carried out that wonderful thing. I can't thank you adequately, dear uncle George, it is just impossible."[4]

After his summer in Dublin, Sam began to frequent the New York theaters. The evening of November 15, ten days after his return to the city, he attended a performance of Daniel Frohman's adaptation of James Barrie's *Peter Pan* at the Empire Theater on Broadway. He wrote Frohman the next day that he had been "interviewed this morning for a syndicate of 62 Western papers" and "closed the interview with the most outspoken praises of the play & said among other strong expression that it hadn't a defect." More to the point, what he told the interviewer was that *Peter Pan* "is a fairy play. There isn't a thing in it which could ever happen in real life. That is as it should be. It is consistently beautiful, sweet, clean, fascinating, satisfying, charming, and impossible from beginning to end. It breaks all the rules of fairyland, and the result is altogether contenting to the spirit." He soon befriended Maude Adams, who starred in the play, and over the weeks he invited a host of children to see it with him. As he wrote Adams, he believed that *Peter Pan* "is a great and refining and uplifting benefaction to this sordid and money-mad age and that the next best play on the boards is a long way behind it, so long as you play Peter. The next time I can spare an evening I am going to attend your performance again, check my practicability with my overcoat, and take a dive into the deep water of Barrie's play." Sam had much the same reaction to the opening-night production of *Hansel and Gretel*—a benefit for the Legal Aid Society of New York—when he saw it at the Metropolitan Opera House the evening of December 6. Adapted from the Brothers Grimm folktale, the *Märchenoper,* or fairy-tale opera, as the composer Engelbert Humperdinck called it, required no advertising, Sam thought, because "the chorus of that lovely masterpiece" was "so deep and satisfying" that "whoso has been under its spell once will come again."[5]

These stage productions, especially *Peter Pan,* served as a catalyst to Sam's recruitment of his aquarium of "angelfish," a club of prepubescent girls. "I collect pets: young girls—girls from ten to sixteen years old," he owned in his autobiography, "girls who are pretty and sweet and naïve and innocent—dear young creatures to whom life is a perfect joy and to whom it has brought no wounds, no bitterness, and few tears. My collection consists of gems of the first water." However bizarre his behavior may have been, no concrete evidence of either immoral or criminal conduct on his part has ever been documented. He "collected" the first of these ten or so girls, fifteen-year-old Gertrude Natkin, after attending a recital at Carnegie Hall by the German soprano Johanna Gadski the afternoon of December 26. As Lyon put it, Sam "was sweet to a little girl in brown who recognized him of course, and they exchanged affectionate salutations" and addresses. "Really he is bubbling over with a sweetness, and simpleness and loveliness which is irresistible." They wrote each other a total of thirty-five letters over the next five months—until Gertrude turned sixteen, when he dismissed her from his life because she had reached the age of consent and become sexually mature by law. In a March 1906 note he called her an "elf" and a week later admonished her, as he did all his angelfish, to stay forever young—or elfin like Peter Pan, "the Boy [played by a girl on stage] Who Would Not Grow Up." "Don't get any older—I can't have it," he pleaded. "Stay always just as you are—youth is the golden time." On April 8, her sixteenth birthday, he grumbled in a note to her, "Oh come, this won't do—you mustn't move along so fast, at this rate you will soon be a young lady and next you will be getting married. . . . *Sixteen*! Ah what has become of my little girl? I am almost afraid to send a blot [kiss], but I venture it. Bless your heart, it comes within an ace of being improper! Now, back you go to 14!—then there's no impropriety." That is, Sam was fully aware of the risks to propriety in maintaining such a relationship. Natkin replied sorrowfully, "Dear Grandpa, please don't love me any less because I am sixteen. . . . I shall always be your little Marjorie [his nickname for her] as long as you wish it." The same dynamic occurred in his preoccupation with eleven-year-old Dorothy Quick, another of the angelfish. "Dorothy is perfect, just as she is," Sam insisted. "Dorothy the child cannot be improved; let Dorothy the woman wait till the proper time comes." He regretted, too, that she "didn't see *Peter Pan*," which had long since closed on Broadway, "but you will see it yet."[6]

Sam was also in the audience at the Lyric Theater the evening of December 11, 1905, the opening night of Sarah Bernhardt's two-week New York run, for a performance of *La Sorcière*, adapted by Victorien Sardou from a history of witchcraft by Jules Michelet. A day or two later, Sam was invited by producers Sam and Lee Shubert to appear with the divine Sarah at a benefit for the victims of anti-Jewish pogroms in Russia at the Casino Theater the afternoon of December 18, and he accepted with alacrity. He was incensed by the practice of ethnic cleansing. "For two years now, the ultra-Christian Government of Russia has been officially ordering and conducting massacres of its Jewish subjects," Sam averred in his autobiographical dictation. "These massacres have been so frequent that we have become almost indifferent to them. . . . The modern Russian Christian and his Czar have advanced to an extravagance of bloody and bestial atrocity undreamed of by their crude brethren of three hundred and thirty-five years ago." He was ready to share the stage in an effort to redress such barbarism. Before the curtain, the actress and Sam, "those rare geniuses" as Lyon called them, chatted, and Sam later told a reporter that he was delighted "to meet Sarah Bernhardt hand to hand, heart to heart. She is the youngest person I ever saw, except myself." Bernhardt played the lead in G. Constant Lounsbury's one-act *L'Escarpolette*, and Sam, who received a three-minute ovation when he walked onstage, spoke for ten minutes. The event raised about $2,500, forwarded by the businessman and philanthropist Jacob Schiff to Jewish groups in the Russian empire.[7]

At the urging of its president, Dan Beard, the Society of Illustrators honored Sam at its monthly meeting in the banquet room of the Aldine Association the evening of December 21. Not only did such artists as Charles Dana Gibson, E. W. Kemble, and Frederic Remington attend but the society also invited a number of special guests, including Andrew Carnegie and publisher Arthur H. Scribner. The odd couple of Beard and Carnegie, one a parlor socialist and the other a captain of industry, sat together at the head table, though according to the Associated Press report of the event Beard began the postprandial talks "with a warning to trust magnates present that they were attending a meeting of a trade union—a union, however, of men who believed in the measure of profit from labor that comes from individual merit." Carnegie replied in his "witty speech" that "he would like to join this young set." As usual, Sam arrived around 10:00 p.m., after the tables were cleared but in time to hear the speeches. When he rose to address the assembly, he was suddenly interrupted "by a medieval fanfare of trumpets" whereupon a young girl attired like Joan of Arc in "a magnificent suit of glistening white armor" appeared and presented him with a bay wreath, which Beard placed on Sam's "frosty old head." Apparently familiar with Sam's infatuation with schoolgirls, Beard had insisted that the society "get the prettiest girl in New York to act the part of the Maid of Orleans." He thought this ritual "would bring a roar of applause" from the audience. Instead, he recalled, "there was a sudden hush, no applause, only a deep and awed silence." Sam "stared at the girl as if he were gazing at a materialized spirit. . . . He stood open-mouthed, transfixed by the vision," before shouting "in that nasal, vibrating, half-comical twang," "Now there is an illustration—a pure and beautiful young woman!"[8]

Though a founding member of the Players, Sam was expelled from the club for nonpayment of dues while he was living in Europe. He was, of course, predictably outraged by this act by an overzealous bookkeeper. The club had "never had anybody in that position there who was intellectually above the grade of an idiot," he complained to Poultney Bigelow. To make amends and entice him back to the fold, some of the members organized a dinner in his honor the evening of January 3, 1906. To simplify matters, he was inducted as "an honorary life member without dues or duties" before an audience that included Frohman, Gilder, Matthews, Millet, and Albert Bigelow Paine. Sam returned home after midnight, when Lyon jotted this note in her daily reminder: "It was a great night . . . because he had stayed away so long."[9]

The event was memorable for another reason, too: it marked the start of Paine's long association with Sam and the Clemenses. The two men had been slightly acquainted for five years, but this night after the dinner Paine, the thirty-four-year-old author of a well-regarded biography of Thomas Nast, chatted with Sam and received his permission to call on him at his home. On Saturday morning, January 6, over cigars at 21 Fifth Avenue, Paine offered his services as Sam's official biographer, and against all odds, Sam accepted. He agreed to dictate to a stenographer, assigned Paine a room where he might live and work, and gave him a key to the house.[10]

Paine returned on January 9 with "a capable stenographer" he had hired—Josephine Hobby, who had previously worked for *Century*, Charles Dudley Warner, and Mary Mapes Dodge—and Sam began the first of about 250 dictations, totaling over half a million words over the next three-plus years, often prompted by questions from his biographer. "He dictated that morning some matters connected with the history of the Comstock mine; then he drifted back to his childhood, returning again to the more modern period, and closed, I think, with some comments on current affairs," Paine remembered.

> It was absorbingly interesting; his quaint, unhurried fashion of speech, the unconscious movement of his hands, the play of his features as his fancies and phrases passed in mental review and were accepted or waved aside. We were watching one of the great literary creators of his time in the very process of his architecture. We constituted about the most select audience in the world enjoying what was, likely enough, its most remarkable entertainment. When he turned at last and inquired the time we were all amazed that two hours and more had slipped away. "And how much I have enjoyed it!" he said. "It is the ideal plan for this kind of work. Narrative writing is always disappointing. The moment you pick up a pen you begin to lose the spontaneity of the personal relation, which contains the very essence of interest. With shorthand dictation one can talk as if he were at his own dinner-table—always a most inspiring place. I expect to dictate all the rest of my life, if you good people are willing to come and listen to it.

Lyon also listened to Sam's monologue and "kept notes of the talk—but I didn't keep notes of his wonderful rising color and his brilliant eyes as he warmed to the subject of the Big Bonanza Mine and its fall to nothing." Three days later, Lyon remarked that "the dictating continues, and Mr. Clemens finds it 'enchanting & an inspiration.' He said, 'I would like to have relays of shorthanders, & keep them at it for six hours on a stretch.'" On January 19, she added that Paine was "'a find.' He is doing the very thing that I have longed to have some worshipping creature do with Mr. Clemens's papers & letters & clippings & autobiographical matter. He is bringing the mess into order—is reducing the great chaos that I have longed to be able to touch, but have never found time for." Sam's dictations "continued steadily from week to week, and always with increasing charm," according to Paine. "We never knew what he was going to talk about, and it was seldom that he knew until the moment of beginning. . . . It was always delightful, and always amusing, tragic, or instructive, and it was likely to be one of these at one instant, and another the next. I felt myself the most fortunate biographer in the world." Paine soon adopted Lyon's nickname for Sam: "Oh, he's the *King*—he's the *King* and it's so glorious to know he is crowned." On his part, Sam composed a standard letter introducing

Paine as "my biographer and particular friend, who is seeking information concerning me for use in his book," in effect granting Paine carte blanche to interview people from his past.[11]

Always intrigued by new technologies, Sam made news merely by touring the auto show at Madison Square Garden on January 16. He was a guest of Roy D. Chapin, a publicist and salesman for Oldsmobile, and announced that "if he were not something like a thousand years old he would drive a machine." He added that he dictated some four thousand words of his autobiography daily and found it "a hard day's work. If I could talk as your salesman talks, talk would be worth money to me." He also met the auto manufacturer A. A. Pope, who chauffeured him on a demonstration ride.[12] But he resisted the temptation to buy or even drive a 'mobile.

To celebrate the twenty-fifth anniversary of the founding of Tuskegee Institute, Booker T. Washington hosted a fundraiser at Carnegie Hall on January 22, 1906. Sam had agreed in mid-December 1905 to address the audience and initially planned to speak about "that thief and assassin, Leopold II King of the Belgians." When he learned that the United States had never ratified the treaty that would have required it to supervise the authority granted to Leopold, he reconsidered his topic and considered canceling his appearance, but Washington pleaded with him to honor his commitment. "It would injure our meeting and disappoint our friends as well as place me in embarrassing position to have you withdraw since your name has already been extensively advertised," Washington telegraphed, and Sam relented: "All right, but don't commit me to talk upon any particular subject." Washington agreed: "Of course we shall expect you to speak in any manner that you see fit." The day before his appearance, Sam was eager to deliver "a devilish speech—full of hypocrisy & sin"—on behalf of a worthwhile charity.[13]

On January 22, despite inclement weather, the hall was filled with three thousand people, including Nicholas Murray Butler, Hobby, Paine, Carl Schurz, and Twichell, with Joseph Choate, Moncure Conway, Gilder, and Sam seated on the stage. In his comments, Sam praised Tuskegee for teaching its students "Christian morals," though he distinguished between "Christian private morals," the "highest and best of all systems," and "Christian public morals," which he declared an oxymoron. "During 363 days in the year the American citizen is true to his Christian private morals, and keeps undefiled the nation's character at its best and highest," he explained; "then in the other two days of the year he leaves his Christian private morals at home, and carries his Christian public morals to the tax office and the polls, and does the best he can to damage and undo his whole year's faithful and righteous work." Isabel Lyon, for one, was impressed: "His speech was fine, he hit the voters, taxpaying citizens, a fearless rap & the whole audience winced and visibly too."[14]

Figure 15. Samuel Clemens seated behind Booker T. Washington at a benefit for the Tuskegee Institute at Carnegie Hall, January 22, 1906. Photograph by Underwood & Underwood, *New York Tribune*, January 28, 1906.

Over the next several weeks Sam made a succession of high-profile public appearances. He traveled to Washington to speak the evening of January 27 at the Gridiron Club dinner at the Willard Hotel with President Roosevelt and Secretaries Root and Taft, with Harvey in the audience. He sat in a draft, however, and refused to move to another seat and lose his view of "pretty women in beautiful garments." While in the city, he and Harvey also lobbied members of both houses of Congress on behalf of revised copyright, met Vice President Charles Fairbanks, hosted an informal reception for congressmen, and twice lunched with Speaker of the House Joe Cannon and other members. "We lunched and lied together," Sam told reporters afterward. "We would take a bit of pie and then indulge in a few flights of imagination." He returned to New York on January 30 "tired, jaded, & with a cold brewing." A week later, he spoke at the second annual dinner of the

Manhattan Dickens Fellowship marking Charles Dickens's ninety-fourth birthday at the New York Press Club. In mid-February he addressed the members of the Ends of the Earth Club, including George Dewey, Arthur Conan Doyle, Rudyard Kipling, and Robert E. Peary, at its annual dinner at the Savoy Hotel. Less than a week later, he was the guest of honor at a Columbia University tea attended by about nine hundred students hosted by Alice Dewey and Marie Boas, wives of Columbia professors John Dewey and Franz Boas. On February 26 he served as a pallbearer at the funeral in Hartford for his former coachman Patrick McAleer, who had died of cancer. While in the city he hosted a luncheon at the Hartford Club for "eleven of my oldest friends," including Charles Clark, E. P. Parker, Charles Perkins, and Twichell, where he praised McAleer without stint—"I have never known a finer human being"—ignoring the fact that he had once fired him for drunkenness. In the intervals between these engagements he found time to raise money to restore Lincoln's birthplace in Kentucky as a trustee of the Lincoln Farm Association and to attend a performance of Benjamin Chapin's *Lincoln* at the Liberty Theatre. He was so impressed by the production that he was blurbed in its later advertisements: "Mr. Chapin's impersonation of the powerful and tender Lincoln is little short of a miracle."[15]

Sam did not, however, find time to aid and comfort Jean, whose condition had worsened over the months. As Clara's health improved in Norfolk, Jean's had deteriorated in Dublin, and Lyon, who considered Sam's youngest daughter her "sacred charge," began to chart the frequency of her seizures. On October 20, 1905, she noted that "Jean is in bad shape. Her malady seems to be increasing in violence." Edward Quintard, the family doctor, who believed that epilepsy was a mental illness, also feared that Jean posed a physical threat and warned Lyon "never to let Jean get between her and the door." Sam was obviously at loose ends to know what to do or how to help. The same day Lyon jotted in her diary that Jean was "in bad shape"—and the day before he left Dublin to spend two weeks in Boston with friends, entrusting his daughter's care to the household staff—Sam wrote Clara that he always kept "in mind that [Jean] is heavily afflicted by that unearned, undeserved & hellish disease, & is not strictly responsible for her disposition & her acts when she is under its influence (if there is ever a time when she is really free from its influence—which is doubtful). She has had 2 attacks today." On November 26, three days after Thanksgiving, Jean again suffered cluster seizures and physically assaulted Katy Leary for the first time. On January 5, 1906, Lyon noted that Jean's "whole physical condition is at a low ebb," and "the child calls . . . for great waves of love from those of us who care." Three weeks later, on January 27, the same day Sam spoke before the Gridiron Club in Washington, Jean attacked Katy again, striking her in the face, the type of violence Lyon had long feared. The secretary described "the wave of passion that swept over [Jean] as being that of an insane person. She knew she couldn't stop. [S]he had to strike & she said that she wanted to kill & was sorry she hadn't. [T]o her mind it doesn't seem right not to finish any job you have begun & she had wanted to kill Katy." At Sam's request, Susan Crane arrived a day or two later to help care for Jean, but Sam remained in Washington for his luncheons with congressmen. Three days after his return, Lyon "had a very plain talk" with Sam "about Jean's condition." She had discussed the issue with Quintard, who had referred her to Dr. Frederick Peterson, a neurologist and professor of psychiatry at Columbia University. Sam's reaction was predictable: "The dreadfulness of it all swept over him as I knew it would," Lyon wrote, "and with that fiercest of all his looks in his face, he blazed out against the swindle of life & the treachery of a God that can create disease & misery & crime, create things that men would be condemned for creating—that men would be ashamed to create." Three days later, on February 5, Lyon—not Sam, though apparently with his consent—escorted Jean to meet Peterson, who agreed to take charge of her case.[16]

Sam continued to deliver talks for charity throughout the spring of 1906. In the afternoon of March 4, he spoke at a benefit for the West Side Y.M.C.A. at the Majestic Theater, an event that sparked a brief street riot. Several hundred would-be attendees milled around Columbus Circle because the doors remained locked until almost time for the lecture to begin. The police were called to control the crowd, and in the melee three men were injured and a plate-glass window smashed. Sam discussed the fracas from the stage, advising the audience to "assert your citizenship. . . . The police are created by you. They are citizens and you share their responsibilities as citizens. If the police fail you, then assert yourself as a citizen, and do those duties which they have neglected." Three weeks later, after an investigation, the police captain in charge when the disturbance occurred was transferred to another precinct. Lyon, who no doubt entered the theater by a stage door, was blissfully unaware of the ruckus. She simply mentioned in her diary that Sam's talk "was lovely, & strong, & brave & instructive & humorous—no one else can combine all those qualities with the charm he possesses."[17]

Over the next month Sam appeared four times on behalf of women's higher education and once at a fundraiser for the blind. On March 7 he spoke at Barnard College, where he enjoyed a "pleasant time with those lassies." After all, as he remarked afterward, "Girls are charming creatures. . . . I shall have to be twice seventy years old before I change my mind as to that." In truth, his age had long since begun to tell. Hamlin Garland at the time thought Sam "looked old and sluggish and congested, his purplish face and bushy yellow-white hair making him a picturesque figure." At lunch with Garland on March 13 "he drank more than he should and ate more than he should. He is old and his work is nearly done." On March 29, in the office of its honorary vice president, he chaired a meeting of the New York Society for Promoting the Interests of the Blind in the ballroom of the Waldorf-Astoria. Before an audience of about fifteen hundred, Sam pleaded for donations to the cause and read a letter from Helen Keller, who was too ill to attend. Lyon thought the appeal "beautifully & bewitchingly done." The event raised about $15,000 for the cause; Sam bragged he had "a very good time there"; and the *Buffalo News* credited Sam with the success of the fundraiser: "He is more than ever golden mouthed." But Waldo Frank remembered the occasion differently in 1919. At the age of fifteen, he had heard Sam speak to the crowd, which "snouted it, guzzled it, roared with delight" at his "ungainly humor." Mistaking Sam's deadpan humor for indifference, Frank admitted he "hated this noble-looking fool." On April 2, Sam bantered at a benefit for the Vassar College Students' Aid Society at the Hudson Theater in New York and afterward "held a reception on the stage for an hour or two" when he greeted students and signed their programs. The event raised over $1,000 for scholarships, and Sam was rewarded for his role. "I was hoping somebody would want to kiss me for my mother," he allowed, "but didn't dare suggest it myself" until one of the students volunteered, and "I did then what I could to make it contagious and succeeded." He received "a kiss every time he wrote his autograph," one paper mused, and "the last heard of the old man he was sending out for more pens." The next afternoon, he addressed an audience of about five hundred at the house of the Women's University Club on Madison Square North. After delivering his remarks, he was reportedly "wreathed about with girls and as happy as a king." He thought most of the women "young and lovely, untouched by care, unfaded by age." One "sweet creature," he said, "wanted to whisper in my ear." She "raised her dainty form on tip-toe, lifting herself with a grip of her velvet hands on my shoulders, and put her lips to my ear and said, 'How do you like being the belle of New York?'" Sam pretended to be embarrassed but, as he admitted later, he was actually thrilled. "I have labored for the public good for thirty-five or forty years," he announced, and "I propose to work for my personal contentment the rest of the time." Then on April 7 he related a brief story at the annual luncheon of the Smith College Club of New York at the

Hotel Astor and declared in the presence of three hundred guests that he was near "seventh heaven," so delighted by the "circumambient loveliness" that he "should like to be elected to the office of Belle of New York" and "have an opportunity of being present at all such lovely affairs as this." He also admitted in his autobiographical dictation at the time that he had "the college-girl habit."[18]

Between March 7 and 10, 1906, nearly four years after President Roosevelt announced a formal end to the insurgency in the Philippines, a division of the U.S. army under the command of "that slimy creature" Major General Leonard Wood "pacified" the Moro region by massacring eight to nine hundred natives of the Moro tribe, including women and children, trapped in an extinct volcano crater on Jolo Island. "They were mere naked savages," Sam noted in his autobiography, "yet there is a sort of pathos about it when that word children falls under your eye, for it always brings before us our perfectest symbol of innocence and helplessness. . . . And if they are frightened and crying and in trouble, our pity goes out to them by natural impulse. We see a picture. We see small forms. We see the terrified faces. We see the tears. We see the small hands clinging in supplication to the mother." Oblivious to the sadism of the slaughter, Theodore Roosevelt cabled Wood to "congratulate you and the officers and men of your command upon the brilliant feat of arms wherein you and they so well upheld the honor of the American flag." Sam scorned Roosevelt's bellicosity—or his fecklessness. "Not a word of what he said came out of his heart," Sam believed. The president "knew perfectly well that to pen" the "helpless and weaponless" Muslim Moros in a hole and butcher them "from a safe position on the heights above was no brilliant feat of arms. . . . He knew perfectly well that our uniformed assassins had not upheld the honor of the American flag but had done as they have been doing continuously for eight years in the Philippines—that is to say, they had dishonored it." Apparently hearing that Sam was disgusted with the Moro massacre, Herbert Welsh, vice president of the Anti-Imperialist League, invited him to become more active in the movement, though Sam demurred. He dictated the outlines of his answer to Lyon: "Interests are full to the brim—cannot find the time to add another one, they poison my life. The woes of the wronged & the unfortunate poison my life & make it so undesirable that pretty often I wish I were 90 instead of 70." Still, as late as December 1907 Sam reiterated his belief in an interview, despite his earlier disclaimers, that American policy in the Philippines was "a stain upon our flag that can never be effaced." The "true citizenship," the true patriotism, he insisted, "is to protect the flag from dishonor—to make it the emblem of a nation that is known to all nations as true and honest and honorable."[19]

Despite Roosevelt's reputation as a "man with the bark on," Sam had long privately criticized TR's "whitewash & slumgullion," his swagger and conceit. "I find him destitute of morals & not respectworthy," he wrote Twichell in February 1905. "It is plain that where his political self and his party self are concerned he has nothing resembling a conscience" and was ever ready "to kick the Constitution into the back yard whenever it gets in his way." Whenever TR "smells a vote" he was "not only willing but eager to buy it, give extravagant rates for it & pay the bill—not out of his own pocket or the party's, but out of the nation's, by cold pillage. As per Order 78 [which granted pensions to all retired soldiers over the age of sixty] & the stealing of the Indian trust funds. A man who will filch trust-money from a pauper Indian to buy votes with is pretty low down." Roosevelt "the man is sane" but Roosevelt the "statesman & politician is insane & irresponsible," the Robespierre of a reign of error, he asserted, and he reiterated the point in his autobiographical dictation: "I think the President is clearly insane in several ways, and insanest upon war and its supreme glories." Not only was he "manifestly brought up on dime-novels," he was "the Tom Sawyer of the political world of the twentieth century; always showing off; always hunting a chance to show off; in his frenzied imagination the Great Republic is a vast Barnum circus with him for a clown and the whole world for an audience; he would go to Halifax for half a chance to show off, and he would go to hell for a whole one." He was "all bluster, all pow-wow, all gas. He hasn't any real courage, he has no staying power," he insisted. In a word, Sam considered Roosevelt "far and away the worst President we have ever had" and "the most formidable disaster that has befallen the country since the Civil War." He did not publicize such views, as he had during the Boxer Rebellion in China and Spanish-American War. Nor did he openly criticize Wood the way he had excoriated Frederick Funston in 1902. He expressed his opinion about the slaughter of the Moro tribe, the general who ordered it, and the president who praised it only in his autobiography and to a few private friends. Instead, he pigeonholed an article about Wood the "Rooseveltian flunky" because "I'm not as free to make enemies now as I was" before he signed his fat contract with Harper & Brothers. "I mustn't make any except when citizenship makes a plain duty of it—& the lousy Wood case doesn't reach up to that. But I shan't destroy it, I'll keep it for my own occasional reading when I am feeling vicious & need a tonic." Nor was Sam pacified by the prospect of the succession to the presidency of William Howard Taft. He told Lyon early in 1906 that he thought Taft was "Roosevelt's miscarriage preserved in alcohol." Nor did he revise that opinion during the campaign of 1908, dismissing Taft as TR's "serf" in his autobiography and adjuring Jean that "no sane person wants Mr. Roosevelt's shadow elected."[20] No doubt Sam would have been appalled by the emergence of his idealized "third party" in 1912 when Roosevelt founded the Bull Moose progressives to oppose Taft's reelection and split the Republican vote.

As early as November 1895, while on tour in New Zealand, Sam rationalized the self-censorship practiced by some professional authors. Why was the world "not full of books that scoff at the pitiful world and the useless universe and violent, contemptible human race"? Or more: "Why don't *I* write such a book? Because I have a family. There is no other reason." Though he risked his popularity by publishing controversial anti-imperialist essays early in the new century, he was reticent to imperil his (family) income by alienating his audience. In late June 1905, a day or two after laying aside the manuscript of "3,000 Years Among the Microbes," Sam admitted to Twichell that he was compelled to write the story because "there was bile in me" and he "had to empty it. . . . If I tried to empty it into the North American Review— oh, well, I couldn't afford the risk." He had "a family to support & I can't afford this kind of dissipation." His opinions had not changed; if anything, he had become more critical of the government. What had changed was his willingness to jeopardize the income his daughters would receive from his writings after his death. To avoid "trouble," he planned to utter his controversial views "from the grave. There is free speech there & no harm to the family." Lyon quoted Sam late in his career to the effect that "we are all slaves in one degree or another" and added that Sam "is a slave" because he had to self-censor; otherwise, "it would be bad for his children." By 1907 Sam was reconciled to the arrangement. "So long as I continue to dig $70,000 a year out of the Harpers on magazine stuff & old copyrights you will always find me acting respectably. Even to the verge of good grammar." He evaded the strictures of the literary market by anonymous publication (as with *What Is Man?*) or posthumous publication ("No. 44, The Mysterious Stranger"). He also adopted a variation on this strategy near the end of his career when he had virtually retired from writing for print. He planned to vent his spleen in letters but not mail them: "I will fire the profanities at Rogers, the indecencies at Howells, the theologies at Twichell."[21]

But a fiasco also erupted in the midst of the clamor. Sam had vehemently opposed Russian tyranny since hearing George Kennan discuss the oppression of serfs and reading Kennan's articles on the subject in 1888. He signed a petition circulated by the Friends of Russian Freedom in June 1891 and hosted the Russian revolutionary Stepniak in his Hartford home. He noted in his journal in September 1891 that "the first gospel of all monarchies should be rebellion; the second should be Rebellion; and the third and all gospels and the only gospel in any monarchy should be Rebellion against Church and State." He arraigned Russian tyranny in his novel *The American Claimant* (1892) and condemned the Treaty of Portsmouth in 1905 because, he believed, it ended the Russo-Japanese War before a climactic Russian defeat that would have sparked a revolution and abolished the monarchy. He had long argued privately that "the first order of business in Russia" should be "to make a bonfire of the Russian throne & fry the Czar." He ridiculed Nicholas II after Bloody Sunday in "The Czar's Soliloquy" and spoke at a fundraiser on behalf of the victims of pogroms. Sam owned a copy of Maxim Gorky's novel *Orlóff and His Wife* (1901), and Gorky publicly thanked Sam in 1905 for signing a petition calling for his release from the Peter and Paul Fortress in St. Petersburg, where he had been briefly imprisoned for fomenting revolution.[22]

So when Gorky landed in New York on April 10, 1906, to raise money for the faltering Russian revolution, not only did the stars seem aligned in his favor but Sam was sympathetic to his cause. Gorky traveled with his common-law wife Maria Andreeva, an actress, and his protégé Zinovy Peshkov, later a distinguished French diplomat and general in the Free French army. On March 27, Sam's "young and delightfulish" near neighbor Charlotte Teller Johnson introduced him to the Russian revolutionary Nikolai Tchaikovsky, brother of the composer and Gorky's advance man. Tchaikovsky "is grizzled, and shows age—as to exteriors—but he has a Vesuvius, inside, which is a strong and active volcano yet," Sam stated in his autobiographical dictation three days later. "He is so full of belief in the ultimate and almost immediate triumph of the revolution and the destruction of the fiendish autocracy that he almost made me believe and hope with him." Sam sent him a letter soon released to the public and copied in newspapers across the country, including the *New York Tribune, New York Herald, New York Times,* New Haven *Journal and Courier, Hartford Courant, Springfield Republican, Los Angeles Times, San Francisco Examiner, Chicago Tribune, Minneapolis Journal, Indianapolis Star, Buffalo Commercial, Washington Post,* and *Washington Star:*

> My sympathies are with the Russian revolution, of course. It goes without saying. I hope you will succeed, and now that I have talked with you, I take heart and believe it will. Government by falsified promises, by lies, by treacheries, and by the butcher-knife for the aggrandizement of a single family of drones and its idle and vicious kin has been borne quite long enough in Russia, I should think, and it is to be hoped that the roused nation, now rising in

> its strength, will presently put an end to it and set up the republic in its place. Some of us, even of the white headed, may live to see the blessed day when Czars and Grand Dukes will be as scarce there as I trust they are in heaven.

On April 9 Sam lunched with his friend Norman Hapgood, editor of *Collier's Weekly*, "to meet the Russian revolutionists" Tchaikovsky and the journalist Ivan Narodny, who in turn invited him to meet Gorky two days later. Narodny, with a fifty-thousand-ruble bounty on his head, had been in hiding in New York for five weeks. Yet incongruously, Sam dined with the oil mogul Rogers the very next evening, April 10, and then attended a world's championship billiard tournament at Madison Square Garden concert hall featuring Willy Hoppe. "I like to remember those old nights," Hoppe reminisced twenty years later, when Sam "with his halo of white hair sat grandly in an arm chair near the table and watched me play."[23]

The next night Sam dined with Gorky and a cadre of thirteen at the cooperative home known simply as "A Club" at 3 Fifth Avenue, about a block from his house. The others included the editor of Hearst's *New York American*, Arthur Brisbane; novelist and *Jewish Daily Forward* editor Abraham Cahan; Finley Peter Dunne; Howells; Narodny; Peshkov; novelist David Graham Phillips; Tchaikovsky; muckraking journalist Ernest Poole; and the so-called millionaire socialist Gaylord Wilshire.

Sam and Gorky recognized each other even before they were introduced, but neither understood the other's language, so "they simply grasped hands and held on more than a minute." They sat together at the table with

Figure 16. A dinner in honor of Maxim Gorky, New York City, April 12, 1906. Left to right: Zinovy Peshkov, Maxim Gorky, Samuel Clemens, and Ivan Narodny. Courtesy of the Mark Twain Papers and Project, Bancroft Library, University of California–Berkeley, PH03508.

Narodny and Peshhov at their sides as translators. "I am most emphatically in sympathy with the movement now on foot in Russia to make that country free," Sam declared to the group. "I am certain that it will be successful, as it deserves to be." On his part, Gorky replied in Russian that he was glad to meet Mark Twain, whose fame was worldwide, and he believed the revolutionaries could depend on Americans for support. According to Poole, Gorky "held us spellbound by the stories which in his deep low voice he told through Narodny." The company also adopted a manifesto pledging to liberate Russia and announced the appointment of a committee, including Sam, Howells, S. S. McClure, and Jane Addams of Hull House in Chicago, to spearhead the appeal for money. The campaign would begin with a fundraising dinner in about two weeks. "We are going to offer Gorky the literary hospitality of the country," Sam told reporters, by hosting a meal for him "with only authors and literary men present. We want to do it in proper style, and will have authors not only from New York, but from Chicago, and we may have some literary geniuses from Indiana, where I believe they breed 'em."[24]

Sam devoted the next few days to his new mission. He and Howells visited Gorky in his suite at the Hotel Belleclaire on Broadway near Central Park, and he wrote another letter to be read before three thousand people during a socialist rally at Grand Central Palace on April 15. In an interview with the *New York Times* he also justified his support for Gorky and the Russian peasantry in terms reminiscent of his defense of violent revolution in *A Connecticut Yankee*:

> We were quite willing to accept France's assistance when we were in the throes of our Revolution & we have always been grateful for that assistance. It is our turn now to pay that debt of gratitude by helping another oppressed people in its struggle for liberty. . . . Inasmuch as we conducted our own Revolution with guns & the sword, our mouths are closed against preaching gentler methods to other oppressed nations. Revolutions are achieved by blood & carnage alone.

To all appearances, Sam was committed to the task. As he told an interviewer for the New York *World*, "Now I'm a revolutionist . . . by birth, breeding, principle, and everything else. I love all revolutions no matter where or when they start." Privately, however, he harbored reservations. On March 30, nearly two weeks before meeting Gorky, he reiterated in his dictation his fear that the Treaty of Portsmouth "had postponed the Russian nation's imminent liberation from its age-long chains indefinitely—probably for centuries" and that Roosevelt by negotiating the treaty "had given the Russian revolution its death-blow, and that I am of that opinion yet." Certainly Gorky's errand became more complicated within a week of his arrival. On April 11, the New York *Evening World* printed a picture of Gorky and his wife. The following Sunday, April 15, the *New York Times* printed a picture of Gorky and the woman who traveled with him to the United States. Trouble is, the women in the pictures were not the same person.[25]

In fact, the New York *Evening World* had broken the story the day before. To sabotage his fundraising tour, the Russian consulate in New York had apparently leaked the news to the paper that Gorky was traveling with a woman not his wife. The *Evening World*, too, had an axe to grind: Gorky had signed a contract with Brisbane to write exclusively for the rival *New York American* while he was in the United States. Gorky responded that the *Evening World* "kicked up a fuss in the American gutter press apropos of my bigamy." In fact, he had divorced Yekaterina Peshkova, his first wife, in Finland in 1903, but their divorce was not recognized in Russia. He had then married Andreeva before a notary, but their union was not considered legal in the Motherland. During the ensuing scandal, Gorky and Andreeva were evicted from the Hotel Belleclaire and refused accommodations in the Lafayette-Brevoort Hotel and the Rhinelander Apartments. They finally accepted the private hospitality of Wilshire and the socialist writer Leroy Scott. In a statement to the press, Gorky exonerated "the American people" for "this disagreeable act. . . . My respect for them does not allow me to suspect that they lack so much courtesy in their treatment of women. I think that this dirt is conspired by the friends of the Russian government." He refused to surrender to the malicious gossip and resolved to fight "against the morality of the petty bourgeois," but the damage had been done. The White House abruptly withdrew an invitation to Gorky to meet the president. H. G. Wells, who was visiting the United States at the time, recalled that the scandal exploded "like a summer thunderstorm. At one moment Gorky was in an immense sunshine, a plenipotentiary from oppression to liberty; at the next was being almost literally pelted through the streets. . . . This change happened in the course of twenty-four hours. On one day Gorky was at the zenith; on the next he had been swept from the world. To me it was astounding—it was terrifying." The reason Gorky was visiting the United States—"the massacres, the chaos of cruelty and blundering, the tyranny, the women outraged, the children tortured and slain"—was forgotten "amidst this riot of personalities." Gorky had compounded his problems, moreover, by sending a telegram to ideological allies at the same time the scandal was erupting. He cabled William Haywood and Charles Moyer, jailed leaders of the International Workers of the World, who had been implicated (falsely) in the murder of the governor of Idaho, as follows: "Greetings to you, my brother Socialists. Courage! The day of justice and deliverance for the oppressed of all the world is at hand." Eugene V. Debs thought Gorky's "real offense" was siding with radical unionists, and Poole shared this view: sending the "telegram just at that time was bound to make trouble." In addition, true or not, the story soon circulated that Gorky's bill for wine in the hotel had been over $100 per day, most extravagant for a "champion of poverty-stricken Russia." Sam was so troubled by these turns of events that he admitted he "would rather die a dog's death than live" them over again.[26]

In recording the "cloud-burst of calamities" that poured over this weekend, Sam remembered that of course the revelation of "the Gorky secret . . . made a sensation." Under the circumstances reporters were as welcome as head lice at 21 Fifth Avenue. Sam was asked by one of them whether he was "a socialist," to which he reiterated a stance he had first taken over twenty years earlier: "No—for it is a *party*. I have never belonged to a party nor to a church. A person cannot be free & belong to either. The party & the church dictate to him; I would rather do my dictating for myself. By nature & training I am a mugwump." Isabel Lyon also spent the day intercepting journalists and went to bed with a sore throat. The "King" was initially uncertain how to react to the news. He recognized that Gorky's "efficiency as a persuader" had been "impaired," but he "would not say that his usefulness has been destroyed." In addition, he was unsure "what effect this publication will have" on his own role in the work of the organizing committee, though he wanted at first to stay the course "until everybody else deserts." Howells resigned immediately from the committee, though he conceded Gorky had been treated with "cruel ignominy." But, he rationalized, "in America it is not the convention for men to live openly in hotels with women who are not their wives. Gorky had violated this convention and he had to pay the penalty; and concerning the destruction of his efficiency as an emissary of the revolution, his blunder was worse than a crime." Poole thought that "if only old Clemens would remain as chairman and come out strong in a public appeal, we felt that his great reputation might even then turn back the tide. He would think it over, he said." Paine recalled Sam remarking at this moment that "American public opinion is a delicate fabric. It shrivels like the webs of morning at the lightest touch." Beard remembered that Sam was heartbroken, lamenting, "Dan, that man should have had a guardian. It's pitiful, pitiful that he was allowed to come over here as he did. Someone should have posted him, someone should have instructed him, in place of allowing him to make a blunder like that. Why, Dan, . . . the man might just as well have appeared in public in his shirttail."[27]

In any event, within two days he concluded that Gorky's mission was likely doomed. He resigned from the committee, the literary dinner was canceled, and he released another statement to the press:

> Laws can be evaded and punishment escaped, but an openly transgressed custom brings sure punishment. The penalty may be unfair, unrighteous, illogical, and a cruelty; no matter, it will be inflicted just the same. Certainly, then, there can be but one wise thing for a visiting stranger to do—find out what the country's customs are and refrain from offending against them. The efforts which have been made in Gorky's justification are entitled to all respect because of the magnanimity of the motive back of them, but I think that the ink was wasted. Custom is custom: it is built of brass, boiler-iron, granite; facts, seasonings, arguments have no more effect upon it than the idle winds have upon Gibraltar.

Three weeks later he still hoped that somehow Gorky might "rectify" his "blunder" because he should have known "that a country's laws are written upon paper & that its customs are engraved upon brass. One may play with the one, but not with the other." He commended an essay in the *Independent* by the Columbia sociologist Franklin H. Giddings in defense of Gorky and Andreeva, but nevertheless conceded that Gorky was "a puzzle & a vexation to me," as he wrote Charlotte Teller Johnson. "He came on a great mission, a majestic mission, the succor of an abused & suffering vast nation," but "he hits the public in the face with his hat & then holds it out for contributions. It is not ludicrous, it is pitiful." He wanted nothing more than to get "the revolution out of my system" and wash his hands of the whole affair. Jane Addams told Sam later that she regretted his failure to support Gorky, and he "waxed warm upon the subject," according to Lyon. In his defense, he contended that because "Gorky came over here as a diplomat" to raise money, "not as an individual or as a literary man," he could not afford to violate the proprieties. In truth, moreover, Sam continued to support the Friends of Russian Freedom and at least pay lip service to the cause of the Russian revolution. In December 1907 he signed a petition to Premier Pyotr Stolypin of Russia urging leniency for Nikolai Tchaikovsky and Catherine Breshkovsky, both of whom had recently been jailed for their political activity, and in April 1908 he reiterated his appeal. The following September he and George Kennan protested the extradition, demanded by the Russian government, of the dissident Jan Pauren. As late as November 1909 he signed a petition demanding a public trial of Tchaikovsky. But in the fallout from the scandal, Sam's reputation on the political left was indelibly stained. In truth, Sam never was a radical leftist. His nephew Jervis Langdon remembered he was once asked what he "really thought of Socialism," and he replied that he could not "believe in it—I can't even hope for it—I know too much about human nature." Even twenty years later, the socialist Upton Sinclair recalled that "in times of stress some of us would go to him for help, for a word of sympathy or backing, and always this strange thing was noticed: he was full of understanding and would agree with everything we said; yes, he was one of us. But when we asked for a public action, a declaration, he was not there." A case in point, according to Sinclair: the planned literary dinner in Gorky's honor to be sponsored by Sam and Howells was canceled when "the storm of scandal broke and these two great ones of American letters turned tail and fled to cover."[28]

Predictably, the imbroglio discouraged Gorky's friends and allies in Russia. The Twentieth Century, formerly the Russ, a group of twenty-five leftist authors including Evgeny Chirikov and Aleksandr Kuprin, passed a resolution critical of Gorky's treatment in the United States, impeached the "Pharisees and fat swine" for "their hypocritical adherence to conventionalities," and specifically blamed Sam for failing to protect him. "The American authors represented by Mark Twain have offended Russian authors in the person of Maxim Gorky and Russian womanhood in the person of Mme Andreeva by interfering with their private affairs. We Russian authors are amazed at such disregard of the principles of privacy recognized by every civilized country, and hereby express our deep indignation. . . . Every book of Mark Twain, whom Russians previously have esteemed, hereafter will be branded as shameful hypocrisy because he joined" Gorky's persecutors. In the end "the miscellaneously married Russian," as one U.S. paper called him, raised only about $10,000—only 1 percent of his goal of $1 million during his seven-month tour of the United States.[29]

Gorky was predictably disgusted and embittered by his experience and wrote a series of six essays critical of the country. Their tone may be inferred from four of their titles: "The Mob," "The City of the Yellow Devil," "The City of Mammon," and "Realm of Boredom." Americans "were just the same spitting, vulgar people that Charles Dickens found," he reportedly cabled his followers. But he never held Sam personally responsible for the debacle. "One does not have to attack the esteemed Mark Twain," he asserted. "He is an excellent man. In this case it occurred that Twain is one of those people who is unclear as to the meaning of facts." Five years later, Gorky urged his ex-wife to read *The American Claimant,* with its indictment of czarist oppression, to their son because, he insisted, "It's a useful and wholesome piece." He also planned eventually to return to the United States now that he better appreciated the customs of the country. He simply had not realized "that a free and democratic country like America" could "be so puritanical." He had "misunderstood America and America misunderstood me." He still cherished the memory of his dinner with Sam and others at the A Club. "I have rarely been more enthusiastic than at that dinner, when Mark Twain in his fiery toast denounced the czar and we drank to Free Russia."[30]

Soon even more sensational news pushed the Gorky story off the front page: an earthquake in San Francisco early in the morning of April 18 and a subsequent fire that killed hundreds of people, destroyed most of the city, and left upward of three hundred thousand homeless. Coincidentally, Sam had agreed a month earlier to speak the evening of April 19 at a fundraiser to build a monument to Robert Fulton. Carnegie Hall was "packed jam-full," Katy Leary recalled, and "that great audience just stood right up on its feet when Mr. Clemens walked onto the platform." Sam concluded his address with "an appeal on behalf of that multitude, of that pathetic army of fathers, mothers, and helpless children, sheltered and happy two days ago, now wandering hopeless, forlorn and homeless—victims of immeasurable disaster—I say I beg of you in your heart and with your purses to remember San Francisco, the smitten city." Two days later, with the city still ablaze, he chaired a hastily organized relief meeting at the Casino. When he left the city in 1866, San Francisco had boasted a population of about 120,000; speaking "in a tear-choked voice," he observed that "there are two and one-half times as many people now without homes as there were in all the city at that time." He was confident that city would be rebuilt, "that the energy and hopeful spirit of California will make a new Colossus in the West," but "what we want to do now is to send food and money." He pleaded for donations to the Salvation Army because it was "the best means I know of to do this work. They are of the poor and they know how to reach the poor. I have seen their work all over the world—always good." Sam also read a telegram at the gathering he later sent to the San Francisco mayor: "San Francisco shall rise more beautiful than ever. We glory in the bravery of her citizens and have unbounded belief in the ability and determination to survive this great catastrophe. The spirit of your fathers still lives in their children and their children's children. The generous and spontaneous aid of the whole country is with you." Finally, he led the crowd in a cheer for the first responders in the city, the firefighters, soldiers, sailors, and especially the doctors. "I don't like physicians' visits myself," he allowed, "but at times like this I believe in giving even this kind of a Satan his due." In the evening of April 24, Sam also appeared at an exhibition billiard tournament in Madison Square concert hall for the relief fund. He spoke briefly and then announced he would attempt a four-cushion carrom, a next-to-impossible trick shot. "He sent the cue ball flying around the table," the *New York Tribune* reported, "and then sat down with the remark, 'Well, I thought I could do it, but I can't.'" The aside "brought down the house."[31]

In the summer of 1906, Sam joined a "People's Lobby" to rally support for liberal causes in Congress. "I am in cordial sympathy with the movement," he wrote in accepting the invitation, "& am as glad to be cordially willing to have my name used." He enlisted in the ranks along with Louis Brandeis, Seth Low, John Mitchell of the United Mine Workers, Lincoln Steffens, University of California president Benjamin Ide Wheeler, and William Allen White.[32] While in the end little came of the nascent organization, it may fairly be considered a precursor of such modern watchdog groups as Public Citizen and Common Cause.

Sam, Jean, and the household staff returned to Dublin for the summer of '06, but the Copley Greene family occupied their residence that season, so Sam rented the Upton House "in the law and science quarter" of the resort. With views "equal to that of Switzerland," the cottage stood "on the edge of a beautiful beech forest some two or three miles from Dublin, just under Monadnock—a good way up the slope." Sam was eager to escape New York because "I have led a turmoilsome life this winter and am tired to the bone," he wrote Thomas Bailey Aldrich. But they were so isolated in the New Hampshire mountains that Sam despised "the House of Mirth" or "Lodge of Sorrow" or "Wuthering Heights," as he variously christened it. "I was never so dismally situated in my life before," he complained. "It is so different from last year!" "We have not a single neighbor who is a neighbor," though he had friends across the region. He took every opportunity to vacation from his holiday, including week-long or longer cruises aboard the *Kanawha* in late July, mid-August, and mid-September. After arriving on May 15, he began a siege of work on his autobiography. He joked that he had "thought of fifteen hundred or two thousand incidents of my life which I am ashamed of, but I have not gotten one of them to consent to go on paper yet." In mid-June he wrote Clara, who had returned to Norfolk, that he dictated "2 hours in the morning, about 4 days per week; and read & revise an hour or two, afternoons, with Miss Lyon for audience. I do nothing, after that, but cripple time—I can't really kill it." He estimated that since January 9 he had "dictated 75 hours in 80 days & loafed 75 days. I've added 60,000 words in the month that I've been here, which indicates that I've dictated during 20 days of that time—40 hours, at an average of 1,500 words an hour." He was more convinced than ever that he had devised a new literary form. "It ranks with the steam engine, the printing press and the electric telegraph," he crowed to Rogers. "I'm the only person who has ever found out the right way to build an autobiography."[33]

He composed it for posterity, he always claimed. Because he initially embargoed its publication until a century after his death, he was free to tell the truth as he saw it "from the grave" without equivocation. It became a type of Proustian project that antedated Proust. "Tomorrow I mean to dictate a chapter which will get my heirs & assigns burnt alive if they venture to print it this side of 2006 A.D.," he alerted Howells on June 17. "There'll be lots of such chapters if I live 3 or 4 years longer. The edition of A.D. 2006 will make a stir when it comes out. I shall be hovering around taking notice, along with other dead pals." The narrative was "perfectly outrageous, in spots, but that's nothing." He predicted "it's going to be worse by & by if I live beyond my appointed date." For four successive days he dictated "some fearful things" that "had been festering for years" and finally "got them out of my system." More to the point, Sam disparaged some fundamental Christian dogmas, particularly the doctrine of the Immaculate Conception; argued that the Bible, rather than the inspired and inerrant Word of God, contained a host of falsehoods; and declared that if there is a hell, "it is nearly dead certain that nobody is going to escape it." Both Paine and Josephine Hobby "expected lightning to strike that room," according to Lyon. Hobby asked her later "what I thought of Mr. Clemens's views & I told her I was used to them & that I'd been an unbeliever for so many years that to me his views of God were a literary criticism & nothing more. My own belief in the eternal isn't weakened any by his terrific words—neither is his own, I think." All the while Sam grew increasingly impatient with Hobby, who compulsively "corrected" his dic(ta)tion. On June 20, during his week of "hell fired" reflections on religion, her trespasses "passed the limit of his endurance," Lyon acknowledged. "Through tightly shut teeth he damned" the editorial interventions of "that idiot" and "devilish woman" and declared that he would "like someone to take her out and have her scalped & gutted." Ironically, Hobby became an immediate audience for a book that supposedly told uncompromising truth because it was narrated from beyond the grave, but the presence of a stenographer in the room, as he admitted, chastened the tone and tenor of his vulgarities.[34]

He was troubled most of the summer, too, by "the Harper treacheries," particularly by the publication of a new four-volume edition of *Mark Twain's Library of Humor* neither authorized nor approved by him. Duneka tried to pass it off as merely a reprint of the earlier single-volume *Library* issued by

Webster and Company in 1888. He offered Sam a piddling royalty of three percent on sales because the original plates had been melted, and Harper would need to reset the work, and Sam agreed, assuming that Duneka accurately represented the project. When the new edition appeared, however, Sam discovered to his dismay that it was "not the one which was compiled by me" but a new work "in whose compilation I have had no part," as he wrote Duneka on June 4. Nor was it a cheap reprint, as Duneka had described it, "with no money in it" for either him or the press, "but is cloth-bound & higher priced than my own book." That is, Harper was exploiting his name for profit. He had

> only consented that you should resurrect my old book, issue a trifling edition in a cheap form, & make ostensible publication to 'save the copyright' from piracy by a Western publisher. This astonishing violation of a plain & simple agreement is most unsatisfactory to me. I would not have consented to a *real* republication of the book which I myself compiled & was responsible for, neither would I have dreamed of allowing anyone to put my name to a book in whose compilation I took no part. I must ask you—in fact I must require you—to take this book out of print immediately & destroy the plates.

He also demanded a twenty percent royalty "on all copies of the book sold between its issue & its suppression" as well as a check for $600 for the failure of the firm to advertise his other books in the January, March, and June issues of the Harper magazines, as their contract required. Two days later, he notified Rogers that "Duneka must arrange a satisfactory compromise with me or I will enjoin that book & sue for damages for unauthorized use of my name for the acquiring of money under false pretenses." At the very least, he planned to publicly repudiate "the book called The Library of Humor." He belatedly realized that "Duneka, that Jesuit," his "secret enemy," "more fool than knave," had conspired against him "from the very beginning" of his contract. "Duneka has defeated several legitimate projects of mine," he carped to Rogers. "His conduct in the 'Library of Humor' matter convicts him of being not merely a thief, but a particularly low-down sneak-thief. I desire his scalp." In truth, Duneka was as duplicitous as Sam suspected. According to Elizabeth Jordan, Duneka "loved and vastly admired" Sam but was "horrified" that Harvey had signed him to an exclusive and expensive contract. "Whenever Clemens lets me know he's ready to write something for us," Duneka told Jordan, "I go to see him and encourage him. After I have encouraged him for a day or two he can't write anything for months! I've saved Harpers thousands and thousands of dollars that way." Sam was so disturbed by Duneka's underhanded conduct, he considered severing his contract with the Harpers and defecting to McClure, Phillips and Company. He entertained an offer from S. S. McClure in early July 1906 to syndicate brief excerpts from his memoirs for $1,000 per installment. Sam had sent him some excerpts from the manuscript, and McClure replied on July 2 that "all are wonderful, but the chapters about the dear dear child [Susy] are the finest I have ever read in literature. I wept & loved & suffered & enjoyed." He wanted to publish "this wonderful thing" in his magazine. Rather than declining on the grounds that he was contractually obligated to the Harpers, Sam temporized by replying that he might "accept your offer, but I can't tell about that yet."[35]

In early July, he railed to New York to consult with Rogers and Rogers's lawyers, another respite from his dull routine in Dublin. "I spend the days in the Standard Oil [building] and the lawyer's office," he wrote Jean, "and my nights on board the yacht where it is cool and noiseless. At 6 p.m. (or 5) we go aboard and drop down about ten miles and anchor out in the open. We come up to East 23d Street in the morning and go ashore right after breakfast." Sam readily allowed at the time that Rogers's "time is worth several thousand dollars an hour, and I have had almost daily use of it for thirteen years; he has not charged me anything for it, therefore I stand morally indebted to him in the sum of several millions of dollars." Booked to address the Associated Press dinner at the Waldorf-Astoria in September, he initially planned to wield "cudgels for Standard Oil" against the muckrakers. For whatever reason, he changed his mind, but a trace of his undelivered remarks appears in a letter to the editor of the *New York Times* he drafted later as a joke but never sent. In the wake of efforts to prevent Standard Oil from forcing rebates from carriers on freight costs, he wondered "what kind of a goddam govment this is that discriminates between two common carriers & makes a goddam railroad charge everybody equal & lets a goddam man charge any goddam price he wants to for his goddam opera box."[36]

Rogers's help—to say nothing about the bookkeeping of Katherine Harrison and the intervention of Rogers's lawyers—was indispensable in squaring Sam's accounts. Sam reported to Lyon from New York in July 1906 that Duneka was "frying in the fire which he prepared for himself & is a very humble & suffering sinner. His sufferings are not going to end just yet. His lawyer & mind were anxious to bring him & me together for a talk, but I objected to intercourse with his grade of criminal." Harvey, loath to lose his star contributor, returned from Europe in mid-July and settled the dispute. "We straightened out our snarl in five minutes," Sam wrote Clara on August 3, because Harvey sweetened the pot. He told Sam he planned "to turn the North American Review into a *fortnightly*" and "make a great & valuable periodical of it. He was always icily indifferent to the Autobiography before but thought he would like to look at it now so I told him to come up. He arrived 3 days ago & has now carefully read close upon a hundred thousand words of it (there are 250,000). He says it is the 'greatest book of the age' & has in it 'the finest literature.' He has done some wonderful editing; for he has selected 5 installments." The individual chapters were satisfactory stand-alone essays "without altering a word. At 10,000 words a month we shall place about 110,000 or 120,000 words before the public in 12 months," Sam estimated. In fact, Harvey published twenty-five installments in the *Review* between September 1906 and December 1907, totaling about a hundred thousand words, for which Sam was paid $30,000. He fully expected his complete, posthumously published autobiography to be "admired a good many centuries" and that several generations of his heirs would receive royalties on it.[37]

Originally designed to be a portrait gallery of his contemporaries, however, the memoir gradually morphed into a ham-handed attempt to settle old scores and manage or massage his public image, though the serialized version mostly omitted his ad hominem attacks. Still, Julius Chambers admitted in the *Brooklyn Eagle* that he was shocked by the first installment of Sam's autobiography in the *Review*. "It is witty enough in places," he conceded, "but the bitterness shown by the author toward the late John T. Raymond mars the effect of the whole rambling composition. The article would be like an after-dinner talk were it not for the contemptuous way in which Raymond is described." Sam had accused the actor, who had played Colonel Sellers in the stage adaptation of *The Gilded Age*, of a number of character faults. The New York *Evening Post* protested after a few chapters that the autobiography "grows more irresponsible as it proceeds" and that Sam was "a fatalist" who "believes the American star is going the way of all previous republics." On the other hand, both the *New York Times* ("fresh, original humor") and the *Boston Transcript* ("Mark Twain at his best . . . as if he had deliberately saved up for us some of his choicest stories for the last") commended Sam's life storytelling. Charles Warren Stoddard considered what "the dear old rogue" wrote about him in the autobiography "both funny and sweet. I think no one ever said sweeter things of me." Helen Keller gushed that she "lately had several chapters of your autobiography read to me. I need hardly tell you with what delighted fingers I listened to them." In chapters 4 to 6, published in October and November 1906, Sam chronicled events early in his marriage, and Keller, who never met either Livy or Susy, wrote him that "you have made me love your dear wife and daughter as if I had indeed held their hands."[38]

Sam earmarked income from the serialization of his autobiography for construction of a house on a seventy-five-acre farm near West Redding, Connecticut, sixty miles or ninety minutes by train from Grand Central Station. He bought the land in March 1906 for $2,000 upon the recommendation of Paine, who had recently purchased adjoining property there. He initially budgeted about $20,000 to build the house, to be designed by John Mead Howells. "You & John Howells can draw . . . up to $15,000" from the bank, he advised Clara in early August, and "then if you find you *must*, you can draw out $5,000 or $6,000 more of it." (He elsewhere in the same letter allowed that the family income "for the next 12 months" from all sources "ought to be $70,000 or $80,000.") Young Howells dined with the family on August 13 and, according to Lyon, "we talked over the plans for the new Redding house. J. H. has good ideas & high ideals." In particular, he planned the house to resemble an Italian villa complete with a loggia and pergola. The next day, Clara, Jean, and John Howells traveled to the property and chose the building site atop "a hill with countryside already planted by nature so that it resembles an Italian garden. There are twenty-three cedar trees all about where the house will be and quantities of bay-bushes." By the end of August, the price Sam was willing to pay had escalated. "If the new house hasn't spaciousness we don't want it." He wanted "a room of my own that would be quiet, a billiard room big enough to play in without jabbing the cues into the wall, and a living room forty by twenty feet" for entertaining and the orchestrelle. "John must build" it "for $25,000 or $30,000," he told Clara. "You will find he can do it." In mid-January 1907 he approved the higher figure. As he told Lyon, the autobiography "*must* pay for the Redding house" and he was willing to devote his entire $30,000 payment for the excerpts of his memoirs in the *Review* toward its construction. He tentatively named it "Autobiography House" because the money from the serialization was to pay for it. Three weeks later, Jean noted in her diary that "the house is to be built as promptly as possible & at a cost of $30,000" but "it won't be absolutely completed for that price." Like the mounting cost of the Hartford mansion over thirty years earlier, the expense of building the villa outside Redding gradually grew. Including the purchase of about 173 acres of additional land, its final price was about $60,000. Asked later if the house was built within budget, Sam joked that half of it was.[39]

Recalling all too vividly the inconveniences the family suffered during the building of the Farmington Avenue house in Hartford, he preferred to be involved as little as possible in the planning, construction, and furnishing of the house in Redding. "I didn't want any of the bother of building," he told an interviewer. "I had enough of that in Hartford when we built a $20,000 house on a $10,000 lot at a cost of $155,000." He never visited the Redding site before he occupied the house; he was "not willing to discuss the plans nor look at the drawings"; he offered no advice or instructions; he would pay the bills and nothing more until the house was finished, and then he would move there. His friends were astounded, Lyon conceded, "to hear him answer 'I don't know' to every question they ask about the house or the property." He insisted "he wouldn't move in till the cats had had their breakfasts and was purrin' on the hearth," Katy Leary remembered. He signed a contract with the builder on May 20, 1907, and then informed Clara and Lyon "to tell him nothing until the house was built & furnished. Then he would go & see it." John Howells, Lyon, and Paine broke ground on the building on May 23, each of them digging a shovelful of earth at the site and then pouring whisky into the hole. Lyon by default supervised the construction and interior decoration of the project over the next many months for no more thanks than the promise of "a strip of land in Redding to build me there a little house" of her own. "Oh, I must be good—monotonously good," she jotted in her journal.[40]

Sam was particularly incensed by the cowardice Roosevelt and others displayed in the so-called Brownsville affair. In mid-August 1906, after two white men were shot, one of them fatally, in Brownsville, Texas, black soldiers from nearby Fort Brown were accused of mayhem and murder. No soldier confessed to the crimes, and no physical evidence except spent military gunshells—suspected to have been planted—was ever produced to support the charges. Nevertheless, an inquiry by the army inspector general based on the eyewitness testimony of some white residents concluded that some unidentified buffalo soldiers were guilty, and Roosevelt ordered 167 men from the fort discharged dishonorably for engaging in a conspiracy of silence. Jean Clemens, for one, was among those who objected to this gross miscarriage of justice. "I think that Roosevelt is a beast and an impertinent bundle of conceit" for smearing so many men because "six or seven may be guilty!" she wrote in her diary. "And I don't think that the investigation made was at all thorough or in any way just." Paine told her that Sam felt just as she did, so she had "a good backing." Publicly, however, Sam was not so forthcoming. "Before I could express an opinion on the subject," he told a reporter in early December 1906, "I should have to study the facts and have a knowledge of military law and custom and civil law, which I do not possess." Eighteen months later, in his autobiographical dictation, he was more candid. He was convinced by then that some "negro soldiers" were responsible for the shooting. But Roosevelt's reputation among southerners had suffered after he dined with Booker T. Washington in the White House in 1901, and, Sam believed, in litigating the Brownsville affair he seized an opportunity to "get himself back into Southern favor" and "instantly made himself as splendidly popular in the South as Alexander VI is in hell. It was the Brownsville incident that gave him his chance." Unable to condemn any of the individual soldiers, Roosevelt "did the next best thing; he convicted the entire command himself, without evidence and without excuse, and dismissed them from the army, adding those malignant and cowardly words, 'without honor.'" If only Sam had said so aloud at the time. The injustice was not "corrected" until 1972, when the federal government issued honorable discharge papers to the heirs of the soldiers, all but one of whom had since died.[41]

Jean's health continued to deteriorate during the spring and summer of 1906. She suffered at least thirty-two seizures between May and October 1906 and was prevented by her epilepsy from joining the other young adults in the neighborhood on hikes to Monadnock and other activities. Worse yet, her antisocial behavior became more pronounced; she "was insolent to her father" and "called Mr. Clemens an old sinner." In September, Lyon thought Jean's disease was worsening by the day, and she confided to her journal that "it isn't safe for me to be alone with her. She could easily lapse into the violence the doctors fear." Sam agreed that Jean "has to have at her elbow an indisputable authority" and that her epilepsy "made her say and do ungentle things." More than once Lyon prohibited her from leaving the house because "she was far too ill" and risked injury or even death if she suffered a seizure away from home. The twenty-six-year-old Jean resented the interference, of course. Gerry Brush, the eighteen-year-old son of the artist George de Forest Brush, visited her on September 29, and Lyon "forbad him to go out walking" with Jean, who "was rabid" and confided to her diary that Lyon was "absolutely & utterly infuriating. . . . She is not my governess & has no right whatsoever to dictate to me in the way she does." Her "ways are terribly irritating to me these days. She is eternally namby-pamby."[42]

Jean yearned to marry, despite the common assumption that epileptics should not bear children lest their offspring inherit the disease. She harbored few illusions about her prospects for happiness under the circumstances.

> Why must I live on aimlessly, with nothing to do, utterly useless, all my life? I who long for the love and companionship that only a man can give, and that man a husband. The affection of friendship between man & woman does not suffice; & of course the love between two women cannot even be considered in the problem of this hunger. Am I never to know what love means because I am an epileptic and shouldn't marry if I had the chance? I seem never to be

> attractive to men. Is that also entirely due to my disease? And if a man that I could love loved me would it really be an actual wrong for me to marry him, because of the possibility of the children inheriting my malady? Will I have to go on indefinitely leading this empty, cheerless life without aim or real interest?

"The older I grow—the nearer & nearer to old-maidhood—I get more & more anxious to marry," she mused. "I know perfectly well that while my illness flourishes I ought not to think of such a thing." Clara believed, too, as Livy had, "that I must never marry." She earned a little money as an artisan and a translator, but she expected to be dependent on her father's estate for a livelihood the rest of her life. The prospect of living with Clara—"we aren't especially sympathetic"—was "perfectly hideous." By late summer 1906, at Frederick Peterson's suggestion after she suffered several seizures, she agreed to submit to a regimen of treatment at Hillbourne Farms in Katonah, New York, a sanitarium in Westchester County, fifty miles north of the city, that specialized in the care (or perhaps more accurately the warehousing) of affluent patients with epilepsy and other "mental" or "nervous disorders" such as alcoholism.[43]

The "treatment," such as it was, was designed to "wear the disease out" by requiring the convalescent to observe a strict routine. Jean agreed to lead "as monotonous and healthy a life as is physically possible—out in the country." She did not "suppose that I shall be very happy in such a place," but "if the result can be at all good I shall be grateful." Sam, Clara, and Lyon all acquiesced in her decision. From all indications, that is, Lyon was not a prime mover in institutionalizing Jean. She simply shared in the unanimous decision of Jean's father, sister, and doctors, though her concurrence is more fully documented than theirs, leaving the impression that she was the driving force. On the contrary, Lyon assured Jean that the facility was not "a rest-cure establishment & that I wouldn't be forbidden to correspond with friends. I should be kept outdoors a good deal—driving & walking—because I would not be a regular invalid, merely a person needing a fixed and unchanged mode of life." Still, when Jean, accompanied by Clara, left on October 25 for "a totally strange place," she tried her "hardest not to cry before them, but as the time of departure began to approach I found it growing more and more difficult to restrain myself, especially when Clara began to cry, too, then it was really hopeless. Poor little Father seemed to feel badly, too, and the whole business was perfectly *horrible* to me." Lyon too thought it "heart stretching to have her go & to see her go." When Clara returned from Katonah two days later she was "much depressed over the place and the great pathos of the situation." Sam tried to put the best face possible on the arrangement, writing Jean on October 29 that he was glad she was "pleased with Katonah; you will be sure to improve there." He visited her a week later—one of only three trips he is known to have made to Katonah during the fifteen months she was a patient there, even though the sanitarium was only about ninety minutes away—and was crestfallen by her "pathetic exile and captivity."[44]

In fact, Jean hated Hillbourne Farms from the start, even though Sam paid extra for her to receive preferential courtesies. Between March 1907 and January 1908, her expenses averaged $274 a month, over five times the advertised minimum rate, plus another $51 in incidentals. The recreation, such as it was, consisted of croquet; bowling; board and card games; dancing; knitting; skiing, skating, and sledding in the winter; boating and canoeing in the spring and summer; tetherball; medicine ball; fishing; gardening; lawn tennis; birding; and squash, "provided I did not go at it violently." She indulged her love for animals—"I always could get on better with an animal than I could with a person," she once wrote in her diary—and in December 1906 she protested the slaughter of songbirds by Italian immigrant farmers near the sanitarium in a letter printed in the *New York Tribune*. She was expected to take a near-freezing bath every morning, even in winter. Edward A. Sharp, the owner and administrator of the health resort, was a dictatorial or patriarchal type who even arranged the seating of his patients at the dining table. He enforced a number of dietary restrictions—no doughnuts or griddle cakes because "they were fried in lard and could affect my condition," no salt or eggs, no more than three cups of tea per week and only then with the amount of sugar monitored. Wherever else he spent money, Sharp economized in the kitchen: Jean complained on one occasion about her "atrocious supper" of soup, sardines, and toast and on another that she failed to "see how I can exist much longer on the fare I get. The soufflé was like bread last night, the mutton at lunch tough & today's beefsteak was like felt & I ate nothing." Sharp forbade men and women from playing cards together behind closed doors, and neither was Jean was allowed to ride a horse, though she might drive a carriage so long as she was not accompanied by a man. Sharp likewise denied Jean permission to visit her family at Christmas. "I had often felt that it would be a relief" to Sam and Clara "to have me out of the way," she wrote in her diary with more than a twinge of self-pity, "because I often caused trouble by being unmanageable when I was ill. . . . I don't for a minute believe that I was sent out here for any such reason, but since it is better for me to be here it at the same time must be a relief to them. Also, the idea that they miss me is absurd. . . . It seems a heartless thing to say, but now that I am accustomed to the place, I don't really miss either of them." She eventually distinguished between Sharp's rules and his therapy: "I can say but little good of the place," but of the medical treatment she received there, "I cannot say enough," especially after, in a classic case of transference, she became infatuated with one of her doctors. "I don't in the least hope to win him, fond as I am growing of him," she confided to her diary, "but I can't help wishing that if he is engaged I didn't have to be thrown with him so incessantly as I am."[45]

Soon after Jean was confined in Katonah, Sam confessed that he had lost his enthusiasm for osteopathy, or at least for osteopaths who offered false hopes for her cure. A bill to legalize the practice of osteopathy was reintroduced in the New York State Assembly in February 1907, and George J. Helmer solicited Sam's support of the law. He replied that he had devoted "2 or 3 days of time" in 1901 to testifying in Albany. He "did for the cause once what [he] wouldn't have done for any other cause for 10000 [dollars]—Didn't do any good & doesn't care to repeat that experience." S. S. McClure similarly solicited "a word about osteopathy" from Sam for publication in his magazine to "give a little upward boost to the good cause." Sam again responded that "for various reasons (& indignations) the subject does not interest me."[46]

On September 22, 1906, Clara debuted professionally in the United States with a solo concert at the Eldridge Gymnasium in Norfolk. She devoted the proceeds from her recital to the purchase of a stained-glass window in Livy's honor installed in the local Episcopal Church of the Transfiguration, where she had worshipped during her rest cure in the city. Though she "dreads to have me present," Sam wrote Mary Rogers, Henry Rogers's daughter-in-law, "she hasn't *asked* me not to come." Clara worried, with good reason, that if he were present, her father would upstage her. He asked her "to let me lead her out before her audience," and she refused because "you'll get all the welcome, and I none." Instead, Sam was seated "in the third row and admonished to keep quiet & not try to attract attention." After Clara's performance—which included songs by Rossini, Schubert, and Haydn and which he judged "a beautiful and blood-stirring and spirit-satisfying triumph"—he "sprang to his feet," jumped onto the boards, "kissed her, so as to make myself conspicuous, & put my arm about her & led her off; but turned at once to answer the call for myself," and "Clara led *me* on by the hand" back to center stage, where he delivered an impromptu twenty-minute address, "the only speech I have ever made that *entirely* satisfied me." He thanked the audience "for your appreciation of [Clara's] singing, which is, by the way, hereditary." The

New York *Sun* devoted ninety percent of its report of the event the next day to Sam's remarks rather than to Clara's recital, confirming her misgivings about her father's (li)ability to overshadow her. When she appeared in Passaic, New Jersey, in mid-November, she refused to be photographed with her father to illustrate an article "a littery person" wanted to write about her. She said "she wouldn't be publicly connected with me," as Sam wrote Jean, "but is going to stand or fall on her own merits." As it happened, her performance was a flop.[47]

Unfortunately, the custodians of culture—local librarians and teachers—sometimes failed to follow the lead of the book critics. In late November 1906, both the Charlton and Worcester, Massachusetts, public libraries barred *Eve's Diary* from their shelves because of the "undraped illustrations." The "horrid" pictures of the First Parents in "Eden's costume" were discovered by a female assistant librarian in Charlton, who, as Sam put it, took "some time to examine them all, but she did her hateful duty!" She then took the book to a member of the library board of trustees, "a male this time, and he, also, took a long time to examine the unclothed ladies. He must have found something of the same sort of fascination in them that I found." The trustee was apparently as enthralled as Sam with the image of Eve "skipping through the bushes unrestrained but not at all afraid." In several interviews, Sam castigated the prudes and philistines—the "clothed but unclean-minded" librarians who censured the illustrations. "If the pictures were so good as to occupy their attention so long," he said, "it seems to me that they were a little selfish not to permit the rest of the city a chance instead of shutting the volume out. Seriously, the pictures in the book are graceful and beautiful. They show fine and delicate feeling. So far from being immodest, I thought them chaste and in good taste." He was so puzzled by the uproar, he "shall be driven to read the book again. There must have been something that I missed the first time." The poetasters seized the moment to lampoon the brouhaha, as in these eighteen lines of stilted iambic sextameter:

> The Diary of Mother Eve, as writ by Sammy Clemens,
> In good old Massachusetts has been handed sundry lemons.
> The Deaconess inspected it, although with proper blushing,
> The Deacon didn't scorn to look, although he kept "tush-tushing."
> They put it on the topmost shelf, nor told what made them do so—
> Except they banished Eve because they didn't like her trousseau.
> If costume is the reason why the blushing folks suspend her,
> Our sympathy's with Eve, and now we hasten to defend her.

Although she is not shown to wear a costume you would call dress,
She never made her debut in a decolletty ball dress,
And while blue-nosed New England finds the pictures of her shocking,
They can't complain that Eve had flashed a saucy screen-door stocking.
Oh, Mother Eve, we'd fain believe there is some spite work lurking,
Because they never caught you in a waist with open working.
We will admit your garb was in the nature of a hummer,
But still you never wore a shrinky bathing suit in summer.
You wouldn't do for Horse Show weeks, but still there is no reason
That you could not make quite a hit in any opera season.

Not only did sales of the book soar as a result of the controversy, the head librarian in Charlton confessed that he had not seen a copy before it was banned, and the librarian who removed it from the Worcester library was fired six weeks later for displaying "arrogance to library patrons and an overbearing attitude toward employees."[48]

Not only was Sam unembarrassed by hubbub over *Eve's Diary*, he often gave inscribed copies of the book to young women after its publication—to Elizabeth Wallace, Dorothy Quick, Corinna Lindon Smith, and Mary Rogers. He even pretended to have drawn the illustrations and modeled them on Rogers, writing her that he thought "it a most remarkable thing that I was able to draw you (as mother Eve) to the very life & all by accident. From the first page to the last, there you are; it is your very self, exactly as you would have looked & acted if you had been Eve, with a spang-new beautiful world to flutter around in—& not a detail of you lacking, so far as I can see, but the tawny hair & the clothes."[49]

Sam often sported white suits in summer but never after Labor Day until the fall of 1906. On October 8, nine days before leaving Dublin to return to New York, he resolved to flaunt sartorial convention. "I hope to get together courage enough to wear white clothes all through the winter," he vowed that day in his autobiographical dictation. "It will be a great satisfaction to me to show off." Lyon remarked the same day in her diary that the King was "filled with the idea of . . . wearing suitable white clothes all winter, so he has bidden me order 5 new suits from his tailor." (Lyon's nickname for Sam, "the King," may allude to the character of the White King in Lewis Carroll's *Through the Looking Glass* [1871]). According to Paine, Sam swore he could not "bear to put on black clothes again" because they reminded him of funeral attire. Instead, he would wear white suits year-round except on formal occasions and "let the critics say what they will." His decision has been variously interpreted. Clara Clemens, for example, "always believed that the reason he took to wearing [white] is that it soothed him and reminded him of bed." John Cooley and Leland Krauth suggest Sam enlisted in the movement for male dress reform. At the most elemental level, of course, Sam wore the iconic white suit as a publicity stunt. Ever sensitive to technological advances in journalism, he understood how to self-advertise when newspapers began to reproduce halftone photographs at the turn of the century. "I don't like to be conspicuous," he told the artist James Montgomery Flagg, "but I *do* like to be the most noticeable person!" He bragged to his daughters in March 1907 that he attended a dinner with friends "in full evening dress of *white broadcloth,* & was as white as a ghost. It is a very beautiful costume—and conspicuous" and "just stunning." He confessed to Earl Grey, the governor-general of Canada, whom he had met at a meeting of the Pilgrims Club in New York in April 1906, that his white garb was "premeditated—I got myself up so to attract attention."[50]

He repeatedly hinted at his purpose in wearing white in late 1906 and 1907. He belonged "to the ancient and honorable society of perfection and purity," he proclaimed in December 1906. "I am the president, secretary, and treasurer. I am the only member" and indeed "I am the only person in the United States who is eligible." "I wear white clothes both winter and summer," he declared in his autobiography, "because I prefer to be clean in the matter of raiment—clean in a dirty world; absolutely the only cleanly-clothed human being in all Christendom north of the Tropics." But if clothes are the badge of lost innocence, as Sam's hero Thomas Paine asserted in *Common Sense,* then undress is an emblem of prelapsarian innocence. At the height of the controversy over the illustrations in *Eve's Diary*—with the naked bodies of Eve and Adam depicted on its pages in white—Sam told interviewers that in his opinion the most "comfortable, delightful," "pleasant," and "beautiful costume is the human skin, but since it isn't conventional or polite to appear in public in that garb alone, I believe in wearing white" in order to be "as immaculate as new fallen snow." He announced that he would wear white year-round "because it corresponded to the original costume" in the Garden before the Fall. He soon dubbed the "snow-white *full dress,* swallow-tail & all," his "dontcareadam suit"—a double-entendre that could mean both "don't care a dam suit" and "don't care adam suit." By June 1909 he owned twenty-four white suits, both linen for summer and flannel for winter.[51]

For the record he read excerpts from *Eve's Diary* to the Dublin Lake Club while attired in a white suit as early as July 1905. But for all practical purposes he debuted his dandy new look on December 7, 1906, at the Library of

Congress. With the temperature in Washington below freezing—he assured reporters that he was wearing "plenty of things underneath"—he and other members of the American Copyright League, including Howells, Edward Everett Hale, Frank Millet, and John Philip Sousa, testified before a joint congressional committee on behalf of new legislation to protect the rights of authors, artists, and musicians (or, as Sam called them, "those hand-organ men who ought to have a bill of their own"). Howells remembered arriving for the hearing when Sam with a dramatic gesture "flung off his long loose overcoat and stood forth in white from his feet to the crown of his silvery head. It was a magnificent coup," and like Tom Sawyer "he dearly loved a coup." Paine had "never seen a more impressive sight than that snow-white figure in that dim-lit, crowded room," he later wrote, and Howells "laughed the buttons off his clothes," according to Sam. His outfit soon inspired a jingle:

> The scribes of old were often cold,
> In shabby garb they wandered;
> I'd like to see Mark Twain's white suit
> Before he has it laundered.

In the course of his comments Sam urged the extension of copyright to the life of the writer plus fifty years and predicted that, if such a measure passed, it would simply feed "some starving author's children. . . . I like the fifty years' extension, because that benefits my two daughters." He was amenable to compromise on the point, later proposing that he would support a forty-year extension on the condition the copyright owner "issue an edition at *one-tenth* the price of the cheapest *existing* edition." Nevertheless, he attracted more attention for his manner of dress than for his testimony, and many newspapers led their reports about the hearing the next day with descriptions of his clothing. From the Willard Hotel, Sam wrote Jean that evening that he was the only person in the meeting room "in snow-white clothes. The others all wore black, & looked gloomy & funereal." Over the next several days, sequestered in the offices of Speaker of the House Cannon and Senator Henry Cabot Lodge, Sam lobbied members of Congress, including 180 U.S. representatives and leaders of both parties. The only way to enact "this improved copyright bill," he thought, was to contact "every member of Congress" individually. "I am the only person that is willing to undertake this formidable enterprise," moreover, "& perhaps the only one who has the gifts to do it 'ansomely." He met with Theodore Roosevelt in the White House, gave his autograph to both First Lady Edith Roosevelt and TR's daughter Ethel, and afterward announced to the press that "the President is one with us on the copyright matter."[52]

At the close of a hectic week, Sam briefly sat in the Senate gallery while that body debated Reed Smoot's eligibility as a Utah Mormon to retain his seat, and in the afternoon of December 12, he and Paine drove to Rock Creek Cemetery to contemplate the Augustus Saint-Gaudens sculpture marking the grave of Clover Adams, Henry Adams's late wife. The pensive figure "is in deep meditation on sorrowful things," he told Paine. When she learned of his trip to Washington, Helen Keller wrote Sam that she hoped "you got the copyright law you wanted and that you will get everything else you want, if it is really good for you. But pray, pray, do not try for a copyright that shall last as long as your books. Three thousand years is quite long enough in all reason." She also wondered whether he had donned "that white costume" for the hearing in order to practice "for the Ascension robe."[53]

A revised copyright law was finally passed in 1909 that extended the period of copyright renewal from fourteen to twenty-eight years, thus permitting a work potentially to be copyrighted a total of fifty-six years. Sam thanked his friend Champ Clark, House minority leader and future U.S. Speaker of the House, for supporting the legislation and assured him it was "the only sane, & clearly-defined, & just & righteous copyright law that has ever existed in the United States."[54]

In September 1906, Harper & Brothers issued yet another compendium of thirty-seven of Sam's articles, most of them published previously, some of them multiple times (e.g., "A Double-Barrelled Detective Story," "A Dog's Tale"), a few dating back decades, dregs resurrected from the bottom of the barrel such as "Advice to Little Girls" (1865), "Post-Mortem Poetry" (1870), and "The Danger of Lying in Bed" (1871). Apparently assembled by Frederick Duneka to tap the holiday trade market, *The $30,000 Bequest and Other Stories* included "Eve's Diary" and a new version of "Extracts from Adam's Diary." "I hate to have the old Adam go out any more—don't put it on the presses again," as Sam advised Duneka. "Let's put the new one in place of it." The title story, a cautionary tale about avarice written after the fact of Sam's own bankruptcy, was in effect a companion piece to "The Man That Corrupted Hadleyburg." In both parables, a stranger exploits the greed of an innocent couple, in this case by tempting them with promises of wealth to invest on margin in the stock market—that is, with money they do not have. "The castle-building habit, the day-dreaming habit—how it grows! what a luxury it becomes," the narrator inveighs. The inevitable stock market crash evaporates their paper fortune and destroys their lives. This piece was one of the redeeming features of the collection, which, according to the *Philadelphia Inquirer,* "in many respects gives a better idea of the versatility of the author than any other that has appeared." Not only was the title story "full of good things," the *San Francisco Chronicle* added, "some of the shorter skits are among the best things Mark Twain has ever written." The same note was struck by most other reviewers, as in the *Nation* ("much . . . entertainment"), *Charleston News* ("charming bits of humorous literature"), New York *Sun* ("a miscellany of stories, grave and gay"), *Brooklyn Eagle* ("full of chuckles"), *American Monthly Review of Reviews* ("500 delightful" pages), *Louisville Courier-Journal* ("entertainment in plenty"), Sydney *World's News* ("typical examples of Mark Twain's humor, power of graphic recital, and aggressively sensible philosophy"), and *Western Morning News* ("inimitable blending of humour and pathos"). The *Baltimore Sun* (the author's "latest scrap basket . . . put out as a potboiler") and London *Morning Post* ("a rather haphazard collection of odds and ends of newspaper articles, squibs, and stories") were less impressed. A pair of religious magazines were even more severe, objecting to the inclusion of "A Monument to Adam," "A Humane Word for Satan," and Adam's and Eve's diaries. The *Congregationalist and Christian World* opined that readers "will miss the element of thoughtfulness" and *Zion's Herald* vilified the volume: the "grossest exaggerations and wildest improbabilities are made to do duty in place of genuine humor and natural sentiment," and the author's opinions "are not such as to make his writings agreeable to religious people."[55]

Clara spent the year-end holidays in 1906 with her father at 21 Fifth Avenue during a hiatus between rest cures and concert tours. Privately, he damned her with faint praise: she was "getting to be a mighty competent singer." They welcomed the new year with a party for sixty friends, including the poet Witter Bynner. Katy Leary remembered that Bynner "wrote lots of poetry," including one poem for Clara, and was "very good-looking, too—tall and dark—a nice, handsome-looking fellow. He was really very charming, I believe." Katy never knew he was gay. To entertain the party guests, Clara burlesqued grand opera in a musical number entitled "Sham," Lyon played a nurse with a baby bottle prop to Sam's screeching infant in a skit named "Pain," and Bynner and Sam reprised the old conjoined twins joke in a sketch called "Champagne." The two men—despite their forty-five-year age difference—were attached by a red ribbon suggesting a ligature. As the younger twin (Bynner) drank from a flask, the older twin (Sam) became intoxicated while delivering a temperance lecture. Sam also prepared a surprise for his guests. Five minutes before midnight, he switched on a telharmonium, a technological advance on the orchestrelle that amplified live piano music—in this case "Auld Lang Syne," "The Star Spangled Banner,

"American Patrol," and a medley of Norwegian songs—piped over the telephone line, according to Sam "the first time this marvelous invention ever uttered its voice in a private house." The music "was clear and sweet and strong, and it broke upon the ears of the assembled company as a weird and charming surprise; there being no musical instruments in sight, they could not guess whence it came." "Next to the day I was put in trousers," Sam joked, "this is the happiest occasion of my life."[56]

CHAPTER 14

Shortcuts

There is more real pleasure to be gotten out of a malicious act, where your heart is in it, than out of thirty acts of a nobler sort.

—*Autobiography of Mark Twain*

SAM, ISABEL LYON, and Joseph Twichell cruised to Bermuda together early in the new year 1907. Sam's doctor Edward Quintard had recommended he travel there in late November, but George Harvey "couldn't go with me," so he had postposed the trip. Lyon had suffered a bout of nervous exhaustion from overwork in the fall and taken some time off, but since her return in mid-December she had resolved never to leave Sam again "unless he sends me." That is, "the King needs the trip away—& I need it." Joe Twichell "needs it too," she thought, "for he was tired out with his Xmas clerical duties." They embarked the morning of January 2 aboard the 425-foot *Bermudian* of the Quebec Steamship Company, a modern steamship launched in July 1904 that accommodated about 240 first-cabin passengers with meals "even the hypercritical could hardly find fault with." To be sure, their holiday was brief: only a week, including three days on the islands, where they registered at the Princess Hotel on the beach in Hamilton, sailed around the harbor, and haunted the tourist traps, including Joyce's Dock Caves and Devil's Hole on the shore of Harrington Sound. "The weather was perfect every day," Twichell remembered, "the company altogether delightful, M. T. being in excellent spirits all the while. . . . We took several long drives, and a lovely sail in the waters about Hamilton, delighting ourselves on the soft balmy air, and in viewing again the scenes that had enchanted us thirty years before." The trio returned to New York on the *Bermudian*, which completed its weekly round trip on January 9. Met at the pier by reporters, Sam assured them that he had "just been for a rest, so please don't say I went down to Bermuda for my health. I have plenty of health—enough to give some away if anybody wants it." In truth, he had been annoyed the entire week by Twichell, who was so deaf he could "only hear when shouted at" yet jabbered about trifles until, as Lyon put it, "the King almost loses patience." Twichell fairly concluded that he had enjoyed the trip more than Sam, who was "encumbered" by fame whereas "I had the freedom of my obscurity—an advantage that has always been mine when traveling in your company."[1]

The day after their return from Bermuda, Sam and Lyon railed to Katonah, his second visit there. But Jean was "in a torrent of impossible moods," according to Lyon, "& distressed her wonderful father until he was ready to weep." Jean had again been denied permission by the staff to ride her horse Scout, and her father had consoled her as best he could. "I do hope you are feeling happier, by this time," he wrote his daughter the next day.

> It wrung my heart to see you so disappointed & I could not help thinking all the time how grieved your mother would have been to see you long for a thing—anything—& have to be denied it. Bear with the situation as well as you can, dear Jean, & call back the gentle spirit you were born with, & believe that all those people mean you well, for it is indeed so. It is your disease that makes you see ill intentions in them—they mean well by you.

But uncharacteristically Sam was still depressed in mid-January. He urged his daughter to enjoy the "healthful outdoor times." But in truth he had abandoned hope that she might someday be cured, instead surrendering to the wishful thought that some form of treatment might eventually mitigate her disorder. "Jean will never be well," he admitted to Rogers, "but is contented and happy where she is." At Sam's request, Lyon confronted Edward Livingstone Hunt, one of the staff physicians, on January 30 to ask for a detailed prognosis of Jean's condition. She reported that Hunt "was hopeful but said this was barely the beginning & that [Jean] mustn't expect any real improvement inside of a year" because it "was very hard to judge a case under six months." Lyon advised Jean to accept the likelihood she "would probably have to be here during the summer" and Jean submitted to the inevitable: "If it is positively the only thing for me to do, then of course I shall stay without raising objections." On February 22 Hunt relayed the hopeful news that Jean had "in the last three weeks suffered from only *one single attack* and that one of the petit mal type. This is the best three weeks she had had since I have taken care of her."[2]

A week after Sam and Lyon returned from Bermuda, Helen Keller and Anne Sullivan Macy, her teacher and "miracle worker," spent the evening at 21 Fifth Avenue. Sam "had not met [Keller] for a long time," and when he greeted his guests at the door, Lyon recalled, she "threw her arms around him & buried her head in his neck & felt of his hair" and "when Mrs. Macy told her that he was still wearing his halo, the King wept." Paine was fascinated by Keller, who against all odds had acquired "a store of knowledge" to light "the black silence of her physical life. To see Mark Twain and Helen

Keller together was something not easily to be forgotten." Lyon expected Keller to be "blasé & spoiled a little because of her great fame; but she isn't spoiled a bit." On the contrary, she was struck by Keller's "nobility & the womanliness & the great play of intellect & affection & emotion & seriousness." Lyon played Schubert's "Der Erlkönig" on the orchestrelle, and Keller discerned the vibrations of the music, especially the "deep trembling of the bass." Sam noted that her "face flushed and brightened on the instant, and the waves of delighted emotion began to sweep across it. Her hands were resting upon the thick and cushion-like upholstery of her chair, but they sprang into action at once, like a conductor's, and began to beat the time and follow the rhythm." A few days later, Keller wrote Sam that she would "always, always remember the evening we spent with you, and had you all to ourselves for two precious hours! I think sometimes that there is nothing in the world so precious as a beautiful memory. . . . How it all comes back—the beautiful room, the music that stole into my soul through my finger-tips." She wished "I could sit beside you oftener. For there is something about you so vital and simple and nothing-withholding that somehow darkness and silence seem no longer to be." Whereas Sam considered her "the eighth wonder of the world," Keller reminisced a generation later in one of her several autobiographies that Sam "talked delightfully, audaciously, brilliantly. His talk was fragrant with tobacco and flamboyant with profanity. I adored him because he did not temper his conversation to any femininity."[3]

Sam had been among the first to congratulate Bret and Anna Harte when their daughter Jessamy was born in 1872. Thirty-five years later, mentally ill and destitute, estranged from her abusive husband, with both of her parents dead, Jessamy desperately needed a benefactor. She was in many respects a tragic figure. Only six years old when her father moved to Europe, she never saw him again. An aspiring artist, she studied with the painter George Wharton Edwards in 1893 and she exhibited some of her sketches at the World's Columbian Exposition in Chicago the same year. She soon earned a modest living as an illustrator for magazines. In 1898 she wed Henry Milford Steele, a midwestern industrialist, owner of a coal mine in Colorado, and later president of an irrigation company headquartered in Chicago, but theirs was a rocky marriage at best. The Steeles separated in 1906, and in late January 1907 Jessamy Harte Steele, now thirty-four years old, was living in an almshouse in Portland, Maine, and suffering from mild dementia. Her pathetic condition and erratic behavior made news across the country. She was taken under wing by the actress Eleanor Robson, then appearing onstage in New York in *Salomy Jane*, adapted from a short story by Jessamy's father. Robson planned a special charity performance of the play at the Liberty Theatre on February 14, with all box office receipts allotted to Jessamy. Robson had enlisted as much support for the benefit as possible. On January 28, Leander Richardson, a theatrical writer, playwright, and the son of Albert D. Richardson, the late associate editor of the *New York Tribune*, asked Sam to permit his name to be included in a testimonial Robson was preparing to publicize the event and, Lyon noted, "the King is willing." The next day Robson personally solicited Sam's help "in a little plan I have" for Jessamy's relief, "knowing that you will be only glad to lend your valuable assistance to Bret Harte's daughter." She urged him to subscribe to the charity fund she had started, whereupon Sam decided that "it might be better taste to leave me out. For the past 30 years we were not friends. In the circumstances I do not want a prominent place—never heard of any member of the family who differed much from Bret Harte. I despised him." Lyon was surprised. A day after granting "permission to have his name used," he withdrew it, "for he sees through the whole thing as being mainly an advertisement for Eleanor Robson. He is so impulsive & continually has to withdraw from propositions that he has gone into with enthusiasm." In Katonah, Jean was no less disappointed. She read in the paper that Jessamy "was in the poorhouse" without a penny. "What a sarcasm! Bret Harte's works have been so generally read & were in such favor at one time & here is his daughter a beggar. It is one of the most pitiful cases I have ever heard of, I think, & I do hope Father will do something to help her." Sam agreed only to issue a vague statement commending the fundraising on Jessamy's behalf. Buried in the back pages of the *New York Times* for January 30, it read: "I feel that the American people owe a debt of gratitude to Bret Harte, for not only did he paint such pictures of California as delighted the heart but there was such an infinite tenderness, such sympathy, such strength, and such merit in his work that he commanded the attention of the world to our country, and his daughter is surely deserving of our sympathy." Despite this lukewarm endorsement, this letter fueled speculation that Sam would attend and perhaps even participate in the benefit at the Liberty Theatre. Two days later he issued a second statement, published in the *New York American*, that quashed the gossip. In fairness, Sam almost certainly did not know that Jessamy had been physically abused. Still, he seemed remarkably callous to her plight. This statement—the last public utterance he would ever make on the subject of the faint Harte—appeared under the headline "Mark Twain's Flat 'No' for Mrs. Steele's Benefit Recalls Feud with Harte" and left little question why he refused to rally to the cause: "If the use of my name as a patron of the benefit which Miss Robson is to give for the daughter of Bret Harte is of any value to those interested in the matter they are welcome to it," he began.

> Further than this I will not go. It has been my habit this Winter to decline to participate in anything of the kind, unless I have felt it to be a most urgent duty. I do not feel that it is in this case. I was never an intimate friend of the Harte family, and have not been thrown into contact with any of them for thirty years. Perhaps if Bret Harte's daughter in her present plight were a single woman, I might feel it more of a duty to aid her further, but as the case stands I do not. I will not attend the benefit performance or occupy a box, as has been stated.

Jessamy Harte Steele was not really indigent, he argued in effect, because she had a husband.[4]

Four days later, on February 4, 1907, as if a fuse had been lit inasmuch as "things are happening which bring Bret Harte to my mind again," Sam began to reminisce at length about Harte in his autobiographical dictation. The published version of his remarks runs to about ten thousand words. "In these days things are happening which bring Bret Harte to my mind again; they rake up memories of him which carry me back thirty and forty years," he mused. Five years after Harte's death, Sam still harbored an irrational animosity toward him. Or as his grand-nephew Samuel Charles Webster once observed, Sam "never forgave anyone he had injured." In San Francisco in the 1860s "I liked Bret Harte," he recalled, "but by and by I got over it. . . . He was bad, distinctly bad; he had no feeling, and he had no conscience. His wife was all that a good woman, a good wife, a good mother, and a good friend, can be; but when he went to Europe as consul he left her and his little children behind, and never came back again." When Harte lived in England, "he was kept, at different times, by a couple of women—a connection which has gone into history, along with the names of those women. He lived in their houses, and in the house of one of them he died." As for Jessamy: "Who is to blame for this tragedy? That poor woman? I think not. She came by her unwise and unhappy ways legitimately; they are an inheritance; she got them from her father, along with her temperament. . . . Bret Harte transmitted his unfortunate temperament to her."[5] She was simply the innocent victim of her ancestry. Most of what is known about Sam's hatred of Harte appears in his dictation this day.

The sequel to this sad story may be briefly told. Eleanor Robson's benefit performance of *Salomy Jane* on February 14 raised about $1,000. Jessamy and Henry Steele divorced in 1909, he alleging desertion and she extreme cruelty and desertion. After a brief, failed career as a cabaret singer, Jessamy was admitted to the mental ward of a hospital in Islip, New York, in 1915. She was transferred to the St. Lawrence State Hospital in Ogdensburg, New York, in 1917, where she died in 1964, forty-seven years later, at the age of ninety-two.[6]

After delaying publication of *Christian Science* for several years, the Harpers finally released the volume in early February 1907. Sam's patience had been exhausted by June 1906, when he asked Rogers to "please get my Christian Science book" from the "slippery" Duneka, an action that lit a fire under the firm. Witter Bynner congratulated Sam when he heard the news: "I hear you've brought 'em to the point of publishing the Christian Science book. Bully for you! You might dedicate it to the subject,—not to Mother Eddy but to *Auntie-Christ*!" The January 1907 issue of *McClure's*, moreover, contained the first installment of a twelve-part debunking biography of Mary Baker Eddy by Georgine Milmine, and the moment seemed propitious to issue a more "balanced" treatment of the subject, or so Jeannette Gilder asserted: "What Mark Twain has said about Mrs. Eddy in his book on Christian Science ought to act as an antidote to the poison in the articles in *McClure's*." Eddy "has on her shoulders the best business head in Christendom—bar none," Sam conceded. "While obscure & without money or influence, she stole [Phineas] Quimby's book & upon it she built her Science, organized its ancient & powerful forces, compacted the whole into a religion, & hitched the religion & Christianity & herself to the Holy Family." His book was not hostile to mind healing "but only to Mrs. Eddy, who is a great & shining & impressive fraud." He took "a strong and indestructible interest in Mrs. Eddy," he avowed, "because she is picturesque and unusual. I take the same interest in Satan." Even a year before his death he asked, "How did that ignorant village-born peasant woman know the human ass so well? She has no more intellect than a tadpole—until it comes to *business*—then she is a marvel!" The actual practice of Christian Science has "the same value now that it had when Mrs. Eddy stole it from Quimby; that its healing principle (its most valuable asset) possesses the same force now that it possessed a million years before Quimby was born." Sam was so convinced of the efficacy of Christian Science that he recommended it to Jean during her illness because "it brings healing to the spirit & is inestimably valuable."[7]

Like his earlier writings on the topic, *Christian Science* was controversial and its notices many and mixed. The prepublication announcements emphasized its gravity; the New York *Sun* called it "a book of serious interest," the *Washington Times* "a book of vital seriousness," and the *New York Times* praised "the serious body of the work." Though the question of whether the book was humorous was broadly debated, most of the pundits concluded that it contained some comedy. On the one hand, the New York *Sun* insisted that "nobody should make the mistake of taking this book for a book of humor." On the other hand, a number of reviewers found comedy aplenty in it, among them the *Christian Observer* ("the serious vein is so intermingled with the author's spontaneous and irresistible humor that the weightier element is altogether secondary"), *Independent* ("extremely funny—in spots"), *Providence Journal* ("humor—of which there is abundance"), *Spectator* ("his great comic powers are unimpaired"), *Pittsburgh Press* ("a lot of delicious, albeit harmless, fun"), Janesville (Wisc.) *Gazette* ("sparkles with wit and drollery"), *Pall Mall Gazette* ("the most ludicrous and laughable word-torturing"), *Book News* ("the cult of Eddyism has become the butt of Mark Twain's inimitable wit and keen satire"), *Congregationalist and Christian World* (exposes "the weaknesses, fallacies and frauds" of Christian Science leaders with "inimitable humor"), and *World Today* (written "with that incisive and not altogether reverent style we have come to associate with its author"). Still other critics equivocated on the point or refused to reach a conclusion, such as the *Los Angeles Herald* (the author "refused to say whether it is a joke or an attempt to riddle the cult by means of barbed arrows of ridicule"), London *Truth* ("humor shows itself time after time" but is "in the main . . . a serious criticism"), the *Boston Herald* and *Chicago Tribune* ("not a work of humor" but "not without humorously entertaining touches"), the *Nation* ("cannot be regarded as either a serious or a humorous contribution to the discussion"), and the *Newcastle Chronicle* ("a somewhat scrappy re-hash of magazine articles which have not been properly edited," though as "an exposure" of "charlatanry" it "leaves very little to be desired").[8]

Most commentators agreed, however, that Sam's study was impartial, as in the New York *Evening Sun* ("we know of no treatise on the hostile side so thorough as this and so little distorted by prejudice"), *Life* ("a frank, nonpartisan, complimentary and pitiless analysis"), *Athenaeum* ("does his work coolly and impartially"), *Brooklyn Times Union* ("a serious, carefully considered investigation and impartial examination and analysis of a movement"), *Australian Star* ("what phrenologists call the bump of reverence would not seem to have been strongly developed at any time in Mark Twain"), and *Nashville Tennessean* ("an earnest, painstaking, and impartial study"). Nor was there any attempt in the mainstream Christian press to defend Christian Science against Sam's assault; the *Christian Advocate* called *Christian Science* "a curious mixture, eminently characteristic of the author, who uses, first, sound argument and then effective ridicule against the great delusion which he labors to dispel," the *Northern Christian Advocate* wrote that he "treats the subject seriously and with no little insight and strength," and the *Catholic World* called the book "a serious attack" in which Sam marshals an "artillery of sarcasm and ridicule."[9]

To be sure, a bloc of critics reproached Sam for wasting his time and talent. Edward Kimball, a member of the Christian Science Board of Education whose opinion was solicited by *Cosmopolitan,* the magazine that had published Sam's original essay mocking Christian Science in 1899, sniffed "an air of venerable staleness about the time-fixed platitudes and the sinuous innuendos" in the book. B. O. Flower, a muckraking journalist who defended the sect in *Christian Science as a Religious Belief and a Therapeutic Agent* (1910), though never a formal adherent, accused Sam of an "intellectual lawlessness" that was "little less than morally criminal." Scarcely less hostile were the *Washington Star* ("58% vituperation, 25% reason, 15% fun, but no trace of brotherly love"), *Springfield Republican* ("will deeply grieve many of the friends of the most beloved of living American authors"), *Hartford Courant* ("too full of reiteration, too vociferous, voluble, prolix"), *Dial* ("adds nothing to the fame of the author"), *Spectator* ("altogether this book is unfortunate"), *Syracuse Post-Standard* ("outspoken to a degree that will strike some as sacrilegious"), *Scotsman* ("when he becomes serious and effective in argument his wit deserts him"), and Melbourne *Argus* ("the book is not an unqualified success from any point of view" because it is "not good humour and can scarcely be regarded as criticism"). The *Brooklyn Eagle* hinted at its disapproval: "powerful and convincing—to the man who does not need to be convinced." The playwright Charles Klein, an occasional contributor to Christian Science publications and a convert to the sect, asserted in the *North American Review* that "from beginning to end" Sam "misunderstands where he does not misstate the beliefs of Christian scientists." Klein's review was followed by a comment in the same issue by the theosophist Charles Johnston, who thought *Christian Science* "a sober, compassionate and very earnest study of a remarkable system, the achievement of a very gifted woman."[10]

Perhaps surprisingly, given its modern reputation as one of Sam's weaker works, the vast majority of the contemporary notices of *Christian Science* were favorable, even laudatory. Some of them applauded in superlatives: "the most damaging indictment of Christian Science yet penned" (*London Tribune*); "the most important contribution to the current discussion of Mrs. Eddy and her creed" (*Albany Argus*); "the most enjoyable Mark Twain book that has come out for some time" (*Brooklyn Standard Union*); and "the most serious and extended criticism of the subject that has yet been made" (*San Jose Mercury News*). Or near-superlatives: "Our Mark Twain has done few things better than this study" (*Louisville Courier-Journal*), and "one of the most interesting [books] that Mr. Clemens has written" (*Cleveland Plain Dealer*). Most of these notices focused on the invective Sam hurled at Eddy or her credulous followers, among them the *Philadelphia Inquirer* ("the sting of the book is in the attack on Mrs. Eddy"), *Sydney Herald* ("exposure of Eddyism is final and convincing"), New York *Outlook* ("mercilessly ridicules certain pretentions of Mrs. Eddy and her disciples"), *Manchester Guardian* ("a very remarkable piece of work" and "entertaining . . . to the student of human gullibility"), Plymouth *Western Evening Herald* ("Mark Twain is far more likely to cure me of the toothache than Mrs. Eddy"), Adelaide *Register* ("analyzes [Eddy's] pretensions and pulverizes them to nothing"), Adelaide *Express and Telegraph* ("exhaustive and remorseless"), and Melbourne *Age* ("a big and unflinching indictment" that "will arouse violent controversy"). No less complimentary to the book or inimical to Eddy were the *San Francisco Chronicle* ("shows very conclusively that the hand that wrote the autobiographical parts of *Science and Health* could not have written the body of this book of doctrine"), Philadelphia *Public Ledger* ("denunciations framed in sentences of fire"), *Current Literature* ("a startling book"), *Chicago Inter Ocean* ("a curious sort of book in every way characteristic of Mark Twain"), St. Joseph (Mo.) *News-Press* ("written with all the author's genial charm"), and *Buffalo Times* ("profound and extended criticism"). The London *Times Literary Supplement* was particularly blunt on this point, with a dash of snobbish nationalism added for flavor:

> The readiness to worship an ordinary living woman, to submit to her autocratic rule, to accept her impossible pretensions, her blasphemous audacities, her nonsensical writings, her puerile scraps of philosophy, her mock science, her shameless commercialism, her pretended cures, her burlesque college, her dummy boards, and the whole paraphernalia of rank imposture—the readiness to swallow all this is possible only in the United States, because people are brought up to it there. The remarkable thing is not Mrs. Eddy but her willing and eager dupes.

Privately, Howells read Sam's "massacre" of Eddy and "gloated on every drop of her blood."[11]

Sam again appeared in public in a serious role when he recited Shelley's "To a Skylark" at a fundraiser in the ballroom of the Waldorf-Astoria on February 14 to benefit the Shelley-Keats House in Rome. "Today I am to appear in public again, to my discomfort," he wrote Jean. "I am weary of public appearances." But he had been asked to appear by Helena de Kay Gilder, Richard Watson Gilder's wife and Rodman and Jeannette's mother, and "I would not refuse" her "any reasonable thing." He had "never done anything of quite so serious a nature before & would rather not be so serious this time—but I must obey orders." Before his reading he drank enough whisky "to bring cobwebs and make him forget the things he planned to say." Performing on the same program as Silas Weir Mitchell, Ellen Terry, and E. C. Stedman, and with Thomas Bailey Aldrich, Frances Cleveland, Richard Watson Gilder, Sarah Orne Jewett, Count Massiglia (the husband of the horrible Countess Massiglia), Eleanor Robson, Augustus Saint-Gaudens, and Booth Tarkington in the audience, Sam began by expressing the hope that "henceforth the public would take him more seriously." During the happiest years of his life, he continued, he read Shelley's lyric "more than any other to my wife. Hers was a beautiful nature. Her heart touched this poem and it was sacred to me." He then recited the poem and, as an encore, Robert Browning's "Memorabilia"—a word, he joked, that he never could pronounce. According to Lyon, Sam "was bored to extinction & hated it all," and after his performance "we all slipped away." A few days later, he took some pride in his recitation "much as I was depressed about it at first. Privately I knew there wouldn't be any other readings there that could come up to it, but I was troubled because I didn't hear anyone *say* so. It's all right, though—plenty have said it since. More than that—I saw more than fifty women crying, but I had forgotten about that." He soon donated the volume from which he had read to the Keats-Shelley House. He crossed paths with William James around this time, and as James wrote his brother Henry and son William Jr., Sam was showing his age. He was "good only for monologue" or "for dialogue at best," but "he's a dear little genius all the same."[12]

Accompanied by pianist Charles Wark and violinist Marie Nichols, Clara launched a concert tour on February 19 that included performances in North Adams, Massachusetts, Elmira, Utica, Hartford, and Bangor, Maine. "I like Mr. Wark & his honest blue eyes ever so much," Sam told Clara. "I think you are fortunate to be in his guardianship." The tour was a financial failure, losing at least $2,500 the first month, not that her father resented the expense. "Pay the bills and tell [Clara] to go ahead," he instructed Lyon, who now was managing the household accounts. He explained that his daughter "was learning her trade" and had she "come home with twenty thousand dollars in her purse it would not be of the value to her that this experience has been; the big enthusiastic audiences are not the ones that are of greatest help—but the smaller cold audiences that you win over are the ones that help you most." Clara sailed for Europe in mid-May with her entourage to tour through September at an even greater cost—they spent nearly $23,000 during the two years Clara tried to launch a singing career. But Sam was resigned to the inevitable expense. Howells wrote his daughter Mildred that "Clara seems to be having a real success" and her father "seems for the first time proud of her."[13]

Much as the Transvaal in 1896 reminded him of the Comstock in the 1860s, Sam thought Bermuda early in the new century resembled the Hawaiian paradise of 1866. On March 10, as Lyon observed in her journal, Sam "was droopy & had a touch of gout, which means that he is tired & he ought to have a change." The next day she reported that he was "restless—the gout seems better" though she painted his foot with iodine, and they began to plan another flying trip to the Caribbean. "I have lost interest in everything and am in deadly need of a change," he wrote Clara. He was so tired of banquets, he wrote Brander Matthews, that he would not attend another one, "not even the Last Supper." They "should have but one night" in the islands because they sailed on the *Bermudian* on Saturday March 16 and returned the following Thursday, Lyon noted, "but the King won't care. He will have 5 days away from home." At their invitation, the nineteen-year-old Paddy Madden, whom they had met on the return voyage from Bermuda in January, joined them. She proved to be "a delightful bait for the very nicest men on board," including President Charles W. Eliot of Harvard. They landed in Hamilton on March 18, the only day they left the ship, and immediately drove to the Princess Hotel to see Mildred Howells, W. D. and Elinor's daughter and John's brother, and then sailed "among the islands in one of the sweet native boats." Sam chaffed the local press when he learned that the humorist Edwin Austin Oliver was also visiting Bermuda; the size of the country, he said, "made it impossible for two great wits to be in it at the same time." Sam, Lyon, and Madden spent the night aboard the ship, which embarked the next day on the return to New York. Sam learned that during his absence his old friend Tom Aldrich had died, and he sent his widow Lilian a telegram expressing his "heartfelt sympathy." Within a week of their return, Sam began to discount the significance of the getaway. "The passages to and fro, and the twenty-four hours' sojourn in those delightful islands," he admitted, "were matters of high importance and enchanting interest for the time being, but already they have shriveled to nothing and taken their place among the rest of the trivialities of life."[14]

In early January 1907, on the advice of his nephew Jervis Langdon, Sam invested $5,000 in the Robert Hope-Jones Organ Company of New York and Elmira, more specifically in a new organ for the Park Church in Elmira. He told Lyon it was "an investment for the children"—that is, his daughters, nieces, and nephews. No doubt he again consulted with Jervis, the president and treasurer of the company, when he visited Elmira in late January 1907 to attend the funeral of Isabella Beecher Hooker. In mid-March, Jervis invited Sam to Elmira on April 3 to attend a demonstration of the organ and—not so coincidentally—assist the company in its advertising by meeting some of the fifty "very delightful" organists and music critics from New York who would hear and play the instrument and tour the factory. Of course, Sam would "enjoy an hour or two" of the music, too. On April 2, Lyon noted in her datebook, Sam left "for Elmira—a sense-of-duty visit," as he described it, "he was sorry that he had to make." It would be his last visit to Elmira, in no small part because "he hates the place now and all the people too—except the Stanchfields [Clara and John] and Mrs. Crane." At least on the surface, however, Sam enjoyed the recital. He requested a program of Wagner music, including the "Pilgrim's Chorus," and according to the *Elmira Star-Gazette* "he appeared to take keen enjoyment in the music," performed on a new type of electronic organ that mimicked the sound of an entire orchestra. Afterward, he addressed the assembled musicians from the pulpit. Max Eastman, the twenty-four-year-old son of Samuel Eastman and Annis Ford Eastman, co-pastors of Park Church, and later a writer, social activist, and editor of the *Masses*, met Sam on April 3 and remembered that in his speech he joked about bouncing the infant Jervis II on his knee and how "now looking back I'm glad . . . I *didn't* sing." After returning to New York, Lyon reported, Sam was "depressed" and "said that he wouldn't go again to Elmira. He couldn't."[15] He was haunted by memories of Livy, Quarry Farm, and happier days.

On June 25, 1906, the millionaire playboy Harry Thaw killed Stanford White in the rooftop theater of Madison Square Garden, which White had designed, by firing three bullets at point-blank range into his face. The most famous architect in America, White had also designed the Washington Square Arch and the rebuilt Rotunda at the University of Virginia. White's apartment on West Twenty-Fourth was a notorious boudoir, with a mirror room where Thaw believed White had raped the underage Evelyn Nesbit, a former model and Gibson Girl, memorialized as "the girl in the red velvet swing." Shaw and Nesbit later married, and when he was arrested, Thaw reportedly said, "I shot him because he ruined my wife."[16]

Thaw was prosecuted for murder in the first twentieth-century "trial of the century." It began in New York on January 23, 1907, and Sam followed the proceedings closely. He had "come into casual contact with Stanford White, now and then, in the course of the past fifteen or twenty years," he observed in his autobiographical dictation on February 28, while the trial was still in session. White "had a very hearty and breezy way with him," Sam recalled, "and he had the reputation of being limitlessly generous—toward men—and kindly, accommodating, and free-handed with his money—toward men; but he was never charged with having in his composition a single rag of pity for an unfriended woman." Evelyn Nesbit Thaw's testimony at trial exposed White's perfidy:

> The witness charges the middle-aged architect—who was rich, of the first renown in his profession, and possessed of a middle-aged wife and a grown-up son—with eagerly and diligently and ravenously and remorselessly hunting young girls to their destruction. These facts have been well known in New York for many years, but they have never been openly proclaimed until now. . . . New York has known for years that the highly educated and elaborately accomplished Stanford White was a shameless and pitiless wild beast disguised as a human being; and few, if any, have doubted that he ought to have been butchered long ago, by some kindly friend of the human race.

Thaw's trial ended after six weeks in a hung jury. His second trial in early 1908, in which his team of lawyers led by Sam's friend Martin Littleton successfully mounted an insanity defense—a legal strategy that was one of Sam's old bugaboos from his years in Nevada and California—ended with a verdict of not guilty. Thaw was then confined in a mental hospital until 1915.[17]

Sam's philo-Semitism assumed a new guise in the spring of 1907 with his renewed support for the Children's Theater of the Educational Alliance, a Jewish community center on East Broadway in New York. The work of the theater among young immigrants "is one of the most remarkable educational developments in the country," he claimed. "Its influence has already spread" throughout the Lower East Side. Justice Samuel Greenbaum once introduced the Yiddish humorist Sholem Aleichem to him there as "the Jewish Mark Twain," to which Sam replied "Please tell him that I am the American Sholem Aleichem." Alice Minnie Herts, the director of the theater, recalled that Sam was invited to a matinee performance of *The Prince and the Pauper* and "his deep interest was immediate and unbounded." On April 14, with Daniel Frohman, president of the Actors' Fund Fair, Howells, Clara, and eight hundred children present, Sam delivered a "half-political, half-theological" curtain speech. "I wish we had forty theaters like this in the city," he said. "The cost to the city would be $2 million a year, but it might save $10 million after a while in graft." "This theater is an influence," and if promoted properly "it would make better citizens, honest citizens." The Children's Theater was "educating 7,000 children & their families." According to Herts, he "grasped the fact that the play" was "only the final expression of the deep, underlying educational principle" of the theater, and after seeing a production "he responded enthusiastically to a request of the players to give a special evening performance for his friends in the hope that some wealthy person or persons might be interested to suitably subsidize this unique and practical method of providing the best means of entertainment for young men, women, and children." In the audience for the special, invitation-only performance were many of Sam's literary friends (Dan Beard, John Burroughs, George Washington Cable, P. F. Collier, Richard Harding Davis, Hamlin Garland, Norman Hapgood, George Harvey, and Matthews), influential power brokers (Police Commissioner Theodore Bingham, Carnegie, Chauncey Depew, Charles Eliot of Harvard, Governor Charles Evans Hughes, District Attorney William Jerome), and businessmen (Solomon Guggenheim, Jacob Schiff, and Elbert H. Gary). "The charming play was finely mounted," the *Brooklyn Eagle* remarked the next day, "finely rendered, finely costumed, and thoroughly enjoyed." A children's theater "is easily the most valuable adjunct that any educational institution for the young can have," Sam testified, and "no otherwise good school is complete without it. It is much the most effective teacher of morals & promoter of good conduct that the ingenuity of man has yet devised, for the reason that its lessons are not taught wearily by book & by dreary homily but by visible & enthusing *action*; & they go straight to the *heart*, which is the rightest of right places for them." But no sponsor emerged to underwrite the work of the Theater of the Educational Alliance, as Sam had hoped, and it failed financially the following year.[18]

Sam's charitable work on behalf of schools was not limited to the Educational Alliance. He was also a patron of Farragut High School in Knoxville, Tennessee, and Lincoln Memorial University in Cumberland Gap, Tennessee. He presided at a benefit for the university at the Metropolitan Opera House in February 1909 at which Ida Tarbell delivered the principal address and the New York Symphony Orchestra performed under the direction of Walter Damrosch.[19]

Sam assured the members of the Friends of Russian Freedom in mid-April 1906 that he would ignore the Russian general Arthur Cherep-Spiridovich, who was on tour in the United States to rally support for the czarist regime. But the two men and General Nelson Miles shared a box at a performance by Ethel Barrymore in *Carrots* at the Hudson Theater on March 12, 1907, and they afterward attended a lunch at the St. Regis Hotel in New York. The New York *Worker*, the organ of the Socialist Party of America, wondered what

> has come over Mark Twain, the fearless, outspoken, stimulating Mark Twain, the Mark Twain whom we had come to look upon as free from the cant that characterizes so many "popular" writers? What does he mean by attending a banquet given by General Spiridovich and there sit, silent and apparently unashamed, as that supporter of the Russian autocracy emits fulsome eulogy of the Tsar and all his detestable court, the same Tsar whom Mark Twain so bitterly satirized a few years ago? Are we to reckon Mark as among the lost from now on? Last year he snubbed Maxim Gorky, when the newspapers opened their mud batteries on that splendid genius. Now he sits at the feet of the Tsar himself and pays homage to a coarse and blatant toady of the infamous regime at St. Petersburg.

Similarly, Nikolai Tchaikovsky wrote to caution Sam about Cherep-Spiridovich: "He is no more 'Count' or 'General' than I am." A week later, Tchaikovsky sent Sam a copy of an article in the *New York Times* that asserted he had "paid compliments to the count" and asked whether Sam thought his "name has been very improperly and unscrupulously used." Tchaikovsky predicted that Spiridovich would make "still further use of it in the European press unless you put an abrupt and public stop to this proceeding."[20]

Between April 19 and 21, Sam and Lyon left on a long-delayed trip to Hartford to celebrate the thirtieth anniversary of the Saturday Morning Club, a forerunner of the angelfish. He had organized the meetings of the young girls in the Hartford house "& for this service was made a member; & to this day I am the only male member it has ever had," he bragged to Jean. While "the signs of age are upon them," they "are still young in their hearts. We had a rousing time, a happy time, a memorable time." In truth, this occasion, when Sam stayed with Harmony and Joe Twichell, ruptured his friendship with Harmony. The night before the reunion, Sam read his newest story

"Wapping Alice" to Joe and Harmony, the tale of the Clemens family maid who in 1877 faked a pregnancy to bamboozle her boyfriend into marrying her—a wedding Joe had conducted. Their son the Reverend Joseph Hooker Twichell remembered fifty years later that as Sam read, "my mother became disgusted and her mouth became set very hard. This caused my father to laugh heartily. The more my father laughed the more disgusted my mother became. Mark Twain thought my father's laughter was excited simply by the story, which was not the case." The next evening Sam read the same story to the grown members of the Saturday Morning Club. Harmony, who had been invited to the meeting, arrived in the midst of the recitation "and marched straight into the house and, without taking her hat off, marched straight upstairs to dad's study and walked in without knocking. She was mad right through. I could not hear what went on, but at one point dad started to laugh, but he quickly choked [it] off." Downstairs the clubwomen were horrified, and some left "in a huff." For the rest of her life, according to Twichell's biographer Leah A. Strong, "Harmony Twichell never completely forgave" Sam. She "could not condone" his "poor taste. . . . The Sam Clemens who had been her neighbor would never have done such a thing."[21]

Sam had hardly returned from Hartford before he sailed on the *Kanawha* on April 24 with Rogers and a few others to witness the naval review opening the Jamestown Exposition, which marked the three-hundredth anniversary of the founding of the Virginia colony. "There's something inspiring about seeing a lot of big warships," he observed. As he embarked, he joked about Rogers's swashbuckling reputation. "I'm going to be a buccaneer," he told reporters at the dock. "No pirate of finance, but just a carefree ocean searcher for havens of pleasure aboard the yacht of a friend of mine." The fleet on review the opening day of the exposition featured twenty-five battleships and cruisers and welcomed President Roosevelt with twenty-one-gun salutes under sunny skies. The "day was very gay & really paid for the excursion," Sam wrote Clara. But on April 28 fog rolled across the cape and effectively blocked all sea travel along the eastern Virginia shore. Rogers and most of the other passengers "deserted & fled home by rail," but Sam adamantly refused to return by train. The navigation officer on the *Kanawha* "won't risk the passage," Sam explained to an interviewer, so he telegraphed Lyon the next day that he was marooned or "delayed indefinitely." He and the crew remained on the yacht at anchor off Old Point "day after day smothered in white fog, & read, talked, smoked, yawned, gaped, & cussed. . . . Once we went ashore & spent a couple of hours with the officers in Fortress Monroe; & once we went ashore to do some shopping." In the Hotel Chamberlain "I saw the most beautiful girl you can imagine; but I was so stupefied by the fog that I couldn't think of anything to say to her, so I didn't speak to her at all. I am still regretting it." Finally, in the predawn hours of May 1 the ship hoisted anchor for its return voyage, arriving in New York late that evening. Meanwhile, Rogers spread a rumor, copied by the *New York Times*, *New York Tribune*, and other papers on May 4, that the *Kanawha* was missing at sea and Sam presumed drowned—all while Sam was lounging at home at 21 Fifth Avenue, where reporters met him the next day. "The rumor of my having been lost at sea is somewhat overdrawn," he explained. (Or as he might have said, "reports of my death have been greatly exaggerated.") "I do not honestly believe that I was drowned, but I shall inaugurate a most rigorous investigation to determine whether I am alive or dead."[22]

Sam returned from Virginia just in time to be involved in yet another brouhaha. At the invitation of Daniel Frohman, he had agreed weeks earlier to deliver the opening address at the Actors' Fund Fair on May 6 at the Metropolitan Opera House. He donated several inscribed copies of his books to be sold at auction, volunteered to autograph more of them at the Century Theater Club booth, and even authorized Frohman to "use my name and use it freely. Use it in any way you can think of that can help to raise money for that fund, which no right feeling and grateful human being can ever hear named without a leaping of the pulses and a warming of the heart. Forge it if you want to." Then trouble. Genie Holtzmeyer Rosenfeld, president of the Century Theater Club, a devout Christian Scientist and wife of Broadway producer Sydney Rosenfeld, Sam's prospective playscript collaborator, objected to Sam's role at the fair and, at a meeting of the club booth committee on April 30, while Sam lingered aboard the *Kanawha* off the coast of Virginia, demanded that the autographed books he had donated be returned to him and his offer to appear in person under the auspices of the club be denied. She issued an ultimatum, threatening to resign from the organization if her demands were not met. After all, "what concord hath Christ with Belial?" Mrs. Rosenfeld "'was very much affected at the committee meeting this morning,' said a club member. . . . 'She told the members that her Jesus and Mrs. Mary Baker Eddy were dearer to her than any club or anything else in the world, and that she would rather give up anything than be associated with persons who publicly said about Mrs. Eddy such things as Mark Twain had said.' The committee was simply dumbfounded."

Its members adopted a formal resolution of apology, and Edith Baker, the committee chair, hand-delivered a personal letter of apology to Sam that he received upon his return. "Mrs. Rosenfeld is an Englishwoman," she wrote, "and does not understand that after the constitution and the emancipation proclamation, you are our biggest native document and our best beloved institution. I cannot imagine the Bartholdi statue trembling when a stone is thrown into the waters at its feet, nor you experiencing any emotion over the affair beyond that of mild amusement." When Frohman heard about the turmoil, he was furious. He considered Sam's scheduled appearance at the fair a public relations coup. But he found a solution: he transferred Sam, with his consent, to the Players Club booth. On his part, Sam accepted Baker's apology with grace. "I am very very sorry, most sincerely sorry," he replied,

> that an incident has troubled & distressed you which has drenched my jaded spirit with the refreshing waters of a pure delight. Cheer up! & be glad, & grateful, & happy, & enjoy your president's attitude at its full value: as the most innocently & impressively & comprehensively humorous thing that has been imagined by a mere uninspired human being these many, many, many centuries! Ah, I wish *I* could be as funny as that. Miss Lyon knew quite well that the episode would only entertain me & would cost me not a pang. . . . Now you must not retire from the field. Daniel Frohman & I are unanimously of that opinion. It is not for victors to retire under fire: that is for the defeated, & you have not been defeated.

After all this drama, the fair was anticlimactic. At noon on May 6, Frohman escorted Sam, adorned in white flannels, to the podium, where he delivered a conciliatory address. "This is not an occasion for talk," he declared. "You are here in the guise of benefactors. The actor has been your benefactor in the past; now it is your turn. The money raised here is to go to his support in his age and infirmity. . . . No creeds are represented here. The only religion is charity." He hoped that the event would raise a quarter of a million dollars for the fund. He then declared the fair open and "threw a few kisses to the actresses as he skipped down."[23]

Sam was the "lion" of the charity the rest of the week, according to the New York correspondent of the *Cleveland Plain Dealer*. He was "surrounded by bevies of beautiful actresses." He studiously avoided the Century Theater Club booth, though some members "were seen to look wistfully at his white serge back, reflecting, probably, on what might have been." On May 8 he spent four hours signing books in the Players booth and helping the socialite Mamie Fish, wife of businessman Stuyvesant Fish, in the flower booth. Ethel Barrymore remembered greeting him "at some big benefit at an opera house where there were booths. He was sitting in the book stall, signing things." On May 10, Sam and James J. Corbett, who had turned to acting after retiring from the boxing ring, umpired a charity baseball game for the Actors' Fund at Hilltop Park in Washington Heights between teams of actors named for two Broadway musicals, *The Red Mill* and *Little Johnny Jones*. The latter squad, "the Yankee Doodle Boys," featured George M. Cohan at shortstop and Barrymore at cheerleader.[24] Cohan admitted to reporters that he had "only read two books in his life," and both were by Mark Twain. The same day, Genie Rosenfeld was removed from the presidency of the Century Theater Club by vote of its members.[25]

Despite his receipt of honorary doctoral degrees from Yale in 1901 and the University of Missouri in 1902, Sam concealed "a secret old sore which has been causing me sharp anguish once a year for many, many years" until he had an "accumulation of bile and injured pride." He was jealous of cohorts who had been honored more often and/or by more prestigious institutions. Howells, for example, had been awarded honorary doctorates from Harvard, Yale, and Columbia and a Litt.D. by Oxford University. Carnegie received three honorary degrees in 1906 alone—from the universities of Pennsylvania, Edinburgh, and Aberdeen. "I'd have gone to the Aberdeen 400th [anniversary celebration] last September," he admitted, "but they didn't offer me a degree & it made me jealous of Carnegie." "In these past thirty-five or forty years," he complained in his autobiographical dictation, "I have seen our universities distribute nine or ten thousand honorary degrees and overlook me every time. . . . This neglect would have killed a less robust person than I am, but it has not killed me; it has only shortened my life and weakened my constitution." In mid-April 1907, C. F. Moberly Bell, the editor of the *Times* of London, asked Sam when he would next visit London, and he replied "When Oxford bestows its degree upon me!" Bell promised to "arrange that." Sam was especially solicitous of an Oxford degree because, as he explained, it was "a loftier distinction than is conferrable by any other university on either side of the ocean and is worth twenty-five of any other, whether foreign or domestic." In this game of one-upmanship, as Lewis Leary has remarked, he was "petty enough to seek an Oxford degree and great enough to deserve it." Even the sycophantic Lyon admitted that the "red Oxford robe was cheapened (for me) because it was asked for!"[26]

So Sam was not entirely surprised when, on May 3, he was notified by his old ex-nemesis Whitelaw Reid, now the U.S. ambassador to the Court of St. James, that he had been awarded a Litt.D. by Oxford contingent on his appearance at graduation ceremonies on June 26 to receive it. After all, as Sam wrote Jean, "these mighty distinctions are not conferred by mail." He accepted on the instant, cabling Reid "I will come with greatest pleasure" and the same day thanking Moberly Bell for his intervention: "Your hand is in it," and though "I wouldn't cross an ocean again for the price of the ship that carried me I am glad to do it for an Oxford degree." In his autobiographical dictation later, he confessed that he took "the same childlike delight in a new degree that an Indian takes in a scalp and I take no more pains to conceal my joy than the Indian does." He publicly announced his receipt of the honor from Oxford on May 10 while the guest of the governor of Maryland and his wife.[27]

Sam was invited to Annapolis, strangely enough, to raise money for a church. On March 4 Emma Warfield, the wife of Governor Edwin Warfield, a dark horse candidate for president in 1908, had invited Sam "to visit us and to give in the spacious drawing room of the Government House a reading or talk (gratis) for the benefit of our struggling Presbyterian Church." She and the governor had "long wished to know you—and it would indeed be a great pleasure to have you come to this quaint, old historical town, doubly interesting because of the Naval Academy in its midst." Though he routinely received dozens of these sorts of overtures, he was open to accepting this one. As he told Lyon, to "boost up a Presbyterian Church" was "right in my line for I'm nothing if I'm not a Presbyterian!" (In all fairness, he was nothing.) He had "never been to Annapolis" and relished the visit. First, however, he wanted to meet his prospective hosts on his turf, and so he invited them to dinner at his Fifth Avenue home on March 22 and they accepted. The governor graciously thanked Sam. "I have for years desired to know you personally, because I have enjoyed your writings and have learned to greatly admire you," he wrote. "I am therefore much pleased that this visit will afford me the opportunity I have so long sought." The dinner, attended not only by the Warfields but by Dorothea Gilder, the daughter of R. W. and Helena; Count Spiridovich; and Melville Stone, the general manager of the Associated Press, was "satisfactory and delightful," Lyon reported, and "the King found Mrs. Warfield very sweet." Afterward Emma Warfield expressed her appreciation. "The evening spent with you in your home and the warm welcome which you extended to the Governor and to me gave *untold* pleasure," she submitted. "The delightful people and charming dinner, but more than all meeting and knowing you will always be a beautiful memory. We appreciate indeed, dear Mr. Clemens, your kindness and hospitality and we earnestly hope we may soon have the great pleasure of having you come to our little Capitol."[28]

Sam soon consented to speak at a benefit for the First Presbyterian Church in Annapolis on May 10. The demand for tickets at $2 apiece was so great that the event was moved from the Executive Mansion to the hall of the House of Delegates, with a seating capacity of almost six hundred. Sam and Lyon were greeted by the governor at Camden Station in Baltimore the afternoon of May 9 and escorted to his mansion in Annapolis, where he was the guest of honor at a dinner that evening. Among the other guests was the classical scholar Basil Gildersleeve of Johns Hopkins University. The next day Sam toured the Naval Academy, observed a parade in his honor from the porch of the superintendent's house, and, sporting his now-characteristic white suit, delivered a medley of anecdotes at the State House. The so-called Bentztown Bard commemorated his appearance with an occasional poem that rhymed "moustache" and "a flash" and ended half of its thirty-six lines with an exclamation point, including this stanza:

> Blow, bugles of morn, o'er the Severn! Roll, river, in ripples of light,
> For the good, gray guest who has come to our door, Immaculate warrior of right!
> Greet him with cornbread and chicken, and rest him from tumult and strife—
> This prophet who comes in the garments of snow, a knight of the blameless life!
> Blow softly your tenderest welcome, bloom sweetly your tenderest rose,
> And let him lie down in the quiet old town, where even the wicked repose!

No doubt the poet lariat would have been proud. At the reception at Government House after his speech, Sam welcomed some two hundred visitors, including three young women: the governor's daughter and niece and the daughter of the Maryland secretary of state. He was "so entranced . . . with their beauty," the *Sun* reported, that he "tried to hug all of them at the same time." By his own testimony, he also "kissed a few girls."[29]

Sam had already resolved to cut short his visit to Annapolis. His stay had been originally scheduled to last five days, but the morning of May 10, Lyon noted, "he was in despair & said we've got to get away from here." He insisted he "never could stay until Monday" on account of the demands on his time and the restrictions on his behavior. Sam fudged the reason for his early departure; as the local press reported, "owing to unforeseen circumstances" he was compelled to leave Annapolis and return home on "important business." He added that "he had enjoyed to the utmost his visit to Maryland's capital and the hospitality that had been extended him." The next day he was accompanied by the governor to his office in the capitol and to the *Baltimore Sun* building before catching a train for New York.[30]

Sam leased a house on the shore of Wee Wah Lake in Tuxedo Park, a wealthy neighborhood about forty miles northwest of New York, from May through October 1907 for $250 a month. By this time Clara and Jean had both begun to regard Lyon, Paine, and Ashcroft as types of sibling rivals for their father's attention if not his affection. Sam had appointed Paine the "editor and executor of my literary remains" in December 1906, a designation he revoked on January 14, 1907, at Clara's insistence. He likewise had entrusted Isabel Lyon with his affairs. "All Tuxedo likes Miss Lyon—the hackmen, the aristocrats and all," he wrote Jean after settling in the town. He regretted that Lyon had failed to win his daughters' esteem—"I wish it were otherwise"—but he offered no apology. Or as Sam advised Rogers at the time, "Miss Lyon runs Clara, and Jean, and me, and the servants, and the housekeeping, and the house-building, and the secretary-work, and remains as extraordinarily competent as ever." On May 7, Sam assigned Lyon power of attorney to handle all matters related to the construction of the house in Redding and "to exercise a general supervision over all my affairs and to take charge of and manage all my property both real and personal and all matters of business relating thereto; to lease, sell and convey any and all real property wheresoever situated which may now or which may hereafter at any time belong to me." On the eve of his departure for England to receive his honorary degree from Oxford, Sam deeded a tumbledown farmhouse, nicknamed "the Lobster Pot" for its squat shape, and twenty acres of his Connecticut land to Lyon in appreciation for her work on behalf of the Clemens clan over the years. One of the local newspapers reported that the house was "an excellent one, needing only some interior repairs to put it into first class shape."[31]

Sam booked a cabin aboard the steamer *Minneapolis* of the Atlantic Transport line for England on June 8—both Clara's thirty-third birthday and the fortieth anniversary of his departure aboard the *Quaker City* on his first transatlantic trip. He wanted to spend a few days around London before the ceremony at Oxford "to see a few English friends & get my gown & hood made. . . . I take Ashcroft with me," as he wrote Jean on May 14, and he assured her that "I shan't leave the country before I've seen you. If you were sound & well & there was *time* for some travel, you & I would go together." He visited her a week later and "came home weary at 7 o'clock," according to Lyon. Five days later he wrote Jean that he was "saddened" to "go away from you," but he hoped "this is the last far journey I shall ever have to take." He also telephoned her in Katonah the day of his departure. "It was fearfully painful to hear his voice & not be able to see or squeeze him," she noted in her diary. "To think of his going abroad without me is *horrible*." At the dock to wish him bon voyage, Clara handed him a note with instructions about "how to act on every occasion" while in England. She emphasized that he should not "wear white clothes on ship or on shore until you get back." Lyon remembered that "there were so many reporters about him that we could not stay very long." Sam well understood that, past the age of seventy-one, it was his valedictory voyage or, as he joked with the cluster of reporters at the gangplank, "I may never go to London again" until he returned "to this sphere . . . after I am dead."[32]

CHAPTER 15

Oxford

I like the degree well enough . . . but I'm crazy about the clothes! I wish I could wear 'em all day and all night.

—Samuel Clemens, quoted by Kate Douglas Wiggin, *My Garden of Memory* (1923)

"We had a lazy, comfortable, homelike, nine-day passage, over smooth seas, with not enough motion in a thousand miles to make a baby sick," Sam recalled later. Among the other hundred and fifty-three passengers were Francis Patton, former president of Princeton University; Archibald Henderson, professor of mathematics at the University of North Carolina and George Bernard Shaw's biographer; and fifty-one college women "going out on vacation to study Europe. This was pleasant to me, who am rather abnormally partial to young girls." From all indications Sam was the center of attention during the crossing. According to a fellow passenger, he was a fixture at the captain's table, where "the ladies continually encircled the humorist." The "pick of the flock," Sam declared, "was a very pretty and very sweet child of seventeen who looked only fourteen, and who seemed only fourteen, and remained only fourteen to me to the end of the voyage." He "formed a solemn compact" with Carlotta Wells, whom he nicknamed "Charley," that "if he would go to her wedding she would go to his funeral," though she resisted his efforts to monopolize her time. "You don't know what you are missing," he wrote her one day in an attempt to entice her from her cabin. "There's more than two thousand porpoises in sight, and eleven whales, and sixty icebergs, and both Dippers, and seven rainbows, and all the battleships of all the navies, and me." On her part, Charley resisted the lure of his celebrity. "I used to get restless and chafed at times at being expected to sit quietly with him when my inclination was to race around," she complained years later. Some of the other passengers were scandalized by his flirtation with an adolescent girl. Elizabeth Kelly expressed her disapproval of his behavior in print. Sam "allowed himself to be completely absorbed by a lass of about fifteen years," she lamented. "He sits next to her at the table, moves his deck chair down by her, walks with her, etc., and consequently has not had much intercourse with other people. Yesterday at lunch he threw bread back and forth across two tables with some young girls, much to the amusement of the dining room." During the customary concert the night before their arrival to benefit the Seaman's Hospital and Orphanage, Charley played a violin solo and, attired for the only time during the voyage in his white suit, Sam spoke. He proposed a sexist toast in honor of the women ("The ladies—second only to the press in the dissemination of news") and related how his daughters routinely cautioned him to behave in public. His "remarks were chiefly foolish," according to Kelly, "and not at all wonderful." Peter Richards, a caricaturist—Sam called him "a jack-legged draughtsman"—drew some sketches of him auctioned on board for charity.[1]

The *Minneapolis* berthed in Tilbury, twenty-five miles upriver from London, early in the morning of June 18. When Sam disembarked, the dock workers welcomed him with an ovation. "A hundred men of my own class, grimy sons of labor, the real builders of empires and civilizations, the stevedores," Sam remembered, "stood in a body on the dock and charged their masculine lungs, and gave me a welcome which went to the marrow of me." He joked with reporters that he had come to England to attend a "funeral" simply to "pick up a few hints from it" to plan for his own memorial. He had not yet "settled on the time or the place," but a fortune-teller had informed him he would "die in a foreign land—maybe New Jersey." The procession "will be five miles long," with brass bands "every fifty yards and each playing a different tune. It'll be a showy funeral, with plenty of liquor for the guests." He and Ralph Ashcroft caught a boat train to St. Pancras Station, where by chance they met Shaw, who was there to greet Henderson. "There was a hasty introduction amid the scramble for luggage," Shaw recalled, "and after a word or two I tactfully took myself and Henderson off." Sam and Ashcroft hastened to the suite they had booked in Brown's Hotel on Dover Street, "a placid, subdued, homelike, old-fashioned English inn" where the Clemens clan had resided for a couple of weeks in the fall of 1900. It was "a blessed retreat of a sort now rare in England, and becoming rarer every year." In truth, the caravansary was often considered "the most exclusive and aristocratic hostelry in the world."[2]

The poet Eden Phillpotts hailed his arrival with a sonnet in the *London Tribune*:

> The voice of England welcomes thee again,
> Thou well beloved son of Freedom, one and all
> Would be thy hosts; and where the way shall fall
> A myriad friends press forward to obtain

The bounty of a smile. There is a chain
Of pure hearts gold that links mankind in thrall
Before the magic sleight of him we call
After the watchful pilot's cry: "Mark Twain!"
Helmsman of joy, thy shining wake doth glow
Beneath the glory of the Westering sun;
And by its gleaming ripple all men know
The steadfast course that thou hast ever run.
Through life's uneven weather—steered to show
Sane laughter and sweet Liberty are one.

Sam immediately thanked Phillpotts for the "moving & beautiful poem! . . . I prize your love, Eden Phillpotts, & glad am I to believe it is the 'Voice of England' speaking!"[3]

As soon as he registered at his hotel, moreover, he began to receive waves of hotel society: Sir Thomas Lipton, Bram Stoker, conservative members of parliament Harry Brittain and John Henniker Heaton, authors Marjorie Bowen and Elizabeth Bisland, and publisher T. Fisher Unwin, to name only a few. He called on the political journalist Henry Lucy at his home in Ashley Gardens and on Dorothy Tennant, Henry Stanley's widow, and he was the guest of honor at a bachelor banquet hosted by Whitelaw Reid at Dorchester House, "the most palatial private residence in London," the evening of June 21. He received a congratulatory telegram from Cornelius Vanderbilt expressing "regards to our Ambassador and his guests," though when he learned who had attended, Sam's doctor Edward Quintard "sputtered finely against Reid and called him splendid, bad names for not giving a better banquet for the King—'only painters and writers, when he might have had dukes there.'" Then again, those who were invited were among the most distinguished contemporary authors and artists living in London, including Edwin A. Abbey, Sir Lawrence Alma-Tadema, the poet laureate Alfred Austin, Arthur Conan Doyle, Edmund Gosse, Kipling, Sidney Lee, the scientist Sir Norman Lockyer, Lucy, the artists John Singer Sargent and Anthony Hope, George Smalley, Stoker, and Hubert von Herkomer. But there was a catch: Sam had prepared a speech, ostensibly one on international copyright "embellished . . . with some bits" of autobiography. Reid called for no speeches except for his own brief welcome to the assembly, however, in effect snubbing the guest of honor. Sam admitted to Lucy later that he carried the manuscript of a speech in his coat pocket and "shared the general surprise" that he was preventing from delivering it. Lest he allow Reid to think he had gotten the better of him, Sam perpetrated a minor hoax. He claimed "a day or two later" to Lucy, who printed the story, that he had sold the speech to a New York newspaper for £120. "I reckon . . . it would have taken me a quarter of an hour to say it all" and receive nothing for it, he crowed. Instead, he was paid the equivalent of "£8 a minute" not to declaim it at the dinner. Sam seems to have invented this version of events in order to save face and poke a proverbial finger in Reid's eye. To be sure, at the time he was selling excerpts of his autobiography to the *North American Review*, but he published no "undelivered" speech on copyright in a New York newspaper during this period, nor did he receive a windfall payment for such a contribution.[4]

In fact, Sam and Reid had never buried the hatchet, and the guest of honor this evening well understood that he had been invited to the soiree because the American ambassador was obliged to observe diplomatic protocol. "He did it because he couldn't help it," Sam snorted in his autobiography, "and he knew I accepted it because I couldn't help it. I was visiting England in the character of an unofficial ambassador, to receive and acknowledge an honor ostensibly conferred upon me, but really—at least mainly—upon the United States, and he, as the official representative of the nation, was obliged to take public notice of me." Reid and Sam were "diplomatically pleasant and friendly" to each other—"and it is quite likely that we shall remain in that condition until Satan wants one of us and the New Jerusalem the other." The journalist John Y. W. MacAlister threw an after-party for Sam at the Hyde Park Hotel, a three-minute horsecar ride from Dorchester House, with dancing by "about a dozen very *pretty young* girls in appropriate costume." Despite all the late-night frolicking, the English comic writer Jerome K. Jerome believed he too had been snubbed. While Sam was in England "not a single humorist was invited to meet him!" Jerome whined, and "it seemed to please him immensely." Nevertheless, some of the custodians of high culture were decidedly displeased by the welcome given a vulgar American humorist whose wit, they thought, was as dry as a legal brief. The *Academy* groaned that "a great deal of unnecessary fuss is being made in various newspapers about the arrival of 'Mark Twain' "; *Blackwood's* groused that "Mark Twain the humourist is a bull in the china-shop of ideas"; the French satirist Ernest Charles growled that Sam was nothing more than an "alcoholic barbarian"; and the *Saturday Review* griped that the "lionizing" and the "shouting with laughter over his improvised wit, and so forth—how absurd it ought to make us look in the eyes of the world." While he had "written one or two capital books," they were "no reason why these antics and absurdities should be indulged in when he happens to be in England."[5]

The morning of June 20 Sam went to some length to violate custom with a publicity stunt. He left his hotel in slippers and a white Turkish bathrobe, crossed Dover Street to the Bath Club for a swim, and returned an hour or so later. As a punster might have said, he schlepped in his pajamas. He feigned surprise at the resulting hullabaloo. "I simply wanted to take a bath," he protested, "and did the same thing I'd often done at the seaside. London is a sort of seaside town, isn't it?" Jerome, for one, suggested that in his advanced age Sam required a guardian. "He really ought to have someone with him nowadays," he told a reporter. "Much worried" by a report of her father's behavior, Clara telegraphed him to "remember proprieties," and he replied in his defense, "They all pattern after me," as if he were setting a new norm of conduct.[6]

In the afternoon of June 22, at the special invitation of the king, Sam attended the annual Windsor Garden Party, one of the ornaments of his sojourn in England.

It was pronounced "the greatest garden party on record" by the *London Tribune*, and Henry Lucy averred that Sam "was undoubtedly the hero" among the estimated eighty-five hundred people present, with the king of

Figure 17. Ralph Ashcroft, Mr. and Mrs. John Henniker Heaton, and Samuel Clemens (left to right) en route to the Windsor Garden Party, June 22, 1907. Published as "Mark Twain Going to the King's Garden Party," *Buffalo Express*, October 20, 1907. Courtesy of the Mark Twain Papers and Project, Bancroft Library, University of California–Berkeley, PH03555.

Siam, who would receive an honorary degree from Cambridge three days later, "quite a secondary personage." Sam "wandered through the crowds for an hour, shaking hands right and left with strangers," listening to music performed by the band of the Royal Horse Guards, and greeting his old friend Sir Henry Campbell-Bannerman, now the British prime minister, Fridtjof Nansen, Ellen Terry, Archdeacon Basil Wilberforce, and other notables. Frank Harris, whose conversation with Sam in Heidelberg in 1878 had been unpleasant, "drew out of the way; I did not want to meet" him again. Sam was escorted by Whitelaw Reid to meet King Edward and Queen Alexandra, and according to observers, he chatted "with them for fully ten minutes—a far longer time than their Majesties spared for any of their other guests." Sam and the king reminisced briefly about their encounter in Homburg fifteen years earlier, and when rain threatened, Sam donned his hat at the insistence of the queen, prompting a report in the London *Daily Express* that he had committed a major faux pas. But, as Sam explained in his defense, "I didn't approach the Queen of England with my hat on, but with it in my hand, where it belonged. I would not wear a hat; I trust I have better sense than that, and better manners than that." Nor had he "put my hat on when first she asked me to put it on; and I neglected that, and then her Majesty told me to put it on. There is a command." Another paper claimed Sam "patted his Majesty on the shoulder" or slapped him on the back, another social "impertinence of which I was not guilty; I was reared in the most exclusive circles of Missouri and I know how to behave. The King rested his hand upon my arm a moment or two while we were chatting, but he did it of his own accord," and Sam in turn "laid my hand on his shoulder. Each of us meant to honor the other in this laying on of hands." Sam felt at home "in that vast multitude in the Castle grounds," as he wrote Jean the next day, "for both sexes introduced themselves to me with a quite American freedom from ceremony." He bragged that he had "climbed all the rounds of the ladder & shaken hands with all the grades, from the stevedores on up to king & queen," all the while behaving admirably, with "but one breach in Clara's instructions: there was one young lady who was so phenomenally beautiful that I couldn't resist—so I shook hands with her & begged her pardon; but she graciously said she had been trying to get up courage enough to make the first advances herself. So Clara will have to overlook that breach." At the close of the bash Sam was motored back to Brown's Hotel by Sir Thomas Lipton.[7]

Over the next several days he filled his dance card, as Paine later declared, like "a débutante in her first season." He was driven hither and yon—to tea with Archdeacon Wilberforce, lunch with Sir Norman and Lady Lockyer, tea with Winston Churchill, David Lloyd George, Hamar Greenwood, T. P. O'Connor, and Philip Stanhope, first Baron Weardale, on the terrace of the House of Commons. Without any publicity, he visited his old friend Joseph Hatton, who was dying at his home in St. John's Wood. Rather than the casual existence he enjoyed in the United States, especially during the summer, at the age of seventy-one he lived according to a strict schedule for four weeks while in England in 1907.

> I breakfasted in bed, then got up and breakfasted with somebody else somewhere else; then took luncheon at somebody's house, and tea and dinner at other people's houses, and was usually home again, and asleep, by half-past ten or eleven. . . . From four o'clock until six, every day, I returned calls. In all previous years the women of the family had attended to this duty, and I had been spared it, and was grateful; but I was alone now and had to carry out this formidable duty myself. The thought of it was irksome and distasteful, and for three days I made excuses and shirked it. I should probably have gone on shirking it but for a happy accident. In the hotel I stumbled upon one of those college girls (there were a bunch of them on the ship coming over); I had not known before that she was in the house. She was a lovely creature of sixteen, and I borrowed her of her mother at once. After that I paid calls every day, and she went with me.[8]

Frances Nunnally of Atlanta, whom Sam nicknamed Francesca, the daughter of a candy manufacturer and an early investor in Coca-Cola, became the newest angelfish.

Sam spoke on June 25 at a luncheon meeting at the Savoy Hotel of the Society of Pilgrims, an organization founded in 1902 by Harry Brittain to promote Anglo-American friendship. Brittain recalled over a half century later that he "saw a great deal of Mark Twain during that last visit to England and, like all who knew him, soon came to love him." Among the hundred and fifty guests—of the thousand who applied to attend—were Augustine Birrill, Chauncey Depew, H. Rider Haggard, Norman Hapgood, Anthony Hope, Lipton, T. P. O'Connor, Henry Rogers, and Beerbohm Tree. In his address, Sam conceded that he occasionally needed to lay aside "the cap and bell" of the jester, though he also played along with the joke circulating in the press that he had stolen the prestigious Ascot Gold Cup, awarded annually to the winner of the two-and-a-half-mile horse race at Ascot racecourse in Berkshire, which coincidentally disappeared the day of his arrival. Sam protested he had "never seen it" and "did not have a chance to get it." Owen Seaman, an editor of *Punch*, also declaimed a brief lyric in Sam's honor which the rival *Academy* soon dismissed as "eight lines of fulsome gush":

Pilot of many Pilgrims since the shout
"*Mark twain*!"—that serves you for a death sign—
On Mississippi's waterway rang out
Over the plummet's line—
Still where the countless ripples laugh above
The blue of halcyon seas long may you keep
Your course unbroken, buoyed up on a love
Ten thousand fathoms deep!

That evening, Sam made his first public appearance in Oxford at the Jesus College Gaudeamus (or "Gaudy," a college feast).[9]

The university exercises the next day climaxed Sam's month in England. The honorary doctoral recipients, who in addition to Sam included General William Booth of the Salvation Army, Rudyard Kipling, Lockyer, Reid, the sculptor Auguste Rodin, and the musical composer Camille Saint-Saëns, gathered at All Souls College in the morning to walk together to the Sheldonian Theater. "When we moved, gowned & mortar-boarded" up the street "between solemn walls of the common people," Sam wrote Jean, "their hearty welcome deeply touched me all the way, & brought back to mind the welcome of the stevedores when I went ashore at Tilbury dock." Trailing him in the parade so that he "could enjoy Oxford's delight," Kipling recalled that "the street literally rose at [Sam]—men cheered him by name on all sides." Sam was "very charming and evidently much impressed" by the pageantry. "All the people cheered Mark Twain. And when they weren't cheering and shouting, you could hear the Kodak shutters click-clicking like gun locks." Sam gloated later that "someone with a camera" tried to photograph Kipling and instead snapped "the best picture I ever had taken" during the procession. "Kipling was behind me" but "the kodak slipped or something happened and it turned out that I had eclipsed him completely and there was nothing left but the tip of his ear." Put another way, he not only upstaged the recipient of the Nobel Prize for Literature in 1907 but literally obscured him from view.[10]

The formalities at the theater were so ponderous that, rather than linger in the wings, Kipling, Lockyer, Sir William Ramsay, and Sam crossed the quadrangle to "a big archway" where, Kipling recalled, they smoked "like naughty boys."

They "were there more than an hour" before they returned to the Sheldonian "happy, content, and greatly refreshed," then "filed into the theatre, under a very satisfactory hurrah" to receive their degrees. "When his mass of white hair was first seen" as he walked in his scarlet gown "up the gangway,"

Figure 18. Samuel Clemens (left) smoking and talking with Sir William Ramsay (right) at Oxford University while waiting to receive his honorary degree, June 26, 1907. Courtesy of the Mark Twain Papers and Project, Bancroft Library, University of California–Berkeley, PH00412.

the *London Tribune* reported, "a storm of cheering broke out which could hardly be controlled." When at last his name was called to be hooded, according to Kipling, "even those dignified old Oxford dons stood up and yelled." The journalist Sydney Brooks remembered that "of all the recipients of degrees" Sam "roused the greatest enthusiasm. The whole building broke into a roar of applause when he stood up to be presented to the Chancellor." The *New York Times* reported that Sam "was the lion of the occasion" and that "when he was escorted up the aisle" and stood before the crowd he was "applauded for a quarter of an hour." He was cheered in particular by the undergraduate students and "was privately very vain of the common remark that [his ovation] was the largest one of the day—for I was born vain, & can't seem to get over it." Lord Curzon, the chancellor of the university, hailed him in Latin—a speech soon parodied in verse:

Vir jocundissime,
Lepidissime,
Facetioussime.
Ego amo kissime,
Doctoris in litteris,

Laughibus sideum splitteris,
Tua hilaritate,
Whoopitupto em hotti,
Markibus on the spotti.
Jokum et chokum,
Nihil fit.
Brother to the Oxford,
You are It.
Sic semper tyrannis!
Turn on the champagne.
E pluribus unum!
Hooray for Doc Twain!

After the commencement the honorees retired to All Souls College for a lunch hosted by Lord Curzon. As they left the theater, according to Brooks, "the people in the streets singled out Mark Twain, formed a vast and cheering bodyguard around him and escorted him to the college gates. But before and after the lunch it was Mark Twain again whom everybody seemed most of all to want to meet." After lunch, they were fe(as)ted at a garden party on the grounds of St. John's College, where once again "everyone pressed forward for an exchange of greetings and a handshake" with Sam. The newly minted doctors dined at another Gaudeamus feast in the Great Hall of Christ Church that evening. At the close of a long day, Sam was obviously exhausted. Whitelaw Reid remembered that "his speech was rather longer than was expected, rambling, and, as the English said, thin in straining for humor to which he did not attain. But the closing sentence redeemed it. He wished them to understand, in spite of the light tone in which he might seem to have spoken, that he fully appreciated and was profoundly grateful for the great honor they had done him—perhaps the greatest he should ever receive." He was flattered to have been "bracketed between a Prince of the Blood (here he turned and bowed to Prince Arthur of Connaught) and a Prince of the Republic of Letters," nodding to Kipling. "And with that he sat down. It struck me as really fine."[11]

The next two days Sam was a guest of Lord Curzon at the Oxford Pageant, a grand reenactment of events in British history from Saxon times "to the powdered wig era of George III." "Oxford was not perfect until pageant day arrived," he later reminisced. "The make-ups of illustrious historic personages seemed perfect, both as to portraiture and costume; one had no trouble in recognizing them." The pageant opened "with A. D. 710; then 1110; then 1284; then 1521; then 1587; then 1607; then 1641; then 1686;

then 1790; then 1810," as he described the spectacle to Clara. The twenty-five hundred members of the cast were local residents.

> At 2 p.m. daily they all swarmed out, in costume, & started for the meadow, outside the town, & went loafing down the quaint old lanes & streets of the venerable city—& dear me they did harmonise with the quaint & mouldy old buildings to perfection! Once I turned a corner & came suddenly upon an ecclesiastic of A.D. 710 & up went his two fingers in prelatic blessing as he called me by name & made me welcome to his long-vanished day; & I met Charles I in the same way—oh, Charles to the life! And he also was cordial. And James I, & Henry VIII, & Friar Bacon, & no end of others—I came upon them everywhere, & always it was a charming & a thrilling surprise.

The cavalcade "was beyond anything I at all imagined. I never meant to journey over any sea again except to my own funeral, but I would cross the Atlantic twice to see it." By comparison grand opera seemed "poor & small & cheap & fictitious. And then the final scene" when the entire cast "were present & mingling, marching & countermarching before us—well, it was a fairy dream!" The "reproduction of bygone English life and achievements by pageantry," Sam decided, "is the most beautiful, most instructive, and most impressive way of portraying history." When Sam returned to the manuscript of "No. 44, the Mysterious Stranger" in September, he depicted an "Assembly of the Dead" in chapter 33 inspired by the Oxford parade. Little Satan "summoned those forlorn wrecks from all the world & from all the epochs & ages," including King Arthur "with all his knights." As late as January 1909, Sam reminisced about observing "the Oxford pageant file by the grandstand, picture after picture, splendor after splendor, three thousand five hundred strong, the most moving and beautiful and impressive historically-instructive show conceivable."[12]

On April 28 Sam was the guest of honor at a luncheon hosted by the journalist Robert Porter, at whose home he stayed while in Oxford. That afternoon he visited the offices of the Oxford University Press as the guest of its superintendent, Horace Hart. In the evening he attended a meeting of the American Rhodes scholars and was almost snarled in controversy. The local fraternity had ostracized a black student from its ranks. Sam agreed to "do my best to convince them that their position was not wise and not just," but instead he sidestepped the issue by refraining "from any reference to the matter in dispute" and confining "my talk to other and cheerfuler things." The young black scholar was Alain Locke, a recent graduate of Harvard College, future editor of *The New Negro* (1925), and a prominent figure in the Harlem Renaissance. Sam reluctantly commended "the Rhodes benefaction" because he "always detested Mr. Rhodes; I never saw him, either in South Africa or in London; I avoided his vicinity; I never met him, and never wanted to meet him; my praises of what he has done must at least be granted the merit of sincerity." He "enjoyed talking to the Rhodes scholars," as he wrote Jean, and in all "I prodigiously enjoyed every hour of my 3 days in Oxford. . . . I enjoyed all the fine old time-worn ceremonies" except the speech-making.[13]

Sam's reminiscences of the Oxford festivities, dictated on July 26, were subsequently excerpted in the *North American Review* for October 1907. As anodyne as the account seemed, he incurred criticism from an Ohio physician in the pages of a medical journal because he published "the fact that when he was awaiting the conferring upon him of the degree at Oxford, his desire for tobacco became so insistent that he knowingly violated the rules of the institution by smoking," according to this Pecksniff. Sam's "obdurant forcing of his tobacco habit upon defenseless Oxford . . . brazenly obtrude[d] itself" upon the innocent people at the ceremony. "I don't mind what they say about me," Sam allowed. "I'm used to it and through it all I've kept my moral character fairly clean." One of his fellow doctoral recipients "said that we could go around to a certain corridor and no one would see us and there would be nothing said." Sam swore he "was not the chief criminal; there were four, one American and three Englishmen, so you see that the crime was pretty well divided up." He wished he could "divide up all my crimes in the same proportion." The Ohio doctor might believe "the excessive use of tobacco is responsible" for certain evils, but Sam did not "think it can quite ruin" a person. "There are about 40 other causes" of his declining health "and tobacco will have to bear only a fortieth part of the blame."[14]

On his return to London on June 29, Sam detoured through Stratford-on-Avon to pay a courtesy call on the American expatriate novelist Marie Corelli. In truth he had little time to spare: he was scheduled to speak that evening at a dinner in his honor hosted by the Lord Mayor of London. But Corelli had admonished him upon his arrival in England that he "mustn't go back across the sea without coming to Shakespeare!" and, despite his aversion to her when they met in Homburg in 1891, he accepted her invitation to lunch on the only date available to him. The side trip "looked like an easy matter" on the map; "the travel connected with it could not amount to much, I supposed," so he agreed to a hasty meal. The mayor of Stratford proposed to host a civic reception, but Sam preferred to pop in and out of town on a private visit without fanfare. Corelli promptly planned a full afternoon of events so that she could show off her trophy guest—at the Bard's birthplace, his grave, Anne Hathaway's house, historic Harvard House, and finally at her home, historic Mason Croft, "where a few of [her] friends" were "invited to meet him." Corelli even attended the garden party at St. John's College in Oxford on June 26 "to make sure of her prey," as Sam put it. He tried to call off the lunch, attempted "to persuade a conscienceless fool to mercifully retire from a self-advertising scheme which was dear to her heart. She held her grip; anyone who knew her could have told us she would." Her plans were too advanced to cancel them, she insisted. "I think there is no criminal in any jail with a heart so unmalleable, so unfazeable, so flinty, so uncompromisingly hard as Marie Corelli's," he reflected six weeks later. He might have added, as he sometimes said of boors, that she was the kind of person who kept a parrot.[15]

Sam was greeted at the Stratford station in midmorning by a throng of people, a band playing Handel's "See, the Conquering Hero Comes," and Corelli in her carriage, ready to parade him through the town. She

> was going to drive us to Shakespeare's church, but I canceled that; she insisted, but I said that the day's program was already generous enough in fatigues without adding another. She said there would be a crowd at the church to welcome me, and they would be greatly disappointed, but I was loaded to the chin with animosity [like the jumping frog with quail shot], and childishly eager to be as unpleasant as possible, so I held my ground, particularly as I was well acquainted with Marie by this time and foresaw that if I went to the church I should find a trap arranged for a speech; my teeth were already loose from incessant speaking, and the very thought of adding a jabber at this time was a pain to me; besides, Marie, who never wastes an opportunity to advertise herself, would work the incident into the newspapers.

Corelli told Sam she was buying Harvard House, once the home of John Harvard, the founder of Harvard University, and

> wanted to stop at that dwelling and show me over it, and she said there would be a crowd there. I said I didn't want to see the damned house. I didn't say it in those words, but in that vicious spirit, and she understood; even her horses understood, and were shocked, for I saw them shudder. . . . As we drove by I saw that the house and the sidewalk were full of people—which meant that Marie had arranged for another speech.

Finally, they reached Mason Croft, "a very attractive and commodious English home." Sam asked "to go immediately to a bedchamber and stretch out and get some rest" and Corelli "was voluble with tender sympathy." First, however, she "deftly steered me into the drawing-room and introduced me to her company." Then she "beguiled me" outdoors to "a stretch of waste ground where stood fifty pupils of a military school, with their master at their head—arrangement for another advertisement. She asked me to make a little speech" and "I complied briefly" with a reminiscence of his abbreviated service in the Ralls County Rangers during the Civil War. They returned to the house, and Sam "got a quarter of an hour's rest" before lunch. "Toward the end of it that implacable woman rose in her place, with a glass of champagne in her hand, and made a speech! With me for a text, of course. . . . When she had finished I said—'I thank you very much'—and sat still." In retrospect, Sam considered her "the most offensive sham, inside and out, that misrepresents and satirizes the human race today."[16]

Sam returned to London late that afternoon in a pouring rain, slept for a few hours at Brown's Hotel, then hurried to the banquet in his honor at Mansion House. Among the two hundred and fifty attendees were Sir William Gilbert, George Grossmith, Fridtjof Nansen, and Bram Stoker. As he entered the room he received a warm reception, and when the Lord Mayor introduced him, "the assembly sprang to its feet and shouted its welcome" and sang "For He's a Jolly Good Fellow." Speaking with bowed head and in a subdued voice, Sam announced that he would return to the United States "in a week or two. I came to get an honorary degree, and I would have compassed seven seas for an honor like that. I cannot feel too grateful to the University and to Lord Curzon for conferring it upon me. I am sure my country must appreciate the honor, for of course it is first and foremost to my country." The degree was "the greatest honor that has ever fallen to my share." Sam closed his address with a parting message to his friends in the audience. "It is unlikely I shall ever see England again," he declared, "but I shall ever retain the recollection of what I have experienced here in the way of generous, most kindly welcomes. . . . And so I must say good-bye, and in saying good-bye I do so not with my lips, but with my whole heart." He returned to his seat amid "loud cheers." Despite his eloquence, Sam thought the speech "a botch" delivered at the end of the "most hateful day my seventy-two years have ever known."[17]

Sam spent his final days in England hewed to a packed social calendar neatly organized around meals. Some of the highlights: dinner on June 30 hosted by Sir Gilbert and Lady Parker, dinner on July 1 at the Garrick Club hosted by the scholar Sir Sidney Lee, lunch the next day with John Henniker Heaton and T. P. O'Connor at the House of Commons, dinner that evening at the Savoy Hotel hosted by Harry Brittain, dinner on July 3 with C. F. Moberly Bell, lunch on July 4 with Sir James Knowles at the Hotel Cecil, dinner on July 5 with the Earl and Countess of Portsmouth, breakfast the next day with Lord Avebury, Lord Kelvin, and Sir Charles Lyell, lunch on July 7 with Sir Norman Lockyer, followed by an afternoon spent returning calls in company with Francesca, dinner on July 8 again with Bell, and lunch the following day hosted by Sir Benjamin Stone in the Harcourt dining room of the House of Commons with former prime minister Arthur Balfour and Baron Komura Jutaro, Japanese ambassador to Britain and one of the negotiators of the Treaty of Portsmouth. Despite Sam's loathing for that diplomatic accord, according to press reports he "was in his happiest vein." He "buzzed around every day & many nights" to a total of at least forty (he estimated) "breakfasts, luncheons, teas & dinners, & have never been fatigued, more than an hour at a time," as he assured Clara.[18] He mixed mostly with conservative members of parliament and the elite or titled class at most of these affairs.

There were some exceptions to this pattern, however. On July 3 he lunched with "that brilliant Irishman, Bernard Shaw," his feminist wife Charlotte Payne-Townshend, Archibald Henderson, and the essayist and political cartoonist Max Beerbohm at the Shaws' apartment in Adelphi Terrace overlooking the Thames. Sam presented the Fabian socialist Shaw with an inscribed copy of *Christian Science* and from all indications the five of them enjoyed a convivial conversation. Beerbohm was struck by Sam's "benign blue eyes." Shaw remembered that Sam "had a complete gift of intimacy which enabled us to treat one another as if we had known one another all our lives, as indeed I had known him through his early books, which I read and reveled in before I was twelve years old." He wrote Sam later that he was "persuaded that the future historian of America will find your works as indispensable to him as a French historian finds the political tracts of Voltaire." On his part, Sam initially admitted that, while he was unfamiliar with Shaw and his writings, "he is a charming and delightful host." In his autobiographical dictation, Sam added that "Shaw is a pleasant man; simple, direct, sincere, animated; but self-possessed, sane, and evenly poised, acute, engaging, companionable, and quite destitute of affectation."[19]

On July 4, Sam replied to the toast "The Day We Celebrate" during a banquet of the American Society in London at the swank Hotel Cecil, virtually the only occasion on this trip when he gathered with countrymen—among them Reid, Oliver Wendell Holmes Jr., and Nicholas Murray Butler. His remarks, which provoked some laughs, were tempered. Americans honor Independence Day "all through the daylight hours," he opined, but "when night comes we dishonor it" with pandemonium and fireworks that "cripple and kill more people than you would imagine." In truth the Fourth of July "is our day of mourning, our day of sorrow.'" Better to celebrate the anniversary of the Emancipation Proclamation in 1863, "which not only set the black slaves free but set the white man free also," than the anniversary of the Declaration of Independence in 1776. Little wonder that in February 1908 Sam joined the Society for the Suppression of Unnecessary Noises, an organization dedicated to regulating Fourth of July revelry.[20]

He was again the guest of honor at a dinner of the Savage Club the evening of July 6, the only time the entire month in England he wore a white suit. In his speech he reminisced about the first meeting of the club he attended in 1872, which had "always remained in my mind as a peculiarly blessed evening, since it brought me into contact with men of my own kind and my own feelings. I am glad to be here, and to see you all, because it is very likely that I shall not see you again." At the close of his remarks he was presented with a gilded plaster facsimile of the Ascot Cup he supposedly had stolen.[21]

"The prettiest incident of my long life," Sam asserted in his autobiography, occurred the afternoon of July 9, when the staff of *Punch* hosted a luncheon in his honor at its editorial offices on Bouverie Street, "and I cannot think of it yet without a thrill at my heart and quickened pulsebeat." He had delayed his return to the United States specifically to attend this function. "In fifty years I am the only stranger unto whom has been extended the privilege of crossing that sacred threshold and sitting at that sacred board," he bragged. At the outset, before the humorist F. C. Burnand, Henry Lucy, and the other guests were seated, Joy Agnew, the young daughter of Philip Agnew, proprietor of the magazine, "a little fairy decked out in pink," "danced out," "made a curtsey to me," and presented Sam with the original Bernard Partridge cartoon that had appeared in *Punch* on June 26, depicting Mr. Punch offering Sam a glass of punch. According to both Lucy and the humorist E. V. Lucas, Sam "was visibly touched" by the gesture and referred to it repeatedly in his speech, once with his voice "broken with emotion."[22]

Sam, Ashcroft, and O'Connor left from Euston Station by express train the next morning for Liverpool, where Sam had been invited by John Japp, the Lord Mayor, to speak that evening at a town hall banquet. The rail authorities provided Sam and his entourage with a special car, usually reserved for the Prince of Wales and nicknamed "the King's carriage," so that they could rest while traveling. As usual, Sam skipped the meal and arrived at the banquet hall only in time for speeches. Sir Edward Russell, editor of

Figure 19. Bernard Partridge, "To the Master of His Art," cartoon in *Punch,* June 26, 1907.

the *Liverpool Post,* had composed an irregular sonnet, "The Health of Mark Twain," to mark the occasion:

Happy the Wit whom humour claims its own.
Happy the Humorist whose wit is prone
To polish every quaintly human stroke
Of paradox; chisel each homely joke
His name Mark Twain—beloved in every land—
Whose subtleties 'tis joy to understand;
His irony all play, his play all wise,
(How wild soever) and his fun a prize
In each mind's luck-bag of bizarre thought.
Long may his life with happiness be fraught.
With grateful memories may his heart be filled:

This wish, the monument his readers build
To one who has enlarged the sphere of mirth,
Of wit, of humour and of lettered worth.

Sam soon thanked Russell for the "beautiful poem" and "the impulse that moved" him to write it. Before an audience of two hundred, Sam spoke eloquently for most of an hour and delivered, as Paine wrote later, "one of the most effective [addresses] of his whole career." He pronounced the Oxford degree "the loftiest honor that has ever fallen to my fortune, the one I should have chosen as outranking any and all others and more precious to me than any and all others within the gift of men and states to bestow upon me," as if he already knew he would be overlooked for the Nobel Prize later in the year. He concluded by citing an incident in Richard Henry Dana's *Two Years before the Mast:*

> There was a presumptuous little self-important skipper in a coasting sloop engaged in the dried-apple and kitchen-furniture trade, and he was always hailing every ship that came in sight. He did it just to hear himself talk and to air his small grandeur. One day a majestic Indiaman came plowing by with course on course of canvas towering into the sky, her decks and yards swarming with sailors, her hull burdened to the Plimsoll line with a rich freightage of precious spices, lading the breezes with gracious and mysterious odors of the Orient. It was a noble spectacle, a sublime spectacle! *Of* course the little skipper popped into the shrouds and squeaked out a hail, "Ship ahoy! What ship is that? And whence and whither?" In a deep and thunderous bass the answer came back through the speaking-trumpet, "The *Begum* of Bengal—142 days out from Canton—homeward bound! What ship is that?" Well, it just crushed that poor little creature's vanity flat and he squeaked back most humbly, "Only the *Mary Ann,* fourteen hours out from Boston, bound for Kittery Point—with nothing to speak of!" Oh, what an eloquent word that "only," to express the depths of his humbleness! That is just my case. During just one hour in the twenty-four—not more—I pause and reflect in the stillness of the night with the echoes of your English welcome still lingering in my ears, and then I am humble. Then I am properly meek, and for that little while I am only the *Mary Ann,* fourteen hours out, cargoed with vegetables and tinware; but during all the other twenty-three hours my vain self-complacency rides high on the white crests of your approval, and then I am a stately Indiaman, plowing the great seas under a cloud of canvas and laden with the kindest words that have ever been vouchsafed to any wandering alien in this world.

Then Sam's "twenty-six fortunate days on this old mother soil seem to be multiplied by six" and he "sang out the words" in a "rich, resonant, uplifted voice," "*I* am the *Begum* of Bengal—142 days out from Canton." O'Connor remembered that "there burst forth a great cheer from one end of the room to the other. It seemed an inopportune cheer" and at the moment it seemed to trouble Sam, "yet it was felicitous in opportuneness. Slowly, after a long pause, came the last two words—like that curious, detached and high note in which a great piece of music sometimes suddenly and abruptly ends—'Homeward bound.' Again there was a cheer; but this time it was lower; it was subdued; it was the fitting echo to the beautiful words." Only "a great littérateur" and great orator could have delivered so dramatic a farewell, according to O'Connor, who realized both "how tremendous was Mark Twain's power over an audience" and that he "ought to have been an orator by occupation as well as a writer." Afterward Sam shook hands with everyone present before leaving for his hotel. "It was my last (public) night in England," he crowed, "and certainly no one has ever had a more uplifting night anywhere, nor one so easy to house and sacredly preserve in the memory." He reported to Rogers that, although "I did most profoundly dread the journey & the banquet & the reception," in the end "I was very glad I went" to Liverpool. He, O'Connor, and Ashcroft returned from the Lime Street Station in Liverpool to London the next day aboard the "King's carriage."[23]

While Sam was carousing in England, he was the subject of some malicious gossip in the States. On July 4 the *New York Herald* reported that he and Isabel Lyon were engaged to be married. The rumor was probably started by Charlotte Teller Johnson in retaliation for similar gossip about her spread by Isabel Lyon several months earlier. Sam later suspected that Ashcroft and/or Lyon had planted the story, but Lyon was the first to gainsay it. She immediately issued an "unqualified denial," explained that she had simply been Sam's private secretary for the five years, "looked after his affairs," and that "the King would be as pained as his secretary to hear of any such report." Sam likewise repudiated the claim: "I have not known and shall never know anyone who could fill the place of the wife I have lost. I shall not marry again," prompting at least one newspaper to quip that he denied the rumor as "vigorously as though he thought many people would care."[24]

During his final two days in London, Sam held court as usual. On July 11 he dined with his publishers Andrew Chatto and Percy Spalding and met his old friend Bram Stoker. The next day he received calls at his hotel from

Hamilton Wright Mabie and Sir Thomas Lipton, lunched with the Earl and Countess of Portsmouth, and spent two hours at the National Gallery with its director Sir Charles Holroyd and Sir Lawrence Alma-Tadema. During the tour he viewed Alma-Tadema's new painting *Caracalla and Geta,* which depicted spectators at a bear fight in the Roman Colosseum, and Anthony van Dyck's portrait of Giovanni Battista Cataneo.[25]

He and Ashcroft departed early in the morning of July 13 from St. Pancras Station for Tilbury, where they embarked on the Atlantic Transport steamer *Minnetonka* for New York. The parting was the epitome of sweet sorrow. Sam issued a statement as they boarded:

> I have led a violently gay life here for four weeks, but I felt no fatigue and have had little desire to quiet down. I'm younger now by seven years than I was, and if I could stay another month I could make it forty years. This has been the most enjoyable holiday I ever had. I'm sorry the end has come. I have met a hundred old friends and made a hundred new ones. It is a good kind of riches to have. There is none better. For two years I have been planning my funeral, but I have changed my mind and postponed it.

His only regret was his failure to revisit Ireland, particularly after he was invited to Dublin by the viceroy of Ireland, his friend Lord Aberdeen. The *Pall Mall Gazette* editorialized that

> we are sorry that he is going, because he might have continued to jest for another month without being at all wearisome. There is a sort of breezy morality about his valetudinarianisms. They suggest the happiness of facing hard facts with serenity, and are quite of a piece with all his gay philosophy; for Mr. Clemens's humour, apart from his earliest books of large buffoonery, may be strictly defined as the playfulness of common sense. May there be no reaction after the "violently gay and energetic life" of this farewell trip.

The *London Tribune* asserted with pardonable hyperbole that Sam had "triumphed and in his all-too-brief stay of a month has done more for the cause of the world's peace than will be accomplished by the Hague Conference," under way at the time, and Sam reiterated in his autobiography that "those four weeks in England were the delightfulest of my life."[26]

On the first day of the voyage he captured another angelfish, eleven-year-old Dorothy Quick of Plainfield, New Jersey, who was traveling with her mother and grandparents. She claimed to have read all his books, which "in the main" was "true enough," and she soon convinced him that she "knew more about his books" than Sam did. She wore white sailor suits the remainder of the voyage to match his white flannels. "We were inseparable," she wrote; Sam "literally wouldn't let me out of his sight." He "laughingly called [her] his business manager" and required the organizers of onboard entertainments to obtain her permission before his performances. The other passengers thought Sam "kindly, affable, an eager watcher of the ship's sports and especially fond of the children, a fondness which centered itself finally upon Dorothy Quick," and they even voted him a Master of Goodfellowship. In the course of the cruise Sam also discussed the impracticality of Prohibition, or "whisky phobia," with a fellow passenger who belonged to the Women's Christian Temperance Union. Temperance was an impossible ideal, he claimed, because the Germans had "just invented a method of making brandy out of sawdust. Now what chance will prohibition have when a man can take a ripsaw and go out and get drunk with a fence rail? What is the good of prohibition if a man is able to make brandy smashes out of the shingles on his roof or if he can get delirium tremens by drinking the legs off the kitchen chairs?"[27]

Early in the morning of July 15, two days out from Tilbury, the *Minnetonka* collided with a fishing schooner in a dense fog. The schooner lost its bowsprit and head sails. The crash punched a hole in the *Minnetonka* above the water line, and the captain ordered deployment of the lifeboats. Sam hurried to the deck in a bathrobe and slippers before learning the ship was in no danger of sinking. He soon enlisted the support of the other passengers in a statement to the directors of the shipping line acquitting the crew of all responsibility for the accident. He also composed a cable report of the collision widely circulated in the American and British press, a reversion to the river notices he contributed a half century earlier to the St. Louis and New Orleans newspapers: "At 6.30 a barque suddenly loomed up close to us, and lost her bowsprit dragging along our side. We received very slight damage. The barque was coming for our broadside, but prompt action on both sides prevented a direct collision. The barque disappeared in the fog. We saw her twice during three hours' hunt, but she was quickly enveloped in fog that we could not speak to her, so we resumed our trail. All well." Dorothy Quick remembered, however, that "some of the passengers slept in their clothes the remainder of the trip." Despite the collision, the *Minnetonka* docked in New York the afternoon of July 22 six hours ahead of schedule.

Sam and Ashcroft were welcomed home by Duneka and David Munro of Harper & Brothers, Isabel Lyon, and a pack of reporters. Lyon noted that "the King stood along at the end of the long line of passengers on the lower deck, with a little girl snuggling up against him." He refused to be photographed without his "*mon amie*," and, as Dorothy recalled, they posed for the paparazzi on the sundeck of the steamer. Attired in her sailor suit, she sat in Sam's lap, leaned her head against his shoulder, and "the next day there wasn't a paper in New York that didn't have one of the pictures in it."[28]

Figure 20. Samuel Clemens and Dorothy Quick upon their arrival in New York City, July 22, 1907. Courtesy of the Library of Congress.

Figure 21. Samuel Clemens and Dorothy Quick in Tuxedo Park, New York, late summer 1907. Photograph by Isabel Lyon. Courtesy of the Mark Twain Papers and Project, Bancroft Library, University of California–Berkeley, PH02055.

CHAPTER 16

Anecdotage

If I drink coffee it gives me dispepsia [sic]; if I drink wine it gives me the gout; if I go to church it gives me dysentery.

—Samuel Clemens to Henry H. Rogers, 7 August 1905

SAM SCURRIED TO Tuxedo Park with Isabel Lyon the morning after his return from England and hibernated for most of the next two months. Jean's health remained a worry, despite Frederick Peterson's rosy reports of her improvement. In truth, she was increasingly miserable in the Katonah sanitarium, where she was a virtual prisoner. In her diary she used the term "rabid" no less than nine times between July 15 and November 8, 1907, to describe her anger, as though she were a caged animal infected with rabies. She was particularly irked by her father's and sister's profligate spending while she was expected to limit her expenses. Sam had subsidized Clara's concert tours, including a salary for her accompanist, Charles Wark, to the tune of thousands of dollars, as well as Clara and Lyon's vacation in June in Nova Scotia, while he had enjoyed the trip to England with Ashcroft, lodging at one of the most exclusive hotels in the world. Meanwhile, Sam begrudged Jean's monthly $16 fee to maintain her pet Saint Bernard, ironically named Prosper. On July 26, four days after Sam returned from England, she received "a rather disagreeable letter from Father" about the cost to feed her dog but "never a word about my birthday" that same day. She resented the "selfish attitude about Prosper's board," blaming both Sam and Lyon, the keeper of the family purse, while they happily covered the cost "of a trip to Europe to receive a great honor or one to Nova Scotia for a little recuperation." Sam finally traveled to Katonah on August 12, only his third and final call on his daughter during her fifteen-month confinement there. They "had a real visit this time, without Miss Lyon & over an hour in length," Jean noted. "When Miss Lyon is about I am always more painfully conscious of my ignorance and stupidities." Still, Sam rued the folly of feeding Prosper. "He tho[ugh]t the dog of no value—no dog had ever been of value that he had known," she complained. "He ought to be destroyed & the money given to the poor." She was affronted by her father's "empty letters, telling me to have a good time," when "he won't really try to rectify bad conditions." Jean sent "a cruel letter" to him around this time "damning" Lyon and "finding fault with him" for neglecting her, though he attributed her grievances to her disease and to "the God who can create such natures."[1]

The same day Sam received this letter, Peterson told Jean he "believed [in] letting well enough alone & that as I had done so well here he tho[ugh]t it a pity to change." The next day Peterson told Lyon he was opposed to discharging Jean from the sanitarium "where she is improving." He also advised, according to Lyon's notes of their conversation, that Jean "must never live with her father again because her affection might easily turn into a violent & insane hatred & she could slay, just by the sudden & terrible & ungovernable revulsion of feeling."[2] Jean was resigned to the inevitable. "Dr. Peterson insists on my staying here, for a while at least!" and if "there's no other convenient place for me to go," she decided, "why then I'll have to make the best of this & feeling mournful & crying constantly aren't going to do me any good or change the situation. I have asked father to allow me sufficient money for occasional trips to Bronxville & I am neither afraid of his refusing it nor of Dr. Peterson's refusals to let me go." She notified her father that under the circumstances she would remain in Katonah, and Sam replied as though she had surrendered in a battle of wills. "Jean dear," he wrote, "I hear that Dr. Peterson is exceedingly well pleased with your year's progress, & certainly I am. It is a wonderful advance. How fortunate it was that fortune put you into his hands." She was incensed by this response. "Father has written & is glad that I was happy & cheerful & willing to help carry out all of Dr. P.'s plans," she groused. "Fool that I was to write that misunderstood letter. I only meant that while I *had* to stay I was trying to make the best of things, but never did I mean to convey that I was contented, happy in such a place. That shows how little he appreciates how I feel or he *could* not write in such a way."[3]

In the immediate wake of his Oxford honors, Sam was victimized by a pair of publishing scoundrels who printed unauthorized interviews with him. Upon his return from England, he spurned all invitations to speak with reporters. The *New York Herald* had offered him "an extravagant sum for an interview upon a respectable topic & I had declined." On July 27, however, Channez Huntington Olney presented a letter of introduction to Sam from Daniel Frohman and asked to see him. "She was not without attraction," Lyon noted, "and succeeded in interesting him when she said she was making a collection of the imprints of the hands of famous men and her collection would not be complete without his." Unfortunately, a month later

Olney printed in the New York *World* a purported interview with Sam and an impression of his right hand. A palm reader would conclude, she asserted, that he was "an artist, a sensitive man, proud, firm willed, impulsive, clear headed." Enraged by this betrayal of his confidence, Sam dictated a letter to Joseph Pulitzer, the owner of the *World*, that "under cover of lies" this "scurvy drab" gained "access to my room" and spoke with him. "There was no interview," he insisted, "the *World* should not have been deceived by this cheap swindle," and "I ought to have been asked about it over the telephone" prior to its publication.[4]

The evening of October 27 Sam met the British writer Elinor Glyn, in the United States to promote her potboiling romance *Three Weeks*. She arrived "upon the stormwind of a vast and sudden notoriety," he remembered, and they arranged to meet again after he read her book. In her autobiography, Glyn recalled that she spent "a thrilling afternoon" at 21 Fifth Avenue with the "exquisitely whimsical" and "dear old man." He considered her novel "a fine piece of writing," but he understood "why the public condemn it and call it immoral." The adulterous couple featured in the story were puppets of their passions and, as Sam explained, "they keep on obeying them and obeying them, to the reader's intense delight and disapproval, and the process of obeying them is described, several times, almost exhaustively, but not quite—some little rag of it being left to the reader's imagination, just at the end of each infraction." A few days later they met again, and Glyn informed Sam that she had transcribed "every word I had said, just as I had said it, without any softening and purifying modifications and that it was 'just splendid, just wonderful.'" She "begged me to let her publish it and said it would do infinite good in the world but I said it would damn me before my time and I didn't wish to be useful to the world on such expensive conditions." Nevertheless, Glyn printed her transcript of their interview and presented Sam with a copy. He immediately repudiated her account of their conversation.

> She put into my mouth humiliatingly weak language, whereas I used exceedingly strong language—much too strong for print, and also much too indelicate for print—a fact which she has fully recognized by not reproducing any of it. . . . Inadequate as was her report of my sermon, she got at a good part of the substance of it, but she left out its only worthwhile feature—which was the argument I offered that her book was a mistake. . . . I am afraid she wants another advertisement of her book. I am sorry, for it is a very harmful and very readable book, though I did not pay it the extravagant compliments which she has put into my mouth.

To be sure, parts of Glyn's text rings true, particularly her reference to *What Is Man?*: "He said he had written a book" that challenged social convention "which would be published at his death, as there was no use in saying such things while alive, as his 'law' was to protect his daughters." But he vehemently protested Glyn's violation of his privacy and the accuracy of her report. He wrote that her record of their chat "reads pretty poorly. I get the sense of it, but it is a poor literary job; however, it would have to be because nobody can be reported even approximately except by a stenographer. . . . If you had put upon paper what I really said, it would have wrecked your type-machine. I said some fetid and over-vigorous things, but that was because it was a confidential conversation. I said nothing for print. My own report of the same conversation reads like Satan roasting a Sunday School."[5]

Even before his venture to Oxford, Sam shared in the planning for Robert Fulton Day on September 23 at the Jamestown exposition. Rogers loaned him the *Kanawha* to make the trip and, as the master of ceremonies, he was responsible for recruiting an orator for the day. He tendered invitations to Grover Cleveland, only to learn that the former president was in failing health, and to Joseph Choate, a member of the U.S. delegation to the Peace Conference at the Hague. "There's going to be inebriousness & general dissipation & a Halifax of a time," he wrote Choate, who declined to sail across the Atlantic merely to deliver a speech. He floated the name of Nicholas Murray Butler, though Rogers soon punctured the trial balloon. "I think you make a mistake in trying to advertise a man like Butler," Rogers notified Sam. "People of Virginia don't want to see him. They want Mark Twain. If you cannot see that, I can." Sam finally persuaded his friend Martin Littleton to fill the role. When he entered the banquet hall in Jamestown, the audience "rose and cheered" for "more than five minutes" despite inclement weather. He then delivered, according to Paine, "a brief, amusing talk on Fulton" before introducing Admiral Purnell Harrington and Littleton. Even the plan for a flotilla of ships in the bay to mark the occasion had fizzled. Rather than "a double line of majestic battleships stretching toward the horizon and fading into spectral forms in the distance," the fleet consisted of a "wee little handful of floaters. . . . Fulton's Festival had turned itself into a funeral." Sam returned to New York aboard the *Kanawha* the next day. While he reported to Dorothy Quick that he had enjoyed "altogether a good time," he was more candid with Rogers: Fulton Day had been "the completest & perfectest fiasco in history." Two weeks later, Sam bragged to Jean that he had kissed "two little girls" while in Jamestown "because he had kissed their sister." Jean was appalled: "to me it's not pleasant. I don't know how old the girls are but it seems a trifle queer, even if he is very old." Dorothy Quick visited Sam in Tuxedo Park about this time, and Quick remembered they posed for pictures "on the porches and in the garden."[6]

Figure 22. Samuel Clemens and Dorothy Quick in Tuxedo Park, New York, late summer 1907. Photograph by Isabel Lyon. Courtesy of the Mark Twain Papers and Project, Bancroft Library, University of California–Berkeley, PH00429.

Henry Rogers was not only Sam's best friend but his financial angel. Over the years Rogers had invested on Sam's behalf in such surefire stocks as Utah Consolidated and Amalgamated Mining, the Brooklyn Gas Company, and Federal Steel. These assets were hardly high-risk gambles; after all, Rogers was a seasoned inside trader. As Greg Zacharias observes, "the whole of Amalgamated stock was manipulated by Rogers and his colleagues for huge gains and thousands of individual investors were swindled of their money." His fortune "piles up faster under your handling of it than it did under my labors on the platform," Sam acknowledged to his adviser. During two weeks in December 1898, for example, his Federal Steel stock under Rogers's management increased in paper value by nearly $5,000, the equivalent of $150,000 in modern dollars. Rogers was nothing less than "a magician who can turn steel and copper and Brooklyn gas into gold," Sam thought. He had "nothing to do but sit around and watch you set the hen"—a pun here on the first syllable of Rogers's first name—"and hatch out those big broods and make my living for me. Don't you wish you had somebody to do the same for you?"[7]

Early in 1907 the stock market began to crumble, and it collapsed in a mid-October panic, threatening to wipe out the modest fortune Sam had recovered over the previous decade. The plunge no doubt revived Sam's memories of the Panic of 1873, when much of his fortune evaporated. As early as August he considered canceling the contracts he had signed to build the house in Redding, but John Howells advised that such a move would cost him "between ten and fifteen thousand dollars" in construction costs with nothing to show for the expense. Credit was so tight in early October that a ditty made the rounds of the press:

> We know there'll be no money
> For quite a little while;
> The outlook isn't funny
> When father reads Carlyle.
> He never seeks those pages
> When good luck comes along;
> Carlyle his woe assuages
> When everything goes wrong.
> Then father looks the queerest
> And glares with knitted frown,
> And when the storm is nearest
> He reads him upside down.
> 'Tis then we cut down closer
> And dine on cheese and bread,
> And dare not meet the grocer—
> The poor house looms ahead.
> But when those days are over,
> Like sunshine after rain,
> The family is in clover
> When father reads Mark Twain.

During the third week in October the market crashed, prompting a run on the banks, including the Knickerbocker Trust Company of New York, the third largest financial institution in the city, which suspended its payments. Lyon and Ashcroft by chance were in the city on October 21 and hurried to the Knickerbocker at Thirtieth Street and Fifth Avenue in a vain attempt to withdraw Sam's $51,000 deposit, only "to see crowds of people there, with bank books in their quivering hands." Before she "could do anything it was too late." She returned "to Tuxedo to find the King in bed and so cheerful and beautiful and brave and trying not to show his anxiety." The next day when Lyon "went to the King's room his face looked grey, but he was brace and cheerful and talked over what we must do. Sell the steel bonds a few at a time to build the Redding house with, for the autobiography money is in the Knickerbocker, and live on what comes from the Harpers." Clara warned Jean that their father was "desperately afraid" he would lose all his money, and if so, she might "not be able to stay" in Katonah. Jean was "scared in case that should mean" she would be obliged to live with her father; "I'm sure that would put me back."[8]

The directors of the Knickerbocker announced on October 23 that its suspension was temporary and that its assets exceeded its liabilities. Meanwhile, J. P. Morgan orchestrated an infusion of liquidity to prop up the stock market, or, as Sam put it, "the millionaire 'bandits' whom the President is so fond of abusing in order to get the applause of the gallery stepped in and stayed the desolation." Roosevelt promptly claimed credit for stabilizing the economy, "and there is much evidence that this inebriated nation thinks he is entitled to it." On November 1 Jean noted in frustration that her father's letter that day "made me tired. He spoke wholly of playing billiards for hours & said not one word regarding the business troubles. . . . I should be used to his peculiarities by now, I suppose, but I can never wholly reconcile myself to some of them." The next day, Sam assured her that "we shall lose nothing but only be temporarily cramped." In the end, no Knickerbocker depositor lost money by the suspension, though twenty-two thousand clients were "more or less inconvenienced." Asked by the New York *World* for a Thanksgiving sentiment at the end of the month, Sam expressed thanks "beyond words that I had only fifty-one thousand dollars on deposit in the Knickerbocker Trust, instead of a million; for if I had had a million in that bucket shop, I should be nineteen times as sorry as I am now." Sam privately scolded the Knickerbacker directors. "You discriminated against me by accepting two deposits from me after some had been warned to take their money out," he complained. "Instead of putting your hands in your pockets & paying your debts like the Lincoln Trust & other respectable concerns, you have been shillyshallying for a month trying to escape your obligations & find some more economical & less reputable way to resume. Why do you wish to resume? Do you suppose any one will risk money with you again? Next time you will bring up in jail, where you probably ought to have been many & many a year ago." The next winter Sam acquiesced to a plan to reorganize and reopen the trust. The alternative was to assign its assets to "a permanent receivership. I have already tried a permanent receivership once and did not like the result. It costs more to keep a permanent receiver than it does to keep a harem." The *Philadelphia Inquirer* mused in response, "Has he tried both?"[9]

At the depth of the fiscal crisis in the fall of 1907, incredibly enough, Charles Parsloe's widow Harriet Parsloe proposed to revive Sam and Bret Harte's play *Ah Sin*, a theatrical flop thirty years earlier. With Sam's permission, she wanted the script rewritten by a competent dramatist and staged under the title *Where the Trail Divides*. He was amenable but unenthusiastic, agreeing in principle but insisting that any publicity for the production include this caveat in order to protect his reputation: "revised & reconstructed by consent of Mark Twain from a play written by Bret Harte & Mark Twain called *Ah Sin*." The failure to credit his collaborator "would not be fair," he explained, because Harte had "constructed the scenario." Whereas Sam had claimed in 1877 that he had "left hardly a footprint of Harte" in the script, in 1907 he admitted that Harte "furnished the main character" and "wrote fully half the play."[10] In the end nothing came of the project.

Before the last installment of his autobiography appeared in the *North American Review* in December 1907, moreover, Sam agreed to permit George Harvey to syndicate the narrative in newspapers across the country. "It will not bring him in a penny," Lyon observed, but "it will be a good advertisement" for his books. The autobiography began to appear serially in such papers as the *New York Tribune*, *Boston Post*, *Washington Star*, *Chicago Record-Herald*, and *Pittsburgh Post* on October 17, and even in Australia the narrative was welcomed for the intimacy and pathos of many passages "which will astonish those readers who think of Mark Twain as merely a humorist."[11]

To add to Sam's financial woes, in the midst of the economic recession that followed the financial panic the Plasmon Company of America went bankrupt. Sam blamed the failure on Henry A. Butters, "a sharper hailing from Long Valley, California," who "robbed" and "skinned" the firm, rather than the faltering economy. He soon consigned Butters, "my heart's detested darling," to the same hell occupied by Elisha Bliss, Bret Harte, Charles Henry Webb, Charley Webster, and a host of other enemies real and imagined. Ironically, even as the American company struggled, plasmon attracted testimonials from the bodybuilder Eugen Sandow and the British medical journal the *Lancet*, which declared that when "added to ordinary food [it] raises the nutritive value enormously." Sam publicly endorsed the latter claim. Nevertheless, the company declared bankruptcy in early December; its remaining assets, including office furniture, were liquidated on December 6; and, after some of its former officers filed claims for back salary, Sam resigned as its acting president on December 12. He estimated later that he lost $32,000 in the defalcation. The joke soon went around that "one good way to locate an unsafe investment is to find out if Mark Twain has been permitted to get in on the ground floor."[12]

Ralph Ashcroft, one of the plaintiffs who sued for back pay when the Plasmon Company of America declared bankruptcy, compensated for his modest financial sacrifice by becoming Sam's full-time business manager. Between 1904 and 1906, at Ashcroft's urging, Sam lost several thousand dollars by investing in a gimmick corkscrew-shaped hat- and hairpin, manufactured by a company largely owned by Ashcroft's uncle. Yet on November 12, 1907, Ashcroft registered "Mark Twain" as a trademark on whisky and tobacco products, ostensibly to protect the Mark Twain facial image and facsimile signature with the U.S. Patent Office. The scheme was not designed to make money, Ashcroft insisted, but to safeguard "the trade value of Mr. Clemens' name." To comply with the law Ashcroft planned limited production of a Mark Twain whisky and a Mark Twain cigar. Sam's willingness to "make his pseudonym into a trademark," Guy Cardwell notes, suggests "that to him his writings very much resembled manufactured goods" or commodities.[13] The patent right filing was a prelude to Ashcroft's incorporation a few months later of the Mark Twain Company.

Meanwhile, Lyon continued to supervise the construction of the house in Redding and the renovation of the adjacent Lobster Pot. She noted in mid-September 1907 that the contractor rebuilding her house had installed triple windows, shingled the roof, and torn "the plaster from the ceiling" in the main room to reveal "what will be a most beautiful old oak ceiling, for the beams are splendid and the flooring above is a darling color. It is going to be glorious." Several months later the contractor "tore the plaster from the stone work around the mantles" to reveal "a lovely old chimney piece of coarse stonework" that Lyon chose to leave exposed. The revamping included the addition of a new kitchen and the conversion of the old kitchen into a parlor. Trouble is, it is unclear who was paying for this work. Lyon insisted that Sam had promised to loan her the money to rebuild the house; Sam claimed he had promised her only $1,000, though without formal paperwork to document the transaction; nevertheless, Lyon claimed to have spent $1,500. Sam forgave $500 of it as a Christmas gift in 1908 and promised to forgive the other $1,000 over time. Unfortunately, the various costs to construct Sam's house and to renovate Lobster Pot or the exact amounts of Sam's gifts and loans to Lyon during this period are impossible to calculate at this distance, mostly as a result of Lyon's slipshod accounting practices. As Hamlin Hill remarks, "on a number of occasions a workman who labored" at both Sam's house and Lobster Pot "was paid by a single check, with no separate accounting." While managing the household account between March 1907 and February 1909, Lyon also wrote checks for $6,789 to pay the wages of the staff and to cover the cost of Clara's concert tours "and many other items." According to Ashcroft, Lyon's ledgers revealed unexplained expenses of only about $5 a week; that is, despite her reputation as a femme fatale in Twain scholarship, she was arguably nothing more than a petty and inept thief and a sloppy bookkeeper.[14]

With his assets in the Knickerbocker Trust frozen, Sam needed money to finance the final stage of construction on the Redding house. After tinkering with "Captain Stormfield's Visit to Heaven" for nearly forty years, he retrieved the "rusty little batch" of manuscript from the safe deposit box where it was stored, "counted the words, and saw that there was enough of them to build the loggia" and Clara's music room and bedroom over it, "so I sent the 'Visit' to *Harper's Monthly* and collected the money." George Harvey had declined the story the previous September, dismissing it as "too damn godly for a secular paper," but he accepted it the next year. Because Sam thought it "a little too freely spoken"—too unpious—he had considered dumping the narrative into his autobiography, where it would appear posthumously, but he "greatly desired that loggia and the suite of rooms over it; so I concluded to make Captain Stormfield pay for it. He could afford it, but I couldn't." Instead of calling the dwelling Autobiography House as originally planned, Sam later chose to christen it Innocence at Home, for the angelfish, and then, at Clara's urging, Stormfield. Stormfield was "the best name anyway," given that it was "set so high" and "all the storms that come will beat upon it," as he wrote Jean.[15]

"Extract from Captain Stormfield's Visit to Heaven," which recounts the arrival of an old tar in the celestial domain, first appeared serially in *Harper's Monthly* for December 1907 and January 1908 and betrayed, as Huck might have said, "orgies of influence." Originally a riff on Elizabeth Stuart Phelps's *The Gates Ajar* (1868), "Stormfield" may also parody Lilian Whiting's *After Her Death* (1897), an account of the hereafter ostensibly narrated by Sam's old acquaintance Kate Field from beyond the grave, a copy of which Sam owned. In any case, Sam's heaven admits "cannibals, Presbyterians, pariahs, politicians, teetotalers, Turks, tramps,—indeed, all sorts of disagreeable people." In the final iteration of

Figure 23. Samuel Clemens sits outside at Stormfield, 1908, from *World's Work* 20, (June 1910).

the fantasy, it includes Jews, First Peoples,[16] and extraterrestrials, though paradise is segregated, offering each group separate but equal space in the next world. "I built a properly and rationally stupendous heaven and augmented its Christian population to 10 per cent of the contents of the modern cemeteries," Sam explained in his autobiography, and "as a volunteer kindness I let in a tenth of 1 per cent of the pagans who had died during the preceding eons."[17]

The installments were reviewed favorably but not widely in the United States, as in the *Brooklyn Eagle* ("one of the most amusing and witty of his later tales"), New York *Bookman* ("the manner is exactly that of" *A Connecticut Yankee* and *The Innocents Abroad*), *Salt Lake Herald* ("the most astonishing of all his humorous fiction"), and *Washington Star* ("remarkable story"). A pair of venues in the Commonwealth—the *Manchester Guardian* ("not in his happiest vein") and the *Sydney Stock and Station Journal* ("the most dreadful matter that ever was compounded for a respectable family magazine")—were more inimical.[18]

Sam was again in demand for banquets during the winter of 1907–8, though he was careful to pick and choose the dates. He readily agreed to speak at the opening of the new Engineers' Clubhouse the evening of December 9 in order to honor Andrew Carnegie, who donated the building on Fortieth Street adjacent to Bryant Park and the New York Public Library. Sam was a longtime but halfhearted convert to Carnegie's pet project of simplified or phonetic (fonetik?) or reformed (sometimes called "deformed") spelling, which he thought (thot?), like chastity, "can be carried too far." The "real disease," Sam quipped, was not the standard spelling of difficult words but the "silly alphabet" used to spell them. "If we had a sane, determinate alphabet, instead of a hospital of compound comingled cripples and eunuchs," he insisted, people "wouldn't have to learn to spell at all." Before he finished he blamed simplified spelling for "sunspots, the San Francisco earthquake, and the recent business depression." In the audience, Thomas Edison jotted on his dinner card that "An American loves his family. If he has any love left over for some other person he generally selects Mark Twain." Two weeks later Sam was the guest of honor and Dorothy Quick his guest at a Pleiades Club dinner at the Hotel Brevoort, a few steps from 21 Fifth Avenue, and on Saturday, December 28, he commuted with seventy other "slaves of Harper & Brothers," including Paine, Lyon, Duneka, Elizabeth Jordan, and Henry Mills Alden, to the posh Laurel House in Lakewood, New Jersey, to lunch with Howells prior to his departure for Italy. In his speech, Howells joked that he and Sam had once made a deal: he would write all of Sam's books if Sam would make all of Howells's speeches. Sam leaped to his feet to deny the allegation. "Howells hasn't written a book of mine for years," he remonstrated.

> But he did use to expurgate them. There was a time when I used to send all my stuff around to Howells and he'd edit it. That was fine. He was a good editor. But he got fresh with my stuff. He saw that his expurgations of my books were winning me fame and fortune. He saw that if he continued to expurgate them he would soon have me on a pinnacle higher than himself. So he began to make interlineations as well as expurgations. I could stand the latter but not his writings. I called a halt. Since then both Howells and I have shown a falling off.

The next night Sam hosted a private dinner party at his home for a few theatrical friends: John Drew, William Gillette, and Billie Burke, best known today for her role as Glinda the Good Witch in the movie *The Wizard of Oz* (1939). In her autobiography Burke remembered with affection Sam's "charming little Sunday night dinners" at his "dear old house on lower Fifth Avenue." He "would shake that beautiful shock of snowy white hair"—once ginger or "red headitary," he called it—and tell her, "Billie, we redheads have to stick together." On January 11 he was the guest of honor before an audience of three hundred, including Rogers, Carnegie, and George Harvey, at "his last great banquet" at the Lotos Club, as Paine put it. At the close of Sam's speech Robert Porter, at whose home he had stayed in Oxford, stepped behind him and threw Sam's Oxford gown across his shoulders and crowned him with the mortarboard to an ovation from the crowd. Sam declared that he "always did like red. The redder it is the better I like it. . . . There is no red outside the arteries of an archangel that could compare with this." Three days later Sam hosted the first of his so-called "doe" luncheons for women (in contrast to his "stag" luncheons for men) at his home. His guests included Lyon, his daughter Clara, Ethel Barrymore, and Kate Douglas Wiggin Riggs, the author of the children's classic *Rebecca of Sunnybrook Farm* (1903).[19]

At long last Jean Clemens left Katonah on January 9, 1908, to live in Greenwich, Connecticut, with a friend, Marguerite Schmitt, and two nurses, sisters Edith and Mildred Cowles. She was still in the care of Frederick Peterson but, at least according to Sam, "much happier than she was in that desolate sanitarium." Privately, however, Jean felt abandoned by her father and sister. "The idea that they miss me is absurd," she confided to her diary.

> Clara's & my interests are too absolutely different for us to be necessary to one another even if we are fond of each other & Father can't possibly find any entertainment or interest in me. I am sure he is fond of me but I don't believe that he any more than Clara really misses me. . . . I do often have a sort of hunger to get hold of him & hug him, but if I were to say I missed him or Clara steadily, I should be lying.

Jean grumbled aloud about how she had been neglected by her family, and Lyon got wind of her complaints. "People have come to me & said, 'Oh, do you know the cruel things that Jean is saying of her father & of her sister?'" Lyon observed. Jean had informed both Lyon and Clara "many times that she doesn't want her father to go & see her." Lyon had concealed from Sam "that Jean has had a serious return of her malady" since moving to Greenwich, "for it depresses him for days. . . . Two letters will come in the same mail—one to me, one to the King—the one to me will be sweet & affectionate, the one to the King will be full of complaints of me & cruel accusations." Sam grieved "that Jean is as she is," according to Lyon, and "groaned to think that his had been the crime of bringing her into the world." Increasingly dissatisfied with her circumstances in Greenwich, Jean moved with her caregivers after a few weeks to Gloucester, Massachusetts. "I hope you will find a place that will be entirely satisfactory to you and your friends," Sam wrote her, "but be sure it is close to New York, because I want you to be near Dr. Peterson." In the past, he allowed, "I would not have expected you to be otherwise than unhappy in a new & strange home, but your spirit & your philosophy have undergone great & beneficent improvement in these latter days, along with your improved physical health." Whereas she was "virtually in prison at Greenwich," he assured her that in Gloucester she "can live out of doors."[20]

Habitually afflicted every spring with bronchitis, Sam as a septuagenarian elected to treat the disease with a home remedy he had discovered in the mining camps of Nevada and California: shots of whisky. In May 1905, for example, Lyon noted that he "was fighting the beginning of a cold so he took his whisky bottle" and "in an hour he was very happily and comfortably drunk." Over the years Carnegie occasionally sent him a keg of his favorite eighty-year-old Scotch—a malt he only shared with a select few, including Presidents Cleveland, Harrison, and Roosevelt. In February 1906 he thanked "Saint Andrew" for the gift: "The whisky arrived in due course from over the water," Sam wrote, and "last week one bottle of it was extracted from the wood & inserted into me, on the instalment plan, with this result: that I believe it to be the best & smoothest whisky now on the planet." With the onset of his annual bout of respiratory trouble in mid-January 1908, Sam began to binge drink. The latest keg "came in very handy," he notified Carnegie. "I had a very wild & exasperating cold, but a pint of the whisky tamed it in 3 minutes by the watch & I did not wake up again for ten hours." He wrote his niece Julia Langdon Loomis the morning of January 16 that, instead of dictating any of his autobiography, he was "half full of whisky—& not yet finished. I have discovered a cold & this is to break it up; for with my bronchial tendencies I dread a cold as the Presbyterian burnt child dreads perdition." Rather than discourage his drinking, moreover, his factotums facilitated it. "The King has written a brilliant letter to Mrs. Loomis under the inspiration of the whisky," Lyon remarked, "and as I sat beside his bed and we discussed the inspirational qualities of whisky he said that there is something in it that strips off the artificialities of man and brings out the real creature. They *are* the cobwebs that cover our brains

& hearts & they are made by the conventionalities." That night Sam, Lyon, and Ashcroft played cards "and the King got drunk," according to his secretary. "He sailed around the room trying to reach the door." He glanced at Lyon and said, "'I'm just practicing,' as he sailed with light footsteps over to the door & up to the bathroom. . . . So much for the whole quart of scotch they—we—drank." The next night, Lyon was awakened by noise and found Sam "in a drunken haze" playing billiards with Paine and unable to "move without reeling." Paine

> was furious with me & told me to clear out but I sat down & said I'd stay until the King started for bed. P[aine] didn't like me—but I didn't care. It was wonderful to see the King pick up a ball & fondle it—& then try to hit it with his cue & be unable to touch it; but he swore splendidly. A. B. left the room & I gently took . . . the King's cue away & led him to his room. He staggered & hit his head against one of the little angels on his bed post & grabbed his dear head with a volley of oaths.

That night he gave new meaning to the phrase "sleep tight." On January 21 he admitted he was "in bed bronchially" and unable to work "because my head is dizzy with drugs." His physician Edward Quintard ordered him to a milder climate so Ashcroft booked staterooms on the *Bermudian* sailing from New York on January 25. "In Bermuda a sick person gets well in 3 days & strong in a week," he wrote Dorothy Quick. He planned to try the "onion cure," as he told reporters at the dock. Raw onions, "if taken plentifully," supposedly strengthened the throat, and "the best onion patch in Bermuda" had been "fenced off for his use." At lunch before sailing, Henry Harper asked him about the "big swelling adorning his forehead," and Sam explained he had fallen into bed while treating his cold with whisky.[21]

He and Ashcroft arrived in Hamilton the morning of January 27 and registered at the Princess Hotel. Among the first Americans he met was Woodrow Wilson, the president of Princeton, who routinely vacationed on the islands. Sam and Wilson had crossed paths at least thrice before: at Yale graduation in October 1901, at Laurence Hutton's house in April 1902, and at Wilson's presidential inauguration six months later. Upon landing in Bermuda, Sam was welcomed by Mary Allen Peck, the mutual friend of both men. Within his first couple of days Sam began to recover from his cold and "added a jewel" to his collection of young girls: twelve-year-old Margaret Blackmer, the daughter of Colorado lawyer and industrialist Henry Myron Blackmer. "We were close comrades—inseparables in fact—for eight days," as he remembered. Elizabeth Wallace remarked with gender specificity in her journal that "If a child of ten or twelve happened to be anywhere within the radius of his glance he is inevitably sure of seeing her. Then begins the most delightful flirtation. The King nods—if that is not effective he beckons with his hand and sometimes he goes up to the child and makes a remark that seems to continue a conversation broken off at some remoter period." Isabel Lyon similarly observed that "the King's interest in children increases—his interest in little girls." While in Bermuda this week Sam also ventured to the village of Somerset to meet Upton Sinclair. He had read *The Jungle* shortly after its publication by Doubleday and wrote the author to congratulate him on "the magnitude & effectiveness of the earthquake" the novel "has set going under the Canned Polecat Trust of Chicago." On his part, Sinclair remembered that Sam "was kind, warm-hearted, and also full of rebellion against capitalist greed and knavery, but he was an old man, and a sick man, and I did not try to probe the mystery of his life. The worm which was gnawing at his heart was not revealed." On February 4 Sam dined with Wilson on West Indian pepper pot at Peck's home in Paget. "He seems to like being with me," Wilson noted. Peck "gathered a most interesting little group of garrison people to meet him. He was in great form and delighted everybody." The *Washington Post* reported that Sam was "enjoying the brilliant sunshine and blue skies of Bermuda. His table in the long and handsome saloon of the Hamilton Hotel" was "always the center of attraction and his gay and witty sallies meet with . . . delight and appreciation." Sam and Ashcroft left Bermuda on February 6 and arrived back in New York thirty hours later. "I am feeling excellently," he told reporters at the dock. "This was just a little jaunt, and it proved a most delightful one."[22]

He returned, he said, to keep a number of pressing social obligations. Accompanied by Charles Wark on piano and Marie Nichols on violin, Clara sang before an audience of about a hundred and forty "very choice people," including the Rogerses, Gilders, Doubledays, and Carnegies, at 21 Fifth Avenue the evening of February 13. Afterward Sam dined at midnight—after the theaters closed—at Sherry's Restaurant at Forty-Fourth Street and Fifth Avenue with Ethel Barrymore, Richard Harding Davis, the Astors, Vanderbilts, and Whitneys, and the poet Helen Hay Whitney, John Hay's daughter, whom he had not seen "since she was a little child." The assembly was amused after the "freak dinner" by the so-called dog ballet and a troupe of chorus girls from the Broadway musical *Top o' th' World*. Sam wrote Jean the next day that he "enjoyed it thoroughly till 4.05 a.m., when I came away with the last of the rioters." The afternoon of February 18 he and Clara attended a staging of the Ben Jonson masque *The Hue and Cry after Cupid* at the Plaza Hotel, and the next evening he dined with publisher Frank Doubleday and his wife Neltje De Graff Doubleday, then proceeded to the famous salon at the home of the British socialite Bridget Guinness on Washington Square. "By eleven a great throng had gathered" there, including the opera star Enrico Caruso, and "there was fine instrumental music and fine singing." Sam even danced with Waldorf Astor's wife Nancy, Viscountess Astor, at her insistence. He left after midnight with the sculptor Prince Paolo Troubetzkoy and the humorist Finley Peter Dunne. The next evening, dining with the Pilgrims at Delmonico's, he gratefully replied to the toast "To Oxford University" by acknowledging that the occasion recalled "the proudest day of my life." The evening of February 21, probably at Caruso's recommendation, he attended a performance of Gaetano Donizetti's *Lucia di Lammermoor* starring Luisa Tetrazzini at the Manhattan Opera House.[23]

Sam convinced Henry Rogers, who had suffered a minor stroke the previous July, that the temperate Bermudan climate would help restore his health, though Rogers agreed to the trip only on the condition that Sam accompany him. Joined by Isabel Lyon and Rogers's son-in-law William Evarts Benjamin, the publisher who bought the *Library of American Literature* from Webster and Company in 1893, they embarked aboard the *Bermudian* on February 22 for a seven-week holiday to the islands. Sam teased reporters at the dock that they would only pose together for pictures if they were paid, and Rogers joked that his notorious business practices were no worse than Sam's threadbare humor. All laughter aside, Lyon noted that Rogers was "a sick, sick man" when he "feebly" boarded the ship.[24]

The four of them registered at the Princess Hotel in Hamilton upon landing on February 24. They were met by Elizabeth Wallace, who recorded her first impression of Isabel Lyon: "a black eyed black haired Italian looking little woman who hovers about him with the tender care of a mother and daughter combined." Wallace realized too that "the Rajah," as she nicknamed the "tall, distinguished" Rogers, and Sam "love each other dearly and manifest their affection by abusing each other whenever the occasion offers." Fortunately, Rogers began to recuperate as soon as they landed. He "is improving every day now & he isn't the gray feeble man he was less than a week ago," Lyon noted on February 28. Sam similarly notified Clara the next day that Rogers was "in better condition than he was in when he left New York," and he reported to Rogers's daughter Mai on March 2 that her father was "ever so much better, & *I* think he improves daily. This is exactly the place for him, & I hope to get him to remain clear into April." To be sure, Rogers "was pretty poorly when we came down here & Miss Lyon was not much better off, but both are in much improved condition now. There was nothing the matter with me, yet I seem to have improved a little myself." Lyon was "getting strong & robust," he advised Dorothy Quick on March 10, "& Mr. Rogers is improving so decidedly that he has stopped talking about going back home." He wrote Emilie Rogers that her husband was "getting along splendidly! This was the very place for him. He enjoys himself & is as quarrelsome as a cat." The Hamilton *Royal Gazette* noted that Sam and Rogers "almost any afternoon, weather permitting," rode in a carriage along Front Street, "chatting cosily and absorbing with shrewd glances from under bushy eyebrows the sights and the scenes." Sam assured Jean that there was "plenty of company in this hotel, & of an excellent sort, & there's a dance twice a week. We are not suffering for a lack of pleasant social life." They toured the local aquarium; visited Spanish Point, Castle Harbor, and Crystal Cave; sailed to the coral reefs and Sea Gardens; attended a garden party at the governor's home and band concerts at the British garrison; enjoyed "driving, walking, lunching"; and "& at night we play billiards & cards." The group often gathered in Sam's room late in the evening to hear him read Kipling's poems. Elizabeth Wallace memorialized the experience in verse:

> When the King reads Kipling
> We grow silent and are still,
> And our hearts begin to thrill,
> For we know we shall be carried to far lands across the seas.
> We shall tramp through tropic forests, we shall rest 'neath banyan trees,
> Where we hear the lazy rustling of palmettos in the breeze.
> We shall feel like happy children, for we haven't any choice
> When we hear the East a-calling with its yearning languorous voice,
> When the King reads Kipling.

On March 27, Sam recited some of the poems at Mary Allen Peck's home for her guests. He declaimed "in a tone and with a depth of feeling that gave to the verses a value seldom recognized," according to the *Royal Gazette*.[25]

Of course, he also found time for other entertainments. He routinely attended baseball games at the Richmond Cricket Ground on Serpentine Road, about a mile from the hotel. He spoke at benefits for the Bermuda Biological Station and Aquarium at the Colonial Opera House and for the local children's hospital at the Princess Hotel. "He was the drawing-card," Wallace remembered, and he packed the hotel parlors "to suffocation." On March 10 he lunched at the officers' mess aboard the HMS *Cressy*, anchored in the harbor, "& had a screaming good time." And he went sailing on March 30 with Nicholas Murray Butler and Earl Grey, governor-general of Canada and "a winning and lovable man and a fine and sterling character."[26]

But as Lyon wrote on February 28, "his first interest when he goes to a new place is to find little girls" and "off he goes with a flash when he sees a new pair of slim little legs appear and if the little girl wears butterfly bows of ribbon on the back of her head then his delirium is complete." Shortly after his arrival, Sam met twelve-year-old Irene Gerken of New York, thirteen-year-old Jean Spurr of Newark, and Helen Allen, thirteen-year-old daughter of William Allen, the U.S. vice-consul in Bermuda, whom he described in his autobiographical dictation a few weeks later as "perfect in character, lovely in disposition, and a captivator at sight!" His preoccupation with these latest angelfish was widely reported in the press. The *Philadelphia Inquirer* noted that his newest "girl" was Irene; the *New York Times* printed a photograph of Sam and Irene; the *New York Tribune* asserted that when he was not with Rogers, he was "usually acting as escort to the little girls at the hotel"; and the *Washington Star* remarked that at a recent dance in Hamilton he had been "the pet partner of all the little girls." On March 23, Sam picnicked with Jean and Helen and "romped in the sand on the sea-shore about 6 hours" with them. On April 10, he went swimming in the ocean with Helen at Bay House, the Allens' home, and Lyon photographed them.

Figure 24. Samuel Clemens swimming with Helen Allen at Bay House, Bermuda, March 1908. Photograph by Isabel Lyon. *Strand* 46 (August 1913): 219.

"I have led a lazy & comfortable life here . . . a most pleasant & useless life," he admitted to Clara.[27]

On April 11, after a holiday of forty-seven days, Sam and his entourage sailed for New York aboard the *Bermudian*. After his departure, he wrote

Helen Allen that he missed Bermuda "but not so much as I miss you; for you were rare, & occasional, & select." As he lounged about the ship he recruited yet another new angelfish to his aquarium: sixteen-year-old Dorothy Sturgis of Boston, granddaughter of the architect Russell Sturgis, one of the founders of the Metropolitan Museum of Art, and daughter of the architect R. Clipston Sturgis. As with Dorothy Quick on the voyage of the *Minnetonka* nine months earlier, Sturgis and Sam "became inseparable," as she remembered almost sixty years later. "He and his dear friend, Mr. H. H. Rogers, and I spent a good deal of time huddled under rugs in our deck chairs" in the spring chill, "but Mr. Clemens and I also used to walk the decks." They were promenading "around the deck, arm in arm, glorying in the elements" on April 12 when, as they approached the stern, the wind blew up. They watched "the huge waves lift the ship skyward then drop her, most thrillingly H—alifaxward," Sam recalled in his autobiographical dictation five days later, "when one of them of vast bulk leaped over the taffrail and knocked us down and buried us under several tons of salt water." Sturgis reminisced that they helped "each other to our feet," "returned laughing and dripping" to their rooms to change clothes, "and thought no more about the matter." Sam added that "Dorothy was not discomposed, nobody was hurt," and they "were on deck again in half an hour." Sam even made light of the incident: "I never knew the ocean was so wet before." Nevertheless, after they docked in New York the next day, they were the subject of scream headlines in the press: "Mark Twain Near Death from Wave" (*Boston Herald*) and "Mark Twain Rescues a Girl as Huge Sea Sweeps the Bermudian" (*New York Herald*). The papers "made a perilous and thundersome event of it, but it wasn't that kind of a thing at all," Sam insisted, and Sturgis concurred that they carried "a garbled and highly dramatized version of the event." These accounts pictured her "swept away" by a wave "in the 60-mile an hour gale into the scuppers" where she "lay gasping and in a half swoon" and Sam rescued her, holding her "until the flood subsided" and then carrying her "safely to a gangway and down into the shelter of the cabin." In a "hairbreadth escape," he had "managed to catch the rail and save himself" from "being swept into the Atlantic Ocean." Sturgis was disgusted by the reporting. "What an insult! I was too much of a tomboy to tolerate the stigma of being rescued by anybody!" she remembered. "In fact, I had supported him against the wind, for he was well along in years and I was concerned about his shivering in the white suit which by then had become his habitual wear."[28]

Even before Sam escaped to Bermuda, the Clemens household was at loggerheads over the privileges to which Albert Bigelow Paine was entitled in his role of official biographer. As early as July 1907, Paine lost in Grand

Central Station in New York a handbag containing "photos of the King" and "the Orion letters [and draft autobiography] he was carrying up to Elmira to read." Lyon had warned "him best not to take them away." The power struggle in the household over the next months resembled nothing so much as an intricate chess match with various actors: Sam the King, Lyon and Clara the would-be Queens, Paine the Knight, Ralph Ashcroft the Bishop (he in fact would soon be nicknamed the "Bishop of Benares" after a character in Charles Rann Kennedy's play *The Servant in the House*), or perhaps a Knave were he a playing card, Jean a sidelined Rook, with Charles Wark, Ossip Gabrilowitsch, and the angelfish mere pawns in the game. On January 22, Sam learned that Sam Moffett had "been lending old letters of mine" to Paine "without first submitting them to me for approval or the reverse, so I've stopped it. I don't like to have those privacies exposed in such a way to even my biographer." Katy Leary also saw Paine rummaging through Sam's private papers and letters, whereupon Sam "insisted that the manuscript box be locked." After all, he had authorized Clara and Jean to compile an edition of his letters, and he feared Paine's official biography would preclude that project if it contained an abundance of his correspondence. He was so concerned that the biography would overlap with the edition of letters that he gave Clara copies of "all letters of mine now obtainable" with "full authority over them" and advised George Harvey that Paine might "merely use extracts, not whole letters" to a total of "10,000 words for the *whole* biography." He likewise wrote Howells to caution him against sharing copies of their correspondence because "a man should be dead before his private foolishnesses are risked in print." Howells replied to Sam that his

> wish about the letters comes, I am sorry to say, two months too late. When a biographer asks me for the biographee's letters, I always give them, if I can find them, which sometimes I can't; and I saw Paine on such intimate terms with you that I should not have hesitated to offer him all your letters. . . . I don't think Paine could abuse the confidence put in him, or would make an indiscreet use of them; but I no more thought of asking you whether I should give them than I thought of asking Mrs. Aldrich whether I should give Aldrich's very intimate letters to his biographer, when he askt for them. Of course Paine will do exactly what you say about them; he spoke to me with entire judgment and good sense.

When Lyon discovered that some of Sam's other letters were missing from his personal archives, she contacted Paine to ask whether he had taken them. "If you haven't got them, then I'm terribly worried," she wrote. "I should not have left them there. . . . I know just about what was in that trunk tray & now it seems to me that I saw you going down the hall with a bundle of letters, but I felt you wouldn't take any without telling me." Receiving no reply, she telephoned Paine "to ask about letters that I am missing and that the King and Santa would hold me responsible for. He was cross and answered in a burst of ill temper" that he had borrowed many letters and would continue to borrow them as he needed them—the same proprietary interest in Sam's literary estate he would exhibit for the rest of his life. Paine not only defended his behavior to Lyon but confessed to his apologetic purpose two days later in a letter that might have served to introduce his hagiography. He in effect threatened to abandon the project unless he received unqualified help and support:

> Nowhere is a man's life and nature so revealed as in his letters; and it is the King's life and . . . nature that I am to preserve as well as the story of his progress. I do not care to prepare what would be a mere resemblance, or even to paint an accurate portrait of him—or a dozen of them. My purpose is to *present* the man *himself*, with all his colossal genius, his strength, and his triumphs; with all his weaknesses and his failures. . . . I have no desire to parade the things he would wish forgotten—to hold them up to the world saying, 'See how weak a strong man may be,' but it is *absolutely necessary* that I should know all there is to know, whatever it may be, in order that I may build a personality so impregnable that those who, in years to come, may endeavor to discredit and belittle will find themselves so forestalled at every point that the man we know . . . will remain known as *we* know him, loved and honored through all time. If I can have the King's fullest confidence and cooperation I feel that I shall have the strength and the understanding and the perseverance and the expression to do this thing. But if, on the other hand, I am to be shut off on one avenue of research, and another; if I am to be handicapped by concealments, and opposition, and suspicion of ulterior motives; if I am to be denied access to the letters written to such men as Howells and Twichell; in a word, if I am to become not *the* biographer but simply *a* biographer—one of a dozen groping, half-equipped men, then I would better bend my energies in the direction of easier performance and surer and prompter return, not only in substance but in credit for us all.

Such statements failed to reconcile Lyon to what she considered Paine's theft of Sam's private documents, and as Hamlin Hill puts it, by early 1908 they "had become so antagonistic to each other that open warfare almost broke out." Lyon alluded vaguely throughout 1908 to "warring outside things" in the home, "the gloom that misunderstandings frequently put into my heart," and the "misunderstandings" rankling the family and domestic staff.[29]

Coincidentally, Lyon's long vacation in company with Sam that spring also seems to have upset Clara, whose anger surfaced two weeks after their return from Bermuda. As Lyon noted in her journal on May 2, "Santa misunderstood all my efforts in working over the house. My anxiety over the furnishings, my interest in my search for the right thing for the King's house has all been misinterpreted, and the child says I am trying to ignore her. All my effort has been to please her." Lyon clearly underestimated Clara's resentment of the part she played in her father's life. "Somebody has put all these sickening ideas into Santa's head," she lamented. However inadvertently, Lyon was caught in a crossfire, the target of both Sam's biographer and daughter. Her simmering feud with "Santa" was curtailed only when she, Wark, and Marie Nichols sailed for England on May 16 to launch a concert tour. Clara hinted at the stress she suffered in an interview with the *London Express*: "Father is, of course, a genius—and that is what makes me so tired. My fatigue is directly caused by the incessant strain—prolonged over some years and induced by trying to find a secret hiding place where I can shroud my identity and be sure of a really comfortable bed." When Clara spoke these words, Laura Skandera Trombley adds, she and her pianist "were certainly enjoying more than a professional relationship and they likely were sexually involved." Clara wrote in June that Wark was "more wonderful all the time but I can't bear the many many months still that separate us from freedom and frank expression of the truth." The unspoken truth was that Wark, though estranged from his wife, was a married man with a family.[30]

Meanwhile, Lyon's dispute with Paine continued to fester. In late July, according to Ashcroft, Paine was spreading rumors that the secretary was abusing phenacetine, ironically the same drug that had killed Charley Webster. In mid-October, Lyon "discovered another of AB's indiscretions. He has had letters written from Mrs. Clemens to Mrs. Crane in his possession for over a year. The King's anger burned furiously," but rather than confront Paine directly, "he bade me go to the telephone and demand those letters. I did so" with Ashcroft "standing beside me to courage me up."[31] Paine promised to return them when he no longer needed them.

Sam kept up appearances throughout the spring and summer of 1908. Five days after his return from Bermuda he spoke at the first annual dinner at Reisenweber's Café on Columbus Circle before a hundred and fifty comic artists, cartoonists, caricaturists, and writers who worked for the humor periodicals of New York. He remarked as he left "that he hadn't had as much fun since the last time he had bronchitis." On April 29 Sam and six thousand children filled St. Patrick's Cathedral for a solemn high mass to mark the hundred anniversary of the founding of the diocese of New York. No adults save Sam were admitted. Ten days later he sat on the reviewing stand with Michael Cardinal Logue, Archbishop John Murphy Farley, and Mayor

George B. McClellan Jr. during the annual police parade. "The policeman is my friend; I know he is," Sam joked. "Of course, it must be a sure sign that he wants to know all that I do since he watches me every time I appear on the street and sometimes follows me in a casual gumshoe sort of way." Less than a week later Sam attended the dedication of the new buildings of the College of the City of New York on St. Nicholas Heights. Some five thousand people assembled on the campus, according to the *Brooklyn Eagle*, and Sam "was the center of attention" in his flamboyant scarlet Oxford gown "and bowed to cheers at every turn." He was joined by "about 200 degree-men in gowns," including Mayor McClellan, Joseph Choate, and President Charles Eliot of Harvard, as he wrote Jean, "but they were black ones; I was glad to have a red one on, because it made me conspicuous." Brander Matthews observed that Sam "wore his scarlet gown "as often as he could and he said he would like to wear it always. No doubt he delighted in the richness of its glowing color, but he delighted even more in the showiness of it." The photographer William Ireland Starr likewise remembered that he "was very proud of the cap and gown he had worn on this occasion and sometimes strutted around in them." Howells also recalled "how proud he was of his Oxford gown, not merely because it symbolized the honor in which he was held by the highest literary body in the world, but because it was so rich and so beautiful. The red and the lavender of the cloth flattered his eyes as the silken black of the same degree of Doctor of Letters, given him years before at Yale, could not do." The gown today is on display at the Mark Twain Boyhood Home and Museum in Hannibal.[32]

The evening of the CCNY convocation Sam addressed the college alumni association at the Waldorf-Astoria. Whereas he had commended Congress at the Pilgrim dinner in February for restoring the motto "In God We Trust" to U.S. coinage, even blaming the economic recession on the omission of the words, he commended the president at the alumni dinner in May for removing the adage because it was "an overstatement." Should "cholera should ever reach these shores we should probably pray to be delivered from the plague," he explained, "but we would put our main trust in the Board of Health." Before the end of May, Sam also addressed the American Booksellers' Association annual meeting, thanking the members for their support; he celebrated Empire Day or Queen Victoria's birthday at Delmonico's with the British Schools and Universities Society; and he retreated for a week to George Harvey's summer home in Deal Beach, New Jersey, where he enticed Harvey's young daughter Dorothy to join his aquarium.[33]

His villa in Redding was finally ready for occupation in mid-June. "The final last tinkering & fussing & finishing" were completed under Lyon's supervision on June 14 "& everything is shipshape & ready now," Sam cackled to Mary Rogers. Lyon "& the servants & the four cats" took possession on June 16, "& I am to follow two days later in the later afternoon." He was "conscious of a steadily augmenting great curiosity to see what the house looks like." After all, as he put it, "I haven't had a real home, until now, since we left the Hartford one 17 years ago. It is a long, long time to be homeless." For nearly two decades he had lived in houses he did not own and owned houses where he did not live. The first piece of furniture installed in the house was the billiard table from the Hartford house, a gift of the Rogerses. Sam, along with Albert Bigelow Paine, his daughter Louise Paine, who was another new member of Sam's aquarium, "a reporter or two," and a photographer arrived via express train at the Redding depot in the late afternoon to a welcome by a crowd of his new neighbors and departed on the three-mile ride to his new home in "a flower-bedecked carriage." When he first spied the house, according to Paine, Sam remarked "How beautiful it all is" and "I did not think it could be as beautiful as this." He assured Helen Allen later that from the first moment he "was glad I built it." After crossing the threshold and standing "in his own home for the first time in seventeen years," he toured its eighteen rooms and pronounced it "a perfect house—perfect, so far as I can see, in every detail. It might have been here always." With 7,600 square feet of space, the house also featured an eight-thousand-gallon cistern, an ice house, a coal furnace with steam heat, and lighting by acetylene torches rather than gas jets or electric bulbs. The orchestrelle was installed in the twenty-one-by-forty-foot ground-floor library. Dorothy Quick remembered that "the whole room was built around it and splendidly furnished with the most comfortable of chairs and couches. There were plenty of tables, lavishly appointed with the smoking accessories that were so necessary to Mark Twain's comfort. The room was the epitome of all anyone could ask for, not only for comfort but for charm."[34]

Though Sam had originally planned only to spend his summers at Stormfield, he soon decided to live there year-round. "I am sorry I did not see this place sooner," he admitted. "I never want to leave it again. If I had known it was so beautiful I should have vacated the house in town and moved up here permanently." He credited John Howells and Isabel Lyon with building and furnishing the villa "without any help or advice from me & the result is entirely to my satisfaction." He congratulated Howells in early July for designing such "a shapely & stately & handsome house," and he gloated to Clara that Lyon had "achieved wonders." Though the Hartford mansion had been "lovely," the "architect damaged many of its comfort-possibilities & wasted a deal of its space." The Fifth Avenue house was "roomy & pleasant," but "sunless" and "not beautiful. This house is roomy & delightful & beautiful & no space has been wasted. The sun falls upon it in such floods that you can hear it."[35]

The first evening in his new residence Sam hosted a small dinner party for Lyon, Ashcroft, Paine, and several others. Two of his neighbors, the artist Dan Beard and the contractor Harry Lounsbury, set off fireworks by the pergola. They were invited to join the guests, and when they reached the house the library "was filled with people in evening clothes, ladies with décolleté gowns with long trains, while we were powder-blackened and bedaubed with paint." Sam closed the day by playing billiards with Paine and Ashcroft until midnight "& had a good time." A few days later, he loosed the latch string by hosting a banquet for the workers who built the house and a housewarming attended by the residents of Redding, including Ida Tarbell, Jeannette Gilder, the playwright Kate V. Saint Maur, and two of Julian Hawthorne's daughters (and Nathaniel Hawthorne's granddaughters), Hildegarde Hawthorne and Imogen Hawthorne Deming. Sam stood at the door and "went down the line shaking hands with everybody." Tarbell remembered that Sam "was a friendly neighbor. He every now and then gave a great party, sending the invitations around by our peripatetic butcher." She treasured her "recollections of days when Jeannette Gilder and I drove over to tea or lunch" at Stormfield and "heard great stories of the doings in his new home." Yet Sam was able to protect his privacy there because, unlike the brownstone in New York, "the nearest *public* road" was "half a mile away, so there is nobody to look in." The seclusion was "perfect," he bragged to Rogers, and he reveled in the "tranquility, this deep stillness, this dreamy expanse of woodsy hill & valley!" Though he hosted twenty-one guests during his first seven weeks and a hundred and eighty people during his first year in Redding, the house was "isolated & not very close to anything & not very easy to get at. But in a way these seeming defects are an advantage. Indeed a very large advantage: in these 40 days no stranger with an axe to grind has called." His new house was "a good place to live in, a good place to die in—presently," as he put it on his second day there.[36]

He only regretted that he had leased the Fifth Avenue town house for another year. He never returned there. "I do so delight in this home," he allowed to Clara, "that the thought of ever going back to that crude & tasteless New York barn, even to stay overnight, revolts me." Predictably, Lyon was charged with dismantling the New York house where the Clemenses "had charming times and gay times," but for the secretary they were "sadder than gay" or "more agonizing." There she "saw the terrible sorrow and grief of the King after Mrs. Clemens's death and I saw the crying rage of servants dismissed by Jean and Clara. I saw Jean in her convulsions and I saw Clara in her agony and in her illness and in her struggles with her career and in her hates and fierce lovings. And while my heart was full of loving for all of them, there was a long long lack of peace, & the stairs I climbed were often pitifully weary ones." After Lyon shipped Clara's furniture and piano to Redding in early August, she closed the New York house. "I have retired from New York for good, I have retired from labor for good," Sam notified Howells, "& have entered upon a holiday whose other end is in the cemetery."[37]

Sam's friend Julian Hawthorne, the father of his near neighbors in Redding, began to tout investments in silver mines in Canada during the summer of 1908. In the jesting parlance of the period, Sam defined a mine as "a hole in the ground owned by a liar." In this case, the liar was Hawthorne. At the height of the scheme, hundreds of letters offering shares in his mining company and bearing his signature—virtually all of them forged by the typists—were mailed each day to people whose addresses appeared in street directories for towns and cities across the country. Sam received one of the letters and, unlike most of the recipients, replied to it in a letter now lost. On August 8 Hawthorne responded to him:

> With a few friends of mine, I have found a silver mine in the Cobalt region up in Canada and we are developing it with a view to living on our dividends. The assays and the general conditions are as good as the best of the big producers up there; and this is the statement not only of our own experts, but of those of capitalists who sent up to find out and, as a consequence, have offered to buy out our control at very liberal figures. But we mean to keep the thing for ourselves and are offering only a small block of our stock for sale to help us out with our preliminary work. We shall keep clear of Wall Street and of all speculation. Of course, you are rich; but you should consider that it is invidious in a literary man to grow rich from his own profession; and it would allay the feeling against you if it were known that you had made an additional fortune out of silver. Get somebody to read the enclosed prospectus to you, and then act promptly. The stock is sold in bunches of not less than 1000 shares at a good reduction from face value. We shall close up about the end of September; but I have my heart set on landing you for a purchaser. I am glad to hear that you are a neighbor of my daughter's up there—which, of course, I could not be if it were my intention to sell you a gold brick.

This manuscript letter includes a penciled note in Lyon's hand apparently dictated by Sam: "I'm not gambling on the mines, because I know people sometimes say things about mines that are not true. I used to do it myself when I had mines to sell—But I am gambling on Julian Hawthorne's integrity & levelheadedness." Fortunately, there is no record that Sam actually invested in the worthless mine. In March 1913 Hawthorne was convicted of mail fraud and sentenced to a year and a day in federal prison.[38]

On June 30, less than two weeks after settling in Redding, Sam railed with Paine to Portsmouth, New Hampshire, for the dedication of the Thomas Bailey Aldrich Memorial Museum, Aldrich's widow Lilian's brainchild. Sam dreaded the ceremony, one of the last gatherings of the old guard, with good reason. "By God, I would rather be hanged" than travel in the dead of summer, he admitted. "However, it is a memorial service in honor of an old friend & I think he would reciprocate by & by, if he could." The editor and author Caroline Ticknor remembered that the day was "a terribly hot one" and the guests—among them Finley Peter Dunne, Richard Watson Gilder, Thomas Wentworth Higginson, Howells, Sarah Orne Jewett, Thomas Nelson Page, and John T. Trowbridge —"mopped their brows and purchased palm-leaf fans." Ticknor was seated next to Sam, who "let fall various droll sayings." He spoke last in Portsmouth and floored the thousand-plus attendees with his irreverence. Paine recalled that the other orators "all said handsome, serious things," but Sam deliberately violated the gravity of the occasion. "This isn't Aldrich's funeral!" he said to Ticknor before he rose to the rostrum "as if it were his one wish to show how truly alive Aldrich was at that moment." Rather than deliver a eulogy, he entertained the crowd "with twelve minutes of lawless and unconfined and desecrating nonsense." He began "by mopping his forehead," then his face, then his throat, "all in slow motion and without a word. Finally he said, with a quaver in his voice: 'Poor Tom! Poor Tom! I hope—he isn't—as hot—as I am now.'" He read aloud from his autobiography a passage about Aldrich that he had dictated in 1904 and published in the *North American Review* in September 1906, concluding that Aldrich "was always brilliant, he will always be brilliant; he will be brilliant in hell." The address, Paine believed,

> certainly would have delighted Aldrich. . . . It was full of the most charming humor, delicate, refreshing, and spontaneous. The audience, that had been maintaining a proper gravity throughout, showed its appreciation in ripples of merriment that grew presently into genuine waves of laughter. He spoke out his regret for having worn black clothes. It was a mistake, he said, to consider this a solemn time—Aldrich would not have wished it to be so considered. He had been a man who loved humor and brightness and wit and had helped to make life merry and delightful.

The memorial "was dreary; it was devilish; it was hard to endure; there were two sweltering hours of it," Sam dictated a week later, "but I would not have missed it for twice the heat and exhaustion and Boston and Maine travel it cost."[39]

Sam and Paine paused in Gloucester to visit Jean en route back to Redding. "We were charmed & surprised to see how well she was, how sound & vigorous in mind & body," and Sam floated the possibility his daughter might join him in Redding, specifically by relocating with her full-time nurses to an abandoned farmhouse on his property. As he recounted the story in the Ashcroft-Lyon manuscript, when he arrived in Stormfield the next day "I broke the good news to Miss Lyon in an outburst of enthusiasm & said Dr. Peterson must cancel her exile & let her come home at once. Miss Lyon did her best to look glad & said she would write the doctor, but there was frost upon her raptures." Rather than follow his instructions, according to Sam, Lyon cabled Peterson "telling him to absolutely refuse his consent to Jean's removal to Stormfield!"—he claimed to know the substance of the message because the local contractor Lounsbury read the telegram before he sent it. "That evening Ashcroft & Miss Lyon"—who were conspiring to cheat him, he was convinced by mid-1909, when he composed the manuscript—"walked the hall in agitated conversation & Paine heard Miss Lyon say with emphasis: 'This is the *last time!* He shall never leave this place again without one of us *with* him!'"[40]

In truth, there is a much less sinister explanation for these events based on reliable contemporary evidence. Sam withdrew his offer of a farmhouse near Stormfield where Jean and her nurses might live on July 2, the day after he tendered it, because it was too dilapidated. "I am disappointed, distressed, & low-spirited," he wrote his daughter the same day he returned from the Aldrich Memorial, "for that dream of yours & mine has come to nothing. That house turns out to be a poor trifling thing, like the rest of the ancient farmhouses in this region, it has no room in it. . . . I am so sorry. I wish I could situate you exactly to your liking, dear child, how gladly I would do it." That is, Lyon, Ashcroft, and Peterson apparently had little or nothing to do with dashing Sam's plan. Peterson soon acceded to Sam's suggestion that Jean sail to Germany to be treated by Hofrath von Reuvers, a specialist in nervous disorders, and Jean was "wildly excited" by the prospect of "seeing Berlin—I saw it last when I was only eleven years old." Accompanied by Anna Sterritt and Marguerite Schmitt, she embarked aboard the *Pretoria* on September 26 with Sam, Lyon, and Dorothy Quick at the dock to bid her adieu. As for the supposed conspiracy by his secretary and business manager never to allow him to leave Stormfield again without an escort, Lyon confided to her diary much less nefariously on August 8, a month after his return from Portsmouth and six weeks before Jean's departure for Germany, that "Benares and I have a moral obligation now in looking after the King. I shall not leave him for an hour unless Benares or another as good is here to look after him and together we must uphold him in our spiritual arms. The plan was for me to take Jean to Germany but I must not go away from the King, ever. He is too wonderful." The artist S. J. Woolf remembered about this time Lyon's "suave manner and the way she laughed at everything he said whether it was really humorous or not. She guarded him too well for my purposes." She was overprotective, "fiercely efficient, haughty to strangers and subservient to Mr. Clemens and his family. She gave the impression that he could not be left alone and all the time I worked she sat guarding him."[41]

Meanwhile, Jean reveled in her newfound freedom. Von Reuvers told her when they first met that "he thou[gh]t he could help me & the next day" that "he thou[gh]t he could cure me." His medicine "is absolutely harmless, he says, & his rules as to food are almost the same as Dr. P[eterson]'s." But there were drawbacks. Above all, the expense: "Living in Berlin is not inexpensive by any means," she notified Lyon two weeks after her arrival. "My room costs 10 M[arks] a day, Bébé's 8 M. & Anna's 5.50 M. That includes food, of course, & may include my milk—in the a.m. & evening but it includes neither baths, heating, lights, nor tea." She pressed Lyon "in haste & speed" to mail her more money. In addition, Marguerite Schmitt apparently was homesick and left Berlin in December, only two months after she arrived. Unwilling to permit Jean to live with a single full-time caretaker, Sam summoned Jean back to New York. In his autobiography, Sam claimed that "Jean was doubtful of the Berlin doctor & sent home one of his prescriptions" upon which Peterson urged him to "order her home at once." In any case, she settled in Babylon, Long Island, in January and in Montclair, New Jersey, a few weeks later.[42]

On August 1, 1908, Sam's nephew and namesake Samuel Moffett died while swimming in the surf off the Jersey shore in full view of his young son. He apparently died not by drowning, because the autopsy revealed no water in the lungs, Sam learned, but as the result of apoplexy "brought on by fright caused by the turbulent seas." Though he had recently suffered a dizzy spell while playing billiards, Sam attended the obsequies on August 4. He was struck, as he wrote Jean, Mary Rogers, and Susan Crane, by the "most moving" and "most heart-breaking" and "pathetic" sight of "that stunned & crushed & inconsolable family." To add to the calamity, the record of Moffett's life has been largely lost in a biographical blind spot. Paine, who accompanied Sam to the funeral, recalled that during their return to Redding "he was much depressed and a day or two later became really ill." Sam blamed his "bilious collapse" or "something akin to a sunstroke" on the summer heat and the heavy dark suit he wore at the funeral. In any case, on the night of August 6 Lyon heard "a groan from the King's room" and she hurried *dishabille* "to find him staggering and vomiting in the bathroom. It was a terrible experience." The rest of the night "I could not sleep and at every little sound from his room I would go in to find him lying like a sick and restless baby; but he had no fever." The next morning she "found him lighting a pipe and feeling as fresh and looking as sweet as a baby." Still, she summoned Edward Quintard from New York, who ordered Sam "not to stir" from Stormfield again "before frost."[43]

Despite all appearances of loyalty to his employer, Ashcroft was guilty of clandestine schemes. He was almost certainly the source of an embarrassing leak to the New York *World*, published on September 7 and widely copied—no doubt to the surprise of Edith Cullis Wark—that Clara and Charles Wark would soon announce their engagement. Lyon had likely shared with "Benares" details of the couple's unconventional relationship, and Ashcroft certainly was the first person to contact Lyon when the item appeared in the *World*. He telephoned her with the news, and she hastily contradicted the rumor when city reporters called long-distance to confirm it—this while Clara and Wark were still at sea and out of contact aboard the Cunard steamship *Caronia*, returning from their lavish and pound-foolish concert tour in Europe. The spree cost Sam a weekly average of about £22, or $110 a week, about $3,000 modern dollars. Whereas Ashcroft managed Sam's money and Lyon disbursed it, Clara spent it. "Unlike Jean," as Hill observes, Clara "was not troubled in the least at her financial drain on her father's income," and as Michael Shelden adds, Ashcroft resented her "prima donna attitude" and luxurious lifestyle, which he charged her father with facilitating. In spring 1908, while Sam vacationed in Bermuda and the diva "warbled" on tour, Ashcroft notified Lyon sarcastically that "the good ship Clara Clemens ran ashore yesterday on the No Money shoals, while bound South. Cost of salvage, $300, which please remit." In March 1909 Sam raised Clara's monthly allowance to $400, an amount eight times greater than Lyon's monthly salary of $50. When Lyon was accused of embezzlement, Ashcroft claimed that most of the allegedly missing money was paid to Clara "for the expenses of concert tours and the delightful experience of paying for the hire of concert halls destined to be mainly filled with 'snow' or 'paper,' for the maintenance of her accompanist, Charles E. Wark, and to defray other cash expenditures." Blindsided by the story of her betrothal upon her arrival in New York on September 9, 1908, Clara vehemently denied it—"It is absurd to say that I am engaged to be married," she told the journalists who met her ship, though she could hardly deny that she and Wark had been traveling together for the past several weeks at her (or Sam's) expense. She immediately left for Stormfield with her father, and Wark discreetly followed the next day.[44]

He was still there when a pair of inept burglars (bunglars?) tried to steal the Clemens silverware shortly after midnight on September 18. Attracted by news reports about the opulent villa, they hid in the shrubs until the lights were off, broke a kitchen window,[45] entered the house, and began to rifle a sideboard. Lyon "was awakened by the crash in the dining room," which was "followed by a second noise, as if something had tumbled off a table, and I decided that something was wrong. I hurried from my apartment, which is just over the dining room, and ran downstairs." She surprised the robbers in the act, "screamed for help," and as they fled with their booty, she dashed back to her room. Her shouts roused the butler, Claude Beuchotte, who scurried downstairs and fired a revolver into the darkness. Sam heard the shots, thought someone was popping the corks on champagne bottles, and went back to sleep. Lyon telephoned the sheriff, who arrived at the house with a posse of deputies within an hour and, joined by Wark (aka "a Stormfield guest" in Paine's account) with a shotgun, tracked the thieves seven miles to the train station in Bethel. After a brief gunfight in which the sheriff was wounded, the burglars were arrested. Sam, Clara, and Wark appeared at their arraignment in Redding later in the day. Sam admonished one of them, who confessed during the proceedings that he was Jewish. "You ought to be ashamed," Sam told him. "I have been at the front as a defender of the Jewish people all my life. I have written defenses of you and have contended that Jews have never, as a rule, been guilty of big crimes—crimes of violence." Or as this culprit recalled in his autobiography, when Sam "entered the courtroom and saw a poor devil sitting there with his head all bandaged up, his wrath instantly changed to pity. 'I have been slaving day and night,' he said to me, 'to refute the vile statement of Mr. [Theodore] Bingham (the then Police Commissioner of New York) that 99 percent of the Jews in New York were crooked, and here you are verifying the very statement I've tried so hard to refute.'"[46]

Dan Beard, who by chance was present at the town clerk's office when Sam arrived for the hearing, described the encounter differently. According to Beard, Sam confronted the yeggs as they waiting for the proceedings to begin:

> "So you're the two young men who called at my house last night and forgot to put your names in my guest-book? Now that was a pretty sort of business

> for you, wasn't it, and a nice way to treat me, after I've been down on the East Side working for just such fellows as you, and after I made Bingham take back what he said about the Jews." "Excuse me, Mr. Clemens," interrupted the battered and wounded prisoner, for the first time showing any interest in the proceedings, "my parents were Jewish." "Then you're a disgrace to your race!" "Well, I guess I am," replied the burglar. "Now you two young men," continued Mr. Clemens, "have been up to my house, stealing my tinware, and got pulled in by these Yankees up here. You had much better have stayed in New York, where you have the pull. Don't you see where you're drifting to? They'll send you from here down to Bridgeport jail, and the next thing you know, you'll be in the United States Senate. There's no other future left open for you."

The loot was found a few days later near the house. In addition, Sam famously posted at his house a notice to the next group of crooks:

> There is nothing to be had in this house henceforth but plated ware. You will find it in that brass thing over in the corner by the basket of kittens. If you want the basket put the kittens in the brass thing. And do not make a noise; it disturbs the family. You will find gumshoes in the front hall by that thing that has umbrellas in it—the thing they call a chiffonier or pergola, or whatever it is. Please close the door when you go away.

Charles Wark moved into a pied-à-terre on the eastern edge of Stuyvesant Square in New York a few days after the heist, and Clara found an apartment in the same building two weeks later. The break-in at Stormfield also terrorized the household staff—"not a woman in this house has had a whole solid hour's sleep since," Sam wrote Howells a week later. In its wake several of them resigned, and Sam ordered a burglar alarm installed. To replace them, Sam rehired a pair of Italian servants who had emigrated with the family to New York in 1904 and recruited "some natives from the farmhouses" in the area. He assured Jean that, as a result, "we are ever so much better off than we have ever been before."[47]

The thieves pleaded guilty at their trial in November. One was sentenced to four years in the crowbar hotel, the other—the shooter who resisted arrest—to nine years. In his autobiographical dictation the day after the trial ended, Sam declared them "not guilty" in accordance with his deterministic beliefs. They simply had "obeyed the law of their temperament and the compulsions of their birth, their training, their associations and their circumstances." He eventually received a letter of apology from "the murderous one," whom Sam considered "a merciless devil, a bloody-minded devil, but softly sentimental, just the same, for he is a German." Though he failed to reply to the entreaty, he bore the men "no malice and put no blame on them, for it is only circumstances and environment that make burglars; therefore, anybody is liable to be one. I don't quite know how I managed to escape myself. Yes I do: my circumstances and environment protected me."[48]

CHAPTER 17

Under the Weather

I suppose we all have a Jackson's island somewhere & dream of it when we are tired.

—Samuel Clemens to Walter Besant, 22 February 1898

In July 1908 Sam professed that his fine kettle of angelfish had become his "life's chiefest interest," and evidence supports the claim. His extant correspondence with adolescent schoolgirls "numbers approximately 300 letters," all of them written between 1905 and 1910, John Cooley calculates, and of all letters Sam "is now known to have written in 1908, 94 were to members of the Aquarium—almost half" of his total for the year, according to Laura Skandera Trombley. Its change of name to Stormfield notwithstanding, Sam insisted, he built his house in Redding "largely, indeed almost chiefly for the comfort & accommodation of the Aquarium. Its members will always be welcome under its roof." So far as the angelfish were concerned, its name remained Innocence at Home, and it was "not misnamed for I know the fishes well and am aware that they can furnish the innocence to make the name good." The billiard room on the second floor, its walls adorned with framed photographs of the girls, became the club's headquarters, and next to it was the double-bedded "angelfish bedroom" reserved for the members and their mothers, which Sam filled as often as possible. He readily conceded in his autobiographical dictation in 1908 to a "worship of school girls—if worship is the right name, and I know it is." "In grandchildren I am the richest man that lives today," he rationalized. "Whereas all other grandfathers have to take them as they come, good, bad and indifferent," he picked his grandchildren. But he only selected girls. The attention of "a school girl gratifies me more than the like from any other source," he elsewhere granted. "I am 73 & grandchildless, & so one might expect the whole left hand compartment of my heart to be empty & cavernous & desolate; but it isn't because I fill it up with schoolgirls." Louise Paine, one of the angelfish and the daughter of Sam's biographer and first literary executor, remembered fondly that he "was especially understanding with little girls."[1]

The question remains in Twain studies, however: How proper were his relationships with these girls? Or as John Cooley frames the question, "At issue is whether or not the Aquarium became for Clemens a perverse obsession, more a harem than a benign collection of surrogate granddaughters." On the one hand, Hamlin Hill contends that "his interest in the Angel Fish was more than avuncular, was even—in those final months when his mind tended to wander, his memory lapsed, and symptoms of senility became obvious—latently sexual." On the other, Shelley Fisher Fishkin insists that "the hundreds of letters that Twain exchanged with these dozen or so 'surrogate granddaughters' reveal nothing of the kind." But according to Cooley, whom Karen Lystra describes as the scholar "most familiar with the Angelfish letters," dozens of the letters he received from the girls have disappeared, presumably destroyed by Clara sometime after she returned from her European concert tour in 1908, thus vitiating Fishkin's argument. On his part, in his official biography Paine asserted that the angelfish simply represented the "youth and feminine beauty" Sam missed and described them as "just another of the harmless and happy diversions" he discovered in retirement. But Paine also privately cautioned Elizabeth Wallace not to reproduce "any '*affectionate*' photographs [of Sam] with young girls" in her book *Mark Twain and the Happy Island* because Clara "feels pretty strongly about that." Certainly Clara disapproved of her father's infatuation with the angelfish. As Paine revealed, Clara "never quite liked her father's attentions to young girls (or old ones, either, for that matter) in public."[2] In any case, Sam continued to befriend young women until the end of his life.

His attraction to beautiful young women was well known, usually tolerated, and sometimes encouraged. Margaret Illington, a popular actress and the young wife of Daniel Frohman, dressed for dinner at Sam's home in May 1908 as a twelve-year-old with pink ribbons in her hair, so he "admitted her as an angelfish" for a day. "There are a lot of lady candidates but I guess we won't let any more in—unless perhaps Billie Burke," who was twenty-four, he promised Dorothy Quick. He invited Dorothy Sturgis, Frances Nunnally, and Nunnally's mother to join him at a matinee performance by Burke in *Love Watches* at the Lyceum Theatre on Broadway on September 26 and afterward escorted them backstage to her dressing room, as Sturgis remembered. Burke remarked in her autobiography that Sam "loved the theater, often occupying a box with friends" at her plays. Burke spent part of the holiday season at Stormfield, and Sam threw a dinner party in her honor. She wrote to thank him for "the great happiness" she had enjoyed, and he glossed on the letter that she possessed "all the charms that the most fortunate of her sex can claim: youth, beauty, sincerity, simplicity, refinement, a good heart and irreproachable character." For two days in mid-October 1908, moreover, Laura Hawkins Frazer, the model for Becky Thatcher, "the very best sweetheart I ever had" and in a sense the original angelfish, and her granddaughter visited Stormfield.

Figure 25. Samuel Clemens and Laura Frazer at Stormfield, mid-October 1908. Courtesy of the Library of Congress.

"One child to whom I paid court when she was five years old and I eight," he reflected a couple of months later, "still lives in Hannibal and she visited me last summer, traversing the necessary ten or twelve hundred miles of railroad without damage to her patience or to her old-young vigor." Frazer remembered that Sam "took me over Stormfield. It must have been a tract of three hundred acres. We went through the fields . . . and across a rustic bridge over a little rushing brook. . . . It was as if the half century had rolled away and we were there looking on the boy and girl we had been."[3]

Ever ready to be a good neighbor, Sam helped to establish the local library with a gift of books, and in the fall he sponsored a pair of benefits for it. At its grand opening on October 28 he welcomed his "fellow farmers," announced that he had levied a tax of a dollar a night per male guest at Stormfield to help support the library association, and read a version of his essay "How I Edited an Agricultural Paper Once," originally published in 1870, in which he assumes the comic pose of a country squire who knows nothing about farming. Privately, he admitted he raised nothing on his land "but sunsets and scenery," and the joke went around that Sam was the only farmer in

Connecticut who could make two blades of grass grow where three had grown before. In fact, rather than cultivate native flora, he sowed his land with gorse seed from England. But he was hospitable to his rural neighbors. He opened "by telling them how he adored farming. That year, of course, he hadn't done much, the bananas hadn't ripened," he had not "planted very much sugar cane," and millions of turnips had been "picked before they were ripe. The proper way to do it was to send a boy up to shake the tree." His audience was bewildered at first, according to his new stenographer Mary Louise Howden. "None of them had ever had the privilege of hearing the king of humorists before. Most of them were elderly country people with all the New England taciturnity and dislike of giving themselves away and Mark Twain's drawling speech and gravity, his inimitable way of apparently not considering himself funny, puzzled them at the outset. But long before he got through they were rocking with delight." He also opened his house the afternoon of November 27, the day after Thanksgiving, to a hundred "of the sterlingest farmers & their families encounterable anywhere," who each paid twenty-five cents toward the local library fund to hear him read "the same old string of yarns." Elizabeth Wallace, visiting from Chicago, recalled that folding chairs had been borrowed from the undertaker and arranged in rows in the library and the loggia. The first person to arrive "had walked five miles." The farmers from the region "came in buggies and in other handy vehicles. They entered the house solemnly and took their places silently, refusing to make themselves comfortable, and held on grimly to fur overcoats and fleece lined jackets. Soon the big living-room was filled to overflowing, and then Mr. Clemens stepped up to the improvised platform at one end of the long room and bade them welcome."[4]

One evening during the Thanksgiving weekend 1908, Wallace remembered, Sam read aloud to his guests from *What Is Man?* It was not exactly holiday fare, but he fervently believed in its tenets, "and when he read aloud to us the clear, trenchant dialogue, we, too, were convinced, for a time, of their truth. He grew so earnest that he would often repeat a phrase, twice, in a deep, solemn voice, and he so utterly forgot his pipe that it went out completely." Sam similarly hosted Helen Keller, Anne Sullivan Macy, and her husband John Macy at Stormfield during a long weekend in early January 1909. He had read Keller's *The World I Live In* (1908) and sent her a note urging them to visit. "As we approached the Italian villa on the very top of the hill," Keller later recounted, "they told me Mr. Clemens was standing on the veranda waiting." Over the next three days Sam led Keller on walks around his property. "He said many beautiful things about Stormfield," she recalled, such as "It is my Heaven. Its repose stills my restlessness." On the evening of January 10, the last night of her visit, Sam donned his Oxford gown at Keller's request and read *Eve's Diary* to her—"an experience, I am sure, no other person in the world had ever had." Mark Twain, "our American, our humorist, the embodiment of our country," who "seemed to have absorbed all America into himself," drew her to him "and kissed me on the brow, as a cardinal or pope or a feudal monarch might have kissed a little child." As he read the story, Lyon recalled, Keller "quivered with delight" and Sam "was shaken with emotion. Could hardly find his voice again. It was a marvel to behold." When, at the end of the story, "Eve sighed her love" and "Adam stood at her grave grieving bitterly," Keller wept. "Perhaps my strongest impression" of Sam that evening, she later wrote, "was that of sorrow. There was about him the air of one who had suffered greatly." Before she and the Macys left the next morning, she inscribed the Stormfield guestbook: "I have been in Eden three days and I saw a King. I knew he was a King the minute I touched him though I had never touched a King before—A daughter of Eve."[5]

"Probably no literary light has been guest of honor in Manhattan with more frequency" during the winter of 1908–9 than Sam, *Brooklyn Life* reported in January. In mid-January, he spoke at a dinner at Delmonico's of the faculty and staff of the Post Graduate Medical School and Hospital, of which both Clarence C. Rice and Rogers were trustees. He announced to the crowd that he would read a paper entitled "On the Three Great Laws to be Observed in the Treatment of Bright's Disease of the Kidneys." A week later, Martin and Maud Littleton hosted a luncheon in his honor at their new home on Fifth Avenue. Among the guests were George B. McClellan Jr. and George W. Harvey. In February, Sam signed petitions in support of women's suffrage likewise endorsed by such people as Jane Addams, Dorothy Dix, Charlotte Perkins Gilman, Sarah Orne Jewett, Hamlin Garland, Julian Hawthorne, Julia Ward Howe, Howells, Lincoln Steffens, and Elizabeth Stuart Ward.[6] He helped to plan a testimonial dinner for district attorney William Travers Jerome at Delmonico's the evening of May 7. Jerome had served eight years in office since 1901, when he was elected on the Fusion ticket, but he had not been nominated for a third term. Sam had donated $25 to his 1905 campaign and mentioned in his speech that "he had voted for Jerome before and wanted to do it again. The diners roared their approval." Among the other dignitaries present were Richard Harding Davis, Harvey, publisher Condé Montrose Nast, and brewer Jacob Ruppert.[7]

Sam had long questioned William Shakespeare's authorship of the plays attributed to him. As early as 1873 he expressed some doubts in a notebook, but as the editors of his autobiography note, "as a rule his adherence to the

Baconian party is not apparent before 1887." Sam's skepticism was fueled by several bits of circumstantial evidence, including the erasure of Shakespeare's life from contemporary records. "It always seemed unaccountable to me," he explained, "that a man could be so prominent in Elizabeth's little London as historians and biographers claim that Shakespeare was and yet leave behind him hardly an incident for people to remember him by." The "Stratford Shakespeare," he insisted, "was a person of no public consequence or celebrity during his lifetime, but was utterly obscure and unimportant." He also argued that a relatively unlettered layman like the Stratford actor could not have known the subtleties of Elizabethan jurisprudence as well as the author of the plays, though more recent scholarship has demonstrated that the plays betray a surprising ignorance of the law. Sam was convinced, finally, that Sir Francis Bacon was the likely playwright by the putative discovery of his coded signature in the earliest printed scripts. John Macy shared the news with him at Stormfield in January 1909 that William Stone Booth in his forthcoming *Some Acrostic Signatures of Francis Bacon, Etc.* had detected Bacon's name "concealed in acrostics in more than a hundred places in the plays and sonnets," such as in the epilogue to *The Tempest,* where it appears "in its Latin form—Francisco Bacono."[8]

Helen Keller urged Sam to join the public debate over the authorship of the plays, and soon after her departure he began to dictate his twenty-one-thousand-word polemical essay *Is Shakespeare Dead?* "After long idleness" he was at work "throwing bricks at Shakespeare," he wrote Jean in February, building the case that the Bard "didn't write a one of the Plays & Poems that pass under his name. I think he & Mother Eddy are just about a pair—a pair of humbugs." Sam had "a good time" puncturing the pretensions of "everybody who is ignorant enough & stupid enough to go on believing Shakespeare ever wrote a play or a poem in his life or even so much as a single line of literature of *any* kind." He read "half a dozen Shakespeare-Bacon controversy-books," including Booth's *Some Acrostic Signatures of Francis Bacon;* Delia Bacon's *The Shakespeare Problem Revealed* (1857), which he first read a half century earlier as an apprentice pilot on the Mississippi; Ignatius Donnelly's *The Great Cryptogram* (1888), which he and Charley Webster had rejected for publication by Webster and Company; and George Greenwood's *The Shakespeare Problem Restated* (1908). He was particularly impressed by Greenwood's book, which he cited at length in *Is Shakespeare Dead?* Privately, he reported to John Macy that he had "read it most carefully and have stolen meat enough from it to stuff yards and yards of sausage-gut in my vast Autobiography and make it look like my own."[9]

Unfortunately, his purpose in writing the essay was unclear. Was it to discredit the claims of "the Shakespearites," "Shakespearoids," and

"Stratfordalators," or to bolster the arguments of "the Baconians"? He elsewhere smeared the orthodox Shakespeareans, aka "thugs, bangalores, troglodytes, hermafrodites [sic], blatherskites, buccaneers, and bandoleers." Even Sam seemed uncertain what he was about. On the one hand, he was intent on lumping "Shakespeare of Stratford-on-Avon" with the Tichborne claimant and Mary Baker Eddy among the famous frauds of history. "*So far as anybody actually knows and can prove*," he asserted, Shakespeare "never wrote a play in his life. *So far as anybody knows and can prove*, he never wrote a letter to anybody in his life. *So far as anyone knows, he received only one letter during his life*. So far as anyone *knows and can prove*, Shakespeare of Stratford wrote only one poem during his life," the doggerel on his gravestone. Privately, Sam was coy. "I wrote [*Is Shakespeare Dead?*] for pleasure," he claimed in a note to Keller, "*not* in the expectation of convincing anybody that Shakespeare did not write Shakespeare." Elsewhere, he contradicted even this modest claim: "All *I* want is to convince sane people that Shakespeare did not write Shakespeare. Who *did* is a question which does not greatly interest me." On yet other occasions he conceded that "the Baconians seem to me" to have the "more reasonable and rational and persuasive" argument, and he acknowledged that while "no evidence at all" indicated that Shakespeare composed the plays, "there was only one man alive [who] *could* have" written them. His nephew Jervis Langdon remembered that on one of his last visits to a theater, to see a performance of *Romeo and Juliet*, moreover, Sam remarked it was "'one of the greatest things Bacon ever wrote.' His belief that Bacon wrote Shakespeare was absolute."[10]

Sam finished the essay in early March and forwarded the manuscript to George Harvey. According to Lyon, Harvey was reluctant to issue it but was contractually obligated to publish anything Sam submitted. Sam's readers wanted "only the beloved humorous side of him," and Harvey worried that he was "slipping intellectually." Nevertheless, the essay appeared as a pamphlet on April 8 to predictably mixed reviews. Like a prizefighter who drops his hands before the bell, Sam was vulnerable to the allegation that Mark Twain had died. Eugene Angert suggested in the *North American Review* that "Mark Twain" could not be the author of the book and that "Twain" must have died in 1906, the year his autobiography began to appear in the pages of the *Review*. Angert also proves by a cipher that his recent work had been written by the popular author Elbert Hubbard. (Similarly, a New York *Sun* editor discovered the name "Theodore Roosevelt" hidden cryptically in Ben Jonson's prologue to the 1623 first folio.) The *Toledo Blade* hinted that "in the years to come somebody will claim that Ella Wheeler Wilcox" wrote Sam's work and, worse yet, the *Tampa Tribune* wondered what would happen "if, several centuries hence, some literary 'smarty' should discover that

Bret Harte wrote Mark Twain?" An editorialist for the *Cleveland Plain Dealer* contended that acrostics proved Sam was the author of "the book of Job, Tom Paine wrote *The Imitation of Christ,* and Theodore Roosevelt *Idylls of the King.*" Another columnist for the Brisbane *Telegraph* discerned a cipher in the lines inscribed to the Martin Droeshout frontispiece of the First Folio indicating that Mark Twain was Shakespeare's pseudonym.[11]

Most of the critics who noticed *Is Shakespeare Dead?* considered it nothing more than an elaborate joke. The *Portland Oregonian,* for example, answered the question in the title with a question: "Do we hear a Twain chuckle?" Many newspapers and magazines followed suit, among them the *Boston Journal* ("witty" with "a vein of seriousness"), *San Francisco Call* ("a running accompaniment of humor and anecdote"), *Sacramento Union* ("quick with humor and pierced with vigilant wit"), *Washington Times* ("humor is irresistible"), *Dallas Morning News* ("force of habit constrains us to take as a joke"), *Philadelphia Inquirer* ("indescribable" and "funny"), *Charleston News and Courier* ("certainly amusing if not convincing"), *American Review of Reviews* ("the argument abounds in humor but it is not for that reason the less convincing"), *New York American* ("an entertaining and thoughtful contribution to the Bacon-Shakespeare controversy"), *San Francisco Examiner* ("a serious book full of quaint humor"), *Springfield Republican* ("an entertaining little book"), *New York Times Saturday Review of Books* ("full of the humor which has never failed him"), *San Francisco Chronicle* ("very entertaining"), *Indianapolis News* ("a rich vein of fun and merriment"), *Harper's Monthly* ("humorous exposition of the mock combat"), London *Telegraph* ("puts the 'Baconian' arguments in a fresh and entertaining way"), *Belfast Telegraph* ("by a man whose translucent common sense is second only to his rich and perennial gift of humor"), London *Globe* ("Mark Twain is wonderful"), *Scotsman* ("hard to beat" among funny things in "all the Shakespeare-Bacon literature"), and Sydney *World's News* ("full of fun"). Champ Clark, a future Speaker of the House of Representatives and an ally in the battle for more equitable copyright, wrote Sam that in his opinion it was "the best book you ever wrote, which is saying a great deal. You did not leave the Shakespeare claimants a leg to stand on and I am glad of it." A pair of Commonwealth periodicals offered oxymoronic responses to the pamphlet: the *New Zealand Times* ("a serious book full of humour") and *St. James's Budget* ("jocularly serious").[12]

On the other hand, the reviewers who panned the pamphlet lacked for neither ammunition nor targets. In effect, in their view, Sam drove his reputation into a ditch. H. L. Mencken, for one, set the tone in *Smart Set*: "Since *Following the Equator,* his decline has been almost pathetic. Once a great artist, he is now merely a public character. . . . Let us try to forget this latter-day Mark Twain, with his potboilers and his wheezes, and remember only the incomparable Mark Twain that was." A large number of pundits shared this perspective, including James Stetson Metcalf in *Life* ("isn't a very good joke and certainly isn't worth the price that the publishers ask"), F. Dana Reed in the *Brooklyn Eagle* ("very sad" and "has a tendency to make one weep"), Edward Fuller in the New York *Bookman* ("he is not even funny when he loses his temper"), the *New Orleans Picayune* ("falls short of Mark Twain at his best"), *Independent* ("a feeble argument"), *Nation* ("occasionally somewhat forced" humor), *Northern Christian Advocate* ("not satisfactory"), *Zion's Herald* ("exceedingly flat and forced and sterile"), *Nation* ("insubstantial"), *Providence Journal* ("a foolish book"), *Boston Transcript* ("strains the rhetorical figure of irony almost to the breaking point"), *Manchester Guardian* ("poor stuff"), *Hereford Times* ("hardly just to his subject"), *Book News Monthly* ("means nothing"), *Independent* ("a feeble argument" that resembles "an exquisite parody"), *Spectator* ("makes a strong demand upon our indulgence"), New York *Outlook* ("a great deal of dreary reading"), *Library* ("not an action that will add to his credit as a writer"), London *Standard* ("disconcerting"), Sydney *Daily Telegraph* ("it seems a pity that Mark gets on to these side tracks"), Perth *Times* ("anti-Shakespeare fizzle"), and Dublin *Irish Times* ("perhaps this is serious work" but "the recommendation of a humourist's work for serious study is scarcely a compliment"). Both Frank Harris ("When Mark Twain decided that the Stratford Shakespeare did not write the plays and that Bacon did, he wrote himself down a bad critic as carefully as he could in fair long-hand") and the actor Beerbohm Tree, whom Sam had met in London in 1907 ("It is absurd to treat [Shakespeare] as a piece of worn-out art"), sneered at the essay. The *American Library Association Booklist* delivered the coup de grâce: "not recommended except where demand necessitates."[13]

As if the equivocal reviews of *Is Shakespeare Dead?* were not damaging enough, the news broke in the *New York Times* on June 9 that Sam had copied verbatim about three thousand words, or fifteen percent of his essay, from *The Shakespeare Problem Restated.* Most of Sam's eighth chapter consists of quotations from Greenwood's thirteenth chapter. Greenwood's London publisher addressed a letter to the editor of the *Times,* which published it under the title "Literary Larceny": no fewer than twenty-two of its 149 pages "are taken bodily" from Greenwood's book. Had Greenwood or his publisher "been applied to, we should have been proud to accord our permission" to Sam to copy those passages. In fact, Harper & Brothers at Sam's request had notified the John Lane Company on March 29 that he "wishes to use" part of Greenwood's book in his "little monograph," and Lane responded that he might "quote from Mr. Greenwood's book as much as he pleased." When Sam's pamphlet appeared, however, Greenwood and Lane were "justly indignant" that Greenwood was not footnoted as a source of the chapter, and they interdicted the sale of *Is Shakespeare Dead?* in England. In his own defense, Sam issued a statement acknowledging that in his pamphlet

> I took the liberty of using large extracts from Mr. Greenwood's book, 'The Shakespeare Problem Restated.' I made use of the extracts because of the great admiration I have for that book and with full permission of the publishers, I added a footnote in which I gave full credit to both author and publishers. The book was put through the press in great haste and somewhere, nobody seems to know where, the footnote was lost, probably in the composing room. That is the sum and substance of the whole story.

Harper & Brothers similarly allowed that Sam's footnote to Greenwood had been inadvertently omitted by a compositor or a proofreader in the haste to release his essay: "At the author's request this book was issued more hurriedly perhaps than any volume we have ever published. Only eighteen days elapsed between the time we received the manuscript and the appearance of the finished book." The publisher promised that the next edition of the pamphlet would rectify the oversight and restore the footnote. But the protests that the requisite credit to Greenwood had been mistakenly "lost" in production is belied by Sam's admission to Macy that he had "stolen meat" from *The Shakespeare Problem Restated* and made "it look like my own." Some critics mentioned the faux pas in their reviews, moreover. The *Spectator* asserted, for example, that Sam's "only serious arguments are 'lifted' avowedly" from Greenwood's book; the *Philadelphia Inquirer* noted the irony "that one who has so violently maintained his own rights should be so careless of the rights of others"; and the *Rochester Democrat and Chronicle* cracked that Sam's "latest sin" had left him "in deep water" and "a bad fix." The London *Referee* even ridiculed Sam's theft in a rhymed couplet:

> Said John Lane to Mark Twain to Mark Twain said he,
> "You've been plucking your fruit from my Greenwood Tree."[14]

In 1905 Sam began to suffer from what he dismissed at the time as chronic indigestion or dyspepsia but was more likely the early symptoms of congestive heart failure, the result of his lifelong smoking habit. He began to "fletcherize" his meals or, as he put it, "to thoroughly masticate one's food and saturate it with saliva." He also "stopped frolicking with mince pie after midnight." Two years later, much as he had consumed fresh watermelon as a home remedy for dysentery, he graduated to a diet of fresh radishes. He ate a "big dish of radishes . . . every night for dinner," Lyon observed, and "had no heartburn." Perhaps inspired by the starving survivors of the shipwrecked *Hornet* in 1866, he soon tried fasting ("a little starvation can really do more for the average sick man than can the best of medicines and the best of doctors") and then consulted an osteopath who "said there was a bone out of true—nothing the matter with the heart. He adjusted the bone; came up again, after 3 days, & readjusted it; same after another interval & re-readjusted it. Then I discarded *him*. But retained the pain."[15]

By October 1908 he had replaced the osteopath with an electric vibrator. "The Arnold electric vibrating machine," he bragged to Emilie Rogers, "seems to do all that the human massageur does with his hands—and more, and better, and pleasanter, and simpler, and more effectively. It stops headaches for Miss Lyon and cures and limbers lame and stiff backs for me. It claims to ease all sorts of pains, and I judge it can do it, for it stirs up the circulation quite competently and tones up the nerves—and that is really *the* essential function of osteopathy and kindred treatments." Though vibrators were "mostly marketed to women as a health and relaxation aid," as Rachel Maines notes, Sam treated his "frequent & protracted heartburn, due to indigestion," with "three applications of a minute each" of the vibrator "with ten-minute intervals between." It abolished "indigestions, sick headaches, & such things." He was so confident in its therapeutic value that he offered to buy Clara a vibrator for Christmas 1908 because "it easily & quickly knocks out my two ailments—indigestion & rheumatism." Sam's endorsement of the Arnold vibrator was even cited in the company advertising.[16]

By summer 1909 he had resorted to drinking hot water to relieve his chest pains. "I drink barrels of boiling water to keep the pain quiet; I read, & read, & read, & smoke, & smoke, & smoke *all* the time," he wrote Elizabeth Wallace. All the while Sam was in denial about the health risks of tobacco. "Smoking doesn't seem to affect my health at all," he told an interviewer in September 1902, and he reiterated that he had "smoked practically all my life . . . and it has never done me any harm" in May 1907. The humorist Oliver Herford teased him about his habit around this time:

> When I recall how first I met
> Mark Twain—an infant barely three,
> Rolling a tiny cigarette
> While cooing on his nurse's knee.
> Since then in every sort of place
> I've met with Mark and heard him joke;

Yet how can I describe his face?
I never saw it for the smoke.
At school he won a smokership—
At Harvard College (Cambridge, Mass.).
His name was soon on every lip,
They made him "smoker of his class."
Who will forget his smoking bout
With Mount Vesuvius—our cheers—
When Mount Vesuvius went out
And didn't smoke again for years?
The news was flashed to England's King,
Who begged Mark Twain to come and stay,
Offered him dukedoms—anything
To smoke the London fog away.
But Mark was firm. "I bow," said he,
"To no imperial command,
No ducal coronet for me,
My smoke is for my native land!"
For Mark there waits a brighter crown!
When Peter comes his card to read—
He'll take the sign "No Smoking" down,
Then Heaven will be Heaven indeed.

In July 1909 Sam finally admitted that he was suffering from a "tobacco heart," and his long-held opinion that "a man could smoke any time or all the time without any injury to his health" was wrong. He could no longer "walk three hundred yards or take an extra smoke or two" without paying a "penalty with a severe pain in my heart." His monumental blunder "will move even the wise to laugh at me," he confessed, "for in my vanity I have often bragged that tobacco couldn't hurt me. . . . However the victory over me is not much of a victory after all, for it has taken 63 years to build this disease. I was immune *that* long, anyway." On Dr. Quintard's orders he briefly cut back his cigars from forty a day to four, though they were the largest cigars he could find. Nevertheless, two months later he again vowed that smoking was "in no way responsible for my malady" and "I'm smoking as much as ever now." He reverted to the belief that his "pain was due to *indigestion*; a curious idea, since nobody's stomach & bowels could beat mine for perfect performance. . . . Still, if I eat moderately, no pain comes; but every time I over-eat, it comes." In January 1910 he again insisted that the source of his chest pain was "digestive" and "not pulmonary," and as late as March he reported to

Clara that "the pain in my breast has attacked me frequently and severely" as the result of "extravagant & inexcusable imprudences" in his diet.[17]

The behind-the-scenes power struggle at Stormfield again erupted openly when Clara returned from Europe in September 1908. As Sam remembered, Clara detested Lyon "most cordially & diligently," and in turn Lyon hated Clara "with her whole heart." The renewed attempts to discredit Lyon included allegations of drug abuse and alcoholism, though all such charges occurred months after the fact. "Miss Lyon took large quantities of whiskey & bromide, reducing herself pretty close to insanity—at times," Jean claimed to Twichell—but not until June 1909, after she was fired. Sam calculated that Lyon drank, perhaps with Ashcroft's help, a total of forty quarts of Scotch in July and August 1908, that she guzzled an entire quart in a single day in September 1908, and that she "always kept a bottle of cocktails in her room"—but he leveled these accusations in his final autobiographical dictation, dated October 21, 1909. Paine joined the attack with ditty he sent Sam in February 1910:

> Who feeds on bromide and on Scotch
> To keep her nerves at highest notch?
> Who makes of business-books a botch?
> *The Bitch.*

In addition, Clara alleged that Lyon embezzled money from Sam during the construction of Stormfield, diverting much more than the $1,500 she claimed to have "borrowed" to remodel Lobster Pot.[18]

Sam turned a blind eye to Clara's criticisms for many months. "I have no suspicions of her," he cautioned his daughter in early March 1909. Lyon "was not trained to business & doubtless has been loose & unmethodical, but that is all. She has not been dishonest, even to a penny's worth. All her impulses are good and fine. . . . She has served me with tireless devotion, & I owe her gratitude for it—& I not only owe it but feel it. I have the highest regard for her character. . . . And what shall I say of Ashcroft? He has served me in no end of ways, & with astonishing competency—brilliancy, I may say. During 7 years he has fought my Plasmon fight against desperate odds—a night-&-day month-in-and-month-out struggle, through lawsuit after lawsuit & machination after machination, never complaining, never losing hope." Ashcroft also invented the Mark Twain Company "to prevent piracy in years to come" by trademarking "in the name of Samuel L. Clemens such things as the 'Mark Twain Cigar,' tobacco, whiskey, shirt, corset, hair-restorer, etc. etc. This would place the issuance or suppression of such things entirely in the hands" of his heirs. To paraphrase a character in Dickens's *David Copperfield*, "Barkus was willing," and the company was incorporated on December 22 with capital of $5,000, its stock owned entirely by Sam, Ashcroft, Lyon, Clara, and Jean. As its president, Sam transferred all of his literary rights to the company, trusting that his daughters would be its long-term beneficiaries, though as usual he failed to understand all the legal implications of the contract he signed. In all, Sam adjured Clara, "I know Ashcroft and Miss Lyon better and more intimately than I have ever known anyone except your mother and I am quite without suspicion of either their honesty or their honorableness." Until she produced "something definitely & demonstrably incriminating," she should call off her lawyer. He would not allow "anyone to say a word in criticism of those worshiped pets of mine. To every man & woman in this region they were a pair of transparent rascals, but to me they were worthy of the kingdom of heaven."[19]

Then Sam learned from Fred Duneka that Lyon had mismanaged the house accounts to a greater extent than he had realized. Albert Bigelow Paine heard from his mother on March 8 that Sam was "being driven almost crazy" by the infighting "and he said that until three weeks ago he thought he was happy and well off, but since then it has been h—and that if things did not get better he would cut his G—D—throat." On March 13, he revoked Lyon's check-writing authority, a right she had enjoyed for nearly two years, authorized her to edit a volume of his letters, raised her salary to a hundred dollars a month, but effectively demoted her from a surrogate daughter to the rank of an employee. She would no longer perform such intimate tasks for him as drying his hair or painting his feet with iodine when he suffered from gout. He alleged no criminal conduct, but he was dismayed by her ineptitude. "Nothing is as it was," he confessed to Clara on March 14. "Everything is changed. Sentiment has been wholly eliminated. All things in this house are now upon a strictly business basis. All duties are strictly defined, under several written contracts, signed before a notary. All services rendered me are paid for, henceforth. But there is no vestige of ugly feeling, no *hostility* on either side. The comradeship remains, but it is paid for; also the friendship. Stormfield was a home; it is a tavern now & I am the landlord." In a word, as he wrote a few days later, "This house has gone to hell." In an attempt to square accounts, Ashcroft gave Sam signed IOUs for $1,000 to cover the balance of the "loan" to Lyon to renovate her house, and Sam signed documents specifying Ashcroft's duties as an officer of the Mark Twain Corporation and promising him a commission to manage Sam's business affairs for two years. Lyon continued to arrive at Stormfield in the morning and to return to Lobster Pot in the afternoon, but "she had nothing official to do" in the meantime.[20]

On March 18, Lyon and Ashcroft were married at the Church of the Ascension in Greenwich Village, New York. They had announced their engagement in late February, and Lyon had assured Sam that she and her new husband could work for him together "and you will have his love joined with mine and my love strengthened by his to stand by you and yours as long as you need us." On his part, Sam thought "it was an insane idea & unbelievable," as "amazing as if . . . they had concluded to hang themselves." Ashcroft admitted "frankly & without blush that he didn't love her, he only wanted to be in a position to take care of her in her persistent & exhausting illness. He knew she got her illness out of a whisky bottle & was drunk a good half of her time." Indeed, "she had proposed the marriage." Counting the bride, groom, minister, Isabel's mother, Ralph's brother, the Holy Trinity, and Sam, as he put it later, nine persons were present at the wedding. He told a reporter that the newlyweds' romance began as a "business association," "ripened into warm friendship, and then grew worse." Forty years later Lyon claimed she wed Ashcroft to "legitimize [or perhaps re-legitimize] her standing in the household" after her demotion and/or to squelch rumors that she was Sam's mistress. (Best Be the Tie That Blinds?) In any case, though eleven years older than Ashcroft's thirty-four, she seemed "girlish" during the ceremony, according to Sam.[21] The Ashcrofts returned to Stormfield that night and occupied separate bedrooms, fueling Sam's later conviction that their union was nothing more than a sham, part of a criminal bargain. As husband and wife, they enjoyed legal immunity from testifying against each other. "Each knew the other's crimes; each knew the other was treacherous by nature & would turn State's evidence at the first hint of danger; they *had* to marry & shut each other's mouths," he asserted. Still, "the Ashcrofts & I were soon friendly & sociable again & I hoped & believed these conditions would continue. Clara hoped the opposite."[22]

Sam had tried to entice Howells to visit his farm since buying the property. As early as August 1906 he offered to sell his friend a ten-acre building lot for only $25, and Howells drolly declined: "I would come and build next to you, but you ask too much for your land." After moving into Stormfield in June 1908, Sam reiterated the invitation to the entire Howells family. "Won't you & Mrs. Howells & Mildred come & give us as many days as you can spare & examine John's triumph?" he asked. "For to my mind it *is* a triumph. It is the most satisfactory house I am acquainted with & the most satisfactorily situated." Howells finally made the trek to the Connecticut countryside in late March 1909 and was struck during his only visit to Stormfield by the amity in the house. The entire staff, on their best behavior, "watch over [Sam] with tender constancy," he noted.[23]

Figure 26. Samuel Clemens and W. D. Howells at Stormfield, late March 1909. Photograph by Isabel Lyon. Courtesy of the Mark Twain Papers and Project, Bancroft Library, University of California–Berkeley, PH01836.

While the Ashcrofts' domestic melodrama was playing out in Redding, Clara and Charles Wark were cohabitating, or at least closely inhabiting nearby apartments, in the same building on Stuyvesant Square in New York. When exactly Sam learned about their affair—and when he learned that Wark was married—is impossible to say. Laura Skandera Trombley is no doubt correct that "Clara was more than loath to tell him," though he likely was aware of the problem no later than mid-January 1909, when the Twichells visited Stormfield. According to Lyon, Harmony Twichell disclosed that "all the Hartford world is talking about Clara's 'reported' engagement to Wark—saying that she is only waiting for Mrs. Wark to get a divorce from him. . . . The Country people around here have got hold of a similar Tale." Ironically, even as Sam valorized the innocence of young girls in his aquarium, his adult daughter was engaged in an adulterous affair. He had coerced at least two other unwed couples into marriage during his life, moreover, the first aboard the *America* while sailing from California to New York in December 1866, the second when he discovered his housemaid's dalliances with a male visitor to the Hartford house in 1877. He may have intervened again in an effort to protect Clara from public scandal. Both Skandera Trombley and Shelden assert that Wark "vanished from the Clemenses' lives," or that he and Clara ended their personal and professional relationship in late November or early December 1908. In fact, Wark accompanied Clara in concert (and continued to be paid with checks signed by Sam) through spring 1909. Isabel Lyon also suggested late in life that she had married Ashcroft as part of a "deal" brokered by Sam that required Clara to break with Wark, though the situations seem utterly unrelated. More likely, when Ossip Gabrilowitsch reappeared on the scene in December 1908, Sam simply encouraged his attentions to his daughter.[24]

Enter the leading man in Clara's romance. In truth, tall and handsome, with charm, talent, and a gentle demeanor, "Gab" or "G'ossip" had never been long absent from their lives. "We have known Gabrilowitsch intimately for 11 years," Sam wrote Elizabeth Wallace, "ever since Vienna days, when he & Clara were pupils of Leschetizky. They were engaged years ago—twice. Broken both times, to Mrs. Clemens's great regret." Gab had debuted in the United States with concerts at Carnegie Hall and Mendelssohn Hall in November 1900 and spent most of the winter in New York, where he was a frequent guest of the Clemens clan. Clara sailed with a chaperon to Paris in April 1902 to visit her beau—one of the periods when they were apparently affianced—and when the pianist toured the United States that fall under the management of Daniel Frohman, he was in occasional touch with the family. Clara and Gab renewed their friendship in early 1907, when he returned from Europe, and he renewed his suit in December 1908 when he spent the holidays at Stormfield. "Clärchen dear," Sam wrote his daughter on December 11, "you & G'ossip will be very welcome" at Stormfield—after all, the young man could not for propriety's sake stay at her apartment in the city—and a week later they arrived together in Redding. The morning of December 20 Gabrilowitsch took Clara for a ride in the snow that ended when the horse bolted and overturned the sleigh—an accident detailed the next day on the front page of the *New York Times*. That afternoon Gab entertained the family at the piano for an hour, much to Lyon's delight. "He is a darling musician & it is so good to have him in the house," she noted in her journal. Dorothy Sturgis remembered that, during one of her visits to Stormfield, the virtuoso "actually played the piano for us to my great delight." Sam wrote Margaret Blackmer, another angelfish, that Gabrilowitsch, Ethel Newcomb, and Clara, all of them Leschetizky's former students, were filling the house with music "all the time, night & day!" Mary Louise Howden remembered that the many members of the household were "thrilled to the very marrow by the harmonies that poured through the house" in "the gathering winter twilight." The "glorious sounds would stop for a while and Mr. Clemens's sonorously clear voice could be heard reading some passages from *Tom Sawyer*" before "the cataract of melody would fill the house again. These two masters of technique, each in his own line, were entertaining each other. It was an entertainment an outsider would have given many dollars to hear." When Clara performed in concert at Mendelssohn Hall on April 13, she sang Gabrilowitsch's "Wasserfahrt," which he dedicated to her on this occasion. Howells "applauded as if he belonged to a paid claque," and Sam presented his daughter with a bouquet of flowers at the close.[25]

At Henry Rogers's invitation, Sam agreed to deliver a series of speeches in early April celebrating the completion of the Virginian Railway, a 446-mile stretch of road between Norfolk and Deepwater, West Virginia, built for about $40 million almost entirely at Rogers's personal expense. The project opened over a million acres of coal fields in western Virginia to mining. "You have carried that giant enterprise through as patiently and quietly and unostentatiously as a geologic period overlays a continent with a new crust—well, it's just great!" Sam congratulated his friend. "That majestic achievement is the triumph of your life, and will be and remain your eulogy and your monument in the far by-and-bye." He and Rogers sailed from New York on the Old Dominion ship *Jefferson* on April 1. Ashcroft accompanied Sam to "take care of me, & baby me, & protect me from drafts, & so-on & so-on, just in the old-time way, the old charming way, the old happy way, & just as if nothing had ever happened to interrupt our heaven-born relations." Weeks later, Sam accused Ashcroft of perpetrating "two or three sly & underhand treacheries, perfidies, & shameless & pathetically small dishonesties—the smallest & shabbiest that have been practiced upon me in my lifetime"—while on the trip. More specifically, he charged that Ashcroft in Norfolk "procured a sum of money from me on false pretenses, by methods distinctly criminal in their character." Nevertheless, he stuck to the script Rogers had written. He addressed an audience of two thousand at the Richmond Board of Trade the evening of April 2 and paid tribute to Rogers for saving him from financial ruin a decade earlier and for his support over the years of Helen Keller—the first public revelation of the role Rogers had played in funding her education—during a banquet at the Monticello Hotel in Norfolk the next night. "Without the public knowing anything about it," he announced, Rogers "rescued, if I may use that term, that marvelous girl, that wonderful southern girl, that girl who was stone deaf, blind and dumb from scarlet fever when she was a baby eighteen months old; and who now is as well and thoroughly educated as any woman on this planet at twenty-nine years of age." Before leaving the city, Sam also spoke at the Norfolk high school and assured the thousand students that if they "went after everything in life as they went after him there would be no doubt of their success." On April 5 Sam and Rogers rode the new railway to Roanoke, where they were entertained by local businessmen, and they arrived back in New York via the liner *Hamilton* two days later. The Virginian Railway was a commercial bust, however, eventually reducing Rogers's fortune by half.[26]

On April 15, at Clara's insistence, Sam gave Isabel Lyon her one-month notice of dismissal and two months' severance pay required by the documents he had signed the month before. He canceled immediately Lyon's contract to edit a volume of his letters. She acknowledged her termination the same day: "Thank you so much for doing in so kind a way the thing that I have been expecting. . . . And I now accept my dismissal from your service, to take place at any time you shall cho[o]se within the month, with thanks inexpressible for the wonder & beauty you have brought into my life." Ashcroft prepared his weekly business statement on April 17 and disappeared from Stormfield "down the road in the distance," and Sam never saw him again. He reviled his former business manager in no uncertain terms in the Ashcroft-Lyon manuscript, a 429-page diatribe he composed between May 2 and October 21, 1909, to extort silence from his former secretary and business adviser: he was "a sneaky little creature, with beady, furtive, treacherous little eyes, & *all* the ways of a lackey—obsequious, watchful, attentive, and looking as if he wanted to lick somebody's boots." Sam wrote a check to Lyon on April 19 for $150 that discharged his obligation to her. In a "burst of affectionate regard" she at once "started to tell me what a sacrifice she had made for my sake in getting married: that she had not wanted to marry, but saw it was the only way that she & Ashcroft could save me from depression in my lonely estate," but Sam cut her off before she could continue. In late April Sam authorized Rogers to commission a complete audit of Lyon's and Ashcroft's books for the previous two years. "I would be very glad to take up the matter, if you desired it," Rogers assured him, "and see if I could straighten it out to your entire satisfaction." Before the end of the month Ashcroft agreed to cooperate with the audit and turn over all records, though he indicted "the ghastly treatment accorded to Miss Lyon during the past few weeks by a member of your family" and insisted that the allegations "emanated from a brain diseased with envy, malice, & jealousy"—that is, from Clara's imagination. Sam instructed Rogers to confiscate the vouchers and other account books on the grounds that they belonged to him. But he was befuddled by one of Ashcroft's accusations: "What was there about Miss Lyon for Clara to envy? Why should she envy my housekeeper? She might as well envy the cook." He failed to understand the extent to which Clara had been alarmed, if by nothing else, by her father's trip to Bermuda with his secretary in spring 1908. Clara readily allowed to a reporter that Sam and "Miss Lyon had always been friendly, and I hardly liked that." She complained once to Katy Leary that, unlike Lyon, "I don't control Father's checkbook." Clara even wanted Lyon's trunks "searched for stolen goods" before her employment ended, and from Sam's point of view the demand was justified. He later claimed that Lyon had filched some carnelian beads belonging to Livy and that Ashcroft stole a dinner jacket from him.[27]

With Lyon's imminent departure, Sam needed to replace her with a trustworthy assistant. He did not look far. On March 14, the day after he demoted Lyon, Sam and Paine asked Frederick Peterson to allow Jean a weeklong trial visit to Stormfield. On April 19, four days after firing Lyon, Sam invited Jean to join him in Redding. "Dear child," he wrote her, "you will be as welcome as if it were your mother herself calling you home from exile!" She arrived on April 26 and soon settled into a routine. As she wrote her "Uncle Joe" Twichell in mid-June, "You can't imagine how thankful I am to get back home again, & in this beautiful place, too"—she had not seen Stormfield before she moved there.

> I don't know when I have been as happy & absolutely contented as now. And I have so many reasons for feeling so, that if I didn't, it would be disgraceful. I am in better health than for a long time; able at last to be of use to Father; permitted once more, after four years, to ride; living in a beautiful country & now (since yesterday) with a farm next to Father's original purchase, to develop & improve after my own desire & ability. I love country life & dislike city life, so that my one & only cause for irritation is the thought of what has happened in the past & the necessity of passing the charming little house still in Miss Lyon's possession every time I leave the house.

Jean alleged in her letter to Twichell that Lyon had told neighbors "that Clara was insane" and "that I was." In fact, Ashcroft repeated the lie to Archibald Henderson in May 1909: "There is a rather distressful situation at

Stormfield. Mr. Clemens has practically abandoned the place, the present occupants being his two semi-insane daughters."[28]

Sam was elated by Jean's return to the fold and did not, at least initially, hold Lyon responsible for their long separation. He gave Jean a hundred and fifty acres adjacent to his property that included a house and gloated that she "maintains perfect health, robust health, now that she is free of the privations & irritations & captivity of the sanitariums. She is outdoors all day, riding, driving, & managing her farm. I believe she could have been with us a year ago as well as not. . . . I suppose Jean's banishment was necessary for her recovery, but I hope it will never have to be repeated." He repeatedly expressed his joy and relief that Jean was "home." She displayed "wisdom, judgment, penetration, practical good sense—like her mother—& character, courage, definiteness, decision; also goodness, a humane spirit, charity, kindliness, pity; industry, perseverance, intelligence, a clean mind, a clean soul, dignity, honesty, truthfulness, high ideals, loyalty, faithfulness to duty—she is everything that Miss Lyon isn't." She "abides with me & runs a farm & keeps my accounts," he bragged to Elizabeth Wallace.[29]

After firing Lyon for alleged financial malfeasance, he gradually evolved the opinion that "that reptile" was responsible "for keeping [Jean] out of her natural home so long." But as Hamlin Hill fairly contends, "Nothing in the surviving record indicates" that Lyon "was instrumental in keeping father and daughter apart. . . . Possibly the secretary used her influence with Dr. Peterson, affecting his decision to restrict the contact between Jean and her father; and indisputably Miss Lyon was terrified, with reason, of the unpredictable quirks in Jean's behavior." Only in the Ashcroft-Lyon manuscript did Sam accuse Lyon of scheming to exile Jean when she was "well enough to have come home," even to the extent of hypnotizing him. The allegation has unfortunately become commonplace in Mark Twain studies."[30] To be sure, Lyon had screened Sam's correspondence, but only at his request because he wanted to be insulated from problems he could not fix. "Clara, Miss Lyon and Mr. Paine keep all sorts of distresses from me, and I am very thankful for it—distresses which they are aware I could not remedy, I mean," he once wrote Jean. "They know I desire this." Had she wanted to register her complaints or requests with her father directly, as Hill notes, she could have done so in her letters, their telephone conversations, or during his occasional visits to her. In some instances, Sam also changed his story to blame Lyon for alleged transgressions, such as the mass resignation of servants the previous September. The servants had been repelled not by fear of burglars but by "Miss Lyon & her slave-driver violences of speech."[31]

"One of the more egregious" of Sam's false accusations in the Ashcroft-Lyon manuscript, as Amanda Gagel asserts, was his "mischaracterization of Lyon" as a disappointed seductress. With money from her boss, Lyon bought a $50 dress to wear to Sam's seventieth birthday celebration at Delmonico's because, she explained, he wished "to have me in rich soft clinging silks of splendid or delicate colors." On his part, Sam described Lyon in the Ashcroft-Lyon manuscript as "a luxurious mendicant. . . . She would get herself up in sensuous oriental silken flimsies of dainty dyes." Sam elsewhere described Lyon in less vampish terms. He "could not go to bed" with "that little old superannuated virgin," he asserted. "I would rather have a waxwork." She was merely "an old, old virgin, and juiceless, whereas my passion was for the other kind." He excoriated Lyon as late as March 1910 in a note to Clara in which he piled on the epithets as was his wont: his former secretary had been "a liar, a forger, a thief, a hypocrite, a drunkard, a sneak, a humbug, a traitor, a conspirator, a filthy-minded and salacious slut pining for seduction and always getting disappointed, poor child."[32] Little evidence outside of Sam's own personal writings supports this view.

On May 19 Sam left Redding and arrived in New York about noon to consult with Rogers about the Ashcroft mess. Clara met him at Grand Central Station with the news that Rogers had died overnight from another stroke. Her father was devastated by the loss of his best friend and financial guru. "This is terrible, terrible," he told reporters. "I cannot talk about it. I am inexpressibly shocked and grieved. I do not know just where I will go. . . . Mr. Rogers was as close to me as a brother." Clara remembered that "the expression of grief on Father's face was pitiful to behold. . . . He looked so delicate, enveloped in this shadow of sorrow." After resting briefly at a hotel he headed to the Rogers home to express his condolences to the family. "The tears streamed down his cheeks as he was greeted by Henry H. Rogers, Jr., at the door," according to the *Washington Times*. He notified Elizabeth Wallace, who had met Rogers during their Bermuda sojourn, that Rogers's death was "a heavy stroke. It bruised many a heart: how many we shall never know, for his helpful kindnesses went far & wide, & made no outward sign. Here we shall not look upon his like again." Rogers had been "the best friend I ever had, and the nearest perfect, as man and gentleman, I have yet met." Sam remained in the city until the funeral at the Church of the Messiah on May 21. He served as a pallbearer along with Elbert H. Gary, one of the founders of U.S. Steel after whom the city of Gary, Indiana, is named; William Rockefeller, John D.'s younger brother; E. H. Harriman, multimillionaire railroad executive; John D. Archbold, vice president of Standard Oil; and

Clarence C. Rice. A false rumor soon circulated that Sam was mentioned prominently in Rogers's will, prompting a wag to joke that

> Mark Twain was benefited by
> The will of Henry Rogers;
> Each humorist should pick him out
> One of these rich old codgers.

More to the point, many of Rogers's obituaries mentioned his philanthropy, especially his "benefactions" to Helen Keller.[33] He was also uniquely qualified to negotiate a discreet settlement between Sam and the Ashcrofts, and unfortunately, his death ended the audit of their accounts.

Ironically, a week after Rogers's funeral Sam discovered almost by accident that Lyon had spent much more than she had claimed to refurbish Lobster Pot and, worse yet, that Ashcroft had schemed to swindle him. On May 29 the contractor Harry Lounsbury casually mentioned to Sam that the remodeling costs had totaled about $3,500, and after an audit of his books confirmed Lounsbury's account, Sam realized that Lyon had paid "about $2000 of my money on her house *before* I had offered to assist her with a loan. This was plain, simple, stark-naked *theft*." The same day, "Ashcroft made one of his 'blunders'" by bragging to Lounsbury that he could sell Stormfield "over [Sam's] head, for a thousand dollars, whenever I want to!" Within three days Paine located in a safety deposit box in the Liberty National Bank of New York a general or comprehensive power of attorney Sam had unwittingly signed on November 14, 1908, assigning "all I own and all I ever *shall* own" to Ashcroft and Lyon. The document appointed them "my true and lawful attorneys" and empowered them

> to exercise a general supervision over all my affairs and to take charge of and manage all my property both real and personal and all matters of business relating thereto; to lease, sell and convey any and all real property wheresoever situated which may now or which may hereafter at any time belong to me; to remand, receive and collect all dividends, interests and moneys due and payable to [me]; . . . to sell, assign and transfer any and all stocks, bonds and mortgages belonging or which may at any time belong to me; to change any or all of my investments and to make any investment of any or all of the moneys belonging to me; to draw checks or drafts upon any banks, banker or Trust Company or any financial institution with which or whom I have or may at any time hereafter have moneys on deposit or to my credit.

Ashcroft and Lyon "had not asked me for a power of attorney & I had not conferred one upon them," Sam wrote, asserting in the Ashcroft-Lyon manuscript that he had not seen the document "so I do not know whether I signed it or whether the signature is forged." But so long as it was enforceable, the pair owned Mark Twain, Inc., lock, stock, and barrel. Still, the attempted deception came at a price. "The Ashcrofts have wrecked their life—& *so* foolishly!" Sam lamented. "Where do you think you could find a poor, & obscure, & inconsequential pair so highly & influentially & promisingly situated as they were? They are in disgrace—in irremediable disgrace—& nothing to blame for it but their own greed & treachery." He had hitherto considered "the Countess Massiglia the lowest-down woman on the planet" but he began to suspect "I have been doing the Countess a wrong." Sam immediately revoked the power of attorney in writing, and Ashcroft promptly acquiesced to his action, since neither he nor Lyon "has used or had cause to use" the legal authority.[34]

Two weeks after revoking the power of attorney, Sam called it "the most amazing document that has seen the light since the Middle Ages." Edward Loomis, the husband of Julia Langdon Loomis, concluded years later that if Sam "hadn't acted when he did, Clara would have inherited zero." Ashcroft had never "asked me for a power of attorney" and until its discovery in a bank vault "I had never heard of that paper—yet I *signed* it." By his own testimony, Sam was "a pretty versatile fool, when it comes to contracts and business and such things."[35] Hill concludes that Sam had simply been "gullible and foolish." Fortunately, he escaped relatively unscathed. During the seven months the power of attorney was in force Ashcroft did not invoke it for any purpose, legal or otherwise. He was apparently planning to claim Sam's postmortem estate. Had Sam died before he revoked Ashcroft's power of attorney, he conceded, "It would have been difficult for a court to find any objection" to his title. Clara and Jean "would have been paupers. However, I didn't die" and Ashcroft's designs were frustrated. Though Lyon was named Sam's co-attorney in the document, she was unaware of Ashcroft's scheme, to judge from all available evidence. Thirty years later, she admitted her marriage had been a "mistake" and blamed her "bad" ex-husband for "laying his own plans" to defraud their former employer. Henry Nash Smith, after interviewing Lyon years later, averred that Sam was unjust to her "at the time she left his employ." She never publicly criticized Sam or his daughters, and while she apparently destroyed her diary covering the crucial year 1909, she shielded her other diaries from public view until after Clara's death.[36]

The Ashcrofts sailed for Europe on June 8—ironically, Clara's thirty-fifth birthday. Sam falsely alleged that the couple "took to the water when the investigation began to get pretty warm" and that "the soiled birds had flown" the coop on "an obscure steamer," perhaps under fake names, to escape jail.

"They were scared. They were in flight, to save Miss Lyon from arrest." In fact, Ashcroft had notified Sam on June 3 that, "owing to the unjust and unfounded accusations made against her," Lyon's health had "been seriously undermined" and "her doctor orders immediately a complete change. As I have important business to attend to in England," the two of them planned to sail for England within a few days "to be gone about four weeks." Sam's assertion "that they fled surreptitiously to avoid prosecution was clearly false," according to Hill.[37] Fairly or not, at the suggestion of his lawyer Sam filed writs of attachment for $4,000 on Lobster Pot on June 19 and on the Lyon family home in Farmington, Connecticut, a day or two later. In effect, he moved to repossess not only the house he had given "the wench" but her other property as well, news that soon exploded in the press on both sides of the Atlantic. The *Brooklyn Eagle* contacted Ralph's brother Herbert Ashcroft, who bluntly blamed Clara for causing the fuss. She had been alarmed by Lyon's "faithful and devoted service" to her father and "determined to get rid of the secretary." The matter of irregularities in the accounts "would have been settled amicably" had Rogers not died. Lyon "was threatened with nervous prostration" and "her physician ordered her to take a trip abroad without delay, thinking that the sea air would calm her and save her health." The suit to seize the house in Redding during their absence "is spite work, that's all it is." In her own defense Lyon likewise faulted Clara, "a young woman of an artistic temperament that is apt to lead her at times into a flighty and wrong direction." Lyon returned immediately to the United States to

> do everything possible to clear myself of the charges which have been made against me. You may rest assured that there is not the least doubt in my mind but that I will disprove to the satisfaction of everyone every charge that has been made. . . . Every step that was taken in the restoration of the farmhouse was with [Sam's] knowledge and approval. . . . For every cent that was expended I did incur liability. Mr. Clemens possesses notes amounting to nearly a thousand dollars. . . . This whole matter will soon be settled, but it is a shame that I should be placed in the improper light in which I have.

While Lyon was in mid-ocean en route to New York, Clara fretted that she would "have long conversations with the newspapers—drat her!" and urged her father to "make a simple statement for all the papers saying that you were grateful to me and my friends for discovering Miss Lyon's dishonesty etc.—because just now before a winter of concerts it may create a harmful atmosphere for me if you remain perfectly silent." Lyon arrived aboard the *Carmania* on July 14 and, as expected, spoke to reporters at the dock. For seven years, she said, her "relations with Mr. Clemens were almost those of a daughter toward her father. . . . I loved him as I would my father." Lyon signed the deed to the house back to Sam, but later insisted she had done so under duress and that, in any case, it was not valid without her husband's signature. Ashcroft followed two weeks later and announced upon his arrival that he was still Sam's "financial representative and will continue to be so far as he knows."[38]

The situation devolved when Ashcroft became embroiled in the controversy and turned the legal strategy from defense to offense. When he returned from England in late July, he expressed his shock in a note to Stanchfield that his wife had been "inveigled into transferring her cottage and land at Redding to Mr. Clemens." In his first formal statement to the press, released on August 3, he alleged that both Clara and Jean were "jealous of Mrs. Ashcroft, were afraid that Mark Twain could marry her, and often attempted to destroy his confidence in her." The only person who had openly charged Lyon with dishonesty was Clara, and with the transfer of title to Lobster Pot "the trouble of the cottage" had been "settled amicably" so far as Sam and the Ashcrofts were concerned. Though there remained a question of the amount of her debt to Sam, Ashcroft reiterated that he was "still manager of the Mark Twain Company and shall so remain for the present. My contract has nearly two years to run." Ashcroft's shot across Sam's bow also hinted at the kind of reprisal he might inflict on the reputation of the family if he was not mollified: "For two years or more after their mother's death, both girls were in sanitaria most of the time, and the younger daughter has been under the care of nerve specialists ever since."[39]

Ashcroft also contacted Sam's lawyers with a not-too-subtle threat to retaliate with a libel suit: "Your client must afford us vindication or face us in court." For a brief period in August and early September the two parties seemed on course to settle their differences: a withdrawal of all pending lawsuits on both sides, a cancellation of the attachment on Lyon's house in Farmington, the departure of Lyon from Lobster Pot and the restoration of the property to the Clemens estate, and an acknowledgment by Ashcroft that Sam "owns and has always owned all of the stock" in the Mark Twain Company and "nominated and elected all of the directors." On September 7, Sam, Clara, and Jean signed a "discharge of all indebtedness and obligations" owed by the Ashcrofts.[40]

But then Ashcroft overstepped, repeatedly claiming "vindication" or "exoneration" in newspaper reports that began to appear on September 11. In Ashcroft's twist on the story, Sam had withdrawn his demand that Lyon repay the $3,000 "loan" to refurbish Lobster Pot (but he had regained ownership of the house, so why would he require reimbursement?); he had instead paid Lyon "a substantial sum of money" in damages, he and Clara had both retracted their allegations and signed documents to that effect, and Sam had asked Ashcroft to remain in office at the Mark Twain Company because "his work has been most satisfactory." One of the articles acquitting Ashcroft appeared in Sam's old nemesis the *New York Times* on September 13. Sam was so annoyed he addressed a reply to Adolph Ochs, the owner of the paper. "The facts in my case are simple," he began. Lyon "had authority to sign checks for me" and "she was caught stealing." She was asked "to hand back the house I had given her" and "she did it." Ashcroft's claims notwithstanding, he had not dropped "any suit for an alleged 'loan'" because "the suit was to *recover stolen money*." No "reparation" had been paid, though Ashcroft's bill for $8,000 in past services rendered was settled for $1,000, and in lieu of the two years' worth of commissions that he demanded he had accepted the equivalent of a half-year payment. Sam sold the manuscripts of *Life on the Mississippi, Pudd'nhead Wilson,* and "The Man That Corrupted Hadleyburg" on September 15 to J. P. Morgan for $2,500, "more than enough to square with Ashcroft." No document "acquitting Mrs. Ashcroft of blame for her treacherous conduct of my affairs" had been signed; Clara had "'retracted' not a word she has uttered about 'that discredited mollusk'"; nor did Ashcroft remain in office as a flack or shill for the Mark Twain Company, because after Sam alleged he was "not a fit person to serve," he had been asked to resign, and he did. Rather than send this letter, however, Sam dispatched Paine to meet with Ochs, who agreed to "let Mr. Clemens alone" in the future "or at least to adhere to facts." At Clara's insistence, he addressed a similar complaint about the Ashcrofts to his friend Melville Stone, general manager of the Associated Press, but in a cover letter he allowed that "if I alone were concerned I wouldn't take any notice of the rotten Ashcrofts. I caught Miss Lyon stealing money (she had been at it more than two years), & I bounced her. That is the whole of the dispute."[41]

During his spin campaign, Ashcroft went so far as to draft a template of the apology he wanted Sam to sign, forwarded a copy to Sam's lawyer, and released it to the press:

> My Dear Mrs. Ashcroft—
>
> With reference to our recent misunderstandings, and the unfortunate airing of the same in the press due to my attachment on your property, I beg to state that I have had the administration of my financial and other affairs investigated and find the same to have been properly and satisfactorily conducted by you, and I regret that any criticism by any one of you in this respect should have occurred.
>
> Yours sincerely,
> S. L. Clemens.

In fact, Ashcroft had agreed to resign from the Mark Twain Company on the conditions that Sam write a letter expressing regret for the loss of his services and "a note clearing Mrs. Ashcroft of dishonesty & regretting that by an unfortunate mistake she has been wrongly charged with it." Sam declined to entertain the latter proviso and jotted on the Ashcrofts' envelope that it contained a "letter from a sniveling hypocrite—who is also a skunk, & a professional liar. It is precious, it has no mate in polecat literature." He complied with Ashcroft's first request, though his lawyer "did not think [the reference] would be satisfactory to Ashcroft" so he suppressed it, too: "Recognizing . . . that [Ashcroft] is a liar, a traitor, a sneak, & a would-be thief, it is matter of deep regret to me that the Mark Twain Company must lose his services as manager & director; for, the above defects aside, he possesses high capacities for those positions, he being notably shrewd, inventive, enterprising, & tirelessly diligent, watchful, & persistent in the administration of all business affairs that interest him & furnish play for his talents." Lyon finally vacated Lobster Pot in late August, to Sam's great relief. He was thankful that she had been "awfully punished" in a variety of ways:

1. She has lost her house & home;
2. She has married *him!* (& he *her!*)
3. She has to live in Brooklyn;
4. She adores Society—& is out of it for good;
5. And he? He's a stevedore, now. Much too respectable a calling for that sandhog.

Though he later conceded "that putrescent pair cost me $50,000," Sam crowed to Elizabeth Wallace that at least "we got shut of those frauds & all settled up, finally & for good."[42]

He reckoned too soon. Ashcroft continued to exploit the commercial value of Sam's name for his own profit. During the weeks he spent in England at midyear, while he was still Sam's business adviser, Ashcroft apparently sold for £25, the equivalent of over $3,600 in modern dollars, a pair of advertisements for Player's Navy Cut to the John Player & Sons tobacco company. These ads featured Sam's likeness and signature on a phony testimonial letter—another example of Ashcroft's talent for grift and fraud—and were reproduced in 1909 in dozens of British newspapers, including the *Manchester Evening News*, London *Telegraph*, *Bristol Times and Mirror*, *Yorkshire Post*, *Sheffield Telegraph*, *Portsmouth News*, *Punch*, London *Graphic*, and *Illustrated Sporting and Dramatic News*.

To satisfy the demand for his autograph, Sam sometimes signed his name multiple times on single sheets of paper that were cut apart, and Sam worried

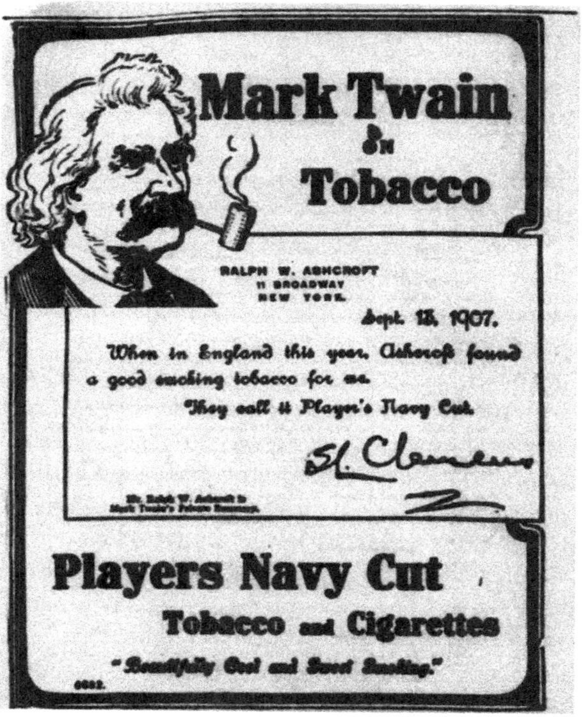

Figure 27. John Player & Sons tobacco company testimonial advertisement, *Manchester Evening News*, June 30, 1909.

that Ashcroft had obtained one of these sheets. "The forgery published by Ashcroft . . . & the tobacco-puff forgery indicate that Ashcroft has a supply of genuine signatures of mine in his possession on blank sheets of paper for I never signed" the advertisements that appeared in the British press. He cautioned Paine and his lawyers to be alert after his death for "swindles & forgeries from the Ashcroft camp: thieving documents purporting to date back to the days of that power of attorney but really concocted since." Even if Ashcroft was Sam's business agent at the time he sold these ads, "he was still not authorized to use his authority to injure me & to steal £25 from me." As Sam explained to Elizabeth Wallace, "In England Ashcroft committed a forgery in the second degree upon me, & sold for £25 my name (& words which I would not have uttered for a hundred times the money.) Sh—! say nothing about it—we hope to catch him & shut him up in a British prison."[43]

To be fair, all parties in the dispute were culpable. Sam may not only have signed documents, including the one granting Ashcroft power of attorney over his financial affairs, without reading them but also libeled the couple, particularly Lyon, in both private correspondence and the Ashcroft-Lyon manuscript. In the absence of definitive financial records, moreover, it is impossible to determine the extent to which Ashcroft was more responsible than Lyon for defrauding the old man, though none of the principal actors in the drama was blameless.

Sam had promised his angelfish Frances Nunnally six months in advance that he would speak at commencement ceremonies at St. Timothy's School for Young Girls in Catonsville, Maryland, on June 10, 1909. He was eager to attend the formalities because, as he told reporters, "I always like the young ladies and would go a long way to be in their company." "Pretty girls—and you almost have a monopoly of them here—are always an inspiration to me," he mused, and "they are all very sweet and make one feel young again to be with them." Not that he was old, he hastened to add. "No, indeed, I am just as young now as I was forty years ago." In truth, he had suffered his first severe attack of angina pectoris two days earlier. He told Paine that it was "a curious, sickening, deadly kind of pain. I never had anything like it." He told "Francesca" later that he was stricken with heart disease, not the kind that "plucks the life out of you and suddenly as by a lightning-stroke" but the kind that "is slow and tedious and procrastinating and you have to wait and wait 'till you get run over by a freight train." Despite his discomfort, Sam left Stormfield with Paine on June 8—ironically, the same day the Ashcrofts sailed for England—overnighted in New York, registered at the Belvedere Hotel in Baltimore the next day, and arrived in Catonsville, twenty miles to the west, the morning of June 10. In his final public appearance, Sam admonished the graduating class, "all in their pretty commencement dresses" according to Paine, not "to smoke or drink or marry—to excess." On the lawn of St. Timothy's, Sam learned from a reporter that his friend Edward Everett Hale had died that morning in suburban Boston, and he offered this comment for the record: "I had the greatest respect and esteem for Edward Everett Hale, the greatest admiration for his work. I am as grieved to hear of his death as I can ever be to hear of the death of any friend, though my grief is always tempered with the satisfaction of knowing that for the one that goes, the hard, bitter struggle of life is ended." Back at Stormfield a week later, he wrote Francesca that he had enjoyed "a very delightful time at your school & remember it with great pleasure. If I were not so inadequate in age & sex I would go there and take a term or two." The jocular comment could not hide the truth, however. After a physical examination on June 23, Sam's doctor Quintard concluded Sam "had no more than two years to live," again admonished him to cut down his smoking, and ordered him "not to stir" from the house "upon any account before autumn." "I am preparing for another world," he joked with George Harvey, "with wings in the morning, parachute in the afternoon." But in letters to two other angelfish he was more candid. He admitted to Dorothy Quick that since his breakdown in Baltimore he had not "had a well day" and "lately I keep to my room almost all the time"; and to Margery Clinton that "the slightest physical exertion gives me a pain in the breast that is not endurable, sitting, standing, or lying down."[44]

Soon after Sam returned from Maryland, Thomas Edison and a crew from his New Jersey studio arrived in Redding to film him. The minute-and-forty second movie they produced depicts Sam in his signature white suit outdoors walking around Stormfield in his typical sloth-like ramble while smoking a cigar and indoors dining with Clara and Jean in the loggia. Claude Beuchotte, Sam's butler, appears in a cameo when he serves the trio. The only known motion picture of Sam Clemens, it is readily available online today.

Ossip Gabrilowitsch was nursed by Clara at Stormfield much of the spring and early summer of 1909 for an ear infection that developed into mastoiditis. He underwent a "terrible operation," as Katy Leary called it, at the Manhattan Eye and Ear Hospital in late June and recuperated in Redding upon his release. He had sufficiently recovered by September 21 to perform at a benefit for the local library along with Clara and David Bispham, formerly with the Metropolitan Opera, that attracted some over five hundred people to Stormfield. Bispham remembered that "every room on the ground floor of the spacious house was filled to the last inch that afternoon by a crowd that spread up the stairways, on the balcony, out into the pergola, anywhere indeed from which the music could be heard, even if we performers could not be seen." "The guests came from long distances," according to Dan Beard. "No distance seemed too great for them to drive." They "came from everywhere," Sam reported to Wallace—"Danbury, New Haven, Norwalk, Redding, Redding Ridge, Ridgefield, and even from New York," some in automobiles, others in buggies and carriages, with "a swarm of farmer-youngfolk on foot from miles around." Had ticket sales not been halted a day and a half before the performance, Sam observed, "we should have been swamped. We jammed 160 into the library (not quite all had seats); we filled the loggia, the dining-room, the hall, clear to the billiard room, the stairs, & the brick-paved square outside the dining room door." Tickets were priced at fifty cents, seventy-five cents, and a dollar, depending on seating, and the event netted a total of $372 for the library and "might have netted a great deal more if the prices had been higher." Sam introduced the performers—"My daughter is not so famous as these gentlemen, but *she's ever so much better looking*!"—and the audience welcomed them, which "woke them up, and I tell you they performed to the Queen's taste! The program was an hour and three-quarters long and the encores added a half-hour to it. The enthusiasm of the house was hair-lifting." Bispham, famous for his renditions of Wagner, sang "Les deux grenadiers." Sam lingered after the program ended because "I wanted to remain & get acquainted" with his visitors—"which I did. It took several hours . . . but I had a good time!" Sam hosted a private tea for a dozen friends after the recital. Jean Clemens, "fine and handsome, apparently full of life and health, danced down that great living-room as care-free as if there was no shadow upon her life," Paine recalled.[45] The evening ended with Clara's announcement that she and Gabrilowitsch were engaged to be married.

CHAPTER 18

The Passing Show

Manifestly, dying is nothing to a really great and brave man.

—Samuel Clemens to Olivia Clemens, 1 July 1885

Clara and Gabrilowitsch tied the knot in the library at Stormfield on October 6, 1909, fifteen days after their engagement was announced. They needed to marry quickly because Gabrilowitsch had scheduled a European concert tour beginning later in the month, and he was not yet recovered entirely from his ear surgery the previous June. "The sudden marriage was decided upon in order that my daughter might go with him and continue to nurse him," Sam explained. Joe Twichell performed the ceremony, much as he had married Sam and Livy almost forty years before, and at Clara's direction he omitted the word "obey" from her vows. She invited "a few intimate friends" and family members, a total of only thirty-two, including Richard Watson Gilder, the Littletons and Paines, Edward Quintard, Clara and John Stanchfield, and Clara Clemens's cousin Julia Langdon Loomis and aunt Susan Crane. Her sister Jean, her maid of honor, wore a white silk dress trimmed with lace, and her cousin Jervis Langdon was the groom's best man. Never shy about upstaging his daughters, Sam sported his Oxford robes over white flannels. Ethel Newcomb performed Wagner's "Bridal Chorus" and Mendelssohn's "Wedding March" on the piano. "I get nearly as much delight out of this marriage as I do out of the irrevocable soldering together of that pair of thieves that nested in my bosom so long," Sam wrote Elizabeth Wallace. The newlyweds left Stormfield late in the afternoon and planned to sail to Germany on October 12, but the honeymoon and Gab's concert tour were abruptly postponed when the groom fell ill (again) and underwent an appendectomy in New York a few days later. The couple finally sailed on November 20, and Sam was unfazed by his son-in-law's health crises. "Gabrilowitsch is an exceedingly fine fellow & I am glad to have him on the family list. He has done me one service for which I am most thoroughly grateful: he has squelched Clara's 'career.' She is done with the concert-stage—permanently, I pray."[1]

Figure 28. Clara Clemens's wedding at Stormfield, October 6, 1909. Left to right: Samuel Clemens, Jervis Langdon II, Jean Clemens, Ossip Gabrilowitsch, Clara Clemens Gabrilowitsch, and Joseph Twichell. Photograph by Frank J. Sprague. Courtesy of the Mark Twain Papers and Project, Bancroft Library, University of California–Berkeley, PH00643.

After the wedding but before their departure for Europe, Clara was harried by a shadow from her past. According to hearsay, Edith Cullis Wark, the estranged wife of her former pianist Charles Wark, was preparing to sue her for alienation of affections. Jean believed the rumor had been planted by Ashcroft. In any event, on October 13, several of the New York dailies printed a card requesting that Mrs. Wark contact Charles J. Campbell, a midtown Manhattan pettyfogger eager to handle her case. Campbell predicted that sensational information about Clara and the Warks would soon emerge that would make "interesting reading for the public." Gabrilowitsch insisted to reporters that he and Clara were "at a loss to know what it all means. There has been no suit for alienation against her nor is she engaged in any other litigation. Mr. Wark is a personal friend of both of us, and I am sure he has nothing to do with it. The report has evidently been circulated through maliciousness." On October 18, however, the day after Gab's remarks appeared in the press, Sam signed a $1,000 check that John Stanchfield, his attorney, presumably paid someone (Campbell? Edith Wark? the Ashcrofts?) to silence the gossip.[2]

Two days before the newlyweds sailed to Germany on their honeymoon, Sam left with Paine for Bermuda on the *Bermudian* to escape the chill of the Connecticut hills, nurse the pain in his chest, and put the Ashcrofts out of mind as well as out of sight. He had just registered at the Hamilton Hotel when Helen Allen and her mother Marion Allen arrived and insisted he join them at Bay House, the vice-consul's home on a nearby beach. "I have been the grateful & contented guest ever since," he wrote Frances Nunnally. "I have driven two or three hours every afternoon with my hosts" and Paine "in a light Victoria" carriage "over these fine roads, in this fine air, with the brilliant blues of the sea always in sight." After dinner he helped Helen, who had grown over the past year but was "as sweet & innocent & unspoiled a child as ever she was," with her homework.[3]

In late October, while Sam was sojourning in Bermuda, Harper issued a 121-page edition of *Extract from Captain Stormfield's Visit to Heaven* to mostly favorable reviews. The hostile notices were the exception, such as in the New York *Sun* ("vents . . . on common ideals of future bliss with no great regard for delicacy or other people's feelings"), *Pall Mall Gazette* ("we like it no better in a book than we did in serial form"), London *Globe* ("will probably shock some of his admirers"), *Yorkshire Post and Leeds Intelligencer* ("the irreverence of the book is rather too audacious even for a licensed jester"), and *Literary Digest* ("somewhat machine-made and always banal," "absolutely lacking in humor," and "does not make any moral or political point"). The *Salt Lake City Intermountain Catholic* notice was even harsher: "Mark Twain has gained a great reputation as a 'funny writer.' But his fun has always been destructive. . . . The most sacred things, human and divine, have been made the target of his jest. He has held up man and God to ridicule." He "is now an old man" and "it is too late for him to repair the evil he has done."[4]

Far more common were complimentary notices of the book on both sides of the Atlantic. They appeared in such venues as the *New York American* ("a clever satire on the old-fashioned, wings-harp-and-halo paradise"), *New York Times Saturday Review of Books* (a "capital piece of half-serious drollery"), New York *Bookman* ("his humor is still of the brand labelled American"), *Times Literary Supplement* ("humor . . . sparkles on its pages"), *Congregational and Christian World* ("Mark Twain is both at his humorous and serious best"), *Book News Monthly* ("while the world will class this seeming absurdity among the funny books, it has a preferential claim to the theological shelf"),

Portland Oregonian ("one of the most remarkable fun-generators of our era"), *Richmond Times-Dispatch* ("a rollicking fabrication from beginning to end"), *Philadelphia Inquirer* ("one of the author's fine pieces of extravagance written with much humor and a little underlying philosophy"), *San Francisco Chronicle* ("very funny" and "very entertaining"), *Queen* ("its form is bizarre but it is worth a good many sermons"), Dublin *Irish Times* ("a spiritual tonic"), *Westminster Gazette* ("keen dry humor with passages of real insight which give it another value"), London *Clarion* ("an audacious, amusing, original, and powerful satire"), and *New Zealand Times* ("innocently mirth-provoking").[5]

While in Bermuda, Sam puttered on a satirical epistolary novel in Satan's voice entitled "Letters from the Earth." A sort of sequel to the Adam and Eve diaries and "A Humane Word from Satan," the narrative was so intentionally sacrilegious that, as Sam admitted to Elizabeth Wallace, it "will never be published—in fact it couldn't be, because it would be felony to soil the mails with it, for it has much Holy Scripture in it of the kind that prostitutes & Christians like, but which can't properly be read aloud, except from the pulpit & in family worship. Paine enjoys it, but Paine is going to be damned one of these days." Not only did the work betray the influence of the Higher Criticism but, as John Bird documents, "one long passage" was plagiarized from the writings of Robert Ingersoll, specifically his essays "Some Mistakes of Moses" (1879) and "Orthodoxy" (1884). Then again, he did never expected his "borrowings" to be detected.[6]

Sam's familiarity with contemporary biblical criticism was also evident in his discussion of the difference between "the two Testaments." "The Old one gives us a picture of these people's Deity as he was before he got religion," he explained, and "the other one gives us a picture of him as he appeared afterward." In conversation with Paine he was more specific in contrasting the God of wrath and the God of mercy. "In the Old Testament He is pictured as unjust, ungenerous, pitiless, and revengeful, punishing innocent children for the misdeeds of their parents; punishing unoffending people for the sins of their rulers, even descending to bloody vengeance upon harmless calves and sheep as punishment for puny trespasses committed by their proprietors," he told Paine. "Think of a God of mercy who would create the typhus germ, or the house-fly, or the centipede, or the rattlesnake, yet these are all His handiwork."[7] So much for the doctrine of benevolent design.

"Letters from the Earth" was also unpublishable at the time of its composition for its forthright treatment of human sexuality. Indeed, Sam rarely valorized chastity save among women in his own family. From all indications he patronized "hog ranches" or brothels near military posts in the West and the whorehouses of Virginia City, and he certainly argued in private in 1896 that Britain military authorities were duty bound to "provide safe women for the soldiers" stationed in India, "clean women subject to rigid inspection," as "to provide wholesome food for them." As many as half of the seventy thousand British soldiers deployed to South Asia were "poxed" and "go home and marry fresh young English girls and transmit a heritage of disease to their children and grandchildren." Sam also insisted to Elinor Glyn a decade later that by rights adultery should not be considered a venal sin. The adulterous hero and heroine in her romance *Three Weeks* "recognize that they were highly and holily created for each other and that their passion is a sacred thing, that it is the master by divine right and that its commands must be obeyed." Sam followed such arguments to their logical ends in "Letters from the Earth." As he wrote from Satan's point of view, the First Pair "knew the Supreme Art" and "practiced it diligently and were filled with contentment." Women were by nature "as competent as the candlestick is to receive the candle. Competent every day, competent every night. Also, she *wants* that candle—yearns for it, longs for it, hankers after it, as commanded by the law of God in her heart. But man is only briefly competent. . . . After 50 his performance is of poor quality, the intervals between are wide, and its satisfactions of no great value to either party; whereas his great-grandmother is as good as new." Should she act in accordance with her innate desires, Sam concluded, a woman was entitled to exercise "the high privilege of unlimited adultery."[8]

On December 20, on the return voyage aboard the *Bermudian,* Sam expressed his gratitude to the Allens for their hospitality. He could not thank them "enough for the perfectly charming time you have given me," he allowed. "I have never had a lovelier time, & I can't get over being sorry that it had to come to an end. This is not a comfortable voyage. We plunged into heavy seas before the waving handkerchiefs & the flag were an hour out of sight, & nine-tenths of the passengers were abed before dinner time. Paine succumbed early, & got extravagantly seasick, & that other pain (the one in my breast) kept me entertained until 3 this morning." He cautioned fifteen-year-old Helen by the same mail to "beware of Arthur," her bartender-boyfriend. "O, beware of that snake in the grass, that precocious criminal, that ultimate decoration of the gallows! What a murderous face he has! For one so young." When the ship landed in New York on December 21, Paine was met at the pier by his wife Dora and Sam by Jean, Martin and Maud Littleton, a gaggle of journalists, and below-freezing temperatures. "His shaggy brows" were "contracted with pain," "his face looked haggard as if from lack of sleep," "his cheeks were hollow," and "he walked with a shuffling step," according to the reporters. He "leaned heavily" on Paine, and "his hands were pressed over his left breast," where, he admitted, "he was suffering great pain." His "work in this life" was over, he announced to the group. "I shall write no more works, attempt no more lectures or new work. I have half a dozen unfinished books that I have hardly touched in three years." In Bermuda "I never feel my age," he added, though he admitted he was "getting too old to play golf and tennis." The breast pain "that constantly annoys me—from dyspepsia, I imagine—I never feel when I am in Bermuda. But the moment I leave the island it returns." He had "not worked for three years" and feared "there will be no new work for me in this world or this life." While speaking with the press, however, and despite "his protestations that he felt very feeble, he puffed away at a long black cigar."[9]

Sam left the harbor with the Littletons for their home, where he rested a day before returning to Stormfield. Martin Littleton told reporters that, "barring the aches and pains that a man of his age has a right to expect, he is in excellent shape. Naturally, leaving Bermuda and striking New York with the temperature only twenty above zero, the cold got in its work, and he was hardly so chipper as in the tropics. But he is feeling all right today." Despite this statement, the story circulated that Sam had become a "most pathetic figure," and Jean urged him to deny the rumor publicly. She "said I must think of Clara," who "would see the report in the German papers," so "I sent a humorous paragraph by telephone to the Associated Press." "I hear the newspapers say I am dying," he observed in his statement. "The charge is not true. I would not do such a thing at my time of life. I am behaving as good as I can. Merry Christmas to everybody!"[10]

Jean met him at the door, "beaming a welcome," when he arrived at Stormfield the evening of December 22. "We had two splendid days together," Sam wrote the Twichells, and in the library after dinner the next evening they planned to take a vacation to Bermuda together in the spring. As they retired, Jean told her father that she could not kiss him good night because she had "a cold and you could catch it," so Sam "bent and kissed her hand. She was moved—I saw it in her eyes—and she impulsively kissed my hand in return." Early the next morning he heard voices outside his bedroom door and thought that Jean was leaving "on her usual horseback-flight to the station for the mail." When the door opened, "I supposed it was Jean coming to kiss me good morning, she being the only person who was used to entering without formalities." Instead, Katy Leary entered "gasping & quaking" and announced "Miss Jean is dead!" Leary remembered that Sam leaped from bed, "put his two hands to his head, and whispered: 'Oh, God! Oh, God!'" He ran to her bathroom and "there she lay, the fair young creature, stretched upon the floor and covered with a sheet. And looking so placid, so natural, and as if asleep." A local doctor was summoned, and his attempts to revive her, "like our previous ones, failed to bring her back to life." Sam tried to console Leary by telling her that Jean was "happy now, she's with her mother and sister; and if I thought I could bring her back by just saying one word, I wouldn't say it." Sam assumed "she had been seized with a convulsion and could not get out of the tub. There was no help near, and she was drowned," the cause of death reported in the obituaries published over the next several days. But little water was found in her lungs during the autopsy, so the most reasonable explanation for Jean's death was not that she suffered a seizure while bathing and drowned but that the shock of the cold bath, a standard ameliorative prescribed by osteopaths to stimulate the nerves and muscles, precipitated a heart attack. That is, she died as the result of an ill-advised form of medical treatment. As Katy Leary put it, "I think she jumped into the tub that morning and the shock must have been too great for her heart." Sam cabled Clara in Germany with the sad news and discouraged her from returning for the funeral. He followed the telegram with a letter:

> O, Clara, Clara dear, I am so glad she is out of it and safe—safe! I am not melancholy; I shall never be melancholy again, I think. You see, I was in such distress when I came to realize that you were gone far away and no one stood between her and danger but me—and I could die at any moment, then *then*—oh then what would become of her! For she was willful, you know, and would not have been governable. You can't imagine what a darling she was, that last two or three days; and how *fine*, and good, and sweet, and noble—and *joyful*, thank Heaven!—and how intellectually brilliant. I had never been acquainted with Jean before.

Her "last act" before they parted the night before her death, Sam allowed to Clara, was to defend Lyon when he "burst out upon her!" He was everlastingly grateful that so charitable a soul "did not meet her fate in the house of a stranger" but "in the loving shelter of her own home."[11]

Then the funeral preparations. Just as Katy Leary had dressed Susy's and Livy's bodies for burial, she dressed Jean's, in this case in the white gown she had worn as maid of honor at Clara's wedding. On Christmas Day her body was carried in her coffin to the library and Sam saw her there, but he had already decided he would not travel to Elmira for her internment. He would never again "look into the grave of any one dear to me." "I saw Livy buried," he wrote Twichell. "I will never consent to see another dear friend put under the ground." In the evening Jervis Langdon arrived with a hearse "to bear away its pathetic burden." At Sam's request, Paine played the orchestrelle as Jean's body was borne from the house: Schubert's "Impromptus" for her, Mascagni's "Intermezzo" for Susy, and Handel's "Largo" for Livy.[12]

And the inevitable recriminations, mostly arraigning Lyon. Jean was "shamefully & criminally abused for three years, through the plots & lies & malignities of that unspeakable person," Sam charged. Jean "had a fine mind, a most competent brain. That shit said she was insane! She & her confederate told that to everybody around here." Jean's death—"her emancipation"—was "the only kindness that God ever did that poor, unoffending child in all her hard life." After enduring an "unspeakable" and "cruel malady" that might have incapacitated her for life,

> she is free & harm can never come to her more. . . . For sixteen years Jean suffered unspeakably under the dominion of her cruel malady, & we were always dreading that some frightful accident would happen to her that would stretch her mutilated upon her bed for the rest of her life—or, worse—that her mind would become affected; but now she is free, & harm can never come to her more. Eight months ago we got her back from her long & bitter exile in sanitariums, & from then until her last moment she was utterly & exultingly happy. I am so happy in this memory, that the very thought of it almost makes me cry. Yesterday evening at 6 I stood at my window & saw her borne away from this home to another, whence she will not return any more. I remained here. I saw her mother buried. I will never endure that shock again.

The same day Jean died, Sam began to write an essay in her memory that he completed two days later. "In her loss I am almost bankrupt, and my life is a bitterness, but I am content," he mourned, "for she has been enriched with the most precious of all gifts—that gift which makes all other gifts mean and poor—death." He handed the manuscript to Paine the evening of December 26 to approve. "I have finished it," he said; "read it. I can form no opinion of it myself. If you think it worthy, some day—at the proper time—it can end my autobiography." Paine printed in his biography of Sam a paragraph omitted from the essay when it was appended to an early edition of the autobiography: "Did I know Jean's value? No, I only thought I did. I knew a ten-thousandth fraction of it, that was all. It is always so, with us, it has always been so. Shall I ever be cheerful again, happy again? Yes. And soon. . . . My temperament has never allowed my spirits to remain depressed long at a time." Whereas he had blamed himself in the past for the deaths of his brother Henry, son Langdon, daughter Susy, and wife Livy, he assumed survivor guilt in this case not for causing Jean's death but for outliving her. Her love "astonished me daily" during the final months, he wrote Clara. "I recognized its sincerity, but could not divine the source of it, nor what had bred it & kept it alive, any more than I can divine why you love me nor how you keep it up. But I was deeply grateful to Jean for that unearned love & I am deeply grateful to you for yours." Three months after Jean's death and only a month before his own, he still rejoiced that she had been released. "I have lost that dear Jean, & my sorrow lies heavy upon me—but I would not bring her back if I could. Nor Livy, nor Susy. Death is the most precious of all the gifts this life has for us—& it is theirs. Peace to their sacred ashes!"[13]

"The pain in my breast has come back," Sam wrote Elizabeth Wallace on New Year's Day, "so I am leaving for Bermuda next Wednesday" to stay with the Allens. Stormfield had become "a desolation, its charm all gone, and I could not stay there," he allowed. Paine mailed the Allens "a bottle of medicine" prescribed by Quintard—probably a narcotic—"to be given him only if the pain in his breast should be very severe indeed." Sam and his butler Claude Beuchotte railed to New York on January 4, and Sam dined with Paine and Howells that evening. Howells remembered that "the last time I saw him alive was made memorable to me by the kind, clear judicial sense with which he explained and justified the labor unions as the sole present help of the weak against the strong." Sam sailed aboard the *Bermudian* with Beuchotte the next day. "I still have that pain in my left breast," he told reporters at the dock, "and I am going back to Bermuda to see if I cannot get rid of it. I am not troubled with the pain when on the island but as soon as I return to this city it attacks me again. I was not as ill as the reporters perhaps imagined when I came back to New York a few weeks ago." He again attributed his pain to indigestion, "not the sort of ailment that causes people to die." He fondled a cigar and said "This is my only friend," inspiring a lyric by John A. Moroso:

Your only pal! Since first you wrote
Your pals began to troop your way,
And Fate has never struck a note
Of sorrow, and the smiling way
Of fortune never opened wide
That we weren't by your side.
Your only pal! Why, Mark, you seem
To overlook ten million folks
Who weep when sorrows 'round you teem—
You can't discard us as old jokes!
Your chasms never opened wide
That we weren't at your side.

Your only pal! Sam Clemens, you!
When you say that, don't treat us right;
Your pals are millions and they're true
Until the coming of the Night.
Mark twain, mark thrice before you chide
Old friends who have not died!

Sam arrived at Bay House on January 7 and professed satisfaction with his life in repose in response to all inquiries. "My ship has gone down, but my raft has landed me in the Islands of the Blest, and I am as happy as any other shipwrecked sailor ever was," he declared.[14]

From all indications, he settled into a pleasant routine. "I am living the ideal life and am immeasurably content," he notified Paine on January 11. Beuchotte lived at the Hamilton House and came to Bay House twice daily to ask "if I need any service. He is invaluable." He could not imagine how to improve the new normal with its "good times, good home, tranquil contentment all day & every day without a break." He toured the recently commissioned research ship *Carnegie*, built to map the earth's magnetic field, within a week of his arrival. He attended a party at Government House in honor of German naval officers in late January, frequented lectures at the British military base, and regularly dined with friends. He enjoyed motorboating and picnics and watching cricket matches and horse races. He even played rounds of "clock golf" with Woodrow Wilson on the Allens' lawn.[15] Wilson wrote his wife afterward that Sam "does not see why he should ever leave Bermuda again. . . . He seems weaker than when I last saw him, but very well. He speaks of the tragical death of his daughter with touching simplicity. He is certainly one of the most human of men. I can easily understand how men like Cleveland and Joseph Jefferson learned to love him."[16] At least twice a week he attended concerts at the hotels, usually the Hamilton Hotel, once asking the bandmaster to conduct Mascagni's "Cavalleria rusticcana intermezzo" in honor of Susy and later presenting him with a copy of *Captain Stormfield's Visit to Heaven*. Other evenings he simply held court in one of the hotel parlors, according to the Hamilton *Royal Gazette*, "surrounded by admiring friends." At a charity event in early March, he sold kisses to "pretty young women," a fact that made news in the United States. Sam's old Hartford friend William Lyon Phelps, now professor of English at Yale, sent him a copy of his new book *Essays on Modern Novelists*, which pronounced him "our foremost living American writer." In reply, Sam thanked Phelps "ever so much for the book, which I find charming indeed, that I read it through in a single night & did not regret the lost night's sleep. I am glad if I deserve what you have said about me; & even if I don't I am proud & well contented since you think I deserve it." W. D. Howells's daughter Mildred, also in Bermuda for her health, visited him occasionally. "Poor old Clemens!" her father wrote her. "I am sorry he suffers so. I'm sure it must comfort him to have you near him." Fearing that Sam was near the end, Howells sent him a joking valedictory letter on January 18. "I hope you are worse. You will never be riper for a purely intellectual life again," Howells assured him, "and it is a pity to have you dragging along with a worn out material body on top of your soul." As for their respective legacies, Howells happily deferred to Sam's superior credentials: "I shall feel it honor enough if they put on my tombstone 'He was born in the same Century and general Section of middle western Country with Dr. S. L. Clemens, Oxon., and had his Degree three years before him through a Mistake of the University.' "[17]

Sam made no immediate plans to return to the United States. "I suppose I shan't see Stormfield again very soon," he wrote one of the angelfish. "I have no sorrowful associations with Bermuda, so I expect to spend a good deal of my time here in future. I am not in any hurry to go back to America." On the islands there were "no newspapers, no telegrams, no mobiles, no trolleys, no trains, no tramps, no railways, no theaters, no noise, no lectures, no riots, no murders, no fires, no burglaries, no politics, no offenses of any kind, no follies but church, and I don't go there. I think I could live here always and be contented." He put the best face possible on his physical impairment in a note to Mary Rogers: "My health is blemishless except for the pain in my breast. That is permanent, I suppose. It doesn't allow me to work, & it doesn't allow me to walk even so much as a hundred yards; but as it lets me do all the things I want to do, it is not an encumbrance."[18]

Sam began to settle his affairs in absentia. He offered the Lobster Pot to Clara and sold Jean's farm for $6,000, money to be used to build a Redding library in her honor. With Paine's help he reduced the expense of maintaining Stormfield inasmuch as he planned to live there "but seldom hereafter & then only flittingly." He promised Clara that he would "take care of myself, for your sake; I shall live as long as I may, for your sake,—not my own, for I believe I was born indifferent to this silly life"—and instructed her to protect his assets in her own interest after his death by retaining his crew of lawyers.[19]

Sam was preoccupied during these weeks in Bermuda with Helen Allen, the daughter of his hosts, more than with any other pastime. He read to her, though she was indifferent to the books he selected; he flirted with her, though she apparently paid little heed; he wrote to her, though she failed to reply, assuming she read his missives; and he dictated his letters for her to transcribe, for which help he contributed $200 toward her "school allowance." He openly admitted his jealousy of "the bloody-minded bandit Arthur," Helen's boyfriend. He "still fetches and carries Helen," he wrote Paine within a week of his arrival, and "presently he will be found drowned." The Allens sometimes joined Sam at the band concerts, where he watched Helen dance. In all, he carped, she took "a strong interest in clothes & dancing & the theatre, & riding & canoeing & picnicking & a prodigious interest in any & all members of the [male] sex, under 45, married or single." She exhibited "absolutely *no* curiosity" and probably had never read a line of verse—except perhaps the poem Sam sent her on Valentine's Day 1910:

> I know a precious little witch,
> And Helen is her name,
> With eyes so blue the asters say
> "They bring *our* blue to shame;"
> And cheeks so pink the eglantine,
> That by the roadway blow,
> Shed all their leaves when so they fail
> To match the dainty glow
> That steals across from ear to ear,
> and down from eyes to chin,
> When that sweet face betrays the thoughts
> That hidden lie within
> Concerning Arthurs and their like
> Who long this maid to win;
> And form so classic in its grace
> Of budding bust and tapering limb
> And rounded hip and slender waist
> And faultless features, that aghast
> The sculptured marbles of the Greek
> Grieving confess their chorus surpassed!
> I am hers, though she's not mine—
> I'm but her loyal
> Valentine.

When Helen's mother printed this poem in a memoir of Sam in 1913, she omitted eight of the final eleven lines, including those about "Arthurs and their like" who "long" to win Helen and the descriptions of her adolescent daughter's "classic" form, "budding bust and tapering limb," "rounded hip and slender waist," and her "faultless features" surpassing the beauties of classical nude sculpture. That is, Marion Allen was evidently troubled by

Sam's rather prurient interest in her daughter, though some of his biographers dismiss his comments as mere "jokes."[20]

Some remarks Sam addressed to Helen after his departure from Bermuda in mid-April are even more odd. They appear in a letter he probably never sent her, though a rough draft survives among his papers in the Bancroft Library. He admits to missing her, wishes he "could trade places with Teddy" (a pet? a stuffed animal? another boyfriend?), and adds in shorthand, as Hamlin Hill notes, "endearments somewhat inappropriate from a 75 year old man to a girl not yet sixteen": "you are very pretty and sweet and dear and cute." He confesses that "out of my jealous heart I drink to your barkeep" Arthur, though he also threatens to "carve him up with his own Excalibur" if he catches him around her again. Finally, he admonishes her to "be cautious, watchful, wary" with her "diamond" or her virginity. Both Hill ("the disturbing excesses of the old man's infatuation") and John Cooley (his "behavior was certainly unusual, even obsessive") have documented in detail Sam's odd fascination with schoolgirls. But the infamous report that "something unprintable" or "very terrible . . . happened in Bermuda" during his final trip there, something presumably involving Helen Allen, has never been verified. Hill speculates that "it is at least possible that Clemens' jealousy erupted into an over expression that frightened or offended the Allens," though Cooley is more cautious, reporting simply that "there is no evidence to suggest real impropriety or scandal in connection with any of the angelfish."[21] Certainly such second- or thirdhand hearsay would have been inadmissible in court.

Sam left Bermuda for only one reason: he was dying. To be sure, he had rallied when he first arrived on the islands. Robert Collier claimed that he saw Sam nearly every day and thought he looked "better than I have seen him at any time during the last four years." In mid-March he wrote Clara that he was only "waiting for the mild weather" or "non-bronchial weather" to return to Stormfield. "I shall be home by the end of April anyway, if not sooner." But within a week his health took a turn for the worse. On March 22, during a day trip to the aquarium on Agar's Island, he suffered an attack of angina so acute that Marion Allen "feared we might not get him home." On March 25 he notified Paine that he and Beuchotte were scheduled to sail on the *Bermudian* for New York on April 23, though "I may have to go sooner if the pain in my breast doesn't mend its way pretty considerably. I don't want to die here for this is an unkind place for a person in that condition. I should have to lay in the undertaker's cellar until the ship would remove me & it is dark down there & unpleasant." He wrote Clara the same day that his chest pain had been severe for three days and attributed it, as usual, to indigestion or "extravagant & inexcusable imprudences in feeding." He resorted to "Quintard's medicine," likely morphine, which he "had never touched" before. Three days later he contacted Paine again: "I have been having a most uncomfortable time for the past four days with that breast pain, which turns out to be an affection of the heart, just as I originally suspected." If he recovered sufficiently to travel, "I may sail for home a week or two earlier than has been proposed." The same day, Paine reported, he received a letter from Sam's host William Allen, "who frankly stated that matters had become very serious indeed. Mr. Clemens had had some dangerous attacks and the physicians considered his condition critical." Paine checked with Edward Quintard, who supplied him with morphine and taught him "the use of the hypodermic needle." The two men cabled Clara and Gabrilowitsch in Rome, where they had traveled for Easter, to urge them to sail for New York "without delay." And Paine sailed the next day for Bermuda.[22]

Paine arrived in Hamilton unannounced on April 4 with plans to return to New York with Sam and Beuchotte in tow aboard the *Oceana* eight days later. Paine's "one purpose" in the interim "was to get [Sam] physically in condition for the trip." He was able to sleep the night of April 8 "only after repeated injections of morphine," and he complained two days later that his "breast pain stands watch all night and the short breath all day" and requested "a jugful of that hypnotic injunction [hypodermic injection] every night and every morning." But he had improved by April 12, when they embarked. "As long as I remember anything I shall remember the forty-eight hours of that homeward voyage," Paine recalled later. When the ship ran into "the more humid, more oppressive air of the Gulf Stream," Sam's breathing became more labored and he asked for more morphine. He even pleaded for a lethal dose (Paine refused) and lodged the equivalent of a modern "do not resuscitate" order. "When I seem to be dying," he told Paine, "I don't want to be stimulated back to life. I want to be made comfortable to go." "I am sorry for you, Paine," he added, "but I can't help it—I can't hurry this dying business." While en route, he worried that "we won't make it." He was heavily sedated and confined to his berth for most of the "dreadful" voyage.[23]

After the *Oceana* docked in New York on April 14, Sam remained asleep in his cabin for three hours. Quintard and his assistant, Dr. Robert H. Halsey, met the ship at the pier, and after seeing his patient Quintard addressed the press:

> I think Mr. Clemens about a week or so ago had a heart attack much more serious than any preceding one. He seems easier just now than he has been for some time. . . . We hope that after his arrival at Stormfield he will continue

> to improve. I have made only a superficial examination of him. When we get him home we will make a thorough examination. As everyone knows angina pectoris is a dangerous affection of the heart. I can say that he looks better than I expected to find him.

Quintard added that Sam "might live five years and might die in five minutes." As Sam was carried from the ship in an invalid chair by Paine and Beuchotte, he stated the obvious to the photographers: "I am not so strong as I was when you snapped me before."

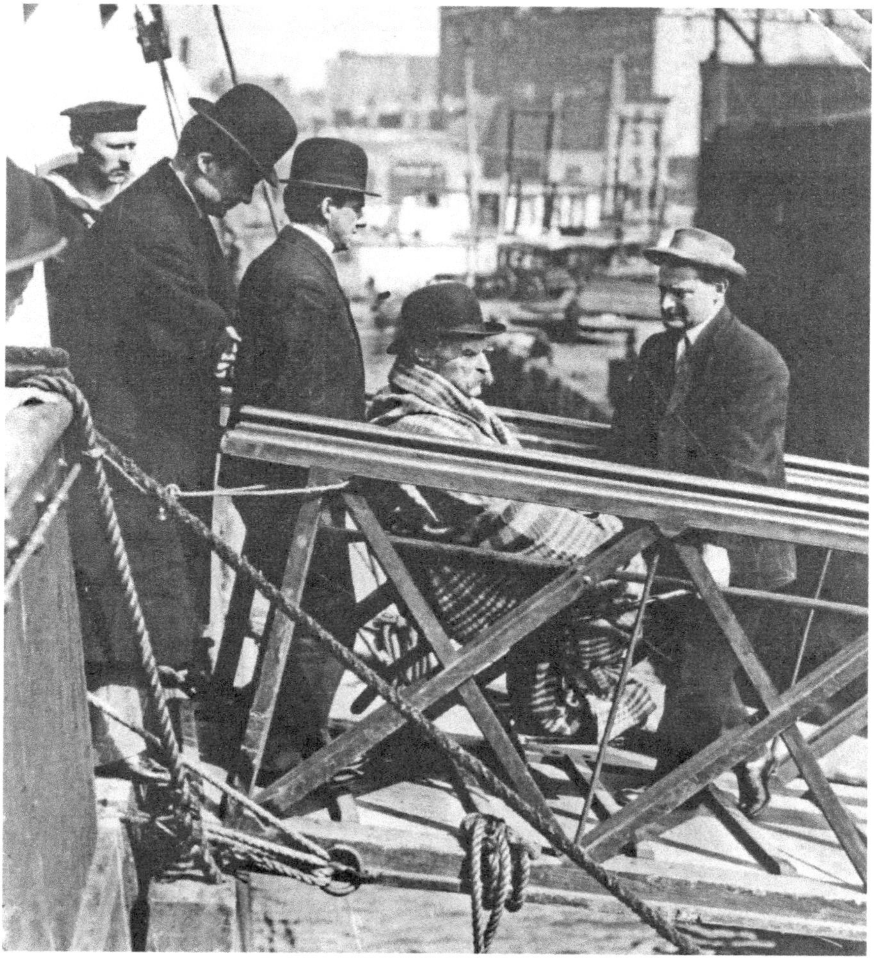

Figure 29. Samuel Clemens carried from the ship in New York, April 14, 1910. Photograph by the National News Association.

At Grand Central Station Sam tried to walk to the express to Redding but abandoned the effort "after finding that he was too feeble to stand alone." Aboard the train he indulged in a bit of denial to reporters. "I am really feeling good now," he told them. "Bully, in fact; I'll be all right as soon as I get my lungs full of this good New England air." In Redding he was again carried to the carriage and driven by Lounsbury to his house. "When we drew up to Stormfield," Paine remembered, Katy Leary and others on the household staff were "waiting to greet him" and "he stepped from the carriage alone with something of his old lightness, and with all his old courtliness, and offered each one his hand." He was then carried upstairs to his room and "to the comforts and blessed air of home." Halsey "never left the house again" for the duration of Sam's care, and Quintard checked on Sam every night.[24]

Over the next few days he was aided by his medical team, who restricted his consumption of morphine because "he no longer suffered acutely" from chest pain. Instead, he was given restoratives—digitalis, strychnine, camphor—and oxygen, albeit to little effect. Paine, Leary, and others on the domestic staff kept vigil at his bedside; Clara and Gabrilowitsch arrived from Europe on April 16; and he was visited late in the week by his nephew Jervis, his niece Julia, and her husband Edward. He read occasionally, in particular Carlyle's *History of the French Revolution*, and on April 19 he asked Clara to sing for him. She performed "three little Scotch songs he had always cared for," presumably the airs the orchestrelle was programmed to play, and she was grateful ever after she had given "Father the serene sense of comfort he evidently received." The large New York dailies sent reporters to Redding to cover his death. They acknowledged "they were turkey buzzards," according to Dan Beard, but "that was part of their duty." Quintard and Halsey issued daily medical bulletins that were variously represented in headlines around the nation. For example, on April 20 alone he was reportedly "dying" (*Bridgeport Farmer*), "improving" (*Canton News*), "not improving" (*Evansville Press*), "better" (*Medford Mail Tribune*), "weaker" (*Washington Post*), "holding his own" (*Galveston News*), "encouraging" (*Telluride Journal*), "fighting for life" (*Salt Lake Tribune*), "nearing death" (*Hawaiian Star*), "unchanged" (*Pittsburgh Press*), "sinking" (*Long Branch Record*), and "failing" (*Hackensack Record*). The morning of April 21 he summoned Paine and instructed him to throw away two of his unfinished manuscripts. He scribbled a brief note to Clara that, though she had not told him, "I have found out that you—Well, I [illegible]." He had learned, perhaps from Gab, that she was pregnant with his first and only grandchild. That afternoon, with Clara at his bedside, he "suddenly opened his eyes, took my hand, and looked steadily into my face. Faintly he murmured, 'Goodbye, dear, if we meet—.'" Katy Leary kept vigil "at the foot of the bed and he was very quiet. Then he just breathed hard—a little bit—twice—and then he turned his head on the pillow—his beautiful head."[25] He slipped into a quiet doze and then fell into the big sleep.

Epilogue

The fun is not in publishing a book but only in writing it.

—*Samuel Clemens to J. L. Bishop, 12 September 1900*

THE NEXT DAY, Albert Bigelow Paine, Dan Beard, and "a sort of voluntary guard of honor" of journalists accompanied Sam's body to New York. The afternoon of April 23, a "brevet Presbyterian" to the end, he lay in repose in one of his signature white suits at the Brick Presbyterian Church on Fifth Avenue. During a twenty-minute ceremony, Henry van Dyke of Princeton University spoke briefly and Joe Twichell offered a prayer. The rosewood coffin was banked with flowers, including a wreath of mountain laurel grown at Stormfield. The front pews were occupied by Sam's family and closest friends—Carnegie, Clara and Ossip Gabrilowitsch, Julian Hawthorne, Howells, Jervis Langdon, Julia and Edward Loomis, the widow and children of Sam Moffett, the Paines—and the church was filled with about fifteen hundred visitors while hundreds of others milled in the street outside. Over three thousand people filed past his open coffin after the obsequies. Early the next morning, accompanied by Clara and Gab, Julia and Edward, Paine, and Duneka, the casket was carried to Elmira in Loomis's private railcar. Twichell hurriedly returned to Hartford to be with his wife Harmony, who had suddenly fallen ill. He was replaced at Sam's funeral the next day in the parlor of the Langdon mansion on Main Street—where Sam and Livy had been married nearly forty years earlier and where the funerals of Langdon, Susy, Livy, and Jean had been held—by the Reverend Samuel Eastman of the Park Church. His son Max Eastman remembered that the minister read a service his mother Annis Eastman had written. Sam was afterward buried beside Livy in the family plot in Woodlawn Cemetery in the midst of a rainstorm. In a cruel twist of fate, both Harmony Twichell and Elinor Howells, the wives of Sam's oldest surviving friends, died within the next three weeks.[1]

Sam had disdained the conventions of obituary verse, and predictably so: he became at his death the subject of reams of drivel and hogwash poetry.

One of the few exceptions was written by the distinguished journalist Arthur B. Krock:

Old Innocence has gone abroad, and the sea is wide between;
I saw his hand on the misty wheel as he steered for the darkened main.
He took his laugh and he took his pipe and the place where his heart had been,
And he crossed the bar where the waters gulped the plumb-line below mark twain.
He has steered from the flats and the yellow flood that he knows from bed to brim
To the greenish gush of a stranger wave that bathes every western star;
And 'Give me my glasses,' I heard him say[2]—for the night of the Lord is dim,
And the salt spray blinds and the wind cuts cold as the ship sails out by the bar.
'Twould be time to weep for the good gray head that is lost in the driving spray
Were there not in my study window here a boy with a puckered lip,
And he whistles shrill, "Oh, Buff'lo gals, ain't you com' out today?"[3]
So I know tonight that he'll join Huck Finn and go for a pirate trip.
'Twould be time to weep for the one that's gone did the boys he loved go, too;
But Tom and Joe and Sid and Huck on my study shelves I spy.
So good-by, Mark Twain, may you steer far out; may the wheel at your helm turn true;
And I'll keep Tom straight while you're off to sea, and for Huck—well, Mark, I'll try.[4]

Krock's tribune was, at the very least, superior to the hackneyed lines that read like Bloodgood Cutter parodies of Whitman's "O Captain! My Captain!" that appeared in many newspapers.[5]

Sam's final will, dated August 17, 1909, left his entire estate to his daughters, though with Jean's death in December 1909 Clara became his sole heir. Her father "was pathetically anxious to inform me about the financial state of affairs," she remembered, "expressing regret that there was less than he had hoped there would be." The will distributed no charitable gifts from an estate probated in Redding in July 1911 totaling $471,000. Sam's stock in the Mark Twain Company, including his copyrights, was appraised at $200,000; Stormfield, with its two hundred and thirty acres, at $66,000; Lobster Pot and its twenty acres at $4,000; his stock in the Utah Consolidated Mining Company at $87,000; and his 375 shares in the British Plasmon Company at about thirty cents each.[6]

Among Sam's other employees, friends, and acquaintances, Katy Leary left Clara's employ on October 19, 1910, six months after Sam's death, after thirty years in the Clemenses' service, to manage a boardinghouse in New York. Clara and Sam "had fixed things up so I could always be comfortable and not worry about money the rest of my life," she acknowledged. Horace Bixby continued to pilot Mississippi river boats until 1912, when he died at the age of eighty-six. Frank Millet, William T. Stead, and Isidor Straus of the Children's Educational Alliance, though unknown to each other, all died together the night of April 16, 1912, aboard the *Titanic*.[7]

Nor did the effort to manage Sam's legacy end with his death. Frederick Duneka and Paine concocted a corrupt version of "The Mysterious Stranger" a few years later. In effect, they bowdlerized the earliest substantial manuscript fragment, "The Chronicle of Young Satan," expurgated the character of the drunken and profane priest Father Adolf, replaced him with a wicked astrologer who would not offend Catholics, sutured the solipsistic final chapter of "No. 44" to the earlier draft, and serialized the jumble in *Harper's Monthly* between May and November 1916 as though it were an authentically new Mark Twain work. The fraud was finally discovered by a team of textual editors led by John S. Tuckey in 1963.

True to his wishes, Clara refused to authorize the publication of her father's "Letters from the Earth," his last book manuscript, until 1962, though Bernard DeVoto had prepared it for publication in 1939, lest the controversial book compromise the commercial value of his "trademark." She finally lifted the embargo shortly before her death in 1962. At Clara's insistence if not with her assistance, Ashcroft and Lyon became personae non gratae, erased from the record of Sam's life almost as thoroughly as victims of a Stalinist purge. Each of them is mentioned by name only once in Paine's 1,673-page official biography ("Mark Twain's secretary, Miss I. V. Lyon, had superintended the furnishing" of Stormfield; and "Clemens engaged a special secretary for the trip" to England in 1907, "Mr. Ralph W. Ashcroft"). Paine whitewashed Sam's life as thoroughly as the boys whitewash the fence in *The Adventures of Tom Sawyer*. Similarly, apparently at Clara's insistence, Elizabeth Wallace, Katy Leary, and Dorothy Quick expunged the Ashcrofts from their respective memoirs *Mark Twain and the Happy Island* (1912), *A Lifetime with Mark Twain* (1925), and *Mark Twain and Me* (1961), Wallace ignoring them entirely and Leary and Quick referring to Lyon in passing merely as "the secretary." Clara tried to prevent Marion Allen from publishing her own memoir because she feared, as Keith Archibald Forbes notes, that "such an intimate portrait might reveal some unpleasantness" about Sam's relationship with her daughter Helen. Allen eventually published her essay in the London *Strand*, which was "beyond the reach of Clara." Similarly, Paine "sequestered" the so-called Helen Allen manuscripts, which Sam wrote in Bermuda or while returning from the islands in 1910, "to protect Twain's reputation," according to John Cooley, and "it is fortunate that Clara, Paine, or others did not destroy them."[8]

From all indications, the Gabrilowitsches' marriage was a blissful one. Their daughter Nina, Sam's only grandchild, was born August 18, 1910, at Stormfield; Clara continued to appear occasionally onstage and to write; and Ossip served as founding director of the Detroit Symphony Orchestra from 1918 until 1935. At his death in 1936, his body was interred literally at Sam's feet in the family plot in Elmira. Clara wed Jacques Samossoud, a Russian musician and gambling addict, in 1944. A convert late in life to Christian Science, she died in 1962 alone in a bungalow at the Bahia Resort Hotel on Mission Bay, near San Diego, where twenty-seven years later the American Literature Association began to convene its annual meetings. Nina Clemens Gabrilowitsch died, an apparent suicide, from a drug overdose in a Los Angeles hotel room in 1966.

The Ashcrofts, who stole some of Sam's manuscripts on their way out the door, offered in the summer 1910 to sell the manuscript of *Is Shakespeare Dead?* to brokers in New York, a theft Clara discovered when dealers contacted her to verify its authenticity. As she observed in a letter to a friend dated August 5, 1910, less than four months after Sam's death,

> Father left me one weapon to use in case they [Ashcroft and Lyon] troubled me anymore & I used it.—He wrote out a full description of their entire story of dishonesty which I was to publish if there was no other way to keep them quiet.—So we sent the lawyer out to Chicago (where they are now), who threatened them with the publication of this M.S. if they did not give back to me all the stuff of Father's that they had in their possession & desist from annoying me in any way. It was successful.

The editors of volume 3 of the *Autobiography of Mark Twain* conclude that "So far as is known, this incident was the last time that Clara was threatened by the Ashcrofts." The couple divorced in 1927, and in a 1950 interview Lyon claimed that, much as Sam had predicted, Ashcroft had made "her life a living hell." He proved to be "fundamentally dishonest," in her words "a forger and all-around crook for whose actions she was equally blamed." He was also "very unsatisfactory" in his marital role. Lyon confessed that her marriage had been "a mistake" and that she had taken "a viper unto her bosom," by analogy taking the part of Cleopatra (thus casting Mark Twain in the role of Mark Antony in her imagination?). She died in her Greenwich Village apartment in 1958 at the age of ninety-four.[9]

Over the years, Sam's houses in Hannibal and Hartford and the farmhouse at Quarry Farm have become tourist destinations. But not Stormfield in Connecticut, his final home. It burned to the ground in July 1923, the blaze perhaps started and certainly accelerated by the acetylene torches installed to light the house in lieu of gas jets or electric bulbs. "I have visited Stormfield since Mark Twain's death," Helen Keller wrote in 1929. "The flowers still bloom; the breezes still whisper and sough in the cedars, which have grown statelier year by year; the birds still sing, they tell me. But for me, the place is bereft of its lover. The last time I was there, the house was in ruins. Only the great chimney was standing erect, a charred shaft of bricks in the bright autumn landscape." Lobster Pot was similarly destroyed by fire in 1953.[10]

At his death, with rare exceptions, Sam was eulogized on all sides, including by U.S. presidents past, present, and future. Theodore Roosevelt declared that he "was not only a great humorist, but a great philosopher, and his writings form one of the assets in America's contributions to the world of achievement." William Howard Taft, Roosevelt's successor, asserted a bit wistfully that not only would Sam's work continue to give "real intellectual enjoyment" to millions of readers "yet to come," but that he "never wrote a line that a father could not read to a daughter." Sam's friend Woodrow Wilson, who would succeed Taft in 1913, observed while "all the world knows" that Sam was "a delightful humorist," "only those who had the privilege of knowing him personally can feel to the full the loss of a man of high and lovely character, a friend quick to excite and give affection, a citizen of the world who loved every wholesome adventure of the mind or heart." Both the plutocrat Andrew Carnegie ("the most original genius of our age and one of the sweetest, noblest men that ever lived') and the labor leader Samuel Gompers ("a deep student of men and events, a profound philosopher") paid tribute to him. In Hannibal, his childhood friends Laura Hawkins Frazer and Barney Farthing wept when they learned he had died. Frazer lived to the age of ninety-one and cherished a picture of Sam he had inscribed to her when she visited Stormfield in 1908 "with the love of her earliest sweetheart." For the rest of his life, Joe Twichell also mourned Sam, "eminently a man 'with the bark on.'" Sam's old nemesis Frank Harris filed one of the few dissenting opinions: "He wrote for the market and the million praised and paid him; he had a gorgeous and easy life, and was a friend of millionaires, and went about at the end like a glorified Hall Caine; but he wrote nothing lifeworthy, not a word that has a chance of living except his boys' books, *Tom Sawyer* and *Huckleberry Finn*, which may live for a generation, or perhaps even two." Harris noted that Algernon Charles Swinburne had "classed Mark Twain with Martin Farquhar Tupper, author of the comic series *Proverbial Philosophy*," and added "that's about his true place." Among other members of the guild, Booker T. Washington avowed that Sam "succeeded in literature as few men in any age succeeded because he stuck close to nature and to the common people." Julia Ward Howe acclaimed him "a man of letters with a very genuine gift of humor"; Brander Matthews paid homage to him as "a great artist in humor and in narrative and in style, a great moralist—and a great man"; Hamlin Garland asserted that Sam's writings epitomized our national literature and were "as closely related to this country as the Mississippi"; and Owen Wister pronounced him "not only the most interesting" American writer "but also the best beloved." Rudyard Kipling declared that in his opinion Sam "was the largest man of his time, both in the direct outcome of his work, and, more important still, as an indirect force in an age of iron Philistinism." Like Howells and Matthews, Kipling later compared Sam to Cervantes, his picaresque novel *Huck Finn* by implication to *Don Quixote*. Keller ranked Sam among the greatest of all Americans. "To me he symbolizes the pioneer qualities," she averred, "the large, free, unconventional, humorous point of view of men who sail new seas and blaze new trails through the wilderness." The American authors Eugene O'Neill and William Faulkner, recipients of the Nobel Prize for Literature in 1936 and 1949, respectively, perhaps uttered his crowning epitaphs, pronouncing Sam the "true father of all American literature" and "the first truly American writer, and all of us since are his heirs."[11]

Abbreviations

AMT	*Autobiography of Mark Twain*
CTSSE	*Collected Tales, Sketches, Speeches, & Essays*
FE	*Following the Equator*
HHR	*Mark Twain's Correspondence with Henry Huttleston Rogers, 1893–1909*
IVLD	Isabel V. Lyon diary
JHT	*Letters of Mark Twain and Joseph Hopkins Twichell*
LLMT	*The Love Letters of Mark Twain*
LMT	*A Lifetime with Mark Twain*
MFMT	*My Father, Mark Twain*
MTB	*Mark Twain: A Biography*
MTCI	*Mark Twain: The Complete Interviews*
MTCR	*Mark Twain: The Contemporary Reviews*
MTHL	*Mark Twain–Howells Letters*
MTJ	*Mark Twain Journal*
MTLP	*Mark Twain's Letters to His Publishers*
MTN	*Mark Twain's Notebook*
MTP	*Mark Twain Papers and Project, Bancroft Library, University of California, Berkeley*
MTSpk	*Mark Twain Speaking*
MyMT	*My Mark Twain*
NYT	*New York Times*
SLC	Samuel Langhorne Clemens
UCCL	*Union Catalog of Clemens Letters*
UCLC	*Union Catalog of Letters to Clemens*

Notes

Chapter 1

1. Zacharias, "Henry Rogers," 2–17; Willis, *Mark and Livy*, 232.

2. "Poverty to Wealth," *Chicago Inter Ocean*, 4 October 1893, supplement, 4; *Tom Sawyer Abroad*, 84; *Elmira Star-Gazette*, 28 January 1893, 4; "An Innocent Abroad," *Trenton Times*, 23 November 1892, 5; "He Was Rich," *Puck*, 12 August 1891, 753; *MTLP*, 278–79.

3. *Mark Twain's Notebooks and Journals*, 3:622; "Travelling Episodes," *New York Tribune*, 10 August 1891, 6; *MTLP*, 277.

4. Katy Leary, quoted in Harrington and Jenn, *Twain and France*, 145; *LMT*, 112–13; Turpin, "Thomas Jefferson Snodgrass," 175–79; Rodney, *Twain Overseas*, 135; *CTSSE*, 11–13.

5. *Portland Oregonian*, 3 December 1891, 10; *MTLP*, 276; Edward Bok, "Leaves of Literary Men," *Weekly Nebraska State Journal*, 4 December 1891, 10.

6. *CTSSE*, 15–28.

7. *What Is Man?* (1917), 210, 223; *LMT*, 114; Jean Clemens diary, 5 August 1891.

8. *What Is Man?* (1917), 214–26; *LMT*, 118.

9. *Europe and Elsewhere*, 113–28; *LMT*, 121; SLC to Clarence C. Buel, 16 August 1891, *UCCL* 04223; SLC to Franklin G. Whitmore, 24 August 1891, *UCCL* 04225; *AMT*, 2:228.

10. *MTLP*, 283; *MFMT*, 88, 90–94; Willis, *Mark and Livy*, 201; Cardwell, *Man Who Was Mark Twain*, 129; "Literary Notes," *San Francisco Call*, 16 September 1894, 20.

11. *LMT*, 180; *MTN*, 217; *CTSSE*, 49–51; SLC to Frank Finlay, 13 September 1891, *UCCL* 04226; *MTLP*, 283–84.

12. *Europe and Elsewhere*, 129, 133, 169–74; "Mark Twain's Guide," *London Daily Mail*, 25 September 1902, 3; IVLD, 5 January 1903; Harrington and Jenn, *Twain and France*, 152, 204; Ferguson, *Twain: Man and Legend*, 248; Olivia Langdon Clemens to SLC, 29 September 1891, *UCCL* 04229.

13. SLC to Olivia Langdon Clemens, 28 September 1891, *UCCL* 04236 and 11719, SLC to Olivia Langdon Clemens, 30 September 1891, *UCCL* 04238; SLC to Clara Clemens, 29 September 1891, *UCCL* 04237; *JHT*, 167; *MTLP*, 352; *Europe and Elsewhere*, 129–68; Scott, "*Innocents Adrift*," 230–37.

14. Rodney, *Twain Overseas*, 138; *Mark Twain's Notebooks and Journals*, 3:623; *LMT*, 123; Austilat, *Tramp in Berlin*, 40–41, 48, 50, 146, 148, 149; *MFMT*, 95; "Vermischtes," *Täglishes Cincinnatier Volksblatt*, 6 November 1891, 4. The error in this report is apparently the result of at least two misunderstandings. In fact, SLC received $1,000 for each of his travel letters for the McClure syndicate. That is, at a one-to-five exchange rate of dollars to marks, he received 5,000 marks per letter. *If* he had written twenty such letters, he would have received $20,000, or 100,000 marks, possibly misrepresented as $100,000. In other words, SLC's actual receipt of $6,000 for six letters was wildly misconstrued as $100,000 for twenty letters.

15. "Income Tax in Europe," *Buffalo Express*, 20 August 1894, 10.

16. "In Financial Difficulties," *San Francisco Call*, 22 November 1891, 1; Harrington and Jenn, *Twain and France*, 159; *MFMT*, 96; *MTB*, 933; *The £1,000,000 Bank-Note and Other New Stories*, 210–32; Fisher, *Abroad with Mark Twain and Eugene Field*, 78, 88, 103; "American Corn and Pork," *Boston Herald*, 1 November 1891, 4; "General News," *St. James's Gazette*, 2 November 1891, 7; Gribben, *Twain's Library*, 394.

17. Susy Clemens to Louise Brownell, 31 October 1891, *UCCL* 09136; Susy Clemens to Louise Brownell, 12 November 1891, *UCCL* 09137; Austilat, *Tramp in Berlin*, 65; "The Meininger Actors Arrive," *New York Sun*, 9 November 1891, 5; "Gotham Gossip," *New Orleans Picayune*, 15 November 1891, 3; "Thanksgiving Day Abroad," *Chicago Inter Ocean*, 27 November 1891, 3; *MTLP*, 294; "Phelps and Mark Twain," *Boston Herald*, 20 December 1891, 6; "Personal," *New York Tribune*, 1 April 1895, 6; *MTLP*, 301; "Court Calls in Berlin," *NYT*, 3 January 1892, 3; Dickie, *In the Kaiser's Capital*, 185–86; Kaplan, *Singular Mark Twain*, 462; *AMT*, 1:190; *MTN*, 222.

18. Austilat, *Tramp in Berlin*, 81; "Income Tax in Europe," *Buffalo Express*, 20 August 1894, 10; *MFMT*, 95; "Court Calls in Berlin," *NYT*, 3 January 1892, 3.

19. *AMT*, 2:310, 2:432; *MTN*, 224; Bigelow, "Ten Years of Kaiser Wilhelm," 457; Carl Dolmetsch, "Berlin, Germany," in LeMaster and Wilson, *Mark Twain Encyclopedia*, 71; Kaplan, *Singular Mark Twain*, 461.

20. Olivia Langdon Clemens to Alice Hooker Day, 7 March 1892, *UCCL* 10526; *Pall Mall Gazette*, 25 March 1892, 5; SLC to Pamela A. Moffett, 21 March 1892, *UCCL* 04275; SLC to Susy Clemens, 22 March 1892, *UCCL* 04276; *Boston Herald*, 24 April 1892, 24; Olivia Langdon Clemens to Harriet E. Whitmore, 5 May 1892, *UCCL* 04287; Susy Clemens to Louise Brownell, 21 April 1892; Susy Clemens to Louise Brownell, *UCCL* 09140; Susy Clemens to Louise Brownell, 29 April 1892, *UCCL* 09141; Jean Clemens diary, April 1892; *Greenock Telegraph and Clyde Shipping Gazette* (Scotland), 16 April 1892, 3.

21. *MTN*, 225; *MFMT*, 118–19; Downing, *Queen Bee of Tuscany*, 194; Susy Clemens to Louise Brownell, 29 May 1892, *UCCL* 09143.

22. Johnson, *Remembered Yesterdays*, 320–24; *MFMT*, 113; Scott, "Letters from Twain to Phelps," 377; *AMT*, 2:506; Olivia Langdon Clemens to Grace King, 1 July 1892, *UCCL* 01558.

23. IVLD, 5 January 1903; "Mark Twain's Courier," *Washington Star*, 23 November 1895, 24; "Mark Twain's Guide," *London Daily Mail*, 25 September 1902, 3; "Talks of Mark Twain," *New Orleans Times-Democrat*, 24 September 1902, 11; SLC to Theodore Stanton, 14 January 1903, *UCCL* 06562.

24. Messent, *Short Works*, 117; *MTCR*, 323–25; "Turning New Leaves," *Boston Post*, 10 May 1892, 2; "Recent Publications," *Cultivator & Country Gentleman*, 14 April 1892, 296; "New Books," *Boston Transcript*, 16 May 1892, 6; "Comment on New Books," *Atlantic Monthly* 70 (October 1892): 563; "Literature of the Day," *Kansas City Times*, 18 April 1892, 5; "Some Mildly Merry Tales," *Kansas City Star*, 21 April 1892, 4.

25. "New Novels," *San Francisco Chronicle*, 28 August 1892, 9.

26. *London Daily News*, 19 October 1892, 4; "Mark Twain's New Book," *London Literary World*, 7 October 1892, 251–52; *MTCR*, 329–34; "Literary Arrivals," *Leeds Mercury*, 10 October 1892, 8; London *Morning Post*, 19 October 1892, 8; "Books Good and Bad," *Once a Week*, 12 November 1892, 15; Edward Bok, "How Beecher Read It," *Philadelphia Times*, 31 July 1892, 19.

27. Scharnhorst, "Bret Harte–Mark Twain Feud," 29–32.

28. Kaplan, *Singular Mark Twain*, 465; SLC to Orion Clemens, 28 June 1892, *UCCL* 04302; Willis, *Mark and Livy*, 196; Olivia Langdon Clemens to Grace King, 1 June 1892, *UCCL* 04292.

29. SLC to unidentified, 19 June 1892, *UCCL* 04300; "Mark Twain Returns," *New York Sun*, 23 June 1892, 10; Gribben, *Twain's Library*, 506; "Paige Type-Setting Machines," *NYT*, 30 March 1892, 3; Kaplan, *Singular Mark Twain*, 466; "Depew and Cleveland," *Philadelphia Times*, 3 July 1892, 2; SLC to Olivia Langdon Clemens, 27 June 1892, *UCCL* 11961; SLC to Orion Clemens, 28 June 1892, *UCCL* 04302; SLC to Marshall H. Mallory, 1 July 1892, *UCCL* 01563; SLC to Fred Hall, 1 July 1892, *UCCL* 12087; SLC to Augustine Daly, 13 August 1892, *UCCL* 01728.

30. "Yale Men Off to Europe," *New Haven Register*, 6 July 1892, 1; E. J. Edwards, "Mark Twain in Irons," *Wilmington Journal*, 3 November 1892, 2; "Twain in Durance Vile," *Nebraska State Journal*, 21 November 1892, 3.

31. Welland, *Twain in England*, 157; Austilat, *Tramp in Berlin*, 56, 118; Messent, *Short Works*, 115; SLC to Orion Clemens, 7 August 1894, *UCCL* 04775; Kaplan, *Mr. Clemens and Mark Twain*, 330–31; "Scissors and Paste," *Windsor and Richmond Gazette*, 2 April 1892, 2; Quirk, *Twain: A Study of the Short Fiction*, 91; SLC to Fred Hall, 24 August 1892, *UCCL* 04594; SLC to Fred Hall, 4–5 September 1892, *UCCL* 04653; Wiggins, "The Original," 355–57; *Scientific American*, 12 December 1891, 374; *MTLP*, 313–14.

32. *Tom Sawyer Abroad*, 9–10, 69, 87–88, 96; Budd, *Twain: Social Philosopher*, 157, 231.

33. Hill, *God's Fool*, 324; *MTLP*, 315–17.

34. SLC to Clara Clemens, 16 October 1893, *UCCL* 05448; *MFMT*, 86; Beard, *Hardly a Man*, 344–45; Cardwell, "Bowdlerizing of Mark Twain," 190; White, "Twain as a Newspaper Reporter," 961; Howden, "Twain as His Secretary Remembers Him," *New York Herald*, 13 December 1925, 1–4.

35. Morris, *Gender Play*, 18; Gribben, *Twain's Library*, 770; *AMT*, 3:98; Rodney, *Twain Overseas*, 146–47.

36. SLC to William W. Phelps, 24 September 1892, *UCCL* 02295; SLC to Susan Crane, 18 September 1892, *UCCL* 02123, 30 September 1892, *UCCL* 04662; Ross, *The Fourth Generation*, 331; Downing, *Queen Bee of Tuscany*, 195; Ishihara, "Twain's Italian Villas," 20.

37. SLC to Susan Crane, 30 September 1892, *UCCL* 04662; *AMT*, 1:245; Rodney, *Twain Overseas*, 148; *Mark Twain's Letters* (1917), 572–73; *MFMT*, 127.

38. *Mark Twain's Letters* (1917), 571; Jean Clemens diary, September 1892; King, *Memories of a Southern Woman*, 176; *AMT*, 1:249; Olivia Langdon Clemens to Alice Hooker Day, 23 February 1893, *UCCL* 10525; "News from Florence," *Hartford Courant*, 29 December 1892, 9; James, *Letters*, 1:333.

39. SLC to Clara Clemens, 21 January 1893, *UCCL* 04328; Clara Clemens to SLC, 23 January 1893, *UCCL* 11570; "Mark Twain's Daughter," *Philadelphia Times*, 29 July 1894, 18; Willis, *Mark and Livy*, 201.

40. King, *Memories of a Southern Woman*, 173, 176–77; Olivia Langdon Clemens to George H. Warner, 1 December 1891, *UCCL* 04258; Susy Clemens to Louise Brownell, 3 September 1893, *UCCL* 09164; Susy Clemens to Louise Brownell, 27 September 1892, *UCCL* 10425; Susy Clemens to Louise Brownell, 7 November 1892, *UCCL* 09150; Susy Clemens to Louise Brownell, 5 March 1893, *UCCL* 09156; James, *Daisy Miller*, 21–22, 73, 108; Susy Clemens to Clara Clemens, 28 February 1893, *UCCL* 04345; Susy Clemens to Clara Clemens, 29 April 1893, *UCCL* 04389; Olivia Langdon Clemens to Harriet E. Whitmore, 5 January 1893,

UCCL 04322; *Mark Twain to Mrs. Fairbanks*, 268–69; SLC to Clara Clemens, 5 November 1892, *UCCL* 02399; *MFMT*, 126; Willis, *Mark and Livy*, 203; Clara Clemens to Susy Clemens, 14 February 1893, *UCCL* 11593.

41. *MTLP*, 296–97, 329, 334, 349; SLC to Fred Hall, 5 May 1893, *UCCL* 04395.

Chapter 2

1. SLC to Susan Crane, 18 September 1892, UCCL 02123; *MTLP*, 319, 321, 328, 336; *Tragedy of Pudd'nhead Wilson*, 310; Wiggins, "*Pudd'nhead Wilson*," 184.

2. Parker, *Flawed Texts and Verbal Icons*, 134; *MTLP*, 354–55; *MTCI*, 354.

3. Galton, *Finger Prints*, 1–2; SLC to Chatto & Windus, 10 November 1892, *UCCL* 04623; Emerson, *Twain: A Literary Life*, 194; *MTLP*, 355.

4. *Tragedy of Pudd'nhead Wilson*, 124; Berger, "Emendations of the Copy-Text," 191; Moss, "Tracing Mark Twain's Intentions," 49; Wood, "Narrative Action and Structural Symmetry in *Pudd'nhead Wilson*," 375.

5. Wigger, "Twain's *Pudd'nhead Wilson*," 94; Gilman, *Concerning Children*, 4; *MTCI*, 287.

6. Regan, *Unpromising Heroes*, 208; *LLMT*, 291.

7. Pettit, *Twain and the South*, 142–43; *Tragedy of Pudd'nhead Wilson*, 1; Leslie Fiedler, "As Free as Any Cretur . . . ," *New Republic*, 22 August 1955, 16; Krauth, *Twain and Company*, 89; *Mark Twain's Letters* (1988–2002), 3:440, 4:53; *"Amongst the Books," Melbourne Leader*, 21 August 1880, 1; Fiedler, *What Was Literature?*, 242; Gribben, *Twain's Library*, 672.

8. Lynn, *Twain and Southwestern Humor*, 265–66; Kiskis, *Twain at Home*, 78; Stowe, *Uncle Tom's Cabin*, 284.

9. *Tragedy of Pudd'nhead Wilson*, 10, 83; Scharnhorst, *Owen Wister and the West*, 20.

10. Susan K. Harris, quoted in Reesman, "Discourses of Faith vs. Fraud," 121; *Mark Twain to Mrs. Fairbanks*, 269; Horn, "Twain, William James, and the Funding of Freedom," 173–94; Morris, "What Is Personal?," 99. SLC took some inadvisable short cuts in the course of composition. As Salomon, *Twain and the Image of History*, 179, notes, he underlined part of a sentence in *La Vierge Lorraine* and later copied it verbatim "into his own manuscript" and borrowed "almost intact" the "Countess's description of Joan before the tribunal at Poitiers."

11. Harper, *House of Harper*, 574; *AMT*, 3:234.

12. *MTLP*, 336; Gillman, *Dark Twins*, 108; Stone, "Twain's *Joan of Arc*," 6; Emerson, *The Authentic Mark Twain*, 213; Harrington and Jenn, *Twain and France*, 169; *MFMT*, 125–27.

13. *Personal Recollections of Joan of Arc*, 349; Wallace, *Twain and the Happy Island*, 21–25; Van Doren, *The American Novel*, 178; Isabel V. Lyon, diary, 1893; Booker T. Washington, "Tributes to Mark Twain," *North American Review* 191 (June 1910): 828–30.

14. *AMT*, 2:197; *Mark Twain to Mrs. Fairbanks*, 268–70; *MTLP*, 335; SLC to Laurence Hutton, 5 February 1893, *UCCL* 04337.

15. *The £1,000,000 Bank-Note and Other New Stories*, 46; SLC to R. W. Gilder, 6–13 November 1898, *UCCL* 05459; *MTHL*, 675.

16. Lynden Behymer, "Among the Authors," *Los Angeles Herald*, 30 April 1893, 13; "Mark Twain's £1,000,000 Bank Note," *American Monthly Review of Reviews* 7 (February 1893): 76; "Literary Talk," *Hartford Courant*, 6 January 1893, 9; "Our Book Table," *Fort Worth Gazette*, 9 January 1893, 4; "Literary Bric-a-Brac," *New Orleans Times-Democrat*, 22 January 1893, 16; "Humorous, in Spots," *Chicago Tribune*, 15 January 1893, 26; *London Standard*, 9 June 1893, 4; *London Standard*, 5 June 1893, 2; *London Post*, 15 May 1893, 8; *Glasgow North British Daily Mail*, 29 May 1893, 2; George Saintsbury, "New Novels," *Academy*, 8 July 1893, 28; *MTCR*,

337–40; *London Graphic*, 26 August 1893, 20; "Mark Twain's Latest," *London Literary World*, 19 May 1893, 454–55; "New Books," *Scotsman*, 8 May 1893, 3; "Literary Notes," *New Zealand Mail*, 14 July 1893, 11.

17. *MTLP*, 342; SLC to Fred Hall, 8 May 1893, *UCCL* 04640; *MTLP*, 356; "Talk about New Books," *Catholic World* 58 (November 1893): 287; "Our London Letter," *Coolgardie (Western Australia) Miner*, 10 July 1896, 7; Edward Bok, "Literary," *Brooklyn Standard Union*, 29 April 1893, 7; *Mark Twain to Mrs. Fairbanks*, 270–71.

18. *MTCR*, 416–21; "Adam's Diary," *Thanet Advertiser* (Ramsgate, England), 19 August 1893, 6.

19. *MTLP*, 344–45, 349; *AMT*, 2:78. SLC jotted on the envelope of Hall's 10 March 1893 letter, "How the spreading of the Bank debt probably occurred."

20. *AMT*, 2:79; *HHR*, 117–18.

21. *MTLP*, 342; "He Is a Lion," *Buffalo News*, 27 March 1893, 5. Afterward, SLC remained in touch with Phelps. He sent a gift when Phelps's daughter wed in Berlin in June; "Ex-Minister Phelps' Daughter Wed," *Seattle Post-Intelligencer*, 2 June 1893, 1.

22. "Italian Commissioners Reach New York," *Chicago Tribune*, 4 April 1893, 5; *New Orleans Times-Democrat*, 8 April 1893, 4; "Mark Twain Travelling Incog," *New York Herald*, 4 April 1893, 11.

23. Kaplan, *Singular Mark Twain*, 472; *MTHL*, 651; "Literary Talk," *Hartford Courant*, 6 May 1893, 6; SLC to Olivia Langdon Clemens, 4 April 1893, *UCCL* 04362.

24. "Mark Twain's Fortune and Paige Machine," *St. Louis Republic*, 21 September 1898, 6.

25. SLC to Susan Crane, 23 April 1893, *UCCL* 04381; SLC to Pamela A. Moffett, 26 April 1893, *UCCL* 04387; Hall, "Tells the Story," 2–3; Fanning, *Twain and Orion Clemens*, 206; Olivia Langdon Clemens to SLC, 23 April 1893, *UCCL* 04382; Ferguson, *Twain: Man and Legend*, 140; DeVoto, *Twain at Work*, 141.

26. *MTLP*, 350; SLC to Orion Clemens, 1 May 1893, *UCCL* 04393; SLC to Ida Langdon, 11 May 1893, *UCCL* 04401; "Personal Jottings," *New Haven Morning and Courier*, 13 May 1893, 2; *MTHL*, 652–53; "Brooklyn People in Lucerne," *Brooklyn Eagle*, 25 June 1893, 6; *JHT*, 179; "Mark Twain Kills a Boy," *St. Louis Republic*, 12 April 1893, 6; Olivia Langdon Clemens to SLC, 9 April 1893, *UCCL* 04368.

27. Csicsila, "'These Hideous Times,'" 129; Hall, "Tells the Story," 2; Fred Hall to SLC, 19 May 1893, *UCLC* 45923; Kaplan, *Singular Mark Twain*, 476; *MTLP*, 343–44.

28. Fred Hall to SLC, 2 June 1893, *UCLC* 45925; Messent, *Short Works*, 243; *Mark Twain's Letters* (1917), 586, 589; *MFMT*, 109.

29. *MTLP*, 348–49, 353; Hall "Tells the Story," 2; *AMT*, 1:287; *MTLP*, 359.

30. SLC to Susan Crane, 20 June 1893, *UCCL* 04418; SLC to Susan Crane, 9–10 July 1893, *UCCL* 04423; Kaplan, *Singular Mark Twain*, 474; Austilat, *Tramp in Berlin*, 126; *MTLP*, 346–47; "'Mark Twain' in Berlin," *Philadelphia Inquirer*, 2 July 1893, 1; Dolmetsch, "Berlin, Germany," in LeMaster and Wilson, *Mark Twain Encyclopedia*, 70; "Prof. E. E. Barnard," *Nashville Banner*, 31 July 1893, 3; "An Astronomer's Travels," *Chicago Inter Ocean*, 11 September 1893, 5.

31. *MTLP*, 352–57; *Mark Twain's Letters* (1917), 594; Kaplan, *Singular Mark Twain*, 391; SLC to unidentified, 1893, *UCCL* 09550.

32. *MTLP*, 352–53, 356–57.

33. *MFMT*, 121; *MTN*, 234; *Brooklyn Eagle*, 8 September 1893, 4; "People Talked About," *San Francisco Call*, 29 September 1893, 6.

Chapter 3

1. *MTLP*, 336, 345, 354; *LLMT*, 267–71, 278–79; SLC to Olivia Langdon Clemens, 15 February 1894, *UCCL* 04693.

2. *LLMT*, 267–68; SLC to Olivia Langdon Clemens, 19 September 1893, *UCCL* 04454; Leary, "Bankruptcy of Mark Twain," 15; SLC to Clara Clemens, 15 September 1893, *UCCL* 04450; *AMT*, 2:158–59; Kaplan, *Singular Mark Twain*, 478; "Mark Twain in Trouble," *Victoria (B.C.) Colonist*, 19 April 1894, 6; Hall, "Tells the Story," 2; *HHR*, 11.

3. Marcosson, "Twain as Collaborator," 24; Halla, "The Plutocrat and the Author," 18; *HHR*, 709; SLC to Olivia Langdon Clemens and Jean Clemens, 4 December 1893, *UCCL* 04518; Beard, *Hardly a Man*, 348; SLC to Clara Clemens, 30 September 1893, *UCCL* 04464; Matthews, *Tocsin of Revolt*, 282.

4. SLC to Olivia Langdon Clemens, 21 September 1893, *UCCL* 04456; SLC to William Carey, 21 September 1893, *UCCL* 04652.

5. "Along Literary Pathways," *New Orleans Times-Democrat*, 24 December 1893, 16; "Notes," *Nation*, 8 February 1894, 103; *Windsor Review*, 1 February 1894, 3; "Magazines," *London Middlesex Courier*, 8 December 1893, 4; "Magazines and Reviews," *Leeds Mercury*, 12 December 1893, 3; William Livingstone Alden, "The Book Hunter," *Idler* 6 (August 1893): 222–23; Martha McCullough Williams, "In Re Pudd'nhead Wilson," 99–102; "New Publications," *NYT*, 2 June 1894, 3.

6. Frank Mayo, "Pudd'nhead Wilson," *Harper's Weekly*, 22 June 1895, 594; SLC to Olivia Langdon Clemens, 7 February 1894, *UCCL* 04689; *LLMT*, 296–97; Fike, *Frank Mayo*, 299; *Early Tales and Sketches*, 1:477.

7. "Mark Twain the Guest," *Brooklyn Eagle*, 18 October 1893, 5; "Mark Twain Dined by Brooklyn Club," *New York World*, 18 October 1893, 7; "Personal and Political," *Boston Advertiser*, 23 October 1893, 4; SLC to Fred Hall, 24 October 1893, *UCCL* 08978; SLC to John Elderkin, 27 October 1893, *UCCL* 04478; *Critic*, 4 November 1893, 294; *LLMT*, 276–77.

8. "Mark Twain in the Lotos' New Home," *New York Herald*, 12 November 1893, 10; "Lotos Dinner to Mark Twain," *NYT*, 10 November 1893, 8; "Mark Twain Their Guest," *New York Sun*, 12 November 1893, 4; "Mark Twain Its Guest," *New York Tribune*, 12 November 1893, 7; *MTSpk*, 265; "Mr. Irving to Sup with the Lotos Club," *New York Tribune*, 17 November 1893, 7; Edward Bok, "A Forgotten Poetess," *Philadelphia Times*, 3 December 1893, 9; *Boston Globe*, 5 December 1893, 4; "Mark Twain Hard Up," *St. Louis Republic*, 17 December 1893, 18.

9. "Edwin Booth," *Boston Journal*, 14 November 1893, 2; SLC to Susy Clemens, 6 November 1893, *UCCL* 04490; Kaplan, *Singular Mark Twain*, 480; *MTHL*, 654.

10. "Fine Display of Fencing," *New York Herald*, 21 November 1893, 8; *LLMT*, 279–80; SLC to Olivia Langdon Clemens, 2 December 1893, *UCCL* 04516; SLC to Olivia Langdon Clemens, 15 December 1893, *UCCL* 04530; *Mark Twain's Letters* (1917), 597; "'Mark Twain' Visits Editor Bunner," *NYT*, 11 December 1893, 1; "'Mark Twain' Too Ill to Lecture," *NYT*, 15 December 1893, 1; "Sons of the Revolution," *New York Sun*, 8 December 1893, 7; "Life Topics about Town," *New York Sun*, 15 December 1893, 7; SLC to Annie Trumbull, 17 December 1893, *UCCL* 11026.

11. SLC to Olivia Langdon Clemens, 19 December 1893, *UCCL* 04532; Matthews, *Tocsin of Revolt*, 278; "Brander Matthews's Friends," *New York World*, 21 December 1893, 7; SLC to Susy Clemens, 27 December 1893, *UCCL* 04540; *MTSpk*, 269.

12. *LLMT*, 267–68, 274–75; SLC to Olivia Langdon Clemens, 18 October 1893, *UCCL* 04476; SLC to T. K. Webster, 31 October 1893, *UCCL* 04480; SLC to Susy Clemens, 6 November 1893, *UCCL* 04490.

13. *HHR*, 17, 148; Kaplan, *Singular Mark Twain*, 483; SLC to Olivia Langdon Clemens, 19 December 1893, *UCCL* 04532; SLC to Olivia Langdon Clemens, 25 December 1893, *UCCL* 04536; *LLMT*, 289–92.

14. SLC to Susy Clemens, 27 December 1893, *UCCL* 04540.

15. SLC to Olivia Langdon Clemens, 30 December 1893, *UCCL* 04545; SLC to Olivia Langdon Clemens, 12 January 1894, *UCCL* 04671; *LLMT*, 286–89; "A Masque of Culture," *Hartford Courant*, 11 January 1894, 6; "Sandow's Lectures," *New York Sun*, 15 January 1894, 7.

16. "Amusement Notes," *Boston Globe*, 25 January 1894, 5; "One Thousand More," *Boston Globe*, 26 January 1894, 4; "Authors' Readings," *Boston Advertiser*, 26 January 1894, 2; SLC to Olivia Langdon Clemens, 25 January 1894, *UCCL* 04677; SLC to Olivia Langdon Clemens, 27–30 January 1894, *UCCL* 04679; SLC to Olivia Langdon Clemens, 7 February 1894, *UCCL* 04689; SLC to Elizabeth Millet, 1 February 1894, *UCCL* 11500; SLC to Clara Clemens, 5 February 1894, *UCCL* 04688; Benson, "Twain's Contacts with Scandinavia," 159–60; SLC to Mr. Hardy, 3 February 1894, *UCCL* 04687.

17. *Mark Twain's Letters* (1917), 611–12; SLC to Olivia Langdon Clemens, 15 February 1894, *UCCL* 04693; *MTHL*, 973; *HHR*, 6; Seybold, "Neoclassical Twain," 83.

18. SLC to Olivia Langdon Clemens, 11–13 February 1894, *UCCL* 04692; SLC to Olivia Langdon Clemens, 23 February 1894, *UCCL* 04697; Dias, "Twain in Fairhaven," 13; "Mark Twain Made a Speech," *Buffalo Enquirer*, 22 February 1894, 1; "Fairhaven's Day," *Boston Globe*, 23 February 1894, 5; *HHR*, 40, 112, 591, 711.

19. *LLMT*, 293–96; SLC to Olivia Langdon Clemens, 11–13 February 1894, *UCCL* 04692; *MTHL*, 659; SLC to William H. Rideing, 11 March 1894, *UCCL* 09936; *CTSSE*, 201–6; SLC to S. S. Rush, 9 August 1893, *UCCL* 11476.

20. SLC to Olivia Langdon Clemens, 20 February 1894, *UCCL* 04695; SLC to Olivia Langdon Clemens, 2 March 1894, *UCCL* 04802; *LLMT*, 296–97; "Mark Twain's Old Stories," *NYT*, 27 February 1894, 4; "Twain and Riley's Readings," *New York Herald*, 27 February 1894, 10; "Mark Twain and Mr. Riley to Read Again," *New York Tribune*, 28 February 1894, 7; "Authors Recite at Chickering Hall," *New York Sun*, 4 March 1894, 4; *HHR*, 126–27; "In the World of Clubs," *New York Tribune*, 11 March 1894, 19.

21. *HHR*, 20, 31; SLC to Olivia Langdon Clemens, 27–30 January 1894, *UCCL* 04679; SLC to Olivia Langdon Clemens, 25–27 February 1894, *UCCL* 04699; SLC to Pamela A. Moffett, 25 February 1894, *UCCL* 04698.

22. *Mark Twain's "Which Was the Dream?,"* 3; *HHR*, 40, 66, 709; Kaplan, *Singular Mark Twain*, 485; SLC to Bram Stoker, 2 February 1894, *UCCL* 08839; *MTCI*, 139, 143.

23. "New York Sails Away," *New York Evening World*, 7 March 1894, 4; *MTCI*, 143, 320–21; "This Morning's News," *London Daily News*, 15 March 1894, 5; "Latest News from Europe," *New York Sun*, 18 March 1894, 1; "Mark Twain's New Books," *San Francisco Morning Call*, 25 March 1894, 15.

24. "Europe's Red Specter," *Brooklyn Eagle*, 27 March 1894, 8; "Notes from Paris," *Truth*, 5 April 1894, 772; "Mark Twain among the Entertainers," *New York Tribune*, 6 April 1894, 1; *HHR*, 51; "Mark Twain Reciting at the British Embassy, Paris," *Penny Illustrated Paper*, 14 April 1894, 233; Gabriel Randon, "Causerie-Conférence de Mark Twain," *Le Figaro*, 6 April

1894, 2; "Our London Correspondence," *Glasgow Herald*, 6 April 1894, 3, 24; SLC to Orion Clemens, 12 April 1894, *UCCL* 04717.

25. "Mark Twain in Town," *New York Sun*, 15 April 1894, 5; "New York Personals," *Philadelphia Inquirer*, 15 April 1894, 5; "Crew Returns," *Boston Post*, 15 April 1894, 8; "She Beat the Campania," *New York Herald*, 15 April 1894, 6; SLC to Olivia Langdon Clemens, 14 April 1894, *UCCL* 04718.

26. SLC to Olivia Langdon Clemens, 20 February 1894, *UCCL* 04695; *LLMT*, 299–300; SLC to Pamela A. Moffett, 25 February 1894, *UCCL* 04698; *MTHL*, 983; "Recent Events," *Brooklyn Eagle*, 19 April 1894, 4; "Mark Twain in Trouble," *Victoria (B.C.) Colonist*, 19 April 1894, 6; "Mark Twain's Failure," *Philadelphia Times*, 20 April 1894, 7; "Examining Mark Twain's Assets," *NYT*, 12 July 1895, 9; "Mark Twain's Failure," *San Francisco Call*, 19 September 1894, 2; "Failure of Mark Twain," *New York Tribune*, 19 April 1894, 1; "Hoping to Resume Business," *New York Tribune*, 20 April 1894, 4.

27. *LLMT*, 300–302; Edward Bok, "Pinero and Sullivan," *Philadelphia Times*, 17 June 1894, 21.

28. Arthur Pettit, *Twain and the South*, 159; Crawford, *How* Not *to Get Rich*, 155; "Mark Twain as a Debtor," *New York Sun*, 12 July 1895, 7.

29. "Among the Authors," *Los Angeles Herald*, 16 September 1894, 15; "Men, Women, and Books," *Critic*, 20 October 1894, 252.

30. "New Book by Mark Twain," *London Daily News*, 18 April 1894, 6; "New Books," *Dundee Advertiser* (Scotland), 10 May 1894, 2; *MTCR*, 343–56; "Literary Notes," *London Morning Post*, 6 June 1894, 6; "Mark Twain in the Clouds," *London Sketch*, 11 July 1894, 15; "The Literary Lounger," *London Sketch*, 2 May 1894, 14; "Books of the Week," *Manchester Guardian*, 15 May 1894, 7; DeVoto, *Portable Mark Twain*, 31–32.

31. SLC to Olivia Langdon Clemens, 16 April 1894, *UCCL* 04720; SLC to Olivia Langdon Clemens, 22 April 1894, *UCCL* 04724; SLC to Olivia Langdon Clemens, 25 April 1894, *UCCL* 11798; *Mark Twain to Mrs. Fairbanks*, 273–74.

32. Cardwell, *Man Who Was Mark Twain*, 77; SLC to Pamela A. Moffett, 25 February 1894, *UCCL* 04698; Kaplan, *Singular Mark Twain*, 487; *LLMT*, 300–302; SLC to Fred Hall, 1 June 1894, *UCCL* 04737; Fred Hall to A. B. Paine, 14 January 1909, *UCLC* 49255.

33. *MTHL*, 984; Zacks, *Chasing the Last Laugh*, 55; *LLMT*, 305–7; Olivia Langdon Clemens to SLC, 31 July 1894, *UCCL* 04768.

34. *MTHL*, 986–87; *LLMT*, 299–300; Olivia Langdon Clemens to SLC, 31 July 1894, *UCCL* 04768; SLC to Orion Clemens, 23 April 1894, *UCCL* 04726.

35. "Mark Twain Still Speaketh," *Boston Journal*, 30 April 1894, 2; SLC to Olivia Langdon Clemens, 16 May 1894, *UCCL* 10490; Joseph Andriano, "Fenimore Cooper's Literary Offenses," in LeMaster and Wilson, *Mark Twain Encyclopedia*, 286; *Letters from the Earth*, 290; *HHR*, 53–54; SLC to R. W. Gilder, 29 April 1898, *UCCL* 05381.

36. "North American Review," *Kansas City Gazette*, 1 July 1895, 2; *Buffalo Express*, 7 July 1895, 12; "Editorial Etchings," *Wilkes-Barre Record*, 20 July 1895, 4; "Twain and Cooper," *Salt Lake Herald*, 8 August 1895, 4; "Fenimore Cooper's Literary Offences," *San Francisco Examiner*, 25 August 1895, 24; "Literary Notes," *New York Tribune*, 21 July 1895, 24; *Chicago Tribune*, 6 August 1895, 6; *Elmira Star-Gazette*, 2 July 1895, 4; "Cooper and Mark Twain," *Chicago Inter Ocean*, 7 July 1895, 26; "Mark Twain, Critic," *Detroit Free Press*, 28 July 1895, 24; "Literary Criticism," *Austin American-Statesman*, 11 July 1895, 4; *Brooklyn Life*, 6 July 1895, 6; "Mark Twain Given a Rap," *Lancaster (Penn.) Examiner*, 31 July 1895, 3; "Personal and General Notes," *New Orleans Times-Picayune*, 8 August 1895, 4.

37. "Queen Victoria," *Boston Advertiser*, 8 June 1894, 5; "Prominent People," *Dublin Herald*, 19 May 1894, 1; "Notes of Foreign Happenings," *New York Sun*, 18 May 1894, 3; "Politics and Persons," *St. James's Gazette*, 18 November 1895, 13; *HHR*, 55; SLC to Laurence Hutton, 26 July 1894, *UCCL* 04762.

Chapter 4

1. SLC to Grace King, 30 April 1894, *UCCL* 04727; *HHR*, 67, 68; *A Family Sketch*, 35.

2. *HHR*, 61–63; "This Morning's News," *London Daily News*, 5 July 1894, 5; SLC to Orion Clemens, 21 June 1894, *UCCL* 04742.

3. *LLMT*, 302, 305; SLC to Olivia Langdon Clemens, 26 July 1894, *UCCL* 04764; SLC to Olivia Langdon Clemens, 31 July 1894, *UCCL* 04767; "Arrived on the Paris," *New York Evening World*, 14 July 1894, 2; Harper, *House of Harper*, 575; *HHR*, 170; SLC to J. Henry Harper, 11–12 September 1894, *UCCL* 04786.

4. SLC to Henry Robinson, 23 July 1894, *UCCL* 11051; "Coney Island's Revival Off," *New York Sun*, 16 July 1894, 5; *Brooklyn Eagle*, 16 July 1894, 5; *LLMT*, 305–7; SLC to Olivia Langdon Clemens, 29 July 1894, *UCCL* 04766; SLC to Olivia Langdon Clemens, 31 July 1894, *UCCL* 04767; SLC to Olivia Langdon Clemens, 3 August 1894, *UCCL* 04769; "At Manhattan Beach," *New York Herald*, 27 July 1894, 9; Wigger, "Twain's *Pudd'nhead Wilson*, 97; SLC to Chatto & Windus, 28 August 1894, *UCCL* 04783.

5. "Mayor Gilroy Sails Today," *New York Sun*, 15 August 1894, 1; "Mark Twain and the Deckhand," *New York Tribune*, 16 August 1894, 2; "Mark Twain Goes Abroad," *New York Sun*, 16 August 1894, 3; "A Mid-Ocean Letter," *Brooklyn Eagle*, 9 September 1894, 5.

6. *HHR*, 71, 73, 77.

7. *HHR*, 80, 103; *MFMT*, 127; *MTB*, 989; Healy, "Twain at Home," 23.

8. *MTCR*, 359–64; "Mark Twain's New Book," *Elgin Courant and Morayshire Advertiser* (Scotland), 25 December 1894, 7.

9. "A Few New Story Books," *Book-Buyer*, n.s. 12 (March 1895): 92; "Mark Twain's New Volume," *NYT*, 27 January 1895, 27; "New Publications," *Washington Star*, 27 July 1895, 19; *MTCR*, 367–73; "Current Literature," *Chicago Inter Ocean*, 9 February 1895, 10; "Novels and Tales," *New York Outlook*, 2 March 1895, 357.

10. Quirk, *Twain: A Study of the Short Fiction*, 108; Bourget, *Outre-Mer*; *MTCR*, 164, 178; *HHR*, 80; SLC to Lloyd S. Bryce, 13 October 1894, *UCCL* 04797; "Mark Twain at Sydney," *Melbourne Argus*, 16 September 1895, 5.

11. Scharnhorst, "Twain and Julian Hawthorne," 48; "Mark Twain on Bourget," *Hartford Courant*, 9 January 1895, 6; "Americanisms," *St. James Gazette*, 21 January 1895, 4; "Reviews and Magazine," *Saturday Review*, 26 January 1895, 137; *NYT*, 9 January 1895, 4; *London Sporting Times*, 6 April 1895, 1; "National Characteristics," *London Globe*, 17 January 1895, 1; "A Frenchman on Mark Twain and His Criticisms of Bourget," *Literary Digest*, 2 March 1895, 521.

12. Max O'Rell, "Twain and Paul Bourget," *North American Review* 160 (March 1895): 302–10.

13. "General News," *Murchison Times* (Australia), 6 November 1897, 2; *How to Tell a Story*, 213–33; *MTCR*, 421, 425–27.

14. "The Biter Bit," *Los Angeles Times*, 6 March 1895, 1; *MTCI*, 200; "That Twain-O'Rell Duel," *Wilkes-Barre (Penn.) Times-Leader*, 27 March 1895, 3; "Said in Fun," *Nebraska State Journal*, 17 March 1895, 12; "Mark Twain Mad," *Helena (Mont.) Independent-Record*, 15 March 1895, 1.

15. "Claimant Clement," *St. Louis Post-Dispatch*, 19 May 1895, 20; *MTCI*, 198.

16. "Dinner Given to Mark Twain," *Boston Herald*, 17 June 1899, 2; "At Broadstairs," *London M.A.P.*, 24 June 1899, 22–23; Grossmith, *From Studio to Stage*, 359–60; Gribben, *Twain's Library*, 658.

17. *MFMT*, 104–6; *LLMT*, 277–78; SLC to Orion Clemens, 3 November 1893, *UCCL* 04487; *Mark Twain to Mrs. Fairbanks*, 272–73.

18. *Tom Sawyer Abroad*, 115; *HHR*, 122, 170; Emerson, *Twain: A Literary Life*, 216; "Tom Sawyer, Detective," *Wellington Evening Post*, 24 October 1896, 2; "Along Literary Pathways," *New Orleans Times-Democrat*, 13 September 1896, 18.

19. *HHR*, 83, 87, 88, 92; Charles E. Davis, "Composing, Line-Justifying, and Distributing," 381; Joseph Csicsila, "'These Hideous Times,'" 132.

20. *HHR*, 26, 104, 106.

21. *HHR*, 108–9, 112; Zacks, *Chasing the Last Laugh*, 53.

22. *HHR*, 26, 115–16, 119, 147; Gold, "*Hatching Ruin*," 42; *AMT*, 1:455; *MTB*, 914; Powers, *Twain: A Life*, 561.

23. *HHR*, 36; "Mark Twain's Fortune and Paige Machine," *St. Louis Republic*, 21 September 1898, 6; "An Expensive Typesetter," *Hartford Courant*, 20 September 1898, 3.

24. *HHR*, 125; *Mark Twain to Mrs. Fairbanks*, 276–77; *Personal Recollections of Joan of Arc*, 461; *Europe and Elsewhere*, 299.

25. SLC to Katharine Harrison, 15 April 1895, *UCCL* 04868; Harrington and Jenn, *Twain and France*, 178; *AMT*, 2:353; "Literary Notes," *Chicago Inter Ocean*, 9 November 1895, 10.

26. *Dial*, 16 February 1895, 123; "Personal," *New York Tribune*, 3 April 1895, 6; "Literary Notes," *New York Tribune*, 14 April 1895, 24; "Literary Notes," *London Anglo-American Times*, 4 May 1895, 2; "Personal and Pertinent," *New York World*, 19 April 1895, 4; Edward Bok, "Next Year Kipling's Year," *Philadelphia Times*, 5 May 1895, 23; "Joan of Arc and Her Latest Executioner," *Boston Sacred Heart Review*, 12 October 1895, 5; "He Did Not Meet Bourget," *Boston Herald*, 19 May 1895, 7; *MTCI*, 153, 155; *Boston Globe*, 24 January 1896, 6.

27. *HHR*, 126, 129; "'Mark Twain' Sails for Home Today," *New York World*, 23 February 1895, 3; "Howard Gould Returns," *New York Evening World*, 2 March 1895, 3; "Mark Twain Mad," *Helena (Mont.) Independent-Record*, 15 March 1895, 1; SLC to Lloyd Bryce, 9 March 1895, *UCCL* 04847; SLC to Franklin G. Whitmore, 8 January 1895, *UCCL* 04834.

28. *LLMT*, 268–69, 274–75; Lorch, *Trouble Begins at Eight*, 184; *Nelson Colonist* (New Zealand), 16 July 1894, 3; "Our Australian Colonies," *London Morning Post*, 14 September 1894, 2; *HHR*, 128, 138.

29. Courtney, *Joseph Hopkins Twichell*, 246; *LLMT*, 312.

30. SLC to Anne Sullivan Macy, 11 January 1909, *UCCL* 09387; "Hears with Her Fingers," *Washington Times*, 25 June 1895, 5; *AMT*, 1:465; Keller, *The Story of My Life*, 111; Wesley Britton, "Keller, Helen Adams," in LeMaster and Wilson, *Mark Twain Encyclopedia*, 427; Chambliss, "Helen Keller and Mark Twain," 306; Sangster, *From My Youth Up*, 285; Hutton, *Talks in a Library*, 390–91; Keller, *Midstream*, 47.

31. *AMT*, 2:279–80; *HHR*, 253–54, 261, 264; SLC to Emilie Rogers, 22 December 1896, *UCCL* 05157; *FE*, 605.

32. "The St. Paul Didn't Budge," *New York Sun*, 26 March 1895, 1.

33. "Americans Going Abroad," *New York Sun*, 27 March 1895, 5; *HHR*, 135, 138.

34. *HHR*, 140–41; SLC to Poultney Bigelow, 25 April 1895, *UCCL* 04870; SLC to J. Henry Harper, 23 April 1895, *UCCL* 04869; SLC to Orion Clemens, 26 May 1895, *UCCL* 04880; *MFMT*, 136.

35. "Mark Twain May Come," *Salt Lake Herald*, 28 May 1895, 3; "Mark Twain Coming Here," *San Francisco Call*, 19 May 1895, 1; "News of the Platform," *Brooklyn Eagle*, 28 April 1895, 4.

36. *HHR*, 143; SLC to John D. Adams, 13 June 1895, *UCCL* 05005; Fred C. Chamberlin, "La Comtesse de Lisne," *Boston Herald*, 26 May 1895, 35; "Amusements," *New York Sun*, 25 May 1895, 5.

37. "Claimant Clemens," *St. Louis Post-Dispatch*, 19 May 1895, 20; "Hill Has the N.P.," *Minneapolis Star Tribune*, 19 May 1895, 1; "Mark Twain Gave Readings," *Brooklyn Eagle*, 18 May 1895, 2; "Mark Twain Sees 'Pudd'nhead,'" *Springfield Republican*, 21 May 1895, 8.

38. "Claimant Clemens," *St. Louis Post-Dispatch*, 19 May 1895, 20; *HHR*, 141; Fike, *Frank Mayo*, 308; "Mr. Mayo and 'Pudd'nhead Wilson,'" *New York Tribune*, 16 April 1895, 7; Pond, *Eccentricities of Genius*, 228–29; "Theatrical Gossip," *NYT*, 16 May 1895, 13; "This Week at the Theatres," *New York Sun*, 19 May 1895, sec. 2, p. 3.

39. "Mark Twain Speaks," *New York Herald*, 19 May 1895, 7; "Mark Twain and the Twins," *New York Tribune*, 23 May 1895, 7; "Mark Twain's Twins," *Brooklyn Eagle*, 23 May 1895, 10.

40. Fike, *Frank Mayo*, 317; "What Frank Mayo Says," *San Francisco Call*, 5 April 1896, 7; *HHR*, 211, 219–20, 267.

41. SLC to Orion Clemens, 26 May 1895; SLC to James B. Pond, 24 May 1895, *UCCL* 04992; SLC to Sam Moffett, 11 June 1895, *UCCL* 04888; *Jamestown (N.D.) Weekly Alert*, 13 June 1895, 7; SLC to Franklin G. Whitmore, 8 January 1896, *UCCL* 04834; Wallace, "Twain on the Great Lakes," 182.

42. *HHR*, 149–52.

43. *HHR*, 249–50, 252.

44. SLC to Robert Underwood Johnson, 30 May 1895, *UCCL* 04882; *HHR*, 150, 163; Kaplan, *Singular Mark Twain*, 503.

45. *HHR*, 159, 161, 165–66, 168–69; "Examining Mark Twain's Assets," *NYT*, 12 July 1895, 9; "Had Mark Twain on the Rack," *New York Herald*, 12 July 1895, 5; "Mark Twain No Financier," *New York Sun*, 13 July 1895, 7; "'Mark Twain' Is Ruined," *Boston Globe*, 12 July 1895, 23; "Mark Twain as a Debtor," *New York Sun*, 12 July 1895, 7; SLC to Sam Moffett, 14–15 August 1895, *UCCL* 04943; *Concord (Mass.) Enterprise*, 25 July 1895, 4; SLC to Pamela A, Moffett, 14 July 1895, *UCCL* 04931.

46. *HHR*, 165–66, 172–73, 176; "Webster & Co.'s Case Closed," *Brooklyn Eagle*, 23 July 1895, 1.

47. *HHR*, 146–48, 167, 169; "Twain Tries On His Lecture," *New York Sun*, 13 July 1895, 7.

48. Bacheller, *Opinions of a Cheerful Yankee*, 7; Sorrentino, *Stephen Crane*, 163.

49. *HHR*, 167, 171; Lorch, *Trouble Begins at Eight*, 354; Parsons, "Clubman in South Africa," 253–54; "Mark Twain's Audiences," *New York Tribune*, 27 December 1903, 6.

50. *MTHL*, 663; *Mark Twain's Letters* (1917), 636.

51. SLC to Sam Moffett, 14–15 August 1895, *UCCL* 04943; Denney, "Next Stop Detroit," 26; Rodney, *Twain Overseas*, 165; "Mark Twain," *Cleveland Plain Dealer*, 16 July 1895, 8.

52. Pond, *Eccentricities of Genius*, 200–201; "Mark Twain Begins His Tour," *NYT*, 23 July 1895, 3; *HHR*, 171; "Amusements," *Seattle Post-Intelligencer*, 13 August 1895, 8; "Mark Twain," *Cleveland Plain Dealer*, 16 July 1895, 8; Lorch, "Twain's 'Morals' Lecture," 58; *Buffalo Enquirer*, 22 July 1895, 4; Denney, "Next Stop Detroit," 26; "Impressions of Mark Twain," *Cleveland Plain Dealer*, 28 July 1895, 17.

53. Wallace, "Twain on the Great Lakes," 183; Pond, *Eccentricities of Genius*, 201; "Society," *Cleveland Plain Dealer*, 21 July 1895, 18.

54. Pond, *Overland with Mark Twain*, 3, 5; Cooper, *Around the World*, 23; Zacks, *Chasing the Last Laugh*, 75–76; Denney, "Next Stop Detroit," 27; *HHR*, 173; "A Packed House," *Petoskey (Mich.) Resorter*, 21 July 1895; "Bay View Cottages Filled," *Chicago Tribune*, 21 July 1895, 28.

55. Pond, *Overland with Mark Twain*, 5; "Mark an Hour Late," *Duluth (Minn.) News Tribune*, 23 July 1895, 5; Flanagan, "Twain on the Upper Mississippi," 379.

56. Pond, *Overland with Mark Twain*, 5–6; "Mark Twain's Lecture," *Minneapolis Journal*, 24 July 1895, 4; "Smiled with Twain," *Minneapolis Tribune*, 24 July 1895, 3; "A Reception to Twain," *Minneapolis Journal*, 20 July 1895, 6; "Mark Twain Tonight," *St. Paul Globe*, 24 July 1895, 4; "Mark Twain's Reading," *St. Paul Globe*, 25 July 1895, 5; Fatout, *Twain on the Lecture Circuit*, 246.

57. *HHR*, 177; Pond, *Overland with Mark Twain*, 6; W. E. Sterner, "Musical and Dramatic," *Winnipeg Tribune*, 27 July 1895, 3; "Mark Twain," *Vancouver World*, 31 July 1895, 5; "Visit to Winnipeg," *Winnipeg Free Press*, 22 April 1910, 1; "Mark Twain, Author and Lecturer," *Winnipeg Tribune*, 26 July 1895, 5. See also Allingham, "Twain in Winnipeg," 2–12.

58. "Mark Twain Talks," *Grand Forks (Mont.) Herald*, 30 July 1895, 4; Pond, *Overland with Mark Twain*, 6; Pond, *Eccentricities of Genius*, 207–8; Fatout, *Twain on the Lecture Circuit*, 246.

59. "About Maj. Pond," *Topeka State Journal*, 27 June 1903, 13; Pond, *Eccentricities of Genius*, 208–9; "Twain Appreciated," *Anaconda (Mont.) Standard*, 2 August 1895, 7.

60. "Mark Twain," *Great Falls (Mont.) Tribune*, 1 August 1895, 4; "In Great Falls," *Anaconda (Mont.) Standard*, 4 August 1895, 9; Zacks, *Chasing the Last Laugh*, 90; "Twain Pleased Them," *Butte Miner*, 2 August 1895, 6; "Mark Twain in Butte," *Helena Independent-Record*, 2 August 1895, 1; "Mark's All Right," *Anaconda (Mont.) Standard*, 2 August 1895, 5; *Butte Post*, 2 August 1895, 2; Pond, *Overland with Mark Twain*, 8.

61. "Funny Mark," *Anaconda (Mont.) Standard*, 3 August 1895, 3; Pond, *Eccentricities of Genius*, 210–12.

62. Pond, *Overland with Mark Twain*, 8–9; "An Evening with Twain," *Helena Independent-Record*, 4 August 1895, 6; Pond, *Eccentricities of Genius*, 212.

63. Pond, *Overland with Mark Twain*, 9, 11; "Twain at the Bennett," *Missoula Missoulian*, 6 August 1895, 1; *Missoula Republican*, 6 August 1895, 4; Pond, *Eccentricities of Genius*, 215–16; "Ninety Minutes with Mark Twain," *Spokane Spokesman-Review*, 8 August 1895, 3. See also Coleman, "Twain in Montana," 9–16.

64. Pond, *Overland with Mark Twain*, 11; Pond, *Eccentricities of Genius*, 218.

65. Pond, *Overland with Mark Twain*, 12; *MTN*, 246; Zacks, *Chasing the Last Laugh*, 99; Pond, *Eccentricities of Genius*, 219; Pease, "Mark Twain at the Marquam," *Portland Oregonian*, 10 August 1895, 8; *Portland (Ore.) Telegram*, 10 August 1895.

66. Hoeltje, "When Mark Twain Spoke in Portland," 76–77; *JHT*, 365–66; "Personal Mention," *Portland Oregonian*, 10 August 1895, 8; Pond, *Eccentricities of Genius*, 218–19; *MTCI*, 173.

67. Pond, *Overland with Mark Twain*, 13; "City News in Brief," *Olympia Washington Standard*, 16 August 1895, 3; "Our Popular Theater," *Olympia Washington Standard*, 4 October 1895, 2; Zacks, *Chasing the Last Laugh*, 99.

68. Tanner and Scharnhorst, "Twain Speaking," 24–25; "A Pleasant Afternoon with Mark Twain," *Tacoma News*, 17 August 1895, 8; "In Honor of Mark Twain," *Seattle Post-Intelligencer*, 18 August 1895, 10; "Coast News in Brief," *San Francisco Call*, 13 August 1895, 4; Rodney, *Twain Overseas*, 166; Lorch, "Twain's 'Morals' Lecture," 58; "Mark Twain Tonight," *Vancouver*

World, 15 August 1895, 7; "Twain Makes a Hit in Tacoma," *Seattle Post-Intelligencer*, 13 August 1895, 8; Pond, *Eccentricities of Genius*, 219–20; *Tacoma Union*, 13 August 1895; "The City in Brief," *Tacoma News*, 13 August 1895, 3; "A Pleasant Afternoon with Mark Twain," *Tacoma News*, 17 August 1895, 8.

69. Wheeler, *Yesterdays in a Busy Life*, 335; Rodney, *Twain Overseas*, 166; "A Continuous Laugh," *Seattle Post-Intelligencer*, 14 August 1895, 8; *Seattle Times*, 14 August 1895; "Mark Twain at the Rainier Club," *Seattle Post-Intelligencer*, 18 August 1895, 9; Pond, *Eccentricities of Genius*, 220; SLC to Sam Moffett, 14–15 August 1895, *UCCL* 04943.

70. Cooper, *Around the World with Mark Twain*, 52–53; Pond, *Overland with Mark Twain*, 13; *HHR*, 181; Pond, *Eccentricities of Genius*, 220; "Mark Twain in Whatcom," *Seattle Post-Intelligencer*, 16 August 1895, 3.

71. Pond, *Eccentricities of Genius*, 221; Allingham, "Twain in Vancouver," 5–6; *HHR*, 181; "Mark Twain," *Vancouver World*, 16 August 1895, 7.

72. *FE*, 15; *HHR*, 183, 186; Pond, *Eccentricities of Genius*, 221–22; "About Maj. Pond," *Topeka State Journal*, 27 June 1903, 13.

73. Pond, *Overland with Mark Twain*, 14–15; Pond, *Eccentricities of Genius*, 222–23; "The Lecture a Treat," *Victoria (B.C.) Times*, 22 August 1895, 4; Burnet, "Twain in the Northwest," 188; "Mark Twain," *Victoria (B.C.) Colonist*, 22 August 1895, 8; Lorch, "Twain's 'Morals' Lecture," 55; *MTN*, 248–49; Gordon, *Canadian Journal of Lady Aberdeen*, 276.

74. *FE*, 25; Fatout, *Twain on the Lecture Circuit*, 252; SLC to James B. Pond, 17 September 1897, *UCCL* 05289; *MTCI*, 185–86, 192; Olivia Langdon Clemens to Susan Crane, 5 September 1895, *UCCL* 04958; "Talk of the Day," *Boston Journal*, 19 September 1895, 10; *Bakersfield Californian*, 20 August 1895, 2; "Chronicle," *Saturday Review*, 7 September 1895, 304; Zacks, *Chasing the Last Laugh*, 109.

75. Pond, *Overland with Mark Twain*, 15.

76. Potts and Potts, "Twain Family in Australia," 48; Zacks, *Chasing the Last Laugh*, 115; Pond, *Eccentricities of Genius*, 224; *FE*, 26–27.

77. Pond, *Eccentricities of Genius*, 221–25; Allingham, "Twain in Vancouver," 10; *FE*, 25–26; *HHR*, 188.

78. "Mark Twain," *Sydney Herald*, 27 August 1895, 5; *Honolulu Hawaiian Gazette*, 23 August 1895, 5, 6; "Mark Twain," *Honolulu Independent*, 29 August 1895, 3; "Local Brevities," *Honolulu Advertiser*, 30 August 1895, 7.

79. Pond, *Overland with Mark Twain*, 2; "Captain Rice Photographed," *Honolulu Pacific Commercial Advertiser*, 4 September 1895, 6; *MTN*, 249–50; Scharnhorst, "A Recovered Mark Twain Letter," 87–88.

80. *FE*, 90–92; Olivia Langdon Clemens to Susan Crane, 5 September 1895, *UCCL* 04958; *HHR*, 187.

81. *HHR*, 187; *MFMT*, 141; Cooper, *Around the World with Mark Twain*, 61.

Chapter 5

1. *MFMT*, 143; *MTCI*, 209–10; "Current Topics," *Sydney Australian Star*, 17 September 1895, 4; "Mark Twain," *Sydney Daily Telegraph*, 19 September 1895, 5; "Our Telephone," *Sydney Times*, 22 September 1895, 5; "Personal," *Sydney Times*, 22 September 1895, 4; Shillingsburg, *At Home Abroad*, 49.

2. *Melbourne Advocate*, 21 September 1895, 15; "Table Talk," *Melbourne Table Talk*, 27 September 1895, 1; *MTCI*, 202–3, 217–18, 238; Shillingsburg, *At Home Abroad*, 36, 44,

47–48; Kate Carew, "12-Minute Interview on 12 Subjects with Bret Harte," *New York World*, 22 December 1901, 5.

3. "A Chat with 'Mark Twain,'" *Ballarat Star*, 21 October 1895, 3; *MTN*, 265.

4. "Mark Twain," *Sydney Herald*, 23 September 1895, 6; *HHR*, 190; Shillingsburg, *At Home Abroad*, 41–43, 53; "Mark Twain," *Sydney Herald*, 20 September 1895, 5; SLC to James B. Pond, 17 September 1897, *UCCL* 05289.

5. *MTSpk*, 665; Cooper, *Around the World with Mark Twain*, 230; SLC to Jack Harrington, 28 August 1895, *UCCL* 11651; Shillingsburg, *At Home Abroad*, 111, 173; "Rhyme with Kangaroo," *Adelaide Herald*, 27 January 1900, 8; "An Adieu to Mark Twain," *Melbourne Australasian*, 11 January 1896, 32.

6. Cooper, *Around the World with Mark Twain*, 94; *MTCI*, 213–15; "Fresh Food and Ice Company," *Sydney Herald*, 21 September 1895, 80; Shillingsburg, *At Home Abroad*, 50, 225; *HHR*, 188; "Mark Twain," *Sydney Herald*, 26 September 1895, 4; "Amusements in Australia," *London Era*, 9 November 1895, 11; "Mark Twain," *Sydney Truth*, 5 January 1896, 4.

7. "Mark Twain in Melbourne," *Adelaide Express*, 27 September 1895, 3; "Theatrical Gossip," *Washington Star*, 5 December 1899, 20; "'Mark Twain' At Home,'" *Melbourne Argus*, 28 September 1895, 7; "Amusements," *Melbourne Leader*, 28 September 1895, 22; "Mark Twain's 'At Home,'" *Melbourne Age*, 28 September 1895, 7; "Mark Twain 'At Home," *Melbourne Herald*, 28 September 1895, 3; "The Theatres &c.," *Australasian*, 5 October 1895, 31; "Melbourne," *Bendigo Advertiser*, 28 September 1895, 5; "Mark Twain in Melbourne," *Sydney Herald*, 30 September 1895, 5; Shillingsburg, *At Home Abroad*, 66–67; "'Mark Twain' At Home," *Melbourne Argus*, 1 October 1895, 6; "Mark Twain 'At Home,'" *Melbourne Herald*, 1 October 1895, 3; "Amusements," *Melbourne Age*, 3 October 1895, 6; Lorch, *Trouble Begins at Eight*, 255; *MTSpk*, 293.

8. Potts and Potts, "Twain Family in Australia," 46; SLC to Henry Huttleston Rogers, 10 November 1895, *UCCL* 11200; *MTSpk*, 298; *HHR*, 190.

9. "Mark Twain," *Adelaide Advertiser*, 12 October 1895, 5; "Amusements in Australia," *London Era*, 28 December 1895, 12; "Our Adelaide Letter," *Newcastle (New South Wales) Herald*, 2 November 1895, 2; Cooper, *Around the World with Mark Twain*, 105; "Mark Twain's At Home," *Adelaide Advertiser*, 14 October 1895, 7; "Mark Twain at Home," *South Australian Register*, 14 October 1895, 6; Shillingsburg, *At Home Abroad*, 81; Parsons, "Twain in Adelaide," 51–54; "A Civic Reception," *Adelaide Express and Telegraph*, 15 October 1895, 4; Horace George Stirling, "Hugh Kalytus on Mark Twain," *Adelaide Journal*, 19 October 1895, 5; *FE*, 184–85; "Essence of Parliament," *Adelaide South Australian Register*, 16 October 1895, 6; "Hottest Wave on Record," *Chicago Inter Ocean*, 29 August 1896, 5.

10. "Mark Twain at the Mechanics' Hall," *Horsham Times*, 18 October 1895, 3; Shillingsburg, *At Home Abroad*, 94–95, 98, 105, 107, 109, 116; *MTCI*, 240; "Mark Twain," *Ballarat Star*, 22 October 1895, 4; "The Minister of Mines at Stawell," *Melbourne Age*, 22 October 1895, 6.

11. "'Mark Twain' at the Royal Princess Theater," *Bendigo Advertiser*, 25 October 1895, 3; Parsons, "Twain in Melbourne," 40–42; *MTSpk*, 298–301; "Mark Twain 'At Home,'" *Geelong Advertiser*, 29 October 1895, 3; "Echoes of the Week," *Prahran Telegraph*, 2 November 1895, 4.

12. "Down South," *Launceston Tasmanian Democrat*, 8 November 1895, 2; *FE*, 284; "Mark Twain," *Sydney Daily Telegraph*, 19 September 1895, 5; Davitt, *Life and Progress in Australasia*, 337–40; *MTSpk*, 303; *MTCI*, 245; SLC to Franklin G. Whitmore, 8 January 1895, *UCCL* 04834.

13. Shillingsburg, *At Home Abroad*, 131, 136, 140; *FE*, 299; Davitt, *Life and Progress in Australasia*, 349–52; Charles Umbers, "To Mark Twain," *Dunedin Star*, 6 November 1895, 2; "Mark Twain 'At Home,'" *Otago Times*, 7 November 1895, 3; "Dunedin Notes," *Tuapeka Times*, 9 November 1895, 3; *Grey River Argus*, 9 November 1895, 2.

14. Parsons, "Twain in New Zealand," 57; *FE*, 209, 256, 265.

15. Zacks, *Chasing the Last Laugh*, 172; "Mark Twain," *Timaru Herald*, 11 November 1895, 3; "The Critic on Mark Twain," *Oamaru Mail*, 12 November 1895, 3; Parsons, "Twain in New Zealand," 58; Potts and Potts, "Twain Family in Australia," 49; "To-Day," *Christchurch Star*, 14 November 1895, 2; "News of the Day," *Christchurch Press*, 16 November 1895, 7; "Mark Twain," *Lyttelton Times*, 15 November 1895, 5; Shillingsburg, *At Home Abroad*, 150, 154; Parsons, "Twain in New Zealand," 61–62; *MTSpk*, 303; *FE*, 297–98.

16. Shillingsburg, *At Home Abroad*, 151; *FE*, 301–3; *Nelson Mail*, 18 November 1895, 2; SLC to Sarah Kinsey, 23 November 1895, *UCCL* 04975; *MFMT*, 150; Parsons, "Twain in New Zealand," 66–67; "Notes by a Quiet Man," *Nelson Mail*, 25 November 1895, 2.

17. Parsons, "Twain in New Zealand," 68; "Mark Twain 'At Home,'" *Auckland Star*, 22 November 1895, 3; Shillingsburg, *At Home Abroad*, 156; "Mark Twain," *New Zealand Herald*, 22 November 1895, 5; "The Lorgnette," *New Zealand Observer*, 30 November 1895, 10; *FE*, 308; "Mark Twain," *Adelaide Express and Telegraph*, 10 November 1900, 7; Olivia Langdon Clemens to Susan Crane, 24 November 1895, *UCCL* 04976.

18. *FE*, 315; Shillingsburg, *At Home Abroad*, 161–64; *JHT*, 184–85; SLC to James B. Pond, 30 November 1895, *UCCL* 05003; "Personalities," *Adelaide Quiz*, 26 December 1895, 6.

19. Parsons, "Twain in New Zealand," 72; *FE*, 318; Shillingsburg, *At Home Abroad*, 168, 171–72; *Hawera Star*, 4 December 1895, 3.

20. "Current and Under-Current," *Hawera Star*, 9 December 1895, 2; "Mark Twain's 'At Home,'" *Taranaki Herald*, 7 December 1895, 2; *MTN*, 261; *FE*, 278–79.

21. "A Lady's Letter," *Manawatu Herald*, 17 December 1895, 2; Rodney, *Twain Overseas*, 168; Shillingsburg, *At Home Abroad*, 173, 178; "Echoes of the Week," *New Zealand Times*, 14 December 1895, 1; "Mark Twain at Home," *New Zealand Times*, 11 December 1895, 2; SLC to Henry Huttleston Rogers, 12 December 1895, *UCCL* 11202.

22. *FE*, 324; *MTN*, 262–63; Shillingsburg, *At Home Abroad*, 185, 187–88; *MFMT*, 145; "District News," *Maitland Mercury*, 21 December 1895, 31; "Mark Twain's Lectures," *Sydney Daily Telegraph*, 21 December 1895, 10; "Mark Twain on the Situation," *Sydney Daily Telegraph*, 21 December 1895, 9; *MTCI*, 338.

23. *FE*, 331; Shillingsburg, *At Home Abroad*, 189; *MFMT*, 144; "Mark Twain," *Melbourne Herald*, 26 December 1895, 1; *Camperdown Chronicle*, 17 December 1895, 2; "Mark Twain's Farewell," *Melbourne Age*, 28 December 1895, 7; Rodney, *Twain Overseas*, 171; Shillingsburg, "Down Under Day by Day," 34.

24. Shillingsburg, *At Home Abroad*, 193; "Notes on Passing Events," *Petersburg Times*, 2 August 1904, 2; "South Australia," *Perth Inquirer*, 3 January 1896, 2; Parsons, "Twain in Adelaide," 52–53.

25. "Mark Twain," *Sydney News*, 7 December 1895, 7; *MTN*, 265; Ahluwalia, "Twain's Lecture Tour in India," 9; *HHR*, 190, 193–94; *MTCI*, 277; *FE*, 336; *MFMT*, 153–54; R. S. Smythe, "Herr Johann Kruse's Farewell," *Melbourne Age*, 30 November 1895, 14.

26. *FE*, 345; Parsons, "Sightseer in India," 76, 78; *MTCI*, 277–78; Ahluwalia, "Twain's Lecture Tour in India," 9; *MFMT*, 158; Rodney, *Twain Overseas*, 181–82; Mutalik, *Twain in India*, 65–66; *Sioux City Journal*, 11 March 1896, 4.

27. In his edition of *Mark Twain's Notebook*, 272, Paine incorrectly asserts that this Gandhi was "our good Mahatma of later years," a mistake parroted in Hoffman, *Inventing Mark Twain*, 408, and Willis, *Mark and Livy*, 234.

28. *FE*, 369; Mutalik, *Twain in India*, 17; Khan, *Memoirs of the Aga Khan*, 57–58.

29. Cooper, *Around the World with Mark Twain*, 205.

30. Ahluwalia, "Twain's Lecture Tour in India," 10, 12; Parsons, "Sightseer in India," 80; *MFMT*, 155; *MTN*, 275.

31. *MTCI*, 284; Ahluwalia, "Twain's Lecture Tour in India," 12; *FE*, 469–70, 473.

32. *FE*, 197–98, 479, 499, 512; *MTCI*, 284–85.

33. *MTCI*, 287, 310; Philippon, "'Following the Equator' to Its End," 6; Scott, *Twain at Large*, 228.

34. *MTCI*, 286–87.

35. Roosevelt, *History as Literature and Other Essays*, 76–77; *MTCI*, 295; *FE*, 625, 690, 692.

36. Kaplan, *Singular Mark Twain*, 521; *FE*, 517, 522; Zacks, *Chasing the Last Laugh*, 248; Rodney, *Twain Overseas*, 184; Ahluwalia, "Twain's Lecture Tour in India," 13–14.

37. *MTCI*, 289; "Mark Twain at Darjiling," *Englishman's Overland Mail*, 26 February 1896, 8; Cooper, *Around the World with Mark Twain*, 239; *HHR*, 194–95; *FE*, 543.

38. "Mark Twain on Tour," *Englishman's Overland Mail*, 26 February 1896, 6; *FE*, 532, 567; Cooper, *Around the World with Mark Twain*, 241; Ahluwalia, "Twain's Lecture Tour in India," 17; *MTN*, 278.

39. Parsons, "Twain in India," 90–91; *FE*, 569–70; *MTCI*, 350.

40. Ahluwalia, "Letters from Olivia and Clara Clemens," 45, 47; *FE*, 570, 578, 580; *HHR*, 202; *AMT*, 2:81.

41. Olivia Langdon Clemens to Susan Crane, 30 March 1896, *UCCL* 05034; SLC to Franklin G. Whitmore, 12 April 1896, *UCCL* 05039; Zacks, *Chasing the Last Laugh*, 280; Olivia Langdon Clemens to Jean Clemens, 10–12 March 1896, *UCCL* 05030; *HHR*, 212; Cooper, *Around the World with Mark Twain*, 257; "Mark Twain," *Bathurst National Advocate*, 29 May 1896, 2.

42. Kaplan, *Singular Mark Twain*, 524; *MTCI*, 295; *FE*, 290; *HHR*, 210.

43. *HHR*, 210; Parsons, "Clubman in South Africa," 235; *FE*, 620, 623, 630. Sam again invoked the phrase "fish-belly white" to describe a dead body in *Mark Twain's "Which Was the Dream?,"* 232.

44. *MTCI*, 299–300; Parsons, "Traveler in South Africa," 4.

45. *FE*, 644, 648; *HHR*, 212; Parsons, "Traveler in South Africa," 5; Philippon, "'Following the Equator' to Its End," 14–15; Godfrey, "More on Mark Twain," 34–35.

46. Parsons, "Paid Performer in South Africa," 3; SLC to Olivia Langdon Clemens, 16 May 1896; Cooper, *Around the World with Mark Twain*, 273.

47. "Mark Twain's Lecture," *Johannesburg Standard & Diggers News*, 19 May 1896, 5; SLC to Olivia Langdon Clemens, 19 May 1896, *UCCL* 05047; SLC to Olivia Langdon Clemens, 21 May 1896, *UCCL* 05050; Parsons, "Paid Performer in South Africa," 4, 9; "Mark's Way," *Johannesburg Star*, 26 May 1896, 3.

48. *HHR*, 215; *MTCI*, 306, 307, 310, 314–15; Hammond, *Autobiography*, 2:398–400; *FE*, 659; "Twain Likes the Vaal," *Chicago Tribune*, 1 August 1896, 3.

49. Hammond, *A Woman's Part*, 47; *MTCI*, 310; Zacks, *Chasing the Last Laugh*, 291–92; *JHT*, 187.

50. *JHT*, 187; Parsons, "Clubman in South Africa," 246; *MTCI*, 352–64; Hillier, *Raid and Reform*, 86–87; SLC to Olivia Langdon Clemens, 23–24 May 1896, *UCCL* 08652; *HHR*, 215.

51. *Mark Twain to Mrs. Fairbanks,* 205–9; Hillier, *Raid and Reform,* 86–87; Parsons, "Clubman in South Africa," 247; *MTN,* 296; Orcutt, *In Quest of the Perfect Book,* 222.

52. *FE,* 657; *MTCI,* 310, 355; Tenney, "Twain and the Reformers," 50; Hammond, *Autobiography,* 2:398–400; Zacks, *Chasing the Last Laugh,* 294; SLC to Olivia Langdon Clemens, 25 May 1896, *UCCL* 05055; "Note and Comment," *Portland Oregonian,* 17 July 1896, 4.

53. *Pretoria Transvaal Advertiser,* 25 May 1896, 2; SLC to Olivia Langdon Clemens, 23–24 May 1896, *UCCL* 08652; Kaplan, *Singular Mark Twain,* 525; *JHT,* 188; Shillingsburg, *At Home Abroad,* 88; *MTCI,* 198.

54. Philippon, "'Following the Equator' to Its End," 17; Parsons, "Paid Performer in South Africa," 4.

55. Parsons, "Paid Performer in South Africa," 5; "A Notable Impresario," *Johannesburg Times,* 29 May 1896, 5; "Mark Twain's Farewell," *Johannesburg Times,* 29 May 1896, 5; *Johannesburg Standard & Diggers' News,* 29 May 1896, 5; Godfrey, "More on Mark Twain," 42, 44; Bigelow, *Seventy Summers,* 2:165–68.

56. Poultney, *Dawn to Dusk,* 75–76; Godfrey, "More on Mark Twain," 46–47; Parsons, "Paid Performer in South Africa," 6; *HHR,* 216.

57. SLC to Olivia Langdon Clemens, 8 June 1896, *UCCL* 05069; SLC to Olivia Langdon Clemens, 12 June 1896, *UCCL* 05073; Parsons, "Traveler in South Africa," 26; Philippon, "'Following the Equator' to Its End," 21; *MTN,* 300; Smythe, "The Real 'Mark Twain,'" 33.

58. Philippon, "'Following the Equator' to Its End," 22; Parsons, "Paid Performer in South Africa," 7, 9, 10; *HHR,* 227; SLC to Olivia Langdon Clemens, 10 June 1896, *UCCL* 05071; Rodney, *Twain Overseas,* 190.

59. Philippon, "'Following the Equator' to Its End," 23; *FE,* 701–2, 710; *MTN,* 310; *MTCI,* 315; Parsons, "Paid Performer in South Africa," 9, 11; Rodney, *Twain Overseas,* 193; Cooper, *Around the World with Mark Twain,* 302.

60. "Mark Twain," *Melbourne Herald,* 21 August 1896, 2; *FE,* 408; Parsons, "Traveler in South Africa," 40; *MFMT,* 170; Lorch, *Trouble Begins at Eight,* 255. Fatout, *Twain on the Lecture Circuit,* 265, estimates that during the world speaking tour SLC netted a total of \$20,000–\$25,000; both Scott, *Twain at Large,* 223, and Emerson, *The Authentic Mark Twain,* 225, estimate \$30,000; see Philippon, "'Following the Equator' to Its End," 4.

Chapter 6

1. "Twain Likes the Vaal," *Chicago Tribune,* 1 August 1896, 3; SLC to James B. Pond, 10 August 1896, *UCCL* 05239; *MTHL,* 660–61.

2. "Books of the Year," *London Morning Post,* 31 December 1896, 2; SLC to J. Henry Harper, 5 August 1896, *UCCL* 05238; "Fiction," *Scotsman,* 18 May 1896, 3; "Literary Notes," *London Morning Post,* 21 May 1896, 3.

3. *MTCR,* 385, 391–92, 399, 405–7; Le Gallienne, "Wanderings in Bookland," 113; "Recent Novels," *London Times,* 20 August 1896, 8; "Mark Twain's 'Joan of Arc,'" *Chicago Inter Ocean,* 10 September 1896, 9; "The Bookman's Table," *Bookman* (London) 10 (July 1896): 124; "Literary Notes," *London Morning Post,* 7 May 1896, 5; *Gentleman's Magazine* 280 (June 1896): 15; "Novels and Stories," *Glasgow Herald,* 21 May 1896, 10; "Books and Writers," *Dublin Herald,* 20 June 1896, 6.

4. *MTCR,* 404; "Books," *Northern Christian Advocate,* 17 June 1896, 10; *New York Tribune,* 11 July 1896, 8; *Bookman* (New York) 3 (June 1896): iii.

5. "Some New Novels," *London Standard,* 25 June 1896, 3; *MTCR,* 402–3, 406; "Reviews," *Manchester Guardian,* 29 July 1896, 1192; "Reviews," *Pall Mall Gazette,* 19 September 1896,

3; "Current Literature," *Sydney Herald*, 20 June 1896, 4; Harris, *Contemporary Portraits*, 164; Cox, *Mark Twain*, 261n19.

6. Harper, *I Remember*, 140–41; *Harper's Monthly* 93 (July 1896): n.p.; "Joan of Arc," *New York Outlook*, 22 August 1896, 335; *MTCR*, 380, 382, 384, 386, 390–91, 401–2, 406; "Literature," *New York Evening Post*, 18 July 1896, 4; "Literary Notes," *Chicago Inter Ocean*, 30 May 1896, 11; "New Books," *New York Sun*, 4 July 1896, 7, and *New York Sun*, 19 September 1896, 7; "Literary Department," *Colorado Springs Gazette*, 7 June 1896, 10.

7. "About a Great Book," *Emporia Gazette*, 27 June 1896, 2; "Literary Notes," *Philadelphia Times*, 9 May 1896, 8; *New York Tribune*, 10 June 1896, 8; "Among the Books," *Boston Post*, 17 May 1896, 14; "The Literary World," *Boston Advertiser*, 7 May 1896, 5; "New Publications," *Indianapolis Journal*, 25 May 1896, 3; "Current Publications," *Salt Lake Tribune*, 8 June 1896, 4; "New Fiction," *Book Buyer*, 1 June 1896, 300; *New York Sun*, 19 September 1896, 7; "Comment upon New Publications," *Philadelphia Inquirer*, 22 June 1896, 11; "Biography," *Baltimore Sun*, 4 July 1896, 6; Vachel Lindsay, "Mark Twain and Joan of Arc," *Poetry* 10 (July 1917): 175; *MTB*, 1034.

8. *MyMT*, 156; Laurence Hutton, "Literary Notes," *Harper's Monthly* 93 (June 1896): 1–2; *MTCR*, 387–89, 393–94, 397–98; "Art and Letters," *Hartford Courant*, 8 May 1896, 6; "Books of the Hour," *St. Paul Globe*, 21 June 1896, 14; "Books," *Minneapolis Star Tribune*, 12 July 1896, 15.

9. Roth, "Madelon and Joan of Arc," *San Francisco Wave*, 16 May 1896, 10; *Personal Recollections of Joan of Arc*, 237, 290, 360; "Books and Magazines," *Buffalo Courier*, 31 May 1896, 16; *MTCR*, 379, 398–99, 403; "The Maid of Orleans," *Dial*, 16 June 1896, 351–56; "Literature," *Milwaukee Weekly Wisconsin*, 11 July 1896, 4; "Mark Twain's Joan of Arc," *San Francisco Call*, 10 May 1896, 23; J. W. Colby, "The Maid of Orleans," *Nation*, 16 July 1896, 52–53; Julian Hawthorne, "Mark Twain," *Pasadena Star-News*, 30 April 1924, 32; "Brander Matthews' Essays," *San Francisco Call*, 1 November 1896, 23; Basil Wilberforce to SLC, 20 April 1900, *UCLC* 32947; Sarah Bernhardt to SLC, 20 December 1905, *UCLC* 35089; SLC to Hélène Picard, 22 February 1902, *UCCL* 06282.

10. SLC to James B. Pond, 10 August 1896, *UCCL* 05239; Andrews, *Nook Farm*, 219; *MTB*, 1020; SLC to Anna Goodenough, 14 August 1896, *UCCL* 12446; *LLMT*, 317–19; SLC to Olivia Langdon Clemens, 19 August 1896, *UCCL* 05096, 05097; SLC to Mrs. Armstrong, 18 August 1896, *UCCL* 11505.

11. King, *Memories of a Southern Woman*, 201–2; *MTN* 321; SLC to Laurence Hutton, 6 September 1896, *UCCL* 05104.

12. Kaplan, *Singular Mark Twain*, 534; SLC to OC, 14 September 1896, *UCCL* 05110; *AMT*, 1:324; SLC to Olivia Langdon Clemens, 19 August 1896, *UCCL* 05096, 05097; *MTHL*, 663; *JHT*, 190–91.

13. SLC to Olivia Langdon Clemens, 19 August 1896, *UCCL* 05096, 05097; 29–30 August 1896, *UCCL* 05102; *LLMT*, 324–26.

14. *LLMT*, 323; "Mark Twain Arrives," *Los Angeles Herald*, 23 August 1896, 1; *MFMT*, 170–71.

15. *LMT*, 138; *AMT*, 1:325.

16. Max Eastman, "Mark Twain's Elmira," *Harper's Monthly* 176 (May 1938): 620–32; King, *Memories of a Southern Woman*, 201–2; *MTHL*, 663; SLC to Edward Bunce, 16 October 1896, *UCCL* 05131; Olivia Langdon Clemens to MMF, 28 December 1896, *UCCL* 05902.

17. *JHT,* 190; *MTN* 314, 316; *HHR,* 235, 255; SLC to Pamela A. Moffet, 7 January 1897, *UCCL* 05166.

18. *HHR,* 235, 238, 259; "Mark Twain's Lecturing Suspended," *San Francisco Examiner,* 19 October 1896, 6; "Mark Twain at Work," *Baltimore Sun,* 23 September 1896, 7; SLC to J. R. Clemens, 6 May 1897, *UCCL* 08845; "Our London Letter," *Sheffield and Rotherham Independent,* 31 August 1896, 5; "Mark Twain," London *Fun,* 20 October 1896, 152; *LMT,* 146; SLC to Poultney Bigelow, October 1896, *UCCL* 05122; SLC to Pamela A. Moffet, 7 January 1897, *UCCL* 05166; *MFMT,* 179, 184.

19. "The Lounger," *Critic,* 3 August 1895, 79; *MTHL,* 663; *MTN* 362; SLC to Laura McQuiston, 26 March 1901, *UCCL* 08868; *MTB,* 1583.

20. Bigelow, *Seventy Summers,* 2:165–68; Robert M. Rodney, *Twain Overseas,* 205; Gribben, *Twain's Library,* 179, 568; "A Talk with Major Pond," *New York Tribune,* 6 August 1897, 5; Frederic, "A Subject for Mark Twain," *NYT,* 21 March 1897, 17; Frank Marshall White, "Will Lunch with Victoria," 1; Arthur L. Scott, *Twain at Large,* 224; *MFMT,* 178; *MTB,* 1038–39; Henry W. Fisher, *Abroad with Mark Twain and Eugene Field,* 194; *LMT,* 158; Le Bourgeois and Evans, "Twain's Secret Mission," 344–47.

21. *HHR,* 235, 244, 255; *MTB,* 1026; *MTHL,* 664; SLC to Frank Bliss, 19 March 1897, *UCCL* 05187; SLC to Frank Bliss, 26 March 1897, *UCCL* 05191; "South Africa in 1950," *Adelaide Chronicle,* 29 March 1902, 11; SLC to Chatto & Windus, 25 March 1897, *UCCL* 05190; SLC to Frank Fuller, 26 March 1897, *UCCL* 08844; SLC to OC, 28 March 1897, *UCCL* 05194.

22. SLC to Frank Bliss, 3–5 May 1897, *UCCL* 05511; SLC to Frank Bliss, 2 July 1897, *UCCL* 05249; SLC to J. Y. W. MacAlister, 14 April 1897, *UCCL* 05507; *HHR,* 276; Philippon, "'Following the Equator' to Its End," 7.

23. "Mark Twain's New Book," *New Haven Register,* 3 July 1897, 8; *HHR,* 276, 309, 374; *MTHL,* 690; SLC to Lyman Powell, 27 May 1907, *UCCL* 07734; *FE,* 710.

24. *FE,* 191, 216, 623; Messent, "Racial and Colonial Discourse," 76.

25. "Some New Novels," *London Standard,* 30 January 1897, 4; *MTCR,* 411, 415–20; *London Standard,* 18 December 1896, 4; "New Books," *Charleston News and Courier,* 6 December 1896, 5; *Spectator,* 19 July 1897, 89; "Literature," *Sydney Daily Telegraph,* 23 January 1897, 3; "Literature," *Sydney Daily Telegraph,* 23 January 1897, 3; "Current Literature," *Sydney Herald,* 23 January 1897, 4; *Sydney Australian Town and Country Journal,* 16 January 1897, 44.

26. "Danes Claim Mark Twain Stole Plot of 'Tom Sawyer, Detective,'" *Boston Herald,* 6 February 1910, 29.

27. "Men and Matters," *London Globe,* 2 March 1897, 7; SLC to J. R. Clemens, 5 March 1897, *UCCL* 05184; *MTN* 327–28; Frank Marshall White, "Mark Twain Amused," *New York Journal,* 2 June 1897, 1; "A Talk with Major Pond," *New York Tribune,* 6 August 1897, 5; White, "Twain as a Newspaper Reporter," 967; "Mark Twain Is Ill in London," *New York Herald,* 1 June 1897, 9; "For Twain Himself," *New York Herald,* 19 June 1897, 5; SLC to James Gordon Bennett, 19 June 1897, *UCCL* 08637.

28. "Mark Twain's Necessities," *Washington Times,* 16 June 1897, 4; "Personal," *New York Tribune,* 20 June 1897, 6; *Town Topics,* 17 June 1897, 13; Macnaughton, *Twain's Last Years as a Writer,* 22; Zacks, *Chasing the Last Laugh,* 347; "An Insult to Mark Twain," *Life,* 24 June 1897, 534.

29. SLC to Frank Fuller, 2 July 1897, *UCCL* 05248; *HHR,* 282–83; SLC to James Gordon Bennett, 19 June 1897, *UCCL* 08637; SLC to James Gordon Bennett, 24 June 1897, *UCCL*

05232; "Mark Twain Declines Help," *New York Herald*, 27 June 1897, I, 8; "Mark Twain," *Brooklyn Eagle*, 30 June 1897, 6; *Indianapolis News*, 29 June 1897, 4; "Notes," *Chap-Book*, 15 July 1897, 151–52.

30. *HHR*, 286; Budd, *Our Mark Twain*, 131; *HHR*, 286.

31. White, "Twain as a Newspaper Reporter," 966; SLC to J. R. Clemens, 3 June 1897, *UCCL* 05225; J. R. Clemens, "Some Reminiscences of Mark Twain," *Overland Monthly and Out West* 87 (April 1929): 105; "Nethersole Brings Suit," *Boston Globe*, 2 July 1897, 4.

32. SLC to Frank Bliss, 22 April 1899, *UCCL* 05581; "Notes About Books," *New York World*, 18 March 1898, 15; "Literary," *Hartford Courant*, 15 May 1897, 12; "Literature," *Washington Times*, 18 April 1897, 20; "Books and Bookmakers," *San Francisco Call*, 25 April 1897, 23; "Mark Twain as an Essayist," *Brooklyn Eagle*, 18 April 1897, 24; "Current Literature," *Chicago Inter Ocean*, 1 May 1897, 11; Hutton, "Literary Notes," *Harper's Monthly* 95 (June 1897): 2; "Books," *Northern Christian Advocate*, 30 June 1897, 10; "Mark Twain's Essays," *Buffalo Express*, 2 May 1897, 18; "Book Notes," *West Chester (Pa.) Citizen* 3, July 1897, 121; "Some Essayists," *New York Tribune*, 25 July 1897, supplement, 12; *MTCR*, 429–30.

33. White, "Twain as a Newspaper Reporter," 961, 963, 966; "Literary Gossip," *New Haven Register*, 6 September 1897, 6.

34. "Mark Twain on the Jubilee Pageant," *Chicago Tribune*, 20 June 1897, 1; "Mark Twain Writes About the Parade," *Chicago Tribune*, 23 June 1897, 1; *MTB*, 1044; Howard Paul, "London Chat and Gossip," London *American Register*, 10 July 1897, 5.

35. SLC to Francis Skrine, 19 January 1897, *UCCL* 05171; *JHT*, 192; *MTHL*, 664; *MTB*, 1063; Garland, *Roadside Meetings*, 450–53.

36. *JHT*, 197; SLC to Wayne MacVeagh, 27 July 1897, *UCCL* 05272.

37. Susan Crane to Sam Moffett, 22 July 1897, *UCLC* 31202; *LMT*, 122; SLC to Wayne MacVeagh, 27 July 1897, *UCCL* 05272; SLC to Wayne MacVeagh, 22 August 1897, *UCCL* 05280; *JHT*, 197; Pond, *Eccentricities of Genius*, 225; *HHR*, 301.

38. *JHT*, 197–98; *MTN*, 336.

39. *CTSSE*, 217–19; SLC to Henry Alden, 22 August 1897, *UCCL* 13156; *JHT*, 202–3.

40. For differences between the British and American editions, see Welland, "Twain's Last Travel Book," 31–48; and chapter 9 of Welland, *Twain in England*.

41. SLC to Chatto & Windus, 22 July 1897, *UCCL* 05267; SLC to Chatto & Windus, 22–24 July 1897, *UCCL* 08644; SLC to Chatto & Windus, 25 July 1897, *UCCL* 05271; SLC to Wayne MacVeagh, 22 August 1897, *UCCL* 05280.

42. *HHR*, 242, 290, 303.

43. *Huck Finn and Tom Sawyer among the Indians*, 289; "A Substitute for Rulloff," *New York Tribune*, 3 May 1871, 2; "Literary Notes," *Baltimore Sun*, 8 January 1903, 8; *Wellington Journal*, 14 February 1903, 2.

44. *HHR*, 291, 294, 296–98, 300, 374; "F. Marion Crawford," *Vancouver World*, 13 April 1898, 4; SLC to James B. Pond, 17 September 1897, *UCCL* 05289; SLC to James B. Pond, 15 March 1898, *UCCL* 05488.

45. Pond, "Anecdotal Side of Mark Twain," 5–6; *HHR*, 370, 379; SLC to James B. Pond, 14 September 1900, *UCCL* 08205.

46. Dolmetsch, *"Our Famous Guest,"* 23. SLC never repented for his blasphemy. As late as 21–23 February 1910, two months before his death, he denounced "that odious Church [of Rome], whose history would disgrace hell & whose birth was the profoundest calamity which

has ever befallen the human race except for the birth of Christ" (SLC to Clara Clemens, 21–23 February 1910, *UCCL* 08561.

47. SLC to J. R. Clemens, 21 October 1897, *UCCL* 05299; *HHR*, 360; *MFMT*, 190.

Chapter 7

1. Dolmetsch, "Twain and the Viennese Anti-Semites," 13; *MTB*, 1049; Dolmetsch, *"Our Famous Guest,"* 32; SLC to J. Henry Harper, 13 October 1897, *UCCL* 11352.

2. "Live Topics of Today," *Chicago Tribune*, 22 December 1896, 6; Dolmetsch, "Twain and the Viennese Anti-Semites," 14; Vogel, *Twain's Jews*, 55.

3. "Journey to an Asterisk" (DV 203); *AMT*, 1:420; *Innocents Abroad*, 269; Kahn, "Twain's Philosemitism," 18–19; SLC to Charles E. S. Wood, 22 January 1885, *UCCL* 11487; Gribben, *Twain's Library*, 796; "Literary Notes and News," *Westminster Budget*, 27 November 1896, 22; "Literary Notes and News," *Westminster Gazette*, 23 November 1896, 3; *Mark Twain's Fables of Man*, 279–82; Dolmetsch, "Twain and the Viennese Anti-Semites," 14; *JHT*, 201; *Man That Corrupted Hadleyburg*, 278.

4. Dolmetsch, "Twain and the Viennese Anti-Semites," 17; Dolmetsch, *"Our Famous Guest,"* 62, 64, 163; *JHT*, 201.

5. Dolmetsch, *"Our Famous Guest,"* 41, 46; Dolmetsch, "Twain and the Viennese Anti-Semites," 16; "Mark Twain Banqueted in Vienna," *Kansas City Star*, 3 November 1897, 6; Hemminghaus, "Twain's German Provenience," 465; "Mark Twain on the Horrors of German," *San Francisco Examiner*, 21 November 1897, 13.

6. *MTN*, 340, 341, 356; *London Standard*, 9 February 1911, 5; Dolmetsch, *"Our Famous Guest,"* 135, 182; Dolmetsch, "Austria," in LeMaster and Wilson, *Mark Twain Encyclopedia*, 50; Austilat, *Tramp in Berlin*, 126; SLC to Chauncey Depew, 2 February 1899, *UCCL* 05541; "Mark Twain in Vienna," *Canterbury Press* (New Zealand), 3 January 1899, 6.

7. Dolmetsch, *"Our Famous Guest,"* 133; *MTHL*, 696; "Hungarian Countess Returns to Stage," *San Francisco Call*, 8 October 1905, 28; *MTN*, 342; *AMT*, 3:275.

8. *MFMT*, 193; *LMT*, 164–65; Kaplan, *Singular Mark Twain*, 558; Fisher, *Abroad with Mark Twain and Eugene Field*, 110; Rodney, *Twain Overseas*, 213; Benson, "Twain's Contacts with Scandinavia," 159–67; Paderewski and Lawton, *Paderewski Memoirs*, 205; Hambourg, *From Piano to Forte*, 98–99; "Music," *Sydney Daily Telegraph*, 3 February 1900, 6.

9. Gabrilowitsch, "Memoir of Leschetizky," 132; *LMT*, 163; Clemens, *My Husband, Gabrilowitsch*, 1; Dolmetsch, *"Our Famous Guest,"* 145; Hapgood, *Victorian in the Modern World*, 146.

10. *AMT*, 2:27; SLC to Mollie Clemens, 11 December 1897.

11. *Man That Corrupted Hadleyburg*, 144, 244; *MFMT*, 130; SLC to Chatto, 19 November 1897; *HHR*, 305.

12. SLC to Chatto & Windus, 19 November 1897; SLC to J. Henry Harper, 8 February 1898, *UCCL* 05245; "Zola and Dreyfus," *New York Herald*, 30 January 1898; *Europe and Elsewhere*, 223; SLC to Chatto & Windus, 8 February 1898, *UCCL* 05346; SLC to Simon Wolf, 15 September 1899, *UCCL* 05677; *Man That Corrupted Hadleyburg*, 170.

13. Dolmetsch, *"Our Famous Guest,"* 184–85, 189; SLC to Walter Besant, 8 April 1898, *UCCL* 03817; SLC to Bertha von Suttner, 17 February 1898, *UCCL* 05351; SLC to Cornelius Cole, 17 May 1898, *UCCL* 05390; *MTB*, 1063; SLC to Theodore Stanton, 26 May 1898, *UCCL* 05395; *Kansas City Star*, 21 June 1898, 4.

14. SLC to Chatto & Windus, 13 May 1898, *UCCL* 05388; *JHT*, 219; Pond, *Eccentricities of Genius*, 228; *MTCI*, 353; "Mark Twain Discusses Spain's Alleged Cruelties," *Chicago Tribune*, 21 June 1898, 2; *MTB*, 1064; "Personal," *New York Tribune*, 4 November 1898, 6; SLC to Mrs. Keenan, 3 November 1899, *UCCL* 12886.

15. *Mark Twain's Letters* (1917), 672; "In Equivalents of Waterloo Men," *War against War*, 20 January 1899, 21.

16. SLC to John Hay, 4 May 1899; SLC to Eduard Pötzl, 26 May 1899, *UCCL* 12360; SLC to Nikola Tesla, 17 November 1898, *UCCL* 05471; *MFMT*, 264; "Mark Twain 'Converted,'" *London Daily News*, 20 October 1898, 5; *JHT*, 239.

17. SLC to William J. Lampton, March 1901, *UCCL* 06011; *Europe and Elsewhere*, 221; *JHT*, 259; *MTCI*, 353; *CTSSE*, 469; *MTCI*, 592; SLC to Laurence Hutton, 3 December 1900, *UCCL* 05925.

18. *CTSSE*, 466; Kinzer, *True Flag*, 215; "On American Imperialism," 49–51; *AMT*, 1:404.

19. Kinzer, *True Flag*, 225.

20. *MTHL*, 844; *AMT*, 2:142. See also Frank Doubleday: "I thought that the whole thing was a crazy piece of business and urged him to forget it, but he thought it the best thing he had ever written. . . . It was, I always thought, a poor thing, and I think so yet." *Memoirs of a Publisher*, 87–88.

21. Jones, "Determinism of *What Is Man?*," 3; *JHT*, 279; *MTHL*, 689; *MFMT*, 208; Hill, *God's Fool*, 41–42.

22. *What Is Man?* (1973), 128; *HHR*, 348; SLC to Carl Thalbitzer, 26 November 1902, *UCCL* 11438; Hill, *God's Fool*, 134.

23. Bird, "Twain and Robert Ingersoll Connection," 47; Gribben, *Twain's Library*, 344; "Ingersoll on 'Mark Twain,'" *Kansas City Star*, 21 June 1897, 5; SLC to Eva Farrell, 12 November 1899, *UCCL* 05706; *MyMT*, 31.

24. IVLD, 2 October 1906; Tuckey, *Mark Twain and Little Satan*, 37; Ozick, "Twain and the Jews," 56–62. SLC borrows the word *pandemonium*, which he invokes to describe the town meeting, from Milton's *Paradise Lost*. See Scharnhorst, "Paradise Revisited," 59–64.

25. "Fresh Literary Notes," *Chicago Tribune*, 18 July 1898, 8; Messent, "Carnival," 218. These pieces are "From the 'London Times' of 1904," "My First Lie and How I Got Out of It," "Concerning the Jews," and "My Boyhood Dreams."

26. *HHR*, 383.

27. "The Humor of Mark Twain," *London Literary World*, 21 September 1900, 192–93; "New Novels," *Manchester Guardian*, 3 October 1900, 3; "Book Reviews," *Public Opinion*, 2 August 1900, 152; "Recent Fiction," *American Monthly Review of Reviews* 22 (October 1900): 505; "A Study in Human Nature," *Baltimore Sun*, 28 July 1900, 6; "Our Book Table," *Zion's Herald*, 22 August 1900, 1076; "Reviews," *Salisbury and Winchester Journal*, 23 December 1899, 3; *MTCR*, 485–87, 500, 502, 504–6, 508–11; F. D. Power, *St. Louis Christian Evangelist*, 21 March 1901, 14.

28. Dolmetsch, *"Our Famous Guest,"* 64, 70; *Man That Corrupted Hadleyburg*, 293.

29. *Man That Corrupted Hadleyburg*, 294; Dolmetsch, *"Our Famous Guest,"* 50.

30. *MTHL*, 672–74; "Notes of the Magazines," *Washington National Tribune*, 10 March 1898, 5; "Mark Twain," *Lexington Herald*, 27 February 1898, 10; "As Mark Twain Saw History," *Springfield Republican*, 4 March 1898, 10; *Man That Corrupted Hadleyburg*, 292, 316.

31. "Frequent Insult," *Boston Journal*, 6 November 1897, 4; *Boston Journal*, 8 November 1897, 4; "Coffee Houses in Vienna," *NYT*, 30 October 1898, 7; Grünzweig, "Comanches in the Austrian Parliament," 5.

32. Dolmetsch, *"Our Famous Guest,"* 71, 75–76; *MTCI*, 352; Kaplan, *Singular Mark Twain*, 563; *Man That Corrupted Hadleyburg*, 333.

33. "Historical Drama," *Boston Globe*, 29 November 1897, 14; *St. Louis Republic*, 28 November 1897, 6; *JHT*, 208; "Mark Twain Assaulted," *Boston Journal*, 27 November 1897, 1; *HHR*, 308, 344; *Man That Corrupted Hadleyburg*, 340; Olivia Langdon Clemens to Sam Moffett, 6 January 1898, *UCCL* 05331.

34. SLC to Chatto & Windus, 16 March 1899, *UCCL* 05564; *HHR*, 390; "The 'Austrian Parliamentary System'?," 59–61.

35. "Out of the Woods," *Boston Journal*, 23 October 1897, 10; "Twain's Debts Paid," *New Haven Journal-Courier*, 23 October 1897, 3; "Mark Twain Out of Debt," *Hartford Courant*, 23 October 1897, 5; "Personal," *New York Tribune*, 2 November 1897, 6; "Mark Twain Deeply in Debt," *Boston Journal*, 6 November 1897, 7; SLC to Frank Bliss, 4 November 1897, *UCCL* 05307; *HHR*, 310, 316; "'Mark Twain' Paying Debts," *New York Tribune*, 18 December 1897, 10.

36. SLC to F. G. Whitmore, 5 May 1898, *UCCL* 05382; SLC to F. G. Whitmore, 9 July 1898, *UCCL* 05410; *HHR*, 462.

37. SLC to Frank Bliss, 4 November 1897, *UCCL* 05307 and *UCCL* 05309; SLC to Frank Bliss, 28 August 1898, *UCCL* 05424; "Mark Twain's Book," *New York Tribune*, 11 October 1897, 3; Scharnhorst, "Had Their Mothers Only Known"; "Mark Twain's New Book," *San Francisco Call*, 24 October 1897, 23; "Mark Twain," *Idaho Statesman*, 18 October 1897, 2; *Dalles (Ore.) Chronicle*, 10 November 1897, 2; "Mark Twain's Last Book," *New York Herald*, 10 October 1897, sec. 5, 6. Justin Kaplan reports that in October 1897, "a month before *Following the Equator* was published, the *Herald* ran a full-page advance review which included, without permission, about 6000 words of quotation as well as six pictures." Kaplan, *Mr. Clemens and Mark Twain*, 349. Bliss obviously authorized the early publication of these excerpts to publicize the book.

38. SLC to R. W. Gilder, 13 January 1898, *UCCL* 05167; SLC to Frank Bliss, 10 December 1898, *UCCL* 05478.

39. *MTCR*, 463, 464, 469, 473, 476, 479; "Twain's Book," *New York Tribune*, 8 February 1898, 8; "Current Literature," *Chicago Inter Ocean*, 11 December 1897, 10; "Mark Twain as a Globe-Trotter," *Literary Digest*, 22 January 1898, 115; "Mark Twain's New Book," *Buffalo News*, 9 January 1898, 4; "New Books," *Nebraska State Journal*, 10 January 1898, 8; "Some New Books," *Dallas Morning News*, 31 January 1898, 4; "Mark Twain and the Equator," *Topeka American Bimetallist*, 3 December 1897, 1; "Literary Notes," *Harper's Monthly* 96 (January 1898): 3–4; SLC to Laurence Hutton, 20 February 1898, *UCCL* 05352.

40. Unfortunately, the travelogue has not stood well the test of time; Van Wyck Brooks called it "drab and weary journalism," Bernard DeVoto "the dullest of [Clemens's] books," Henry Nash Smith "merely a travel diary," Kenneth Lynn "a sorry affair," Louis Budd "not a happy or great book," and Richard Bridgman "a flat and uninspired work." See DeVoto, *Twain at Work*, 143; Budd, *Twain: Social Philosopher*, 168; and Philippon, "'Following the Equator' to Its End," 6.

41. "New Books," *New York Sun*, 11 December 1897, 7; *HHR*, 311; "Mark Twain's New Book," *New Haven Register*, 26 November 1897, 6; "Books and Bookmakers," *Louisville Courier-Journal*, 18 December 1897, 7; *MTCR*, 466, 478, 481; "A Corner for Books," *Minneapolis Star Tribune*, 23 January 1898, 17; "Books and Their Makers," *Los Angeles Herald*, 3 April 1898, 22; "Mark Twain's New Book," *Rockford (Ill.) Star*, 2 November 1897, 2; "Mark Twain's Newest Book," *Omaha Bee*, 20 January 1898, 9; "A New Book by Mark Twain," *Cottonwood*

Falls News-Courant, 2 December 1897, 3; "Mark Twain's Latest," *San Francisco Call*, 16 January 1898, 22; "New Literature," *Boston Globe*, 31 December 1897, 8; Charles de Kay, "Mark Twain's Mixed Pickles," *New York Times Book Review*, 15 January 1898, 40.

42. *MTCR*, 467, 469–70, 474, 476–78, 480; *Munsey's* 19 (April 1898): 148; "Books of the Weeks," *Chicago Tribune*, 18 December 1897, 10; "Mark Twain's 'Following the Equator,'" *Hartford Courant*, 1 December 1897, 8; "Mark Twain's New Book," *Washington National Tribune*, 2 December 1897, 3; "Mark Twain's Latest," *Burlington (Vt.) Free Press*, 16 November 1897, 5; "Current Publications," *Salt Lake Tribune*, 29 November 1897, 4 ; "Following the Equator," *Arkansas Gazette*, 9 January 1898, 4; "Following the Equator," *Augusta Chronicle*, 14 February 1898, 4; "Mark Twain," *Lexington Herald*, 27 February 1898, 10; "Mark Twain's New Book," *Vancouver Province*, 26 March 1898, 371; "Our Book Table," *Christian Observer*, 22 June 1898, 3; "Publications Received," *Rio de Janeiro News*, 17 May 1898, 8; *HHR*, 306; Foner, *Twain: Social Critic*, 245; *MTHL*, 707, 816; *MyMT*, 184.

43. *MTCR*, 438–43, 445–58, 456–57; "Mark Twain on the British Empire," *St. James's Gazette*, 6 January 1898, 5; "Mark Twain's *More Tramps Abroad*," *Review of Reviews* (London) 17 (January 1898): 79–82.

44. "Mark Twain on Australia," *Brisbane Courier*, 3 January 1898, 6; "Mark Twain on Australia," *Melbourne Age*, 1 January 1898, 5; "Mark Twain on Australia," *Wagga Wagga Express*, 22 January 1898, 2; "Our Numerous Critics," *Coolgardie Miner*, 11 January 1898, 8; Shillingsburg, *At Home Abroad: Mark Twain in Australasia*, 227; "Review," *Wellington Post*, 15 January 1898, 10; "Literary Gossip," *Clare's Weekly*, 5 February 1898, 20; "Mark Twain on South Australia," *Adelaide Weekly Herald*, 22 January 1898, 11.

45. *MTCR*, 438, 443–45, 450–55, 457–59; "The Bookman's Table," *Bookman* (London) 13 (February 1898): 164; "Mark Twain's New Book," *Auckland Star*, 31 December 1897, supplement, 1; "Mark Twain's New Book," *Sydney Herald*, 1 January 1898, 5; "More Tramps Abroad," *Westminster Budget*, 4 February 1898, 22; "Books of the Day," *London Morning Post*, 2 December 1897, 2; "Day by Day," *Sydney Australian Star*, 11 February 1898, 4; "More Tramps Abroad," *Westminster Gazette*, 24 January 1898, 3; "Mark Twain's Latest," *London Globe*, 1 December 1897, 4; "More Tramps Abroad," *Otago Witness*, 27 January 1898, 52; "Mark Twain on Australia," *Sydney Daily Telegraph*, 29 December 1897, 9.

46. *MTCR*, 435, 439–40, 448–49, 453–55; "Gift Books," *Manchester Guardian*, 22 December 1897, 22; "Literature," *Colonies and India*, 18 December 1897, 21; *London Standard*, 5 January 1898, 6; Shillingsburg, *At Home Abroad*, 227; *London Standard*, 8 December 1897, 8; *Manchester Guardian*, 26 January 1898, 32; "The Booksellers' Books of the Week," *Booksellers' Review*, 2 December 1897, 4; "Mark Twain on Australia," *Perth Daily News*, 22 January 1898, 2; "Reviews," *Pall Mall Gazette*, 1 December 1897, 9; "More Tramps Abroad," *Truth*, 9 December 1897, 52; "Travellers' Tales," *London Graphic*, 8 January 1898, 25; *HHR*, 309; "Literary Chit-Chat," *Adelaide Critic*, 15 January 1898, 7; "Mark Twain on Australia," *Melbourne Australasian*, 15 January 1898, 49; "As Others See Us," *Chiltern Leader*, 15 February 1898, 3.

47. "To Help Mark Twain Out of Debt," *Kansas City Journal*, 27 March 1897, 1; "Literary," *New Haven Register*, 10 February 1898, 10; *Buffalo Commercial*, 29 December 1897, 7; Welland, *Twain in England*, 182; *AMT*, 2:80.

48. *HHR*, 307, 310, 312, 315–21, 349.

49. *HHR*, 191, 206, 223; "Mark Twain's Noble Achievement," *Pall Mall Gazette*, 1 March 1898, 8; *Boston Globe*, 5 March 1898, 12.

50. *HHR*, 300, 384, 389, 408–9; *MTHL*, 684; Gribben, "Twain, Business Man," 24–43; *MTCI*, 331–32.

51. *Publishers' Weekly*, 19 February 1898, 376; "Mark Twain and Messrs. Webster's Debts," *London Times*, 1 March 1898, 5; SLC to J. Y. W. MacAlister, 12 March 1898, *UCCL* 05362; "Mark Twain's Debts as Paid," *New York Times Saturday Review of Books*, 12 March 1898, 169; "Tributes to Mark Twain," *North American Review* 191 (June 1910): 827; Carnegie, *Autobiography*, 296; *MyMT*, 55; Vorpahl, "'Very Much Like a Fire-Cracker,'" 88; MacGrath, "Twain," *Buffalo Enquirer*, 6 December 1900, 5; *MTCI*, 355; "Tribunes to Mark Twain," *North American Review* 191 (June 1910): 833; "Local and General," *Feilding Star*, 23 August 1907, 2.

52. *New Haven Register*, 19 January 1898, 6; "Russian Sculptress," *New York Tribune*, 20 August 1900, 7; Dolmetsch, *"Our Famous Guest,"* 69, 87, 97–100, 112–14, 270; "Mark Twain in Vienna," *New York Tribune*, 7 November 1897, 8; *Man That Corrupted Hadleyburg*, 250; "Miss Hallock's Success Abroad," *Philadelphia Inquirer*, 12 December 1897, 14; "Men of Note," *Los Angeles Times*, 23 January 1898, 14; *LMT*, 165; Kaplan, *Singular Mark Twain*, 557; "Things in Vaudeville," *New York Sun*, 13 December 1897, 5; "Personal," *New York Tribune*, 23 December 1897, 6.

53. *MTHL*, 670; White, "Twain as a Newspaper Reporter," 966–67; Macnaughton, *Twain's Last Years as a Writer*, 78; *HHR*, 318, 324, 326, 358; "Mark Twain Writes a Comedy," *New Haven Register*, 3 February 1898, 3; Klaw & Erlanger to Alf Hayman, 2 February 1899, *UCLC* 46219.

54. E. C. Martin, "Outlook for Literature," *Omaha Bee*, 24 April 1898, 14; "Stage Whispers," *Westminster Budget*, 6 May 1898, 14; "Things at the Theater," *New York Sun*, 21 March 1898, 2; *HHR*, 333, 345, 353; Schirer, *Twain and the Theatre*, 94–106; "Literary Notes," *Philadelphia Times*, 4 June 1898, 7; Hemminghaus, "Twain's German Provenience," 466.

55. "Shackleford's Ghost" (DV 318); "Literature," *Washington Times*, 29 May 1898, 16; "Frawley to the Rescue," *San Francisco Call*, 12 June 1898, 29; "Mark Twain as Playwright," *NYT*, 21 October 1900, 11; "At the Theater," *Los Angeles Herald*, 28 October 1900, 13; "Dollar Theatre Seats Soon," *New York Tribune*, 28 December 1903, 12.

56. *Man That Corrupted Hadleyburg*, 235–51; *MTHL*, 685–86n7.

57. Schönemann, "Twain and Adolf Wilbrandt," 372–74; *AMT*, 1:204; *Man That Corrupted Hadleyburg*, 254; *Mysterious Stranger Manuscripts* , 35–36, 55; *Mark Twain on Potholes and Politics*, 162.

58. "Personal Points," *Cleveland Plain Dealer*, 21 February 1898, 4; *HHR*, 318; Lederer, "Twain in Vienna," 6; *MTSpk*, 665; "Twain Lectures in Vienna," *Chicago Tribune*, 2 February 1898, 2; *AMT*, 1:118–19; *London Times*, 3 February 1898, 6; Vogel, *Twain's Jews*, 58–59; "Chips," *Middlesbrough North-Eastern Gazette*, 4 February 1898, 4; *JHT*, 212.

59. *MTB*, 1057; *HHR*, 308, 332, 337, 343; Balicer, "Szczepanik's 'Portrait' of Mark Twain," 968; SLC to R. W. Gilder, 2 April 1898, *UCCL* 05373; *MTN*, 358.

60. *HHR*, 342, 344; *New York Sun*, 12 June 1898, 2.

61. *NYT*, 9 February 1903, 14; *MTCI*, 369–70; *MyMT*, 82; van Onselen, *Cowboy Capitalist*, 361; *HHR*, 439, 436; Hill, *God's Fool*, 10.

62. *Man That Corrupted Hadleyburg*, 148–49; *HHR*, 318, 344, 346; SLC to Heinrich Obersteiner, 5 October 1897, *UCCL* 05294; Dolmetsch, *"Our Famous Guest,"* 222; SLC to Mollie Clemens, 16 May 1898, *UCCL* 11916.

63. *Who Is Mark Twain?*, 61; *JHT*, 254; "Home from Europe," *Hartford Courant*, 13 August 1898, 3; Olivia Langdon Clemens to Mary Cheney, 7 October 1898, *UCCL* 05445; Dolmetsch, *"Our Famous Guest,"* 147; *Man That Corrupted Hadleyburg*, 153.

64. "Fourth of July in Berlin," *NYT*, 24 July 1898, 15.

65. *MFMT,* 204; *Man That Corrupted Hadleyburg,* 252–83; Phipps, *Twain's Religion,* 192; Vogel, "Concerning Mark Twain's Jews," 155; *HHR,* 354; Vogel, *Twain's Jews,* 82.

66. Jordan Lesslie, *Our Misunderstanding Concerning the Jews* (New York: Cooke, 1908), 11; Mayer S. Levy, "A Rabbi's Reply to Mark Twain," *Overland Monthly* 34 (October 1899): 364–67; *American Israelite,* 1 August 1901, P4; "Speaks for the Jews," *Richmond Dispatch,* 23 September 1899, 1; Cyrus L. Sulzberger, "Mark Twain Writes His Chapter," *American Hebrew,* 6 October 1899, 549–50; Foner, *Twain: Social Critic,* 225–36; Vogel, *Twain's Jews,* 84; "A Friendly Critic," *Jewish World,* 29 September 1899, 12; "Concerning the Jews," *Indianapolis Journal,* 6 September 1899, 4; Kravitz, "Philo-Semitism as Anti-Semitism ," 1–12; Richmond, "Freud's 'Comment on Anti-Semitism,'" 563–74; Frank Bliss to SLC, 15 September 1899, *UCLC* 46275; "Magazines," *Chicago Advance,* 21 September 1899, 375; *Jewish Herald,* "Our Home Letter," 13 October 1899, 3; "Mark Twain and the Jews," *Southern Cross,* 1 December 1899, 6.

67. *MTHL,* 676; *CTSSE,* 248, 252, 258.

68. *MTN,* 365; *Mark Twain's "Which Was the Dream?,"* 104; DeVoto, *Twain at Work,* 122.

69. *HHR,* 335, 352, 358, 360–61; *MTHL,* 676, 685; Dolmetsch, *"Our Famous Guest,"* 104; *New York Tribune,* 22 April 1899, 5.

70. Dolmetsch, *"Our Famous Guest,"* 81–82; *JHT,* 221; Olivia Langdon Clemens to Susan Crane, 11 September 1898, *UCCL* 12842; *HHR,* 363; *What Is Man?* (1917), 170.

71. SLC to Chatto & Windus, 13 November 1898, *UCCL* 01289; *Mammoth Cod,* 11; Welland, *Twain in England,* 196.

72. *Mysterious Stranger Manuscripts,* 428–29; SLC to Frank Finlay, 25 April 1900, *UCCL* 05799; *MTHL,* 698–99.

73. Lorch, *Trouble Begins at Eight,* 268; Pond, *Eccentricities of Genius,* 226; Dolmetsch, *"Our Famous Guest,"* 118; "Mark Twain's New Word," *Kansas City Star,* 14 April 1899, 13; "Gossip from Abroad," *Baltimore Sun,* 18 April 1899, 6; "Mark Twain in Vienna," *Melbourne Age,* 22 April 1899, 4.

74. SLC to Frank Bliss, 31 March–2 April 1899, *UCCL* 05571; SLC to Laurence Hutton, 12 March 1899, *UCCL* 05561; Katona, "Interview with Mark Twain," 73–81; *MTB,* 1078; Scott, *Twain at Large,* 238; Katona, "Twain's Reception in Hungary," 113–14; *MTHL,* 690; SLC to James B. Pond, 4 April 1899, *UCCL* 05603; Dolmetsch, *"Our Famous Guest,"* 57; *MTSpk,* 319–20; *JHT,* 236; "Mark Twain at Buda-Pesth," *Chicago Tribune,* 26 March 1899, A1.

75. IVLD, 9 October 1907; Dolmetsch, *"Our Famous Guest,"* 155–56; William J. Tucker, "Minister Tower's Dinner," *Philadelphia Times,* 26 November 1898, 7; *Louisville Courier-Journal,* 12 March 1899, 22; "Tower's Farewell Dinner," *Philadelphia Times,* 4 March 1899, 7. See also Brunet, *Nellie and Charlie,* 78.

76. SLC to Charles Dudley Warner, 15 February 1899, *UCCL* 05546; Dolmetsch, *"Our Famous Guest,"* 156; "American Representation in Vienna" (DV 237).

77. Dolmetsch, *"Our Famous Guest,"* 214, 301; *MTCI,* 332; *JHT,* 239; *LMT,* 162.

78. IVLD, 9 October 1907; Dolmetsch, *"Our Famous Guest,"* 306–9; Lederer, "Twain in Vienna," 8–9; "Mark Twain Is Decidedly Rattled," *San Francisco Call,* 26 May 1899, 2; *MTB,* 1079; "Compliment to Mark Twain," *Omaha Bee,* 28 May 1899, 1.

79. *MFMT,* 214.

Chapter 8

1. "Mark Twain in Prague," *Topeka State Journal,* 31 May 1899, 4; Clemens, *Gardens and Books,* 212; *HHR,* 398–99.

2. *MTSpk*, 323, 666; Katherine Clemens, *Gardens and Books*, 212; Lillie Planner to SLC, 12 June 1899, *UCLC* 46265; *MTHL* 700, 710.

3. Stoker, *Personal Reminiscences*, 166. SLC championed William S. Gilbert, who composed the librettos of such light operas as *Pinafore* and *The Pirates of Penzance*. He "seems to me a perfectly delightful and exquisite humorist. How perfectly charming is the lambent play of his fancy! and when I read his operas I am struck dumb with astonishment. It seems to me marvelous that a man should have this gift of saying not only the funniest things, but of saying them in verse!" *MTCI*, 205.

4. "Dinner to Mark Twain," *NYT*, 17 June 1899, 6; "Mark Twain Dined at White Friars Club," *San Francisco Call*, 17 June 1899, 2; "Mark Twain at the Whitefriars Club," *London Standard*, 17 June 1899, 5; "Dinner Given to Mark Twain," *Boston Herald*, 17 June 1899, 2; "On Motoring," *London Morning Post*, 13 April 1906, 3.

5. "The News of Two Capitals," *New York Tribune*, 18 June 1899, 2; "War Rumors are Thick in London," *Philadelphia Times*, 25 June 1899, 11; "'Mark Twain' at Lambeth Palace," *London Morning Post*, 23 June 1899, 6; *MTSpk*, 334; "Six Senators Meet in London," *New York Sun*, 29 June 1899, 2; "This Morning's News," *London Daily News*, 16 June 1899, 5; "Senator Hanna Talks Politics in London," *Brooklyn Eagle*, 2 July 1899, 1; "At U.S. Embassy," *Boston Globe*, 5 July 1899, 13; Budd, "Twain Sounds Off," 276–77.

6. SLC to Wayne MacVeagh, 20 April 1899, *UCCL* 12035; "Vienna Politics Worse Than Ours," *New York Sun*, 20 May 1899, 1; Hill, *God's Fool*, 7; Bigelow, *Seventy Summers*, 2:167; SLC to R. W. Gilder, 22 August 1899, *UCCL* 05663; SLC to John Brisben Walker, 30 July 1899, *UCCL* 05658; *HHR*, 400, 402–7, 430, 433; SLC to Sam Moffett, 15 September 1899, *UCCL* 05674; *JHT*, 245; Cyriax, *Kellgren's Manual Treatment*, 396.

7. SLC to Edmund Gosse, 6 July 1899, *UCCL* 05651; SLC to William James, 23 April 1900, *UCCL* 05796; *JHT*, 245–46; SLC to Sam Moffett, 15 September 1899, *UCCL* 05674; *HHR*, 408–9.

8. SLC to Sam Moffett, 15 September 1899, *UCCL* 05674; Lystra, *Dangerous Intimacy*, 50; *HHR*, 490; SLC to Susan Crane, 22 December 1899, *UCCL* 05723; SLC to Mollie Clemens, 18 May 1900, *UCCL* 11225; Jean Clemens diary, 26 September 1906.

9. SLC to Laurence Hutton, 13 July 1899, *UCCL* 05654; SLC to Willard Fiske, 15 July 1899, *UCCL* 11373; SLC to R. W. Gilder, 23 July 1899, *UCCL* 05657; Benson, "Twain's Contacts with Scandinavia," 163; Anderson, "Twain in Sweden," 87–88.

10. SLC to John Brisben Walker, 30 July 1899, *UCCL* 05658; SLC to Andrew Chatto, 24 September 1899, *UCCL* 05620; SLC to Sam Moffett, 15 September 1899, *UCCL* 05674; *JHT*, 246; SLC to William James, 17 April 1900, *UCCL* 05792. Kellgren treated him for "piles" or hemorrhoids with digital "vibrations." "No physician has ever helped my semi-annual itching piles with even a moment's relief. . . . These manipulations here relieved it promptly every day for a week." *HHR*, 406.

11. Anderson, "Twain in Sweden," 85; *HHR*, 426; *JHT*, 258; SLC to William James, 17 April 1900, *UCCL* 05792; "The Case of Sir Henry M. Stanley" and "Postscript—Osteopathy" (DV13); *MTB*, 1087.

12. SLC to Susan Crane, 22 December 1899, *UCCL* 05723; SLC to Susan Crane, 8 February 1900, *UCCL* 05758; *JHT*, 258.

13. *HHR*, 404, 412; SLC to Douglas B. Sladen, 30 October 1899, *UCCL* 09108; SLC to Frank Bliss, 27 February 1899, *UCCL* 05552; SLC to R. W. Gilder, 23 July 1899, *UCCL* 05657; *JHT*, 245, 247, 250.

14. *What Is Man?* (1973), 661; Macnaughton, *Twain's Last Years as a Writer,* 118; "Magazine Mention," *Omaha Bee,* 12 October 1899, 7; "Literary Notices," *Hampshire Advertiser,* 21 October 1899, 7; *MTB,* 1068; "Christian Science: Has It a Future?" *T. P.'s Weekly,* 9 January 1903, 274; "Abjures Judaism," *Fort Wayne Sentinel,* 10 February 1900, 13; Wertheimer, *Why I Left Christian Science.*

15. SLC to E. E. Hale, 1 November 1899, *UCCL* 05698; *JHT,* 240; "The Chatterer," *Boston Herald,* 29 December 1899, 6; "Would-Be Murderess, Fraud, Charlatan," *Santa Cruz Evening News,* 1 September 1909, 5.

16. *MTHL,* 698; *Mysterious Stranger Manuscripts,* 79; SLC to R. W. Gilder, 22 August 1899, *UCCL* 05663; *Mark Twain's "Which Was the Dream?,"* 278.

17. SLC to James B. Pond, 26 September 1899, *UCCL* 05622; SLC to Laurence Hutton, 18 September 1899, *UCCL* 05679; SLC financial file for 1899, *MTP*; "Mark Twain at Berlin," *Sacramento Union,* 1 October 1899, 12; *HHR,* 412, 430, 448.

18. *HHR,* 414, 443; *JHT,* 257; SLC to Susan Crane, 22 December 1899, *UCCL* 05723; SLC to Pamela A. Moffet, 25 April 1900, *UCCL* 05800; *MTB,* 1088.

19. SLC to Sam Moffett, 23 April 1900, *UCCL* 05797; SLC to Sam Moffett, 17–19 May 1900, *UCCL* 05807; SLC to Sam Moffett, 1 July 1900, *UCCL* 05830.

20. *HHR,* 123–25, 424; SLC to Poultney Bigelow, 19 December 1898, *UCCL* 05481; Olivia Langdon Clemens to Grace King, ca. spring 1900, *UCCL* 05728.

21. *HHR,* 427, 431–32, 442, 444, 449; SLC to S. S. McClure, 1 February 1900, *UCCL* 08735; *AMT,* 2:197.

22. *HHR,* 446, 448; "Mark Twain Settled in England," *Kansas City Star,* 29 July 1900, 5; *AMT,* 2:449; *MTN,* 373; *JHT,* 269; Baetzhold, *Twain and John Bull,* 111; SLC to J. R. Clemens, 25 July 1900, *UCCL* 12864; Burdette, *Robert J. Burdette,* 427–28; W. H. Helm, "Mornings with Mark Twain," *London Daily News,* 22 April 1910, 4; W. H. Helm, *Memories* (London: Richards, 1937), 77–79.

23. "'Mark Twain' Returns to America," *Pall Mall Gazette,* 6 October 1900, 8; *Chicago Tribune,* 2 November 1900, 7; *JHT,* 263–64; *Manchester Guardian,* 16 March 1900, 5; Gribben, *Twain's Library,* 325; *London Standard,* 6 July 1900, 4; "Our London Letter," *Sheffield and Rotherham Independent,* 17 March 1900, 7; SLC to J. Y. W. MacAlister, 24 March 1900, *UCCL* 09426; "From Our London Correspondent," *Leeds Mercury,* 10 July 1900, 4; "London Day by Day," *London Telegraph & Courier,* 27 June 1900, 10; L. H. Moore, "For a New Nation," *Washington Star,* 30 May 1900, 13; "Mark Twain on Copyright," *Brooklyn Eagle,* 4 April 1900, 3; "Perpetual Copyright," *New York Tribune,* 21 April 1900, 8; "Mark Twain Tilts at Copyright Wrong," *Brooklyn Eagle,* 23 April 1904, 11; Chapin, *Their Trackless Way,* 184–85; Henry Lucy, "London Letter," *Gloucester Journal,* 7 February 1903, 5; Henry Lucy, "Mark Twain," *Bathurst Argus,* 13 February 1909, 3.

24. "Royal Literary Fund," *London Daily News,* 3 May 1900, 2; *MTSpk,* 337; "Twain for President," *Salt Lake Herald,* 17 May 1900, 4; "Howe, Vice President," *Topeka State Journal,* 8 May 1900, 1.

25. "Choate and Mark Twain," *St. Louis Republic,* 10 June 1900, 6; Max Eliot, "Chats About Folks," *Boston Herald,* 24 June 1900, 14; "Editorial Points," *Boston Globe,* 13 June 1900, 20; "Tribunes to Mark Twain," *Overland Monthly* 87 (April 1929): 123; *MTSpk,* 338; I. N. F[ord], "News of Two Capitals," *New York Tribune,* 17 June 1900, 2; "London's Rapid Transit," *Chicago Tribune,* 28 June 1900, 3; "England," *Cleveland Plain Dealer,* 27 August 1900, 4.

26. SLC to Frank Bliss, 2 February 1899, *UCCL* 05539; *MTCR*, 491, 504–5.

27. "Mark the Evergreen," *Pall Mall Gazette*, 5 October 1900, 9; "Recent Fiction," *American Monthly Review of Reviews* 22 (October 1900): 505; *MTCR*, 485, 487–90, 492, 497–98, 503–5; "Fiction in a Variety of Forms," *Cleveland Plain Dealer*, 1 July 1900, 20; "Notes about New Books," *New York Observer and Chronicle*, 5 July 1900, 29; "Book Reviews," *Public Opinion*, 2 August 1900, 152; "Mark Twain's Latest Book," *Washington Times*, 24 June 1900, II, 8; "Literature," *Christian Advocate*, 26 July 1900, 1221; "New Books," *Minneapolis Star Tribune*, 5 August 1900, 20; "In the Literary World," *Detroit Free Press*, 23 June 1900, 11; "Mark Twain's Stories," *Buffalo Express*, 1 July 1900, 22; "Stories and Sketches by Mark Twain," *Review of Reviews* (London) 22 (September 1900): 398; "Mark Twain's New Volume," *London Globe*, 17 September 1900, 6; "More Mark Twainisms," *London Evening News*, 17 September 1900, 1; "Our London Letter," *Belfast News-Letter*, 18 September 1900, 6.

28. *MTCR*, 485–86, 490–91, 506, 508–11; "New Books," New York *Sun*, 16 June 1900, 7; "Mark Twain's New Stories," *Brooklyn Life*, 28 July 1900, 8; "Books of the Week," *New York Outlook*, 30 June 1900, 510; "New Novels," *Manchester Guardian*, 3 October 1900, 3; "Fiction," *Literature*, 29 September 1900, 238–39; "Literature," *Melbourne Arena*, 10 November 1900, 12; "Mark Twain's Latest," *Hampshire Telegraph and Naval Chronicle*, 1 September 1900, 11; "Current Literature," *Sydney Herald*, 3 November 1900, 4; "Mark Twain's Joan of Arc," *Literary Digest*, 5 September 1896, 603; "Twain Humor Rot!" *Buffalo Enquirer*, 27 October 1908, 7.

29. *Who Is Mark Twain?*, 103; *JHT*, 267–69; "Twain's with the Boxers," *New York Sun*, 24 November 1900, 2; *MTSpk*, 361–62; *MTCI*, 350.

30. SLC to H. F. Gordon Forbes, 15 September 1899, *UCCL* 05673; *MTHL*, 715–17; *JHT*, 260, 263; *Who Is Mark Twain?*, 59; *MFMT*, 216.

31. *MTB*, 1105; *JHT*, 267; *St. Louis Post-Dispatch*, 4 October 1900, 16; *HHR*, 445.

32. SLC to Pamela A. Moffett, 25 April 1900, *UCCL* 05800; *MyMT*, 76; *MTHL*, 692, 689; *JHT*, 257, 271, 285.

33. *MTCI*, 336; SLC to Richard Watson Gilder, 31 July 1900, *UCCL* 05841; *Mysterious Stranger Manuscripts*, 112, 136–37.

34. *HHR*, 433; SLC to Andrew Still, 23 February 1900, *UCCL* 05762; *JHT*, 269; Still, *Mechanical Principles of Osteopathy*, 199, 304.

35. *HHR*, 430; Woodall, *Manual of Osteopathic Gynecology*, 36; Clark, *Diseases of Women*, 325, 349; "Epilepsy and Retroversion of Uterus," *Osteopathic Physician* 11 (April 1907): 14; Maines, *Technology of Orgasm*, 12; Jean Clemens to Isabel V. Lyon, 27 October 1908, *UCCL* 08147; Jean Clemens diary, 16 November 1900.

36. "Mark Twain Is Coming Home," *Chicago Tribune*, 28 September 1900, 2; "'Mark Twain' at Kensal Rise," *London Daily News*, 28 September 1900, 6; *AMT*, 3:73; *MTB*, 1382; *Mark Twain's Letters* (1917), 700; "Mark Twain at the Whitefriars Club," *Westminster Gazette*, 6 October 1900, 4.

37. *AMT*, 2:81; "Mark Twain Goes Home," *London Daily Mail*, 6 October 1900, 3.

38. Emerson, *Twain: A Literary Life*, 219; *HHR*, 244, 361; SLC to J. Henry Harper, 30 August 1898, *UCCL* 05429.

39. *HHR*, 362, 373, 517; SLC to J. Y. W. MacAlister, 27 August 1901, *UCCL* 06121; SLC to American Publishing Company, 10 June 1903, *UCCL* 10877; "Mark Twain," *Hartford Courant*, 1 May 1899, 8; "Mark Twain's Next Book," *Brooklyn Eagle*, 29 May 1899, 4.

40. *New York Sun*, 16 June 1901, 27; *HHR*, 472, 526.

Chapter 9

1. *MTCI*, 350–51, 353.

2. Messent, *Short Works*, 254; George Harvey to H. H. Rogers, 17 October 1900, *UCLC* 40084; SLC to John Y. W. MacAlister, 6 September 1902, *UCCL* 06427; "Bloodgood Cutter Bursts into Rhyme," *Brooklyn Eagle*, 25 November 1900, 31; S. E. Kiser, "Mark Twain," *Honolulu Republican*, 11 November 1900, 2; *MTCI*, 355–56, 369.

3. *LMT*, 194; "Mark Twain Closes Bazaar," *New York Tribune*, 18 October 1900, 6.

4. "'Mark Twain' Mourns Death of Mr. Warner," *Chicago Tribune*, 22 October 1900, 4; "City Personals," *Hartford Courant*, 24 October 1900, 3; "Funeral of Mr. Warner," *New York Tribune*, 24 October 1900, 8; *Mark Twain's Letters* (1917), 701; *AMT*, 3:315.

5. SLC to John Y. W. MacAlister, 27 October 1900, *UCCL* 05887; SLC to John Y. W. MacAlister, 31 December 1900, *UCCL* 05943; "A Talk by Mark Twain," *New York Tribune*, 28 October 1900, 23; "Twain at the Lotos Club," *New York Sun*, 11 November 1900, 4; "Mark Twain Has Fun with Lotos Club," *Philadelphia Inquirer*, 12 November 1900, 1; "Mark Twain at the Lotos," *New York Tribune*, 11 November 1900, 4; W. D. Howells to T. B. Aldrich, 4 November 1900, *UCLC* 43529.

6. "Mark Twain at the Press Club," *New York Sun*, 13 November 1900, 7; "Mark Twain with the Authors," *New York Sun*, 16 November 1900, 1; *MTCI*, 376.

7. *LMT*, 196–99; "Mark Twain at the City Hall," *Brooklyn Eagle*, 21 November 1900, 18.

8. *Man That Corrupted Hadleyburg*, 349; "It Pays to Kick," *Boston Globe*, 20 May 1895, 5; *MTB*, 1125; Charles Edgerton Carpenter, "Mark Twain in Vienna," *Louisville Courier-Journal*, 12 March 1899, 22.

9. "Mark Twain, Reformer, Calls Cabman Pirate," *New York Evening World*, 22 November 1900, 1; "Mark Twain Easy," *Boston Globe*, 29 November 1900, 9; *MTB*, 1125; *Springfield Republican*, 2 December 1900, 8; "An Act of Plain Justice," *Brooklyn Eagle*, 23 November 1900, 4; "Mark Twain, American Citizen," *New York Evening Post*, 26 November 1900, 6.

10. Clemens, *My Husband, Gabrilowitsch*, 115; "Mark Twain Forgives," *Boston Globe*, 29 November 1900, 8; "Mark Twain Ill," *St. Louis Republic*, 30 November 1900, 6; "A Cabman's Estimate of Twain," *New York Tribune*, 2 May 1901, 5; "The Master," *Cleveland Plain Dealer*, 5 December 1900, 4; "Editorial Suggestions," *Boston Advertiser*, 4 December 1900, 4.

11. "Mark Twain on Schools," *New York Tribune*, 24 November 1900, 7; "Aldine Entertains Mark Twain," *New York Tribune*, 5 December 1900, 9; "Mark Twain at the Aldine Club," *New York Times Saturday Review*, 15 December 1900, 916; Ellsworth, *Golden Age of Authors*, 243–4; *Boston Globe*, 6 December 1900, 6.

12. "Twain Tweaked Them," *New York Sun*, 7 December 1900, 2; "Twain's Satire on City," *New York Tribune*, 7 December 1900, 1; *San Francisco Call*, 16 December 1900, 30.

13. *Chicago Tribune*, 2 November 1900, 7; Churchill, *My Early Life*, 360–62; "Twain Introduces Churchill," *New York Sun*, 13 December 1900, 3; *MTSpk*, 367–69; "Winston Churchill's Lecture," *Brooklyn Eagle*, 13 December 1900, 4; "Mr. Churchill's Lecture," *New York Tribune*, 13 December 1900, 9; *New York Evening Post*, 13 December 1900, 8; *Detroit Free Press*, 14 December 1900, 4.

14. "Miss Clemens' Debut," *Philadelphia Times*, 23 January 1901, 1; "Amusements," *Washington Star*, 23 January 1901, 12; "Music and the Drama," *Chicago Tribune*, 23 January 1901, 7; Olivia Langdon Clemens to Grace King, 15–24 February 1901, *UCCL* 05999.

15. *CTSSE*, 456; Gibson, "Twain and Howells," 451; SLC to Abner C. Goodell, 31 December 1900, *UCCL* 05942; SLC to John Y. W. MacAlister, 31 December 1900, *UCCL* 05943.

16. "Croker Sought Peace," *New York Sun*, 5 January 1901, 1–2; "City Club Discusses Municipal Misrule," *Brooklyn Eagle*, 5 January 1901, 5; *Twain's Weapons of Satire*, 67.

17. *MTCI*, 389; "Topics of the Times," *NYT*, 7 January 1901, 6; "City Club's Banquet," *Boston Herald*, 5 January 1901, 4; "Kept His Ballot 'Clean,'" *Washington Times*, 5 January 1901, 1; SLC to George Gates, 21 January 1901, *UCCL* 05969; Conway, "Mark Twain, Literature, and War," *NYT*, 11 January 1901, 8; *New York Evening Post*, 7 January 1901, 6; Jerome, Wisbey, and Snedecor, *Twain in Elmira*, 206–7; *MTB*, 1165.

18. SLC to Edward Ordway, 13 January 1901, *UCCL* 06982; "Erving Winslow Petitions," *New York Sun*, 5 February 1902, 6; "For Suspension of Hostilities," *Springfield Republican*, 5 February 1902, 7; *Twain's Weapons of Satire*, xxiv; Zwick, " 'Prodigally Endowed with Sympathy,'" 8.

19. *CTSSE*, 457–73; *JHT*, 277.

20. Foner, *Twain: Social Critic*, 279; "Meet Peace Envoys Today," *New York Sun*, 24 December 1900, 1; "Loot and Indemnity in China," *NYT*, 26 January 1901, 8; *MTB*, 1129.

21. *JHT*, 277–78; *Twain's Weapons of Satire*, 18; O. O. Howard to SLC, 2 February 1901, *UCLC* 33139.

22. *JHT*, 278–79; Foner, *Twain: Social Critic*, 269.

23. Olivia Langdon Clemens to Grace King, 15 February 1901, *UCCL* 05999; Hill, *God's Fool*, 25–26; "Certainly False, But Probably Funny," *NYT*, 7 February 1901, 8; "Mark Twain May Cheer Up," *Washington Post*, 10 February 1901, 16.

24. Powers, *Twain: A Life*, 605; "A Humorist Astray," *Boston Journal*, 12 February 1901, 4; *Duluth News Tribune*, 25 February 1901, 4; "Errancy of Mark Twain," *Portland Oregonian*, 13 February 1901, 3; "Note and Comment," *Springfield Republican*, 15 February 1901, 6; "The Matter with Mark Twain," *Hartford Courant*, 16 February 1901, 14; "Mark Twain's 'Person,'" *Hartford Courant*, 11 February 1901, 10; "Mark Twain's Apology," *Des Moines News*, 2 April 1901, 4; " 'Loot' Once More," *Independent*, 18 July 1901, 1690–91; "China's Responsibility," *Portland Oregonian*, 9 March 1901, 3; "Mark Twain on His Country," *Brooklyn Eagle*, 2 February 1901, 4; *St. James's Gazette*, 25 February 1901, 12; *Aberdeen Press and Journal*, 3 April 1901, 6; "The Literary Lounger," *London Sketch*, 10 April 1901, 18; "Mark Twain as a Moralist," *Chicago Advance*, 11 April 1901, 505; *Yorkshire Post and Leeds Intelligencer*, 19 February 1901, 4; *Westminster Budget*, 1 March 1901, 14; "Mark Twain on the Blessings of Civilisation," *Wellington Evening Post*, 4 May 1901, supplement, 2; "Mark Twain's Latest," *Norwich Mercury*, 23 February 1901, 4; "To a Person Sitting in Darkness," *New York Outlook*, 16 February 1901, 387; "Fair Play for China Missionaries," *Congregationalist*, 16 February 1901, 245; "Mark Twain as Moral Poseur," *Zion's Herald*, 3 April 1901, 424.

25. "Is the Philippine Policy of the Administration Just? Yes," *Harper's Weekly*, 9 February 1901, 155; Poultney Bigelow to SLC, 19 February 1901, *UCLC* 33189.

26. "Mark Twain Getting Serious," *Baltimore Sun*, 4 February 1901, 4; "Periodical Literature," *Baltimore Sun*, 14 February 1901, 8; "An Ex-Humorist," *Syracuse Post-Standard*, 9 February 1901, 4; "Current Literature," *Buffalo Courier*, 10 February 1901, 11; "Turned on M'Kinley," *Boston Herald*, 2 February 1901, 5; *Boston Literary World*, 1 March 1901, 46; "Clemens Was on the Move," *Boston Post*, 18 January 1901, 2; "Political," *New York Evening Post*, 8 February 1901, 6; " 'Treason' from Mark Twain," *Boston Globe*, 9 February 1901, 6; *Springfield Republican*, 3 February 1901, 8; "The Blessings of Civilization," *New Orleans Times-Democrat*, 23 April 1901, 4; *Review of Reviews* (London) 23 (March 1901): 254–56; "Mark Twain, Preacher and Satirist," *City and State*, 7 February 1901, 90–91; "Mark Twain on M'Kinley," *New York Evening Post*, 2 February 1901, 6; Watterson, "Mark Twain, Reformer," *Louisville*

Courier-Journal, 1 April 1901, 4; "Mark Twain on Missionaries," New York *People*, 29 April 1901, 1; *Life*, 7 March 1901, 184; Howells, *Life in Letters*, 142; "Mark Twain on M'Kinley," *Nation*, 7 February 1891, 104–5; *MTB*, 1133; Kolb, *Gift of Humor*, 312; Zwick, "'Prodigally Endowed with Sympathy,'" 7.

27. E. L. Godkin to SLC, 22 March 1901, *UCLC* 33231; Adams, *Letters*, 326–27; "Current Topics," *Sheffield Telegraph*, 5 April 1901, 4; "Adam's Diary," *Review of Reviews* (London) 23 (March 1901): 379; "Literary Notes," *Paisley & Renfrewshire Gazette*, 20 April 1901, 2; "American Magazines of the Month," *London Daily News*, 9 April 1901, 6; "Calls Christian Scientists Cheats," *New York Tribune*, 13 June 1901, 14.

28. Erving Winslow to Herbert Welsh, 12 February 1901, *UCLC* 50323; "Mark Twain Must Apologize," *Detroit Free Press*, 16 April 1901, 5; "Score Belgians and Mark Twain," *San Francisco Call*, 15 October 1901, 11; "Letter to Mr. Clemens," *Hartford Courant*, 12 February 1901, 8; "Mark Twain Says Not I," *New York Tribune*, 15 February 1901, 3; *JHT*, 281; SLC to Henry Chamberlain, 20 February 1901, *UCCL* 10662.

29. *Boston Globe*, 20 February 1901, 9; "Dr. Ament in Fighting Mood," *Boston Post*, 2 June 1901, 10; William Scott Ament, "Mark Twain's Criticism Is Not Justified," *Success* 4 (July 1901): 896; *Europe and Elsewhere*, 278–80; Porter, *William Scott Ament*, 236; "Editorial Points," *Boston Globe*, 22 February 1901, 6; "An Apology Due from Mr. Clemens," *Colorado Springs Gazette*, 9 March 1901, 4; "Dr. Ament's Vindication," *Zion's Herald*, 15 May 1901, 630; SLC to Judson Smith, 10 March 1901, *UCCL* 06018; SLC to Rudolf Lindau, 24 April 1901, *UCCL* 06042; *MTSpk*, 394; SLC to Edward Ordway, 4 January 1903, *UCCL* 12871; *JHT*, 408.

30. *HHR*, 478–79, 560; Tarbell, *All in the Day's Work*, 10, 211–12; Tarbell, *Standard Oil Company*, 2:110, 2:225.

31. "Favors Forest Park Site," *Brooklyn Eagle*, 28 February 1901, 5; SLC to Andrew Biggs, 11 January 1905, *UCCL* 06981; *MTSpk*, 385; "Topics of the Times," *NYT*, 28 February 1901, 8; *MTN*, 344.

32. "Twain Arises Ire of Preachers," *San Francisco Call*, 22 March 1901, 2; *Europe and Elsewhere*, 289; "Mark Twain's 'Apology,'" *New York Tribune*, 30 March 1901, 5; "The North American Review," *Sheffield Telegraph*, 24 April 1901, 3.

33. "The Missionaries Defended," *NYT*, 25 April 1901, 2; "Missionaries Did No Looting," *New York Tribune*, 27 April 1901, 7; "Mark Twain and the Missionaries," *Modern Culture* 1 (July 1901): 401–2; "The Charges against the Missionaries," *Independent*, 9 May 1901, 1051; "Missionaries Not Guilty of Looting Houses," *San Francisco Call*, 26 April 1901, 1; "'Loot' Once More," *Independent*, 18 July 1901, 1690–91; "He Won't Sue Mark Twain," *Detroit Free Press*, 2 May 1901, 7; "Ament at Y.M.C.A.," *Chicago Tribune*, 14 May 1901, 4; *JHT*, 281.

34. Washington Gladden to SLC, 22 February 1901, *UCLC* 33194; "Dr. Burrell Attacks Yonkers Jury," *New York Tribune*, 17 June 1901, 2; "Mark Twain Criticised," *Brooklyn Eagle*, 29 April 1901, 13; "Mark Twain and the Devil," *NYT*, 6 June 1901, 1; "Mission Work in China," *Brooklyn Eagle*, 30 April 1901, 12; Sheldon, "The Use and Abuse of Fiction," *Independent*, 24 April 1902, 966; "Priest Attacks Mark Twain," *St. Louis Post-Dispatch*, 15 November 1903, 10; "Ministers Attack Twain," *New York Sun*, 23 April 1901, 2; "Twain's Retort to Dr. Spaulding," *New York Sun*, 29 April 1901, 1; "Religious Comment," *Brooklyn Eagle*, 4 May 1901, 4.

35. *Iowa City Press-Citizen*, 9 April 1901, 2; Chapin, "A Mark Twain Convert," *New York Tribune*, 8 April 1901, 3; "Why, Why, Bishop Potter!" *Boston Globe*, 20 June 1901, 6.

36. SLC to Charles E. S. Wood, 24 June 1901, *UCCL* 06079; Walter H. Larom, "Mark Twain in the Adirondacks," *Bookman* (New York) 58 (January 1924): 538; "Ampersand, N.Y.," *Brooklyn Eagle*, 21 July 1901, 32; *AMT*, 2:82; Alexander, "Writer in Residence," 18.

37. "Mark Twain's Latest Speech," *Hartford Courant*, 8 August 1901, 10; SLC to Olivia Langdon Clemens, 3 August 1901, *UCLC* 06106; "The Provinces," *Worcester Spy*, 19 August 1901, 7; "Mark Twain in Town," *Charleston News and Courier*, 6 April 1902, 16; "Mark Twain Fleeced," *Elmira Star-Gazette*, 17 August 1901, 1; "Stories of Thomas B. Reed," *NYT*, 13 December 1902, 10; *HHR*, 467–68; "Lost, One 97-Cent Umbrella," *New York Sun*, 24 September 1901, 24; Rice, "Twain as His Physician Knew Him," 48; *JHT*, 285; "Mark Twain at the Race," *New York Sun*, 4 October 1901, 3.

38. *MTCI*, 394–98. SLC echoed the comment in his story: "the Extraordinary Man who had filled the world with the fame of his more than human ingenuities." *Man That Corrupted Hadleyburg and Other Essays and Stories*, 333–34. Doyle refers to Holmes as an "extraordinary man" in "The Adventure of the Cardboard Box" (1893).

39. Jean Clemens diary, 10 November 1900; *JHT*, 287–88.

40. "Notes," *New York Evening Post*, 8 February 1902, 19; "Along Literary Pathways," *New Orleans Times-Democrat*, 29 December 1901, 20; "Among the Magazines," *Minneapolis Star Tribune*, 29 December 1901, 19; "The February Magazines," *Richmond Times*, 2 February 1902, 13.

41. "Books and Authors," *New York Sun*, 26 March 1902, 7; *MTCR*, 517–18, 522–23; "Satirical Humour," *New Zealand Mail*, 3 September 1902, 30; "About Books," *Lyttelton Times*, 6 September 1902, 3; "Books and Bookmen," *Sydney World's News*, 9 August 1902, 31.

42. "Harper's for January," *Brooklyn Eagle*, 27 December 1901, 10; *MTCR*, 515–21, 523–25; "Magazine Notes," *Hartford Courant*, 9 January 1902, 10; "On the Book Table," *Hartford Courant*, 3 May 1902, 18; "Fiction," *Baltimore Sun*, 1 May 1902, 8; "A Double-Barrelled Detective Story," *Brooklyn Life*, 19 April 1902, 10; "Books of the Week," *New York Outlook*, 10 May 1902, 133; "A Terrible Story," *London Daily News*, 3 July 1902, 8; "Novels of the Day," *London Standard*, 23 July 1902, 4; "Letters on Books," *Truth*, 3 July 1902, 47; "Rapid Reviews," *St. James's Gazette*, 30 June 1902, 18; "Book Gossip," *Yorkshire Post and Leeds Intelligencer*, 2 July 1902, 4; "Some Fiction of Minor Importance," *Chicago Tribune*, 17 May 1902, 20; *Buffalo Commercial*, 26 April 1902, 9; "Mark Twain's Book," *Buffalo Review*, 8 May 1902, 4; "A Half Dozen New Books," *Dayton News*, 26 April 1902, 21; "Tragedy and Farce," *New York Tribune*, 12 April 1902, 10; "Mark Twain's New Story," *San Francisco Chronicle*, 8 June 1902, 4; "New Books," *Brooklyn Standard Union*, 7 June 1902, 4; "Notes on Novels," *Chicago Dial*, 1 June 1902, 390; "Both Triggers at Once," *Springfield Republican*, 27 July 1902, 19; "Recent Publications," *New Orleans Picayune*, 11 May 1902, 20; "Mark Twain's Latest Effort," *Grand Rapids Press*, 17 May 1902, 13; "Mark Twain's 'Double-Barrelled Detective Story," *Philadelphia Times*, 3 May 1902, 19; "Sherlock Holmes in Burlesque," *Boston Advertiser*, 17 April 1902, 8; "Fiction," *Sydney Daily Telegraph*, 9 August 1902, 16; "Mark Twain's Story Called 'Literary Junk,'" *New York American*, 24 April 1907, 1; *San Francisco Call*, 12 May 1907, 52.

43. *HHR*, 470; *JHT*, 287, 289.

44. *JHT*, 289–91.

45. Scott, *Poetry of Mark Twain*, 129–31; *Boston Globe*, 19 September 1901, 1; *JHT*, 370.

46. SLC to Rose Hawthorne Lathrop, 19 October 1901, *UCCL* 06161; *JHT*, 294.

47. *MTHL*, 732; *LLMT*, 330–31; "Mark Twain at the Hyperion," *New Haven Journal and Courier*, 23 October 1901, 1; *AMT*, 3:257; Matthews, "Memories of Mark Twain," 81; "Were

Given Degrees," *New Haven Journal and Courier*, 24 October 1901, 12; Kaplan, *Mr. Clemens and Mark Twain*, 364; *Hartford Courant*, 23 October 1901, 2.

48. *AMT*, 3:257; SLC to Miss Meyer, 25 October 1901, *UCCL* 10476; Chapin, *Their Trackless Way*, 216–17; *MTB*, 1144.

49. SLC's note: "Manila the Government has placed a certain industry [prostitution] under the protection of our flag."

50. *CTSSE*, 1006; *Mark Twain's Fables of Man*, 403–19; "The Yale Birthday," *Hartford Courant*, 23 October 1901, 1.

51. SLC to Frank Bliss, 29 August 1901, *UCCL* 06126; SLC to Frank Bliss, 8 September 1901, *UCCL* 06131; Oggel, "Speaking Out about Race," 124. Foner in *Twain: Social Critic* observes that "unfortunately, the book [on the history of lynching] was never finished" (221), though Foner fails to note the reason—that SLC feared the loss of his Southern audience.

52. Clemens, *My Husband, Gabrilowitsch*, 14; SLC to Frank Bliss, 26 August 1901, *UCCL* 06119; Oggel, "Speaking Out about Race," 119–20; *Europe and Elsewhere*, 249; "The Mississippi Lynchings," *Chicago Tribune*, 3 August 1901, 12; *CTSSE*, 479–86; *JHT*, 281.

53. *Twain's Weapons of Satire*, 95, 106; *AMT*, 1:93.

Chapter 10

1. *AMT*, 1:603, 2:262; SLC to Olivia Langdon Clemens, 2 August 1901, *UCCL* 06105; SLC to John Y. W. MacAlister, 27 August 1901, *UCCL* 06121; SLC to Muriel Pears, 4 December 1901, *UCCL* 06182; "Novelist Howells Visits His Old Home," *St. Louis Republic*, 30 March 1902, 9; Hill, *God's Fool*, 36; Ade, *One Afternoon with Mark Twain*, 5–13; *MyMT*, 83; *HHR*, 465; "Mark Twain and Burglars," *Duluth News-Tribune*, 17 November 1901, 2.

2. *JHT*, 279; "Mark Twain to Women," *New York Tribune*, 21 January 1901, 7; Cooley, *Twain's Aquarium*, 242; Lystra, *Dangerous Intimacy*, 301; "New Plays for a New Year," *New York Sun*, 28 December 1902, sec. 3, 7; "Mark Twain Read to Them," *Brooklyn Eagle*, 12 May 1901, 28; *MTCI*, 401, 405, 410; "Mark Twain Is in It," *Boston Herald*, 18 October 1901, 3; *MTSpk*, 404; *MTB*, 1145; Scott, *Twain at Large*, 263; "Low Will Construe Laws in a Broad, Liberal Way," *Brooklyn Eagle*, 29 October 1901, 1.

3. "Final Slogan from Jerome," *New York Sun*, 5 November 1901, 2; "Humorous Side of American Public Life," *Baltimore Sun*, 11 November 1901, 4; Macnaughton, *Twain's Last Years as a Writer*, 142, 175; "The 'Acorns' Hold an Election Jubilee," *NYT*, 7 November 1901, 3.

4. *MTSpk* 421; "Explained by Carnegie," *New York Tribune*, 17 November 1901, 3; "Dinner to Dr. Ettinger," *Brooklyn Eagle*, 24 November 1901, 45; *MTHL*, 735; *CTSSE*, 512–23; *AMT*, 2:314.

5. Luscher, "Italian Accounts of Mark Twain," 220; *AMT*, 3:183, 3:189; SLC to Andrew Carnegie, 6 February 1901, *UCCL* 05990; Orcutt, *In Quest of the Perfect Book*, 174–75; Matthews, *Tocsin of Revolt*, 271–72.

6. SLC to T. B. Aldrich, 30 December 1901, *UCCL* 06199; "Yale Alumni," *Hartford Courant*, 1 February 1902, 2; SLC to Laurence Hutton, 20 December 1902, *UCCL* 06523; SLC to William Winter, 8 December 1901, *UCCL* 06185; SLC to James B. Pond, 30 October 1902, *UCCL* 06476.

7. "Says There's Room at the Top," *New York Tribune*, 29 January 1902, 16; Budd, *Twain: Social Philosopher*, 195; *AMT*, 3:96.

8. SLC to Olivia Langdon Clemens, 14 March 1902, *UCCL* 06300; SLC to Olivia Langdon Clemens, 21 March 1902, *UCCL* 06308; SLC to Olivia Langdon Clemens, 22 March 1902,

UCCL 06310; SLC to Olivia Langdon Clemens, 24 March 1902, *UCCL* 06311; SLC to Olivia Langdon Clemens, 29 March 1902, *UCCL* 06313; *LLMT*, 336–37; Reckford, "Mark Twain in South Florida," 2–3; *MTSpk* 455; *Mammoth Cod*, 19; "With a Lavish Hand," *Washington Star*, 10 December 1904, 9; "Great Days in Charleston," *Winston-Salem Journal*, 13 April 1902, 5; "Mark Twain in Town," *Charleston News and Courier*, 6 April 1902, 16; "Mark Twain Calls with Thomas B. Reed," *Columbia (S.C.) State*, 6 April 1902, 9; Leon, "Mark Twain at the Charleston Exposition," 4–7; "Mark Twain at Old Point," *New York Evening World*, 7 April 1902, 8; *Brooklyn Eagle*, 13 April 1902, 14; *HHR*, 485.

9. *Twain's Weapons of Satire*, 113. Funston has been widely quoted in histories of the Philippine-American War as declaring, "All Americans who had recently petitioned Congress to sue for peace in the Philippines should be dragged out of their homes and lynched." I have been unable to locate a reliable original source for this assertion and comparable quotations from the speech. The earliest source I have located is Miller, *Benevolent Assimilation*, 234–35, where the passage is attributed to a transcript of the speech in the *New York Sun* ("Bravo! Gen. Funston," 10 March 1902, 4–5). But the passage nowhere appears in this transcription. Another version of the passage appeared in the *San Francisco Call*: "It would have been more an act of justice had we hanged people who signed the recent petition to Congress asking that we confer with the Philippine leaders in an effort to secure peace." "Funston Advises Hanging," *San Francisco Call* 12 March 1902, 1.

10. "Gen. Funston at Lotos Club," *New York Sun*, 9 March 1902, 1.

11. *HHR*, 484; *London Morning Post*, 16 May 1902, 9; *Twain's Weapons of Satire*, 119–32.

12. *Emporia Republican*, 8 May 1902, 4; "Mark Twain Wrong," *Leavenworth Times*, 18 May 1902, 2; *Chanute Sun*, 13 May 1902, 2; "Mark Twain on Fred Funston," *Wichita Eagle*, 19 May 1902, 4; "War Is Not a 'Social Function,'" *Topeka Capital*, 16 May 1902, 4; "Is Mark Twain Joking?" *Topeka Capital*, 21 May 1902, 3; "A Literary Freak," *Topeka Capital*, 25 May 1902; *Topeka Capital*, 28 May 1902, 5, and 30 May 1902, 4; "Mark and Fred," *Nebraska State Journal*, 23 May 1902, 6; "Honor the Army and Navy," *Rochester Democrat and Chronicle*, 4 May 1902, 6; "Mistaking Their Vocations," *Chicago Tribune*, 8 May 1902, 4; "A Call Upon Mark Twain," *Wilmington (Del.) News*, 23 June 1906, 9; "Funston and Mark Twain," *Duluth News-Tribune*, 13 May 1902, 4; *Buffalo Courier*, 6 May 1902, 4; "Mark Twain on Funston," *Kansas City Gazette*, 10 May 1902, 2; *St. Joseph (Mo.) News-Press*, 3 May 1902, 4; "The Philippine Infamy," *Columbia (S.C.) Sunday State*, 5 May 1902, 4; "Twain on Funston," *Charlotte Observer*, 11 May 1902, 12; "A Defence of Funston," *Houston Post*, 7 May 1902, 4.

13. "Mark Twain Hutton's Guest," *Philadelphia Times*, 21 April 1902, 3; "Princeton," *Worcester Spy*, 13 May 1901, 7; Keller, *Midstream*, 48–49; Zwick, " 'Prodigally Endowed with Sympathy,'" 10; *Twain's Weapons of Satire*, 115; "Mark Twain Would Reform the World," *Philadelphia North American*, 10 May 1901, 3; *JHT*, 304.

14. Helen Keller to Olivia Langdon Clemens, 5 April 1903, *UCLC* 33750; Chambliss, "Helen Keller and Mark Twain," 307–8; *AMT*, 2:279; Keller, *Midstream*, 47.

15. SLC to Hélène Picard, 22 February 1902, *UCCL* 06282.

16. *AMT*, 2:647–48; *CTSSE*, 550–53.

17. SLC to Richard Jesse, 14–19 April 1902, *UCCL* 06322; *MTCI*, 423, 436.

18. *Brooklyn Eagle*, 30 May 1902, 11; *MTCI*, 424, 427, 429, 464; *LLMT*, 337–38.

19. *MTB*, 1167–68; *MTCI*, 436.

20. *MTCI*, 439, 441; Sorrentino, "Twain's 1902 Trip to Missouri," 28.

21. *MTCI*, 436, 438, 441; *MTB*, 1167; "Mark Twain's Way of Distributing Diplomas," *St. Louis Post-Dispatch*, 31 May 1902, 1; *St. Louis Post-Dispatch*, 1 June 1902, 15.

22. "Mark Twain Muses on the Years Gone By," *San Francisco Examiner*, 1 June 1902, 2; Hastings MacAdam, "Address Before Labinnah Club," *St. Louis Republic*, 1 June 1902, 27; *MTCI*, 448, 455; *MTB*, 1168.

23. *AMT*, 1:401; *MTB*, 1169; *St. Louis Post-Dispatch*, 1 June 1902, 15; SLC to Everett Gill, 1 June 1902, *UCCL* 06349; Newton, *River of Years*, 89–90; "Mark Twain's First Sermon," *Chicago Tribune*, 6 June 1902, 12; *MTCI*, 449, 462.

24. *AMT*, 1:401; SLC to John RoBards, 3 June 1902, *UCCL* 06354.

25. *MTCI*, 446, 449; *MTB*, 1168–71; *MTSpk*, 457; *St. Louis Globe-Democrat*, 1 June 1902, 4.

26. "Hannibal, Mo.," *St. Louis Republic*, 8 June 1902, 20; Sorrentino, "Twain's 1902 Trip to Missouri," 14.

27. "Ovations to Humorist," *St. Louis Globe-Democrat*, 4 June 1902, 7; *AMT*, 1:353.

28. "Good-Bye to Mark Twain," *Hannibal Courier-Post*, 3 June 1902, 1; "Twain Says Farewell," *Decatur (Ill.) Herald*, 4 June 1902, 1; "Ovations to Humorist," *St. Louis Globe-Democrat*, 4 June 1902, 7; *MTSpk*, 431; SLC to W. H. Dulany, 17 June 1902, *UCCL* 08881.

29. *MTB*, 1172; "Twain's Tomcat Story His Best," *Hartford Courant*, 25 November 1905, 16; "Huck Finn in Tears Revives Days of Old," *St. Louis Republic*, 22 April 1910, 3; "Ovations to Humorist," *St. Louis Globe-Democrat*, 4 June 1902, 7; Garland, *Companions on the Trail*, 192–94.

30. *MTSpk*, 671; "Mark Twain's Gift to Missouri University," *Kansas City Star*, 22 June 1902, 4.

31. "Missouri University Makes Mark Twain Doctor of Laws," *St. Louis Republic*, 5 June 1902, 2; "Mark Twain Honored," *New York Sun*, 5 June 1902, 1; *MTSpk*, 435; "Twain's Vow of Silence," *Chicago Tribune*, 6 June 1902, 5; "Make Twain an LL.D.," *Anaconda Standard*, 5 June 1902, 6; "How Twain Feels as an LL.D.," *Charlotte Observer*, 15 June 1902, 15.

32. "Mark Twain," *Mexico Missouri Message*, 12 June 1902, 1; Clemens, *Gardens and Books*, 213; *MTCI*, 453–56.

33. *MTCI*, 453, 450, 459; *MTSpk*, 440; *MTB*, 1174.

34. *MTCI*, 461, 462; "Mark Twain So," *Chicago Tribune*, 11 June 1902, 4; "Sailing of French Guests," *New York Evening Post*, 12 June 1902, 3.

35. *St. Louis Republic*, 2 August 1902, 2; "Mark Twain's New Work," *St. Louis Post-Dispatch*, 25 December 1906, 4; Rolla Wells to SLC, 27 March 1907, *UCLC* 36280.

36. *MTSpk*, 442; "Memorial Table Unveiled at Eugene Field's Birthplace," *St. Louis Republic*, 7 June 1902, 4; *MTCI*, 463; Sorrentino, "Twain's 1902 Trip to Missouri," 14.

37. SLC to Eugene Field II, 12 June 1902, *UCCL* 12126; Cuoco and Gass, *Literary St. Louis*, 74.

38. *MTCI*, 456, 462–63, 466; Clemens, *Gardens and Books*, 213; "Mark Twain Talks to Art Students," *St. Louis Republic*, 8 June 1902, 27; Love, "To Mark Twain," *St. Louis Post-Dispatch*, 8 June 1902, 29.

39. *MTB*, 1181; *AMT*, 2:214, 2:552.

40. *MTB*, 1203; SLC to Laura Stephens, 12 June 1902, *UCCL* 06362.

41. SLC to F. G. Whitmore, 2–3 March 1902, *UCCL* 06290; SLC to Poultney Bigelow, 12 March 1902, *UCCL* 06295; Leary, "Twain Did Not Sleep Here," 15; *HHR*, 484, 499.

42. *JHT*, 287; SLC to F. G. Whitmore, 27 August 1901, *UCCL* 06122; SLC to F. G. Whitmore, 7 December 1901, *UCCL* 06184.

43. *HHR*, 485; Hill, *God's Fool*, 33; *Vancouver World*, 19 July 1902, 12; SLC to F. G. Whitmore, 14 June 1902, *UCCL* 06366.

44. SLC to F. G. Whitmore, 14 June 1902, *UCCL* 06366; *HHR*, 490; *New York Tribune*, 27 April 1902, 13; Kaplan, *Singular Mark Twain*, 593; William H. Hoyt & Co. and George W. Reeves to SLC, 14 May 1902, *UCLC* 33464; *MTCI*, 474; Leary, "Twain Did Not Sleep Here," 13–16; "Mark Twain's Assessment," *New York Tribune*, 3 May 1903, 6.

45. *LMT*, 220; Emerson, "Smoking and Health," 557; "Mark Twain at Kittery," *Portsmouth (N.H.) Herald*, 27 June 1902, 6; *HHR*, 489–90; Hill, *God's Fool*, 45–46; *MyMT*, 90; Messent, *Twain and Male Friendship*, 206.

46. SLC to Klaw & Erlanger, 27 July 1902, *UCCL* 06391; SLC to Klaw & Erlanger, 7 August 1902, *UCCL* 12225; *HHR*, 493; SLC to Charles Dillingham, 2 August 1902, *UCCL* 11706; "Stage Matters," *Boston Post*, 7 August 1902, 8; "World of Players," *New York Clipper*, 9 August 1902, 508; "Mark Twain Helping Author," *St. Louis Republic*, 8 August 1902, 6; "Miss Clipper's Anecdotes, Personalities, and Comments," *New York Clipper*, 23 August 1902, 554; "Bustle at Parson's," *Hartford Courant*, 10 November 1902, 4; "'Huckleberry Finn' Presented," *New Haven Journal and Courier*, 12 November 1902, 6; "Mark Twain, Playwright," *Brooklyn Sunday News*, 30 November 1902, 14; "Mark Twain as Dramatist," *Canterbury Press* (New Zealand), 27 January 1903, 5.

47. "Old York Celebrates," *Boston Herald*, 6 August 1902, 3; "Maine Town 250 Years Old," *New York Tribune*, 6 August 1902, 12; *MTHL*, 744.

48. *HHR*, 496–97, 499, 505–6, 508; *AMT*, 2:99; SLC to Susan Crane, 15 August 1902, *UCCL* 06407; *LMT*, 220; SLC to F. G. Whitmore, 21 August 1902, *UCCL* 06409; SLC to John Y. W. MacAlister, 6 September 1902, *UCCL* 06409; SLC to John Y. W. MacAlister, 23 September 1902, *UCCL* 06439; SLC to Charley Langdon, 11 September 1902, *UCCL* 06431; *JHT*, 307.

49. *HHR*, 499, 509, 522; SLC to Fred Duneka, 6 October 1902, *UCCL* 06454; SLC to F. G. Whitmore, 6 October 1902, *UCCL* 06455; SLC to F. G. Whitmore, 18 October 1902, *UCCL* 06466; SLC to F. G. Whitmore, 24 November 1902, *UCCL* 06492; SLC to F. G. Whitmore, 16 January 1903, *UCCL* 06565; SLC to F. G. Whitmore, 7 March 1903, *UCCL* 06592; SLC to F. G. Whitmore, 5 April 1903, *UCCL* 10142; SLC to F. G. Whitmore, 11 April 1903, *UCCL* 11602; SLC to Wilson Hawkes, 23 April 1903, *UCCL* 06629; *JHT*, 307; "Mark Twain's House Sold," *New York Sun*, 8 May 1903, 9; "Mark Twain's House," *Hartford Courant*, 8 May 1903, 5.

50. "Local Works," *Manawatu Standard*, 8 October 1902, 2; *Portland (Ore.) Journal*, 13 August 1902, 4; "Huck Finn Tabooed by Denver," *Washington Times*, 7 September 1902, 24; "Mark Twain Scores Men Who Don't Like 'Huck,'" *Denver Post*, 18 August 1902, 1; "Mark Twain's Immorality," *Collier's Weekly*, 24 December 1904, 7.

51. *Ames (Neb.) Times*, 5 January 1905, 9; "Mark Twain in Iowa," *Fort Wayne News*, 11 January 1905, 9; *Santa Cruz Sentinel*, 3 June 1905, 4; Lentz, "Twain in 1906," 30; "Mark Twain's Boys Disliked," *Philadelphia Inquirer*, 5 December 1904, 16; SLC to Asa Dickinson, 21 November 1905, *UCCL* 07215; SLC to Harriet Whitmore, 7 February 1907, *UCCL* 07645.

52. *Leavenworth Times*, 21 August 1902, 4; *Fort Scott Monitor*, 15 October 1902, 2; *Topeka Capital*, 20 August 1902, 3; *Topeka Capital*, 21 August 1902, 4; *Topeka Capital*, 22 August 1902, 4; *Elmira Star-Gazette*, 23 September 1902, 4; "Is 'Huckleberry Finn' Good for the Children?" *Omaha World-Herald*, 24 August 1902, 14; "Mark Twain on 'Huck Finn,'" *Omaha World-Herald*, 31 August 1902, 17; "Stray Scraps," *Alton (Ill.) Telegraph*, 3 October 1902, 2.

53. *Mark Twain's Fables of Man*, 322, 327, 388, 391; Schrager, "Mark Twain and Mary Baker Eddy," 43; *MTB*, 1164.

54. SLC to Muriel Pears, 13 October 1902, *UCCL* 06460; *HHR*, 505, 511; *AMT*, 2:99.

55. SLC to John Y. W. MacAlister, 18 October 1902, *UCCL* 06466; SLC to Muriel Pears, 13 October 1902, *UCCL* 06460; *AMT*, 2:99–100; SLC to T. B. Aldrich, 22 December 1902, *UCCL* 06524.

Chapter 11

1. Hill, *God's Fool*, 93, 111; "City Personals," *Hartford Courant*, 26 September 1902, 7; *AMT*, 3:333, 3:429; Skandera Trombley, *Twain's Other Woman*, 20, 25; Clara Clemens to Harriet Whitmore, 10 December 1902, *UCCL* 06509; Isabel V. Lyon to Harriet Whitmore, 8 January 1905, *UCCL* 10951.

2. "Mark Twain in Want of Fuel," *Buffalo Enquirer*, 21 October 1902, 1; *Lawrence Journal*, 22 October 1902, 2; "A Public Nuisance," *Wellington (Kans.) Journal*, 22 October 1902, 1; "Harlem Flat for Mr. Twain," *New York Evening World*, 22 October 1902, 1. See also "The Man in the Street," *New York Times Magazine*, 11 January 1903, 1.

3. "At Princeton's Helm," *Boston Herald*, 26 October 1902, 4; "Mr. Cleveland's Guest," *New York Evening World*, 17 October 1902, 6; "Football Notes," *Boston Globe*, 29 October 1902, 5.

4. *MTCI*, 486, 489, 490; Lucy, *Sixty Years in the Wilderness*, 221–23; Henry Lucy, "Mark Twain," *Bathurst Argus*, 3; Henry Lucy, "Mark Twain," *Lyttelton Times*, 6.

5. *The $30,000 Bequest*, 230–33; *MTB*, 1155.

6. *LLMT*, 339–40; Scharnhorst, *Owen Wister and the West*, 20; *Elmira Star-Gazette*, 3 December 1902, 4; "In Honor of Mark Twain," *Brooklyn Eagle*, 29 November 1902, 4; W. D. Howells, "In Honor of Mark Twain," *Harper's Weekly*, 23 December 1902, 1943–44; Harper, *I Remember*, 105; "Tribunes to Mark Twain," *North American Review* 191 (June 1910), 833; *MTSpk*, 458.

7. "Niece of Mark Twain Weds," *Brooklyn Eagle*, 30 November 1902, 53.

8. "The Country Has Not Bred a Nobler Man," *Boston Journal*, 7 December 1902, 2; SLC to Susan Reed, 7 December 1902, *UCCL* 06505; *Europe and Elsewhere*, 297–98.

9. Tuckey, *Mark Twain and Little Satan*, 90; SLC to Edward Everett Hale, 1 November 1899, *UCCL* 05698; SLC to John Greenall, 6 April 1906, *UCCL* 08891; SLC to Fred Duneka, 11 September 1902, *UCCL* 08228.

10. "Postscript," *Larne Times*, 24 January 1903, 8; "Mark Twain on Christian Science," *Toronto Saturday Night*, 31 January 1903, 5; "Mark Twain on Christian Science," *Pittsburgh Post*, 7 December 1902, 26; "Wanted, a Few More Humorists," *Nebraska State Journal*, 12 December 1902, 4; "Mark Twain on Christian Science," *Philadelphia Medical Journal* 11 (January 1903): 5; "Mark Twain on Eddyism," *American Medicine*, 10 January 1903, 43; William D. McCrackan, "Mrs. Eddy's Relation to Christian Science," *North American Review* 176 (March 1903): 353; *Christian Science*, 357.

11. SLC to SC, 7 February 1896, *UCCL* 05018; Willis, *Mark and Livy*, 230; *AMT*, 2:66; "Mark Twain Talks about Osteopathy and Christian Science," *New York Tribune*, 3 March 1901, 3. Five years later, SLC admitted that "I have never tried Christian Science myself, but it is not because I am prejudiced against it. I have no prejudices." SLC to John Greenall, 6 April 1906, *UCCL* 08891.

12. *MTB*, 1195; *Christian Science*, 55; SLC to W. D. McCrackan, 5 December 1902, *UCCL* 06498; SLC to Frederick W. Peabody, 5 December 1902, *UCCL* 06499; SLC to Edward Day, 21 March 1903, *UCCL* 06606.

13. *Christian Science*, 119, 134, 292; SLC to Livingstone Wright, 17 April 1903, *UCCL* 06623; SLC to Millard Sewall, 3 May 1903, *UCCL* 12956; *MyMT*, 83.

14. *Christian Science*, 47; "Mrs. Eddy to Mark Twain," *New York Sun*, 17 January 1903, 6; SLC to John Greenall, 6 April 1906, *UCCL* 08891; *Roughing It*, 130, 132, 135.

15. *Christian Science*, 45, 69, 102; Scharnhorst, "A Sheaf of Recovered Mark Twain Letters," 11; Garland, *Companions on the Trail*, 194.

16. SLC to Frederick W. Peabody, 5 December 1902, *UCCL* 06499; *Christian Science*, 72, 229, 241; *MyMT*, 83; SLC to John Greenall, 6 April 1906, *UCCL* 08891; *AMT*, 2:136.

17. SLC to Percy Spalding, 15 December 1902, *UCCL* 06519; Fred Duneka to SLC, 28 January 1903, *UCLC* 33692; *AMT*, 2:144; SLC to Lyman Powell, 27 May 1907, *UCCL* 07734; "Literary and Trade Notes," *Publishers' Weekly*, 11 April 1903, 984; *HHR*, 607; Hill, *God's Fool*, 54; SLC to Edwin H. Anderson, 20 April 1903, *UCCL* 06624; SLC to John Greenall, 6 April 1906, *UCCL* 08891; SLC to unidentified, 24 February 1906, *UCCL* 13127.

18. "A Philippine Petition," *New York Evening Post*, 13 February 1903, 7; SLC to Edward Ordway, 4 January 1903, *UCCL* 12871.

19. SLC to Sam Moffett, 26 August 1902, *UCCL* 06415; *JHT*, 312–19; *CTSSE*, 533; "Mark Twain on Lying," *Baltimore Sun*, 2 December 1902, 4; *MFMT*, 231; *AMT*, 2:100; *MTHL*, 760, 757; SLC to Muriel M. Pears, 14 January 1903, *UCCL* 06560; SLC to John Y. W. MacAlister, 7 April–8 May 1903, *UCCL* 06617.

20. Garland, *Companions on the Trail*, 181; W. D. Howells, "Editor's Easy Chair," *Harper's Monthly* 108 (December 1903): 158; *MTHL*, 774–75.

21. "Mark Twain Will Live in Italy," *New York Herald*, 10 June 1903, 5; "Music and Musicians," *Buffalo Express*, 29 March 1903, 27; SLC to Laurence Hutton, 18 March 1903, *UCCL* 06600; "Long Deaf Able to Hear," *New York Sun*, 27 March 1903, 12; SLC to Poultney Bigelow, 17 April 1903, *UCCL* 06622; SLC to William Winter, 28 April 1903, *UCCL* 06639.

22. SLC to John Y. W. MacAlister, 7 April–8 May 1903, *UCCL* 06617; SLC to Willard Fiske, 1 June 1903, *UCCL* 11375; SLC to Henry Lucy, 4 October 1903, *UCCL* 06735; SLC to Poultney Bigelow, 17 April 1903, *UCCL* 06622; SLC to Susan Crane, 20 April 1903, *UCCL* 06625; *HHR*, 527–28, 532; "Mark Twain to Speak at Fairhaven," *New York Tribune*, 23 May 1903, 7.

23. SLC to Eleanor and Laurence Hutton, 2 July 1903, *UCCL* 06688; SLC to Hélène Picard, 11 July 1903, *UCCL* 06697; *LMT*, 222; Willis, *Mark and Livy*, 275; *JHT*, 322.

24. "Mark Twain at Quarry Farm," *Elmira Star-Gazette*, 10 July 1903, 5; "'Mark Twain' on Sport and Vivisection," *London Daily News*, 1 March 1900, 6; "Mark Twain on Vivisection," *St. Louis Post-Dispatch*, 22 April 1900, 42.

25. *MTHL*, 777; "Short Notes of New Books," *San Francisco Chronicle*, 2 October 1904, 8; Peattie, "Among the New Books," *Chicago Tribune*, 8 October 1904, 10; "A New Book," *London Standard*, 23 February 1905, 2; *Saturday Review*, 1 April 1905, 525; "Literature," *Northern Chronicle and General Advertiser for the North of Scotland*, 16 December 1903, 3; "Mark Twain's Latest," *Sydney Herald*, 22 April 1905, 4.

26. "The Christmas Numbers," *New York Tribune*, 28 November 1903, 10; "New Books," *Charleston News and Courier*, 25 September 1904, 21; "New Books and Magazines," *Brooklyn Standard Union*, 25 September 1904, 21; "Mark Twain's Story of a Dog," *Philadelphia Inquirer*, 23 September 1904, 5; *MTCR*, 541; "Mark Twain's Dog Story," *Buffalo Express*, 1 October 1904, 8; *Hartford Courant*, 8 December 1904, 16; "Books and Reading," *New York Evening Post*, 3 December 1903, 6; "A Dog's Tale," *Pittsburgh Press*, 8 October 1904, 14; "Recent Publications," *New Orleans Times-Picayune*, 23 October 1904, 32; "Mark Twain's Plea," *Salt Lake Tribune*, 30 October 1904, 27; "Reviews," *Bath Chronicle and Weekly Gazette*, 17 December

1903, 6; "Books of the Day," *Newcastle Chronicle*, 31 March 1905, 8; "Recent Fiction," *Yorkshire Post and Leeds Intelligencer*, 29 March 1905, 4.

27. "Too Noisy for Mark Twain," *New York Sun*, 10 September 1903, 2; *New York Herald*, 30 August 1903, sec. 2, 3; "Steam Fliers Face Home," *New York Sun*, 28 August 1903, 2.

28. SLC to Muriel Pears, 17 October 1903, *UCCL* 06744; "Murder by the Wholesale," *New York Tribune*, 16 October 1903, 2; "The Cause Is Just," *New York World*, 23 October 1903, 3; "Mark Twain Sails," *New York Evening World*, 24 October 1903, 4.

29. "City Personals," *Hartford Courant*, 5 June 1903, 13; "Mark Twain's Plans," *Hartford Courant*, 8 June 1903, 7; Hill, *God's Fool*, 66; *HHR*, 540, 691–708; James B. Morrow, "Mark Twain's Exclusive Publisher Tells What the Humorist Is Paid," *Washington Post*, 3 March 1907, 87; *Brooklyn Citizen*, 24 December 1907, 6; Kaplan, *Singular Mark Twain*, 601; *AMT*, 3:234.

30. Luscher, "Italian Accounts of Mark Twain," 219; "A Dinner to Mark Twain," *Springfield Republican*, 23 October 1903, 3; "Good-by to Mark Twain," *New York Sun*, 23 October 1903, 7; Alden, "Mark Twain: Personal Impressions," *Book News Monthly* 28 (April 1910): 582; *MTHL*, 774.

31. *MTCI*, 484; *JHT*, 323; SLC financial file for 1903, *MTP*; "Immigration's Ebb Tide," *Rockford (Ill.) Morning Star*, 21 November 1903, 4; "Perfectly Natural," *St. Louis Post-Dispatch*, 10 November 1903, 10; *HHR*, 546; SLC to Mary Mapes Dodge, 18 December 1903, *UCCL* 06770; Simboli, "Twain from an Italian Point of View," 518.

32. SLC to Muriel M. Pears, 17 October 1903, *UCCL* 06744; "Mark Twain to Reform the Language of Italy," *NYT*, 10 April 1904, 11; "Mark Twain's Winter Home," *San Francisco Call*, 9 November 1903, 9; Simboli, "Twain from an Italian Point of View," 521; Orcutt, *From My Library Walls*, 230; Hill, *God's Fool*, 70, 82; *JHT*, 326; *MTHL*, 775; "Topics in Paris," *New York Tribune*, 10 April 1904, 4; Phelps, "Some Notes on Mark Twain," *Independent*, 5 May 1910, 958.

33. *JHT*, 330; *CTSSE*, 578; "Mark Twain to Reform the Language of Italy," *NYT*, 10 April 1904, 11; Luscher, "Italian Accounts of Mark Twain," 218; *MTHL*, 774; "In European Cities," *San Francisco Call*, 27 November 1903, 2; Downing, *Queen Bee of Tuscany*, 219; Orth, "George Gregory Smith and Mark Twain," 29; "Painted Twain's Picture," *Philadelphia Inquirer*, 29 May 1904, 13; "Banquet to Mark Twain," *Boston Globe*, 5 June 1904, 8; "Mark Twain at Florence," *Chicago Tribune*, 31 January 1904, 13; "Mark Twain Writing an Autobiography," *St. Louis Republic*, 31 January 1904, sec. 4, 11; *Mark Twain's Letters* (1917), 756; "Mark Twain Hankers for Prize from World's Fair," *Chicago Tribune*, 14 June 1904, 6.

34. "Notes of the Stage," *New York Tribune*, 10 July 1904, 10; "May Reach Adjustment," *New York Tribune*, 11 June 1904, 4; Downing, *Queen Bee of Tuscany*, 219; "Encourage Such Lying, Says Mark Twain," *Boston Post*, 3 April 1904, 65; Orcutt, *From My Library Walls*, 222; Orcutt, *In Quest of the Perfect Book*, 171; James, *Letters*, 2:342; Bosha, "Mark Twain–William James Friendship," 7–8; "Mark Twain to Reform the Language of Italy," *NYT*, 10 April 1904, 11; "Literary Chat," *San Francisco Call*, 7 April 1904, 8.

35. "Mark Twain's Candidacy," *Boston Globe*, 29 November 1903, 8; "Mark Twain for President," *New York Evening Post*, 19 December 1903, 4; "Mark Twain for President," *New York Tribune*, 8 January 1904, 7; "Mark Twain for President," *Biloxi Herald*, 18 November 1905, 4.

36. "Signor M. Twain a Jolly Neighbor," *St. Louis Post-Dispatch*, 16 August 1904, 9; *The $30,000 Bequest*, 172, 189.

37. Zwonitzer, *The Statesman and the Storyteller*, 254; SLC to Fred Duneka, 5 January 1904, *UCCL* 06782; *Europe and Elsewhere*, 326–38; Brodwin, "Mark Twain's Masks of Satan," 216–17.

38. *MTHL*, 778–79; *AMT*, 1:1, 1:441; IVLD, 1904; *MTCI*, 333.

39. *MTCR*, 531–32, 536–37; "The Humorists," *NYT*, 16 April 1904, 29; "Books and Authors," *Montreal Gazette*, 9 April 1904, 6; "New Books and Magazines," *Brooklyn Standard Union*, 1 May 1904, 21; *NYT*, 23 April 1904, 27; "When Adam Kept a Diary," *Philadelphia Inquirer*, 6 May 1904, 14; "The Diary of Adam," *Des Moines Register*, 24 April 1904, 17; "Extracts from Adam's Diary," *Pittsburgh Press*, 3 May 1904, 20; "Briefer Notices," *Public Opinion*, 28 April 1904, 539; "Literature and Art," *Hartford Courant*, 30 April 1904, 18; "New Novels," *Manchester Guardian*, 22 June 1904, 4; "Books of the Week," *New York Outlook*, 30 April 1904, 1044; "Adam," *Boston Journal*, 7 June 1904, 8; "Books of the Week," *Syracuse Post-Standard*, 16 April 1904, 11; *Brooklyn Eagle*, 11 April 1904, 8; "Extracts from Adam's Diary," *Chicago Inter Ocean*, 21 May 1904, 7; "Reviews of New Books," *Washington Post*, 23 April 1904, 13; "Rendered from Adam," *Boston Advertiser*, 14 April 1904, 8; "Spring Fiction," *New York Sun*, 16 April 1904, 7; "Mark Twain on Adam," *Washington Times*, 23 April 1904, 5; Peck, "As to Mark Twain," *Bookman* (New York) 12 (January 1901): 441–42.

40. "New Novels," *Manchester Guardian*, 22 June 1904, 4; "Books of the Day," *London Telegraph*, 22 June 1904, 12; *MTCR*, 533; "New Books," *London Globe*, 1 June 1904, 10; "Mark Twain as Adam," *Yorkshire Post and Leeds Intelligencer*, 22 June 1904, 10; "Adam's Diary," *London Daily News*, 11 June 1904, 4; "Mark Twain's Latest," *Sydney Herald*, 16 July 1904, 4; "Adam's Diary," *London Morning Post*, 1 June 1904, 5; "Mark Twain's New Book," *Westminster Gazette*, 2 July 1904, 14; "Adam's Diary," *St. James's Gazette*, 11 June 1904, 19; "Among the New Books," *Sydney World's News*, 30 July 1904, 28.

41. SLC to John Y. W. MacAlister, 17 November 1903, *UCCL* 06759; *MTB*, 1211, 1213; *AMT*, 1:75.

42. *AMT*, 1:74, 1:239; "Signor M. Twain a Jolly Neighbor," *St. Louis Post-Dispatch*, 16 August 1904, 9; *LMT*, 223; IVLD, 1903–4.

43. *HHR*, 557–59; Hill, *God's Fool*, 73; "Signor M. Twain a Jolly Neighbor," *St. Louis Post-Dispatch*, 16 August 1904, 9; *LMT*, 223–24; Kaplan, *Mr. Clemens and Mark Twain*, 371; Kaplan, *Singular Mark Twain*, 605; IVLD, 25 August 1906; SLC to Raffaello Stattesi, 19 February 1905, *UCCL* 07004; *AMT*, 1:239, 1:241; *MTB*, 1213.

44. SLC to Fred Duneka, 8 February 1904, *UCCL* 06791; SLC to T. B. Aldrich, 14 February 1904, *UCCL* 06793; SLC to Mary Mapes Dodge, 18 December 1903, *UCCL* 06770; *HHR*, 545, 558; "Putting a Happy Face on an Often Unhappy Twain," *NYT*, 22 April 2000, B13; Hill, *God's Fool*, 83; Orth, "George Gregory Smith and Mark Twain," 33; SLC to Susan Crane, 17 February 1904, *UCCL* 06796; SLC to John Y. W. MacAlister, 21 March 1904, *UCCL* 06811; SLC to John Y. W. MacAlister, 25 April 1904, *UCCL* 06825; Skandera Trombley, *Twain's Other Woman*, 38; *MFMT*, 242–43, 246; SLC to Poultney Bigelow, 4 May 1904, *UCCL* 06827.

45. SLC to Susan Crane, 6 June 1904, *UCCL* 06858; *AMT*, 2:107–8; *Mark Twain's Letters* (1917), 761; SLC to Muriel M. Pears, 23 October 1904, *UCCL* 06935; Orth, "George Gregory Smith and Mark Twain," 34; *LMT*, 228.

Chapter 12

1. SLC to Susan Crane, 6 June 1904, *UCCL* 06858; *MTHL*, 785; *LMT*, 228–30; *MTB*, 1218, 1350.

2. *HHR*, 569–71; SLC to Susan Crane, 6 June 1904, *UCCL* 06858; *AMT*, 1:324; SLC to T. B. Aldrich, 6 June 1904, *UCCL* 06856; *JHT*, 338.

3. SLC to Thomas Lounsbury, 21 July 1904, *UCCL* 06896; *JHT*, 337; Helen Keller to SLC, 14 June 1904, *UCLC* 39138; SLC to Keller, 26 July 1904, *UCCL* 06904.

4. "Mark Twain Will Bring Wife's Body," *Boston Journal*, 8 June 1904, 8; *HHR*, 569–71; SLC to Charley Langdon, 8 June 1904, *UCCL* 06865; *MTHL*, 787; Orth, "George Gregory Smith and Mark Twain," 34–35; Yurán, "Twain at Norfolk," 5; Hill, *God's Fool*, 81; Kaplan, *Singular Mark Twain*, 614; SLC to Frank Mason, 23 July 1904, *UCCL* 06900.

5. SLC to Frank Mason, 23 July 1904, *UCCL* 06900; SLC to Moses Starr, 26 February 1905, *UCCL* 06994; IVLD, 5 July 1904.

6. *LMT*, 231; SLC to Clara Clemens, 21–23 February 1910, *UCCL* 08561; *HHR*, 572; Skandera Trombley, *Twain's Other Woman*, 41; "Mrs. Clemens Laid at Rest," *Boston Journal*, 15 July 1904, 6; SLC to Edward Loomis, 15 July 1904, *UCCL* 06885; SLC to Thomas Lounsbury, 21 July 1904, *UCCL* 06896; Hill, *God's Fool*, 88.

7. *HHR*, 570; IVLD, 1904; SLC to Clara Clemens, 26 July 1904, *UCCL* 06903; SLC to Sam Moffett, 6 August 1904, *UCCL* 06909; Hill, *God's Fool*, 96–97; SLC to Susan Crane, 9 September 1904, *UCCL* 06919; *LMT*, 233; SLC to Muriel Pears, 23 October 1904, *UCCL* 06935; SLC to Frank Doubleday, 10 November 1904, *UCCL* 06942; *JHT*, 350.

8. SLC to John Y. W. MacAlister, 9 November 1904, *UCCL* 06948; *HHR*, 573; *JHT*, 346–48.

9. SLC to Susan Crane, 25 July 1904, *UCCL* 11450; SLC to Susan Crane, 22 August 1904, *UCCL* 06915; SLC to Susan Crane, 23 October 1904, *UCCL* 06936; SLC to Susan Crane, 9 May 1905, *UCCL* 07040; Skandera Trombley, *Twain's Other Woman*, 41–42; *AMT*, 3:201; Keller, *Midstream*, 50; SLC to Mai Coe, 27 December 1909, *UCCL* 08524.

10. *MTB*, 1224; IVLD, 1904; "Mark Twain's Daughter Has Narrow Escape from Death," *Berkshire Eagle*, 1 August 1904, 1; SLC to Carolyn Wells, 15 April 1906, *UCCL* 10941; SLC to Sam Moffett, 6 August 1904, *UCCL* 06909; "Lenox," *Boston Herald*, 21 August 1904, 33.

11. SLC to Muriel Pears, 23 October 1904, *UCCL* 06935; *HHR*, 579.

12. *MTHL*, 789; "Personal," *Wall Street Journal*, 15 September 1904, 8; "Rogers Memorial Church at Fairhaven Dedicated," *Boston Globe*, 5 October 1904, 4.

13. SLC to Elizabeth Wallace, 12 March 1910, *UCCL* 08570; *MTCR*, 552; "Literature," *Melbourne Leader*, 21 October 1905, 31; Hawkins, "Twain's Involvement with the Congo Reform Movement," 155; Gribben, *Twain's Library*, 484; Hawkins, "King Leopold's Soliloquy," in LeMaster and Wilson, *Mark Twain Encyclopedia*, 430; Giddings, "Twain and King Leopold of the Belgians," 210–11; *JHT*, 351; Foner, *Twain: Social Critic*, 297; *MTCI*, 499, 529; *AMT*, 2:134, 2:307.

14. Kaplan, *Mr. Clemens and Mark Twain*, 366; "Congo Lobby Is Still Busy in Spite of Expose," *San Francisco Examiner*, 12 December 1906, 1; Giddings, "Twain and King Leopold of the Belgians," 215–16; *CTSSE*, 661–85.

15. Hawkins, "Twain's Involvement with the Congo Reform Movement," 155; *AMT*, 2:145; IVLD, 7 July 1905; Wuliger, "Twain on *King Leopold's Soliloquy*," 235–36; SLC to Fred Duneka, 16 June 1905, *UCCL* 07064.

16. L. Call Barnes, "Fresh Light on the Dark Continent," *American Journal of Theology* 10 (January 1906): 198; *MTCR*, 549; "King Leopold's Defense," *Baltimore American*, 2 October 1905, 11; "King Leopold's Soliloquy," *Washington Times*, 4 October 1905, 4; "Mark Twain and Leopold," *Chicago Inter Ocean*, 8 October 1905, 27; *Montgomery (Ala.) Times*, 7 October 1905, 4; *Sioux City Journal*, 11 March 1906, 16; "King Leopold's Soliloquy," *Buffalo Commercial*, 2 October 1905, 6; "On the Book Table," *Chicago Advance*, 14 December 1905, 718; "New Publications," *New Haven Journal and Courier*, 28 December 1905, 10; *Nashville Tennessean*,

30 October 1905, 10; A. W. Halsey, "King Leopold and Mark Twain," *New York Observer and Chronicle*, 1 February 1906, 143; T. B. Aldrich to SLC, 25 October 1905, *UCLC* 34710.

17. SLC to Thomas Barbour, 23 September 1905, *UCCL* 07146; Hawkins, "Twain's Involvement with the Congo Reform Movement," 163–65; IVLD, 7 December 1905; SLC to Robert Bacon, 6 December 1905, *UCCL* 07235; Hill, *God's Fool*, 119; SLC to T. B. Aldrich, 26 December 1905, *UCCL* 07272; SLC to Charles Alexander, 31 January 1906, *UCCL* 12133; Booker T. Washington, "Tributes to Mark Twain," *North American Review* 191 (June 1910): 829.

18. IVLD, 27 December 1905; *MTCI*, 529; *AMT*, 2:8, 2:461–62; Hawkins, "Twain's Involvement with the Congo Reform Movement," 166–67, 169.

19. *MTCR*, 549–53; "Mark Twain's Terrible Book," *T. P.'s Weekly*, 7 June 1907, 709; "Charivaria," *Punch*, 19 June 1907, 439; "The Congo Atrocities," *Bristol Western Daily Press*, 31 May 1907, 6; "Mark Twain in Earnest," *Newcastle Chronicle*, 2 August 1907, 8; *Truth*, 22 May 1907, 1294; "Mark Twain Satirizes Leopold," *London Clarion*, 7 June 1907, 4; "Mark Twain and Congo Horrors," *Sheffield Telegraph*, 4 July 1907, 5; "Miscellaneous," *Belfast News-Letter*, 25 July 1907, 11; "Europe and the Congo," *Perthshire Advertiser*, 17 July 1907, 4; "King Leopold's Soliloquy," *Stroud News and Gloucestershire Advertiser*, 2 November 1906, 8; "King Leopold's Soliloquy," *Sydney World's News*, 20 July 1907, 28; "A Reader's Notes," *Manitoba Free Press*, 1 July 1907, 12; "Miscellaneous," *Aberdeen Press and Journal*, 10 June 1907, 3; "Mark Twain's Satire on the Congo Free State," *Perth Western Mail*, 27 July 1907, 49; "Mark Twain and King Leopold," *Adelaide Advertiser*, 3 August 1907, 12; "Mark Twain on King Leopold," *Australian Christian Commonwealth*, 8 December 1905, 4; "Literature," *Melbourne Leader*, 21 October 1905, 31; "King Leopold Denounced by Mark Twain," *Lithgow Mercury*, 30 August 1907, 7; "Mark Twain on Congoland," *Sydney Daily Telegraph*, 27 July 1907, 4; "New Leaves," *London Justice*, 22 June 1907, 4; "King Leopold's Soliloquy," *Sydney Stock and Station Journal*, 13 September 1907, 3; *An Answer to Mark Twain*, 5–6.

20. *MTB*, 1231.

21. Hawkins, "Twain's Involvement with the Congo Reform Movement," 174; Scharnhorst, "A Sheaf of Recovered Mark Twain Letters," 93.

22. SLC to Frank Doubleday, 10 November 1904, *UCCL* 06942; IVLD, 30 November 1904.

23. Quick, *Enchantment*, 51–52, 96; IVLD, 1 March 1905, 13 July 1905, 15 August 1905, 10 October 1905, 23 January 1906, 25 January 1906, 4 February 1906, 24 February 1906, 25 June 1906, 15 July 1906, 11 August 1906, 6 October 1907, and 23 January 1908; SLC to Clara Clemens, 3 September 1905, *UCCL* 07127; *Horse's Tale*, vii; Harding, "Twain Lands an Angel Fish," 9; Lentz, "Twain in 1906," 26; Skandera Trombley, *Twain's Other Woman*, 47, 278; SLC to E. B. Proudfit, 3 October 1905, *UCCL* 08671; Hill, *God's Fool*, 94. See also SLC to Jean Clemens, 27 October 1904: "What is your favorite piece of music, dear? Mine is Beethoven's 5th Symphony. I've found that out within a day or two."

24. Dickie, *In the Kaiser's Capital*, 187; "The Man in the Street," *New York Times Magazine*, 1 September 1901, 1; "Famous Men at Luncheon," *Carbondale Free Press*, 23 December 1903, 2; "Mark Twain on Friends and Fighters," *Philadelphia North American*, 1 January 1906, 14; Berkove, *Insider Stories*, 1039.

25. SLC to Charley Langdon, 19 June 1904, *UCCL* 06875; "Mark Twain's Wife Leaves Him Her Estate," *San Francisco Examiner*, 16 August 1904, 3; "Mark Twain's Home for Sale," *New York Tribune*, 11 June 1903, 16; Kaplan, *Singular Mark Twain*, 603.

26. *The $30,000 Bequest*, 49; "Mark Twain's 'Bequest,'" *San Francisco Call*, 27 December 1904, 6.

27. SLC to John Y. W. MacAlister, 10 March 1900, *UCCL* 05774; SLC to John Y. W. MacAlister, 24 April 1901, *UCCL* 06043; SLC to John Y. W. MacAlister, 27 August 1901, *UCCL* 06121; SLC to John Y. W. MacAlister, 17 March 1902, *UCCL* 06304; *HHR*, 440, 445; Crawford, *How Not to Get Rich*, 183.

28. Hill, *God's Fool*, 63; *AMT*, 3:270, 3:332; SLC to John Y. W. MacAlister, 21 March 1904, *UCCL* 06811; SLC to John Y. W. MacAlister, 22 November 1904, *UCCL* 06953; *HHR*, 557, 561; SLC to Howard Wright, 5 February 1903, *UCCL* 11940.

29. *AMT*, 3:332; John Hays Hammond to SLC, 15 September 1904, *UCCL* 12884; "Mark Twain Forwards Prosaic Deposition," *Brooklyn Eagle*, 16 October 1907, 18; "Plasmon Libel Suit Fails," *New York Sun*, 27 February 1910, 8; "Mark Twain's Testimony Was Very Prosaic," *Brooklyn Standard Union*, 16 October 1907, 9; SLC to John Y. W. MacAlister, 9 November 1904, *UCCL* 06948; Hill, *God's Fool*, 13; "Mark Twain Witness in Libel Suit," *New York Tribune*, 16 October 1907, 11; SLC to A. B. Paine, 4 March 1910, *UCCL* 11844; SLC to Hammond, 22 March 1910, *UCCL* 12915.

30. SLC to Augustus Gurlitz, 12 December 1900, *UCCL* 12189; SLC to Augustus Gurlitz, 7 April 1901, *UCCL* 12196; Quick, *Enchantment*, 148; "Mark Twain Again a Witness," *New York Tribune*, 18 May 1901, 7; "Mark Twain as a Witness," *New York Tribune*, 14 March 1901, 7; "Mark Twain Enters Suit," *Brooklyn Eagle*, 26 March 1901, 7.

31.*MTCI*, 493, 572; *CTSSE*, 627–34; "Note and Comment," *Springfield Republican*, 9 February 1905, 6; SLC to Edward Everett Hale, 28 March 1905, *UCCL* 07023.

32. *CTSSE*, 642–47; IVLD, 30 January 1905, 3 February 1905; Skandera Trombley, *Twain's Other Woman*, 61; Foner, *Twain: Social Critic*, 316.

33. "Mark Twain Holds the Czar Up to Scorn," *Minneapolis Journal*, 8 March 1905, 4; "Features in the Magazines," *Decatur (Ill.) Herald*, 12 March 1905, 11; "The Magazines," *Salt Lake Tribune*, 12 March 1905, 26; "Literary Notes of the Week," *Oakland Tribune*, 25 March 1905, 18; "The Czar's Soliloquy," *Sydney News*, 8 May 1905, 8; "Some April Magazines," *London Standard*, 23 March 1905, 2; "Further Notes on the Magazines," *New York Evening Post*, 4 March 1905, 23; "Mark Twain Misses Aim," *Buffalo News*, 5 March 1905, 4; "Among the Magazines," *Washington Post*, 18 March 1905, 43; "The Ethics of Invective," *Spectator*, 25 March 1905, 434–35; "The Czar's Soliloquy," *Australian Christian Commonwealth*, 14 July 1905, 5; "If Emperors Were All Stripped Naked," *Review of Reviews* (London) 31 (April 1905): 375.

34. *JHT*, 364; IVLD, 10–11 March 1905, 21 March 1905, 30 May 1905; *Europe and Elsewhere*, 394–98; Elizabeth Jordan to SLC, 22 March 1905, *UCLC* 33978; SLC to Dan Beard, 30 March 1905, *UCCL* 12539; "Here's Mark Twain's War Prayer," *Boston American*, 6 September 1914, sec. 2, 2.

35. *JHT*, 366; SLC to Clara Clemens, 2 September 1905, *UCCL* 07125; "'Russian Liberty Has Had Its Last Chance,' Says Mark Twain," *Boston Globe*, 30 August 1905, 4; *Boston Globe*, 31 August 1905, 6; *Mark Twain's Letters* (1917), 775, 776.

36. *AMT*, 1:364; *JHT*, 364; *MTB*, 1335.

37. *Mark Twain's Fables of Man*, 157–249; *Who Is Mark Twain?*, 55–60; *AMT*, 2:196.

38. IVLD, 26 July 1905; *LMT*, 283; *MTB*, 1237; SLC to John Y. W. MacAlister, 16 July 1905, *UCCL* 07085; SLC to Muriel Pears, 11 October 1905, *UCCL* 07172; SLC to T. B. Aldrich, 27 October 1905, *UCCL* 10845; SLC to Clara Clemens, 20 October 1905, *UCCL* 07184.

39. *MTB*, 1237–38; "Table Gossip," *Boston Globe*, 27 August 1905, 42; *MTCI*, 513–14; SLC to Helena de Kay Gilder, 28 July 1905, *UCCL* 12056; Barrymore, *Memories*, 154–55; Smith 191–92.

40. *FE*, 132; *MTB*, 1354; *Mark Twain's "Which Was the Dream?,"* 433–554.

41. *Mark Twain's "Which Was the Dream?,"* 433–554; IVLD, 22 May 1905, 24 May 1905; SLC to Clara Clemens, 8 June 1905, *UCCL* 07060; SLC to William Benjamin, 1 June 1905, *UCCL* 07056; SLC to Fred Duneka, 6 June 1905, *UCCL* 12898; SLC to Fred Duneka, 16 June 1905, *UCCL* 07064; SLC to Fred Duneka, 24 June 1905, *UCCL* 09660; *Mark Twain's Letters* (1917), 782–83; *JHT*, 371; *AMT*, 2:196.

42. SLC to Clara Clemens, 29 June 1905, *UCCL* 07073; SLC to Hamlin Garland, 30 June 1905, *UCCL* 07075; IVLD 30 June 1905, 1 July 1905, 3 July 1905, 12 July 1905; *HHR*, 589; Tuckey 69.

43. *Mysterious Stranger Manuscripts*, 165, 307, 383–84; Michelson, *Printer's Devil*, 217–18.

44. SLC to John Y. W. MacAlister, 16 July 1905, *UCCL* 07085; SLC to Helena de Kay Gilder, 28 July 1905, *UCCL* 12056; Higginson, *Story of His Life*, 373–74; "In Bed," *Detroit Free Press*, 28 May 1907, 4; SLC to Fred Duneka, 16 July 1905, *UCCL* 08240; *Eve's Diary*, 109; SLC to Charley Langdon, 19 June 1904, *UCCL* 06875; Fred Duneka to SLC, 27 July 1905, *UCLC* 34551; "Observations of a Woman," *Scranton Republican*, 27 November 1905, 2.

45. SLC to Fred Duneka, 20 March 1906, *UCCL* 08253; SLC to Charlotte Teller, 16–18 June 1906, *UCCL* 08261; SLC to Martha S. Bensley, 14 June 1906, *UCCL* 07459.

46. *MTCR*, 557–62; "Literary Notes," *Belfast Northern Whig*, 14 July 1906, 10; *Brooklyn Eagle*, 8 June 1906, 27; "Eve's Diary by Mark Twain," *Houston Post*, 10 June 1906, 29; "Eve's Diary," *Fort Worth Telegram*, 15 July 1906, 4; "A Glimpse of the Book Table," *New York Observer and Chronicle*, 23 August 1906, 245; "Among the New Books," *Cincinnati Enquirer*, 11 June 1906, 5; "New Books Reviewed," *Hartford Courant*, 7 July 1906, 18; "Eve's Diary," *Philadelphia Inquirer*, 9 July 1906, 5; "The Book-Buyer's Guide," *Critic* 49 (September 1906): 288; "Summer Reading," *New York Times Saturday Review of Books*, 16 June 1906, 386; *Independent*, 16 August 1906, 397; "Comment on Current Books," *New York Outlook*, 18 August 1906, 910; "Notes among the Publishers," *Springfield Republican*, 18 June 1906, 13; "Eve's Diary," *Boston Journal*, 2 July 1906, 6; "Eve's Diary," *Woman's Standard* 19 (August 1906): 4; *MTCR*, 557; "Mark Twain in Eden," *Sydney Daily Telegraph*, 29 September 1906, 6; "Eve's Diary," *Sydney World's News*, 6 October 1906, 29; "Literature and Art," *New Zealand Herald*, 25 August 1906, supplement, 4; "Literary Gossip," *New Zealand Mail*, 29 August 1906, 43; "Our Literary Page," *Perth Daily News*, 10 November 1906, 14; "A Terrible Book," *Otago Witness*, 7 August 1907, 87; "Fiction for Summer Reading," *New York Sun*, 16 June 1906, 7; "Our Book Table," *Zion's Herald*, 1 August 1906, 984; "American Humor," *Providence Journal*, 15 July 1906, sec. 4, 7; "New Novels," *Manchester Guardian*, 22 August 1906, 3; *AMT*, 2:167.

47. SLC to Fred Duneka, 16 September 1905, *UCCL* 07137; SLC to Fred Duneka, 19 September 1905, *UCCL* 07140; *Brooklyn Eagle*, 6 November 1905, 11; "Among the Books," *Louisville Courier-Journal*, 21 October 1905, 5; "The New Books," *New Orleans Times-Picayune*, 29 October 1905, 27; "Editorial Wild Oats," *Santa Cruz Sentinel*, 29 October 1905, 9; *New York Sun*, 3 November 1905, 9; "Twain's New Book," *Elmira Star-Gazette*, 25 September 1905, 4; "Mark Twain," *Portland Oregonian*, 9 October 1905, 6; "New Books and Magazines," *Brooklyn Standard Union*, 8 October 1905, 14; "Mark Twain as a Journalist," *Chicago Tribune*, 30 September 1905, 9; "Editorial Wild Oats," *Pittsburgh Press*, 13 October 1905, 32; "Mark Twain's New Book," *San Francisco Chronicle*, 5 November 1905, 8; "New Publications," *Hartford*

Times, 17 October 1905, 11; *New York Outlook*, 28 October 1905, 524; "Some Books of the Week," *Spectator*, 16 June 1906, 952; *MTCR*, 545; "The Latest Books under Brief Review," *Richmond Times-Dispatch*, 24 December 1905, 7; "Other Books," *New York Sun*, 7 October 1905, 8; "Our Bookshelf," *Adelaide Observer*, 17 February 1906, 4; "Books and Their Writers," *Queen*, 9 December 1905, 50.

48. *HHR*, 590; *JHT*, 375, 377.

49. SLC to Minnie Maddern Fiske, 18 September 1905, *UCCL* 07141; IVLD, 26 September 1905; SLC to Clara Clemens, 1 October 1905, *UCCL* 07156; SLC to Clara Clemens, 6 October 1905, *UCCL* 07163; SLC to Fred Duneka, 2 October 1905, *UCCL* 08244; *HHR*, 601; *Horse's Tale*, 56; Boewe 10–11; *AMT*, 2:189–90.

50. *MTCR*, 587–89; "Literature," *Independent*, 5 December 1907, 1377; *New York Sun*, 2 November 1907, 7; "Magazine Notes," *Brooklyn Citizen*, 9 September 1906, 21; "New Fiction and Books for Little Folks," *Nashville Tennessean*, 1 December 1907, 32; "Books," *Northern Christian Advocate*, 12 December 1907, 11; "New Books of the Season," *Trenton Times*, 14 December 1907, 4; "New Books of the Autumn Season," *New York Times Saturday Review of Books*, 19 October 1907, 665; "Books and Authors," *Pittsburgh Press*, 8 September 1906, 5; *San Francisco Examiner*, 19 January 1908, 39; Boewe, "A Horse's Tale," in LeMaster and Wilson, *Mark Twain Encyclopedia*, 368; "Literary News and Gossip," *Buffalo Express*, 15 July 1906, 24; "Books of the Year," *Hartford Courant*, 9 November 1907, 19; "The New Books," *Chicago Inter Ocean*, 9 November 1907, 5; "By Mark Twain: 'A Horse's Tale,'" *Brooklyn Eagle*, 7 December 1907, 5; "Books and Authors," *Launceston Telegraph*, 14 December 1907, 5; "On the Book Table," *Chicago Advance*, 14 November 1907, 602; "Recent Publications," *New Orleans Picayune*, 22 December 1907, 32; "Fiction," *Scotsman*, 31 October 1907, 3; "General Reader," *Field*, 23 November 1907, 41.

51. John B. Stanchfield to SLC, 21 April 1908, *UCLC* 37764; Hill, *God's Fool*, 129; *AMT*, 3:270–71.

52. *JHT*, 363; IVLD, 31 August 1905; SLC to Lillian G. Kimball, 2 March 1902, *UCCL* 12484.

53. *CTSSE*, 731; *AMT*, 2:332, 3:126; IVLD, 24 May 1906; SLC to Frank Doubleday, before May 1906, *UCCL* 12907; SLC to Frank Doubleday, 23 May 1906, *UCCL* 07445.

54. Frank Doubleday to SLC, 17 December 1906, *UCLC* 35776; Elia W. Peattie, "Among the New Books," *Chicago Tribune*, 27 July 1907, 9; SLC to Helen Roberts, 8 November 1909, *UCCL* 08485; Jones, "Determinism of *What Is Man?*," 1–17; *AMT*, 2:314.

55. Frank, *Our America*, 43; Mencken, *Chrestomathy*, 487; Kaplan, *Mr. Clemens and Mark Twain*, 347.

56. *Springfield Republican*, 3 June 1905, 14; *Mark Twain's Letters* (1917), 771–72; SLC to unidentified, ca. June 1905, *UCCL* 07053; Yurán, "Twain at Norfolk," 14; SLC to Clara Clemens, 11 June 1905, *UCCL* 07061; IVLD, 7 June 1905.

57. Isabel V. Lyon to Raffaello Stiattesi, 12 August 1905, *UCCL* 11749; *HHR*, 589, 596. 598; "Mark Twain in Poor Health," *Springfield Republican*, 20 August 1905, 8; "Mark Twain in Norfolk," *New Haven Journal and Courier*, 14 August 1905, 5; "Mark Twain and the Gout," *Logansport Reporter*, 1 September 1905, 12; Hill, *God's Fool*, 114; *JHT*, 379; Andrews 222–23; "Mark Twain Banqueted," *Berkshire Eagle*, 29 August 1905, 9.

58. *CTSSE*, 660; "Independents Greet Ivins," *New York Tribune*, 4 November 1905, 2.

59. SLC to Clara Clemens, 15 October 1905, *UCCL* 07177; *HHR*, 602; IVLD, 21 October 1905, 24 October 1905; "Twain Makes Authors Forget Jerome," *Boston Journal*, 26 October

1905, 12; "Reception to Mark Twain," *Boston Globe*, 26 October 1905, 14; "Table Gossip," *Boston Globe*, 29 October 1905, 44; Richards et al., *Julia Ward Howe*, 341; "Mark Twain the Guest," *Boston Herald*, 27 October 1905, 14; "At the Round Table Club," *Boston Globe*, 27 October 1905, 3; *AMT*, 3:242; "Mark Twain Talks Peace," *Chicago Tribune*, 5 November 1905, 1; SLC to Clara Clemens and Jean Clemens, 1 November 1905, *UCCL* 13130; SLC to Hamilton Osgood, 24 November 1905, *UCCL* 13049; "The Observant Citizen," *Boston Post*, 8 November 1905, 6.

60. *The Devil's Race-Track* 369–72; "Journey to an Asterisk" (DV 203).

61. "The Argument Against Acceptance," *New York Outlook*, 8 April 1905, 868; *CTSSE*, 656–57; *JHT*, 366.

62. *JHT*, 408–9.

63. SLC to Clara Clemens, 8 June 1905, *UCCL* 07060; SLC to Clara Clemens, 18 June 1905, *UCCL* 07063; SLC to Clara Clemens, 18 October 1905, *UCCL* 07179; Skandera Trombley, *Twain's Other Woman*, 56–58, 81, 84; *AMT*, 3:340; IVLD, 2 September 1905, 1 November 1905, 8 December 1905; "'Football' Barney Weds," *Trenton Times*, 5 September 1905, 6; *MTB*, 1339.

Chapter 13

1. "Mark Twain to Move," *Baltimore Sun*, 2 May 1906, 10; *MTCI*, 359; "What Mark Twain Said," *Richmond Times-Dispatch*, 27 October 1908, 4; *MTCI*, 508–9; SLC to Herbert Putnam, 21 November 1905, *UCCL* 07216; "The New Rasselas Abroad," *Upper Des Moines Republican*, 29 November 1905, 4; "Mark Twain Here; Will See President," *Washington Times*, 27 November 1905, 1; "Mark Twain at White House," *New Haven Journal and Courier*, 28 November 1905, 1; IVLD, 28 November 1905; SLC to Edith Roosevelt, 28 November 1905, *UCCL* 07221; "America's Greatest Humorist and His Thanksgiving Message," *Washington Times*, 27 November 1905, 1; "Silhouettes," *Portland Oregonian*, 29 November 1905, 8.

2. SLC to George Harvey, 7 October 1905, *UCCL* 12900; W. D. Howells to T. S. Perry, 10 December 1905, *UCLC* 37053; *MTSpk*, 462; *Trenton Times*, 3 December 1905, 4; "Twain's Birthday," *Waterbury Democrat*, 6 December 1905, 6; *MTB*, 1258; Skandera Trombley, *Twain's Other Woman*, 89; SLC to Andrew Carnegie, 6 December 1905, *UCCL* 07242.

3. W. D. Howells to T. S. Perry, 10 December 1905, *UCLC* 37053; "Compliment to Mark Twain," *Chicago Inter Ocean*, 7 January 1906, 38; Theodore Roosevelt to George Harvey, 28 November 1905, *UCLC* 48335; "Twain's Birthday," *Waterbury Democrat*, 6 December 1905, 6; Burroughs, *Life and Letters*, 88; "Mark Twain on Friends and Fighters," *Philadelphia North American*, 1 January 1906, 14.

4. Orcutt, *In Quest of the Perfect Book*, 177; *MTSpk*, 464; Matthews, *Tocsin of Revolt*, 274; Bellamy, *Twain as a Literary Artist*, 23; IVLD, 18 January 1906; SLC to George Harvey, 24 December 1905, *UCCL* 07270. Matthews quotes Tennyson's tribute to Wellington ("good gray head that all men knew").

5. SLC to Daniel Frohman, 16 November 1905, *UCCL* 07209; *MTCI*, 528; IVLD, 4 February, 6 April, 4 February, and 25 August 1906; "Gossip of the Stage," *Baltimore American*, 16 June 1906, 10; Wagenknecht, *Twain: The Man and His Work*, 37; "Mark Twain on Peter Pan," *Washington Star*, 13 October 1907, 6; "New York Society," *New York Tribune*, 7 December 1905, 6; SLC to Louis Windmüller, 12 December 1905?, *UCCL* 07248; "Greets Mrs. Roosevelt," *New York Tribune*, 16 March 1906, 6.

6. *AMT,* 3:202; IVLD, 26 December 1905; SLC to Gertrude Natkin, 4–9 March 1906, *UCCL* 07375; SLC to Gertrude Natkin, 18 March 1906, *UCCL* 07393; SLC to Gertrude Natkin, 8 April 1906, *UCCL* 07421; Cooley, "Twain's Aquarium," 20–21; Cooley, *Twain's Aquarium,* 242.

7. "$50,000 Advance Sale," *Montreal Gazette,* 9 December 1905, 4; Sam and Lee Shubert to SLC, 13 December 1905, *UCLC* 35044; *AMT,* 2:133; IVLD, 18 December 1905; "Sarah Bernhardt and Mark Twain," *Baltimore American,* 19 December 1905, 5; "Literary Notes," *New York Tribune,* 18 December 1905, 5; "Sarah and Mark Benefit a Benefit," *New York Evening World,* 19 December 1905, 17.

8. "Mark Twain Crowned," *Waterbury Democrat,* 22 December 1905, 8; Beard, *Hardly a Man,* 342–43, 348–49; Morris, *Confessions in Art,* 202–3; "Dinner Given to Mark Twain," Santa Barbara *Morning Press,* 23 December 1905, 1.

9. SLC to Poultney Bigelow, 21 February 1903, *UCCL* 06584; *MTB,* 1260; "Players Welcome Mark Twain," *New York Tribune,* 4 January 1906, 7; IVLD, 3 January 1906.

10. *MTB,* 1262–65.

11. *MTB,* 1266–68; IVLD 9 January 1906, 12 January 1906, 19 January 1906; 20 February 1906; Gold 65.

12. "The 'Auto' Holds Sway," *New York Tribune,* 17 January 1906, 10; "Automobile Topics," *Hartford Courant,* 22 January 1906, 2.

13. *AMT,* 2:8; Booker T. Washington to SLC, 28 December 1905, *UCLC* 35127; Booker T. Washington to SLC, 4 January 1906, *UCLC* 35306; *HHR,* 604; Lentz, "Twain in 1906," 18.

14. *MTSpk,* 478–49; IVLD, 22 January 1906.

15. Lentz, "Twain in 1906," 20; "Mark Twain and the Senators Swap Lies," *Indianapolis News,* 30 January 1906, 5; "Mark Twain Sees Congress," *San Francisco Call,* 30 January 1906, 6; "From Ends of Earth," *New York Tribune,* 17 February 1906, 7; "Brander Matthews Praises Mark Twain," *Topeka Capital,* 24 February 1906, 2; "Of Social Interest," *New York Tribune,* 25 February 1906, 51; *AMT,* 1:413; *MTCI,* 535; "Mr. Clemens Lunches with Friends," *Hartford Courant,* 2 March 1906, 4; "Lincoln Farm Will Be National Park," *San Francisco Call,* 12 February 1906, 6; "Notes of the Stage," *New York Tribune,* 14 April 1906, 7; *Cleveland Plain Dealer,* 30 June 1907, 7. See also "The Theater," *Washington Star,* 24 June 1906, 11.

16. Kaplan, *Singular Mark Twain,* 607; IVLD, 20 October 1905, 5 January 1906, 27 January 1906; Skandera Trombley, *Twain's Other Woman,* 81, 83; SLC to Clara Clemens, 20 October 1905; Skandera Trombley, "'She Wanted to Kill,'" 230–31; Hill, *God's Fool,* 120–21.

17. "Police Use Clubs and Start Riot," *San Francisco Call,* 5 March 1906, 1; "Fight to See Twain," *New York Tribune,* 5 March 1906, 1; "Captain Daly Shifted," *New York Tribune,* 24 March 1906, 10; Lentz, "Twain in 1906," 27.

18. Leary, "Twain at Barnard College," 13, 15–17; Garland, *Diaries,* 191–92; "Meeting to Aid Blind," *New York Tribune,* 30 March 1906, 7; IVLD, 29 March 1906; *AMT,* 1:464; *AMT,* 2:16; *Buffalo News,* 31 March 1906, 2; Frank, *Our America,* 42; "New Plays for Vassar Aid," *New York Sun,* 3 April 1906, 7; Monterey, Va., *Highland Recorder,* 13 April 1906, 2; "Lion at University Club," *New York Tribune,* 4 April 1906, 4; "Twain Guest of 300 Women," *Trenton Times,* 9 April 1906, 2.

19. *AMT,* 1:403–5; McFarland 206; Herbert Welsh to SLC, 15 December 1906, *UCLC* 35774; *MTCI,* 657.

20. *JHT,* 356, 369; *AMT,* 2:9, 3:136, 3:162, 3:173, 3:187; SLC to Fred Duneka, 30 December 1903, *UCCL* 06773; Kaplan, *Mr. Clemens and Mark Twain,* 372; SLC to Jean Clemens, 12 October 1908, *UCCL* 08136.

21. *JHT*, 371; *Who Is Mark Twain?* 60; IVLD, 14 March 1907; SLC to Lyman P. Powell, 27 May 1907, *UCCL* 07734; *MTHL*, 845.

22. "Friends of Russian Freedom," *NYT*, 13 June 1891, 8; *MTN* 217; Foner, *Twain: Social Critic*, 316; *JHT*, 366; Gribben, *Twain's Library*, 269; Robert Crozier Long, "Gorky in Prison Writes a Play," *San Francisco Examiner*, 2 March 1905, 4.

23. IVLD, 28 March 1906; *MTB*, 1283; *AMT*, 1:462; SLC to Clara Clemens, 8 April 1906, *UCCL* 07420; "Russian Republic Near, Declares Leader Here," *NYT*, 7 April 1906, 1; "Hoppe Beats Cutler," *New York Tribune*, 12 April 1906, 5; Hoppe 114.

24. Poole 80; "Gorky and Mark Twain Meet," *New York Sun*, 12 April 1906, 2; *MTSpk*, 513; "Gorky and Twain Plead for Revolution," *NYT*, 12 April 1906, 4; "Maxim Gorky Visits the Tomb of Grant," *NYT*, 13 April 1906, 2.

25. *MTB*, 1282; "Mark Twain's Position," *NYT*, 15 April 1906, 3; *MTCI*, 541; *AMT*, 1:462–63; "Maxim Gorky, Russian Patriot and His Wife," *New York Evening World*, 11 April 1906, 3; "Maxim Gorky on the Russian Revolution," *New York Times Magazine*, 15 April 1906, 1.

26. Kaplan, *Mr. Clemens and Mark Twain*, 367; "Hotels Turn Gorky Away," *New York Sun*, 15 April 1906, 1; "M. Gorky Is Hostile," *Washington Star*, 15 April 1906, 1; Gorky, *Selected Letters*, 111: Poole 79, 81; Wells, "Maxim Gorky in America," *Otago (N.Z.) Star*, 23 October 1906, 8; Foner, *Twain: Social Critic*, 123; "Maxim Gorky Snubbed," *Brisbane Telegraph*, 7 June 1906, 2; "A Cloud-Burst of Calamities" (DV 246).

27. "A Cloud-Burst of Calamities" (DV 246); "Gorky Sent from Hotel," *New York Tribune*, 15 April 1906, 2; "Gorky and Actress are Driven from Their Hotel," *New York Evening World*, 14 April 1906, 2; *MyMT*, 95; Poole 82; *MTB*, 1285; Beard, *Hardly a Man*, 347.

28. *MTB*, 1285; SLC to Charlotte Teller, 4 May 1906, *UCCL* 08256; SLC to Charlotte Teller, 6 May 1906, *UCCL* 08257; Giddings, "The Social Lynching of Gorky and Andreiva," *Independent*, 26 April 1906, 976–78; IVLD, 26 August 1906; "Cheer Slav Patriots," *New York Tribune*, 5 March 1907, 5; Isabel Hapgood to SLC, 5 March 1907, *UCLC* 36193; Arthur Bullard to SLC, 27 February 1907, *UCLC* 36160; Nikolai Tchaikovsky to SLC, 1 April 1907, *UCLC* 35995; "Mark Twain Leads Appeal to Liberate Noted Nihilists," *Los Angeles Herald*, 27 December 1907, 1; "Cable Appeal for Tchaykovsky," *New York Tribune*, 17 April 1908, 4; "Should Pauren Be Sent Back?" *Buffalo Times*, 27 September 1908, 45; "Americans Active for Tchaykovsky," *NYT*, 2 December 1909, 6; Langdon, *Clemens: Some Reminiscences*, 12; Sinclair, *Mammonart*, 328.

29. "Russian Authors Amazed," *Washington Post*, 23 April 1906, 1; "Gorky in America," *Washington Star*, 23 April 1906, 4; "Gorky's Joke on Mark Twain," *Scranton Truth*, 17 April 1906, 6.

30. "The Fall of an Idol," *Wairarapa Age*, 5 June 1906, 7; Foner, *Twain: Social Critic*, 124; Gorky, *Selected Letters*, 159; "Gorky to Return to America Once More," *San Diego Union*, 10 April 1910, 15.

31. *LMT*, 276; *MTSpk*, 517, 519–20; "Natives of California Give Way to Feeling," *Brooklyn Eagle*, 21 April 1906, 3; "Mark Twain's Plea," *Brooklyn Eagle*, 22 April 1906, 7; "Californians Here Meet," *New York Sun*, 22 April 1906, sec. 2, 3; "City Rushes Relief," *New York Tribune*, 22 April 1906, 4; "Californians Arrange to Give Aid to Victims," *New York Evening World*, 21 April 1906, 2; "A Shot That Failed," *New York Tribune*, 25 April 1906, 5.

32. SLC to Samuel Merwin, 24 July 1906, *UCLC* 35513; "Bureau to Watch All Legislation," *Washington Times*, 19 September 1906, 3.

33. SLC to Fred Duneka, 2 October 1905, *UCCL* 08244; "'Mark Twain' at His Home Among the Granite Hills," *Boston Herald*, 23 September 1906, 36; *MTB*, 1307; SLC to T.

B. Aldrich, 26 April 1906, *UCCL* 07435; IVLD, 8 June 1906; SLC to Clara Clemens, 18–19 June 1906, *UCCL* 07462; SLC to Jean Clemens, 1 July 1906, *UCCL* 04682; SLC to Charlotte Teller, 10 June 1906, *UCCL* 08260; *MTB*, 1315; "Rogers' Yacht Wins," *Fort Worth Star-Telegram*, 25 July 1906, 1; *MTHL*, 810, 819; *JHT*, 387; *AMT*, 2:27; *HHR*, 611.

34. *MTHL*, 811, 815; IVLD, 19 June 1906; Lentz, "Twain in 1906," 36.

35. Fred Duneka to SLC, 11 October 1905, *UCLC* 34687; SLC to Duneka, 4 June 1906, *UCCL* 07448; *HHR*, 609–12; IVLD, ca. 22 June 1906; Jordan 220–21; S. S. McClure to SLC, 2 July 1906, *UCLC* 35495; Hill, *God's Fool*, 142; Lentz, "Twain in 1906," 33.

36. *HHR*, 613; *AMT*, 2:158–59, 161; IVLD, 28 July 1906; *MTHL*, 827.

37. SLC to Isabel V. Lyon, 10 July 1906, *UCCL* 07478; SLC to Clara Clemens, 3 August 1906, *UCCL* 07489; *MTB*, 1322; Kiskis xxv.

38. Chambers, "Walks and Talks," *Brooklyn Eagle*, 8 September 1906, 24; "Books and Reading," *New York Evening Post*, 7 January 1907, 6; "Topics of the Week," *New York Times Book Review*, 29 September 1906, 602; *New York Sun*, 19 January 1907, 7; George Wharton James, "Charles Warren Stoddard," 668–69; Helen Keller to SLC, 18 December 1906, *UCLC* 36128.

39. "Mark Twain Buys Farm Home," *New York Tribune*, 10 April 1906, 6; Hill, *God's Fool*, 126; "Mark Twain Joins Redding's Literary Colony," *New Haven Journal and Courier*, 7 April 1906, 8; SLC to Clara Clemens, 3 August 1906, *UCCL* 07489; SLC to Clara Clemens, 28 August 1906, *UCCL* 07510; IVLD, 13 August 1906, 16 January 1907; Jean Clemens diary, 20 August 1906, 4 February 1907; Doubleday, "Stormfield," 608; "Mark Twain Buys Farm," *New York Tribune*, 14 March 1907, 1; "Redding News of General Interest to Our Readers," *Bridgeport Farmer*, 2 April 1909, 8; Skandera Trombley, *Twain's Other Woman*, 116.

40. Doubleday, "Stormfield," 608; IVLD, 6 August 1906, 9 April 1907, 23 May 1907; *LMT*, 289; Jean Clemens diary, 21 May 1907.

41. Jean Clemens diary, 23 November 1906; *MTCI*, 559; *AMT*, 3:257–58.

42. Skandera Trombley, *Twain's Other Woman*, 106; IVLD, 9 June 1906, 26 July 1906, 20 September 1906, 29 September 1906, 2 October 1906; *AMT*, 3:316; Jean Clemens diary, 29 September 1906, 5 October 1906, 8 October 1906.

43. Hill, *God's Fool*, 148; Jean Clemens diary, 4 July 1906, 4 October 1906, 5 January 1907; Kaplan, *Singular Mark Twain*, 623.

44. Jean Clemens diary, 26 September 1906, 27 September 1906, 18 October 1906, 25 October 1906; IVLD, 27 September 1906, 25 October 1906, 27 October 1906; Hill, *God's Fool*, 155: SLC to Jean Clemens, 29 October 1906, *UCCL* 07558; *HHR*, 620.

45. Skandera Trombley, *Twain's Other Woman*, 118; Jean Clemens diary, 20 November 1900, 14 January 1907, 2 February 1907, 8 May 1907, 12 October 1907, and 1 December 1907; "Miss Clemens's Plea," *New York Tribune*, 24 December 1906, 9; Shelden, *Twain: Man in White*, 231; Hill, *God's Fool*, 167.

46. SLC to George J. Helmer, 23 February 1907, *UCLC* 36150; S. S. McClure to SLC, 28 February 1907, *UCLC* 36165; SLC to S. S. McClure on or after 28 February 1907, *UCCL* 13383.

47. SLC to Mary Rogers, 21–23 September 1906, *UCCL* 07528; Hill, *God's Fool*, 147; SLC to Jean Clemens, 23 September 1906, *UCCL* 07529; SLC to Jean Clemens, 13 November 1906, *UCCL* 07568; *MTSpk*, 529; "Twain's 'First Appearance,'" *New York Sun*, 24 September 1906, 3; "Mark Twain's Daughter Here," *Passaic News*, 16 November 1906, 1.

48. "Twain's 'Eve's Diary' Barred," *Waterbury Democrat*, 24 November 1906, 8; *Chicago Tribune*, 30 November 1906, 8; "Library Bars 'Eve's Diary,'" Santa Cruz *Sentinel*, 26 November 1906, 1; SLC to Mary Rogers, 26 November 1906, *UCCL* 07576; *MTCI*, 558–59; Walter A.

Sinclair, "Eve: Her Diary," *Washington World*, 26 November 1906, 14; "Starbeams," *Kansas City Star*, 30 November 1906, 10; "Has Not Seen Twain's Eve," *Boston Herald*, 25 November 1906, 3; *Duluth News-Tribune*, 17 January 1907, 8.

49. Wallace, *Twain and the Happy Island*, 122; Quick, *Enchantment*, 19; Smith, *Interesting People*, 189; SLC to Mary B. Rogers, 14 August 1906, *UCCL* 07499.

50. *AMT*, 2:250; IVLD, 25 June 1905, 8 October 1906; Isabel V. Lyon to Harriet E. Whitmore, 12 November 1906, *UCCL* 10962; *MTB*, 1342; "Mark Twain as His Daughter Sees Him," *Boston Herald*, 14 June 1908, 3; Gillman, *Dark Twins*, 146; Cooley, "Twain's Heroic Maidens," 42; Krauth, *Proper Mark Twain*, 257; Flagg, *Roses and Buckshot*, 168–70; SLC to Jean Clemens, 5 March 1907, *UCCL* 07670; SLC to Clara Clemens, 5 March 1907, *UCCL* 07671; SLC to Clara Clemens, 5 April 1908, *UCCL* 07969; "Earl Grey Banqueted in New York," *Sheffield Telegraph*, 2 April 1906, 6.

51. *MTCI*, 556, 562–63; *AMT*, 3:253; "Mark Twain Has Now Taken Up Dress Reform," *San Francisco Examiner*, 8 December 1906, 1; "Mark Twain Has Suit of White," *Boston Globe*, 15 February 1907, 5; SLC to Jean Clemens, 14 May 1907, *UCCL* 07720; Skandera Trombley, *Twain's Other Woman*, 112–13. SLC similarly approved peek-a-boo skirts and blouses for women for their "obvious advantages of being cool and comfortable."

52. IVLD, 22 July 1905; *MTSpk*, 533–34, 538; *MTB*, 1343; *MyMT*, 96; SLC to Jean Clemens, 7 December 1906, *UCCL* 07582; "The Contrast," *Washington Herald*, 3 March 1907, 6; SLC to Champ Clark, 11 December 1908, *UCCL* 11688; "Mark Twain in White Attire," *New York Sun*, 8 December 1906, 4; "Mark Twain, Lobbyist," *NYT*, 11 December 1906, 1; SLC to Kate Douglas Wiggin, 7 December 1906, *UCCL* 08271; *Buffalo Commercial*, 15 April 1907, 15; *Brooklyn Eagle*, 12 July 1908, 27; *MTCI*, 568.

53. "Puerto Rico Message," *Waterbury Democrat*, 12 December 1906, 8; *MTCI*, 571; *MTB*, 1351; Helen Keller to SLC, 18 December 1906, *UCLC* 36128.

54. SLC to Champ Clark, 5 June 1909, *UCCL* 08415.

55. SLC to Fred Duneka, 16 July 1905, *UCCL* 08240; *The $30,000 Bequest*, 20; "Good Things by Mark Twain," *Philadelphia Inquirer*, 18 November 1906, 11; *MTCR*, 567–68; "New Books," *New York Sun*, 6 October 1906, 10; "Stories and Sketches by Mark Twain," *Brooklyn Eagle*, 13 October 1906, 10; "The Novels of the Season," *American Monthly Review of Reviews* 35 (January 1907): 127; "Books and Their Writers," *Louisville Courier-Journal*, 3 November 1906, 5; "The 30,000 Dollar Bequest," *Sydney World's News*, 23 February 1907, 28; "New or Recent Books," *Western Morning News*, 2 April 1907, 8; "Fiction," *Baltimore Sun*, 23 January 1907, 12; "A Mark Twain Miscellany," *London Morning Post*, 14 February 1907, 3; "Our Book Table," *Zion's Herald*, 21 November 1906, 1490.

56. *HHR*, 620; *LMT*, 201; IVLD, 30 December 1907, 1 January 1907; "Twain Gives Guests Music over a Wire," *San Jose Mercury News*, 7 January 1907, 9; *AMT*, 2:447; *MTCI*, 575.

Chapter 14

1. SLC to John Y. W. MacAlister, 29 November 1906, *UCCL* 07577; IVLD, 12 December 1906, 1 January 1907, 6 January 1907, 7 January 1907; Hoffmann, *Twain in Paradise*, 76; *JHT*, 342, 391; "Mark Twain Was Resting," *Brooklyn Eagle*, 9 January 1907, 18; Hill, *God's Fool*, 160–61.

2. IVLD, 10 January 1907, 12 January 1907; SLC to Jean Clemens, 11 January 1907, *UCCL* 07625; SLC to Jean Clemens, 26 January 1907, *UCCL* 07635; *HHR*, 625; Jean Clemens diary, 4 February 1907; E. L. Hunt to Isabel V. Lyon, 22 February 1907, *UCLC* 36148.

3. *AMT*, 2:374–76; IVLD, 16 January 1907, 17 January 1907; *MTB*, 1365; Helen Keller to SLC, 18 February 1907, *UCLC* 36133; Keller, *Midstream*, 56–57.

4. "Bret Harte," *San Francisco Argonaut*, 5 February 1894, 5; IVLD, 28 January 1907, 30 January 1907; Eleanor Robson to SLC, 29 January 1907, *UCLC* 35880; SLC to Eleanor Robson, 30 January 1907, *UCCL* 12538; Jean Clemens diary, 30 January 1907; "Aid for Harte's Daughter," *NYT*, 30 January 1907, 18; "Benefit for Bret Harte's Daughter," *New York Tribune*, 30 January 1907, 6; "Mark Twain's Flat 'No,'" *New York American*, 1 February 1907, 7.

5. *AMT*, 2:415, 2:417, 2:422, 2:427; Webster, *Twain: Business Man*, viii.

6. "Benefit for Bret Harte's Daughter," *New York Tribune*, 15 February 1907, 3; Scharnhorst, "Bret Harte–Mark Twain Feud," 29–32.

7. *HHR*, 610; Witter Bynner to SLC, 2 January 1907, *UCLC* 35810; "Gossip of Books and People Who Make Them," *San Francisco Call*, 28 April 1907, 13; SLC to John Greenall, 6 April 1906, *UCCL* 08891; SLC to Florence Jones, 27 May 1907, *UCCL* 07732; SLC to J. Wylie Smith, 7 August 1909, *UCCL* 08440; SLC to Jean Clemens, 17 January 1907, *UCCL* 07615.

8. "Books and Authors," *New York Sun*, 11 January 1907, 9; "Mark Twain on Christian Science," *Washington Times*, 12 January 1907, 6; "Mark Twain's Latest," *New York Times Saturday Review of Books*, 12 January 1907, 21; "M. Twain on Christian Science," *New York Sun*, 16 February 1907, 8; "Our Book Table," *Christian Observer*, 20 March 1907, 7; *MTCR*, 573, 576–77, 581–82; *New York Sun*, 12 October 1907, 7; "Mark Twain on Christian Science," *Spectator*, 6 April 1907, 536–37; "Books and Authors," *Pittsburgh Press*, 23 February 1907, 16; *Janesville (Wisc.) Gazette*, 13 May 1907, 4; "Christian Science," *Book News* 25 (May 1907): 624; "Books and Magazines," *Los Angeles Herald*, 28 April 1907, sec. 3, 6; "Letters on Books," *Truth*, 1 May 1907, 1100–1101; "Mark Twain Pictures Mrs. Eddy and Dollar," *Boston Herald*, 3 Feb 1907, 1; "Mark Twain on Mrs. Eddy's Cult," *Chicago Tribune*, 3 February 1907, sec. 8, 16; "Books of the Day," *Newcastle Chronicle*, 31 July 1907, 8.

9. *New York Tribune*, 12 October 1907, 7; "Literature," *Athenaeum*, 20 April 1907, 467; "Books and Bookmen," *Brooklyn Times Union*, 2 March 1907, 27; "Mark Twain and Mrs. Eddy," *Sydney Australian Star*, 18 May 1907, 9; "Notes on the New Books," *Nashville Tennessean*, 17 February 1907, 34; *MTCR*, 568; "Library Table," *Northern Christian Advocate*, 9 May 1907, 290; "New Books," *Catholic World* 86 (November 1907): 244–46.

10. Edward A. Kimball, "Mark Twain, Mrs. Eddy, and Christian Science," *Cosmopolitan* 43 (May 1907): 38; B. O. Flower, "Mark Twain's Attack on Christian Science," *Arena* 38 (November 1907): 567; Charles Klein and Charles Johnston, "Mark Twain and Christian Science," *North American Review*, 15 March 1907, 636–45; "The Law of Pure Literature," *Washington Star*, 30 August 1907, 14; "Books, Authors and Arts," *Springfield Republican*, 17 February 1907, 23; "New Books Reviewed," *Hartford Courant*, 6 March 1907, 19; *MTCR*, 579; *Spectator*, 6 April 1907, 536; "Among Books and Writers," *Syracuse Post-Standard*, 9 March 1907, 4; "New Books," *Scotsman*, 25 March 1907, 2; "Mark Twain and Mrs. Eddy," *Melbourne Argus*, 11 May 1907, 6; "Mark Twain's New Book," *Brooklyn Eagle*, 23 February 1907, 10; "Mark Twain and Christian Science," *North American Review*, 15 March 1907, 642.

11. *Manchester Guardian*, 18 April 1907, 5; *New York Tribune*, 12 October 1907, 5; "Mark Twain on Mrs. Eddy," *Brooklyn Standard Union*, 28 April 1907, 23; "New Books at the Library," *San Jose Mercury News*, 24 March 1907, 20; Carl T. Robertson, "Mark Twain, Investigator of Christian Science," *Cleveland Plain Dealer*, 24 February 1907, magazine, 7; "Mark

Twain on Mrs. Eddy," *Philadelphia Inquirer*, 4 March 1907, 9; "Mark Twain on Mrs. Eddy," *Sydney Herald*, 11 May 1907, 4; "Is Mrs. Eddy Sane?" *New York Outlook*, 9 March 1907, 545; "Mark Twain on Christian Science," *Manchester Guardian*, 1 April 1907, 3; *Plymouth Western Evening Herald*, 6 April 1907, 2; "Literary Notes," *Adelaide Register*, 20 April 1907, 9; *MTCR*, 576–80; "Mark Twain's Opinion of Mrs. Eddy," *Melbourne Age*, 20 April 1907, 6; "Christian Science," *Adelaide Express and Telegraph*, 20 April 1907, 5; "Are We Standing at the Birth of a Great Religion?" *Current Literature* 42 (March 1907): 321; "Books and Men Who Make Them," *Chicago Inter Ocean*, 2 March 1907, 5; "Books and Their Makers," *St. Joseph (Mo.) News-Press*, 2 March 1907, 8; "Mark Twain's New Book," *Buffalo Times*, 3 February 1907, 47; "Mark Twain on Mrs. Eddy," *Times Literary Supplement*, 5 April 1907, 108; *MTHL*, 847.

12. SLC to Jean Clemens, 14 February 1907, *UCCL* 07649; Hill, *God's Fool*, 164–65; "Men, Women and Affairs," *Springfield Republican*, 17 February 1907, 6; "New York Society," *New York Tribune*, 15 February 1907, 6; "Keats-Shelley Matinee," *New York Sun*, 15 February 1907, 6; IVLD, 14 February 1907; SLC to Clara Clemens, 5 March 1907, *UCCL* 07671; Robert Underwood Johnson to SLC, 1 March 1907, *UCLC* 36172; William James, *Letters*, 2:264.

13. Hill, *God's Fool*, 170; SLC to Clara Clemens, 24 February 1907, *UCCL* 07662; IVLD, 28 March 1907; Lystra, *Dangerous Intimacy*, 15; Messent, *Twain and Male Friendship*, 147.

14. IVLD, 10 March 1907, 17 March 1907, 18 March 1907; SLC to Clara Clemens, 12 March 1907, *UCCL* 07675; Hill, *God's Fool*, 181–82; "Mark Twain at Bermuda," *Fort Worth Star-Telegram*, 3 April 1907, 7; SLC to Lilian Aldrich, 21 March 1907, *UCCL* 07676; *AMT*, 3:13.

15. *HHR*, 624; IVLD, 12 January 1907, 2 April 1907, 5 April 1907; "Noted Men at Hooker Funeral," *Boston Herald*, 27 January 1907, 14; Jervis Langdon II to SLC, 12 March 1907, *UCLC* 36230; Jervis Langdon II to SLC, 31 March 1907, *UCLC* 36291; "Plays for Mark Twain," *Elmira Star-Gazette*, 5 April 1907, 5; Max Eastman, "Mark Twain's Elmira," *Harper's Monthly* 176 (May 1938): 620.

16. Samuels, *Girl in the Red Velvet Swing*, *passim*.

17. *AMT*, 2:454–55; *CTSSE*, 550–53.

18. *MTCI*, 655–56; Waife-Goldberg, *My Father, Sholom Aleichem*, 187; Budd, *Our Mark Twain*, 191; "The Drama in Young Hands," *New York Sun*, 15 April 1907, 3; "Mark Twain Tells of Being an Actor," *NYT*, 15 April 1907, 9; SLC to Amelia Hookway, October 1908, *UCCL* 08096; Heniger, *Children's Educational Theatre*, 60; "Mark Twain's Theater Party," *Cleveland Plain Dealer*, 24 November 1907, 57; "Greet Mark Twain," *New York Tribune*, 20 November 1907, 4; "At Educational Alliance," *Brooklyn Eagle*, 20 November 1907, 4; *MTSpk*, 596; "The Stage to Remain Unelevated," *Kansas City Star*, 10 August 1909, 4.

19. "News of the Clubs," *New York Tribune*, 13 May 1907, 5; "Lincoln's Acts are Lauded by Miss Tarbell," *Detroit Times*, 9 February 1909, 1.

20. SLC to Nikolai Tchaikovsky, 16 April 1906, *UCCL* 10748; IVLD, 12 March 1907; "Count Spiridovich Gives a Luncheon," *NYT*, 28 March 1907, 9; *New York Worker*, 27 April 1907, 4; Nikolai Tchaikovsky to SLC, 1 April 1907, *UCLC* 35995; "Spiridovich's Mission," *NYT*, 7 April 1907, V, 17.

21. SLC to Jean Clemens, 22 April 1907; interview with Joseph Hooker Twichell, 14 August 1957, *MTP*; Strong, *Twichell: Mark Twain's Friend and Pastor*, 138–39.

22. *MTCI*, 583–86; SLC to Clara Clemens, 2 May 1907, *UCCL* 07705; SLC to Isabel V. Lyon, 29 April 1907, *UCCL* 07698; "Joke on Mark Twain," *Washington Post*, 5 May 1907, 14; "Mark Twain and Yacht Missing," *New York Tribune*, 4 May 1907, 1.

23. *Brooklyn Eagle*, 13 May 1907, 26; "Mark Twain Fuss at Actors' Fair," *NYT*, 1 May 1907, 2; "Warm Apologies to Mark Twain," *NYT*, 2 May 1907, 11; "Nice Little Row over Mark Twain," *Hartford Courant*, 3 May 1907, 9; SLC to Edith Baker, 2 May 1907, *UCCL* 07706; "Actors' Fair Set Going by Roosevelt and Twain," *New York Evening World*, 6 May 1907, 3.

24. "New York Letter," *Cleveland Plain Dealer*, 11 May 1907, 4; *New York Tribune*, 7 May 1907, 4; "Flower Booth the Favorite," *New York Tribune*, 9 May 1907, 4; Barrymore, *Memories*, 154–55. The following August SLC attended a baseball game in New York along with John Philip Sousa, Chauncey Depew, and Richard Harding Davis. Bozeman Bulger, "Real Fan Neither a 'Boob' Nor a 'Bug,'" *New York Evening World*, 15 August 1907, 10.

25. "Mark Twain to Umpire Umpires," *New York Tribune*, 10 May 1907, 14; "Mrs. Rosenfeld Out," *New York Tribune*, 11 May 1907, 10.

26. *AMT*, 3:54; SLC to John Y. W. MacAlister, 29 November 1906, *UCCL* 07577; Hill, *God's Fool*, 166; Eble, *Old Clemens and W.D.H.*, 164.

27. SLC to Jean Clemens, 14 May 1907, *UCCL* 07720; *AMT*, 3:53, 3:468; SLC to C. F. Moberly Bell, 3 May 1907, *UCCL* 12070; "Oxford Degree for Twain," *NYT*, 11 May 1907, 1.

28. Emma Warfield to SLC, 4 March 1907, *UCLC* 36191; Emma Warfield to SLC, 27 March 1907, *UCLC* 36279; IVLD, 9 March 1907, 22 March 1907; Edwin Warfield to SLC, 14 March 1907, *UCLC* 36248.

29. *MTCI*, 604; "Mark Twain in Clover," *Baltimore Sun*, 10 May 1907, 14; Nolan and Tomlinson, "Mark Twain's Visit to Annapolis," 4–7; "Mark Twain at Annapolis," *Baltimore Sun*, 11 May 1907, 4; "Annapolis Laughs," *Baltimore Sun*, 11 May 1907, 10; SLC to Jean Clemens, 14 May 1907, *UCCL* 07720.

30. IVLD, 10 May 1907; *MTCI*, 605.

31. Skandera Trombley, *Twain's Other Woman*, 190–91, 126, 133; "Mark Twain at Tuxedo," *Boston Herald*, 11 May 1907, 2; Hill, *God's Fool*, 159; "Ashcroft Accuses Miss Clara Clemens," *NYT*, 4 August 1909, 1; *HHR*, 625; "Redding News," *Bridgeport Farmer*, 2 April 1909, 8.

32. SLC to Jean Clemens, 14 May 1907, *UCCL* 07720; SLC to Jean Clemens, 26 May 1907, *UCCL* 07730; IVLD, 21 May 1907, 8 June 1907; Jean Clemens diary, 8 June 1907; *MTB*, 1381; *MTCI*, 611.

Chapter 15

1. *AMT*, 3:72; "Good Tales of Notables," *Sacramento Union*, 25 August 1907, 5; *MTCI*, 616; Cooley, *Twain's Aquarium*, 40; Hill, *God's Fool*, 173; "Mark Twain 'Chiefly Foolish,'" *San Antonio Light*, 11 July 1907, 4; "Good Tales of Notables," *Sacramento Union*, 25 August 1907, 5; *MTB*, 1381.

2. *MTB*, 1382; *Edinburgh Dispatch*, 20 June 1907, 5; *MTCI*, 619; Shaw, "Letters to the Editor," 15; "Hotel of the Aristocrats Selected by Mark Twain," *Atlanta Constitution*, 14 July 1907, 4.

3. Phillpotts, "To Samuel Langhorne Clemens," sec. 3, 2; SLC to Eden Phillpotts, 21 June 1907, *UCCL* 09402.

4. Lathem, *Twain's Four Weeks in England*, 140, 145–46, 148; Lucy, *Diary of a Journalist*, 269; *AMT*, 3:113–14; "Congratulates Twain," *Brooklyn Eagle*, 23 June 1907, 45; IVLD, 25

June 1907; "U.S. Ambassador Reid Dined Mark Twain," *Macon Telegraph*, 22 June 1907, 1; "Twain in Pajamas," *Washington Star*, 21 June 1907, 11; *MTB*, 1384; Lucy, "Life in London," 7; Lucy, "Mark Twain," *Bathurst Argus*, 3.

5. *AMT*, 3:113–14; John Y. W. MacAlister to SLC, 21 June 1907, *UCLC* 36642; "Jerome K. Jerome's Explanation of Himself," *New York Times Sunday Magazine*, 20 October 1907, 7; "The Literary Week," *Academy*, 22 June 1907, 596; "Musings without Method," *Blackwood's* 182 (August 1907): 283; "Vanderbilt Marriage Talk," *New York Sun*, 13 October 1907, 3; "Notes of the Week," *Saturday Review*, 22 June 1907, 767–68.

6. "Twain Startles London," *NYT*, 21 June 1907, 1; "Jerome K. Jerome's Explanation of Himself," *New York Times Sunday Magazine*, 20 October 1907, 7; *MTB*, 1385.

7. "Royal Garden Party," *London Tribune*, 24 June 1907, 7; Lucy, *Diary of a Journalist*, 269; *AMT*, 3:144–45; Lathem, *Twain's Four Weeks in England*, 28; Harris, *Contemporary Portraits*, 163; Sydney Brooks, "England's Ovation to Mark Twain," *Harper's Weekly*, 27 July 1907, 1086; *MTSpk*, 607; *MTCI*, 630–31; SLC to Jean Clemens, 23 June 1907, *UCCL* 07767.

8. *MTB*, 1384; Lathem, *Twain's Four Weeks in England*, 156, 158; "Twain at House of Commons," *New York Sun*, 25 June 1907, 3; "Mark Twain Hears Debate," *New York Tribune*, 25 June 1907, 3; "Will the Plan Work?" *Cardiff Western Mail*, 25 June 1907, 4; "Our London Letter," *Gloucester Citizen*, 1 August 1907, 4; *AMT*, 3:74.

9. Brittain, "My Friend Mark Twain," 3; "Mark Twain Has Lunch with London Pilgrims," *Brooklyn Eagle*, 25 June 1907, 3; *MTSpk*, 558; "Mark Twain and the Pilgrims," *London Times*, 26 June 1907, 3; Owen Seaman, "To Mark Twain," *Punch*, 26 June 1907, 463; "The Fool's Reproach," *Academy*, 6 July 1907, 653; "Mark Twain Is Dined at Oxford," *Pawtucket Times*, 26 June 1907, 10.

10. SLC to Jean Clemens, 30 June 1907, *UCCL* 07771; Kipling, *Letters*, 242, 248–49; Wallace, *Twain and the Happy Island*, 37–38. Coincidentally (or not), Kipling's receipt of the Nobel Prize for Literature in 1907 was announced in late October 1907 even as SLC's autobiographical chapter about the festivities at Oxford was appearing in the *North American Review*. According to news reports, SLC lost because the Nobel judges considered him "too flippant and frivolous," especially in light of his humorous denial while in England that he had not stolen the Ascot Cup ("Mark Twain Too Flippant," *North Scot and Moray & Nairn Express*, 26 October 1907, 3).

11. *AMT*, 3:83; Lathem, *Twain's Four Weeks in England*, 50; Jerome, Wisbey, and Snedecor, *Twain in Elmira*, 210; Sydney Brooks, "England's Ovation to Mark Twain." *Harper's Weekly*, 27 July 1907, 1089; "Mark Twain, D.Litt., Oxon.," *NYT*, 27 June 1907, 1; SLC to Jean Clemens, 30 June 1907, *UCCL* 07771; "Mark Twain at Oxford," *Washington Post*, 30 June 1907, 56; Cortissoz, *Life of Whitelaw Reid*, 380–81.

12. "Pageant in the Mist," *London Express*, 28 June 1907, 1; *AMT*, 3:86–87; SLC to Clara Clemens, 30 June 1907, *UCCL* 07773; "Pageant at Oxford," *Washington Herald*, 28 June 1907, 9; SLC to Jean Clemens, 30 June 1907, *UCCL* 07771; "Indorsed by Mark Twain," *Charleston News and Courier*, 24 May 1908, 8; *Mysterious Stranger Manuscripts*, 400, 402; *Mark Twain's Letters* (1917), 827.

13. *AMT*, 3:96, 3:488; SLC to Jean Clemens, 30 June 1907, *UCCL* 07771.

14. Tracy, "Psychology of the Tobacco Habit," 366–67; "Mark Twain Gives Answer," *Meadville Republican*, 3 August 1909, 4; *MTCI*, 689.

15. Marie Corelli to SLC, 23 June 1907, *UCLC* 36672; Ralph Ashcroft to Marie Corelli, 24 June 1907, *UCCL* 07768; *AMT*, 3:98–100; "Court Circular," *London Times*, 1 July 1907, 10; "Local News," *Stratford-Upon-Avon Herald*, 28 June 1907, 8.

16. "Twain's Quiet Times," *Washington Herald*, 7 July 1907, 3; *AMT*, 3:99–100; "Court Circular," *London Times*, 1 July 1907, 10.

17. "Mark Twain and the Savage Club," *London Times*, 1 July 1907, 14; "Mark Twain's Stories," *London Mail*, 1 July 1907, 5; *MTSpk*, 556; *AMT*, 3:101, 3:490.

18. Lathem, *Twain's Four Weeks in England*, 79, 82, 85, 102, 106; "Entertaining Mark Twain," *NYT*, 3 July 1907, 4; *MTB*, 1399; "Komura Meets Twain," *New York Sun*, 10 July 1907, 3; "Travelling with Mark Twain," *Charleston News and Courier*, 4 August 1907, 21; SLC to Clara Clemens, 12 July 1907, *UCCL* 07783.

19. *AMT*, 3:73, 3:109; "Bernard Shaw's Biography," *Springfield Republican*, 25 August 1907, 12; Alan Dent, "Max Is Eighty," *Saturday Review*, 30 August 1952, 20; Shaw, "Letters to the Editor," 15; Shaw, *Collected Letters*, 696–97; "Shaw Baffles Twain," *New York Sun*, 4 July 1907, 3.

20. Baetzhold, *Twain and John Bull*, 247; *MTSpk*, 568–70; "Suppressors of Noise," *New York Sun*, 27 February 1908, 3.

21. *MTSpk*, 575; Lathem, *Twain's Four Weeks in England*, 105.

22. *AMT*, 3:122, 3:124; *MTSpk*, 608–9; "E. V. Lucas and Twain at a '*Punch* Dinner,'" *Bookman* (London) 38 (June 1910): 16–19; Lucy, "Life in London," 7.

23. Lathem, *Twain's Four Weeks in England*, 220; SLC to Edward Russell, 12 July 1907, *UCCL* 07772; *MTSpk*, 582; *MTB*, 1401–2; T. P. O'Connor, "Twain as an Orator," *T.P.'s Weekly*, 19 July 1907, 85; "Liverpool Hears Mark Twain's Best," *Boston Herald*, 11 July 1907, 4; *HHR*, 631; Rodney, *Twain Overseas*, 272.

24. Hill, *God's Fool*, 173; IVLD, 1 July 1907, 25 July 1907; Skandera Trombley, *Twain's Other Woman*, 137, 138, 140; "Denies Betrothal to Mark Twain," *New York Herald*, 3 July 1907, 4; "Note and Comment," *Springfield Republican*, 6 July 1907, 8; "Old Hickory Chips," *Colusa (Calif.) Sun*, 21 September 1907, 4.

25. Welland, *Twain in England*, 229–30; SLC to Jean Clemens, 12 July 1907, *UCCL* 07782; Lathem, *Twain's Four Weeks in England*, 117; "Mark Twain 7 Years Younger," *New York Sun*, 13 July 1907, 1; SLC to Clara Clemens, 12 July 1907, *UCCL* 07783; "Personal," *Pawtucket Times*, 26 July 1907, 6.

26. *MTCI*, 637; SLC to Jean Clemens, 30 June 1907, *UCCL* 07771; "Mark Twain at Sea Promenading the Deck," *Brooklyn Eagle*, 7 August 1907, 22; "Mark Twain's Good-bye," *Pall Mall Gazette*, 13 July 1907, 2; *MTB*, 1403; *AMT*, 3:150.

27. *MTCI*, 638; "Travelling with Mark Twain," *Charleston News and Courier*, 4 August 1907, 21; Quick, "Little Girl's Mark Twain," 342–48; "Mark Twain on Prohibition," *Washington Star*, 22 December 1907, 4.

28. "Mark Twain at Sea," *London Daily News*, 18 July 1907, 7; Lathem, *Twain's Four Weeks in England*, 222; IVLD, 22 July 1907; *MTCI*, 645; Quick, *Enchantment*, 18; Quick, "Little Girl's Mark Twain," 342–48.

Chapter 16

1. Hill, *God's Fool*, xxvi, 185; Jean Clemens diary, 26–27 July and 12 August 1907; Shelden, *Twain: Man in White*, 101; Jean Clemens to SLC, 28 August 1907, *UCCL* 11547; IVLD, 2 October 1907.

2. Jean Clemens diary, 2 October 1907; IVLD, 5 October 1907. Karen Lystra asserts that Lyon was "almost certainly inventing dialogue and disguising her personal bias as a medical dictum when she has Peterson declare authoritatively: 'Jean must never live with her father again.' It was the secretary, not the doctor, who wished to keep Jean and her father separated."

Lystra, *Dangerous Intimacy*, 108. Trouble is, Lyon's comment appears in her private diary, for which she had no reason to invent dialogue or disguise her bias.

3. Jean Clemens diary, 7–8, 12 October 1907; SLC to Jean Clemens, 8 October 1907, *UCCL* 07849. No letters written by Jean Clemens to SLC between 28 August 1907 and 26 May 1908 are extant.

4. SLC to Joseph Pulitzer, 1 September 1907, *UCCL* 07825; IVLD, 27 July 1907, 2 September 1907; *MTCI*, 649.

5. *AMT*, 3:195, 3:198; Glyn, *Romantic Adventure*, 144; Elinor Glyn, *Mark Twain on Three Weeks* (London: privately printed, 1908); Charles Henry Meltzer, "Twain Says He Told Her 'Book a Mistake,'" *New York American*, 27 September 1908, sec. 2, 1.

6. SLC to Joseph Choate, 3 August 1907, *UCCL* 12081; *HHR*, 636, 639; *MTB*, 1406; *AMT*, 3:142; Quick, *Enchantment*, 100; IVLD, 14 October 1907; Jean Clemens diary, 2 November 1907. This letter from SLC to Jean Clemens is now missing. No letters from SLC to Jean Clemens dated between 8 October and 15 November 1907 are extant.

7. *HHR*, 300, 384, 389, 479; Zacharias, "Henry Rogers," 4. See also "Utah Consolidated and Its Owners," *Hartford Courant*, 19 October 1908, 5.

8. John Howells to SLC, 8 August 1907, *UCLC* 37144; McLandburgh Wilson, "The Family Index," *New York Sun*, 6 October 1907, 8; IVLD, 22–23 October 1907; Hill, *God's Fool*, 183; Jean Clemens diary, 23 October 1907.

9. *AMT*, 3:178–79, 3:535; Jean Clemens diary, 1–2 November 1907; *Brooklyn Eagle*, 19 January 1908, 6; "Editorial Comment," *Philadelphia Inquirer*, 20 January 1908, 8.

10. SLC to A. E. Sunderhauf, 15 October 1907, *UCLC* 37334.

11. IVLD, 9 September 1907; "Literary Notes," *Bendigo Independent*, 21 November 1907, 5.

12. *HHR*, 557; *AMT*, 3:122, 270; *MTCI*, 659–60; "Plasmon," *Adelaide Register*, 18 July 1905, 4; "A Mark Twain Company Broke," *New York Sun*, 21 December 1907, 9; *Washington Post*, 27 January 1908, 6.

13. Hill, *God's Fool*, 102; SLC to Isabel V. Lyon, 7 October 1904, *UCCL* 10888; Kaplan, *Singular Mark Twain*, 620; Edward Morris to SLC, 4 December 1907, *UCLC* 37487; "'Mark Twain' Whisky under Patent Rights," *Brooklyn Eagle*, 5 January 1908, 1; "Mark Twain Idea," *Grand Rapids Press*, 7 February 1908, 8; Cardwell, *Man Who Was Mark Twain*, 93.

14. IVLD, 12 September 1907, 1 May 1908; Skandera Trombley, *Twain's Other Woman* 146; Kaplan, *Singular Mark Twain*, 645; Hill, *God's Fool*, 226, 235–37.

15. George Harvey to SLC, 7 September 1906, *UCCL* 08813; Doubleday, "Stormfield," 611; *MTHL*, 811; Cooley, *Twain's Aquarium*, 238–39; SLC to Jean Clemens, 2 October 1908, *UCCL* 08118.

16. Gribben, *Twain's Library*, 763; *Mark Twain's Notebooks and Journals*, 2:369. See also SLC to Jean Clemens, 26 February 1909, *UCCL* 08355: "That poor old Geronimo! I am glad his grand old patriot heart is at peace, no more to know wrong & insult at the hands of the Christian savage"; and "The Dervish and the Offensive Stranger" (1902), in *Europe and Elsewhere*, 312: "And they hunted and harried the original owners of the soil, and robbed them, beggared them, drove them from their homes, and exterminated them, root and branch."

17. *AMT*, 2:194.

18. "The December Harper's," *Brooklyn Eagle*, 19 November 1907, 4; *Bookman* (New York) 26 (December 1907): 323; "Magazines for January," *Salt Lake Herald*, 19 January 1908, 14; "January Magazines," *Washington Star*, 21 December 1907, 11; "Christmas Numbers," *Manchester Guardian*, 13 December 1907, 4; "Mark Twain on Heaven," *Sydney Stock and Station Journal*, 3 April 1908, 2.

19. *MTSpk*, 598–99, 606; "Carnegie, Edison, and Twain," *New York Sun*, 10 December 1907, 4; Cooley, *Twain's Aquarium*, 87–88; "Mark Twain Joshes Howells," *Trenton Times*, 31 December 1907, 2; *MTB*, 1432; Burke, *Feather on My Nose*, 70; "Honor for Mark Twain," *New York Tribune*, 12 January 1908, 9.

20. Hill, *God's Fool*, 196; SLC to Charley Langdon, 11 February 1908, *UCCL* 07934; Skandera Trombley, "Twain's Last Work of Realism," 42; IVLD, 16 February 1908; SLC to Jean Clemens, 20 May 1908, *UCCL* 08005; SLC to Jean Clemens, 21 May 1908, *UCCL* 08006.

21. IVLD, 26 May 1905, 16 January 1908; "Carnegie Finds Pleasure in Giving," *San Francisco Chronicle*, 12 March 1910, 1; Skandera Trombley, *Twain's Other Woman*, 49, 183; SLC to Andrew Carnegie, 10 February 1906, *UCCL* 07337; SLC to Andrew Carnegie, 22 January 1908, *UCCL* 08897; SLC to Julia Langdon, 16 January 1908, *UCCL* 07916; SLC to Joseph Twichell, 21 January 1908, *UCCL* 07923; Cooley, *Twain's Aquarium*, 99; "Twain to Visit Bermuda," *Brooklyn Eagle*, 24 January 1908, 18; Harper, *I Remember*, 145.

22. Hoffmann, *Twain in Paradise*, 95–96; *AMT*, 3:203; Hill, *God's Fool*, 204; IVLD, 8 February 1908; "Mark Twain on 'The Jungle,'" Eau Claire, Wisc., *Leader-Telegram*, 7 August 1906, 4; Sinclair, *Mammonart*, 328; Shelden, *Twain: Man in White*, 211; Wallace 68; *Washington Post*, 3 February 1908, 7; "Mark Twain Home," *Elmira Star-Gazette*, 7 February 1908, 1.

23. SLC to Jean Clemens, 14 February 1908, *UCCL* 07938; "Miss Clemens's Musicale," *NYT*, 14 February 1908, 7; *AMT*, 3:210–11; "Collier Ballet for Collier," *NYT*, 14 February 1908, 7; "Debutantes Give Charity Pantomime," *NYT*, 19 February 1908, 7; "Reid, Guest of Pilgrims," *New York Sun*, 20 February 1908, 5; *MTSpk*, 607–12; IVLD, 21 February 1908.

24. "Two Jokers, One Deck," *New York Tribune*, 23 February 1908, 8; "Rogers Pits His Humor Against Mark Twain's," *New York Evening World*, 22 February 1908, 1; *HHR*, 645.

25. Hill, *God's Fool*, 203–5; Wallace, *Twain and the Happy Island*, 55, 98; IVLD, 28 February 1908; SLC to Clara Clemens, 29 February 1908, *UCCL* 07951; SLC to Clara Clemens, 23 March 1908, *UCCL* 07962; SLC to Mai Coe, 2 March 1908, *UCCL* 07906; Cooley, *Twain's Aquarium*, 118; SLC to Emilie Rogers, 2 March 1908, *UCCL* 07953; SLC to Jean Clemens, 2 March 1908, *UCCL* 07952; Hoffmann, *Twain in Paradise*, 108, 119, 123, 173.

26. "H. H. Rogers Very Feeble," *Philadelphia Inquirer*, 6 March 1908, 1; "Mark Twain Is Rooter," *Cleveland Plain Dealer*, 8 March 1908, 28; "Mark Twain," *Port of Spain Gazette*, 14 May 1908, 5; *MTSpk*, 616; Wallace, *Twain and the Happy Island*, 87; Cooley, *Twain's Aquarium*, 115–16, 119–20; *AMT*, 3:213.

27. Hill, *God's Fool*, 195; *AMT*, 3:220; "H. H. Rogers Very Feeble," *Philadelphia Inquirer*, 6 March 1908, 1; "Mark Twain's Outing in Bermuda," *NYT*, 19 April 1908, 4; "Pursue H. H. Rogers," *New York Tribune*, 12 April 1908, 5; "Mark Twain Having Fun," *Washington Star*, 27 March 1908, 23; IVLD, 23 March 1908; SLC to Clara Clemens, 23 March 1908, *UCCL* 07962; SLC to Clara Clemens, 5 April 1908, *UCCL* 07969; Hoffmann, *Twain in Paradise*, 119, 126; Cooley, *Twain's Aquarium*, 144.

28. Hoffmann, *Twain in Paradise*, 126; *MTCI*, 664–67; *AMT*, 3:221; Harding, "Twain Lands an Angel Fish," 5–10; "Mark Twain Near Death from Wave," *Boston Herald*, 14 April 1908, 16; "Ocean Is Very Wet," *Buffalo Express*, 14 April 1908, 3; "Mark Twain a Hero?" *New York World*, 14 April 1908, 16; "Mark Twain Rescues a Girl as Huge Sea Sweeps the Bermudian," *New York Herald*, 14 April 1908, 5.

29. IVLD, 11 July 1907, 3 January 1908, 22 January 1908, 21 October 1908, 26 October 1908; Kaplan, *Singular Mark Twain*, 639; SLC to Clara Clemens, 30 July 1908, *UCCL* 08066; SLC to George Harvey, 30 July 1908, *UCCL* 08065; SLC to George Harvey, 10 August 1908,

UCCL 08079; *MTHL*, 828–29; Hill, *God's Fool*, 200–201; Skandera Trombley, *Twain in the Company of Women*, 191; *AMT*, 3:619.

30. IVLD, 2–4 May 1908; Skandera Trombley, *Twain's Other Woman*, 146; "Mark Twain as His Daughter Sees Him," *Boston Herald*, 14 June 1908, 3; Clara Clemens to Isabel V. Lyon, 24 June 1908, *UCCL* 08040.

31. IVLD, 26 July 1908; Hill, *God's Fool*, 208–9.

32. "Funny Men Eat Steak," *New York Tribune*, 19 April 1908, 7; "Mark Twain and 6,000 Tots at Mass," *Trenton Times*, 29 April 1908, 1; "Whole City Arrested," *New York Tribune*, 10 May 1908, 1, 5; "City College Dedicates Its Fine New Buildings," *Brooklyn Eagle*, 14 May 1908, 2; SLC to Jean Clemens, 15 May 1908, *UCCL* 07999; Matthews, "Memories of Mark Twain," 81; Starr, "Twain at Stormfield," n.p.; *MyMT*, 97.

33. "Twain Discharges Morgan," *San Francisco Call*, 20 February 1908, 2; "Jubilee Dedication for City College," *NYT*, 14 May 1908, 5; "Twain for Citizenship," *New York Tribune*, 15 May 1908, 2; "Mark Twain's Big Sale of Books," *New York Tribune*, 21 May 1908, 1; "Queen Victoria Birthday Dinner," *New York Tribune*, 24 May 1908, 7; "Twain Visits Allaire," *Monmouth (N.J.) Inquirer*, 4 June 1908, 1.

34. SLC to Mary Rogers, 15 June 1908, *UCCL* 08030; *HHR*, 650; Jeanette Gilder, "The Lounger," *Putnam's* 4 (August and September 1908): 627, 760; "Nothing Said of Any Moving Picture Shows," *Wilkes-Barre Times-Leader*, 19 June 1908, 10; *MTB*, 1450; SLC to Helen Allen, 13 August 1908, *UCCL* 11334; Quick, *Enchantment*, 185.

35. *MTB*, 1452; Cooley, *Twain's Aquarium*, 179; SLC to John Howells, 3 July 1908, *UCCL* 08899; SLC to Clara Clemens, 20 June 1908, *UCCL* 08037.

36. Beard, "Twain as a Neighbor," 706; Beard, *Hardly a Man*, 346–50; SLC to Jean Clemens, 19 June 1908, *UCCL* 08035; *Brooklyn Eagle*, 4 July 1908, 9; "Nutmeg Villagers Greet Mark Twain," *Hawaiian Star*, 8 July 1908, 3; Tarbell, *All in the Day's Work*, 265; *HHR*, 652; SLC to Susan Crane, 12 August 1908, *UCCL* 08083; SLC to Emilie Rogers, 6 August 1908, *UCCL* 08076; Skandera Trombley, *Twain's Other Woman*, 180; SLC to Joe Goodman, 30 July 1908, *UCCL* 08064; SLC to John Brown, Jr., 20 June 1908, *UCCL* 08036.

37. SLC to Clara Clemens, 18 July 1908, *UCCL* 08055; Skandera Trombley, *Twain's Other Woman*, 152; Cooley, *Twain's Aquarium*, 198; *MTHL*, 833.

38. Scharnhorst, "Twain and Julian Hawthorne," 47–54.

39. SLC to Jean Clemens, 14 June 1908, *UCCL* 08028; Ticknor, *Glimpses of Authors*, 149–50; *MTB*, 1456; *MTHL*, 831; *MTSpk*, 679; *AMT*, 1:229, 3:251.

40. *AMT*, 3:343.

41. SLC to Jean Clemens, 2 July 1908, *UCCL* 08051; Skandera Trombley, *Twain's Other Woman*, 179; IVLD, 8 August 1908; Woolf, *Drawn from Life*, 10, 78–80.

42. Jean Clemens to Isabel V. Lyon, 19 October 1908, *UCCL* 08138; *AMT*, 3:342. Hamlin Hill wonders why Jean Clemens "was suddenly separated from the teenaged Marguerite Schmitt, her closest friend" (*God's Fool*, 214), but the separation was only temporary. They were reunited not long after both of them returned to the United States. See also SLC to Jean Clemens, 6 December 1909, *UCCL* 08507.

43. SLC to Emilie R. Rogers, 6 August 1908, *UCCL* 08076; SLC to Emilie R. Rogers, *Mark Twain's Letters* (1917), 815–16; IVLD, 7 August 1908; SLC to Jean Clemens, 9 August 1908, *UCCL* 08077; SLC to Mary Rogers, 17 August 1908, *UCCL* 08069; SLC to Susan Crane, 12 August 1908, *UCCL* 08083; *MTB*, 1458; *HHR*, 657.

44. Skandera Trombley, *Twain's Other Woman*, 162–63, 165; "Engagement of Miss Clemens Is Denied," *Winston-Salem Journal*, 8 September 1908, 1; IVLD, 7 September 1908,

10 September 1908; Shelden, *Twain: Man in White*, 263; Hill, *God's Fool*, 200; Lystra, *Dangerous Intimacy*, 164; "Ashcroft Accuses Miss Clara Clemens," *NYT*, 4 August 1909, 1–2; "Absurd, Says Mark Twain's Daughter," *San Francisco Call*, 10 September 1908, 3.

45. In his memoir, Charles Hoffman, one of the burglars, denied that they broke into the house: one of the kitchen windows "had been left partly open. . . . I entered by the front door, like a gentleman." Hoffman, *In the Clutch of Circumstance*, 171.

46. "Miss Lyons's Story," *New York Evening World*, 18 September 1908, 2; IVLD, 3 October 1908; *MTB*, 1462; "Bold Burglars Rob Mark Twain House," *Brooklyn Eagle*, 18 September 1908, 1; *MTCI*, 670; Charles Hoffman "More from the Burglar," 12. According to New York police commissioner Theodore Bingham, "perhaps half of the criminals" in the city were "Hebrews" (383).

47. Beard, "Twain as a Neighbor," 708–9; *MTCI*, 669; Hill, *God's Fool*, 210; Skandera Trombley, *Twain's Other Woman*, 169; *MTHL*, 835; SLC to Margaret Blackmer, 6–9 October 1908, *UCCL* 08123; SLC to Jean Clemens, 30 November 1908, *UCCL* 08289.

48. *AMT*, 3:278; Cooley, *Twain's Aquarium*, 238–39.

Chapter 17

1. Cooley, *Twain's Aquarium*, 185–86; Cooley, "Twain's Aquarium," 19; Skandera Trombley, *Twain's Other Woman*, 195; "The Aquarium Manuscript" (DV 375; *AMT*, 3:214, 3:219; SLC to Nettie Brockley, 7–10 December 1908, *UCCL* 08166; Moore 3).

2. Cooley, "Twain's Angel-Fish," 4; Hill, *God's Fool*, xxvii, 268; Fishkin, "Twain and Women," 68; Cooley, "Twain's Aquarium," 23; *MTB*, 1440; Hoffmann, *Twain in Paradise*, 129.

3. Cooley, *Twain's Aquarium*, 154, 212–16; IVLD, 26 September 1908; "Theatrical Notes," *NYT*, 27 September 1908, 11; Harding, "Twain Lands an Angel Fish," 9; Burke, *Feather on My Nose*, 70; *Springfield Republican*, 10 January 1909, 21; Billie Burke to SLC, 3 January 1909, *UCLC* 38554; SLC to Laura Frazer, 4 November 1908, *UCCL* 08154; *Is Shakespeare Dead?*, 64; "Mark Twain's Childhood Sweetheart Recalls Their Romance," *Literary Digest*, 23 March 1918, 74.

4. *MTSpk*, 630; Doubleday, "Stormfield," 608, 652; Howden, "Twain as His Secretary Remembers Him," 1–4; *MTHL*, 838; Wallace, *Twain and the Happy Island*, 115–17.

5. Wallace, *Twain and the Happy Island*, 121; Keller, *Midstream*, 63; Shelden, *Twain: Man in White*, 314; IVLD, 11–12 January 1909; Keller, "Mark Twain," 51, 80–81; Alison Leigh Cowan, "Mark Twain as Entertainer and Color Commentator," *NYT*, 25 April 2010, NJ8.

6. "The Week in Society," *Brooklyn Life*, 30 January 1909, 20; "Mark Twain to Attend Dinner," *New York Tribune*, 20 January 1909, 4; *MTSpk*, 632; "Mark Twain Signs Woman Suffrage Petition," *Cleveland Plain Dealer*, 21 February 1909, 39; "Authors and Woman Suffrage," *Washington Post*, 23 April 1909, 6; "Campaign for Suffrage," *Washington Star*, 20 October 1909, 22. Despite his public support for women's rights, as Guy Cardwell remarks, SLC "never developed an appreciation of gender equality and throughout most of his life, for all the customary, evasive reasons, he opposed having women play full political roles." Cardwell, *Man Who Was Mark Twain*, 223. Even in some of his late comments he perpetuated some stereotypes about "the weaker sex," opining that "when a man goes out to buy a collar he comes back with a collar and perhaps a necktie or two. When a woman starts out to buy a collar she returns exhausted with a new silk waist, a pair of gloves, some skirt binding, a cake of soap, a paper of pins, some window curtains, a sewing-machine, and a refrigerator." "Mainly about People," *Perth Daily News*, 24 June 1908, 4.

7. *AMT*, 3:559; "Jerome at Dinner with His Friends," *New York Tribune*, 8 May 1909, 1; *MTSpk*, 643; "A Great Night for Jerome," *New York Sun*, 8 May 1909, 1.

8. *AMT*, 3:298, 3:303, 3:603.

9. Macnaughton, *Twain's Last Years as a Writer*, 232; SLC to Jean Clemens, 26 February 1909, *UCCL* 08355; SLC to Jean Clemens, 3 March 1909, *UCCL* 08358; SLC to John Macy, 25 February 1909, *UCCL* 10685.

10. "Is Shakespeare Dead?" *Brisbane Truth*, 23 January 1910, 7; *Is Shakespeare Dead?*, 35, 51; SLC to Helen Keller, 29 June 1909, *UCCL* 08429; Keller, *Midstream*, 58; SLC to M. B. Colcord, 18 May 1909, *UCCL* 08397; SLC to James Beck, 25 April 1909, *UCCL* 08389; Langdon, *Clemens: Some Reminiscences*, 12.

11. Hill, *God's Fool*, 217–18; Angert, "Is Mark Twain Dead?" *North American Review* 190 (September 1909): 319–29; *Brooklyn Eagle*, 9 September 1909, 4; "The Latest Sin of Samuel Clemens," *New York Sun*, 13 May 1909, 6; "Pickups from the Papers," *San Diego Union*, 17 July 1909, 4; *Tampa Tribune*, 30 April 1909, 6; Carl T. Robertson, "On the Book Shop Shelves," *Cleveland Plain Dealer*, 3 July 1909, 6; "Mark Twain on Shakespeare," Brisbane *Telegraph*, 31 July 1909, 12.

12. "Books," *Portland Oregonian*, 2 May 1909, 11; "New Books," *Boston Journal*, 18 May 1909, 2; "The Insider," *San Francisco Call*, 24 May 1909, 6; "Books and Authors," *Sacramento Union*, 19 April 1909, 6; "Mark Twain for Bacon," *Washington Times*, 15 May 1909, 4; "Mark Twain Takes Sides in Shakespeare Question," *Dallas Morning News*, 24 May 1909, 4; "Mark Twain on Shakespeare," *Philadelphia Inquirer*, 31 May 1909, 5; "New Books," *Charleston News and Courier*, 9 May 1909, 15; "Books about the Stage," *American Review of Reviews* 39 (June 1909): 768; *MTCR*, 593–95, 597, 601; "Is Shakespeare Dead?" *San Francisco Chronicle*, 2 May 1909, Sunday supplement, 10; "Editor's Study," *Harper's Monthly* 119 (July 1909): 316; "Is Shakespeare Dead?" *London Telegraph & Courier*, 3 June 1909, 8; "Mark Twain on Shakespeare," *Belfast Telegraph*, 7 June 1909, 4; *Westminster Gazette*, 22 June 1909, 2; "Mark Twain on the Shakespeare Riddle," *London Globe*, 15 May 1909, 4; *Scotsman*, 27 May 1909, 2; "Is Shakespeare Dead?" *Sydney World's News*, 17 July 1909, 31; Champ Clark to SLC, 13 September 1909, *UCLC* 40300; "Books," *New Zealand Times*, 17 July 1909, 4; "Shakespeare's Legal Knowledge," *Wellington Evening Post*, 2 October 1909, 13.

13. *MTCR*, 597–604; Metcalfe, "Drama," *Life*, 20 May 1909, 696; Reed, "Mark Twain on Shakespeare," *Brooklyn Eagle*, 15 May 1909, 5; Fuller," Much Ado About Nothing," *Bookman* (New York) 29 (August 1909): 633–36; "The New Books," *New Orleans Picayune*, 25 July 1909, 43; "Literature," *Independent*, 8 July 1909, 90; "Drama," *Nation*, 22 April 1909, 422; "Library Table," *Northern Christian Advocate*, 16 September 1909, 2 "Our Book Table," *Zion's Herald*, 26 May 1909, 660; *Spectator*, 6 November 1909, 716; "Is Shakespeare Dead?" *New York Outlook*, 8 May 1909, 69; "Is Shakespeare Dead?" *Hereford Times*, 7 August 1909, 8; "Shakespeare and the School of Assumption," *Western Daily Press*, 26 July 1909, 3; "Shakespeare—and Mark Twain," *London Standard*, 30 July 1909, 5; "Mark Twain on the Shakespeare Problem," *Sydney Daily Telegraph*, 17 July 1909, 4; "Books and Their Builders," *Perth Times*, 15 August 1909, 1; "Mark Twain and Shakespeare," *Irish Times*, 16 July 1909, 9; Harris, *Contemporary Portraits*, 168; "Sir H. B. Tree," *Sydney Star*, 14 August 1909, 4; *A. L. A. Booklist* 5 (June 1909): 158.

14. "Can Mark Twain Be a Literary Pirate?" *NYT*, 9 June 1909, 1; "Mark Twain Comes Back at Accusers," *Washington Times*, 10 June 1909, 1; *MTCI*, 679; Hill, *God's Fool*, 217; *MTB*, 1497; *MTCR*, 604; "Mark Twain a Pirate?" *Philadelphia Inquirer*, 17 June 1909, 8;

"Mark Twain's Neglect to Give Credit to Englishman in His Latest Book Starts Trouble," *Rochester Democrat and Chronicle*, 9 June 1909, 1; *Referee* (London), 13 June 1909, 11.

15. *MTCI*, 511; Hulbert, *Story of Mrs. Peck*, 177; "Mince Pie After Midnight," *London Mirror*, 3 January 1906, 11; IVLD, 2 January 1908; "Mark Twain Has Fasting Fad," *New York Tribune*, 21 June 1908, 3; SLC to William Henry Bishop, 11 October 1909, *UCCL* 08466.

16. *HHR*, 655; Maines, *Technology of Orgasm*, 19; SLC to Margery H. Clinton, 25 November 1908; SLC to Jean Clemens, 30 November 1908, *UCCL* 08289; SLC to Clara Clemens, 11 December 1908, *UCCL* 08179; "Prominent Users of the Arnold Vibrator," *Springfield Republican*, 2 May 1909, 14; "Prominent People Recommend It," *Cleveland Plain Dealer*, 16 May 1909, 7; *Boston Globe*, 28 March 1909, 40; "This Remarkable New Invention," *Chicago Tribune*, 28 March 1909, 25.

17. *MTB*, 1497–98, 1505, 1527, 1528; SLC to Elizabeth Wallace, 27 August 1909 and 22 September 1909; *MTCI*, 471, 597, 680, 689, 694; Herford, "Mark Twain," 10; Cooley, *Twain's Aquarium*, 261–62; SLC to William Henry Bishop, 11 October 1909, *UCCL* 08466; SLC to Clara Clemens, 24–25 March 1910, *UCCL* 08574.

18. *AMT*, 3:309–10, 3:353; Bush, "'The Pandemonium That Went On,'" 71; Hill, *God's Fool*, 268. As Isabel V. Lyon notes in her diary for 12 June 1906, "I have to sleep on Bromidia."

19. *AMT*, 3:343, 3:398; Hill, *God's Fool*, 183, 212; "Mark Twain Company," *Boston Herald*, 24 December 1908, 1.

20. Skandera Trombley, *Twain's Other Woman*, 206, 208; Cooley, *Twain's Aquarium*, 235; SLC to Clara Clemens, 11 March 1909, *UCCL* 08370; Hill, *God's Fool*, 221, 226; *AMT*, 3:367.

21. In a widely published photo of SLC standing with the couple after the wedding (*Washington Herald*, 28 March 1909, IV, 4), Michael Shelden notes that he "looks more like a passerby than a friend of the bride and groom." Shelden, *Twain: Man in White*, 334–35. In truth, the photo is a "fakeograph," a primitive form of photoshopping.

22. "Ashcroft-Lyon," *Boston Herald*, 19 March 1909, 3; Ralph Ashcroft to SLC, 28 February 1908, *UCLC* 37693; *AMT*, 3:346, 3:354; Skandera Trombley, *Twain's Other Woman*, 204, 253; SLC to Elizabeth Wallace, 27 August 1909, *UCCL* 08446; Hill, *God's Fool*, 222; "Mark Twain's Secretary to Wed," *New York Tribune*, 18 March 1909, 7.

23. *MTHL*, 820, 832–33, 842–43.

24. Skandera Trombley, "Twain's Annus Horribilis," 117, 119–20; Skandera Trombley, *Twain's Other Woman*, 197; Shelden, *Twain: Man in White*, 301; "Clara Clemens Sings," *Brooklyn Eagle*, 7 May 1909, 4.

25. SLC to Elizabeth Wallace, 10 November 1909, *UCCL* 08487; Lystra, *Dangerous Intimacy*, 31; Jean Clemens diary, 6 and 12 November 1900; Hill, *God's Fool*, 44; "News of the Players," *Hartford Courant*, 8 August 1902, 3; IVLD, 19 January 1907, 13 February 1907, 20 December 1908; SLC to Clara Clemens, 11 December 1908, *UCCL* 08179; "Saves Miss Clara Clemens," *NYT*, 21 December 1908, 1; Harding, "Twain Lands an Angel Fish," 9; Cooley, *Twain's Aquarium*, 246; Howden, "Twain as His Secretary Remembers Him," 1–4; "Easter Concerts Promise to be Good," *Brooklyn Eagle*, 10 April 1909, 9; "Clara Clemens Sings," *Brooklyn Eagle*, 14 April 1909, 11; *MTHL*, 846.

26. "Ready to Begin Big Celebration," *Richmond Times-Dispatch*, 2 April 1909, 3; "Opens Road He Personally Built," *San Diego Tribune*, 2 April 1909, 1; *HHR*, 7, 658; "To Open H. H. Rogers's Road," *New York Sun*, 2 April 1909, 1; *AMT*, 3:414; SLC to the board of directors, Mark Twain Co., after 25 September 1909, *UCCL* 12344; "Great Coal Road Formally Opened," *Richmond Times-Dispatch*, 3 April 1909, 1; *MTSpk* 640–43; "Mark Twain

Kidnapped by Dixie Schoolboys," *Detroit Times*, 8 April 1909, 4; "Rogers and Mark Twain," *Montgomery Advertiser*, 6 April 1909, 6; *MTCI*, 676.

27. *AMT*, 3:366–67, 3:438; *HHR*, 662; "Twain Denies Power of Attorney Held by His Now Wedded Secretaries," *Bridgeport Times*, 21 June 1909, 1; Hoffman, *Inventing Mark Twain*, 487; Zuppello, "Visit with Mark Twain," 82; Ralph Ashcroft to SLC, 10 May 1909, *UCLC* 50366. Hill describes the Ashcroft-Lyon manuscript as "a geyser of bias, vindictiveness, and innuendo." Hill, *God's Fool*, 231.

28. SLC to Jean Clemens, 19 April 1909, *UCCL* 08385; Bush, "'The Pandemonium That Went On,'" 71–72; Hill, *God's Fool*, 227.

29. SLC to F. G. Whitmore, 21 June 1909, *UCCL* 08423; SLC to Clara Clemens, 18 July 1909, *UCCL* 08435; SLC to Elizabeth Wallace, 10 November 1909, *UCCL* 08487.

30. *JHT*, 411; Hill, *God's Fool*, 215, 230; *AMT*, 3:343; Skandera Trombley, "Twain's Last Work of Realism," 42. SLC fails to mention his 1908 vacation in Bermuda with Henry Huttleson Rogers and Isabel V. Lyon in the Ashcroft-Lyon manuscript.

31. SLC to Jean Clemens, 21 May 1908, *UCCL* 08006; *AMT*, 3:337.

32. Gagel n.p.; Skandera Trombley, *Twain's Other Woman*, 89; *AMT*, 3:338, 3:437; SLC to Clara Clemens, 6 March 1910, *UCCL* 08567.

33. "Mark Twain Overcome by News of Death," *Brooklyn Eagle*, 19 May 1909, 2; *MTCI*, 678; *MFMT*, 278; "Family at Side of Bed as Death Claims Rogers," *Boston Journal*, 20 May 1909, 2; "H. H. Rogers Taken by Death in Gotham Home," *Washington Times*, 19 May 1909, 2; SLC to Elizabeth Wallace, 26 May 1909, *UCCL* 08403; *AMT*, 3:312; *Brooklyn Eagle*, 21 May 1909, 2; "Mark's Example," *Houston Post*, 6 June 1909, 28; *Boston Herald*, 22 May 1909, 11.

34. *AMT*, 3:339, 3:379, 3:390–91; Hill, *God's Fool*, 227; SLC to William Coe, 16 June 1909, *UCCL* 08421; SLC to Elizabeth Wallace, 7 June 1909, *UCCL* 08418; Shelden, *Twain: Man in White*, 359.

35. Hill, *God's Fool*, 212–13, 241; *AMT*, 3:391. SLC acknowledged that his past business experiences "stand as abiding proof that when it comes to examining a contract and understanding it, I am an incapable. I have shown that I misread and misunderstood those contracts in every instance." *AMT*, 2:143.

36. Hill, *God's Fool*, 232; *AMT*, 3:394; Shelden, *Twain: Man in White*, 296; Emerson, *Singular Mark Twain*, 340; Rafferty, "'The Lyon of St. Mark,'" 54.

37. SLC to William Coe, 27 June 1909, *UCCL* 08428; *AMT*, 3:395; Ralph Ashcroft to SLC, 3 June 1909, *UCLC* 50372; Hill, *God's Fool*, 228. Shelden echoes Sam's baseless allegation: the Ashcrofts "quietly slipped away on a passenger freighter. . . . It wasn't the kind of ship that someone looking for them might think to search." Shelden, *Twain: Man in White*, 359.

38. "Mark Twain Now Wants His Money," *Portland Oregonian*, 20 June 1909, 4; SLC to the board of directors, Mark Twain Co., after 25 September 1909, *UCCL* 12344; "Mark Twain Is Suing Woman He Long Trusted," *Brooklyn Eagle*, 21 June 1909, 16; "Mrs. Ashcroft Blames Mark Twain's Daughter," *Brooklyn Eagle*, 14 July 1909, 3; Hill, *God's Fool*, 232–33; "Wants Mark Twain to Explain to Her," *NYT*, 15 July 1909, 16; "Mark Twain's Financial Man Back," *New York Tribune*, 28 July 1909, 7.

39. Skandera Trombley, *Twain's Other Woman*, 220; "Mr. Ashcroft's Side," *New York Tribune*, 4 August 1909, 2.

40. "Ashcroft Serves Ultimatum on Twain's Daughters; Scores Daughters in Press Statement," *Bridgeport Farmer*, 4 August 1909, 1, 3; *Bridgeport Farmer*, 19 August 1909, 3; "Mark Twain Company," *Bridgeport Farmer*, 20 August 1909, 12; Hill, *God's Fool*, 238–39.

41. "Vindication for Ashcrofts," *Bridgeport Farmer*, 11 September 1909, 1; SLC to J. P. Morgan, 15 September 1909, *UCCL* 13044; SLC to the Mark Twain Co. board of directors, 5–9 September 1909, *UCCL* 12344; "Mark Twain Suits All Off," *NYT*, 13 September 1909, 8; Lystra, *Dangerous Intimacy*, 239; SLC to Melville Stone, 14 September 1909, *UCCL* 08451.

42. "Vindication of the Ashcrofts," *Bridgeport Farmer*, 16 September 1909, 4; *AMT*, 3:437, 3:613; *JHT*, 411–12; SLC to John Hays Hammond, 22 March 1910, *UCCL* 12915; SLC to Elizabeth Wallace, 22 September 1909, *UCCL* 08457.

43. SLC to A. B. Paine, 17–18 February 1910, *UCCL* 1184; SLC to A. B. Paine, 2 March 1910, *UCCL* 11843; SLC to Elizabeth Wallace, 26 and 29 January 1910, *UCCL* 08548.

44. *MTCI*, 680, 682, 687; Kaplan, *Singular Mark Twain*, 648; Cooley, *Twain's Aquarium*, 260–62; *MTB*, 1498; Emerson, "Smoking and Health," 561; *JHT*, 411; SLC to George Harvey, 12 August 1909, *UCCL* 08443; Cooley, *Twain's Aquarium*, 263.

45. "Gabrilowitsch Operated on for Mastoiditis," *Hartford Courant*, 30 June 1909, 11; *LMT*, 306; Bispham, *Quaker Singer's Recollections*, 340–41; Beard, *Hardly a Man*, 346–50; SLC to Elizabeth Wallace, 22 September 1909, *UCCL* 08457; Jeanette Gilder, "The Lounger," *Putnam's* 7 (December 1909): 369–70; Skandera Trombley, "Twain's Annus Horribilis," 126; *LMT*, 308; *MTB*, 1522; SLC to Augusta Ogden, 22 September 1909, *UCCL* 08458.

Chapter 18

1. Skandera Trombley, "Twain's Annus Horribilis," 126, 127, 131; SLC to Richard E. Johnston, 12 October 1909, *UCCL* 11924; Skandera Trombley, *Twain's Other Woman*, 311; *LMT*, 312, 316; *MTB*, 1523; "Miss Clemens to Wed," *New York Sun*, 6 October 1909, 4; "Gabrilowitsch Doing Well," *Brooklyn Eagle*, 19 October 1909, 20; SLC to Augusta Ogden, 13 October 1909, *UCCL* 08467; SLC to Elizabeth Wallace, 10 November 1909, *UCCL* 08487.

2. Shelden, *Twain: Man in White*, 381; "Young Bride, Twain's Daughter, Featured in Strange Suit," *Oakland Tribune*, 13 October 1909, 20; Skandera Trombley, "Twain's Annus Horribilis," 127–28, 130; "Wife of Pianist at His Bedside," *Washington Times*, 17 October 1909, 8; Skandera Trombley, *Twain's Other Woman*, 231–32.

3. Cooley, *Twain's Aquarium*, 267; SLC to Clara Clemens, 26 November 1909, *UCCL* 08500; SLC to Clara Clemens, 6 December 1909, *UCCL* 08506; SLC to Elizabeth Wallace, 10 November 1909, *UCCL* 08487.

4. *MTCR*, 609–12; "Mark Twain's Latest," *London Globe*, 20 November 1909, 4; "Miscellaneous Publications," *Yorkshire Post and Leeds Intelligencer*, 5 January 1910, 4; "A Popular Idol," *Salt Lake City Intermountain Catholic*, 20 November 1909, 4.

5. "Fiction," *Times Literary Supplement*, 4 November 1909, 405; "Books," *Portland Oregonian*, 7 November 1909, 9; "Recent Publications," *Richmond Times-Dispatch*, 21 November 1909, 21; "Mark Twain on Heaven," *Philadelphia Inquirer*, 28 November 1909, 33; "A Visit to Heaven," *San Francisco Chronicle Sunday Magazine*, 28 November 1909, 6; "Some Notable Books," *Queen*, 25 December 1909, 1172; "Recent Fiction," *Irish Times*, 3 December 1909, 9; "A Clever Satire," *Westminster Gazette*, 20 November 1909, 17; "First Impressions," *London Clarion*, 24 December 1909, 2; "Writers and Readers," *New Zealand Times*, 15 January 1910, 9.

6. SLC to Elizabeth Wallace, 13 November 1909, *UCCL* 08490; Bird, "Twain and Robert Ingersoll Connection," 51, 55.

7. *Letters from the Earth*, 44; *MTB*, 1356.

8. *AMT*, 3:195; *Letters from the Earth*, 40.

9. SLC to Marion Allen, 19 December 1909, *UCCL* 11779; SLC to Helen Allen, 18–20 December 1909, *UCCL* 11780; "Mark Twain Says His Work Is Done," *San Francisco Call*, 21 December 1909, 8; *MTCI*, 692; "Personal Items," *Wellington Dominion*, 2 February 1910, 4; "Twain Says He'll Write No More," *Boston Herald*, 21 December 1909, 5.

10. "Twain Is Laughing at Retiring Talk," *Washington Times*, 21 December 1909, 9; "Good Old Mark Twain," *Portsmouth (N.H.) Herald*, 23 December 1909, 4; *AMT*, 3:312; "Twain's Merry Christmas," *NYT*, 24 December 1909, 6.

11. *AMT*, 3:311, 3:313, 3:317; SLC to Mai H. Coe, 27 December 1909, *UCCL* 08524; *JHT*, 414; *LMT*, 321–22; "Miss Jean Clemens Drowned in Bath Tub," *Buffalo Enquirer*, 24 December 1909, 1, 4; *Mark Twain's Letters* (1917), 835; Harrington and Jenn, *Twain and France*, 205; "Mark Twain Bereft of Young Daughter," *Eugene (Ore.) Register*, 25 December 1909, 1; "Mark Twain's Daughter Dies," *Fresno Republican*, 25 December 1909, 2; Skandera Trombley, *Twain's Other Woman*, 235; Ferguson, *Twain: Man and Legend*, 320; Clemens, *My Husband, Gabrilowitch* 52; Hill, *God's Fool*, 253; SLC to Clara Clemens, 29 December 1909, *UCCL* 08527.

12. *LMT*, 229, 324; *AMT*, 3:318; *JHT*, 414; *MFMT*, 284–85.

13. Skandera Trombley, *Twain's Other Woman*, 236; SLC to Harriet Whitmore, 28 December 1909, *UCCL* 08526; *JHT*, 414; *MTB*, 1552, 1559; SLC to Mai Coe, 27 December 1909, *UCCL* 08524; *AMT*, 3:314–15; SLC to Clara Clemens, 23 February 1910, *UCCL* 08561; Hill, *God's Fool*, 255; SLC to Katharine Clemens, 24 March 1910, *UCCL* 08575.

14. SLC to Elizabeth Wallace, 1 January 1910, *UCCL* 08532; Cooley, *Twain's Aquarium*, 270–71; Hoffmann, *Twain in Paradise*, 144; *MyMT*, 100; "Mark Twain Leaves Home," *New York Tribune*, 6 January 1910, 7; "Clemens Sails for Bermuda," *Washington Star*, 6 January 1910, 8; "Mark Twain Chooses Bermuda as Home," *Salt Lake Telegram*, 10 January 1910, 2; John A. Moroso, "To S. L. Clemens," *NYT*, 15 January 1910, 8.

15. *Mark Twain's Letters* (1917), 837–38; SLC to A. B. Paine, 24 January 1910, *UCCL* 08546; SLC to A. B. Paine, 5–7 February 1910, *UCCL* 08555; Hoffmann, *Twain in Paradise*, 148. Rather than "clock golf" on a single green, SLC and Woodrow Wilson played "miniature golf." Hoffmann, *Twain in Paradise*, 151; Lystra, *Dangerous Intimacy*, 261; and Powers, *Twain: A Life*, 626.

16. Hoffmann, *Twain in Paradise*, 148.

17. SLC to Mr. Roberts, 7–31 January 1910, *UCCL* 08533; *Brooklyn Eagle*, 30 January 1910, 36; "Note and Comment," *Springfield Republican*, 11 March 1910, 8; Phelps, *Essays on Modern Novelists*, 102; SLC to William Lyon Phelps, 12 March 1910, *UCCL* 08571; *MTHL*, 851, 853.

18. Cooley, *Twain's Aquarium*, 271; Wallace, *Twain and the Happy Island*, 138–39; SLC to Mary Rogers, 21 February 1910, *UCCL* 08562; Hoffmann, *Twain in Paradise*, 149.

19. SLC to A. B. Paine, 5–7 February 1910, *UCCL* 08555; SLC to A. B. Paine, 17–18 March 1910, *UCCL* 11845; Paine to SLC, 11 February 1910, *UCLC* 50442; *Mark Twain's Letters* (1917), 843; SLC to Clara Clemens, 21–23 February 1910, *UCCL* 08561; Skandera Trombley, "Twain's Annus Horribilis," 130.

20. *Mark Twain's Letters* (1917), 837–38; Cooley, *Twain's Aquarium*, 272, 276–77; Allen 170; Shelden, *Twain: Man in White*, 467.

21. Cooley, "Mark Twain's Angel-Fish," 15; Cooley, *Twain's Aquarium*, 278–79, 282; Hill, *God's Fool*, 260, 261, 292; Julian Street to A. B. Paine, 2 January 1912, *UCLC* 47777.

22. "Robert J. Collier Returns from Bermuda," *NYT*, 22 March 1910, 9; SLC to Clara Clemens, 12 March 1910, *UCCL* 08569; SLC to Clara Clemens, 24–25 March 1910, *UCCL*

08574; Shelden, *Twain: Man in White*, 405; *MTB*, 1563; "Visitors Crowd Rome," *Washington Post*, 3 April 1910, 39.

23. *MTB*, 1565, 1571, 1573; Beard, *Hardly a Man*, 346–50.

24. "How Mark Twain Wrote His Books," *Pawtucket Times*, 16 April 1910, 3; "Mark Twain Home Very Ill," *New York Sun*, 15 April 1910, 9; "Mark Twain's Heart Failing," *Baltimore American*, 15 April 1910, 9; "Mark Twain Pines for Puff of Smoke," *Sacramento Union*, 16 April 1910, 6; *MTB*, 1574; *LMT*, 328.

25. "Mark Twain Dead," *Washington Post*, 22 April 1910, 21; "Mark Twain While Weaker Still Smokes," *Bridgeport Farmer*, 21 April 1910, 1; Gribben, *Twain's Library*, 128; *MFMT*, 290, 291; Beard, *Hardly a Man*, 346–50; *MTB*, 1577; Hill, *God's Fool*, 265; *LMT*, 331.

Epilogue

1. Beard, *Hardly a Man*, 350; "Last Glimpse Here of Mark Twain," *NYT*, 24 April 1910, 3; Max Eastman, "Mark Twain's Elmira," *Harper's Monthly* 176 (May 1938): 620.

2. According to the Associated Press report of his final hours, SLC wrote a note to Clara Clemens on his deathbed: "Give me my glasses." See, for example, "Mark Twain Is Dead at 74," *NYT*, 22 April 1910, 1.

3. This standard minstrel song is sung by characters in both *The Adventures of Tom Sawyer* and "The Chronicle of Young Satan."

4. Arthur B. Krock, "Mark Twain," *Washington Post*, 24 April 1910, 4.

5. For example, S. E. Kiser, *Pittsburgh Post*, 24 April 1910, "Mark Twain," 10: "His hands fall from the wheel; he looks no more / To see what reef or shoal may be ahead, / What narrow channel there may be to thread, / What jagged rocks may jut out from the shore!"

6. Cardwell, *Man Who Was Mark Twain*, 65; LeMaster and Wilson, *Mark Twain Encyclopedia*, 256; Budd, *Twain: Social Philosopher*, 235; Wagenknecht, *Twain: The Man and His Work*, 161; "Mark Twain Left $611,136," *Brooklyn Eagle*, 26 October 1910, 1.

7. Harnsberger, *Twain: Family Man*, 268; *LMT*, 337.

8. Hill, *God's Fool*, 44; *MTB*, 1379, 1446; Keith Archibald Forbes, "Mark Twain and Bermuda," bermuda-online.org/twain.htm; Cooley, "Twain's Aquarium," 18.

9. Skandera Trombley, *Twain's Other Woman*, 246; Lystra, *Dangerous Intimacy*, 310n6; *AMT*, 3:326–27; Hill, *God's Fool*, 241.

10. Keller, "Mark Twain," 51, 80–81; Harnsberger, *Twain: Family Man*, 268.

11. "Tributes to Mark Twain," *Harper's Weekly*, 14 May 1910, 35; "Tributes to Mark Twain," *North American Review* 191 (June 1910): 827–35; "Hannibal Wants Body Buried at Boyhood Home," *Brooklyn Eagle*, 22 April 1910, 2; Messent, *Twain and Male Friendship*, 41; Harris, *Contemporary Portraits*, 172; "Leading Men of America Pay Tribute to the Memory of Mark Twain," *Boston Post*, 22 April 1910, 16; Baetzhold, *Twain and John Bull*, 195; Vorpahl, "'Very Much Like a Fire-Cracker,'" 83; Kipling to Frank Doubleday, 13 October 1903, *UCLC* 41899; *MTHL*, 668; Keller, "Mark Twain," 51, 80–81; Keller, *Midstream*, 48–49; www.biblio.com/mark-twain/author/174.

Bibliography

Writings by Samuel L. Clemens, aka Mark Twain

The American Claimant. New York: Webster, 1892.

"The 'Austrian Parliamentary System'? Government by Article 14." *Lords and Commons* 25 (February 1899): 59–61.

Autobiography of Mark Twain. Edited by Harriet Elinor Smith and Benjamin Griffin. 3 vols. Berkeley: University of California Press, 2010–15.

Christian Science. New York: Harper, 1907.

Collected Tales, Sketches, Speeches, and Essays, 1891–1910. Edited by Louis J. Budd. New York: Library of America, 1992.

The Devil's Race-Track: Mark Twain's Great Dark Writings. Edited by John S. Tuckey. Berkeley: University of California Press, 1980.

Early Tales and Sketches. Edited by Edgar Marquess Branch, Robert Hirst, and Harriet E. Smith. 2 vols. Berkeley: University of California Press, 1979.

Eve's Diary. New York: Harper, 1906.

Europe and Elsewhere. Edited by Albert Bigelow Paine. New York: Harper, 1923.

A Family Sketch and Other Private Writings. Edited by Benjamin Griffin. Berkeley: University of California Press, 2014.

Following the Equator. Hartford, Conn.: American Publishing, 1897.

A Horse's Tale. New York: Harper, 1907.

How to Tell a Story and Other Essays. New York: Harper, 1897.

Huck Finn and Tom Sawyer among the Indians and Other Unfinished Stories. Berkeley: University of California Press, 1989.

The Innocents Abroad. Hartford, Conn.: American Publishing, 1869.

The £1,000,000 Bank-Note and Other New Stories. New York: Webster, 1893.

King Leopold's Soliloquy. Boston: Warren, 1905.

Letters from the Earth. Edited by Bernard DeVoto. New York: Harper & Row, 1962.

The Letters of Mark Twain and Joseph Hopkins Twichell. Edited by Harold K. Bush, Steve Courtney, and Peter Messent. Athens: University of Georgia Press, 2017.

The Love Letters of Mark Twain. Edited by Dixon Wecter. New York: Harper, 1949.

The Mammoth Cod and Address to the Stomach Club. Milwaukee: Maledicta, 1976.

The Man That Corrupted Hadleyburg and Other Stories and Essays. New York: Harper, 1900.

Mark Twain: The Complete Interviews. Edited by Gary Scharnhorst. Tuscaloosa: University of Alabama Press, 2006.

Mark Twain–Howells Letters. Edited by Henry Nash Smith and William Gibson. Cambridge, Mass.: Belknap, 1960.

Mark Twain on Potholes and Politics. Edited by Gary Scharnhorst. Columbia: University of Missouri Press, 2014.

Mark Twain Speaking. Edited by Paul Fatout. Iowa City: University of Iowa Press, 1976.

Mark Twain to Mrs. Fairbanks. Edited by Dixon Wecter. San Marino, Calif.: Huntington Library, 1949.

Mark Twain's Correspondence with Henry Huttleston Rogers, 1893–1909. Edited by Lewis Leary. Berkeley: University of California Press, 1969.

Mark Twain's Fables of Man. Edited by John S. Tuckey. Berkeley: University of California Press, 1972.

Mark Twain's Letters. Edited by Albert Bigelow Paine. 2 vols. New York: Harper, 1917.

Mark Twain's Letters. 6 vols. Vol. 1, *1853–1866*, edited by Edgar Marquess Branch, Michael B. Frank, Kenneth M. Sanderson, Harriet Elinor Smith, Lin Salamo, and Richard Bucci; vol. 2, *1867–1868*, edited by Harriet Elinor Smith, Richard Bucci, and Lin Salamo; vol. 3, *1869*, edited by Victor Fischer, Michael B. Frank, and Dahlia Armon; vol. 4, *1870–1871*, edited by Victor Fischer, Michael B. Frank, and Lin Salamo; vol. 5, *1872–1873*, edited by Lin Salamo and Harriet Elinor Smith; vol. 6, *1874–1875*, edited by Michael B. Frank and Harriet Elinor Smith. Berkeley: University of California Press, 1988–2002.

Mark Twain's Letters to His Publishers, 1867–1894. Edited by Hamlin Hill. Berkeley: University of California Press, 1967.

Mark Twain's Notebook. Edited by Albert Bigelow Paine. New York: Harper, 1935.

Mark Twain's Notebooks and Journals. Edited by Frederick Anderson, Michael Berry Frank, and Kenneth M. Sanderson. 3 vols. Berkeley: University of California Press, 1975–80.

Mark Twain's Speeches. Edited by Albert Bigelow Paine. New York: Harper, 1923.

Mark Twain's Weapons of Satire: Anti-Imperialist Writings on the Philippine-American War. Edited by Jim Zwick. Syracuse, N.Y.: Syracuse University Press.

Mark Twain's "Which Was the Dream?" and Other Symbolic Writings of the Later Years. Edited by John S. Tuckey. Berkeley: University of California Press, 1966.

The Mysterious Stranger Manuscripts. Edited by William M. Gibson. Berkeley: University of California Press, 1969.

"On American Imperialism." *Atlantic Monthly* 269 (April 1992): 49–51.

Personal Recollections of Joan of Arc. New York: Harper, 1896.

Roughing It. Hartford, Conn.: American Publishing, 1872.

The $30,000 Bequest and Other Stories. New York: Harper, 1906.

Tom Sawyer Abroad; Tom Sawyer, Detective; and Other Stories. New York: Harper, 1896.

The Tragedy of Pudd'nhead Wilson and the Comedy Those Extraordinary Twins. Hartford, Conn.: American Publishing, 1894.

What Is Man? and Other Essays. New York: Harper, 1917.

What Is Man? and Other Philosophical Writings. Edited by Paul Baender. Berkeley: University of California Press, 1973.

Who is Mark Twain? Edited by Robert H. Hirst. New York: HarperStudio, 2009.

Major Print Sources

Ahluwalia, Harsharan Singh. "Itinerary of Mark Twain's Lecture Tour in India, January 18–April 5, 1896." *MTJ* 34 (Spring 1996): 8–20.

———. "Letters from Olivia and Clara Clemens." *MTJ* 34 (Spring 1996): 43–47.

Alexander, Charles. "Writer in Residence: Mark Twain's Saranac Summer." *Adirondack Life* 24 (July/August 1998): 16–24.

Allingham, Philip V. "Mark Twain in Vancouver, British Columbia, August 1895." *MTJ* 28 (Fall 1990): 2–14.

———. "Mark Twain in Winnipeg, Manitoba, July 26–28, 1895." *MTJ* 36 (Fall 1998): 2–12.

Anderson, Carl L. "Mark Twain in Sweden: An Interview and Commentary." *American Literary Realism* 11 (Spring 1978): 80–91.

Andrews, Kenneth R. *Nook Farm: Mark Twain's Hartford Circle*. Cambridge, Mass.: Harvard University Press, 1950.

An Answer to Mark Twain. Brussels: Bulens Bros., 1907.

Austilat, Andreas. *A Tramp in Berlin*. New York: Berlinica, 2013.

Bacheller, Irving. *Opinions of a Cheerful Yankee*. Indianapolis: Bobbs-Merrill, 1925.

Baetzhold, Howard G. *Mark Twain and John Bull*. Bloomington: Indiana University Press, 1970.

Bellamy, Gladys. *Mark Twain as a Literary Artist*. Norman: University of Oklahoma Press, 1950.

Benson, Adolph B. "Mark Twain's Contacts with Scandinavia." *Scandinavian Studies and Notes* 14 (August 1937): 159–67.

Berger, Sidney E. "Emendations of the Copy-Text: Substantives." In *Pudd'nhead Wilson and Those Extraordinary Twins*, 183–92. New York: Norton, 1980.

Bird, John. "The Mark Twain and Robert Ingersoll Connection: Freethought, Borrowed Thought, Stolen Thought." *Mark Twain Annual* 11 (2013): 42–61.

Boewe, Mary. "Smouching towards Bedlam; or, Mark Twain's Creative Use of Some Acknowledged Sources." *MTJ* 29 (Spring 1991): 8–12.

Bosha, Francis J. "The Mark Twain–William James Friendship." *MTJ* 21 (Fall 1983): 7–8.

Brittain, Harry. "My Friend Mark Twain." *MTJ* 11 (Fall 1961): 1–3.

Brodwin, Stanley. "Mark Twain's Masks of Satan: The Final Phase." *American Literature* 45 (May 1973): 206–27.

Budd, Louis J. *Mark Twain: Social Philosopher*. Bloomington: Indiana University Press, 1962.

———. "Mark Twain Sounds Off on the Fourth of July." *American Literary Realism* 34 (Spring 2002): 265–80.

———. *Our Mark Twain: The Making of His Public Personality*. Philadelphia: University of Pennsylvania Press, 1984.

———, ed. *Mark Twain: The Contemporary Reviews*. New York: Cambridge University Press, 1999.

Burnet, Ruth A. "Mark Twain in the Northwest, 1895." *Pacific Northwest Quarterly* 42 (July 1951): 187–202.

Bush, Harold K., Jr. "'The Pandemonium That Went On': An Unpublished Letter by Jean Clemens." *American Literary Realism* 44 (Fall 2011): 68–73.

Cardwell, Guy. "The Bowdlerizing of Mark Twain." *ESQ* 21 (1975): 179–93.

———. *The Man Who Was Mark Twain*. New Haven, Conn.: Yale University Press, 1991.

Chambliss, Amy. "The Friendship of Helen Keller and Mark Twain." *Georgia Review* 24 (1970): 305–10.

Clemens, Clara. *My Father, Mark Twain*. New York: Harper, 1931.

Clemens, Cyril. "Some Unpublished Letters by Mark Twain." *Overland Monthly* 87 (April 1929): 99–108.

Coleman, Rufus A. "Mark Twain in Montana." *Montana Magazine of History* 3 (Spring 1953): 9–16.

Cooley, John. "Mark Twain's Angel-Fish: Innocence at Home?" *Mississippi Quarterly* 38 (Winter 1984–85): 3–19.

———. "Mark Twain's Aquarium: Editing the Mark Twain–Angelfish Correspondence." *MTJ* 27 (Spring 1989): 18–24.

———. *Mark Twain's Aquarium: The Samuel Clemens Angelfish Correspondence, 1905–1910*. Athens: University of Georgia Press, 1991.

———. "Mark Twain's Heroic Maidens: Angelfish, Androgyny, and the Transvestite Tales." *MTJ* 34 (Fall 1996): 38–42.

Cooper, Robert L. *Around the World with Mark Twain*. New York: Arcade, 2000.

Courtney, Steve. *Joseph Hopkins Twichell: The Life and Times of Mark Twain's Closest Friend*. Athens: University of Georgia Press, 2008.

Cox, James M. *Mark Twain: The Fate of Humor*. Princeton, N.J.: Princeton University Press, 1966.

Crawford, Alan Pell. *How Not to Get Rich: The Financial Misadventures of Mark Twain*. New York: Houghton Mifflin Harcourt, 2017.

Csicsila, Joseph. "'These Hideous Times': Mark Twain's Bankruptcy and the Panic of 1893." In *Mark Twain and Money*, 139–52. Tuscaloosa: University of Alabama Press, 2017.

Denney, Lynn. "Next Stop Detroit: A City's Views of Mark Twain's Evolution as a Literary Hero, 1868–1895." *MTJ* 31 (Spring 1993): 22–28.

DeVoto, Bernard. *Mark Twain at Work*. Cambridge, Mass.: Harvard University Press, 1942.

———, ed. *The Portable Mark Twain*. New York: Viking, 1946.

Dias, Earl J. "Mark Twain in Fairhaven." *MTJ* 13 (Summer 1967): 11–15.

Dolmetsch, Carl. "Mark Twain and the Viennese Anti-Semites: New Light on 'Concerning the Jews.'" *MTJ* 23 (Fall 1985): 10–17.

———. *"Our Famous Guest": Mark Twain in Vienna*. Athens: University of Georgia Press, 1992.

Doubleday, Neltje De Graff. "Stormfield, Mark Twain's New Country Home." *Country Life in America* 15 (April 1909): 607–11, 650–52.

Eastman, Max. "Mark Twain's Elmira." *Harper's Monthly* 176 (May 1938): 620–32.

Eble, Kenneth E. *Old Clemens and W.D.H.: The Story of a Remarkable Friendship*. Baton Rouge: Louisiana State University Press, 1985.

Emerson, Everett. *The Authentic Mark Twain*. Philadelphia: University of Pennsylvania Press, 1984.

———. *Mark Twain: A Literary Life*. Philadelphia: University of Pennsylvania Press, 2000.

———. "Smoking and Health: The Case of Samuel L. Clemens." *New England Quarterly* 70 (December 1997): 548–66.

Fanning, Philip. *Mark Twain and Orion Clemens*. Tuscaloosa: University of Alabama Press, 2003.

Fatout, Paul. *Mark Twain on the Lecture Circuit*. Bloomington: Indiana University Press, 1960.

Feinstein, Herbert. "Mark Twain's Lawsuits." Ph.D. diss., University of California, Berkeley, 1968.

Ferguson, DeLancey. *Mark Twain: Man and Legend*. Indianapolis: Bobbs-Merrill, 1943.

Fisher, Henry W. *Abroad with Mark Twain and Eugene Field*. New York: Brown, 1922.

Flanagan, John T. "Mark Twain on the Upper Mississippi." *Minnesota History* 17 (December 1936): 369–84.

Foner, Philip S. *Mark Twain: Social Critic*. New York: International, 1958.

Gagel, Amanda. "Letters as Critical Texts: A Consideration of Mark Twain's 'Ashcroft-Lyon Manuscript.'" *Scholarly Editing* 36 (2015): n.p.

Gibson, William M. "Mark Twain and Howells: Anti-Imperialists." *New England Quarterly* 20 (December 1947): 435–70.

Giddings, Robert. "Mark Twain and King Leopold of the Belgians." In *Mark Twain: A Sumptuous Variety*, edited by Giddings, 199–221. Towana, N.J.: Barnes & Noble, 1985.

Gillman, Susan. *Dark Twins: Imposture and Identity in Mark Twain's America*. Chicago: University of Chicago Press, 1989.

Godfrey, Dennis. "More on Mark Twain in the South African Press." *MTJ* 40 (Spring 2002): 34–48.

Gold, Charles H. *"Hatching Ruin"; or, Mark Twain's Road to Bankruptcy*. Columbia: University of Missouri Press, 2003.

Gribben, Alan. "Mark Twain, Business Man: The Margins of Profit." *Studies in American Humor* 1 (June 1982): 24–43.

———. *Mark Twain's Library: A Reconstruction*. Boston: Hall, 1980.

Grünzweig, Walter. "Comanches in the Austrian Parliament: Austria as a Metaphor for Mark Twain's Disillusionment with Democracy." *MTJ* 23 (Fall 1985): 3–9.

Hall, Fred J. "Tells the Story of His Connection with Charles L. Webster & Co." *Twainian* 6 (November–December 1947): 2–3.

Halla, Robert C. "The Plutocrat and the Author: Mark Twain and H. H. Rogers." *MTJ* 18 (Winter 1976–77): 18–19.

Harding, Dorothy Sturgis. "Mark Twain Lands an Angel Fish." *Columbia Library Columns* 16 (February 1967): 3–12.

Harnsberger, Caroline. *Mark Twain: Family Man*. New York: Citadel, 1960.

Harrington, Paula, and Ronald Jenn. *Mark Twain and France*. Columbia: University of Missouri Press, 2017.

Hawkins, Hunt. "Mark Twain's Involvement with the Congo Reform Movement: 'A Fury of Generous Indignation.'" *New England Quarterly* 51 (June 1978): 147–75.

Healy, Chris. "Mark Twain at Home." *Grand Magazine* 6 (August 1907): 20–28.

Hemminghaus, Edgar H. "Mark Twain's German Provenience." *Modern Language Quarterly* 6 (December 1945): 459–78.

Hill, Hamlin. *Mark Twain: God's Fool*. New York: Harper & Row, 1973.

Hoffman, Andrew J. *Inventing Mark Twain: The Lives of Samuel Langhorne Clemens*. New York: Morrow, 1997.

Hoffmann, Donald. *Mark Twain in Paradise*. Columbia: University of Missouri Press, 2006.

Hoeltje, Hubert H. "When Mark Twain Spoke in Portland." *Oregon Historical Quarterly* 55 (March 1954): 73–81.

Horn, Jason G. "Mark Twain, William James, and the Funding of Freedom in *Joan of Arc*." *Studies in American Fiction* 23 (Autumn 1995): 173–94.

Howells, W. D. *My Mark Twain*. New York: Harper, 1910.

Ishihara, Tsuyoshi. "Mark Twain's Italian Villas." *MTJ* 52 (Spring 2014): 18–39.

Jerome, Robert D., Herbert A. Wisbey Jr., and Barbara E. Snedecor, eds. *Mark Twain in Elmira*. 2nd ed. Elmira, N.Y.: Elmira College Center for Mark Twain Studies, 2013.

Jones, Alexander E. "Mark Twain and the Determinism of *What Is Man?*" *American Literature* 29 (March 1957): 1–17.

Kahn, Sholom J. "Mark Twain's Philosemitism: 'Concerning the Jews.'" *MTJ* 23 (Fall 1985): 18–25.

Kaplan, Fred. *The Singular Mark Twain*. New York: Doubleday, 2003.

Kaplan, Justin. *Mr. Clemens and Mark Twain*. New York: Simon and Schuster, 1966.

Katona, Anna B. "An Interview with Mark Twain." *Hungarian Studies Review* 9 (Spring 1982): 73–81.

———. "Mark Twain's Reception in Hungary." *American Literary Realism* 16 (Spring 1983): 107–20.

Kiskis, Michael. *Mark Twain at Home*. Tuscaloosa: University of Alabama Press, 2016.

Kolb, Harold H., Jr. *Mark Twain: The Gift of Humor*. Lanham, Md.: University Press of America, 2015.

Kravitz, Bennett. "Philo-Semitism as Anti-Semitism in Mark Twain's 'Concerning the Jews.'" *Studies in American Culture* 25 (October 2002): 1–12.

Krauth, Leland. *Mark Twain and Company*. Athens: University of Georgia Press, 2003.

———. *Proper Mark Twain*. Athens: University of Georgia, 1999.

Langdon, Jervis. *Samuel Langhorne Clemens: Some Reminiscences*. Elmira, N.Y.: privately printed, 1938.

Lathem, Edward C. *Mark Twain's Four Weeks in England, 1907*. Hartford, Conn.: Mark Twain House and Museum, 2006.

Lawton, Mary. *A Lifetime with Mark Twain: The Memories of Katy Leary*. New York: Harcourt, Brace, 1925.

Leary, Lewis. "The Bankruptcy of Mark Twain." *The Carrell: Journal of the Friends of the University of Miami Library* 9 (1968): 13–20.

———. "Mark Twain at Barnard College." *Columbia Library Columns* 10 (1961): 12–17.

———. "Mark Twain Did Not Sleep Here: Tarrytown, 1902–1904." *MTJ* 17 (Summer 1974): 13–16.

Le Bourgeois, John Y., and Jonathan Evans. "Mark Twain's Secret Mission to the London Hospital." *New England Quarterly* 81 (June 2008): 344–47.

Lederer, Max. "Mark Twain in Vienna." *Mark Twain Quarterly* 7 (Summer–Fall 1945): 1–12.

LeMaster, J. R., and James D. Wilson, eds. *The Mark Twain Encyclopedia*. New York: Garland, 1993.

Lentz, Laurie. "Mark Twain in 1906: An Edition of Selected Extracts from Isabel V. Lyon's Journal." *Resources for American Literary Study* 11 (Spring 1981): 1–36.

Leon, Philip W. "Mark Twain at the Charleston Exposition." *MTJ* 23 (Spring 1985): 4–7.

Lorch, Fred W. "Mark Twain's 'Morals' Lecture during the American Phase of His World Tour in 1895–1896." *American Literature* 26 (March 1954): 52–66.

———. *The Trouble Begins at Eight*. Ames: Iowa State University Press, 1968.

Luscher, Robert. "Italian Accounts of Mark Twain." *American Literary Realism* 17 (Autumn 1984): 216–24.

Lynn, Kenneth S. *Mark Twain and Southwestern Humor*. Boston: Little, Brown, 1979.

Lystra, Karen. *Dangerous Intimacy: The Untold Story of Mark Twain's Final Years*. Berkeley: University of California Press, 2006.

Machlis, Paul. *Union Catalog of Clemens Letters*. Berkeley: University of California Press, 1986.

Machlis, Paul, and Deborah Ann Turner. *Union Catalog of Letters to Clemens*. Berkeley: University of California Press, 1992.

Macnaughton, William R. *Mark Twain's Last Years as a Writer*. Columbia: University of Missouri Press, 1979.

McFarland, Philip. *Mark Twain and the Colonel: Mark Twain, Theodore Roosevelt, and the Arrival of a New Century*. Lanham, Md.: Rowman & Littlefield, 2012.

Marcosson, Isaac F. "Mark Twain as Collaborator." *Mark Twain Quarterly* 2 (Winter 1937–38): 7, 24.

Matthews, Brander. "Memories of Mark Twain." *Saturday Evening Post*, 6 March 1920, 14–15, 77–81.

———. *The Tocsin of Revolt and Other Essays*. New York: Scribner's, 1922.

Messent, Peter. "Carnival in Mark Twain's 'Stirring Times in Austria' and 'The Man That Corrupted Hadleyburg.'" *Studies in Short Fiction* 35 (Summer 1998): 217–32.

———. *Mark Twain and Male Friendship*. New York: Oxford University Press, 2013.

———. "Racial and Colonial Discourse in Mark Twain's *Following the Equator*." *Essays in Arts and Sciences* 22 (October 1993): 67–83.

———. *The Short Works of Mark Twain: A Critical Study*. Philadelphia: University of Pennsylvania Press, 2001.

Michelson, Bruce. *Mark Twain on the Loose*. Amherst: University of Massachusetts, 1995.

———. *Printer's Devil: Mark Twain and the American Publishing Revolution*. Berkeley: University of California, 2006.

Morris, Linda. *Gender Play in Mark Twain*. Columbia: University of Missouri Press, 2007.

———. "What Is Personal about *Personal Recollections of Joan of Arc?*" *American Literary Realism* 51 (Winter 2019): 97–110.

Moss, Robert. "Tracing Mark Twain's Intentions: The Retreat from Issues of Race in *Pudd'nhead Wilson*." *American Literary Realism* 30 (Winter 1998): 43–55.

Mutalik, Keshav. *Mark Twain in India*. Bombay: Noble, 1978.

Nolan, Charles, Jr., and David O. Tomlinson. "Mark Twain's Visit to Annapolis." *MTJ* 25 (Fall 1987): 2–8.

Oggel, Terry. "Speaking Out about Race: 'The United States of Lyncherdom' Clemens Really Wrote." *Prospects* 25 (2000): 115–38.

Orth, Ralph H. "George Gregory Smith and Mark Twain: Florence, 1903–4." *MTJ* 41 (Fall 2003): 27–36.

Ozick, Cynthia. "Mark Twain and the Jews." *Commentary* 99 (May 1995): 56–62.

Paine, Albert Bigelow. *Mark Twain: A Biography*. New York: Harper, 1912.

Parsons, Coleman O. "Mark Twain: Clubman in South Africa." *New England Quarterly* 50 (June 1977): 234–54.

———. "Mark Twain in Adelaide, South Australia." *MTJ* 21 (Spring 1983): 51–54.

———. "Mark Twain in Melbourne." *MTJ* 22 (Spring 1984): 40–42.
———. "Mark Twain in New Zealand." *South Atlantic Quarterly* 61 (1962): 51–76.
———. "Mark Twain: Paid Performer in South Africa." *MTJ* 19 (Summer 1978): 2–11.
———. "Mark Twain: Sightseer in India." *Mississippi Quarterly* 16 (1963): 76–93.
———. "Mark Twain: Traveler in South Africa." *Mississippi Quarterly* 29 (Winter 1975–76): 3–41.

Pettit, Arthur. *Mark Twain and the South*. Lexington: University Press of Kentucky, 1974.

Philippon, Daniel J. "'Following the Equator' to Its End: Mark Twain's South African Conversion." *MTJ* 40 (Spring 2002): 3–13.

Phipps, William E. *Mark Twain's Religion*. Macon: Mercer University Press, 2003.

Pond, James B. "The Anecdotal Side of Mark Twain." *Ladies' Home Journal* 15 (October 1898): 5–6.
———. *Eccentricities of Genius*. New York: Dillingham, 1900.
———. *Overland with Mark Twain: James B. Pond's Photographs and Journal of the North American Lecture Tour of 1895*. Edited by Alan Gribben and Nick Karanovich. Elmira, N.Y.: Elmira College Center for Mark Twain Studies, 1992.

Potts, E. Daniel, and Annette Potts. "The Mark Twain Family in Australia." *Overland* 70 (1978): 46–50.

Powers, Ron. *Mark Twain: A Life*. New York: Free Press, 2005.

Quick, Dorothy. *Enchantment: A Little Girl's Friendship with Mark Twain*. Norman: University of Oklahoma Press, 1961.
———. "A Little Girl's Mark Twain." *North American Review* 240 (September 1935): 342–48.

Quirk, Tom. *Mark Twain: A Study of the Short Fiction*. New York: Twayne, 1997.

Rafferty, Jennifer L. "'The Lyon of St. Mark': A Reconsideration of Isabel Lyon's Relationship to Mark Twain." *MTJ* 34 (Fall 1996): 43–55.

Reckford, Philip. "Mark Twain in South Florida." *MTJ* 23 (Spring 1985): 2–3.

Reesman, Jeanne Campbell. "Discourses of Faith vs. Fraud in *Personal Recollections of Joan of Arc* and *Christian Science*." *American Literary Realism* 51 (Winter 2019): 111–35.

Regan, Robert. *Unpromising Heroes: Mark Twain and His Characters*. Berkeley: University of California Press, 1966.

Rice, C. C. "Mark Twain as His Physician Knew Him." *Mentor* 12 (May 1924): 48–49.

Richmond, Marion A. "The Lost Source of Freud's 'Comment on Anti-Semitism': Mark Twain." *Journal of the American Psychoanalytic Association* 28 (1980): 563–74.

Rodney, Robert M. *Mark Twain Overseas*. Washington, D.C.: Three Continents, 1993.

Salomon, Roger B. *Twain and the Image of History*. New Haven, Conn.: Yale University Press, 1961.

Scharnhorst, Gary. "The Bret Harte–Mark Twain Feud: An Inside Narrative." *MTJ* 31 (Spring 1993): 29–32.
———. "Had Their Mothers Only Known: Horatio Alger Jr. Rewrites Cooper, Melville, and Twain." *Journal of Popular Culture* 15 (Winter 1981): 175–82.
———. "'He Is Amusing but Not Inherently a Gentleman': The Vexed Relations of Kate Field and Samuel Clemens." *Legacy* 18 (Spring 2002): 193–204.
———. "Mark Twain and Julian Hawthorne." *Mark Twain Annual* 10 (2012): 47–54.
———. "Paradise Revisited: Twain's 'The Man That Corrupted Hadleyburg.'" *Studies in Short Fiction* 18 (Winter 1981): 59–64.

———. "A Recovered Mark Twain Letter to Henry M. Whitney in 1895." *American Literary Realism* 39 (Fall 2006): 87–88.
———. "A Sheaf of Recovered Mark Twain Letters." *American Literary Realism* 52 (Fall 2019): 89–94.
Schirer, Thomas. *Mark Twain and the Theatre*. Nuremberg: Hans Carl, 1984.
Schönemann, Friedrich. "Mark Twain and Adolf Wilbrandt." *Modern Language Notes* 34 (June 1919): 372–74.
Schrager, Cynthia D. "Mark Twain and Mary Baker Eddy: Gendering the Transpersonal Subject." *American Literature* 70 (March 1998): 29–61.
Scott, Arthur L. "*The Innocents Adrift* Edited by Mark Twain's Official Biographer." *PMLA* 78 (June 1963): 230–37.
———. "Letters from Mark Twain to William Walter Phelps, 1890–1893." *Huntington Library Quarterly* 27 (1964): 375–81.
———. *Mark Twain at Large*. Chicago: Regnery, 1969.
———. *On the Poetry of Mark Twain*. Champagne: University of Illinois Press, 1966.
Seybold, Matt. "The Neoclassical Twain: The Zombie Economics of Col. Sellers." *Mark Twain Annual* 13 (2015): 78–90.
Shelden, Michael. *Mark Twain: Man in White*. New York: Random House, 2010.
Shillingsburg, Miriam. *At Home Abroad: Mark Twain in Australasia*. Jackson: University Press of Mississippi, 1988.
———. "Down Under Day by Day with Mark Twain." *MTJ* 33 (Fall 1995): 6–34.
Simboli, Raffaele. "Mark Twain from an Italian Point of View." *Critic* 44 (June 1904): 518–24.
Skandera Trombley, Laura. *Mark Twain in the Company of Women*. Philadelphia: University of Pennsylvania Press, 1997.
———. "Mark Twain's Annus Horribilis of 1908–1909." *American Literary Realism* 40 (Winter 2008): 114–36.
———. "Mark Twain's Last Work of Realism: The Ashcroft-Lyon Manuscript." *Essays in Arts and Sciences* 23 (October 1994): 39–48.
———. *Mark Twain's Other Woman*. New York: Knopf, 2010.
———. "'She Wanted to Kill': Jean Clemens and Postictal Psychosis." *American Literary Realism* 37 (Spring 2005): 225–37.
Smythe, Carlyle. "The Real 'Mark Twain.'" *Pall Mall Magazine* 16 (September 1898): 29–36.
Sorrentino, Paul. "Mark Twain's 1902 Trip to Missouri: A Reexamination, a Chronology, and an Annotated Bibliography." *Mark Twain Journal* 38 (Spring 2000): 13–44.
Stone, Albert E., Jr. "Mark Twain's *Joan of Arc*: The Child as Goddess." *American Literature* 31 (March 1959): 1–20.
Tanner, Louis, and Gary Scharnhorst. "Mark Twain Speaking: Three New Documents." *MTJ* 30 (Fall 1992): 23–25.
Tenney, Thomas. *Mark Twain: A Reference Guide*. Boston: Hall, 1977.
———. "Mark Twain and the Reformers." *MTJ* 40 (Spring 2002): 49–51.
Tuckey, John S. *Mark Twain and Little Satan: The Writing of The Mysterious Stranger*. West Lafayette, Ind.: Purdue University Press, 1963.
Turpin, Zachary. "Thomas Jefferson Snodgrass Goes to England." *American Literary Realism* 49 (Winter 2017): 175–79.

Vogel, Dan. "Concerning Mark Twain's Jews." *Studies in American Jewish Literature* 17 (1998): 152–55.
———. *Mark Twain's Jews*. Jersey City, N.J.: KTAV, 2006.
Vorpahl, Ben M. "'Very Much Like A Fire-Cracker': Owen Wister on Mark Twain." *Western American Literature* 6 (Summer 1971): 83–98.
Wagenknecht, Edward. *Mark Twain: The Man and His Work*. Norman: University of Oklahoma Press, 1967.
Wallace, Elizabeth. *Mark Twain and the Happy Island*. Chicago: McClurg, 1914.
Wallace, Robert. "Mark Twain on the Great Lakes." *Inland Seas* 17 (1961): 181–86.
Webster, Samuel Charles. *Mark Twain: Business Man*. Boston: Little, Brown, 1946.
Welland, Dennis. *Mark Twain in England*. Atlantic Highlands, N.J.: Humanities Press, 1978.
———. "Mark Twain's Last Travel Book." *Bulletin of the New York Public Library* 69 (1965): 31–48.
White, Frank Marshall. "Mark Twain as a Newspaper Reporter." *New York Outlook* 24 December 1910: 961–67.
Wigger, Anne. "The Composition of Mark Twain's *Pudd'nhead Wilson* and 'Those Extraordinary Twins': Chronology and Development." *Modern Philology* 55 (November 1957): 93–102.
Wiggins, Robert A. "The Original of Mark Twain's *Those Extraordinary Twins*." *American Literature* 23 (November 1951): 355–57.
———. "*Pudd'nhead Wilson*: 'A Literary Caesarean Operation.'" *College English* 25 (December 1963): 182–86.
Willis, Resa. *Mark and Livy*. New York: Athenaeum, 1992.
Wood, Barry. "Narrative Action and Structural Symmetry in *Pudd'nhead Wilson*." In *Pudd'nhead Wilson and Those Extraordinary Twins*, edited by Sidney E. Berger, 370–81. New York: Norton, 1980.
Wuliger, Robert. "Mark Twain on *King Leopold's Soliloquy*." *American Literature* 25 (May 1953): 234–37.
Yurán, Robin R. "Mark Twain at Norfolk, 1904–1906." *MTJ* 45 (Spring 2007): 4–16.
Zacharias, Greg W. "Henry Rogers, Public Relations, and the Recovery of Mark Twain's 'Character,'" *MTJ* 31 (Spring 1993): 2–17.
Zacks, Richard. *Chasing the Last Laugh: Mark Twain's Raucous and Redemptive Round-the-World Comedy Tour*. New York: Doubleday, 2016.
Zuppello, Maria. "A Visit with Mark Twain in 1909." *American Literary Realism* 41 (Fall 2008): 79–83.
Zwick, Jim. "'Prodigally Endowed with Sympathy for the Cause': Mark Twain's Involvement with the Anti-Imperialist League." *MTJ* 32 (Spring 1994): 2–25.
Zwonitzer, Mark. *The Statesman and the Storyteller: John Hay, Mark Twain, and the Rise of American Imperialism*. Chapel Hill, N.C.: Algonquin, 2017.

Reviews and Other Print Sources

Ade, George. *One Afternoon with Mark Twain*. Chicago: Mark Twain Society, 1939.
Allen, Marion Schuyler. "Some New Anecdotes of Mark Twain." *Strand* 46 (August 1913): 166–72.
Andriano, Joseph. "Fenimore Cooper's Literary Offenses." In *The Mark Twain Encyclopedia*, edited by J. R. LeMaster and James D. Wilson, 286–87. New York: Garland, 1993.

Balicer, Hermann C. "Szczepanik's 'Portrait' of Mark Twain." *Publishers' Weekly*, 20 February 1937, 68–69.

Beard, Dan. "Mark Twain as a Neighbor." *American Review of Reviews* 41 (June 1910): 705–9.

Boewe, Mary. "A Horse's Tale." In *The Mark Twain Encyclopedia*, edited by J. R. LeMaster and James D. Wilson, 368. New York: Garland, 1993.

Britton, Wesley. "Keller, Helen Adams." In *The Mark Twain Encyclopedia*, edited by J. R. LeMaster and James D. Wilson, 427–28. New York: Garland, 1993.

Brooks, Sydney. "England's Ovation to Mark Twain." *Harper's Weekly*, 27 July 1907, 1086–89.

Carew, Kate. "12-Minute Interview on 12 Subjects with Bret Harte." *New York World*, 22 December 1901, 5.

Chamberlin, Fred C. "La Comtesse de Lisne." *Boston Herald*, 26 May 1895, 35.

Dent, Alan. "Max Is Eighty." *Saturday Review*, 30 August 1952, 20.

Dolmetsch, Carl. "Berlin, Germany." In *The Mark Twain Encyclopedia*, edited by J. R. LeMaster and James D. Wilson, 70–71. New York: Garland, 1993.

Eastman, Max. "Mark Twain's Elmira." *Harper's Monthly* 176 (May 1938): 620–32.

Fiedler, Leslie. "As Free as Any Cretur . . ." *New Republic*, 22 August 1955, 16–18.

Flower, B. O. "Mark Twain's Attack on Christian Science." *Arena* 38 (November 1907): 567–74.

Forbes, Keith Archibald. "Mark Twain and Bermuda." bermuda-online.org/twain.htm.

Gabrilowitsch, Ossip. "Memoir of Leschetizky." *New York Times*, 7 December 1930, 132.

Gilder, Jeannette. "The Lounger." *Putnam's* 4 (August 1908): 627; 4 (September 1908): 760; 7 (December 1909): 369–70.

Glyn, Elinor. *Mark Twain on Three Weeks*. London: privately printed, 1908.

Hawkins, Hunt. "King Leopold's Soliloquy." In *The Mark Twain Encyclopedia*, edited by J. R. LeMaster and James D. Wilson, 430–31. New York: Garland, 1993.

Helm, W. H. *Memories*. London: Richards, 1937.

———. "Mornings with Mark Twain." *London Daily News*, 22 April 1910, 4.

Herford, Oliver. "Mark Twain." *Collier's Weekly*, 26 December 1908, 10.

Howden, Mary Louise. "Mark Twain as His Secretary at Stormfield Remembers Him." *New York Herald*, 13 December 1925, 1–4.

Howells, W. D. "Editor's Easy Chair." *Harper's Monthly* 108 (December 1903): 153–59.

———. "In Honor of Mark Twain." *Harper's Weekly*, 23 December 1902, 1943–44.

Kimball, Edward A. "Mark Twain, Mrs. Eddy, and Christian Science." *Cosmopolitan* 43 (May 1907): 35–41.

Kiser, S. E. "Mark Twain." *Honolulu Republican*, 11 November 1900, 2.

———. "Mark Twain." *Pittsburgh Post*, 24 April 1910, 10.

Krock, Arthur B. "Mark Twain." *Washington Post*, 24 April 1910, 4.

Larom, Walter H. "Mark Twain in the Adirondacks." *Bookman* 58 (January 1924): 536–38.

Le Gallienne, Richard. "Wanderings in Bookland." *Idler* 10 (August 1896): 113.

LeMaster, J. R., and James D. Wilson. "Estate of Samuel L. Clemens." In *The Mark Twain Encyclopedia*, edited by J. R. LeMaster and James D. Wilson, 256. New York: Garland, 1993.

Lesslie, Jordan. *Our Misunderstanding Concerning the Jews*. New York: Cooke, 1908.

Levy, Mayer S. "A Rabbi's Reply to Mark Twain." *Overland Monthly* 34 (October 1899): 364–67.
Lucy, Henry. "Life in London and Thereabout." *Sydney Morning Herald*, 24 August 1907, 7.
———. "London Letter." *Gloucester Journal*, 7 February 1903, 5.
———. "Mark Twain." *Bathurst Argus*, 13 February 1909, 3.
———. "Mark Twain." *Lyttelton Times*, 23 July 1904, 6.
Mayo, Frank. "Pudd'nhead Wilson." *Harper's Weekly*, 22 June 1895, 594.
McCrackan, William D. "Mrs. Eddy's Relation to Christian Science." *North American Review*, 176 (March 1903): 349–64.
Moore, Louise Paine. "Mark Twain as I Knew Him." *Twainian* 18 (January–February 1959): 3–4.
O'Connor, T. P. "Mark Twain as an Orator." *T.P.'s Weekly*, 19 July 1907, 85.
Paul, Howard. "London Chat and Gossip." *London American Register*, 10 July 1897, 5.
Phillpotts, Eden. "To Samuel Langhorne Clemens." *Washington Herald*, 21 July 1907, sec. 3, 2.
Randon, Gabriel. "Causerie-Conférence de Mark Twain." *Le Figaro*, 6 April 1894, 2.
Seaman, Owen. "To Mark Twain." *Punch*, 26 June 1907, 463.
Shaw, George Bernard. "Letters to the Editor." *Saturday Review of Literature*, 12 August 1944, 15.
Starr, William Ireland. "My Three Meetings with Mark Twain at Stormfield." twainproject.blogspot.com/2009/11/new-stormfield-articles.html.
"Tribunes to Mark Twain." *North American Review* 191 (June 1910): 827–35.
White, Frank Marshall. "Mark Twain Amused." *New York Journal*, 2 June 1897, 1.
———. "Will Lunch with Victoria." *St. Louis Republic*, 24 June 1897, 1.
Williams, Martha McCullough. "In Re Pudd'nhead Wilson." *Southern Magazine* 4 (February 1894): 99–102.
Wilson, McLandburgh. "The Family Index." *New York Sun*, 6 October 1907, 8.

Manuscripts and Scrapbooks (MTP)

"The Aquarium Manuscript" (DV 375)
"American Representation in Vienna" (DV 237)
"The Case of Sir Henry M. Stanley" and "Postscript—Osteopathy" (DV13)
Clara Clemens manuscript letters
"A Cloud-Burst of Calamities" (DV 246)
Interview with Joseph Hooker Twichell, 14 August 1957
Isabel V. Lyon diary
Jean Clemens diary
"Journey to an Asterisk" (DV 203)
"Shackleford's Ghost" (DV 318)
SLC financial records

General Studies

Adams, Henry. *Letters, 1892–1918*. Edited by Worthington Chauncey Ford. Boston: Houghton Mifflin, 1938.
Barrymore, Ethel. *Memories: An Autobiography*. New York: Harper, 1955.
Beard, Dan. *Hardly a Man Is Now Alive*. New York: Doubleday, 1939.

Berkove, Lawrence I. *Insider Stories of the Comstock Lode and Nevada's Mining Frontier, 1859–1909*. Lewiston, N.Y.: Edwin Mellen, 2007.
Bigelow, Poultney. *Seventy Summers*. 2 vols. London: Edward Arnold, 1925.
———. "Ten Years of Kaiser Wilhelm." *Century* 56 (July 1898): 450–58.
Bingham, Theodore. "Foreign Criminals in New York." *North American Review* 188 (September 1908): 383–94.
Bispham, David. *A Quaker Singer's Recollections*. New York: Macmillan, 1920.
Bourget, Paul. *Outre-Mer: Impressions of America*. New York: Scribner's, 1895.
Brunet, Helen Tower. *Nellie and Charlie: A Family Memoir of the Gilded Age*. New York: iUniverse, 2005.
Burdette, Clara Bradley. *Robert J. Burdette: His Message*. Philadelphia: Winston, 1922.
Burke, Billie. *With a Feather on My Nose*. New York: Appleton-Century-Crofts, 1949.
Burroughs, John. *Life and Letters*. Edited by Clara Barrus. Boston: Houghton Mifflin, 1925.
Carnegie, Andrew. *Autobiography*. Boston: Houghton Mifflin, 1920.
Chapin, Adèle. *Their Trackless Way*. New York: Holt, 1932.
Churchill, Winston. *My Early Life: A Roving Commission*. New York: Scribner's, 1930.
Clark, Marion Edward. *Diseases of Women*. Kirksville, Mo.: Journal Print, 1901.
Clemens, Clara. *My Husband, Gabrilowitsch*. New York: Harper, 1938.
Clemens, Katharine. *Gardens and Books*. Webster Groves, Mo.: International Mark Twain Society, 1938.
Cortissoz, Royal. *The Life of Whitelaw Reid*. New York: Scribner's, 1921.
Cuoco, Lorin, and William H. Gass, eds. *Literary St. Louis: A Guide*. St. Louis: Missouri Historical Society Press, 2000.
Cyriax, Edgar F. *The Elements of Kellgren's Manual Treatment*. New York: Wood, 1904.
Davis, Charles E. "Composing, Line-Justifying, and Distributing." In *Typographical Printing-Surfaces*, edited by Lucien Alphonse Legros and John Cameron Grant, 378–86. London: Longmans, Green, 1916.
Davitt, Michael. *Life and Progress in Australasia*. London: Methuen, 1898.
Dickie, James F. *In the Kaiser's Capital*. New York: Dodd, Mead, 1910.
Doubleday, Frank. *The Memoirs of a Publisher*. New York: Doubleday, 1972.
Downing, Ben. *Queen Bee of Tuscany*. New York: Farrar, Straus and Giroux, 2013.
Ellsworth, William W. *A Golden Age of Authors*. Boston: Houghton Mifflin, 1919.
Fiedler, Leslie. *What Was Literature?* New York: Simon and Schuster, 1982.
Fike, Duane Joseph. *Frank Mayo: Actor, Playwright, and Manager*. Ph.D. diss., University of Nebraska-Lincoln, 1980.
Fishkin, Shelley Fisher. "Mark Twain and Women." In *The Cambridge Companion to Mark Twain*, edited by Forrest G. Robinson, 52–73. New York: Cambridge University Press, 1995.
Flagg, James Montgomery. *Roses and Buckshot*. New York: Putnam's, 1946.
Frank, Waldo. *Our America*. New York: Boni and Liveright, 1919.
Galton, Francis. *Finger Prints*. London: Macmillan, 1892.
Garland, Hamlin. *Companions on the Trail*. New York: Macmillan, 1931.
———. *Diaries*. Edited by Donald Pizer. San Marino, Calif.: Huntington Library, 1968.
———. *Roadside Meetings*. New York: Macmillan, 1931.
Gilman, Charlotte Perkins. *Concerning Children*. Boston: Small, Maynard, 1900.
Glyn, Elinor. *Romantic Adventure*. New York: Dutton, 1936.

Gordon, Ishbel. *The Canadian Journal of Lady Aberdeen, 1893–1898*. Edited by John T. Saywell. Toronto: Champlain Society, 1960.
Gorky, Maksim. *Selected Letters*. Edited by Andrew Barratt and Barry P. Scherr. Oxford: Clarendon, 1997.
Grossmith, Weedon. *From Studio to Stage*. New York: John Lane, 1913.
Hammond, John Hays. *The Autobiography of John Hays Hammond*. 2 vols. New York: Farrar & Rinehart, 1935.
Hammond, Natalie. *A Woman's Part in a Revolution*. London: Longmans, Green, 1897.
Hapgood, Hutchins. *A Victorian in the Modern World*. New York: Harcourt, Brace, 1939.
Harper, J. Henry. *The House of Harper: A Century of Publishing in Franklin Square*. New York: Harper, 1912.
———. *I Remember*. New York: Harper, 1934.
Harris, Frank. *Contemporary Portraits: Fourth Series*. London: Richards, 1923.
Heniger, Alice Minnie Herts. *The Children's Educational Theatre*. New York: Harper, 1911.
Higginson, Mary Thacher. *T. W. Higginson: The Story of His Life*. Boston: Houghton Mifflin, 1914.
Hillier, Alfred P. *Raid and Reform*. London: Macmillan, 1898.
Hambourg, Mark. *From Piano to Forte: A Thousand and One Notes*. London: Cassell, 1931.
Hoffman, Charles. *In the Clutch of Circumstance*. New York: Appleton, 1922.
———. "More from the Burglar." *MTJ* 25 (Spring 1987): 12.
Hoppe, Willy. *Thirty Years of Billiards*. New York: Putnam, 1925.
Howells, Mildred, ed. *Life in Letters of William Dean Howells*. Garden City, N.Y.: Doubleday, Doran, 1928.
Hulbert, Mary Allen. *The Story of Mrs. Peck*. New York: Minton, Balch, 1933.
Hutton, Laurence. *Talks in a Library with Laurence Hutton*. New York: G. P. Putnam's Sons, 1907.
James, George Wharton. "Charles Warren Stoddard." *National Magazine* 34 (August 1911): 659–72.
James, Henry. *Daisy Miller*. New York: Harper, 1900.
James, William. *Letters*. Edited by Henry James. 2 vols. Boston: Atlantic Monthly Press, 1920.
Johnson, Robert Underwood. *Remembered Yesterdays*. Boston: Little, Brown, 1923.
Jordan, Elizabeth. *Three Rousing Cheers*. New York: Appleton, 1938.
Khan, Aga, III. *The Memoirs of the Aga Khan*. New York: Simon and Schuster, 1954.
Keller, Helen. "Mark Twain as Revealed by Himself." *American Magazine* 108 (July 1929): 51, 81–82.
———. *Midstream: My Later Life*. Garden City, N.Y.: Doubleday, 1929.
———. *The Story of My Life*. New York: Doubleday, 1954.
King, Grace. *Memories of a Southern Woman of Letters*. New York: Macmillan, 1932.
Kinzer, Stephen. *The True Flag: Theodore Roosevelt, Mark Twain, and the Birth of American Empire*. New York: Holt, 2017.
Kipling, Rudyard. *Letters, 1900–1910*. Edited by Thomas Pinney. New York: Palgrave Macmillan, 1996.

Lucy, Henry W. *The Diary of a Journalist*. London: Murray, 1920.
———. *Sixty Years in the Wilderness*. New York: Dutton, 1909.
Mac Donnell, Kevin. "Stormfield: A Virtual Tour." *MTJ* 44 (Spring–Fall 2006): 1–68.
Maines, Rachel P. *The Technology of Orgasm*. Baltimore: Johns Hopkins University Press, 1999.
Mencken, H. L. *Chrestomathy*. New York: Knopf, 1949.
Miller, Stuart. *Benevolent Assimilation*. New Haven, Conn.: Yale University Press, 1982.
Morris, Harrison. *Confessions in Art*. New York: Sears, 1930.
Newton, Joseph Fort. *River of Years*. Philadelphia: Lippincott, 1946.
Orcutt, William Dana. *In Quest of the Perfect Book*. Boston: Little, Brown, 1926.
———. *My Library Walls*. London: Longmans, Green, 1945.
Paderewski, Ignace, and Mary Lawton. *The Paderewski Memoirs*. New York: Scribner's, 1939.
Parker, Hershel. *Flawed Texts and Verbal Icons*. Evanston: Northwestern University Press, 1984.
Phelps, William Lyon. *Essays on Modern Novelists*. New York: Macmillan, 1910.
Poole, Ernest. "Maxim Gorki in New York." *Slavonic and East European Review* 22 (May 1944): 77–83.
Porter, Henry Dwight. *William Scott Ament: Missionary of the American Board to China*. New York: Revell, 1911.
Poultney, Dora Ortlepp. *Dawn to Dusk*. London: Cassell, 1936.
Richards, Laura, Maud Howe, and Florence Howe Hall. *Julia Ward Howe, 1819–1910*. Boston: Houghton Mifflin, 1915.
Roosevelt, Theodore. *History as Literature and Other Essays*. New York: Scribner's, 1913.
Ross, Janet. *The Fourth Generation*. New York: Scribner's, 1912.
Samuels, Charles. *The Girl in the Red Velvet Swing*. New York: Fawcett, 1953.
Sangster, Margaret. *From My Youth Up*. New York: Revell, 1909.
Scharnhorst, Gary. *Owen Wister and the West*. Norman: University of Oklahoma Press, 2015.
Shaw, George Bernard. *Collected Letters, 1898–1910*. Edited by Dan H. Lawrence. London: Reinhardt, 1972.
Sinclair, Upton. *Mammonart*. Pasadena: privately printed, 1925.
Smith, Corinna Lindon. *Interesting People*. Norman: University of Oklahoma Press, 1962.
Sorrentino, Paul. *Stephen Crane: A Life of Fire*. Cambridge, Mass.: Harvard University Press, 2014.
Still, Andrew T. *The Philosophy and Mechanical Principles of Osteopathy*. 1902.
Stoker, Bram. *Personal Reminiscences of Henry Irving*. New York: Macmillan, 1906.
Stowe, Harriet Beecher. *Uncle Tom's Cabin*. Boston: Jewett, 1852.
Strong, Leah A. *Joseph Hopkins Twichell: Mark Twain's Friend and Pastor*. Athens: University of Georgia Press, 1966.
Tarbell, Ida. *All in the Day's Work*. New York: Macmillan, 1939.
———. *History of the Standard Oil Company*. 2 vols. New York: McClure, Phillips, 1904.
Ticknor, Caroline. *Glimpses of Authors*. Boston: Houghton Mifflin, 1922.
Tracy, James L. "The Psychology of the Tobacco Habit." *American Medicine*, n.s. 4 (July 1909): 359–72.

Van Doren, Carl. *The American Novel*. New York: Macmillan, 1921.
van Onselen, Charles. *The Cowboy Capitalist: John Hays Hammond, the American West, and the Jameson Raid*. Charlottesville: University of Virginia Press, 2018.
Waife-Goldberg, Marie. *My Father, Sholom Aleichem*. New York: Simon and Schuster, 1968.
Wertheimer, Max. *Why I Left Christian Science*. Findlay, Ohio: Fundamental Truth, 1916.
Woodall, Percy Hogan. *A Manual of Osteopathic Gynecology*. Nashville, Tenn.: Rundle, 1902.
Woolf, S. J. *Drawn from Life*. New York: Whittlesey House, 1932.
Wheeler, Candace. *Yesterdays in a Busy Life*. New York: Harper, 1918.

Index

B

C

M

S